Roger Ebert's Movie Yearbook 2012

Andrews McMeel Publishing, LLC
Kansas City • Sydney • London

This book is dedicated
to Robert Zonka, 1928–1985.
God love ya.

Andrews McMeel Publishing, LLC
an Andrews McMeel Universal company
1130 Walnut Street, Kansas City, Missouri 64106

www.andrewsmcmeel.com

11 12 13 14 15 MLY 10 9 8 7 6 5 4 3 2 1

ISBN: 978-1-4494-0813-8

Library of Congress Control Number: 2011926181

All the reviews in this book originally appeared in the *Chicago Sun-Times*.

Contents

Introduction

The dominant trend in the past twelve months was the ascendency of 3-D. My views on the process are well known and briefly summarized: It is an unnecessary distraction, inflicts a dim picture upon us, and is a marketing gimmick. Only a process such as true IMAX seems capable of projecting a strong enough beam to handle it. Since the illusion of three dimensions exists already in 2-D, calling attention to the visual plane is a mistake.

In the year since the last *Yearbook*, almost every weekend has featured a 3-D movie, all of them action pictures, many aimed at children or superhero fans. Thus far no serious drama except *Avatar* and very few live-action comedies have used the process, possibly because directors feel it would be a distraction in that genre. In the first half of 2011, a backlash began to take form, with a majority of customers for many movies choosing the cheaper alternative of 2-D.

This is good news. It is encouraging to me because, as a movie lover, I hope anyone who buys a ticket enjoys themselves. This is entirely apart from whether I personally admire a movie; all of my reviews are subjective and intended only to express my opinion, not dictate anyone else's. I must say that as my weekly routine of screenings comes to require at least one weekly annoyance with the 3-D glasses, the pleasure with which I always begin watching a film has been diminished; I'm already displeased as I look at the studio logo.

One thing I'm learning about movies based on comic book heroes: Their fans study the sources with the devotion and intensity of Shakespearean or biblical scholars. My reviews of these films are subjected to analysis I would appreciate more if it were carried over into more challenging films. I am often lectured on having made plot mistakes, or being unfamiliar with the provenance and relationships of the characters.

This is fair enough. Since the plots of comic book movies are by definition preposterous and arbitrary, one must really care in order to follow them. In the case of a really good movie, such as *The Dark Knight*, *Iron Man*, or *Spider-Man II*, that happens effortlessly. In the case of something like *Thor* or *The Green Lantern*, frankly, my attention sometimes drifts. I don't give enough of a damn. I can no longer be absorbed in new ways of regarding loud and hyperkinetic special effects.

This feeling has reached its zenith with the second and third of the *Transformers* movies, which did not even begin with comic books but with toys. Obviously, a moviegoer who grew up with the toys has a special feeling about them, but their mythology and genealogy afflict me with profound indifference.

Is this a weakness for a movie critic? I would rather describe it as an attribute. I am a critic who doesn't care much about Transformers. Other critics do. You take your pick. My opinion is of some interest specifically because it originates from outside the fan base.

When I write a blog entry and attract the fury of some fans, I am pleased for them that they care that much. Yet I suspect some of their anger is inspired simply because my review doesn't validate their experience. They went to the movie, they liked it, and now I have the temerity to say I didn't. Does that mean I think they were wrong? Of course not. It means I disagree. Some of these films are loved with an intensity that I suspect will evaporate over time—sometimes as quickly as a few weeks later, when the latest franchise product comes out of the chute.

Movie critics these days find themselves reviewing two kinds of films: real movies and consumer products. Sometimes these categories overlap. Often they're not even intended to. Artistic considerations take second place to marketing concerns, which grow all the more urgent as studios deplete the ranks of available superheroes. Batman, Superman, and Spider-Man, yes, certainly. But . . . the Green Hornet and his magic ring?

* * *

My sincere thanks to Dorothy O'Brien, who has been the book's valued editor at Andrews McMeel Publishing for many years. Also to Sue Roush, my editor at Universal Uclick, and to Laura Emerick, Amanda Barrett, Miriam Dinunzio, Darel Jevens, Teresa Budasi, Thomas Conner, and all the other heroes at the *Chicago Sun-Times*, and Jim Emerson and the Web staff at rogerebert.com. Many others are thanked in the acknowledgments.

In autumn 2011, Grand Central published *Life Itself: A Memoir*, my autobiography. Late last year, the University of Chicago Press published *The Great Movies III*. And Andrews McMeel will follow up *I Hated, Hated, Hated This Movie* and *Your Movie Sucks* by publishing a third volume of my collected reviews of bad movies, but for now I'm keeping the title to myself.

Roger Ebert

Acknowledgments

My editor is Dorothy O'Brien, tireless, cheerful, all-noticing. My friend and longtime editor Donna Martin suggested the yearbook approach to the annual volume. The design is by Cameron Poulter, the typographical genius of Hyde Park.

My thanks to production editor Christi Clemons Hoffman, who renders Cameron's design into reality. John Yuelkenbeck at Alias Creative Group is the compositor who has worked diligently on the series for years. I have been blessed with the expert and discriminating editing of Laura Emerick, Miriam DiNunzio, Darel Jevins, Jeff Johnson, and Teresa Budasi at the *Chicago Sun-Times*; Sue Roush at Universal Uclick; and Michelle Daniel and David Shaw at Andrews McMeel Publishing. For much advice and counsel, thanks to Jim Emerson and John Barry of www.rogerebert.com.

Many thanks are also due to Marsha Jordan at WLS-TV. My gratitude goes to Carol Iwata, my expert personal assistant, and to Gregory Isaac, who is a computer whiz and invaluable aide-de-camp. I must also thank those who have given me countless observations and corrections, including Peter Debruge, Jana J. Monji, and Troylene Ladner.

And special thanks and love to my wife, Chaz, who was always at my side during a difficult illness, helped see three books through the press during that time, and was a cheerleader for this one. I am so grateful to her as we once again, relieved, enter a period of good health.

ROGER EBERT

Key to Symbols

★★★★	A great film
★★★	A good film
★★	Fair
★	Poor
	G, PG, PG-13, R, NC-17: Ratings of the Motion Picture Association of America
G	Indicates that the movie is suitable for general audiences
PG	Suitable for general audiences but parental guidance is suggested
PG-13	Recommended for viewers 13 years or above; may contain material inappropriate for younger children
R	Recommended for viewers 17 or older
NC-17	Intended for adults only
141 m.	Running time
2010	Year of theatrical release
☞	Refers to "Questions for the Movie Answer Man"

Reviews

A

Accomplices ★ ★ ★

NO MPAA RATING, 93 m., 2010

Gilbert Melki (Herve Cagan), Emmanuelle Devos (Karine Mangin), Cyril Descours (Vincent Bouvier), Nina Meurisse (Rebecca Legendre), Joana Preiss (Esther). Directed by Frederic Mermoud and produced by Damien Couvreur and Tonie Marshall. Screenplay by Mermoud and Pascal Arnold.

Accomplices coils through two stories, cutting between them as they converge, as we know they will, because the film has opened with a corpse floating in the river Seine. This body, as a flashback establishes, belongs to a boy about nineteen, and the film will watch as he meets a cute girl in a cyber café and leads her into his dangerous world. The other story involves two police inspectors, who begin with the corpse.

Sometimes when a movie cuts between parallel stories it's tiresome. Not this one. The director, Frederic Mermoud, does an interesting thing with time: As the cops are working their way back from the dead body, the other story works its way forward to the point that the body became dead. Then the stories join up and conclude in a surprising and particularly satisfying way.

Vincent (Cyril Descours) is a hustler who meets his male clients in hotel rooms. He meets Rebecca (Nina Meurisse), likes her, gets her phone number, and they start seeing each other. He says he works in real estate—unlikely, given his scruffy appearance and the shabby mobile home he lives in. She is bourgeois but ready for the wild side, and they fall truly in love, like Bonnie and Clyde and other couples where crime is in the mix.

Vincent eventually tells Rebecca what he really does, and the way the movie charts her reaction is touchingly realistic. She learns of his world and stirs the jealousy of his pimp—or *friend,* as he considers him. It's thrilling for her to glimpse his outlaw life, and fun when they use prostitution income to pay cash for sneakers.

Herve (Gilbert Melki) and Karine (Emmanuelle Devos) are like a long-established couple, skilled in police work, functioning expertly together, sharing personal feelings. We think it's a possibility they might hook up, but the plot isn't that obvious. The film is a police procedural explaining how they begin with a nameless body and find their way back to Vincent's associates and clients. One interview, with a businesswoman who shared Vincent with her husband, is startling: The woman is forthcoming, matter-of-fact, defiant.

Without making a big deal out of it, *Accomplices* puts several plausible murder suspects onstage, including Rebecca, who disappeared the day of Vincent's murder. It's like an Agatha Christie in which lots of people have the opportunity and the motive. But Mermoud works so close to the characters, sees them in such detail, that only later do we pull back and observe the workings of the plot.

The original English title of the film was *Partners,* and that would have been accurate. It's about two partnerships. The one is the sad, doomed story of Vincent and Rebecca, incapable of dealing with the risks they run. The other is about how Herve and Karine shy away from risks in their lonely personal lives; how police routine creates a way for them to spend most of their waking hours together without having to deal with the sleeping hours.

I appreciate the way French films, in particular, often approach their characters at eye level. There's no artificial heightening. No music pounding out emotional instruction. They're cool, curious, looking for performances with the tone of plausible life. All four of these actors are completely natural in front of the camera.

You may have seen Emmanuelle Devos in films such as *Read My Lips* (2001) or *The Beat That My Heart Skipped* (2005); she's in the wonderful *L'Origin,* still unreleased, about a small-town mayor and a desperate con man. She's always attractive, never distractingly so, and comes equipped with intelligence and hidden motives. I like actors who make me want to figure them out.

Accomplices is technically a murder mystery. But the murder is only what happens. A lot of other things could have happened, and the story plays fair with the fateful role that chance takes. You would even argue that no one is actually murdered in this movie, and that when they die it is simply the result of bad decisions.

Adam ★ ★ ½

PG-13, 97 m., 2009

Hugh Dancy (Adam Raki), Rose Byrne (Beth Buchwald), Frankie Faison (Harlan), Mark Linn Baker (Mr. Klieber), Amy Irving (Rebecca Buchwald), Peter Gallagher (Marty Buchwald). Directed by Max Mayer and produced by Leslie Urdang, Miranda de Pencier, and Dean Vanech. Screenplay by Mayer.

Adam seems to be a good catch for a young woman. He's good-looking, works as an engineer, has a big, comfy apartment, is fascinated by astronomy, and knows lots and lots of stuff. On the other hand, he has Asperger's syndrome. Beth has never met anyone like him. He behaves in social situations with an honesty that approaches cruelty and doesn't seem much aware of that.

Adam, the story of a romance involving this unlikely couple, would seem even more unlikely if Beth herself weren't self-centered. Perhaps it takes a man even less outgoing to inspire her nurturing side. At first Adam simply offends her with his baffling objectivity. Then he explains, "I have Asperger's," and she understands. If she knows the term, it's surprising she hasn't already arrived at that diagnosis.

Asperger's is sometimes described as high-functioning autism, although some argue the conditions are not related. The syndrome produces people who can be quite intelligent and functioning, but lack ordinary social skills or insights. Adam (Hugh Dancy) does not know, for example, that when a proud young mother shows off her cute new baby, he should ooh and aah. There is not a single ooh or aah in him.

Yet he feels a perplexing attraction to Beth (Rose Byrne). He even—what's this?—experiences sexual feelings for another person for perhaps the first time in his life. Beth is touched. Adam's condition draws her out of her own self-absorption. When he faces a daunting job interview, she coaches him: "Look the other person in the eye. Seem interested. Don't go on autopilot with one of your streams of information. Look like you want the job."

In a way, she could be coaching him about how to behave toward herself. And indeed such coaching is one of the forms of therapy used with Asperger's. He responds slowly, awkwardly, with breaches of behavior that at times infuriate her. The film somehow extracts from their situation a sweet, difficult relationship, although it's a good question how she finds the will to persist.

The film complicates their story with one about Beth's parents, Rebecca and Marty (Amy Irving and Peter Gallagher). They're concerned that she broke up with a suitable young man and now brings Adam home. They're also worried by a court case charging that Marty, an accountant, misrepresented a client's books. There are even courtroom scenes touching on this separate drama that I'm not sure really relate to the central story.

Adam himself seems completely isolated except for Beth and his only other friend, Harlan (Frankie Faison). Harlan gives him lifts, has lunch with him, advises him, instinctively understands him. These two accept each other without question, and Adam needs Harlan, although it's unclear if he realizes just how much.

Hugh Dancy and Rose Byrne, he from England, she from Australia, have seamless American accents, and make a pleasant couple. You may remember her as Diana, the grown-up daughter of the little girl at the beginning of *Knowing,* who wrote down the numbers. As her parents, Irving and Gallagher are always plausible, never over the top, showing that her father, too, has had his difficulties in communicating and her mother knows all about that.

The film has a storybook ending—literally, from a children's book Beth writes. It's unclear how much of a storybook lifetime the two will have together. *Adam* wraps up their story in too tidy a package, insisting on finding the upbeat in the murky, and missing the chance to be more thoughtful about this challenging situation.

The Adjustment Bureau ★ ★ ★

PG-13, 105 m., 2011

Matt Damon (David Norris), Emily Blunt (Elise Sellas), Anthony Mackie (Harry Mitchell), John Slattery (Richardson), Michael Kelly (Charlie Traynor), Terence Stamp (Thompson). Directed by George Nolfi and produced by Nolfi, Bill Carraro, Michael Hackett, and Chris Moore. Screenplay by Nolfi, based on the short story "Adjustment Team" by Philip K. Dick.

Here I go again. I'll be helpless to stop myself. *The Adjustment Bureau* is about the conflict between free will and predestination, and right there you have the whole dilemma of life, don't you? Either it makes a difference what you choose to do, or the book has already been written and all you can do is turn the pages.

That these questions are raised in a science-fiction thriller with a romance at its core should not be surprising. Sci-fi offers storytellers the freedom of tinkering with realism, and few writers did that with more complexity than Philip K. Dick. This movie, written and directed by George Nolfi, is based on a Dick story about a legion of "adjusters" who move a strange thing there and a known thing here, just to be sure everything proceeds according to plan. Whose plan? The adjusters aren't big on explanations. They're like undercover agents for the higher power of your choice.

But the best-laid plans of mice and men sometimes stray. Random chance barges in, and its interference must be corrected. In *The Adjustment Bureau*, Matt Damon plays a congressional candidate named David Norris, who walks into a men's room he has every reason to believe is empty, and who should emerge from one of the stalls but Elise Sellas (Emily Blunt). What was she doing there? You don't cross-examine a Meet Cute. The important thing is, these two people, who were never intended to meet, have that particular chemistry that means they're a perfect romantic match. They know it, we know it, and when their eyes and lips meet, their stories become entangled.

Philip Dick was intrigued by devices that allowed him to examine the mechanisms by which life unfolds. I think he voted for free will in the short run (the span of intelligent life on Earth, say), evolution for the middle distance (things develop according to underlying principles), and predestination in the long run (the universe will entropy and cease). A man and a woman whose eyes Meet Cute need only be concerned about the very short run.

In the movie, David Norris becomes aware of certain men wearing suits and fedoras who strangely appear in his life. He meets two of these: Mitchell and Richardson (Anthony Mackie and John Slattery). They explain that they work for a bureau that makes corrections when things go slightly wrong. For example, David and Elise were not intended to meet. What was she doing in the men's room, anyway? For her sake and his, David must not see her again.

OK, so this is where it gets intriguing. They do meet again, once again by pure chance. But *this* time, they recognize each other, you see, because they had met earlier. It is possible the second time they see each other was intended to be the first time, in which case (if you follow me) they would not necessarily even notice each other. Seeing a woman on the bus isn't the same thing as getting into a conversation with her in a men's room. So answer me this: When the adjusters urge David to forget about Elise and never see her again, aren't they asking him to exercise his free will? Aren't they implying he has a choice?

So you might think, but *The Adjustment Bureau* reveals a hidden level of reality by which players can be yanked out of the game. David is confronted in a cavernous industrial space and warned that if he doesn't straighten up, his memory will be erased. This space is reached through a doorway to a place that has no logical possibility of existence; it must be like the bedroom beyond Jupiter in *2001*, which was summoned by a greater intelligence to provide the illusion of a familiar space for an unwitting subject.

The plot develops into a cat-and-mouse game of the mind, in which David and Elise, in love and feeling as if they're destined for each other, try to outsmart or elude the men in the suits and hats. This is fun, and because Matt Damon and Emily Blunt have an easy rapport, it doesn't seem as preposterous as it is. Beneath its apparent sci-fi levels, a romantic comedy lurks here.

If you're like me, you're thinking the universe in this movie is run by a singularly inefficient designer. There is no room for chance in predestination. If there is a plan, you can't allow tinkering. There's a well-known sci-fi precept that warns if you travel back far enough in time and step on the wrong insect, you could wipe out the future. By the time we meet a very, very serious senior adviser named Thompson (Terence Stamp), we begin to suspect that his employer has delusions of grandeur. Thompson gives the appearance of being firmly in control and knowing all the right buttons to push, but his problem is David and Elise have seen behind the curtain and realize they need not be instruments of a plan. There's even the intriguing possibility that the adjusters themselves have some freedom of choice.

The Adjustment Bureau is a smart and good movie that could have been a great one if it had been a little more daring. I suspect the filmmakers were reluctant to follow its implications too far. What David and Elise signify by their adventures, I think, is that we're all in this together, and we're all on our own. If you follow that through, the implications are treacherous to some, not all, religions. In the short term, however, the movie is a sorta heartwarming entertainment.

Adoration ★ ★ ★

R, 101 m., 2009

Arsinee Khanjian (Sabine), Devon Bostick (Simon), Scott Speedman (Tom), Rachel Blanchard (Rachel), Noam Jenkins (Sami), Kenneth Walsh (Morris). Directed by Atom Egoyan and produced by Egoyan, Simone Urdl, and Jennifer Weis. Screenplay by Egoyan.

Atom Egoyan is fascinated by the way life coils back on itself. He uses coincidences and chance meetings not as plot devices but as illustrations of the ways we are linked across generations and national boundaries. His characters are often not completely connected to where they find themselves, and they bring along personal, sometimes secret, associations. These often reflect much larger realities in the outer world.

Adoration circles around a central event or nonevent. A report is read about a woman who falls in love with a man from the Middle East. His family is in Israel, he says, although I am not sure that is true. She becomes pregnant. He is unhappy at first but later overjoyed. They seem deeply in love. He wants her to fly to meet his parents in Bethlehem. For business reasons, he must take a later flight.

In an age of terrorism, this triggers alarms, but not for her. What becomes of these people and the flight is not for me to relate now. We see them only in flashbacks. The story presents more than one way they possibly did meet. The film is about other people in their lives—before, and after, they met. It is also about how these other people think about what they did and didn't do.

The buried issues involve nationalism, religion, and prejudice. But this is not a message film. It is about people trying to find their way through emotional labyrinths. We are not always sure what these are, or what really happened, or what these people really feel about it, or their motives. Neither are they. *Adoration* isn't confusion; it's about confused people. Most movies make it easy for us. The central characters know what they want, and we understand.

Here there is the illusion that we are feeling our way along with these people. The most important connection, although we don't realize it for a while, is a Toronto high school drama teacher named Sabine (Arsinee Khanjian, Egoyan's muse). She reads a story about the original air travel incident as an exercise in French class. Why that story? An exercise in comprehending spoken French. And something more . . .

A student named Simon (Devon Bostick) transforms this into a first-person story, with his mother as the pregnant woman and his father as the treacherous fiancé. Simon's parents are dead, and he lives with his Uncle Tom (Scott Speedman). Sabine encourages him to read his story to the class as if it were true—as an acting exercise, she says. The story is picked up in Internet chat rooms involving Simon's high school friends.

I don't want to say too much about what is

real or imagined here, and nothing at all about the secret connection the teacher Sabine is hiding. Egoyan contrives meetings between Sabine and Tom with two rather brilliant sequences that keep us guessing even while played out in full view. And there are flashbacks to the couple in Simon's story and to his actual parents, played by the same actors, so that, as it frequently does in Egoyan's films, reality takes on uncertain implications.

Throbbing beneath are ideas about terrorism, about Israeli-Palestinian feelings, about Muslims in Canada, and about the role of the Internet in creating factoids that might as well be real. Statements are made involving these subjects, but they're all suspended in an incomplete resolution; the movie withholds closure. There are areas only suggested: the boy's anger at his father, the use of the original story to him, the circumstances of two deaths, the placing of blame.

Some viewers may find the film confusing; I found it absorbing. One problem with reviewing an Egoyan film is that you find yourself struggling to describe a fractured plot line and what characters (and we) may believe at one point and not later. This can be confusing and unsatisfactory. Yet the film presents emotions that are clear. Why does Egoyan weave a tangled web? Because his characters are caught in it. Our lives consist of stories we tell ourselves about our lives. They may be based on reality, but not necessarily, and maybe they shouldn't always be. If you couldn't do a little rewriting, how could you stand things?

Adventureland ★ ★ ★

R, 107 m., 2009

Jesse Eisenberg (James Brennan), Kristen Stewart (Em Lewin), Martin Starr (Joel Schiffman), Bill Hader (Bobby), Kristen Wiig (Paulette), Ryan Reynolds (Mike Connell), Margarita Levieva (Lisa P.). Directed by Greg Mottola and produced by Ted Hope, Anne Carey, and Sidney Kimmel. Screenplay by Mottola.

It is a truth of twenty-somethings that if you have a crappy summer job with other twenty-somethings, the way to take your mind off work is daydreaming of sex with your workmates. You are trapped there together, eight or ten hours a day for three months, right, so what else is there to make you dance to unheard melodies?

Take James. Here he is, all set to move to New York, and his dad loses his job and he's forced to take a job at a shabby Pittsburgh amusement park. All of the rides look secondhand, all of the games are rigged, and all of the prizes look like surplus. Your job is to encourage customers even more luckless than you are to throw baseballs at targets that are glued down, while inflamed with hopes of taking home a Big Ass Panda. That's what Bobby the owner calls them when he instructs you, "Nobody *ever* wins a Big Ass Panda."

Director Greg Mottola, who made the rather wonderful *Superbad*, is back now with a sweeter story, more quietly funny, again about a hero who believes he may be a virgin outstaying his shelf life. Jesse Eisenberg, from *The Squid and the Whale*, plays James, who has a degree in Renaissance studies. (The movie is set in the 1980s, and there may still be a few jobs around.) He's out of his element at Adventureland; Bobby has to coach him to fake enthusiasm when he announces the horse race game, where you advance your horse by rolling balls into holes. His performance reminded me uncannily of my last visit to Dave & Buster's.

Most of the male employees in the park lust for Lisa P. (Margarita Levieva), whose Adventureland T-shirt unfortunately advertises Rides Rides Rides. James is much more interested in Em (Kristen Stewart), who is quieter and deeper (Games Games Games). She's smart, quirky, and seems more grown-up than the others. A quick rapport springs up, despite her edge on James in sexual experience. She thinks he's kinda sweet. They talk about subjects that require more than one sentence.

This romance takes fragile bloom while Mottola, also the screenwriter, rotates through a plot involving James's friends, one of whom expresses his devotion by hitting him in the netherlands every time he sees him. We cut often to the owner, Bobby, and his wife, Paulette (Kristen Wiig), who are lovebirds and have firm ideas about how every job at the park should be performed, which doesn't endear them to the employees because they're usually right. Oh, and then there's Connell (Ryan Reynolds), the good-looking maintenance man, who is married, and why am I telling you that?

As the summer lurches between deadly boredom and sudden emergencies (someone wins a Big Ass Panda), James and Em grow closer. This is absorbing because they reveal themselves as smarter than anyone else realizes. From his earlier work, I expected to like Eisenberg. What surprised me was how much I admired Kristen Stewart, who in *Twilight* was playing below her grade level. Here is an actress ready to do important things. Together, and with the others, they make *Adventureland* more real and more touching than it may sound.

I worked two summers at Crystal Lake Pool in Urbana. I was technically a lifeguard and got free Cokes, but I rarely got to sit in the lifeguard chair. As the junior member of the staff, I was assigned to Poop Patrol, which involved plunging deep into the depths with a flyswatter and a bucket. Not a lot of status when you were applauded while carrying the bucket to the men's room. ("No spilling!" my boss, Oscar Adams, warned me.) But there was another lifeguard named Toni and—oh, never mind. I don't think she ever knew.

After.Life ★ ★ ½

R, 97 m., 2010

Liam Neeson (Eliot Deacon), Christina Ricci (Anna Taylor), Justin Long (Paul Conran), Chandler Canterbury (Jack), Josh Charles (Tom Peterson), Celia Weston (Beatrice Taylor). Directed by Agnieszka Wojtowicz-Vosloo and produced by Brad Michael Gilbert, Bill Perkins, and Celine Rattray. Screenplay by Wojtowicz-Vosloo, Paul Vosloo, and Jakub Korolczuk.

"You people!" says Eliot Deacon sadly, and with a touch of frustration. He is referring to the dead. They are whiners. They're not ready to die, they've got unfinished business, there are things they still desire, the death certificate is mistaken, and on and on and on. Deacon, as a mortician, has to put up with this.

Take Anna as an example. She drove away from a disastrous dinner with her boyfriend, was speeding on a rainy night, and was killed in a crash. Now here she is on a porcelain slab in his prep room, telling him there's been some mistake. Deacon tries to reason with her. He even shows her the coroner's signature on the death certificate. But no. She's alive, as he can clearly see. Besides, if he's so sure she's dead, why does he carefully lock the door from the outside whenever he leaves the room?

After.Life is a strange movie that never clearly declares whether Anna (Christina Ricci) is dead or alive. Well, not alive in the traditional sense, but alive in a sort of middle state between life and death. Her body is presumably dead. She has no pulse, and we assume her blood has been replaced by embalming fluid. Yet she protests, argues, can sit up and move around. Is Deacon (Liam Neeson) the only one who can see this? Maybe he's fantasizing? No, the little boy Jack (Chandler Canterbury) sees her, too, through a window.

Jack tells her boyfriend, Paul (Justin Long). He believes it. He's had a great deal of difficulty accepting her death. He still has the engagement ring he planned to offer her on that fateful night. He tries to break into the funeral home. He causes a scene at the police station. He sounds like a madman to them.

After.Life is a horror film involving the familiar theme of being alive when the world thinks you're dead. It couples that with a possibility that has chilled me ever since the day when, at far too young an age, I pulled down Poe from my dad's bookshelf, looked at the table of contents, and turned straight to "The Premature Burial." From Anna's point of view, she's still alive when the earth starts thudding on the coffin. From Deacon's point of view? Yes, I think from his POV, too.

From ours? The director, Agnieszka Wojtowicz-Vosloo, says audiences split about half and half. That's how I split. Half of me seizes on evidence that she's still alive, and the other half notices how the film diabolically undercuts all that evidence. I think the correct solution is: Anna is a character in a horror film that leaves her state deliberately ambiguous.

Neeson's performance as Deacon is ambiguous but sincere. He has been working with these people for years. He explains he has the "gift" of speaking with them. And little Jack, the eyewitness? Oh, but Deacon thinks he has the gift, too. So once again, you don't know what to believe. Perhaps the gift is supernatural, or perhaps it's madness or a delusion.

The film has many of the classic scenes of horror movies set in mortuaries. The chilling stainless steel paraphernalia. The work late at night. The moonlit graveyard. The burial. The opened grave. Even her desperate nails shredding the lining inside the coffin—although we see that from Anna's POV and no one else's.

I think, in a way, the film shortchanges itself by not coming down on one side or the other. As it stands, it's a framework for horror situations, but cannot be anything deeper. Yes, we can debate it endlessly—but pointlessly, because there is no solution. We can enjoy the suspense of the opening scenes and some of the drama. The performances are in keeping with the material. But toward the end, when we realize that the entire reality of the film is problematical, there is a certain impatience. It's as if our chain is being yanked.

Agora ★ ★ ★

NO MPAA RATING, 141 m., 2010

Rachel Weisz (Hypatia), Max Minghella (Davus), Oscar Isaac (Orestes), Ashraf Barhom (Ammonius), Michael Lonsdale (Theon), Rupert Evans (Synesius), Homayoun Ershadi (Aspasius), Sammy Samir (Cyril), Richard Durden (Olympius), Omar Mostafa (Isidorus), Oshri Cohen (Medorus). Directed by Alejandro Amenabar and produced by Alvaro Augustin and Fernando Bovaira. Screenplay by Amenabar and Mateo Gil.

I went to see *Agora* expecting an epic with swords, sandals, and sex. I found swords and sandals, some unexpected opinions about sex, and a great deal more. This is a movie about ideas, a drama based on the ancient war between science and superstition. At its center is a woman who in the fourth century A.D. was a scientist, mathematician, philosopher, astronomer, and teacher, respected in Egypt although women were not expected to be any of those things.

Hypatia (Rachel Weisz) was born into the family business. Her father, Theon (Michael Lonsdale), was the curator of the Library of Alexandria, which had as its mission "collecting all the world's knowledge." Scholars traveled there from across the ancient world, doing research and donating manuscripts. It was destroyed by Christians in 391 A.D., and *Agora* takes place in the years surrounding that incalculable loss.

The film's title refers to the name for the public assembly places in ancient Greek city-states. The library was such an agora, and we see Hypatia teaching a class of young men, who listen to her with open admiration. There's an early indication that this won't be a routine *Troy*-like exercise in CGI action scenes: Hypatia actually *does* teach something, using the first scale model of planetary motion to deduce, centuries before Galileo, that the earth cannot be the center of the universe.

Hypatia has three students completely under her spell: Davus (Max Minghella), Synesius (Rupert Evans), and Orestes (Oscar Isaac). All make the error of feeling lust, Orestes least subtly. Hypatia seems devoid of sexual feeling; perhaps she believes her vocation prohibits it. Her method of rejecting Orestes is brutally direct. Although Rachel Weisz may be beautiful, in the performance she makes no effort to exploit that, and is single-minded in her dedication to knowledge.

The director, Alejandro Amenabar, re-creates the Alexandria of Hypatia's time with a mixture of sets and effects, showing it at the tipping point between Greek and Roman paganism and the new religion of Christianity. As she studies with and under her father, drawing from countless parchment scrolls in the library, outside in the city the Christians burn with a fearful intensity. Hypatia herself is not interested in religion; she feels passion only for her ideas.

Neither pagans nor Christians are pacifists. Both sides possess that peculiar certainty that their opponents must by definition be evil. Blood is shed. Foolishly believing they hold the upper hand, the pagans led by Orestes sponsor a bloodletting, only to learn in a savage lesson that there are now more Christians than they imagined. This warfare culminates in the destruction of the library. Hypatia races with her students to rescue armloads of scrolls, a few of which may literally have been responsible for our surviving texts from Aristotle and other Greeks.

In sword-and-sandal epics, the Christians are without fail the good guys. Not here. Christians and pagans are equally blinded by the conviction that those who disagree deserve death. After the rise of the Christians, they grow even more militant; one group wears black robes and searches the streets for dissenters, heretics, and Jews.

There is historical truth here. The actual teachings of Jesus are often imperfectly observed by his followers. The film also has unmistakable parallels to militant Islam and to the sectarian conflicts in the Middle East and elsewhere. The movie doesn't make as much as you might expect about Hypatia's gender; possibly the subjugation of women was so unconsciously and universally accepted that, in some sense, she was seen less as a woman than as a daughter teaching the lessons of her father.

That Hypatia was a genius seems beyond question. Her invention, the hydrometer, is being used in the Gulf of Mexico at this moment to distinguish oil from water by their specific densities. Although *Agora* avoids the temptation to sneak in a romantic subplot, it gets mileage out of her character as a focus of emotional intrigue for her male students, who would have never seen a woman anything like her.

Alejandro Amenabar seems drawn to stories about the determination of the intellect to work in the real world. His *The Sea Inside* (2004) starred Javier Bardem as a paralyzed man who fought for the right to die. In *Open Your Eyes* (1997), a disfigured man struggles to express his love for a woman. The underrated *The Others* (2001) starred Nicole Kidman as a woman compelled to prove her ideas of ghosts have objective reality. Here a woman finds the earth circles the sun, but moves in indifference to her ideas.

Ajami ★ ★ ★

NO MPAA RATING, 120 m., 2010

Shahir Kabaha (Omar), Ibrahim Frege (Malek), Fouad Habash (Nasri), Youssef Sahwani (Abu Elias), Ranin Karim (Hadir), Eran Naim (Dando), Scandar Copti (Binj). Directed by Scandar Copti and Yaron Shani and produced by Moshe Danon, Thanassis Karathanos, and Talia Kleinhendler. Screenplay by Copti and Shani.

Americans didn't know we had the right idea, but we did. We welcomed those from foreign lands (or, in some cases, forced them to come here). Then we shook them up together and left them to sort things out. We have every race, ethnicity, and religion, and that helps. Unhappy are those who live in a land with only a few.

Consider Israel, where Jews, Arabs, Muslims, and Christians by and large think it is extremely important that they are Jews, Arabs, Muslims, and Christians. There is a growing minority that says, hey, here we all are together, and since nobody is budging, let's get along. Most people apparently think someone should budge and it's not them.

Ajami is the latest and one of the most harrowing films set along the religious divides in Israel. It was cowritten and codirected by an Israeli and a Palestinian, and set in Jaffa, technically a part of Tel-Aviv, which has high crime and unemployment rates. The focus is on mean streets that Scorsese might understand. Gangsters, cops, and drug dealers are tossed in with religious conflicts and the ancient Romeo and Juliet dilemma. God help anyone who marries outside their tribe.

I have never seen a film from either Israeli or Palestinian filmmakers that makes a case for anything other than coexistence. There are probably such films. But the dominant theme is the tragedy of the social divides, the waste, the loss, the violence that often claims innocent victims.

Why, in an area where tension and indeed hatred runs so high, aren't there more partisan or sectarian films? Beginning with the advantage of ignorance, I'll speculate that those Palestinians and Israelis who are inclined to make feature films are drawn from the elites of their societies. They see more widely and clearly. They may be better educated. They are more instinctively liberal. They've grown beyond the group mentality.

Ah, but there is still family. No matter how advanced your views, blood ties run deep, especially when reinforced by religion. A young couple may fall in love outside their tribe, but their fathers and uncles and cousins to remote degrees will feel threatened by their love, and God will be invoked on both sides. It is the same when a relative is murdered. Instincts demand revenge.

Ajami is about an interlocking series of such situations, starting in the first place when a man is shot dead. Then another man is mistakenly killed in revenge. Was he mistaken for the original killer? No, he was mistaken for a member of the original killer's family—which he was, although not the correct member. Now two people are dead, more vengeance is required, nothing has been proven, and everyone involved is convinced they are in the right.

Calm heads try to prevail and stop the killing. The actual original killer (are you following?) is levied with a fine. To pay it, he finds he must sell drugs. That means we are now headed into gang territory. The source of the drugs is a Palestinian in love with a Jewish girl. An Israeli cop becomes involved in the case. I won't describe more. I'm not sure I can. It's clear enough in the film who is who, but I suspect even the characters lose track of the actual origins of their vendetta. What happens is that hatred continues to claim lives in a sort of domino effect.

The film doesn't reduce itself to a series of Mafia-style killings, in which death is a way of doing business. There are situations in which characters kill as a means of self-defense. And the filmmakers, Scandar Copti and Yaron Shani, by and large show characters on all sides who essentially would like simply to be left alone to get on with their lives. Few of them possess the *personal* hatred necessary to fuel murder. But the sectarian divide acts as an artery to carry murder to everyone downstream. Was that a mixed metaphor, or what?

The specifics of the plot in *Ajami* aren't as important as the impact of many sad moments built up one after another. Hatred is like the weather. You don't agree with the rain but still you get wet. What justifies this is the "honor" of your family, your religion, your tribe. The film deplores this. So do we all, when we stand back. The film has no solution. Nor is there one, until people find the strength to place more value upon an individual than upon his group. Sometimes I fear we're all genetically programmed not to do that. One solution is the mixing of gene pools so that groups are differently perceived. I'm not holding my breath.

Alice in Wonderland ★ ★ ★

PG, 108 m., 2010

Johnny Depp (Mad Hatter), Mia Wasikowska (Alice), Anne Hathaway (Mirana, the White Queen), Helena Bonham Carter (Iracebeth, the Red Queen), Crispin Glover (Stayne, the Knave of Hearts), Matt Lucas (Tweedledee/Tweedledum). And the voices of: Stephen Fry (Cheshire Cat), Michael Sheen (White Rabbit), Alan Rickman (Absolem), Timothy Spall (Bayard), Barbara Windsor (Dormouse), Christopher Lee (Jabberwocky). Directed by Tim Burton and produced by Burton, Joe Roth, Jennifer Todd, Suzanne Todd, and Richard D. Zanuck. Screenplay by Linda Woolverton, based on the books *Alice's Adventures in Wonderland* and *Through the Looking-Glass* by Lewis Carroll.

As a young reader, I found *Alice in Wonderland* creepy and rather distasteful. Alice's adventures played like a series of encounters with characters whose purpose was to tease, puzzle, and torment her. Few children would want to go to Wonderland, and none would want to stay. The problem may be that I encountered the book too young and was put off by the alarming John Tenniel illustrations. Why did Alice have such deep, dark eye sockets? Why couldn't Wonderland be cozy like the world of Pooh? Watching the 1951 film, I feared the Cheshire Cat was about to tell me something I didn't want to know.

Tim Burton's new 3-D version of *Alice in Wonderland* answers my childish questions. This has never been a children's story. There's even a little sadism embedded in Carroll's fantasy. I think of uncles who tickle their nieces until they scream. *Alice* plays better as an adult hallucination, which is how Burton rather brilliantly interprets it until a pointless third act flies off the rails. It was a wise idea by Burton and his screenwriter, Linda Woolverton, to devise a reason why Alice (Mia Wasikowska) is now a grown girl in her late teens, revisiting a

Wonderland that remains much the same, as fantasy worlds must always do.

Burton is above all a brilliant visual artist, and his film is a pleasure to regard; I look forward to admiring it in 2-D, where it will look brighter and more colorful. No artist who can create these images is enhancing them in any way by adding the annoying third dimension. But never mind that.

He brings to Carroll's characters an appearance as distinctive and original as Tenniel's classic illustrations. These are not retreads of familiar cartoon images. They're grotesques, as they should be, from the hydrocephalic forehead of the Red Queen (Helena Bonham Carter) to Tweedledee and Tweedledum (Matt Lucas), who seem to have been stepped on. Wonderland itself is not limited to necessary props, such as a tree limb for the Cheshire Cat and a hookah for the caterpillar, but extends indefinitely as an alarming undergrowth beneath a lowering sky. Why you can see the sky from beneath the Earth is not a fair question. (The landscape was designed by Robert Stromberg of *Avatar.*)

When we meet her again, Alice has decidedly mixed feelings about her original trip down the rabbit hole, but begins to recall Wonderland more favorably as she's threatened with an arranged marriage with Hamish Ascot (Leo Bill), a conceited snot-nose twit. At the moment of truth in the wedding ceremony, she impulsively scampers away to follow another rabbit down another rabbit hole, and finds below that she is actually remembered from her previous visit.

Burton shows us Wonderland as a perturbing place where the inhabitants exist for little apparent reason other than to be peculiar and obnoxious. Do they reproduce? Most species seem to have only one member, as if Nature quit while she was ahead. The ringleader is the Mad Hatter, played by Johnny Depp, that rare actor who can treat the most bizarre characters with perfect gravity. Whomever he plays (Edward Scissorhands, Sweeney Todd, Jack Sparrow, Willy Wonka, Ichabod Crane), he is that character through and through.

This is a Wonderland that holds perils for Alice, played by Mia Wasikowska with beauty and pluck. The Red Queen wishes her ill and the White Queen (Anne Hathaway) wishes her well, perhaps because both are formed according to the rules of Wonderland queens. To be sure, the insecure White Queen doesn't exhaust herself in making Alice welcome. The Queens, the Mad Hatter, Alice, the Knave of Hearts (Crispin Glover), and presumably Tweedledee and Tweedledum are versions of humans; the others are animated, voiced with great zest by such as Stephen Fry (Cheshire), Alan Rickman (Absolem the Caterpillar), Michael Sheen (White Rabbit), and Timothy Spall, Barbara Windsor, and Christopher Lee.

The film is enchanting in its mordant way until, unfortunately, it arrives at its third act. Here I must apologize to faithful readers for repeating myself. Time after time I complain when a film develops an intriguing story and then dissolves it in routine and boring action. We've *seen* every conceivable battle sequence, every duel, all carnage, countless showdowns, and all-too-long fights to the finish.

Why does *Alice in Wonderland* have to end with an action sequence? Characters not rich enough? Story run out? Little minds, jazzed by sugar from the candy counter, might get too worked up without it? Or is it that executives, not trusting their artists and timid in the face of real stories, demand an action climax as insurance? Insurance of what? That the story will have a beginning and a middle but nothing so tedious as an ending?

Alien Trespass ★ ★

PG, 90 m., 2009

Eric McCormack (Ted Lewis/Urp), Jenni Baird (Tammy), Robert Patrick (Vern), Dan Lauria (Chief Dawson), Jody Thompson (Lana Lewis). Directed by R. W. Goodwin and produced by Goodwin and James Swift. Screenplay by Steven P. Fisher.

Alien Trespass is a sincere attempt to make a film that looks like one of those 1950s B movies where a monster from outer space terrorized a small town, which was almost always in the desert. Small, to save on extras and travel. In the desert, because if you headed east from Hollywood that's where you were, and if you headed west you were making a pirate picture.

The movie is in color, which in the 1950s was uncommon, but otherwise it's a knowing replication of the look and feel of those pictures, about things with jaws, tentacles, claws, weapons that shot sparks, and eyes that shot laser beams at people, only they weren't known as laser beams but as Deadly Rays. Facing them are plucky locals, dressed in work clothes from Sears, standing behind their open car doors and looking up to watch awkward special effects that are coming—coming!—this way!

The movie doesn't bend over backward to be "bad." It tries to be the best bad movie that it can be. A lot of its deliberate badness involves effects some viewers might not notice. For example: bad back projection in shots looking back from the dashboard at people in the front seat. In the 1950s, before CGI, the car never left the sound stage, and in the rear window they projected footage of what it was allegedly driving past. Since people were presumed not to study the rear window intently, they got away with murder. In *Casablanca,* Rick and Ilsa drove from the Champs-Elysées to the countryside instantly.

The plot: Astronomer Ted Lewis (Eric McCormack) and his sexpot wife, Lana (Jody Thompson), are grilling cow-sized steaks in the backyard when something shoots overhead and crashes in the mountains. The sexpot wife is an accurate touch: The monster genre cast pinups like Mamie Van Doren and Cleo Moore, who were featured on the posters with Deadly Rays shooting down their cleavage.

Ted goes to investigate. When he returns, his body has been usurped by Urp, an alien. Urp means well. He needs help to track down another alien who arrived on the same flying saucer, named the Ghota, which has one eye, enough to qualify it as a BEM, or a Bug-Eyed Monster. The Ghota consumes people in order to grow, divide, and conquer. Sort of like B.O.B. in *Monsters vs. Aliens,* which is *also* a send-up of 1950s BEM movies. So far, Todd Haynes's *Far from Heaven* (2002) is the only movie ever made in tribute to a *great* movie of the 1950s.

The Ghota is battled by Urp and his plucky new buddy Tammy (Jenni Baird), a local waitress who is a lot more game than Lana. As nearly as I can recall, in the 1950s good girls were never named Lana and bad ones were never named Tammy. There are also hapless but earnest local cops (Robert Patrick and Dan Lauria) and an assortment of Threatened Townspeople. Also great shots of the Lewis family home, separated from the desert by a white picket fence, surrounded by the age-old story of the shifting, whispering sands.

Alien Trespass, directed by R. W. Goodwin (*The X Files* on TV) from a screenplay by Steven P. Fisher, is obviously a labor of love. But why? Is there a demand for cheesy 1950s sci-fi movies not met by the existing supply? Will younger audiences consider it to be merely inept, and not inept with an artistic intention? Here is a movie more suited to Comic-Con or the World Science Fiction Convention than to your neighborhood multiplex.

If you must see a science fiction movie about a threat from beyond Earth, there's one right now that I think is great: *Knowing.* If you're looking for a *bad* sci-fi movie about a threat, etc., most of the nation's critics mistakenly believe it qualifies. How can you lose? "From beyond the stars—a mysterious force strikes terror into the hearts of men!"

All About Steve ★ ½

PG-13, 98 m., 2009

Sandra Bullock (Mary Horowitz), Thomas Haden Church (Hartman Hughes), Bradley Cooper (Steve), Ken Jeong (Angus). Directed by Phil Traill and produced by Sandra Bullock and Mary McLaglen. Screenplay by Kim Barker.

It is not much fun to laugh at a crazy person. None, I would say. Sandra Bullock plays a character who is bonkers in *All About Steve,* which is billed as a comedy but more resembles a perplexing public display of irrational behavior. Seeing her run around as a basket case makes you appreciate Lucille Ball, who could play a dizzy dame and make you like her. Overacting is risky even in a screwball comedy. Perhaps especially.

Bullock plays Mary Horowitz, a crossword puzzle constructor who knows a vast number of words and how they're spelled, but not much about how they might enlighten her. Because her apartment has to be fumigated, she moves back home with her parents. The headline here is how she earned enough to move out in the first place. I may be mistaken, but I think of crossword puzzle construction as more of a second job for smart people.

Anyway, Mary is fortyish and still single, perhaps in part because she wears extraordinarily clumpy shiny red disco boots everywhere, all the time—even on a 5K charity hike, I can only assume. Her parents arrange a blind date with Steve (Bradley Cooper of *The Hangover*), a television cameraman for a cable news network. The network must not be as big as CNN because there's only evidence of one crew: Steve and his on-air talent Hartman Hughes (Thomas Haden Church).

Mary lays her eyes on Steve and wants to lay everything else. This isn't love at first sight; it's erotomania. On their first date, she gives his tonsils a tongue massage. Soon he's fleeing from sightings of her, and she's in hot pursuit. Her desperation extends to a scene where she runs in her disco boots beside the TV news van, breathlessly small-talking to Steve through the window. If Steve had mercy, he would stop or speed up—anything would be better than playing her along.

The crew is assigned to the site of a big breaking story. A group of small deaf children has fallen into a well. Why deaf? Diversity in casting, I guess. It's not like they have to do anything other than be rescued. Mary pursues them to the accident scene, and in a shot destined to go viral on YouTube, she runs across the field behind Steve, waving wildly, and falls into the hole herself.

You see what I mean. The point comes when we're rolling our eyes right along with Mary. But don't get me wrong. I am fond of Sandra Bullock. I've given her some good reviews, as recently as this summer (*The Proposal*). But how does she choose her material? If she does it herself, she needs an agent. If it's done by an agent, she needs to do it herself. The screenplay by Kim Barker requires her to behave in an essentially disturbing way that began to wear on me. It begins as merely peculiar, moves on to miscalculation, and becomes seriously annoying. One of its most unfortunate elements is seeing Bullock so stranded and helpless in a would-be comic frenzy. An actress should never, ever be asked to run beside a van in red disco boots for more than about half a block, and then only if her child is being kidnapped.

All Good Things ★ ★ ★ ½

R, 101 m., 2010

Ryan Gosling (David Marks), Kirsten Dunst (Katie Marks), Frank Langella (Sanford Marks), Lily Rabe (Deborah Lehrman), Philip Baker Hall (Malvern Bump), Michael Esper (Daniel Marks), Diane Venora (Janice Rizzo). Directed by Andrew Jarecki and produced by Jarecki, Michael London, Bruna Papandrea, and Marc Smerling. Screenplay by Smerling and Marcus Hinchey.

All Good Things is based on one of those true stories like Dominick Dunne used to tell so intriguingly in *Vanity Fair.* Let me begin with a brief summary, based on the film because I know nothing about the reality. It involves David Marks, the son of a New York family that owned valuable Forty-second Street real estate in the 1970s. The property at that time was rented to strip clubs, porno shops, massage parlors, and so on. The family, wealthy and private, moved in the best circles, and the nature of its holdings was not widely known. The patriarch, Sanford Marks (Frank Langella), is a commanding man who is hands-on. He often collects the rent in cash. He expects his son to enter the family business. David (Ryan Gosling) wants nothing to do with it. A free spirit of the Woodstock era, he meets Katie (Kirsten Dunst), and together they escape from New York and open a twee Vermont health foods and organic products store named, yes, All Good Things.

Sanford ratchets up the pressure. David caves in and returns to Manhattan, where his wife enjoys a luxurious but unhappy existence. She eventually discovers the nature of the family business. David, meanwhile, begins to change from the loving hippie she fell in love with. Their marriage comes apart. Katie disappears. She is never found again. David is suspected of being involved but never charged, because he appears to have an unquestionable alibi. And I will not reveal more.

The film is the work of Andrew Jarecki, who in 2003 made the remarkable Sundance-winning documentary *Capturing the Friedmans,* about a family and its secrets; the father and one son were charged with child molestation. It's easy to see why this story appealed to him.

The key to the film is in the character of David. One can imagine a scenario in which an overbearing father drives the son to rebellion, but what happens here is more complex and sinister. David seemingly adapts to the lifestyle forced upon him. He plays a role like his father played among Manhattan power brokers and establishment members. He and Katie live in an expensive condo, attend charity events, and so on. Perhaps it is self-hatred that drives him to insist they have an abortion.

Kirsten Dunst is so good here as a woman at a loss to understand who her husband really is and what the true nature of his family involves. The man she married and trusted has undergone the transformation of a Mr. Hyde. What happens is the sort of thing that develops only in fantastical horror stories, but this story apparently did happen in one form or another, and the most incredible details of David's transformation are specifically based on facts revealed during two murder investigations. I choose not to reveal how or where David meets the wonderfully named Malvern Bump (Philip Baker Hall).

The nature of their relationship goes along with where they meet—the place both their lives have bottomed. Hall is one of those actors who seem to have inhabited their characters for years. He needs no explanation because he *exists.* Jarecki offers a possible solution for the enigma of Katie's disappearance and David's alibi. It involves his enigmatic friendship with Janice Rizzo (Diane Venora), and that's enough about that. This film reminded me of Barbet Schroeder's *Reversal of Fortune* (1990), based on the Dominick Dunne-able Klaus von Bulow case.

In both stories, there is every reason to focus on the obvious suspect, except the impossibility of explaining how he could have committed the crime—indeed, if there even *was* a crime. I don't understand David Marks after seeing this film, and I don't know if Andrew Jarecki does. It occurs to me that on my first visits to New York of course I was drawn to Forty-second Street, the port of entry for many a young man from the provinces, and I might have even laid eyes on Sanford or David Marks. Little would I have known.

Amelia ★ ★ ★

PG, 111 m., 2009

Hilary Swank (Amelia Earhart), Richard Gere (George Putnam), Ewan McGregor (Gene Vidal), Christopher Eccleston (Fred Noonan), Joe Anderson (Bill), Cherry Jones (Eleanor Roosevelt), Mia Wasikowska (Elinor Smith). Directed by Mira Nair and produced by Lydia Dean Pilcher, Kevin Hyman, and Ted Waitt. Screenplay by Ronald Bass and Anna Hamilton Phelan.

I am drawn to every news story about the attempts, which still continue, to solve the mystery of Amelia Earhart's disappearance on July 2, 1937. It's pretty clear she ditched at sea, but you just never know. Those clues found on a Pacific atoll are tantalizing. It is not her disappearance but her life that fascinates me.

She was strong, brave, and true, and she looked fabulous in a flight suit. No ladylike decorum for her; before she wed George Putnam she wrote him their marriage would have "dual controls," and said neither one should feel bound to "a medieval code of faithfulness." Maybe she was keeping a loophole for Gene Vidal (Ewan McGregor), the founder of TWA and father of Gore, who told his son he loved her but didn't marry her "because I didn't want to marry a boy."

Hilary Swank uncannily embodies my ideas about Earhart in Mira Nair's *Amelia.* She looks like her, smiles like her, evokes her. Swank is an actress who doesn't fit in many roles, but when she's right, she's right. The tousled hair, the freckles, the slim figure, the fitness, the physical carriage that says: "I know precisely who I am and I like it—and if you don't, bail out." Not only was she the first person after Lindbergh to fly solo across the Atlantic, she even looked like him.

Amelia tells this story with sound performances and impeccable period detail. It deals with her final flight so accurately that many of the radio transmissions between her and the Coast Guard cutter *Itasca,* stationed off Howland Island, are repeated verbatim. (They could hear her but she couldn't hear them.) It ends on exactly the correct note. As Red River Dave sang in the lyrics of the first song ever broadcast on U.S. television:

Half an hour later, her SOS was heard,
Her signal's weak, but still her voice was brave.
In shark-infested waters, her aeroplane went down that night
In the blue Pacific to a watery grave.

She was an early feminist role model, an American hero not tainted like Lindbergh by chumminess with the Nazis. A few years after her death, U.S. women would be asked to hang up their aprons, put on overalls, and work on the production lines of the war. She was the real thing. Yes, she signed contracts to endorse chewing gum, soap, and a fashion line, but she needed the money to finance her flights, and she always chewed the gum, used the soap, wore the clothes.

I suppose I vaguely knew she married the famous New York publisher G. P. Putnam (Richard Gere). It never registered. The film reports, correctly, that Putnam was instrumental—promoting her, booking her lectures, publishing her book, raising money for flights. The movie doesn't much deal with how a small-town Kansas tomboy got along with the famous New York socialite who published Lindbergh's *We*. It was love at first sight for George, and forever after for both of them.

That's the trouble with Amelia Earhart's life, seen strictly as movie material. What we already know is what we get. To repeat: She was strong, brave, and true, she gained recognition for women fliers, and she looked fabulous in a flight suit. She flew the Atlantic solo, she disappeared in the Pacific, she died too young, and there was no scandal or even an indiscretion. She didn't even smoke, although Luckies wanted her for an endorsement.

I'm not suggesting that Mira Nair and her writers, Ronald Bass and Anna Hamilton Phelan, should have invented anything. It is right that they resisted any temptation. It's just that there's a certain lack of drama in a generally happy life. At least by treating her big flights as chapters in a longer life, they sidestepped the dilemma that defeated Billy Wilder when he starred Jimmy Stewart in *The Spirit of St. Louis* (1957). Lindbergh's life offered such promising details as a 1930s decoration by the Nazis and the kidnapping of his baby, but Wilder focused on the long flight itself, during which the most exciting event is the appearance of a fly in the cockpit.

Amelia is a perfectly sound biopic, well directed and acted, about an admirable woman. It confirmed for me Earhart's courage—not only in flying, but in insisting on living her life outside the conventions of her time for well-behaved females. The next generation of American women grew up in her slipstream.

There's a beautiful, beautiful field
Far away in a land that is fair.
Happy landings to you, Amelia Earhart
Farewell, first lady of the air.

Note: Listen to "Amelia Earhart's Last Flight" at www.youtube.com/watch?v=xRMu3dEHCaM.

The American ★ ★ ★ ★

R, 105 m., 2010

George Clooney (Jack/Edward), Violante Placido (Clara), Thekla Reuten (Mathilde), Paolo Bonacelli (Father Benedetto), Johan Leysen (Pavel). Directed by Anton Corbijn and produced by Clooney, Anne Carey, Jill Green, Grant Heslov, and Ann Wingate. Screenplay by Rowan Joffe, based on the novel *A Very Private Gentleman* by Martin Booth.

The American allows George Clooney to play a man as starkly defined as a samurai. His fatal flaw, as it must be for any samurai, is love. Other than that, the American is perfect: sealed, impervious, and expert, with a focus so narrow it is defined only by his skills and his master. Here is a gripping film with the focus of a Japanese drama, an impenetrable character to equal Alain Delon's in *Le Samourai*, by Jean-Pierre Melville.

Clooney plays a character named Jack, or perhaps Edward. He is one of those people who can assemble mechanical parts by feel and instinct, so inborn is his skill. His job is creating specialized weapons for specialized murders. He works for Pavel (Johan Leysen, who looks like Scott Glenn left to dry in the sun). Actually, we might say he "serves" Pavel, because he accepts his commands without question, giving him a samurai's loyalty.

Pavel assigns him a job. It involves meeting a woman named Mathilde (Thekla Reuten) in

Italy. They meet in a public place, where she carries a paper folded under her arm—the classic tell in spy movies. Their conversation begins with one word: "Range?" It involves only the specifications of the desired weapon. No discussion of purpose, cost, anything.

He thinks to find a room in a small Italian hilltop village, but it doesn't feel right. He finds another. We know from the film's shocking opening scene that people want to kill him. In the second village, he meets the fleshy local priest, Father Benedetto (Paolo Bonacelli). Through him he meets the local mechanic, walks into his shop, and finds all the parts he needs to build a custom silencer.

In the village he also finds a whore, Clara (Violante Placido), who works in a bordello we are surprised to find such a village can support. Jack or Edward lives alone, does push-ups, drinks coffee in cafés, assembles the weapon. And so on. His telephone conversations with Pavel are terse. He finds people beginning to follow him and trying to kill him.

The entire drama of this film rests on two words, "Mr. Butterfly." We must be vigilant to realize that once, and only once, they are spoken by the wrong person. They cause the entire film and all of its relationships to rotate. I felt exaltation at this detail. It is so rare to see a film this carefully crafted, this patiently assembled like a weapon, that when the word comes it strikes like a clap of thunder. A lesser film would have underscored it with a shock chord, punctuated it with a sudden zoom, or cut to a shocked close-up. *The American* is too cool to do that. Too Zen, if you will.

The director is a Dutchman named Anton Corbijn, known to me for *Control* (2007), the story of Ian Curtis, lead singer of Joy Division, a suicide at twenty-three. Corbijn has otherwise made mostly music videos (and is a famous photographer of the bands U2 and Depeche Mode). Here he paints an idyllic Italian countryside as lyrical as his dialogue is taciturn. There is not a wrong shot. Every performance is tightly controlled. Clooney is in complete command of his effect. He sometimes seems to be chewing a very small piece of gum, or perhaps his tongue.

His weakness is love. Clara, the prostitute, should not be trusted. We sense he uses prostitutes because he made a mistake in the relationship that opens the film. In his business, he cannot trust anybody. But perhaps Clara is different. Do not assume from what I've written that she isn't different. It is very possible. The film ends like a clockwork mechanism arriving at its final, clarifying tick.

American Violet ★ ★ ★

PG-13, 103 m., 2009

Nicole Beharie (Dee Roberts), Tim Blake Nelson (David Cohen), Will Patton (Sam Conroy), Michael O'Keefe (Calvin Beckett), Xzibit (Darrell Hughes), Charles S. Dutton (Reverend Sanders), Alfre Woodard (Alma Roberts). Directed by Tim Disney and produced by Bill Haney. Screenplay by Haney.

You may recall the story from the news in 2000. The cops in a small Texas town arrested forty black people on drug charges in a sweep of a public housing project. They were working on a tip from a single informant, a former mental patient who had good reason to cooperate with them. Dee, a young mother of four, who was not found with drugs and had no history of drug use, was arrested primarily because she went outside to drag her little girl to safety. She, along with the others, is offered a plea bargain: If she pleads guilty, she gets probation. She refuses to plead guilty.

American Violet is clear about the motivation for such raids with little or no evidence. A guilty plea helps the district attorney build up a record as a crime fighter, even though he is the one who has committed the crime. A defendant who pleads guilty cannot continue to live in public housing and will always have a felony on her record. But if Dee caves in, she goes free and is reunited with her children. Her snaky ex-husband has snatched his kids and moved them in with his new girlfriend, who has a history of child abuse.

This is all based on an actual case (the names have been changed). This stuff happens all the time and is far from rare in Texas, a state with a shameful record of law enforcement practices. The movie occasionally intercuts commercials from the Gore-Bush campaign then under way, to no particular purpose except to remind me that as Texas governor, Bush commuted the sentence of only one of the 131 people put to death under his reign, even though public defenders presented no defense at all for 41 of them and a third of their defense attorneys were later disbarred or sanctioned.

American Violet stars Nicole Beharie, a recent Juilliard graduate in her second role, as Dee Roberts. It is a stunning performance: She is small, vulnerable, fearful for her children, but damned if she will plead guilty to a crime she did not commit. She stands firm even as her mother, Alma (Alfre Woodard), begs her to take the plea; Alma argues the harsh racial realities of their small town. When Dee vows to stay in jail, she attracts the attention of the ACLU, which sends a lawyer named David Cohen (Tim Blake Nelson) down to defend her. Because he needs a local partner, he persuades the lawyer Sam Conroy (Will Patton), himself a former DA, to join him; Sam refuses at first but agrees out of guilt because he knows full well how the system works.

The DA is Calvin Beckett (Michael O'Keefe), a man of whom it can fairly be said that he has no interest at all in whether the people he has arrested are guilty. How would it look in an election year if he went around dropping drug charges? And now the stage is set for a docudrama that may have an outcome we already know but is a loud lesson about truth, justice, and the Texas Way. I know I'll hear complaints from Texans of a certain stripe. They won't see this film. They know all they want about the ACLU from their favorite broadcasters.

Some critics have found *American Violet* to be too mainstream, too agenda-driven, too much like made-for-TV, not enough "suspense." Say what? Dee is innocent, her lawyers are putting themselves at risk because of their outrage, and the DA is a heartless scofflaw. If the movie tries to have fun concealing that, it's jerking our chain.

What worked for me was the strength of the performances, beginning with Nicole Beharie as the convincing heroine. Alfre Woodard in attack mode is formidable; Tim Blake Nelson underplays as a determined, methodical lawyer, not a showboat, and Will Patton in some ways steals the show as a good man who has done bad in the past, knows it, and is trying to make up. As Beckett, Michael O'Keefe is rock-solid as a man who has more important things on his mind than justice.

American Violet, it's true, is not blazingly original cinema. Tim Disney's direction and the screenplay by Bill Haney are meat and potatoes, making this story clear, direct, and righteous. But consider the story. How would you feel if this happened to you? What if cases like this were to lead to disregard of due process of law at even the highest levels? I wish I could convince . . . hell, never mind. I can't. That district attorney? Still in office.

Amreeka ★ ★ ★ ½

PG-13, 96 m., 2009

Nisreen Faour (Muna Farah), Melkar Muallem (Fadi Farah), Hiam Abbass (Raghda Halaby), Alia Shawkat (Salma Halaby), Yussef Abu Warda (Nabeel Halaby), Joseph Ziegler (Mr. Novatski). Directed by Cherien Dabis and produced by Christina Piovesan and Paul Barkin. Screenplay by Dabis.

Muna is a nonreligious Palestinian, which makes her an outsider on both sides of the Israeli checkpoint she has to pass daily on the way to her job as a bank accountant. She dreams of immigrating to America with her teenage son, Fadi, so he can grow up in a less sectarian society. When against all odds she wins the U.S. lottery for green cards, they leave for a new life that is more, and less, than they expected.

So begins Cherien Dabis's heartwarming and funny first feature, with a title using the Arabic word for *America.* Muna and Fadi have the misfortune to arrive soon after the start of the war in Iraq, when Homeland Security is in a lather and anti-Arab sentiment runs high. Her life savings are confiscated by customs at O'Hare airport, along with the cookie tin she kept them in. She arrives in a distant Chicago suburb with no money but high hopes. "Occupation?" asks the immigration official. "Yes, we are occupied," she smiles proudly.

They move in with her sister and her husband, a doctor. Muna (Nisreen Faour, from *The Visitor*) is fully qualified in accounting, but her race causes her to lose a bank job. She finds work at a nearby White Castle, hiding this comedown from her family. She can't understand why anybody would want to eat one of those greasy sliders. If it is any consolation to the good sports at White Castle, who allowed a real restaurant to be used as a location, they looked mighty appetizing to me.

Her son, Fadi (Melkar Muallem), finds an ally in Salma (Alia Shawkat), a cousin about the same age. She masterminds an American teenage wardrobe for him and is a friend at school, where he is bullied as an Arab (i.e., possible teenage terrorist). At home, his uncle the doctor (Yussef Abu Warda) sees his practice decline for the same reason. Does it occur to xenophobic Americans that almost all immigrants, like their own ancestors, come here because they admire America? Explain that to Lou Dobbs. *Amreeka* isn't a story of American prejudice, but of American reality, the good and the bad. When Fadi is bullied, fights back, and is called into the principal's office, his mother sheds her White Castle uniform and hurries to the school, deeply concerned. Here she finds the Jewish principal (Joseph Ziegler) not only sympathetic but responding to her own warmth and charisma. He wonders if she'd like to join him for coffee . . .

Cherien Dabis incorporates some of her own story in her film. A Jordanian raised in Dayton, Ohio, during the years of the Gulf War, she was discriminated against. American anti-Arab prejudice apparently considers all Arabs to be on the wrong side of every problem. To explain that Palestinians had no involvement with Saddam's invasion of Kuwait would be a waste of time with such people, who seem to believe Arabs shouldn't exist at all, or at the very least should stay at home. My Irish-American ancestors faced similar discrimination, my German-American father was bullied during World War I, Japanese-Americans were locked up during World War II, and the ancestors of African-Americans scarcely came here voluntarily. How soon we forget.

Amreeka is a heartwarming film, not a political dirge. Much of this warmth comes from the actress Nisreen Faour. To see her in action is to smile. Some people are blessed with being quickly likable. As for Melkar Muallem, who plays her son, set aside his Arabic origins and he could be the hero of any American high school film. Joseph Ziegler, as the principal, is not demonstrating his open-mindedness by expressing affection for Muna, but is responding as any man in his shoes might naturally feel. When this woman smiles, you want it to be on you.

Angels & Demons ★ ★ ★

PG-13, 138 m., 2009

Tom Hanks (Professor Robert Langdon), Ewan McGregor (Camerlengo Patrick McKenna), Ayelet Zurer (Dr. Vittoria Vetra), Stellan Skarsgard (Commander Richter), Pierfrancesco Favino (Ernesto Olivetti), Nikolaj Lie Kaas (Assassin), Armin Mueller-Stahl (Cardinal Strauss). Directed by Ron Howard and produced by Howard, Brian Grazer, and John Calley. Screenplay by David Koepp and Akiva Goldsman, based on the novel by Dan Brown.

Since *Angels & Demons* depends on a split-second schedule and a ticking time bomb that could destroy the Vatican, it's a little distracting when the Camerlengo, a priest entrusted with the pope's duties between papacies, breaks into the locked enclave of the College of Cardinals and lectures them on centuries of church history.

These men, many of them elderly, may face death in minutes, which the Camerlengo knows. The commander of the Swiss Guard *thinks* he can evacuate the Vatican and the hundreds of thousands of faithful waiting in St. Peter's Square in fifteen minutes before an explosion vaporizes "a big chunk of Rome," but frankly, we in the audience think a lot of monsignors back home are going to receive promotions real soon.

Since very few plot details in the film are remotely plausible, including its desperate chase across Rome, the history lesson is excusable. Having been told about the long war between the Church and the Illuminati, and religion and science, we are grateful for the briefing, even if the cardinals already know most of the history. This kind of film requires us to be very forgiving, and if we are, it promises to entertain. *Angels & Demons* succeeds.

It's based on a novel that came before *The Da Vinci Code* in Dan Brown's oeuvre, but is set afterward. Professor Robert Langdon (Tom Hanks) is back at Harvard when he is summoned from a swimming pool by an emissary from the Vatican and flown to Rome to face a crisis. Earlier, we learned, a rare sealed vial of antimatter was stolen from the CERN Large Hadron Collider in Geneva, and a note taking credit comes from the Illuminati, a secret society that has long hated the Church because of the days when it persecuted Galileo and other scientists.

A "popular and progressive" pope has just died. The cardinals have been summoned to elect his successor. Four of them, the *preferati*, the favorites to be the next pope, have been kidnapped. One will be executed at 8, 9, 10, and 11 p.m., until the battery on the antimatter vial runs out of juice at midnight, and the faithful will see more than a puff of white smoke above the Vatican. I don't recall if the Illuminati had any demands. Maybe it just wants revenge.

In that case, why hide the vial at the end of a trail that can be followed only by clues discovered or intuited by Professor Langdon? Why not just blow up the place? What is the purpose of the scavenger hunt? Has it all been laboriously constructed as a test of professor Langdon's awesome knowledge? Are the Illuminati trying to get even after Langdon foiled Opus Dei, another secret society, in *The Da Vinci Code*?

I don't know, and, reader, there is no time to care. Langdon uses his knowledge of Illuminati symbols to follow the trail through four Rome churches. He has uncanny luck. He spots and correctly identifies every clue, even though they're very well hidden. Just as well because one dungeon overlooked or one statue pointing the wrong way, and he loses. For his companion he has the beautiful and brilliant Vittoria Vetra (Ayelet Zurer) from CERN. Her father was murdered in the antimatter theft. Her purpose is (a) to explain that the battery will indeed run down, (b) request her father's secret journals from Geneva, although they are never read, and (c) run along everywhere with Tom Hanks to provide him with urgent conversation.

Meanwhile, there is intrigue within the Vatican and lots of red herrings among all the red hats. The young Camerlengo (Ewan McGregor) joins the professor's desperate quest, as does the commander of the pope's protectors, the Swiss Guard (Stellan Skarsgard). Inside the conclave, Cardinal Strauss (Armin Mueller-Stahl) is in charge of the election. Because of his sinister mien (I love the phrase "sinister mien"), German accent, and absolutist views on Church tradition, he seems set up to be a suspect, since the progressive pope's death may have been an inside job. (I forgot to mention that there has also been time to exhume the pontiff's remains and discover evidence of poisoning.)

All of this happens at breakneck speed, with little subtlety but with fabulous production values. The interiors of the Sistine Chapel, the Pantheon, churches, tombs, and crypts are rendered dramatically; the College of Cardinals looks both (a) very impressive and (b) like a collection of elderly extras from Cinecittà.

The film by no means tilts the conflict between science and religion one way or the other. The professor is not religious, indeed seems agnostic, but the Church, on the other hand, is not portrayed as antiscience. Galileo would be happy that there is now a Vatican Observatory. If the Illuminati are indeed scientists, they would better employ themselves not avenging ancient deeds, but attacking modern fundamentalist cults.

The professor has a fascinating exchange with the Camerlengo, who asks him if he believes in God. He believes, he says, that the existence of God is beyond his mind to determine. "And your heart?" asks the priest. "My heart is not worthy." Agnostics and believers can both find something to agree with there; director Ron Howard does an even-handed job of balancing the scales.

So good, indeed, that even after Howard accused the Church of refusing him access to Vatican locations, and although the dependable William Donohue of the Catholic League has attacked his film, *Angels & Demons* received a favorable review from the official Vatican newspaper *L'Osservatore Romano*, which wrote it is a "harmless entertainment which hardly affects the genius and mystery of Christianity."

And come on, Ron: Would you *expect* the Church to let you shoot a Dan Brown thriller in the Sistine Chapel? Get real.

Another Year ★ ★ ★ ★

PG-13, 129 m., 2011

Jim Broadbent (Tom), Ruth Sheen (Gerri), Lesley Manville (Mary), Oliver Maltman (Joe),

Peter Wight (Ken), David Bradley (Ronnie), Karina Fernandez (Katie). Directed by Mike Leigh and produced by Georgina Lowe. Screenplay by Leigh.

Not quite every year brings a new Mike Leigh film, but the years that do are blessed with his sympathy and penetrating observation, and with his instinct for human comedy. By that I don't mean "comedy" as in easy laughter. I mean that comedy that wells up from movies allowing us to recognize ourselves in characters both lovable and wretched. Leigh's *Another Year* is like a long, purifying soak in empathy.

He begins with Tom and Gerri, a North London couple who have been happily married for years. Immediately you can see the risks Leigh is prepared to take. A happy married couple? Two wise and lovable people? Who are intelligent and alert to the real world? Not caricatures, not comforting, not clichés, but simply two people I wish I knew? I'd look forward to them every time I visited their house, and be slow to leave.

That's also how Mary (Lesley Manville) feels. She has worked for years in the office of Gerri, a behavioral counselor. Many people have a friend like Mary. Many people are a friend like Mary: unmarried, not getting any younger, drinking too much, looking for the perfect spouse as a way of holding any real-world relationship at arm's length. Mary drops in on Tom (Jim Broadbent) and Gerri (Ruth Sheen) a lot. Every time she visits, we're reminded of Robert Frost: "Home is where, when you have to go there, they have to take you in."

Mary needs healing. She badly requires sobriety. She wears an invisible sign around her neck: "Needy." Tom and Gerri don't lecture. Sometimes they drop gentle hints. "It's a shame," Tom observes to Gerri after Mary has ended yet another sad visit, and that's all he has to say. No criticisms, no anger, just a factual statement. In their own lives, they're in complete accord. They garden, they work, they feed their friends dinners, they hope their son will find the right girl, they are in love. Remarkably, in this age, their thirty-year-old son, Joe (Oliver Maltman), loves them and is happy.

Leigh has a gift for scenes involving embarrassment in social situations. We squirm, not because the characters are uneasy, but because we would be, too. In *Another Year*, Tom and Gerri and their son attend the funeral of Tom's sister-in-law. We have never been to a funeral quite like it, yet it is like many funerals. The uninvolved clergyman, the efficient undertakers, the remote father, the angry son, the handful of neighbors who didn't know the deceased all that well, the family skeletons. He sees the ways people display their anguish without meaning to.

The movie doesn't require this scene. It has no obligatory scenes. Like life, it happens once you plug in the people. Mary lives in a very small world, where it's unlikely she'll find happiness. She buys a car to give her more "freedom," but no one who drinks like she does will find freedom that way. She fantastically begins to think of the son, Joe, as a possible partner. Joe brings home Katie (Karina Fernandez) to meet his parents, and they love her. When Mary meets Katie and understands who she is, it is devastating.

All the actors are pitch perfect. Lesley Manville is virtuoso in making Mary pathetic and yet never a caricature. Listen to the way her cadences vary with drink. Notice the way Tom and Gerri's responses to her modulate during the course of a visit. Even, for that matter, observe Ken (Peter Wight), Tom's friend. Ken is no prize, but might be happy to date Mary and maybe marry her; and after all, could Mary do any better? She persists in the delusion that she could.

Now we come to the matter of the chins, and here we touch on something central to the appeal of Mike Leigh. He is not afraid to star imperfect people. Jim Broadbent has a little too much chin, and Ruth Sheen not quite enough. In most movies everybody has about the right chinnage. At the risk of offending many of his many actor-collaborators, I'll say that not once in forty years has Mike Leigh ever starred a conventionally handsome or beautiful movie-star type. Instead, he has enriched the British cinema by his use of unconventional types, also including Imelda Staunton, Sally Hawkins, Timothy Spall, Marianne Jean-Baptiste, Brenda Blethyn, and David Thewlis.

Another Year gave me characters I could love, feel uneasy about, identify with, or be appalled by. I see a lot of movies where the characters have no personalities, only attributes. I like James Bond, but I ask you: In what way is he human? Every single character in *Another Year* is human, and some of them all too human. I saw it and was enriched.

The Answer Man ★ ★

R, 95 m., 2009

Jeff Daniels (Arlen Faber), Lauren Graham (Elizabeth), Lou Taylor Pucci (Kris Lucas), Kat Dennings (Dahlia), Olivia Thirlby (Anne), Nora Dunn (Terry Fraser), Tony Hale (Mailman). Directed by John Hindman and produced by Kevin Messick. Screenplay by Hindman.

Anyone writing a book titled *Me & God* has a big idea of himself or a small idea of God. Yet Arlen Faber's best-seller has captured 10 percent of the "God market" and held that position for twenty years. During those two decades his idea of himself has grown smaller. He tries to do his daily meditation, he really tries, but when the doorbell interrupts, he instinctively reacts with a string of fairly impressive swear words, strung together as if he's had practice.

Here is a man in deep spiritual doo-doo. One day he throws out his back and is in such pain he must crawl on his hands and knees to the new local chiropractor. She pushes here and probes there and soon he's back on his feet. He was in such pain when he crawled in that he gave his real name, having long been under deep cover and avoiding his fellow man. Elizabeth the doctor (Lauren Graham) has never heard of him, but her receptionist Anne (Olivia Thirlby) certainly has, and this is the start of his gradual recovery as a social being.

Arlen (Jeff Daniels) does an excellent job of portraying a misanthrope with back pain, but not so much as a man on a first-pronoun basis with God. Everything we see of him leads us to suspect that readers whose lives were changed by his book did the heavy lifting themselves. What's amazing is that his book is still read after twenty years and yet no one in the film, no one, repeats a single thing to be learned from it. Inquiring minds need to know: "What did he tell God?"

This is not a movie about spirituality, however, but a romantic comedy, with a clunky subplot involving a book seller (Lou Taylor Pucci) who has just graduated from rehab and needs advice only this shambling, foul-mouthed wreck Arlen can give. Arlen is thus reluctantly hauled into the problems of another human being, while meanwhile gradually becoming involved in the life of Elizabeth and her young son, Alex (Max Antisell).

Early sequences in the film seem inspired by outtakes from a manic Jim Carrey comedy. That's not such a bad thing. Later the movie follows the timeworn pathways of countless romcoms before it. How much more interesting is a film like *500 Days of Summer*, which is about the complexities of life, in comparison with this one, which cheerfully cycles through the clichés?

Now about that God business. It is necessary for me to share one of my favorite journalism stories. It's said that Richard Harding Davis was dispatched by William Randolph Hearst to cover the Johnstown flood. Here was his lead: "God stood on a mountaintop here and looked at what his waters had wrought." Hearst cabled back: "Forget flood. Interview God."

A wonderful story. Checking out the quote online, I found a blog entry by Dennis G. Jerz of Seton Hill University, reporting that I have related this same story four times in print since 1993, sometimes changing it slightly. Good gravy! My only defense for using it once again is that it's more interesting than anything else I could write about *The Answer Man.*

Antichrist ★ ★ ★ ½

NO MPAA RATING, 105 m., 2009

Willem Dafoe (He), Charlotte Gainsbourg (She). Directed by Lars von Trier and produced by Meta Louise Foldager. Screenplay by von Trier.

The term "antichrist" is commonly used to mean "the opposite of Christ." It actually translates from the Greek as "opposed to Christ." This is a useful place to begin in considering Lars von Trier's new film. The central character in *Antichrist* is not supernatural, but an ordinary man who loses our common moral values. He lacks all good and embodies evil, but that reflects his nature and not his theological identity.

This man, known only as He, is played by Willem Dafoe as a somber, driven, tortured soul. The film opens with He and his wife, She (Charlotte Gainsbourg), making passionate love. This is a moment of complete good. In the next room, their infant son begins to crawl around to explore and falls to his death. This in itself is a neutral act. It inspires the rest of the film, which labels itself in three stages: Grief, Pain, and Despair.

We must begin by assuming that He and She are already at psychological tipping points. She has been doing research on witchcraft, and it leads her to wonder if women are inherently evil. That may cause her to devalue herself. He is a controlling, dominant personality, who I believe is moved by the traumatic death to punish the woman who delivered his child into the earth.

Their first stage, Grief, is legitimate. Their error is in trying to treat it instead of accepting it and living it through. Of course they blame themselves for having sex when they should have been attentive to the infant. Guilt requires punishment. She mentally punishes herself. For reasons he may not be aware of, he is driven to deal with her guilt as a problem, lecturing her in calm, patient, detached psychobabble. Her grief is her fault, you see, and he will blame her for it. This leads to Pain, most directly when he insists, at this of all times, on them going to their remote cabin in a dark wood that she fears at the best of times. The cabin is named Eden; make of that what you will. They have already eaten of the fruit, and it will never be Eden for them again.

The psychic pain of his counseling and their removal to the forest are now joined by pain inflicted upon them by nature and each other. The woods are inhabited by strange animals that look ordinary—a deer, a fox, a crow—but are possessed and unnatural. He and She don't much seek refuge in their cabin but increasingly find themselves outside in the wilderness. They begin to inflict pain on each other in unspeakable and shockingly intimate ways.

These passages have been referred to as "torture porn." Sadomasochistic they certainly are, but porn is entirely in the mind of the beholder. Will even a single audience member find these scenes erotic? That is hard to imagine. They are extreme in a deliberate way; von Trier, who has always been a provocateur, is driven to confront and shake his audience more than any other serious filmmaker—even Bunuel and Herzog. He will do this with sex, pain, boredom, theology, and bizarre stylistic experiments. And why not? We are at least convinced we're watching a film precisely as he intended it, and not after a watering-down by a fearful studio executive.

That said, I know what's in it for von Trier. What was in it for me? More than anything else, I responded to the performances. Feature films may be fiction, but they are certainly documentaries showing actors in front of a camera. Both Dafoe and Gainsbourg have been risk takers, as anyone working with von Trier must be. The ways they're called upon to act in this film are extraordinary. They respond without hesitation. More important, they convince. Who can say what von Trier intended? His own explanations have been vague. The actors take the words and actions at face value and invest them with all the conviction they can. The result, in a sense, is that He and She get away from von Trier's theoretical control and act on their own, as they are compelled to.

We don't know as much as we think we do about acting. I asked Dafoe what discussions he had with Gainsbourg before their most difficult scenes. He said they discussed very little: "We had great intimacy on the set but the truth is we barely knew each other. We kissed in front of the camera the first time, we got naked for the first time with the camera rolling. This is pure pretending. Since our intimacy only exists before the camera it makes it more potent for us."

So it is a documentary in one way. What does it document? The courage of the actors, for one thing. The realization of von Trier's images, for another. And on the personal level, our fear that evil does exist in the world, that our fellow men are capable of limitless cruelty, and that it might lead, as it does in the film, to the obliteration of human hope. The third stage is Despair.

Anton Chekhov's The Duel ★ ★

NO MPAA RATING, 95 m., 2010

Andrew Scott (Laevsky), Fiona Glascott (Nadia), Tobias Menzies (Von Koren), Niall Buggy (Samoylenko). Directed by Dover Koshashvili and produced by Mary Bing and Donald Rosenfeld. Screenplay by Bing, based on the novella by Anton Chekhov.

What strikes you immediately about *Anton Chekhov's The Duel* are the visuals. The cinematography of Paul Sarossy composes shots as soft impressionist romance, the colors tastefully softened, the elements arranged in classical symmetry. Unfortunately, this combined with the unwavering progress of the story results in much of a muchness, and we wouldn't object to the occasional taste of vulgarity.

The film, as you have guessed, is based on a story by Chekhov. That accounts for the textbook quality of the title. I suppose it was out of the question to use *Steven Spielberg's The Duel—Not!* The story involves two indolent lovers and a fierce Darwinian zoologist creating a love triangle of theory, not practice, on the beautiful coast of the Black Sea. Maybe after the rigors of the Russian winter they are all driven a little mad by the good weather.

Laevsky (Andrew Scott) is one of those civil servants of nineteenth-century Russian literature who seems high up on an insignificant ladder. He's shacked up in this seaside resort with his married mistress, Nadia (Fiona Glascott), who has lost her appeal now freed of her husband. I've been reading a lot of Balzac lately, and am struck that absent husbands in European classics seem to play much like noises off. Laevsky expresses his discontents to the local physician; Chekhov often provides such learned listeners to sit gravely through anguished monologues. Dr. Samoylenko is required not for his diagnosis but for his ears. Also for his money: Laevsky is a gambler and drunk who desperately hopes for a loan.

Into this powder keg comes the zoologist Von Koren (Tobias Menzies), inflamed with the revolutionary principles of Darwinism that were then being embraced by the intelligentsia in all the wrong ways. Rare is the man not convinced that all evolution points like an arrow to his door. Von Koren is too refined to enter a horse of his own in the race, but he observes with scientific precision the willingness of the locals to respond to Nadia's underemployed sexuality. All comes to a head at a party one night when the overserved Laevsky temporarily goes barking mad, and Von Koren determines he isn't fit to survive.

The zoologist then faces one of the two choices open to him, given his rudimentary grasp of Darwin's theory. If he wants little Von Korens to prevail over little Laevskys, he can either seduce the female or kill the man. *Anton Chekhov's The Duel* is by no means shy about portraying sex in a forthright manner, and director Dover Koshashvili has gratifying taste in nudity, which has grown sadly rare as Friday night audiences lose their interest in it. But Von Koren is too much of a lardass to seduce Nadia and he knows it, so he challenges Laevsky to a duel.

One of two men will die over this woman: Man Number One, who no longer desires her, or Man Number Two, who knows what he would do if only he were in Man Number One's shoes. For Nadia, this must not be quite as exciting as Rhett Butler calling out Ashley Wilkes. The doctor saw it all coming, but then doctors are always seeing it all coming.

Koshashvili is a good filmmaker. His *Late Marriage* (2002) involved some of the more practical difficulties of an arranged marriage in Israel among immigrants from Soviet Georgia. Its characters had the advantage of caring strongly about who they did or didn't sleep with. In *The Duel* and much of Chekhov, lust seems to be a matter best approached by the introspection of the world-weary.

Anton Chekhov's The Duel isn't exactly a bad film. It's very well made and acted in English by a mostly Irish cast in a polished Chekhovian tone. But it somehow isn't as exciting as a duel over a woman should be. If you're not well rested before entering the theater, it could put you under.

Anvil! The Story of Anvil ★ ★ ★

NO MPAA RATING, 90 m., 2009

Featuring Steve "Lips" Kudlow, Robb Reiner, G5, Ivan Hurd, Tom Araya, Chris Tsangarides, Tiziana Arrigoni, Cut Loose, Mad Dog, Lars

Ulrich, Lemmy, Scott Ian, Slash. A documentary directed by Sacha Gervasi and produced by Rebecca Yeldham.

This is the sound of optimism: "Everything on the tour went drastically wrong. But at least there was a tour for it to go wrong on." The optimist is Steve "Lips" Kudlow, lead guitarist in Anvil, a band you've never heard of. In 1973, he made a friend named Robb Reiner in Toronto, who had a drum set, and they vowed to make rock 'n' roll until they were old. Now they are old, at least for heavy metal rockers.

Anvil! The Story of Anvil is a documentary about the moderate rise and long, long fall of their band, where musicians in the two other slots came and went, but Lips and Robb rocked on. "How many bands stay together for thirty years?" asks Slash of Guns N' Roses, in a backstage interview. "You've got the Stones, the Who, U2—and Anvil." Yeah. And Anvil.

Anvil had one modestly successful album (*Metal on Metal*), is credited as an influence by lots of heavy metal bands, had bad management and lousy record labels, and was Canadian at a time (as now) when that didn't feel synonymous with heavy metal. "I was raised to be polite," says Reiner, after he fails at a job in telephone hard selling.

Reiner is also seen working on a demolition project. Kudlow drives a delivery truck carrying school meals, and explains the menu. One day maybe lamb stew and meat loaf. Then meat loaf and pizza. Then pizza and lamb stew. He burns with the original fire: The band will, will, will win the success it deserves.

There are still loyal fans. One, Tiziana Arrigoni of Sweden, books a European tour for them. This was the tour that went drastically wrong. They missed trains. Couldn't find the club in Prague. Weren't paid. Were invited to the Monsters of Transylvania, a heavy metal concert. Lips shares the news that the venue seats 10,000: "I hear the mayor of Transylvania is going to be there!" The audience numbers 178.

The documentary, directed by Anvil fan (and *The Terminal* screenwriter) Sacha Gervasi, spends time in Toronto with Lips's and Robb's spouses, siblings, children. The wives are loyal but not optimistic. The rockers are good family men. They were apparently spared the heavy metal plague of heavy drugs, although there is a little weed in one shot.

Down and down they fall. They get the veteran producer Chris Tsangarides to cut their thirteenth album ("our best work"—Lips), but have to release it themselves. One CD finds its way to Japan, and they are invited to a Tokyo concert with a venue seating (an ominous omen) 10,000. They play at the unheavy-metal hour of 9:45 a.m. How many people turn up?

I don't know if their music is any good. Their fans think so. The doc doesn't show one song all the way through. But they swore a pledge when they were fourteen, and they're still honoring it, and at fifty-one Lips knows he still has it and that Anvil will be back on the charts. Maybe there is hope for Susan Boyle.

Araya ★ ★ ★ ½

NO MPAA RATING, 90 m., 2010

Featuring the Pereda, Salazar, and Ortiz families. A documentary directed by Margot Benacerraf and produced by Henry Nadler. Screenplay by Benacerraf.

To be born here is to be born into hell. That must have happened for more than three hundred years, because no one would ever want to come to live here. *Araya* tells the story of life on the remote, barren Araya peninsula of Venezuela, where Spanish conquistadors found salt about 1550. Salt was treasure in Europe, to the misfortune of those whose lives were devoted to it.

This astonishing documentary, so beautiful, so horrifying, was filmed in the late 1950s, when an old way of life had not yet ended. It was the belief of the filmmaker, Margot Benacerraf, that the motions of the salt workers became ritualized over the decades, passed down through the generations, and that here we could see the outcome of the endless repeating of arduous tasks that would destroy others.

The salt cake is taken up from the floor of a shallow marsh, loaded into flat-bottomed wooden boats, broken up, carted onto land in wheelbarrows, and loaded into 120-pound baskets to be balanced on the heads of workers who trudge up the side of an ever-growing pyramid to deposit it. At the top, a man with a rake forms each mound into a towering, geometrically perfect shape. Now it is ready to be hauled away in trucks.

The workers, bronzed by the sun, all muscle and sinew, work in a blazing sun in a land where nothing grows. Food comes from the sea and from corn meal that is carted in. They live in small rude shacks. They get their water from a tank truck. Some work all day. Some work all night. Such is their life.

And just such a phrase, *such is their life,* is used in the doc's narration, which seems to hover in detachment above the sweat on the ground. I imagine Benacerraf's purpose was to make the toilers of Araya seem heroic in a "land where nothing lives." Where the sun is hot and pitiless so often it becomes a mantra. The effect is odd at first, but then we grow accustomed: The idea is to see these not as individuals but almost as a species evolved to take salt from the sea, build it into pyramids, watch it hauled away, and start again.

We learn something about salt along the way. It was so prized that the Spanish built their largest overseas fortress on the peninsula to guard it. The men who died building it were the first of many who paid for salt with their lives. The working conditions of the salt workers were brutal; their feet and legs were ulcerated by the salt, and if they faltered, they had no income. Their existence is agonizing, and we feel no regret that their way of life is ending. They have been reduced to robots. Small wonder the film contains so little dialogue. Yet these people lived and died, and we had salt in our shakers. It would be too sad if they were not remembered.

This black-and-white doc, so realistic in its photography, so formal in its words, played at Cannes in 1959 and shared the critics' prize with Alain Resnais's *Hiroshima, Mon Amour.* Benacerraf, a Venezuelan director born in 1926, it still alive and much honored. Her work was almost lost in the years since it was made. Now it has been restored to pristine beauty by Milestone Films, and is on a national tour of art venues.

Around a Small Mountain ★ ★ ★

NO MPAA RATING, 85 m., 2010

Jane Birkin (Kate), Sergio Castellitto (Vittorio), Andre Marcon (Alexandre), Jacques Bonnaffe (Marlo), Julie-Marie Parmentier (Clemence), Helene de Vallombreuse (Margot). Directed by Jacques Rivette and produced by Martine Marignac and Maurice Tinchant. Screenplay by Rivette, Pascal Bonitzer, Christine Laurent, and Shirel Amitay.

Sometimes a film is simply a story we might have found interesting to live. Its message may be no more than that we all have to weather hard times. To ordinary life may be added some style and artifice, allowing the filmmaker to tweak reality into a more pleasing form. Maybe that's what Jacques Rivette has in mind with *Around a Small Mountain.* One of the founders of the French New Wave, Rivette is still very much active at eighty-two.

At the center of his film is a shabby little circus, playing to sparse crowds in villages. It becomes the stage on which his two characters live, and they meet on their way to it. Kate (Jane Birkin) is driving down a road when her car stalls. Vittorio (Sergio Castellitto) happens along and fixes it for her: a Meet Cute as old as time. He doesn't even speak. He drives on, slows, and turns back. Something about Kate has struck him.

We learn that she is returning to the little circus after fifteen years. It was her father's. Her lover was killed in a performance. Vittorio sizes up the situation and books the room above a local café on the spur of the moment. At the performance that has never worked, he breaks the silence by suddenly laughing. Even the clowns are startled.

When the circus caravan leaves town, he follows. It's not that he and Kate begin a love affair. It's that they've both run off to join the circus. He apparently has nowhere to go and nothing else to do, and the same might be said of her. We learn of the buried past of the circus and the buried careers of its performers. Little one-ring circuses like this set up in town squares in rural districts. They still exist. On the Lido in Venice one night we attended one smaller than this—so small that after the show the clown came over to our granddaughter Raven and gave her a ride on his mule.

Jane Birkin has a sculpted, intelligent face that might not get her far on a U.S. soap opera, but I think she's sexy. She's a woman who looks like she's up to something. She's had quite a life. She's sixty-four, looks nowhere near that, was actually one of the two "birds" who frolicked nude in David Hemmings's photo studio in *Blow-Up*. What else? She was a famous model during the Swinging London days. Hermes named its Birkin bag after her, she once played Brigitte Bardot's lover in a film, was once married to John Barry, was the long-time lover of Serge Gainsbourg, and is the mother of Charlotte Gainsbourg, who underwent such rigors in Lars von Trier's *Antichrist.* It has been quite a life for anybody who seems so open and vulnerable.

Here she exudes the loss of her father, her lover, the circus. I doubt if she's experienced love since her lover died. Vittorio becomes a sort of passive counselor, coaxing her to face her wounds and let go of them. Their relationship is ever so much more interesting than if Rivette had reduced it to romance. This man and woman, strangers, actually find themselves talking to each other. How often do you see that?

The movie is the shortest one Rivette has ever made. His *La Belle Noiseuse* (1991), also with Birkin and one of my Great Movies, runs 236 minutes, and not a second too long. This one clocks in at 85 minutes, again the right length. Some men when they grow old feel a need to be profound. Rivette embodies the New Wave in that he needs to be playful.

Arthur ★ ★ ★

PG-13, 110 m., 2011

Russell Brand (Arthur), Helen Mirren (Hobson), Greta Gerwig (Naomi), Jennifer Garner (Susan), Geraldine James (Vivienne), Luis Guzman (Bitterman), Nick Nolte (Burt Johnson). Directed by Jason Winer and produced by Chris Bender, Russell Brand, Larry Brezner, Kevin McCormick, J. C. Spink, and Michael Tadross. Screenplay by Peter Baynham.

Arthur is a fairly close remake of the great 1981 Dudley Moore movie, with pleasures of its own. It shares some of the same strengths and virtues, and if it lacks Dudley Moore as Arthur and John Gielgud playing his butler, Hobson, well, it has Russell Brand and Helen Mirren playing his nanny, Hobson. That's not a trade-off, but it's a good try.

The thing about Moore, whom people persisted in calling "Cuddly Dudley," although he hated it, is that he was just plain lovable. The thing about Russell Brand is that he isn't, not much, and he should get credit here for at least being a good deal more likable than he usually chooses to seem. He plays the alcoholic zillionaire Arthur Bach as a man who wants to party with the world and pick up the check.

Helen Mirren has the presence and authority of John Gielgud, but not the same aloof dignity. Gielgud's Hobson was a man so reserved you sometimes wanted to knock and see if anyone answered. Then again, they've made Hobson into a nanny still loyal from Arthur's childhood, so she should be expected to love him in a more tender way.

The main plot beats are roughly the same: Arthur is drunk more or less all the time, and steadfast in his irresponsibility. He inadvertently falls in love with a sweet young woman named Naomi (Greta Gerwig), just as his controlling mother, Vivienne (Geraldine James), is arranging his marriage with a very rich woman named Susan (Jennifer Garner). Susan wants him for his name; she may be rich, but she's not welcomed into the upper crust because her daddy (Nick Nolte) worked his way up in construction.

Naomi cares little about such matters, and supports herself as an unlicensed guide, giving bootleg tours of Grand Central Terminal. She's remarkably forgiving of Arthur's irregularities, considering he has the self-discipline and tact of a Charlie Sheen. But then, neither *Arthur* deals with alcoholism as other than a colorful character trait. No one could possibly drink like Arthur and not be dead at the end of twenty-four hours.

The casting of Greta Gerwig works nicely. Did you see her as the assistant to Ben Stiller's brother in *Greenberg* (2010)? The thing about her is that she is indeed cuddly. We sometimes talk about personal chemistry as something that happens in casting. It probably begins at birth. She's a woman you instinctively feel good about, like Amy Adams in *Junebug.* This quality goes a long way toward filling in the psychological gaps in her relationship with Arthur. Nice people can get away with more, and take bigger chances.

Russell Brand isn't doing a Dudley Moore imitation, but you can tell he's studied the movie, and carefully resists any temptation to go over the top. Just as well, since the whole role resides over the top. I confess I haven't regarded him as a particularly subtle actor, but here he has a lot of smile moments when he quickly and quietly reacts. I'll mention an almost invisible one. In the scene in the library at the end, when the kiddies are saying rude things, note how he hushes and dismisses them without much seeming to even notice them. That's good acting. Bad acting would be to respond directly and lose the focus of the scene, which must be on the woman he loves.

This *Arthur* is not as laugh-out-loud funny as the earlier one; its scene of a dinner in a staid hotel dining room isn't as successful, and it doesn't have as much fun with the father of the Naomi character. But the dialogue is well written—witty and quick, and not clunky. The visuals in the Grand Central Terminal scene may be overdone, but they are impressive (when did architecture lose its faith in grandeur?). And Russell Brand takes on a thankless task and earns at least some thanks.

The Art of Getting By ★ ★ ½

PG-13, 84 m., 2011

Freddie Highmore (George Zinavoy), Emma Roberts (Sally Howe), Michael Angarano (Dustin), Elizabeth Reaser (Charlotte Howe), Rita Wilson (Vivian Sargent), Blair Underwood (Principal Martinson), Alicia Silverstone (Ms. Herman), Sam Robards (Jack Sargent), Jarlath Conroy (Harris McElroy). Directed by Gavin Wiesen and produced by Kara Baker, P. Jennifer Dana, Darren Goldberg, and Gia Walsh.

George, the hero of *The Art of Getting By*, is a high school senior who has decided to stop doing homework and paying any attention to tests. He isn't tortured, depressed, addicted, or anything like that. It has occurred to him that he will die, and therefore, what use is homework? This is more sophisticated than my theory, which was that homework would kill me.

George is played by Freddie Highmore, who only yesterday was the kid in *August Rush*. He could make a durable leading man because he looks good, and by that I don't mean handsome, I mean kind and likable. He's nice even when he explains to his parents and teachers that he doesn't see the point in graduating from school. He's the spiritual kin of Melville's Bartleby the scrivener, who patiently informed people, "I would prefer not to."

By not assigning a fixable reason for George's behavior, the movie sidesteps some of the clichés of the teen problem picture. Not all of them. There's always romance. George, for example, is attracted by Sally (Emma Roberts), a classmate who he assumes is somehow beyond his reach. In this he isn't being defeatist but, he thinks, simply realistic. If he were a little more perceptive, he'd realize Sally likes him a whole lot. His life seems stuck on Pause.

His passivity is both interesting and frustrating because George possesses the answers to all of his problems, and freely chooses to be unhappy. As a result, most of the tension generated by the movie is in ourselves and not in the plot. We want George to succeed, we want him together with Sally, and we even like Dustin (Michael Angarano), an older artist who likes Sally and likes George, too. Dustin is so nice he would step aside from Sally if he thought George was ever going to make a move. Not likely in romance, but there you have it.

George's parents (Rita Wilson and Sam Robards) are concerned, but curiously distant. The family is obviously affluent, but isn't obsessed with George graduating or getting into a good school. He is spared counseling or diagnosis, and we later learn about their distractions. But his school is very engaged, especially his principal (Blair Underwood), his English teacher (Alicia Silverstone), and his bearded and irascible art teacher (Jarlath Conroy). They come up with a deadline that would provide more tension if it were not so clear that a film like this requires George to meet it.

That leads to a rather sadistic scene in which George must actually attend his school graduation ceremony to find out if he's graduating. This last-instant verdict has been brought about by the principal, who until this point in the film has been unfailingly kind and understanding. I fear the scene exists for the single purpose of concocting an ending for the screenplay. It shouldn't be so obvious.

Another problem involves certain details of the relationship between Sally and Dustin that I don't want to spoil for you. Let me use evasive language. With what is implied by her apparent decision, we must assume emotional decisions on her part that aren't consistent with her eventual choices. You'll see what I mean.

The Art of Getting By is pleasant and well acted, and easy to watch. I wouldn't advise against seeing it because it showcases Freddie Highmore and Emma Roberts (Julia's niece), and they are likely to do greater things, but at the end I was wondering, what is the point? Nice people lead enviable lives, the hero can solve most of his own problems, and the villain is a sweetheart. It's custard without the lemon.

The Art of the Steal ★ ★ ★ ½

NO MPAA RATING, 101 m., 2010

Featuring John Anderson, Colin B. Bailey, Julian Bond, Carolyn T. Carluccio, David D'Arcy, Richard Feigen, D. Michael Fisher, Tom L. Freudenheim, Jim Gerlach, Richard H. Glanton, Nancy Herman, Walter Herman, Christopher Knight, Meryl Levitz, Bruce H. Mann, Robert Marmon, Toby Marmon, Ross Mitchell, Barry Munitz, Irvin Nahan, Marcelle Pick, David W. Rawson, Jay Raymond, Edward G. Rendell, Mark D. Schwartz, Harry Sefarbi, Richard Segal, Nick Tinari, Robert Zaller. A documentary directed by Don Argott.

Dr. Albert C. Barnes accomplished two things for which we must be grateful: He invented a treatment for VD, and he founded the Barnes Foundation in the Philadelphia suburb of Lower Merion. The first paid for the second, so the wages of sin were invested wisely. In his imposing private structure, far from the power brokers of the city, Barnes created an oasis for serious students, who could learn from his collection without rubbing elbows with crowds of art tourists.

How important was the Barnes Collection? I learn from the press notes of *The Art of the Steal* that it included 181 Renoirs, 69 Cezannes, 59 Matisses, 46 Picassos, 16 Modiglianis, and 7 Van Goghs. Barnes collected these during many trips to Paris at a time when establishment museums, such as the Philadelphia Museum of Art, considered these artists beneath their attention. Some of the paintings are today literally priceless; one estimate of the worth of the collection is $25 billion.

That was a lot of art to be sitting in Merion. Barnes knew it was. He designed every detail of his collection with personal care, grouping paintings to reflect and comment on one another, placing period furniture and wall ornaments near them, and filling walls with a richness of paintings close, but not too close, together. He loved his collection, and he hated the Philadelphia Main Line establishment—most particularly, the Museum of Art, which had scorned his collection in its early days.

Barnes was a rich man. He hired himself some Philadelphia lawyers and drew up an iron-clad will, endowing the foundation with funds enabling it to be maintained indefinitely where it was and how it was. It was his specific requirement that the collection not go anywhere near the Philadelphia Museum of Art. And that is exactly where it is today.

He hated the museum. He hated its benefactors, the Annenberg family, founded by a gangster, enriched by *TV Guide*, chummy with the Nixon administration. The Annenbergs published the *Philadelphia Inquirer*, which consistently and as a matter of policy covered this story with slanted articles and editorials.

Don Argott's *The Art of the Steal* is a documentary that reports the hijacking of the Barnes Collection with outrage, as the Theft of the Century. It was carried out in broad daylight by elected officials and Barnes trustees, all of whom justified it by placing the needs of the vast public above the whims of a dead millionaire.

The film explains in great detail the chain of events that began after the death of Barnes at the wheel of his own car in 1951. It involves Lincoln University, the small African-American college to which he entrusted control of the foundation, no doubt to piss off the establishment. It involves how the president of Lincoln, Richard H. Glanton, sidestepped the wishes of Barnes by taking many of the treasures on tour, bringing honor to himself for such a benefaction. But Glanton is not the final villain. As he perhaps overspent and depleted Barnes's endowment, the vultures from Philadelphia were hovering, ready to pounce and fly off with their masterpieces to their nest in the museum—yes, at the top of the same great stairs Rocky Balboa ran up in *Rocky*. It is not difficult to imagine them at the top, their hands in triumph above their heads.

Well, was this such a bad thing? The Renoirs and Picassos can now be seen by anyone visiting the museum, instead of by a limited number of art students. That is good, I suppose, although I've seen tourists jogging past the *Mona Lisa* in Paris just to check it off their itinerary. The film could do a better job of allowing the public access issue to be defended. But what it does is tell a cautionary tale.

It is perfectly clear exactly what Barnes specified in his will. It was drawn up by the best legal minds. It is clear that what happened to his collection was against his wishes. It is clear that the city fathers acted in obviation of those wishes, and were upheld in a court of appeals. What is finally clear is this: It doesn't matter a damn what your will says if you have $25 billion and politicians and the establishment want it.

Astro Boy ★ ★ ★

PG, 94 m., 2009

With the voices of Freddie Highmore (Astro, Toby), Kristen Bell (Cora), Nathan Lane (Hamegg), Eugene Levy (Orrin), Matt Lucas (Sparx), Bill Nighy (Dr. Elefun), Donald Sutherland (President Stone), Charlize Theron (*Our Friends* Narrator), Nicolas Cage (Dr. Tenma). Directed by David Bowers and produced by Maryann Garger. Screenplay by Bowers and Timothy Hyde Harris.

Astro Boy is yet another animated comedy in which the hero, who is about the same age as his target audience, is smarter, braver, and stronger than the adults in his world. Toby is also a quick learner; after he dies in an accident, he's reborn inside a robot that looks just like him and retains all of his memories. His father, in fact, treats him just like the original Toby. But "Toby is dead!" my inner logician insisted. Here's a good question: Does Astro Boy with Toby's memory wonder why he is a robot and can fly?

No time to ask questions. Metro City is in upheaval. Astro Boy (voice by Freddie Highmore) is powered by a Blue energy source discovered by his dad (Nicolas Cage); it's safe and clean, but its opposite is Red energy, which is dirty and dangerous and desired by the warmonger president (Donald Sutherland), who wants to use it to seize complete control. That seems like a shame, because Metro City is in peaceful orbit around the earth, its citizens waited on hand and foot by robots.

Below on Earth, there is devastation as garbage piles high. The precocious Astro Boy does battle with the president and then vamooses to Earth, where he meets some scavenger human kids, led by the Faginesque Hamegg (Nathan Lane), who builds fighting robots out of scrap parts. Apparently BattleBots still thrives.

All builds up to Astro Boy, back up in Metro City, leading the Blues against the evil, polluting Reds, in an apocalypse where any thoughts of Blue and Red states would of course be completely inappropriate.

The movie contains less of its interesting story and more action and battle scenes than I would have preferred. Has market research discovered our children are all laboring with attention deficits, and can only absorb so much story before brightly colored objects distract them with deafening combat? Still, *Astro Boy* is better than most of its recent competitors, such as *Monsters vs. Aliens* and *Kung Fu Panda*.

It may have a building audience because of loyalty to the Astro Boy character, first introduced in a Japanese manga and then adapted into two generations of TV cartoons. Daffy Duck, he ain't; in fact, he's a boy robot of few words and simple ideas, but he has pluck, and cannons built into his chest and butt. You don't see that every day.

Now try this test. *Astro Boy* was filmed in glorious 2-D. Take the kids if they insist on going, and afterward ask them if there was anything missing. I'll bet not a single kid says, "I wish it had been in 3-D." So the kids are happy, plus you've saved $3 a ticket and didn't have to wear those damned glasses.

The A-Team ★ ½

PG-13, 121 m., 2010

Liam Neeson (Hannibal), Jessica Biel (Charisa), Bradley Cooper (Face), Sharlto Copley (Murdock), Quinton "Rampage" Jackson (B.A.), Patrick Wilson (Lynch). Directed by Joe Carnahan and produced by Stephen J. Cannell, Jules Daly, Tony Scott, Spike Seldin, Iain Smith, and Alex Young. Screenplay by Joe Carnahan, Brian Bloom, and Skip Woods, based on the TV series by Cannell and Frank Lupo.

The A-Team is an incomprehensible mess with the 1980s TV show embedded inside. The characters have the same names, they play the same types, they have the same traits, and they're easily as shallow. That was OK for a TV sitcom, which is what the show really was, but at over two hours of queasy-cam anarchy it's punishment.

The movie uses the new style of violent action, which fragments sequences into so many bits and pieces that it's impossible to form any sense of what's happening, or where, or to whom. The actors appear in flash-frames, intercut with shards of CGI and accompanied by loud noises, urgent music, and many explosions. This continues for the required length, and then there's some dialogue. Not a lot. A few words, a sentence, sometimes a statement that crosses the finish line at paragraph length.

The plot: Wrongly framed for counterfeiting, the team members, all Iraq veterans, bust out of various prisons and go after the engraving plates, which would be pretty much worn out while printing enough $100 bills to pay for the millions in property damage they cause in the process.

Bored out of my mind during this spectacle, I found my attention wandering to the subject of physics. *The A-Team* has an action scene that admirably demonstrates Newton's Third Law, which instructs us that for every action there is always an equal and opposite reaction.

The movie illustrates this as the heroes fall from an exploding airplane while inside an armored tank. As the tank hurtles to the ground (cf. Newton's Law of Gravity), the team leader, Hannibal Smith (Liam Neeson), looks out an opening and barks out commands for the tank's gun. I am paraphrasing: "Turn forty-five degrees to the left! Fire! Twenty-five degrees to the right! Fire!" etc. In this way he is able to direct the fall of the tank and save their lives. This is very funny.

The action scenes also benefit from everyone having had a glance at the choreography beforehand. Consider a scene when a team member is confronted by a Talking Killer. This is, of course, a killer who only has to pull the trigger but pauses to sneer and boast. He and his target are standing in the middle of a jumble of dozens of freight shipping containers that have been spilled onto a dock. He talks just a little too long, and B. A. Baracus ("Rampage" Jackson) comes roaring to the rescue through the air on his motorcycle and wipes him out.

I know there are Harley lovers among my devoted readers. Am I right in assuming that it is difficult to get enough speed for a good aerial jump while biking across a crooked heap of freight containers? I ask because, as I hinted above, no action in this movie necessarily has any relationship to the actions surrounding it.

The characters here have that annoying ability to precisely predict what will happen and coordinate their response to it. An example. A slimy double-dealer is about to kill another team member, never mind who, when suddenly behind him a container is lifted into the air, and behind it are revealed all of the other team members lined up in a row, with choice words and brief phrases to say.

I don't want to be tiresome, but (1) how did they know the two guys were behind precisely that container; (2) how did they line up a crane and hook up the container without being heard or noticed; (3) how were they able to gather the members so quickly after the chaos of the preceding action; and (4) was someone eavesdropping to give the cue at the right moment to lift the container? Ten seconds later, and it might have been too late. Ten seconds earlier, and dialogue would have been stepped on.

Are my objections ridiculous? Why? How is it interesting to watch a movie in which the "action" is essentially colorful abstractions? Isn't it more satisfying if you know where everyone is and what they're doing and how they're doing it in real time? In other words, isn't *The Hurt Locker* more interesting than *The A-Team*?

To give it credit, the movie knows it is childish. The PG-13 is appropriate. There's little actual gore, no sex beyond a chaste kiss, no R-rated language, but—ohmigod—there's smoking! Alert to preteens: Try one of those fat cigars Hannibal smokes and you won't feel like dinner.

Atlas Shrugged: Part 1 ★

PG-13, 97 m., 2011

Taylor Schilling (Dagny Taggart), Grant Bowler (Henry Rearden), Matthew Marsden (James Taggart), Graham Beckel (Ellis Wyatt), Edi Gathegi (Eddie Willers), Jsu Garcia (Francisco D'Anconia), Michael Lerner (Wesley Mouch). Directed by Paul Johansson and produced by John Aglialoro and Harmon Kaslow. Screenplay by Aglialoro and Brian Patrick O'Toole, adapted from the novel by Ayn Rand.

I feel like my arm is all warmed up and I don't have a game to pitch. I was primed to review *Atlas Shrugged*. I figured it might provide a parable of Ayn Rand's philosophy that I could discuss. For me, that philosophy reduces itself to: "I'm on board; pull up the lifeline." There are, however, people who take Ayn Rand even more seriously than comic book fans take *Watchmen*. I expected to receive learned and sarcastic lectures on the pathetic failings of my review.

And now I am faced with this movie, the most anticlimactic nonevent since Geraldo Rivera broke into Al Capone's vault. I suspect only someone very familiar with Rand's 1957 novel could understand the film at all, and I doubt they will be happy with it. For the rest of us, it involves a series of business meetings in luxurious retro leather-and-brass boardrooms and offices, and restaurants and bedrooms that look borrowed from a hotel no doubt known as the Robber Baron Arms.

During these meetings, everybody drinks. More wine is poured and sipped in this film than at a convention of oenophiles. There are conversations in the English language after which I sometimes found myself asking, "What did they just say?" The dialogue seems to have been ripped throbbing with passion from the pages of *Investor's Business Daily*. Much of the excitement centers on the tensile strength of steel.

The story involves Dagny Taggart (Taylor Schilling), a young woman who controls a railroad company named Taggart Transcontinental (its motto: "Ocean to Ocean"). She is a fearless and visionary entrepreneur, who is determined to use a revolutionary new steel to repair her train tracks. Vast forces seem to conspire against her.

It's a few years in the future. America has become a state in which mediocrity is the goal and high-achieving individuals the enemy. Laws have been passed prohibiting companies from owning other companies. Dagny's new steel, which is produced by her sometimes lover Hank Rearden (Grant Bowler), has been legislated against because it's better than other steels. The Union of Railroad Engineers has decided it will not operate Dagny's trains. Just to show you how bad things have become, a government minister announces "a tax will be applied to the state of Colorado in order to equalize our national economy." So you see how governments and unions are the enemy of visionary entrepreneurs.

But you're thinking, railroads? Yes, although airplanes exist in this future, trains are where it's at. When I was six, my Aunt Martha brought me to Chicago to attend the great Railroad Fair of 1948, at which the nation's rail companies celebrated the wonders that were on the way. They didn't quite foresee mass air transportation. *Atlas Shrugged* seems to buy into the fair's glowing vision of the future of trains. Rarely, perhaps never, has television news covered the laying of new railroad track with the breathless urgency of the news channels shown in this movie.

So OK. Let's say you know the novel, you agree with Ayn Rand, you're an objectivist or a libertarian, and you've been waiting eagerly for this movie. Man, are you going to get a letdown. It's not enough that a movie agree with you, in however an incoherent and murky fashion. It would help if it were, like, you know, entertaining?

The movie is constructed of a few kinds of scenes. (1) People sipping their drinks in clubby surroundings and exchanging dialogue that sounds like assorted corporate lingo; (2) railroads, and lots of 'em; (3) limousines driving through cities in ruin and arriving in front of vast, ornate buildings; (4) city skylines; (5) the beauties of Colorado. There is also a love scene, which is shown not merely from the waist up but from the ears up. The man keeps his shirt on. This may be disappointing for libertarians, who I believe enjoy rumpy-pumpy as much as anyone.

Oh, and there is Wisconsin. Dagny and Hank ride blissfully in Taggart's new high-speed train, and then Hank suggests they take a trip to Wisconsin, where the state's policies caused the suppression of an engine that runs on the ozone in the air, or something (the film's detailed explanation won't clear this up). They decide to drive there. That's when you'll enjoy the beautiful landscape photography of the deserts of Wisconsin. My free advice to the filmmakers: If you want to use a desert, why not just refer to Wisconsin as "New Mexico"?

Atlas Shrugged closes with a title card saying, "End of Part One." Frequently throughout the film, characters repeat the phrase, "Who is John Galt?" Well they might ask. A man in black, always shot in shadow, is apparently John Galt. If you want to get a good look at him and find out why everybody is asking, I hope you can find out in Part Two. I don't think you can hold out for Part Three.

The Audition ★ ★ ★

NO MPAA RATING, 107 m., 2009

Featuring Jamie Barton, Kiera Duffy, Michael Fabiano, Disella Larusdottir, Ryan McKinny, Angela Meade, Nicholas Pallesen, Matthew Olenk, Alek Shrader, Ryan Smith, Amber Wagner, Conductor Marco Armiliato, General Manager Peter Gelb, and Brian Dickie of the Lyric Opera of Chicago, a judge. A documentary directed by Susan Froemke and produced by the Metropolitan Opera.

Attending the Metropolitan Opera's annual National Council Auditions must be one of the great pleasures of operagoing. From forty-five districts of the nation, hopeful young singers compete to advance to fifteen regionals, from which they advance to semifinals in New York, and ten become national finalists. Of these, five become grand winners after public performances with the Met's full orchestra. "I sang on the Met stage with their orchestra!" exults Ryan Smith, one of the singers. "That's enough!"

The Audition is a backstage and onstage documentary observing this process as it unfolded two years ago. A sad element in the film is the fact that Ryan Smith, blessed with a sunny presence and a magnificent tenor voice, died at thirty-one, since the film was made. Chosen for the Lyric's Ryan Opera Center ensemble, he was diagnosed with lymphoma soon after. He speaks briefly about himself; he's older than the other finalists and actually stopped singing for three years, he says, before telling his parents he was going to give it two years of his best effort. That was good enough. It doesn't get any better than winning at this level.

I am far from being a music critic, but I am an opera lover; we've had season tickets at Chicago's Lyric for twenty years, and my love of opera began when I was twenty and drove a rental Vespa to the Baths of Caracalla in Rome, where I was delighted to see elephants and camels under the stars and discover that the Italians sold *glace* during the performance.

It goes without saying that any singer making it to the national auditions is gifted. The film is centered on their performances, as we follow them up the final steps of their ascent. The Met has produced the film, allowed access to backstage, rehearsals, costume fittings, and so on, and (most interesting) allows us to listen in on some of the jury's deliberations; the judges include Brian Dickie of Chicago's own Lyric.

However, and this is a big however, what we eavesdrop on is almost entirely complimentary. A gingerly discussion on the sensitive topic of the weights of singers is only fleetingly followed. Visiting dressing rooms and rehearsals, we see only pleasant, smiling, sometimes nervous faces. I suppose we shouldn't expect fiascos, breakdowns, or temper tantrums—and at this level, maybe there were none. The American opera stars I've met, such as Sam Ramey, are absolutely down-to-earth. I doubt if Maria Callas would have been a delight at the National Council.

I suspect the director, Susan Froemke, may have had some inside information. As the winners are being announced, her camera stays focused on one of them as if she knows what's going to happen. Speaking of that camera, I wonder why she chose a wide lens if she was going to do so much panning; the stretching at the sides of shots becomes distracting.

As a documentary, *The Audition* isn't cutting-edge. As an introduction to a new generation of American opera stars and an opportunity to hear them sing, it is splendid.

Avatar ★ ★ ★ ★

PG-13, 163 m., 2009

Sam Worthington (Jake Sully), Zoe Saldana (Neytiri), Sigourney Weaver (Grace Augustine), Stephen Lang (Colonel Miles Quaritch), Michelle Rodriguez (Trudy Chacon), Giovanni Ribisi (Parker Selfridge), Joel David Moore (Norm Spellman), CCH Pounder (Mo'at), Wes Studi (Eytukan), Laz Alonso (Tsu'tey). Directed by James Cameron and produced by Cameron and Jon Landau. Screenplay by Cameron.

Watching *Avatar*, I felt sort of the same as when I saw *Star Wars* in 1977. That was another movie I walked into with uncertain expectations. James Cameron's film has been the subject of relentlessly dubious advance buzz, just as his *Titanic* was. Once again, he has silenced the doubters by simply delivering an extraordinary film. There is still at least one man in Hollywood who knows how to spend $250 million, or was it $300 million, wisely.

Avatar is not simply sensational entertainment, although it is that. It's a technical breakthrough. It has a flat-out Green and antiwar message. It is predestined to launch a cult. It contains such visual detailing that it would reward repeated viewings. It invents a new language, Na'vi, as *The Lord of the Rings* did, although mercifully I doubt this one can be spoken by humans, even teenage humans. It creates new movie stars. It is an Event, one of those films you feel you must see to keep up with the conversation.

The story, set in the year 2154, involves a mission by U.S. armed forces to an Earth-sized moon in orbit around a massive star. This new world, Pandora, is a rich source of a mineral Earth desperately needs. Pandora represents not even a remote threat to Earth, but we nevertheless send in the military to attack and conquer it. Gung-ho Marines employ machine guns and pilot armored hover ships on bombing runs. You are free to find this an allegory about contemporary politics. Cameron obviously does.

Pandora harbors a planetary forest inhabited peacefully by the Na'vi, a blue-skinned, golden-eyed race of slender giants, each one perhaps twelve feet tall. The atmosphere is not breathable by humans, and the landscape makes us pygmies. To venture out of our landing craft, we use avatars—Na'vi look-alikes grown organically and mind-controlled by humans who remain wired up in a trancelike state on the ship. While acting as avatars, they see, fear, taste, and feel like Na'vi, and have all the same physical adeptness.

This last quality is liberating for the hero, Jake Sully (Sam Worthington), who is a paraplegic. He's been recruited because he's a genetic match for a dead identical twin, whom an expensive avatar was created for. In avatar state he can walk again, and as his payment for this duty he will be given a very expensive operation to restore movement to his legs. In theory he's in no danger because if his avatar is destroyed, his human form remains untouched. In theory.

On Pandora, Jake begins as a good soldier and then goes native after his life is saved by the lithe and brave Neytiri (Zoe Saldana). He finds it is indeed true, as the aggressive Colonel Miles Quaritch (Stephen Lang) briefed them, that nearly every species of life here wants him for lunch. (Avatars are not made of Na'vi flesh, but try explaining that to a charging thirty-ton rhino with a snout like a bullet-head shark.)

The Na'vi survive on this planet by knowing it well, living in harmony with nature, and being wise about the creatures they share with. In this and countless other ways they resemble Native Americans. Like them, they tame another species to carry them around—not horses, but graceful, flying dragonlike creatures. The scene involving Jake capturing and taming one of these great beasts is one of the film's greatest sequences.

Like *Star Wars* and *LOTR*, *Avatar* employs a new generation of special effects. Cameron said it would, and many doubted him. It does.

Pandora is largely CGI. The Na'vi are embodied through motion-capture techniques, convincingly. They look like specific, persuasive individuals, yet sidestep the eerie Uncanny Valley effect. And Cameron and his artists succeed at the difficult challenge of making Neytiri a green-skinned giantess with golden eyes and a long, supple tail, and yet—I'll be damned—sexy.

At 163 minutes, the film doesn't feel too long. It contains so much. The human stories. The Na'vi stories, for the Na'vi are also developed as individuals. The complexity of the planet, which harbors a global secret. The ultimate warfare, with Jake joining the resistance against his former comrades. Small graceful details like a floating creature that looks like a cross between a blowing dandelion seed and a drifting jellyfish, and embodies goodness. Or astonishing floating cloud-islands.

I've complained that many recent films abandon storytelling in their third acts and go for wall-to-wall action. Cameron essentially does that here but has invested well in establishing his characters so that it *matters* what they do in battle and how they do it. There are issues at stake greater than simply which side wins.

Cameron promised he'd unveil the next generation of 3-D in *Avatar*. I'm a notorious skeptic about this process, a needless distraction from the perfect realism of movies in 2-D. Cameron's iteration is the best I've seen—and more important, one of the most carefully employed. The film never uses 3-D simply because it has it and doesn't promiscuously violate the fourth wall. He also seems quite aware of 3-D's weakness for dimming the picture, and even with a film set largely in interiors and a rain forest, there's sufficient light. I saw the film in 3-D on a good screen and was impressed.

It takes a hell of a lot of nerve for a man to stand up at the Oscarcast and proclaim himself king of the world. James Cameron just got reelected.

Away We Go ★ ★ ★ ½

R, 97 m., 2009

John Krasinski (Burt), Maya Rudolph (Verona), Jeff Daniels (Jerry), Maggie Gyllenhaal (LN), Allison Janney (Lily), Chris Messina (Tom), Catherine O'Hara (Gloria), Paul Schneider (Courtney), Carmen Ejogo (Grace), Jim Gaffigan (Lowell). Directed by Sam Mendes and produced by Edward Saxon, Marc Turtletaub, and Peter Saraf. Screenplay by Dave Eggers and Vendela Vida.

Burt and Verona are two characters rarely seen in the movies: thirty-something, educated, healthy, self-employed, gentle, thoughtful, whimsical, not neurotic, and really truly in love. Their great concern is finding the best place and way to raise their child, who is a bun still in the oven. For every character like this I've seen in the last twelve months, I've seen twenty, maybe thirty, mass murderers.

Sam Mendes's *Away We Go* is a film for nice people to see. Nice people also go to *Terminator: Salvation,* but it doesn't make them any nicer. The movie opened June 5, 2009, in New York and Los Angeles, and then rolled out after lukewarm reviews accusing Verona and Burt of being smug, superior, and condescending. These are not sins if you have something to be smug about and much reason to condescend. Are the supporting characters all caricatures or simply a cross-section of the kinds of grotesques we usually meet in movies? I use the term "grotesque" as Sherwood Anderson does in *Winesburg, Ohio*: a person who has one characteristic exaggerated beyond all scale with the others.

Burt (John Krasinski) and Verona (Maya Rudolph) live in an underheated shabby home with a cardboard window. "We don't live like grown-ups," Verona observes. It's not that they can't afford a better home, so much that they are stalled in an impoverished student lifestyle. Now that they're about to become parents, they can't keep adult life on hold.

Away We Go is about an unplanned odyssey they take around North America to visit friends and family and essentially do some comparison shopping among lifestyles. Her parents are dead, so they begin with his: Gloria (Catherine O'Hara) and Jerry (Jeff Daniels). The parents truly *are* self-absorbed, and have no wish to wait around to welcome their first grandchild. They're moving to Antwerp.

Verona is of mixed race, and Gloria asks her

conversationally, "Will the baby be black?" Is this insensitive? Why? Parents on both sides of an interracial couple would naturally wonder, and the film's ability to ask the question is not racist, but matter-of-fact in an America slowly growing tolerant. In moments like that the married screenwriters, Dave Eggers and Vendela Vida (both novelists and magazine editors), reflect a society in which race is no longer the primary defining characteristic.

After the parents vote for Belgium, Burt and Verona head for Phoenix and a visit with her onetime boss Lily (Allison Janney) and her husband, Lowell (Jim Gaffigan). Lily is a monster, a daytime alcoholic whose speech is grossly offensive and whose husband and children are in shock. Burt and Verona flee to Madison, where Burt's childhood friend Ellen (Maggie Gyllenhaal) has changed her name to "LN" and become one of those rigid campus feminists who have banned human nature from their rule book.

Then to Montreal and friends from college, Tom and Munch (Chris Messina and Melanie Lynskey), who are unhappily convinced they're happy. And next down to Miami and Burt's brother (Paul Schneider), whose wife has abandoned her family. Not a single example of healthy parenting in the lot of them.

The almost perfect relationship of (the unmarried) Verona and Burt seems to survive inside a bubble of their own devising, and since they can blow that bubble anywhere, they, of course, find the perfect home for it, in a scene of uncommon sunniness. They have been described as implausibly ideal, but you know what? So are their authors, Eggers and Vida. Consider: Thirty-somethings. Two children. Novelists and essayists. He publishes *McSweeney's*; she edits *The Believer.*

They are playful and at the same time socially committed. Consider his wonderful project 826 Valencia, a nonprofit storefront operation in San Francisco, Chicago, Los Angeles, New York, Seattle, Boston, and Ann Arbor. It runs free tutoring and writing workshops for young people from six to eighteen. The playful part can be seen in San Francisco, where the front of the ground floor is devoted to a Pirate Store. Yes. With eye patches, parrots' perches, beard dye, peg legs, planks for walking—all your needs.

I submit that Eggers and Vida are admirable people. If their characters find they are superior to many people, well, maybe they are. "This movie does not like you," sniffs Tony Scott of the *New York Times.* Perhaps with good reason.

B

The Baader Meinhof Complex ★ ★ ½

R, 149 m., 2009

Martina Gedeck (Ulrike Meinhof), Moritz Bleibtreu (Andreas Baader), Johanna Wokalek (Gudrun Ensslin), Bruno Ganz (Horst Herold), Nadja Uhl (Brigitte Mohnhaupt), Jan Josef Liefers (Peter Homann), Stipe Erceg (Holger Meins). Directed by Uli Edel and produced by Bernd Eichinger. Screenplay by Eichinger and Edel, based on the book by Stefan Aust.

In the 1970s, Germany was transfixed by the outlaw Baader Meinhof Gang, terrorists who robbed banks, set off explosives, kidnapped, assassinated, and otherwise attempted to bring the government to its knees. What were they against? The usual: American imperialism and German capitalist oppression. What were their politics? Marxist, they thought, but actually reflecting the anarchist theory that random acts of violence could destroy the fabric of a society. They resembled the Weathermen, but were longer lived and much more destructive.

The Baader Meinhof Complex is an ambitious attempt to chart the group's rise, fall, and tentative rebirth over the course of a decade, when it called itself the Red Army Faction. The film is historically accurate, I gather—perhaps too accurate, with too many names and places and dates and victims to easily comprehend. No doubt a German who lived through those years would understand it more easily.

As it is, we grasp at a handful of high-profile characters and relate to the others only in general terms. The central figures are Andreas Baader (Moritz Bleibtreu), Gudrun Ensslin (Johanna Wokalek), and Ulrike Meinhof (Martina Gedeck). Baader and Ensslin are lovers and radicals, inflamed by Vietnam, German industrialism, an attempt on the life of a left-wing leader, and a laundry list of other causes that lead them to conclude that violence is the only effective form of opposition.

Entering their world near the beginning is the well-known journalist Meinhof, who comes to share their convictions. She's the most enigmatic figure in the film. At first a confidante and adviser, she becomes a participant, disappears from view, abandons her husband and their two children. This decision is not satisfactorily examined by the film; because it was actually taken, I suppose we're intended to accept it as granted.

The film is an impressive period re-creation, directed by Uli Edel, whose best work involves Jennifer Jason Leigh's astonishing performance in *Last Exit to Brooklyn* (1989). The screenplay is by Edel and Bernd Eichinger, who wrote the great *Downfall* (2004), about Hitler's last days in his Berlin bunker. That film was intensified by its limitations of time and space. *The Baader Meinhof Complex* is diluted by too many events and characters distributed over too much time.

The unifying character, supplying a sort of focus, is Horst Herold (Bruno Ganz), the top law enforcement officer in West Germany, who makes an attempt to understand the thought processes of the terrorists. He patiently tries to argue why some police tactics are futile and counterproductive. He certainly doesn't agree with Baader Meinhof, but he comprehends them. That's the Sherlock Holmes theory: Understand the mind of the criminal.

Ganz effortlessly brings all the weight of his distinguished career to this role. There is a quality in his face that adds authenticity to everything he says. Hard to believe this is the same actor who played the trembling, disintegrating, paranoid Hitler. As event piles on event, he supplies an observer who assists us.

I suspect that Uli Edel finds some sympathy, in abstract principle anyway, with the cause of the gang. Yes, but their tactics are murderous and futile. At the very beginning, after it is agreed that no guns will be used in a bank robbery, one conspirator brings one and kills someone, and after that, murder becomes part of the Baader Meinhof charter. I submit that it is insane to judge an ordinary citizen as directly responsible for the activities of his government. Yes, we all "share some blame" for what our nations do, but to set off a bomb is to execute a random passerby. That is the evil of terrorism in general, although, of course, in the classic theory of anarchism it is theoretically justified. I understand anarchy expressed in art, literature, or film that seeks the downfall of an establishment. But to take a price in blood? You must be very full of yourself.

The film meanders but finds focus again toward the end, after the first members of the gang are rounded up and held in prison. They go on a hunger strike, are forcibly fed, find the means to commit suicide. Exactly how and why—and even if—some of them take this action is left in some doubt. No doubt it was the same in life. The film would have benefited by being less encompassing and focusing on a more limited number of emblematic characters—Meinhof and Herold, for starters.

Babies ★ ★ ★

PG, 79 m., 2010

Featuring Ponijao, Bayar, Mari, and Hattie. A documentary directed by Thomas Balmes and produced by Amandine Billot, Alain Chabat, and Christine Rouxel.

Babies is the perfect film for anyone who has never had the opportunity to interact with humans at an early age. You may never have had one, held one, or baby-sat one, yet remained curious about the infants you see in a park, on the beach, or in baby carriers at the mall. Now a French documentarian has traveled to Africa, Asia, and America to bring back charming footage of babies in their natural habitats.

If, however, you've raised children and/or grandchildren, or had little brothers and sisters, the movie may resemble seventy-nine minutes of unpaid baby-sitting. When Baby Mari starts screaming, you're wishing you could turn on the TV and use something bright and noisy as a distraction. But no, you're at a movie. On the other hand, *Babies* may be fascinating viewing for babies, just as many dogs and cats have their favorite programs. At last, programming for the Mommy & Me screenings.

The babies are cute. Well, all babies are cute. That's just as well, because how could filmmakers audition a baby and wait six months to give it a callback? It's not a baby anymore. The director, Thomas Balmes, has found exemplary babies in Namibia, Mongolia, Tokyo, and San Francisco, and observes them lovingly as they nurse, play, doze, poke kittens, and happily hit one another. The movie is really about the babies, not their parents, and in most cases we see only those parts of the parents ranking highest on the infant's interest scale: nipples, hands, arms, and male and female chests. Not all of the nipples are real, but the babies don't discriminate as long as they work.

Two of the babies come from poor parts of the world, and two from rich. They seem equally happy and healthy. The Japanese and American babies are subjected to an awesome array of baby training strategies so they can begin climbing the success ladder as early as possible. I have no argument against baby yoga classes, but I have never known a baby that wasn't naturally able to contort itself into alarming positions and get lost in meditation on the spur of the moment.

The African baby, Ponijao, lives in a forest hut with an earth floor, but this is Home and here is Mother and there are sticks to play with that may not be made of plastic and ornamented with Disney creatures but are excellent sticks nonetheless, and satisfying. Bayar, whose family lives in a yurt in Mongolia, passes time by becoming expert in sibling rivalry. Mari, from Japan, and Hattie, from America, are surrounded by a baffling array of devices to entertain them, serve them, shelter them, protect them, and help them grow up big and strong. Can the epidemic of attention deficit disorder be explained by the First World's lack of opportunities for babies to be bored? How can babies concentrate when things are forever being jingled and dangled at them? Is there too much incoming?

I dunno. What I do know is that babies are miraculous. From a sprawling, bawling start, they learn to walk, talk, plan, scheme, play, and figure stuff out. Generations of scientists have hurled themselves at the question of exactly how babies learn to talk. They must be getting so frustrated by the fact that the babies just go ahead and do it with no training.

Did I like the movie? Aw, yeah, I did. How could I not? Did I feel I needed to see it? Not really. I appreciated the fact that there was no narrator to explain what I was seeing; no voice-overs like "little Bayar learns early to appreciate the mystery of yogurt." No parents asking, "Are you a good little boy?" and answering, "Yes, he's good little boy." Just babies. Wonderful. I was once in that state myself. I remember being flat on my stomach with my eyes an inch away from ants all crawling in a line on the front sidewalk. I've never been so entertained in my life.

The Back-up Plan ★

PG-13, 104 m., 2010

Jennifer Lopez (Zoe), Alex O'Loughlin (Stan). Directed by Alan Poul and produced by Todd Black, Jason Blumenthal, and Steve Tisch. Screenplay by Kate Angelo.

Some movies are no better than second-rate sitcoms. Other movies are no better than third-rate sitcoms. *The Back-up Plan* doesn't deserve comparison with sitcoms. It plays like an unendurable TV commercial about beautiful people with great lifestyles and not a thought in their empty little heads. So timid is this film that when it finally arrives at its inevitable childbirth scene, it bails out after two "pushes"!

Jennifer Lopez has never looked better. That's about all she does here, is look better. She is talented and deserves more than this birdbrained plot about characters who have no relationship to life as it is lived by, you know, actual people. The movie deals with artificial insemination, romance, sex, and organic goat cheese, which are promising areas for investigation, but it's so watered down it approaches homeopathy.

Lopez plays Zoe, a Manhattan pet shop owner who despairs of finding the perfect inseminator and decides to become artificially impregnated. Leaving the doctor's office, she is so happy she finds herself singin' in the rain. Then she hails a cab and a strange man pops into the backseat the same moment she does. As a Meet Cute, this ranks right down there with two characters bending over to pick up the same thing and bumping heads, which is what Tony Randall is always doing whenever I think of Meet Cutes.

This stranger is Stan (Alex O'Loughlin). We know, according to the Law of Conservation of Dramatic Resources, that (a) Zoe will become pregnant, and (b) she and Stan will fall in love. Consider the alternatives: (a1) she doesn't become pregnant, and (b2) they never see each other again. Anyway, fate brings them together, and then again, and soon they're falling for each other.

This Stan is a prime catch. Not only does he personally sell organic goat cheese in a ridiculously upscale farmers' market, but he produces it himself, on his own upstate farm. I am at a loss to explain why the movie squandered an opportunity to show Lopez milking a goat. Or having a goat eat her shoes, or whatever goats usually do in movies of this sort.

Obviously, the only way to make this feature-length is for Zoe and Stan to break up and get back together again, which they do, I think, three times. Their breakups tend toward communications difficulties, as one or the other idiotically misunderstands dialogue that is crystal clear to everyone in the audience. In Little Movie Glossary lore this is Damon Knight's famous Idiot Plot, in which all difficulties could be resolved by the uttering of one or two words.

I don't believe *The Back-up Plan* is intended to be set in the real Manhattan. Take a close look at the farmers' market. It's more of a Farmer's Faire at a church benefit in a rich suburb. Farmer Stan and his goats, indeed. But consider the scene where Zoe is a bridesmaid at a wedding, and her water breaks. What does she do? Rush to the hospital? No, she commandeers the wedding's rented white Bentley and is driven to the market, where the auto shoulders its way right down the middle of the street and halts before the organic goat cheese stall, where Zoe can leap out and make up with Stan right there in public, while onlookers all smile and listen like benevolent insiders, instead of New Yorkers wondering who the hell these jerks are. Does Stan happen to have one of those little boxes with a ring in it handy? What does a goat do in the woods?

I have neglected poor little Nuts, Zoe's Boston terrier. Nuts follows her everywhere, and whenever he gets a close-up, he barks appropriately, as if he understands what is said. When was the last time in a movie where somebody said something, and there was a cut to a dog who barked, and you thought, "That's so funny!" Nuts is paralyzed from the waist down and pulls himself everywhere on his little cart, without the benefit of much loving and cooing from his mistress, who relates to him as exactly what he is, a prop. But the little tyke can really wheel around and is always there when he's needed on camera.

This movie is desperately boring. No one says much of anything interesting. They have extremely limited ranges of interest. There are older characters: Zoe's Nana (Linda Lavin) and grandpa (Tom Bosley) and gynecologist (Robert Klein). They seem human, so the camera cuts away lest they get started on something. At the playground where Stan hangs out (allegedly fascinated by the prospect of fatherhood), there's "Playground Dad" (Anthony Anderson), a proud black father who gives Stan pep talks on the joys of parenting. African-Americans are so wise in movies like this, always playing proud dads and wise advisers and God and so forth, it's a wonder the movies are about anyone else.

Bad Lieutenant: Port of Call New Orleans ★ ★ ★ ★

R, 122 m., 2009

Nicolas Cage (Terence McDonagh), Eva Mendes (Frankie Donnenfield), Val Kilmer (Stevie Pruit), Alvin "Xzibit" Joiner (Big Fate), Fairuza Balk (Heidi), Shawn Hatosy (Armand Benoit), Jennifer Coolidge (Genevieve), Tom Bower (Pat McDonagh). Directed by Werner Herzog and produced by Stephen Belafonte, Nicolas Cage, Randall Emmett, Alan Polsky, Gabe Polsky, Edward R. Pressman, and John Thompson. Screenplay by William Finkelstein.

Werner Herzog's *Bad Lieutenant: Port of Call New Orleans* creates a dire portrait of a rapist, murderer, drug addict, corrupt cop, and degenerate paranoid, very apprehensive about iguanas. It places him in a devastated New Orleans not long after Hurricane Katrina. It makes no attempt to show that city of legends in a flattering light. And it gradually reveals itself as a sly comedy about a snaky but courageous man.

No one is better at this kind of performance than Nicolas Cage. He's a fearless actor. He doesn't care if you think he goes over the top. If a film calls for it, he will crawl to the top, hand over hand, with bleeding fingernails. Regard him in films as various as *Wild at Heart* and *Leaving Las Vegas*. He and Herzog were born to work together. They are both made restless by caution.

In the gallery of bad cops, Terence McDonagh belongs in the first room. Everyone will think of Harvey Keitel's lieutenant in Abel Ferrara's 1992 masterpiece *Bad Lieutenant* for the obvious reason. I hope this film inspires you to seek out that one. It deserves to be sought. Ferrara is Shakespearean in his tragedy, Herzog more like Cormac McCarthy. Sometimes on the road to hell, you can't help but laugh.

In a city deserted by many of its citizens and much of its good fortune, McDonagh (Cage) roams the midnight streets without supervision. He serves and protects himself. He is the law, and the law exists for his personal benefit. Lurking in his prowler outside a night club, he sees a young couple emerge and follows them to an empty parking lot. He stops them, searches them, finds negligible drugs on the man, begins the process of arrest. The man pleads. He's afraid his father will find out. He offers a bribe. McDonagh isn't interested in money. He wants the drugs and the girl, whom he rapes, excited that her boyfriend is watching.

The film's only similarities with the Ferrara film are in the title and the presentation of a wholly immoral drug addict. It's not what a movie is about, but how it's about it. Ferrara regards his lieutenant without mercy. Herzog can be as forgiving as God. An addict in need can be capable of about anything. He will betray family, loved ones, duty, himself. He's driven. Because addiction is an illness (although there is debate), we mustn't be too quick to judge. Drugs and alcohol are both terrible, but drugs can drive a victim more urgently to ruin.

Herzog shows McDonagh lopsided from back pain. He begins with prescription Vicodin and moves quickly to cocaine. As a cop, he develops sources. He steals from other addicts and from dealers. In the confusion after Katrina, he steals from a police evidence room. George Carlin said: "What does cocaine feel like? It makes you feel like some more cocaine."

McDonagh has a girlfriend named Frankie (Eva Mendes). She's a hooker. He's okay with this. He gives her drugs; she sometimes has them for him. They share something an addict craves: sympathy and understanding. They stand together against the horrors. He's also close to his sixtyish father, Pat (Tom Bower), not close to Pat's fortyish partner, Genevieve (Jennifer Coolidge). His father has a history with AA. Genevieve is a bosomy all-day beer drinker. They live in a slowly decaying rural manse somewhere in the parish. Pat knows what to look for in his son and sees it.

Colorful characters enrich McDonagh's tunnel-visioned life. There's Alvin "Xzibit" Joiner as Big Fate, a kingpin who holds the key to the execution of five Nigerian drug dealers. Fairuza Balk as a cop and his sometime lover. Brad Dourif as his bookie (he gambles, too). Val Kilmer as his partner, in an uncharacteristically laid-back performance. Maybe we couldn't take Cage and Kilmer both cranked up to eleven. Tom Bower plays his father as a troubled man but one with good instincts. Jennifer Coolidge, with great screen presence as always, changes gears and plays an MI-wouldn't-LF.

The details of the crimes need not concern us. Just admire the feel of the film. Peter Zeitlinger's cinematography creates a New Orleans unleavened by the picturesque. Herzog, as always, pokes around for the odd detail. Everyone is talking about the shots of the iguanas and the alligator, staring with cold, reptilian eyes. Who else but Herzog would *hold* on their gaze? Who else would foreground them, placing the action in the background? Who but Cage could regard an iguana sideways in a look of suspicion and disquiet? You need to keep an eye on an iguana. The bastards are always up to something.

Bad Lieutenant: Port of Call New Orleans is not about plot but about seasoning. Like New Orleans cuisine, it finds that you can put almost anything in a pot if you add the right spices and peppers and simmer it long enough. Yet, surely, *Bad Lieutenant: Port of Call New Orleans* is an odd title, isn't it? Let me give you my fantasy about that.

Herzog agrees with Ed Pressman to do a remake of the 1992 film, which Pressman also produced. Pressman is no fool and knows a Werner Herzog remake will be nothing like the original. Abel Ferrara is outraged, as well he might be. Martin Scorsese picked *Bad Lieutenant* as one of the ten best films of the 1990s.

"Gee, I dunno," Pressman says. "Maybe we *should* change the title. How about taking a line from the screenplay? How about calling it *Port of Call New Orleans*?"

"We will compromise," Herzog says with that precision he uses when explaining something he needs to make clear. "We will call it *Bad Lieutenant: Port of Call New Orleans.*" He's not going to back down from Ferrara. These are proud men.

Bad Teacher ★ ★

R, 92 m., 2011

Cameron Diaz (Elizabeth Halsey), Justin Timberlake (Scott Delacorte), Lucy Punch (Amy Squirrel), John Michael Higgins (Principal Wally Snur), Jason Segel (Russell Gettis), Phyllis Smith (Lynn Davies), Dave (Gruber) Allen (Sandy Pinkus), Jillian Armenante (Ms. Pavicic). Directed by Jake Kasdan and produced by Jimmy Miller. Screenplay by Gene Stupnitsky and Lee Eisenberg.

Jake Kasdan's *Bad Teacher* immediately brings *Bad Santa* to mind, and suffers by the comparison. Its bad teacher is neither bad enough nor likable enough. The transgressions of Elizabeth Halsey (Cameron Diaz) are more or less what you'd expect, but what's surprising is that she's so nasty and unpleasant. Billy Bob Thornton, as the bad Santa, was more outrageously offensive and yet more redeemed by his desperation. He was bad for urgent reasons. Elizabeth seems bad merely as a greedy lifestyle choice.

As the film opens, the Diaz character is engaged to a rich guy she leeches on but doesn't love. She's dumped and has to return to middle school teaching, an occupation she has no talent for or interest in, and passes the time showing DVDs to her students and napping, drinking, and doing drugs at her desk. This creates astonishment and indignation in the charmingly named Amy Squirrel (Lucy Punch), whose classroom is right across the hall.

The school characters also include the backup teacher Scott Delacorte (Justin Timberlake), amiable but juiceless; the veteran teacher Ms. Pavicic (Jillian Armenante), a sweet dumpling; the hunky gym teacher Russell Gettis (Jason Segel); and the dolphin-obsessed Principal Wally Snur (John Michael Higgins).

Of these characters, the rival played by Lucy Punch is the most colorful because she's the most driven and obsessed. The others seem curiously inconsequential, content to materialize in a scene, perform a necessary function, and vaporize. There's no urgency, and that was the one quality *Bad Santa* dripped with.

None of the film's major characters is a student, which seems odd. Yes, there's a kid who writes bad poetry and has a crush on the class sexpot, but his desperation seems well within comic bounds. There are no vindictive students, none with aggressive behavior, no little Omens in training. The casting of the children seems lacking in imagination, but then what does the screenplay give them to do?

Cameron Diaz has proven that she is gifted with comedy. But here her Elizabeth is a mean, antagonistic money-grubber on autopilot. Where did she come from? Why did she get into teaching in the first place? Has she no heart? There are times in *Bad Santa* when we feel sorry for the poor SOB, but nothing in *Bad Teacher* inspires more than distaste for the character.

Other problems: There is no chemistry, or indeed even much mutual awareness, between Diaz and Timberlake. You know those annual Bad Sex Awards for the worst sex scene in a movie? Their dry-humping scene deserves an award for the decade. The scene itself is pathetic. The shot it ends on—the wet spot on Timberlake's blue jeans—had the audience recoiling.

Whole chunks of the plot seem to have gone missing. And how, oh how, can we possibly understand the eventual development between Elizabeth and Russell the gym teacher? You know what that feels like? It feels like they called Diaz and Jason Segel in for one additional day of shooting to provide a preposterous happy ending. Jolly music keeps elbowing its way onto the sound track in an unconvincing attempt to cue us that we've seen a good comedy.

Bandslam ★ ★ ★

PG, 111 m., 2009

Aly Michalka (Charlotte Banks), Vanessa Hudgens (Sa5m), Gaelan Connell (Will Burton), Scott Porter (Ben Wheatly), Lisa Kudrow (Karen Burton), Ryan Donowho (Basher Martin), Charlie Saxton (Bug). Directed by Todd Graff and produced by Elaine Goldsmith-Thomas, Ron Schmidt, and Marisa Yeres. Screenplay by Graff and Josh A. Cagan.

Will Burton lives within himself. A high school kid, new in town, he's too much of a geek to have any hope of dating the girls he notices in school. He lives in a room where he has made a shrine to David Bowie (with whom he has a daily one-way e-mail correspondence) and wishes he had been born soon enough to frequent CBGB, a legendary New York club that was the launching pad for punk rock.

Not that you'd think he was a punk if you saw him. He's just an ordinary kid, always joined with his iPod until one day his life changes when his musical expertise is recruited by the popular Charlotte (Aly Michalka, of Aly & AJ). She has a three-piece group that will compete in an upcoming tristate battle of the bands, and Will thinks (correctly) it doesn't have a chance.

He in turn spots a loner girl named Sa5m ("the five is silent"). She's played by Vanessa Hudgens (*High School Musical*) as withdrawn, usually in black, keeping secrets. One of them is that she has musical talent. Will adds her to the band, along with other side musicians, including a very quiet Asian girl named Kim Lee (Lisa Chung), who is a classical pianist but plays a great pop keyboard even if it looks like it might kill her to smile.

Charlotte's band is called the Glory Dogs. Will renames it "I Can't Go On I'll Go On," which inevitably reflects a situation that comes up in the film. He throws himself into reshaping the group's music, to the concern of his hovering single mom (Lisa Kudrow)—who comes to hear for herself and is converted.

Will knows zip about girls. When Charlotte says she really likes him, he believes it, even though a former head cheerleader is unlikely to choose a nerd like him. Sa5m expresses great disinterest in the subject of romance, and, of course, is obviously the girl for him. Also in the picture is the handsome senior Ben (Scott Porter), whose own group won Bandslam last year, and who used to be Charlotte's b.f. He's the kind of jerk who accidentally bangs against you in the corridor.

The movie leads up to the tristate Bandslam, of course, at which many relationships are settled and problems solved. So the plot conceals no surprises. What makes the film work is its feeling for the characters and the appeal of the leads. Gaelan Connell has been compared to the young John Cusack and Tom Hanks, with reason; he's attractive but a little quirky, not too handsome, good at replacing his down-on-himself attitude with newfound confidence as a band producer. It does wonders for his high school rep that everyone believes Charlotte likes him.

The student body is, of course, oblivious to the qualities of Sa5m, which is often the case. Look around a school for the bright misfits and you will find those destined to make more of themselves than the "popular crowd"; it's not a foolproof indicator, but useful. You will also find someone who, if they say they like you, probably means it.

Both Aly Michalka and Vanessa Hudgens are gifted musicians, which makes the rehearsal and performance segments convincing. They also possess beauty and presence, and yet look plausible, and Lisa Kudrow avoids the pitfalls of the hysterically overprotective mother; we learn some of the reasons for her concern. This isn't a breakthrough movie, but for what it is, it's charming, and not any more innocuous than it has to be.

The Bang Bang Club ★ ★

NO MPAA RATING, 109 m., 2011

Ryan Phillippe (Greg Marinovich), Malin Akerman (Robin Comley), Taylor Kitsch (Kevin Carter), Frank Rautenbach (Ken Oosterbroek), Neels Van Jaarsveld (Joao Silva). Directed by Steven Silver and produced by Adam Friedlander, Daniel Iron, and Lance Samuels. Screenplay by Silver, based on the book *The Bang-Bang Club: Snapshots from a Hidden War* by Greg Marinovich and Joao Silva.

Many of the photos of the bloody final months of apartheid were taken by four photographers who became famous as "The Bang Bang Club," because of their willingness to risk death for great pictures. Two of them won Pulitzers. One of them was killed, one committed suicide, one was shot four times before retiring. The word often used about them was "courageous," but another word that occurs is "foolhardy."

In the opening scene, we meet Greg Marinovich (Ryan Phillippe), who pulls his car to the side of a highway and clambers down an embankment to follow an angry mob into a riot in Soweto, the African township outside Johannesburg. He joins three other photographers, all of them white, as they run, crouch low, and shoot photos in the middle of mob violence. They seem almost reckless.

Why do the blacks largely ignore these whites in their midst? Why is their attention so focused on their enemies of the same color? This question, which will instinctively occur to many viewers, is never quite dealt with in the film. The photographers sometimes drive into the middle of violent situations, hold up a camera, and say "Press!"—as if that will solve everything. Sometimes it does.

We know with the benefit of history that South Africa's president F. W. de Klerk was even then in talks with Nelson Mandela of the African National Congress that would lead to free elections, Mandela as president, and today's South Africa. In 1994, the white minority was still involved in forcibly fighting black demonstrations, but almost all of the fighting filmed by the Bang Bang Club was black against black. The movie explains in a cursory way that the ANC was being opposed by the Inkatha Freedom Party, made of Zulus who opposed Mandela's mostly Xhosa membership.

Inkatha fighters did more actual violence against the ANC than the whites did. I'm not referring to the overarching, crushing daily violence of apartheid itself, but to specific murders. The Zulus introduced the practice of "necklacing," in which a tire would be tied around a victim's head and set on fire. This war between two tribes was doubly ironic in a nation ruled by a white tribe.

The Bang Bang Club will not leave its

viewers with much of an insight into that. Some audience members may come out of the movie wondering why they didn't see much apartheid, except implicitly. The focus is on the four photographers, Marinovich (Phillippe), Kevin Carter (Taylor Kitsch), Ken Oosterbroek (Frank Rautenbach), and Joao Silva (Neels Van Jaarsveld). Young, fit, hip, they compete for photos but run as a pack, sometimes sharing the same VW van. At nights in Jo'berg they hang out in bars and seem to attract a generous share of good-looking women.

One of these is Robin Comley (Malin Akerman), the photo editor of the *Johannesburg Star*, who buys Marinovich's photos and then buys into a relationship. Ryan Phillippe is effective in the lead—the newcomer to the club, protected by an indifference to personal danger that seems naive if not suicidal. But they all act like immortals: Consider a scene where one sprints across a street during a fierce gun battle to bring back a couple of liters of Coke.

Did these four men ever have extended discussions among themselves about the South African situation and apartheid itself? I'm sure they did, but there's little of that here. Were their photos intended to strengthen or weaken the government? I can't tell if they care. They like the money and the glory, they thrive on adrenaline, they buy into their Bang Bang legend. For them, in a sense, the reality of apartheid is only a photo op. Later, most of them will shoot films under fire in Sudan, the Middle East, and Bosnia. They live only to take pictures.

Well, that's their job, their craft, and their passion. But it evades a question: What is their investment as human beings? Kevin Carter takes a photo of a little girl, bent over with hunger and dehydration, as she is eyed by a nearby vulture. The picture won the Pulitzer Prize. At a press conference, he's asked what happened to the girl. He doesn't know. Didn't he do anything to help her? No. This is a universal dilemma for journalists in the face of tragedy. How many of them would frighten away the vulture and help the child? How many would take the photograph?

The film poses the question raised by the photo, but offers no answer. Perhaps there is none, or it is depressingly obvious. *The Bang Bang Club* seems curiously oblivious to South Africa as a whole. If this were your only film about that nation, you would leave with meager information. You would recall four good-looking guys who took a lot of chances and had some good times and some bad ones. But the big story wasn't about them. Bang Bang.

Barney's Version ★ ★ ★ ½

R, 132 m., 2011

Paul Giamatti (Barney), Rosamund Pike (Miriam), Minnie Driver (Second Mrs. P.), Rachelle Lefevre (Clara), Scott Speedman (Boogie), Dustin Hoffman (Izzy), Bruce Greenwood (Blair), Macha Grenon (Solange). Directed by Richard J. Lewis and produced by Robert Lantos. Screenplay by Michael Konyves, based on the novel by Mordecai Richler.

Barney's Version tells the story of a man distinguished largely by his flaws and the beautiful woman who loves him in spite of them. What she sees in him I am not quite sure. He is a precariously functioning alcoholic and chain-smoker of cigars, a man balding and with a paunch, a producer of spectacularly bad television shows, and a fanatic hockey fan. Since he lives in Montreal, many good women might forgive the hockey, but he is also hostile toward her friends, rude at dinner parties, and has bad taste in ties.

Barney Panofsky is played by Paul Giamatti, who just won a Golden Globe for his performance. It is a successful performance not simply because of his acting but because of his exuding. He exudes a sweet quality that just barely allows us to understand why three women, the last of them a saint, would want to marry him. It's not money: He's broke when he marries the first, the second is rich in her own right, and the third is so desirable that Barney actually walks out of his own wedding reception to chase her to the train station and declare his love at first sight.

Barney's Version is based on a 1997 novel by Mordecai Richler, whose *The Apprenticeship of Duddy Kravitz* (1959) is also the life story of a flawed but lovable Jewish character from Montreal. Barney's story is told in retrospect, in the form of a response to a book written by a cop who is convinced Barney murdered his best friend. How the friend probably did die is suggested in a nicely handled late scene that Barney himself, by the time he experiences it, is not able to understand.

Having once in middle age forgotten where he parked his car, Barney progresses rather rapidly into Alzheimer's, although most of the film involves scenes before that happens. Since this isn't a movie about the disease, we might ask why it's included at all, but I think it functions as a final act in a life that was itself forgettable. Nothing distinguishes Barney except his romanticism and the woman who inspires it.

She is Miriam (Rosamund Pike), an ethereal beauty with a melodious voice and a patience with Barney that surpasses all understanding. They have two children, they live happily, Barney remains a mess, and at important moments in her career he would rather be getting drunk in a bar while watching hockey than being there for her. Yet he cannot live without her, and when she goes to New York for a week, he becomes reckless with loneliness.

I haven't read the much-loved novel by Richler, which is told in Barney's voice and has been compared by some to Saul Bellow's *Herzog*. The novel is said to be richer and more complex than the movie, but having only seen the movie, I can respond favorably to what it does achieve.

Giamatti's performance is one of those achievements. He is making a career of playing unremarkable but memorable men; remember his failed wine lover in *Sideways*, his schlubby Harvey Pekar in *American Splendor*, and his soul transplant victim in *Cold Souls*. (What he plans in his announced project *Bubba Nosferatu: Curse of the She-Vampires* is a question worthy of consideration.) Giamatti's Barney is not especially smart, or talented or good-looking, but he is especially *there*—a presence with a great depth of need that apparently appeals to the lovely Miriam. She's one of those women who seems unaware that everyone must constantly be asking, "What does she see in him?" That women persist in seeing things in us, as men, we must be grateful.

Dustin Hoffman is very good here as Barney's father, a retired Montreal detective who imparts wisdom, but not too excessively, and love, but not too smarmily. The bond between elderly father and aging son is cemented by good cigars, which I have seen work in other cases. There is a lot of truth in *Barney's Version*. It is a mercy that Barney cannot see most of it.

Battle for Terra ★ ★ ★

PG, 85 m., 2009

With the voices of: Luke Wilson (Jim Stanton), Evan Rachel Wood (Mala), Brian Cox (General Hemmer), James Garner (Doron), Chris Evans (Stewart Stanton), David Cross (Giddy), Justin Long (Senn), Dennis Quaid (Roven). Directed by Aristomenis Tsirbas and produced by Keith Calder, Ryan Colucci, Jessica Wu, and Dane Allan Smith. Screenplay by Evan Spiliotopoulos.

Battle for Terra is a bewitchingly animated story about an invasion from outer space by aliens who threaten to destroy all life on the planet so they can claim it as their own. I know what you're thinking. Here's the surprise: The aliens are the human race. The inhabitants of Terra look like cute tadpoles, combined with features of mermaids and seahorses.

The planet Terra (so named by the Terrans) is one of the stars of the film. A world where nearly everything seems to be organic, it has a unique scale. Although a Terran is of considerable size, about as large as a human child of six of seven, the vegetation grows on a much larger scale, so that a hollow reed can be used for high-rise living. The civilization includes certain mechanical features (helicopter chairs, ultralight aircraft), but seems very much a part of nature.

The thinking that went into this other world is typical of classic science fiction, both in its physical details and its sociological ones. The atmosphere is apparently dense enough that the Terrans can hover with a minimal effort by their tadpole tails. It can also support huge, friendly sky leviathans, who float among the clouds like peaceful whales. The planet is ruled by a well-meaning thought-control autocracy, which enforces strict conformity and discourages independent thought.

When a vast human vessel appears in the

sky, the Terrans assume it is God. The bright, rebellious Mala (voice by Evan Rachel Wood) thinks otherwise. When her light aircraft is pursued by a human fighter plane, she lures it into a crash, then rescues its pilot, Jim Stanton (Luke Wilson). Helped by Jim's chirpy robot companion, Giddy (David Cross), she saves his life and builds a dome within which he can breathe oxygen.

Oxygen is the problem. The humans, exhausted after a generations-long voyage through the cosmos, intend to replace Terra's atmosphere with oxygen, thus providing a new Earth for themselves, but alas, killing all life forms on Terra. This gaiacide is directed by the militarist General Hemmer (Brian Cox), who brushes away Jim's arguments that the two races can peacefully coexist.

All leads to war, which was a disappointment to me, because a film that offers invention and originality reduces itself to essentially just another aerial battle with, however, some nice touches. Are kids taught to require combat at the end? Could they perhaps be trusted to accept a character-based resolution?

The movie contains a subtle level of sociopolitical commentary, involving the blind faith encouraged by the leaders on both sides, the questioning of orthodoxy by Mala and her friend Senn (Justin Long), and the nuke-the-enemy strategy of General Hemmer. The assumption that the Earthlings are gods shows the pitfalls of imposing a supernatural solution to a natural problem.

The animation is nicely stylized and the color palette well chosen, although the humans are so square-jawed they make Dick Tracy look like Andy Gump. The voice performances are persuasive. The obvious drawback is that the film is in 3-D. If you can find a theater showing it in 2-D, seek out that one. The 3-D adds nothing and diminishes the light intensity, as if imposing a slightly cloudy window between the viewer and a brightly colored wonderland. Take off the glasses to see how much you're losing.

Battle: Los Angeles ½ ★

PG-13, 116 m., 2011

Aaron Eckhart (Staff Sergeant Michael Nantz), Michelle Rodriguez (Technical Sergeant Elena Santos), Ramon Rodriguez (Second Lieutenant William Martinez), Bridget Moynahan (Michele), Ne-Yo (Corporal Kevin Harris), Michael Peña (Joe Rincon). Directed by Jonathan Liebesman and produced by Jeffrey Chernov, Ori Marmur, and Neal H. Moritz. Screenplay by Christopher Bertolini.

Battle: Los Angeles is noisy, violent, ugly, and stupid. Its manufacture is a reflection of appalling cynicism on the part of its makers, who don't even try to make it more than senseless chaos. Here's a science-fiction film that's an insult to the words "science" and "fiction," and the hyphen in between them.

Meteors fall to Earth near the coasts of the world's major cities (and in Ireland's Dingle Bay—that meteor must have strayed off course). They contain alien troops, which march up from the beach with their weapons of war and attack mankind. No reason is given for this, although it's mentioned they may want our water. We meet the members of a U.S. Marine platoon and its battle-scarred staff sergeant. They're helicoptered into Santa Monica and apparently defeat the aliens. Since all of Los Angeles is frequently seen in flames, it's not entirely clear how the Santa Monica action is crucial, but apparently it is.

The aliens are hilarious. Do they give Razzies for special effects? They seem to be animal/machine hybrids with automatic weapons growing from their arms, which must make it hard to change the baby. As the marines use their combat knives to carve into an alien, they find one layer after another of icky, gelatinous, pus-filled goo. Luckily, the other aliens are mostly seen in long shot, where they look like stick figures whipped up by apprentice animators.

Aaron Eckhart stars as Staff Sergeant Nantz, a twenty-year veteran who has something shady in his record that people keep referring to, although the screenwriter, Christopher Bertolini, is too cagey to come right out and describe it. Never mind. Eckhart is perfectly cast, and let the word go forth that he makes one hell of a great-looking action hero. He is also a fine actor, but acting skills are not required from anyone in this movie.

The dialogue consists almost entirely of terse screams: "Watch it! Incoming! Move!

Look out! Fire! Move!" The only characters I remember having four sentences in a row are the anchors on cable news. Although the platoon includes the usual buffet of ethnicities, including Hispanics, Asians, and a Nigerian surgeon, none of them get much more than a word or two in a row, so as characters they're all placeholders.

You gotta see the alien battleships in this movie. They seem to have been assembled by the proverbial tornado blowing through a junkyard. They're aggressively ugly and cluttered, the product of a planet where design has not been discovered and even the Coke bottles must look like pin cushions. Although these ships presumably arrived inside the meteors, one in particular exhibits uncanny versatility, by rising up from the earth before the very eyes of the startled marines. How, you may ask, did it burrow for ten or twelve blocks under Santa Monica to the battle lines at Lincoln Boulevard? And well you may ask.

There is a lazy editing style in action movies these days that assumes nothing need make any sense visually. In a good movie, we understand where the heroes are and where their opponents are and why, and when they fire on one another we understand the geometry. In a mess like this, the frame is filled with flashes and explosion and shots so brief that nothing makes sense. From time to time there'll be a close-up of Aaron Eckhart screaming something, for example, and on either side of that shot there will be unrelated shots of incomprehensible action.

When I think of the elegant construction of something like *Gunfight at the OK Corral*, I want to rend the hair from my head and weep bitter tears of despair. Generations of filmmakers devoted their lives to perfecting techniques that a director like Jonathan Liebesman is either ignorant of or indifferent to. Yet he is given millions of dollars to produce this assault on the attention span of a generation.

Young men: If you attend this crap with friends who admire it, tactfully inform them they are idiots. Young women: If your date likes this movie, tell him you've been thinking it over and you think you should consider spending some time apart. ☞

The Beaches of Agnes ★ ★ ★ ★

NO MPAA RATING, 110 m., 2009

With Agnes Varda, Rosalie Varda, Mathieu Demy, Jim McBride, Zalman King, Jane Birkin, and others. A documentary produced and directed by Agnes Varda. Screenplay by Varda.

Dear Agnes Varda. She is a great director and a beautiful, lovable, and wise woman, through and through. Her face is still framed by a cap of shining hair. Her eyes are still merry and curious. She is still brimming with energy, and in *The Beaches of Agnes* you will see her setting up shots involving mirrors on the beach, or operating her own camera, or sailing a boat single-handedly down the Seine under the Pont Neuf, her favorite bridge.

And she has given us the most poetic shot about the cinema I have ever seen, where two old fishermen, who were young when she first filmed them, watch themselves on a screen. Yes, and the screen and the 16 mm projector itself are both mounted on an old market cart that they push through the nighttime streets of their village.

If you have never seen a single film by Agnes Varda, perhaps it is best to start with *The Beaches of Agnes*. This is not an autobiography, although it is about her lifetime. She closes it by saying, "I am alive, and I remember." The film is her memories, evoked by footage from her films and visits to the places and people she filmed. But that makes it sound too straightforward. The film is a poem, a song, a celebration. Although she's in robust health, she accepts, as she must, that she's approaching the end. She expresses no thoughts about an afterlife, and only one great regret about this one: that Jacques and she could not complete the journey together, as they had planned.

She doubts she had seen ten films by the time she was twenty-five, when she made her first film. She had no theory and never desired any. She filmed as she felt, even in her first work, which boldly brings together two story lines. Its visual compositions are compared to Bergman's in an enormously useful IMDb user comment. It starred the great actor Philippe Noiret in his first role. Coming before the first films of Godard, Truffaut, Chabrol, Demy, Rivette, and Resnais, Varda is sometimes called the grandmother, not the mother, of the New Wave.

For Varda, film has been a family business. Her husband, Jacques Demy, of course, is most famous for *The Umbrellas of Cherbourg,* the all-singing musical that won the Palme d'Or at Cannes. Varda's *Vagabond* won the Golden Lion at Venice. They supported each other when needed, but kept a "respectful" distance from each other's work.

Their great collaboration came at the end, when Demy started to write down memories of his youth in Nantes, and Agnes said, "Jacques, do you want me to make a film of these?" Jacques said he did, and Agnes began immediately, that very day. The story is in *Beaches.* Calling on friends and collaborators, she started to film with Demy at her side and everyone aware he was dying. It was a period piece, with actors playing young Demy and the others. *Jacquot* was finished with a few days to spare. She must have had a personal agenda for beginning work so quickly; right to the end of his life, Demy was needed. There is no use in waiting passively to die.

In *The Beaches of Agnes,* there is a sequence in which all of her children and grandchildren, dressed in white, perform a slow ballet on the beach, and Varda dances behind them, dressed all in black. And that's all I need to say about that. Many times when we see her in the film, she is walking backward, as the film itself walks backward through her life, and as she perhaps sees herself receding from our view. But her films will not recede, and neither will Varda. There is absolutely no hint to suggest this will be her last film.

The film most central to her life in many ways is *The Gleaners and I,* where she ennobles a trade she traces back to the Middle Ages: the trade of moving through the places of Man and rescuing those things that can usefully be used again. When I see men moving down our alley with grocery carts, searching garbage bins for items of value, I do not think of the words "homeless," "mendicants," "vagrants." Having been taught by Varda, I think "gleaners." They have a life to live and a living to make, and are of greater actual use to society than some who make millions a year.

In that way all of Varda's films have been gleanings. Although she is happy when one of them is successful ("*Vagabond* was a big hit," she recalls cheerfully), I don't believe a single one was made because of its commercial prospects. They were made out of love of the art form, and constructed by what fell to hand and seemed good to her. And now at eighty-one she can walk backward with more serenity than most of us, because she will not stumble.

Beautiful Boy ★ ★ ★

R, 100 m., 2011

Maria Bello (Kate), Michael Sheen (Bill), Alan Tudyk (Eric), Moon Bloodgood (Trish), Austin Nichols (Coop), Kyle Gallner (Sam), Meat Loaf Aday (Motel Clerk). Directed by Shawn Ku and produced by Lee Clay and Eric Gozlan. Screenplay by Ku and Michael Armbruster.

The death of a child is a calamity. When that child has gone on a killing rampage at his campus and then taken his own life, it must be a tragedy so fundamental that it paralyzes thought. *Beautiful Boy* gives us a glimpse of the young student on the night before his murders, and then is about how his parents live with what he has done.

No rational response seems possible. They cannot reason with madness. Their son fits all the clichés of sudden killers: He was quiet, shy, kept to himself, never caused trouble. In scenes before his death we see that his home was an arid minefield. His parents were closed off from each other and on the edge of divorce. When he telephones them on his last night, their advice is "study hard." His mother speaks with him longer than his father, but neither picks up what we see: The boy (Kyle Gallner) is on the edge of tears.

Beautiful Boy is a sincere attempt to imagine the aftermath of tragedy for the parents. Maria Bello and Michael Sheen play Kate and Bill, two people living in a daze. The news of their son's death is followed immediately by the news about his rampage. Ordinary grief is stunned senseless. Their home is immediately placed under siege by reporters and TV news crews demanding a statement. This is always the case. I always wonder what the reporters are hoping for. What can be said? When Bill finally reads out a statement of regret, it is perfunctory and useless.

Shawn Ku's film follows them. Bill tries to continue working at his office, but his coworkers stare and wonder. Kate is an editor and works on the manuscript of a new author. In her attention to minute details she deadens herself. Driven from their home, they move in with her sister (Moon Bloodgood) and husband (Alan Tudyk). This can't last. Finally they are alone in the world, checking into a hotel where the night clerk (Meat Loaf Aday) becomes the first person in the film to treat them as if they were ordinary people.

They were ready to divorce. Now they are together because no one else in the world can share this devastating new fact with them. Were the killings their fault? Did their marriage produce a disturbed boy? Do they deserve more guilt than they already feel? It's here, I believe, that the film fails, almost by default. In a way, it must fail. Ku, who is also the cowriter of the screenplay, has posed himself questions without answers. His story permits no catharsis. There are moments when some minuscule contentment creeps back into the lives of Kate and Bill, in a scene at the hotel where they have a dinner of snack food and whisky and remember a little why they were once in love. But there can never again be joy.

A film like this can end honestly in only one way, and Ku is true to it. Life will go on, one baffling day after another. There can be no release, only a gradual deadening. So it must be with most parents of children who commit horrible deeds. People do things for which there are no reasons, and if they don't kill themselves, they must live, like Mark David Chapman, in the debris of their madness.

There is a film that dealt with such an incident from the killer's point of view. Gus Van Sant's *Elephant* (2003) was about the shooters at a high school massacre like Columbine. It dared to suggest no explanation, no insight, no theories. Shawn Ku does the same. Here is the crucial difference: Van Sant focused on the killers. Ku focuses on the parents. They are alive, and are forced to live with the fact that there is no reason and no consolation. The parents of their son's victims are at least given the consolation of someone to hate.

The Beaver ★ ★ ½

PG-13, 91 m., 2011

Mel Gibson (Walter Black), Jodie Foster (Meredith Black), Anton Yelchin (Porter Black), Jennifer Lawrence (Norah), Riley Thomas Stewart (Henry Black). Directed by Jodie Foster and produced by Steve Golin, Keith Redmon, and Ann Ruark. Screenplay by Kyle Killen.

The Beaver is almost successful despite the premise of its screenplay, which I was simply unable to accept. I concede it is possible that a man in depression might be able to heal himself by projecting his personality into a hand puppet. I am not sure it is possible, or even advisable, to make a serious movie about that. We go through the movie with Mel Gibson wearing a toothy beaver on his left hand, and that creates a whole lot of disbelief for us to suspend.

Yet here is another of Mel Gibson's fine performances, a reminder that he is after all a superb actor. His personal life is in ruins because of the disease of alcoholism, which he is still struggling with. When he's responsible for outrageous acts and statements, I think, this is not the good man I have met many times. From what I know about alcoholism, I believe he goes through personality changes, that he is content on some days and consumed by rage and madness on others, and that such changes are symptoms of the disease. Make your own diagnosis.

It took some courage on the part of Jodie Foster to direct this film. I believe she knows Gibson's good side and respects his talent. He was certainly the right choice for this material. All of his troubles through recent years are summed up by her opening shot, of an exhausted man floating on a raft in a swimming pool, his arms wide like the crucified Christ. A voice (later revealed to be the Beaver's) informs us this is Walter Black, a man so deep in depression he has alienated his family and nearly destroyed his business.

We meet his much-suffering wife, Meredith (Jodie Foster), his resentful son, Porter (Anton Yelchin), and his disbelieving colleagues. Meredith finally throws him out, not without love. He buys a bottle, checks into a motel, tries to kill himself, and is interrupted by the hand puppet. Finding that the puppet has a voice of its own, he allows it to speak for him, and begins to reenter his life. Foster, Gibson, and the writer, Kyle Killen, make not the slightest attempt to employ the illusion of ventriloquism; Gibson manipulates the puppet and speaks from his own mouth, in an admirable if inexplicable Cockney accent.

His life improves in ways I leave for you to discover. I also leave you to wonder if Matt Lauer on a real *Today* program would chat with a hand puppet quite as he does here. A parallel plot involves Porter, the son, whose gift is to ghostwrite papers for classmates that read as if written by themselves. The class valedictorian asks him to write her speech. If she's that smart, why can't she write it herself? She's going through problems, which Porter will discover in a story that tends to lead us, however interestingly, away from the through-line.

What sort of movie would have resulted with the same characters but not the beaver? We will never know. On the other hand, without *The Beaver* we would never have witnessed a sexual threesome involving a hand puppet. Foster and Gibson must have gone through some serious times while making this film, but don't you suppose that while filming that sex scene they had to suppress the urge to giggle?

That is the fatal flaw in this sincere endeavor. As good as Gibson is, his character is still caught between the tragedy of the man and the absurdity of the beaver. Fugitive thoughts of Señor Wences crept into my mind. I'm sorry, but they did.

Beginners ★ ★ ★ ½

R, 105 m., 2011

Ewan McGregor (Oliver), Christopher Plummer (Hal), Melanie Laurent (Anna), Goran Visnjic (Andy), Kai Lennox (Elliot), Mary Page Keller (Georgia), Keegan Boos (Young Oliver). Directed by Mike Mills and produced by Miranda de Pencier, Lars Knudsen, Leslie Urdang, Jay Van Hoy, and Dean Vanech.

Six months after his mother dies, Oliver's father tells him something startling: "I am gay." His father is seventy-five and was married for thirty-eight years. Oliver himself is about thirty-eight when he learns this news, and is in a different sort of closet: Afraid of failing, afraid of commitment, afraid to trust, he has never had a meaningful relationship. *Beginners* is about how both men find love. It is a film in which only a dog named Arthur seems to hold everything in perspective.

No, this isn't a comedy about a talking dog. Arthur has only a bit part and communicates in subtitles, thinking the kinds of thoughts that dogs, who are obsessed with the study of humans, might indeed think. But the presence of this wise Jack Russell terrier provides a perspective apart from sexuality and personality, one that perceives merely when everything is, or is not, as it should be.

Oliver, played by the engaging Ewan McGregor, is an artist whose work, apparently successful, communicates a reluctance to be sure and bold. His father, Hal, is played by Christopher Plummer as a man who arrived at an agreement with his wife, Georgia (Mary Page Keller), many years ago, and has been true to it. He has always known he is gay, and his revelation to his son conveys pride, relief, and a kind of joy. Perhaps he has arrived at an age when only his son could be expected to care about this unexpected information.

The film moves easily within three time frames. There is the period between his father's announcement and his death a few years later, the period in Oliver's life after the death, and flashbacks to Oliver's memories of childhood. If we must extract a meaning from *Beginners*, it may be that it is never too late to make a fresh start, and the father sets an example for his son.

Christopher Plummer, an actor filled with presence and grace, brings a dignified joy to his new gay lifestyle. He delights in the Gay Pride rainbow, dances in clubs, throws parties, and introduces Oliver to his boyfriend, Andy (Goran Visnjic). This Andy is so improbably handsome that the liaison seems unlikely, but we grow convinced that Andy truly and deeply loves the old man, with a fullness that almost shames Oliver. The film pays due attention to Hal's happiness and to the process of his death, which he approaches with the consolation that at last there is nothing he must keep secret.

Some months later, deep in idleness and distraction, sad in his bones, Oliver attends a costume party dressed as Freud. He stations himself next to a sofa and acquires a patient named Anna (Melanie Laurent). She communicates by writing notes in little spiral notebooks. She can't speak because she has laryngitis. In a curious sense, her notes and the dog's subtitles convey the same kinds of bottom-line observation: "Why," she writes, "did you come to a party when you were so sad?" She knows that he is sad, just as a dog doesn't need to be told such things.

One of the pleasures of *Beginners* is the warmth and sincerity of the major characters. There is no villain. They begin by wanting to be happier and end by succeeding. The person left out is the dead mother, Georgia. She spent years in a pointless marriage. If Hal and Georgia were sticking it out for the sake of Oliver, that doesn't seem to have turned out well. And once he was an adult and had left home—why did they persist? Did Hal lack the moral courage to declare himself? He could have been happier years sooner, and she could have had her chance, too. Hal is not quite as nice as he seems.

Another question occurs. Both Hal and Oliver find ideal romantic partners, who are breathtakingly good-looking, unflaggingly nice, deeply warmhearted, and loyal. Everyone who goes to gay bars or costume parties should be so lucky. That makes it all too neat, but then this isn't a deep drama, anyway. It's a hopeful fable with deep optimism and a cheerful style that kids itself. Like many dogs, it shrugs off setbacks and keeps hoping it can go outside and play.

Behind the Burly Q ★ ★

NO MPAA RATING, 98 m., 2010

Alan Alda, Tempest Storm, Beverly Arlynne, Lou Costello, Sally Rand, Betty Rowland, Lili St. Cyr, Kitty West, Blaze Starr, and others. A documentary directed by Leslie Zemeckis and produced by Zemeckis, Sheri Hellard, and Jackie Levine. Screenplay by Zemeckis.

My entry in the 1959 essay contest of the United Republican Fund won me a free trip to Chicago and the chance to shake Richard Nixon's hand during a banquet at the Chicago Amphitheater. What I remember about that trip is stepping into a cab in front of the Conrad Hilton Hotel and telling the driver, "Take me to the best burlesque show in town." He threw down the flag on his meter and drove me one block, to the Rialto on South State Street.

In those days both the Rialto and the Follies survived as part of the last gasp of American burlesque. The Rialto had once been owned by Harold Minsky, Broadway's legendary burlesque impresario. There I beheld striptease artistes and a team of two comedians who told bawdy jokes about body parts, pulled improbable objects out of their pockets, and slapped each other with rubber chickens.

Burlesque survived there until the theaters were booked as porn houses. It made fitful revivals here and there around town, including at the Town, now the Park West, where in a seedy dressing room I interviewed the legendary Tempest Storm and found her kind and patient. Now it is gone and almost forgotten. Once it was known as the poor man's Broadway.

A new documentary named *Behind the Burly Q* recalls those days, but that's about all it accomplishes. It gathers an impressive series of talking head interviews with surviving stars, including Tempest Storm herself, looking pretty damned good for a redhead aged eighty-two. In 1999, San Francisco mayor Willie Brown proclaimed a Tempest Storm Day. Catch Michael Bloomberg doing that.

In its heyday a top-flight burlesque show would run ninety minutes and feature a large cast, elaborate costumes, energetic choreography, and a nice little orchestra. Young comics got a start there, including Abbott and Costello. Alan Alda appears in this film to remember his father, Robert, a straight man on Forty-second Street. Burlesque was considered a step down from vaudeville, although it was a lot classier than the nude revues and lap dances that replaced it.

There wasn't total nudity, for one thing, although Sally Rand caused a sensation at the 1933 Chicago World's Fair with her celebrated fan dance, during which she was apparently completely nude, but manipulated her fans so adroitly that you could never be absolutely sure. This proves the principle that it is more erotic to be about to see everything than it is to actually see it. Miss Rand died in 1979 at the age of seventy-five, and was still dancing in that decade. I know that for a fact because my friend John McHugh has a photograph of himself with her to prove it. In the picture he is conducting himself as befits a reporter from the *Chicago Daily News* while her perky nipples wink at him.

Behind the Burly Q, written and directed by the burlesque historian Leslie Zemeckis (wife of Robert), settles too easily for an editing formula that alternates talking heads, too-cursory performance footage, and montages of headlines and photographs. The timeline is unclear and the structure seems too random, but a composite picture emerges as young girls, often out of poverty, dream of stardom but end by taking it off. The successful ones had gimmicks. Lili St. Cyr appeared to make love with a parrot and Babette Bardot was allegedly Brigitte Bardot's sister. Their names showed some invention, for example Blaze Starr's; she famously had an affair with Louisiana governor Huey P. Long, and is in this film via telephone, refusing to be photographed.

The many burlesque veterans who do appear in the film look, it must be said, like attractive seniors, and in their faces and voices we glimpse a spirit and defiance. They were overworked and underpaid and generally considered to be hookers, but they supported themselves, some from the age of fourteen. You hear some nostalgia, but with most of them you don't get the idea that if they had the chance they'd do it all again.

Note: My interview with Tempest Storm is at http://j.mp/b7GnZb.

Best Worst Movie ★ ★ ★

NO MPAA RATING, 91 m., 2010

George Hardy, Claudio Fragasso, Margo Prey, Jason Steadman, and Darren Ewing. A documentary directed by Michael Paul Stephenson and produced by Mary Francis Groom, Brad Klopman, Jim Klopman, Jim McKeon, Lindsay Rowles Stephenson, and Michael Paul Stephenson.

I bought the DVD of *Troll 2* because a friend advised me to see it. "You're busy," he told me. "You don't have time to see every bad movie. So you might as well see the worst of all time." Yes, reader, *Troll 2* has a coveted 0 percent rating on the Tomatometer: the lowest-rated film ever made. A critic could become the most-hated person in fan circles by awarding it even half a star and spoiling the perfection of that zero.

I always intended to view *Troll 2* but, I dunno, never found the time. Now comes *Best Worst Movie* to save me the trouble. This is a documentary about what happens to you when you appear in *Troll 2*. It stars the star of the original film, a dentist from a small town in Alabama named George Hardy. This is one nice guy. Even his ex-wife says so. He has a Harrison Ford head of hair and a smile so wide it's like a toothpaste billboard. He treats poor kids for free.

He made the movie twenty years ago when he was living in Utah. It was being directed by an Italian named Claudio Fragasso, who didn't speak-a the English but said he understood Americans better than they understood themselves. The movie was named *Goblin*, but then the title was changed to *Troll 2* because that sounded more commercial. It is only a technicality that there was no movie named *Troll*. You could go out and make one, but then this would be the sequel.

We catch glimpses of *Troll 2* in *Best Worst Movie*. Don't ask me to explain it. It's about vegetarian goblins who cause their human victims to start growing branches and leaves. The special effects make the victims look like people who have tree limbs strapped to their arms with duct tape. The goblins wear homemade masks a child wouldn't be caught dead wearing on Halloween. The budget was so small the actors had to provide their own clothes. One actor recalls a scene where it was necessary to nail his shoe to the ground. "They used my own shoe," he moans.

For some time, George Hardy forgot all about having made the movie. Then some of his patients started looking at him strangely and asking him if he'd appeared in this horror film they'd seen on cable. The film had been discovered and embraced by the bottom-feeders of horror film fandom, and soon Hardy found himself being invited to revivals and horror conventions. The other actors were also suddenly in demand.

One of them, Michael Paul Stephenson, who played the kid in the movie, is the director of this documentary. Neither he nor anyone else knew what Fragasso was attempting or even if he was quite serious. One actor explains he was out on a pass from a mental institution when he was cast as the ominous store owner: "The actor they hired didn't turn up and they said, 'OK, you've got the job.' Watching himself in a scene, he says, 'You can see I was crazy.'"

If the film didn't make much of an impression at the time, its rediscovery certainly did. The actors got standing ovations and started autographing photos, T-shirts and body parts at conventions. Claudio Fragasso himself, who looks very slightly like an embittered Fellini, attended revivals at the Nuart in Los Angeles and in Salt Lake City, and said his actors were morons then and are morons today. He adds that to make the worst film is as great an honor as making the best one.

But there is a bittersweet ending in this curiously touching doc. Stephenson follows George Hardy to conventions where only half a dozen people attend his panel. He films him standing at the *Troll 2* table at a horror exhibition, completely ignored. Hardy is reduced to drumming up business: "Have you heard of *Troll 2*? You haven't? You should see it! It's the worst movie of all time!" Depressed, he observes, "There's a lot of gingivitis in this room."

There's something irresistible about the movies. If you've been the star of a famous one, that means something, doesn't it? Even if it's the worst? How many people get even that far? The lesson, I guess, is that you can only be the flavor of the month for about thirty days, sometimes thirty-one. *Troll 2* was February.

Big Fan ★ ★ ★ ½

R, 88 m., 2009

Patton Oswalt (Paul Aufiero), Kevin Corrigan (Sal), Marcia Jean Kurtz (Theresa Aufiero), Michael Rapaport (Philadelphia Phil), Matt Servitto (Detective Velardi), Gino Cafarelli (Jeff Aufiero), Serafina Fiore (Gina Aufiero), Jonathan Hamm (Quantrell Bishop). Directed by Robert Siegel and produced by Elan Bogarin and Jean Kouremetis. Screenplay by Siegel.

Paul is a short, chubby thirty-five-year-old man who lives with his mother and works the night shift as an attendant at a parking garage. His mother screams at him that he only dates his own right hand. But there is another Paul, "Paul of Staten Island," who is a regular caller to a sports radio station, defending his beloved New York Giants against the hated Eagles fan "Philadelphia Phil." This Paul is proud, articulate, and happy.

He and his best (or only) friend, Sal, never miss a Giants home game. They're tailgaters. They park in the Giants parking lot and watch the game on a TV set that runs off his car battery. Behind them inside the towering stadium walls, the great quarterback Quantrell Bishop leads the Giants toward a championship.

Big Fan, one of the more thought-provoking sports movies I've seen, is the directorial debut of Robert Siegel, who wrote *The Wrestler.* It's a comedy with dark undertones that asks: What kind of a man listens to and calls sports talk radio compulsively, even in the middle of the night? Even out of season? Even on, say, Thanksgiving, or Election Day? He should get a life, do you think? That's what his mother thinks. Paul believes he has a life, a glorious life, as a Fan.

I've known such people. They identify so strongly with their idols that it's a kind of derangement. They *are* their city, their team, their heroes. When their team loses, they bleed. Supporters of a rival team are their enemies. Pro athletes get paid. Pro fans work pro bono. For anyone to describe himself as a team's "number one fan" is kind of pathetic.

One night Paul (Patton Oswalt) and Sal (Kevin Corrigan) are out late eating pizza when they see the great Quantrell Bishop (Jonathan Hamm) at a gas station. They tail him. He is driven to a dicey neighborhood in Staten Island for murky purposes (a cocaine buy, is my guess). Then he drives into Manhattan, and Paul and Sal follow him into a lap-dance emporium. They approach "QB" to praise him, and he's nice enough at first. Then they recklessly tell him they've been following him all the way from the shady neighborhood. Are they implying a shakedown? QB explodes and hammers Paul, who awakens three days later in a hospital after emergency surgery for bleeding in the brain.

QB is suspended. Paul is not eager to testify against him. A detective (Matt Servitto) tries to question him. He says he can't remember. "Can't—or won't?" the cop asks. His hunch is correct. When Paul's shyster brother files a multimillion-dollar lawsuit against QB, Paul refuses to cooperate. He can't think of Quantrell Bishop as the man who nearly killed him. That's because, in a sense, Paul *is* Quantrell Bishop. Without QB, there is no Paul there.

And then the film follows Paul more deeply into the consequences of his obsession. I will leave you to discover for yourself what happens. I've seen films about fanatic sports fans before, in particular frightening films about British football hooligans, who organize into armed gangs and battle with one another. Paul is a more common American type, one who is especially tiresome to sportswriters, whom they zero in on with a combination of fascination and resentment: Who are you to pass judgment on my team?

Patton Oswalt, best known as a stand-up comedian, brings a kind of brilliance to his performance. He plays a man limited in curiosity, confidence, and ambition. He sounds good on the radio because he's listened to thousands of hours of sports radio, which largely comes down to the same verbal formulas repeated time and again. Alone in his toll booth late at night, he scripts words for "Paul from Staten Island" and reads from legal pads, striding back and forth in his bedroom while his mother, next door, shouts for him to shut up so she can get some sleep.

This isn't only, or even, a sports movie. It's about leading a life vicariously. There's a movie called *Surrogate,* about a future time when people recline at home hooked up to brain sensors, and lead their lives through more attractive and younger android versions of themselves. This practice is going on now. Quantrell Bishop is Paul's surrogate. Disconnect him, and Paul is a body on a bed, dreaming with his right hand.

Big Man Japan ★ ★ ★ ½

PG-13, 113 m., 2009

Hitosi Matumoto (Dai Sato), Riki Takeuchi (Jumpy Monster), Ua (Sato's Manager), Ryunosuke Kamiki (Baby Monster), Itsuji Itao (Smelly Monster). Directed by Hitoshi Matsumoto and produced by Akihiko Okamoto. Screenplay by Matsumoto and Mitsuyoshi Takasu.

Well, I guess this is the movie I've been asking for. Whenever I see a superhero epic, I'm always nagged by logical questions—like, when the Incredible Hulk becomes enormous, how do his undershorts also expand? *Big Man Japan* answers that question with admirable clarity. Before Big Man grows, workers winch an enormous pair of undershorts up on two poles, and he straddles the crotch. Then he expands to fill them. Had to be something like that.

The movie, which is very funny in an insidious way, takes the form of a slice-of-life documentary about Dai Sato (Hitosi Matumoto), the latest generation in a Tokyo dynasty of monster killers. He is a quiet, introverted, unhappy man, whose wife has left him and taken away their daughter. He lives alone in cluttered bachelor squalor. Nothing much happens, but he's always on call, and when the Department of Defense needs him, he has to rush to the nearest power plant, be zapped with massive bolts of electricity, and grow into a giant ready to battle the latest monster with his only weapon, a steel club.

These are some monsters. One has expanding cables for arms, embraces skyscrapers, pulls them out of the ground, and throws them over his back. Then he has to flick his comb-over back in place. One consists of a giant body and one foot, with which he jumps on things. One exudes an overpowering stink. One breathes fire and looks like Hellboy. One has a single giant eyeball on a long stem hanging from its crotch, and wields it like a bola.

These monsters come from who knows where, and when they die we see their souls take flight and ascend to heaven. Their battles take place in cities that look gloriously like phony special effects, and unlike most monster movies with terrified mobs, these streets and buildings do not have a single person visible.

In contrast with the action scenes, the movie takes the form of a downbeat doc about the nightmare of being Big Man. Dai Sato never gets time off. He isn't paid much. He raises cash from TV specials about his fights and selling advertising space among his tattoos. People hate him for stepping on things, soiling the environment, and disturbing the peace. His TV ratings are down. He wonders why his agent, a chain-smoking, cell phone–addicted woman, has a new car but he takes the train. His only company comes from professional geishas.

Matumoto plays the role absolutely on the straight and level. So do all of the human characters. He is as concerned about the practical problems of being a superhero as I am. The film takes, or seems to take, his dilemma with utter seriousness. Matumoto is also the writer and director, and it becomes clear that he is satirizing three genres: the personal documentary, monster movies, and reality TV. And he does this slyly, with a scalpel instead of a hatchet. Only the monsters are over the top, and are they ever. The weird thing is that, thanks to CGI, some of them have worried, middle-age human faces on their grotesque bodies.

Note: Something has been nagging you. That name Matumoto doesn't seem quite right. You would be correct. Hitosi Matumoto's real name is Hitoshi Matsumoto, but he misspells both names in the credits. Little joke. Think Ada Sadler. He's a popular Japanese comedian. I hope all his overseas viewers get the joke.

The Big Uneasy ★ ★

NO MPAA RATING, 98 m., 2011

Harry Shearer, Maria Garzino, Ivor Van Heerden, Robert Bea, John Goodman, and the voices of Brad Pitt, Jennifer Coolidge, Wendell Pierce, and Will Lyman. A documentary directed by Harry Shearer. Screenplay by Shearer.

What Hurricane Katrina did to New Orleans was not an act of God, a "natural disaster," or a failure by FEMA. It was the almost inevitable result of years of incompetent and dangerous work by the Army Corps of Engineers, which then used its power to cover its ass. That is the message, much repeated, in Harry Shearer's documentary *The Big Uneasy.*

Using soil and flood-control experts, Google maps, new footage, and damning video, Shearer builds a compelling case against the corps's flawed planning and leaky levees. I was convinced. Unfortunately, I was also convinced that trapped within this ninety-eight-minute film is a good thirty-minute news report struggling to get out. Shearer, who is a bright and funny man, comes across here as a solemn lecturer.

His facts are depressing. The Army Corps constructed levees on sand that was water permeable and unable to hold concrete walls in place under the pressure of flood waters. He shows large sections of levees not "breeched," as we were told, but actually pushed aside by the flooding. He documents—with the aid of a corpswoman whose whistle-blowing was disregarded at the time—that pumps installed to handle flood waters were inadequate and malfunctioning. He shows that the lovely city was set up for destruction, and that with wiser planning it might have suffered no worse than "wet ankles." Incredibly, we learn that one of the contractors whose company was constructing the levees even went into court to argue the corps's plans were flawed—and lost.

His view of the army engineers is thoroughly depressing. Far from welcoming advice and analysis from academic experts, they installed barbed-wire fences to block their access to crucial areas. They spent more than $1 million on a public relations campaign to repair their image. They were responsible directly or indirectly for the firing, demotion, or silencing of many of their critics. They stand indicted—and, Shearer says, their similar mistakes may mean the city of Sacramento is vulnerable to flood damage on a similar scale.

This is important and needs to be made known. Unfortunately, Shearer as a documentarian is not the right man for the job. *The Big Uneasy* lacks the dramatic impact and artistic imagination of many recent docs about environmental issues. An attempt to liven things up by shoehorning John Goodman into the action fails, when he appears out of any context to introduce awkward segments in which

Shearer and other New Orleans residents answer criticisms of their city. *The Big Uneasy* plays way too much like an educational film.

Bill Cunningham New York ★ ★ ★ ★

NO MPAA RATING, 84 m., 2011

Bill Cunningham, Tom Wolfe, Anna Wintour, Carmen Dell'Orefice, Annette de la Renta, John Kurdewan, Iris Apfel, Josef Astor, Editta Sherman, Anna Piaggi, Shail Upadhya, and Thelma Golden. A documentary directed by Richard Press and produced by Philip Gefter.

Here is a movie about a happy and nice man. Bill Cunningham was lucky to find what he loves to do, and do it, and win universal affection from all who know him, and to make a contribution to our lives and times. Doing what he loves is very nearly *all* he does, except to sleep and eat.

Ever since reading Thoreau's *Walden* I have been teased by the notion of leading a life with only the bare essentials of life and peacefulness. I lacked the nerve to find that little cottage and plant those rows of beans. Bill Cunningham lives a life as pure and idealistic as Thoreau, and he does it in the middle of Manhattan. Until a couple of years ago, when he was evicted by the landlord, Bill lived in a tiny rent-controlled apartment in Carnegie Hall. Yes, Carnegie Hall, in one of the artists' studios on the upper floors set aside when greed didn't decide everything.

Bill celebrates his eightieth birthday in the movie. Every day of his life he still pedals around Manhattan on his bicycle, taking photographs of what people are wearing. He has been famous for many years for doing this, and his work has been featured in such places as *Women's Wear Daily*, *Vogue*, and the original *Details* magazine, which once devoted forty-one pages to a portfolio. These days you can find him featured in big spreads in the *New York Times*, whose publisher, Arthur Sulzberger, was among those at his birthday party.

Do not make the mistake of calling Bill Cunningham a "fashion photographer." He is a photographer of people and what they wear. Don't call him a "paparazzo." He doesn't know who half the celebrities are, and doesn't care. He's genuinely fascinated by what people wear—not by haute couture, but by what makes people feel good about themselves. He cycles to social events and openings, to street fairs and parades, to parks and markets, and will stop in the middle of the street if he spots an interesting hat.

Sometimes his photos don't even show faces. "I've always loved clothes," he says. And shoes. And individualistic looks. Fashion editors study his work because he seems to be early to notice a developing trend. In Bill's view, fashion begins with creative individuals and not "tastemakers," and he is as interested in T-shirts as evening wear. It's not that he's a snob about the high and mighty; it's that he's sincerely affectionate about whatever people wear and whoever they are.

Bill lives the life of a monk. His Carnegie Hall apartment was so filled with file cabinets of his decades of negatives that there was literally nothing else there but a mattress on top of some files. No kitchen. Bathroom down the hall. When he was relocated to another rent-controlled apartment overlooking Central Park, he had the landlord remove the kitchen appliances to make room for more filing cabinets.

"Who needs a kitchen?" he asks. And yet here is a man who never tastes the free food and drink at so many of the functions he covers. That would be crossing some line in his mind. Nor, despite his life of the love of clothing, does he own many clothes. He dresses in black tie when the job requires it, but otherwise always wears one of the cheap blue smocks he finds in Paris—the ones garbagemen wear—because they have lots of pockets for his film. He works pretty much all day every day, taking off a little time every Sunday to attend Mass.

Cunningham is vague about his life. He seems to have all the money he needs, but he didn't come from a rich family. Richard Press, the director of this documentary, asks: "You don't need to answer this, but, have you ever had a romantic relationship?" Bill is delighted by the question, and laughs spontaneously: "Are you asking if I'm gay?" He doesn't say if he is or not, but his reply seems to suggest that he wasn't raised to think much about sex, and doesn't. He loves his work too much.

I mentioned his laugh. This is a man who seems always delighted. He smiles and laughs warmly and easily. Does that make him sound simple? There is nothing simple about Bill Cunningham, who is an artist and a philosopher. Here's what it is: Bill is happy. He has invented an occupation he does better than anyone else ever has, he has simplified his life until nothing interferes with that vocation, and now, at over eighty, he is still biking around Manhattan in his blue smock of many pockets and taking photos of people who had a little extra fun when they got dressed today.

It doesn't matter if you care nothing at all about clothing, fashion, or photography. You might still enjoy *Bill Cunningham New York,* because here is a good and joyous man who leads a life that is perfect for him, and how many people do we meet like that? This movie made me happy every moment I was watching it.

Birdwatchers ★ ★ ★

NO MPAA RATING, 102 m., 2010

Claudio Santamaria (Roberto), Alicelia Batista Cabreira (Lia), Chiara Caselli (Beatrice), Abrisio da Silva Pedro (Osvaldo), Ademilson Concianza Verga (Ireneu), Ambrosio Vilhalva (Nadio), Fabiane Pereira da Silva (Maria), Leonardo Medeires (Lucas Moreira). Directed by Marco Bechis and produced by Bechis, Caio Gullane, Fabiano Gullane, and Amedeo Pagani. Screenplay by Bechis and Luiz Bolognesi.

There's an opening overhead shot of the Brazilian rain forest, dense and limitless. As a tourist boat slides along a river, native Indians materialize on the banks to regard it reproachfully. They hold bows and arrows and don't seem fond of these visitors. But hold on; one of the young men has a layered haircut with the top blond.

As recently as the 1970s, when Herzog filmed *Aguirre* in such a forest, these Indians would have been "real." But the time is the present and the forest a preserved facade shielding fields, which have been stripped of trees and devoted to farming. The Indians can, if they want, pile into the back of a truck and hire out as day laborers. But all of their traditions center on the forest and its spirits, and this new life is alienating. Some simply commit suicide.

This is all true, as we have been told time and again, and meanwhile the Brazilian government remains benevolent toward the destruction of the planet's richest home of life forms and its crucial oxygen source. Indians have been stripped of ownership of their ancestral lands and assigned to reservations far from the bones of their parents; it is the same genocide the United States practiced, for those with power have not developed a conscience in the years since.

Marco Bechis's *Birdwatchers* is a ground-level drama involving a group of Indians that packs up one day, leaves "their" federal land, and builds shelters of tree limbs and plastic sheets on farmland that once was their tribe's. This goes down badly with the farmer, who with his family lives in a spacious home with a pool and (Indian) servants.

The film portrays the descendants of colonialists very broadly; its strength is in the directness of the performances by Indians. I assume their performances are informed by actual life experience, because Bechis shot on location with local nonactors. They're cohesive in the group, grow depressed when separated from it, are attuned to spirit omens (or believe they are, which amounts to the same thing). Without conversational preludes, they say bluntly what they mean: "I want to be with you, you're a big dick man, you must leave here and never return."

This doesn't mean they lack subtlety. It means they keep a lot of things to themselves. We follow two adolescent boys, Osvaldo (Abrisio da Silva Pedro) and Ireneu (Ademilson Concianza Verga), the first the son of the leader, the second he of the haircut and a yearning for sneakers. The leader, Nadio (Ambrosio Vilhalva), is strong enough to lead the group onto the farmlands, enforce discipline, and deal with many newcomers. But he's an alcoholic, his booze happily supplied by a merchant who controls them by giving credit. Shades of the company store.

Sex is in the air. The farmer's teenage daughter, in a bikini, and one of the boys, in a loincloth, begin meeting at the river, he to collect water, she to swim, and although they don't get very far, an intriguing tension is there between them. On both sides there is the allure of unfamiliarity.

The group is chronically low on food and funds, and Nadio correctly realizes that day labor is a form of bondage. He begins to call his followers "the movement." Sooner or later there will be a clash and there is, but one that unfolds in a way unique to these people.

Birdwatchers is impressively filmed and never less than interesting. If it has a weakness, it's that this is a familiar sermon: Save the rain forest. Respect its inhabitants. Bechis and his cowriter, Luiz Bolognesi, don't really develop the characters much beyond their functions. But the reality of the Indians and the locations adds its own strength.

Note: I learn from the press notes that the European-sounding sacred music was composed by Domenico Zipoli, an Italian Jesuit who lived with this same Guarani tribe in the 1700s.

Biutiful ★ ★ ★

R, 148 m., 2011

Javier Bardem (Uxbal), Maricel Alvarez (Marambra), Eduard Fernandez (Tito), Diaryatou Daff (Ige), Cheng Tai Shen (Hai), Luo Jin (Liwei). Directed by Alejandro Gonzalez Inarritu and produced by Inarritu, Fernando Bovaira, and Jon Kilik. Screenplay by Gonzalez Inarritu, Armando Bo, and Nicolas Giacobone, based on a story by Inarritu.

Alejandro Gonzalez Inarritu's *Biutiful* stars Javier Bardem as a low-level criminal in Barcelona who is told by his doctor he has very little time to live. He works as a middleman in an industry that makes fake luxury items in sweatshops and sells them to tourists through sidewalk vendors. You've seen the Gucci bags lined up on pavements. He's also involved in importing and housing the undocumented Chinese workers who exist in poverty and manufacture the items. Both fake Gucci and real Gucci are made by poor people, but the real Guccis are made in China.

Uxbal's life is a mess. He is separated from his bipolar wife. He tries to care for the sons he loves. He is under urgent pressure from his criminal associates. He sees after the living conditions of his illegal immigrants. There is blood in his pee. He works in crime but is not a bad man, and indeed under sentence of death he is moved, like the hero of Kurosawa's *Ikiru*, to try to do something good.

One gesture he makes ends in tragic consequences. His workers are cold in their crowded basement, and he tries to alleviate that. He also tries to make some money in the process. He's devastated. Surely few actors have faces that project sorrow more completely than Bardem.

Gonzalez Inarritu follows Uxbal's last days with great intimacy, burying his camera in the seamy street life Uxbal lives, introducing many characters in sharp and colorful relief. He grants his characters the dignity of having feelings and reasons, and not simply behaving as mechanical inhabitants of a crime plot.

The moral sense of the film is heartfelt, but not especially daring; by giving us a good man as his hero, Gonzalez Inarritu possibly weakens his case against the general sense of injustice in his film. Uxbal is so wholly sympathetic that it's hard for us to assign blame for his sins, and yet surely they are sins. Perhaps the idea is that he inhabits a world so lacking in goodness that his possibilities for choice are limited. Everyone he comes into contact with is flawed, with the exception of his children and Ige (Diaryatou Daff), a Senegalese woman he hires as a nanny for his children. And her love for them (and to a degree for him) is warm but almost obligatory in a story of this sort; one more unworthy character would be unthinkable.

What drew me into the film and engaged my sympathy was the presence of Bardem himself. He is a vastly human actor. He can be handsome, ugly, hard, tender, or a monster (as he was in *No Country for Old Men*). Here he suffers, and is good, and suffers partly simply because he cannot do good things. That isn't a complex message, but I see films every day like *The Mechanic* that will entertain millions with cold, amoral violence, and sometimes it's good to simply see a man who cares about the consequences of his actions.

The Black Balloon ★ ★ ★

PG-13, 97 m., 2009

Rhys Wakefield (Thomas Mollison), Luke Ford (Charlie Mollison), Gemma Ward

(Jackie Masters), Erik Thomson (Simon Mollison), Toni Collette (Maggie Mollison). Directed by Elissa Down and produced by Tristram Miall. Screenplay by Down and Jimmy Jack.

At the center of *The Black Balloon* is Toni Collette's performance as the mother of an autistic son. The way she meets this challenge opens a way to understand all the other characters. Her son, Charlie, can be sweet and lovable. He can also make life for his family all but unbearable. Collette, as his mother, Maggie, has been dealing with him for seventeen years and seems to have long ago made her peace with the fact that Charlie is who he is and is not going to change. As his mother, she loves him.

The film is concerned largely with how her other son, Thomas (Rhys Wakefield), exists with his brother. Tom is a military brat, used to new towns and new schools, affable but shy. He shares the burden of Charlie (Luke Ford), cares for him, loves him, but is ashamed of him. Thomas is at just that point in adolescence when he's acutely conscious of all his defects, and in teenage social terms, Charlie is a defect.

In an acutely embarrassing scene, Thomas is revealed during a swimming class as a sixteen-year-old who cannot swim. This makes him a target for other students, who like many teenagers are quick to mock. One girl is nice to him. This is Jackie (Gemma Ward), a tall blonde who quietly makes it clear that she likes Thomas. Thomas doesn't really know how to deal with this, but his first instinct is to try to hide Charlie from her. And a crisis is building at home; his mom is pregnant again, his dad, Simon (Erik Thomson), insists on bed rest for her, and when Simon is away the burden of running the household falls on Thomas.

The Black Balloon establishes this family with a delicate mixture of tenderness and pain. Charlie is not made into a cute movie creature. He cannot speak, he cannot control his rages, he can have instant, violent mood changes. He runs through the neighborhood in his underpants. He throws a tantrum in a supermarket. He rubs his feces into the carpet. Thomas is supposed to protect Charlie from himself and perform the damage control.

The story elements of *The Black Balloon* could have been manipulated to make the film false and cute. In some circles, that would be interpreted as upbeat. The film tries to be true. The uplift comes in how the family, and Jackie, respond to Charlie. Maggie and Simon are strongly bonded in a marriage that has survived Charlie. They have no time for nobility; they are focused on doing what needs to be done. Charlie is theirs and will not be stored in a "facility." Thomas agrees with this, but he has a breaking point.

It is Jackie who turns out to be special. Although Gemma Ward, who plays her, is a well-known model and this is her first substantial role, there is nothing of the professional model in her performance. She creates a spontaneously warm young woman who cares for Thomas, sympathizes with him, accepts Charlie without question, and helps Charlie accept himself.

Luke Ford's performance as Charlie is a convincing tour de force. You may recall him as Brendan Fraser's heroic son in *The Mummy: Tomb of the Dragon Emperor.* Rhys Wakefield, in his first feature role, is a good casting decision, suggesting inner turmoil without overacting. But it is Toni Collette who explains, without even seeming to try, why this family is still together at all.

Elissa Down, who directed and cowrote the film, reportedly has two autistic brothers. Her experience informs this story, particularly in the way enormous pressure is brought to bear on the family. Perhaps she wrote from experience about how the two parents begin with unconditional love; how rare to see a happy, long-surviving marriage in a movie, where so often the father is flawed. Rare, too, and a tribute to the Australian film industry, to see a film that doesn't allow star power to compromise its vision.

The mainstream cinema would no doubt be eager to employ Gemma Ward in a no-brainer teeny romcom. She made the right choice here and seems poised to follow the example of another onetime model, Nicole Kidman, in treating herself seriously and not getting lost in the soul-deadening life of a professional model.

Black Dynamite ★ ★ ★

R, 90 m., 2009

Michael Jai White (Black Dynamite), Kym Whitley (Honey Bee), Tommy Davidson (Cream Corn), Kevin Chapman (O'Leary), Byron Minns (Bullhorn), Salli Richardson (Gloria), Cedric Yarbrough (Giddy Up), Mykelti Williamson (Chicago Wind), Brian McKnight (Sweet Meat), Bokeem Woodbine (Back Hand Jack), Arsenio Hall (Tasty Freeze), John Salley (Kotex), James McManus (Richard M. Nixon), Nicole Sullivan (Patricia Nixon). Directed by Scott Sanders and produced by Jenny Wiener Steingart and Jon Steingart. Screenplay by Sanders, Michael Jai White, and Byron Minns, from a story by White and Minns.

I've seen a *lot* of 1970s blaxploitation films, and I'm here to tell you that *Black Dynamite* gets it mostly right, and when it's wrong, it's wrong on purpose and knows just knows what it's doing. It's one of those loving modern retreads of older genre movies.

It's built around a pitch-perfect leading man, Michael Jai White, who has been kicking around in movies for twenty years and apparently building those muscles in his time. That means he effortlessly evokes real blaxploitation stars such as Fred Williamson, who kicked around in thankless roles before hammering villains to death in urban action movies. White has a *Shaft* moustache and like all of the characters is dressed in 1970s gaucherie: oversize hats, bell bottoms, bling, shades, and unbuttoned or missing shirts in patterns resembling a hippie's ideal of wallpaper.

The women are also dressed in period, and many have big Afros. I am happy to say it brings back an element sadly missing in recent movies, gratuitous nudity. Sexy women would "happen" to be topless in the 1970s movies for no better reason than that everyone agreed, including themselves, that their breasts were a genuine pleasure to regard—the most beautiful naturally occurring shapes in nature, I believe. Now we see breasts only in serious films, for expressing reasons. There's been such a comeback for the strategically positioned bedsheet you'd think we were back in the 1950s.

The plot is deliberately fashioned to seem familiar. Michael Jai White plays Black Dynamite, a one-man street army who wants vengeance for the death of his kid brother (named Jimmy, as so many kid brothers are). Jimmy was killed by drug dealers, protected by The Man, of course. Black Dynamite has lethal chops, socks, fists, kicks, elbows, forearms, and, it goes without saying, a .44 Magnum, which you will recall from Dirty Harry "is the most powerful handgun in the world." He's a formidable fighter and a charming playa, leading to gratifying interludes with such babes as Gloria (Salli Richardson) and Honey Bee (Kym Whitley).

Honey Bee's name reminds us that many 1970s characters had names that were actually more like titles. Nobody was ever "Mike" or "Phil." Here we get Cream Corn (Tommy Davidson as a wildly politically incorrect gay man), and such others as Bullhorn, Giddy Up, Chicago Wind, Sweet Meat, Back Hand Jack, Tasty Freeze, Kotex, and Richard M. Nixon. No, wait, Richard M. Nixon isn't a nickname, as Dynamite discovers during a showdown in the Oval Office. One would like to know more about how these nicknames were earned, especially in the case of Chicago Wind.

The movie looks and sounds so much like 1970s blaxploitation that anyone finding it while cable surfing could be excused for assuming it is one. Technical expertise has been used to meticulously reproduce such details as an oversaturated color scheme, bonus camera moves, smash cuts to close-ups on big lines, and dramatic camera angles. There's also "Mickey Mouse music," so called because whatever the hero does, the music does it too. Black Dynamite even has his own theme—three fearsome chords whenever *Dynamite* needs to underlined.

Why the plot leads us to the White House is actually less interesting than how. There is a pathetic orphanage where the children use drugs, perhaps to train them as users who will be dealers. So you see the kind of evil Black Dynamite is up against. But he's the man to Take Back the Streets.

Black Swan ★ ★ ★ ½

R, 108 m., 2010

Natalie Portman (Nina Sayers), Vincent Cassel (Thomas Leroy), Mila Kunis (Lily), Barbara

Hershey (Erica Sayers), Winona Ryder (Beth MacIntyre). Directed by Darren Aronofsky and produced by Scott Franklin, Mike Medavoy, Arnold Messer, and Brian Oliver. Screenplay by Mark Heyman, Andrew Heinz, and John McLaughlin.

Darren Aronofsky's *Black Swan* is a full-bore melodrama, told with passionate intensity, gloriously and darkly absurd. It centers on a performance by Natalie Portman that is nothing short of heroic, and mirrors the conflict of good and evil in Tchaikovsky's *Swan Lake.* It is one thing to lose yourself in your art. Portman's ballerina loses her mind.

Everything about classical ballet lends itself to excess. The art form is one of grand gesture, of the illusion of triumph over reality and even the force of gravity. Yet it demands from its performers years of rigorous perfectionism, the kind of physical and mental training that takes ascendancy over normal life. This conflict between the ideal and the real is consuming Nina Sayers, Portman's character.

Her life has been devoted to ballet. Was that entirely her choice? Her mother, Erica (Barbara Hershey), was a dancer once, and now dedicates her life to her daughter's career. They share a small apartment that feels sometimes like a refuge, sometimes like a cell. They hug and chatter like sisters. Something feels wrong.

Nina dances in a company at Lincoln Center, ruled by the autocratic Thomas Leroy (Vincent Cassel). The reach of his ego is suggested by his current season, which will "reimage" the classics. Having cast off his former prima ballerina and lover, Beth MacIntyre (Winona Ryder), he is now auditioning for a new lead. *Swan Lake* requires the lead to play opposite roles. Nina is clearly the best dancer for the White Swan. But Thomas finds her too "perfect" for the Black Swan. She dances with technique, not feeling.

The film seems to be unfolding along lines that can be anticipated: There's tension between Nina and Thomas, and then Lily (Mila Kunis), a new dancer, arrives from the West Coast. She is all Nina is not: bold, loose, confident. She fascinates Nina, not only as a rival but even as a role model. Lily is, among other things, a clearly sexual being, and we suspect Nina may never have been on a date, let alone slept with a man. For her Lily presents a professional challenge and a personal rebuke.

Thomas, the beast, is well known for having affairs with his dancers. Played with intimidating arrogance by Cassel, he clearly has plans for the virginal Nina. This creates a crisis in her mind: How can she free herself from the technical perfection and sexual repression enforced by her mother, while remaining loyal to their incestuous psychological relationship?

No backstage ballet story can be seen without *The Red Shoes* (1948) coming into mind. If you've never seen it, of course eventually you will. In the character of Thomas, Aronofsky and Cassel evoke Boris Lermontov (Anton Walbrook), the impresario in that film, whose autocratic manner masks a deep possessiveness. And in Nina there is a version of Moira Shearer's ingénue, so driven to please.

Black Swan will remind some viewers of Aronofsky's previous film, *The Wrestler.* Both show single-minded professionalism in the pursuit of a career, leading to the destruction of personal lives. I was reminded also of Aronofsky's brilliant debut with *Pi* (1998), about a man driven mad by his quest for the universal mathematical language. For that matter, his *The Fountain* (2007) was about a man who seems to conquer time and space. Aronofsky's characters make no little plans.

The main story supports of *Black Swan* are traditional: backstage rivalry, artistic jealousy, a great work of art mirrored in the lives of those performing it. Aronofsky drifts eerily from those reliable guidelines into the mind of Nina. She begins to confuse boundaries. The film opens with a dream, and it becomes clear that her dream life is contiguous with her waking one. Aronofsky and Portman follow this fearlessly where it takes them.

Portman's performance is a revelation from this actress who was a thirteen-year-old charmer in *Beautiful Girls* (1996). She has never played a character this obsessed before, and never faced a greater physical challenge (she trained for ten months). Somehow she goes over the top and yet stays in character: Even at the extremes, you don't catch her acting. The other actors are like dance partners holding her aloft. Barbara Hershey provides a perfectly calibrated performance as a mother whose love is real, whose shortcomings are not signaled, whose own perfectionism has all been focused on the creation of her daughter.

The tragedy of Nina, and of many young performers and athletes, is that perfection in one area of life has led to sacrifices in many of the others. At a young age everything becomes focused on pleasing someone (a parent, a coach, a partner), and somehow it gets wired in that the person can *never* be pleased. One becomes perfect in every area except for life itself.

It's traditional in many ballet-based dramas for a summing-up to take place in a bravura third act. *Black Swan* has a beauty. All of the themes of the music and life, all of the parallels of story and ballet, all of the confusion of reality and dream come together in a grand exhilaration of towering passion. There is really only one place this can take us, and it does. If I were you, I wouldn't spend too much time trying to figure out exactly what happens in practical terms. Lots of people had doubts about the end of *The Red Shoes,* too. They were wrong, but they did. ☞

Blood Done Sign My Name ★ ★ ★

PG-13, 128 m., 2010

Rick Schroder (Vernon Tyson), Nate Parker (Ben Chavis), Nick Searcy (Robert Teel), Lela Rochon (Roseanna Allen), Afemo Omilami (Golden Frinks), Darrin Dewitt Henson (Eddie McCoy), Michael Rooker (Billy Watkins), Gattlin Griffith (Tim Tyson). Directed by Jeb Stuart and produced by Mel Efros, Jeb Stuart, and Mari Stuart. Screenplay by Jeb Stuart, based on the book by Tim Tyson.

In 1970 in Oxford, North Carolina, it was perfectly possible for a young black man to be beaten and clubbed by three whites, and shot dead by one of them. And for an all-white jury to hear from two eyewitnesses, and watch the white defendant's young son break down in tears and confess his testimony had been forced on him by his father's lawyers. And for the jury to vote unanimously that the white man was not guilty.

Blood Done Sign My Name tells the story of that murder, and how it was a catalyst for change in Oxford and in the lives of those who lived there. It's based on a memoir by the son of a liberal white Methodist preacher, and there's a scene in the film that has details I'm pretty sure the son witnessed when he was a boy.

His father said he wanted to show him something. They crept behind a rock and observed a Ku Klux Klan meeting. A cross was being erected. "It's a revival!" young Tim Tyson said. "No, it's not a revival," his father said, and that night they watched the cross being burned. The part I believe he remembers was this: The whole event was treated as a family picnic, with kids playing and mothers unpacking picnic hampers, and the sickness of racism almost *looking* like a revival.

The film tells two parallel stories. One involves a young black man who graduates from college and comes home to Oxford to teach at a black high school (black, although the schools had in theory been integrated). This is Ben Chavis (Nate Parker), who later became the president of the NAACP. The other is Vernon Tyson (Rick Schroder), the minister, who lost his congregation because of his liberal views, but found other churches in North Carolina and retired only recently. His son, Tim, went on to become a scholar of African-American studies and now teaches at Duke.

I go into biographical details because the events in 1970 are clearly remembered by Chavis and the younger Tyson as the turning points in their lives. The civil rights movement sent Golden Frinks (Afemo Omilami), an "outside agitator," to Oxford to organize the black community after the murder. He led a historic march fifty miles from Oxford to Raleigh, the state capital, where the governor refused to meet with the marchers—but the point had been made.

Unlike a more conventional film, *Blood Done Sign My Name* doesn't end with the courtroom verdict. It starts there, as Chavis leads an economic boycott of stores that took black dollars and valued black customers but hired no blacks in a county that was 40 percent African-American.

The movie tells this story in a traditional, straightforward way. No fancy footwork. No chewing the scenery. Meat and potatoes, you could say, but it's thoughtful and moving. The writer and director, Jeb Stuart, focuses on the events and people and lets them speak for themselves. He uses a level, unforgiving gaze.

Apart from the Oxford racists, his only major white characters are the minister and his family. And they're rather remote from the turmoil. Rev. Tyson invites the president of a black college to speak to his congregation, which clears out half the Christians pretty quickly, and then his son recorded these momentous days in his book.

Ben Chavis is energized and angered, but it's clear the prime mover was Golden Frinks, also a real man, whose full-time job, you could say, was outside agitating. The day of the trial, he tells Chavis he's on his way to another town: "It's up to you now." And that's what happened, essentially: The civil rights marchers led the way for the rise of a black middle class in the South.

In the opening scenes of the film, you assume the stories of Chavis and the Tyson family will connect. They don't. Each man undoubtedly knew about the other, but they were on paths that didn't intersect. I guess that's the way it was. By the time Oxford began to change, Rev. Tyson had an African-American congregation elsewhere in the state. One story at a time, things change.

Those born in 1970 will be forty this year. The acquittal of white racists by all-white juries is no longer the Southern routine. It took unpopular and courageous actions by a lot of people to bring about that change, and it is not yet complete. But it happened, and I think Tim Tyson, who isn't fifty yet, wrote his book to say it happened. If you know how to look, history doesn't take place too fast to be seen.

Blood: The Last Vampire ★ ★ ★

R, 89 m., 2009

Gianna (Saya), Allison Miller (Alice McKee), Liam Cunningham (Michael), J. J. Feild (Luke), Koyuki (Onigen), Yasuaki Kurata (Kato Takatora), Larry Lamb (General McKee). Directed by Chris Nahon and produced by William Kong and Abel Nahmias. Screenplay by Chris Chow, based on the 2001 anime film.

Saya is sixteen and has been sixteen for a very long time. What's interesting about teenage vampires, such as the hero of *Twilight,* is that they're frozen in time while old enough to be sexy, but too young to have developed a complex sensibility. Apparently your maturation is put on hold along with your appearance, since Saya is four hundred years old.

In *Blood: The Last Vampire,* her life has been a thankless slog through the extermination of demons that have plagued Japan down through the centuries. Whether these demons are vampires is a good question. I suppose so; the movie is a little hazy on its definition of vampires. Saya, for example, must be a vampire since she drinks bottled blood supplied to her by a shadowy Council.

Saya (Gianna) doesn't personally sink fangs into anyone, but there must be sad goings-on back at the bottling works. No matter; since the demons/vampires prey on human victims and she eviscerates them with her invincible swordplay, she can fairly be considered the solution and not the problem. They must not be quick studies if they haven't figured out after four hundred years of immortality that Saya never loses. They are witless creatures, and Saya is bright and attractive, perhaps because she's half vampire and half human (never mind the rules say the two don't mix).

The movie is surprisingly entertaining. It's an international hybrid. Filmed in Hong Kong and Argentina, set in Japan, mostly in English, with a French director, a Chinese writer, a beautiful Korean star (Gianna, known in her homeland as Jeon Ji-hyun), a Japanese villainess (Koyuki as the evil Onigen), and an otherwise American cast, it has a plot that conveniently explains why this is: The Council has assigned Saya to an American military base where the vampires have been focusing their attention.

The plot makes sense, I guess, but is inconsequential, serving as a laundry line on which to hang action sequences. These are mostly cut too quickly to emulate the grace of classic martial arts films, which can approach a sort of impossible ballet. That may be because Gianna is never really convincing as a martial artist, although she sure looks great.

What we're seeing is the price we pay for CGI. When computer graphics make anything seem possible, they are overused to the point where they make everything look impossible.

In classic kung fu films, we knew the actors were shot from angles to enhance their movements, were suspended from invisible wires, were often stuntmen, but were in some sense really there. Now they're essentially replaced in action scenes by very realistic animation. This devalues actual achievement. I remember praising Ang Lee for the "astonishing realism" of his treetop swordfight in *Crouching Tiger, Hidden Dragon,* only to be told: Those were the actors themselves, suspended by wires from cranes. The rooftop chase was really happening, too.

Blood: The Last Vampire is essentially a CGI fantasy, pleasing to the eye, and indeed based on a well-known 2001 Japanese anime. Gianna holds it together with a sympathetic performance, trying to win acceptance as the only Japanese girl in an otherwise all-American student body in the school on the U.S. military base. It doesn't help her fit in when she dresses for her first day in a sailor suit; her wardrobe ideas must have become fixed in the *Madame Butterfly* era. Still, you gotta admit she's fetching.

This isn't a great movie. But it's sincere as an entertainment, it looks good, it's atmospheric, and I will perk up the next time I hear Gianna is in a picture. There probably cannot be a sequel, however, since in this film she seems to be putting herself out of a job. Oops, I gave away the title.

Blue Valentine ★ ★ ★ ½

R, 120 m., 2011

Ryan Gosling (Dean), Michelle Williams (Cindy), Faith Wladyka (Frankie), Mike Vogel (Bobby), John Doman (Jerry), Ben Shenkman (Dr. Feinberg), Jen Jones (Gramma), Maryann Plunkett (Glenda). Directed by Derek Cianfrance and produced by Lynette Howell, Alex Orlovsky, and Jamie Patricof. Screenplay by Cianfrance, Joey Curtis, and Cami Delavigne.

Who was it who said we get married because we want a witness to our lives? That may provide an insight into the troubled minds of the married couple in *Blue Valentine,* which follows them during their first six years of mutual witness. Did Dean and Cindy get married because they wanted to be sure someone was watching? Or was that Dean's need, and did Cindy lose the thrill of the watch?

Here is a film that watches pretty well itself. Derek Cianfrance, the director, observes with great exactitude the birth and decay of a relationship. This film is alive in its details. Toward the end of the six years, when Cindy is hardly able to remember why she wanted to marry Dean, Cianfrance observes the physical and mental exhaustion that have overcome her. And the way that Dean seems hardly to care—just so long as Cindy remains his wife and his watcher, which in his mind was the deal. Dean thinks marriage is the station. Cindy thought it was the train.

They're played by Ryan Gosling and Michelle Williams as a Pennsylvania working couple with a daughter, Frankie. She was born right at the start. Cindy is a nurse. Dean is a house painter. When they met, and for some time after, work was hardly central to their lives. It was where they went to and where they returned from. In effective physical transformations, Williams and Gosling give us Dean and Cindy at two ages: their age at present, and at the beginning, when they were filled with that dreamy knowledge that the touch of the other brings quick sensuality. It is easier for an actor to play the same character at twenty-four and sixty than at twenty-four and thirty. Although some bodily change takes place, what really happens is a transformation of inner certainty. Williams plays a woman who sits inside her body and no longer knows what it's for and what she wants to do with it.

All marriages have legendary milestone moments, events of startling clarity that allow the new lovers to see themselves as a couple that has been defined. Dean is capable of grand, goofy romanticism, and Cindy likes that. She yearns toward it. They first meet at her grandmother's retirement home. Have you ever had one of those chance meetings with a stranger in a place neither one of you belongs? A space empty of your lives, so that you start new with your first conversation, and plunge straight ahead into a suddenly new future?

That's what it's like that day. Soon they're playing at this new toy, their love. They do things together as if they were children doing them. Then they get married and have (the unplanned but welcomed) Frankie, and the realities of making a living and work schedules and child raising and *real* marriage settle in. Dean seems stuck. He seems to stay fixed at the initial stage. Can you see the difference between (1) "He loves me as much as he always did," and (2) "He loves me exactly like he always did"?

Blue Valentine moves between past and present as if trying to remember what went wrong. From Dean's point of view, maybe nothing did. He wanted to be married to Cindy, and he still does and he still is. Cindy can't stand that. He never signed off on the "grow old along with me" part. He doesn't think the best is yet to be. He thinks it's just fine now.

Williams plays Cindy as a woman who has lost her pride of body and self. No, she doesn't become a drunk—he's the one who drinks too much. But that's not the problem. It's his infuriating inability to care for this Cindy, right here, right now, because when she married him she became exactly the Cindy he required.

I wonder what kind of script conferences Cianfrance had with his cowriters, Joey Curtis and Cami Delavigne. They were writing about something ineffable, a void, a need. This wasn't a story with convenient hooks involving things like, you know, disease—things stories are familiar with. It was about inner defeat and the exhaustion of hope. I've read reviews saying Cianfrance isn't clear about what went wrong as they got from there to here. Is anybody?

The Book of Eli ★ ★ ★

R, 118 m., 2010

Denzel Washington (Eli), Gary Oldman (Carnegie), Mila Kunis (Solara), Ray Stevenson (Redridge), Jennifer Beals (Claudia), Frances de la Tour (Martha), Michael Gambon (George). Directed by the Hughes brothers and produced by Broderick Johnson, Andrew A. Kosove, Joel Silver, and David Valdes. Screenplay by Gary Whitta.

I'm at a loss for words, so let me say these right away: *The Book of Eli* is very watchable. You won't be sorry you went. It grips your attention, and then at the end throws in several WTF! moments, which are a bonus. They make everything in the entire movie impossible and incomprehensible—but, hey, WTF.

Now to the words I am at a loss for. The story involves a lone wanderer (Denzel Washington) who wears a name tag saying, "Hi! My name is Eli." It may not be his name tag, but let's call him Eli anyway. Eli has been walking west across the devastated landscape of America for thirty years, on his way to the sea. I haven't walked it myself, but I'm pretty sure it doesn't take that long.

On the other hand, maybe Eli only thought he was walking west. On his final trek, he walks from right to left across the screen, which in movie shorthand is walking east. "How do you know you're walking the right way?" he's asked. "Faith," he says, a reply that takes on added resonance later in the film.

Eli is a quick hand with knives, pistols, rifles, shotguns, and karate. He needs to be. After a catastrophe has wiped out most of the earth's population and left ruin and desolation behind, the remaining humans are victimized by roaming motorcycle gangs of hijackers and thieves. These gangs are each issued with a perquisite tall bald man, a short hairy scruffy one, and their gofers.

The Hughes brothers, Albert and Allen, film this story in sunburned browns and pale blues, creating a dry and dusty world under a merciless sky. Water is treasure. This wasteland Eli treks at an implacable pace. Set upon in an ambush, he kills all his attackers. He's got one of those knives that makes a "snicker-snack" noise all by itself, and is a one-man army. Why don't the bad guys just shoot at him? Later in the film, they try that.

Denzel and the Hughes brothers do a good job of establishing this man and his world, and at first *The Book of Eli* seems destined to be solemn. But then Eli arrives at a Western town ruled by Carnegie (Gary Oldman), who, like all the local overloads in Westerns and gangster movies, sits behind a big desk flanked by a tall bald guy and of course a short scruffy one. How are these guys recruited? "Wanted: Tall bald guy to stand behind town boss and be willing to sacrifice life. All the water you can drink."

In this town, desperate and starving people live in rusty cars and in the streets. We meet

Carnegie's abused wife, Claudia (Jennifer Beals), and her daughter, Solara (Mila Kunis), named for some reason after the cause of all the destruction. She's a prostitute in Carnegie's bar, having made the mistake of coming on Take Your Child to Work Day. Carnegie hurts Claudia to control Solara. How he controls the fearsome bald guy is hard to say.

The third act is recycled, but done well, out of many Westerns in which the hero and the girl hole up and are surrounded. So many other movies are quoted that we almost miss it when their hideout house is perforated by bullets, *L.A. Confidential* style. That allows countless beams of sunlight to shine in and function as a metaphor.

Carnegie needs Eli because Eli has maybe the last remaining copy of a book that Carnegie believes will allow him to expand and rule many more towns. I am forbidden by the Critic's Little Rule Book from naming the volume, but if you've made a guess after seeing numerous billboards stating "Religion Is Power," you may have guessed right.

The Hughes brothers have a vivid way with imagery here, as in their earlier films such as *Menace II Society* and the underrated *From Hell.* The film looks and feels good, and Washington's performance is more uncanny the more we think back over it. The ending is "flawed," as we critics like to say, but it's so magnificently, shamelessly, implausibly flawed that (a) it breaks apart from the movie and has a life of its own, or (b) at least it avoids being predictable.

Now do yourself a favor and don't talk to *anybody* about the film if you plan to see it.

The Boondock Saints II: All Saints Day ★

R, 121 m., 2009

Sean Patrick Flanery (Connor MacManus), Norman Reedus (Murphy MacManus), Billy Connolly (Poppa M), Clifton Collins Jr. (Romeo), Julie Benz (Agent Eunice Bloom), Peter Fonda (The Roman), Judd Nelson (Concezio Yakavetta). Directed by Troy Duffy and produced by Chris Brinker and Don Carmody. Screenplay by Duffy.

The Boondock Saints II: All Saints Day is an idiotic ode to macho horseshite (to employ an ancient Irish word). It is, however, distinguished by superb cinematography. It's the first film in ten years from Troy Duffy, whose original *Boondock Saints* (1999) has become a cult fetish. It's such a legendary cult film, a documentary was even released about it.

No, not one of those "the making of" jobs. One made by two of Duffy's former pals who got pissed off during the filming. They show him as a possibly alcoholic egomaniac. You know you're in trouble when your movie scores 16 percent on the Tomatometer, and the documentary about it scores 79 percent.

To quote from my review of the 2004 doc: "*Overnight* tells a riches-to-rags story, like *Project Greenlight* played in reverse. *Greenlight,* you will recall, is the Miramax contest to choose and produce one screenplay every year by a hopeful first-time filmmaker. In *Overnight,* the director starts out with a contract and money from Miramax, and works his way back to no contract, no film, and no money. Call it *Project Red Light.*"

The documentary validates Gene Siskel's favorite verdict on a film: "I'd rather see a documentary of the same people having lunch." In this case, you see the same people getting drunk. After Duffy signs with the William Morris Agency, he brags to his pals, "I get drunk at night, wake up the next morning hung over, go into those meetings in my overalls, and they're all wearing suits." Being Hollywood agents, they were probably more familiar with the danger signals of alcoholism than Duffy was.

The Boondock Saints cost $7 million and grossed $25,000 in two weeks in five theaters. Then a miracle occurred. It became a big hit on DVD—so big, this sequel was justified. It's a well-photographed picture with extensive special effects and good actors (Sean Patrick Flanery, Norman Reedus, Billy Connolly, Clifton Collins Jr., Julie Benz, Judd Nelson, and an unrecognizable Peter Fonda).

Flanery and Reedus are back from the original, as Connor and Murphy MacManus, two Irish Catholic brothers who executed countless Boston villains with bullets through the head and pennies on their eyes. Brothers? To me they look like twins. They now lead a quiet life in Ireland, herding sheep and smoking. Brokeback bachelors. After ten years, still unmarried, they live at home with old Poppy MacManus (Billy Connolly) in a cottage perhaps once inhabited by Ryan's Daughter's great-grandmother.

Word comes that a beloved Irish-American priest has been executed back in Boston, with pennies on his eyes. This calls for revenge: Someone is imitating their style! Electrified, the lads rush back to the States on a freight ship and go into action killing, oh, I'd say, hundreds of people, easily. This is done very well, in the way of stunts, f/x, and heavy metal cranked up to twelve.

The lads borrow a page from their old Poppy and don leather vests with built-in holsters for either four or six handguns, I forget. These they typically use while leaping in slo-mo off concealed trampolines while firing two guns each at the camera. If they always jump side by side, does that make it harder for their enemies to miss at least one? Can you fly forward through the air while firing two heavy-duty handguns without your arms jerking back and smacking you in the chin? Would that violate one of Newton's laws? Just askin'.

There's a lot of pious Roman Catholic iconography in the movie, although no one except the beloved executed priest ever goes into a church for purposes other than being murdered. The lads are loyal to the church in the same way fans are loyal to Da Bears. They aren't players themselves, but it's their team and don't mess with it. They do hold a quasi-religious ceremony, however, standing in a circle with a pal and vowing to never, ever stop smoking or drinking or attend an AA meeting. Drinking doesn't bother them anyway. They chug Irish whiskey like Gatorade. The only thing that bothers them, and they're super sensitive about this, is the slightest suggestion that they're gay.

The Bounty Hunter ★ ½

PG-13, 110 m., 2010

Jennifer Aniston (Nicole Hurly), Gerard Butler (Milo Boyd), Christine Baranski (Kitty Hurley). Directed by Andy Tennant and produced by Neal H. Moritz. Screenplay by Sarah Thorp.

I'm on the brink of declaring a new entry for Ebert's Little Movie Glossary: No comedy not titled *Caddyshack* has ever created a funny joke involving a golf cart. The only thing preventing me is that I can't remember if *Caddyshack* had golf cart jokes. In any event, if there is a golf cart, it will sooner or later drive into a water hazard. The funny angle here is that the filmmakers went to all that trouble because they trusted the audience to laugh.

I stared with glazed eyes at *The Bounty Hunter.* Here is a film with no need to exist. Among its sins is the misuse of Jennifer Aniston, who can be and has been very funny, but not in dreck like this. Lacking any degree of character development, it handcuffs her to a plot of exhausted action comedy clichés—and also to a car door and a bed.

The handcuffer is her former husband, Milo (Gerard Butler), a former cop who is now a bounty hunter and draws the assignment of tracking down his ex-wife, who has skipped bail. Have I lost touch here, or are bounty hunters routinely deployed to track down criminals accused of no more than a nonfatal traffic violation? Never mind.

Let's do a little mental exercise here, the same sort that the screenplay writer, Sarah Thorp, must have done. Remember the ground rules: The movie must contain only clichés. I used to test this exercise on my film class. I'd give them the genre, and begin sentences ending with an ellipsis. They'd compete to be first to shout out the answer.

1. The story involves a formerly married couple. He is a bounty hunter tracking her down for . . .
2. They dislike one another. Therefore by the end of the movie . . .
3. He drives a . . .
4. Because . . .
5. And his beloved . . .
6. He loves to gamble. Their road trip takes them to . . .
7. Where he . . .
8. And gets into trouble with . . .
9. Inspiring . . .
10. In a golf cart, they . . .
11. During the movie, he gets kicked . . .
12. She wears clothes so we can . . .

Well, I already gave you number ten. To the others, clever students would answer: (1) a nonserious crime, since this is a comedy; (2) they will fall back in love; (3) vintage convertible; (4) movies like them because older cars look like real cars, and with a convertible you can more easily light the characters and show the landscape at the same time; (5) gets damaged; (6) you can be excused for guessing Las Vegas, but it's Atlantic City; (7) wins big or loses big, but either way . . . ; (8) gangsters; (9) chase scenes, CGI sequences, impossible action, and lots of shots of her running in high heels; (10) you know; (11) in the crotch; (12) peek down her neckline.

Why, oh why, was this movie necessary? Could it have been redeemed by witty dialogue? Perhaps, but neither character is allowed to speak more than efficient sentences serving to further the plot. Hollywood movies started to simplify the dialogue when half the gross started to roll in from overseas. Has anyone noticed the great majority of nations dub foreign movies, so that subtitles aren't a problem?

Gerard Butler is a handsome hunk who can also act; he's currently starring in Ralph Fiennes's *Coriolanus.* Jennifer Aniston is a gifted comedienne. If you could pay their salaries, wouldn't you try to put them in a better movie than this? I saw the poster and had a sinking feeling the title gave away the whole story.

The Box ★ ★ ★

PG-13, 113 m., 2009

Cameron Diaz (Norma Lewis), James Marsden (Arthur Lewis), Frank Langella (Arlington Steward), James Rebhorn (Norm Cahill), Holmes Osborne (Dick Burns). Directed by Richard Kelly and produced by Kelly, Dan Lin, Kelly McKittrick, and Sean McKittrick. Screenplay by Kelly, based on the short story "Button, Button" by Richard Matheson.

I know, I know, *The Box* triumphantly qualifies for one of my favorite adjectives, "preposterous." But if you make a preposterous movie that isn't boring, I count that as some kind of a triumph. This one begins as traditional science fiction and branches out into radio signals from Mars, nosebleeds, Sartre's theories about free will, amputated toes, NASA, the National Security Agency, wind tunnels, murders, black Town Cars, obnoxious waiters, and a mysterious stranger.

His name is Arlington Lewis Steward (Frank Langella). He drops a box on the front porch of Norma and Arthur Lewis and returns with an offer: If they push the button on top of the box, they will be paid $1 million in crisp $100 bills ("nontaxable"), but unfortunately, someone not known to them will die. Well, what would you do? Norma (Cameron Diaz) has just learned their son's tuition is going up, and Arthur (James Marsden) has been dropped from astronaut training. The hell with it: Norma, so sweet and earnest, pushes the button.

This sets into motion a chain of events that I will not describe for you even if I could. The writer-director, Richard Kelly, goes from A to Z using fifty-two letters, but his transitions flow so uncannily it's only when you look back you realize you're off the road. Everything, including some impressive high-tech rocket science, is taken so seriously that you get sucked in. There's also the matter of the 360-degree camera that Arthur Lewis has designed for the Mars Lander. Well, what about it? After you've seen the movie, you tell me. At least the nosebleeds are explained.

The Box is based on the story "Button, Button" by Richard Matheson, published by *Playboy* in 1970. It inspired a simpler adaptation for a *Twilight Zone* episode in 1986, which had a different ending but a very similar box design. Well, what can you do with a box with a button on top? Matheson, who has three films in preproduction at eighty-three, has inspired or written at least twenty-three films (*I Am Legend* has been made three times) and countless TV episodes.

Here he seems motivated by the Milgram Experiment, one of the most famous psychological tests ever conducted. You've heard of it. Professor Stanley Milgram of Yale told volunteers he was testing the limits of human pain endurance. He showed them a dial and said it would administer electrical shocks to test subjects. The high range on the dial was painted red, indicating danger. The volunteers could hear the subjects screaming. They were told by the test supervisor it was *essential* to continue administering shocks (even though the dial indicated they might become fatal). In one round of experiments, 65 percent of the volunteers followed orders even when it meant a fatal shock.

What *would* you do? And what if the victim wasn't a person you had met who was screaming in another room, but someone unknown to you? And the reward wasn't helping out Yale with its research, but a cool million? Norma and Arthur Lewis aren't bad people—pretty nice ones, in fact. They regret her impulsive action immediately. But then the plot grows sinister, coiling around to involve them, which we expect, but also venturing into completely unanticipated directions and inspiring as many unanswered questions as *Knowing*, which I loved.

Many readers hated *Knowing*, and many will hate *The Box*. What can I say? I'm not here to agree with you. This movie kept me involved and intrigued, and for that I'm grateful. I'm beginning to wonder whether, in some situations, absurdity might not be a strength.

The Boys Are Back ★ ★ ½

PG-13, 103 m., 2009

Clive Owen (Joe Warr), Emma Booth (Laura), Laura Fraser (Katy), George MacKay (Harry), Nicholas McAnulty (Artie). Directed by Scott Hicks and produced by Greg Brenman and Timothy White. Screenplay by Allan Cubitt, based on the memoir *The Boys Are Back in Town* by Simon Carr.

An opening shot in *The Boys Are Back* shows a small boy balanced on the hood of an SUV, which his father is driving on a beach. No, his father isn't drunk; he's simply a man whose idea of giving his son freedom comes recklessly close to endangerment. Surprisingly, the film considers him to be a good dad.

His name is Joe Warr (Clive Owen). He's a British sportswriter who moved to Australia to follow his second wife, Katy (Laura Fraser). After her sudden death, he becomes the single parent of Artie (Nicholas McAnulty), who is six and doesn't quite understand how his mom could die, although he acts out erratically. During Artie's earlier years, his dad, one of Australia's top sportswriters, was away frequently covering events or working on deadline. His mom provided a secure home. Joe is new to the day-after-day responsibility of fatherhood and running a household (how *do* rooms get themselves cleaned and straightened?).

Joe's belief is that kids need to be challenged, trusted, and given as much freedom as possible. That may sound good in theory, but children also require structure and rules. They don't always want their parents screaming at them that they're going to break their necks, but on the other hand, it can be unsettling to have a dad who almost seems OK with neck breaking.

I believe in the benefits of raising "free-range children"—within reason. When I was a kid, we ran around the neighborhood and could be away from home all day without anyone calling the police—just so we were home when the street lights went on. At the same time, we knew all the parents in the neighborhood had an eye on us through a window or from a porch chair, we knew there were rules, we knew we were loved and worried about.

Artie is treated by Joe almost like a college buddy. This suits Joe's personality, but doesn't work so well with the uncertain kid, and also not with Laura (Emma Booth), a woman he eventually starts dating, who is a single mom with more sensible ideas about parenting. The film seems to regard Joe with affection, and Owen certainly portrays him as a nice man. But why are his unformed theories about raising Artie supposed to fill us with affection and sentiment?

There's a problem, too, when Joe's teenage son, Harry (George MacKay), from his first marriage comes out from England for a summer with Dad. Harry and Artie bond quickly, but Harry was raised in a more structured way (too structured, judging from what we see) and has big problems with Joe's child-rearing theories. Some of the film's more successful passages involve the ways Harry becomes the father his poor little brother doesn't have.

There's something a little too absent about Joe. I want to call it selfishness. With Artie, he needs to look and listen more closely. Just because Joe thinks things are fine doesn't mean they are. Clive Owen can be a likable actor, but the character is working against him. *The Boys Are Back* was directed by Scott Hicks, whose *Shine* remains a moving experience, but here he has all the pieces in place (cast, cinematography, music) and doesn't quite have the story he thinks he has. And please, please, give us a break from the scenes where the ghost of the departed turns up and starts talking as if she's not dead.

Bran Nue Dae ★ ★ ½

PG-13, 85 m., 2010

Rocky McKenzie (Willie), Jessica Mauboy (Rosie), Ernie Dingo (Uncle Tadpole), Missy Higgins (Annie), Geoffrey Rush (Father Benedictus), Deborah Mailman (Roxanne), Tom Budge (Slippery), Magda Szubanski (Roadhouse Betty). Directed by Rachel Perkins and produced by Graeme Isaac and Robyn Kershaw. Screenplay by Perkins, Reg Cribb, and Jimmy Chi.

Here's something I wasn't expecting: an Aboriginal musical from Australia, set in a late hippie era and featuring production numbers with a dash of Bollywood. It isn't a masterpiece, but it is a good-hearted, sweet comedy, featuring an overland chase that isn't original but sure is energetic.

The movie opens with its two young lovers shyly making eyes at each other. These are the young teenagers Willie (Rocky McKenzie) and Rosie (Jessica Mauboy). They daringly peek into a local saloon, and the singer invites the pretty Rosie (but pointedly not Willie) inside. Rosie can't resist a chance at a microphone, and magically becomes the center of the movie's first dance number. The way everyone in the room seems to have rehearsed the choreography is the hint of Bollywood, where characters seem to arrange themselves instinctively into chorus lines.

Willie's pious mother is determined to see her son win respect and get a good job as a priest. She whisks him away from his hometown to a rather strange seminary, ruled by Father Benedictus (Geoffrey Rush), who has a German accent but not overmuch of the holy spirit.

Willie yearns for home and Rosie, and runs away, finds a hobo camp, and is befriended by Uncle Tadpole (Ernie Dingo), who claims to be a relative but forgets about that in the morning. No matter. Uncle Tadpole comes along for the trip, and they hitch a ride in a van painted in a psychedelic 1960s style and piloted by two jolly hippies. Father Benedictus follows in unconvincing and not very clerical fashion as he goes in pursuit, having forgotten, I guess, that Willie must want to be a priest and not be captured and forced.

And so on. I learn *Bran Nue Dae* was a hit on the Australian stage in 1990. Many of the songs, some with serious undertones, reflect the treatment of Aborigines, who were treated as cruelly as Native Americans, and in such recent decades you'd think a more enlightened vision might have seeped into Australia, not that we have anything to feel smug about.

The two leads are sweet and attractive, their roles don't place great demands, and the movie skips along happily, if a little disorganized. Its look is striking; the cinematography, by Andrew Lesnie of *The Lord of the Rings*, gives the exteriors an almost Day-Glo brightness, as if the sun is shining through the screen.

Bride Flight ★ ★ ★

R, 130 m., 2011

Waldemar Torenstra (Frank), Karina Smulders (Ada), Anna Drijver (Esther), Elise Schaap (Marjorie), Petra Laseur (Older Marjorie), Pleuni Touw (Older Ada), Willeke van Ammelrooy (Older Esther), Rutger Hauer (Older Frank). Directed by Ben Sombogaart and produced by Hanneke Niens and Anton Smit. Screenplay by Marieke van der Pol.

Bride Flight derives its title from an actual flight in 1953 between London and Christchurch, New Zealand—part of the Last Great Air Race. The Dutch plane in the race carries many women flying to New Zealand to meet current or prospective husbands, and the movie will follow the fortunes of three of them for many tumultuous years, using two actors to portray each of them as younger and older.

The events in the plot are the stuff of soap opera, but the movie treats it seriously, and the acting is convincing enough that we forgive the story and begin to care about the characters. Four people on the flight will find their lives linked in New Zealand. Ada (Karina Smulders) and Marjorie (Elise Schaap) are flying out to meet their husbands. Esther (Anna Drijver), a Holocaust survivor, is a fashion designer hoping to start a new business. Frank (Waldemar Torenstra) is a hunky rancher. During the flight, Ada, who has met her new husband only once, finds that she and Frank are falling in love.

In Christchurch they all find an optimistic postwar city that's filled with opportunity, especially in contrast with war-torn Holland. Ada stays with her husband (Micha Hulshof), a fiercely censorious Calvinist. Esther opens a design studio. Marjorie finds she can't have children. Esther finds she can but doesn't want to; her career comes first. And Frank—well, Frank is a genial lad, well liked, and if he isn't with the one he loves, he loves the one he's with.

Bride Flight takes this melodrama and adds details of period, of behavior, of personality, to somewhat redeem its rather inevitable conclusion. The key figure is Ada, who has three children and then arrives at a momentous decision that colors everything else that happens. Esther and Marjorie find that their own decisions are not so easily left in the past.

You can sense I'm not describing much of the story. It wouldn't be fair. A film like *Bride Flight* works because we want to see it unfolding. We observe the pieces going into place and want to see how it will all work out. That it works out more or less inevitably is to be expected, I suppose, but you'd be upset if I revealed some of the twists and turns.

This is the biggest-budgeted film ever made in Holland, not least because the story of the real bride flight is well known and involves a period fraught with emotion. So considerable is the production that Rutger Hauer has returned to Dutch films after thirty years to play the older Frank. The young actresses who play the three leads are all capable, and Karina Smulders much more than that, in a role that takes her more deeply than the others.

Three observations. (1) There's a danger in assigning a mannerism to a character and enforcing it too relentlessly. Esther smokes using a little cigarette holder, which she *always* holds next to her face. This begins to be a glitch. (2) In a scene at an airport, a crucial piece of information is imparted in a subtle and rather elegant understatement. You'll see what I mean. (3) There is a love scene of real urgency and passion. Often movie sex scenes seem to be merely energetic exercise.

Bridesmaids ★ ★ ★ ½

R, 128 m., 2011

Kristen Wiig (Annie), Maya Rudolph (Lillian), Rose Byrne (Helen), Wendi McLendon-Covey (Rita), Ellie Kemper (Becca), Melissa McCarthy (Megan), Chris O'Dowd (Rhodes). Directed by Paul Feig and produced by Judd Apatow, Barry Mendel, and Clayton Townsend. Screenplay by Annie Mumolo and Kristen Wiig.

Three of my good female friends, who I could usually find overcoming hangovers at their Saturday morning Recovery Drunches at Oxford's Pub, once made pinpricks in their thumbs and performed a ceremony, becoming blood sisters. They were the only people I have actually known who could inspire a Judd Apatow buddy movie, and all three could do what not all women do well, and that is perfectly tell a dirty joke.

Maybe I liked *Bridesmaids* in their honor. Kristen Wiig's new comedy is about a group of women friends who are as unbehaved as the guys in *The Hangover.* Don't tell me "unbehaved" isn't a word. It is now. And Wiig is rather brilliant in her physical comedy as she flies to Vegas as part of her BFF's bachelorette party; if it were not the wedding of her BFF, this trip would get her thrown out of the wedding. Her motto: "What happens in Vegas, starts on the plane."

Wiig plays Annie, whose Milwaukee bakery shop has just gone bust, who rooms with a surpassingly peculiar British brother and sister, and whose longtime friend Lillian (Maya Rudolph) is getting married. Naturally, she expects to be maid of honor, but begins to fear a rival in Helen (Rose Byrne), the rich and overconfident trophy wife of the groom's boss. You see that can lead to trouble.

Helen is one of those people who at birth was placed in charge of everything for everyone. It's not that she's trying to steal Annie's thunder, it's just that she can't comprehend that she isn't running the wedding. This leads finally to Annie's explosion at a bizarre French-themed bridal shower with an item of pastry that would strike even an editor of the *Guinness Book of World Records* as, well, excessive.

The movie, written by Wiig and Annie

Mumolo and directed by Paul Feig (*The Office*), does a good job of introducing a large cast, and in particular, keeping all the members of the bridal party in play. These include Rita (Wendi McLendon-Covey), a mother of three adolescent sons ("My house is covered in semen"), and (my favorite) Megan (Melissa McCarthy), who has the sturdiness and the certainty of a fireplug.

Did I mention the movie was produced by Apatow? Love him or not, he's consistently involved with movies that connect with audiences, and *Bridesmaids* seems to be a more or less deliberate attempt to cross the chick flick with the raunch comedy. It definitively proves that women are the equal of men in vulgarity, sexual frankness, lust, vulnerability, overdrinking, and insecurity. And it moves into areas not available to men, for example the scene when they're all trying on dresses at a bridal shop and the lunch they've just shared suddenly reappears, if you get my drift.

Not everybody can do physical comedy. Wiig's behavior on the flight to Vegas would win the respect of Lucille Ball. I don't even want to start describing what happens. In these days when you can get arrested on a plane for taking out your car keys, her behavior is a throwback to the good old days of airborne slapstick.

Yet the movie has a heart. It heals some wounds, restores some hurt feelings, confesses some secrets, and in general ends happily, which is just as well, because although there are many things audiences will accept from women in a comedy, ending miserably is not one of them. That may be sexist, but there you are.

Bride Wars ★ ★

PG, 90 m., 2009

Kate Hudson (Liv), Anne Hathaway (Emma), Kristen Johnston (Deb), Bryan Greenberg (Nate), Candice Bergen (Marion), Steve Howey (Daniel), Chris Pratt (Fletcher). Directed by Gary Winick and produced by Julie Yorn, Alan Riche, and Kate Hudson. Screenplay by Greg DePaul, Casey Wilson, and June Diane Raphael.

Is there anyone old enough to care about weddings and naive enough to believe *Bride Wars*? Here is a sitcom about consumerism, centering on two bubble-brained women and their vacuous fiancés, and providing them with not a single line that is smart or witty. The dialogue is fiercely on-topic, dictated by the needs of the plot, pounding down the home stretch in clichés, obligatory truisms, and shrieks.

Kate Hudson and Anne Hathaway, who play the would-be brides, are good actors and quick-witted women, here playing characters at a level of intelligence approximating HAL 9000 after he has had his chips pulled. No one can be this superficial and survive without professional care. Compare this film with the wonderful *Rachel Getting Married,* for which Hathaway won an Oscar nomination as Rachel's sister, and now see how she plays a prenuptial Stepford Wife.

I am sure there are women who will enjoy *Bride Wars,* as a man might enjoy a film about cars and Hooters girls. It's like a moving, talking version of *Brides* magazine. Hudson and Hathaway play Liv and Emma, girlhood friends who made a vow to realize their dreams of both getting married at the Plaza. They're serious. They've been saving up the money for their big days for more than ten years. No daddies are around to fork over.

Liv is a lawyer and has perhaps made some money. Emma, without parents, is a schoolteacher. They both go to the most famous wedding planner in Manhattan (Candice Bergen) and, with *three months' notice,* are able to nail down dates at the Plaza for a June wedding. This is before Madoff forced the wholesale cancellation of reservations.

Do you have any idea what such weddings would cost, after flowers and table decorations, invitations, gowns, limos, a reception, dinner, music, the sweets table, the planner, the event room at the Plaza, and rooms for the wedding parties to get dressed? Plus tips? For enough room to get the bride and her bridesmaids whipped into shape, I think you could all squeeze into an Edwardian Park suite, 1,000 square feet with a king-size bed, which next June 7 will go for $2,195. Family of the bride? Impecunious out-of-town relatives? Groom and his best men? Have them wait in the hallway.

At least there will be no expenses for a honeymoon, since neither couple ever discusses one. The movie is about the brides and their weddings, and that's that. The grooms are, in fact, remarkably inconsequential, spending a lot of time sitting on couches and watching their brides act out romantic and revenge fantasies. That's because after both weddings are scheduled for the same time, Emma and Liv forget their lifelong bonds of friendship, start feuding, and play practical jokes involving a deep orange suntan, blue-dyed hair, and a projected video from their bachelorette party. They end up in a cat fight in the aisle. Fortunately neither one thinks of introducing E. coli into the punch bowl.

Women and men have different visions of wedding ceremonies. This I know from *Father of the Bride* (1991), with Steve Martin and Diane Keaton as the parents. Martin envisions the swell ceremony he will provide for his daughter: lots of balloons in the backyard and him manning the barbecue grill. Keaton gently corrects him. Even at the time I reviewed the movie, there was a newspaper story about a father who offered his daughter the choice of a nice ceremony or a condo.

Bride Wars is pretty thin soup. The characters have no depth or personality, no quirks or complications, no conversation. The story twist is so obvious from the first shot of two characters talking that they might have well been waving handkerchiefs over their heads and signaling: "Watch this space for further developments." The whole story is narrated by Candice Bergen as the wedding coordinator, who might as well have been instructing us how to carve bars of Ivory Soap into little ducks.

Bright Star ★ ★ ★ ½

PG, 119 m., 2009

Abbie Cornish (Fanny Brawne), Ben Whishaw (John Keats), Paul Schneider (Mr. Brown), Kerry Fox (Mrs. Brawne). Directed by Jane Campion and produced by Jan Chapman and Caroline Hewitt. Screenplay by Campion.

John Keats wasn't meekly posing as a Romantic poet. He was the real thing, and the last-born of the group that also included Blake, Wordsworth, Coleridge, Byron, and Shelley. He died at twenty-five and remains forever young.

The great and only love of his life was Fanny Brawne, the daughter of his landlady. He lived with his friend Charles Brown and she with her mother, sister, and brother in the two halves of a Hampstead cottage so small it gives meaning to the phrase "living in each other's pockets." Their love was grand and poetic and—apart from some sweet kisses—platonic, for he had neither the means nor the health to propose marriage, and they were not moved to violate the moral code of what was not yet quite the Victorian era.

Jane Campion's beautiful and wistful new film shows them frozen in courtship, like the young man Keats wrote about in "Ode on a Grecian Urn"—the youth who is immortalized forever in pursuit of a maid he is destined never to catch. He could have been writing about himself and Fanny: "Bold Lover, never, never canst thou kiss, / Though winning near the goal—yet, do not grieve; / She cannot fade, though thou hast not thy bliss, / For ever wilt thou love, and she be fair!"

It is almost as if they were spiritually inflamed by their doomed love. She was not shy but she was proper, and he loved her, but perhaps he had some difficulty in thinking of her as physical. When his younger brother Tom died and his own health began to fail, he immortalized his loss of that which he had never possessed. (From his deathbed in Italy, however, he did indeed write Brown that he wished he had "had her" when he had a chance.) Dr. Johnson observed to Mr. Boswell: "Marriage, sir, is a state with few pleasures. Chastity, with none." Yet Keats and Fanny seemed quite pleased enough.

I have visited the Keats House many times, and I can tell you it is shockingly small. The dividing wall between the two households was knocked out in the mid-1880s, but propriety must have erected a stouter wall. John and Fanny court and flirt as if they live in neighboring counties. It's to Campion's credit that she doesn't heat up the story or go for easy emotional payoffs, and we're spared even the pathetic deathbed scene that another director might have felt necessary.

The key figure is Fanny, played by Abbie Cornish with effervescence. "I confess I do not find your poems easy," she tells Keats (Ben Whishaw). But she studies at them earnestly, with a touching faith that they must contain clues to the stirrings in her heart. He requires her as a muse. For a reader, he has the bearded, gruff Brown (Paul Schneider), possessive, demanding, a taskmaster. Brown is hostile to Fanny's appeal to his friend and resents it when she interrupts them "working," which seems to consist of him scowling morosely at a manuscript while Keats idly dreams. Brown is a poet himself, but to his credit he recognizes the better craftsman and behaves like a coach or an agent.

There might be some question whether Brown felt sexual stirrings of his own involving Keats, but I think he is oblivious to such a possibility. He knows the real thing, he wonders if Keats would daydream his career away, as always at his back he hears time's winged chariot hurrying near. When Keats leaves for Italy, it is Brown who accompanies him—not Fanny, of course, who waits forlornly for the postman to approach down the little lane beneath the tree where Keats perhaps heard the nightingale sing. (The tree now growing on the spot is not the same one, but don't tell everyone.)

What Campion does is seek visual beauty to match Keats's verbal beauty. There is a shot here of Fanny in a meadow of blue flowers that is so enthralling it beggars description. Hampstead in those days was a village on the slopes north of London, almost rural, where shepherds could graze their flocks on the public land of Hampstead Heath. Coleridge lived not far way in Highgate, and the two met during their rambles on the heath. To support oneself seems to have been relatively possible, despite Dickens's portraits of poverty at the time. Mrs. Brawne (Kerry Fox) observes to her daughter that he has "no living and no income," the volumes of verse brought in only a few pounds, but when it is time for Keats to live in Italy, he finds the means. It appears that an English gentleman could support himself on air and credit.

It is famously impossible for the act of writing to be made cinematic. How long can we watch someone staring at a blank sheet of paper? It is equally unenlightening to show the writer seeing something and dashing off to scribble down impassioned words while we hear him reading them in his mind. Campion knows all this, and knows, too, that without the poetry John Keats is only a moonstruck young man. How she works in the words is one of the subtle beauties of the film. And over the end credits, Whishaw reads the "Ode" and you will want to stay.

Note: Tom O'Bedlam reads the poem Keats wrote about Fanny Brawne, "Bright Star": www.youtube.com/watch?v=QyymuJqZJtM.

Broken Embraces ★ ★ ★ ★

R, 128 m., 2009

Penelope Cruz (Lena Rivero), Lluis Homar (Harry Caine), Jose Luis Gomez (Ernesto Martel), Blanca Portillo (Judit Garcia), Ruben Ochendiano (Ray X), Tamar Novas (Diego Garcia). Directed by Pedro Almodovar and produced by Esther Garcia. Screenplay by Almodovar.

Pedro Almodovar loves the movies with lust and abandon and the skill of an experienced lover. *Broken Embraces* is a voluptuary of a film, drunk on primary colors, caressing Penelope Cruz, using the devices of a Hitchcock to distract us with surfaces while the sinister uncoils beneath. As it ravished me, I longed for a freeze frame to allow me to savor a shot.

The movie confesses its obsession up front. It is about seeing. A blind man asks a woman to describe herself. Since we can see her perfectly well, one purpose of this scene is to allow us to listen to her. How to describe the body, the hair, the eyes? Movies are really about the human body more than anything else. I was recently faulted for lingering overmuch on Ingrid Bergman's lips in *Casablanca*. Anyone, man or woman, who doesn't want to linger on Ingrid Bergman's lips is telling us something about themselves we'd rather not know.

The blind man is Harry Caine (Lluis Homar). Harry Lime and Citizen Kane, get it? Both played by Orson Welles, the great man of the cinema. Welles's *Magnificent Ambersons* was infamously botched by being re-edited in his absence.

Harry Caine is the name Mateo Blanco took after being blinded in an automobile accident. Perhaps only he knew why. As Blanco, he directed a film named *Girls and Suitcases.* It was produced by a man named Ernesto Martel (Jose Luis Gomez). Harry/Mateo hates Martel for reasons that will be explored. One day he's visited by Ray X (Ruben Ochandiano). X-Ray: Yeah, you got it. X despises the memory of his father and wants to enlist Caine, now a famous writer, to do the screenplay. Perhaps he has hidden reasons for contacting Caine.

Guarding Caine in his blindness is Judit (Blanca Portillo), who was his trusted aide when he could see and has now become indispensable. It is clear, although she has never revealed it to him, that she loves him. We sense her feelings go beneath love, however, into realms he doesn't guess.

Penelope Cruz has been Almodovar's constant muse since *Live Flesh* (1997). When Martel and Blanco/Caine were preparing *Girls and Suitcases,* the producer hired Lena (Cruz) as his assistant. In the time-honored tradition of such arrangements, in particular when the woman has been a prostitute, he arranges for Lena to audition for a role in the new picture. The director falls in love with her during the screen test.

Martel is enraged as only a rich middle-aged man who has purchased love can be. He sics his son on them. Yes, the future Ray X follows them with his camera like a nerdy fanboy. That it's unwholesome to spy on the behavior of your father's mistress goes without saying; can the boy be blamed for growing up to hate Martel? His videos are screened for the father, who combines jealousy with voyeurism, a common enough mixture.

I've really only scratched the surface of where *Broken Embraces* goes and what it discovers. To find that this passion comes to fruition in a blind man's editing room is to demonstrate that all films, and all of us, are blind until the pieces are put together. There are two, or really four, movies within this one: Martel's film in its first and second cuts, and Ray X's video seen one way and then another. The nature of each film changes in transition, and the changes have deep meaning for the characters.

Look at Almodovar's command of framing here. There's one unbroken shot so "illogical" it may even slip past you. There's urgent action on a sofa in the foreground and then a character stands and moves to the right, talking, and dawdles slightly and then moves to the left, and now we see for the first time the next room completely open to this one, and there is a young man seated at a table in there.

What? He must have been there all along, yet the foreground action took no notice of him, the camera didn't establish him, and now no acknowledgment is made of his incongruous presence. I *think* this shot may be about the ability of camera placement and film editing to dictate absolutely what is and is not in a scene. I'm sure it also has meaning in terms of the characters, but I don't know what. It shows Almodovar saying he'll do things just for the hell of it and keep a straight face.

Mention must be made of red. Almodovar, who always favors bright primary colors, drenches this film in red: in the clothing, the decor, the lipstick, the artwork, the furnishings—everywhere he can. Red, the color of passion and blood. Never has he made a film more visually pulsating, and Almodovar is not shy. Never has Penelope Cruz been more clearly the brush he uses, the canvas he covers, and the subject of his painting. To see this film once is to experience his deliberate abandon. To see it twice, as I've been able to, is to understand that his style embodies his subject. That subject is this: Film and life rush ahead so heedlessly that the frames are past before we can contemplate them.

Bronson ★ ★ ★

R, 92 m., 2009

Tom Hardy (Michael Peterson/Bronson), Matt King (Paul Daniels), Amanda Burton (Mum), James Lance (Phil). Directed by Nicolas Winding Refn and produced by Daniel Hansford and Rupert Preston. Screenplay by Refn and Brock Norman Brock.

Michael Peterson tells us he was born into a normal middle-class family. He doesn't blame his childhood or anything else for the way he turned out, and neither does this film. It regards him as a natural history exhibit. No more would we blame him on his childhood than we would blame a venomous snake's. It is their nature to behave as they do.

At an early age, after seeing *Death Wish*, young Michael took the name of Charles Bronson. And as Bronson, he has become the U.K.'s most famous prisoner and without any doubt its most violent. With a shaved head and a comic-opera mustache, he likes to strip naked and grease himself before going into action.

His favorite pastime is taking a hostage and then engaging in a bloody battle with the guards who charge to the rescue, swinging clubs and beating him into submission. He has triggered this scenario many times, perhaps because he enjoys it so much. Originally sentenced to seven years ("You'll be out in three," his mother calls to him in the courtroom), he has now served thirty-four uninterrupted years, thirty of them in solitary confinement.

Why? We don't know. The movie doesn't know. If Bronson knows, he's not telling. The movie takes on a fearsome purity, refusing to find reasons, indifferent to motives, not even finding causes and effects. It is ninety-two minutes of rage, acted by Tom Hardy. This is a versatile actor. As you'd expect, he's made a lot of British gangster movies (*RocknRolla, Layer Cake, Sucker Punch*), but he's also played Bill Sikes in *Oliver Twist* and Heathcliff in a TV adaptation of *Wuthering Heights*.

Hardy brings a raw physicality to the role, leaping naked about his cell, jumping from tables, hurtling himself into half a dozen guards, heedless of pain or harm. It must hurt him, because it makes us wince to watch. The word is animalistic.

They say one definition of insanity is when you repeat the same action expecting a different result. Bronson must therefore not be insane. He repeats the same actions expecting the same results. He goes out of his way to avoid different outcomes. During one stretch of comparative passivity, he's allowed to go to the prison art room and work with an instructor. He enjoys this, I think. He isn't a bad artist. When it appears he may be showing progress, what does he do? He takes the instructor hostage, and is beaten senseless by guards.

"I showed magic in there!" he shouts after one brawl, bleeding in triumph. How's that? Magic, like an opening night? Does he expect a standing ovation? I believe most of us, no matter how self-destructive, expect some sort of reward for our behavior. It may not be some people's idea of a reward, but it's ours. Is Bronson then an extreme masochist, who wants only to be hurt? They say there are masochists like that, but surely there's a limit. What kind of passionate dementia does it require to want to be beaten bloody for thirty-four straight years?

I suppose, after all, Nicolas Winding Refn, the director and cowriter of *Bronson*, was wise to leave out any sort of an explanation. Can you imagine how you'd cringe if the film ended in a flashback of little Mickey undergoing childhood trauma? There is some human behavior beyond our ability to comprehend. I was reading a theory the other day that a few people just happen to be pure evil. I'm afraid I believe it. They lack any conscience, any sense of pity or empathy for their victims. But—Bronson is his own victim. How do you figure that?

Brooklyn's Finest ★ ★ ★

R, 140 m., 2010

Richard Gere (Eddie), Don Cheadle (Tango), Ethan Hawke (Sal), Wesley Snipes (Caz), Will Patton (Hobarts), Lili Taylor (Angela), Shannon Kane (Chantel), Ellen Barkin (Smith). Directed by Antoine Fuqua and produced by Elie Cohn, Basil Iwanyk, John Langley, Avi Lerner, and John Thompson. Screenplay by Michael C. Martin.

Three cops, three journeys to what we suspect will be doom. No good can come of the lives they lead. They aren't bad guys, not precisely, but they occupy a world of such unremitting violence and cynicism that they're willing to do what it takes to survive. In the kind of coincidence provided only by fate or screenplays, each one will mean trouble for the other two.

Richard Gere gets top billing as Eddie, a veteran with one week left before retirement. It is a movie convention that anyone who has a week to go before retirement must die before that week is up, but Eddie seems impatient. As the film opens, he wakes up, chugs some whiskey from a bottle, and points a revolver into his mouth, never a good sign.

Don Cheadle is Tango, who is completely embedded undercover in Brooklyn's toughest drug precinct, where he has blended in so well with the bad guys that it's a fine line separating him from crime. His friend is Caz (Wesley Snipes), a dealer trying to go straight after prison; they share one of those inexplicable bonds between two tough guys, causing them to consider each other brothers when they should really be nothing of the kind.

The third cop, Sal (Ethan Hawke), is a narc whose wife (Lili Taylor) provides him with more of a melodramatic emergency than we are perhaps prepared to believe. They have seven kids, live in a house too small for them, and the mold in the walls provokes potentially dangerous asthma attacks. Oh, and she's pregnant. Having twins.

Sal has made an offer on a new place for which he cannot make the first payment. He desperately needs cash, and there's a lot of it around in his work. Tango needs to somehow use Caz and yet spare him. Eddie needs to negotiate an alcoholic haze for seven more days before he can go fishing.

The film and the actors do a good job of establishing these characters in their own lives. Indeed, the best things about *Brooklyn's Finest* are the one-on-one scenes. These are fine actors. The milieu involves a tough, poker-playing, substance-abusing, hard-bitten world where the law meets crime and the two sides have more in common with each other than with civilians. I don't believe it's like this for most cops, but somehow it is for the great majority of movie cops.

Cheadle and Snipes have some very good scenes involving what is left unsaid but not unsuspected. Ethan Hawke has a fierce loyalty to his wife and family, and Lili Taylor does her usual touching job with what's basically a soap opera role. Hawke is especially effective in desperate scenes where he takes crazy risks because he needs to raise cash quickly. Richard Gere's character is not as rich as the other two, is more depressed, is on a more predictable trajectory.

What is rather startling is the level of the violence and killing. Although cops-vs.-drugs movies are traditionally awash in blood, *Brooklyn's Finest* demonstrates a trope I've seen with disturbing frequency: the scene in which one character lifts a firearm and peremptorily blows away another one—almost casually or unemotionally, like cleaning house. I complained for years about the Talking Killer Syndrome, in which the shooter delays in order to explain himself to a man who will presumably be dead soon. But Instant Killers are not the answer. The fact of taking life is robbed of weight and meaning. The gun becomes the instrument of merciless self-will.

The director of *Brooklyn's Finest,* Antoine Fuqua, made *Training Day* (2001), the film Denzel Washington won an Oscar for. That powerfully costarred Ethan Hawke. This film has the same level of savage violence and the same cops operating outside the same law, but the human stakes are more obvious and less convincing. The lives of the three cops intersect through a series of coincidences and inevitabilities, and I think we become a little too conscious that they're being guided less by chance than by a screenwriter. The film has a basic strength in its performances and craft, but falls short of the high mark Fuqua obviously set for himself.

Brothers ★ ★ ★ ½

R, 104 m., 2009

Tobey Maguire (Captain Sam Cahill), Jake Gyllenhaal (Tommy Cahill), Natalie Portman (Grace Cahill), Sam Shepard (Hank Cahill), Bailee Madison (Isabelle Cahill), Taylor Geare (Maggie Cahill). Directed by Jim Sheridan and produced by Michael De Luca, Ryan Kavanaugh, and Sigurjon Sighvatsson. Screenplay by David Benioff, based on the motion picture *Brothers* written by Susanne Bier and Anders Thomas Jensen.

Brothers is the new film by Jim Sheridan, a director who has a sure hand with stories about families (*In America, In the Name of the Father, The Boxer*). This one is about a family twisted from its natural form when the father leaves for service in Afghanistan just after his brother comes home from prison. The good brother goes into harm's way while the bad brother is shielded by his own misbehavior.

The brothers are played by two leading young actors I hadn't thought of as plausible brothers before, but I do now. Tobey Maguire is Captain Sam Cahill, very warmly married to Grace (Natalie Portman), father of Isabelle and Maggie. Jake Gyllenhaal is his brother, Tommy, out after a term for armed robbery. Their father, Hank Cahill (Sam Shepard), makes little secret of his pride in Sam and his contempt for Tommy.

But Tommy in his own way is trying to avoid more trouble. Word arrives that Sam has died in a helicopter crash in Afghanistan. Portman handles this blow, and the whole movie, in a touchingly mature way; it redoubles her love for her daughters. Tommy, awkwardly, almost fearfully, tries to help her out with jobs around the house that Sam would have done. She doesn't want this help, but over a time she softens. She knows all about Tommy's history, but she married into it; she didn't grow up with it.

I will try to avoid unnecessary detail. You will have anticipated that with Sam dead, the mother raising the girls and Tommy trying to help, there is the possibility that the two survivors will grow close. Whether they do is not the subject of the picture. That becomes whether Sam suspects they do and what he thinks about it.

It's not a spoiler to observe that Sam didn't die in the crash because from the very first *Brothers* shows him alive in Afghanistan. The film cuts between life at home and the cruel tortures of the Taliban. The prisoner scenes are handled with a ruthless realism, showing Sam placed in the grip of a moral and emotional paradox that makes it, I would say, necessary that he commit acts he will never forgive himself for.

He returns home. He's greeted with love and joy. He feels no joy in return. Sam is so deeply scarred that ordinary emotion is unavailable to him, and he is strange even toward his children. He makes little secret that he suspects Grace and Tommy may have been sleeping together. What can set his mind at ease, especially when, if he had died, that might have been something he desired? And there is always his own unbearable guilt locked within.

Sheridan and his screenplay sources make *Brothers* much more than a drama about war and marriage. It is about what we can forgive ourselves for—and that, too, has been a theme running through Sheridan's films. As an Irish Catholic of sixty, he was raised to feel a great deal about guilt. This becomes Tobey Maguire's film to dominate, and I've never seen these dark depths in him before. Actors possess a great gift to surprise us, if they find the right material in their hands.

The principal actors, with Shepard's well-timed and not overacted appearances, make this a specific story about particular people, and avoid temptations toward melodrama. It's about guilt and happiness, and how Tommy treats his guilt by righteous action, and Sam sinks into self-destruction. As a mother who seeks to preserve her daughters in the middle, Portman is the emotional heart of the story, as mothers are for so many families.

Brothers is a very close remake of a 2005 Danish film by Susanne Bier, which starred as the mother Connie Nielsen, that remarkable Danish actress equally at home in English (*Gladiator*, *The Ice Harvest*). Same story, same characters, same moral crisis. I cannot fault the Sheridan remake except in a way that perhaps only an experienced filmgoer would understand.

It is too finished. It is smooth Hollywood craftsmanship, cinematography, editing. The Danish film, loosely associated with the Dogma movement, was rougher, shakier, and more improvised: therefore, more reality, less fiction. You might find it interesting to see the two films together. If it's true that a film is not what it's about but how it's about it, these two will cause you to ask yourself how a film should be about this story.

Brothers at War ★ ★ ★

R, 110 m., 2009

Featuring Jake Rademacher, Captain Isaac Rademacher, Sergeant Joe Rademacher, Jenny Rademacher, Claus Rademacher, Mahmoud Hamid Ali, Edward Allier, Zack Corke, Danelle Fields, Ben Fisher, Kevin Keniston, Frank McCann, Brandon "Mongo" Phillips, and Robert Smallwood. A documentary directed by Jake Rademacher and produced by Rademacher and Norman S. Powell.

I've been waiting for this film since the early days of the war in Iraq. *Brothers at War* is an honest, on-the-ground documentary about the lives of Americans fighting there. It has no spin. It's not left or right. I don't recall if it even mentions President Bush. It's not pro- or antiwar, although obviously the two brothers fighting there support it. It is simply about men and women.

The film is about the men in the Rademacher family from Decatur, Illinois. Jake, the oldest, always planned to go into the military but didn't make it into West Point and found himself as an actor. Isaac, the next, graduated top of his class at West Point and married his classmate Jenny. Joe, next in line, enlisted and was top of his class at Army Ranger school. The brothers were very close growing up, but Jake sensed a distance growing as they came home on leave. He felt he could never know their experience.

What Jake decided to do was visit them in Iraq and film a documentary of them at work—easier because Sergeant Joe was assigned to Captain Isaac's unit. This sounds simple enough, but it involved investment, logistical problems, and danger under fire. The result is a film that benefits from an inside view, as Jake is attached to Isaac's group and follows them for extended periods under fire in the Sunni Triangle and on patrol on the Syrian border. It is clear that the brothers are expert soldiers.

But this is not a war film. It is a life film, and its scenes filmed at home are no less powerful than those filmed in Iraq. Jenny Rademacher served in Kuwait and elsewhere, then has their child. Isaac is deployed to Iraq soon after, and when he returns home it's to a daughter who has never met him. Jake films the homecomings and departures of both brothers, attends family gatherings, and watches Isaac as he trains troops of the Iraqi Army. The filmmakers are often under fire, and a man is killed on one mission by a roadside bomb.

Jake's entree gives him access to many moments of the kind you never see on the news. Nicknamed "Hollywood" and such an accustomed daily sight that soldiers are not self-conscious around his camera, he listens in on small talk, shop talk, and gab sessions. He watches during meals. He walks along on a door-to-door operation. He looks at houses and roadsides in a way that recognizes they may harbor his death. He gives a stark idea of the heat, the dust, the desolate landscape.

I've reviewed many documentaries about Iraq. All of them have been antiwar. "Why don't you ever review a pro-war documentary?" readers asked me. The answer was simple: There weren't any. There still aren't, because no one in this film argues in favor of the war—or against it, either. What you hear is guarded optimism, pride in the work, loyalty to the service. This is deep patriotism. It involves risking your life for your country out of a sense of duty.

Every time he saw Isaac or Joe deployed, Jake says, he wondered if he would ever see them again. In filming his documentary, he feels he has walked a little way in their shoes. As is often the case among men, the brothers leave these things unspoken. But now Jake sees their war as more of a reality and less of an abstraction. He invites his audience to do the same.

Bruno ★ ★ ★ ½

R, 82 m., 2009

Sacha Baron Cohen (Bruno), Gustaf Hammarsten (Lutz). Cameos, knowingly or not, by Paula Abdul, Harrison Ford, Ron Paul, Bono, Chris Martin, Elton John, Slash, Snoop Dogg, Sting. Directed by Larry Charles and produced by Sacha Baron Cohen, Jay Roach, Dan Mazer, and Monica Levinson. Screenplay by Cohen, Anthony Hines, Mazer, and Jeff Schaffer.

Bruno is a no-holds-barred comedy permitting several holds I had not dreamed of. The needle on my internal Laugh Meter went haywire, bouncing between hilarity, appreciation, shock, admiration, disgust, disbelief, and appalled incredulity. Here is a film that is eighty-two minutes long and doesn't contain thirty boring seconds. There should be a brief segment at the next Spirit Awards with John Waters conferring the Knighthood of Bad Taste to Sacha Baron Cohen. If he decides to tap Cohen on each shoulder with his sword, I want to have my eyes closed.

To describe Baron Cohen's character Bruno as flamboyantly gay would be an understatement. He makes Bruce Vilanch seem like Mike Ditka. Bruno is disgraced in his native Austria when he wears a Velcro suit to Fashion Week and sticks to backdrops, curtains, and models. It's slapstick worthy of Jerry Lewis. Then he flies to Los Angeles with his loyal worshipper Lutz (Gustaf Hammarsten), vowing to become a celebrity.

As in his 2007 hit *Borat,* Baron Cohen places his character into situations involving targets who may not be in on the joke and have never heard of Bruno or, for that matter, Sacha Baron Cohen. Some of the situations may be set up with actors, but most are manifestly the real thing. I include an interview in which Bruno lures Congressman Ron Paul into a hotel room, his appearance on a Dallas TV morning show, the screening of a TV pilot before a focus group, counseling with two Alabama ministers dedicated to "curing" homosexuals, and a gay wrestling match before a crowd that is dangerously real.

The setups include an interview with Paula Abdul and originally included one with La Toya Jackson, which was cut because of her brother's death. That accounts for the running time being three minutes shorter than at the movie's London opening. I also believe those are real parents at interviews trying to get their babies hired for a proposed film—mothers who say their babies are ready to work with pyrotechnics, dress as Nazis, or be strapped to a cross. These moms want their babies to be stars.

One incredible scene involved a darling little black boy Bruno claims to have adopted in Africa. He appears with this child on the *Richard Bey Morning Show* in Dallas, before a manifestly real, outraged, and all-black studio audience. The host is indeed Richard Bey, but I suspect he was in on the gag. I learn that the audience wasn't. Shows like Jerry Springer and Maury Povich have dredged up such astonishing lowlifes that audiences are prepared to believe almost anything.

Certainly it takes sheer nerve for Baron Cohen to walk into some of these situations, knowing he'll only get one take—if he's lucky. He plays an allegedly gay-hating straight wrestler in a scene promising gay bashing, and then shows the two men in the cage getting turned on as they grapple. There is also an eerie tension in a scene where Bruno the gay new hunter sits around a campfire with macho hunters who are very, very silent.

It is no doubt unfair of Baron Cohen to victimize an innocent such as Ron Paul. Watching Paul trying to deal with this weirdo made me reflect that, as a fringe candidate, he has probably been subjected to a lot of strange questions on strange TV shows, and is prepared to sit through almost anything for TV exposure. On the other hand, he has made a lot of intolerant comments about homosexuals, so by shouting "Queer!" as he stalked out along a hotel corridor, he blew his chance of making amends. Helpful rule: If you find you have been the subject of a TV ambush, the camera is probably still rolling.

The movie is directed by Larry Charles, who in *Borat,* Bill Maher's *Religulous,* and his TV series *Curb Your Enthusiasm* has specialized in public embarrassment. Come to think of it, this may explain his outstandingly awful feature film debut, the Bob Dylan vehicle *Masked and Anonymous* (2003). In that one, stars such as Jeff Bridges, Penelope Cruz, Angela Bassett, John Goodman, Val Kilmer, and Luke Wilson appeared as straight men while Dylan occasionally deigned to utter brief and enigmatic proverbs. Maybe they were told, ha ha, they were going to appear in a real movie.

Note: The R rating is very, very hard.

Buck ★ ★ ★

PG, 88 m., 2011

Buck Brannaman, Reata Brannaman, Mary Brannaman, Betsy Shirley, Shayne and Jo-Anne Jackson, Betty and Craig Staley, Robert Redford, Bibb Frazier, Gwynn Turnbull Weaver, Annette Venteicher, and Nevada Watt. A documentary directed by Cindy Meehl and produced by Julie Goldman.

Buck Brannaman was the original "horse whisperer," the character Nicholas Evans based his novel on and Robert Redford used as the on-set consultant for his film. He has a way with horses, and Cindy Meehl's documentary is moving as she shows them engaged in dances of understanding. W. G. Sebald wrote, "Men and animals regard each other across a gulf of mutual incomprehension," but Buck and his animals seem to have bridged it.

We see footage of Buck and his brother, Bill,

in childhood as "Buckshot and Smokie, the Idaho Cowboys." They appeared onstage, at rodeos, and even on a TV game show, and were being beaten regularly by their father. They were well trained. They could do rope tricks while blindfolded, but in the footage, we see they never look happy but more like frightened robots.

One of the most affecting moments in the film comes when Buck remembers a high school coach telling him to undress and take a shower, and then seeing the welts on his back and legs. A deputy sheriff was called in, and Buck was taken away from his father and placed in a foster home. Curiously, the movie makes no mention of Bill.

There was an older approach to horse training that resembled Buck's father's cruelty as he trained his boys. Standing against this trend, we learn, were two legendary horse trainers named Tom Dorrance and Ray Hunt, and when young Buck saw Hunt at work, one must assume he powerfully yearned to have been treated with as much gentleness and compassion.

The key to this approach involves empathy for the feelings of the horse. Buck understands how horses read humans, how they interpret gestures, and how they're "so sensitive they can feel a fly land." I was reminded of Temple Grandin, the autistic designer of cattle-handling chutes, whose secret was identifying the feelings of cattle with her own.

Buck Brannaman spends most of every year on the road, giving four-day workshops on horse handling. Sometimes his wife, Mary, travels with him, and his daughter Reata comes along every July and August, sometimes sleeping in a tent next to the big horse trailer. Reata seems calm and happy as her father never was as a child; he recalls being made to sit at a kitchen table until he almost had the grain of the wood memorized.

The film perhaps goes too far in visiting the sins of a horse upon its owner. There's a beautiful but dangerous stud toward the end of the film who is a "predator," Buck warns. This horse's dam died while giving birth, and in a cold winter the foal was raised in the house. That sounds kind, but something went wrong, perhaps oxygen deprivation during birth, and the horse is very aggressive. Advising its owner to have the horse castrated, Brannaman learns she has a field full of twelve more studs at home: "That's looking for trouble."

In some of his commentaries during workshops, it seemed to me that Buck attributed qualities to the horses and their owners that owed as much to his abusive childhood as anything. Well, why not? We meet Robert Redford, who talks about the trainer's contribution to *The Horse Whisperer* (1998), and see in one scene how Buck's own horse is used to perform in a way a highly trained Hollywood "trick horse" is incapable of.

What I was left with was the goodness of Buck Brannaman as a man. He was dealt a hand that might have destroyed him. He overcame his start and is now a wise and influential role model. He does unto horses as he wishes his father had done unto him.

Buried ★ ★ ★ ½

R, 95 m., 2010

Ryan Reynolds (Paul Conroy). Directed by Rodrigo Cortes and produced by Adrian Guerra and Peter Safran. Screenplay by Chris Sparling.

Buried alive. It must be a universal nightmare. I read Edgar Allan Poe's *The Premature Burial* when I was seven or eight, and the thought troubled me for many a dark night. You are alive, you can move, you can scream, but no one will hear.

Paul Conroy is a truck driver working for a private contractor in Iraq. He comes to consciousness in blackness. He reaches out, feels, realizes. He finds a lighter. In its flame his worst fears are realized. He finds a cell phone. He learns he has been kidnapped and is a hostage.

Obviously his captors want him to use the phone. They want to prove he is alive because they plan to demand ransom. And by now we are identifying with Conroy's desperate thinking. Who can he call who can rescue him before the oxygen in the coffin runs out? Thankfully the coffin is longer than usual, allowing it to contain more air and also permitting certain camera angles that enhance the action.

Because there is action. Although the entire movie takes place in the enclosed space, director Rodrigo Cortes and writer Chris Sparling are ingenious in creating more plausible action than you would expect possible. They also allow themselves a few POV shots from outside the coffin—not on the surface, but simply from undefined darkness above the space.

Paul (Ryan Reynolds) uses the phone to call 911. The Pentagon. His employer's office. His wife. He receives calls from his kidnappers. These calls are exercises in frustration. There is nothing quite like being put on hold while you're buried alive.

It is their wise decision to omit any shots of the action at the other end of the calls. No shots of 911 operators, Pentagon generals, or corporate PR types. No shots of his desperate kidnappers. No flashbacks to the ambush and kidnapping itself. No weeping wife. The movie illustrates the strength of audiobooks and radio drama: The images we summon in our minds are more compelling than any we could see. A seen image supplies satisfaction. An imagined one inspires yearning. Along with Paul, we're trying to transport ourselves to the other end of each call.

It would not be fair to even hint at some of the events in the coffin. Let it be said that none of them is impossible. There is no magic realism here. Only the immediate situation. The budget for *Buried* is said to be $3 million. In one sense, low. In another sense, more than adequate for everything director Cortes wants to accomplish, including his special effects and the voice talents of all the people on the other end of the line.

Ryan Reynolds has limited space to work in, and body language more or less preordained by the coffin, but he makes the character convincing if necessarily limited. The running time, 95 minutes, feels about right. The use of 2:35 widescreen paradoxically increases the effect of claustrophobia. I would *not* like to be buried alive.

Notes: My top ten reasons for wanting to be cremated are at http://j.mp/dpQwYu. Read The Premature Burial *by Edgar Allan Poe at http://j.mp/bput7O.*

Burlesque ★ ★

PG-13, 116 m., 2010

Cher (Tess), Christina Aguilera (Ali), Eric Dane (Marcus), Cam Gigandet (Jack), Julianne Hough (Georgia), Alan Cumming (Alexis), Peter Gallagher (Vince), Kristen Bell (Nikki), Stanley Tucci (Sean). Directed by Steven Antin and produced by Donald De Line. Screenplay by Antin.

The burlesque shows in *Burlesque* feature no nudity, no striptease, no baggy-pants comedians, and no performers with names like Porsche Galore. Other than that, the shows are identical to the offerings at the Rialto and Follies burlesque houses that flourished on South State Street when I first visited Chicago as a sin-seeking teenager.

This is burlesque if it died and went to heaven. Behind a tawdry side entrance on Sunset Strip, a club exists that would make a Vegas casino proud. It has the eerie expanding and contracting dimensions of fantasy. At first, the stage is the right size for an intimate cabaret; later, there's enough space to present a production number with dozens of (unaccounted for) dancers descending a staircase worthy of Busby Berkeley. The audience is all shadowy extras, whose friends will have to look real hard to spot them.

The Burlesque Lounge attracts the attention of Ali (Christina Aguilera), the proverbial small-town girl just off the bus from Iowa. She walks in just in time to see Tess (Cher) conveniently performing the number "Welcome to Burlesque." In this scene and throughout the movie, Cher looks exactly as she always does. Other people age. Cher has become a logo.

The movie has a limited cast of broadly drawn characters, used to separate song and dance numbers. Tess co-owns the club with her ex-husband, Vince (Peter Gallagher). As a couple, they inspire games of What Is Wrong with This Picture? His function is to eagerly hope they can sell out to Marcus (Eric Dane), the real-estate developer who wants to tear down the club and put up condos. The club bartender is Jack (Cam Gigandet), who wears eyeliner but turns out to be straight. He allows Ali to crash on his sofa, but there's no sex because he has a fiancée in New York and also because the film has a PG-13 rating. The stage manager is Sean (Stanley Tucci). He's gay, except for one unforgettable night with Tess in Reno. Or Lake Tahoe. She forgets.

The star dancer is Nikki (Kristen Bell), who grows instantly angry with Ali after the farm girl tells her she looks like a drag queen. They must not see many drag queens in Iowa. There is also the nice girl named Georgia (Julianne Hough), who . . . well, a plot like this only leaves one thing for her, doesn't it?

Sorry, I got distracted again, thinking of the condo tower Marcus wants to build. How big a footprint will it need? We get repeated shots of the exterior of the lounge, which consists of an arch of lightbulbs next to what looks like the side of a modest frame building with outside steps to a second floor that doesn't seem to exist inside.

On the landing of those steps on that first night, Ali sees a black girl standing, who smiles nicely to her. We see this same girl repeatedly during the film, but she never gets a name or any dialogue. She has the role of the Black Girl Who Is Seen but Not Heard as a Member of the Club Family. She shouldn't complain. No other dancer gets to be anything at all.

In the film, both Cher and Christina Aguilera are showcased in big song numbers, which I enjoyed on a music video level. Aguilera has an unforced charm in her early scenes, but as she morphs into a glamorous star, she becomes increasingly less interesting. We learn she is an orphan. That simplifies the backstory.

You know how in Bollywood musicals the star actress will be all by her lonely self on a mountaintop, and when she starts to sing and dance, a dozen male singer-dancers materialize out of thin air? That happens here in the big final number. The girls form a perfect chorus line, a stairway to the stars appears, and a dozen male dancers descend. Where did they come from? Where will they go? Remember, this club is so small there is only one clothing rack backstage for all the costumes.

Is this the movie for you? It may very well be. You've read my review, and you think I'm just making snarky comments and indulging in cheap sarcasm. Well, all right, I am. *Burlesque* shows Cher and Christina Aguilera being all that they can be, and that's more than enough. ☞

The Burning Plain ★ ★ ½

R, 106 m., 2009

Charlize Theron (Sylvia), Kim Basinger (Gina), Jennifer Lawrence (Mariana), John Corbett (John), Joaquim de Almeida (Nick), Danny Pino (Santiago), J. D. Pardo (Young Santiago), Jose Maria Yazpik (Carlos). Directed by Guillermo Arriaga and produced by Laurie MacDonald and Walter F. Parkes. Screenplay by Arriaga.

The Burning Plain involves events perhaps twenty years and one thousand miles apart, with many of the same characters. Told chronologically, it might have accumulated considerable power. Told as a labyrinthine tangle of intercut timelines and locations, it is a frustrating exercise in self-indulgence by the writer-director, Guillermo Arriaga.

He is familiar with intercut story lines. As the favorite writer of Alejandro Gonzalez Inarritu, he wrote *Amores Perros, Babel,* and *21 Grams,* three splendid films that moved among people and places. They were all different characters, and it was clear where everything was happening. That made it easier. And the human drama in each place had continuity and integrity; the story strands might even have been reassembled as self-contained short films.

In *The Burning Plain,* his first film as a director, Arriaga should have asked harder questions of his screenwriter, himself. I don't know if it's a spoiler or just merciful assistance to tell you that many of the characters we see are the same people at different times in their lives, and that some of the men at different ages are hard to tell apart.

Certainly a time comes when you figure that out for yourself—before, I hope, the movie belatedly relents and makes it clear. Given the Law of Economy of Characters, you eventually realize that there would be no need for separate stories apparently destined never to meet. You can see there are two main locations—New Mexico and Oregon—and you decide that years must have passed, although the visual cues (cars, clothes) don't provide clues.

What is Arriaga's purpose in this construction? Search me. He's being too clever for his own good. That's a shame, because his actors provide him with effective performances, even though they must emotionally build up or refer back to the same characters played by different actors.

Having possibly diminished your experience (or maybe enhanced it) by tipping off the two time periods, I will deliberately avoid additional details and simply describe the characters we meet. In New Mexico, Gina (Kim Basinger) is a married woman, passionately in love with Nick (Joaquim de Almeida), a man not her husband. They live in separate towns, and he places a house trailer midway so they can meet. This mobile home is isolated enough that traffic never passes, and close enough that Mariana (Jennifer Lawrence), Gina's teenage daughter, can reach it by bicycle. Coincidentally, Mariana meets Santiago (J. D. Pardo), Nick's son. These coincidences have a way of happening in Arriaga's screenplays.

In Oregon, Sylvia (Charlize Theron) manages a chic seaside restaurant and is deeply unhappy. She has quick, meaningless sex with, seemingly, almost any man, and has a way of leaving her job at key hours and smoking morosely above the waves. A mysterious man named Carlos (Jose Maria Yazpik) follows her and insists they must meet. Perhaps he desires sex? No, it is more complicated.

And that's all I'll say. Basinger and Theron have the key roles and are excellent, although by the nature of the story construction, their characters are denied continuity, and that's something leading characters usually require. Theron is one of the film's producers. She is intelligent and daring in her choice of roles, and must have trusted that the author of those three great screenplays and *The Three Burials of Melquiades Estrada* would know how to negotiate this tangle. Unfortunately, he doesn't.

C

The Cake Eaters ★ ★ ★

NO MPAA RATING, 95 m., 2009

Kristen Stewart (Georgia), Aaron Stanford (Beagle), Bruce Dern (Easy), Elizabeth Ashley (Marge), Jayce Bartok (Guy), Melissa Leo (Ceci), Miriam Shor (Stephanie). Directed by Mary Stuart Masterson and produced by Masterson, Allen Bain, Darren Goldberg, Elisa Pugliese, and Jesse Scolaro. Screenplay by Jayce Bartok.

Kristen Stewart has been in feature films since 2003, but this year, still only eighteen, she became a big star as a vampire's girlfriend in *Twilight.* Now comes her remarkable performance in *The Cake Eaters,* made two years ago, showing her as a very different kind of lover in a very different kind of film. It's the directorial debut of Mary Stuart Masterson, herself a fine actress (*Fried Green Tomatoes*).

Stewart plays Georgia, a high school student who has a degenerative muscular disease. It causes her to walk unsteadily, stand crookedly and, as Beagle tells her, talk like she's had a few beers. Beagle (Aaron Stanford) is the kid she meets at a flea market. She asks him to come over to her house that evening. Beagle says, uh . . . ah . . . yeah, sure. He has no problems with her condition; it's just that he's terrified of girls.

Beagle is going through a rough time emotionally. His mom has recently died after a long ordeal with cancer. His dad, Easy (Bruce Dern), is a good guy and in his corner. His brother, Guy (Jayce Bartok, writer of the screenplay), sat out the entire illness in New York, seeking success as a rock or folk star, and has returned just too late for the funeral. Beagle is enraged at him. Beagle cared for his mom the whole three years.

Georgia, as played by Stewart, is not looking for sympathy. She's looking for sex and is very forthright about that. When a hairdresser asks her if she isn't rushing things, she says simply, "I don't have a lot of time." Why did she choose Beagle? He's OK-looking, he's not bothered by her disability, you can see he's gentle, and perhaps she suspects she can get him to do what she wants.

Masterson and her cast make these characters, and others, into specific people and not elements in a docudrama. Nobody is a "type," certainly not Georgia's grandmother Marge (Elizabeth Ashley), the kind of woman you know once raised some hell and hasn't completely stopped. When Beagle happens to see his dad kissing Marge, so soon after the funeral, he's devastated. This creates enormous tension among all three men in the family and a connection between Beagle and Georgia they're not aware of.

Beagle is three or four years older than Georgia, but behind her in emotional development, I sense. He's very naive. Georgia's mother (Melissa Leo) is suspicious of him but has no hint of her daughter's plans for the unsuspecting boy. And Beagle's father is reassuring: "My boy has no game in that area, I promise you."

So there are three simultaneous romances: Beagle and Georgia, Easy and Marge, and I forgot to mention Guy, who has a local girl named Stephanie (Miriam Shor), furious at him because he proposed marriage and then left for New York without even saying good-bye.

You might think with all of these plot lines and colorful characters, the movie turns into a carnival. Not at all. I won't say why. I'll only say it all leaves us feeling good about most of them. Masterson, like many actors, is an assured director even in her debut; working with her brother Pete as cinematographer, she creates a spell and a tenderness, and pushes exactly as far as this story should go.

Capitalism: A Love Story ★ ★ ★ ½

R, 117 m., 2009

A documentary directed by Michael Moore and produced by Michael Moore and Anne Moore. Screenplay by Michael Moore.

The loudest voice in Michael Moore's new film speaks to us from the grave. It belongs to Franklin Delano Roosevelt, less than a year before his death, calling for a Second Bill of Rights for the American people. He says citizens have a right to homes, jobs, education, and health care. In measured, judicious words, he speaks gravely to the camera.

Until a researcher for Moore uncovered this footage, it had never before been seen publicly. Too ill to deliver his State of the Union address to Congress in person, Roosevelt delivered it on the radio, and then invited in Movietone News cameras to film it. It was included in no newsreels of the time. Today, eerily, it still seems relevant, and the improvements he calls for are still unachieved.

In moments like that, Moore's *Capitalism: A Love Story* speaks eloquently. At other times his message is a little unclear. He believes that capitalism is a system that claims to reward free enterprise but in fact rewards greed. He says it is responsible for accumulation of wealth at the top: The richest 1 percent of Americans have more than the bottom 95 percent. At a time when America debates legalized gambling, it has long been practiced on Wall Street.

But what must we do to repair our economy? Moore doesn't recommend socialism. He has faith in the ballot box, but believes Obama has been too quick to placate the rich and has not brought about substantial reforms. The primary weapon Moore employs is shame. That corporations and financial institutions continue to exploit the majority of Americans, including tea-baggers and Town Hall demonstrators, is a story that hasn't been told.

Here are two shocking revelations Moore makes. The first involves something that is actually called "peasant insurance." Did you know that companies can take out life insurance policies on their workers so that *they* collect the benefits when *we* die? This is one form of employee insurance they don't have a problem with. Companies don't usually inform a surviving spouse of the money they've made from a death.

The second is the reckless, immoral gambling referred to as "derivatives." I've read that derivatives are so complex they're created by computers, and not even the software authors really understand them. Moore asks three experts to explain them to him. All three fail. Essentially, they involve bets placed on the expectation that we will default on our mortgages, for example. If we do, the bets pay off. What if we don't? Investors can hedge their bets, by betting that *they* will fail. They hope to win both ways.

Our mortgages are the collateral for these bets. Moore says they are sliced and diced and rebundled and scattered hither and yon. He has an interview with Congresswoman Marcy Kaptur, D-Ohio, who advises her constituents: If a bank forecloses, don't move, and demand they produce a copy of your mortgage. In many cases, they can't. Your mortgage is no longer a signed document in a safety deposit box. It has been fragmented into scattered bits on the world financial markets.

You may have seen that weirdo screaming on the financial cable show about shiftless homeowners who obtained mortgages they couldn't afford. Moore says that in fact two-thirds of all American personal bankruptcies are caused by the cost of health care. Few people can afford an extended illness in this country. Moore mentions his film *Sicko* (cough).

Capitalism is most effective when it explains or reveals these outrages. It is less effective, but perhaps more entertaining, when it shows Michael being Michael. He likes to grandstand. On Wall Street, he uses a bullhorn to demand our money back. He uses bright yellow police crime scene tape to block off the stock exchange. He's a classic rabble rouser. Love him or hate him, you gotta give him credit. He centers our attention as no other documentarian ever has.

He is also a working-class kid, no college education, still with the baseball cap and saggy pants, who feels sympathy for victims. Watch him speaking with a man who discovered his wife's employer collected "peasant insurance." Listen to him speak with a family that is losing a farm after four generations. Consider that a great deal of wealth in America has been earned from *our* failures. When union-busting companies move jobs overseas, workers lose but the companies don't.

The film's title is never explained. What does Moore mean by *Capitalism: A Love Story*? Maybe he means that capitalism means never having to say you're sorry.

Carlos ★ ★ ★ ½

NO MPAA RATING, 165 m., 2010

Edgar Ramirez (Carlos), Juana Acosta (Girlfriend), Alexander Scheer (Johannes Weinrich), Nora von Waldstatten (Magdalena

Kopp), Ahmad Kaabour (Wadie Haddad), Christoph Bach (Hans-Joachim Klein), Rodney El-Haddad (Khalid), Julia Hummer (Nada). Directed by Olivier Assayas and produced by Jens Meurer. Screenplay by Assayas and Dan Franck.

The man known as Carlos the Jackal said that Marxism was his religion and he was dedicated to the Palestinian cause. Having seen the long version of Olivier Assayas's remarkable *Carlos*, I conclude that for Carlos, his religion and his cause were the same, and they were himself. This is a terrifying portrait of an egomaniac who demands absolute obedience, and craves it even more when his power and relevance are drained away. All he has left at the end are a few pathetic nonentities who obey him.

If Carlos is a shabby excuse for a great man, *Carlos* is nonetheless a powerful film from recent history, considering in (largely fictionalized) detail how the myth of Carlos shadowed the years from 1975, when he led a raid on OPEC oil ministers in Vienna, until 1994, when he was betrayed by former comrades, arrested in Sudan, and returned to France for trial. He is now serving a life sentence, and from prison has complained that this film is inaccurate.

I have no knowledge of the real Carlos and can only review the film. On that basis, Ilich Ramirez Sanchez, a Venezuelan born in 1949 and educated at a Cuban training camp and Patrice Lumumba University in Moscow, used his ideology primarily to dominate others and excuse his megalomania. Toward the end, even his superiors in the Palestinian liberation movement were fed up with him, and after exhausting the hospitality of Libya, Syria, and Iraq, he became a man without a country.

Carlos is played by Edgar Ramirez, an actor of great vitality and conviction. I learn he speaks five languages, and in *Carlos* he performs dialogue in even more, as he functions in France, Spain, Germany, Egypt, Iraq, Russia, and North Africa. (The film is largely in English, the international language of terrorism.) Without using any apparent makeup tricks, he successfully ages from a young hothead to a middle-age "Syrian businessman" with a nice little pot belly, while passing through a period when he is lean and muscular after guerrilla training. His sideburns flourish and disappear, beards and mustaches come and go, and yet clearly he is Carlos if you take a good look at him. He passed through countless passport controls where apparently nobody did, although once years ago at London Heathrow I was pulled aside on suspicion of being Carlos. He ran on the plump side, for a jackal.

In notes and anonymous phone calls taking blame (or "credit") for bombings, murders, and missile attacks, he identified his group as "the armed branch of the Palestinian Liberation Struggle." I have no idea what the reality was. In the film, this organization seems to consist largely of himself as the autarch of a small group of submissive followers who had loose connections with better-organized cells in Germany and France. He was well financed by mischievous governments, including Russia, East Germany, and Iraq; shipped crates of weapons by using diplomatic immunity; and lived in swank hotels or sometimes in safe houses or borrowed apartments.

His "operations" seem almost anarchic. He and his followers have the strategy of walking in armed and doing what they intend. In a public observation area at an airport, surrounded by others, they attempt to deploy a rocket launcher to blow up airplanes. Their getaway strategy usually comes down to get the hell outta there. He got his nickname from the Frederick Forsyth novel *The Day of the Jackal*, but the hero of the excellent Fred Zinnemann film of that name takes meticulous care in his planning. Carlos seems impulsive. It's extraordinary how long he survived on the run.

His major operation was the OPEC raid. He took forty-two hostages and demanded an airplane to take them to Algiers. That led to an odyssey on to Baghdad and Tripoli before returning to Algiers. Assayas is at his best showing this undertaking, during which Carlos fails to execute two of the oil ministers as ordered and is berated by his superior in the movement, Wadie Haddad (Ahmad Kaabour). Then as later, his personal fame and publicity were felt to distract from the focus of the Popular Front for the Liberation of Palestine.

Did he care deeply about Palestine? I get the

impression that he cared deeply about seeming to care deeply. His personality would have been equally well suited to any other revolutionary struggle. He hated any authority except his own, and granted himself life and death power over others because—well, because he was Carlos. Given the opportunity, he might have made a Stalin, Hitler, or Pol Pot.

Much of the film is devoted to the periods between action. We meet the private Carlos, whose sexuality depends on the conquest and domination of women. He is enabled by a long-suffering girlfriend and wife, Magdalena Kopp (Nora von Waldstatten), before they have a child and she walks out for the child's sake. Also by a series of mistresses, especially Nada (Julia Hummer), who stands by him during a painful illness with a testicular tumor. It is an insight into Carlos's ego that he postponed tumor surgery for a more important operation: liposuction.

That he satisfies women sexually there seems no doubt. They accept, not always happily, his many affairs with others, including prostitutes. He is such a great man he is exempt from ordinary behavior. All along the way he is accompanied by his sidekick Hans-Joachim Klein (Christoph Bach), an uncertain man with a wispy mustache, who has a way of drinking himself unconscious, not a valuable trait in a terrorist. When the two of them party with hookers in East Berlin, they're too naive to suspect they're plants by the secret police.

Carlos exists in three formats. The theatrical version runs 165 minutes; there's a road-show version in two parts totaling 332 minutes. The full three-part miniseries, totaling 5:35, played on the Sundance Channel. I saw the longest, and I was not bored. Olivier Assayas doesn't make the mistake of wearing us out with action, which in excess is simply boring; he's fascinated by the minutiae of daily routine in the life of a wanted and hated man.

There is a detail I must mention. I have never seen more smoking in a movie. Every character smokes heavily, and Carlos constantly, indeed distractingly. No doubt this is based on fact, but what does Assayas mean by depicting it so pointedly? It shows Carlos addicted to quick and constant fixes. He never shows any pleasure in smoking. He simply has to do it. It may be a metaphor for terrorism.

Cars 2 ★ ★ ★ ½

G, 107 m., 2011

With the voices of Larry the Cable Guy (Mater), Owen Wilson (Lightning McQueen), Michael Caine (Finn McMissile), Emily Mortimer (Holley Shiftwell), Eddie Izzard (Miles Axlerod), John Turturro (Francesco Bernoulli). Directed by John Lasseter, codirected by Brad Lewis, and produced by Denise Ream. Screenplay by Ben Queen.

While I was watching *Cars 2*, an elusive nostalgia tugged at my mind. No, I wasn't remembering Pixar's original *Cars* from 2006. This was something more deeply buried, and finally, in the middle of one of the movie's sensational grand prix races, it came to me: I was sitting on the floor of my bedroom many years ago, some toy cars lined up in front of me, while I used my hands to race them around on the floor and in the air, meanwhile making that noise kids make by squooshing spit in their mouths.

In this memory I was completely engrossed with my cars. They were as real as people, and I played favorites and identified one car as my surrogate. Maybe my hands were swooping around with toys, but my imagination was somewhere else, and I performed the dialogue for the cars: "Oh yeah?" "Take that!" "We'll see!" "Eeeeyowww!"

This memory was not random. I think it was inspired by the spirit of John Lasseter's movie. I believe in some sense the great animator was sitting Indian style on the floor of his Pixar playroom and hurtling his cars through time and space with sublime, reckless delight. We learned from *Cars* that Lasseter loves automobiles, and here we learn that they can serve him as avatars in an international racing-and-spying thriller as wacky as a Bond picture crossed with Daffy Duck.

I have no idea what kids will make of the movie. At a time when some "grown-up" action films are relentlessly shallow and stupid, here is a movie with such complexity that even the cars sometimes have to pause and explain it to themselves. It mixes concerns about fossil fuels with spy craft and a lot of grand prix racing where more is at stake than who wins. And it has a new hero: The shiny red

Lightning McQueen (voice by Owen Wilson) is eclipsed by a rusty, buck-toothed tow truck named Mater (Larry the Cable Guy), who was only a supporting vehicle in the first film.

A plot synopsis would spin us into bafflements, and the movie isn't about a plot so much as the action it involves. Briefly, Sir Miles Axlerod (Eddie Izzard) has invented a new fuel that doesn't deplete the planet's shrinking oil reserves, and wants to prove it in a World Grand Prix to be run in England, Japan, and Italy. This is a masterful way of introducing new backdrops into the races, and the movie is so visually complex that I imagine Lasseter and his colleagues slipped details in just for fun.

At one point, in a shot so brief you don't want to blink, we even learn that the Popemobile travels in its own Popemobile. This inspires the theological puzzle of whether the one inside is the pope. One of my fellow viewers said she didn't even see a Popemobile. Maybe I dreamed it. In any event, there are no humans in the movie who could be the pope, although much is made of the dinosaurs who are a source of fossil fuels. Actually, I believe oil originated from ancient plants and microorganisms and not so much from dinosaurs, but in the Lasseter universe, it no doubt comes from gas-guzzling dinosaurs like in those old Rambler ads.

But I digress. Lightning McQueen ends up in a championship duel with the Italian car Francesco Bernoulli (John Turturro at full throttle). He and Mater the tow truck find themselves in the middle of a clandestine war between the forces of fossil and alternative fuels, also involving the British secret agents Finn McMissile (Michael Caine) and Holley Shiftwell (Emily Mortimer). Having recently admired Steve Coogan and Rob Brydon doing dueling Michael Caine imitations in *The Trip*, I noted that Michael Caine does a pretty good one himself.

The original film was an elegy to a past when America spun out along Route 66 and now-classic cars occupied an iconic role in American lives. The cars in *Cars 2* have developed an array of new bells and whistles; they extrude so many wires, spikes, weapons, and gimmicks they must really be shape-shifters, and Mater in particular is expert at disguising himself. This is not surprising because a lot of the guys you find around tow trucks are pretty good using paint jobs to dress up beaters.

Anyway, *Cars 2* is fun. Whether that's because John Lasseter is in touch with his inner child or mine, I cannot say. There remains one bone to pick. Although the hero of the 2006 film was a Hudson with the step-down design and there are AMC Gremlins in this film, as nearly as I can tell you, Lasseter entirely ignores the greatest independent American automaker of them all, Studebaker. Maybe I missed one. Maybe I stepped out to pee. I don't think so. There is a more obvious reason. Introducing a Studebaker Golden Hawk into this film would make all of the other characters look shabby.

Casino Jack ★ ★ ★

R, 108 m., 2010

Kevin Spacey (Jack Abramoff), Barry Pepper (Michael Scanlon), Kelly Preston (Pam Abramoff), Rachelle Lefevre (Emily Miller), Jon Lovitz (Adam Kidan), Maury Chaykin (Big Tony). Directed by George Hickenlooper and produced by Gary Howsam, Bill Marks, and George Zakk. Screenplay by Norman Snider.

Political movies often play cute in drawing parallels with actual figures. They drop broad hints that a character is "really" Dick Cheney or Bill Clinton and so on. *Casino Jack* is so forthright it is stunning. The film is "inspired by real events," and the characters in this film have the names of the people in those real events: Jack Abramoff, Michael Scanlon, Representative Tom DeLay, Ralph Reed, Karl Rove, George W. Bush, Representative Bob Ney, and Senator John McCain.

This decision to name names by the director George Hickenlooper seems based on boldness, recklessness, or perhaps iron-clad legal assurances. His film uses a fictional sledgehammer to attack the cozy love triangle involving lobbyists, lawmakers, and money. It stars Kevin Spacey in an exact and not entirely unsympathetic performance as Abramoff, once one of the most powerful lobbyists in Washington, who was convicted on charges involving the funds he stole from wealthy Indian casinos while arranging laws for their convenience on Capitol Hill.

The first press screening of the film at the Toronto International Film Festival was witnessed in a sort of stunned silence by a capacity audience, interrupted slightly by an undercurrent of incredulous murmurs and soft laughter when Spacey, as Abramoff, in a fantasy sequence, explodes at a Senate hearing being chaired by McCain. Having invoked the Fifth Amendment repeatedly, he's unable to restrain himself any longer and jumps to his feet to accuse the very members of the panel of having taken campaign contributions and favors from his Indian clients, and voting in their favor. Abramoff shows some degree of honor among thieves by not pulling such a stunt.

Astonishingly, Hickenlooper intercuts real footage of the real hearing and the real John McCain with Spacey's performance. Can he get away with this? I guess so. The distributors, ATO, have no doubt had the film scrutinized by their attorneys. Apart from that, there's the likelihood (which lawyers may think but cannot say) that no one named in this film is very likely to sue. The Abramoff scandal was called at the time the biggest since Watergate (both were broken by the *Washington Post*), but in the years since his sentencing in 2006, his name has faded from everyday reference, and it's doubtful anyone desires to make it current again. With Alex Gibney's current doc *Casino Jack and the United States of Money* also around, those deep waters are being sufficiently stirred.

The film's story line can be briefly summarized: The lobbyist Abramoff was a dutiful family man and Republican standard bearer who defrauded Indian tribes out of millions to lobby for their casinos. That enriched him and his partner, Michael Scanlon (Barry Pepper), and a good many members of Congress, not all of them Republicans. He worked out every day, was an observant member of his temple, and a smooth and elegant dresser. And somehow at his core there were no principles and no honesty.

If Casino Jack put up a good front, George Hickenlooper's film is merciless with Scanlon, a venal and vulgar man with the effrontery to flaunt his corruption. It is Spacey's performance that contains most of the mystery of the movie, because although Abramoff's actions left little room for justification, in Spacey's performance there is some. He used much of the stolen money for good works, which made him appear charitable. His principal charity was himself, but there you are.

There are scenes here that make you wonder why the Abramoff scandals (plural) didn't outshine Watergate as the day does the night. Within Abramoff there is some small instinct for simple justice, and the film's most dramatic scene comes as he snaps at that hearing, ignores his lawyer, forgets the Fifth Amendment, and tells the panel members to their faces that they were happy to take his cash.

The overall message of *Casino Jack* has become familiar. Corporate and industry lobbyists are the real rulers in Washington, and their dollars are the real votes. Both parties harbor corruption, the Republicans grabbing the breasts and thighs, the Democrats pleased to have the drumsticks and wings. Jack Abramoff didn't invent this system. He simply gamed it until Scanlon's boldness betrayed them and another generation of lobbyists took over. Have you heard the banks are broke again?

Catfish ★ ★ ★

PG-13, 86 m., 2010

Nev Schulman, Ariel Schulman, Henry Joost, Angela Pierce, Vince Pierce, and Abby Pierce. A documentary directed by Ariel Schulman and Henry Joost and produced by Schulman, Joost, Andrew Jarecki, and Marc Smerling.

Here's one way to look at *Catfish:* Some filmmakers in New York City, who think they're way cool, get taken apart by an ordinary family in Ishpeming, Michigan. You can also view it as a cautionary tale about living your emotional life on the Internet. Or possibly the whole thing is a hoax. At Sundance 2010, the filmmakers were given a severe cross-examination and protested their innocence, and indeed everyone in the film is exactly as the film portrays them.

To go into detail about that statement would involve spoiling the film's effect for you. I won't do that because the effect is rather lovely. There's a point when you may think you know what I'm referring to, but you can't appreciate it until closer to the end. The facts in the film are slippery, but the revelation of a human personality is surprisingly moving.

The film opens in the Manhattan office of Nev Schulman, Ariel Schulman, and Henry Joost, who make videos and photographs of modern dancers. I'm going to guess they're thirtyish. Nev has received a painting of one of his photographs from Abby Pierce, an eight-year-old girl. They enter into a correspondence—or, more accurately, Abby's mom, Angela Pierce, e-mails for her. Just as well. Would you want your eight-year-old daughter in a chat room with some strange adult Facebook friend?

Never mind. Nev, a wholesome, even naive man, is touched by Abby's paintings, and begins to identify with the whole family. He learns of school plans, pie baking, Sunday family breakfast, and the horse farm Abby's nineteen-year-old sister, Megan, is buying. I doubted that detail. It would take a New Yorker to believe horse farms in Michigan are cheap enough for a nineteen-year-old to buy. She could afford a horse, farm not included.

Nev and Megan correspond and talk on the phone. Megan composes songs for Nev. They begin a cyber-romance. Nev begins to wonder if this could possibly be the girl for him. There are dozens of photos on her Facebook site, and he even starts using software to put himself and Megan in the same photos. In anyone over, oh, fourteen, this is a sign of immaturity, wouldn't you say?

The three videographers have to fly to Vail to shoot a dance event. On the way back east, they decide to make a detour to Ishpeming. Were they born yesterday? Do they think you drop in unannounced on strangers? Using ever-helpful GPS navigation, they pay a midnight visit to Megan's horse farm, and find . . . no horses. In Ishpeming they do indeed find the Pierce home and family, and I suppose are welcomed with as much grace as possible under the circumstances.

The key to the human qualities in the film can be found in Angela, the mother, and in a couple of thoughtful statements by Vince, the father. You'll see what I mean. Living in Ishpeming may not be the ideal choice for people with an artistic temperament. I haven't been there and can't say. But this family has adapted to realities and found ways of expression, and who are we to say making dance videos in New York is preferable?

Angela Pierce comes across as an essentially good person, as complex as the heroine of a novel. At the end of the day, I believe she humbles Nev and his friends. I wonder if they agree. They all seem to be nice people. Let's agree on this: We deserve to share happiness in this world, and if we supply it in the way it's sought and nobody gets hurt, is that a bad thing?

Note: Angela Pierce's Web site is at http://www.artbyapierce.com.

Cave of Forgotten Dreams ★ ★ ★ ½

NO MPAA RATING, 90 m., 2011

A documentary directed by Werner Herzog and produced by Adrienne Ciuffo and Erik Nelson. Screenplay by Herzog.

About thirty-two thousand years ago, in a limestone cave above the Ardeche River in southern France, humans created the oldest cave paintings known to exist. They spring from the walls with boldness and confidence, as if the artists were already sure what they wanted to paint and how to paint it. Perhaps twenty-five thousand years ago, a child visited the cave and left a footprint, the oldest human footprint that can be accurately dated. At some time after the child's visit, a rock slide sealed the entrance to the cave. In 1994, French archaeologists, searching for air plumes that might reveal the presence of a cave, found it again.

They had to descend a narrow opening to its floor, far below on the original entrance level. It is their entry route that Werner Herzog follows in his spellbinding new film, *Cave of Forgotten Dreams.* Herzog filmed in 3-D to better convey how the paintings follow and exploit the natural contours of the ancient walls. The process also helps him suggest how the humans of the Upper Paleolithic era might have seen the paintings themselves, in the flickering light of their torches.

Access to Chauvet Cave, named for one of its discoverers, was immediately closed off by the French government, and a locked steel door now bars the way to the air shaft. Behind that door the cave's guardians enforce a strict regime. Herzog is allowed a four-man crew, including himself. They are limited to four cold-panel lights, powered from battery belts. They dare step only on two-foot-wide aluminum pathways that have been installed. They are allowed four hours. If anyone has to leave for any reason—even to get a screwdriver—that day's visit is over; the guardians want to shield the cave's air supply.

Surely men must have been painting somewhere before these cave walls were covered. It is hard to believe that these confident lines and shapes came into being without prelude. Or was there something innate in these forms? Accurate carbon dating suggests that other artists returned to the cave at least two thousand years after the first ones, and continued the work in the same style.

Only two very small sculptures in the cave show human forms. One is a woman, her sexual organs exaggerated to dramatize her fertility. The paintings themselves are all of animals, an astonishing variety, providing a bestiary of the valley at the time. Mammoths, cave bears, lions, bison, panthers, horses, rhinos. The rhinos have what are surely exaggerated horns, suggesting a desire to emphasize their power. Some of the drawings repeat horns and legs in an obvious attempt to depict movement.

In addition to the footprint, there are poignant signs that humans were here. Near the original entrance, where outside light was still present, many visitors left their palm prints on a wall in red ochre. Were these the artists' marks? Calling cards? Why did many leave them? A palm print stands out: One man had a damaged little finger. Farther back in the cave, they found another mark with the same finger. His two visits and a child's footprint remain after twenty-five millennia.

Herzog's limitation of four small portable light panels works to his advantage; as they move they suggest how the flickering torches might have created an illusion of movement in those repeated features. The space was so limited it was impossible for his crew to stay out of many shots, and their shadows dance on the walls, just as the shadows of forgotten ancestors must have danced in the torchlight. Herzog's inspiration is to show us the paintings as the cave's original visitors must have seen them. I have seen perfectly lighted photographs of other cave paintings that are not so evocative.

Herzog says that in general he dislikes 3-D. But he believes there are occasions when 3-D is appropriate, and his film is one of them. It was shown with bright, well-focused digital projection. Apart from a one-shot joke at the very end, he never allows his images to violate the theater space; he uses 3-D as a way for us to enter the film's space, instead of a way for it to enter ours. He was correct to realize how useful it would be in photographing these walls. To the degree that it's possible for us to walk behind Herzog into that cave, we do so.

Note: Based on my blog entry from the Toronto 2010 film festival.

Cedar Rapids ★ ★ ★

R, 87 m., 2011

Ed Helms (Tim Lippe), John C. Reilly (Dean Ziegler), Anne Heche (Joan Ostrowski-Fox), Sigourney Weaver (Miss Vanderhei), Isiah Whitlock Jr. (Ronald Wilkes), Stephen Root (Bill Krogstad), Kurtwood Smith (Orin Helgesson), Alia Shawkat (Bree), Rob Corddry (Gary). Directed by Miguel Arteta and produced by Jim Burke, Alexander Payne, and Jim Taylor. Screenplay by Phil Johnston.

You are making the mistake of thinking of Cedar Rapids as a small town. In *Cedar Rapids*, a sweet comedy with a dirty mind, it is the metropolis, a sinkhole of sex, sin, and high living at an annual insurance industry convention. Into this pit of depravity descends the innocent and naive Tim Lippe (Ed Helms), who never before in his life has left his hometown of Brown Valley, Wisconsin.

Helms, from *The Office*, is assigned to take the big trip after his boss dies in embarrassing circumstances. His character is a bachelor who still lives in his childhood home, although excitement has recently entered his life with his first affair. Yes, he's sleeping with his grade school teacher Miss Vanderhei, who is played by Sigourney Weaver as a woman who has seen it all—if it's in Brown Valley, anyway.

Lippe's assignment: Attend the convention and come home with the coveted Two Diamonds Award. I immediately flashed on the older son in *Gates of Heaven*, sitting proudly behind and in front of plaques and statuettes and observing that he is displaying "the maximum trophies" to impress young recruits into—yes, it was the insurance business there, too. Apparently, the folks in Brown Valley prefer to deal with Two Diamonds winners.

The coveted award is the gift of Orin Helgesson (Kurtwood Smith), a mighty figure at the convention. I recall from my days as a cub reporter the self-importance of "industry legends" who lovingly spoke at length to their captive audiences. Helgesson is very public with his piety, and it would be a disaster if he discovers how Lippe's boss died. Lippe's job is to stay out of trouble. Since he doesn't smoke or drink and his sexual adventures are possibly limited to Miss Vanderhei, this should be easy.

The director, Miguel Arteta, understands that real laughter grows from characters. He has a rich start with Lippe, played by Helms as a man who is thrilled even to go through security at the airport. He calls Miss Vanderhei with breathless reports that his hotel has a swimming pool and that there is, gasp, an African-American in his room! This turns out to be his roommate, Ronald Wilkes (Isiah Whitlock Jr.), who is an old hand at the convention and a useful ally. His other roommate, Dean Ziegler (John C. Reilly), is trouble—a hard-drinking womanizer and client poacher.

Now we know the story arc. Ziegler will lead Lippe into temptation, Wilkes will try to caution him, Orin Helgesson will be outraged, and the hotel pool will be involved in an unseemly way. All of this works out to be pretty funny, especially with the intervention of the sexy Joan Ostrowski-Fox (Anne Heche), whose trips to the convention are the highlight of her sex life, I hope.

Cedar Rapids has something of the same spirit of *Fargo* in its approach to the earnest natures of its small-towners. The two films, otherwise so different, like their characters. Some of them do unspeakable things, especially in *Fargo*, but none of them *want* to be evil. They just hope to get out in one piece.

It is a relief, for example, that Reilly's Dean Ziegler isn't a malicious buffoon, but simply a nice guy, terminally immature. And Ed Helms makes an ideal leading man because he always seems to be searching for someone to stand behind. The problem with so many madcap comedies is that their heroes cannot fully embrace cluelessness. It is funnier for a second banana to play the lead than for a lead to pretend to second bananahood.

Cell 211 ★ ★ ★ ½

NO MPAA RATING, 111 m., 2010

Luis Tosar (Malamadre), Alberto Ammann (Juan Oliver), Antonio Resines (Jose Utrilla), Manuel Moron (Ernesto Almansa), Marta Etura (Elena), Carlos Bardem (Apache). Directed by Daniel Monzon and produced by Alvaro Augustin, Juan Gordon, and Borja Pena. Screenplay by Monzon and Jorge Guerricaechevarria, based on the novel by Francisco Perez Gandul.

Cell 211 is a thriller about a man's attempt to save his life by thinking quickly. It never explains. It simply sets out the situation and shows us what he does and what the results are. You might be surprised by how much more exciting this is than conventional action.

The film won eight Goya awards, the Spanish Oscars, this year. It deserves them. In addition to its effectiveness as a thriller, it is also a film showing a man in the agonizing process of changing his values. And it is a critique of a cruel penal system. It doesn't preach, it doesn't end with a message, but it makes us think.

The story involves Juan Oliver (Alberto Ammann), a serious young man who reports a day early for his new job as a prison guard. We spend a little time with him at home with his wife, Elena (Marta Etura). She is pregnant. They are head over heels in love. They don't have much money, but his new job will be a big help.

As other guards are taking him on a tour of the prison, he is knocked unconscious in an accident. They carry him to a bunk in an empty cell, Cell 211, and are calling for help when a violent prison riot breaks out. Their lives are in danger, and they must leave him behind when they flee. He regains consciousness and hears what is going on outside. He doesn't know why he's been left behind—he probably doesn't recall the falling debris that knocked him unconscious—but he knows his shoes, shoelaces, and belt are fatal giveaways that he's not a prisoner.

And now we enter into real time with him, as he boldly walks into a public area and passes himself off as a new prisoner who was admitted only shortly before. The rioting prisoners are desperate. They're led by a brutal strongman, a lifer with nothing to lose named Malamadre (Luis Tosar). Juan reads the situation immediately and improvises. Instinctively he takes the role of a man siding with his fellow prisoners. When he makes canny strategic suggestions, he seems to prove his worth.

I don't want to describe any more than that in specific terms. Those really would be spoilers because in *Cell 211* it is actually impossible to anticipate what will happen. The story follows no established formula. It discourages attempts at anticipation. It unfolds convincingly at every stage, but unpredictably. As Juan faces more stringent tests, he continues to improvise, sometimes devising masterstrokes.

The events in the cellblock are paralleled by two other stories: In the prison office, the warden and security staff monitor the security cameras. And in the city, Elena does some shopping and then learns of the riot in the prison where she knows her husband went that morning. Another strand consists of flashbacks to their loving moments together, which are much more effective dropped in like this than coming before everything.

The dynamic in the film happens between Juan and Malamadre. In a subtle way, the director, Daniel Monzon, shows an understanding developing. Malamadre is relentless and unforgiving, resentful when Juan takes the lead in making suggestions but admiring of the new man's courage. Very gradually, in the midst of the chaos, they exchange personal information. As Malamadre's understanding of the full situation changes, his interpretation of it keeps pace. He isn't a stupid man. Given his information, he makes logical decisions. When his information changes, he responds sanely and not without reason.

The term "mounting tension" is an overused cliché. To use it here would be appropriate. Little by little, one development at a time, the situation becomes more critical and the options for Juan and Malamadre grow more limited. And Juan's life always hangs in the balance. There is a moment, indeed, when he says something on a walkie-talkie that would have betrayed him if anyone had been listening.

The actors are well chosen. Luis Tosar, as Malamadre, is a powerful man, shorter than Juan but more muscular, his head shaved, his mustache and beard somehow ominous. Alberto Ammann, as Juan, is of medium build, not aggressive, a convincing mimic in the role he adopts. He is not too heroic and Tosar is not too villainous. They are trapped in this situation, and unwittingly they come to share it.

Certifiably Jonathan ★

NO MPAA RATING, 80 m., 2011

Themselves: Jonathan Winters, Jeffrey Tambor, Ryan Stiles, Sarah Silverman, Rob Reiner, Gary Owens, Howie Mandel, Robert Klein, Jimmy Kimmel, Kevin Dunn, Nora Dunn, Tim Conway, Rosanna Arquette, Patricia Arquette, David Arquette, Robin Williams, Jim Carrey. Directed by Jim Pasternak and produced by Richard Marshall. Screenplay by Pasternak.

Jonathan Winters is a fine and funny fellow, and deserves better than this. Out of the goodness of his heart, he agreed to be at the center of a mockumentary directed by Jim Pasternak. The result is not merely a bad film, but a waste of an opportunity. As he approaches eighty-six, Winters is still active, still funny, enthusiastically involved in painting, and could have been the subject of a good film. This isn't it.

The mockumentary form has many possibilities. They usually depend on satirizing the tone and feeling of a genre. The simple fact that it's fake doesn't make one successful. This one purports to show Winters at a crucial moment in his late flowering as an artist, during which he gets a gallery opening, is championed by a famous art critic, and promised a show at the Museum of Modern Art. None of these nonevents is staged with style or conviction. They are simply walked through as if really happening.

At the gallery, one of his paintings is stolen from a wall and Winters goes into a depression, finding himself unable to paint. It was, you see, his favorite painting. Pasternak leads a team that includes Winters himself to go to the house of the alleged thief. The house is unlocked, they walk in and find the painting, and Winters can paint again. Is there anyone reading this who can't think of an approach that isn't so lame?

Consider, too, the "curator" at the Museum of Modern Art. She is a pleasant woman who looks at negatives of Winters's sub-Dali paintings through a little magnifier and declares him worthy of a show. No effort is made to make her character or her process funny.

It appears one reason for this film was for Pasternak to gain access to Jonathan Winters, spend an excess amount of time personally on camera, and use Winters as bait to lure his famous friends into the film. These include Robin Williams, Howie Mandel, Nora Dunn, Jim Carrey, Sarah Silverman, Tim Conway, Jeffrey Tambor, Jimmy Kimmel, Robert Klein, Ryan Stiles, Rob Reiner, Kevin Dunn, David Arquette, Patricia Arquette, and Rosanna Arquette.

All of these friends are seen briefly and forgettably. Only Robin Williams is funny. The others seem to be paying courtesy calls. With that much talent on the screen, it's significant that the funniest moments belong to Winters, seen on old TV shows.

Much is made, in the title and by Winters himself, of his history of bipolar disorder. It's assumed that today's audiences will know what's being referred to. In general, they won't. It's sad but true that many younger viewers won't quite know the range of Winters's brilliance. What would have been more appropriate: a tour through film and TV archives, memories of friends rather than testimonials, a real documentary instead of a fake one, and Jim Pasternak nowhere to be seen.

Certified Copy ★ ★ ★ ½

NO MPAA RATING, 106 m., 2010

Juliette Binoche (Woman), William Shimell (James Miller). Directed by Abbas Kiarostami and produced by Kiarostami, Charles Gillibert, Marin Karmitz, and Nathanael Karmitz. Screenplay by Kiarostami.

Certified Copy invites us into an intriguing story and then strands us. Yes, we can consider various explanations for what we see, and yes, the film's mystery is apparently its purpose. For me, it is too clever by half, creating full-bodied characters but inserting them into a story that is thin soup. I enjoy puzzles like Antonioni's *Blow-Up* or *L'Avventura*, about characters who don't understand what has happened, but here there seems to be no underlying reality at all, and Abbas Kiarostami is playing with us. That he does it so well is a consolation.

A woman (Juliette Binoche) attends a lecture in Italy by an art historian (William Shimell). He speaks on the difference between original art and its copies. Is there, in fact, any difference? The woman would like to meet him. She leaves the address of her antiquities shop. He appears, they engage in talk that is immediately flirtatious, and she offers to drive him to a nearby village in Tuscany. In the course of the drive, and at a café after they get there, their apparent relationship seems to shift. The café owner hears them arguing, assumes they're married, and then they begin to behave as if they're married.

Which is the real relationship, and which is the counterfeit? Were they a couple pretending to meet for the first time, or a new couple pretending to be married? I believe that to begin with they are really meeting for the first time, and later they are really an established couple. Perhaps Kiarostami's intention is to demonstrate how the reality is whatever the artist chooses, and that he can transfer from original art to a copy in midstream. Or perhaps that's not possible. Perhaps I have no idea what he's demonstrating.

The woman, who is not named, and the historian, named James Miller, are articulate, playful, and devious. I enjoyed watching them, whatever they were up to. Binoche and Shimell always stay in the moment and never signal us what they're up to. Binoche seems so attracted to the man in the early scenes that it seems they must have some history. But it's certainly not the history they later seem to reveal. Throughout *Certified Copy* there's the sense of offscreen dimensions or untold side stories.

Kiarostami is rather brilliant in the way he

creates offscreen spaces. Consider the opening scene. We clearly see that Binoche has a seat in the front row of the lecture hall, directly in front of the historian. Then the POV changes around to regard her, and we never see him again. Her son is standing at one side, trying to get her attention, eager to leave. She communicates with him using sign language and mouthing words. He comes over to her. She gives the man next to her a note with the address of her shop. She and the boy leave together.

All this commotion is taking place, distractingly, close in front of the speaker—but we never see him react! Kiarostami creates an implied drama involving what Miller *must* be experiencing, but refuses to see it. There's also implied offscreen activity during the long drive they take. The camera regards them through the windshield for extended dialogue passages, sometimes cutting to inside the car. Filming people as they drive is one of Kiarostami's trademarks, and I wonder why. It is a way to explain why you're showing two people side by side and looking ahead; if you put them on a park bench that would look odd. It's also a way to imply offscreen events on the road and involving the passing scenery.

What it comes down to is this: We assume there's more going on here than meets the eye, but maybe what meets the eye is *all* that's going on, and there is no complete, objective reality. Does that also apply to a copy of a masterpiece of art? Is a skillful copy of the *Mona Lisa* less valuable than the original painting? What if the original had been lost? Would we treasure the copy?

Such questions are raised by *Certified Copy* and not answered. Is raising them the point? Does Kiarostami know the answer? Does he care? At least we are engaged, and he does it well. Is that enough? I can explain *Blow-Up* and *L'Avventura* to my own satisfaction. This is the best I can do with *Certified Copy.* Perhaps it was wrong of me even to try.

Chandni Chowk to China ★ ★

NO MPAA RATING, 168 m., 2009

Akshay Kumar (Sidhu), Deepika Padukone (Sakhi/Meow Meow), Mithun Chakraborty (Dada), Ranvir Shorey (Chopstick), Gordon Liu (Hojo), Roger Yuan (Chiang). Directed by Nikhil Advani and produced by Mukesh Talreja, Rohan Sippy, and Ramesh Sippy. Screenplay by Rajat Aroraa and Shridhar Raghavan.

Chandni Chowk is a historic marketplace in the walled city of old Delhi, so now you understand the title of *Chandni Chowk to China,* and because the plot is simplicity itself there is nothing else to understand but its origins. This is the first Bollywood movie to get a North American release from a major studio, and was chosen, I suspect, because it is a slapstick comedy containing a lot of kung fu. That, and maybe because it stars Akshay Kumar, described in the publicity as "the heartthrob of Indian cinema and current reigning king of Bollywood."

I would need to see Kumar in something other than this to understand his fame. He comes across here as a cross between Jerry Lewis and Adam Sandler, but less manic than Jerry and not as affable as Sandler. What I can understand is that his costar, Deepika Padukone, abandoned a promising start as a badminton champion to become a model and actress. She is breathtaking, which of course is standard in Bollywood, where all the actresses are either breathtaking or playing mothers.

The story plays as though it could be remade as a Sandler comedy with no changes except for length. When you go to a movie in India, you get your money's worth, in what takes the time of a double feature. As my Mumbai friend Uma da Cunha told me, big Bollywood movies give you everything: adventure, thrills, romance, song, dance, stunts, the works. In India, when you go to the movies, you go to *the movies. Chandni Chowk to China* plays at 168 minutes, having been shortened, I learn, for the American release. It would be safe to say few viewers will complain of its brevity.

Kumar stars as Sidhu, a lowly potato and onion chopper in his father's potato pancake stand. He adores his Dada (Mithun Chakraborty), despite the old man's propensity for kicking him so high over Delhi that he's a hazard to low-flying aircraft. As eager to please as a puppy, he has a gift for getting into trouble, but all that changes the day he finds the image of a god on one of his potatoes. This image, to my eye, makes the eBay portraits on grilled cheese sandwiches look like Norman Rockwells.

No matter. He exhibits the potato and collects donations, which are stolen by the nefarious Chopstick (Ranvir Shorey), while meanwhile, in China, a village is menaced by an evil hoodlum named Hojo (Gordon Liu), no relation to the U.S. pancake vendor. Two villagers happen upon Sidhu in Chandni Chowk and are convinced he is the reincarnation of the mighty kung fu warrior who saved them from bandits in times long past. Sidhu is soon lured to their village, being promised wealth and voluptuous pleasures, but is now expected to defeat Hojo, who uses his bowler hat as a flying guillotine and may plausibly be related to Odd Job.

Enter the ravishing Deepika Padukone, in a dual role of Sakhi and Meow Meow, an Indian home shopping network hostess and Chinese tigress. As you see the film, you may reflect that the opportunities of an Indian actress to achieve dramatic greatness are limited by the industry's practice in filming them only as spectacular beauties, preferably with the wind rippling their hair. Kissing in public is severely frowned upon in India, so that the greatest tension in all romances comes as a heroine is maybe, just maybe, *about* to kiss someone. This is always spellbinding and illustrates my maxim that it is less erotic to snoggle for sixty minutes than spend sixty seconds wondering if you are almost about to be snoggled.

I gather that Akshay Kumar usually plays more stalwart heroes, with the obligatory unshaven look, wearing his testosterone on his face. It's unlikely he could have become the heartthrob of Indian cinema playing doofuses like this. He becomes involved with both Sakhi and Meow Meow, whose surprise relationship might have been more surprising had they not been played by the same actress. There are lots of martial arts sequences, and of course several song-and-dance numbers, including an Indian rap performance. It's done with great energy but with a certain detachment, as if nothing really matters *but* the energy.

My guess is that *Chandni Chowk to China* won't attract many fans of kung fu—or Adam Sandler, for that matter. The title and the ads will cause them to think for a second, an unacceptable delay for fanboys. The movie will appeal to the large Indian audiences in North America and to Bollywood fans in general, who will come out wondering why this movie of all movies was chosen as Hollywood's first foray into commercial Indian cinema. I don't know a whole lot about Bollywood, and even I could name some better possibilities.

The Chaser ★ ★ ★ ½

NO MPAA RATING, 124 m., 2010

Kim Yoon-suk (Jung-ho), Ha Jung-woo (Young-min), Seo Young-hee (Mi-jin), Koo Bon-woong (Meathead). Directed by Na Hong-jin and produced by Choi Moon-su. Screenplay by Na Hong-jin, Hong Won-chan, and Lee Shin-ho.

The Chaser is an expert serial killer film from South Korea and a poster child for what a well-made thriller looked like in the classic days. Its principal chase scene involves a foot race through the deserted narrow nighttime streets of Seoul. No exploding cars. The climax is the result of everything that has gone before. Not an extended fight scene. This is drama, and it is interesting. Action for its own sake is boring.

The film is a police procedural with a difference: The hero is an ex-cop named Jung-ho (Kim Yoon-suk), now a pimp, and he is not a nice man. He is angered because a client of his call-girl service has been, he believes, kidnapping his girls and selling them. When another girl disappears, a phone number raises an alarm, and he sets out to track down the client—who didn't give an address but arranged a street rendezvous.

What we know is that the client, Young-min (Ha Jung-woo), is a sadistic murderer. The girl, named Mi-jin (Seo Young-hee), is driven in his car to an obscure address that she is not intended to ever leave alive. It is a characteristic of South Korean films that they display the grisly details of violence without flinching; the rights to this film have been picked up by Warner Bros., and it's dead certain the violence and the shocking outcome itself will be greatly toned down. Let me simply note that Young-min's tools of choice are a hammer and a chisel, for reasons a police psychiatrist has much to say about.

The film's structure is relentless in maintaining suspense. We have reason to suspect the prostitute may still be alive, but dying. Both the pimp and the killer are arrested. A ludicrous attack on the mayor of Seoul becomes a media sensation and puts pressure on the cops to charge someone with something to change the headlines. The killer, a calm psychopath, claims first nine murders, then twelve, but changes his story and says he has no idea what he did with the bodies. He's released on lack of evidence.

The story is an exercise in audience manipulation, especially with the corruption and incompetence of the police. The director, Na Hong-jin, knows exactly what he's doing. Like the master, Hitchcock, he gives the audience precisely enough information to be frustrated. It is obvious to us what the characters should be doing, but there are excellent reasons why it isn't obvious to them. If you can contrive that in a screenplay, you have already surpassed the level of the modern thriller.

Another strength of the film is in its attention to characters. The killer is seen as a mental dead zone, a man without conscience to whom good and evil are equally meaningless. The pimp begins as a merchant of sex, goes looking for Young-min for simple mercenary reasons, and very gradually expands his concerns in response to the presence of the call girl's young daughter. The daughter follows the Glossary Rule, which instructs us that all children in movies, told to stay put, quickly wander away into danger. Well, can we blame the director? How interesting would it be if she obediently stayed put?

What I responded to was the street-level reality of the film. There are no supermen and no sensational stunts. When the actors run, we see that they are running. These shots extend in time and are not constructed of baffling editing. The spatial realities of the chases are respected; we begin to learn our way around the neighborhood. The cops are not stock characters, but just your average officers. No one in *The Chaser* seems on autopilot.

When I see a film like this, it reminds me of what we're missing. So many recent movies are all smoke and mirrors. A thriller is opening soon in which the star cannot be clearly seen to complete any physical act in an action sequence. We might as well be reading a comic strip, where our minds are expected to fill in the movement between the frames. You sit there and *The Chaser* unfolds and the director knows what he wants and how to do it without insulting us. In addition to remaking this movie, Hollywood should study it.

Che ★ ★ ★ ½

R, 258 m., 2009

Benicio Del Toro (Che Guevara), Demian Bichir (Fidel Castro), Santiago Cabrera (Camillo Cienfuegos), Elvira Minguez (Celia Sanchez), Jorge Perugorria (Joaquin), Edgar Ramirez (Ciro Redondo), Victor Rasuk (Rogelio Acevedo), Catalina Sandino Moreno (Aleida Guevara). Directed by Stephen Soderbergh and produced by Benicio Del Toro and Laura Bickford. Screenplay by Peter Buchman and Benjamin A. van der Veen.

Che Guevara is conventionally depicted either as a saint of revolution or a ruthless executioner. Stephen Soderbergh's epic biography *Che* doesn't feel the need to define him. It is not written from the point of view of history, but from Guevara's own POV on a day-to-day basis in the process of overthrowing the Batista regime in Cuba and then failing to repeat his success in Bolivia. Both parts of the film are based on his writings, including a diary in Bolivia written in the field, day to day.

The film plays in two parts, named *The Argentine* and *Guerrilla.* It resists the temptation to pump up the volume, to outline Che (Benicio Del Toro) against the horizon, to touch conventional biographical bases. In Cuba, we join him in midstream. We learn that he is a doctor but not how and why he became one. It is a given that he is a revolutionary. He is a natural leader of men. Fidel Castro is his comrade, but the film does not show them in a detailed relationship; much of the time, they are apart.

There isn't an explanation of why he chose to secretly leave Cuba after the revolution, no reference to his time in the Congo, no explanation about why he chose Bolivia as his next field of operation, no reference to the political decisions he made as a young man motorcycling across South America (as described in the 2004 film *The Motorcycle Diaries*).

Che is all in the present tense. He has made an irrevocable decision to overthrow governments. He explains why in his descriptions of injustice; he identifies with peasants and not with his own ruling class, and although he is nominally a Communist, we do not hear discussion of theory and ideology. He seems completely focused on the task immediately before him. His method is to give voice to popular resentment against a dictator, win the support of the people, and demoralize opposing armies of unenthusiastic soldiers. He needs few men because he has a powerful idea behind him.

That method worked in Cuba and failed in Bolivia. Soderbergh's 258-minute film works as an arc: upward to victory, a pause with his family in Argentina, downward to defeat. The scenes in Argentina show him with his second wife, Aleida (Catalina Sandino Moreno), and children but do not engage in why he left them, how his wife really feels, how he feels about them. A wanted person, he has disguised himself so successfully that his children do not recognize him as he presides over the dinner table. His wife shared his political ideas but must have had deep feelings about a man who would leave his children to lead a revolutionary war in another country; but we don't hear them, and in a way it's a relief to be spared the conventional scenes of recrimination. It is all as it is.

That helps explain another peculiarity of the film. Surprising attention is given to Che meeting the volunteers who join his guerrilla bands. Names, embraces. But little effort is made to single them out as individuals, to develop complex relationships. Che enforces an inviolable rule: He will leave no wounded man behind. But there is no sense that he is *personally* emotionally involved with his men. It is *a man* he will not leave behind, not *this* man. It is the idea.

In Cuba, the rebels are greeted by the people of the villages, given food and cover, cheered on in what becomes a triumphal tour. In Bolivia there seems little sympathy. Villagers betray him. They conceal government troops, not his own. When he lectures on the injustice of the government medical system, his audience seems unresponsive. You cannot lead a people into revolution if they do not want to follow. Soderbergh shows U.S. military advisers working with the Bolivians but doesn't blame the United States for Che's failure. Che chose the wrong war at the wrong time and place.

In showing both wars, Soderbergh does an interesting thing. He doesn't structure his battle scenes as engagements with clear-cut outcomes. Che's men ambush and are ambushed. They trade fire with distant enemies. There is usually a cut to the group in the aftermath of battle, its casualties not lingered over. This is not a war movie. It is about one man's unrealistic compulsion to stay his course.

Soderbergh made the film himself, directing, photographing, editing. There is no fancy camera work; he looks steadily at Che's dogged determination. There are very few subjective shots, but they are effective; Che's POV during his last moments, for example. There is a lot of the countryside, where these men live for weeks at a time. The overwhelming impression is of exhaustion, and Guevara himself has malaria part of the time and suffered from asthma. There is nothing more powerful than an idea whose time has come, and more doomed than one whose time is not now.

Benicio Del Toro, one of the producers, gives a heroic performance, not least because it's self-effacing. He isn't foregrounded like most epic heroes. In Cuba he emerges in victory; in Bolivia he is absorbed in defeat and sometimes almost hard to recognize behind a tangle of beard and hair. He embodies not so much a personality as a will.

You may wonder if the film is too long. I think there's a good reason for its length. Guevara's experience in Cuba and especially Bolivia was not a series of events and anecdotes, but a trial of endurance that might almost be called mad.

Cheri ★ ★ ★ ½

R, 92 m., 2009

Michelle Pfeiffer (Lea de Lonval), Rupert Friend (Cheri), Kathy Bates (Charlotte Peloux), Felicity Jones (Edmee), Iben Hjejle (Marie-Laure). Directed by Stephen Frears and produced by Andras Hamori, Bill Kenwright, Thom Mount, and Tracey Seaward. Screenplay by Christopher Hampton, based on the novels *Cheri* and *The Last of Cheri* by Colette.

Near the beginning of Colette's novel *Cheri,* Lea gives her young lover a necklace with forty-nine pearls. We can imagine there is one pearl for every year of her age. Her lover is twenty-four years younger than she. Therefore, twenty-five. Six years pass. In a way, the movie is about how twenty-five and forty-nine are not the same as thirty-one and fifty-five. Colette tells us their tragedy is that they were destined to be the only perfect love in each other's lives, yet were not born on the same day.

The success of Stephen Frears's film *Cheri* begins with its casting. Michelle Pfeiffer, as Lea, is still a great beauty, but nearing that age when a woman starts counting her pearls. Rupert Friend, as her lover Cheri, is twenty-seven and looks younger—too young to play James Bond, although he was considered. They are both accomplished actors, which is important, because *Cheri* tells a story of nuance and insinuation, concealed feelings and hidden fears.

Lea is a courtesan, currently without court. She has a lot of money and lives luxuriously. Cheri is the son of a courtesan, Charlotte Peloux (Kathy Bates). She and Lea have been friends for years; courtesans may be rich and famous, but they cannot really talk freely with women not like themselves. Lea was constantly in the life of her friend's son, named Fred but called Cheri ("darling") by one and all. One day Madame Peloux comes to her and asks her to take in the boy. She does not quite say (as Lee Marvin tells a whore in *Paint Your Wagon*), "I give you the boy. Give me back the man," but she might as well have.

Cheri is far from a virgin, but he needs some reining in. It turns out he accepts Lea's saddle quite willingly. What begins as lovemaking quickly becomes love, and they float in a perfumed world of opulent comfort, Lea paying all the bills. The two things a courtesan cannot ever do are really fall in love, and reveal what she is really thinking. Lea fails at the first.

You need not be told what happens in the story, or how thoughtless and cruel Cheri can be when it suits him. Be content to know that Lea knows sooner and Cheri later that what they had was invaluable and irreplaceable. *Cheri* became Colette's most popular book because of its air of describing familiar lives with detached regret, and that is the tone Frears goes for: This is not a tearjerker, but a record of what can happen when people toy with their hearts.

How well I remember that day in 1983 when I walked across Blackfriars Bridge in London and came upon an obscure little used book shop, and inside discovered a set of the works of Colette, small volumes, bound in matching maroon leatherette with cloth bookmarks. I have been in awe of her writing ever since. When Donald Richie, the great authority on Japanese cinema, was moving to a smaller flat in Tokyo and had to perform triage on his library, he gave away Shakespeare, because he felt he had internalized him, but could not bring himself to give away Colette.

Colette, who was eighty-one when she died in 1954, is probably best known to you as the author of *Gigi.* After leaving an unfaithful first husband, Colette, already a successful author, supported herself as a music hall performer, knew many courtesans in the era of La Belle Epoque, had affairs with women, shocked *tout le monde* with the first onstage kiss between two women, married the editor of *Le Matin,* and was divorced at fifty-one after she had an affair with her twenty-year-old stepson. So *Cheri* is not entirely a work of the imagination.

Colette's many books are considered difficult to film because much of what happens is based on emotions rather than events. This is a challenge Frears and his screenwriter, the playwright Christopher Hampton, have accepted. The film is about how to behave when you live at a distance from your real feelings. It is fascinating to observe how Pfeiffer controls her face and voice during times of painful hurt. It is bad to feel pain, worse to reveal it; a courtesan has her pride.

The performances seem effective to me, including Bates as Charlotte, who like many an older prostitute plays a parody of her profession. Laugh, and the world laughs with you. The cinematography by Darius Khondji and costumes by Consolata Boyle are meticulous in evoking decadence. The most emotional moments at the end occur offscreen and are related by the narrator (Frears himself). That is as it should be. Some things don't happen to people. They happen about them.

Chicago Heights ★ ★ ★

NO MPAA RATING, 90 m., 2010

William Gray (Sherwood Anderson/Old Nathan), Keisha Dyson (Elizabeth Walker), Andre Truss (Nathan Walker), Benny Stewart (Dr. Reefy), Jay Johnson (Reverend Curtis Hartman), Ron Jarmon Jr. (Wash Williams), Simone Wilson (Louise Trunnion). Directed by Daniel Nearing and produced by Sanghoon Lee. Screenplay by Nearing and Rudy Thauberger, based on the novel *Winesburg, Ohio*, by Sherwood Anderson.

Sherwood Anderson's *Winesburg, Ohio*, is sometimes named as a great work of fiction that cannot be filmed. Daniel Nearing demonstrates in *Chicago Heights* that that's not necessarily true. The book is a collection of twenty-two short stories connected by the character George Willard, who comes of age in Winesburg and reflects on the citizens he has grown to know. Perhaps one could make twenty-two short films. Nearing finds an approach that in ninety minutes accomplishes the uncanny feat of distilling the book's essence.

Anderson's Winesburg is a town with roads that can be walked along a short distance into the country. His time frame spans the twentieth century's first quarter. Nearing's Chicago Heights is a distant southern suburb of Chicago, bordering on farmland. His time is the present and recent decades. His central character is Nathan Walker (Andre Truss), also played as Old Nathan by William Gray, and at that age is named in the credits as Sherwood Anderson. Anderson's characters were all white. Nearing's characters are all African-American. Race is not really a factor. We are concerned with inner selves.

It's helpful, maybe essential, to be familiar with the book before seeing the movie. Anderson explains his theory of grotesques, by which he means not sideshow freaks but people who have one aspect of their body or personality exaggerated out of proportion to the whole. Wing Biddlebaum, for example, has hands so expressive they flutter like birds, and these beautiful hands are the cause of his isolation and hatred by the community. All of the characters have some special reason they don't fit in. This attribute is why their inner thoughts and dreams never become known. They are judged by the uncaring and will be buried never understood.

What Nearing does, and it is rather brilliant, is show us Nathan in old age, under a blanket on his bed, remembering, dreaming, or hallucinating about the people he has known. A narrator explains his thoughts. Remarkably for a film of average length, Nearing touches on almost every one of Anderson's characters, and because of his meditative stylistic approach the film never feels rushed or choppy.

The film is mostly in contrasty black and white, sometimes slipping into color. Dialogue slips in and out, too, as it does in the book, but we're not intended to think it's being said now. It's being heard in memory. Chicago Heights is seen as a not particularly lovely place, drowsing near the prairie with the skyline of modern Chicago in the distance. Much of it was shot on location, and Nearing succeeds in establishing it as a place like Winesburg where the countryside is always in walking distance, and one can go there with one's grotesqueries and feel at peace.

When I say it helps to have read the book, I don't mean to frighten you. Perhaps you could read just a few of the stories to begin with. They won't take long, and once you understand their workings, the whole film will come into focus. Nearing is not the first artist to be drawn to *Winesburg*. It inspired a made-for-TV film and a Broadway musical, and influenced authors such as Hemingway, Faulkner, Steinbeck, and Salinger. It is a beautiful book and has inspired this beautiful film.

Chloe ★ ★ ★ ½

R, 96 m., 2010

Julianne Moore (Catherine Stewart), Liam Neeson (David Stewart), Amanda Seyfried (Chloe), Max Thieriot (Michael Stewart), R. H. Thomson (Frank), Nina Dobrev (Anna). Directed by Atom Egoyan and produced by Jeffrey

Clifford, Joe Medjuck, Ivan Reitman, Simone Urdl, and Jennifer Weiss. Screenplay by Erin Cressida Wilson, based on the motion picture *Nathalie,* directed by Anne Fontaine.

Looking down from her office window, she sees a young woman who has the manner and routine of a high-priced call girl. This she stores in her memory. When her husband says he missed his flight back to Toronto and she finds a disturbing photo on his iPhone, she goes to the hotel where she saw the girl, makes eye contact with her in a bar, contrives a conversation in the powder room. The girl, with perfect calm, explains that single women are not usually her clients. Couples, maybe.

Atom Egoyan finds intrigue at the edges of conventional sex. *Chloe,* like his great film *Exotica* (1994), is about sexual attraction confused by financial arrangements. It centers on a powerfully erotic young woman with personal motives that are hidden. It is not blatant but seductive, depending on the ways that our minds, more than our bodies, can be involved in a sexual relationship. It's not so much what we're doing as what I'm thinking about it—and what you're thinking, which may be more complex than I realize.

Catherine Stewart (Julianne Moore) is a gynecologist, a successful one, judging by the house she inhabits fresh from the cover of *Architectural Digest.* Her husband, David (Liam Neeson), is an expert on opera. The call girl she saw from her window is Chloe (Amanda Seyfried), young, red-lipped, intelligent. Catherine explains to Chloe that she suspects her husband of adultery and wants to test if he would try to pick up another woman. She tells Chloe where her husband always has lunch.

Early in the film, talking with a patient uncertain about her sex life, Catherine explains that an orgasm is a simple muscular contraction, quite natural, nothing to be frightened of or make mysterious. Orgasms for Catherine, however, involve a great deal more than muscles, and a great deal depends on whom they are experienced with, and why. Chloe tells her about entering a café, boldly asking David if she can take the sugar from his table, and returning to her own. David understands that Chloe is not interested in sugar.

Chloe meets with Catherine to relate this encounter. Chloe is good at this. She informs us early in the film that she is skilled at what she does. It's not a matter of renting her body. She uses her intelligence to intuit what a client desires—really desires, no matter what the client might claim. And she knows how to provide this in a way that will provoke curiosity, even fascination. Now she describes details to Catherine that do a great deal more than provoke a wife's jealousy about her husband. They provoke an erotic curiosity about her husband.

Chloe is perhaps twenty-five years younger than Catherine, but in many ways wiser and more experienced. She is certainly more clear about what it is she really wants. She enjoys the psychological control of her clients, and her own skill in achieving that. She looks so young and innocent, but her life has taught her many lessons. Seyfried plays Chloe as a woman in command of her instrument—her body, which is for sale, and her mind, which works for itself. Moore, that consummate actress, undergoes a change she only believes is under her control. Neeson is an enigma to his wife and in a different way to us.

Egoyan follows his material to an ultimate conclusion. Some will find it difficult to accept. Is it arbitrary? Most of life's conclusions are arbitrary. I am not sure this particular story should, or can, be wound up in a conventional manner. It's not the kind of movie that depends on the certainty of an ending. It's more about how things continue. I have deliberately withheld much of the story, which he leaves for you to understand. His central fascination is with Chloe's motives. Does she act only for money? Does she do only what is requested? Does she remain emotionally detached? Does she get anything for herself besides money?

At one point she's asked how she can relate to some of her clients, who might seem unattractive, even repugnant. A call girl has no idea who will open the door after her knock, and the ground rules are that she will gratify the client's desires, if he can pay and she doesn't feel in personal danger. But how can she endure some of them? "I try to find something I can love," she says.

After you see the movie, run through it again in your mind. Who wants what? Who gets what? Who decides what? Whose needs are gratified? Atom Egoyan never makes a story with one level. He never reveals all of the motives, especially to his characters. He invites us to be voyeurs of surfaces that may not conceal what they seem. Fundamental shifts can alter all the relationships. All the same, their sexuality compels his characters to make decisions based on their own assumptions. It is a tangled web he weaves.

A Christmas Carol ★ ★ ★ ★

PG, 95 m., 2009

Jim Carrey (Scrooge/Ghosts of Christmas), Robin Wright Penn (Belle/Fan), Gary Oldman (Cratchit/Marley/Tiny Tim), Colin Firth (Fred), Cary Elwes (Dick Wilkins/Fiddler/Businessman), Bob Hoskins (Fezziwig/Old Joe), Fionnula Flanagan (Mrs. Dilber). Directed by Robert Zemeckis and produced by Zemeckis, Steve Starkey, and Jack Rapke. Screenplay by Zemeckis, based on the story by Charles Dickens.

A Christmas Carol by Robert Zemeckis (and Charles Dickens, of course) is an exhilarating visual experience and proves for the third time he's one of the few directors who knows what he's doing with 3-D. The story that Dickens wrote in 1838 remains timeless, and if it's supercharged here with Scrooge swooping the London streets as freely as Superman, well, once you let ghosts into a movie there's room for anything.

The story I will not repeat for you. The ghosts of Christmas Past, Present, and Future will not come as news. I'd rather dwell on the look of the picture, which is true to the spirit of Dickens (in some moods) as he cheerfully exaggerates. He usually starts with plucky young heroes or heroines and surrounds them with a gallery of characters and caricatures. Here his protagonist is the caricature: Ebenezer Scrooge, never thinner, never more stooped, never more bitter.

Jim Carrey is in there somewhere beneath the performance-capture animation; you can recognize his expressive mouth, but in general the Zemeckis characters don't resemble their originals overmuch. In his *Polar Express*, you were sure that was Tom Hanks, but here you're not equally sure of Gary Oldman, Robin Wright Penn, and Bob Hoskins.

Zemeckis places these characters in a London that twists and stretches its setting to reflect the macabre mood. Consider Scrooge's living room, so narrow and tall just as he is. The home of his nephew, Fred, by contrast, is as wide and warm as Fred's personality.

Animation provides the freedom to show just about anything, and Zemeckis uses it. Occasionally, he even seems to be evoking the ghost of Salvador Dali, as in a striking sequence where all the furniture disappears and a towering grandfather clock looms over Scrooge, a floor slanting into distant perspective.

The three starring ghosts are also spectacular grotesques. I like the first, a little elfin figure with a head constantly afire and a hat shaped like a candlesnuffer. Sometimes he playfully shakes his flames like a kid tossing the hair out of his eyes. After another (ahem) ghost flies out through the window, Scrooge runs over to see the whole street filled with floating spectral figures, each one chained to a heavy block, like so many Chicago mobsters sleeping with the fishes.

Can you talk about performances in characters so much assembled by committee? You can discuss the voices, and Carrey works overtime as not only Scrooge but all three of the Christmas ghosts. Gary Oldman voices Bob Cratchit, Marley, and Tiny Tim.

I remain unconvinced that 3-D represents the future of the movies, but it tells you something that Zemeckis's three 3-D features (also including *Beowulf*) have wrestled from me eleven of a possible twelve stars. I like the way he does it. He seems to have a more sure touch than many other directors, *using* 3-D instead of being used by it. If the foreground is occupied by close objects, they're usually looming inward, not out over our heads. Note the foreground wall-mounted bells we look past when Scrooge, far below, enters his home; as one and then another slowly starts to move, it's a nice little touch.

Another one: The score by Alan Silvestri sneaks in some traditional Christmas carols, but you have to listen for such as "God Rest Ye, Merry Gentlemen" when its distinctive cadences turn sinister during a perilous flight through London.

So should you take the kiddies? Hmmm. I'm not so sure. When I was small, this movie would have scared the living ectoplasm out of me. Today's kids have seen more and are tougher. Anyway, *A Christmas Carol* has the one quality parents hope for in a family movie: It's entertaining for adults.

The Chronicles of Narnia: The Voyage of the Dawn Treader ★ ★ ★

PG, 115 m., 2010

Skandar Keynes (Edmund), Georgie Henley (Lucy), Will Poulter (Eustace), Ben Barnes (King Caspian), Gary Sweet (Ship's Captain), Tilda Swinton (White Witch). And the voices of Simon Pegg (Reepicheep), Liam Neeson (Aslan the Lion). Directed by Michael Apted and produced by Andrew Adamson, Mark Johnson, and Philip Steuer. Screenplay by Christopher Markus, Stephen McFeely, and Michael Petroni, based on the novel by C. S. Lewis.

The alarming thing about Narnia is that you might be in the same room with it. It could be inside that old cupboard. Or, this time, inside that painting with the nautical theme. Those waves look so real. In fact, says Lucy, they almost look like they're moving. The next thing we hear is, "I'm inside the painting!"

Indeed she is, and the *Dawn Treader* is approaching over the waves. Her nuisance of a cousin Eustace unwisely pulls the painting from the wall, and seawater rushes out and fills the room until they seem in danger of drowning, but no, they surface and are rescued by sailors from the ship, captained by Caspian (Ben Barnes), who almost seems to have been expecting them.

The Chronicles of Narnia: The Voyage of the Dawn Treader, third of the films inspired by the C. S. Lewis tales, once again requires the services of English children to rescue an alternate universe. How a universe is possible that requires participation from a parallel universe I will leave to theoretical physics. If you don't ask a question, it's not a question.

On board the sailing vessel, Lucy (Georgie Henley), her brother Edmund (Skandar Keynes), and young Eustace (Will Poulter) ask no questions. They're too blissful to be back in Narnia, despite the hair-raising adventures they had in the earlier films. Lucy and Edmund, now in their midteens, seem uncommonly calm about being yanked from their everyday lives and put on a strange ship in uncharted seas, but these kids have pluck.

They're briefed on the situation: Narnia is threatened by evil forces from the mysterious Dark Island, which no one has seen but everyone has heard about. There is a matter of seven missing magical swords representing the Lords of Telmar, which were given to Narnia by Aslan the Lion and must be brought together again to break a spell that imprisons the lords. Obviously, these kids can do it. Eustace is perhaps seven years old, but, hey, bring the kid along.

On board the ship is a peppy little swashbuckling rat named Reepicheep (voice of Simon Pegg). He walks upright, speaks assertively, falls squarely into the semiobligatory Cute Little Sidekick role, has a heroic heart, and a cute little sword he is unafraid to brandish. Why the little fella has never been stepped on and squished goes unexplained.

It's a rough voyage. There is a tempest. There is a horrifying battle with a sea monster. The monster looks big enough to send the *Dawn Treader* to the bottom with its tail, but the Narniaites prevail, not least because Reepicheep scampers up the rigging and imparts a nasty flesh wound. As they sail from one Narnian island to another seeking the swords, a series of other challenges confronts them, including an ominous sea fog as alarming as Stephen King's *The Mist.*

A climactic voyage to the Dark Island becomes necessary, and it is fraught with hazards. Half-rations of food and water for all on board! No one knows how far it is. Lucky thing they know in which direction to sail. If they overshoot the island they may sail off the edge of the earth, Columbus having not existed in Narnia.

The island, first glimpsed from a distance, looks ominously like a skull, with the glow of possible volcanoes in its skeleton eyes. Skull Island comes to mind. Here the fate of Narnia will be sealed. The island, we're told, is the habitation and embodiment of pure Evil; I suppose, since Lewis intended his books as Christian allegory, it is Hell. The kids and the crew of the *Dawn Treader* are up against it, and Eustace is greatly pleased by being transformed into a fire-breathing dragon.

If I've lingered overmuch on the story, it's because mostly what you have is a series of opportunities for special effects. The characters have characteristics rather than personalities, and little self-consciousness. They spring to the service of the plot—which, not particularly coherent, boils down to one damn thing after another.

Still, this is a rip-snorting adventure fantasy for families, especially the younger members who are not insistent on continuity. Director Michael Apted may be too good for this material, but he attacks with gusto. Nor are the young actors overly impressed by how nobly archetypal they are; Lucy (who is really the lead) could give lessons to Harry Potter about how to dial down the self-importance. A universe may hang in the balance, but hey, it's only a movie.

I'm afraid it's in 3-D. I will say it has the best rendition of 3-D I've seen in one of these action spectaculars; Apted uses it and is not driven by it. The light level is dimmed. It always is in 3-D. I wish I could have seen it in 2-D. If you can, try to.

Cirque du Freak: The Vampire's Assistant ★ ½

PG-13, 108 m., 2009

John C. Reilly (Larten Crepsley), Ken Watanabe (Mr. Tall), Josh Hutcherson (Steve), Chris Massoglia (Darren), Ray Stevenson (Murlaugh), Patrick Fugit (Evra the Snake Boy), Willem Dafoe (Gavner Purl), Salma Hayek (Madame Truska), Michael Cerveris (Mr. Tiny). Directed by Paul Weitz and produced by Ewan Leslie and Lauren Shuler Donner. Screenplay by Weitz and Brian Helgeland, based on the Cirque du Freak series of books by Darren Shan.

Cirque du Freak: The Vampire's Assistant includes good vampires, evil Vampaneze, a wolfman, a bearded lady, a monkey girl with a long tail, a snake boy, a dwarf with a four-foot forehead, and a spider the size of your shoe, and they're all boring as hell. The movie has good special effects and suitably gruesome characters, but it's bloodless.

It's also a mess. The movie is shot through with curious disconnects. Often within a single sequence of events, we won't know where we are or how they're related in space or time. Characters like the bearded lady (Salma Hayek) drop in and out at random. Willem Dafoe plays a man who keeps intensely bursting in, but I didn't know who he was or where he went when he wasn't on the job. His name, I learn, is Gavner Purl, which doesn't ring a bell.

There is a mannered giant named Mr. Tiny (Michael Cerveris), who has flaming gay affectations for no purpose, since anyone who can evoke purple gas to shrink humans into living mummies already has, you would think, sufficient interest. Cerveris gives the only really interesting performance in the movie. And there's a paternal vampire named Larten Crepsley (John C. Reilly), who is proud of having developed a system of feeding off humans without killing them or turning them into vampires (i.e., "blooding them").

All of these characters travel with the Cirque du Freak, which comes to town for a one-night stand in an abandoned and shuttered theater. You slide your money into a slot at the bottom and something tries to bite you. Inexplicably, there is a small audience of normal customers who apparently don't object to this treatment.

Oh, and I almost forgot the two high school kids (Josh Hutcherson and Chris Massoglia) who are allegedly the hero and the antihero. They're equally bland, for my money. Turns out there are warring vampire factions: The followers of Larten Crepsley, who don't kill when they dine, and the evil Vampanese, who don't need to kill but do anyway, apparently because the habits of centuries are hard to break. The lads end up on opposing teams.

All of this gruesome grotesquerie is incredibly wrapped up into a story that grunts and groans and laboriously offers up a moral at the end, which is, and I quote: "It's not about what you are, it's about who you are." I could have told you that.

City Island ★ ★ ★

PG-13, 103 m., 2010

Andy Garcia (Vince Rizzo), Julianna Margulies (Joyce Rizzo), Steven Strait (Tony Nardella), Alan Arkin (Michael Malakov), Emily Mortimer (Molly Charlesworth), Ezra Miller (Vinnie

Rizzo), Dominik Garcia-Lorido (Vivian Rizzo). Directed by Raymond de Felitta and produced by Felitta, Andy Garcia, Zachary Matz, and Lauren Versel. Screenplay by Felitta.

Vince is a man with a dream. Marlon Brando is his god. He would like to become an actor. This is not likely. He's well into his forties, a prison guard living with his family on City Island, a bucolic outcrop of the Bronx known mostly to its residents. Telling his wife he's going to a poker game, he attends acting classes in Manhattan. In one class, Vince creates a spot-on imitation, not of Marlon Brando, but of bad Brando imitators.

Vince, played by Andy Garcia with brawny blue-collar dialogue, is married to Joyce (Julianna Margulies), who's convinced the poker games mean a mistress. His children hide secret lives. His daughter, Vivian (Dominik Garcia-Lorido), has dropped out of college and is working as a stripper in hopes of saving money to reapply. His son, Vinnie (Ezra Miller), is hooked not just on any old Internet porn, but on sites featuring fat women who eat on camera. The younger son in so many movie families is somehow weird.

Two life-changing experiences happen to Vince. At work, he gets a new prisoner whose name he has reason to recognize. He pulls the kid's file to confirm it: Tony (Steven Strait) is the son he fathered in a long-ago affair. Meanwhile, in acting class, his teacher (Alan Arkin) assigns the students to pair up and share their biggest secret in order to prepare for a monologue. He draws Molly (Emily Mortimer), who slowly draws this secret from him. They meet often in the city—not to have an affair, but because they become friends and confidants.

Tony is eligible to be released into the community, but has no family member to sign for him. Vince determines to bring him home for a month. This is the catalyst for upheaval in the long-established pattern of his life. *City Island*, written and directed by Raymond de Felitta, has a serious side but is essentially a human comedy, at times almost a gentle farce, as discoveries and revelations drop like explosives. You can imagine this story as the outline for an opera.

Garcia and Margulies, who worked so well together in George Hickenlooper's *The Man from Elysian Fields* (2001), show a sure feel for comedy here, especially after he introduces an unexplained stranger into his home: "You just decided to bring a prisoner home to *live* with us?" Convinced the poker games are a cover-up, she toys with the idea of fooling around with the hunky Tony. Molly, meanwhile, convinces Vince to try his luck at an open audition for a new movie.

There's a jolly subplot involving their next-door neighbor on City Island, a fat woman who Vinnie was following on the Web when—OMG!—he sees her on the way to the grocery store, and she asks if he wants to come along. This cheerful woman, played by an actress not listed on IMDb, defuses any awkwardness or discomfort and invites Vinnie and Tony over for some lasagna. Thus Felitta sidesteps a story hazard.

The last scene of the movie could indeed be used in an opera, with all of the leads onstage. It may strike you as a tad coincidental. So it is. Felitta has the good sense not to make it realistic, which it could not be. In the satisfactory tradition of comic melodrama, he tidies up all the loose ends. But don't get the idea *City Island* is a laugh riot. For this story about these people, it finds about the right tone. They're silly and foolish, as are we all, but deserve what happiness they can negotiate.

Note: City Island *won the Audience Award at the Tribeca Film Festival 2009.*

Clash of the Titans ★ ★ ★

PG-13, 106 m., 2010

Sam Worthington (Perseus), Gemma Arterton (Io), Mads Mikkelsen (Draco), Alexa Davalos (Andromeda), Jason Flemyng (Calibos/King Acrisius), Ralph Fiennes (Hades), Liam Neeson (Zeus). Directed by Louis Leterrier and produced by Kevin De La Noy and Basil Iwanyk. Screenplay by Travis Beacham, Phil Hay, and Matt Manfredi, based on the 1982 screenplay by Beverley Cross.

There are too many Greek gods for me to keep straight, since as a child I didn't have action figures as a learning tool. I was prepared to take notes during *Clash of the Titans*, but only wrote down a single one: "'Release the

Kraken!'—Conan O'Brien." I know I was intended to be terrified by the release of the Kraken, but all I could think of was O'Brien shouting "Release the bear!" and then some guy in a bear suit runs out and sits on the lap of a guest. In this case, the Kraken is the nuclear option for Zeus, who has been persuaded by Hades to put down a revolt by the upstart mortals of Argos.

The mortals are fed up with the whims of the gods. It would be one thing if they stayed on Olympus and killed time leaning on pillars and addressing one another in thundering ultimatums. Now they meddle in the affairs of men. King Acrisius of Argos declares war and enlists the aid of a demigod who has been found at sea. This is Perseus (Sam Worthington), son of Zeus (Liam Neeson) and a human mother. He didn't ask to be a savior, but would be happier as a simple fisherman. You know the type.

Zeus, it should be explained, disguised himself as the husband of Perseus's mother and stole into her bedchamber to father the boy. So he is a rapist. Just sayin.' Perseus so loved his mother and adoptive father that he will never forgive Poseidon for drowning them, and wants nothing to do with gods. Yet such is his destiny.

The outcome is told in *Clash of the Titans* with impressive technical mastery and somewhat lesser dramatic command. For its intended audience I suspect this will play as a great entertainment. I enjoyed myself, particularly after they released the Kraken. There's no particular dramatic conflict in the movie: Perseus has to wrestle with his demigod ambiguity; Hades (Ralph Fiennes) nurses a resentment against Zeus; he demands the sacrifice of King Acrisius's daughter Andromeda (Alexa Davalos) to spare the city, and the citizens seem prepared to get along very nicely without her. That's about it.

It's strange how the sacrifice of one person makes us uneasy. Earlier in the film, the entire fleet of Argos is lost at sea, with the exception of the vessel holding Perseus. The king is philosophical: They were patriots. But the sacrifice of his own daughter—now you're talkin' real death.

Most of the film involves terrifying battles between mortals and special effects. After Calibos has a hand chopped off, his fingers grow into claws. Later, his blood drops start growing, creating a crowd of huge lobster-monsters that come crawling over rocks and snapping at everyone. Later in the film, inexplicably, these lobsters appear to be tame and walk obediently across the desert, bearing little houses on their backs for the mortals. What, did they forget they were the blood of Calibos?

There's worse to come. Perseus and his comrades must invade the lair of Medusa, one of the three Gorgon girls, whose hair is a writhing mass of snakes and body is a long, lethal snake's tail. Look at her, and you'll turn to stone! Maybe this explains the high quality of Greek sculpture. The struggles with Medusa take place on ledges over a flaming lake of lava far below. She must be beheaded, which Perseus does, thoughtfully keeping the head, which he carries around like the head of Alfredo Garcia. Is that a spoiler? The story has been out since 490 B.C.

The climax is classic, with the fair Andromeda hung by her wrists and suspended in a clinging white gown over a flaming pit at the edge of the sea. Meanwhile, Perseus flies to the rescue on the wings of the great flying horse Pegasus. The townspeople clamor for her death, but lose their enthusiasm after the Kraken rears up from the sea.

I like this kind of stuff. I don't say it's good cinema, although I recognize the craftsmanship that went into it. I don't say it's good acting, when the men have so much facial hair they all look like Liam Neeson. I like the energy, the imagination, the silliness. I even like the one guy who doesn't have a beard. That's Perseus. From the first moment we see him as an adult until his last scene in the movie, he has the Standard Regulation Macho-Length Stubble on his chin. And in a city where all the men go to Jerry Garcia's barber, he has a burr cut on the short clipper setting.

So do I recommend the movie? Yes, if you intuit that this review is affectionate and have the same tolerance for goofy Greek gods as I do. One word of consumer advice, however. Explain to kids that the movie was not filmed in 3-D and is only being shown in 3-D in order to charge you an extra five dollars a ticket. I saw it in 2-D, and let me tell you, it looked terrific. Split the difference: "We see it in 2-D, I save five bucks, and I increase your allowance by $2.50 this week."

The Class ★ ★ ★ ★

PG-13, 128 m., 2009

Francois Begaudeau (Francois), Wei Huang (Wei), Esmeralda Ouertani (Esmeralda), Franck Keita (Souleymane), Carl Nanor (Carl), Arthur Fogel (Arthur). Directed by Laurent Cantet and produced by Carole Scotta, Caroline Benjo, Barbara Letellier, and Simon Arnal. Screenplay by Cantet, Francois Begaudeau, and Robin Campillo, based on the novel *Entre les Murs* by Francois Begaudeau.

The Class might have been set in any classroom in the Western world, and I believe most teachers would recognize it. It is about the power struggle between a teacher who wants to do good and students who disagree about what "good" is. The film is so fair that neither side is seen as right, and both seem trapped by futility.

In a lower-income melting pot neighborhood in Paris, Francois, the teacher, begins a school year with high hopes and a desire to be liked by his students. They are a multiethnic group of fifteen- and sixteen-year-olds, few of them prepared by the educational system to be promising candidates for Francois' hopes. None of them seems stupid, and indeed intelligence may be one of their problems: They can see clearly that the purpose of the class is to make them model citizens in a society that has little use for them.

The movie is bursting with life, energy, fears, frustrations, and the quick laughter of a classroom hungry for relief. It avoids lockstep plotting and plunges into the middle of the fray, helping us become familiar with the students, suggesting more than it tells, allowing us to identify with many points of view. It is uncannily convincing.

The reason for that, I learn, involves the method of the director, Laurent Cantet, one of the most gifted new French directors. He began with a best-selling autobiographical novel by a teacher, Francois Begaudeau. He cast Begaudeau as the teacher. He worked for a year with a group of students, improvising and filming scenes. So convincing is the film that it seems documentary, but all of the students, I learn, are playing roles and not themselves.

There is a resentful Arab girl, who feels she is being undervalued by the teacher. A high-spirited African boy, very intelligent, but prone to anger. An Asian boy, also smart, who has learned (from his family's culture, perhaps) to keep a low profile and not reveal himself. Others who are confederates, pals, coconspirators.

A lot of grief in the classroom has to do with the rote teaching of French. As the students puzzle their way through, I don't know, the passive pluperfect subjunctive or whatever, I must say I sided with them. Despite the best efforts of dedicated and gifted nuns, I never learned to diagram a sentence, something they believed was of paramount importance. Yet I have made my living by writing and speaking. You learn a language by listening and speaking. You learn how to write by reading. It's not an abstraction. Do you think the people who first used the imperfect tense felt the need to name it?

The title of the original novel translates as *Between the Walls*, and indeed the film stays for the most part within the classroom. We know from Jack London that the members of a dog pack intensely observe one another. There can only be one top dog, and there are always candidates for the job. A school year begins with the teacher as top dog. Whether it ends that way is the test of a good teacher. Do you stay on top by strict discipline? With humor? By becoming the students' friend? Through psychology? Will they sense your strategy? Sometimes I think the old British public school system was best: Teachers were eccentric cranks, famous for their idiosyncrasies, who baffled their students.

Cloud Nine ★ ★ ★

NO MPAA RATING, 97 m., 2009

Ursula Werner (Inge), Horst Rehberg (Werner), Horst Westphal (Karl), Steffi Kuehnert (Petra). Directed by Andreas Dresen and produced by Peter Rommel. Screenplay by Dresen, Cooky Ziesche, Laila Stieler, and Jorg Hauschild.

When I was much younger, I would experience an "oh, no!" feeling if I realized I was falling in love. It was a mixture of joy in the moment and dread of the usual complications that had, around the age of nineteen, tutored me that there was no such thing as living happily ever after—usually, anyway. I suspect that feeling never entirely leaves us. Consider Inge (Ursula Werner), who is sixty-seven and has been married with reasonable happiness for thirty years to Werner (Horst Rehberg), and finds herself knocking hopefully on the door of a seventy-six-year-old man she hardly knows.

This is Karl (Horst Westphal), who had dropped off his pants to be altered. Inge is a seamstress, working on a sewing machine in the bedroom, living in a nice little apartment with Werner, who in the evenings likes to listen to recordings of steam engines arriving in train stations. His idea of a nice day out for the two of them is taking a train to no particular place while they look out the window.

Werner is not presented as a boring monster, because he isn't. Looking out a train window is often the occasion for dreamy reveries, and as I watched this film I felt the desire, easily suppressed, to go to the Amtrak station and buy a ticket to no particular place. Werner helped Inge raise her family, her daughter Petra (Steffi Kuehnert) considers him her father, and they carry out a soothing ritual of drinking coffee and watching TV.

What came over Inge when she was measuring Karl for his pants? Why did she deliver them herself? Why did he invite her in, and why did they fall into each other's arms a moment later and find themselves losing their underwear so quickly? There's no accounting for such things. The French call it a *coup de foudre,* a lightning bolt to the heart.

Petra advises her not to confess to Werner. "Go ahead, Mother, enjoy yourself—but tell no one!" Sound advice. Inge, however, finds confession necessary. Werner doesn't take the news at all well. "I didn't want to!" she cries out. "I didn't want this to happen to me!" One of those "oh no!" moments.

We shy away from details about elder sex. I had a friend who protested: "Dad, I don't want to know!" Inge and Karl are like a couple of kids, enjoying each other's bodies and presence. She's no beauty, never wears makeup, and apparently goes through the whole film without washing her hair, unless the time she skinny-dips with Karl counts. But when she smiles: Well, everyone has a beautiful face when they look at you with love in their eyes. In this film without deeply complex characters, so much depends on how Karl and Werner look at Inge and how she looks at them.

The director, Andreas Dresen, presents the sex scenes as if they involve two twenty-year-olds, as she should. During sex you have only two ages: immortal or dead. She regards their total nudity with all the detachment we might feel in a steam room. There is a scene where the actress stands naked in front of a mirror and looks at herself. Such a moment of honesty is common enough in the movies, but she does it for so long that our minds begin to supply her thoughts about the inexorable fading of youth.

Paul Cox's great film *Innocence* also considers a late-life romance and is deeper than *Cloud Nine,* I think, because its characters are more sensitive and thoughtful. Inge and Werner in their late sixties don't seem to know much more about such matters than they did when they were teens. About Karl we can't be sure. Yet these performances are so quietly effective that we watch, absorbed. I'm not sure, however, that where this film comes from quite earns the place it goes to.

Note: Cloud Nine *was the winner of the Un Certain Regard jury prize at Cannes 2008.*

Cloudy with a Chance of Meatballs ★ ★ ½

PG, 90 m., 2009

With the voices of: Bill Hader (Flint Lockwood), James Caan (Tim Lockwood), Anna Faris (Sam Sparks), Andy Samberg (Brent McHale), Mr. T (Earl Devereaux), Bruce Campbell (Mayor Shelbourne). Directed by Phil Lord and Chris Miller and produced by Pam Marsden. Screenplay by Lord and Miller, based on the book by Judi Barrett and Ron Barrett.

Let me search my memory. I think—no, I'm positive—this is the first movie I've seen where the hero dangles above a chasm lined with razor-sharp peanut brittle, while holding onto a red licorice rope held by his girlfriend, who has a peanut allergy, so that when she gets cut by some brittle and goes into anaphylactic shock and her body swells up, she refuses to let go, and so the hero bites through the licorice to save her. You don't see that every day.

Cloudy with a Chance of Meatballs is a 3-D animated comedy based on a children's book popular in the 1980s, about a kid named Flint who survives on an island in the Atlantic by catching and canning sardines. When the sardine market collapses and the citizens grow tired of eating their own sardines, he decides to save his island by creating a machine that can convert ordinary water into any food on Earth: hamburgers, ice cream, jelly beans, you name it. As the only practicing film critic who has visited an actual sardine cannery on the coast of Namibia, I am here to tell you that a large cannery on a small island would make you yearn for such a machine.

Flint wants to be an inventor, but his dad insists he help out in the family fishing tackle and sardine store. His dad possibly needs help because he has no visible eyes, only one bushy eyebrow growing straight across his face like a hairy hedge. But Flint works late at night in his tree house, which eventually grows into the largest structure in town, and eureka!

Kids eat jelly beans all day long. Gummi bears frolic. Hamburgers grow on trees. The machine seems to create only food kids like. Pizza, but no broccoli. There is a problem. Because of an error, the machine runs out of control, deluging the island in a cascade of edibles.

It's a good thing the movie is animated. That makes it easier to create a tornado funnel cloud made of spaghetti and meatballs. Its velocity causes meatballs to spin off and rain down upon the town, looking like—well, never mind what they look like.

There is a giant refuse heap outside town, looking like a slag heap and held back by a dam. In an attempt to stop the food storm, Flint, his girlfriend, and his buddy tunnel into a candy mountain, leading to the peanut brittle crisis. There are other characters, including the town's bombastic mayor, a Herculean mascot for the sardine ad campaigns, a monkey, and so on.

It seemed to me the mountains of fudge, ice cream, and pancakes overshot the mark and looked silly, and the airborne food cast a pall over the city, but by golly those kids are plucky. They look a little odd, however; Flint seems to be all nose, like his dad is all eyebrow.

This is the first outing for the new Sony digital 3-D imaging software. I continue to find 3-D a distracting nuisance, but it must be said that the Sony process produces a sharp, crisp picture, with no visible imprecision between the matches of the images. There is clear definition between closer and farther elements. I've seen a lot of 3-D recently, and in terms of technical quality, this is the best.

Coco Before Chanel ★ ★ ★ ½

PG-13, 110 m., 2009

Audrey Tautou (Gabrielle "Coco" Chanel), Benoit Poelvoorde (Etienne Balsan), Alessandro Nivola (Arthur "Boy" Capel), Marie Gillain (Adrienne Chanel), Emmanuelle Devos (Emilienne). Directed by Anne Fontaine and produced by Caroline Benjo, Philippe Carcassonne, and Carole Scotta. Screenplay by Anne Fontaine and Camille Fontaine, with Christopher Hampton and Jacques Fieschi, adapted from the book *L'Irreguliere ou Mon Itineraire Chanel* by Edmonde Charles-Roux.

We talk about people "inventing themselves." That assumes they know who they want to invent. *Coco Before Chanel* begins with an abandoned orphan girl, watches her grow into a music hall chanteuse, and then sidestep prostitution by becoming a mistress. All the while from behind the clouds of her cigarettes she regards the world with unforgiving realism and stubborn ambition. She doesn't set out to become the most influential fashion icon of the twentieth century. She begins by designing a hat, making a little money, and striving to better herself. She wants money and independence. One suspects she would have been similarly driven if she had invented a better mousetrap and founded a home appliance empire.

The naturalism of Anne Fontaine's film would be at home in a novel by Dreiser. Her star, Audrey Tautou, who could make lovability into a career, avoids any effort to make Coco Chanel nice, or soft, or particularly sympathetic. Her fashions may have liberated women from the hideous excesses of the late nineteenth century, but she creates them not out of idealism, but because they directly reflect her inalterable personality. She didn't put women in sailor shirts out of conviction. She liked to wear them.

Perhaps because of its unsentimental approach to Chanel's life, *Coco Before Chanel* struck me as less of a biopic, more of a drama. It's not about rags to riches but about survival of the fittest. Is Coco, young and poor, used by the rich playboy Etienne Balsan (Benoit Poelvoorde)? Perhaps he thought so early in their relationship, but she uses him as well. She likes him, but she signed aboard for money, status, and entrée, not merely sex and romance. She sees theirs as a reasonable transaction. She isn't a brazen temptress but a capitalist, who collects on her investment.

Through Balsan she meets the bold actress Emilienne (Emmanuelle Devos) and Boy Capel, an Englishman. It's clear that to Chanel, love with a man or a woman is pretty much the same, but Boy truly does love her, and this is a unique experience for Coco. Things might have proceeded quite differently in her life if that relationship had survived. Baron Balsan, not blinded by love, sees Boy as exactly what he is—something Coco, for once, hasn't done.

Tautou isn't stereotypically beautiful but more uniquely fetching. It's her spirit as much as her face, and the tilt of her upper lip more than her curves. Coco is above all a disciplinarian of herself; at the end of the film we learn she died in 1971—"on a Sunday," at work, just as she worked every day of her life. She had an original vision of fashion, yes, but we get the feeling she didn't depend on it for her success. She worked hard, dealt with people realistically, drove hard bargains, and saw fashion as a job, not a career or a vocation.

By underlining that, the movie becomes more absorbing. We've seen enough films about heroines carried along by the momentum of their blessed fates. That's not how it works. To the winner belongs the spoils, even if in life you started pretty far back from the starting line. In the case of little Gabrielle Chanel and her sister Adrienne (Marie Gillain), the orphanage probably gave them better chances in life than the parents they missed. They got an education, and it's possible Chanel's fashion sense was influenced by the unadorned, severe lines of the black and white habits of the nuns. Did she start identifying simplicity in dress with women in power?

The young teenage girls break into the lowest rungs of music halls, performing songs in a duet of which it must be said their youth is more appealing than their talent. Music halls attract sugar daddies, and they both size up the situation and make their choices. The film loses some of its fascination, for me, when Coco Chanel is unmistakably launched on her career path. But that's when the story ends; this is titled *Coco Before Chanel* for a reason.

Note: Her story continues in an entirely different film, Coco Chanel & Igor Stravinsky.

Cold Souls ★ ★ ★

PG-13, 101 m., 2009

Paul Giamatti (Paul Giamatti), David Strathairn (Dr. Flintstein), Dina Korzun (Nina), Emily Watson (Claire), Katheryn Winnick (Sveta), Lauren Ambrose (Stephanie). Directed by Sophie Barthes and produced by Andrij Parekh, Dan Carey, Elizabeth Giamatti, Paul Mezey, and Jeremy Kipp Walker. Screenplay by Barthes.

Would an actor sell his own soul for a great performance? No, but he might pawn it. Paul Giamatti is struggling through rehearsals for Chekhov's *Uncle Vanya* and finds the role is haunting every aspect of his life. His soul is weighed down, it tortures him, it makes his wife miserable. He sees an article in the *New Yorker* about a new trend: People are having their souls extracted for a time, to lighten the burden.

The man who performs this service is Dr. Flintstein, whose Soul Storage service will remove the soul (or 95 percent of it, anyway) and hold it in cold storage. As played by a droll David Strathairn, whose own soul seems in storage for this character, Flintstein makes his service sound perfectly routine. He's the type of medical professional who focuses on the procedure and not the patient. Giamatti, playing an actor named after himself, has some questions, as would we all, but he signs up.

Cold Souls is a demonstration of the principle that it is always wise to seek a second opinion. The movie is a first feature written and directed by Sophie Barthes, whose previous film was a short about a middle-aged condom tester who considers buying a box labeled "Happiness" at the drugstore. Clearly this is a filmmaker who would enjoy having dinner with Charlie Kaufman. Perhaps inspired by Kaufman's screenplay for *Being John Malkovich,* she also credits *Dead Souls,* the novel by Gogol about a Russian landowner who buys up the souls of his serfs.

Gogol was writing satire, and so is Barthes. We hope that medical intervention can help us do what we cannot do on our own: focus better, look younger, lose weight, cheer up, be smarter. If only it were as simple as taking a pill. Or, in Giamatti's case, lying on his back to be inserted into a machine looking uncannily like a pregnant MRI scanner.

His soul is successfully extracted and kept in an airtight canister. He's allowed to see it. It has the size and appearance of a chickpea. Lightened of the burden, he becomes a different actor: easygoing, confident, upbeat, energetic—and awful. Rehearsals are a disaster, and he returns to Flintstein demanding his old soul back.

This is not easily done, for reasons involving Nina (Dina Korzun), a sexy Russian courier in the black market for souls. A Russian soul is made available to Giamatti, with alarming results. All of this is dealt with in the only way that will possibly work, which is to say, with very straight faces. The material could be approached as a madcap comedy, but it's funnier this way, as a neurotic, self-centered actor goes through even more anguish than Chekhov ordinarily calls for.

I suppose *Cold Souls* is technically science fiction. There's a subset of SF involving a world just like the one we inhabit, with only one element changed. In an era of Frankenscience, *Cold Souls* objectifies all the new age emoting about the soul and inserts it into the medical care system. Certainly if you have enough money to sidestep your insurance company, a great many cutting-edge treatments are available. And soul extraction is not such a stretch when you reflect that personality destruction, in the form of a prefrontal lobotomy, was for many years medically respectable. Insert an ice pick just so, and your worries are over.

I enjoy movies like this, that play with the logical consequences of an idea. Barthes takes her notion and runs with it, and Giamatti and Strathairn follow fearlessly. The movie is rather evocative about the way we govern ourselves from the inside out. One of Nina's problems is that she has picked up little pieces from the souls of all the other people she has carried. Don't we all?

Cold Weather ★ ★ ★ ½

NO MPAA RATING, 96 m., 2011

Cris Lankenau (Doug), Trieste Kelly Dunn (Gail), Raul Castillo (Carlos), Robyn Rikoon (Rachel). Directed by Aaron Katz and produced by Lars Knudsen, Brendan McFadden, and Ben Stambler. Screenplay by Katz.

Cold Weather is good in so many subtle ways I despair of doing them justice. It's a thriller involving the personalities of its characters, who we get to know surprisingly well. It remains low-key, even during its final big chase scene, which involves only one car. The acting is so good you may not notice it. Although the characters stumble over the plot at least forty minutes into the film, it's as ingenious as a high-tech Friday night special.

The tone is established by Doug (Cris Lankenau), a midtwenties guy who was studying forensics in college but dropped out for no reason he ever explains. In an opening scene he tells his parents "it's a possibility" he may return to school. For now, he's returned to Portland, Oregon, and is sleeping on the sofa of his sister's apartment. He finds a job in a factory that makes those plastic bags filled with ice, and spends his time shifting bags from one place to another.

Doug and his sister, Gail (Trieste Kelly Dunn), get along fine. No sibling problems. At work, he makes a friend named Carlos (Raul Castillo) and lends him a book of Sherlock Holmes stories. Carlos likes it. Doug's former girlfriend Rachel (Robyn Rikoon) comes to town from Chicago and gets a motel room while she trains for a job, she says. The four characters spend some time together. No big deal. Carlos asks Rachel to a Star Trek convention. Doug is fine with that. He remains friends with Rachel but their romance is over with.

Why am I telling you these inconsequential things? Because the movie seems quite willing to spend its running length following the daily lives of nice, low-key, ordinary, even endearing twenty-somethings. All four actors, unknown to me, are natural and convincing, like people you would cast with Catherine Keener, if you know what I mean. Cris Lankenau and Raul Castillo as Doug and Carlos do a very difficult thing here, which is to play young male friends without the slightest shadow of Buddy Movie Syndrome.

Carlos grows alarmed. Rachel stood him up on a date. Possibly inflamed by Sherlock Holmes and Doug's studies in forensics, he talks him into an investigation of what he is convinced is a mysterious disappearance. Now at last there is a plot. About the plot I will tell you nothing, except that I could believe in it. I'm not sure Rachel would use the code described here, or that Doug would figure out how to break it, but never mind. Carlos sensibly says, "We need some common sense," they both enlist Gail, and Doug and Gail find themselves trailing a man in a cowboy hat after having an absolutely realistic sibling conversation about which of them will drive Gail's car.

That's it. Aaron Katz's direction is just about flawless. It's a matter of finding the right tone, established by Doug at the outset, and following it through. It's about a distaste for artificial tension-heightening devices. It's about love of these characters. It's about seeing if smoking a pipe, like Sherlock Holmes did, might help. It's about how an ice factory gets rid of its excess ice. Some people will find this movie boring. That may be because they've been deadened by thrillers that don't pay any more attention than they do.

Collapse ★ ★ ★ ★

NO MPAA RATING, 80 m., 2009

A documentary featuring Michael Ruppert. Directed by Chris Smith and produced by Smith and Kate Noble.

If this man is correct, then you may be reading the most important story in today's paper.

I have no way of assuring you that the bleak version of the future outlined by Michael Ruppert in Chris Smith's *Collapse* is accurate. I can only tell you I have a pretty good built-in BS detector, and its needle never bounced off zero. There is controversy over Michael Ruppert, and he has many critics. But one simple fact at the center of his argument is obviously true, and it terrifies me.

That fact: We have passed the peak of global oil resources. There are only so many known oil reserves. We have used up more than half of them. Remaining reserves are growing smaller, and the demand is growing larger. It took about a century to use up the first half. That usage was much accelerated in the most recent fifty years. Now the oil demands of giant economies such as India and China are exploding. They represent more than half the global population, and until recent decades had small energy consumption.

If the supply is finite and usage is potentially doubling, you do the math. We will face a global oil crisis, not in the distant future, but within the lives of many now alive. They may well see a world without significant oil.

Oh, I grow so impatient with those who prattle on about our untapped resources in Alaska, yada yada yada. There seems to be only enough oil in Alaska to power the United States for a matter of months. The world's great oil reserves have been discovered.

Saudi Arabia sits atop the largest oil reservoir ever found. For years the Saudis have refused to disclose any figures at all about their reserves. If those reserves are vast and easy to tap by drilling straight down through the desert, then ask yourself this question: *Why are the Saudis spending billions of dollars to develop off-shore drilling platforms?*

Michael Ruppert is a man ordinary in appearance, on the downhill slope of middle age, a chain-smoker with a mustache. He is not all worked up. He speaks reasonably and very clearly. *Collapse* involves what he has to say, illustrated with news footage and a few charts, the most striking of which is a bell-shaped curve. It takes a lot of effort to climb a bell-shaped curve, but the descent is steep and dangerous.

He recites facts I knew, vaguely. Many things are made from oil. Everything plastic. Paint. Eight gallons of oil in every auto tire. Oil supplies the energy to convert itself into those by-products. No oil, no plastic, no tires, no gas to run cars, no machines to build them. No coal mines except those operated by men and horses.

Alternative energies and conservation? The problem is the cost of obtaining and using it. Ethanol requires more energy than it produces. Hybrid and battery cars need engines, tires, and batteries. Nuclear power plants need to be built with oil. Electricity from wind power is most useful near its source. It is transmitted by grids built and maintained by oil. Wave power is expensive to collect. Solar power is cheap and limitless, but we need a whole hell of a lot more solar panels and other collecting devices.

Like I say, you do the math. Ruppert has done his math, and he concludes our goose is cooked. He doesn't have any answers. We're passing the point of diminishing returns on the way to our rendezvous with the point of no return. It was nice while it lasted. People lived happily enough in the centuries before oil, electricity, and steam, I guess. Of course, there were fewer than six billion of us. And in this century, Ruppert says, there will be a lot fewer than six billion again. It won't be a pretty sight.

I'm not going to mention his theories about global warming, because that's a subject that inflames too many zealots. About peak oil, his reasoning is clear, simple, and hard to refute.

So you can stop reading now. That's the heart of Ruppert's message, delivered by a calm guy who could be Wilford Brimley's kid brother, lives alone with his dog, and is behind on his rent.

I was fascinated by some of the directions peak oil takes him into. For him, he says, it was the key to understanding many seemingly unconnected geopolitical events. The facts he outlines are known to world leaders. They don't talk a lot about them in alarmist terms, but they explain why Bush/Cheney were happy to have an excuse to invade Iraq. And why our embassy compound in Baghdad is the largest we've ever built, larger than the Vatican City. And why we're so much more worried by Iran than North Korea. They may also explain Obama's perplexing decision to increase troops in Afghanistan. An undeclared world war for oil is already under way.

I don't know when I've seen a thriller more frightening. I couldn't tear my eyes from the screen. *Collapse* is even entertaining, in a macabre sense. I think you owe it to yourself to see it.

The Company Men ★ ★ ★

R, 115 m., 2011

Ben Affleck (Bobby Walker), Chris Cooper (Phil Woodward), Kevin Costner (Jack Dolan), Tommy Lee Jones (Gene McClary), Maria Bello (Sally Wilcox), Rosemarie DeWitt (Maggie Walker), Craig T. Nelson (James Salinger). Directed by John Wells and produced by Wells, Claire Rudnick Polstein, and Paula Weinstein. Screenplay by Wells.

The happiest people I come into contact with seem to be those who have real jobs. In the last few weeks, I've talked with a Macintosh tutor, a doctor, a set designer, a stagehand, a heating and air-conditioning man, a lawyer, a Web designer, my editor, an animator, and Millie Salmon, the woman who is my caregiver, although that job description makes me sound more decrepit than I am.

All of these people work hard, know what they're doing, think it's worth doing, enjoy it, and take pride in it. There is the same serenity I sensed from my father, who was an electrician and a damned good one. I do not, on the other hand, pick up good feelings from those people I know who are largely involved in "making money for the stockholders." They focus on moving money around, hiring and firing, cutting costs, serving the bottom line. They are caregivers for corporations, which would be more satisfactory if corporations were not essentially balance sheets. I know the Supreme Court has ruled that corporations are individuals, but when did one ever tell you a good joke?

The Company Men follows the stories of characters who have oriented their lives around a corporation named GTX. Years ago this company involved two men who began building ships; small ones at first, and then big ones. Now it's called General Transportation Systems, which is how we spell Acme these days. Caught in the economic downturn, GTX is downsizing, and some of its employees are discovering their primary occupation was making and spending a lot of money, and that without those jobs there isn't much they really know how to do.

We focus at first on Bobby Walker (Ben Affleck), who drives a Porsche and has a nice golf handicap, a big suburban house, and a wife, named Maggie (Rosemarie DeWitt), who is an expert consumer. Bobby loses his job. His severance and "savings cushion" can't support his overhead. He enters, with great displeasure, the shadow world of the unemployed. His company has paid for temporary office space at a job search center that helps with his résumé. He attends sessions in group therapy where he learns how to present himself and think positively. He loathes them.

Phil Woodward (Chris Cooper), an older man at GTX, is also fired. If there is no great demand for Bobby, there is none for an unemployed executive around sixty. He was literally his job. Without it, in economic terms, he is a man with no buyers and nothing to sell. He was under the impression he had importance and value. He realizes that was a fiction. Employees of corporations are like free-ranging scavenger cells. When the corporation inhales in good times, they find themselves in a warm place with good nurture. When it exhales in bad times, they go spinning into the vast, indifferent world.

GTX was started by Salinger (Craig T. Nelson) and McClary (Tommy Lee Jones). McClary preserves the belief that a corporation owes its employees some loyalty, and that it should serve a useful function. Salinger has outgrown that phase and realizes a corporation survives only by maximizing its profits and producing one primary product: income. As Salinger's vision prevails over McClary's old-fashioned idealism, the inexorable task of "working for the shareholder" is reduced to "sacrificing the jobs and lives of others for the bottom line."

Although the actors are convincing and the film well crafted, *The Company Men* delivers few satisfactory character portraits because the movie isn't really about characters; it's about economic units. When a corporation fires you, it doesn't much care whether you're a good friend, a loving father, a louse, or a liar. You are an investment it carries on its books, or not. The impact of the movie comes when these people realize that, in economic terms, it doesn't matter who they are.

There's one character who really does something. This is Jack Dolan (Kevin Costner), Bobby's brother-in-law, who owns a small construction company that builds one house at a time. He and his workers know how to make house siding lie true, how to use materials efficiently, how to—well, how to drive a nail. Bobby has always dismissed Jack as a "working man," but when you're out of work, that looks pretty good.

Written and directed by John Wells, *The Company Men* offers no great elation or despair. Its world is what it is. We all live in it. In good times young people go to the movies and dream of becoming Gordon Gekko. In bad times, a housebuilder looks more like a Master of the Universe. It happens I've been talking with a few young people who are trying to make career decisions. My advice involves the old cliché, "Find what you really love doing and make that your profession." I think this is true. If you have to be unemployed, it might seem less bleak if you hated doing the job anyway.

Conan O'Brien Can't Stop ★ ★ ★

R, 89 m., 2011

Conan O'Brien, Andy Richter, Steve Kroft, Eddie Vedder, Stephen Colbert, Jon Stewart, Jim Carrey, and Jack White. A documentary directed by Rodman Flender and produced by Rachel Griffin and Gavin Polone.

Conan O'Brien Can't Stop has a title of piercing accuracy. After NBC and Jay Leno pulled the rug out from under him, O'Brien went overnight from hosting *The Tonight Show* to being banned from television for six months. To be sure, NBC paid him $40 million in a send-off package, but the O'Brien we see in the film wasn't in it for the money. He was in it because he can't stop.

I appeared many times on his original program, most memorably being attacked by a man in a bear suit. I always liked him. I've also been on Carson, Oprah, Letterman, Leno, Regis, Arsenio, Joan Rivers, and a.m. here and a.m. there. You arrive at least an hour early, finish with makeup, leave your dressing room door open, and watch what happens in the corridor. Carson, Conan, and Leno would drop by to say hello. I don't remember seeing the others before airtime. Letterman in particular seems to build up steam in private. It has nothing to do with who's nice and who isn't. It's showbiz.

Watching this documentary, I realize that when Conan lost *The Tonight Show* he was like Wile E. Coyote, chasing the Road Runner of his dreams off the edge of a cliff and afraid to look down. Enraged at Leno and NBC, he quickly undertook "The Legally Prohibited from Being Funny on Television Tour," which covered thirty-two cities, from Radio City Music Hall to the Bonnaroo Music Festival in Tennessee—where inside a tent in one-hundred-degree heat he was expected to introduce every act, and did. You get the notion he would have introduced them anyway.

Here is a man driven to assert himself. He waited five years for *The Tonight Show,* lost it in months, and needed to say to the universe, "Sir! I exist!" The film, directed by Rodman Flender, watches him before and after shows and en route between cities, seeing a man incapable of giving himself a break. Overworked, exhausted, assaulted by demands, he cannot say no to an autograph, patiently hosts waves of visitors in his dressing room, drums up work on his days off, and at times seems on the edge of madness.

Everyone around him pays a price. He relentlessly nibbles away at his support system, picks on his personal assistant, needles his sidekick Andy Richter, and dominates his "writers" so compulsively that I can hardly recall one of them being allowed to say anything at meetings. He seems to consider them more of an audience.

Why these people stay with him is a mystery. My guess is that they know him better than we do and realize he's undergoing a crisis. He's driven. After shows, exhausted, he insists on going out to sign autographs and pose for photos with fans. The photos in particular are a version of the Water Torture Test for celebrities. The fan hands a camera to a friend or bystander, who *inevitably* doesn't know how to operate it. The celebrity remains in position, his mouth frozen in the rictus of a smile, while the fan explains how the camera operates: "You push this button."

In addition to telling jokes, O'Brien plays guitar and joins a backup band and various guest stars to perform country-rock. He's surprisingly good, for a talk show host. He fantasizes receiving a text message from Jay Leno ("What's it like to have a soul?"). I can only imagine how well he sleeps. We see his wife in only one brief, early scene, and I suspect she was well advised not to come along.

This is not to say Conan O'Brien is a bad man. In fact, after the movie, I rather admired him. What we are seeing is a man determined to vindicate himself after a public humiliation. People attend his shows, cheer him, like him. That proves something, doesn't it?

What we don't see are the details of what must have been going on all this time in negotiations to find a new television home after the end of the six-month banishment. He and his agents must have been talking about a lot of possibilities, including TBS, where he ended up. Those would have added a maddening level of frustration to his exhausting existence.

O'Brien started out as a writer. He must have been driven to become a performer. It is a need in some people. One of the almost unbelievable stories in talk show history is how Johnny Carson was able to retire at the height of his popularity, and mean it, and stick to it. Maybe one of the reasons people liked him so much is that he never seemed to *need* to perform.

Other people do. I once observed Henny Youngman taping a TV show in the old NBC studios at the Merchandise Mart in Chicago. We got into an elevator together. It stopped at the second floor, a private club. A wedding was under way. Youngman got off the elevator, asked to meet the father of the bride, and said, "I'm Henny Youngman. I'll do ten minutes for a hundred dollars."

Confessions of a Shopaholic ★ ★ ½

PG, 112 m., 2009

Isla Fisher (Rebecca Bloomwood), Hugh Dancy (Luke Brandon), Joan Cusack (Jane

Bloomwood), John Goodman (Graham Bloomwood), John Lithgow (Edgar West), Kristin Scott Thomas (Alette Naylor), Leslie Bibb (Alicia Billington), Fred Armisen (Ryan Koenig), Julie Hagerty (Hayley), Krysten Ritter (Suze Cleath-Stewart), Robert Stanton (Derek Smeath). Directed by P. J. Hogan and produced by Jerry Bruckheimer. Screenplay by Tracey Jackson, Tim Firth, and Kayla Alpert, based on the books by Sophie Kinsella.

I liked *Confessions of a Shopaholic* about as much as I disliked *Sex and the City.* Both are about clueless women, but this one knows it. *SATC* is about women searching for love in most of the wrong places, and *Shopaholic* is about a woman searching for happiness in the places that are absolutely right for her: Prada, Gucci, Macy's, Barneys, Saks, and on down the avenue.

The plotting is on automatic pilot. It needs Chesley B. Sullenberger III. There is not a single unanticipated blip in the story arc. But here's what sort of redeems it: It glories in its silliness, and the actors are permitted the sort of goofy acting that distinguished screwball comedy. We get double takes, slow burns, pratfalls, exploding clothes wardrobes, dropped trays, tear-away dresses, missing maids of honor, overnight fame, public disgrace, and not, amazingly, a single obnoxious cat or dog.

At the center of this maelstrom is a genuinely funny comedienne named Isla Fisher. She reminded me of Lucille Ball, and not only because she's a redhead. She does one of the most difficult things any actress can do, which is physical comedy: walk into doors, drop trays, fall into people, go ass over teakettle. She plays a Perfect Ditz in the sense of the Perfect Storm, carrying all before her. Give her a fan and twenty seconds of tango lessons, and get off the floor.

It is to the credit of the director, P. J. Hogan of *My Best Friend's Wedding,* that he gives Fisher freedom and yet modulates it, so her character's earnest desire to please shines through. It was the same on *I Love Lucy.* Lucy wasn't a klutz because she was trying to look funny. She was a klutz because she was trying not to.

Fisher plays Rebecca Bloomwood, the only child of blue-collar parents (Joan Cusack and John Goodman), who has been reborn as a Most Preferred Customer through the miracle of credit cards. She begins with a narration describing the nearly erotic bliss she feels while shopping, and we follow her through store after store in an endless cycle of accessorizing outfits, and then buying outfits to match the accessories. It's like the dilemma of the ten hot dogs and eight buns: You can never come out even at the end.

She dreams of working for a famous fashion magazine but stumbles, literally, into a money management magazine published by the same company. How does this woman who knows nothing about money or its management get the job? By impressing the editor (Hugh Dancy) with her eccentric brilliance. Everything she does that's wrong turns out right. Also she benefits from a brave roommate, Suze (Krysten Ritter), who plays the Ethel Mertz role: coconspirator and occasional voice of reason.

Meanwhile, the villainous bill collector Derek Smeath (Robert Stanton) is on her trail, hints that breaking her legs is not out of the question, and eventually has one of the funnier scenes in the movie. After she gains (highly improbable) international fame overnight on the basis of her writing, it would destroy her, she fears, to be unmasked. Whether it does or not, I leave it to your experience of cinematic plotting to determine.

Look, *Confessions of a Shopaholic* is no masterpiece. But it's funny, Isla Fisher is a joy, and—of supreme importance—it is more entertaining to a viewer with absolutely no eagerness to see it (like me) than *Sex and the City* was. Also, no movie can be all bad where the heroine attends a Shopaholics Anonymous meeting and meets a former Chicago Bulls star.

The Conspirator ★ ★ ★

PG-13, 121 m., 2011

James McAvoy (Frederick Aiken), Robin Wright (Mary Surratt), Kevin Kline (Edwin M. Stanton), Evan Rachel Wood (Anna Surratt), Danny Huston (Joseph Holt), Justin Long (Nicholas Baker), Colm Meaney (General David Hunter), Alexis Bledel (Sarah), Tom Wilkinson (Reverdy Johnson). Directed by Robert Redford and

produced by Redford, Brian Peter Falk, Bill Holderman, Greg Shapiro, Robert Stone, and Webster Stone. Screenplay by James Solomon.

In the period following the assassination of Abraham Lincoln, those holding together the wounded federal government were desperate to bring charges against the guilty. Their problem was they couldn't find them. John Wilkes Booth, the gunman, was captured soon after the deed and shot by a Union soldier who was acting against orders. Prosecutors felt he was part of a conspiracy including about eight people.

The Conspirator, Robert Redford's new film, takes up the story in a postwar Washington convincingly shot on location in Savannah, Georgia. He approaches it as a legal procedural, concerned not only with the case but also with the legal precedents it established, which we are still dealing with today. Crucially, it tried a civilian in a military tribunal, denying her the right to a jury of peers that is guaranteed in the Constitution.

This civilian was named Mary Surratt (Robin Wright). She owned a boardinghouse in Washington, where Booth and his fellow plotters met. They were brought there by her son, John. Surratt was charged as a coconspirator. Secretary of War Edwin M. Stanton (Kevin Kline), the de facto power in Washington despite the presence of President Andrew Johnson, wanted her tried and convicted quickly, to placate an enraged population. He gave the assignment to defense attorney Reverdy Johnson (Tom Wilkinson), who passed it to a young Union veteran named Frederick Aiken (James McAvoy).

Aiken wanted nothing to do with it. He felt Surratt must certainly be guilty. Johnson, a Southerner, felt he couldn't take the case with passions running so high, and forced the job upon the Northerner Aiken, explaining that Surratt had a right to a competent defense. Surratt is certainly not helpful to her young attorney, because her only thought is to protect her son. Gradually, however, Aiken begins to believe it is possible she was not involved in the meetings of the conspirators.

Redford considers this material in an unusually literate and thoughtful historical film, working from years of research by his screenwriter, James Solomon. I found it absorbing and relevant today. It is useful to reflect that it isn't *her* constitutional rights that are being violated, but our own, because the Constitution must be seen to work equally for all or it loses its strength for everyone. The language and reasoning of Stanton echo with similar statements by George W. Bush and Dick Cheney in defense of the Patriot Act, and Reverdy Johnson in this reading would represent Barack Obama, more a compromiser than an idealist.

The film depends on Robin Wright and James McAvoy for its human appeal. Wright's performance is deliberately withdrawn and restrained. Having apparently concluded she is certain to be found guilty, she's reluctant to cooperate with her attorney. In a sense, because of his ambivalent feelings about her, he's trying his case against himself. His conversion to her cause is essentially his conversion to the underlying constitutional principles involved. As he argues in the military tribunal, he is arguing about its very presence in a case involving a civilian woman with no role in the military.

Redford could have vulgarized this material. He and Wright certainly have the skills to make Mary Surratt a passionate, heroic victim. They choose not to. They require us to think our own way through the case, and arrive at our own opinions, and that is the value of *The Conspirator.* In most historical dramas, the opinions are already in and the conclusions already reached. Redford and his producers, the American Film Company of the Ricketts family, show respect in their treatment of a little-known footnote to a well-known story.

Well, was Mary Surratt a conspirator? I put the question point blank to Redford recently, and he said he thought she must surely have known what her son was discussing with the others under her roof. But her guilt isn't the issue. The film is about the correct means of determining guilt—or innocence. If the Constitution says you can't do something, if it guarantees a due process, then it must be obeyed.

All of this requires a lot of theory, a lot of philosophy, and a lot of dialogue. Those most interested in American history will probably find it most valuable. Those who want a historical romance or a courtroom potboiler will be disappointed. You have to give credit to Redford, Wright and McAvoy, and the other filmmakers. Not many films this smart can be made.

Conviction ★ ★ ★

R, 96 m., 2010

Hilary Swank (Betty Anne Waters), Sam Rockwell (Kenny Waters), Minnie Driver (Abra Rice), Melissa Leo (Nancy Taylor), Peter Gallagher (Barry Scheck), Juliette Lewis (Roseanne Perry). Directed by Tony Goldwyn and produced by Goldwyn, Andrew S. Karsch, and Andrew Sugerman. Screenplay by Pamela Gray.

Kenny Waters might not have been a very nice man, but he was an innocent one. By considering his innocence and not his personality, *Conviction* puts the focus where it belongs: on the sister who reshaped her entire life to win his freedom. Her determination is fierce, her rebirth is inspiring, and in Hilary Swank the film finds the right actress to embody gritty tenacity.

You can hardly imagine anyone else playing Betty Anne Waters. She's a working-class woman from a hard childhood. She and her brother Kenny (Sam Rockwell) had an absent father and a mother who might as well have been absent, and were shuffled through a series of dismal foster homes. But they stuck together and helped each other, almost as Dickensian survivors. Her gratitude to him is boundless.

The movie doesn't avoid the fact that Kenny gets wild when he gets drunk. He displays the personality changes of an alcoholic. He can be mean, and everybody knows it. In many circles this is seen as a trait and not a symptom. A local woman is murdered; he's arrested on suspicion and makes the mistake of behaving insultingly to a cop (Melissa Leo, from *Frozen River*). He will pay for that. A couple of local women, including a ditzy witness (Juliette Lewis), sorta are kinda sure they musta seen him at the crime scene, and the vengeful cop railroads him into jail.

(Some spoilers ahead.)

Swank dedicates her life to proving her brother's innocence. This involves reinventing herself. She gets a high school diploma and a college degree and enrolls in law school. One cost of this is her marriage. It's an intriguing possibility, untouched by the movie, that after a certain point in her reeducation she simply outgrew her earlier life, and carried on for her own sake as well as her brother's.

In law school she bonds with another student named Abra (Minnie Driver), who also dedicates her life to the case. The movie never really explains why; is it just the goodness of her heart? Driver is very good, in any event, and the two women involve us in their investigation.

Courtroom scenes just about always work for me. It must be built into the situation. *Conviction* has good ones, especially when the Juliette Lewis character comes back into play. It is good to see Melissa Leo again, not so good that her vengeful cop has one dimension, but she's effective at how well she evokes it.

This is all based on a true story, including the lucky break when DNA testing is introduced and proves Kenny innocent. The story generates the kind of urgency we feel when a character is obviously right and is up against stupidity and meanness. It delivers.

What it doesn't reveal during the "where are they now?" crawl at the end is that six months after his release, according to The Associated Press, Kenny was killed when he "fractured his skull when he fell from a 15-foot wall while taking a shortcut to his brother's house after a dinner with his mother." Tragic. But Betty Anne Waters is still working for wrongfully convicted prisoners.

Cop Out ★ ½

R, 110 m., 2010

Bruce Willis (Jimmy Monroe), Tracy Morgan (Paul Hodges), Adam Brody (Barry Mangold), Kevin Pollak (Hunsaker), Ana de la Reguera (Gabriela), Guillermo Diaz (Poh Boy), Michelle Trachtenberg (Ava), Seann William Scott (Dave). Directed by Kevin Smith and produced by Polly Cohen Johnsen, Marc Platt, and Michael Tadross. Screenplay by Robb Cullen and Mark Cullen.

Jimmy and Paul are cops hunkered down across the street from a stakeout when they see a mysterious figure run across rooftops and break into a house. Seconds later, he can clearly be seen in an upper window, sitting on a toilet and reading a magazine. "What kind-ofa guy breaks into a house and takes a crap?" asks Paul, or words to that effect.

Paul explains he always delays this elementary function until he gets home. He's not relaxed until then. But once he's home—ooohhh boy! Then he lets loose. He describes the results in great detail. The walls, the ceilings. All right! I'm thinking, all right, already! I got it! Mudslide! Paul isn't finished. Now he's talking about the reaction of the neighbors.

How do you know this is a scene from a Kevin Smith film? The imitation of a nine-year-old describing bodily functions might be a clue. But the clincher is when that mysterious guy runs across the rooftops. Paul (Tracy Morgan) explains to his partner Jimmy (Bruce Willis): "That's known as 'parkour.' It's a new martial art." Well, thanks, Paul. I didn't know that until yesterday, when it was explained in *District 13: Ultimatum*. What synchronicity. That other movie costars the man who gave "parkour" its name. The movie is filled with it. I suspect its presence as a brief walk-on in *Cop Out* can be explained this way: Kevin found out about it, thought it was cool, and slipped in a little quick "parkour" for fun.

If you combine the enthusiasms of a geek with the toilet humor of a third-grader, you'll be pretty close to defining the art of Kevin Smith. Hey, I'm not complaining. If we lose our inner third-grader, we begin to die. When the muse visits him, Smith gets inspired and makes fun movies like *Zack and Miri Make a Porno*. Alas, *Cop Out* is not one of those movies. Tracy Morgan is forced to go way over the top; Bruce Willis seems eager to have a long, sad talk with his agent; and Kevin Pollak, who gets costar billing, does at least appear for longer than a quark at Fermilab.

Cop Out tells your standard idiotic story about buddy cops who screw up, get suspended by the captain, and redeem themselves by overthrowing a drug operation while searching for the valuable baseball card Jimmy wants to sell to pay for his daughter's wedding. Paul spends an unreasonable amount of time dressed as a cell phone, considering there is nothing to prevent him from taking it off.

A lot of the dialogue is intended to be funny, but man, is it lame. Many of the gags possibly looked good on paper, but watching Willis and Morgan struggle with them is like watching third-graders do Noel Coward, if Noel Coward had been rewritten by Kevin Smith. At St. Joseph's Boys' Camp there was this Chicago kid named Bob Calvano who was naturally hilarious around the campfire every night. Then I'd get up and flop with my memorized bits from Buddy Hackett records. "Ebert," he advised me kindly, "it isn't funny if you act like it's supposed to be funny. Act like you don't know." All I can do is pass along Calvano's advice.

Coraline ★ ★ ★

PG, 101 m., 2009

With the voices of: Dakota Fanning (Coraline Jones), Teri Hatcher (Mother/Other Mother), John Hodgman (Father/Other Father), Ian McShane (Mr. Bobinsky), Jennifer Saunders (Miss Spink), Dawn French (Miss Forcible), Robert Bailey Jr. (Wybie Lovat). Directed by Henry Selick and produced by Claire Jennings and Mary Sandell. Screenplay by Selick, based on the novel by Neil Gaiman.

The director of *Coraline* has suggested it is for brave children of any age. That's putting it mildly. This is nightmare fodder for children, however brave, under a certain age. I know kids are exposed to all sorts of horror films via video, but *Coraline* is disturbing not for gory images but for the story it tells. That's rare in itself: Lots of movies are good at severing limbs but few at telling tales that can grab us down inside where it's dark and scary.

Even more rare is that Coraline Jones (Dakota Fanning) is not a nice little girl. She's unpleasant, complains, has an attitude, and makes friends reluctantly. Nor does she meet sweet and colorful new pals in her adventure, which involves the substitution of her parents by ominous doubles with buttons sewn over their eyes. She is threatened with being trapped in their alternate world, which is reached by an alarming tunnel behind a painted-over doorway in her own house.

Not that Coraline's own parents are all that great. They're busy, distracted, bickering, and always hunched over their computers. They hardly hear her when she talks. That's why she recklessly enters the tunnel and finds her Other Mother and Other Father waiting with roasted chicken and a forced cheerfulness. All she needs to stay there is to have buttons sewn into her own eye sockets.

Coraline is the new film by Henry Selick, who made *The Nightmare Before Christmas* and again combines his mastery of stop-motion and other animation with 3-D. The 3-D creates a gloomier image (take off the glasses and the screen is bright), but then this is a gloomy film with weird characters doing nasty things. I've heard of eating chocolate-covered insects, but not when they're alive.

The ideal audience for this film would be admirers of film art itself, assuming such people exist. Selick creates an entirely original look and feel, uses the freedom of animation to elongate his characters into skeletal specters looming over poor Coraline. Her new friend Wybie (Robert Bailey Jr.) is a young hunchback whose full name is Wyborn, and it doesn't take Coraline long to wonder why his parents named him that.

Other Mother and Other Father (voices by Teri Hatcher and John Hodgman, who are also Mother and Father) essentially want to steal Coraline from her real but distracted parents and turn her into some kind of a Stepford Daughter. Their house, which looks like Coraline's own, has two old ladies (Jennifer Saunders and Dawn French) in the basement, boarders who seem in retirement from subtly hinted careers in the adult entertainment industry. The upstairs boarder is Mr. Bobinsky (Ian McShane), a sometime vaudevillian who has a troupe of trained mice. One of the rooms of the house has insects bigger than Coraline who act as living furniture.

It's more or less impossible, for me anyway, to be scared by 3-D animation. The process always seems to be signaling, "I'm a process!" I think it's harder to get involved in a story when the process doesn't become invisible. I hear from parents who say, "My kids didn't even notice the 3-D!" In that case, why have it in the first place?

Kids who will be scared by the story may not all be happy to attend, 3-D or not. I suspect a lot of lovers of the film will include admirers of Neil Gaiman, whose Hugo Award–winning novel inspired Selick's screenplay. Gaiman is a titan of graphic novels, and there's a nice irony that one of his all-words books has been adapted as animation.

I admire the film mostly because it is good to look at. Selick is as unconventional in his imagery as Gaiman is in his writing, and this is a movie for people who know and care about drawing, caricature, grotesquery, and the far shores of storytelling. In short, you might care little about a fantasy, little indeed about this story, and still admire the artistry of it all, including an insidious score by Bruno Coulais, which doesn't pound at us like many horror scores, but gets under our psychic fingernails.

Credit is due to those who backed this film. I'm tired of wall-to-wall cuteness like *Kung Fu Panda* and wonder if Selick's approach would be suited to films for grown-ups adapted from material like stories by August Derleth or Stephen King. And perhaps I didn't make it clear that it's fine with me that Coraline is an unpleasant little girl. It would be cruelty to send Pippi Longstocking down that tunnel, but Coraline deserves it. Maybe she'll learn a lesson.

Country Strong ★ ★ ½

PG-13, 116 m., 2011

Gwyneth Paltrow (Kelly Canter), Tim McGraw (James Canter), Garrett Hedlund (Beau Hutton), Leighton Meester (Chiles Stanton). Directed by Shana Feste and produced by Tobey Maguire and Jenno Topping. Written by Feste.

Country Strong is one of the best movies of 1957, and I mean that sincerely as a compliment. Lee Remick would have been terrific in this movie—as good as Gwyneth Paltrow is. We live now in more fraught times, with Natalie Portman mentally disemboweling herself for her art while slipping into madness. And I admire her and she deserves her Oscar. But *Country Strong* is a throwback, a pure, heartfelt exercise in '50s social melodrama, using such stock elements as a depressed heroine, her manipulating husband, an ambivalent Other Man, and, tapping her toe impatiently in the wings, young Eve Harrington eager to swoop in and gnaw the heroine's courage from her bones.

This is filmed in a straightforward meat-and-potatoes style, beautifully photographed by John Bailey. It takes place in what could be the Texas of *The Last Picture Show*, except for some performances in a modern arena. It stars Paltrow as Kelly Canter, a troubled country singer who has been released from alcohol rehab too soon. Tim McGraw plays James, the man she married when they were in love and who now stays on as her controlling manager. Garrett Hedlund is Beau Hutton, a singer who "just likes to play music for people" and doesn't care about money. And Leighton Meester is Chiles Stanton, a former Miss Dallas who dreams of stardom.

Beau and Chiles. Man, are those '50s names. The plot does not neglect the tragic loss of Kelly's child, when while pregnant and drunk she fell from a stage. Nor Beau and James, who *both* fool around with Chiles, and *both* are probably in love with Kelly. After Beau (apparently) resigns his day job as an orderly at Kelly's rehab institution, these people move in unison across Texas on a tour route scattered with emotional land mines. Kelly is in the big customized bus. The rest bring up the rear in an old van.

It is a given that Kelly is a great star. Beau is a damn fine country singer, too good to play in bars that can't even afford enough extras to make up a crowd. Chiles is a promising singer but an emotional basket case because of deep insecurities from childhood. She's got herself one of those pinched-up fearful faces with her red lips all forced into a perfect bow and her hair too stiff. She's like a caricature of mama's little beauty pageant contestant until at the end, wow, she scrubs off the makeup and shampoos that hair spray off her head, and we realize Leighton Meester is a beauty and not a victim of a cosmetics counter makeover.

Now it may seem from this that I am finding fault with *Country Strong*. Quite the opposite. We must see a movie for what it is, not for what we think another film might have been. This is a movie into which Lee Remick and Rock Hudson and Sandra Dee would have slipped without shoehorns, and Douglas Sirk would have known where to march them. Its emotions are strong and visible. Its motives are clear. Its music performances are so good we wish they lasted longer. Gwyneth Paltrow is so beautiful and just really nice that she brings enormous sympathy to her role. And Garrett Hedlund's Beau would do anything for a woman—or two women, in this case.

I eat this stuff up. Don't get all on your high horse. Here are big emotions sprayed across the somewhat crowded quarters of a limited number of small sets, punctuated by second-unit drive-bys and grizzly good ol' boys filling out the frame. The only truly realistic character in the movie has hardly a line. That would be the tall middle-age woman who is apparently Kelly Canter's wardrobe woman, and follows her everywhere like those well-paid and not indifferent support people in the lives of stars. She sees everything and knows everything and keeps her mouth shut, which is what you want. She's got your back.

Another thing that places this movie in the 1950s milieu is its understanding of alcoholism. It thinks being drunk comes on people in sudden spurts, like a sneezing fit, and goes away when the plot needs it to. Kelly will be waving a vodka bottle at one moment and morosely pondering at the next. Paltrow has a lovely scene where she coaches young Chiles on what she needs to know about sweat stains, high heels, and love.

Beau tells James his mistake was to take Kelly out of rehab before the rehab was finished. James is not a man of deep insights into drinking or sobriety. Three days after Kelly gets out of rehab, Beau catches her choking down pills in the dressing room. He confronts James about this. "I know!" says James. "I put them in her pillbox myself! They're not dangerous unless she drinks!" I know I didn't hear you say that, James. Tell me you didn't.

Couples Retreat ★ ★

PG-13, 107 m., 2009

Vince Vaughn (Dave), Jason Bateman (Jason), Faizon Love (Shane), Jon Favreau (Joey), Malin Akerman (Ronnie), Kristen Bell (Cynthia), Kristin Davis (Lucy), Kali Hawk (Trudy), Tasha Smith (Jennifer), Carlos Ponce (Salvadore), Peter Serafinowicz (Sctanley), Jean Reno (Marcel), Temuera Morrison (Briggs). Directed by Peter Billingsley and produced by Scott

Stuber and Vince Vaughn. Screenplay by Vaughn, Jon Favreau, and Dana Fox.

Couples Retreat tells the story of four troubled couples and how they're healed by sitcom formulas. Why are they troubled? Because the screenplay says so. It contains little comedy except for freestanding one-liners, and no suspense except for the timing of the obligatory reconciliation. It doesn't even make you think you'd like to visit its island paradise.

The couples are apparently all from Buffalo Grove, which supplies nothing visual except for a T-shirt. Three of them think they're reasonably happy, but their friends Jason (Jason Bateman) and Cynthia (Kristen Bell) beg them to join them for a week at a resort devoted to healing relationships (if four couples go, it's half price).

Jason and Cynthia are anguished because they haven't had a child. The other couples are Dave (Vince Vaughn) and Ronnie (Malin Akerman); Joey (Jon Favreau) and Lucy (Kristin Davis); and Shane (Faizon Love) and Trudy (Kali Hawk). Their troubles: (1) Parenting duties distract from romance; (2) Joey's wandering eye; (3) Shane has split from his wife and is dating a twenty-year-old bimbo.

They fly to the Eden resort, which uses locations on Bora Bora, a truly enchanted place that's reduced to the beach party level. Eden is run by Monsieur Marcel (Jean Reno), a martial arts mystic, and managed by Sctanley (Peter Serafinowicz), who explains his name is spelled with a C. Other staff include Salvadore (Carlos Ponce), doubling for a model on the cover of a lesser romance novel.

The formula itself might have supported hilarity, but the story lacks character specifics. Each couple behaves relentlessly as an illustration of their problem. The movie depends for excitement on a shark attack during a scuba-diving exercise, featuring clueless sharks and an enormous pool of blood apparently leaked from a tiny superficial scratch. Salvadore charms the wives somewhat ambiguously with his oiled pecs and bottles of pineapple-rum drinks. The men don't bond so much as stand together on-screen and exchange bonding dialogue.

There is a twin resort named East Eden, which has all swinging singles as opposed to troubled couples. It's a party scene every night; as nearly as I could tell, our four couples are the only clients on West Eden, so no wonder there was a 50 percent off deal, despite Sctanley's talk of the long waiting list.

Among the better things in the movie, I count Vaughn's well-timed and smart dialogue; the eccentricity of Love and Hawk in contrast to the cookie-cutter couples; and Serafinowicz's meticulous affectations, which suggest psychotropic medication.

The concluding scenes are agonizing in the way they march through the stages dictated by an ages-old formula. We know all four couples must arrive at a crisis. We know their situations must appear dire. We expect a transitional event during which they realize the true nature of their feelings. This is a wild party night at East Eden. We expect sincere confessions of deep feelings. And we know there must be a jolly conclusion that wraps everything up.

In the context of the film, the jolly conclusion must be seen to be believed. Were all the transitional events anticipated, even planned, by the all-seeing Monsieur Marcel? Marcel hands each couple an animal representing their true inner animal spirits. These are carved from a dark wood, which I deduced after seeing the second, third, and fourth animals. The first was a rabbit, which looked like nothing else than a chocolate bunny. That would have been strange.

The Cove ★ ★ ★ ★

PG-13, 94 m., 2009

Featuring Richard O'Barry, Louie Psihoyos, Simon Hutchins, Mandy-Rae Cruickshank, Kirk Krack, David Rastovich, and Scott Baker. A documentary directed by Louie Psihoyos and produced by Fisher Stevens and Paula DuPre Pesman. Screenplay by Mark Monroe.

Flipper was smiling on the outside but crying on the inside. That's what Richard O'Barry thinks. He's the man who trained five dolphins for use on the *Flipper* TV show, and then began to question the way dolphins were used in captivity. In the years since, he has become an activist in the defense of captive dolphins exploited in places such as Sea World.

The dolphins who are captured are luckier than the thousands harpooned to death. In a hidden cove near the Japanese coastal village of Taiji, sonar is used to confuse dolphins and lead them into a cul-de-sac where they're trapped and killed. Since their flesh has such a high concentration of mercury that it's dangerous to eat, why slaughter them? To mislabel them as whale meat, that's why. Having long ignored global attempts to protect whales from being fished to extinction, the Japanese have found dolphins easier to find. But who would eat the meat? Japanese children, whose school lunches incredibly include mislabeled dolphin.

Is it necessary to mention that dolphins are not fish, but mammals? Indeed, they're among the most intelligent of mammals and seem naturally friendly toward man. They're even tool-users, employing sponges to protect their snouts in some situations, and teaching that learned behavior to their offspring.

The Cove, a heartbreaking documentary, describes how Richard O'Barry, director Louie Psihoyos, and a team of adventurers penetrated the tight security around the Taiji cove and obtained forbidden footage of the mass slaughter of dolphins. Divers were used to sneak cameras into the secret area; the cameras, designed by Industrial Light and Magic, were hidden inside fake rocks that blended with the landscape.

The logistics of their operation, captured by night vision cameras at times, has the danger and ingenuity of a caper film. The stakes are high: perhaps a year in prison. The footage will temper the enjoyment of your next visit to see performing dolphins.

It is an accident of evolution that dolphins seem to be smiling, the film informs us. They just happen to look that way. Their hearing is incredibly more acute than a human's, and the sounds of loudspeakers and recorded music, rebounding off the walls of their enclosures, can cause them anxiety and pain. O'Barry believes one of the dolphins he trained for *Flipper* literally died in his arms of depression.

There are many documentaries angry about the human destruction of the planetary peace. This is one of the very best—a certain Oscar nominee. It includes a great many facts about the craven International Whaling Commission and many insights into the mistreatment of dolphins; Simon Hutchins is especially helpful.

But when all of the facts have been marshaled and the cases made, one element of the film stands out above all, and that is the remorse of Richard O'Barry. He became rich and famous because of the TV series, which popularized and sanitized the image of captive dolphins. He has been trying for twenty-five years to make amends. But why, you may ask, are performing dolphins so willing to perform on cue? Well, you see, because they have to, if they want to eat.

The Crazies ★ ★ ½

R, 101 m., 2010

Timothy Olyphant (David Dutton), Radha Mitchell (Judy Dutton), Joe Anderson (Russell Clank), Danielle Panabaker (Becca Darling), Christie Lynn Smith (Deardra Farnum), Brett Rickaby (Bill Farnum), Preston Bailey (Nicholas), John Aylward (Mayor Hobbs). Directed by Breck Eisner and produced by Michael Aguilar, Rob Cowan, and Dean Georgaris. Screenplay by Scott Kosar and Ray Wright.

The Crazies is a perfectly competent genre film in a genre that has exhausted its interest for me, the zombie film. It provides such a convenient storytelling device: Large numbers of mindless zombies lurch toward the camera and the hero, wreaking savage destruction, and can be quickly blown away, although not without risk and occasional loss of life. When sufficient zombies have been run through, it's time for a new dawn.

I know there can be good zombie films. I've seen some: *Dawn of the Dead, 28 Days Later, Shaun of the Dead,* and so on. If I saw another one, I'd like it. But all depends on good living characters and a director with something new to say about zombies, who are a subject easily exhausted.

Are the zombies in *The Crazies* real zombies? Maybe, maybe not. Is there an agreed definition of what is a zombie, and how they get that way? Not that I know of. I think zombies are defined by behavior and can be "explained" by many handy shortcuts: the supernatural, radiation, a virus, space visitors, secret weapons, a Harvard education, and so on. I suppose it would be a "spoiler" if I revealed why the Crazies are lurching, but come on, does it matter? What if I revealed they got that way because of, oh, say, eating Pringles? Would that spoil things for you? What difference does it make? All that matters is that they got to be zombies *somehow*. Before that, they were your friends and neighbors. Then they started in on the damn Pringles.

The protagonists, of course, have to be healthy. I cannot imagine a zombie as a leading character. Vampires, now, I grant you. Werewolves. But a zombie doesn't bring much to the party. So we start in sweet little Ogden Marsh, Iowa, described on its Web site as "the friendliest place on Earth," and no wonder. Its sheriff is so good-looking he could be the star of this movie. Must be a quiet place. The sheriff's office is open only from eight to five Monday through Friday.

One day after work Sheriff David Dutton (Timothy Olyphant) and his deputy, Russell Clank (Joe Anderson), are watching a local school baseball game when the town drunk comes lurching into the outfield holding a shotgun. When the autopsy shows he had a 0.0 blood alcohol level, that's the first signal something is wrong in Ogden Marsh. For one thing, their town drunk is a slacker.

The sheriff's wife, Judy (Radha Mitchell), is the local doctor. She starts treating some strange cases. I don't want to spoil anything, so I'll simply say the sheriff and Deputy Russell discover the probable origin of this plague, but of course can't get the mayor to declare an emergency, because he learned the mayoring trade from *Jaws*. Meanwhile, it's up to Dave, Judy, and Russell to defend themselves from zombies and survive after the town is isolated and quarantined and the cure seems worse than the disease.

That requires many scenes involving people and objects that jump out from the sides of the screen with loud noises and alarming musical chords. I'm thinking, so what? The last thing I need is another jump out/loud noise/alarming chord movie. Even a well-made one—like this one, directed by Breck Eisner. It was inspired by George Romero's 1973 movie of the same name, although I can't tell you if the zombies match because that would be a spoiler.

Here is what I can say to aspiring young screenwriters: Movies like this are fairly simple to write. You need zombies. You need heroes. At first there's a mystery, and then the horror. You describe lots of jump/noise/chord situations. When you figure you're up to around ninety minutes, the sun can rise. You'll get an R rating, so throw in a little nudity. Not too much, because if there's a combination that gives me the creeps, it's zombies and nudity. Especially when—but never mind. That's enough for today.

Crazy Heart ★ ★ ★ ★

R, 112 m., 2009

Jeff Bridges (Bad Blake), Maggie Gyllenhaal (Jean Craddock), Robert Duvall (Wayne Kramer), Ryan Bingham (Tony), Colin Farrell (Tommy Sweet), James Keane (Manager). Directed by Scott Cooper and produced by T-Bone Burnett, Judy Cairo, Rob Carliner, Cooper, and Robert Duvall. Screenplay by Cooper, based on the novel by Thomas Cobb.

Some actors are blessed. Jeff Bridges is one of them. Ever since his first starring role in *The Last Picture Show* in 1971, he has, seemingly without effort, created a series of characters whom we simply believe, even the alien in *Starman*. He doesn't do this with mannerisms but with their exclusion; his acting is as clear as running water. Look at him playing Bad Blake in *Crazy Heart*. The notion of a broke-down, boozy country singer is an archetype in pop culture. We've seen this story before. The difference is, Bad Blake makes us believe it happened to *him*.

That's acting. There's a line of dialogue in the movie that I jotted down at the time, and it's been cited by several critics. Bad Blake is being interviewed in his shabby motel room by Jean Craddock (Maggie Gyllenhaal), a reporter for a newspaper in Santa Fe. She's taking him, gently, to places he doesn't want to go. He's been interviewed about the subject too many times. He doesn't say that. He says, "I want to talk about how bad you make this room look."

It's such a good line I can hardly believe I've never heard it before. Bad Blake perhaps knows it sounds like an old movie. It's also the kind of line written by a singer-songwriter, the masking of emotion by ironic displacement, the indirect apology for seedy circumstances. She blushes. I can't think of a better way for the movie to get to where it has to go next. No shy apologies. No cynicism. Just that he wrote a great line of a country song, and it was for her.

Bridges, Gyllenhaal, and Scott Cooper, the first-time writer-director, find that note all through the movie. It's like a country-and-western cliché happening for the first time. Bridges doesn't play drunk or hung over or newly in love in the ways we're accustomed to. It's like Bad has lived so long and been through so much that he's too worn out to add any spin to exactly the way he feels.

Bad Blake was a star once, years ago. He has lyrics that go, "I used to be somebody, but now I'm somebody else." His loyal manager (James Keane) once booked him in top venues. As *Crazy Heart* opens, Bad is pulling up to a bowling alley. "It's this year's *The Wrestler,*" one of my colleagues observed after the screening. Yes. Bad still has a few loyal fans, but you get the feeling they've followed him to the bottom. He has a son he's lost touch with, and he hasn't written a good song in a long time. In the old days he toured with a kid named Tommy Sweet (Colin Farrell). Now Tommy is a big star, but contrary to the conventions of such stories, hasn't forgotten his old teacher and remains loyal.

Maybe, we're thinking, with the love of a good woman he can turn it around. It's not that simple in *Crazy Heart.* Jean is a good woman, but can she afford to love this wreck twenty-five years older than she is? Certainly not if he continues to drink, and maybe not in any case. And it's not easy for Bad to stop drinking; he's descended below his bottom.

How does Bridges do this without making the character some sort of pitiful and self-pitying basket case? The presence of Robert Duvall here, playing his old friend and acting as one of the producers of this movie, is a reminder of Duvall's own *Tender Mercies* (1983), another great film about a has-been country singer and a good woman (Tess Harper). It's a measure of Bridges and Duvall, and Gyllenhaal and Harper, that they create completely different characters.

One of the ways the movie might have gone wrong is if the singing and the songs hadn't sounded right. They do. Bridges has an easy, sandpapery voice that sounds as if it's been through some good songs and good whiskey, and the film's original songs are by T-Bone Burnett and Stephen Bruton (who died of cancer in May 2009 at Burnett's home). Bridges conveys the difficult feelings of a singer keeping his dogged pride while performing in a bowling alley.

The movie knows more about alcoholism than many films do and has more of that wisdom onscreen, not least from the Duvall character. Gyllenhaal's character, too, is not an enabler or an alibi artist, but a woman who feels with her mind as well as her heart. Watch her as she and Bridges find the same level of mutual confidence for their characters. One of the reasons we trust the film is that neither Bad nor Jean is acting out illusions. Colin Farrell, too, is on the same page. We understand why he stays loyal, to the degree that he can. This is a rare story that knows people *don't* always forget those who helped them on the way up.

Jeff Bridges is a virtual certainty to win his first Oscar, after four nominations. The movie was once set for 2010 release (and before that, I hear, for going straight to cable). The more people saw it, the more they were convinced this was a great performance. Fox Searchlight stepped in, bought the rights, and screened it extensively in December for critics' groups, who all but unanimously voted for Bridges as the year's best actor. We're good for something.

Creation ★ ★ ★

PG-13, 108 m., 2010

Paul Bettany (Charles Darwin), Jennifer Connelly (Emma Darwin), Jeremy Northam (Rev. Innes), Toby Jones (Thomas Huxley), Benedict Cumberbatch (Joseph Hooker), Martha West (Annie Darwin). Directed by Jon Amiel and produced by Jeremy Thomas. Screenplay by John Collee, based on the book *Annie's Box* by Randal Keynes.

Darwin, it is generally agreed, had the most important idea in the history of science. Thinkers had been feeling their way toward it for decades, but it took Darwin to begin with an evident truth and arrive at its evident conclusion: Over the passage of many years, more successful organisms survive better than less successful. The result is the improvement of future generations. This process he called "natural selection."

It worked for bugs, birds, and bees. It worked for plants, fish, and trees. In 1859, when he published *On the Origin of Species,* it explained a great many things. Later, we would discover it even explained the workings of the cosmos. But—and here was the question even Darwin himself hesitated to ask—did it explain Man?

Emma Darwin didn't think so. Darwin's wife was a committed Christian who believed with her church that God alone was the author of Man. And for her it wasn't God as a general concept, but the specific God of Genesis, and he created Man exactly as the Old Testament said he did. He did it fairly recently, too, no matter that Darwin's fossils seemed to indicate otherwise.

Creation is a film about the way this disagreement played out in Darwin's marriage. Charles and Emma were married from 1830 until his death in 1882. They had ten children, seven of whom survived to beget descendants who even today have reunions. They loved each other greatly. Darwin at first avoided spelling out the implications for Man of the theory of evolution so as not to disturb her. But his readers could draw the obvious conclusion, and so could Emma: If God created Man, he did it in the way Darwin discovered, and not in the way a four-thousand-year-old legend prescribed.

The problems this created in the Darwin marriage were of interest primarily to Emma and Charles, probably their children, and few others except in the movie business, which seldom encounters an idea it can't dramatize in terms of romance. It helps to know that going in. *Creation* will give you an idea of the lives and times of the Darwins, but unless you bring a knowledge of evolution to the movie you may not leave with much of one.

The film stars the real-life couple Paul Bettany and Jennifer Connelly, as Charles and Emma, who a few years before the publication of *Origins* are grieving the death of their ten-year-old, Annie (Martha West). This loss has destroyed Darwin's remaining faith in God and reinforced his wife's. But it is to Charles that Annie reappears throughout the film, in visions, memories, and perhaps hallucinations.

The film suggests that Darwin was forced almost helplessly toward the implications of his theory. He had no particular desire to stir up religious turmoil, especially with himself as its target. He famously delayed publication of his theories as long as he could. Two close friends tell him he owes it to himself to publish, and Thomas Huxley, who called himself "Darwin's bulldog," tells him: "Congratulations, sir! You've killed God!"

Not every believer in evolution, including the pope, would agree. But Huxley's words are precisely those Darwin feared the most. Consider that he had no idea in the 1850s how irrefutably correct his theory was, and how useful it would be in virtually every hard science. Emma and their clergyman, Rev. Innes (Jeremy Northam), try to dissuade him from publishing, but his wife finally tells him to go ahead because he must. If he hadn't, someone would have: The theory of evolution was a fruit hanging ripe from the tree.

The director Jon Amiel tells his story with respect and some restraint, showing how sad and weakened Charles is and yet not ratcheting up his grief into unseemly melodrama. One beautiful device Amiel uses is a series of digressions into the natural world, in which we observe everyday applications of the survival of the fittest. What's often misunderstood is that Darwin was essentially speaking of the survival of the fittest genes, not the individual members of a species. This process took millions of years, and wasn't a case of humans slugging it out with dinosaurs.

Both Darwins understood and agreed about the role that inheritance (later to be known as genetics) played in health. As first cousins, they wondered if Annie's life expectancy had been compromised. She died of complications from scarlet fever, which wasn't their fault—but did they know and believe that?

I have a feeling that the loss of their child and the state of their marriage were what most interested the backers of this film. They must have wanted to make a film about Darwin the man, not Darwin the scientist. The filmmakers do their best to keep Darwin's theory in the picture, but it sadly isn't fit enough to struggle against the dominant species of Hollywood executives.

Cropsey ★ ★ ★

NO MPAA RATING, 84 m., 2010

Donna Cutugno, Karen Schweiger, David Novarro, and Ralph Aquino. A documentary directed by Joshua Zeman and Barbara Brancaccio and produced by Zeman, Brancaccio, and Zachary Mortensen. Screenplay by Zeman.

Cropsey is a creepy documentary with all the elements of a horror film about a demented serial killer, and an extra ingredient: This one is real, and you see him handcuffed in the film, not merely empty-eyed, shabby, and stooped, but actually drooling. "I've never seen a perp walk like that," says a TV newsman.

The killer's name is Andre Rand, and he's currently doing time in a New York penitentiary. He was the real-life embodiment of "Cropsey," a bogeyman who figured in the campfire stories and nightmares of many children in Pennsylvania, New Jersey, and along the Eastern Seaboard. In the legends, he lived in the woods and ventured out to abduct children. In the early 1980s, Rand was convicted for the kidnapping and murder of two young girls and suspected in the disappearance of three more.

The man fit the legend. Andre Rand was a worker in the Willowbrook State School for the mentally handicapped on Staten Island, a New York borough isolated from the city for many years before a bridge was constructed. Willowbrook, one of the largest mental institutions in the world, was also one of the worst; Geraldo Rivera won fame for a TV special with footage of its half-naked children scattered on the floor, rocking back and forth in misery. Sanitary facilities were pitiful, filth was everywhere, abuse was common. Willowbrook was shut down, but some of its staff and inmates returned, living in a forgotten network of tunnels under the grounds. Among these was Andre Rand.

Already convicted of sexual abuse against a minor, he attracted the attention of searchers after the disappearance of Jennifer Schweiger, a young girl with Down syndrome. Rand was then living in a campsite on the heavily forested grounds of Willowbrook, and was arrested on suspicion. The charges were expanded to include the disappearance of little Holly Ann Hughes.

He made an ideal suspect. Rumors spread of Satan worship in the tunnels. Staten Island was convinced. He was a bogeyman from central casting. There were only a few problems. There was no physical evidence. Jennifer Schweiger's body was found, but here's the funny thing: The grounds of Willowbrook were combed by hundreds of police and volunteers who found nothing, and then a later search found a grave so shallow a hand was sticking out of the earth. It was near Rand's campsite. It wasn't found on the earlier search, and he'd been in jail ever since.

Was he framed? Did he have a partner in murder? Was some eyewitness testimony suspect because he'd already been convicted in the public eye? *Cropsey* raises these questions in a doc that interviews the original detectives on the case, Jennifer's parents, Rand's defense attorneys, and members of the public. It surrounds this footage with the sparse available video of Rand, and uses many letters Rand wrote to the filmmakers claiming his innocence and suggesting unanswered questions.

The people of Staten Island heard in the film seem unconcerned by the possibility of Rand's innocence. They ask, Would you feel safe knowing that man was roaming free? No, but that alone is not the best reason for locking someone away. At the end I was prepared to agree that Rand seemed like an awfully convincing suspect if he happened to be innocent.

I was reminded of the continuing outrage of the West Memphis Three. Three teenagers were arrested, tried, and convicted amid hysterical rumors they were Satanists who sacrificed young boys. This in the face of their alibis and actual physical evidence suggesting the identity of another possible killer, who makes self-incriminating statements in two famous documentaries about the case, *Paradise Lost* and *Paradise Lost 2: Revelations.* Sometimes a perfect suspect is not guilty.

Crossing Over ★ ★ ½

R, 114 m., 2009

Harrison Ford (Max Brogan), Ray Liotta (Cole Frankel), Ashley Judd (Denise Frankel), Jim Sturgess (Gavin Kossef), Cliff Curtis (Hamid Baraheri), Alice Braga (Mireya Sanchez), Alice Eve (Claire Sheperd), Justin Chon (Yong Kim), Summer Bishil (Taslima Jahangir), Ogechi Egonu (Alike). Directed by Wayne Kramer and produced by Frank Marshall. Screenplay by Kramer.

We spend a lot of time talking about the American Dream and have too much suspicion about those who want to live it. Feelings against immigrants are so freely expressed even in polite society that you'd think they all came here for the free lunch. *Crossing Over* creates a mosaic, too simplistic to be sure, of recent arrivals who came here for admirable reasons and will be valuable citizens if they get the chance. Most of them will, anyway. Some were damaged goods at home and have not traveled well.

It is hard to immigrate to this country legally and potentially fatal to do it illegally. That's why I speculate we get some of the best and the brightest; it takes determination, ambition, and skill to get into America either way. Many of those who arrive want to improve themselves, and in the process they will improve us.

I've been taking a lot of cabs the last couple of years, and I've noticed something. Most of the drivers are obviously immigrants, from India, Pakistan, Africa, the Philippines, the Middle East, and the Americas. Without a single exception they all have their car radios tuned to the same station, the best station we have, National Public Radio. It tells you something.

Crossing Over borrows the structure of *Crash* to tell interlocking stories about several immigrants, their problems, and their families. All of their lives connect in some way, if only through U.S. immigration officials. *Crash* wove its pattern fairly naturally. *Crossing Over* seems to strain, with too many characters, too many story strands, and too much of an effort to cover the bases. We meet immigrants new and established, legal and illegal, from Mexico, Nigeria, Bangladesh, Iran, England, Korea, and Australia. It feels like a list.

The connecting links are two immigration officers played by Harrison Ford and Cliff Curtis, an adjudicator (Ray Liotta), and an immigration defense attorney (Ashley Judd). The stories involve a Mexican woman separated from her child in a raid; an Iranian family, well established, which is about to be naturalized; a Muslim teenager who attracts an FBI investigation by reading an outspoken (but legitimate) paper about 9/11 in class; a Korean teenager (Justin Chon) who is being pressured to join a Korean gang; an Australian would-be actress; an atheist Jew from the United Kingdom who poses as a teacher whose presence is needed in a Hebrew school; and a little Nigerian orphan who has been stranded in a holding center and will be sent back to Africa and danger.

Some of these stories are fascinating and some are heartbreaking, but together they seem too contrived. It's too neat the way they mingle, like the traffic on freeway interchanges seen in overhead shots that separate the passages. I was especially moved by Ford's involvement with the Mexican woman (Alice Braga), who is hauled away pleading with him to retrieve her child from the babysitter. He plays a decent man whose conscience won't let him forget, and he ends up uniting the child with grandparents in Mexico. And there's more to it than that. It's hard for him to leave his job at work.

Harrison Ford supplies the strong central strand in the story, but sometimes it grows so implausibly melodramatic we're distracted. Ashley Judd's character provides insights in the way our legal system handles immigration, and the Australian actress (Alice Eve) shows what she is willing to do for the venal official (Liotta) who happens to be Judd's husband. There is a contrast between an Iranian father who thinks of himself as a good Muslim, and a daughter (Summer Bishil) who thinks of herself as a good Muslim and a good American.

Yes, the film is "flawed"—that prissy film critic's complaint. If you're looking for plausibility and resist manipulation, you'll object to it. But sometimes movies are intriguing despite their faults, and you want to keep on watching. This one is like that.

Cyrus ★ ★ ★ ½

R, 91 m., 2010

John C. Reilly (John), Jonah Hill (Cyrus), Marisa Tomei (Molly), Catherine Keener (Jamie), Matt Walsh (Tim). Directed by Mark Duplass and Jay Duplass and produced by Michael Costigan. Screenplay by Mark Duplass and Jay Duplass.

Marisa Tomei plays warm and friendly as well as anyone, and those qualities are essential to *Cyrus,* a film about her grown son and her new boyfriend waging what amounts to war over the possession of her body. There's no incest, but a photo in her bedroom suggests the son was still getting to second base well into his adolescence. The boyfriend is pathetically happy to get on base at all, and this creates a comedy of awkwardness, private thoughts, passive aggression, and veiled hostility. All Molly (Tomei) wants is for everybody to like one another and get along.

Her boyfriend, John (John C. Reilly), is fine with that goal, but her son, Cyrus (Jonah Hill), is jealous and possessive, and very intelligent about how to use his feelings in a sneaky way, so it's not always obvious what he's up to. Not obvious to Molly, anyway, because she doesn't really want to know. More obvious to John, who's on such thin ice he's slow to admit how unpleasant the situation has become.

I can imagine how a sex comedy could spring from this premise, or even an Oedipal drama. What's intriguing about *Cyrus* is the way it sort of sits back and observes an emotional train wreck as it develops. The movie doesn't eagerly jump from one payoff to another, but attunes itself to nuance, body language, and the habitual politeness with which we try to overlook social embarrassment. With only three people, however, it's a problem when one is deliberately creating embarrassment.

Jonah Hill, who is a fairly large man, is able to morph himself somehow into a big baby here; he cleverly uses immature conduct to excuse inappropriate behavior. When he hugs his mommy, for example, there's the not-so-slight suggestion that he does so not as her son but as her smoocher. There's no suggestion that actual sex has ever been involved, but to poor John (and to us), he's over the top. Molly seems oblivious.

Cyrus pretends to welcome and like John. His very welcome outreaches the bounds of propriety. Then little things happen. John's shoes disappear. If Cyrus took them, he could easily throw them away. But *whoever* took them, they're left where they will eventually be found, a ticking time bomb. Little things like that.

Marisa Tomei has the trickiest role here. She's lonely, she's been single too long, and she likes John, the big lug. She befriends him at a party where he's desperately unhappy. She discovers him peeing in the shrubbery and says what, under these circumstances, is a remarkably tactful thing to relieve the embarrassment: "Nice penis." He needs a woman like this. He's apart from his first wife (Catherine Keener), who was maybe too smart for him. Molly isn't dumb, but she's—well, sometimes she's improbably clueless. She is also very sexy, so you can understand that a boy the age of Cyrus (but not her son) would be attracted. That avoids possible Eww Moments.

Cyrus was written and directed by the Duplass brothers, Mark and Jay, who up until now have been identified with "mumblecore," a term I hope I never have to use again. Let's put it this way: If a movie is mumblecore, it probably doesn't much want to be enjoyed, and if it isn't, why call it failed mumblecore? Their previous film, *Baghead* (2008), was not beloved by me. Now here is a film that uses very good actors and gives them a lot of improvisational freedom to talk their way into, around, and out of social discomfort. And it's not snarky. It doesn't mock these characters. It understands they have their difficulties and hopes they find a way to work things out. There's your suspense: How can they?

D

Daddy Longlegs ★ ★ ★

NO MPAA RATING, 100 m., 2010

Ronnie Bronstein (Lenny), Sage Ranaldo (Sage), Frey Ranaldo (Frey), Victor Puccio (Principal Puccio), Eleonore Hendricks (Leni), Leah Singer (Paige), Sean Williams (Dale). Directed by Josh Safdie and Benny Safdie and produced by Casey Neistat and Tom Scott. Screenplay by Josh Safdie and Benny Safdie.

Lenny isn't a bad father. He's no father at all. He doesn't understand the concept. I don't believe he ever will. He doesn't understand being an adult. He doesn't understand anything. The question at the heart of *Daddy Longlegs* is, why did his former wife ever think she could trust him with two weeks a year of child custody? Lenny shouldn't even have custody of himself.

He's in constant motion during *Daddy Longlegs.* If he has role models at all, they're provided by his two sons, Sage and Frey. Lenny acts like their playmate, not their father. "Guys," he calls them. "Guys." I heard him call Sage by name once. Frey, I don't remember even once. They are a unit, the Child Unit, to be plunged into his idea of a good time.

Lenny is played by Ronnie Bronstein, who directed *Frownland,* a 2008 film about a man all bottled up inside. Lenny is the opposite. He projects an almost relentless upbeat enthusiasm, until sometimes he loses it and we see the anger. He tries to babysit the kids, who are five and seven, while at the same time working as a movie projectionist and dating, or breaking up, with his current girlfriend (Eleonore Hendricks). With one kid riding his shoulders and another tagging behind, he rushes out on unclear missions.

For parents, this may play like a horror film. At one point he actually gives these two children fifty-five dollars and sends them by themselves to a supermarket some blocks away in New York City to buy supplies for dinner. At another time, he talks a complete stranger into taking the three of them along on a trip with her boyfriend to upstate New York.

He jumps on the bed with the "guys" and wrestles them. He forgets to pick them up after school. He takes them to work and they print out a thousand Xeroxes. And then, in an unbelievable act of criminal irresponsibility, he figures out a way for them to stay out of trouble for two, maybe three days, while his big mouth manages to get himself arrested.

The Safdie brothers, Benny and Josh, have a dedication on the film that may or may not refer to their own father. Their cinematic father is obviously John Cassavetes, whose own manic heroes ran crazy loops around their lives. If *Daddy Longlegs* is influenced by Cassavetes, well, that's not a bad thing. Few filmmakers have the nerve to travel that path.

Bronstein's performance is crucial. It's difficult to make a manic character plausible, but he does. He never goes over the top. His mania seems devoted more to lifting off from the bottom. How he ever convinced his wife (Leah Singer) to marry him is hard to explain, most of all, probably, to herself.

Note: This film is available in some markets via Video on Demand.

The Damned United ★ ★ ★ ½

R, 97 m., 2009

Michael Sheen (Brian Clough), Timothy Spall (Peter Taylor), Colm Meaney (Don Revie), Henry Goodman (Manny Cussins), Maurice Roeves (Jimmy Gordon), Jim Broadbent (Sam Longson), Stephen Graham (Billy Bremner), Brian McCardie (Dave Mackay). Directed by Tom Hooper and produced by Andy Harries and Grainne Marmion. Screenplay by Peter Morgan, based on the 2006 novel *The Damned Utd* by David Peace.

Imagine if Al Lopez, not long after leading the White Sox to their pennant, had resigned to take Casey Stengel's job at the Yankees, insulted the players and fans, and plummeted the team into a losing streak. That would parallel the career of Brian Clough, who led the underdog Derby County to British football glory, and then took the manager's job at its hated archrival, Leeds United, and informed the players they were hooligans.

That we haven't heard of Brian Clough in

this country is no reason not to see *The Damned United,* the story of a man and the nature of professional sports. Football, known as soccer on this side of the waves, inflames passions in a way unknown to American football fans. To insult a Brit's team is to defame his mother. It's more democratic than U.S. football, because all it really requires to play is a ball. What must they think of us around the world when they witness pro football with its fearsome protective equipment and brief spurts of activity? "How do you find the *patience* to watch it?" I was asked by a London friend. I countered with cricket, the nearest thing in sports to a timeout.

Clough was the youngest manager in history when he took over Derby County. He was funny and friendly, and once before a match tousled the hair of a young man and told him, "You will never forget this day." That fan grew up to be the novelist David Peace, who wrote *The Damned Utd* about the Shakespearean tragedy of Clough.

Clough was a helpless partisan. He identified with Derby so deeply that when he took over Leeds it became almost an act of revenge. Even as their leader, he hated them. And he was stepping into the shoes of their legendary manager Don Revie, who had been named manager of the English national team. Revie, who once neglected to shake his hand after a match. He hated Leeds, Revie, and the team's management, and it's believed by some that Leeds players deliberately lost matches to sabotage him.

The enigma of Brian Clough has long fascinated British fans. *The Damned United* offers no easy explanation, but plunges into the mysteries of the personality. It stars Michael Sheen, who now in three films has embodied modern British icons so uncannily that he's all but disappeared into them. He was Prime Minister Tony Blair in *The Queen,* David Frost in *Frost/Nixon,* and now Brian Clough. He completes these transformations largely without the disguise of makeup, primarily by seeming so intensely *them. The Damned United* again unites Sheen with screenwriter Peter Morgan and producer Andy Harries of the other two. Tom Hooper directs.

Clough is a nervous man. His passion eats at him. During one match with Leeds, he cannot force himself onto the field, but remains in the locker room, trying to interpret the cheers of the crowd. His tortured psyche gains a measure of balance from Peter Taylor (Timothy Spall), his loyal assistant, who is quiet, wise, and prudent, and acts as his drag anchor. Tactless to the core, Clough insults this good man, who doesn't follow him to Leeds. That is the start of his undoing.

Spall is one of three first-rank supporting actors who bring the film richness. Colm Meaney plays Revie, a Woody Hayes or Vince Lombardi type who has the confidence of royalty. Jim Broadbent plays Sam Longson, owner of Derby, who is a Jerry Reinsdorf type, if you see what I mean. At some level, professional sports must be considered, after all, as a retail business.

The Damned United avoids all sports movie clichés, even the obligatory ending where the team comes from behind. Is this the first sports movie where the hero comes from ahead and loses? David Peace says before writing his novel he reread the great proletarian Angry Young Men fictions circa 1960, such as *Look Back in Anger, Saturday Night and Sunday Morning,* and *Loneliness of the Long Distance Runner.* He has a hero who is most comfortable as underdog—indeed, almost needs to be.

The film is not primarily concerned with showing the game. It skillfully uses some archival footage, which evokes the pitch of feeling during a match. Soccer crowds are a mass of unanimous emotion and not so much a collection of individuals. Fans lose themselves in the surging collective like Japanese men at an annual festival of a god.

The film focuses squarely on Brian Clough. We sense what wounded love his admirers felt. He was so good, so true, and fell so swiftly after joining the other side; today in Britain, all you have to do is mention "the forty-four days" and everyone will know you mean Clough's brief tenure at the damned Leeds United. *Therefore the flight shall perish from the swift, and the strong shall not strengthen his force, neither shall the mighty deliver himself.*

Note: In educating myself about Brian Clough, I came across an extraordinary passage by William Thomas in Empire *magazine. He writes that soccer is "a sport that defeats a cinematic treatment—that swift, Brownian motion transformed into Keystone Cop capering as soon as a camera rolls."*

"Brownian motion"? I looked it up on Wikipedia: "the seemingly random movement of particles suspended in a fluid (e.g., a liquid or gas)." Yes! The players on a soccer field are guided at all times by their own free will—unlike American football, with its offensive plays and defensive patterns. The whole field is always in play. The action is too quick on too large a scale to be contained on a screen. Thomas explains something I'd wondered about but never articulated.

Date Night ★ ★ ★ ½

PG-13, 88 m., 2010

Steve Carell (Phil Foster), Tina Fey (Claire Foster), Mark Wahlberg (Holbrooke), Taraji P. Henson (Detective Arroyo), Common (Collins), James Franco (Taste), Mila Kunis (Whippit), Ray Liotta (Mob Boss). Directed by Shawn Levy and produced by Levy and Tom McNulty. Screenplay by Josh Klausner.

Steve Carell and Tina Fey play a nice, unassuming couple in *Date Night,* and that's one of the reasons the movie works so well. Their Phil and Claire Foster are a normal, overworked, sincere, good-natured New Jersey couple whose lives have become routine. But they love each other, and all they really want is to hire a babysitter and enjoy a nice night out on the town.

We believe that. We're halfway prepared for a low-key romantic comedy when all hell breaks loose. They pretend to be an absent couple in order to grab a reservation at a trendy restaurant, and two hit men assume they *are* that couple and topple them into a screwball comedy. Yet all the time Phil and Claire seem like the kind of people who don't belong in a screwball comedy. That's why it's funny. They're bewildered.

Date Night supplies them with the *real* Tripplehorns (James Franco and Mila Kunis), two mob-employed cops (Jimmi Simpson and Common), a mob boss (Ray Liotta), and a muscular security expert (Mark Wahlberg) who never wears a shirt. These characters are also somewhat believable. Plots like this have a way of spinning over the top with insane, manic behavior. It's as if the characters are desperately signaling, "Look at us! Aren't we hilarious?" But the audience has to bring hilarity to you. It can't be assumed.

So what we have is a situation set in motion because a couple named the Tripplehorns don't turn up for a restaurant reservation. The Fosters, mistaken for the Tripplehorns, find themselves in way over their heads with the Tripplehorns' potentially fatal problems. The criminal characters aren't simply stupid, but bright enough to perceive this causes a problem for everyone. And the security agent (Wahlberg) is not simply a muscle-bound goon. He's a caricature, all right, but one living in a condo out of *Architectural Digest* and capable of feeling some sympathy for these pathetic New Jerseyites who've lost their way.

Carell and Fey are both natural comic performers who know (as Second City teaches) that a comedian must never seem to know that it's funny. They play Phil and Claire as nearly as possible like plausible people trapped by this nightmare misunderstanding. Yes, things heat up a little, and yes, there is an obligatory chase scene, and yes, it's a little unlikely how they end up appealing to the security expert. That goes with the territory.

But they know, as great comic actors like Cary Grant and Jack Lemmon knew, that their job in a comedy is to behave with as much realism as possible and let the impossibilities whirl around them. To begin with, Carell and Fey *look* like they might be a pleasant married couple. Attractive, but not improbably so. Young, but not that young. Fit, but they don't reveal unexpected skills. And frightened when they need to be. Do you ever wonder why the characters in some movies are never gobsmacked in the face of what seems like certain death?

All of this is a way of saying that *Date Night* is funny because, against all odds, it is involving. Each crazy step in the bizarre plot made a certain sense because it followed from what went before; it's like the Scorsese masterpiece *After Hours.* The director is Shawn Levy, who committed the two *Night at the Museum* movies, and here shows that he is much more successful when he stays far away from CGI. Remember that he also made the entertaining

Cheaper by the Dozen with Steve Martin and Bonnie Hunt as a hard-pressed married couple.

A movie like *Date Night* encourages Hollywood comedy to occasionally dial down and realize that comedy emerges from characters and situations and can't be manufactured from manic stunts and overkill. If you don't start out liking the Fosters and hoping they have a really nice date night, not much else is going to work.

Daybreakers ★ ★ ½

R, 98 m., 2010

Ethan Hawke (Edward Dalton), Willem Dafoe (Elvis), Claudia Karvan (Audrey Bennett), Michael Dorman (Frankie Dalton), Vince Colosimo (Christopher Caruso), Isabel Lucas (Alison Bromley), Sam Neill (Charles Bromley). Directed by Peter Spierig and Michael Spierig and produced by Chris Brown, Bryan Furst, and Sean Furst. Screenplay by the Spierig brothers.

Ten years in the future, a global epidemic has infected most of the population with vampirism. The few remaining humans are on the run, hunted down by the militant Vampire Army, which doesn't hate them but mostly is just hungry. This depletion of the planet's food supply might be an opening for a parable about our dwindling resources, but no: Instead of making the humans a breeding stock for blood harvesting as practiced by the giant Bromley Marks Corp., the army members eat them. Al Gore must have a chart showing how that's self-defeating.

Bromley Marks is a major supplier of human blood, but is spending a fortune to develop a synthetic blood substitute. Like so many big companies in agribusiness, it wants to wean us off that healthy organic food and sell us a substitute, no doubt sweetened by corn syrup. The B-M's chief hematologist is Edward (Ethan Hawke), who like some of the atomic scientists at Los Alamos feels guilty about his work. He pushes for a cure for vampirism, not just a handy new product.

That sets the stage for this grave new world where life is designed to be lived at night. Underground moving walkways replace sidewalks, curfew starts before dawn, and so on. Edward has ethics and believes it is wrong to exploit comatose humans for their blood. He's one of those damned lefties who years ago probably was against eating beef. He's a vampire with a conscience.

Edward hooks up with the human underground, notably the cute Audrey (Claudia Karvan), and is introduced to Lionel, code name Elvis (Willem Dafoe), who has a cheap and easy vampirism antidote but is being hunted by Edward's hothead brother Frankie (Michael Dorman), because—I dunno. Because Frankie's not about to give up blood for a healthier lifestyle, I guess.

The movie, directed by Australia's twin Spierig brothers (*Undead,* 2003), looks good in its gray, sunless scenes evoking twilight (cough). The newspapers and TV anchors report on hopes for a vaccine, apparently because the constant demands of vampirism maintenance are a grind. Imagine if the price of blood was beyond the pocketbook of the average family of four, and you had to go out human hunting every day to feed the kids. A homeless person holds up a cardboard sign: "Hungry. Will work for blood."

This intriguing premise, alas, ends as so many movies do these days, with fierce fights and bloodshed. Inevitably, the future of the planet will be settled among the handful of characters we've met and a lot of extras with machine guns. I guess, but can't be sure, that audiences will enjoy the way these vampires die. They don't shrivel up into Mr. and Mrs. Havisham but explode, spraying blood all over everyone. Toward the end, their heads blow off like human champagne corks. Well, not human.

Dead Snow ★ ★ ½

NO MPAA RATING, 91 m., 2009

Vegar Hoel (Martin), Stig Frode Henriksen (Roy), Charlotte Frogner (Hanna), Lasse Valdal (Vegard), Evy Kasseth Rosten (Liv), Jeppe Beck Laursen (Erlend), Orjan Gamst (Colonel Herzog). Directed by Tommy Wirkola and produced by Tomas Evjen and Terje Stromstad. Screenplay by Wirkola and Stig Frode Henriksen.

They've finally assembled a horror film entirely from clichés. They even know they're doing it. As a carload of young medical students drives to a secluded cabin in a snowy forest, they find their cell phones don't work. "That's just like *Friday the 13th,*" one says but is corrected: "*They didn't have cell phones then.*"

Yes, they are in a cabin so far in the woods, they have to leave their car behind and follow snowmobile tracks, all except for Sara, who decides to trek overland. We suspect Sara will not be getting a lot of dialogue in this movie. The others settle in and break out the beer but are disturbed by a scary, whiskery old-timer who warns them of a vicious Nazi unit that lurked in these mountains during the war, *and probably froze to death.* Not with seventy-five minutes left in the movie, they didn't.

But how would the Nazis survive until the present day? Well, of course they are zombies, which the kids recognize when their cabin is attacked by shambling decaying men in Nazi uniforms. This crisis throws the threatened students into overdrive, clicking off as many items from *Ebert's Little Movie Glossary* as they possibly can.

I will not list all of them because to do so would summarize the plot. I was especially happy to hear "Let's split up," and later, after two girls wander off alone, to hear them discuss splitting up themselves. One bitter student says, "We should have gone to the beach like I said." I do not recall if he is the same one who sets his backpack on fire to cauterize his wound after amputating his own arm with the obligatory chainsaw.

One thing about the director, Tommy Wirkola. He's thrifty. Once his actors have their faces completely spattered with blood, he lets it stay on for hours. Your average medical students, when they get splattered with blood, they clean it off. It's part of their training. Especially with zombie blood.

One girl, wearing bright red, tries to hide from the Nazi zombies by climbing a tree. Remember that in winter there are no leaves. Yet the zombies, who are not the swiftest corpses in the mortuary, miss spotting her red ski jacket until she disturbs the eggs in a crow's nest, the crow screeches at her, and the Nazis hear her shushing it. In my opinion, shushing a crow is a fool's errand.

But practical details should not concern us. Particularly not after one of the guys disembowels a Nazi and then another Nazi grabs him and they both topple off a high cliff, but the guy holds on by grabbing the dead Nazi's large intestine, which is many yards long. If you have a large intestine that will support the weight of two men, you can forget about the colonoscopy. Apparently zombies evolve such intestines, since when a disemboweled human is seen earlier in the film, he is clearly grasping greasy frankfurter links.

Dead Snow, as you may have gathered, is a comedy, but played absolutely seriously by sincere, earnest young actors. At no point, for example, do they notice that the snow is dead. The movie is pretty funny. One of the guys discovers his cell phone is working and calls 911. "We've been attacked by what look like Germans from the Second World War!" he shouts. "And we set our cabin on fire by accident!" He removes his phone from his ear and stares at it vengefully: "The bitch hung up on me!"

The film comes to us from Norway, which no doubt explains the snow. Nazi ski patrols did once haunt these slopes. It is the second feature by the director-writer team of Tommy Wirkola and Stig Frode Henriksen. Their first film was a satire of Tarantino's *Kill Bill* named *Kill Buljo: The Movie* ("In Kautokeino no one can hear you scream"). If *Mystery Science Theater 3000* had never existed, *Dead Snow* would have had to invent it.

Dear John ★ ★

PG-13, 105 m., 2010

Channing Tatum (John Tyree), Amanda Seyfried (Savannah Curtis), Henry Thomas (Tim), Scott Porter (Randy), Richard Jenkins (Mr. Tyree). Directed by Lasse Hallstrom and produced by Marty Bowen, Wyck Godfrey, and Ryan Kavanaugh. Screenplay by Jamie Linden, based on a novel by Nicholas Sparks.

Lasse Hallstrom's *Dear John* tells the heartbreaking story of two lovely young people who fail to find happiness together because they're trapped in an adaptation of a Nicholas Sparks novel. Their romance leads to bittersweet loss that's so softened by the sweet characters that it feels like triumph. If a Sparks story ended in happiness, the characters might be disappointed. They seem to have their noble, resigned dialogue already written. Hemingway wrote one line that could substitute for the third act of every Sparks story: "Isn't it pretty to think so?"

Channing Tatum stars as John Tyree, a handsome Army Special Forces specialist home on two weeks' leave at the South Carolina shore. Amanda Seyfried plays Savannah, an ethereal beauty whose purse falls off a pier. John dives in and retrieves it, and we guess it could have been worse. He could have gotten her kitten down from a tree. In the few precious days they share, they fall deeply into PG-13 love.

John was raised by his father (Richard Jenkins), a quiet man who wears white gloves while admiring his coin collection, and cooks chicken every Saturday and lasagna every Sunday. Savannah meets him and casually observes to John that he is autistic—a mild case, she gently suggests. John is angered by this insult. Did he never, by the age of twenty-two, observe that his father was strangely mannered? Did no one else? What was his (now absent) mother's thinking? Did the movie mention any employment history for Mr. Tyree? I could have missed it.

In a Sparks story, as we know from *The Notebook,* problems like autism and Alzheimer's are never seen in their tragic stages, but always allow the good souls of their victims to visibly glow. Diseases don't destroy and kill, but exist primarily to inspire admirable conduct by nexts of kin. John and Savannah get over his unhappiness, and he pledges that he'll be back at the end of twelve months so they can wed.

But then 9/11 happens, and like every man in his group he re-enlists. And continues to reenlist until the movie's title hints at what he receives in the mail. Because Savannah is a true-blue heroine, her new love is of course a nice and decent man, someone John can accept, so that we can smile sadly and not get all messy and depressed. That's the note Sparks aims for: the sad smile. First love is not to be, but the moon still looks so large when it rises, and people treat each other gently, and if someone should die, that is very sad, but perhaps it will provide an opportunity for someone else to live a little longer before they, too, must travel to that undiscovered country from whose bourne no traveler ever returns.

John and Savannah are awfully nice. She comes from a rich family who have a mansion, and John and his dad live in a humble but cozy frame house that in its South Carolina island location might easily be purchased for less than $500,000. That would leave a portion of Mr. Tyree's unspecified income free to invest in rare coins and amass a collection worth a fortune. I am just enough of a numismatist to know that you need to invest money to collect rare coins. You don't just find them in your spare change.

I know I'm being snarky. I don't get much pleasure from it. *Dear John* exists only to coddle the sentiments of undemanding dreamers, and plunge us into a world where the only evil is the interruption of the good. Of course John is overseas on a series of missions so secret that Savannah cannot be told where, exactly, he is. In the years after 9/11, where, oh where, could he be? Apparently not in Iraq or Afghanistan, because it can hardly be a military secret that the men of Special Forces are deployed there. But somewhere, anyway, and he re-enlists for a good chunk of her early childbearing years, perhaps because, as *The Hurt Locker* informs us, "war is a drug."

It matters not. In this movie, war is a plot device. It loosens its grip on John only long enough to sporadically renew his romance, before claiming him again so that we finally consider Savannah's Dear John letter just good common sense. And now that I've brought that up: Considering that the term "Dear John Letter" has been in constant use since World War II, and that the hero of this movie is inevitably destined to receive such a letter, is it a little precious of Sparks to name him "John"? I was taught in Dan Curley's fiction class that when the title of a story is repeated in the story itself, the story's spell is broken. But then Sparks never took Curley's class.

Death at a Funeral ★ ★ ★ ½

R, 92 m., 2010

Chris Rock (Aaron), James Marsden (Oscar), Loretta Devine (Cynthia), Peter Dinklage (Frank), Martin Lawrence (Ryan), Regina Hall

(Michelle), Zoe Saldana (Elaine), Kevin Hart (Brian), Danny Glover (Uncle Russell), Keith David (Reverend Davis), Ron Glass (Duncan), Tracy Morgan (Norman), Columbus Short (Jeff), Luke Wilson (Derek), Regine Nehy (Martina). Directed by Neil LaBute and produced by William Horberg, Sidney Kimmel, Laurence Malkin, Chris Rock, and Share Stallings. Screenplay by Dean Craig.

Oh, I know a lot of *Death at a Funeral* is in very bad taste. That's when I laughed the most. I don't laugh at movies where the characters are deliberately being vulgar. But when they desperately don't want to be—now that's funny. Consider the scene when Uncle Russell eats too much nut cake and is seized by diarrhea. And Norman wrestles him off his wheelchair and onto the potty, and gets his hand stuck underneath. Reader, I laughed. I'm not saying I'm proud of myself. That's not the way I was raised. But I laughed.

I laughed all the way through, in fact. This is the best comedy since *The Hangover,* and although it's almost a scene-by-scene remake of a 2007 British movie with the same title, it's funnier than the original. For the character of Frank, the mysterious guest who wants to speak privately with the dead man's sons, it even uses the same actor, Peter Dinklage, and he's funnier this time. Maybe that's because when a comedy gets on a roll, everything is funnier.

The funeral is taking place at home, because that's how the deceased wanted it. Also living at home are his oldest son, Aaron (Chris Rock), Aaron's wife, Michelle (Regina Hall), and his mother, Cynthia (Loretta Devine). Both Michelle and Cynthia are on his case for having not yet fathered a child. Aaron dreams of publishing a novel, while his younger brother Ryan (Martin Lawrence) has published several, which sound like porn to me, but hey, they're in print.

The mourners arrive after various adventures of the cadaver, and get into all sorts of bizarre and dire trouble in ways that the screenplay carefully explains. How was Elaine (Zoe Saldana) to know that a bottle labeled "Valium" contained a next-generation hallucinogen when she gave one to her boyfriend, Oscar (James Marsden)? It's an old gag, the guy accidentally freaked out on drugs, but Marsden elevates it to bizarre heights with a rubber face that reflects horror, delight, nausea, and affection more or less simultaneously.

There's no use in my providing a blow-by-blow of the plot, since it's deliriously screwball and it doesn't much matter what happens, as long as something always is. But I can mention what deft timing and high energy this cast has, each actor finding the rhythm for each character instead of all racing about in manic goofiness. Dinklage, for example, is as good at playing dead serious as Tommy Lee Jones, and here he's always on tone for a man who has come for compelling personal reasons. The brothers and Norman don't really wish harm to befall him, but you can see how it does. Then there is a certain logic to how they react. They're only human.

Loretta Devine has a possibly thankless role as the surviving matriarch, but her timing is delicious as she associates the death of a husband with the absence of a grandchild. Both Regina Hall and Zoe Saldana are steadfast in their love in the midst of chaos, and Danny Glover goes over the top as the cantankerous uncle because, well, that's what the role requires.

British actors are rightly known for their skill, and there were some good ones in the 2007 version of the same Dean Craig screenplay. But playing proper upper-crust characters tends to restrain them. The family in *Death at Funeral* is obviously wealthy, but loose—more human. Their emotions are closer to the surface, and these actors work together like a stock company.

Notice, too, the way director Neil LaBute directs traffic. Because the action is screwball doesn't mean it can be confusing. Screwball depends crucially on our knowing where key characters are, and why. LaBute juggles parallel actions in the big family home so we understand who's in the bathroom and who's in the living room and why everybody is out on the lawn. There's a smooth logic to it that works like spatial punch lines.

LaBute is a brilliant playwright and director who is usually the director of very dark comedies (*In the Company of Men, Your Friends and Neighbors*). But a good director is a good director, and LaBute here, like David Gordon

Green with *Pineapple Express*, masters the form. And oooh, that's a mean line about R. Kelly.

Defiance ★ ★ ½

R, 136 m., 2009

Daniel Craig (Tuvia Bielski), Liev Schreiber (Zus Bielski), Jamie Bell (Asael Bielski), Alexa Davalos (Lilka Ticktin), Allan Corduner (Shimon Haretz), Mark Feuerstein (Isaac Malbin), Mia Wasikowska (Chaya). Directed by Edward Zwick and produced by Zwick and Pieter Jan Brugge. Screenplay by Zwick and Clayton Frohman, based on the book *Defiance: The Bielski Partisans* by Nechama Tec.

Defiance is based on the true story of a group of Jews in Belarus who successfully defied the Nazis, hid in the forest, and maintained a self-contained society while losing only about 50 of their some 1,200 members. The "Bielski Partisans" represented the war's largest and most successful group of Jewish resisters, although when filmmakers arrived on the actual locations to film the story, they found no local memory of their activities and, for many reasons, hardly any Jews. Edward Zwick's film shows how they survived, governed themselves, and faced ethical questions, and how their stories can be suited to the requirements of melodrama.

This story has all the makings of a deep emotional experience, but I found myself oddly detached. Perhaps that's because most of the action and principal characters are within the group. The Nazis are seen in large part as an ominous threat out there somewhere in the forest, like "Those We Don't Speak Of" in M. Night Shyamalan's *The Village*. Do I require a major Nazi speaking part for the film to work? No, but the drama tends to focus on issues, conflicts, and romances within the group, and in that sense could be a very good reality show but lacks the larger dimension of, say, *Schindler's List*.

What the film comes down to is a forest survival story with a few scenes of Nazis trying to find and destroy them and a few battle scenes, which furnish the trailer and promise more of an action film. The survival story may contain omens for our own time. In the most fearsome of future scenarios, we may all have to survive in the wilderness, and we should be so lucky to have the Bielski brothers to help us. They were farmers, strong, fierce, skilled in survival skills, pragmatic.

The brothers are Tuvia Bielski (Daniel Craig), Zus Bielski (Liev Schreiber), and Asael (Jamie Bell). After they flee from genocide into the forest, others come hoping to join them, and word of their encampment spreads through the refugee underground. Tuvia decides early on that they must take in all Jews, even the helpless ones who cannot contribute; Zus, a firebrand, is less interested in saving Jews than killing Nazis, which he reasons will save more Jews. This conflict—between helping our side or harming theirs—is seen even today in the controversy over the invasion of Gaza, with Israel playing the role of the Bielski settlement.

The refugees sort out into leadership and support roles, feed their growing group largely by stealing food, establish such institutions as a hospital, a court, and even a tannery. Romance blossoms, which is common in life but indispensable in a movie, and there are tender scenes that are awfully warmly lit and softly scored, under the circumstances. Craig and Schreiber bring conviction to their roles, differing so sharply that they even come to blows before the younger brother leaves to join the Russians (who hate Jews every bit as much as the Nazis do).

Early in the film there's a scene where a feckless middle-aged man named Shimon Haretz (Allan Corduner) hopes to join the group and is asked what he does. He thinks maybe he's an intellectual. This is no use to the partisans, although he is allowed to stay. At the time of the story, the region was largely agrarian and peasant, and many were skilled craftsmen, artisans, and laborers. I thought, I'm also an . . . intellectual. Of what use would I be in the forest? The film works in a way as a cautionary tale. Most of us live in a precarious balance above the bedrock of physical labor. Someday we may all be Shimon Haretz.

The best performance, because it's more nuanced, is by Liev Schreiber. His Zus Bielski is more concerned with the big picture, more ideological, more driven by tactics. Daniel Craig is very effective as Tuvia, the group leader, but his character, perhaps of necessity, is concerned primarily with the organization, discipline, and planning of the group. A farmer, he becomes an administrator, chief authority, and court of last resort.

As a Nazi observes, not without admiration, the Bielskis set up a self-sustaining village in the wilderness. Their situation is more precarious because they are surrounded by anti-Semites not only from Germany but also from Russia and Poland. They cooperate with Soviet forces from necessity but cannot delude themselves. Their efforts prevailed, and today there are thousands who would not have been born if they had not succeeded.

Departures ★ ★ ★ ★

PG-13, 130 m., 2009

Masahiro Motoki (Daigo Kobayashi), Ryoko Hirosue (Mika, his wife), Tsutomu Yamazaki (Ikuei Sasaki), Kazuko Yoshiyuki (Tsuyako Yamashita), Takashi Sasano (Shokichi Hirata), Kimiko Yo (Yuriko Kamimura). Directed by Yojiro Takita and produced by Yasuhiro Mase, Toshiaki Nakasawa, and Toshihisa Watai. Screenplay by Kundo Koyama, based on the novel *Coffinman* by Shinmon Aoki.

"Death is for the living and not for the dead so much." This observation from the mourner of a dead dog in Errol Morris's *Gates of Heaven* strikes me as simple but profound. It is the insight inspiring *Departures*, the lovely Japanese movie that won this year's Oscar for best foreign film.

The story involves a young man who apprentices to the trade of "encoffinment," the preparation of corpses before their cremation. As nearly as I can recall, there is no discussion of an afterlife. It is all about the living. There is an elaborate, tender ceremony carried out before the family and friends of the deceased, with an elegance and care that is rather fascinating.

The hero is a man who feels he is owed a death. The father of Daigo (Masahiro Motoki) walked out on his mother when the boy was six, and ever since Daigo has hated him for that abandonment. Now about thirty, Daigo is a cellist in a small classical orchestra that goes broke. He and his wife, Mika (Ryoko Hirosue), decide to move back to a small town in the north of Japan and live in his childhood home, willed to him by his recently departed mother. He finds no work. He answers a want ad for "departures," which he thinks perhaps is from a travel agency.

The company serves clients making their final trip. Daigo is shocked to discover what the owner (Tsutomu Yamazaki) does; he cleans and prepares bodies, and painstakingly makes them up to look their best. The ritual involves undressing them behind artfully manipulated shrouds in front of the witnesses. The boss is a quiet, kind man, who talks little but exudes genuine respect for the dead.

Daigo doesn't tell his wife what he does. They need the money. His job is so low-caste that an old friend learns of it and snubs him. The clients are generally grateful; one father confesses cheerfully that the process freed him to accept the true nature of his child.

A lot is said about the casting process for a movie. Director Yojiro Takita and his casting director, Takefumi Yoshikawa, have surpassed themselves. In a film with four principal roles, they've found actors whose faces, so very human, embody what *Departures* wants to say about them. The earnest, insecure young man. The wife who loves him but is repulsed by the notion of him working with the dead. The boss, oracular, wise, kind. The office manager, inspirational but with an inner sadness. All of these faces are beautiful in a realistic, human way.

The enterprise of undertaking is deadly serious but has always inspired a certain humor, perhaps to mark our fears. The film is sometimes humorous, but not in a way to break the mood. The plot involves some developments we can see coming, but they seem natural, inevitable. The music is lush and sentimental in a subdued way, the cinematography is perfectly framed and evocative, and the movie is uncommonly absorbing. There is a scene of discovery toward the end with tremendous emotional impact. You can't say it wasn't prepared for, but it comes as a devastating surprise, a poetic resolution.

Some of the visual choices are striking. Observe the way Takita handles it when the couple are given an octopus for their dinner and are surprised to find it still alive. See how vividly Daigo recalls a time on the beach with his dad when he was five or six, but how in his memory his father's face is a blur. And how certain compositions suggest that we are all in waiting to be encoffined.

In this film, Kore-Eda's *After Life*, and, of course, Kurosawa's great *Ikiru*, the Japanese reveal a deep and unsensational acceptance of death. It is not a time for weeping and the gnashing of teeth. It is an observation that a life has been left for the contemplation of the survivors.

Desert Flower ★ ★ ½

R, 124 m., 2011

Liya Kebede (Waris Dirie), Sally Hawkins (Marylin), Timothy Spall (Terry Donaldson), Juliet Stevenson (Lucinda), Craig Parkinson (Neil), Anthony Mackie (Harold Jackson), Meera Syal (Pushpa Patel), Soraya Omar-Scego (Waris at twelve). Directed by Sherry Hormann and produced by Peter Herrmann. Screenplay by Hormann, based on the autobiographical novel by Waris Dirie.

Desert Flower tells an extraordinary story in an ordinary way. It has a compelling message and surrounds it with biopic scenes that appear to be brought in from a different kind of movie. The effect is rather unsettling.

The film is based on the life of Waris Dirie, an international supermodel who began life as a member of a nomadic tribe in Somalia. At the age of five, she was circumcised, as is the custom in many African lands. An old woman in the desert cut away those parts that could someday allow her to feel sexual pleasure, and sewed shut her vagina—so her husband could be sure he had married a virgin when he cut it open.

Many die during or because of this barbaric mutilation, still widely practiced today, although not mentioned in the Quran or any other holy book. It is the practice of subjugating women, making them commodities and denying them the full lives they deserve. It rises from the woman-hating men who propagate it by refusing to marry any woman who hasn't been "cut."

When Waris was sold as a young teenager to an old man who already had three wives, she simply left one day, walking hundreds of miles across desert and scrubland to seek her grandmother in Mogadishu. Amazingly, she found her—and was hired by an aunt in London to work as a maid. The film cuts between her experiences as a young girl and what happened in London, where she ran away, lived on the streets, and was befriended by a ditzy shop girl named Marylin (Sally Hawkins).

Marylin found her a job in a fast-food restaurant mopping floors, and that's where she was "discovered" by the fashion photographer Terry Donaldson (Timothy Spall). Through him and a mercenary modeling agent named Lucinda (Juliet Stevenson), she rose not without difficulties to the top ranks of models. She eventually denounced genital mutilation before the United Nations and became its spokesperson against the practice.

So it is a rags-to-riches story, but it plays like two stories in conflict. Everything involving Waris in Africa or in London before her success feels true and heartfelt. Many later details are badly handled.

Waris is played by another model, Liya Kebede, herself a spectacular beauty (a question that arises: Why did it take so long for her to be "discovered"?). The film, written and directed by Sherry Hormann, lingers unnecessarily on several sexualized modeling sessions and teases us with nude scenes. Two supporting characters, Lucinda and a janitor named Neil (Craig Parkinson), undergo puzzling personality changes at the convenience of the plot. A character named Harold Jackson (Anthony Mackie) exists exclusively for Idiot Plot purposes. And a jacket materializes after the point has been made that it was left behind.

Still, there are good things here. Sally Hawkins and Timothy Spall, familiar from Mike Leigh films, make their characters original and plausible. Meera Syal, as a rooming-house owner, steps in with some nice moments. And it's a compliment, I think, that Liya Kebede is more convincing as Waris the waif than as Waris the model.

Despicable Me ★ ★ ★

PG, 95 m., 2010

With the voices of Steve Carell (Gru), Jason Segel (Vector), Russell Brand (Dr. Nefario), Julie

Andrews (Gru's Mom), Will Arnett (Mr. Perkins), Kristen Wiig (Miss Hattie), Miranda Cosgrove (Margo), Dana Gaier (Edith), Elsie Fisher (Agnes). Directed by Chris Renaud and Pierre Coffin and produced by John Cohen, Janet Healy, and Christopher Meledandri. Screenplay by Cinco Paul and Ken Daurio.

Despicable Me begins with the truth that villains are often more fascinating than heroes, and creates a villain named Gru who freeze-dries the people ahead of him in line at Starbucks and pops children's balloons. Although he's inspired by many a James Bond bad guy, two things set him apart: (1) His vast mad scientist lair is located not in the desert or on the moon, but in the basement of his suburban home, and (2) he dreams not of world control so much as merely dominating the cable news ratings as The Greatest Villain of All Time.

Gru is voiced by Steve Carell, who gives him an accent halfway between a Russian mafioso and a crazed Nazi. His life is made more difficult because his mother (Julie Andrews) sometimes gets on his case. Memories stir of Rupert Pupkin in his basement, yanked from his fantasies by his mother's voice. Gru's most useful weapon is the Insta-Freeze Gun, but now, with the help of his genius staff inventor Dr. Nefario (Russell Brand), he can employ a Shrink Ray.

Just as global-scale villainy is looking promising, Gru is upstaged by his archrival, Vector (Jason Segel), who steals the Great Pyramid. Since that pyramid was previously pounded to pieces by the Transformers, the Egyptians should establish a CGI-free zone around it.

Gru is cheered ever onward by his faithful minions, who are, in fact, called the Minions, and look like yellow exercise balls with one or two eyes apiece. The principal responsibility of the Minions is to cheer for Gru, who addresses them as if he's running for office. He hatches a plan to use the Shrink Ray to steal no less than the moon itself, and explains it to the Minions with a plan that reminded me of nothing so much as the guy in the joke who plans to get the gorilla down out of the tree using only a broomstick, a pair of handcuffs, and a savage Dalmatian dog.

To make a villain into the hero of an animated comedy is daring, but the filmmakers bring in three cute kids to restore good feelings. These are Margo (Miranda Cosgrove), Edith (Dana Gaier), and Agnes (Elsie Fisher). Gru finds them at his friendly neighborhood orphanage, run by the suspicious Miss Hattie (Kristen Wiig). His plan is to keep them at his home until his moon scheme is ready to hatch, and then use them to infiltrate Vector's home by subterfuge—pretending to sell cookies, say. It follows as the night does the day that the orphans will work their little-girl magic on Gru, and gradually force the revelation that the big lug has a heart after all.

Despicable Me lacks a franchise to ride into town on, but it may establish one. I'm not sure how Gru can think up anything more sensational than stealing the moon, but I'm sure Dr. Nefario is working on that as we speak. The film is funny, energetic, teeth-gnashingly venomous, and animated with an eye to exploiting the 3-D process with such surefire techniques as a visit to an amusement park.

The sad thing, I am forced to report, is that the 3-D process produces a picture more dim than it should be. *Despicable Me* is technically competent and nowhere near the visual disaster that was *The Last Airbender*, but take my word for it: Try to find it in 2-D. Or, if you see it in 3-D, check out the trailers online to see how bright and cheery it would look in 2-D. How can people deceive themselves that 3-D is worth paying extra for?

Diary of a Wimpy Kid ★ ★ ★ ½

PG, 92 m., 2010

Zachary Gordon (Greg Heffley), Robert Capron (Rowley Jefferson), Rachael Harris (Susan Heffley), Steve Zahn (Frank Heffley), Devon Bostick (Rodrick Heffley), Chloe Moretz (Angie Steadman), Grayson Russell (Fregley). Directed by Thor Freudenthal and produced by Nina Jacobson and Bradford Simpson. Screenplay by Jackie Filgo, Jeff Filgo, Gabe Sachs, and Jeff Judah, based on the books by Jeff Kinney.

It is so hard to do a movie like this well. *Diary of a Wimpy Kid* is a PG-rated comedy about the hero's first year of middle school, and it's nimble, bright, and funny. It doesn't dumb down. It doesn't patronize. It knows something about human nature. It isn't as good as *A Christmas Story,* as few movies are, but it deserves a place in the same sentence. Here is a family movie you don't need a family to enjoy. You must, however, have been a wimpy kid. Most kids are wimpy in their secret hearts. Those who never were grow up to be cage fighters.

Greg Heffley isn't the shortest student in his class. That would be Chirag Gupta. Greg (Zachary Gordon) is only the second shortest. He's at that crucial age when everybody else has started to grow. There's a funny slide show illustrating how his class looked in sixth grade, and how they look now—some with mustaches. The girls, of course, are taller than the boys.

The onset of adolescence is an awkward age, made marginally easier for Greg because he still hasn't developed an interest in girls. Even his best friend, Rowley (Robert Capron), is flattered to be noticed by a girl, and Rowley is so out of it he thinks that at his age kids still *play,* when, as we all know, they *hang.*

The girl who notices Greg and Rowley is Angie (Chloe Moretz), who seems wise beyond her years. We first see her under the bleachers, reading *Howl* by Allen Ginsberg. Keep your eye on her in high school. She looks way older than her two new friends, but I checked, and Moretz was only twelve when she made the movie.

In middle school we find cliques, cruelty, and bullying. The pack is poised to pounce. *Diary* is especially funny about a slice of Swiss cheese that was dropped on a playground sometime in the distant past, and has grown an alarming coating of mold. Some kid poked it once, and all the other kids avoided him like the plague. He had the dreaded Cheese Touch. He only got rid of it by touching another kid. Then that kid had the Touch, until . . . and so on. The cheese nicely symbolizes the hunger kids have for an excuse, any excuse, to make other kids pariahs. Remember what happened to anyone who wore green on a Thursday?

Where do they find these actors? They come up on TV, I guess. Chloe Moretz has been acting since she was seven. Zachary Gordon has the confidence and timing of an old pro; he plays wimpy as if it's a desirable character trait. Robert Capron, as the pudgy Rowley, pulls off the tricky feat of being an inch or two taller than Greg and yet still childish; wait until you see his Halloween costume. Greg's parents (Rachael Harris and Steve Zahn) aren't major characters because what happens in school consumes all of Greg's psychic energy. His older brother, Rodrick (Devon Bostick), is, of course, a sadistic teaser who makes life miserable. But at that age, so it goes.

The movie is inspired by the books of Jeff Kinney, and the titles reproduce his hand-lettering and drawing style. The movie reproduces his charm. The director, Thor Freudenthal, made *Hotel for Dogs* (2009), received affectionately in some circles, but this time his touch is more sure and his humor more sunny.

Did You Hear About the Morgans? ★ ½

PG-13, 107 m., 2009

Hugh Grant (Paul Morgan), Sarah Jessica Parker (Meryl Morgan), Sam Elliott (Clay Wheeler), Mary Steenburgen (Emma Wheeler), Elisabeth Moss (Jackie), Michael Kelly (Vincent), Wilford Brimley (Earl Granger). Directed by Marc Lawrence and produced by Liz Glotzer and Martin Shafer.

What possible reason was there for anyone to make *Did You Hear About the Morgans?* Or should I say "remake," because this movie has been made over and over again, and oh, so much better. Feuding couple from Manhattan forced to flee town, find themselves Fish Out of Water in Strange New World, meet Colorful Characters, survive Slapstick Adventures, end up Together at the End. The only part of that formula that still works is The End.

I grant you Hugh Grant and Sarah Jessica Parker evoke charm in the right screenplay. This is the wrong screenplay. I concede that Sam Elliott is always welcome, except in that one eerie role he played without his mustache. I agree Mary Steenburgen is a merry and fetching lass. I realize yet once again the durable validity of Siskel's Question: Is this movie more entertaining than a documentary of the same actors having lunch?

Grant and Parker play Paul and Meryl Morgan, a wealthy Manhattan couple, childless, but they hope to adopt. This virtually guarantees a cute little orphan in the final reel. She is Manhattan's number-one "boutique Realtor." One night they're going together to show one of her multimillion-dollar properties when they witness her client being pushed from its balcony by a mean-looking villain.

He gets a good look at them. It was an important murder. Of course they must be sealed inside the Witness Protection Program and shipped out west, to where the men are men and the women are happy of it. In this strange new world where the men wear cowboy hats and the women wear cowboy hats and bake, will they find themselves in a rodeo? Let's put it this way: The close-up of a local rodeo poster and the matching shot of Hugh Grant squinting at it virtually guarantee that.

Saints preserve us! Not another one of those movies where Hugh Grant and Sarah Jessica Parker end up as the front and back halves of the rodeo clowns' cow suit! What's that you say? This is the first one where they've been inside the cow? Does it feel that way to you? What's that you say? You bet they'll be chased by a bear? Come on, now: Surely only one of them!

Paul and Meryl (unusual name, that; where did they find it?) end up as the houseguests of Clay and Emma Wheeler (Elliott and Steenburgen), the local sheriff and his deputy. Now that's clever thinking! Where better to hide Protected Witnesses than as the guests of the local law enforcement couple. Of course, Clay and Emma are hard to spot as they patrol on their horses with rifles and cowboy hats and mustaches and whatnot.

Paul and Meryl are dudes without a ranch. The small town embraces them. It's in Wyoming, I think someone said, and of course it has all of Wyoming's friendliness: The locals turn out with open arms, as they always do when two East Coast elites hit town and start asking people in the local cafe to refrain from smoking. Why, look! There, at the next table! It's Wilford Brimley! Smoking! It's not every day one movie offers the two most famous mustaches in Hollywood.

Well, you'll never be able to guess what happens then. And whether the villain turns up. And whether anyone is chased by a bear. And whether Paul and Meryl go to the rodeo. And what kind of an animal they wind up playing the front and back halves of. And whether they adopt a cute little orphan. And whether that mean old Wilford Brimley ends up grudgingly liking them after all. And whether he ever stops smoking. But one thing's for sure. You'll feel like you've already heard about the Morgans.

Dinner for Schmucks ★ ★ ★

PG-13, 114 m., 2010

Steve Carell (Barry Speck), Paul Rudd (Tim Conrad), Jemaine Clement (Kieran Vollard), Jeff Dunham (Lewis), Bruce Greenwood (Lance Fender), Ron Livingston (Caldwell), Zach Galifianakis (Therman), Stephanie Szostak (Julie). Directed by Jay Roach and produced by Roach, Laurie MacDonald, and Walter F. Parkes. Screenplay by David Guion and Michael Handelman, inspired by the French film *Le Diner de Cons* (*The Dinner Game*) directed and written by Francis Veber.

The truly goofy comes shrouded in innocence. If a man is trying to be goofy, it's just an act that quickly grows old. But if he lacks the slightest notion of his peculiarity, there's the secret. The blissful ignorance of Barry Speck is beyond pitiful and ascends to a kind of nobility. He's one of those who truly don't have a clue.

In *Dinner for Schmucks,* a group of arrogant rich men use him as part of an elaborate joke, but the joke is on them. You can't insult a man who is always happy to be just exactly who he is. In the film, the millionaires have a dinner party every year that is a secret joke: Each guest invites another guest who is, whether he realizes it or not, in a contest to determine which guest is the biggest idiot. This is plain cruel.

Dinner for Schmucks was inspired by Francis Veber's French film named *The Dinner Game,* which was an enormous hit in France but seemed a shade on the mean side. The genius of this version depends on the performance by Steve Carell, who plays Barry Speck as a man impervious to insult and utterly at peace with himself. And a transcendent idiot.

The hero of the film is Tim Conrad (Paul Rudd), an ambitious young man dreaming of promotion to the corner office. His boss is Lance Fender (Bruce Greenwood), who invites him to bring a guest to the dinner. This chance to hobnob with his boss's powerful friends is attractive, but at first Tim says no; he has an important date scheduled with his fiancée, Julie (Stephanie Szostak). Then he meets Barry, a man whose hobby is populating enormous dollhouses and model landscapes with elaborately costumed dead mice. Barry is too good to pass up. He looks like a sure winner.

The subplot between Julie and Tim is essentially the MacGuffin; there needs to be something important to Tim that comes into conflict with the dinner. The film itself settles down, or stirs itself up, at the long dinner scene, at which we meet several other perfect idiots, but none in the running with Barry.

Barry is such a specimen it's hard to describe him. Yes, he wears a toupee. Yes, he seems to have mice secreted about his person. But it's more that he's the only happy man in the room. One of the reasons we love the great eccentrics in Dickens, I believe, is that they're so pleased with themselves. You cannot be a great eccentric if you're not a happy one; otherwise there's no fun in it.

The dinner turns into farce and finally descends into slapstick, but Carell sails through these choppy seas with a steadfast belief in human nature. He doesn't perceive insult to himself perhaps because he can't imagine anyone acting that way. Jay Roach, who is no stranger to raunchy comedy (*Austin Powers, Meet the Fockers*), makes a good strategic decision on how he handles this: Not only is Barry an innocent, but so is Tim, who invited him to the party for reasons of ambition but not cruelty. So the villain is at three removes. That would be Bruce Greenwood as the sadistic boss.

The guests at the dinner are a strange lot. To describe them would be to give away their jokes, and one of the pleasures of the movie is having each one appear. I wonder if it occurs to anyone to reflect that the hosts of this dinner are the biggest idiots in attendance. Oh, and those elegant little mice remind me of the white mice in Charlie Kaufman's *Human Nature,* being taught their table manners by scientists.

Disgrace ★ ★ ★ ★

NO MPAA RATING, 118 m., 2009

John Malkovich (David Lurie), Jessica Haines (Lucy), Eriq Ebouaney (Petrus), Fiona Press (Bev), Antoinette Engel (Melanie). Directed by Steve Jacobs and produced by Jacobs, Anna-Maria Monticelli, and Emile Sherman. Screenplay by Monticelli, based on the novel by J. M. Coetzee.

I awaited the closing scenes of *Disgrace* with a special urgency because the story had gripped me deeply but left me with no idea how it would end. None—and I really cared. This is such a rare movie. Its characters are uncompromisingly themselves, flawed, stubborn, vulnerable. We feel we know them pretty well, but then they face a situation of such pain and moral ambiguity that they're forced to make impossible decisions. It's easy to ask them to do the right thing. But what is the right thing?

David Lurie (John Malkovich) teaches the Romantic poets at the University of Cape Town. He lingers over Wordsworth's word choices before a classroom of distracted students. One seems to care: Melanie (Antoinette Engel). He offers her a ride home in the rain. She accepts. I spent a year in that university on the slopes of Table Mountain. When someone offers you a ride home in the rain, you accept.

This is South Africa in the years soon after the fall of apartheid. Sexual contact between the races is no longer forbidden by law, and indeed the film opens with a liaison between David and a black prostitute. Melanie is Indian. David is white, at least thirty-five years older, very confident, sardonic, determined. They have sex. We don't see exactly how they get to that point, but it is clear afterward that Melanie is very unhappy. It was probably not literal rape, we're thinking, but it was a psychological assault.

David should be content with his conquest, but he's a cocky and deeply selfish man, and Malkovich, in one of his best performances, shows him acting entirely on his desires. There's a scene where he faces a university disciplinary board; the board obviously hopes to avoid scandal and offers him a graceful exit. He cheekily tells them he is guilty, accepts blame, requests punishment.

Now the divorced David goes to visit his daughter Lucy (Jessica Haines), a lesbian who owns a remote farm and supports herself with a market garden and dog breeding. Her farm manager is an African named Petrus (Eriq Ebouaney, who played the lead in *Lumumba*). This man is more independent than years in South Africa have led David to expect. He doesn't believe Lucy is safe living on the farm with him.

Now events take place I will not describe, except to say that Lucy is indeed not safe, and that David becomes locked in essentially a territorial dispute with Petrus. This dispute has a background in the old and new South Africas, strong racial feelings, and difficult moral choices. The nature of the personalities of David, Lucy, and Petrus are deeply tested.

The film is based on a novel by Nobel laureate J. M. Coetzee, which won the Booker Prize. I read it in 1999, remembered it well, but not the details of the ending. Now I understand why. It isn't so much about what happens, as about the way things are. The final shot by the director Steve Jacobs is in its own way perfect. There cannot be a resolution, apart from the acceptance of reality.

I imagine those seeing *Disgrace* will find themselves in complex discussions about right and wrong. In any sense, what David did with Melanie was wrong, and what happens later to Lucy is wrong. We agree. But whose response is better? David's or Lucy's? To ask that question is the whole purpose of this story. There are two more questions: What does it mean when David decides to put down a dog he feels affection for, and what has happened within him by the time of the final scene? As the last shot begins, you will be asking yourself. The shot will not make it easy for you. I know what I think, but it isn't a comfortable conclusion.

This is one of the year's best films. Before discussing Malkovich, I want to mention four other performances. Fiona Press as Bev, a warm, comfortable middle-aged woman who runs the animal shelter in town, is a necessary center of comfort and calm. Jessica Haines plays Lucy with unbending, clear-eyed conviction. Eriq Ebouaney has a crucial role and plays it wisely, not signaling what we should think of him but simply playing a man who is sure of his ground. Antoinette Engel has a smaller role, also crucial, with perfect pitch: She, too, doesn't parade her feelings. After the film is over, it may occur to you that Melanie and Lucy have undergone similar experiences.

Then there is Malkovich, an actor who is so particular in the details of voice and action. After you see *Disgrace*, you may conclude no other actor could possibly have been cast for the role. He begins as a cold, arrogant, angry man, accustomed to buying his way with his money and intelligence. He is also accustomed to being a white man in South Africa. In no sense does David think of himself as a racist, and he probably always voted against apartheid. But at least it was always there for him to vote against. Now he undergoes experiences that introduce him to an emerging new South Africa—and no, I don't mean he undergoes conversion and enlightenment. This isn't a feel-good parable. I simply mean he understands that something fundamental has shifted, and that is the way things are.

District 9 ★ ★ ★

R, 111 m., 2009

Sharlto Copley (Wikus van der Merwe), Jason Cope (voice of Christopher Johnson), David James (Koobus Venter), Mandla Gaduka (Fundiswa Mhlanga), William Allen Young (Dirk Michaels), Vanessa Haywood (Tania van der Merwe), Kenneth Nkosi (Thomas). Directed by Neill Blomkamp and produced by Peter Jackson and Carolynne Cunningham. Screenplay by Blomkamp and Terri Tatchell.

I suppose there's no reason the first alien race to reach Earth shouldn't look like what the cat threw up. After all, they love to eat cat food. The alien beings in *District 9*, nicknamed "prawns" because they look like a cross between lobsters and grasshoppers, arrive in a spaceship that hovers over Johannesburg. Found inside, huddled together and starving to death, are the aliens, who benefit from a humanitarian impulse to relocate them to a location on the ground.

Here they become not welcomed but feared, and their camp turns into a prison. Fearing alien attacks, humans demand they be resettled far from town, and a clueless bureaucrat named Wikus van der Merwe (Sharlto

Copley) is placed in charge of this task. The creatures are not eager to move. A private security force, headed by van der Merwe, moves in with armored vehicles and flamethrowers to encourage them, and van der Merwe cheerfully destroys houses full of their young.

Who are these aliens? Where did they come from? How did their ship apparently run out of power (except what's necessary to levitate its massive tonnage)? No one asks: They're here, we don't like them, get them out of town. There doesn't seem to be a lot to like. In appearance they're loathsome, in behavior disgusting, and evoke so little sympathy that killing one is like—why, like dropping a seven-foot lobster into boiling water.

This science fiction fable, directed by newcomer Neill Blomkamp and produced by Peter (*The Lord of the Rings*) Jackson, takes the form of a mockumentary about van der Merwe's relocation campaign, his infection by an alien virus, his own refuge in District 9, and his partnership with the only alien who behaves intelligently and reveals, dare we say, human emotions. This alien, named Christopher Johnson—yes, Christopher Johnson—has a secret workspace where he prepares to return to the mother ship and help his people.

Much of the plot involves the obsession of the private security firm in learning the secret of the alien weapons, which humans cannot operate. Curiously, none of these weapons seem superior to those of the humans and aren't used to much effect by the aliens in their own defense. Never mind. After van der Merwe grows a lobster claw in place of a hand, he can operate the weapons, and thus becomes the quarry of both the security company and the Nigerian gangsters who exploit the aliens by selling them cat food. All of this is presented very seriously.

The film's South African setting brings up inescapable parallels with its now-defunct apartheid system of racial segregation. Many of them are obvious, such as the action to move a race out of the city and onto a remote location. Others will be more pointed in South Africa. The title *District 9* evokes Cape Town's historic District 6, where Cape Coloureds owned homes and businesses for many years before being bulldozed out and relocated. The hero's name, van der Merwe, is not only a common name for Afrikaners, the white South Africans of Dutch descent, but also the name of the protagonist of van der Merwe jokes, of which the point is that the hero is stupid. Nor would it escape a South African ear that the alien language incorporates clicking sounds, just as Bantu, the language of a large group of African apartheid targets.

Certainly this van der Merwe isn't the brightest bulb on the tree. Wearing a sweater vest over a short-sleeved shirt, he walks up to alien shanties and asks them to sign a relocation consent form. He has little sense of caution, which is why he finds himself in his eventual predicament. What Neill Blomkamp somehow does is make Christopher Johnson and his son, Little CJ, sympathetic in spite of appearance. This is achieved by giving them, but no other aliens, human body language, and little CJ even gets big wet eyes, like E.T.

District 9 does a lot of things right, including giving us aliens to remind us not everyone who comes in a spaceship need be angelic, octopod, or stainless steel. They are certainly alien, all right. It is also a seamless merger of the mockumentary and special effects (the aliens are CGI). And there's a harsh parable here about the alienation and treatment of refugees.

But the third act is disappointing, involving standard shoot-out action. No attempt is made to resolve the situation, and if that's a happy ending, I've seen happier. Despite its creativity, the movie remains space opera and avoids the higher realms of science fiction.

I'll be interested to see if general audiences go for these aliens. I said they're loathsome and disgusting, and I don't think that's just me. The movie mentions Nigerian prostitutes servicing the aliens, but wisely refrains from entertaining us with this spectacle.

District 13: Ultimatum ★ ★ ★

R, 100 m., 2010

Cyril Raffaelli (Damien), David Belle (Leito), Philippe Torreton (President), Daniel Duval (Gassman), MC Jean Gab'1 (Molko), La Fouine (Ali-K), James Deano (Karl). Directed by Patrick Alessandrin and produced by Luc Besson. Screenplay by Besson.

There is a limit to how far down you can jump and land on your feet and not break an ankle. Well, isn't there? I ask because these limits don't seem to apply to the cops who are the heroes of *District 13: Ultimatum*. Nor, incredibly, do they apply to the bad cops who chase them across the rooftops of Paris while burdened with full SWAT team uniforms, including bulletproof vests. There isn't a single character who lands badly, and limps away.

I know, I know. It's all done with special effects. Yes, but . . . well, see the movie. The height of a jump can be exaggerated by oblique camera angles and lenses. Hong Kong experts use wires and trampolines. Hollywood sidesteps the issue by editing so quickly no physical movement is ever quite entirely seen. Yes. But consider that the costar of *District 13* is a thirty-five-year-old Frenchman named David Belle, famed as the man who named "parkour," which is "the art of flight." This is a hot modern martial art. Not only do the shots look convincing, not only are they held long enough to allow us to see an entire action, but Belle in real life does a version of this stuff.

The stuff is what intrigues me. The screenplay is another of the countless works of Luc Besson, who is the most productive person in modern action movies. It's a sequel to his 2004 film in which a walled-off segment of Paris in 2010 was run by black, white, Asian, and Arab warlords, with a fifth one left over I couldn't categorize. There is a plot within a crooked high-level security agency to destroy the district and rebuild it. This massive work will be accomplished by the corporation that has bribed them, named Harriburton, which does not remind you of anything, of course.

The president of the French republic is not in on the plot. He believes in liberty, equality, fraternity, and the constitution, which would make him unpopular with Harriburton. Anyway, after they luckily see a citizen video showing bad cops murdering good cops and blaming it on gangs in District 13, it's up to Damien (Cyril Raffaelli) and Leito (David Belle) to single-handedly stop the evil scheme.

This they do in many ways, but mostly by running away. Parkour is the "art of flight," you recall. So they grab incriminating tapes and computer drives, the bad cops want to catch them, and this leads to the real point of the movie, which is one chase scene after another. These actors are clearly in superb physical shape. I'm not going to believe they actually do all these stunts, but I believe we clearly see them doing parts of them, which all by themselves would be awesome.

They leap, fall, tumble, twist, climb up and down walls and buildings, swing from wires, slide down wires, and have an alarming eagerness to jump out of buildings without knowing what is below. (Luckily, there are nice comfy landing spots like the roofs of cars.) At one point, after Damien comes home to his girlfriend (Sophie Ducasse), he complains he feels "stiff." Ha. This man needs an intensive care unit. Still, the parkour motto is "*etre et duress*," which means "to be and to endure," or in other words, not to get yourself killed or twist an ankle.

If anyone is going to convince fanboys to attend a movie with French subtitles, that man is Luc Besson. They'll catch on that Besson, working without enormous budgets and A-list stars, knows what he's doing. A movie like *District 13: Ultimatum* may be as preposterous as the lame *From Paris with Love*, but it delivers the goods. You want an action movie where you can see that the actors are really there, and not concealed by editing that looks like someone fed the film through an electric fan? Here's your movie. For that matter, although the characters indeed speak French, they don't talk much, and sometimes the SWAT teams use English they learned from cop movies, like "Go! Go! Go!"

Dogtooth ★ ★ ★

NO MPAA RATING, 94 m., 2010

Christos Stergioglou (Father), Michelle Valley (Mother), Aggeliki Papoulia (Older Daughter), Hristos Passalis (Son), Mary Tsoni (Younger Daughter), Anna Kalaitzidou (Christina). Directed by Yorgos Lanthimos and produced by Yorgos Tsourgiannis. Screenplay by Lanthimos and Efthimis Filippou.

Dogtooth is a bizarre fantasy that takes the concept of homeschooling to squirmy extremes. Some homeschoolers try to limit what their children can learn, and others to broaden it. The parents in *Dogtooth* have passed far beyond such categories into the realms of home psychopathology.

No name is given for the family or any of its members. These involve a father, a mother, a brother, and two sisters. They live in a large, affluent home behind a very high wall and a gate that is always locked. Only the father ever leaves, driving to the factory he owns.

The others are prisoners, the mother apparently by choice. There is a large lawn and a swimming pool. The television set is used only to watch the family's home videos. The children have no idea of the outside world, where they are told man-eating cats roam. On the other side of the wall they believe another brother lives, who they've never seen or heard.

Man-eating cats? Who knows? The film begins with a tape-recorded language lesson in which they're taught the *wrong* words for things. "Sea," for example, is the word for the big leather armchair in the living room. Father is a stern taskmaster, free with stern reprimands and a hard slap or two. He also teaches all of his family members to get down on all fours and bark like dogs. He and Mother seem in complete agreement about their child-rearing methods but never discuss them in detail.

The son is about twenty, the daughters in their teens. To slake the boy's sexual needs, Father brings home a security guard from his factory, who has sex with the son with all the spontaneity and joy of tooth removal. This woman also trades a daughter some cheap jewelry in exchange for some illicit licking.

The kids are so innocent, they decide that it's much the same no matter where you lick, and trade favors for licking legs, elbows, and ears. Sex seems to have no meaning, not even when incest is suggested. The sickness of this family surpasses all understanding, and some have even described the film as a comedy. I wasn't laughing. All I can say of the ending is that it is certainly a possible outcome of the film, and gets much more than you would think out of a shot of the family car.

There is this. *Dogtooth* is like a car crash. You cannot look away. The Greek director Yorgos Lanthimos tells his story with complete command of visuals and performances. His cinematography is like a series of family photographs of a family with something wrong with it. His dialogue sounds composed entirely of sentences memorized from tourist phrase books. The message I took away was: God help children whose parents insanely demand unquestioning obedience to their deranged standards.

Note: The film won the Un Certain Regard section of Cannes 2009.

Drive Angry 3-D ★ ★

R, 104 m., 2011

Nicolas Cage (John Milton), Amber Heard (Piper), William Fichtner (The Accountant), Billy Burke (Jonah King). Directed by Patrick Lussier and produced by Rene Besson and Michael De Luca. Screenplay by Todd Farmer and Lussier.

Drive Angry 3-D opens with a muscle car racing across a burning bridge out of hell, while we hear a famous twelve-letter word used three or four times. So right away we know where we're at. Here is an exercise in deliberate vulgarity, gross excess, and the pornography of violence, not to forget garden variety pornography. You get your money's worth.

A movie review should determine what a movie hoped to achieve and whether it succeeded. The ambition of *Drive Angry 3-D* is to make a grind house B movie so jaw-droppingly excessive that even Quentin Tarantino might send flowers. It succeeds. I can't say I enjoyed it. But I can appreciate it. It offends every standard of taste except bad. But it is well made.

Of course it stars Nicolas Cage. Is there another actor who could or would have dared to sign on? Cage is a good actor in good movies, and an almost indispensable actor in bad ones. He can go over the top so effortlessly he rests up and makes lemonade for everybody. Here he plays a man named John Milton, a reference I fear will be lost on the film's target audience. Milton is hell-bent to rescue his baby granddaughter. A satanic cult enslaved and murdered his daughter, and now plans to sacrifice the infant by the light of the full moon. This Milton cannot abide.

The cult is led by Jonah (Billy Burke), who is obeyed by slavish followers he seems to have recruited from porn movies and guests on Jerry Springer shows about redneck incest.

Their idea of partying is a topless orgy around a fire in an abandoned prison yard, while swigging Jack Daniels and warming up for a midnight infanticide. Their ranks are swelled by the usual shaved-headed and tattooed fatsos. There must be a pool of Hollywood extras who play big bald guys who can take three steps forward and glower into the camera.

Anyway, Milton's quest begins in a bar named Bull by the Balls, where he meets a barmaid named Piper (Amber Heard). After inconceivable violence, they link destinies. You've heard of girls attracted to the wrong kinds of guys? Piper inexplicably stays with Milton, despite many questions which are even better than she thinks. Heard makes a plucky heroine who, although Piper's sexy and Milton likes the ladies, doesn't fall into the usual abyss of "love interest," but slugs it out like a cage fighter.

On their trail is the enigmatic Accountant (William Fichtner). This seemingly (spoiler alert) supernatural figure is relentless in pursuit, yet moves with the speed of a plodding gumshoe when he's not at the wheel of a muscle car or, oh, say, a tanker truck filled with liquid hydrogen. (The movie, of course, contains the official quota of walking-away-from-fiery-explosions-in-slo-mo shots.) As Milton chases Jonah and the Accountant chases Milton, Jonah's followers chase Milton, which is a great convenience, allowing *Drive Angry 3-D* to be more or less nothing but chase scenes, except for some interior gun battles and much portentous dialogue. (Cage brings an inimitable personal touch to, "The bullet is still in there." Pause. "I can feel it.")

Gene Siskel drew the line at children in danger. As a father, he disapproved of thrillers that exploited violent scenes involving kids. What would he have made of an extended sequence here where Jonah commands one of his followers to sacrifice an infant? He would have despised it, I believe. The only justification for it is that this entire movie is so broadly, grotesquely over the top that the baby is more of a prop than a human child. And *Drive Angry 3-D* trusts its audience to put every principle of Western civilization on hold.

So my review is a compromise. I'm giving it two stars. That's halfway between three stars (well made) and one star (loathesome). Nic Cage once again provides the zeal and energy to wade through a violent morass. William Fichtner makes the Accountant so intriguing that, although all CPAs aren't from hell, we know this one is. He has a nice twitchy reserve. Amber Heard and Billy Burke do everything that can possibly be done with their characters, and don't stop there.

Oh, and the 3-D? For an extra charge you get to wear glasses that make it look like it was shot where the sun don't shine.

Due Date ★ ★ ½

R, 95 m., 2010

Robert Downey Jr. (Peter Highman), Zach Galifianakis (Ethan Tremblay), Michelle Monaghan (Sarah Highman), Jamie Foxx (Darryl), Juliette Lewis (Heidi). Directed by Todd Phillips and produced by Phillips and Daniel Goldberg. Screenplay by Phillips, Alan R. Cohen, Alan Freedland, and Adam Sztykiel.

Due Date is as near as makes no difference to a down-market retread of *Planes, Trains, and Automobiles.* It pairs up Robert Downey Jr. and Zach Galifianakis in the Steve Martin and John Candy roles, puts them in a car together, sends them down the highway, and doesn't neglect to rip off one but two car doors.

The first film by director Todd Phillips since his blockbuster *The Hangover* cheerfully includes some of the same raunchy humor and the same dogged persistence in the face of overwhelming character defects. It's not as funny, but few films could be, and it does have some very big laughs. Unfortunately, the story holding them together isn't as successful.

Peter Highman (Downey) and Ethan Tremblay (Galifianakis) have a Meet Cute, or more of a Meet Brute, at the Atlanta airport, when Ethan's beater knocks off the door of Peter's town car. Peter is a neat, precise architect with a schedule to meet. Ethan is a shaggy man-child who confesses that on the way to the airport he and his buddy split a six-pack—of forties.

Ethan is like Joe Btfsplk, that character in *Li'l Abner* who always had a black rain cloud over his head, with the difference that the cloud is over the head of whomever he's standing next to. He efficiently destroys Peter's trip by switching carry-ons with him, shoving his hairy belly into his face (under stress, to be sure), and getting them both thrown off the flight by insisting on using the words "bomb" and "terrorist." That scenario leads to a run-in with TSA agents (who, oddly enough, seem to be morphing into Hollywood's villains du jour).

All cross-country trips involving odd couples require deadlines. Peter agrees to accept a ride in Ethan's rental car only because he must be back in Los Angeles with his wife, Sarah (Michelle Monaghan), who will deliver their child very soon by C-section. Ethan needs to go to Los Angeles because he dreams of becoming an actor. If you doubt Ethan Tremblay has a future in acting, simply consider Zach Galifianakis.

There are stops along the way to visit Western Union, Peter's old buddy (Jamie Foxx), and Ethan's practitioner in "herbal medicines," a pot dealer played by the scene-stealer Juliette Lewis. Those visits are funny. There are also running gags involving Ethan's beloved pet dog and a coffee can containing the ashes of his father. When Ethan performs the rather private act of pleasuring himself in the car's front seat, it's not funny, but when the dog is inspired to copy him, it is. No matter how much I think, I can't decide whether training a dog to do that is cruelty to an animal.

So the movie probably contains enough laughs to satisfy the weekend audience. Where it falls short is in the characters and relationships. *Due Date* may offer enough, but with the example of the classic *Planes, Trains, and Automobiles,* it could have offered more.

Downey and Steve Martin are more or less a standoff. But John Candy (and director John Hughes) made his character earnest, inept, and lovable. The Galifianakis character seems more an exercise in passive aggression. He lacks social skills so urgently it's hard to believe he doesn't know what he's up to. Surely no one could be that obnoxious by accident. In comedy it helps if we have a bottom line of affection for the characters, and Galifianakis and Phillips make affection awfully hard to feel for Ethan.

There's a moment in *PTA* when the Steve Martin character thinks he has seen the last of John Candy, and then pauses, reconsiders, and returns. There's a moment something like that here, but frankly, we don't know why the Downey character returns.

Note: My Great Movie review of Planes, Trains, and Automobiles *is at http://j.mp/9HhHGU.*

Duplicity ★ ★ ★

PG-13, 125 m., 2009

Julia Roberts (Claire Stenwick), Clive Owen (Ray Koval), Tom Wilkinson (Howard Tully), Paul Giamatti (Richard Garsik). Directed by Tony Gilroy and produced by Jennifer Fox, Kerry Orent, and Laura Bickford. Screenplay by Gilroy.

Julia Roberts and Clive Owen generate fierce electricity in *Duplicity,* but we (and they) don't know if it's romantic or wicked. They're Claire and Ray, government spies (she CIA, he MI6) who meet on assignment in Dubai; she sleeps with him, then steals his secret documents. They both enter the private sector, working for the counterespionage departments of competing shampoo giants. At stake: the formula for a top-secret product that, when revealed, does indeed seem to be worth the high-tech games being played to steal and protect it.

The movie resembles *Mad* magazine's Spy vs. Spy series, elevated to labyrinthine levels of complexity. Nothing is as it seems or even as it seems to seem; triple-crosses are only the warm-up. What's consistent through all of the intrigues is the (certain) lust and (possible) love between them. The theory is, they'll scheme together to steal the formula, sell it in Switzerland, split millions, and spend the rest of their lives spying on each other under the covers.

They're both such incurable operatives that neither one can trust the other. We're not even sure they trust themselves. They play an emotional cat-and-mouse game, cleverly scripted by director Tony Gilroy (*Michael Clayton*) to reflect classic romcoms; both actors seem to be channeling Cary Grant.

Claire and Ray seem to have hollow hearts. Can they, in their trade, sincerely love anyone? Knowing all the tricks, they know the other one knows them, too. This removes some of the romantic risk from the story, replacing it with a plot so ingenious that at the end we know more or less what happened, but mostly less. That's fun but deprives Roberts of her most winning note, which is lovability.

This isn't a two-hander; Gilroy uses his supporting cast for key roles. Tom Wilkinson and Paul Giamatti play the two enemy soap tycoons, both consumed by desperate intensity. Carrie Preston steals a scene from Roberts with her hilarious role as a company travel agent who may have been seduced by Ray but bubbles over about how glad she is that it happened. Roberts is amusingly inscrutable as she listens.

Duplicity is entertaining, but the complexities of its plot keep it from being really involving: When nothing is as it seems, why care? The fun is in watching Roberts and Owen fencing with dialogue, keeping straight faces, trying to read each other's minds. That, and admiring the awesome technology that goes into corporate espionage. I don't understand why Wall Street executives deserve millions, but I can see why these two might. All the money they hope to steal, added together, wouldn't amount to an annual bonus for one of the bankruptcy masterminds.

E

The Eagle ★ ★ ★

PG-13, 114 m., 2011

Channing Tatum (Marcus Aquila), Jamie Bell (Esca), Donald Sutherland (Uncle Aquila), Mark Strong (Guern), Tahar Rahim (Seal Prince), Denis O'Hare (Lutorius). Directed by Kevin Macdonald and produced by Duncan Kenworthy. Screenplay by Jeremy Brock, based on Rosemary Sutcliff's novel *The Eagle of the Ninth.*

The Eagle is a rip-snorting adventure tale of the sort made before CGI, 3-D, and alphabet soup in general took the fun out. So much does it evoke the energy of traditional sword-and-shield movies that I had to bring the term "rip-snorting" out of retirement; it's rarely needed in this era of sleek technology. Here we see for the most part the actual actors trekking through real locations, instead of quasi animation.

The story is one I dimly recall, about the disappearance of the Roman Ninth Legion, which marched north from the colony of England into the unknown wilds of Scotland and was never heard from again. It tells of an uneasy bond between a centurion named Marcus (Channing Tatum) and a slave named Esca (Jamie Bell), who join a mission to discover what happened to the Ninth and its proud symbol, a golden eagle.

Some Americans find it quaint that the Scots and Welsh don't think of themselves as English. A Yank can receive the occasional fat lip for that mistake. Scotland was an independent kingdom until well over a millennium after the time of this story, which is set in about AD 140. So fearsome were the Scots warriors that the Roman emperor Hadrian threw up his hands and decreed that a border wall be erected in his name, whether to keep the Scots out or administer a full-body pat-down I am not sure.

In *The Eagle*, Marcus is assigned to lead a minor Roman outpost in England some twenty years after the death of his father, who is still blamed for having lost the eagle. Seriously wounded, he returns to Italy, as it was not then known, to heal at the villa of his Uncle Aquila (Donald Sutherland). Attending a deadly fight of gladiators, he decrees that the life of the courageous slave Esca be spared, and takes him along when he returns to England and takes up a more important command.

Marcus burns with the need to find the solution to the missing legion and find the lost eagle, and against all sane advice determines that he and Esca will cross the wall on a low-profile mission. They discover some answers, not without a great deal of bloodshed. One secret of the film's success is that their quest and the battle scenes are on a more or less plausible human scale. The editing is so rapid that we can't really follow the strategy of the swordplay, but at least a finite number of physical humans seem involved, instead of the absurd tidal waves of warriors in a CGI-fest like *300*.

I think we've possibly seen the last of choreographed sword fights, anyway. They reached their peak in classic Hollywood films and samurai dramas, and those in *Rob Roy* (1995) were among the best ever performed. I understood them. These days, in scenes where there's a berserk human traffic jam of sword fighters on the screen, don't you think that more or less everyone would be left with a number of limbs not divisible by two?

The Eagle has two strengths. One is that it is interested in its period, and what kinds of Romans and barbarians might have lived then. The second is that it really comes down to the relationship of Marcus and Esca, who risk their lives for each other but remain conscious that they are master and slave, and never become buddies. I suppose it is a negative strength that there are no major female characters; this is not the sort of world where women would be expected, and the insertion of romantic interest so obligatory in lesser movies would seem awkward here.

The Eagle is rated R, and that's about right. The blood and gore is kept to a reasonable level, and the battle scenes are about heroism and strategy, not special effects. *The Eagle* attempts to create characters with some dimension and complexity. In Donald Sutherland's interlude as the wise uncle, it provides some notion of the function of empire, then and later. And Tatum and Bell do a good job of sculpting the heroes to a fairly human scale, and not indulging in foolish poses against the horizon. The movie goes a little over the top in finally showing us the eagle, but what can you expect?

Earth ★ ★ ★

G, 99 m., 2009

A documentary directed by Alastair Fothergill and Mark Linfield and produced by Sophokles Tasioulis and Alix Tidmarsh. Screenplay by Fothergill, Linfield, and Leslie Megahey.

Made between 1948 and 1960, Walt Disney's *True Life Adventures* won three Oscars for best documentary feature, and several others won in the since-discontinued category of two-reel short features. Now the studio has returned to this admirable tradition with *Earth*. It's a film that younger audiences in particular will enjoy.

To be sure, Disney didn't produce the film. It is a feature-length compilation from the splendid BBC and Discovery channel series *Planet Earth*, utilizing the big screen to make full use of its high-def images. The feature's original narrator, Patrick Stewart, has been replaced by James Earl Jones.

What we see is astonishing. Polar bear cubs tumble their way to the sea. Birds of paradise make displays of ethereal beauty. Storks fly above the Himalayas. Elephants trek exhausted across a bone-dry desert. Humpback whales swim three thousand miles to their summer feeding grounds off Antarctica. A predator cat outruns a springbok. Ducklings leap from their nest to fly and plummet to the ground—a learning experience.

The most poignant sequence in the film shows a polar bear, lost at sea and searching for ice floes in a time of global warming, finally crawling ashore exhausted and starving. Desperate for food, he hopelessly attacks a herd of walruses, fails, and slumps dying to the earth; nearby walruses are indifferent.

In the tradition of such favorites of my childhood as Disney's *The Living Desert* and *The Vanishing Prairie*, the narration provides these animals with identities. It opens with a mother polar bear and two cubs. The desperate polar bear is identified as their father, although I will bet a shiny new dime that the authors of the narration have absolutely no evidence of its paternal history. I'm not complaining; in a film like this, that goes with the territory.

The film is filled with unexpected facts. Did you know the fir trees beginning at the northern tree line circle the globe with an almost unbroken forest, harbor almost no birds and mammals because they are not edible, and supply more of the planet's oxygen than the rain forests? Or that baby whales have to be taught to breathe?

Earth is beautiful and worthwhile. At its pre-opening press screening, cosponsored by the Lincoln Park Zoo in Chicago, we were supplied not with free popcorn but tiny evergreens to take home and plant.

Easy A ★ ★ ★ ½

PG-13, 93 m., 2010

Emma Stone (Olive Penderghast), Penn Badgley (Woodchuck Todd), Amanda Bynes (Marianne Bryant), Dan Byrd (Brandon), Thomas Haden Church (Mr. Griffith), Patricia Clarkson (Rosemary), Cam Gigandet (Micah), Lisa Kudrow (Mrs. Griffith), Malcolm McDowell (Principal Gibbons), Aly Michalka (Rhiannon), Stanley Tucci (Dill). Directed by Will Gluck and produced by Gluck and Zanne Devine. Screenplay by Bert V. Royal.

Easy A offers an intriguing middle ground to the absolute of sexual abstinence: Don't sleep with anybody, but say you did. It's a funny, engaging comedy that takes the familiar but underrated Emma Stone and makes her, I believe, a star. Until actors are matched to the right role, we can never quite see them clearly.

Stone embodies Olive Penderghast, a girl nobody much notices at Ojai North High School. The biggest surprise about this school (apart from the fact that there is an Ojai North) is that it is scandalous to lose one's virginity in high school. I hesitate to generalize, but I suspect such a thing is not unheard of in Ojai North and elsewhere. I'm not recommending it. I only know what I'm told.

It is a rule with all comedies involving virginity, going back to Doris Day and long before, that enormous misunderstandings are involved and virginity miraculously survives at the end. In this case, Olive is simply embarrassed to admit she spent a whole weekend at home alone, and improvises a goofy story about having lost her virginity to a college boy. That seems safe; nobody in school would know him. But she's overheard by Miss Bryant (Amanda Bynes), a self-righteous religious type, who passes the story round as an object lesson to wayward girls: Don't become a fallen woman like Olive.

Easy A takes this misunderstanding and finds effortless comic variations in it. The news is taken with equanimity by Olive's parents, Dill and Rosemary (Stanley Tucci and Patricia Clarkson), who join Juno's parents in the Pantheon of Parental Admirability. And at Ojai North High, Olive finds that in having lost one reputation, she has gained another. Previously no one noticed her at all (hard to believe about Emma Stone, but there you have it). Now she is imagined to be an experienced and daring adventuress, and it can be deduced that a great many in the student body envy her experience.

Olive puts her notoriety to use. She has a gay friend named Brandon (Dan Byrd), who has been hassled at school (hard to believe in Ojai but, again, there you have it). By allowing word to get out that she and Brandon have shared blissful congress, she is able to bring an end to the bullying (hard to believe no one in Ojai North has heard of a gay and a straight having sex, but this Ojai is one created specifically for the convenience of a movie comedy, and people believe what the plot requires them to believe).

Now that she has become established as the school authority, she begins issuing a sort of Olive's Seal of Approval on various outsiders, misfits, and untouchables in the student body, outfitting them all with credentials of sexmanship. Does anybody wonder why she only sleeps with gays, nerds, and college students? Why should they? Lots of people do.

Easy A, like many good comedies, supplies us with a more or less conventional (movie) world in which one premise—Olive's transformation by gossip—is introduced. She becomes endowed overnight with a power to improve reputations, confer status, and help the needy. Her new power might even work for adults, such as the teacher Mr. Griffith (Thomas Haden Church) and his estranged wife (Lisa Kudrow), the guidance counselor, who become entangled in embarrassments.

The movie works because it's funny, yes, but also because it's smart. When Olive begins wearing the Scarlet Letter "A" on her clothing, borrowing it from the Nathaniel Hawthorne novel they still read in Ojai North, she shows a level of irony that I'm afraid is lost on the student body, but not on us. I think it may always be necessary that we like the hero or heroine of a comedy. I certainly liked Olive. I'm pretty sure that's also how an actor becomes a movie star.

Easy Virtue ★ ★ ★

PG-13, 96 m., 2009

Jessica Biel (Larita), Colin Firth (Mr. Whittaker), Kristin Scott Thomas (Mrs. Whittaker), Ben Barnes (John), Kris Marshall (Furber), Kimberley Nixon (Hilda), Katharine Parkinson (Marion). Directed by Stephan Elliott and produced by Joseph Abrams, James D. Stern, and Barnaby Thompson. Screenplay by Elliott and Sheridan Jobbins, based on the play by Noel Coward.

Unusually for a play by Noel Coward, love has a struggle conquering all in *Easy Virtue,* a subversive view of British country house society between the wars. That era has been described as the most blessed in modern history (assuming you were upstairs and not down), but not here, where the Whittaker family occupies a moldering pile in the countryside. It is said that nothing in a country house should look new. Nothing in this one looks as if it were ever new.

To his ancestral seat, a fresh young man named John (Ben Barnes) brings his great love, Larita (Jessica Biel), to meet his hostile mother (Kristin Scott Thomas), his shambling father (Colin Firth), and his unfortunate sisters Marion (Katharine Parkinson) and Hilda (Kimberley Nixon), one snobbish, the other fawning. Perhaps the innocent John never realized how toxic his mother and elder sister were until Larita arrived to attract their poison.

Larita is an auto racer, the recent winner of

the Monaco Grand Prix. It's worth remembering that in the 1920s racing drivers and pilots were admired almost like astronauts (see Shaw's *Man and Superman*), and females were goddesses. Yet Larita, an American unschooled in the labyrinth of the British upper crust, earnestly hopes to make her alliance with John a success. She does everything an American girl is taught to do, even supervising the preparation of what may be the first edible meal ever served in the stately home (all-purpose 1920s Brit recipe: "Cook until dead").

Scott Thomas and Firth are old hands at their characters, the one brittle and unpleasant, the other depressed, disillusioned, and unhappily wed. Ben Barnes is your prototypical fresh young man. Jessica Biel will surprise some with her skill; she takes to Coward as if to the manner (if not manor) born. She has certainly left her work in *The Texas Chainsaw Massacre* (2003) far behind. She makes Larita independent and able, yet capable of a love more sincere than the feckless John can comprehend. She would be the best thing that ever happened to him, and the story is essentially about whether he can get that through his head.

Mr. and Mrs. Whittaker are both more nuanced than the clichés they first seem. She has her urgent reasons for wishing her son to marry elsewhere. He is a member of that generation where most of the best and brightest died in the trenches of France—including, we learn, all of the men under his command. The matriarch clings desperately to the shreds of her fading family. Her husband retreats into dotty distraction and a studied casual evasiveness that masks despair.

Easy Virtue is being presented, and was no doubt intended by Coward, as a comedy. As we'd expect, the dialogue has an edgy wit, although it has no ambitions to be falling-down funny. Here is the *Odd Couple* formula applied in a specific time and place that make them feel very odd indeed.

Eat Pray Love ★ ★

PG-13, 141 m., 2010

Julia Roberts (Liz Gilbert), James Franco (David Piccolo), Richard Jenkins (Richard), Viola Davis (Delia Shiraz), Billy Crudup (Stephen), Javier Bardem (Felipe), Hadi Subiyanto (Ketut Liyer). Directed by Ryan Murphy and produced by Dede Gardner. Screenplay by Ryan Murphy and Jennifer Salt, based on the memoir by Elizabeth Gilbert.

Elizabeth Gilbert's book *Eat Pray Love*, unread by me, spent 150 weeks on the *New York Times* best-seller list and is by some accounts a good one. It is also movie material, concerning as it does a tall blonde (Gilbert) who ditches a failing marriage and a disastrous love affair to spend a year living in Italy, India, and Bali, seeking to find the balance of body, mind, and spirit. During this journey, great-looking men are platooned at her, and a wise man, who has to be reminded who she is, remembers instantly, although what he remembers is only what she's just told him.

I gather Gilbert's "prose is fueled by a mix of intelligence, wit and colloquial exuberance that is close to irresistible" (*New York Times Book Review*), and if intelligence, wit, and exuberance are what you're looking for, Julia Roberts is an excellent choice as the movie's star. You can see how it would be fun to spend a year traveling with Gilbert. A lot more fun than spending nearly two and a half hours watching a movie about it. I guess you have to belong to the narcissistic subculture of Woo-Woo.

Here is a movie about Liz Gilbert. About her quest, her ambition, her good luck in finding only nice men, including the ones she dumps. She funds her entire trip, including scenic accommodations, ashram, medicine man, guru, spa fees, and wardrobe, with her advance to write this book. Well, the publisher obviously made a wise investment. It's all about her, and a lot of readers can really identify with that. Her first marriage apparently broke down primarily because she tired of it, although Roberts at (a sexy and attractive) forty-three makes an actor's brave stab at explaining they were "young and immature." She walks out on the guy (Billy Crudup), and he still likes her and reads her on the Web.

In Italy, she eats such Pavarottian plates of pasta that I hope one of the things she prayed for in India was deliverance from the sin of gluttony. At one trattoria she apparently orders the entire menu, and I am not making this up. She meets a man played by James Franco, about whom, enough said. She shows moral fiber by leaving such a dreamboat for India, where her quest involves discipline in meditation, for which she allots three months rather than the recommended lifetime. There she meets a tall, bearded, bespectacled older Texan (Richard Jenkins) who is without question the most interesting and attractive man in the movie, and like all of the others seems innocent of lust.

In Bali she revisits her beloved adviser Ketut Liyer (Hadi Subiyanto), who is a master of truisms known to us all. Although he connects her with a healer who can mend a nasty cut with a leaf applied for a few hours, his own skills seem limited to the divinations anyone could make after looking at her, and telling her things about herself after she has already told him.

Now she has found Balance and begins to dance on the high-wire of her life. She meets Felipe (Javier Bardem), another divorced exile, who is handsome, charming, tactful, forgiving, and a good kisser. He explains that he lives in Bali because his business is import-export, "which you can do anywhere"—although later, he explains, "I live in Bali because my business is here." They've both forgotten what he said earlier. Unless perhaps you can do import-export anywhere, but you can only import and export from Bali when you live there. That would certainly be my alibi.

The audience I joined was perhaps 80 percent female. I heard some sniffles and glimpsed some tears, and no wonder. *Eat Pray Love* is shameless wish fulfillment, a Harlequin novel crossed with a mystic travelogue, and it mercifully reverses the life chronology of many people, which is Love Pray Eat. ☞

The Eclipse ★ ★ ★

R, 88 m., 2010

Ciaran Hinds (Michael Farr), Aidan Quinn (Nicholas Holden), Iben Hjejle (Lena Morelle), Jim Norton (Malachy McNeill), Eanna Hardwicke (Thomas), Hannah Lynch (Sarah). Directed by Conor McPherson and produced by Robert Walpole. Screenplay by McPherson and Billy Roche, based on Roche's *Tales from Rainwater Pond.*

The supernatural never seems far out of sight in Ireland, and it creeps in here and there during *The Eclipse,* a dark romance set at a literary festival in the County Cork cathedral town of Cobh. I'm not sure it's required, but it does little harm. The story centers on a quiet, enduring man named Michael Farr (Ciaran Hinds), who has lost his wife to cancer and is raising their two children. He volunteers to drive two visiting authors around town.

The authors have a history that is fondly recalled by only one of them. Nicholas Holden (Aidan Quinn) is a best-selling American novelist not a million miles removed from Nicholas Sparks. Lena Morelle (Iben Hjejle) is a British writer of upscale ghost stories. Once, at another festival, they had a brief fling, which only Nicholas thinks was a wise idea. Lena is warm and curious, a good person, and Nicholas, who after all is married, considers himself entitled to her comforts on the basis of her earlier mistake. Nicholas, when he drinks, can become quite unpleasant.

Of the other two key characters, one is dead and the other nearly so. Michael's late wife, Sarah (Hannah Lynch), is alive in his memory, and also occasionally turns up to offer advice or share his problems. She's simply there, seemingly in the flesh. Her father, Thomas (Eanna Hardwicke), his father-in-law, is still alive, but begins manifesting to Michael as a ghostly figure in the still of the night. Michael doesn't deserve this. His steadfast quality throughout the movie is goodness. Is he seeing a ghost, or is the old man prowling around?

Daytimes, Michael dutifully ferries Nicholas or Lena to their festival events, and shows them something of the town and its idyllic setting. He quickly picks up on the tension between them. If he were not so recently widowed, he might warm to Lena himself, but he isn't operating on that frequency. They slowly begin to bond in mutual sympathy.

Nicholas is a bit of an ass. Full of himself, fond of attention, lacking in insight, imperious. Michael, on the other hand, is almost too humble. He sees himself as an attendant, not a celebrant. And Lena? Smart, nice, increasingly worried about Nicholas's urgency, grateful for Michael as a port in the storm. All of this arrives at what I suppose is an inevitable crescendo involving lust, drinking, threats, and confusion, complicated by the increasingly dire supernatural manifestations Michael has experienced.

The Eclipse is needlessly confusing. Is it a ghost story or not? Perhaps this is my problem. Perhaps people who think they perceive the supernatural must simply incorporate that into their ordinary lives. Michael is a steady soul, and essentially does that. On another level, Aidan Quinn is superb at creating a man with the potential to behave as a monster, but with a certain buried decency. What of Lena and Michael? They deserve each other and will probably someday work that out.

Edge of Darkness ★ ★ ½

R, 117 m., 2010

Mel Gibson (Thomas Craven), Ray Winstone (Darius Jedburgh), Danny Huston (Jack Bennett), Bojana Novakovic (Emma Craven), Shawn Roberts (Burnham). Directed by Martin Campbell and produced by Tim Headington, Graham King, and Michael Wearing. Screenplay by William Monahan and Andrew Bovell.

Can we think of Mel Gibson simply as an action hero? A star whose personal baggage doesn't upstage his performances? I find that I can. He has made deplorable statements in recent years, which may be attributed to a kind of fanatic lunacy that can perhaps be diagnosed as a disease. The fact remains that in *Edge of Darkness* he remains a likable man with a natural screen presence.

Here he plays a Boston cop named Craven (always a dependable movie name). The great love of his life is his daughter, Emma (Bojana Novakovic). She works for a giant secretive corporation named Northmoor. Few corporations with *moor* in their titles are wholly trustworthy; we think too much about bodies being buried there.

Emma comes home for a visit rather unexpectedly. She is having nosebleeds. A bleeding nose can be a symptom of numerous disorders, but in a thriller, as we all know, there's only one possible diagnosis. Emma has hardly arrived when there's a knock on the door, they answer it together, and a man in a hood screams "Craven!" and shoots her dead.

It is assumed that the detective Thomas Craven was the intended target. Craven's not so sure. His investigation leads him to Northmoor and its silky, sinister chairman, Jack Bennett (Danny Huston, ominously courteous just as his father was in *Chinatown*). Bennett tears himself away from planning Northmoor's campaign contributions long enough to greet Craven in his office, atop a towering aerie overlooking his feudal lands.

Because much of the movie is a cranked-up thriller with chases, fights, conspiracies, and all that stuff, permit me a digression on secretive, shadowy corporations. What kinds of headquarters buildings do they inhabit? I Googled. Blackwater, which supplies our mercenaries in Iraq, has a drab two-story building outside Cleveland with eight cars parked out in front. Halliburton, Dick Cheney's old company, recently moved from Houston to an anonymous skyscraper in Dubai, closer to its place of business.

I mention this because Northmoor, which you will not be surprised to learn traffics in illegal, traitorous, and dangerous activities, occupies a spectacular structure atop a tall riverside hill, visible from miles around: its tower, its modernistic design, and its curious enormous gleaming globe suggesting a planetarium. It is a building worthy of magazine covers, not least *Architectural Digest.*

One purpose of corporate architecture is to impress. Northmoor's desire is to impress us, the moviegoer. Its structure looks left over from a James Bond movie, and indeed, the *Edge of Darkness* director, Martin Campbell, made *Casino Royale* (2006). It's the kind of edifice that inspires such questions as, "What do they *do* in there?" Much of what they do takes place in enormous buried spaces within the hill. This low-profile corporation undertook a construction project on a par with a subway line.

I explain this not merely to avoid discussing the off-the-shelf thriller plot, but to illustrate that *Edge of Darkness,* like so many recent thrillers, has no ambition to be taken seriously. If the corporation were more realistic, the movie would be, too. And then the fate of the world wouldn't depend yet once again on One Cop . . . With Nothing to Lose . . . On a Personal Mission.

Gibson inhabits this gazebo with as much conviction as is probably possible. He's joined in this by the superb British actor Ray Winstone, as an intriguing free agent who turns up in Craven's garden one night with a cigar and an enigmatic line of patter. Whom does he work for? Why does he know so much? Why does he work alone? He reminds me of a man I know, Jean-Jacques de Mesterton, who told me: "If you have a problem, you go to the cops. If they can't help you, you go to the FBI. If they can't help you, you go to the CIA. If they can't help you, you come to me."

Winstone's interaction with Gibson provides the movie with much of its interest. For the rest, it's a skillful exercise in CGI and standard-order thriller supplies. Gibson is a credible, attractive hero, as he has always been, so if you want fast-food action, here's your movie.

It does have a useful subtext. It serves as a reminder that the purpose of a corporation is not to be patriotic, but to maximize profits for its officers and shareholders. This is required by its bylaws. I suppose if we, as shareholders, don't agree with its profit-making strategies, we can always sell our stock, assuming we can find out what those strategies are.

An Education ★ ★ ★ ★

PG-13, 100 m., 2009

Carey Mulligan (Jenny), Peter Sarsgaard (David), Dominic Cooper (Danny), Rosamund Pike (Helen), Alfred Molina (Jack), Cara Seymour (Marjorie). Directed by Lone Scherfig and produced by Finola Dwyer and Amanda Posey. Screenplay by Nick Hornby, based on a memoir by Lynn Barber.

An Education tells the story of a sixteen-year-old girl who is the target of a sophisticated seduction by a thirty-five-year-old man. This happens in 1961, when sixteen-year-old girls were a great deal less knowing than they are now. Yet the movie isn't shabby or painful, but romantic and wonderfully entertaining.

It depends on a British actress named Carey Mulligan, who in her first major feature role is being compared by everyone with Audrey Hepburn. When you see her you can't think of anyone else to compare her with. She makes the role luminous when it could have been sad or awkward. She has such lightness and grace you're pretty sure this is the birth of a star.

All very well and good, you're thinking, but how is this a romance? Oh, it's not so much a romance between the teenager and the middle-aged man. That only advances to the level of an infatuation. It's a romance between the girl, named Jenny, and the possibilities within her, the future before her, and the joy of being alive. Yes, she sheds a few tears. But she gets better than she gives, and in hindsight this has been a valuable experience for her.

But wait. Doesn't this girl have parents? She certainly does. Jack and Marjorie (Alfred Molina and Cara Seymour) are proper, traditional middle-class parents in the London suburb of Twickenham, and there's nothing but love in the home. They aren't wealthy or worldly, but they wish the best for their girl and are bursting with pride that she's won a scholarship to Oxford. Then she springs David (Peter Sarsgaard) on them.

This is a smooth operator. He sees her standing at a bus stop in the rain holding her cello case. He offers her a lift in his sports car. He engages her in conversation about classical music. He "happens" to run into her again, and they have a nice chat. He wonders if she might enjoy . . .

You see how it goes. He opens a door she eagerly wants to enter, to concerts, plays, restaurants, double dates with his fascinating friends, talk about the great world when the boys at school have nothing to say. At some point it must become clear to her that he intends to sleep with her if he can, but by now she's thinking that he very possibly can.

I forgot to tell you about her parents. They dote and protect, but are very naive. David is good-looking, well dressed, well spoken, and very, very polite. He has *taken an interest* in Jenny because, why? He is impressed by this young woman's mind and enjoys sharing his advantages. He offers implicit guarantees of her safety, and they're so proud of her they believe a wealthy older man would be interested for purely platonic motives. They're innocents. Jenny will be safe with him for a weekend in Paris—because he has an aunt who lives there and will be her chaperone.

Paris! The city embodies Jenny's wildest

dreams! And to see it with a worldly dreamboat like David, instead of going there on the boat-train with a grotty, pimply seventeen-year-old! Is she cynically taking advantage of David for her own motives? Well, yes. Now close your eyes and remember your teens, and tell me you don't forgive her at least a little.

Part of the genius of *An Education* is it unfolds this relationship at a deliberate pace. Sarsgaard plays an attractive, intelligent companion. He is careful to keep a distance. Must be a good trout fisherman. To some degree he's truthful: He enormously enjoys this smart, pretty girl. He loves walking along the Seine with her. He knows things about the world that she eagerly welcomes.

Yes, he's also a rotter, a bounder, a cad, a dirty rotten scoundrel. But you can't get far in any of those trades if you're not also a charmer. To some degree, Jenny welcomes being deceived. The screenplay by Nick Hornby (*About a Boy, High Fidelity*) is based on a memoir by a real person, the British journalist Lynn Barber. It became well known in the United Kingdom that when she was sixteen, she had a two-year affair with a man named Simon in his late thirties.

There are many scene-by-scene parallels between book and movie, and much closely adapted dialogue. We know that Lynn Barber is smart and that she was pretty when she was sixteen. But her affair wasn't such a great experience, at least not in its second year. What transforms it in *An Education* is Carey Mulligan, who has that rare gift of enlisting us on her side and making us like her. She's so lovable that whatever happens must be somehow for Jenny's benefit. She glows.

So, young women, let this movie offer useful advice. When a man seems too good to be true, he probably isn't—good or true. We all make mistakes when we're growing up. Sometimes we learn from them. If we're lucky, we can even learn during them. And you must certainly see Paris. Do *not* count on meeting the aunt.

Lynn Barber writes: "What did I get from Simon? An education—the thing my parents always wanted me to have. . . . I learned about expensive restaurants and luxury hotels and foreign travel. I learned about antiques and Bergman films and classical music. But actually there was a much bigger bonus than that. My experience with Simon entirely cured my craving for sophistication. By the time I got to Oxford, I wanted nothing more than to meet kind, decent, straightforward boys my own age, no matter if they were gauche or virgins. I would marry one eventually and stay married all my life and for that, I suppose, I have Simon to thank."

Note: Lynn Barber's full account: www.guardian.co.uk/culture/2009/jun/07/lynn-barber-virginity-relationships.

El Camino ★ ★ ★

NO MPAA RATING, 87 m., 2009

Leo Fitzpatrick (Elliot), Christopher Denham (Gray), Elisabeth Moss (Lily), Wes Studi (Dave), Richard Gallagher (Matthew), Amy Hargreaves (Sissy). Directed by Erik S. Weigel and produced by Fran Giblin and Jason Noto. Screenplay by Weigel and Salvatore Interlandi.

El Camino is a pure American road movie, freed of the requirements of plot, requiring only a purpose and a destination. It is so pure that it involves two men and a woman, all in their twenties, all in the same station wagon, and there is *not* a romantic triangle. All three have different needs in life, and have joined only for this journey.

They meet for the first time when their friend Matthew (Richard Gallagher) dies. Elliot (Leo Fitzpatrick) and Matthew were in foster care together. Lily (Elisabeth Moss) was his former girlfriend. Gray (Christopher Denham) met him and felt an immediate bond. After the funeral, Gray and Lily decide to steal Matthew's ashes and scatter them in Mexico. Elliot insists on going along, and he will pay. That's the deal maker.

What did Matthew really mean to them? The movie lacks the usual heart-spilling confessions. All three are reticent, revealing themselves in elliptical asides. Nor do they spill the beans about their own lives. They pound on, mile after mile, North Carolina to Mexico, one cheap motel after another, lots of cigarettes, desultory talk, honky-tonk bars, a fight, unhappy telephone calls.

Road movies require colorful people along the way. This one has a couple. Wes Studi plays a self-employed man who repairs their car, invites them to dinner, has strong political opinions (not the ones you might expect), and contempt for Gray's cynicism. Amy Hargreaves plays an older woman in a bar who smiles at Gray and ends up listening to his introspections. And no, she's not a hooker; she's lonely and nice.

Mystery surrounds Elliot. Flashbacks suggest a confused childhood. We have no idea where he lives now, what he does, where he gets his money. I first saw the gawky Leo Fitzpatrick in the breakthrough movie *Kids* (1995), which also introduced Rosario Dawson, Chloe Sevigny, Justin Pierce, and Jon Abrahams. Fitzpatrick is gawky no more. He only gradually sheds his funeral suit and tie, tends to lean forward thoughtfully, gives the impression of not saying a lot of things that he could.

We begin to wonder what ashes will be scattered: only Matthew's, or perhaps the ashes of the false starts and undirected lives of the living? There are moments of self-discovery along the way, but not underlined with fraught dialogue or painfully intense acting. All three characters seem to be focusing mostly on themselves. In the way this confounds our road movie expectations, it becomes quietly absorbing.

The film is elegantly shot by Till Neumann in rarely seen 2.35:1 widescreen, good for the big boat they're driving in and for the landscape they're driving through. This is the opposite of queasy-cam, and it makes sense that one of those thanked by the filmmakers is the contemplative Terrence Malick (another is Gus Van Sant, himself a master of uncertain journeys). At the end, one of the characters has a next destination in mind. The other two seem prepared to simply move away from, not toward, their lives until now—and that, too, is in keeping with the tone. At a time of life when everything is still tentative, there's insight in a film that doesn't force them into corners.

The End of the Line ★ ★ ★

NO MPAA RATING, 90 m., 2009

A documentary directed by Rupert Murray and produced by George Duffield and Claire Lewis. Based on the book by Charles Clover.

It once was said that the cod were so populous off the coast of Nova Scotia that you could walk on the sea on their backs. Now they have virtually disappeared. The cod, the fish in fish 'n' chips, has been overfished to near extinction. Other fish species are following.

There is heartfelt footage in *The End of the Line,* circa 1992, of angry, panicked fishermen besieging a hearing room where a government minister is calling for a moratorium on cod fishing. The Canadian prime minister, Brian Mulroney, declares it a necessity. These fishermen have depended on the cod for a living, and in many cases, so have their fathers back for many generations. The Canadian maritime provinces were largely settled because of the fishing industry.

The moratorium was imposed. But in 1992 it was already too late. The cod did not come back. They are virtually gone from those waters. Many documentaries about ecology issue dire warnings of crises that will strike at some point in the future. Opponents of these films scoff at them. But *The End of the Line* in large part is about what has already, irrefutably, happened.

Factory fishing grew too quickly, unsupervised, and damaged some fish populations so severely that their very sustainability was put into question. Giant trawlers prowled the seas halfway around the world from their ports. They used technology such as sonar to pinpoint schools of fish, and bottom trawling to capture great masses of them, while incidentally wreaking havoc with the seabed.

Some nations continue outlaw behavior. Japan continues its whaling in the face of international opprobrium. The role of other nations has been more subtle. International fishery experts were puzzled, for example, by the paradox that regional catches were down everywhere but the global catch remained steady.

How could this be? It appeared that all nations posted losses except China, which had steady gains. Were the Chinese overfishing? Just the contrary: Scientists discovered they were making up their numbers, as regional party officials supplied fake growth statistics to look better in Beijing.

The End of the Line documents what threatens to become an irreversible decline in aquatic populations within forty years. Opportunist species move in to take advantage. Oddly, the disappearance of cod has resulted in an explosion of the lobster population, as they lose their chief rival for food.

There are some bright spots. The state of Alaska, for example, is praised for its fishing policies, which restrict fishing waters, the number of boats, the length of the season, and the size of the catch. These policies contribute to "sustainable populations." Walmart, which sells enormous quantities of fish, is switching to sustainable sources. Ninety percent of the fish in McDonald's fish sandwiches is from sustainable sources.

For every bright spot, there is an omen. Fish farms, for example, seem like progress, but their fish are fed the ground-up bodies of captured free-range fish. It takes five kilos of anchovies to produce one of salmon. Bluefin tuna is an endangered species. A lot of retail tuna is not tuna at all. Some of it is dolphin, itself a threatened species.

The famous sushi restaurant Nobu declines to remove bluefin from its menu but promises to add a consumer advisory for consumers, comparing the situation to the health warnings on cigarettes. Not precisely a parallel: Eating bluefin is dangerous to *their* health, not ours.

The question arises: If fish are threatened, and beef production requires much more land and crop consumption than justified in terms of feeding the Earth's population, what are we to eat? The answer is staring us in the face: We should eat a more largely vegetarian diet, using animal proteins as humans have traditionally used them, as a supplement, rather than a main course.

The End of the Line, directed by Rupert Murray, based on a book by Charles Clover, is constructed from interviews with many experts, a good deal of historical footage, and much incredible footage from under the sea, including breathtaking vistas of sea preserves, where the diversity of species can be seen to grow annually. We once thought of the sea as limitless bounty. I think I may even have heard that in school. But those fantasies are over.

Enlighten Up! ★ ★ ★

NO MPAA RATING, 82 m., 2009

Featuring Nick Rosen, Norman Allen, B. K. S. Iyengar, Pattabhi Jois, Gurusharananda, Cyndi Lee, Alan Finger, Dharma Mittra, Shyamdas, Sharon Gannon, David Life, Joseph Alter, David Gordon White, Diamond Dallas Page, Madan Kataria. A documentary directed and produced by Kate Churchill. Screenplay by Churchill and Jonathon Hexner.

An unemployed journalist and a documentary filmmaker spend six months traveling far enough to circle the globe, and they discover that the secret of yoga is the same as how to get to Carnegie Hall: practice, practice, practice. Apart from that, apparently, there is no secret at all to yoga. At least, they don't find a yogi who will admit to one.

Kate Churchill and her subject, Nick Rosen, travel from New York to Boulder to California to Hawaii, and then on to India. Nick practices under masters ranging from the legendary Yogacharya B. K. S. Iyengar, ninety-one, named by *Time* as one of the one hundred most influential people in the world, to Diamond Dallas Page, named by *Pro Wrestling Illustrated* as the most hated wrestler of the year (1999).

All of these teachers, young and old, male and female, Eastern and Western, refuse to define or even really name the ultimate state one hopes to reach. When you get there, you will know it. You will find it within yourself. You just have to do it. Practice does not make perfection, but it makes improvement. One must not focus on the destination but on the journey. Live in the moment. Live in eternity. Find God. Let the body flow into a yoga position as light fills a diamond (Iyengar). Your reward will be tits and ass (Diamond Dallas).

This was all fine with me because I wasn't much interested in arriving at ultimate answers, and neither, it must be said, is Nick Rosen. He does, however, log a lot of miles and has a particularly interesting time in India. He practices fervently. His body assumes positions on which, unlike a diamond, the sun don't shine. He begins as a skeptic about the spiritual side of yoga, and ends the same way, and doesn't find any yogis who try to proselytize him.

Instead, they offer variations of "Just do it!" Nick just does it, and at the end of his trial he tells Kate that he feels good, sleeps better, is stronger, has an improved digestive system, and in theory a better sex life (in practice, he tells her, "I haven't been alone with a woman for months—except you").

He also has better breath control, an area of particular interest to me. Once at Rancho La Puerta I was taking a yoga class, and we were all told to close our eyes and emit the sound "ahhhhhhh." I did so. When I opened my eyes, everyone was staring at me. "You sustained that three times as long as anyone else in the room," the yoga instructor told me. "In fact, I've never seen anyone holding out that long." Chaz theorized it had something to do with my ability to keep talking without letting anyone get a word in edgeways.

Enlighten Up! may prove a disappointment to anyone seeking to discover the secrets of yoga, or have their own beliefs confirmed. Apparently it does all come down to practice. Some seem addicted to it, which seems a shame to me, because a discipline should be a path to a fuller life, not an alternative. If you spend the rest of your life practicing yoga, well, that's what you did with the rest of your life. It's healthier than sinning, but that's about the best you can say.

And yet this is an interesting movie, and I'm glad I saw it. I enjoyed all the people I met during Nick's six-month quest. Most seemed cheerful and outgoing, and exuded good health. They smiled a lot. They weren't creepy true believers obsessed with converting everyone. They seemed happy with where they were, and they assumed Nick wanted to be there, too. And for the most part they seem to live contented lives, although Diamond Dallas advises yoga as a way to meet chicks, and (a sharp shake of the wind chime, please) that man will never find tranquillity who has not divested himself of subterfuge in meeting chicks.

Kate Churchill's role is intriguing. At the outset she tells us she's a yoga practitioner who thought there would be a documentary in recruiting a novice and exposing that person to yoga, then filming what happened. She obviously hopes Nick will take to yoga more than he does, and sounds wistful in her off-camera questions. Is he beginning to find something more in it? Does he have a favorite teacher? Has his appreciation deepened?

Nick is an affable man who goes along with her plan. Recently downsized, he has little better to do than be flown around the world to yoga experiences. But he's not cut out to practice, practice, practice, and he's so laid back that few sparks fly. This is a peaceful kind of film, not terribly eventful, but I suppose we wouldn't want a yoga thriller. Relax. Let it happen. Or not.

Even the Rain ★ ★ ★

NO MPAA RATING, 104 m., 2010

Luis Tosar (Costa), Gael Garcia Bernal (Sebastian), Juan Carlos Aduviri (Daniel), Karra Elejalde (Anton), Carlos Santos (Alberto), Raul Arevalo (Juan). Directed by Iciar Bollain and produced by Juan Gordon. Screenplay by Paul Laverty.

The genre of movies about movies coils back on itself in *Even the Rain.* The film involves the making of a film about Columbus and his discovery of America. That story shows how his arrival began centuries of exploitation of the native Americans he found. *Even the Rain* is about how the filming of this story begins yet another cycle of exploitation.

As the film opens, a cast and crew have arrived on location in the mountains of Bolivia, far from the Caribbean shores first found by Columbus. Here, as the producer Costa (Luis Tosar) boasts, the local Indians can be hired as extras for two dollars a day and count themselves lucky. They can also be used for manual labor, and Costa is happy to use them to haul a giant crucifix into position, saving the cost of tractor rental.

You may begin to glimpse some symbolism coming into view. The film will exploit the Indians just as Columbus did. The difference is that Columbus evoked Christianity as his excuse, while the modern film thinks it is denouncing him while committing the same sins. This is more clear to us than the characters, including Gael Garcia Bernal as Sebastian, the director, who has vague sympathies for his low-paid workers, but places his film above everything.

An opening scene establishes the poverty in the district. A casting call for extras draws a line of hopefuls that reaches out of sight. One of these is Daniel (Juan Carlos Aduviri), a worker who protests when the auditions are cut short. Sebastian ends up casting him in an important role, and then discovers that in real life Daniel is a leader in a local revolt against the privatization of the local water resources. A California company has bought land rights and plans to charge the Indians for water from their own wells.

A memory stirred uneasily within me. The James Bond movie *Quantum of Solace* (2008) involved a scheme to corner the Bolivian water supply, and this seemed ridiculous to me ("Ohooo! Nooo!" I wrote). A reader informed me that there was indeed such a scheme, and that in Cochabamba the Bechtel Corp. lost its fight to charge the locals for the water. *Even the Rain* has been filmed in Cochabamba, is based on that real event, and instead of James Bond, has Daniel as a Christ figure.

The personal dynamics of a movie location can be tricky. Here Sebastian faces not only a crusading local actor but an alcoholic leading man and a penny-pinching producer. Costa is obsessed with saving money, Sebastian thinks of himself as more humanitarian, but it is Costa who is eventually humanized by the plight of the workers. He grows fond of Daniel's sweet little daughter, and when local forces are brought in to subdue the demonstrations, the girl is injured and Costa suddenly sees things in a different light. This is not absolutely convincing, and depends too heavily on a race through riot-torn streets, but it provides a plot device to explain Costa's rediscovery of conscience.

The performance by Luis Tosar as the producer is confident and sturdy. Gael Garcia Bernal, as the director, is wimpy and not clearly defined, but that's in the nature of the character. The movie is brave to raise the questions it does, although at the end I looked in vain for a credit saying, "No extras were underpaid in the making of this film."

Everlasting Moments ★ ★ ★ ★

NO MPAA RATING, 131 m., 2009

Maria Heiskanen (Maria Larsson), Mikael Persbrandt (Sigfrid Larsson), Jesper Christensen (Sebastian Pedersen), Callin Ohrvall (Maja Larsson). Directed by Jan Troell and produced by Thomas Stenderup. Screenplay by Niklas Radstrom, based on a story by Agneta Ulfsater Troell.

Rarely is there a film that evokes our sympathy more deeply than *Everlasting Moments.* It is a great story of love and hope, told tenderly and without any great striving for effect. It begins in Sweden in 1911 and involves a woman, her daughter, her husband, a camera, and the kindness of a stranger. It has been made by Jan Troell, a filmmaker whose care for these characters is instinctive.

The woman is named Maria Larsson. She lives with her husband, Sigfrid, in Malmo, a port city at the southern tip of Sweden. They eventually have seven children. "Sigge" is a laborer on the docks who takes the pledge time and again at the Temperance Society but falls back into alcoholism. He is a loving and jovial man when sober, but violent when he is drunk, and the children await his homecomings with apprehension.

The movie is not really about Sigge. It is about Maria, who is a strong woman, resilient, complex. She raises the children, works as a house cleaner, copes with the family's poverty. Once, when newly married, she won a camera in a lottery. Now she finds it and takes it to a photo shop to pawn it and buy food. There she meets Sebastian Pedersen, and he finds an undeveloped plate still in the camera. He develops it, and something about the photograph or Maria causes him to say he will buy the camera, but she must hold it for him and continue to take pictures.

Maria is not sophisticated and may have little education, but she is a deep and creative woman and an instinctively gifted photographer. She has no theory, but her choices of subjects and compositions are inspired. And perhaps Mr. Pedersen inspires her, too. He is much older and always polite and proper with her, but over a time it becomes clear that they have fallen in love.

No, the film is not about how she leaves her drunken husband and becomes a famous photographer. It is about how her inner life is transformed by discovering that she has an artistic talent. She continues to be committed to Sigge by a bond deeper than marriage or obligation. But she tentatively takes steps toward personal independence that were rare in that time. When Sigge goes to fight in the war, she supports the family by taking marriage photographs.

Maria Heiskanen, who plays Maria, makes her a shy woman who is almost frightened to take a larger view of herself. She is strong when she needs to be but unaccustomed to men like Mr. Pedersen, who treat her as something more than she conceives herself. One of the film's mysteries is how clearly she defines her marriage to Sigge, which endures, even though she fully feels the possibilities that Sebastian never quite offers. Mikael Persbrandt makes Sigge not a bad man but powerless over alcohol. His labor is back-breaking. And look at the tact of Jesper Christensen as Sebastian, who loves Maria from the moment he sees her but wants to protect her from the problems that could bring. The movie is intensely observant about these gradations of love.

Everlasting Moments reflects the great self-assurance of Jan Troell, whose work includes such masterpieces as *The Emigrants, The New Land,* and *Hamsun.* All of his films are about lives striving toward greater fullness. He respects work, values, and feelings. He stands apart from the frantic hunger for fashionable success. After I saw this film, I looked through a few of the early reviews of it and found critics almost startled by its humanism. Here is Todd McCarthy of *Variety:* "Beholding Troell's exquisite images is like having your eyes washed, the better to behold moving pictures of uncorrupted purity and clarity."

The story comes from the heart. Troell, who showed *Everlasting Moments* at Telluride 2008, adapted it from a novel by his wife, Agneta, who based it on one of her own family members, Maria Larsson. Maria lived this life and took some of the photographs we see. The film is narrated by her daughter, Maja Larsson (Callin Ohrvall), and in my imagination I hear Maja telling the story to Agneta, for Jan was born in Malmo, and the dates work out that they might both have known her well and always thought hers was a story worth telling.

Everybody's Fine ★ ★ ½

PG-13, 95 m., 2009

Robert De Niro (Frank Goode), Drew Barrymore (Rosie), Kate Beckinsale (Amy), Sam Rockwell (Robert). Directed by Kirk Jones and produced by Vittorio Cecchi Gori, Ted Field, Glynis Murray, and Gianni Nunnari. Screenplay by Jones, based on Giuseppe Tornatore's 1990 film *Stanno tutti bene.*

A man in his sixties after the death of his wife is a leaky ship without a bailer. Frank Goode has everything above deck shipshape, but he's sinking. The garden is his pride and joy. Everything inside is mopped, scrubbed, polished, dusted, arranged, and alphabetized. He buys big steaks and a new electric grill to cook them on. He selects a wine with the advice of a clueless stock boy. He reclines in his lawn chair on his manicured lawn and awaits the arrival of his four children.

At the last minute, none of them can make it. One can't even be bothered to call, but his regrets are passed along. Frank (Robert De Niro) steers a steady course to his doctor, saying he plans to do some traveling. His doctor says this is a bad idea. Frank decides not to drive, and by train, plane, and automobile visits the homes of his family diaspora. He is not greeted with unalloyed joy. He was a distant disciplinarian, often critical, a chilly alternative to the wife who held them together. They don't hate him, but they have their lives to lead.

Everybody's Fine tells the story of his journey and his discoveries along the way. If we have seen a dozen movies in our lifetime, we can feel pretty safe in predicting that each child will reveal, and present, a different kind of problem. That Frank will discover things he didn't know about himself and them. That he will reevaluate his life in the process. That a great deal of the American landscape will pass by on the screen. And, since all story pegs exist to hang things from, his lifetime of manufacturing telephone cables will result in many, many shots of telephone lines stringing along the way, symbolizing lines of communication. What will we do when the need for landlines disappears?

All that could redeem this thoroughly foreseeable unfolding would be colorful characters and good acting. *Everybody's Fine* comes close, but not close enough. The children are David, an artist who seems not to be at home in his marginal New York apartment building, but whose work is on display in the gallery downstairs; Amy (Kate Beckinsale), a Chicago advertising woman with a high-flying lifestyle; Robert (Sam Rockwell), a classical musician in Denver; and Rosie (Drew Barrymore), a successful professional dancer in Las Vegas with a luxurious apartment.

The more the children feed him vague evasions about David, the more Frank realizes how much they have always concealed from him. He isn't stupid, and picks up on stray dialogue and other clues to realize their lives are all deceptive fictions. And so is his own?

Everybody's Fine is based on a 1990 Giuseppe Tornatore film named *Stanno tutti bene,* which starred Marcello Mastroianni as a man in the same situation. Mastroianni and De Niro are not interchangeable. Mastroianni is effortlessly relaxed and embracing, the life source in a body. De Niro is not. There are many things he does better than anyone else alive, but playing nice isn't one of them.

What he does do is play Frank with respect and affection. There are no De Niro trademarks visible. He builds Frank from the ground up as a man who always tried to do the right thing, usually in the wrong way. He's like an actor singing well after much vocal coaching; Mastroianni in these matters was born pitch-perfect. Of modern comparable actors, I think above all of Jack Lemmon.

Of the actors playing the children, everybody's fine. Drew Barrymore has the central role and as always is a magnet for our affection. In twenty-five years she'd be right for a remake of this story about a widow, not a widower. In general, however, my advice would be, not "rent it" (you know how I feel about that), but the more realistic "check it out if you come upon it by accident while channel-surfing."

Every Little Step ★ ★ ★

PG-13, 96 m., 2009

A documentary directed and produced by James D. Stern and Adam Del Deo.

Every Little Step is a documentary about the casting process starting in 2006 for a Broadway revival of *A Chorus Line,* a musical that has been running somewhere in the world since its premiere in 1975 and inspired Richard Attenborough's 1985 film. The musical is about seventeen dancers who audition for their roles. The doc honors countless more who auditioned but were not chosen.

As I watched the film, one thought above all others was inspired: These people must love dancing to the point of abandon to submit themselves to this ordeal. Dancers must be in physical shape as good as most pro athletes and better than many. In fact, they *are* professional athletes, because although what they perform in is art, what they do is demanding physical work.

Often starting as young children, they practice, rehearse, and at some point forgo ordinary lives to submerge themselves in this process. It's the same with Olympians. They train and condition and focus and sacrifice. They turn up by the hundreds for auditions (the shots of the lineup outside the open call in Manhattan would make a doc in themselves). To get a call-back means they are superbly talented. Even then, the odds are they won't be chosen. Then it's back to more painstaking preparation, another job done for the paycheck, more dreams, more lines, more auditions, and usually more disappointments.

What we sense in the film is the camaraderie among these hopeful dancers. They've all been through the process before, all have been disappointed before, all know better than anyone else what it takes, all believe the best candidates don't always win the jobs.

The stakes are so high that to be one of the judges must cause restless dreams. Among them are Bob Avian, Michael Bennett's fellow choreographer in the 1975 production, and a vivacious force of nature named Baayork Lee, a dancer who played Connie, many people's favorite character, in that production. She handles the lineups, leads routines, and is, in her presence and energy, a testimony that it is possible to survive and find joy in this world.

I was reminded of *The Audition,* a film I saw last month, about the Metropolitan Opera's annual National Council Auditions. The art forms are different; the ordeals are the same. Then we buy our tickets and attend, and make dinner plans, and worry about parking, and chat at intermission, and admire what we see, when admiration is not adequate. We should be kneeling on concrete to remind ourselves what dues these artists pay.

Everything Must Go ★ ★ ★

R, 97 m., 2011

Will Ferrell (Nick Halsey), Rebecca Hall (Samantha), Laura Dern (Delilah), Christopher Jordan Wallace (Kenny Loftus), Michael Peña (Frank Garcia). Directed by Dan Rush and produced by Marty Bowen and Wyck Godfrey, based on the short story "Why Don't You Dance?" by Raymond Carver.

I found myself thinking during *Everything Must Go* that Will Ferrell is a gifted dramatic actor. That's sometimes the case with actors who specialize in comedy. Consider Robin Williams, Jack Lemmon, Jackie Gleason, Jim Carrey. Remember Adam Sandler in *Punch-Drunk Love.* To be good in comedy you need to be very skilled indeed, but talent doesn't always transfer to the heavy stuff. It's partly the matter of the physical presence. Ferrell has a presence. He reminds me sometimes of Fred MacMurray in his noir films.

Everything Must Go is not all the film it could have been, but is more worth seeing than a lot of other recent releases. It held my attention through Ferrell's performance as Nick Halsey, a man who drinks his way out of a job and a marriage. He isn't one of those flamboyant drunks, just a contained, dutiful man whose drinking has become the priority in his life. These are the kinds of alcoholics who break your heart: They mean to do well, they're not mean or violent, but over the years the need for booze has moved into the foreground.

They say you need to find your bottom before you're likely to stop. Every bottom is different. Nick finds his on the front lawn of his house, along with his furniture, his clothing, his keepsakes, and his life as a man whose wife has left him. He's locked out. His credit cards don't work. He deals with this by buying some beer and settling into his La-Z-Boy recliner. Fortunately, the nights can be mild in Arizona.

The idea for the movie, written and directed by Dan Rush, is based on the Raymond Carver short story "Why Don't You Dance?" Carver was an alcoholic who lost most of the things in his life and then found them again through recovery and the love of his wife, the poet Tess Gallagher. In his story, the hero simply has a sale to sell everything he owns, which as we all know is better than dealing with the movers. In the film, the (never seen) wife is the deciding factor, but as the days and nights slide past, Nick Halsey gradually clears out not only his valued possessions but his excess inventory.

Of course neighbors complain. When a cop comes, it's Frank Garcia (Michael Peña), who was Nick's sponsor during an unsuccessful whirl through AA. Nick argues that he has a perfect right to use his lawn as he chooses, and I suppose if the law permits pink flamingos, anything goes. There is also the matter of the young woman named Samantha (Rebecca Hall), who has just moved in across the street, is pregnant, and is awaiting her husband. "What kind of a man lets his pregnant wife move halfway across the country by herself?" protests Nick, whose own wife may have been left on her own a time or two.

Into this situation comes an African-American teenager named Kenny (Christopher Jordan Wallace), a nice kid who rides up on his bike, asks the obvious questions, and enters into a tacit understanding to become Nick's business partner in the yard sale. This character is very well handled. He is not tiny and cute. He is not a cutup. He is not what Spike Lee calls a Magic Negro, one of those black people who enter into the lives of whites with wise advice. No, he is a normal kid, self-possessed, even thoughtful, who keeps his opinions to himself and has an instinctive tact. (Wallace is the son of late Notorious B.I.G., and played his dad as a kid in a movie about the rapper's life.)

The movie doesn't trick up this story much more than it needs. The spartan solemnity of the Carver story seems buried within it. Ferrell plays Nick straight from the shoulder, without spin, respectfully. What it amounts to is for you to decide. At the end I was expecting more of an emotional payoff; making a movie calm is one thing, and making it matter-of-fact is another. But make a note about Will Ferrell. There is depth there.

Exit Through the Gift Shop ★ ★ ★ ½

R, 86 m., 2010

A documentary narrated by Rhys Ifans. Featuring Thierry Guetta, Banksy, Space

Invader, Shepard Fairey, Neckface, and Swoon. Directed by Banksy and produced by Holly Cushing, Jaimie D'Cruz, and James Gay-Rees.

The widespread speculation that *Exit Through the Gift Shop* is a hoax only adds to its fascination. An anonymous London graffiti artist named Banksy arrives to paint walls in Los Angeles. He encounters an obscure Frenchman named Thierry Guetta, who has dedicated his life to videotaping graffiti artists.

The Frenchman's hundreds of tapes have been dumped unorganized into boxes. Banksy thinks they might make a film. Guetta makes a very bad one. Banksy takes over the film and advises Guetta to create some art himself. Guetta does, names himself Mr. Brainwash, and organizes an exhibition of his work, through which he makes a fortune in sales.

Surely Thierry Guetta cannot be real? With his dashing mustache and Inspector Clouseau accent, his long-suffering wife and his zealous risk taking to film illegal artists by stealth? Surely he didn't rent a former CBS television studio and transform it into an exhibition space? Surely people didn't line up at dawn to get in—and pay tens of thousands of dollars for the works of an artist who had never held a show, sold a work, or received a review? Surely not if his work looked like art school rip-offs of the familiar styles of famous artists?

Even while I sat spellbound during this film, that's what I was asking myself. But Thierry Guetta surely did. His art exhibition was written up in a cover story in *L.A. Weekly* on June 12, 2008. It mentions this film, which Banksy was "threatening to do." Common sense dictates that no one would rent a CBS studio and fill it with hundreds of artworks in order to produce a hoax indie documentary. Nor would they cast Guetta, indubitably a real person, as himself. Right? Right?

The film depends entirely on Guetta, a cross between a TV pitchman, a cartoon Frenchman, and a chatty con man. Its footage really has been edited from a decade of tapes made clandestinely while L.A. graffiti artists risked arrest and death to create their paintings in spectacular places. Guetta fearlessly followed them right out onto ledges and helped them carry supplies to places a human fly might balk at. And all the time he's talking, talking, telling his life story and his hero worship for these artists.

There are all kinds of graffiti. Much of it is ugly defacement, the kind of territorial marking a dog does so much more elegantly. Chicago mayor Richard Daley's Graffiti Busters have my support and admiration. Some graffiti, however, is certainly art, as Norman Mailer was one of the first to argue in his book *The Faith of Graffiti* (1974). Banksy and others at his level, such as Guetta's hero Shepard Fairey, find ways to visually reinvent public spaces and make striking artistic statements.

But what does Guetta do? One of his artworks, inspired by Andy Warhol's Campbell's soup can, shows a can of tomato paint spray. OK, that's witty enough for a nice editorial cartoon. How many thousands would you spend to have it in your house? Or a morph of Joan Crawford and Warhol's Marilyn? Then again, at the time, people said Andy Warhol wasn't creating art either. Surely Warhol's message was that Thierry Guetta has an absolute right to call his work art and sell it for as much as he can.

There are currently more than 3,600 comments on my recent blog headlined "Video Games Can Never Be Art." At least 95 percent of them inform me I am a fool and that "art is in the eye of the beholder." I believe video games are not an art *form*, for reasons I am certainly not going to bring up again. I am quite willing to agree that graffiti is Art, but I don't believe the act of painting them is an art form, if you see what I mean. Or maybe you don't. You may be too old to understand my argument.

Anyway, comment No. 3,307 on my blog was from Kristian, and it said: "The wafting smell of dried mung beans pervades my nostrils." That's kind of . . . poetic, don't you think? But I stray from my thoughts, which are (1) *Exit Through the Gift Shop* is an admirable and entertaining documentary; (2) I believe it is not a hoax; (3) I would not much want a Thierry Guetta original; (4) I like Thierry Guetta; and (5) Banksy, the creator of this film, is a gifted filmmaker whose thoughts, as he regards Guetta, must resemble those of Victor Frankenstein when he regarded his monster: It works, but is it Art?

Extract ★ ★ ½

R, 91 m., 2009

Jason Bateman (Joel), Mila Kunis (Cindy), Kristen Wiig (Suzie), Ben Affleck (Dean), J. K. Simmons (Brian), David Koechner (Nathan), Clifton Collins Jr. (Step), Dustin Milligan (Brad), Gene Simmons (Joe Adler). Directed by Mike Judge and produced by Michael Rotenberg and John Altschuler. Screenplay by Judge.

Granted that they're now human beings and not cartoons, Mike Judge's characters may never grow much smarter than Beavis and Butthead, who launched him on his career. The people in *Extract* are not as stupid as the ones in *Idiocracy* (2006), his previous film, but then those idiots had the benefit of a few hundred extra years during which to refute Darwin by evolving less intelligence. The *Extract* people work in a bottling plant that's up for sale when everything goes wrong in the life of its owner, Joel (Jason Bateman, of *Juno*).

Joel suffers in an unhappy marriage with Suzie (Kristen Wiig), whose potential sex life closes every evening at the moment when she tugs tight the drawstring on her sweatpants. That works better for her than a chastity belt. He shares his frustrations with the friendly bartender Dean (Ben Affleck), who advises him to cheat. But Joel can't bring himself to do that to Suzie. All right then, Dean says: Hire a gigolo to seduce her. Once Suzie has cheated, Joel's conscience will be clear.

Many of the other problems in Joel's life stem from the bottling plant, whose floor he overlooks from a high window. One involves a potential lawsuit from an employee named Step (Clifton Collins Jr.) who loses a testicle in a most unfortunate accident. Others come from a lazy and racist woman who does as little work as possible but resents the good workers, especially the Mexican-Americans.

Then there's the arrival of Cindy (Mila Kunis), a sexy con woman who is working far below her competence level on the bottling line, but precisely at her morality level. She understands that almost any man will believe it when a desirable woman says she's attracted to him. Hey, some babes have a fetish for schleppers.

Cindy, who is superb at putting two and two together and putting money in her pocket, convinces Step to sue the company. He hires a lawyer famous for his ads on the benches at bus stops, Joe Adler (Gene Simmons, no more subtle than when he was in Kiss). Meanwhile, Joel recruits a gigolo (Dustin Milligan), who even in this crowd isn't the brightest bulb.

There are some good stretches in the film, Bateman is persuasive as the overwhelmed factory owner, and Mila Kunis brings her role to within shouting distance of credibility. The funniest element for me was supplied by Joel's neighbor Nathan (David Koechner), a pest who lurks in the shrubbery to burst forth with undesired friendliness. He is a case study of a bore, as once defined by John D. MacDonald: "Someone who deprives you of solitude without providing you with companionship." It cannot be easy for an actor to be as inspired as Koechner in the timing and facial language of a man who *cannot* comprehend urgent conversational signals that he get lost immediately.

The movie otherwise is sort of entertaining but lacks the focus and comic energy of Judge's *Office Space* (1999), and to believe that Suzie would be attracted to the gigolo requires not merely the suspension of disbelief but its demolition. A comedy need not be believable. But it needs to seem as if it's believable at least to itself.

Extraordinary Measures ★ ★

PG, 105 m., 2010

Brendan Fraser (John Crowley), Harrison Ford (Robert Stonehill), Keri Russell (Aileen), Meredith Droeger (Megan), Diego Velazquez (Patrick), Sam Hill (John Jr.). Directed by Tom Vaughn and produced by Carla Santos Shamberg, Michael Shamberg, and Stacey Sher. Screenplay by Robert Nelson Jacobs, based on *The Cure* by Geeta Anand.

Extraordinary Measures is an ordinary film with ordinary characters in a story too big for it. Life has been reduced to a Lifetime movie. The story, based on fact, is compelling: Two sick children have no more than a year to live when their father determines to seek out a maverick scientist who may have a cure. This is *Lorenzo's Oil* with a different disease, Pompe disease, although it fudges the facts to create a better story. The film centers on two dying children, nine and seven. In life, most children with Pompe die before age two, and those in the real story were fifteen months and seven days old when they got sick, and five and three when they were treated.

With children that young, the drama would have focused on the parents. By making Megan Crowley (Meredith Droeger) a wise and cheerful nine-year-old, *Extraordinary Measures* improves her as a story element. Her father is John Crowley (Brendan Fraser), an executive at Bristol-Myers. Her mother is Aileen (Keri Russell). Neither is developed any more deeply than the story requires. Their personal relationship is defined by their desperation as the deadlines for their children grow nearer.

Crowley discovers on the Internet a professor at the University of Nebraska named Dr. Robert Stonehill (Harrison Ford). He's working on a controversial cure for Pompe that the medical establishment rejects, and when he won't return messages, Crowley impulsively flies to Nebraska to confront him.

Dr. Robert Stonehill doesn't exist in life. The Pompe cure was developed by Dr. Yuan-Tsong Chen and his colleagues while he was at Duke University. He is now director of the Institute of Biomedical Science in Taiwan. Harrison Ford, as this film's executive producer, perhaps saw Stonehill as a plum role for himself; a rewrite was necessary because he couldn't very well play Dr. Chen. The real Chen, a Taiwan University graduate, worked his way up at Duke from a residency to professor and chief of medical genetics at the Duke University Medical Center. He has been mentioned as a Nobel candidate.

I suspect Dr. Chen might have inspired a more interesting character than "Dr. Stonehill." The Nebraskan seems inspired more by Harrison Ford's image and range. He plays the doctor using only a few spare parts off the shelf. (1) He likes to crank up rock music while he works. (2) He doesn't return messages. (3) He's so feckless he accidentally hangs up on Crowley by pulling the phone off his desk. (4) He likes to drink beer from longneck bottles in a honky-tonk bar and flirt with the waitress. (5) "I'm a scientist, not a doctor." He's not interested in Pompe patients, only the chemistry of the disease.

This becomes tiresome. Later he becomes invested in the Crowleys, but of course he does. They hope to fund a high-tech startup and deal with venture capitalists whose scenes are more interesting than many of the medical ones. Contrast this with the character of Augusto Odone, played by Nick Nolte in *Lorenzo's Oil*—a self-taught parent who discovers his own cure for a rare nerve disease. Ford is given no lines that suggest depth of character, only gruffness that gradually mellows.

The film also fails to explain that the cost of the medication is $300,000 a year for life, which limits its impact in the United States because many American insurance companies refuse to pay for it. According to Wikipedia: "The vast majority of developed countries are providing access to therapy for all diagnosed Pompe patients."

Make no mistake. The Crowleys were brave and resourceful, and their proactive measures saved the lives of their children—and many more with Pompe. This is a remarkable story. I think the film lets them down. It finds the shortest possible route between beginning and end. And it sidesteps the point that the U.S. health care system makes it unavailable to many dying children; they are being saved in nations with universal health coverage.

F

Fair Game ★ ★ ★

PG-13, 105 m., 2010

Naomi Watts (Valerie Plame), Sean Penn (Joseph Wilson), Sam Shepard (Sam Plame), Noah Emmerich (Bill), Michael Kelly (Jack), Bruce McGill (Jim Pavitt). Directed by Doug Liman and produced by Liman, Jez Butterworth, Akiva Goldsman, Bill Pohlad, Janet Zucker, and Jerry Zucker. Screenplay by Jez Butterworth and John-Henry Butterworth, based on the memoirs *The Politics of Truth* by Joseph Wilson and *Fair Game* by Valerie Plame Wilson.

It seems to come down to this: The Bush administration had decided to go to war in Iraq. Scrambling to find reasons to justify the war, it seized on reports that the African nation of Niger had sold uranium to Iraq. Joseph Wilson, a former ambassador to Niger, was sent to seek evidence. He found none. In fact, he found such sales would have been physically impossible.

His report was ignored. We went to war. The nonexistent uranium sales were cited. He wrote an article in the *New York Times* reporting on what he found, or didn't find, in Niger. In an attempt to discredit him, someone in the administration leaked the information to *Chicago Sun-Times* columnist Robert Novak that Wilson's wife, Valerie Plame, was a CIA agent.

Cheney's aide, Scooter Libby, was tried and convicted of obstruction of justice and perjury, sentenced to prison, and had his sentence quickly commuted by Bush. Cheney was angry he wasn't pardoned outright. In the film, we see that Plame, under a variety of aliases, ran secret networks of informants in Baghdad and other Middle Eastern cities. When the administration blew her cover, several of her informants were killed; some reports say seventy. Then the Bush spin doctors leaked the story that she was only a CIA "secretary."

The spinning is still going on. Doug Liman's *Fair Game*, based on memoirs by Valerie Plame and Joseph Wilson and starring Sean Penn and Naomi Watts, is unusually bold for a fictionalization based on real events. Using real names and a good many facts, it argues: (1) Saddam had no WMD; (2) the CIA knew it; (3) the White House knew it; (4) the agenda of Cheney and his White House neocons required an invasion of Iraq no matter what; and (5) therefore, the evidence was ignored and we went to war because of phony claims.

Well. That's what the film says. There will no doubt be dissent. Few people are happy to be portrayed as liars and betrayers. What amazes me is that *Fair Game* doesn't play the game of using fictional names. They're all right there, including Cheney personally ordering the intelligence to be falsified.

Naomi Watts looks uncannily like the real-life Plame, but that's beside the point; what I related to was the serious, workmanlike tone of her Plame, who doesn't see herself as a heroine but as a skilled operative. She has scenes where she devastates other characters with what she knows about them, and how she can use that information. Sean Penn plays Ambassador Wilson, more combative than his wife, outraged by the way administration leakers try to destroy them. The film is realistic about the ways the Plame-Wilson marriage almost failed.

What's effective is how matter-of-fact *Fair Game* is. This isn't a lathering, angry attack picture. Wilson and Plame are both seen as loyal government employees, not particularly political until they discover the wrong information. The implication is that if the Bush administration hadn't suppressed their information and smeared them, there might have been no Iraq war, and untold thousands of lives would have been saved.

This topic has been so poisoned by misinformation that a rational discussion seems impossible. I suppose the question becomes, How well does *Fair Game* work as a movie? I suspect it will work better the more you walk in agreeing with it. The portrait it paints of the Wilson-Plame marriage is a very personal one, based on conflicting personalities under pressure. Penn plays Wilson as a hotheaded idealist, fueled by outrage. Watts makes Plame an ideal spy: secretive, concealing, under the radar. Perhaps she would rather her husband had bitten the bullet like a good soldier. They're surrounded by press attention, and she finds her CIA work belittled by the administration spin doctors and her contacts overseas trashed. Joe obviously didn't prevent the war. If he'd kept quiet, her own CIA work would not have been destroyed.

One interesting element in the movie's version is the cluelessness of George W. Bush. In this version, it's possible he didn't fully realize how flawed his information on Niger was. The Svengali is Cheney. That's the collective narrative that emerges from a group of such films, such as Rod Lurie's *Nothing but the Truth* and Oliver Stone's *W.* The implication was that Cheney wanted Scooter pardoned because Scooter was acting on his orders. It's unlikely Scooter would have been acting on his own.

Fame ★ ★

PG, 107 m., 2009

Naturi Naughton (Denise), Kay Panabaker (Jenny), Anna Maria Perez de Tagle (Joy), Megan Mullally (Fran Rowan), Bebe Neuwirth (Lynn Kraft), Charles S. Dutton (Alvin Dowd), Kherington Payne (Alice), Debbie Allen (Principal Simms), Walter Perez (Victor Taveras), Paul McGill (Kevin), Paul Iacono (Neil Baczynsky), Asher Book (Marco), Collins Pennie (Malik), Kelsey Grammer (Joel Cranston). Directed by Kevin Tancharoen and produced by Mark Canton, Gary Lucchesi, Tom Rosenberg, and Richard S. Wright. Screenplay by Allison Burnett, based on the 1980 film written by Christopher Gore.

Why bother to remake *Fame* if you don't have a clue about why the 1980 movie was special? Why take a touching experience and make it into a shallow exercise? Why begin with an R-rated look at plausible kids with real problems and tame it into a PG-rated after-school special? Why cast actors who are sometimes too old and experienced to play seniors, let alone freshmen?

The new *Fame* is a sad reflection of the new Hollywood, where material is sanitized and dumbed down for a hypothetical teen market that is way too sophisticated for it. It plays like a dinner theater version of the original. That there are some genuinely talented actors in the film doesn't help, because they're given little to build on or work with.

Do we, at this point, need another version of the creaky scene where a boyfriend misunderstands the way his girl smiles at another guy, and gets mad? Do we require parents who want their daughter to be a classical pianist and don't understand the need in her soul to perform hip-hop? Above all, do we need a big finale so elaborate and overproduced it looks like a musical number on the Oscars and could not possibly be staged in any high school?

As an admirer of Alan Parker's 1980 film, I was interested to see what would be done with this one. I suspect its director, Kevin Tancharoen (*Britney Spears Live from Miami*), didn't understand the Parker film. It was not an excuse for a musical. It was a film with great musical performances growing out of tangible dramatic situations.

The new screenplay by Allison Burnett is shallow and facile. No personal or family relationships are dealt with in other but clichés. Some of the student-teacher scenes are expected, but effective, because such adult actors as Charles S. Dutton, Bebe Neuwirth, Megan Mullally, and Debbie Allen (from the original film and TV series) speak from conviction and not plot contrivance.

The film, like the original, is broken into segments: "Freshman Year," and so on. In 1980 we got a sense of time passing and characters changing. In the new film these years relentlessly follow the standard screenplay formula: Introduction, Development, Problems, Resolution, Happy Ending. As "Junior Year" started, I looked at my watch to confirm how little time had passed. The film feels hurried. It is perhaps evidence of postproduction cutting that the fourth-billed Kelsey Grammer, playing a teacher, is on screen so rarely (his first dialogue is nice, however).

I got little sense of who these kids were. Some of them I liked a lot. They don't parallel the original characters or use their names, but I gather that Naturi Naughton, as Denise, is intended to function like Irene Cara, as Coco. Naughton is touching and talented, but the scenes involving her controlling father are written on autopilot. And is it plausible that such a gifted classical pianist would have so little feeling for her art?

Kay Panabaker, as Jenny, makes a sort of Molly Ringwald impression, but her character isn't gifted enough to convince us she'd make it through auditions. Anna Maria Perez de Tagle, as Joy, looks so fetching we wish she had been given more substantial scenes. Collins Pennie, as Malik, has the thankless role of the kid angry about childhood memories; that he is twenty-five makes his adolescent angst less convincing.

The filmmakers have stacked the deck, with several experienced actors in their twenties looking very little like fourteen-year-old freshmen and dancing like Broadway veterans. Their inexperience is acted, not felt. The irony is that Dutton's character in the film provides advice the film should have taken to heart.

Fanboys ★ ½

PG-13, 90 m., 2009

Sam Huntington (Eric), Christopher Marquette (Linus), Dan Fogler (Hutch), Jay Baruchel (Windows), Kristen Bell (Zoe). Directed by Kyle Newman and produced by Evan Astrowsky, Dana Brunetti, Matthew Perniciaro, and Kevin Spacey. Screenplay by Ernest Cline and Adam F. Goldberg.

A lot of fans are basically fans of fandom itself. It's all about them. They have mastered the *Star Wars* or *Star Trek* universes or whatever, but their objects of veneration are useful mainly as a backdrop to their own devotion. Anyone who would camp out in a tent on the sidewalk for weeks in order to be first in line for a movie is more into camping on the sidewalk than movies.

Extreme fandom may serve as a security blanket for the socially inept, who use its extreme structure as a substitute for social skills. If you are Luke Skywalker and she is Princess Leia, you already know what to say to each other, which is so much safer than having to ad lib it. Your fannish obsession is your beard. If you know absolutely all the trivia about your cubbyhole of pop culture, it saves you from having to know anything about anything else. That's why it's excruciatingly boring to talk to such people: They're always asking you questions they know the answer to.

But enough about my opinions; what about *Fanboys*? Its primary flaw is that it's not critical. It is a celebration of an idiotic lifestyle, and I don't think it knows it. If you want to get in a car and drive to California, fine. So do I. So did Jack Kerouac. But if your first stop involves a rumble at a *Star Trek* convention in Iowa, dude, beam your ass down to Route 66.

The movie, set in 1999, involves four *Star Wars* fanatics and, eventually, their gal pal, who have the notion of driving to Marin County, breaking into the Skywalker Ranch, and stealing a copy of a print of *Star Wars Episode 1: The Phantom Menace* so they can see it before anyone else. This is about as plausible as breaking into the U.S. Mint and stealing some money so you can spend it before anyone else.

Fanboys follows in the footsteps of *Sex Drive* by allowing one of its heroes to plan a rendezvous with an Internet sex goddess. To avoid revealing any plot secrets in this movie, I will recycle my earlier warning: In a chat room, don't be too hasty to believe Ms. Tasty.

This plot is given gravitas because one of the friends, Linus (Christopher Marquette), is dying of cancer. His buddy Eric (Sam Huntington) is in favor of the trip because, I dunno, it will give Linus something to live for, I guess. The other fanboys are Hutch (Dan Fogler), who lives in his mother's garage/coach house, and Windows (Jay Baruchel), who changed his name from MacOS. Just kidding. Windows, Hutch, and Linus work in a comic book store, where their favorite customer is Zoe (Kristen Bell). She's sexy *and* a *Star Wars* fan. How cool is that? She's almost better than the date who turns into a pizza and a six-pack when the deed is done.

The question of Linus's cancer became the subject of a celebrated Internet flame war last summer, with supporters of *Fanboys* director Kyle Newman running Anti-Harvey Web sites opposing Harvey Weinstein's alleged scheme to cut the subplot out of the movie. The subplot survived, but it's one of those movie diseases that is mentioned occasionally so everyone can look solemn, and then dropped when the ailing Linus dons a matching black camouflage outfit and scales the Skywalker Ranch walls with a grappling hook.

Fanboys is an amiable but disjointed movie that identifies too closely with its heroes. Poking a little more fun at them would have been a great idea. They are tragically hurtling into a cultural dead end, mastering knowledge that has no purpose other than being mastered, and too smart to be wasting their time. When a movie's opening day finally comes and fanboys leave their sidewalk tents for a mad dash into the theater, I wonder who retrieves their tents, sleeping bags, portable heaters, and iPod speakers. Warning: Mom isn't always going to be there to clean up after you.

Fantastic Mr. Fox ★ ★ ★ ½

PG, 88 m., 2009

George Clooney (Mr. Fox), Meryl Streep (Mrs. Fox), Jason Schwartzman (Ash), Eric Anderson (Kristofferson), Bill Murray (Badger), Wally Wolodarsky (Kylie), Owen Wilson (Coach Skip), Willem Dafoe (Rat). Directed by Wes Anderson and produced by Anderson, Allison Abbate, Jeremy Dawson, and Scott Rudin. Screenplay by Anderson and Noah Baumbach, based on the book by Roald Dahl.

Some artists have a way of riveting your vision with the certitude of what they do. This has nothing to do with subject or style. It's inexplicable. Andy Warhol and Grandma Moses. The spareness of Bergman and the Fellini circus. Wes Anderson is like that. There's nothing consistent about his recent work but its ability to make me go *zooinng*! What else do *The Darjeeling Limited* and *The Life Aquatic with Steve Zissou* have in common?

Now here's *Fantastic Mr. Fox,* an animated picture with nothing in common with traditional animation, except that it's largely in one of the oldest animation styles of all—stop motion, the one used in *King Kong.* The animals aren't smaller than people, but often larger and more mature.

They live in a sometimes flat dimension; the cameras are happier sliding back and forth than moving in and out. It's sometimes like an old-fashioned slide projector. The landscapes and structures of this world are mannered and picture-booky. Yet the extraordinary faces of the animals are almost disturbingly human (for animals, of course). We venture into the UnCanny Valley, that no man's land dividing humans from the devised. Above all their fur is so *real.* I've rarely seen such texture in a film.

The story involves a valley somewhere, by which is meant the world, which is ruled by,

Boggis and Bunce and Bean
One fat, one short, one lean
These horrible crooks
So different in looks
Were nonetheless equally mean.

Nor are the animals all saints. Mr. Fox, voiced by George Clooney, was a flourishing chicken thief until times grew risky. Then, like a bootlegger after repeal, he went straight—or, more precisely, into journalism. He's the Walter Winchell of the valley, until he slips back into dining on takeout chicken, taking them out himself. This he keeps a secret from the upright Mrs. Fox (Meryl Streep).

His deception is blown, to everyone's great disappointment, when the fat, short, and lean ones all turn mean ones and declare war. Leading a team of other animals, Mr. Fox starts tunneling like the heroes of *The Great Escape*—but in, rather than out.

These adventures provide the setting for personal drama, as an uncertainty arises between Mr. Fox's callow son, Ash (Jason Schwartzman), and a cousin named Kristofferson (Eric Anderson). Kristofferson is all a fox should be, as with that name how could he not be? He's the family golden child, or fox. Does Mr. Fox admire the cousin more than his son? What kind of pop has he been, anyway?

All of the animals have excellent tailoring, which adds to their stature. They're not forced to wear silly sailor suits or, like Donald Duck, to never put on pants. The art design is a large part of the film's appeal. It stays fresh all the way through. Think back to the color palettes of *Darjeeling* and *Life Aquatic.*

The film's based on the famous children's book by Roald Dahl, which like all of his work has ominous undertones, as if evil can steal in at any moment. These animals aren't catering to anyone in the audience. We get the feeling they're intensely leading their own lives without slowing down for ours.

Like the hero of *Willy Wonka and the Chocolate Factory,* also based on one of his books, the creatures of Dahl's valley seem to know more than they're letting on, perhaps even secrets we don't much want to know. Children, especially, will find things they don't understand and things that scare them. Excellent. A good story for children should suggest a hidden dimension, and that dimension, of course, is the lifetime still ahead them. Six is a little early for a movie to suggest to kids that the case is closed. Oh, what if the kids start crying about words they don't know?—"Mommy, mommy! What's crème brûlée?" Show them, for goodness' sake. They'll thank you for it. Take my word on this.

Fast and Furious ★ ½

PG-13, 107 m., 2009

Vin Diesel (Dominic Toretto), Paul Walker (Brian O'Conner), Michelle Rodriguez (Letty), Jordana Brewster (Mia Toretto), John Ortiz (Campos), Laz Alonso (Fenix). Directed by Justin Lin and produced by Neil Moritz, Michael Fottrell, and Vin Diesel. Screenplay by Chris Morgan.

Fast and Furious is exactly and precisely what you'd expect. Nothing more, unfortunately. You get your cars that are fast and your characters that are furious. You should. They know how to make these movies by now. Producer Neil Moritz is on his fourth, and director Justin Lin on his second in a row. Vin Diesel and other major actors are back from *The Fast and the Furious* (2001). All they left behind were two definite articles.

This is an expertly made action film, by which I mean the special effects are good and the acting is extremely basic. The screenplay rotates these nouns through various assortments of dialogue: Race. Driver(s). Nitro. Meth. Sister. FBI. Border. Dead. Mexico. Murder. Prison. Traffic violations. Tunnel. Muscle car. Import. Plymouth. Funeral. Helicopter(s). Toretto. Ten seconds. Corona. Cocaine.

The plot. Dom Toretto (Vin Diesel) has been in the Dominican Republic for the last six years but now returns to America, where he is a wanted man. Probable charges: vehicular homicide, murder, smuggling, dating an FBI agent's sister. Reason for return: Letty (Michelle Rodriguez), the girl he loved, has been killed.

After Toretto's arrest all those years ago, he was allowed to escape by FBI agent Brian O'Conner (Paul Walker), for reasons explained in this film. Now Brian is back, on a task force to track down Toretto and the leader of a drug cartel.

This provides a scaffolding on which to hang the body of the movie, which involves a series of chase scenes, fights, explosions, and sexy women who would like to make themselves available to Toretto, to no avail. He is single-minded.

The pre-title chase scene is pretty amazing. Toretto and his group team up in four racing vehicles to pursue a truck hauling not one, not two, not three, but *four* enormous tanks of gasoline. Their method: Toretto drives close behind fourth tank, girl climbs out of sun roof, stands on hood, leaps to ladder on back of tank, climbs on top, runs to front of tank, leaps down, uncouples tank from third one. The reason the girl does this while Toretto drives is, I guess, well, you know what they say about women drivers.

Ever seen a truck hauling four enormous gas containers? I haven't. On a narrow mountain road? With a sudden, steep incline around a curve, when it narrows to one lane? Not me. Why are they going to this trouble? So their buddies can have free gas for a street race that night in L.A. I say let them buy their own damn gas. The race is down city streets with ordinary traffic on them. Then the wrong way on an expressway. Not a cop in sight. Where are the TV news choppers when you want them? This would get huge ratings.

I dunno. I admire the craft involved, but the movie leaves me profoundly indifferent. After three earlier movies in the series, which have been transmuted into video games, why do we need a fourth one? Oh. I just answered my own question.

Faster ★ ★ ½

R, 98 m., 2010

Dwayne Johnson (Driver), Billy Bob Thornton (Cop), Oliver Jackson-Cohen (Killer), Maggie Grace (Lily), Moon Bloodgood (Marina), Carla Gugino (Cicero). Directed by George Tillman Jr. and produced by Tony Gayton, Liz Glotzer, Martin Shafer, and Robert Teitel. Screenplay by Tony Gayton and Joe Gayton.

Faster is a pure thriller, all blood, no frills, in which a lot of people get shot, mostly in the head. Rotate the plot, change the period, spruce up the dialogue, and this could have been a hard-boiled 1940s noir. But it doesn't pause for fine touches, and efficiently delivers action for an audience that likes one-course meals.

Dwayne Johnson stars, in the kind of role he's possibly been avoiding up until now. Once known as The Rock, he has developed a kinder, gentler screen persona that more closely fits him in real life. It's a melancholy fact of Hollywood today that *Faster* could be a good career move for him, moving him onto the trail blazed by Schwarzenegger and Bruce Willis. He has very broad shoulders, wicked tattoos, and a gun that seems to grow from his hand.

As the film opens, he's being released from prison after a ten-year term. He walks out the gate into a desert wilderness and begins to run—run—to a nearby city, where a circa 1970 Chevelle is waiting for him in a junkyard. This is because modern cars all look boring and most action heroes drive classics. He whips off the tarp and peels outta there. A private eye gives him a list of names, and he sets out to murder everyone on the list.

His character is named Driver. A clue to this, and the title, is that he invariably drives at the top possible speed, and obviously never took driver's ed in high school because he doesn't know how to turn around and drive in the other direction except by slamming on the brakes, twisting the wheel, and whipping through 180 degrees.

Driver is soon wanted for one, then two, then three murders. The cops know who he is. His photo is on the TV news. This all takes place in Bakersfield. What are the odds a tattooed killer with a shaved head could elude the Bakersfield police for long while piloting a classic Chevelle at 80 mph and laying rubber all over town? Excellent.

The cop on the case is Cicero (Carla Gugino). She finds herself saddled with a partner known as Cop (Billy Bob Thornton). He's two weeks from retirement. As we all know, anyone two weeks from retirement, be he cop, fireman, stuntman, prison guard, or kindly old dad, will never make it. Cop is also mainlining heroin, for no better reason than to show him doing it. One fix lasts him for the rest of the film.

Cicero and Cop try to track down Driver, who seeks vengeance on those who squealed about a bank heist and killed his brother. These people have moved into other lines of work, most notably Preacher (Buzz Belmondo), who runs revival tent meetings. We find out more about them. And we meet the fatuous Killer (Oliver Jackson-Cohen), a British addict of extreme sports, who is a professional hit man for fun. This is some guy. He informs his girlfriend, Lily (Maggie Grace), that he has "beaten" yoga, having mastered the most difficult three positions, and is ready to move on.

As Driver tracks his victims, Killer tracks Driver, and Cop and Cicero track them all. Director George Tillman does a lean, efficient job of creating stark action scenes. Driver shows vestiges of a personality, reluctantly. Billy Bob creates a cop who looks like it's been all downhill for him since *Bad Santa*. Gugino, a good actress, gamely pretends to be in a more nuanced movie. And the hits keep coming.

Fast Five ★ ★ ★

PG-13, 130 m., 2011

Vin Diesel (Dominic Toretto), Paul Walker (Brian O'Conner), Dwayne Johnson (Luke Hobbs), Jordana Brewster (Mia Toretto), Tyrese Gibson (Roman Pierce), Chris "Ludacris" Bridges (Tej), Matt Schulze (Vincent), Sung Kang (Han), Gal Gadot (Gisele), Joaquim de Almeida (Reyes), Elsa Pataky (Elena). Directed by Justin Lin and produced by Vin Diesel, Michael Fottrell, and Neal H. Moritz. Screenplay by Chris Morgan.

I don't think you can do this. I don't think you can take two midsize sedans, chain them to a bank vault, and haul it behind you on a high-speed chase through the streets of Rio de Janeiro while being chased by the cops. I think the traffic would be too bad.

I also don't think you can steal cars from a speeding train by driving a truck beside the tracks, cutting the side out of a freight car with an acetylene torch, flipping the cars onto the truck bed, tilting the bed, letting them roll to the ground, and then driving them away. I think there are more practical ways to steal cars.

I also think that while Houdini might have been able to make a bank vault disappear from the stage of the New York Hippodrome (and escape from it in the process), bank vaults in general tend to be hard to mess around with, as may occur to you during *Fast Five.* But you know what? It sort of doesn't matter. The movie is made of sheer preposterous nonstop impossible action, muscular macho guys, hot chicks, and platoons of bad guys who are eliminated by the dozens while the leading characters escape certain death so easily it gets to be a habit.

This is the third of the *Fast and the Furious* series, starring Vin Diesel, Paul Walker, and Jordana Brewster, and here they're joined by Dwayne Johnson, making it a sort of convention of reckless drivers. Apparently some of these characters have had, in the past, long conversations about their goals, dreams, abilities, and values, saving time at the present for terse verbal shorthand. When you hear as many as six words in a row, you suspect it's a tagline for a trailer ("We need to assemble a team.").

Justin Lin is emerging as a first-rate director in this second-rate genre, having shelved, temporarily I trust, the ambition suggested in his remarkable *Better Luck Tomorrow* (2002). Unlike a certain other maker of crash-crash-bang-bangs, whose name I trust you to summon effortlessly, Lin devotes attention to a story line that devises ingenious new things to do instead of obsessively blowing up things. He storyboards his impossible action sequences, instead of editing them with incomprehensible speed. And he hauls in fresh faces (played by such as Tyrese Gibson, Chris "Ludacris" Bridges, Matt Schulze, Sung Kang, Gal Gadot, Elsa Pataky, and Joaquim de Almeida) and gives them a specialty and a chance to demonstrate it. You couldn't say the supporting characters are developed beyond their defining labels, but at least they're in the mix.

The villain (de Almeida), a Rio drug kingpin, makes the usual error of ordering his flunkies into hot pursuit and then following them into danger. There's a reason generals don't fight in the trenches. His character, Reyes, is set up as a criminal tycoon, but $100 million is not, after all, very much drug money to have in a bank, not when Wachovia Bank (now absorbed by Wells Fargo) was recently revealed to have laundered drug money equal to a third of the Mexican GDP. One thing you know is that the United States will spend less time trying to put those bankers behind bars than the Brazilians do here, and lose many fewer squad cars in the process.

But facts will get me nowhere in reviewing a movie of this sort. What you want is advice about your genre expectations. The 2001 movie was sorta fun with its energy and ambition, placing Diesel and Walker in a Los Angeles street-racing story. The 2009 film, which made an impenetrable leap from the plot of the first one, was much more routine. Both made plenty of money. The *F&F* titles got confusing with the unrelated *The Fast and the Furious: Tokyo Drift* and John Singleton's *2 Fast 2 Furious,* which is why, I suppose *Fast Five* drops the *furious.* But it isn't technically the fifth *F&F* unless you count the outliers. So I don't know what *Five* refers to. That doesn't bother me.

What it all comes down to is a skillfully assembled 130 minutes at the movies, with actors capable of doing absurd things with straight faces, and action sequences that toy idly with the laws of physics. That can be amusing for some people, not so much for me. What I missed were laughs, although I got a good one right at the end, when we were warned that the driving in the movie was done in a controlled environment by professionals, and we shouldn't try those stunts ourselves. Someday I would like to meet a driver who was planning to race his Hummer into a reinforced concrete wall before being persuaded otherwise by the closing credits.

The Father of My Children ★ ★ ★ ½

NO MPAA RATING, 110 m., 2010

Louis-Do de Lencquesaing (Gregoire), Chiara Caselli (Sylvia), Alice de Lencquesaing (Clemence), Alice Gautier (Valentine), Manelle Driss (Billie), Eric Elmosnino (Serge). Directed by Mia Hansen-Love and produced by Oliver Damian, Philippe Martin, and David Thion. Screenplay by Hansen-Love.

"How much do I owe you?" the producer asks someone on his cell phone. He chuckles. "That much?" He is amused, busy, filled with energy. He handles two phones at a time while threading through Paris traffic and heading for a country weekend with his family. He smokes. He drives. He tells his wife, "I'm almost on the highway." He's stopped by the cops, who ask if he knows why they stopped him. "I have a vague idea," he says.

In the opening sequence, we meet a plausible human being. A French film producer, an honest hustler, a loving father and husband, confident of his powers, enjoying his work. *The Father of My Children* will watch this man come to pieces. It will not be dark melodrama or turgid psychology. It will simply be the story of a good man, well loved, who runs into a dead end.

The man is named Gregoire (Louis-Do de Lencquesaing). The actor, like many French actors, is good-looking without being improbable. He runs his business in his head. He explains, "I don't work with the kinds of directors who do television." He commits to a filmmaker and goes to the limit for the film not because he has lofty ideas about Art, but because that's the kind of man he is.

In the movie, he is plunging into debt while producing an obscure project of a temperamental auteur not a million miles distant from Lars von Trier. He gets phone reports from the set from his trusted assistant, hears of troublesome actors and bad weather, deals with money and debt, and loves his wife, Sylvia (Chiara Caselli), and three daughters, Clemence (Alice de Lencquesaing), Valentine (Alice Gautier), and Billie (Manelle Driss). Their country house evokes quiet family togetherness, which is the idea, but Gregoire's mind is often elsewhere, trying to find a way out of his troubles.

When very busy men are also essentially good men and working at something worthwhile, they tend to find themselves surrounded by supporters and enablers. Gregoire's office is also a family, in a way, and his employees share his vision. When calamity strikes, even his wife pitches in to help salvage his dream. The second half of the film is the most touching, because it shows that our lives are not merely our own, but also belong to the events we set in motion.

Louis-Do de Lencquesaing is effective here at *not* going into a manic mode. He runs his business while improvising from moment to moment, he has some plans for getting through, he tries some scenarios, and he doesn't need anyone to tell him when they're not working. I appreciate the ability of the director, Mia Hansen-Love, to allow the situation to develop through observation of her hero, not dialogue explaining everything.

Chiara Caselli, as Gregoire's wife, is, like many wives of workaholic men, better informed on his business than he can imagine. She believes in him, therefore in his hopes, and touchingly relates with the members of his office family as they all try to move things along. And the film gives due attention to the children, particularly Clemence (played by de Lencquesaing's own daughter), who negotiate unfamiliar emotional territory with their mother. The title (in French, *Le pere de mes enfants*) is appropriate.

SPOILER WARNING: The story is said to be inspired by the life of the real-life producer Humbert Balsan, who made Lars von Trier's *Manderlay* (2005). Balsan had considerable success, making nearly seventy films, including three by James Ivory, and even acting for Bresson. He committed suicide when his business imploded.

Note: The film won the special jury prize in the Un Certain Regard section of Cannes 2009.

Fifty Dead Men Walking ★ ★ ★

R, 118 m., 2009

Ben Kingsley (Fergus), Jim Sturgess (Martin), Rose McGowan (Grace), Kevin Zegers (Sean), Natalie Press (Lara). Directed by Kari Skogland and produced by Skogland, Stephen Hegyes, Peter La Terriere, and Shawn Williamson. Screenplay by Skogland, inspired by the book by Martin McGartland and Nicholas Davies.

Belfast, 1988. The height of the Troubles. British troops occupy the city and are at war with the Irish Republican Army. The British want to retain Northern Ireland as part of the United Kingdom. The IRA considers them invaders. Martin McGartland doesn't much care.

Like many young criminals, he is devoutly nonpolitical. He's a two-bit hustler, stealing and reselling clothing or whatever else he can move. A wise guy, he moves confidently on the mean streets. McGartland (Jim Sturgess) doesn't like the British, but when the IRA breaks his friend's legs with a baseball bat, he likes that even less.

He's recruited by Fergus (Ben Kingsley), an officer in the Special Branch of the British police, to become a double agent, an informer. Fergus has noticed how he moves through Belfast, known to the IRA, unintimidated by the British troops. Both sides already think they know who he is.

Informing on the IRA was, of course, a nearly certain death sentence. It seems incredible that anyone would take such a risk, and very few did. McGartland's information is credited with saving the lives of at least fifty men, and you'd think the IRA might have noticed parallels between their assassination operations and McGartland's participation, but apparently not. Only at the end of the film is there a situation where his role will be betrayed, and by then he already realizes that he will be living for the rest of his life in hiding.

The Troubles were a messy business. The British troops were acting under orders that not all of them necessarily appreciated. They were not fighting in a foreign land, but against those who spoke and lived much as they did. The Protestant/Catholic hatred involved also muddied the water. To step into the middle of this is almost a foolhardy act, and *Fifty Dead Men Walking* never really explains McGartland's decision. Still, it is a fact that he made it, even with the risk to his girlfriend and their child.

The performance of Jim Sturgess as McGartland helps place his decision into the day-by-day process of acting on it. He meets clandestinely with Fergus, rises in the trust of the IRA, is able to use information he gets from Fergus to enhance his position. The two men become not friends, exactly, but mutually dependent, and as the net grows tighter toward the end, their dependence takes on an urgent desperation.

The writer and director is Kari Skogland, a young Canadian whose previous film, *The Stone Angel* (2007), could not be more different. It stars Ellen Burstyn as an old lady who runs away from the children who want to place her in a nursing home. In this film, Skogland, like Kathryn Bigelow does in *The Hurt Locker,* demolishes the notion that women can't direct action.

This movie is based on real events and a book written by McGartland and Nicholas Davies. It presents the usual disclaimers that "some of the events, characters, and scenes in the film have been changed." And McGartland himself has made a statement from hiding that he doesn't endorse the film and it was "inspired by," not "adapted from" the book. Does this reflect his hope that the IRA won't take it personally? Setting entirely aside the accuracy of the film, the IRA still has him marked for death, and indeed there was an attempt on his life in Canada ten years after he fled. He's still out there somewhere.

The Fighter ★ ★ ½

R, 115 m., 2010

Mark Wahlberg (Micky Ward), Christian Bale (Dicky Eklund), Amy Adams (Charlene Fleming), Melissa Leo (Alice Ward). Directed by David O. Russell and produced by Dorothy Aufiero, David Hoberman, Ryan Kavanaugh, Todd Lieberman, Paul Tamasy, and Mark Wahlberg. Screenplay by Tamasy, Scott Silver, and Eric Johnson.

Micky Ward has less personality than the hero of any other boxing movie I can remember. Maybe that's because he can't get a word in edgeways. He has a motormouth crackhead for a half-brother, a mom who acts as his manager, and seven blond sisters who seem to be on a break from a musical being filmed on the next soundstage. It's easy to imagine Micky growing up in this family and sitting ignored in the corner.

David O. Russell's *The Fighter* is based on Ward's true story, and perhaps Micky (Mark Wahlberg) is flat and withdrawn here because he is in life. His family is spectacularly dysfunctional. Dicky Eklund (Christian Bale), his half-brother, is the failed version of what Micky hopes to become: a poor kid from Lowell, Massachusetts, who wins because of his ability to outlast savage punishment and finally land a winning blow.

Micky grew up hero worshipping Dicky,

who lost a lot of fights but allegedly knocked over Sugar Ray Leonard once upon a time. Then Dicky got hooked on crack, and now we see him as a goofy, scrawny guy with a Skeezix haircut, a cigarette behind his ear, and an arm around his brother's shoulders. They're being filmed for an HBO documentary, which Dicky thinks is about his own unlikely comeback, and everybody else knows is about his decline and fall. Crackheads sometimes get the two confused.

As the movie opens, Micky doggedly begins a series of defeats in bad matchups. Then his life changes when he meets a sweet-faced, tough-talking barmaid named Charlene (Amy Adams). She knows the neighborhood, knows the story, and knows that Micky's problem is his family. His mother, Alice (Melissa Leo in a teeth-gratingly brilliant performance), sees both boys as performers in a long-running tribute to herself. She presides in a living room filled with her seven daughters, who smoke so much and use so much hair spray they must be considered fire hazards.

When Micky gets a chance to train seriously in Vegas, Charlene more or less forces him to take it. When Dicky and Alice follow him out there, it's showdown time and Charlene threatens to leave. But the movie is imprecise about how this plays out, and they're all at ringside at the end.

The weakness of the film is the weakness of the leading role. That's not a criticism of Mark Wahlberg, who has a quite capable range, but of how he and Russell see the character. Micky comes across as a proud, not very bright, very determined man who has apparently never given his family much constructive thought. To say of your family "They're my family!" is true enough, but may not be sufficiently analytical. His love for Charlene is real, but he never quite realizes he really must choose between her vision and his mother's. His character remains strangely unfocused.

That's not the case with Dicky, Alice, and Charlene, and those characters are where the life is. Christian Bale, who has played Batman *and* John Connor in *Terminator Salvation*, and for Werner Herzog played a man who survived in the jungles of Laos, so successfully transforms himself that you foresee a career as a cutup in the *Jackass* movies. Melissa Leo (*Frozen River*) is merciless in her depiction of Alice; steering her son to failure is more rewarding than having him succeed on his own. She's one of those women, you know the type, who likes the way she looks posing with a freshly lit cigarette. And look at Amy Adams, our beloved *Junebug* and the nun in *Doubt*, who is clear-headed and has a strong will and tries to lend those qualities to the man she loves.

There are a lot of fight scenes, not as visceral as those in *Raging Bull*, *Rocky*, or *The Wrestler*, but designed more to represent the POV of a sportswriter or fan. Because we aren't deeply invested in Micky, we don't care as much as we should, and the film ends on a note that should be triumph but feels more like simple conclusion.

Fighting ★ ★ ★

PG-13, 105 m., 2009

Channing Tatum (Shawn MacArthur), Terrence Howard (Harvey Boarden), Luis Guzman (Martinez), Zulay Henao (Zulay Valez), Brian White (Evan Hailey), Altagracia Guzman (Lila). Directed by Dito Montiel and produced by Kevin Misher. Screenplay by Montiel and Robert Munic.

I like the way the personalities are allowed to upstage the plot in *Fighting*, a routine three-act fight story that creates uncommonly interesting characters. Set in the streets of Manhattan, Brooklyn, and the Bronx, involving a naive kid from Alabama and a mild-mannered hustler from Chicago, it takes place in a secret world of street fighting for high cash stakes. Do rich guys really bet hundreds of thousands on a closed-door bare-knuckle brawl? I dunno, but it's cheaper than filming a prize-fight arena.

Channing Tatum plays Shawn, whose dad was a wrestling coach near Birmingham. Terrence Howard plays Harvey, whom everybody seems to know. Shawn is a hot-tempered kid not doing very well at selling shoddy merchandise on the sidewalks. Harvey is soft-spoken, with a gentle voice and an almost passive personal style even though he works as an illegal fight promoter. He sees Shawn in a fight, recruits him, and lines up fights with $5,000, $10,000 and finally $100,000 purses.

He does this with stunning speed, even though at the first fight no one has ever seen Shawn before. The movie offers that and other problems of plausibility and logic, but I don't care about them because the director, Dito Montiel, doesn't. Possibly hired to make a genre picture, he provides the outline and requirements, and then focuses on his characters. Terrence Howard's Harvey is the most intriguing: He's too laid back to be in the profession, so philosophical that he even faces what seems to be his own inevitable murder with calm resignation. He knows his world, is known in it, moves through it, yet seems aloof from it.

Channing Tatum, convincing as a former school athlete (which he was), quickly agrees to the fights, even against terrifying opponents. But *Fighting* invests much more feeling in his tentative relationship with Zulay (Zulay Henao), a single mom who works as a waitress in a private club where the private fight world hangs out. He approaches her like a well-raised southern boy would, politely, respectfully.

This arouses greater interest because of the screen presence of Zulay Henao, who sidesteps countless hazards suggested by her character and makes her sweet, sensuous, and perceptive. And then look at Altagracia Guzman as Lila, playing Zulay's elder relative (grandmother?), who was a great audience favorite as she guarded her beloved from the threat of a male predator. The way her talent is employed in the film is an ideal use of a supporting actress.

Listen also to the dialogue by Robert Munic and Montiel, which is far above formula boilerplate and creates the illusion that the characters might actually be saying it in the moment. An extended flirtation between Zulay and Shawn isn't hurried through for a bedroom payoff, but grows sweeter and more tender the longer it continues. This scene illustrates my theory that it is more exciting to wonder if you are about to be kissed than it is to be kissed.

Fighting is not a cinematic breakthrough, but it is much more involving than I thought it would be. The ads foreground the action, no doubt because that's what sells. The film transcends the worldview that produced the ad campaign and gives audiences a well-crafted, touching experience. Sometimes you can feel it when an audience is a little surprised by how deeply they've become involved.

Film Socialisme ★

NO MPAA RATING, 101 m., 2011

Most of the characters are not named. They are played by Catherine Tanvier, Christian Sinniger, Jean-Marc Stehle, Agatha Couture, Eye Haidara, Marie-Christine Bergier, Nadege Beausson-Diagne, Mathias Domahidy, Quentin Grosset, Olga Riazanova, Maurice Sarfati, Dominique Devals, Louma Sanbar, Gulliver Hecq, Marine Battaggia, Elizabeth Vitali, Patti Smith, Lenny Kaye, Alain Badiou, Bernard Maris, Elias Sanbar, Robert Maloubier, and Dominique Reynie. Directed by Jean-Luc Godard and produced by Ruth Waldburger. Screenplay by Godard.

One sunny day at Cannes, I sat at lunch with the British director Ken Russell, who had been well served and was feeling relaxed. As far as he was concerned, he said, he was pleased home video had been invented because now films could be watched on fast-forward, saving everyone's time. There was a quiet smile on Russell's face as he dozed off. "You're kidding!" I said. He awoke with a start. "Certainly not!" he said, and pushed back from the table.

I suppose it was only a matter of time until Russell's insight reached Jean-Luc Godard. The great director began with films that we would all agree fit the definition of "movie," and has relentlessly been putting more and more distance between himself and that form. With *Film Socialisme,* made in his seventy-ninth year, the pioneer of the French New Wave has been swept out to sea.

This film is an affront. It is incoherent, maddening, deliberately opaque, and heedless of the ways in which people watch movies. All of that is part of the Godardian method, I am aware, but I feel a bargain of some sort must be struck. We enter the cinema with open minds and good will, expecting Godard to engage us in at least a vaguely penetrable way. But in *Film Socialisme* he expects us to do all the heavy lifting.

When the film premiered at Cannes 2010, it was received with the usual bouquet of cheers, hoots, and catcalls. Defenders of Godard wrote at length about his content and purpose, while many others frankly felt insulted. In the spirit of Ken Russell, Godard actually posted an online video that used fast-forward to show his entire film in about four minutes. That, I concede, showed wit. You can see it here: http://bit.ly/lznp1u.

In the film, he shows us fragmented scenes on a cruise ship traveling the Mediterranean, and also shots which travel through human history, which for the film's purposes involve Egypt, Greece, Palestine, Odessa (notably its steps), Naples, Barcelona, Tunisia, and other ports. Then we see fragments of a story involving two women (one a TV camerawoman) and a family living at a roadside garage. A mule and a llama also live at the garage. There are shots of kittens, obscurely linked to the Egyptians, as well as parrots. The cruise ship is perhaps a metaphor for our human voyage through time. The garage is anybody's guess.

There is also much topical footage, both moving and still. Words are spoken, some of them bits of language from eminent authors. These words appear in uppercase subtitles, and are mostly nouns. These subtitles, Godard explained, are what he calls Navajo English. I guess he learned it from old Westerns.

His Navajo speakers touch on socialism, gambling, nationalism, Hitler, Stalin, art, Islam, women, Jews, Hollywood, Palestine, war, and other large topics. It all seems terrifically political, but there is nothing in the film to offend the most devout Tea Party communicant, and I can't say what, if anything, the film has to say about socialism.

Godard has sent my mind scurrying between ancient history and modern television, via Marxism and Nazism, to ponder—well, what? In addition to standard digital video, Godard uses a state-of-the-art iteration of high-def video; some shots, especially aboard the cruise ship, are so beautiful and glossy they could be an advertisement for something, perhaps a cruise ship. Other shots seem taken with cell phones, and there are bits and pieces from old movies.

The film closes with large block letters: NO COMMENT. I would have looked forward to attending Godard's press conference, but of course he didn't attend it. Once, at Montreal, I sat next to him at a little dinner for film critics, at which he arranged his garden peas into geometric forms on his plate and told us, "Cinema is the train. It is not the station." Or perhaps my memory has tricked me, and he said, "Cinema is the station. It is not the train." Both are equally true. Or not.

Fired Up ★

PG-13, 89 m., 2009

Nicholas D'Agosto (Shawn Colfax), Eric Christian Olsen (Nick Brady), Sarah Roemer (Carly), Molly Sims (Diora), Danneel Harris (Bianca), David Walton (Dr. Rick), Adhir Kalyan (Brewster), AnnaLynne McCord (Gwyneth), Juliette Goglia (Poppy), Philip Baker Hall (Coach Byrnes), Hayley Marie Norman (Angela). Directed by Will Gluck and produced by Matthew Gross, Peter Jaysen, and Charles Weinstock. Screenplay by Freedom Jones.

After the screening of *Fired Up*, one of my colleagues grimly observed that *Dead Man* was a better cheerleader movie. That was, you will recall, the 1995 Western starring Johnny Depp, Robert Mitchum, Billy Bob Thornton, and Iggy Pop. I would give almost anything to see them on a cheerleading squad. Here is a movie that will do for cheerleading what *Friday the 13th* did for summer camp.

The story involves two callow and witless high school football players, Shawn and Nick, who don't want to attend summer football training camp in the desert. They also want to seduce the school cheerleaders, so they decide to attend cheerleading camp, ha ha. Their high school is in Hinsdale, Illinois, whose taxpayers will be surprised to learn the school team trains in the desert just like the Cubs, but will be even more surprised to learn the entire film was shot in California. And they will be puzzled about why many of the cheers involve chants of the letters *F!U!*—which stand for *Fired Up*, you see.

Oh, is this movie bad. The characters relentlessly attack one another with the forced jollity of minimum-wage workers pressing you with free cheese samples at the supermarket. Every conversation involves a combination of romantic misunderstandings, double entendres, and flirtation that is just sad. No one in the movie has an idea in their bubbly little brains. No, not even Philip Baker Hall, who plays the football coach in an eruption of obligatory threats.

The plot involves a cheerleading competition along the lines of the one in *Bring It On* (2000), the *Citizen Kane* of cheerleader movies. That movie involved genuinely talented cheerleaders. This one involves ungainly human pyramids and a lot of uncoordinated jumping up and down. Faithful readers will recall that I often ask why the bad guys in movies wear matching black uniforms. They do in this one, too. The villains here are the Panther cheerleading squad. How many teams play in all black?

I could tell you about Carly, Bianca, Gwyneth, Poppy, and the other sexy cheerleaders, but I couldn't stir myself to care. There is an old rule in the theater: If the heroine coughs in the first act, she has to die in the third. In this movie, the cutest member of the squad is Angela (Hayley Marie Norman). She also has the nicest smile and the best personality and is on screen early and often, so I kept expecting her big scene, but no: She seems destined to be the cheerleader's cheerleader, pepping them up, cheering them on, smiling, applauding, holding up the bottom of the pyramid, laughing at funny lines, encouraging, bouncing in sync, and projecting with every atom of her being the attitude *You go, girls!* You've got a problem when you allow the most intriguing member of the cast to appear in that many scenes and never deal with her. That is not the movie's fatal flaw, however. Its flaw is that I was thinking about things like that.

Fish Tank ★ ★ ★ ★

NO MPAA RATING, 123 m., 2010

Katie Jarvis (Mia), Michael Fassbender (Connor), Kierston Wareing (Joanne), Rebecca Griffiths (Tyler), Harry Treadaway (Billy). Directed by Andrea Arnold and produced by Kees Kasander. Screenplay by Arnold.

Andrea Arnold's piercing *Fish Tank* is the portrait of an angry, isolated fifteen-year-old girl who is hurtling toward a lifetime of misery. She is so hurt and lonely we pity her. Her mother barely even sees her. The film takes place in a bleak British public housing estate and in the streets and fields around it. There is no suggestion of a place this girl can go to find help, care, or encouragement.

The girl is Mia, played by Katie Jarvis in a harrowing display of hostility. She's been thrown out of school, is taunted as a weirdo by boys her age, converses with her mother and sister in screams, and retreats to an empty room to play her music and dance alone. She drinks what little booze she can get her hands on.

And where is her mother? Right there at home, all the time. Joanne (Kierston Wareing) looks so young she may have had Mia at Mia's age. Joanne is shorter, busty, dyed blond, a chain-smoker, a party girl. The party is usually in her living room. One day she brings home Connor (Michael Fassbender), a good-looking guy who seems nice enough. Mia screams at him, too, but it's a way of getting attention.

Joanne seems happiest when Mia isn't at home. The girl wanders the streets and gets in a fight when she tries to free a horse chained in a barren lot near some shabby mobile homes. She has no friends. She surfs in an Internet café, goes to an audition for sexy dancers, breaks into a house at random.

One day differs from the routine. Connor takes Mia, her mom, and her little sister, Tyler (Rebecca Griffiths), on a drive to the country. This isn't an idyllic picnic; they simply park in a field and hike to a river, Joanne staying with the car. Connor takes Mia in wading ("I can't swim"). Walking back barefoot she gets a ride on his back and rests her chin on his shoulder and what was in the air from the first is now manifest.

Some reviews call Connor a pedophile. I think he's more of an immoral opportunist. *Fish Tank* in any event isn't so much about sex as about the helpless spiral Mia is going through. The film has two fraught but ambiguous scenes—one when she goes to Connor's home, another involving a young girl—that we can make fairly obvious assumptions about. But the movie doesn't spell them out; Arnold sees everything through Mia's eyes and never steps outside to explain things from any other point of view. She knows who the young girl is, and we are left to assume. Whatever she thinks after the visit to Connor's house we are not specifically told. The film so firmly identifies with Mia that there may even be a possibility Joanne is better than the slutty monster we see. A slim possibility, to be sure.

In a film so tightly focused, all depends on Katie Jarvis's performance. There is truth in it. She lives on an Essex housing estate like the one in the movie, and she was discovered by Arnold while in a shouting match with her boyfriend at the Tilbury train station, which is seen in the movie. Now eighteen, she gave birth to a daughter conceived when she was sixteen.

We can fear, but we can't say, that she was heading for a life similar to the one Mia seems doomed to. Her casting in this film, however, led to Cannes, the Jury Prize, and contracts with British and American agents. She is a powerful acting presence, flawlessly convincing here. And Arnold, who won an Oscar for her shattering short film *Wasp* (2003), also about a neglectful alcoholic mother, deserves comparison with British director Ken Loach.

500 Days of Summer ★ ★ ★ ★

PG-13, 95 m., 2009

Joseph Gordon-Levitt (Tom Hansen), Zooey Deschanel (Summer Finn), Geoffrey Arend (McKenzie), Matthew Gray Gubler (Paul), Chloe Grace Moretz (Rachel Hansen), Clark Gregg (Vance), Rachel Boston (Alison), Minka Kelly (Girl). Directed by Marc Webb and produced by Jessica Tuchinsky, Mark Waters, Mason Novick, and Steven J. Wolfe. Screeplay by Scott Neustadter and Michael H. Weber.

We never remember in chronological order, especially when we're going back over a failed romance. We start near the end, and then hop around between the times that were good and the times that left pain. People always say "start at the beginning," but we didn't know at the time it was the beginning. *500 Days of Summer* is a movie that works that way.

Some say they're annoyed by the way it begins on Day 488 or whatever and then jumps around, providing utterly unhelpful data labels: "Day 1," "Day 249." Movies are supposed to reassure us that events unfold in an orderly procession. But Tom remembers Summer as a series of joys and bafflements. What kind of woman likes you perfectly sincerely and has no one else in her life but is *not* interested in ever getting married?

Zooey Deschanel is a good choice to play such a woman. I can't imagine her playing a clinging vine. Too ornery. As Summer, she sees Tom with a level gaze and is who she is. It's Tom's bad luck she is sweet and smart and beautiful—it's not an act. She is always scrupulously honest with him. She is her own person, and Tom can't have her. Have you known someone like that? In romance, we believe what we want to believe. That's the reason *500 Days of Summer* is so appealing.

Tom (Joseph Gordon-Levitt) is in love with Summer from the moment he sees her. His thoughts on love may not run as deeply as, say, those of the Romantic poets. He writes greeting cards, and you suspect he may believe his own cards. It's amazing people get paid for a job like that. I could do it: "Love is a rose, and you are its petals." Summer is his new assistant. He needs an assistant in this job? She likes his looks and makes her move one day over the Xerox machine.

Can he accept that she simply likes him for now, not for forever? The movie, which is a delightful comedy, alive with invention, is about Tom wrestling with that reality. The director, Marc Webb, seems to be casting about for templates from other movies to help him tell this story; that's not desperation but playfulness. There's a little black-and-white, a little musical number, a little Fellini, which is always helpful in evoking a man in the act of yearning. Tom spends this movie in the emotional quandary of Mastroianni in *La Dolce Vita,* his hand always outstretched toward his inaccessible fantasies.

Summer remains mysterious all through the film, perhaps because we persist with Tom in expecting her to cave in. When we realize she is not required to in this movie because it's not playing by the Hollywood rules, we perk up; anything could happen. The kaleidoscopic time structure breaks the shackles of the three-act grid and thrashes about with the freedom of romantic confusion.

One thing men love is to instruct women. If a woman wants to enchant a man, she is wise to play his pupil. Men fall for this. Tom set out in life to be an architect, not a poet of greeting cards. He and Summer share the same favorite view of Los Angeles (one you may not have seen before), and he conducts for her an architectural tour. This is fun not because we get to see wonderful buildings, but because so rarely in the movies do we find characters arguing for their aesthetic values. What does your average character played by an A-list star believe about truth and beauty? Has Jason Bourne ever gone to a museum on his day off?

Joseph Gordon-Levitt has acted in a lot of movies, ranging from one of the *Halloween* sequels to the indie gem *Brick*. He comes into focus here playing a believable, likable guy, hopeful, easily disappointed, a little Tom Hanksian. He is strong enough to expect love, weak enough to be hurt. Zooey Deschanel evokes that ability in some women to madden you with admiration while never seeming to give it the slightest thought. She also had that quality in the overlooked *Gigantic* (2008), although the movie's peculiar supporting characters obscured it.

Tom opens the film by announcing it will not be your typical love story. Are you like me, and when you realize a movie is on autopilot you get impatient with it? How long can the characters pretend they don't know how the story will end? Here is a rare movie that begins by telling us how it will end, and is about how the hero has no idea why.

Note: The movie's poster insists the title is (500) Days of Summer. *Led by* Variety, *every single film critic I could find has simply ignored that. Good for them.*

Five Minutes of Heaven ★ ★ ★

NO MPAA RATING, 89 m., 2009

Liam Neeson (Alistair), James Nesbitt (Joe), Anamaria Marinca (Vika), Richard Dormer (Michael), Mark Davison (Young Alistair), Kevin O'Neill (Young Joe), Gerard Jordan (Jim). Directed by Oliver Hirschbiegel and produced by Eoin O'Callaghan and Stephen Wright. Screenplay by Guy Hibbert.

One of the characteristics of films about the Troubles in Northern Ireland, a period when members of the Protestant Ulster Volunteer Force and the Catholic Irish Republican Army were mounting assassinations against one another, is that we never see anyone at church, or in prayer. Their hatred was not theological but tribal. The Protestants were allied with the British, who consider Northern Ireland a part of the United Kingdom, and the IRA called for the unification of all Ireland. Protestants feared Catholic majority rule.

The dispute inflamed passions on both sides. Consider seventeen-year-old Alistair Little, who wants to gain stature within the UVF and agrees to kill a nineteen-year-old Catholic dock worker because of sectarian rivalry over jobs on the docks. He's given a gun, driven to the man's house, shoots him three times through the glass of the front door, and only then notices a small boy standing transfixed on the sidewalk. This is Joe, the victim's little brother. Alistair, wearing a black hood, regards him for many seconds, spares his life, and then hurries away.

Five Seconds of Heaven leads toward an eventual meeting of these two men thirty-three years later. They are being driven in separate cars to a confrontation arranged by a reality TV show, and as they drive and talk with their drivers, we see in flashbacks what led up to this day. Alistair (Liam Neeson) served twelve years in prison, repented of the murder, now works in conflict resolution. Joe (James Nesbitt) spent a tortured youth being blamed by his mother for his brother's death. "Why didn't you save him?" she screams, as if there was any way the little boy could have.

This story is inspired by real events; the filmmakers, director Oliver Hirschbiegel and writer Guy Hibbert, spent much time talking with the actual Alistair and Joe, who in life have never met. Joe has spent years talking of the "five minutes of heaven" it would mean to him to kill Alistair in revenge.

The film looks for a resolution that has not, perhaps could not, taken place in life. It is very well acted, by Neeson as a large, solemn, reformed man, and by Nesbitt as a sweaty, desperately unhappy one. Because of their acting, the intercut scenes in the two cars are more involving than they might have been. Knowing that Nesbitt is bringing a knife to the meeting staged for television creates considerable tension.

It is the reality show itself that feels wrong. The entire genre is contemptible to some degree. It sidesteps the cathartic function of drama by preying on the lives of real people. We are asked not to identify but to be voyeurs—to be entertained by another's misfortune.

What are the producers of the TV show in *Five Minutes of Heaven* hoping for? If Joe were to murder Alistair on camera, that would certainly be unplanned, but it would make sensational "tragic" footage.

Joe considers the whole project simply a convenience for placing him within striking range. What does Alistair think? If he is indeed the international expert in conflict resolution portrayed in the film, wouldn't he consider the program a cheap stunt? Yes, he deeply regrets the crime he committed against Joe's family. But is there no other way to express this?

The scenes involving the taping of the show nevertheless work on their own terms, not least because of the performance of Anamaria Marinca as an assistant producer assigned to handle *talent.* You may recall her as the best friend in *4 Months, 3 Weeks, and 2 Days,* the Romanian film that won Cannes 2007. Her fraught scenes show an active sympathy at work and draw out the trembling Joe.

It is on the levels of acting and drama that the film works, and also in showing how religious "convictions" can be reduced to completely unspiritual hatred. A final confrontation between the two men is unlikely but well handled. Neeson's ultimate appeal to Joe is effective. But the film seems based on the fabrication of unlikely events. It is true that Alistair and Joe have never met. I learn that if they ever do, Joe would still hope for his five minutes of heaven.

Flame and Citron ★ ★ ★

NO MPAA RATING, 132 m., 2009

Thure Lindhardt (Flammen), Mads Mikkelsen (Citronen), Stine Stengade (Ketty Selmer), Peter Mygind (Aksel Winther), Mille Hoffmeyer Lehfeldt (Bodil), Christian Berkel (Karl Heinz Hoffmann). Directed by Ole Christian Madsen and produced by Lars Bredo Rahbek. Screenplay by Madsen and Lars K. Andersen.

Murder takes an emotional toll, no matter how righteous the motivation. We might all be capable of pulling the trigger on Hitler, but would we reach the point when our willingness to kill others runs out? What if you're a Danish Resistance fighter, executing your fellow countrymen who are Nazi collaborators? I suppose the purpose of war is to provide a reality in which killing is objectified.

Flame and Citron takes place in Copenhagen in 1944, as the approaching Nazi defeat looms ever more clearly. It involves a two-man Resistance hit squad: the red-headed Flame (Thure Lindhardt) and the introverted, nervous, sweaty Citron (Mads Mikkelsen, who played the Bond villain Le Chiffre in the 2006 *Casino Royale*). Flame is empowered by killing, even grows reckless with shadings of omnipotence. For Citron, their lives, lived always on the run and in hiding, gnaw at his soul. The more Flame takes bold chances, the more Citron feels dread.

At first they kill men. Eventually, they become capable of killing women. There comes a point when even Flame is moved to make a small gesture of mercy toward a victim. By now they are in so deep the only way out is ahead.

The SS knows their identities. It has their descriptions. There is a foolhardy scene where they enter a bar filled with Nazis but escape detection. Flame seems almost oblivious to the giveaway of his hair color. They kill a great many collaborators, mostly by simply walking up to them and shooting them dead. The day comes when they kill a German officer. They were already living under a death sentence, but that seems to bring their execution date closer. The Nazi dragnet is under the command of Karl Heinz Hoffmann (Christian Berkel), a complex man with an unsettling way of drawing out the ambiguities of the situation.

It seems a simple matter, in outline: You are a patriot, you are a Dane with hatred of the Nazi occupation, you kill Danes who are collaborating, they have it coming to them. Flame is born to the task. Citron feels they are in the right, but he is disintegrating. And who can they trust? Who is giving their orders? What if there has been insidious infiltration and their skills are being misused? Is romance an unacceptable danger in this world?

Flame and Citron, based on the lives of two actual Resistance heroes, is a taut, handsome production—the most expensive Danish film to date—and it looks like a film noir, as indeed the costumes, cars, guns, and fugitives force it to. The director, Ole Christian Madsen, has said he was influenced by *Army of Shadows,* Jean-Pierre Melville's film about the French Resistance. Melville was himself a Resistance fighter and knew the life from inside. It is a messy business, killing your civilian countrymen. Better a uniformed man, speaking another language, who hopes to kill you. And in a world of duplicity and disguise, whose motives are pure?

Note: Army of Shadows *is in the Great Movies Collection at rogerebert.com.*

Flipped ★ ★ ★ ½

PG, 90 m., 2010

Madeline Carroll (Juli Baker), Callan McAuliffe (Bryce Loski), Rebecca De Mornay (Patsy Loski), Anthony Edwards (Steven Loski), John Mahoney (Chet Duncan), Penelope Ann Miller (Trina Baker), Aidan Quinn (Richard Baker). Directed by Rob Reiner and produced by Reiner and Alan Greisman. Screenplay by Reiner and Andrew Scheinman, based on the novel by Wendelin Van Draanen.

There are moments in adolescence when your feelings about romance turn on a dime. Maybe it's hormonal. The girl you thought was a pest becomes the object of your dreams. The boy you've had a crush on for years begins to seem like a jerk. The timing is off. Sometimes you can look back half a lifetime and see how things might have happened differently if you hadn't been so stupid. Rob Reiner's *Flipped* does the looking.

Here is a lovely movie about a girl who has adored a boy ever since he moved into the neighborhood in the second grade. She even likes his smell, and it is true we cannot love someone who isn't aromatic to our hearts. All through grade school and into high school she pursues him; they're like the runners in Keats's "Ode on a Grecian Urn" who pursue each other for eternity without ever drawing closer. In Reiner's film they flip and start running in the other direction.

Madeline Carroll is Juli Baker, who was determined to get Bryce Loski (Callan McAuliffe) to like her when they were kids, but in eighth grade has turned her attention to more urgent matters, like sparing the life of the beautiful sycamore tree in her front yard. It is threatened with being chopped down by the forces of evil, and she climbs it and won't come down. That shows some character, muses Bryce's grandfather Chet (John Mahoney). If he were Bryce he'd notice a girl like that. Bryce begins to catch on.

There are difficulties and the possibility of heartbreak. There always are in high school. You wear your sleeve on your heart. There are parents. Not everybody has parents like Juno did. If Juno had ordinary parents, her story would be a grim morality play. But *Flipped* doesn't haul in standard Parents of Teenagers, either. Reiner wisely casts gifted actors (Aidan Quinn and Penelope Ann Miller as the Bakers, Anthony Edwards and Rebecca De Mornay as the Loskis). He knows that Mahoney can save a wise grandfather from cornball with sheer brute force of niceness.

There's a screenplay device used by Reiner and Andrew Scheinman, based on the novel by Wendelin Van Draanen, that could be arduous but works here because it has been thought through. The key events in the film are seen from both points of view: Bryce's and Juli's. Teenagers often lose the beat emotionally, and these two need John Philip Sousa. There isn't trickery: The scenes happen as they seem to, and not in alternate universes. But they *seem* so different depending on who is seeing them. There's one of those events so beloved by teenage girls in which they can exact excruciating embarrassment on boys while seeming to be blithely unaware. The boys are auctioned off to the girls as lunchroom partners to raise money for charity. Yeah, that's what a guy wants, to stand on the stage while the most patronizing teacher in the school handles the bidding. Of course, it all goes tragically wrong for Juli and Bryce, but for what seems like different reasons.

Reiner begins the movie in 1959, the same year as his classic *Stand by Me,* and I don't think it's just for nostalgia. In a way, that's the last year of American teenage innocence, before the '60s took hold. Madeline Carroll and Callan McAuliffe, who both look teeth-achingly vulnerable, who are sincere and pure and wholesome, are characters we believe can be hurt. Some of today's teenagers are more wounded and cynical than their parents ever were. And for some of them sex is not an undiscovered country.

Maybe what makes *Flipped* such a warm entertainment is how it re-creates a life we wish we'd had when we were fourteen. That's true for adults, and also I suspect true for some fourteen-year-olds. In a way the audience flips, too.

Food, Inc. ★ ★ ★ ½

PG, 94 m., 2009

A documentary directed by Robert Kenner and produced by Kenner and Elise Pearlstein.

The next time you tuck into a nice T-bone, reflect that it probably came from a cow that spent much of its life standing in manure reaching above its ankles. That's true even if you're eating it at a pricy steakhouse. Most of the beef in America comes from four suppliers.

The next time you admire a plump chicken breast, consider how it got that way. The egg-to-death life of a chicken is now six weeks. They're grown in cages too small for them to move, in perpetual darkness to make them sleep more and quarrel less. They're fattened so fast they can't stand up or walk. Their entire lives they are trapped in the dark, worrying.

All of this is overseen by a handful of giant corporations that control the growth, processing, and sale of food in this country. Take Monsanto, for example. It has a patent on a custom gene for soybeans. Its customers are *forbidden* to save their own soybean seed for use next year. They have to buy new seed from Monsanto. If you grow soybeans outside their jurisdiction but some of the altered genes sneak into your crop from your neighbor's fields, Monsanto will investigate you for patent infringement. They know who the outsiders are and send out inspectors to snoop in their fields.

Food labels depict an idyllic, pastoral image of American farming. The sun rises and sets behind reassuring red barns and white frame farmhouses, and contented cows graze under the watch of the Marlboro Cowboy. This is a fantasy. The family farm is largely a thing of the past. When farmland comes on the market, the corporations outbid local buyers. Your best hope of finding real food grown by real farmers is at a local farmers' market. It's not entirely a matter of "organic" produce, although usually it is. It's a matter of food grown nearby, within the last week.

Remember how years ago you didn't hear much about E. coli? Now it seems to be in the news once a month. People are even getting E. coli poisoning from spinach and lettuce, for heaven's sake. Why are Americans getting fatter? A lot of it has to do with corn syrup, which is the predominant sweetener. When New Coke failed and Coke Classic returned, it wasn't to the classic recipe; Coke replaced sugar with corn sweeteners.

Cattle have been trained to eat corn instead of grass, their natural food. The Marlboro Cowboys should be riding through cornfields. Corn, in fact, is an ingredient in 80 PERCENT of supermarket products, including batteries and Splenda. Processing concentrates it. You couldn't eat enough corn kernels in a day to equal the calories in a bag of corn chips. Corn syrup can be addictive. Also fat and salt. A fast food meal is a heart attack in a paper bag. Poor families can't afford to buy real food to compete with the cost of $1.00 burgers and $1.98 "meals."

If this offends you, try to do something about it. The Texas beef growers sued Oprah. She won in court because she had the money to fight teams of corporate lawyers. You don't. Consider Carol Morrison, who refused to seal her chicken houses off from the daylight and opened them to the makers of this documentary. Morrison's chickens are not jammed into cages, but we see chickens that are unable to stand up. A giant chicken processor canceled her contract and refused to do any more business with her. She was getting sick of how she treated chickens, anyway.

Good food is not a cause limited to actresses on talk shows. Average people are getting concerned. Amazingly, Wal-Mart signed up with Stonyfield Farm. Consumer demand. When you hear commentators complaining about how the "government is paying farmers to not grow food," understand that "farmers" are corporations, and that the government is buying their surpluses to undercut local farmers around the world. The farmers who grew

Bermuda onions are just about out of business because of the dumping of American onions. "Socialized agriculture" benefits megacorporations, which are committed to the goals of most corporations: maximizing profits and executive salaries.

This doesn't read one thing like a movie review. But most of the stuff I discuss in it, I learned from the new documentary *Food, Inc.*, directed by Robert Kenner and based on the recent book *The Omnivore's Dilemma* by Michael Pollan. I figured it wasn't important for me to go into detail about the photography and the editing. I just wanted to scare the bejesus out of you, which is what *Food, Inc.* did to me.

It's times like these I'm halfway grateful that after surgery I can't eat regular food anymore, and have to live on a liquid diet out of a can. Of course, it contains soy and corn products, too, but in a healthy form. They say your total cholesterol level shouldn't exceed your age plus one hundred. Mine is *way* lower than that. And I don't have to tip.

For Colored Girls ★ ★ ½

R, 134 m., 2010

Janet Jackson (Jo), Loretta Devine (Juanita), Michael Ealy (Beau Willie), Kimberly Elise (Crystal), Omari Hardwick (Carl), Hill Harper (Donald), Thandie Newton (Tangie), Phylicia Rashad (Gilda), Anika Noni Rose (Yasmine), Tessa Thompson (Nyla), Kerry Washington (Kelly), Whoopi Goldberg (Alice). Directed by Tyler Perry and produced by Perry, Roger M. Bobb, and Paul Hall. Screenplay by Perry, based on the stage play *For Colored Girls Who Have Considered Suicide When the Rainbow Is Enuf* by Ntozake Shange.

Some plays resist filming. They exist as stage fantasies that can't survive the greater realism of the cinema. When a stage character performs a soliloquy, we understand exactly what's happening. When a film character does it, it can feel strange. A monologue on film, sure—but not a poetic construction unlike the ordinary speech in the same film.

Tyler Perry's ambitious *For Colored Girls* is based on the famous play *For Colored Girls Who Have Considered Suicide When the Rainbow Is Enuf* by Ntozake Shange. Many in the audience will have seen it onstage, and that will be an advantage; they'll understand what Perry is attempting. Ordinary moviegoers, accustomed to Perry's mainline films, are likely to be thrown off by the unconventional approach here. Perry tries to be faithful to the stage play and also to his own boldly and simply told stories, and the two styles don't fit together.

He also paints a cluttered canvas. The play featured seven characters in seven places with seven kinds of problems. He adds three other significant roles in order to flesh out actions that the play described in prose. This is too literal. His actors do an effective job with their soliloquies, but the audience is tugged back and forth between the stylized speech and the straight dramatic material.

Too bad. What a cast he has assembled: Kimberly Elise (Crystal), Janet Jackson (Jo), Loretta Devine (Juanita), Thandie Newton (Tangie), Anika Noni Rose (Yasmine), Kerry Washington (Kelly), Tessa Thompson (Nyla), and Whoopi Goldberg (Alice). Then there's Phylicia Rashad as a wise woman who lives in the same apartment house with six of the others, sees all, and provides a running commentary.

The Rashad character is new. So are Beau Willie (Michael Ealy), a war veteran and victim of posttraumatic stress syndrome who obsesses about Crystal; and Carl (Omari Hardwick), a rich, closeted gay conducting a doomed marriage with Jo. Crystal works for Jo, an imperious magazine editor, establishing some class conflict. The movie, like the play, distributes other problems among the women, so that we seem to be moving among episodes of a soap opera.

The award-winning Ntozake Shange play is justly respected, but I'm not sure it's filmmable, and I'm pretty sure it wasn't a wise choice for Perry. He seems more at home with everyday, human-comedy types of people, and here I think he is, if anything, too wary of his material. If he'd gone all the way in rewriting it into more conventional drama, he might have been criticized by lovers of the play, but he might have made a more entertaining and accessible film.

That's not to say *For Colored Girls* doesn't

have its virtues. Seeing these actresses together is a poignant reminder of their gifts, and of the absence of interesting roles for actresses in general and African-American ones in particular. A generation has been often shut out of fruitful roles. I saw the movie twice, and although it never worked for me as a whole, the second time I found myself appreciating many of its parts more. The soliloquies don't fit, but taken as freestanding dramatic entries, they're strongly done. So there are elements here, but not a fully rounded film.

Forget Me Not ★ ★ ½

NO MPAA RATING, 92 m., 2011

Tobias Menzies (Will), Genevieve O'Reilly (Eve), Gemma Jones (Eve's grandmother). Directed by Alexander Holt and Lance Roehrig and produced by Rebecca Long. Screenplay by Mark Underwood.

Forget Me Not seemed for an hour as if I had walked this way before, and then it took me in a new direction. The film is about a thirtyish couple who Meet Sorta Cute and end up sharing an all-night meander through London. They banter, they share, they separate and join up again, they even take a ride on the London Eye; and all the while I was wondering why *Before Sunrise* needed to be remade. Then the sun rose and the buried nature of the story became transformed.

The movie begins in a pub, where Will (Tobias Menzies) is the singer and Eve (Genevieve O'Reilly) is tending bar. He leaves, he walks to his nearby flat, and a very private moment is interrupted by a call from Eve: He forgot his guitar. Then he sees out the window that she's in a tussle with a drunk, hurries downstairs to rescue her, and they begin their all-night walk.

They are friendly. They exchange some personal information, not much. They're both taciturn, although she conceals that with cheerfulness. We know he is sad—more than she realizes. They have a small encounter with a bachelorette party, split, and later find themselves at the same club. The opening of the club scene is intriguing, showing dancers seemingly dancing to the sounds of their own shoes, until we figure it out.

They walk some more. They pretty much wander from above St. Paul's down the embankment, the streets mostly deserted, the Houses of Parliament making a background appearance. Like many Londoners, they seem impervious to the wonders they walk past. I'm glad I never lived in London after all. I would hate to ever get used to it.

On the next day, he goes along with her to the care home where her grandmother (Gemma Jones) will be taking one of those tests that ominously open by asking you what year it is, and how old you are. And now I will take a big step back from the plot and let it unfold on its own.

A couple of points: (1) If your hero is going to sing in the movie, give him better songs. (2) Although the cinematography is handsome, a couple of shots fall to the temptation of being about themselves and not the story—the foreground chess game in the coffee shop, for example, which has nothing to do with anything.

This is a civilized and empathetic film, but Will and Eve are so reserved and cautious, and as it moves along too deliberately you realize what a brilliant job Richard Linklater, Ethan Hawke, and Julie Delpy did with *Before Sunrise.* The ending conceals an emotional impact, sad and carefully orchestrated, but the film isn't very compelling.

Forks Over Knives ★ ★ ★

PG, 90 m., 2011

Dr. T. Colin Campbell, Dr. Caldwell Esselstyn Jr., Dr. Neil Barnard, Dr. John McDougall, and others. A documentary directed by Lee Fulkerson and produced by John Corry. Screenplay by Fulkerson.

Here is a film that could save your life. So you'd better stop reading now, because you don't want to go to the trouble. You are addicted to fat, salt, sugar, and corn syrup. Your body has established a narcoticlike dependence on them, and you're comfortable with that, just like smokers know why they keep on smoking. If you have to die ten or twenty-five years sooner than necessary, if you need Viagra because your vascular system is compromised, if you're overweight, you can live with that.

Hey, I'm not going all holier-than-thou on you. Think how fat I was for years. I knew the solution; I was weak and lazy. Over twelve years I was eventually able to lose about seventy pounds with a proper diet, but my current weight and superb physical condition can be attributed to my illness. I am unable to eat or drink anything, and my (therefore) perfect diet of canned nutrition has given me an ideal weight and incredibly good blood numbers. I don't recommend that you get sick to get well, however.

What every human being should do is eat a vegetarian diet based on whole foods. Period. That's it. Animal protein is bad for you. Dairy is bad for you. Forget the ads: Milk and eggs are bad for you. Skim milk is no better because it contains proportionately more animal protein. What you're trying to avoid is dietary cholesterol. You also need to cut way down on salt and sugar, and run like hell from high fructose corn syrup.

Forks Over Knives is a documentary in which Lee Fulkerson enacts a mirror image of the journey taken by Morgan Spurlock in *Super Size Me.* Instead of eating only at McDonald's for a month and nearly killing himself, he eats a plant-based whole-food diet for six months, gets off all of his cholesterol and blood pressure medications, drops a lot of weight, sleeps better, and has more energy.

His film follows three other sick people, one with breast cancer, one given less than a year to live because of heart problems, one with murderously high cholesterol. All are well again after following the vegetarian diet. The movie opens with a warning that no one should take such steps without consulting a physician, and I quite agree; I would not have depended on nutrition to cure my cancer, but I'm convinced that I would always have been healthier if I'd eaten correctly.

The film hammers us with information. It centers on the work of the famed nutritionists Dr. T. Colin Campbell of Cornell and Dr. Caldwell Esselstyn Jr. of the Cleveland Clinic. Campbell conducted the awesome China-Oxford-Cornell study, which followed millions of Chinese over decades and found that increases in their incidence of cancer and heart disease directly paralleled their adoption of a Western diet. Short-term studies show the same thing: When Nazis commandeered all the food animals in Norway, and rationing forced Brits away from meat, disease rates plummeted. After the war, they moved up again. On the traditional Japanese diet, breast and prostate cancers are all but unknown.

These facts have long been established, not only by Campbell and Esselstyn but by such as Dean Ornish, John McDougall, and the researchers at Pritikin. There is a catch-22. The federal government subsidizes such crops as corn, which is used for lethal corn syrup and to feed animals that we then eat. It puts bad foods in school lunches. The lobbyists of agribusiness control national farm policy. The government spends millions to subsidize an unhealthy diet. We are raising the first generation of children who will not live as long as their parents.

Over the years I tried vegan and low-protein vegetarian diets, benefitted from them and enjoyed them. I found by experience that all one needed was a rice cooker, a knife, a chopping block, whole grains, and fresh fruits and vegetables. I got all the protein and calcium I needed. I enjoyed it. But I was tempted. I strayed into the elysian fields of pizza, steaks, hamburgers, and soft drinks. I once was blind and now I see.

Forks Over Knives is not a subtle film. It plays as if it had been made for doctors to see in medical school. Few doctors seem prepared to suggest proper nutrition as an alternative to pills, stents, and bypasses. Although regular exercise, especially walking, is invaluable, the film shows only a little exercise and focuses single-mindedly on nutrition.

The bottom line: I am convinced this message is true. A plant-based whole-foods diet is healthy. Animal protein is not necessary, or should be used sparingly as Asians did, as a flavoring and not a main course. This adds the advantage of allowing us to avoid the chemicals and carcinogens pumped into livestock and poultry. Fast food is lethal. Parents who feed it to their children are helping them get hooked on fat, salt, and sugar. The facts are in. Didn't I warn you to stop reading?

P.S. I have recently decided to ditch my canned nutrition and switch to a liquid diet based on fresh fruits and vegetables. Yes, I consulted my physician.

Formosa Betrayed ★ ★ ½

R, 100 m., 2010

James Van Der Beek (Jake Kelly), Will Tiao (Ming), Kenneth Tsang (General Tse), Tzi Ma (Kuo), Wendy Crewson (Susan Kane), John Heard (Tom Braxton), Leslie Hope (Lisa Gilbert). Directed by Adam Kane and produced by Kane, David Allen Cluck, and Will Tiao. Screenplay by Tiao, Charlie Stratton, Yann Samuell, Brian Askew, Nathaniel Goodman, and Katie Swain.

Formosa Betrayed is a political thriller with an agenda. It argues that Formosa, now known as Taiwan, has been the pawn of great powers for centuries. Occupied by Japan in the prewar years, it was claimed by the Nationalists of Chiang Kai-shek after the war, and his army retreated there after its defeat by Red China. Although Americans have long been schooled that Chiang flew the banner of freedom, the film says he seized property, killed thousands of native Formosans, wiped out the leadership class, and established a dictatorship.

This history is related to an FBI agent named Kelly (James Van Der Beek), who has been sent to Taiwan to act as "liaison" in the search for the murderer of a prominent Taiwanese professor in Lake Forest, Illinois. Why Kelly—who speaks no Chinese and scarcely knows that Taiwan was once named Formosa? Perhaps precisely because of his ignorance. In the Cold War years, neither Washington nor Taipei want a scandal. The story takes place in 1983, but that hasn't changed.

Kelly flies in, is greeted by an American official named Susan Kane (Wendy Crewson), and is whisked off to a lavish welcome party while his key witness is being murdered. Secretly contacted by friends of the dead Lake Forest professor, he realizes their lives, and his, are in danger from the police state. At this point, the movie takes hold. Earlier, it seemed to linger overmuch on past history, including even newsreel footage from World War II and Chiang meeting Roosevelt and Churchill.

We realize, somewhat to our surprise, that *Formosa Betrayed* is a thriller that's actually *about* something. Most thrillers are about the good guy trying to outshoot and outrun the bad guys, and their settings are incidental. This one has a bone to chew. One of the screenplay writers is Will Tiao, who also plays Ming, the film's Taiwanese hero, an underground activist committed to regaining control of the island for its original Formosans.

I sense that his desire to make a point about history was equally or more important for the filmmakers than making a taut thriller. That explains the title *Formosa Betrayed,* which is completely accurate in terms of the story, but uses a name for the island that hasn't been current for fifty years. That it works fairly well as a thriller is a tribute to the actors, particularly Tiao, whose emotion can be felt as he relates his homeland's history.

James Van Der Beek's FBI agent might be skilled enough at domestic crime, but Kelly is out of his element in Taiwan. It's when he realizes this that the movie engages. One detail struck me: Van Der Beek insists on the official three-day beard required by all action heroes to signal their pumping testosterone. But in 1983, the FBI required its agents to be clean-shaven. And the action is set in the year before the first season of *Miami Vice,* which popularized the obligatory stubble.

Wendy Crewson's role seems thankless at first: She's limited to advising Kelly to cool it and asking him to keep his nose out of Taiwan's business. Turns out that she and Kelly's boss (John Heard) know many things the agent doesn't. As a result, *Formosa Betrayed* begins as rather clunky, but ends by making a statement that explains a great many things. One question left unasked: Why did we promise to defend Taiwan with nuclear weapons, but refuse to recognize it as a sovereign nation?

45365 ★ ★ ★ ★

NO MPAA RATING, 91 m., 2010

Featuring the townspeople of Sidney, Ohio. A documentary directed by Bill Ross IV and Turner Ross. Produced by Bill Ross IV.

The first shot tells us "45365 is the zip code of this city." In this achingly beautiful film, that zip code belongs to Sidney, Ohio, a handsome town of about twenty thousand residents. The brothers Bill and Turner Ross were born there perhaps thirty years ago. Of course they knew everybody in town, and when they spent seven months of 2007 filming its daily life, their presence must have eventually become commonplace. Their film evokes what *Winesburg, Ohio* might have looked like as a documentary.

Take me for an example. I knew everyone in the film. I grew up there. Well, actually in zip code 61802, which is Urbana, Illinois. My hometown was close to Sidney, Illinois, just as 45365 is not far from Urbana, Ohio. There are also towns named Homer and Philo near both towns named Urbana. East central Illinois was settled by people from Ohio.

In my midwestern town, I knew these people, their homes, their friendliness, the trouble some of them got into, and I knew why after the high school football game some of the kids hung out under the arc lamps and others were in the shade of the bleachers with the hoods pulled up on their sweatshirts. I even recognized, because I once covered the police beat, exactly the tone of voice a policeman will use after stopping a drunk driver he's known for ten years.

The film is privileged. No one is filmed with a hidden camera. The camera must have been right there, in the living room, the riverbank, the barbershop, the backseat, the football practice, the front lawn when a man agrees to put up a sign supporting a judge running for reelection. The Rosses must have filmed so much they became both trusted and invisible. They know this town without even thinking about it.

There is a beautiful shot during a church service that pans slowly to the right over the congregation and pauses looking into a door to a stairwell. A woman and small girl come up the stairs. The camera follows them back to the left until the girl is deposited back in her pew, having obviously just been taken to the potty. Were those two people cued? Obviously not. I suggest the cameraman, Bill or Turner, observed them getting up, intuited where they were going and why, and composed the camera movement instinctively. A brief shot you may not even consciously notice, but a perfect shot, reading the room as our minds do. All human life is in it.

I've never seen a barbershop like the one in the film. All three barbers are surprisingly young; one seems to be a teenager. Yet there is the order and routine of a small-town barbershop with barbers as old as Moses. Do these kids own the shop? Well, why not? It would cost less than a Supercuts franchise. What do they talk about? What all barbers talk about: the Friday night football game.

Sidney has what can only be described as a great radio station. Local human beings sit before the mics and run the boards. This station isn't a robot from Los Angeles. They play hits of the '80s and '90s, they make announcements, they have a sports talk show about the Sidney Yellowjackets. The team has a chicken-dinner benefit coming up. Adults seven dollars, kids three dollars.

It looks like rain on the day of the parade, but the station's reporter is on the spot. He's hooked up via his cell phone, and interviews a woman on the street with a tiny mic he holds up to his mouth and then to hers. He tells everyone to come on downtown, the skies are clearing. At the carnival, Elvis Junior is onstage. It's pouring rain. A guy uses a broom to push up the canvas roof of the tent and spill out the rainwater. A mobile home has been painted up as an exhibit for "LIVE! The World's Smallest Woman!"

Trains rumble through Sidney on business of their own. The radio station is used for the judicial candidate to record ". . . and I approve of this message." A man goes to court for sentencing. Drunk. We've seen two of his former wives agreeing that he needs to get his act together. They argue over whether he left the one *for* the other, or left the one and *then* married the other. They don't exactly seem to be fighting over him.

Spring, summer, autumn, winter. Summer showers. The first snow falling out at the abandoned drive-in theater. Music on Radio 105.5. Lawns. Good-looking old buildings. Sidney still looks like a town, not a squatter's camp of fast-food outlets. One extraordinarily stupid review of the film complains "all of these situations are filmed as if we already know the story of who these people are. We don't even learn anyone's names." This isn't that kind of a documentary. If you need to know everybody's name, you'll never, ever understand this film. Hell, I could go to Sidney, Ohio, tomorrow and feel right at home.

Note: 45365 *won the $25,000 Roger and Chaz*

Ebert Truer Than Fiction Award at the 2010 Independent Spirits. The contest was independently judged.

Four Lions ★ ★ ★

R, 101 m., 2010

Riz Ahmed (Omar), Arsher Ali (Hassan), Nigel Lindsay (Barry), Kayvan Novak (Waj), Adeel Akhtar (Faisal), Preeya Kalidas (Sofia). Directed by Chris Morris and produced by Mark Herbert and Derrin Schlesinger. Screenplay by Morris, Jesse Armstrong, and Sam Bain.

There's a difference between blowing up people and blowing up things. When the African National Congress in South Africa was bombing power pylons, that made strategic sense. When terrorists blow up people (and themselves), it strikes me as self-defeating idiocy. Believing in heaven is commonplace. But surely only a stupid person would blow himself up to get there sooner.

Four Lions is a transgressive comedy about five such people. They live in an anonymous British suburb and dream of jihad. They speak such a fluent mixture of working-class Brit slang and argot, in such fluent accents, that it's odd to hear their radical beliefs in such commonplace slang.

All are Muslims. Four have Pakistani roots. One is a red-bearded Brit whose ideas are the most aggressive. They conduct a scheme to strap bombs to their bodies and strike against society. In this scheme they are so amateurish they fly below the radar of British intelligence. Nor do they have a very clear plan; Barry, the convert, believes they should blow up a mosque to radicalize Muslim moderates. The catch-22 here is that therefore the bomber should be a white Westerner. Hello, Barry.

Four Lions is impossible to categorize. It's an exceedingly dark comedy, a wicked satire, a thriller where the thrills center on the incompetence of the villains. It's fueled by both merriment and anger. It shows characters so dazzled by the prospect of the next life that they have no care for their present lives—or ours. It is about Muslims but also about the fundamentalist mind-set in general, which admits no doubt.

Consider Omar (Riz Ahmed), who I suppose is the film's closest thing to a hero. He has a loving wife, named Sofia (Preeya Kalidas), and a sweet child. He works as a security guard. He has a comfortable flat, where he studies terrorist videos on his laptop. He despairs of the ignorance of some of his comrades (one has "special needs"), but perhaps thinks even the stupid are useful as suicide bombers. Omar and his wife openly discuss his plans without a shred of doubt.

The others seem to be average blokes, apart from their fanaticism. They all seem serene about the prospect of blowing themselves up; they attach much importance to entering heaven with smiles on their faces. They have either not received or were unable to benefit from an education preparing themselves for reality. This is sad, and all the more so because the "four lions" (and a young recruit they pick up) are so satisfied with themselves.

There are elements of slapstick, particularly involving an unfortunate sheep (who was "harmed during the making of this film" the end titles tell us). And the climactic sequence involves the four men dressing up in bizarre clown costumes to run in the London Marathon. Why? To blow up other marathoners?

In the course of this plan, one lion locks himself inside a kebab shop, taking the owner and three customers hostage. When he's reached by a police negotiator and asked for his demands, he . . . doesn't have any. He seems, indeed, to have little idea why he has a bomb strapped to himself. The importance of blowing himself up and arriving in heaven with a smile has overshadowed any mundane considerations.

Four Lions was directed by Chris Morris, a British TV and radio satirist, and cowritten by Morris, Sam Bain, and Jesse Armstrong (who wrote the political satire *In the Loop*). They have made the film with heedless abandon. Its strategy is to regard imbecility with a poker face, and permit horrifying acts to occur absentmindedly. Sometimes this is funny and sometimes not at all, but you can't call it boring.

The Fourth Kind ★ ½

PG-13, 98 m., 2009

Milla Jovovich (Abigail), Elias Koteas (Psychologist), Will Patton (Sheriff), Corey

Johnson (Tommy), Olatunde Osunsanmi (Professor). Directed by Olatunde Osunsanmi and produced by Paul Brooks, Joe Carnahan, and Terry Robbins. Screenplay by Osunsanmi.

Boy, is the Nome, Alaska, chamber of commerce going to be pissed off when they see *The Fourth Kind*. You don't wanna go there. You can't drive there, that's for sure. The only ways in are by sea, air, dogsled, or birth canal. Why the aliens chose this community of 9,261 to abduct so many people is a mystery, as is why owls stare into bedroom windows.

Nome has been the center of an alarming series of strange disappearances, we learn. So many, the FBI has sent agents there ten times more than to big Anchorage. *The Fourth Kind* is based on the testimony of a psychologist who found, circa 2000, that many of her patients reported waking at 3 a.m. with the sense that something was wrong and seeing an owl with its eyes on them.

The film goes to great lengths to be realistic. "I am the actress Milla Jovovich," Jovovich tells us at the outset, explaining that in the film she plays the psychologist Abigail, whose testimony was videotaped. Other fact-based characters are her colleague (Elias Koteas), the local sheriff (Will Patton), and a professor who interviews her (Olatunde Osunsanmi). "Every scene in this movie is supported by archived footage," she says, and to prove it, Osunsanmi, who's also the director, uses split screen to show Jovovich and the *real* Abigail talking almost simultaneously. The real Abigail's name has been changed, but since she's right there on the screen, how much of a mystery can she be in Nome?

It was with crushing disappointment that my research discovered this is all made up out of whole cloth, including the real Abigail. It wasn't even shot in Nome, but mostly in Bulgaria. And Dallas Massie, a retired state trooper who's acting police chief, says he's heard nothing about aliens. I learn all this from the blog of an *Anchorage Daily News* reporter, Kyle Hopkins, who says about twenty people have indeed disappeared in the area since the 1960s, and writes: "The FBI stepped in, reviewing two dozen cases, eventually determining that excessive alcohol consumption and the winter climate were a common link in many of the cases. Some of the dead were killed by exposure or from falling off a jetty into the frigid Snake River."

All right then, *The Fourth Kind* is a pseudo-documentary like *Paranormal Activity* and *The Blair Witch Project*. But unlike those two, which just forge ahead with their home video cameras, this one encumbers the flow of the film with ceaseless reminders that it is a dramatization of real events. When we see Will Patton, for example, there's a subtitle informing us: "Will Patton, actor." Oh! I already know well that Will Patton and Elias Koteas are actors, and Jovovich identifies herself at the start. I wish they'd had a really big-name star. It might have been funny to read "Bruce Willis: Actor."

Now here's a good question. In the film we see the "real" footage of the "actual" client interviews with "Abigail." Why would an actual psychologist release confidential videotapes to a horror film, especially tapes showing the clients having seizures? Who *are* those "actual clients," really? The end credits don't thank them, although the film claims to account for them. Remember, even in a movie "based on a true story" (like *Fargo*), nothing before the actual end credits needs to be true. You want to watch those like a hawk. My theory is, the "actual" clients are played by the actors playing their fictional versions. Of course, I can't be sure of that. Think about it.

Jovovich is good, actually. It's a broad, melodramatic role with lots of screaming, and after two *Resident Evil* movies, she's good at being an endangered heroine and makes a competent psychologist. And a successful one, too. Her log cabin arts and crafts office looks like it was surely subleased from a (Bulgarian) millionaire. We see there's a lot of business in Nome for a specialist in owl staring.

Free Style ★ ★

PG, 94 m., 2009

Corbin Bleu (Cale Bryant), Madison Pettis (Bailey Bryant), Sandra Echeverria (Alex Lopez), Penelope Ann Miller (Jeanette Bryant), Jesse Moss (Justin Maynard), Matt Bellefleur (Derek Black), David Reivers (Dell). Directed by William Dear and produced by Corbin Bleu, Rob Cowan, Michael Emanuel, Dean E. Fronk, Donald Paul

Pemrick, and David Reivers. Screenplay by Jeffrey Nicholson and Joshua Leibner.

There are some charming actors in this movie, all dressed up but with no place to go. *Free Style* is remorselessly formulaic, with every character and plot point playing its assigned role. That it works is primarily because of the charisma of Corbin Bleu (did his parents meet in a French restaurant?) and Sandra Echeverria, as a boy who likes to ride motorcycles and a girl who likes to ride horses.

Bleu plays Cale, a teenager who delivers pizza and races for a motocross team. His best friend runs off the track and crashes during a race, and he turns his bike around and drives upstream to the rescue. I am not a motocross expert, but doesn't this seem idiotic?

The sponsor of his bike withdraws his support, as indeed he should. One day Cale delivers a pizza to a farm and two things catch his eye: a beaten-up old motorcycle, and Alex (Sandra Echeverria), who is not old nor the least bit beaten-up. He's given the bike and goes to work fixing it up, and Alex becomes his girlfriend—although not without the exhausted scene where she sees him with his former girl and leaps to the wrong conclusion. This scene is so obligatory, I think sometimes they even create an old girlfriend just to make it possible.

Cale and his mom (Penelope Ann Miller) argue about his career track. He dreams of making the professional motocross tour. His mom thinks he should focus on school. I think she's right. But noooo—he has a Dream. When will there be a film about a motocross racer or skateboarder, say, who decides, the hell with it, I could break my neck. I think I'll just go to college.

You may know that Penelope Ann Miller is white, and that Corbin Bleu (star of all the *High School Musical* films) is biracial. Why do I mention this? Because the movie makes a big point of it, even providing an absent black father Cale seeks out, perhaps because then, God help us, the father can turn up at the end of the Big Race and nod approvingly. Why not simply provide the kid with two parents? Because the Single Mom is also a beloved cliché, you say? Two for the price of one.

Anyway, all leads up to the Big Race, etc., and the False Dawn, the Fake Crisis, and the Real Dawn, all following the recipe. My primary enjoyment was entertaining myself by mentally casting Corbin Bleu and Sandra Echeverria in other movies. Well, there's hope. Echeverria has the lead in three upcoming movies from Mexico. Bleu (who is handsome and not merely cute) works constantly. In later years people won't be wearing out their DVDs of a movie like this, but as a career step, it's a good one. Better than pro motocross.

Friday the 13th ★ ★

R, 91 m., 2009

Jared Padalecki (Clay Miller), Amanda Righetti (Whitney Miller), Arlen Escarpeta (Lawrence), Danielle Panabaker (Jenna), Travis Van Winkle (Trent), Aaron Yoo (Chewie), Derek Mears (Jason Voorhees). Directed by Marcus Nispel and produced by Michael Bay, Andrew Form, Brad Fuller, and Sean Cunningham. Screenplay by Damian Shannon and Mark Swift.

Friday the 13th is about the best *Friday the 13th* movie you could hope for. Its technical credits are excellent. It has a lot of scary and gruesome killings. Not a whole lot of acting is required. If that's what you want to find out, you can stop reading now.

OK, it's just us in the room. You're not planning to see *Friday the 13th,* and you wonder why anyone else is. Since the original movie came out in 1980, there were ten more films—sequels, retreads, fresh starts, variations, whatever. Now we get the 2009 *Friday the 13th,* which is billed as a "remake" of the original.

That it is clearly not. Let me test you with a trick question: How many kids did Jason kill in the first movie? The answer is none, since Mrs. Voorhees, his mother, did all of the killings in revenge on the camp counselors who let her beloved son drown in Crystal Lake.

Mrs. Voorhees is decapitated at the end of number one and again in the new version, so the new movie is technically a remake up until that point—but the decapitation, although preceded by several murders, comes *before* this movie's title card, so everything after that point is new.

It will come as little surprise that Jason still

lives in the woods around Crystal Lake and is still sore about the decapitation of his mom. Jason must be sore in general.

So far in the series, he has been drowned, sliced by a machete in the shoulder, hit with an ax in the head, supposedly cremated, aped by a copycat killer, buried, resurrected with a lightning bolt, chained to a boulder and thrown in the lake again, resurrected by telekinesis, drowned again, resurrected by an underwater electrical surge, melted by toxic waste, killed by the FBI, resurrected through the possession of another body, returned to his own body, thrown into hell, used for research, frozen cryogenically, thawed, blown into space, freed to continue his murder spree on Earth 2, returned to the present, faced off against Freddy Krueger of *A Nightmare on Elm Street,* drowned again with him, and made to emerge from Crystal Lake with Freddy's head, which winks.

I know what you're thinking. No, I haven't seen them all. Wikipedia saw them so I didn't have to. The question arises: Why does Jason continue his miserable existence, when his memoirs would command a seven-figure advance, easy? There is another question. In the 1980 movie, twenty years had already passed since Jason first went to sleep with the fishes. Assuming he was a camper aged twelve, he would have been thirty-two in 1980, and in 2009 he is sixty-one. That helps explain why one of my fellow critics at the screening was wearing an AARP T-shirt.

SPOILER WARNING: At the end of this film, Jason is whacked with an ax and a board, throttled with a chain, and dragged into a wood chipper, although we fade to black just before the chips start to fly, and we are reminded of Marge Gunderson's immortal words. The next day brings a dawn, as one so often does, and two survivors sit on the old pier with Jason's body wrapped and tied in canvas. Then they throw him into Crystal Lake. Anyone who thinks they can drown Jason Voorhees for the fifth time is a cockeyed optimist.

Note: In my research, I discovered that the scientific name for fear of Friday the 13th is "paraskavedekatriaphobia." I envision a new franchise: Paraskavedekatriaphobia: A New Beginning, Paraskavedekatriaphobia: Jason Lives, Paraskavedekatriaphobia: Freddy's Nightmare, *etc.*

From Paris with Love ★ ★

R, 92 m., 2010

John Travolta (Charlie Wax), Jonathan Rhys Meyers (James Reece), Kasia Smutniak (Carolina), Richard Durden (Ambassador Bennington). Directed by Pierre Morel and produced by Luc Besson and India Osborne. Screenplay by Adi Hasak, based on a story by Besson.

Pauline Kael has already reviewed this movie in her book *Kiss Kiss Bang Bang,* and it only took her the title. I could go through my usual vaudeville act about chase scenes and queasycams and Idiot Plots, but instead I'd like you to join me in the analysis of something that increasingly annoys me.

Imagine we are watching *From Paris with Love* on a DVD with a stop-action button. We look at an action scene all the way through. John Travolta stars as Charlie Wax, an American Mr. Fix-It with a shaved head and goatee, who has been sent to Paris on a mysterious assignment. Not mysterious to him, mysterious to us. It involves Asian drug dealers and/or terrorists from the Middle East. Doesn't matter who they are or what they do, because their only function here is to try to kill Charlie and his fall-guy partner James Reece (Jonathan Rhys Meyers).

OK. We're on the sofa. We look at the scene. We take a second look. We focus on Travolta. This is an athlete. His reflexes are on a hair-trigger. He can deal with several enemies at a time. He can duck, jump, hurdle, spin, and leap. One slight miscalculation, and he's dead. He doesn't miss a beat. He's in superb condition, especially for a guy whose favorite food is Cheese Royales. That's a little joke reminding us of *Pulp Fiction,* and the *last* thing you should do is remind the audience of a movie they'd rather be watching.

Now we go through the scene a frame at a time. We don't miss much in the way of continuity because it's pretty much glued together a frame at a time. We see a dizzying cascade of images, but here's a funny thing: We don't see Travolta completing many extended physical movements, and none involving any danger.

The shots of him involve movement, but in bursts of a few frames, intercut with similar bursts of action by his attackers. There is no sense of continuous physical movement taking place within a defined space. No overall sense of the choreography.

I hasten to say this is not criticism of John Travolta. He succeeds in this movie by essentially acting in a movie of his own. The fight construction is the same with most modern action movies. In past decades studios went so far as to run fencing classes for swordfights. Stars like Buster Keaton, Douglas Fairbanks Sr., and Errol Flynn did their own stunts and made sure you could see them doing them. Most of the stunts in classic kung fu movies, starring such as Bruce Lee and Jackie Chan, were really happening. Sure, they used camera angles, trampolines, and wires, but you try it and see how easy it is.

CGI makes that unnecessary. The stunt work is done by computers and the editing process. I fear that classic action sequences would be too slow for today's impatient action fans, who have been schooled on impossibilities. The actual stunt driving done in such chase landmarks as *The French Connection* and *Bullitt,* where you could observe real cars in real space and time, has been replaced by what is essentially animation.

I mention this because last week I saw a good South Korean thriller named *The Chaser,* and its best scene involved a foot chase through the narrow streets of Seoul by two actors who, you could see, were actually running down streets. In modern actioners, the only people who work up a sweat are the editors.

Anyway, that's what I had on my mind. As for *From Paris with Love,* it's mostly bang bang and not kiss kiss, and as an actress once asked Russ Meyer, what's love got to do with it?

Funny People ★ ★ ★ ½

R, 146 m., 2009

Adam Sandler (George Simmons), Seth Rogen (Ira Wright), Leslie Mann (Laura), Eric Bana (Clarke), Jonah Hill (Leo), Jason Schwartzman (Mark), Aubrey Plaza (Daisy), Torsten Voges (Dr. Lars). Directed by Judd Apatow and produced by Apatow, Clayton Townsend, and Barry Mendel. Screenplay by Apatow.

Stand-up comics feel compelled to make you laugh. They're like an obnoxious uncle, with better material. The competition is so fierce these days that most of them are pretty good. I laugh a lot. But unlike my feelings for Catherine Keener, for example, I don't find myself wishing they were my friends. I suspect they're laughing on the outside but gnashing their teeth on the inside.

Judd Apatow would possibly agree with this theory. I e-mailed him a bunch of questions, and that was the only one he ignored. He was writing material for comics when he was a teenager, and his insights into the stand-up world inform *Funny People,* his new film that has a lot of humor and gnashing. It's centered on Adam Sandler's best performance, playing George Simmons, a superstar comic who learns he has a very short time to live.

He is without the resources to handle this news. He doesn't have the "support group" they say you need when you get sick. He's made a dozen hit movies and lives in opulence in a house overlooking Los Angeles but is so isolated he doesn't even seem to have any vices for company. Sandler modulates George's desperation in a perceptive, sympathetic performance; I realized here, as I did during his *Punch Drunk Love,* that he contains an entirely different actor than the one we're familiar with. His fans are perfectly happy with Sandler's usual persona, the passive-aggressive semi-simpleton. This other Sandler plays above and below that guy, and more deeply.

Funny People is not simply about George Simmons's struggle with mortality. It sees that struggle within the hermetically sealed world of the stand-up comic, a secret society that has merciless rules, one of which is that even sincerity is a joke. "No—seriously!"

Here is a man without confidants. When you depend on your agent for emotional support, you're probably only getting 10 percent as much as you need. On the circuit, he meets a hungry, ambitious kid named Ira Wright (Seth Rogen), who has written some good material. George hires him to write for him, and then gives him a chance to open for him, and then finds himself pouring out his worries to him.

There was a girl once in George's past named Laura (Leslie Mann). She was the one who got away. He encounters her again, married to an obnoxious macho Aussie named Clarke (Eric Bana, playing him as a guy who seems to be weighing the possibility of hitting everyone he meets). George apparently was once able to sort of confide in Laura, until success shut him down, and now he finds he still sort of can.

The thing about *Funny People* is that it's a real movie. That means carefully written dialogue and carefully placed supporting performances—and it's *about something.* It could have easily been a formula film, and the trailer shamelessly tries to misrepresent it as one, but George Simmons learns and changes during his ordeal, and we empathize.

This is a new Seth Rogen on the screen. Much thinner, dialed down, with more dimensions. Rogen was showing signs of forever playing the same buddy-movie costar, but here we find that he, too, has another actor inside. So does Jason Schwartzman, who often plays vulnerable but here presents his character as the kind of successful rival you love to hate.

Rogen and Leslie Mann find the right notes as George's impromptu support group. The plot doesn't blindly insist that George and Laura must find love; it simply suggests they could do better in their lives. Eric Bana makes a satisfactory comic villain, there is a rolling-around-on-the-lawn fight scene that's convincingly clumsy, and Mann mocks him with a spot-on Aussie accent (not the standard pleasant one, more of a bray).

Apatow understands that every supporting actor has to pull his weight. The casting director who found him Torsten Voges to play George's doctor earned a day's pay. Voges is in some eerie, bizarre way convincing as a cheerful realist bringing terrible news: miles better than your stereotyped grim movie surgeon.

After an enormously successful career as a producer, this is Apatow's third film as a director, after *The 40-Year-Old Virgin* and *Knocked Up.* Of him it can be said: He is a real director. He's still only forty-one. So here we go.

G

Gentlemen Broncos ★ ★

PG-13, 89 m., 2009

Michael Angarano (Benjamin Purvis), Jennifer Coolidge (Judith Purvis), Jemaine Clement (Dr. Ronald Chevalier), Hector Jimenez (Lonnie Donaho), Halley Feiffer (Tabitha), Sam Rockwell (Bronco/Brutus). Directed by Jared Hess and produced by John J. Kelly and Mike White. Screenplay by Jared Hess and Jerusha Hess.

As an amateur collector of the titles of fictional novels in movies, I propose that this one has the worst of all time: *Yeast Lords: The Bronco Years.* You say you smiled? Me, too, and there are precious few smiles and laughs in *Gentlemen Broncos,* which is not a very good movie title either, although it might work for an X-rated film. The author of *Yeast Lords* is a teenager named Benjamin who hopefully writes science fiction and idolizes a famous sci-fi novelist named Dr. Ronald Chevalier as much as I once, and still do, admire the good doctor Asimov.

Benjamin Purvis (Michael Angarano) lives in a Buckydome house with his mother, Judith (Jennifer Coolidge), and let's pause right here to observe that Jennifer Coolidge, here and in Werner Herzog's forthcoming *Bad Lieutenant,* possesses what I like to think of as the Walken Factor. That is, her appearance in any scene immediately inspires our particular interest because we sense something unexpected and amusing is about to happen. So it was with her iconic appearance as Stifler's mom in *American Pie* (1999), in which she had the rare honor of inspiring the Internet acronym *MILF.* If you doubt me, look it up in Wiktionary. Hard as it is to believe, *MILF* was not used until Stifler's mom appeared.

Here she is Purvis's mom, and she encourages his budding writing skills by allowing him attend the Cletus Fest, a teenage authors' event that offers the awesome presence of Dr. Ronald Chevalier (Jemaine Clement). He's a science-fiction author with writer's block, and when Benjamin presses a copy of *Yeast Lords: The Bronco Years* into his hands, in a moment of desperation he snatches it up, makes some changes, and submits it as his own work.

That sounds, I suppose, as if *Gentlemen Broncos* might tell a good story. Perhaps the Hollywood gurus who advise, "story, story story" might add: "but don't stop there." The director, Jared Hess, who made *Napoleon Dynamite,* a film I admit I didn't get, has made a film I don't even begin to get. He invents good characters: Purvis, Purvis's mom, Dr. Ronald Chevalier, and Tabitha (Halley Feiffer, daughter of the immortal Jules), who is a wannabe romance novelist, as are we all. Mike White turns up toward the end, providing another Walken Factor moment. But then Hess loses them in a jumbled plot that sometimes seems to mystify the characters. A character-driven plot, if it isn't *The Big Lebowski,* involves people who know what they want and when they want it.

Benjamin sells the film rights to his work to Tabitha and her friend Lonnie (Hector Jimenez), who is the Masha to her Rupert Pupkin. They plan a production that promises to be a mumblecore version of *Star Wars,* and, of course, there are problems with Dr. Ronald Chevalier. This film, Benjamin's novel, and the doctor's rewrite inspire different versions of the fictional hero under various names, and these fantasy sequences are sometimes amusing, but they seem freestanding and a little forlorn. They do suggest that the worst movie title in history would be *Yeast Lords: The Bronco Years: The IMAX Experience.*

Get Him to the Greek ★ ★ ★

R, 108 m., 2010

Jonah Hill (Aaron Green), Russell Brand (Aldous Snow), Elisabeth Moss (Daphne Binks), Rose Byrne (Jackie Q), Colm Meaney (Jonathan Snow), Sean Combs (Sergio Roma). Directed by Nicholas Stoller and produced by Judd Apatow, David L. Bushell, and Rodney Rothman. Screenplay by Stoller.

Aldous Snow is the sort of rock star who can seriously propose himself for the role of White African Jesus. What would his duties be? He has no idea. It's just the sort of thing he throws out to keep people on their toes. Aldous was first seen as a rock star, clean and sober, in *Forgetting Sarah Marshall* (2008), and he returns in *Get Him to the Greek* as a wild man deep into a relapse.

It is the task of an earnest and square young man, Aaron Green, to fly to London and in exactly three days get him to New York for a *Today* show appearance and then to Los Angeles for a comeback concert at the Greek Theater. *Get Him to the Greek* is the story of those three days, and nights, which pass in a blur for the innocent Green. They are a blur for Aldous as well, but then, that's his lifestyle.

The movie is funny in the way of *The Hangover* about what trouble lads can get into when their senses are whirling. Unlike some depictions of binges, it doesn't shortchange vomit. The adventures of Aldous and Aaron remind me of a friend I used to meet on Saturday mornings for what we called Drunch. "Sometimes," she said, "it can be really exhausting having a good time." Aaron (Jonah Hill), who has been threatened with flaying if he doesn't deliver Aldous (Russell Brand) on time, panics when he can't get him to Heathrow airport for the right flight, can't get him to the *Today* show on time, can't get him to the sound check at the Greek, and very nearly can't get him to the Greek. Aldous, for the most part, floats benevolently above these small misunderstandings. When it comes to himself, he's a very understanding man.

There are really two movies here. One is a gross-out comedy that grows lyrical in its exuberant offensive language, its drug excesses, its partying, its animal behavior. The other movie, which comes into focus, so to speak, in the last half, is surprisingly sweet, and shows that Aldous and Aaron arrive at a friendship that has been tempered in the forge of their misbehavior. Both movies were produced by Judd Apatow, who does a nice line in gross-out comedies.

The lads share loneliness and a feeling of failure with women. Aaron is in love with Daphne Binks (Elisabeth Moss of *Mad Men*), a hospital intern who works endless shifts and gets a great job offer in Seattle, far from the music biz. Aldous has split from Jackie Q (Rose Byrne) as a consequence of his spectacular fall from sobriety. We learn they earlier collaborated on an album voted the worst of all time, but while Aldous has plunged, Jackie Q has soared. In a movie jammed with celebrity cameos (Paul Krugman?), we see bits of her music videos, which, incredible as they may be, aren't entirely improbable. We are so deep into post-irony that it's hard to be sure if a video is *intended* to be bad.

The reason the friendship works is that Russell Brand and Jonah Hill are good actors. Hill's character is required to be blotto half of the time, but there's the sense that he's desperately trying to do the right thing. Russell Brand is convincing as a rock star, imperious, self-destructive, smarter than he seems, calculating, measuring out wretched excess in survivable portions. When it comes time for him to sing, he does it convincingly, with songs that sound like real rock songs. I was reminded a little of Rod Stewart.

The urgency of Aaron's mission depends entirely on his fear of Sergio Roma (Sean Combs), the owner of Aldous's record label. Combs is convincing in an early scene as an egotistical, hard-driving music executive. Then his character has a comic flowering in later scenes, as he reveals his true rock 'n' roll roots. He can party at top speed *and* send Aldous onstage at the Greek despite a bleeding wound from a jump from a rooftop. That Aldous may collapse onstage doesn't occur to him. And indeed Aldous rises to the occasion, as from many reports a lot of rock stars are able to do. They may not remember their performances, but they were great.

What I'm backing into here is that under the cover of slapstick, cheap laughs, raunchy humor, gross-out physical comedy, and sheer exploitation, *Get Him to the Greek* is also fundamentally a sound movie. The writer-director, Nicholas Stoller, who also directed *Forgetting Sarah Marshall*, carefully places the foundations of the story and restrains himself from making Aldous and Aaron into *completely* unbelievable caricatures. The fundamentals are in place.

Get Low ★ ★ ★

PG-13, 102 m., 2010

Robert Duvall (Felix Bush), Bill Murray (Frank Quinn), Sissy Spacek (Mattie Darrow), Lucas Black (Buddy Robinson), Gerald McRaney (Revered Gus Horton), Bill Cobbs (Reverend Charlie Jackson). Directed by Aaron Schneider and produced by David Gundlach and Dean Zanuck. Screenplay by Chris Provenzano and C. Gaby Mitchell.

We're asked to take Felix Bush on faith, and since he's played in *Get Low* by Robert Duvall, we must. Duvall is authentic right down to the bone, and lends his credibility to almost every character he plays. Felix requires a lot of credibility. He's a backwoods hermit with the kind of beard that suggests he took a box of Smith Brothers Cough Drops into the barber and said, "Give me one of those." He lives with a mule, a shotgun, and his secrets.

The film opens with a murky scene of a farmhouse on fire and a man running away through the night. Who could this man be? Given the Law of Economy of Characters, it must be Felix, and therefore at the end, the movie must account for this scene. Since Felix is an ornery rascal, it follows as the night the day that by the end he will be downright amenable to folks. We don't require him to shave off his beard, but he obliges.

In the present (the 1930s), Felix learns of the death of an old friend, and this inspires him to make his own plans. He makes a rare visit to town to meet with Frank Quinn, the undertaker (Bill Murray), and explains how he wants to "get low." He plans his burial plot, his stone, his farewell send-off, and even the designated speaker. He intends this all to happen now, while he's still alive and can enjoy getting the value for his money.

Frank, who is oleaginous even for a movie undertaker, has a fresh-faced young assistant, Buddy (Lucas Black), who has a wife and baby and ends up as Felix's unofficial minder. Frank dreams up a real corker of a getting low party, many of the townsfolk will come, and Felix gets a new spring in his step. He meets for the first time in years Mattie Darrow (Sissy Spacek), whom he used to be sweet on, and Frank even pulls Reverend Charlie Jackson (Bill Cobbs) out of his hat—or at least out of southern Illinois. The reverend may be the only man alive who knows what happened on that dark night.

All leads up to the big day, during which hearts are healed, truths told, secrets revealed, misunderstandings set straight, and Felix delivers a speech he must have been rehearsing for years. The movie, which opened in an unexpected and intriguing way, has by now long since been on autopilot. That's where Duvall comes in—and Murray.

After you get to a certain point with an actor, you don't much care what he does; you just want to watch him doing it. So it is with Duvall and Murray. They've played versions of these characters not a million miles distant. Duvall is a sly old twinkler, and Murray would take the bills out of your billfold before screwing you in, explaining he doesn't want you to spend eternity with a bump under your butt.

All of this is just plain enjoyable. I liked it, but please don't make me say it's deeply moving or redemptive and uplifting. It's a genre piece for character actors, is what it is, and that's an honorable thing for it to be. Perhaps Robert Duvall is the only man alive who could make his big speech here sound like the truth, and sincere. But he does.

G-Force ★ ★ ½

PG, 89 m., 2009

Voices of animated characters: Nicolas Cage (Speckles), Sam Rockwell (Darwin), Jon Favreau (Hurley), Penelope Cruz (Juarez), Steve Buscemi (Bucky), Tracy Morgan (Blaster).
Homo sapiens: Bill Nighy (Leonard Saber), Will Arnett (Kip Killian), Zach Galifianakis (Ben Kendall), Kelli Garner (Marcie), Tyler Patrick Jones (Connor), Piper Mackenzie Harris (Penny), Gabriel Casseus (Agent Trigstad), Jack Conley (Agent Carter). Directed by Hoyt Yeatman and produced by Jerry Bruckheimer. Screenplay by Cormac and Marianne Wibberley, Ted Elliott, Terry Rossio, and Tim Firth.

G-Force is a pleasant, inoffensive 3-D animated farce about a team of superspy guinea pigs who do battle with a mad billionaire who wants to conquer the earth by programming all the home appliances made by his corporation to follow his instructions. It will possibly be enjoyed by children of all ages.

The film is nonstop, wall-to-wall madcap action. It's possible to imagine Jerry Bruckheimer, the producer, and his cast and crew side by side with the little creatures on their whirling hamster wheels. But be careful what you say out loud. The guinea pigs resent being mistaken for hamsters, as do we all.

The evil billionaire is named Saber and played by Bill Nighy in what we might describe as a one-of-a-kind performance. The FBI has been on his trail for two years, but in one single night the G-Force is able to save the planet by stealthily introducing a worm, or virus, or something into his diabolical software. All of the cyber work is done by a keyboard whiz with the intensity appropriate for a programmer racing to key in code to outwit the program. You should see that little fella type. Man, oh man.

There are a limited number of other creatures in the film, including the gaseous hamster Hurley (Jon Favreau), who is loudly and frequently flatulent. I thought I heard some of his pals calling him "Farty," but that could be just me. The G-Force also includes Darwin (Sam Rockwell), Juarez (Penelope Cruz), and Bucky (Steve Buscemi). Nicolas Cage plays a mole named Speckles with a wise lack of his usual intensity. You don't want a hyperactive mole. I didn't know they had those twitchy pink feelers on their noses. Must tickle. Juarez (Cruz) provides the animal sex appeal, although, if you ask me, one guinea pig looks about like another.

Now here is the neat part. How will the remote-controlled home appliances conquer the earth? Well, sir, they will all fly together and amalgamate themselves into gigantic robots made of assorted mechanical parts. We see one of these metal monsters, and why, if I didn't know better, I'd have to say it looks like a . . . yes, I think so . . . a . . . Transformer! Except made from Cuisinarts instead of Chevys. How will they all conquer the earth? By stomping on things.

These slave appliances can be dangerous. Hurley becomes entrapped in a microwave oven, which cycles itself through several settings, from Cake to Chicken, yet is unable to cook its captive. I had a microwave like that once. It wouldn't cook doodley-squat.

There is also a human cast, including not only Bill Nighy but Kelli Garner as a veterinarian, Zach Galifianakis as a big, shaggy guy, Will Arnett as a thin, not shaggy guy, and Gabriel Casseus as Agent Trigstad. Anything else you need to know?

Ghosts of Girlfriends Past ★ ★

PG-13, 100 m., 2009

Matthew McConaughey (Connor Mead), Jennifer Garner (Jenny Perotti), Michael Douglas (Uncle Wayne), Breckin Meyer (Paul Mead), Lacey Chabert (Sandra Volkom), Robert Forster (Sergeant Volkom), Anne Archer (Vondra Volkom), Emma Stone (Allison Vandermeersh). Directed by Mark Waters and produced by Jon Shestack and Brad Epstein. Screenplay by Jon Lucas and Scott Moore.

Remember *Harry, the Rat with Women*? This time his name is Connor Mead, but he's still a rat. A modern Scrooge who believes marriage is humbug, he is taught otherwise by the ghosts of girlfriends past, present, and future, and one who spans all of those periods. Just like Scrooge, he's less interesting after he reforms.

Matthew McConaughey plays Connor as a rich and famous *Vanity Fair* photographer whose ambition is to have sex with every woman he meets, as soon as possible. Sometimes this leads to a logjam. Impatient to sleep with his latest quarry, a model who just allowed an apple to be shot off her head with an arrow, Connor actually arranges an online video chat session to break up with three current girlfriends simultaneously, but is bighearted enough to allow them to chat with one another after he logs off.

Connor appears on the eve of the wedding of his younger brother Paul (Breckin Meyer), who lives in the mansion of their late Uncle Wayne (Michael Douglas), a structure designed roughly along the lines of Versailles. (Actually, it's Castle Hill, in Ipswich, Massachusetts, built by the Crane family of Chicago, whose toilets you may have admired.) Connor is attending the wedding only to warn against it; he has a horror of getting hitched and extols a lifetime of unrestrained promiscuity.

The movie is apparently set in the present. I mention that because every woman Connor meets knows all about his reputation for having countless conquests, and yet is nevertheless eager to service him. These days, I suspect a great many of those women, maybe all of them, would view him primarily as a likely carrier of sexually transmitted diseases. To be fair, in a fantasy scene, his used condoms rain from the heavens, an event not nearly as thought-provoking as the raining frogs in *Magnolia.*

Attending the wedding is Jenny (the lovely Jennifer Garner, from *Juno*), who was his first girlfriend and the one he should have married. The ghost of Uncle Wayne materializes as a spirit guide and takes Connor on a guided tour of his wretched excess, after which he bitterly regrets his loss of Jenny, leading to a development which I do not have enough shiny new dimes to award to everyone who can predict it.

Michael Douglas is widely said to have modeled his hair, glass frames, and general appearance on the noted womanizer Bob Evans, but actually he reminded me more of Kirk Douglas playing Bob Evans. It's an effective performance either way you look at it.

The potential is here for a comedy that could have been hilarious. But the screenplay spaces out some undeniably funny lines in too much plot business, and Matthew McConaughey, while admirably villainous as a lecher, is not convincing as a charmer. Just this weekend a new Michael Caine movie is opening, which makes me remember his Alfie, a performance that is to lechers as Brando is to godfathers.

Maybe the movie's problem runs a little deeper. It's not particularly funny to hear women described and valued exclusively in terms of their function as disposable sexual partners. A lot of Connor's dialogue is just plain sadistic and qualifies him as that part of an ass it shares with a doughnut.

The Ghost Writer ★ ★ ★ ★

PG-13, 124 m., 2010

Ewan McGregor (The Ghost), Pierce Brosnan (Adam Lang), Kim Cattrall (Amelia Bly), Olivia Williams (Ruth Lang), Tom Wilkinson (Paul Emmett), Timothy Hutton (Sidney Kroll), Robert Pugh (Richard Rycart), James Belushi (John Maddox), Eli Wallach (Old Man). Directed by Roman Polanski and produced by Polanski, Robert Benmussa, and Alain Sarde. Screenplay by Polanski and Robert Harris, based on a novel by Harris.

In Roman Polanski's movie *The Ghost Writer,* a man without a past rattles around in the life of a man with too much of one. He begins by reading the work of an earlier ghost who mysteriously drowned, and finds it boring and conventional. Hired to pep it up to justify a $10 million advance, he discovers material to make it exciting, all right, and possibly deadly.

This movie is the work of a man who knows how to direct a thriller. Smooth, calm, confident, it builds suspense instead of depending on shock and action. The actors create characters who suggest intriguing secrets. The atmosphere—a rain-swept Martha's Vineyard in winter—has an ominous, gray chill, and the main interior looks just as cold.

This is the beach house being used by Adam Lang (Pierce Brosnan), a former British prime minister so inspired by Tony Blair that he might as well be wearing a name tag. Lang has one of those households much beloved by British authors of country house mysteries, in which everyone is a potential suspect—of something, anyway. His wife, Ruth (Olivia Williams), smart and bitter, met Lang at Cambridge. His assistant, Amelia (Kim Cattrall), smart and devious, is having an affair with him. The wife knows and isn't above referring to it before the Ghost (Ewan McGregor). Security men lurk about, and a serving couple look rather sinister.

Just as his ghost writer starts work, Lang is accused by his former foreign minister of sanctioning the kidnapping and torture of suspects. The World Court prepares an indictment. It would be unwise for him to return to Britain, and he flees to Washington for a photo op with the U.S. administration, unnamed, although the secretary of state looks a whole lot like Condi Rice.

The story is based on a best-seller by Robert Harris, who cowrote the screenplay with Polanski. He implies parallels between his story and the Blair and (both) Bush administrations, but uses a light touch and sly footwork so that not every viewer will necessarily connect the dots. There is also a loud, clanging alarm inviting comparison between Lang, an exile sought by a court, and Polanski himself. This is also the fourth thriller in recent months to make a villain of a corporation obviously modeled on Halliburton.

The Ghost is left to his own devices in a house haunted by the unsaid, and Polanski slips into a pure filmmaking mode. I won't describe what the Ghost searches for, but I will tell you that Polanski evokes Hitchcock in a conversation with an elderly local (Eli Wallach) and some forbidding beach scenes. And that he is masterful in the way he shows the dead former ghost providing the new one with directions, so to speak, leading to a possible source.

There is also a Hitchcock touch in visuals where an incriminating note is passed from hand to hand; the scene is so well done that it distracts from the fact that the Ghost didn't need the information in the note to arrive at the same inference.

There are a few other loose ends. The film seems to have a high incidence of black cars designed to be used as murder weapons. It's far from clear what Ruth Lang's emotional state is on one rainy night. The Ghost himself seems too much a lightweight to explain his daring sleuthing. But the performances are so convincing in detail that they distract us from our questions. McGregor's character has no family, little pride, and much insouciance, but is very smart and doesn't enjoy his intelligence being insulted. And Olivia Williams projects the air of a wife who is committed to her husband in more than expected ways.

The Ghost Writer is handsome, smooth, and persuasive. It is a Well Made Film. Polanski at seventy-six provides a reminder of directors of the past who were raised on craft, not gimmicks, and depended on a deliberate rhythm of editing rather than mindless quick cutting. The film immerses you in its experience. It's a reminder that you can lose yourself in a story because all a film really wants to do is tell it.

Gigante ★ ★ ★

NO MPAA RATING, 88 m., 2010

Horacio Camandule (Jara), Leonor Svarcas (Julia). Directed by Adrian Biniez and produced by Fernando Epstein. Screenplay by Biniez.

We are all voyeurs, although some people fondly describe themselves as "people watchers." Going to the movies is at some level pure voyeurism—if they involve people, that is. Transformers don't count. I admire films that consist only or in large part of watching. *Vertigo* is the classic example, and *The Lives of Others* was voyeurism by eavesdropping.

Gigante is a film that has little meaningful dialogue; just incidental comments along the stream of a boring life. Jara (Horacio Camandule), is a big, strong, lonely man, who works the night shift in a huge supermarket in Montevideo, watching security monitors. He lives alone, and his social life is restricted to messing around with his young nephew. In the company lunchroom, he doesn't chat. Nor does he drink, smoke, watch TV, or much of anything else. He sometimes works as a nightclub bouncer.

One night on his video monitors, Jara notices Julia (Leonor Svarcas). She's a member of the corps of cleaning women, mopping the aisles. He observes her shoplifting something. He doesn't care. Clicking on his cameras, he's able to follow her around the store. Almost immediately, he starts following her around her life.

Since Julia is heard to say nothing until the very end of the film, all depends on the performance of Camandule. Since he says so little, it depends in turn on his presence, his aura. He is tall, broad, overweight, taciturn. He isn't the "gentle giant" type. On the other hand, because he can (as we see) efficiently wallop anyone, he has no need to act intimidating. He just sits or walks around, absorbed in his thoughts.

Of course he wants to ask Julia out. Of course he lacks the nerve. He follows her everywhere—shopping, home, to the movies, to an Internet café, even on a date with a pudgy nerd. Jara is innovative. Later he manages to strike up a conversation with the nerd and discovers the nerd doesn't think Julia liked him. It was their first date. Their tastes didn't match. For one thing, she likes heavy metal, and the nerd can't stand it.

This news is Tabasco for Jara. He has Metallica posters on his wall, listens to metal on his iPod, keeps rhythm with his hands. Does this give him courage? Not exactly. Is it creepy that he follows her? Technically, yes, but we sense he's no threat; his presence reads more as protective, and sad. We have no idea if they have a future together, but we hope he'll work up the courage to at least speak to her.

Because of the limitations imposed by the nature of *Gigante,* and because of Jara's simple, almost childish shyness, the film doesn't transcend its characters. Like Jara, it waits and watches. I kept watching. I was curious. We were both wondering if he would ever ask her out. I think I wanted him to more than he did.

Gigantic ★ ★ ½

R, 98 m., 2009

Paul Dano (Brian Weathersby), Zooey Deschanel (Harriet Lolly), Ed Asner (Mr. Weathersby), Jane Alexander (Mrs. Weathersby), John Goodman (Al Lolly), Sean Dugan (Gary Wynkoop), Brian Avers (Larry Arbogast). Directed by Matt Aselton and produced by Christine Vachon and Mindy Goldberg. Screenplay by Aselton and Adam Nagata.

On the basis of *Gigantic,* Matt Aselton can make a fine and original film. This isn't quite it, but it has moments so good all you wish for is a second draft. Nor is it ever boring. You can't say that about a lot of debuts. I suspect he was trying too hard to be terrific and not hard enough to get organized.

His hero, Brian Weathersby (the willfully bland Paul Dano), is a young and feckless mattress salesman. He was a late son in a tribe of unconventional brothers. When they all get together with Dad (Ed Asner) in the family's cottage in the woods, Dad bonds with him by consuming hallucinogenic mushrooms. How Brian would know he was hallucinating is a good question, because much of his life unfolds on the border of reality.

The Swiss mattress showroom occupies a vast upper floor of a warehouse. Into this space one day marches Al Lolly (John Goodman), a big man with a painful back problem. Brian shows him the high-end $14,000 mattress, which uses real horsehair, which is a big deal in the mattress universe. The mattress also inspires an inspection by Al's daughter Harriet (Zooey Deschanel), a beautiful girl with startling blue-green eyes. Although you might expect to find her on magazine covers, she is as inward as Brian; they speak in minimalist murmurs, as when she asks if he feels like having sex with her, and he confides that he does. Later he tells a friend that he doesn't know if he likes her or not. More accurately, probably, he doesn't know if he liked being jolted out of his lifelong dubiousness.

Ever since he was a little boy, Brian has been obsessed with the idea of adopting a Chinese baby. He doesn't understand why; he just is. Harriet might upset that dream in some obscure way. She invites him to her home, and he enters into a strange world ruled by Al Lolly, a rich, opinionated eccentric, who is driven everywhere flat on his back in the rear of a Volvo station wagon. The great open spaces of their apartment have been decorated by spending a great deal of money on a limited selection of furniture.

Brian's life is complicated by a berserk madman who ambushes him with assaults. This man seems imaginary, until Brian receives facial wounds that don't go away. To summarize: A loser mattress salesman with a peculiar father meets a beautiful lost girl with an eccentric millionaire father, and is attacked by a loony while trying to evade love and adopt a Chinese baby. Does this sound like a screenplay or a contest entry? In the UK it would be described as too clever by half, and "clever" is not a compliment over there.

The strange thing is, the characters are interesting. You could make a movie about them. That Brian's very sane mother is played by Jane Alexander is an example of how well the film is cast. The delicate relationship between Harriet and Brian is beautifully played by Deschanel and Dano, but the movie jars us out of it with bizarre sidetracks such as a scene set in a massage parlor; it's intended as funny but is finally a toss-up between odd and sad.

Gigantic is an example of a certain kind of "Sundance movie" made after the ship has sailed. The pendulum is swinging back toward the more classical forms of filmmaking. It's not enough to add, "Oh—and this homeless guy keeps attacking him." If you want a homeless guy, do something meaningful with him, as Mike Leigh did in *Happy-Go-Lucky.* Wackiness for its own sake is not a substitute for humor or much of anything else.

And yet look at the things here that are really good: the conversation between Brian and Harriet in the doctor's waiting room. The way the parents take to the Chinese baby. The way John Goodman modulates his performance to make Al Lolly a character and not a caricature. The way Harriet falls asleep on the $14,000 mattress, and what they say after she wakes up. Matt Aselton's next film might be a marvel.

G.I. Joe: The Rise of Cobra ★ ½

PG-13, 118 m., 2009

Adewale Akinnuoye-Agbaje (Heavy Duty), Christopher Eccleston (McCullen/Destro), Joseph Gordon-Levitt (The Doctor/Rex), Byung-hun Lee (Storm Shadow), Sienna Miller (Ana/Baroness), Rachel Nichols (Scarlett), Ray Park (Snake Eyes), Jonathan Pryce (U.S. President), Said Taghmaoui (Breaker), Channing Tatum (Duke), Marlon Wayans (Ripcord), Dennis Quaid (General Hawk). Directed by Stephen Sommers and produced by Sommers, Lorenzo di Bonaventura, and Bob Ducsay. Screenplay by Stuart Beattie, David Elliot, and Paul Lovett.

G.I. Joe: The Rise of Cobra is a 118-minute animated film with sequences involving the faces and other body parts of human beings. It is sure to be enjoyed by those whose movie appreciation is defined by the ability to discern that moving pictures and sound are being employed to depict violence. Nevertheless, it is better than *Transformers: Revenge of the Fallen.*

The film is inspired by Hasbro's famous line of plastic action figures. The heroes are no longer exclusively Americans, but a multinational elite strike force from many nations, which provides Paramount the opportunity to give top billing to an actor named Adewale Akinnuoye-Agbaje. And to think there was a time when Maurice Micklewhite was not considered a good name for a star. At last Hollywood allows actors to possess their real names.

The Joes, as they are called, are needed to counter "nanomites," a secret weapon that eats up people and buildings and stuff. This weapon has been invented by the evil disfigured scientist named McCullen (Christopher Eccleston), who steals it *back* from the people he sold it to and plans to use it to conquer the world. Why is McCullen so pissed off? His Scottish clan was insulted centuries ago. Those Scots.

His conquest plans are not sophisticated. He launches four nano-missiles at world capitals. Two of them are Moscow and Washington. The third one is destroyed, and if I'm not mistaken the fourth one is forgotten by the plot and is still up there somewhere. But that's the kind of detail I tend to get wrong because that's more fun than getting it right.

How fast are these missiles? They rocket into space and zoom down to Earth. A Joe named Ripcord (Marlon Wayans) commandeers the enemy's rocket airplane, and even though he's never seen it before, flies it so well that he catches up to the Moscow missile and destroys it, and *then* he turns around and flies halfway around the globe to catch up with the missile headed for Washington. He uses verbal commands to fire his air-to-air weapons, after a fellow Joe named Scarlett (Rachel Nichols) intuits that McCullen would have programmed his plane to respond to Celtic, which, luckily, she happens to speak.

These plot details are not developed at great depth, because the movie is preoccupied with providing incomprehensible wall-to-wall computer-generated special effects. I should have been carrying a little clicker to keep count, but I believe that director Stephen Sommers has more explosions in his movie than Michael Bay had in *Transformers 2* only last month. World records don't last long these days.

What is Cobra? What nationality are its leaders, other than Scottish? What will it gain by destroying world capitals? Reader, I do not know. Even the U.S. president (Jonathan Pryce) asks incredulously, "Don't they have any demands?" His role is otherwise limited to being briefed about the Joes.

Cobra has a woman named the Baroness (Sienna Miller) to match Scarlett of the Joes. These women are interesting. They have leather fetishwear and are seductively made up, but are otherwise honorary boys, because us Joe fans don't like to watch a lot of spit swapping. But because us fans liked the two jive-talkin' robots in *Transformers, G.I. Joe* gives us Ripcord, who is comic relief, says black stuff, and can't control his high-tech armored suit, so he runs into things. We guess he's a contrast to the calm, macho heroism of Adewale Akinnuoye-Agbaje.

The two teams also each have a skilled Ninja fighter from Japan. Why is this, you might ask? Because Japan is a huge market for CGI animation and video games, that's why. It also has a sequence set in the Egyptian desert, although there are no shots of dead robots or topless pyramids. And Cobra headquarters are buried within the miles-deep ice of the Arctic. You think construction costs are high here. At one point, the ice cap is exploded real good so it will sink and crush the G.I. Joes' submarine. We thought ice floated in water, but no, you can see big falling ice chunks real good here. It must be only in your Coke that it floats.

There is never any clear sense in the action of where anything is in relation to anything else. You get more of a binary action strategy. You see something, it fires. You see something else, it gets hit. Using the power of logic, you deduce that the first thing was aiming at the second thing.

Yet I say this movie is certainly better than *Transformers: Revenge of the Fallen.* How so? Admittedly, it doesn't have as much cleavage. But the high-tech hardware is more fun to look at than the transforming robots, the plot is as preposterous, and although the noise is just as loud, it's more the deep bass rumbles of explosions than the ear-piercing bang of steel robots pounding on each other.

I mentioned the lack of pyramids. We do, however, see the Eiffel Tower as it is eaten up by nano technology and topples over onto the Place de la Concorde. Missiles also strike Mount Rushmore. No, wait! That was during one of the Coming Attractions.

The Girlfriend Experience ★ ★ ★

R, 77 m., 2009

Sasha Grey (Chelsea), Chris Santos (Chris), Peter Zizzo (Wealthy Client). Directed by Steven Soderbergh and produced by Mark Cuban, Gregory Jacobs, and Todd Wagner. Screenplay by Brian Koppelman and David Levien.

This film is true about human nature. It clearly sees needs and desires. It is not universal, but within its particular focus it is unrelenting. Steven Soderbergh's *The Girlfriend Experience* is about a prostitute and her clients. In such a relationship, the factor of money makes the motives fairly direct on both sides.

In the language of escort advertising, "GFE" promises a "girlfriend experience." Sometimes sex may not even be involved, although it is implicitly permitted. A man seeking a girlfriend experience offers to pay for companionship, conversation, another human being in his life. The women offering a GFE are acting a role, but in some ways it can be a therapeutic one. We know what sexual surrogates do. A "girlfriend" may be playing a human surrogate.

The film involves a woman named Chelsea and the men in her life. She has been living with one of them for eighteen months, and in a way he may be a boyfriend experience. He doesn't seem much more meaningful to her than a client. The other men are of various ages and backgrounds, but they all have one thing in common: They are wealthy, and Chelsea is not inexpensive. Typically they take her to an expensive restaurant and then a luxury hotel. They may send a limousine for her.

We listen to them talking. We watch them talking. Most of them want to talk about what she does for a living. There is the polite fiction that she is talking about other men, hypothetical men, and not the one she is with. They like to give her advice about how to invest her money and who to vote for (the story takes place during the 2008 campaign). Each one has some reason for thinking he is somehow special. Set during the run-up to the stock market crash, it shows both sides more interested in investing than sex.

These men don't want a girlfriend experience. They want a boyfriend experience. They want to feel as if they're on a date. They will be listened to. Their amazing comments will be smiled at. Their hair will be tousled. They will be kidded. They have told Chelsea about their wives and children, and she remembers their names. They can kiss her. There is no illusion that they are leaving their wives, and none that she wants them to. She simply empowers them to feel younger, more looked up to, more clever than they are.

What draws a powerful man to pay for a woman outside of marriage? It's not the sex. In fact, sex is the beard, if you know what I mean. By paying money for the excuse of sex, they don't have to say: "I am lonely. I am fearful. I am growing older. I am not loved. My wife is bored with me. I can't talk to my children. I'm worried about my job, which means nothing to me." Above all, they are saying: "Pretend you like me."

The film was written by Brian Koppelman and David Levien. Believe it or not, the same two wrote the screenplay for Soderbergh's *Ocean's Thirteen.* I imagine the three of them sitting around on the *Ocean's* set and asking, "What could we be doing instead of this?"

Chelsea is played by Sasha Grey. She is twenty-one. Since 2006, according to IMDb, she's made 161 porn films, of which only the first title can be quoted here: *Sasha Grey Superslut.* No, here's another, which makes me smile: *My First Porn No. 7.* I haven't seen any of them, but now I would like to see one, watching very carefully, to see if she suggests more than one level.

Grey wasn't hired because of her willingness to have sex on the screen; there's no explicit sex in the movie, and only fleeting nudity. I suspect Soderbergh cast her because of her mercenary approach to sex—and her acting talent, which may not be ready for Steppenwolf but is right for this film. She owns her own agency and Web site, manages other actresses, has a disconnect between herself and what she does for a living. So does Chelsea.

The film is intent on her face. It often looks over the shoulder of her clients. She projects precise amounts of interest and curiosity, but conceals real feelings. It is a transaction, and she is holding up her end. Notice the very small nods and shakes of her head. Observe her word choices as she sidesteps questions without refusing to answer them. When her roommate/boyfriend insists on knowing the name of one of her clients, she is adroit in her reply.

Once she allows her mask to slip: a surprising moment when she reveals what she may feel. Sasha Grey perfectly conveys both her hope and her disappointment, keeping both within boundaries. You wonder how a person could look another in the eye and conceal everything about themselves. But the financial traders who are her clients do it every day. Their business is not money, but making their clients feel better about themselves.

The Girl from Monaco ★ ★ ★

R, 94 m., 2009

Fabrice Luchini (Bertrand Beauvois), Roschdy Zem (Christophe Abadi), Stephane Audran (Edith Lassalle), Gilles Cohen (Louis Lassalle), Louise Bourgoin (Audrey Varela). Directed by Anne Fontaine and produced by Philippe Carcassonne and Bruno Pesery. Screenplay by Fontaine, Benoit Graffin, and Jacques Fieschi.

Casting can be the reason one movie works and another doesn't. It is the first reason for the success of *The Girl from Monaco,* the kind of romantic thriller with a twist that used to star Jack Lemmon. That kind of role is played this time by Fabrice Luchini, a fifty-seven-year-old veteran French character actor whose first significant role was thirty-nine years ago in *Claire's Knee.*

He plays Bertrand, a smooth, powerful defense attorney, confident, well known, who is hired for a difficult case. The millionaire widow Edith Lassalle (Stephane Audran) is on trial for murder in Monaco, charged with killing a reputed member of the Russian mafia, and she refuses to utter a single word in her own defense. From the day he arrives in Monaco, Bertrand finds himself shadowed constantly by Christophe (Roschdy Zem), behind sunglasses, a tall, dark young man in a black suit and tie.

This is, he discovers, his bodyguard, hired by Edith's son, Louis (Gilles Cohen), because the Russians may represent a threat. Bertrand believes he is in no danger, doesn't want a bodyguard, finds it absurd how Christophe insists on entering his hotel room first and "checking the perimeter." Christophe is indifferent to his objections. He has to follow "protocol."

This odd couple works because its members are so different. Bertrand is not tall, not handsome, very busy, suave. Christophe is tall, handsome, formal, and distant. No attempt is made to supply them with banter. They are both focused on doing their jobs. Into this mix comes a fiercely ambitious weather girl from Monaco TV named Audrey (Louise Bourgoin). She sees Bertrand as her meal ticket to get a better TV job and wants to do an exclusive feature about the famous man down from Paris.

Audrey, young and sexy, means trouble. Bertrand can see that. Yet when she claims to be in love with him—that they were destined for each other—he goes along, no doubt because her explorations in his bed discover uncharted lands. Audrey is known to Christophe, and indeed perhaps to many of the men in Monaco. He warns his boss away: This woman is a slut, she'll damage him, she's not worth the time of day.

An interesting dynamic takes place. Christophe himself has fallen a little in love with Bertrand, not for sexual reasons, but out of admiration for the older man's work ethic. Since he represents a threat to Audrey's plans, tension grows. Meanwhile, the murder trial marches ahead, and some of the Russians make an appearance.

The director and cowriter, Anne Fontaine, makes no attempt to make this situation cute or sitcommy. As Billy Wilder did with Lemmon, she makes Luchini an everyman, wearied, fearful, not getting any younger, who like all men finds it plausible that a beautiful younger woman would fall for him. Because Luchini's character is so convincingly mundane, the situation grows interesting. And when Christophe's determination to keep her away grows, the plot discovers shadows—even an element of evidence that could be taken two ways, in a Hitchcockian twist.

The Girl from Monaco is no more than an entertainment, but an assured and well-oiled one. It is about its characters, not its stars. It assumes an audience that appreciates complex motivations and an adult situation. Nobody gets shot, and a "chase" down Monaco's lovely mountain roads takes place within the speed limit. We almost don't notice as Christophe becomes the most interesting character, but he surely does.

The Girl on the Train ★ ★ ★

NO MPAA RATING, 101 m., 2010

Emilie Dequenne (Jeanne), Catherine Deneuve (Louise), Michel Blanc (Samuel Bleistein), Ronit Elkabetz (Judith Bleistein), Mathieu Demy (Alex Bleistein), Nicolas Duvauchelle (Franck), Jeremy Quaegebeur (Nathan). Directed by Andre Techine and produced by Said Ben Said. Screenplay by Techine, Odile Barski, and Jean-Marie Besset, based on the play *RER* by Besset.

The girl in Andre Techine's *The Girl on the Train* is Jeanne, who has never fully engaged in the society she occupies. She Rollerblades through French suburbs with her iPod blocking out other sounds, as the world glides past unobserved. Was it the job interview with the lawyer Bleistein that put Jews into her mind? One doubts she had given them, or anything else, much thought.

Jeanne (Emilie Dequenne) is sent to Samuel Bleistein by her mother, Louise (Catherine Deneuve). He was once in love with her. One of the nation's most powerful lawyers, he makes time to see the girl because of old memories. His secretary pages through her résumé and observes there isn't much there. Nor does the interview itself go well. Jeanne doesn't know much, hasn't done much, doesn't even realize how little she's done or what there is to be known. She lives in a cocoon of electronic distraction.

She doesn't care. She's having a romance with a young athlete, a wrestler, tattooed and a little strange. They break up. Now she's jobless, alone, and with her mother on her case—Louise, who provides home care for toddlers, works in the garden, and is gentle enough with her—but anything that interrupts Jeanne's reverie is annoying.

For no particular reason, perhaps hoping to win Bleistein's sympathy, perhaps not, perhaps she doesn't know, she makes up a false story of being assaulted on a train by North Africans who taunted her as a Jew, beat her, and carved a swastika on her stomach. She isn't Jewish, not that it's a point. The case becomes a national scandal. The French president can't get on the phone fast enough to express his sympathy and solidarity.

The police are not as sympathetic because there is absolutely no evidence to back up her claims. No witnesses, no evidence on security cameras—and why is the swastika drawn backward? Well, it can be difficult for the inexperienced. I don't know if I could draw one correctly.

These events occupy the first movement of the film, titled "Circumstances." The second is titled "Consequences," and is really the reason for the first. It deals more fully with Bleistein (the shortish, quite bald Michel Blanc) and his family: his son, Alex (Mathieu Demy), and son's wife, Judith (Ronit Elkabetz), and their child, Nathan (Jeremy Quaegebeur), who is preparing for his bar mitzvah.

The movie seems likely to be about anti-Semitism, but that's more the occasion than the subject. Bleistein gets involved in the case, sees there is nothing to do, doesn't consider Jeanne's lie a case of anti-Semitism so much as a case of utter cluelessness. Within his family, tensions uncoil that are typical of all families. What the film is really about is social embarrassment, and Bleistein's clear-headed, calm understanding that his old friend has a stupid daughter who has caused fraudulent trouble for a great many people.

The story, I understand, is based on a real French case not long ago. I can think of two similar cases—Tawana Brawley, the black girl who said she was attacked by whites, and Ashley Todd, who scratched a B on her face and made up a story that a black man robbed her and was angered by her McCain sticker.

Do these stories inspire others? Do dim TV viewers see them and come away with the impression that such stories inspire sympathy? Don't they hear about the later disgrace? Are they hungry for attention? Who knows? The perpetrators don't inspire much interest, but the effects do: How the media handles them, how politicians jump aboard, how false incidents reveal real racism.

Techine is a French master about the same age as Scorsese. His credits include such splendid films as *My Favorite Season* and *Les Voleurs.* He's worked before with Deneuve, who here strikes a nice balance of sweetness and vagueness. Perhaps she simply forgot to raise a girl with an idea in her head.

The Girl Who Kicked the Hornet's Nest ★ ★ ★

R, 148 m., 2010

Noomi Rapace (Lisbeth Salander), Michael Nyqvist (Mikael Blomkvist), Lena Endre (Erika Berger), Annika Hallin (Annika Giannini), Anders Ahlbom Rosendahl (Dr. Peter Teleborian), Mikael Spreitz (Ronald Niedermann). Directed by Daniel Alfredson and produced by Soren Staermose. Screenplay by Ulf Rydberg, based on the novel by Stieg Larsson.

Lisbeth Salander makes a transfixing heroine precisely because she has nothing but scorn for such a role. Embodied here for the third time by Noomi Rapace, she's battered, angry, and hostile, even toward those who would be her friends. Some of the suspense in the final courtroom showdown of *The Girl Who Kicked the Hornet's Nest* comes from the excellent question of whether she would rather be found guilty than provide anyone with the satisfaction of hearing her testify in her own defense.

By the time she comes to what is essentially a sanity hearing, she has returned to the ranks of punk fashionistas, with the black leather pants and jacket, the boots, the studs and buckles, the spikes, the body piercings, the eyeliner that looks like protective armor, and the stark black crest of her hair. She sits sullen and silent in the courtroom, as if saying, "I care nothing for you, although I have spent hours working on my look in front of the mirror."

She is formidably smart and deeply wounded from childhood, as we know from the earlier two films in the Stieg Larsson trilogy. Worse, she can't leave her pain behind in childhood. Again in her life are her freakish, gigantic half-brother Niedermann (Mikael Spreitz) and the psychologist who fabricated her incarceration in an asylum. And the murderous members of "the Section," a rogue killing unit within the Swedish national police, are determined to eliminate her once and for all.

The outlines of her dilemma will be clear to those who've seen *The Girl with the Dragon Tattoo* and *The Girl Who Played with Fire,* but this film has enough quick flashbacks to orient the first-timer. It begins literally when the second one ended, after the bloody confrontation in the barn with her father and half-brother. She's taken to the hospital with a bullet in her brain, and spends much of the film's first half in intensive care and refusing to speak.

That frees the director, Daniel Alfredson, to focus more time on Mikael Blomkvist (Michael Nyqvist), the investigative journalist who collaborated with her in the first film and has become her fierce defender—and perhaps more, a man who loves her. Their mutual affection was an intriguing subtext in the first film, but has been on hold ever since, while Mikael continues his relaxed intimacy with his editor, Erika Berger (Lena Endre). There are said to be two more Larsson novels in various stages of completion, but even if they're not publishable, Lisbeth Salander is too good a character to suspend after three films, and my guess is there must be sequels.

The sequels need not fret overmuch about plot. These films are really about personality, dialogue, and the possibility that the state has placed itself outside the law. That leads to an oppressive, doomy atmosphere that the characters move through with apprehension. We understand the basics of the Section conspiracy, we recognize most of the faces, but few of us could pass a test on exactly who is who. No problem; neither could Lisbeth nor Mikael.

The tension—and there is a lot of it—grows from the danger that Lisbeth brings upon herself by refusing to act sensibly for her own welfare. She has such a burned-in distrust of authority that even a friend like Mikael gets closed out, and Rapace takes a simple friendly "see you" and invests it with the effort it costs Lisbeth to utter. Her battle with herself is more suspenseful than her battle against her enemies, because enemies can be fought with and that provides release, but we spend much of *The Girl Who Kicked the Hornet's Nest* straining against Lisbeth's fear and sending her urgent telepathic messages about what she should do.

These are all very well made films. Like most European films, they have adults who are grown-ups, not arrested adolescents. Mikael and Erika, his boss and lover, have earned the lines in their faces and don't act like reckless action heroes. They make their danger feel so real to us that we realize the heroes of many action movies don't really believe they're in any danger at all. Lisbeth is in grave danger, but in great part because of her damaged obstinacy, and that scares us more than any number of six-foot-four Nordic blond homicidal half-brothers.

So what has happened is this uptight, ferocious little gamin Lisbeth has won our hearts, and we care about these stories and think there had better be more. The funny thing is I've seen the "real" Noomi Rapace on TV, and she has a warm smile and a sweet face. What a disappointment.

The Girl Who Played with Fire ★ ★ ★ ½

R, 129 m., 2010

Noomi Rapace (Lisbeth Salander), Michael Nyqvist (Mikael Blomkvist), Lena Endre (Erika Berger), Annika Hallin (Annika Giannini), Per Oscarsson (Holger Palmgren), Malin Erikson (Sofia Ledarp), Peter Andersson (Nils Bjurman), Yasmine Garbi (Miriam Wu), Johan Kylen (Jan Bublanski), Tanja Lorentzon (Sonja Modig), Paolo Roberto (Himself), Georgi Staykov (Zalachenko). Directed by Daniel Alfredson and produced by Soren Staermose and Jon Mankell. Screenplay by Jonas Frykberg, based on the novel by Stieg Larsson.

The girl is an enigma. She has a dragon tattoo, she plays with fire, she kicks a hornet's nest. These are not personality traits. We learn in the second movie based on a Stieg Larsson thriller a little more about her childhood, and her fiery relationship with her father. What we don't learn is why she is content to live the life of a hermit, requiring very little human company. Even when she lends a woman her apartment for a year and makes love with her the night she moves in, it seems more like a social gesture.

Noomi Rapace returns as Lisbeth Salander in *The Girl Who Played with Fire.* She was electrifying in last year's *The Girl with the Dragon Tattoo.* She didn't look like your average young heroine. She was lean but not skinny, taut but not muscular, a solemnity rather than a gamin. Her mastery of computers allowed her to hack into almost any information, and the hatred of men's violence against women gave her a motive.

If you saw the earlier film, or have read the novels, you'll recognize some of the key players here. But you can walk in as a first-timer and understand. Mikael Blomkvist (Michael Nyqvist) is back as an investigative journalist. His *Millennium* magazine is negotiating with a researcher and her boyfriend to learn the names and details of trafficking in women between Russia and Sweden, and famous men are implicated as clients. Larsson paints a portrait of a corrupt Swedish climate in politics, the law, and business.

Although Mikael and Lisbeth are the leads, they don't meet until even later in this film than the last one. As before, they sense each other by tracks in cyberspace. Lisbeth has returned to Stockholm after learning of a case she has a personal interest in and finds herself on the trail of a killer. This trail grows complex as it leads back into her own past, and to the introduction of a onetime Soviet bad man and a hulking freak. In a Bond picture these would be stereotypes, but the Larsson stories aim closer to human dimensions and locate them firmly in a well-seen Sweden of cities and isolated country homes.

I suppose at its base this is a police procedural (although the police are on the wrong track all along). But Lisbeth and Mikael are quirky individuals and make up their detective work as they go, so it's hard to predict the story arc. It's also an advantage that the actors are *not* conventional star types. That will be the tricky part in the Hollywood versions. Carey Mulligan and Daniel Craig are cast for David Fincher's 2012 remake of *Dragon*, and they're very good, but are they too mainstream? How about, oh, say, Ed Norton and the non-*Twilight* Kristen Stewart?

The film is filled with strong supporting roles. Peter Andersson plays a twisted attorney. Georgi Staykov is the malevolent Russian, incredibly verbally cruel in one scene. I noted how good Lisbeth's old legal protector, Palmgren, was in an old people's home, as she allowed a little tenderness to show through. I discovered later he was played by Per Oscarsson, a great Swedish actor since 1944, star of *Hunger* and *Here's Your Life* (both 1966), who, incredibly, never worked with Bergman. Someone like that adds texture to a thriller, and with an actress like Rapace, creates an audience sympathy that pays off long after the scene is over.

The Girl Who Played with Fire is very good, but a step down from *The Girl with the Dragon Tattoo*, if only because that film and its casting were so fresh and unexpected. A thriller is incomparably more arresting when it involves plausible people doing plausible things, rather than archetypes costarring with animation.

The Girl with the Dragon Tattoo ★ ★ ★ ★

NO MPAA RATING, 152 m., 2010

Michael Nyqvist (Mikael Blomkvist), Noomi Rapace (Lisbeth Salander), Lena Endre (Erika Berger), Sven-Bertil Taube (Henrik Vanger), Peter Haber (Martin Vanger), Peter Andersson (Nils Bjurman), Marika Lagercrantz (Cecilia Vanger), Ingvar Hirdwall (Dirch Frode). Directed by Niels Arden Oplev and produced by Soren Staermose. Screenplay by Nikolaj Arcel and Rasmus Heisterberg, based on the novel by Stieg Larsson.

The Girl with the Dragon Tattoo is a compelling thriller to begin with, but it adds the rare quality of having a heroine more fascinating than the story. She's a twenty-four-year-old Goth girl named Lisbeth Salander, with body piercings and tattoos: thin, small, fierce, damaged, a genius computer hacker. She smokes to quiet her racing heart.

Lisbeth is as compelling as any movie character in recent memory. Played by Noomi Rapace with an unwavering intensity, she finds her own emotional needs nurtured by the nature of the case she investigates, the disappearance of a young girl forty years earlier. As this case is revealed as part of a long-hidden pattern of bizarre violence against women, her own abused past returns with a vengeance.

Rapace makes the character compulsively interesting. She plays against a passive forty-something hero, Mikael Blomkvist (Michael Nyqvist), an investigative journalist who has six months of freedom before beginning a prison sentence for libel against a Swedish tycoon. Mikael, resourceful and intelligent, is hired by an elderly billionaire named Henrik Vanger (Sven-Bertil Taube), who inhabits a gloomy mansion on a remote island and broods about the loss of his beloved niece, Harriet. She vanished one day when the island was cut off from the mainland. Her body was never found. Because the access bridge was blocked, the killer must have been a member of Vanger's large and greedy family, which he hates. Three brothers were Nazi sympathizers during the war.

The notion of a murder with a limited list of suspects was conventional even before Agatha Christie. Niels Arden Oplev's *The Girl with the Dragon Tattoo* pays it lip service, with Mikael covering a wall with photos of the suspects. But this is a new age, and in addition to his search of newspaper and legal archives, he uses the Internet. That's how he comes across Lisbeth, who has been investigating *him*. She's described as Sweden's best hacker, a claim we have no reason to doubt, and the intensity of her focus, contrasted to her walled-off emotional life, suggests Asperger's.

They team up on the case, and might become lovers if not for Mikael's diffidence and her secretive hostility. They become efficient partners. Scenes involving newspaper photographs and Internet searches create sequences like a *Blow Up* for the digital age. The film is unique in my memory for displaying screen shots of an actual computer operating system, Mac OS X, and familiar programs like Google, e-mail, and iPhoto. Ever notice how most movie computers work like magic?

The forbidding island setting, the winter chill, the frosty inhabitants, all combine with dread suspicions to create an uncommonly effective thriller. It's longer than average, but not slow, not after we become invested in the depravity of the case. There are scenes involving rape, bondage, and assault that are stronger than most of what serves in the movies for sexual violence, but these scenes are not exploitation. They have a ferocious feminist orientation, and although *The Girl with the Dragon Tattoo* seems a splendid title, the original Swedish title was the stark *Men Who Hate Women.*

The novel, one of a trilogy that Stieg Larsson completed before his untimely death at forty-four, was an international best-seller. It is destined to be remade by Hollywood. That may be a good film, but if I were you, I'd be sure to watch this version. The Hollywood version will almost certainly tone down the sexual violence. I can't think of an American actress who could play Lisbeth. Kristen Stewart, whom I respect, has been mentioned. Dakota Fanning. I dunno. A younger Jodie Foster, maybe. Someone able to play hard as nails and emotionally unavailable. Make her a Swede, and simply cast Noomi Rapace.

This is not a deep, psychological study. But it's a sober, grown-up film. It has action, but not the hyperkinetic activity that passes for action in too many American movies. It has sex, but not eroticism. Its male lead is brave and capable, but not macho. Its female lead is sexy in the abstract, perhaps, but not seductive or alluring. This is a movie about characters who have more important things to do than be characters in an action thriller.

Gomorrah ★ ★ ★ ★

NO MPAA RATING, 136 m., 2009

Marco Macor (Marco), Ciro Petrone (Piselli/Ciro), Salvatore Abruzzese (Toto), Toni Servillo (Franco), Carmine Paternoster (Roberto), Gianfelice Imparato (Don Ciro), Maria Nazionale (Maria), Salvatore Cantalupo (Pasquale). Directed by Matteo Garrone and produced by Domenico Procacci. Screenplay by Garrone, Maurizio Braucci, Ugo Chiti, Gianni Di Gregorio, Massimo Gaudioso, and Roberto Saviano, based on the book by Saviano.

It is all so sordid. *Gomorrah* is a film about Italian criminals killing one another. One death after another. Remorseless. Strictly business. The question arises: How are there enough survivors to carry on the business? Another question: Why do willing recruits submit themselves to this dismal regime?

The film is a curative for the romanticism of *The Godfather* and *Scarface.* The characters are the foot soldiers of the Camorra, the crime syndicate based in Naples that is larger than the Mafia but less known. Its revenues in one year are said to be as much as $250 billion—five times as much as Madoff took years to steal. The final shot in the film suggests the Camorra is invested in the rebuilding of the World Trade Center. The film is based on fact, not fiction.

Gomorrah, which won the grand prize at Cannes 2008 and the European Film Award, is an enormous hit in Europe. It sold five hundred thousand tickets in France, which at ten dollars a pop makes it a blockbuster. There was astonishment that the Academy passed it over for foreign film consideration. I'm not so surprised. The Academy committee more often goes for films that look good and provide people we can care about. *Gomorrah* looks grimy and sullen and has no heroes, only victims.

That is its power. Here is a movie about the day laborers of crime. Somewhere above them are the creatures of the $250 billion, so rich, so grand, so distant, with no apparent connection to crime. No doubt New York and American officials sat down to cordial meals with Camorra members while deciding the World Trade contracts and were none the wiser.

Roberto Saviano, who wrote the best-seller that inspired the movie, went undercover, used informants, even (I learn from John Powers on NPR) worked as a waiter at their weddings. His book named names and explained exactly how the Camorra operates. Now he lives under twenty-four-hour guard, although as the Roman poet Juvenal asked, "Who will guard the guards?"

Matteo Garrone, the director, films in the cheerless housing projects around Naples. "See Naples and die" seems to be the inheritance of children born here. We follow five strands of the many that Saviano unraveled in his book, unread by me. There is an illegal business in the disposal of poisonous waste. A fashion industry that knocks off designer lines and works from sweatshops. Drugs, of course. And then we meet teenagers who think they're tough and dream of taking over locally from the Camorra. And kids who want to be gangsters when they grow up.

None of these characters ever refer to *The Godfather.* The teenagers know De Palma's *Scarface* by heart. Living a life of luxury, surrounded by drugs and women, is perhaps a bargain they are willing to make even if it costs their lives. The problem is that only the death is guaranteed. No one in this movie at any time enjoys any luxury. One of them, who delivers stipends to the families of dead or jailed Camorra members, doesn't even have a car and uses a bicycle. The families moan that they can't make ends meet, just like Social Security beneficiaries.

Garrone uses an unadorned documentary style, lean, efficient, no shots for effect. He establishes characters, shows their plans and problems, shows why they must kill or be killed—often, be killed because of killing. Much is said about trust and respect, but little is seen of either. The murders, for the most part, have no excitement and certainly no glamour—none of the flash of most gangster movies. Sometimes they're enlivened by surprise, but it is the audience that's surprised, not the victims, who often never know what hit them.

The actors are skilled at not being "good actors," if you know what I mean. There is no sizzle. Only the young characters have much life in them. Garrone directs them to reflect the bleak reality of their lives, the need and fear, the knowledge that every conversation could be with their eventual killer or victim. Casual friendship is a luxury. Families hold them hostage to their jobs. The film's flat realism is correct for this material.

You watch the movie with growing dread. This is no life to lead. You have the feeling the men at the top got there laterally, not through climbing the ladder of promotion. The Camorra seems like a form of slavery, with the overlords inheriting their workers. The murder code and its enforcement keep them in line: They enforce their own servitude.

Did the book and the movie change things? Not much, I gather. The film offers no hope. I like gangster movies. *The Godfather* is one of the most popular movies ever made—most beloved, even. I like them as movies, not as history. We can see here they're fantasies. I'm reminded of mob bosses like Frank Costello walking into Toots Shor's restaurant in that fascinating documentary *Toots.* Everyone was happy to see him—Jackie Gleason, Joe DiMaggio, everyone. At least they knew who he was. The men running the Camorra are unknown even to those who die for them.

Goodbye Solo ★ ★ ★ ★

NO MPAA RATING, 91 m., 2009

Souleymane Sy Savane (Solo), Red West (William), Carmen Leyva (Quiera), Diana Franco Galindo (Alex), Lane "Roc" Williams (Roc), Mamadou Lam (Mamadou). Directed by Ramin Bahrani and produced by Bahrani and Jason Orans. Screenplay by Bahrani and Bahareh Azimi.

Two actors. One from Africa. The other who was a bodyguard for Elvis. Who but Ramin Bahrani would find these men and pair them in a story of heartbreaking depth and power? Bahrani is the new great American director. He never steps wrong. In *Goodbye Solo* he begins with a situation that might unfold in a dozen different ways and makes of it something original and profound. It is about the desire to help and the desire to not be helped.

In Winston-Salem, North Carolina, a white man around seventy gets into the taxi of an African immigrant. He offers him a deal. For $1,000, paid immediately, he wants to be driven in ten days to the top of a mountain in Blowing Rock National Park, to a place so windy that the snow falls up. He says nothing about a return trip. The driver takes the money but is not happy about this fare. He asks some questions and is told to mind his own business.

Now look at these actors. They aren't playing themselves, but they evoke their characters so fully that they might as well be. Red West plays William, the white man. His face is a map of hard living. He was a Marine and a boxer. He became a friend of Elvis in high school. He was his bodyguard and driver from 1955—a charter member of the "Memphis Mafia." He split with Elvis after breaking the foot of the cousin who was bringing Elvis drugs and telling him he would work his way up to his face.

Souleymane Sy Savane plays Solo, the taxi driver. He is from the Ivory Coast, although the character is from Senegal. Savane was a flight attendant for Air Afrique. Solo is studying for just such a job. Solo lives in Winston-Salem, is married to a Mexican-American woman, adores the woman's young daughter, and acts as her father. William's face was made to look pissed off. Solo's face was made to smile. We are not speaking of an odd couple here. We're speaking of human nature. You can't learn acting like this.

Bahrani worked with these actors for months. Savane drove a taxi in Winston-Salem. Red West spent a lifetime rehearsing William (although in real life he is said to be kind and friendly). Bahrani and his cinematographer, Michael Simmonds, discussed every shot. Although *Goodbye Solo* is an independent film in its heart and soul, it is a classical film in its style. It is as pure as something by John Ford. Only its final shot might call attention to itself—but actually, we aren't thinking about the shot, we're thinking about what has happened, and why.

Don't get the idea the whole film takes place in the taxi. It takes place in Winston-Salem, a city it wears with familiarity because Bahrani was born and raised there. We feel the rhythms of Solo's life. Of his relationship with his wife, Quiera (Carmen Leyva), and their pride in her daughter, Alex (Diana Franco Galindo). Like many taxi drivers, Solo knows where you can find drugs or a sexual partner. But he isn't a pusher or a pimp; he's a one-man service industry, happy to help.

The film sees cars being repaired in front yards, a few customers at a downtown movie theater on a weekday night, a lonely motel room, a bar. The next few times William calls a cab, he begins to notice the driver is always Solo. What's up with that? With almost relentless good cheer, Solo insinuates himself into William's life—becomes his chauffeur, his protector, his adviser, even for a few nights his roommate and almost his friend. It occurred to me that Red West may have performed similar functions for Elvis, another man pointed to doom.

Neither William nor Solo ever once speaks about their real subject, about what William seems to be about to do. It hangs in the air between them. Alex, the stepdaughter, comes to love old William, who has the feel of a grandfather about him. But no, Alex is not one of those redeeming movie children. She doesn't understand everything and brings in an innocence that Solo and William both respect.

Goodbye Solo is not finally about what William and Solo do. It is about how they change, which is how a great movie lifts itself above plot. These two lives have touched, learned, and deepened. Not often do we really *care* this much about characters. We sense they're not on the automatic pilot of a plot. They're feeling their way in life. This is a great American film.

This is Bahrani's third feature, after *Man Push Cart* (2005) and *Chop Shop* (2007). His films are about outsiders in America: a Pakistani who operates a coffee-and-bagel wagon in Manhattan, Latino kids who scramble for a living in an auto parts bazaar in the shadow of Shea Stadium. Now a Senegalese who wants to help an American whose weathered face belongs in a Western. Bahrani, whose parents immigrated from Iran, felt like an outsider when he was growing up in Winston-Salem: "There were blacks, whites and my brother and me." He loves the city, and you can tell that in this film. He is curious about people, and you can tell that from all his films. He told me he asks the same question of all of his characters: How do you live in this world?

A film like this makes me wonder if we are coming to the end of the facile, snarky indie films. We live in desperate times. We are ready to respond to films that ask that question. How do you live in this world? Bahrani knows all about flashy camera work, tricky shots, visual stunts. He teaches film at Columbia. But like his fellow North Carolinian David Gordon Green, he is drawn to a more level gaze, to a film at the service of its characters and their world. Wherever you live, when this film opens, it will be the best film in town.

The Good Guy ★ ★ ★

R, 90 m., 2010

Scott Porter (Tommy), Alexis Bledel (Beth), Bryan Greenberg (Daniel), Anna Chlumsky (Lisa), Aaron Yoo (Steve-O), Andrew McCarthy (Cash), Andrew Stewart-Jones (Shakespeare). Directed by Julio DePietro and produced by DePietro, Rene Bastian, and Linda Moran. Screenplay by DePietro.

The Good Guy creates the interesting notion that Wall Street trading involves a gang of hard-partying goofs who pass their days playing video games with our money. They trade too fast to know much about the stocks they're selling—and besides, they mostly trade funds and may only vaguely know how the portfolios are weighted.

That at least is the impression given by *The Good Guy,* which contains not a moment in which any trader knows much about the fundamentals of a stock, but much about the dance of the numbers on a screen and the mind games he's playing with other traders. At the end of the day, all that matters is the score. Well, I guess that's the way it works.

At Morgan & Morgan, no relation to JPMorgan or Morgan Stanley, we meet a team of traders bossed by the legendary Cash (Andrew McCarthy). His team leader is Tommy (Scott Porter), who's making money hand over fist while leading the pack on sorties into bars that have a high babe count. These guys get drunk and play adolescent games and plow through conquests and keep laughing so it doesn't get quiet. There is charm in being seventeen, and pathos in being twenty-seven and acting as if you're seventeen.

The crew includes Shakespeare (Andrew Stewart-Jones), a black guy with a British accent who may realize, but doesn't care, that any babe impressed by a British accent belongs on Jaywalking. There's Steve-O (Aaron Yoo), master trader. And there's the new guy, Daniel (Bryan Greenberg), who, odd as it may seem, prefers not to horse around but stay home, fix himself some dinner, and read a good novel. You know, maybe by Dickens, whom many people don't know is about as much fun as any novelist who ever lived.

The section's top hotshot bails out to join another firm, and Cash orders Tommy to fill his chair. On a hunch, Tommy promotes Daniel. Everyone including Daniel is disbelieving. Under the delusion that a star trader must party hard and conquer the dollies, Tommy takes Daniel into the field for training; the Forty-Year-Old Virgin becomes a Twenty-Seven-Year-Old Reader.

During this process Daniel meets Beth (Alexis Bledel), Tommy's girlfriend. Beth isn't precisely Tommy's type; she belongs to a book club. Tommy is like one of those guys who might read if the library weren't always closed. Beth is a serious Green and believes Tommy's line that he is, too, but he has a line for every girl and is a serious liar. Daniel observes this dynamic.

Young men, let your old dad here impart some advice. If a woman has a choice of a man who makes sacks of money on the trading floor and a man who likes to stay home at night reading *Lolita*, and she's more attracted to the reader, choose that woman. She needs to pass one more test: Does she believe (a) *Lolita* is a sex novel, or (b) it's one of the greatest works of modern literature? Find that out on the second date. If she answers (b), there's your girl.

The Good Guy could have been just a dumb comedy, but actually it has a nice feel to it. It looks carefully at a lifestyle many people might thoughtlessly envy. The writer-director, Julio DePietro, is a former trader from Chicago, and he convinces us he knows that world. I hasten to add that I know some traders who are nice guys. I also add that I would trade the same way the guys in the movie do, because their clients care less about how much money they'll retire with than how rich they'll be tomorrow. Investing myself, I've trusted value guys over performance. That and buying Apple, just because I loved Macs, has turned out all right.

Readers may pick up on the clue that the title and some of the story are inspired by Ford Madox Ford's novel *The Good Soldier.* It opens with a famous line that makes it impossible to stop reading: "This is the saddest story I have ever heard." Tommy's story is another one.

I keep drifting off course. Will you like *The Good Guy*? I think you might. It has smart characters and is wise about the ones who try to tame their intelligence by acting out. And Beth and her friends are the women all these guys should be so lucky as to deserve.

Good Hair ★ ★ ★

PG-13, 95 m., 2009

A documentary featuring Chris Rock, Maya Angelou, A'Lelia Bundles, Vanessa Bell Calloway, Joe Dudley, Eunice Dudley, Eve, Meagan Good, Vijay Madupali Gupta, Andre Harrell, Ice-T, Nia Long, Paul Mooney, Willie Morrow, Valerie Price, Tracie Thoms, Salli Richardson, Salt-n-Pepa, Al Sharpton, and Raven-Symone. Directed by Jeff Stilson and produced by Stilson, Kevin O'Donnell, and Jenny Hunter. Screenplay by Stilson, Chris Rock, Lance Crouther, and Chuck Sklar.

Good Hair is a documentary about black women and their hair. Chris Rock, the host and narrator, is a likable man, quick, truly curious, with the gift of encouraging people to speak openly about a subject they usually keep private. He conveys a lot of information, but also some unfortunate opinions and misleading facts. That doesn't mean the movie isn't warm, funny, and entertaining.

The film had its start for Rock when his little daughter asked him, "Daddy, how come I don't have good hair?" He wonders how she got that idea. He discovers that some children even younger than her are already having their hair straightened—and that for children that is a bad idea. He talks to a great many black women about their hair, beginning with the matriarch Maya Angelou and including such celebrities as Nia Long, Eve, Tracie Thoms, Salli Richardson, Salt-n-Pepa, and Raven-Symone.

He discovers that for some black women, attaining "good hair" means either straightening or extensions. Straightening involves the application of products containing sodium hydroxide, which a dermatologist and a chemist describe as potentially dangerous to the scalp and even to inhale in quantity (your lungs might get straightened). Leave it on too long, and your scalp or face can be burned—something that has happened to some of the women here.

I imagine a good many black women would tell Chris Rock that having "good hair" simply means having hair that is healthy and strong. For African-American women, that can mean versatile hair that can be worn in a variety of styles: natural, Afros, braids, dreads, African knots, pressed, chemically relaxed, or with extensions. They look great. Often they go back and forth among hairstyles; that is the way of women, unlike us male clods who settle on a hairstyle in grade school and stick with it like Rod Blagojevich.

Extensions involve braiding long hair to rows of existing hair. Think Beyonce. Where does this hair come from? India, mostly, where some women cut off their hair before marriage or for religious purposes, and can sell it for amounts that mean a lot in a poor nation.

What about the hazards of straightening? Rock shows a hair-raising demonstration of an aluminum Coke can literally being eaten up in a bath of sodium hydroxide. It may help to recall that another name for sodium hydroxide is "lye." God forbid a woman should put that on her head! What Rock doesn't mention is that few women do. If he had peeked at Wikipedia, he would have learned: "Because of the high incidence and intensity of chemical burns, chemical relaxer manufacturers have now switched to other alkaline chemicals." Modern relaxers can also burn if left on too long, but they won't eat up your Coke cans.

The popularity of Afros in the 1960s and '70s asserted that natural hair was beautiful just the way it grew (and was styled, cut, and shaped, of course; Angela Davis didn't look that good without effort). Classic Davis-style Afros have grown rare, but another "natural" style, braiding, is seen all the time. Many black men also use braids and dreads as a fashion statement.

The use of the word "natural hair" is, in any event, misleading. Take a stroll down the hair products aisle of a drugstore, or look at the stock price of Supercuts. Few people of any race go without hair grooming. If they did, we would be a nation of Unabombers.

Black hair is a $9 billion industry. Rock plunges in. He visits Dudley Products in Atlanta, a black-owned hair products empire, and is fascinated by the Bronner Bros. International Hair Show, an annual convention in Atlanta. Here a vast convention hall is jammed with the booths of hair-care companies, and there's an annual competition to name the hairdresser of the year. The contest is fascinating, not least because it seems to have little to do with actually taking care of someone's hair. Would you want your hair done by a stylist hanging upside down from a trapeze? Or joining you inside a giant aquarium? Showmanship is everything; one of the four finalists is a young white man who is treasured by his clients.

What Rock does is create a film with much good feeling and instinctive sympathy for our desire to look as good as we can. He asks direct questions, but doesn't cross-examine; he reacts with well-timed one-liners, and he has a hilarious, spontaneous conversation with some black men in a barber shop that gets into areas that are rarely spoken about. The movie has a good feeling to it, but why do I know more about this subject than Chris Rock does? Smile.

The Good Heart ★ ½

R, 98 m., 2010

Brian Cox (Jacques), Paul Dano (Lucas), Isild Le Besco (April). Directed by Dagur Kari and produced by Skuli Fr. Malmquist and Thor Sigurjonsson. Screenplay by Kari.

Every once in a while a movie comes along and you watch it and the credits come up and you sit there feeling a certain sadness. The actors are good ones and they work hard and the look and feel of the film are evocative—but good gravy! Where did that plot come from? The actors cast themselves adrift on the sinking vessel of this story and go down with the ship.

Few people know the name of Horatio Alger anymore. He was long outdated when I heard of him, but in those ancient times people still referred to "a Horatio Alger story." That would be a story sopping wet with cornball sentimentalism, wrapped up in absurd melodrama, and telling some version of the rags-to-riches story. Poor farm boy stops runaway carriage carrying banker's daughter, they fall in love, he inherits bank. I believe Alger used that actual plot.

The Good Heart isn't that obvious, but it's that corny. Poor homeless lad named Lucas (Paul Dano) lives in cardboard shack under the freeway, befriends forlorn kitten. Kitten is found hanged, lad attempts suicide, wakes up in intensive care next to nasty old banker. Sorry! Nasty old tavern owner. This barkeep, named Jacques (Brian Cox), has just had his fifth heart attack and is so foul-tempered even the nurses hate him. Jacques finds out the lad is homeless, brings him home, gives him a garret room above the bar, and tells him he can have the bar after he dies.

In my extensive research into the world of

bars, I have observed that they survive by selling drinks at retail. The House of Oysters doesn't follow this time-tested model. Jacques has three business policies he drums into Lucas: (1) No walk-ins from the street. (2) No women allowed—and BTW it's not a gay bar. (3) No being nice to the customers.

Rule No. 1 seems paradoxical. If no walk-in customers are allowed, how does anybody ever get to be a regular? Presumably the regulars have all been there since Jacques got the place from a man who sold oysters. One of the oysters killed someone, the guy sold out, Jacques took over, discontinued food, and inherited the regulars.

They are a group who need fumigating. The bar itself is a skanky dump. Jacques throws customers out regularly, but they come back, maybe because they're barred everywhere else. One day the beautiful April (Isild Le Besco) walks in and orders champagne. She has a sad story. No, she's not a fallen woman with a heart of gold. She's a flight attendant from France, who can't go home again or find a job because, I kid you not, she's afraid to fly.

Lucas and April fall in love, Jacques hates her for violating all the rules, and now I am biting my hand hard enough to make it bleed in order to prevent myself from blurting out more plot details. No, I will not—I must not—tell you what happens at the end of this movie, except to say I was stupefied that anyone in modern times (i.e., since 1910) would have the gall to sell such cornball at retail.

So now my review must end. But wait. I haven't even mentioned the bar's pet goose. This goose is kept in a sturdy cage, but escapes from time to time and must be chased down by Lucas. The ending of *The Good Heart* is supposed to be sad, but for me the saddest thing in this movie is that Lucas didn't chop off the head of that goose when he had the chance. No animals are harmed during the filming of a picture, and look where it gets you.

The Goods: Live Hard, Sell Hard ★ ★ ★

R, 90 m., 2009

Jeremy Piven (Don Ready), Ving Rhames (Jibby Newsome), James Brolin (Ben Selleck), David Koechner (Brent Gage), Kathryn Hahn (Babs Merrick), Ed Helms (Paxton Harding), Jordana Spiro (Ivy Selleck), Craig Robinson (DeeJay), Charles Napier (Dick Lewiston), Ken Jeong (Teddy Dang), Rob Riggle (Peter Selleck), Alan Thicke (Stu Harding). Directed by Neal Brennan and produced by Adam McKay, Will Ferrell, Kevin Messick, and Chris Henchy. Screenplay by Andy Stock and Rick Stempson.

The Goods: Live Hard, Sell Hard is a cheerfully, energetically, very vulgar comedy. If you're OK with that, you may be OK with this film, which contains a lot of laughs and has studied political correctness only enough to make a list of groups to offend. It takes place after a failing car dealer calls in a hired gun and his team to move goods off the lot over the Fourth of July.

The hotshot is Don Ready (Jeremy Piven), a hard charger who lives on the road and exists only to close deals. On his team: Babs (Kathryn Hahn), a lustful slut; Jibby (Ving Rhames), a sweet man who has never been in love; and Brent (David Koechner), who does not respond well when the failing auto dealer caresses his thigh.

They walk into a seething hotbed of problems in the small-town dealership of Ben Selleck (James Brolin). Let's see. His son, Peter, is ten years old, but because of a hormonal problem looks thirty. His daughter, Ivy (Jordana Spiro), is engaged to the air-headed son (Ed Helms) of his hated rival (Alan Thicke). His sales team includes Dick Lewiston (Charles Napier), who swears at customers and goes after them with a baseball bat, and Teddy Dang (Ken Jeong), a Korean-American who is assaulted by Dick, who blames him for Pearl Harbor.

Romantic entanglements and personal crises spring up overnight, including Don Ready's conviction that he has met the son he fathered with the third runner-up in the local beauty contest twenty-three years earlier. Babs becomes infatuated by the fully grown, lightly bearded ten-year-old. Jibby experiences love for the first time. Ben pursues the hostile Brent. Flashbacks involve an orgy on an airplane and the tragic death of Don's best friend (an uncredited Will Ferrell).

That's all another way of saying the screenplay moves at a breakneck pace. If a gag doesn't work, another one is on its heels.

There are also countless details about auto sales scams, and a definition of the most awesome possible feat of salesmanship, named in honor of Nigeria, which in this film and *District 9* seems to be taking a place as a world leader in con games.

Jeremy Piven might not seem the obvious choice to play the ringleader of this menagerie, but he shows a side of himself I haven't seen before: the pep-talking, superconfident, ultracynical salesman. With no life of his own, as Ivy correctly informs him, he lives only to sell cars. It isn't even the money. It's the imposition of his will on a reluctant customer. His triumph of salesmanship at the end of the film is, at least on its own terms, almost even plausible.

I liked Kathryn Hahn as the potty-mouthed teammate, and Brolin's work as the deeply confused but ever-hopeful car dealer. And it was fun to see Chuck Napier, whose career began as a member of the Russ Meyer stock company, in a mad dog role that gets the film off to a rip-roaring start. He still looks like he could fight a wolf for a T-bone.

The Great Buck Howard ★ ★ ★ ½

PG, 90 m., 2009

John Malkovich (Buck Howard), Colin Hanks (Troy Gable), Emily Blunt (Valerie Brennan), Steve Zahn (Kenny), Griffin Dunne (Jonathan Finerman), Ricky Jay (Gil Bellamy), Tom Hanks (Mr. Gable). Directed by Sean McGinly and produced by Tom Hanks and Gary Goetzman. Screenplay by McGinly.

Is there anyone better than John Malkovich at barely containing his temper? He gravitates toward characters who do not suffer fools lightly, and that would include the Great Buck Howard, who once was Johnny Carson's favorite guest. Buck was dropped from Johnny's guest list and now tours the provinces, taking his magic act from small stages to smaller ones, but he still has his dignity.

"I LOVE this town!" he shouts with outstretched arms in Akron, and Akron still loves him. He is famous for his "signature effect," in which his evening's fee is given to an audience member and he uses his psychic powers to find it. He has never failed, and no one has ever discovered how he does it.

Buck was named "the Great" by Carson and still maintains a facade of greatness, even in front of Troy (Colin Hanks, Tom's son), his newly hired road manager. Malkovich invests him with self-importance and yet slyly suggests it's not all an act; you believe at some level Buck really does love that town, and also when he says, as he always does, "I LOVE you people!"

The story is told from Troy's point of view. His father (Tom Hanks) fervently wants him to enter law school, but he wants to test showbiz, and this is his first contact with any degree of fame. He never penetrates the Great Buck Howard's facade (and neither do we), but he sure does learn a lot about showbiz, some of it intimately from Valerie (Emily Blunt), a new PR person hired for Buck's spectacular new illusion in Cincinnati. Troy learns to carry bags, open doors, deal with local reps, and supply mineral water, not distilled ("I'm not an iron," Buck crisply tells Troy's eventual replacement).

We see Buck as Troy does, as an impenetrable mystery. Buck is far from forgotten (he guests on shows hosted by Regis Philbin and Kelly Ripa, Jon Stewart, and Martha Stewart, all playing themselves). He can still fill a room, even if it's a smaller room. His manager, Gil (Ricky Jay, who always seems to know the inside odds), even gets him a Las Vegas booking. What happens there, and how it happens, is perceptive about showbiz and even more perceptive about Buck and his "signature effect."

Well, how *does* he find the person in the room holding the money—every time? Rumors are common that he uses a hidden spotter, whispering into a mic hidden in his ear. When Troy tells him this, Buck invites two doctors onstage to peer into his ears, then turns his back to the room and covers his head with a black cloth. Does he still find the money?

If he does, it can't be because of psychic powers, can it? I firmly believe such illusions are never the result of psychic powers, but I am fascinated by them anyway. The wisdom of this film, directed and written by Sean McGinly, is to never say. Troy practically lives with the man and doesn't have a clue. He's asked if Buck is gay, and he replies truthfully, "I don't know. I've never seen him with anybody." Colin Hanks is affecting as a man young enough and naive enough to be fascinated by whatever it is Buck represents. Emily Blunt is sweetly kind to him. No one else could have played Buck better than Malkovich. I LOVE this guy.

I've read one review that complains we never meet the real Buck Howard. Of course we don't. There may *be* no real Buck Howard. But the film is funny and perceptive in the way it shows the humiliations for a man with Buck's tender vanity. The ladies singing on stage. The many who have no idea who he is. Being bumped off the news by Jerry Springer. Being bumped off *Jay Leno* for Tom Arnold. Distilled water.

Note: McGinly's screenplay is based on his observations as road manager for the Amazing Kreskin, to whom the film is dedicated.

The Greatest ★ ★

R, 100 m., 2010

Pierce Brosnan (Allen Brewer), Susan Sarandon (Grace Brewer), Carey Mulligan (Rose), Johnny Simmons (Ryan), Aaron Johnson (Bennett), Zoe Kravitz (Ashley), Michael Shannon (Jordan Walker). Directed by Shana Feste and produced by Lynette Howell and Beau St. Clair. Screenplay by Feste.

The Greatest includes a great performance and a very good one at the center of vagueness and confusion. The film's people and situation are perfectly clear, and with this cast might have made a powerful film, but the screenplay contains baffling omissions, needless confusions, and questions we should not be thinking of.

The film opens with two teenagers deeply, joyously in love. It's the kind of love where they've flirted with their eyes and their hearts since they started school, and now, on the last day of their senior year, he finally finds the courage to speak to her, and her face lights up, and this is all they dreamed of, and they make love, and then he's killed when their car is hit by a truck.

Not a spoiler. It's the setup for the whole film. The girl is Rose (Carey Mulligan, the Oscar nominee from *An Education*). The boy is Bennett (Aaron Johnson, on screen briefly but with all the presence necessary to make their love significant). We cut to the funeral, and then to an extraordinary shot of three people in the backseat of a funeral limousine: Bennett's father, Allen (Pierce Brosnan), his mother, Grace (Susan Sarandon), and his kid brother, Ryan (Johnny Simmons).

They do not speak. They do not look at one another. They do not offer comfort. The shot lasts maybe a minute. It establishes that these people are grieving in their own private ways. Bennett was a wonderful boy, known as "the Greatest" since grade school because . . . well, he was. Grace is inconsolable. They all are, but she's the most intense, and Allen tries to hold the family together while Ryan disappears into his room and drugs and who knows.

Three months pass in this way. Rose appears at their door and tells Allen she is pregnant. It was the first time for both Rose and Bennett. She didn't even know you could get pregnant the first time. She moves in with them because—well, I don't know exactly. Apart from one enigmatic phone call late in the film, perhaps involving a mother, she seems to have no one. She attended high school in an affluent neighborhood for three years, she was a gifted pianist, she's in a fatal crash, and now she has no one? No family, no friends, not one single person, and this is never explained?

Maybe she comes from a troubled background? Hard to see. Carey Mulligan plays Rose as upbeat, cheerful, able to cope. Grace is cold and distant; Sarandon plays her as unforgiving. Rose overhears her saying she wishes it was Rose, and not Bennett, who had been killed. She doesn't give a damn about Bennett's child. She wants her own child back.

Allen tries to be friendly. There are a couple of scenes, indeed, that are oddly handled because there's no question of Allen and Rose growing intimate, but the film's staging allows such a question to occur. Meanwhile, Ryan starts attending a grief support group where the leader does what no support group leader should ever do, and offers a diagnosis and recommendation to members after one comment.

In this group, a young woman named Ashley (Zoe Kravitz) reaches out to Ryan, and he responds and improves emotionally, and they like each other, and a romance seems to be in the works, and then he knocks on her door and her sister (I guess) answers and says something (I'm not sure what) and he runs off, and Ashley runs after him but that's the end of that subplot. What's that about?

And what about the scene where Ryan consumes what may be Ecstasy and then smokes pot. OK . . . and then? Nothing. He gets high and comes down, I guess. Meanwhile, Grace sits at the bedside of Jordan (Michael Shannon), the truck driver who hit her son's car. She knows her son lived for seventeen minutes after the crash and that Jordan spoke to him, and she's obsessed to know what he said. But after the conversation Jordan went into coma. Some months later, we see her at his bedside, hearing the story of the seventeen minutes.

I will omit certain additional details involving Allen and Rose (separately), and I suppose I shouldn't describe the melodrama of the closing scenes, except to say they're an anthology of clichés. And there's a car ride in which way too much communication takes place, at long last, in a much too facile fashion.

So the screenplay is a soap operatic mess, involving distractions, loose ends, and sheer carelessness. Yet Sarandon creates a wrenching performance of a woman torn apart by grief, and Brosnan is convincing as a man holding it together as long as he can. As for Mulligan and Simmons, what can I say? There is nothing they do wrong, but this film written and directed by Shana Feste leaves both characters deprived of explanation, development, and revelation. And you can't get me to believe that after you have sex one time and get pregnant, and your lover is killed, and you have absolutely *nobody* to turn to except his parents, and his mother hates you, a teenage girl can have this much self-confidence. Even Juno would have disintegrated under the pressure.

The Greatest Movie Ever Sold ★ ★ ½

PG-13, 86 m., 2011

A documentary directed by Morgan Spurlock and produced by Spurlock, Jeremy Chilnick, Abbie Hurewitz, and Jessica Wu. Screenplay by Chilnick and Spurlock.

Once, long ago, movie stars were trained to hold a can of beer or a pack of cigarettes in such a way that the brand could not be seen. Now when we notice a brand name in a movie we think "product placement!" and get on with it. Names like United Center and Staples Center may be so ingrained that we don't even think of airlines or office supplies stores anymore. Wrigley Field wasn't named for a chewing gum but for a family. I wonder if Chicagoans will allow it to be branded? Nothing is sacred. Just look at the new name on Marshall Field's.

Morgan Spurlock's new documentary, *The Greatest Movie Ever Sold*, finances itself by its own bootstraps. It is a movie about making a movie paid for by product placements. In fact, its official title is *Pom Wonderful Presents The Greatest Movie Ever Sold*, named in honor of the pomegranate juice that is, I now know, 100 percent pomegranate juice—unlike Minute Maid, which is mostly apple and grape juice, with pomegranate finishing under 2 percent.

The film also makes mention of Hyatt Hotels, Mini Coopers, OK Go, Old Navy, and JetBlue. (No promotional consideration was received by me for mentioning these products.) Spurlock is the star, just as he was when he ate only at McDonald's for a month in *Super Size Me*. He talks to agents, lawyers, product reps, movie directors, musicians, and placement specialists, and then makes calls on a series of would-be sponsors, some of whom are extremely wary of his scheme.

He strikes pay dirt with Pom Wonderful, which agrees to be a major sponsor, and then some of the other pieces fall into place. He raised $1.5 million and spent it on this film, he says, although this would be a perfect opportunity for a con of the sort exploited in *The Producers*.

Along the way he consults various learned experts, including Ralph Nader, Noam Chomsky, and Donald Trump (of the Trump Towers franchise), who appear as talking heads in so many docs these days they might almost be product placements for themselves. He finds directors such as Brett Ratner willing to talk on the record—and Quentin Tarantino, who complains he wanted to shoot scenes for *Reservoir Dogs* and *Pulp Fiction* in Denny's, but they wouldn't let him. Spurlock begins as almost serious about his subject, but about the time one of his authorities advises him to take the money and run, we realize that's what he's doing.

The movie is quick and cheerful, and Spurlock is engaging onscreen. I already knew what he was telling us, and I think many people do. I'm not sure Spurlock himself ever defined a purpose greater than raising the money on camera, but then he never claimed to. I can't exactly recommend the movie, but I do recommend drinking Pom Wonderful. Did you know it's a powerful antioxidant, and can provide some of the benefits of Viagra? Maybe if Minute Maid used more pomegranates it would be Ten Minute Maid.

Greenberg ★ ★ ★ ½

R, 107 m., 2010

Ben Stiller (Roger Greenberg), Greta Gerwig (Florence Marr), Rhys Ifans (Ivan Schrank), Jennifer Jason Leigh (Beth), Brie Larson (Sara), Juno Temple (Muriel), Chris Messina (Phillip Greenberg), Susan Traylor (Carol Greenberg), Mark Duplass (Eric Beller). Directed by Noah Baumbach and produced by Jennifer Jason Leigh and Scott Rudin. Screenplay by Baumbach.

When you're angry with the world and yourself to the same degree, you're running in place. It takes a great deal of energy. It can be exhausting. You lash out at people. You're hard on yourself. It all takes place in your head. After a time people give up on you. They think you don't give a damn and don't care about yourself. If they only knew.

That's Roger Greenberg. I never knew who Ben Stiller was born to play, but now I do. I don't mean he *is* Greenberg, but that he makes him a convincing person and not a caricature. The hero of Noah Baumbach's new film was once, years ago, part of a rock band on the brink of a breakthrough. He walked away from it, stranding his bandmates, and never explained why. He fled Los Angeles and became a carpenter in New York.

He's been struggling. There has been some sort of vague period in an institution. Now he's returned to L.A. to house-sit his brother's big home and look after the dog. He glares out of the windows like old man Fredricksen in *Up*. He can live alone no more successfully than with others. He calls Florence Marr (Greta Gerwig), his brother's family assistant, who knows where everything is and how everything works. And the dog knows her.

Florence is someone we know. A bright, pleasant recent college graduate for whom the job market, as they say, has no use. We see her interacting with the family of Greenberg's brother; she does all the planning for them that she should be doing for herself. In a more conventional movie, Florence would be the love interest, and Greenberg would be fated to marry her. But Florence isn't looking for a man. She just broke up. "I don't want to go from just having sex to sex to sex," she says. "Who's the third 'sex'?" asks Greenberg. "You."

I have a weakness for actresses like Greta Gerwig. She looks reasonable and approachable. Some actresses are all edges and polish. This one, you could look up and see her walking dreamily through a bookstore, possibly with a Penguin Classic already in her hand. Greenberg treats her badly. He has no notion of his effect on people. When they end up having sex, and they do, it's like their right hands don't know what their left hands are doing.

Noah Baumbach made the inspired film *The Squid and the Whale* (2005), about a formidably articulate family torn apart by a divorce. Both parents were at fault to various degrees, and both sons could have done more in their own way to help the situation. Everyone obsessed on their grievances. Greenberg takes this a step further: He obsesses on the grievances against him.

He has a reunion with a former bandmate, Ivan (Rhys Ifans), a calm Brit, troubled by a trial separation, happy enough to see Greenberg and help him if he can. But Ivan is troubled that Greenberg *still* doesn't get it, doesn't understand how he crushed the dreams of his bandmates. Then there's Beth (Jennifer Jason Leigh), whom Greenberg once loved and was loved by. Life has moved on. She has a family. Does he recognize the look a woman gets in her eyes when she's thinking how that just would have never, ever worked out? Does he have enough self-knowledge to see how impossible he is?

The important relationship is the one between Greenberg and Florence. We look upon her and see wholesome health and abundant energy. She's happy when she has a purpose. She wishes she had a direction in life, but can be happy enough in the moment. It's as if when Greenberg moves a little in the direction of happiness, he gets jealous because that draws attention away from his miserable uniqueness. People driven to be constantly unique can be a real pain in the ass.

This is an intriguing film, shifting directions, considering Greenberg's impossibility in one light and then another. If he's stuck like this at forty, is he stuck for good? What Ben Stiller does with the role is fascinating. We can't stand Greenberg. But we begin to care about him. Without ever overtly evoking sympathy, Stiller inspires identification. You don't have to like the hero of a movie. But you have to understand him—better than he does himself, in some cases.

The Green Hornet ★

PG-13, 108 m., 2011

Seth Rogen (Britt Reid/Green Hornet), Jay Chou (Kato), Christoph Waltz (Chudnofsky), Cameron Diaz (Lenore Case), Edward James Olmos (Michael Axford), Tom Wilkinson (James Reid), David Harbour (Scanlon). Directed by Michel Gondry and produced by Neal H. Moritz. Screenplay by Seth Rogen and Evan Goldberg.

The Green Hornet is an almost unendurable demonstration of a movie with nothing to be about. Although it follows the rough story line of previous versions of the title, it neglects the construction of a plot engine to pull us through. There are pointless dialogue scenes going nowhere much too slowly, and then pointless action scenes going everywhere much too quickly.

Seth Rogen deserves much of the blame. He cowrote the screenplay giving himself way too many words, and then hurls them tirelessly at us at a modified shout. He plays Britt Reid, a spoiled little rich brat who grows up the same way, as the son of a millionaire newspaper publisher (Tom Wilkinson, who apparently remains the same age as his son ages from about ten to maybe thirty). After his father's death, he shows little interest in running a newspaper but bonds with Kato (Jay Chou), his father's auto mechanic and coffee maker. Yes.

Kato is the role Bruce Lee played on TV. Jay Chou is no Bruce Lee, but it's hard to judge him as an actor with Rogen hyperventilating through scene after scene. Together, they devise a damn fool plan to fight crime by impersonating criminals. This they do while wearing masks that serve no purpose as far as I could determine except to make them look suspicious. I mean, like, who wears a mask much these days?

The crime lord in the city is Chudnofsky (Christoph Waltz, the Oscar winner from *Inglourious Basterds*). That provides the movie with a villain but hardly with a character. The war between Chudnofsky and the Hornet is played out in a great many vehicle stunts and explosions, which go on and on and on, maddeningly, as if screenwriter Rogen tired of his own dialogue (not as quickly as we, alas) and scribbled in: "Here second unit supplies nine minutes of CGI action."

There is a role in the film for Cameron Diaz as Lenore Case, would-be secretary for young Reid, but nothing for her to *do*. She functions primarily to allow us to cut to her from time to time, which is pleasant but unsatisfying. Diaz has a famously wonderful smile, and curiously in her first shot in the film she smiles for no reason all, maybe just to enter the smile in the record.

The director of this half-cooked mess is Michel Gondry, whose *Eternal Sunshine of the Spotless Mind* is as good as this one is bad. Casting about for something to praise, I recalled that I heard a strange and unique sound for the first time, a high-pitched whooshing scream, but I don't think Gondry can claim it because it came from the hand dryers in the men's room.

Green Lantern ★ ★ ½

PG-13, 105 m., 2011

Ryan Reynolds (Hal Jordan/Green Lantern), Blake Lively (Carol Ferris), Peter Sarsgaard (Hector Hammond), Mark Strong (Sinestro), Angela Bassett (Dr. Amanda Waller), Tim Robbins (Senator Hammond), Temuera Morrison (Abin Sur), Jay O. Sanders (Carl Ferris). Directed by Martin Campbell and produced by Greg Berlanti and Donald De Line. Screenplay by Berlanti, Michael Green, Marc Guggenheim, and Michael Goldenberg.

Green Lantern presents yet another case of a human being given the responsibility of leading the battle of good versus evil, or, in this case, of the will versus fear. We learn that an ancient race of aliens has divided the universe into segments to enforce peace, but is being resisted by an alien named Parallax, who went off on his own, committed the sin of pride, and became a prince of darkness. If he reminds you of Satan, that can't be helped. Every superhero requires a malevolent egomaniac to battle.

The movie stars Ryan Reynolds as Hal Jordan, a test pilot who proves that humans are better at flying fighter planes than computers are. His fellow pilot is Carol Ferris (Blake Lively), the daughter of the tycoon Carl Ferris (Jay O. Sanders), who manufactures the fighters. Does Carl worry about his daughter flying in catfights at supersonic speeds? To answer that question would require him to reveal emotion, and he is locked immobile in superhero tycoon mode.

Far away in the universe, the benign aliens have created the Green Lantern Corps to spread out and combat the evil Parallax. One of these corpsmen is sent on a mission to find a worthy man on Earth to become a member of the Corps. His spaceship, which has survived a journey across the cosmos, crash-lands, and he lives long enough to hand over a green ring and a lantern to, of course, Hal Jordan. Hal learns that the ring gives him great power, but he must believe in the triumph of his will and conquer the weakness of fear.

If this sounds childish, of course it is. One of the absurdities of many modern superhero movies is how they adorn silly plots with great solemnity and millions of dollars in special effects. Nor does *Green Lantern* shortchange us on dialogue; indeed, it spends a great deal of time at the impossible task of explaining the logic and rules of its plot. I am amazed at how calmly humans absorb and accept the incredulities of these stories ("Waitaminit! I wear this magic green ring and I'm a superhero? Gee, that's every kid's dream!").

Green Lantern does not intend to be plausible. It intends to be a sound and light show, assaulting the audience with sensational special effects. If that's what you want, that's what you get. Among these are numerous split-second journeys across galaxies by speeding green spheres that shuttle between Earth and the domain of the aliens, while dismissing all technicalities of the speed of light. I nostalgically recalled *Thor*, in which Thor commutes to Earth to do battle with the avatars of his own satanic malevolent egomaniac.

The problem with many of these special effects is that they don't take on the gravity and substance of real events; they are an obvious extrusion of animation into the physical world. Often they take forms created by Hal Jordan's imagination, because whatever he wills becomes real. I suppose that goes with the territory.

Parallax, it must be said, is a well-imagined malevolence. Although he manifests a diabolical face, he seems otherwise to consist mostly of roiling tendrils of foul, polluted matter. There is a scene where the foreground is filled with terrified humans who are fleeing toward the camera, while behind them Parallax causes skyscrapers to tumble. Was it less than ten years ago that we wondered if movies could ever use such images again after 9/11?

The movie has a character I found interesting, if inconsistent. This is Hector Hammond (Peter Sarsgaard), a brilliant scientist nerd with a wispy mustache and a servile superiority. What becomes of Hector I will not say, but Sarsgaard gives him a dimension lacking in the cookie-cutter heroics of Hal Jordan. A subplot about Hector's mind-reading abilities is not developed very well. I also liked the fierce determination of Dr. Amanda Waller (Angela Bassett) and the composure with which Senator Hammond (Tim Robbins) deals with a haywire helicopter.

The bottom line: This is a comic book movie. Fans of the Green Lantern (in his intergalactic story mode and not his earthbound TV series) will no doubt enjoy its visualizations and its references to details of the backstory that escaped me. There's a whole lot going on. We don't really expect subtle acting or nuanced dialogue. We appreciate an effective villain. We demand one chaste kiss between hero and heroine, but no funny stuff. We enjoy spectacular visuals like the Green elders, who are immortal and apparently spend eternity balancing on top of towering pillars. *Green Lantern* delivers all of those things, and for what it's worth, I liked it more than *Thor.*

Perhaps there was a reason for that. The movie, as you know, was filmed in 3-D. But a screening was made available in 2-D, and I chose to attend the 2-D screening. The colors were bright, the images were crisp and clear, the impact was undeniable, the greens were . . . real green. I didn't see the 3-D version, so can't compare the two. I will be looking forward with interest to how other critics around the country describe it.

Green Zone ★ ★ ★ ★

R, 114 m., 2010

Matt Damon (Roy Miller), Jason Isaacs (Briggs), Brendan Gleeson (Martin Brown), Greg Kinnear (Clark Poundstone), Amy Ryan (Lawrie Dayne), Khalid Abdalla (Freddy), Igal Naor (General Al Rawi). Directed by Paul Greengrass and produced by Tim Bevan, Eric Fellner, and Lloyd Levin. Screenplay by Brian Helgeland, inspired by the book *Imperial Life in the Emerald City* by Rajiv Chandrasekaran.

Green Zone looks at an American war in a way almost no Hollywood movie ever has: We're not the heroes, but the dupes. Its message is that Iraq's fabled "weapons of mass destruction" did not exist, and that neocons within the administration fabricated them, lied about them, and were ready to kill to cover up their deception.

Is this true? I'm not here to say. It's certainly one more element in the new narrative that has gradually emerged about Iraq, the dawning realization that we went to war under false premises. It's a thriller that makes no claim to be based on fact, but provides characters and situations that have uncanny real-life parallels. Its director made two of the Bourne films, and imports his approach to Baghdad, starring Matt Damon as an unstoppable action hero.

But this isn't merely a thriller. It has a point to argue: Critical blunders at the outset made a quick and easy victory impossible, and turned Bush's "Mission Accomplished" photo-op into a historic miscalculation. *Green Zone* argues, as many observers have, that the fatal error of the United States was to fire the officers and men of the Iraqi army and leave them at large with their weapons. The army had no great love of Saddam, and might have been a helpful stabilizing force. Instead, it was left unemployed, armed, and alienated.

Damon, playing Chief Warrant Officer Roy Miller, is seen at the outset leading a raid on a suspected storage site for WMDs. Nothing there. Another raid, intended to find weapons of chemical warfare, turns up years-old pigeon droppings. Because some of the raids produce casualties, he begins to question the intelligence reports the raids are based on. He speaks out at a briefing, and rather improbably finds himself face-to-face with a U.S. intelligence agent named Poundstone (Greg Kinnear). He's fed the usual line and told to perform his duty, but is overheard by Brown, a hulking, grizzled CIA man who's an old Middle East hand. Soon he's meeting with Brown to pass on his doubts. *Green Zone* indicates that the CIA, which lacked (as in real life) any evidence to back up the WMD claims, has been cut out of the loop, and that Poundstone is not only the architect of the neocon fictions, but their enforcer; he even has a military group answering directly to him.

Chief Miller also meets a New York newspaperwoman named Lawrie Dayne (Amy Ryan), whose reports about a secret Iraqi informer have given credence to the WMD claims. From her he discovers that General Al Rawi (Igal Naor) of the Iraqi army met with Poundstone in Jordan, but unlike the source Poundstone cited, flatly told him Saddam had no WMDs. So the bad intel was cooked up to justify the war the neocons desired.

Have I made the plot sound complex? Greengrass works with the screenwriter, Brian Helgeland, to tell it with considerable clarity. By limiting the characters and using typecasting, he makes a web of deceit easy to understand. Also a great help to Chief Miller is a local named Freddy (Khalid Abdalla), who risks his life to help him, acts as a translator, and is given the film's key line of dialogue.

The action in *Green Zone* is followed by Greengrass in the queasycam style I've found distracting in the past: lots of quick cuts between handheld shots. It didn't bother me here. That may be because I became so involved in the story. Perhaps also because unlike the Bourne films, this one contains no action sequences that are logically impossible. When we see a car chase that couldn't take place in the real world, we naturally think about the visual effects. When they could take place, and it's a good movie, we're thinking about the story.

Green Zone will no doubt be under fire from those who are still defending the fabricated intelligence we used as an excuse to invade Iraq. Yes, the film is fiction, employs far-fetched coincidences, and improbably places one man at the center of all the action. It is a thriller, not a documentary. It's my belief that the nature of the neocon evildoing has by now become pretty clear. Others will disagree. The bottom line is: This is one hell of a thriller.

Grown Ups ★ ★

PG-13, 102 m., 2010

Adam Sandler (Lenny Feder), Kevin James (Eric Lamonsoff), Chris Rock (Kurt McKenzie), David Spade (Marcus Higgins), Rob Schneider (Rob Hilliard), Maria Bello (Sally Lamonsoff), Salma Hayek (Roxanne Chase-Feder), Maya Rudolph (Deanne McKenzie), Joyce Van Patten (Gloria), Ebony Jo-Ann (Mama Ronzoni), Di Quon (Nanny Rita), Steve Buscemi (Wiley). Directed by Dennis Dugan and produced by Jack Giarraputo and Adam Sandler. Screenplay by Sandler and Fred Wolf.

Grown Ups is a pleasant, genial, good-hearted, sometimes icky comedy that's like spending a weekend with well-meaning people you don't want to see again any time real soon. They're the kind of people where, in the car driving home, you ask, "What was that all about?" Try to imagine the Three Stooges slapping one another's faces with dehydrated reconstituted bananas. No, really.

The pretense for the story: Five kids were on a basketball team in middle school. Their beloved old coach has died. To mourn him they return to the lakeside cabin where they celebrated their victory all those years ago. Wouldn't you know, the five kids on the team they beat are at the same lake for the same weekend.

The five buddies are played by Adam Sandler, Rob Schneider, Kevin James, Chris Rock, and David Spade. Sandler's wife is a famous designer (Salma Hayek). Schneider's much older wife is Joyce Van Patten. Rock's pregnant wife is Maya Rudolph. His Madea-style mother is Ebony Jo-Ann. James's wife is Maria Bello, who is still breast-feeding their four-year-old at every opportunity. Spade is unmarried, which, given the size of the cast, is just as well, since the characters have five children (I think), and there are also roles for Steve Buscemi as a guy who ends up in a body cast, Di Quon as Sandler's Asian nanny, and, of course, Schneider's three daughters from two previous marriages, two of them towering models, the third short and stout. There are so many characters in the movie that some scenes look like everyone lined up for a group shot.

The physical humor is not sophisticated. One character ends up with her face in a cake, and another has his face pushed twice into doggy-doo. The nursing mother squirts milk here and there, and her son is warned that if he doesn't wean himself soon he'll have a "got milk?" mustache with real hair. The gang all goes to a water park. There's a basketball game to settle old scores. And so on.

What's strange is how laid-back it all is. The five old pals at times sound positively like they're idly remembering old times. Lots of stuff seems intended only to be pleasant. When it looks like Sandler and his wife will be given the bedroom with the water mattress, for example, he says, naw, let the kids all share it. Does that sound like the set-up for a joke? There isn't one.

Joyce Van Patten (who is seventy-five) and Rob Schneider (who is forty-six) play a married couple, which generates some laughs, mostly on the nice side, and no vulgarities. See, they really like each other. And during the obligatory scene where every character makes a confession or relates one of life's lessons, she makes a warm and genuine speech that is well delivered, but hardly seems to belong in this movie.

The comedy talent here is seen but not much heard, given the human traffic jam of the cast. Chris Rock and Kevin James are underutilized. Maria Bello is reduced to breast-feeding and milk-pumping scenes. The character of Ebony Jo-Ann, with her farts, bunions, and pratfalls, comes perilously close to an insulting caricature. Maya Rudolph spends much of her time reacting to others and caressing her pregnancy. Adam Sandler plays a good guy who never does much more than be a good guy.

The direction by Dennis Dugan never overcomes the ungainly size of the cast. It's such a challenge to keep all the characters alive that he sometimes does round-robins of reaction shots—a fatal strategy when it comes to timing. Some of the dialogue is broken down into one-shots; some of the characters spend stretches of merely responding. It's all, as I said, pleasant and good-natured, but it feels too much as if all these nice people are trying to keep the conversation going. A comedy it is, but *The Hangover* or *Death at a Funeral* it isn't.

Gulliver's Travels ★ ★ ★

PG, 85 m., 2010

Jack Black (Lemuel Gulliver), Jason Segel (Horatio), Emily Blunt (Princess Mary), Amanda Peet (Darcy Silverman), Billy Connolly (King Theodore), Chris O'Dowd (General Edward). Directed by Rob Letterman and produced by Jack Black, Ben Cooley, John Davis, and Gregory Goodman. Screenplay by Joe Stillman and Nicholas Stoller, not based very much on the novel by Jonathan Swift.

I want to tread carefully here, and not because I might step on a Lilliputian and squish him. I want to explain who *Gulliver's Travels* is for, and who it might not be for. One person it is definitely for is Gloria DeMent, the eighty-four-year-old grandmother who wrote Associated Press film critic Christy Lemire in horror after spending $96 to take four generations of her family to see *The Nutcracker in 3-D*. She wrote: "It broke my heart when we left the theatre that my little great-granddaughters (5-13) had sad little, confused faces." Believe me, Auntie Glo, there would have been smiles on those faces after this movie.

On the other hand, this is not really a movie for Jack Black fans—not of the Jack Black of *School of Rock*, for sure. They're used to seeing Jack with his shirt off, but to see their bad boy getting tiny cannonballs embedded in his belly may not be what they have in mind, not even when he sticks out his gut and the cannonballs pop out again and demolish an enemy armada.

He is standing up to his waist in the ocean at the time. No, not near the shore. Way out where a big enemy navy has massed its warships. Not only is Gulliver a giant in the land of Lilliput, but the sea surrounding their land is apparently Lilliputian as well—about three feet deep, I'd guess, judging by Jack Black's not towering stature.

As the film opens, Black is celebrating his tenth year in the mail room of a New York newspaper. He has a crush on Darcy the travel editor (Amanda Peet), who is a good sport and gives him an assignment to write a piece from Bermuda. Jack falls asleep on board his speedboat and enters the Bermuda Triangle, which, come to think of it, of course is where Lilliput must be. In the land of these six-inch people, he awakens to find himself tied down with ropes staked to the ground, which is also what happened in Jonathan Swift's classic, but boy, would Swift ever not recognize the rest of this story.

Jack, or Lemuel Gulliver, soon finds himself not a captive but more like a hero, god, adviser, and warrior for the Lilliputians, whose society resembles an Arthurian, not a Swiftian, fantasy. On an island centered on a seaside castle, they wear the costumes and play the roles of medieval romantic swashbucklery. And they talk the talk. To paraphrase one Lilliputian, "Whyeth musteth we always speaketh with all these ETHS?"

The kingdom centers on the beloved and beautiful Princess Mary (Emily Blunt), and the rivals for her affection: King Theodore (Billy Connolly) and General Edward (Chris O'Dowd). Lemuel is able to participate in these intrigues by peering over ramparts or taking a seat on battlements. He is about twelve times as tall as they are. I wonder how he can so easily hear their little voices; if he said, "Speak up!" they'd be blown away. No matter. Darcy, of course, turns up in search of Lemuel, battles are waged, tables are turned, romances blossom, and so on.

It just occurred to me that you may be imagining this is an animated film, and that Jack Black is voicing Lemuel Gulliver. Not at all. This is live action, and despite the 3-D, it's sorta old-fashioned, not that that's a bad thing. The problem is to contain Lemuel and the Lilliputians in the same frame when he towers over them. Makes for (1) long shots, or (2) shots of Black's enormous face peering at the little folks from over the edge of something. As he stood on the beach with the little fellas, I was immediately reminded of the genie in Michael Powell's masterpiece *The Thief of Bagdad* (1940).

I wouldn't describe the special effects as seamless. Far from it. But that brings us back around to our grandmother, Gloria DeMent. Do you think her great-grandchildren are going to be sitting there saying, "You can see that's done with green screen"? I don't think so. They're gonna be saying, "Thanks, Grandma Glo! This is ever so much better than that scary Nutcracker movie! There isn't a single Holocaust anywhere in it!"

(Well, in all fairness, the entire Earth is ripped to pieces in a brilliant cartoon that plays before the feature. *Scrat's Continental Crack-Up* stars the manic creature from the first *Ice Age,* who would destroy the globe to save a nut.)

H

Hall Pass ★ ★ ½

R, 105 m., 2011

Owen Wilson (Rick), Jason Sudeikis (Fred), Jenna Fischer (Maggie), Christina Applegate (Grace), Richard Jenkins (Coakley). Directed by Bobby Farrelly and Peter Farrelly and produced by Mark Charpentier, Bobby Farrelly, Peter Farrelly, J. B. Rogers, Bradley Thomas, and Charles B. Wessler. Screenplay by Pete Jones, Kevin Barnett, Peter Farrelly, and Bobby Farrelly.

I was just reading an article about the oddly prolonged adolescence of American males, especially those in the movies. There's a common fantasy where the guys get away from their wives and girlfriends and escape to where they're free to guzzle beer, eat sloppy, belch, fart, leave pizza boxes on the floor, scratch their butts, watch sports on TV, and in many other ways become irresistible to hot chicks. When was the last time you saw a man under thirty in the movies who had a stable marriage, a job, children, and a life where he valued his wife above his buddies?

Hall Pass extends the twenties and thirties into the forties, and imagines a world in which there are no grown-up men at all. We meet two pals named Rick and Fred (Owen Wilson and Jason Sudeikis) who are well married to Maggie and Grace (Jenna Fischer and Christina Applegate) and yet lust improbably after every nubile woman who strays into their target zone. Rick in particular is always being caught by his wife while checking out the passing parade.

It is perhaps hardwired into men that their eyes are constantly on the prowl. Maybe it's an evolutionary trait, and our species has developed it to encourage the sowing of human seed in many fields. Women, by contrast, have evolved to be sure their mates gaze in admiration at them alone and nobody else. There's a famous story by Irwin Shaw, "The Girls in Their Summer Dresses," about an estranged couple who decide to make up. They go for a stroll down Fifth Avenue, but break up all over again because the man can't prevent his eyes from straying. He loves her, yes he really does, but you see, the girls are so pretty in their summer dresses.

Maggie and Grace eventually get fed up with the vagrant eyeballs of their husbands and decide to call the bluff. They issue week-long "hall passes," which are permission slips to allow both men seven days of unsupervised and guiltless sexual freedom. Maybe then they'll get desire out of their systems? Rick and Fred rejoice, and so do the members of their posse, because of course, men when set free seek the protection of the pack. Any real man would hunt alone, the better to sneak up on his prey. A woman does not respond eagerly to flattery emanating from a booth jammed with guys at Fuddrucker's.

Hall Pass is the new comedy by the Farrelly brothers, Bobby and Peter, who are in the unfortunate position of forever being judged against the impossible standard of their movie *There's Something About Mary* (1998). That remains the only movie where I literally, cross my heart, saw a man laugh so hard he fell out of his chair. One of the essential qualities of *Mary* was the performance by Ben Stiller as a man with much dignity, easily offended. Stiller can evoke a kind of vulpine cunning that is funny when thwarted.

A problem with *Hall Pass*, I think, is that both Owen Wilson and Jason Sudeikis are affable, and the movie wants us to like them. It is often more useful for a comedy to have characters whose embarrassment we enjoy. I suspect we're expected to empathize with the lads here, in their inept attempts to plunder the netherlands of steamy chicks. The truest words in the film are spoken by Joy Behar, as a more experienced older woman who tells the two wives that their husbands, like all men, believe only marriage is preventing them from being irresistible to women. It is probably a good thing for the species that so many men believe they're irresistible because so few are.

The plot of the movie is meh. It involves the lads and their posse being cycled through several unsuccessful and quasi-slapstick situations showing their cluelessness, their immaturity, and how women easily see straight through them. Meanwhile, the wives and their posses have a great time on a getaway retreat. Women seem to get along perfectly well when set free without men, but men seem uncomfortable without women. It probably all involves which sex has the greater need to be reassured.

The Hangover ★ ★ ★ ½

R, 100 m., 2009

Bradley Cooper (Phil), Ed Helms (Stu), Zach Galifianakis (Alan), Heather Graham (Jade), Justin Bartha (Doug), Jeffrey Tambor (Sid). Directed by Todd Phillips and produced by Phillips and Dan Goldberg. Screenplay by Jon Lucas and Scott Moore.

Now this is what I'm talkin' about. *The Hangover* is a funny movie, flat out, all the way through. Its setup is funny. Every situation is funny. Most of the dialogue is funny almost line by line. At some point we actually find ourselves caring a little about what happened to the missing bridegroom—and the fact that we almost care is funny, too.

The movie opens with bad news for a bride on her wedding day. Her fiancé's best buddy is standing in the Mohave Desert with a bloody lip and three other guys, none of whom is her fiancé. They've lost him. He advises her there's no way the wedding is taking place.

We flash back two days to their road trip to Vegas for a bachelor party. Her future husband, Doug (Justin Bartha), will be joined by his two friends, the schoolteacher Phil (Bradley Cooper) and the dentist Stu (Ed Helms). Joining them will be her brother, Alan (Zach Galifianakis), an overweight slob with a Haystacks Calhoun beard and an injunction against coming within two hundred feet of a school building.

The next morning, Doug will be missing. The other three are missing several hours: None of them can remember a thing since they were on the roof of Caesars Palace, drinking shots of Jagermeister. They would desperately like to know: How in the hell do you wake up in a $4,200-a-night suite with a tiger, a chicken, a crying baby, a missing tooth, and a belly button pierced for a diamond dangle? And when you give your parking check to the doorman, why does he bring around a police car? And where is Doug?

Their search provides a structure for the rest of the movie, during a very long day that includes a fact-finding visit to a wedding chapel, a violent encounter with a small but very mean Chinese mobster, a sweet hooker, an interview with an emergency room doctor, and an encounter with Mike Tyson, whose tiger they appear to have stolen, although under the circumstances he is fairly nice about it. There is never an explanation for the chicken.

Despite these events, *The Hangover* isn't simply a laugh riot. I won't go so far as to describe it as a character study, but all three men have profound personality problems, and the Vegas trip works on them like applied emergency therapy. The dentist is rigidly ruled by his bitchy girlfriend. The schoolteacher thinks nothing of stealing the money for a class trip. And Alan . . .

Well, Zach Galifianakis's performance is the kind of breakout performance that made John Belushi a star after *Animal House.* He is short, stocky, wants to be liked, has a yearning energy, was born clueless. It is a tribute to Galifianakis's acting that we actually believe he is sincere when he asks the clerk at the check-in counter: "Is this the real Caesar's palace? Does Caesar live here?"

The film is directed by Todd Phillips, whose *Old School* and *Road Trip* had their moments but didn't prepare me for this. The screenplay is by Jon Lucas and Scott Moore, whose *Ghosts of Girlfriends Past* certainly didn't. This movie is *written,* not assembled out of off-the-shelf parts from the Apatow Surplus Store. There is a level of detail and observation in the dialogue that's sort of remarkable: These characters aren't generically funny, but specifically funny. The actors make them halfway convincing.

Phillips has them encountering a mixed bag of weird characters, which is standard, but the characters aren't. Mr. Chow (Ken Jeong), the vertically challenged naked man they find locked in the trunk of the police car, is strong, skilled in martial arts, and really mean about Alan being fat. He finds almost anything a fat man does to be hilarious. When he finds his clothes and his henchmen, he is not to be trifled with. Jade (Heather Graham), a stripper, is forthright: "Well, actually I'm an escort, but stripping is a good way to meet clients." She isn't the good-hearted cliché, but more of a sincere young woman who would like to meet the right guy.

The search for Doug has them piecing together clues from the ER doctor, Mike Tyson's security tapes, and a mattress that is impaled on the uplifted arm of one of the Caesars Palace statues. The plot hurtles through them. If the movie ends somewhat conventionally, well, it almost has to: Narrative housecleaning requires it. It began conventionally, too, with uplifting music and a typeface for the titles that may remind you of *My Best Friend's Wedding.* But it is not to be. Here is a movie that deserves every letter of its R rating. What happens in Vegas stays in Vegas, especially after you throw up.

The Hangover Part II ★ ★

R, 101 m., 2011

Bradley Cooper (Phil), Ed Helms (Stu), Zach Galifianakis (Alan), Justin Bartha (Doug), Ken Jeong (Mr. Chow), Paul Giamatti (Kingsley), Jamie Chung (Lauren), Mason Lee (Teddy), Mike Tyson (Himself). Directed by Todd Phillips and produced by Phillips and Daniel Goldberg. Screenplay by Phillips, Craig Mazin, and Scot Armstrong.

Is this some kind of a test? *The Hangover Part II* plays like a challenge to the audience's capacity for raunchiness. It gets laughs, but some of them are in disbelief. As if making sure no one was not offended, it has a montage of still photos in the closing titles that includes one cruel shot that director Todd Phillips should never, ever have used. The MPAA's elaboration of the R rating says the movie has "pervasive language, strong sexual content including graphic nudity, drug use, and brief violent images." Also other stuff. Maybe their space was limited.

It's not that I was shocked. This is a raunchfest, yes, but not an offense against humanity (except for that final photo, which is a desecration of one of the two most famous photos to come out of Vietnam). The movie has its share of laughs. There's a wedding toast that deserves some sort of award for deliberate social embarrassment. And Alan (Zach Galifianakis), the character who stole much of the original 2009 film, walks off with a lot of this one, too.

If you saw that earlier film (which grossed $485 million, so you may have), there's not much need for me to describe the plot this time. It's the same story. Phillips seems to have taken the *Hangover* screenplay and moved it laterally from Las Vegas to Bangkok while retaining the same sequence of scenes: call to bewildered bride-to-be, flashback to wedding plans, ill-advised bachelor party, four friends waking up with terminal hangovers in unfamiliar hotel room, ominous signs of debauchery, desperate quest to discover what happened, etc.

As the picture opens, a few years have passed. The dentist, Stu (Ed Helms), is now the prospective groom. He's engaged to a beautiful Thai woman named Lauren (Jamie Chung). Her father (Nirut Sirichanya) is not happy. His son Teddy (Mason Lee) is a brilliant sixteen-year-old pre-med student at Stanford, and the father tells Stu: "In this country, we do not consider dentist a doctor." At a pre-wedding feast, he calmly and implacably offers a toast comparing Stu to a flavorless rice pudding.

Then the lads go down to the beach for one (1) beer, and the next thing they know, they're regaining consciousness in a sleazy Bangkok fleabag, Stu has a facial tattoo, and young Teddy is missing, except for a severed finger wearing a Stanford class ring. That sets off their search through the city's underbelly for people who might be able to help them reconstruct the missing hours? days? Let me just observe that no search of the Bangkok underbelly that involves Ping-Pong balls is going to be altogether reassuring.

Their adventures are punctuated by a series of behavioral eruptions by Alan (Galifianakis), who links passive aggression with clueless troublemaking. These interventions have a certain charm, but Alan's funniest scene takes place in his own bedroom before he ever gets to Thailand. Describing himself as a "stay-at-home son," he issues commands to his mother through a speaker system and seems determined to remain a fanboy for life. This character, as seen in this scene, could inspire a movie of its own that I would pay good money to see. (Galifianakis should regrow his hair, however; I like him looking like a shaggy bear more than like the bouncer in a biker bar.)

I'm no expert, but I've been to Bangkok, and while the city no doubt has a seamy side, let it be said that much of *The Hangover Part II* plays like an anti-travelogue paid for by a rival tourist destination—Singapore, maybe. Some of its surprises would shock only those who know little about the city's sex workers, but others are truly unexpected, including the appearance of Paul Giamatti as a crime boss, and Nick Cassavetes as a tattoo artist. The gangster Mr. Chow (Ken Jeong) is back for the second film, still in need of serious tranquilizing.

While many weekend comedies these days seem too timidly in search of the PG-13, *The Hangover* embraced its R, and *Part II* seems to be testing the MPAA's patience. I wonder if there will be an unrated director's cut. The sequel repeats the medical miracle of the first film, in that the characters are able to regain consciousness after horrifying debauches and quickly return to the land of the living. In real life, they'd check themselves into an emergency room.

Hanna ★ ★ ★ ½

PG-13, 111 m., 2011

Saoirse Ronan (Hanna), Eric Bana (Erik Heller), Cate Blanchett (Marissa Wiegler), Tom Hollander (Isaacs), Olivia Williams (Rachel), Jason Flemyng (Sebastian), Jessica Barden (Sophie). Directed by Joe Wright and produced by Marty Adelstein, Leslie Holleran, and Scott Nemes. Screenplay by Seth Lochhead and David Farr.

Hanna is a first-rate thriller about the drawbacks of homeschooling. As it opens, a teenage girl is in the act of killing a deer with her bow and arrow, and then, as she's gutting the carcass, a man sneaks up behind her and says, "You're dead!" She engages in a fierce hand-to-hand battle with this man, who turns out to be her father. He has raised her, as they lived alone deep in the forest in a house that looks like it was inspired by lots of gingerbread.

Gradually most—not all—of the details come clear. Hanna (Saoirse Ronan) has been taught advanced and ruthless killing skills as a means of self-defense against her enemies, who are legion. Her father, Erik (Eric Bana), fears for her safety and his own. He is apparently an agent whose skills and knowledge are so formidable that a CIA officer named Marissa (Cate Blanchett) is obsessed with capturing him—and the child.

Hanna decides she is ready for the real world, and the two of them plunge back into a confrontation with the CIA. And then we get an odd cross between a fairy tale and a high-tech action movie. It could have been a fairly strained attempt at either, but director Joe Wright (*Atonement*) combines his two genres into a stylish exercise that perversely includes some sentiment and insight.

Consider how hard it is to be Hanna. You have never known anyone your own age. You have apparently never met a woman. You speak several languages fluently. You are the master of martial arts and adept at many weapons. Your dad has drilled you to memorize every word in a one-volume encyclopedia that looks like it came as a free gift for opening a new account at the savings and loan. So you are all topped up on facts, but have no knowledge at all of the real world.

Of course, the movie reminded me of *Kick-Ass*, the 2010 action fantasy about a deadly young girl. I like *Hanna* a good deal more, because in its quirky way it has something to say, a certain wit, and a command of the visual poetry of action. There is nevertheless something disturbing about the conversion of little girls into ruthlessly efficient fighters who can kill dozens of people and not give it a second thought. If Hanna were a sixteen-year-old boy, how would that feel?

Marissa, the CIA boss, is essentially a wicked step-mother figure. Why she hates and fears Hanna and Erik is hinted at in many ways, and they all amount to this: The father and daughter represent a threat to American security so great that millions of dollars are gladly spent in the effort to capture and neutralize them. Is there a more personal motivation? Is Hanna by any chance the daughter of Marissa and Erik? The thought occurs because Saoirse Ronan and Cate Blanchett resemble each other in their facial bone structures, and also because—well, there are vibes.

Joe Wright has been known until now for civilized literary adaptations, including the wonderful Keira Knightley version of *Pride and Prejudice.* He's not a vulgarian. He has a purpose here, and I think it's to stir some of the same fundamental emotional parts that are reached by fairy tales, especially of the Grimm variety. He demonstrates that action movies need not be mindless. There is a role for creative choreography in them, even in largely CGI scenes like a chase sequence involving shipping containers on a dock. Even when human bodies are not really there, their apparent movements must be choreographed, and that sequence is a beauty.

Wright and his writers, Seth Lochhead and David Farr, do something else that's effective. They introduce an element of reality. Too many action films exist always at the same unremitting level of violent fantasy. Here, he arranges for Hanna to come across an ordinary British family on vacation. There is a daughter named Sophie (Jessica Barden), who I believe must be the first girl her age Hanna has met. Indeed, this is her first encounter with a family, and it's all strange and unfamiliar. The touch of reality brings into focus how peculiar her life has been.

Cate Blanchett seems strange. She allows little humanity into her Marissa; she's as personable as Ilsa, She Wolf of the SS. Perhaps that's wise. A more human Marissa would introduce tones that might not fit. Her job is to command her minions and focus on the capture of the father and daughter. A chamber in which Hanna is held for a while amusingly reminds us of the James Bond convention that an extraordinary captive demands an extraordinary cell, apparently constructed at great expense for the occasion.

Hanna is good, sound filmmaking. It depends on stylistic order and discipline, a clear story map, and ingenious action sequences. It is not all banging and flashing. Saoirse Ronan takes on a difficult role and aces it with as much confidence as she did playing a much different character in *Atonement.* To see a movie like this is to gain a new understanding of the mindless confusion of something like *Battle: Los Angeles.*

Happy Tears ★ ★ ★

R, 95 m., 2010

Parker Posey (Jayne), Demi Moore (Laura), Rip Torn (Joe), Ellen Barkin (Shelly), Christian Camargo (Jackson). Directed by Mitchell Lichtenstein and produced by Joyce M. Pierpoline. Screenplay by Lichtenstein.

In *Happy Tears,* two sisters—one poor, one rich, one steady, one obsessed with possessions—deal with their old dad's approach to senility and his girlfriend's approach to his money. This story takes on an eerie resonance with the performance by Rip Torn as the aging father. He was recently in the news for being arrested, at the age of seventy-eight, for breaking into a bank while intoxicated and carrying a firearm.

To be sure, it was late at night, he had apparently forgotten he had the firearm, and after all, the bank looked a lot like a house. Nor is senility his problem. He is now in alcohol rehab, and I wish him good fortune because he is a fine actor. Ann Landers wrote about the danger signals of alcoholism. His arrest in the bank is surely one of them. Still, to stir up such a scandal at seventy-eight is perhaps even a tiny accomplishment, when so many his age are no longer physically able to break into banks.

Even more worthy is Torn's work here as Joe, cantankerous, stubborn as a mule, and oblivious to the fact that his "nurse," Shelly (Ellen Barkin), does not practice medicine but a far older profession. This is evident to his daughter Laura (Demi Moore), who has flown in from San Francisco to decide what should be done with him. Of course he insists he's perfectly fine and will stay right at home, thank you.

As the film opens, Laura is on the phone with her sister, Jayne (Parker Posey), telling her it's her duty to fly east and help with Joe. Jayne is a shopaholic, and we see her buying a pair of boots so expensive that if it were my money I'd just buy a car. Posey is an actress with a nice line in flightiness, and here she blends it interestingly with selfishness and irresponsibility. Soon after her arrival, the need to tidy up after Joe's problems with number two becomes the first of several life lessons she'll learn.

Happy Tears centers on these two women, who have been opposites all their lives and yet like each other, and share a fondness for pot. Jayne can be infuriating, but Laura deals with it. Demi Moore is interesting here. In the role of a dialed-down, capable woman, she suggests dramatic possibilities for future roles. She projects a kind of calm, and it's attractive.

I was also intrigued by Ellen Barkin's work as the "nurse" Shelly, who optimistically believes that by wearing a stethoscope around her neck she can pass herself off. It's abundantly clear to Jayne and Laura that she learned her nursing on TV, but Joe is sold on her and cannot comprehend the possibility that he won't get his way. Instead of keeping Shelly at Level One of character complexity, writer-director Mitchell Lichtenstein wisely makes her a little more than she might seem. Barkin, a force of nature in such films as *Sea of Love,* here wades into a character role with zeal.

We assume the movie will mostly concern what the daughters should do with Joe. These scenarios are common enough, when estranged siblings are brought back together for the one reason it's hard to deny: the shared responsibility of family.

It's as well, too, that Joe is seen as a fairly clear-cut case. You want my opinion? He belongs in a home. In many films considering this question, the parents don't actually *need* such care, but it's such a convenience, you see, for their children. Joe presents not so much a problem for Jayne and Laura as an opportunity. It's time to grow up and be daughters and sisters. They've waited long enough. All of this, I must add, is done with a nice, screwy, sometimes stoned humor.

Harry Brown ★ ★ ★

R, 103 m., 2010

Michael Caine (Harry Brown), Emily Mortimer (D. I. Frampton), Charlie Creed-Miles (D. S. Hicock), Ben Drew (Noel Winters), Liam Cunningham (Sid Rourke), Iain Glen (S. I. Andrew Childs), David Bradley (Leonard Attwell), Jack O'Connell (Marky Hathaway). Directed by Daniel Barber and produced by Keith Bell, Matthew Brown, Kris Thykier, and Matthew Vaughn. Screenplay by Gary Young.

Harry Brown is a revenge thriller poised somewhere between *Death Wish* and *Gran Torino.* All three depend on the ability of an older actor to convince us he's still capable of violence, and all three spend a great deal of time alone with their characters, whose faces must reflect their inner feelings. Charles Bronson, Clint Eastwood, Michael Caine. Those are faces sculpted by time.

Caine plays an old man with a dying wife. He lives in a London housing estate used by a drug gang as its own turf. Pedestrians are terrorized and beaten, drugs are openly sold, there are some areas understood as no-go. From his high window, Harry hears a car alarm and looks down to see the car's owner come out and be beaten by thugs. This is the daily reality.

Caine is a subtle actor who builds characters from the inside out. His voice has become so familiar over the years that it's an old friend. In this film he begins as a lonely, sad geezer, and gradually an earlier persona emerges, that of a British marine who served in Northern Ireland. All of that has been put in a box and locked away, he says, and thinks.

There's a pub on the estate, quiet in the daytime, where he and his old friend Leonard (David Bradley) meet for studious games of chess. The thugs have been shoving dog mess through Leonard's mail slot. His life is miserable. He shows Harry a gun. One day when the gang pushes burning newspapers through the slot, he goes to confront them in an underpass they control. Later Frampton, a young police inspector (Emily Mortimer), comes to tell Harry that Leonard has been killed.

The inspector is human, and sympathetic. Harry tells her the police have no control over the area, and she cannot disagree. Her superior officer has his own notions. And then the film takes the turn that we expect, and in the process takes on aspects of a more conventional police procedural.

What Caine is successful at, however, is always remaining in character. Like Eastwood, and unlike Bronson, he is always his age, always in the same capable but aged body. The best scene in the movie involves his visit to the flat of a drug dealer, where Harry plans to buy a gun. There's a semi-comatose girl on the sofa. The situation is fraught. How Harry handles it depends not on strength but on experience and insight. He carefully conceals his cards.

The police investigation is misdirected for political motives. Frampton has an excellent notion of who may be responsible for the killings of neighborhood hoods, but cannot get a hearing. It would not do for a geezer to outdo the police. Vigilante activity is, of course, not the answer to urban crime, but what is? In Chicago, Mayor Richard Daley floods one area with cops, and shootings continue nearby. It's all fueled by drugs and drug money, of course. You know, one of the areas where I think Libertarians may be right is about the legalization of drugs. There would be less of them with no profit motive for their sale. Less money for guns. Fewer innocent bystanders would die. Who knows?

This movie plays better than perhaps it should. Directed as a debut by Daniel Barber, it places story and character above manufactured "thrills," and works better. We are all so desperately weary of CGI that replaces drama. With movies like this, humans creep back into crime films. There is a clear thread connecting this Michael Caine and the Caine of *The Ipcress File*. You may not be able to see it, but it's there.

Harry Potter and the Deathly Hallows: Part 1 ★ ★ ★

PG-13, 146 m., 2010

Daniel Radcliffe (Harry Potter), Rupert Grint (Ron Weasley), Emma Watson (Hermione Granger), Helena Bonham Carter (Bellatrix Lestrange), Robbie Coltrane (Rubeus Hagrid), Ralph Fiennes (Lord Voldemort), Brendan Gleeson (Alastor "Mad Eye" Moody), Rhys Ifans (Xenophilius Lovegood), Jason Isaacs (Lucius Malfoy), Bill Nighy (Rufus Scrimgeour), Alan Rickman (Severus Snape), Imelda Staunton (Dolores Umbridge), Julie Walters (Mrs. Weasley), Mark Williams (Arthur Weasley), Michael Gambon (Albus Dumbledore), Richard Griffiths (Vernon Dursley), John Hurt (Ollivander), Fiona Shaw (Petunia Dursley), Timothy Spall (Wormtail), David Thewlis (Remus Lupin). Directed by David Yates and produced by David Barron, David Heyman, and J. K. Rowling. Screenplay by Steve Kloves, based on the novel by Rowling.

Harry, Hermione, and Ron have grown up. The horrors they met at Hogwarts are but nostalgic memories. They are cast out now into the vastness of the world, on their own, and Voldemort and his Death Eaters draw ever closer. Also drawing near is an equally unsettling phenomenon, sexual maturity. Both are barely kept at bay in this first installment of the last installment of the saga Harry Potter.

David Yates's *Harry Potter and the Deathly Hallows* is a handsome and sometimes harrowing film, and will be completely unintelligible for anyone coming to the series for the first time. At 146 minutes, it confronts us with a roll call of the many, many characters in the series, and requires a nearly encyclopedic recall of the previous chapters of the epic. I've seen all the films, and there were times when I had no idea what they were talking about here. Indeed, there are times when Hermione has to explain to Harry.

My cluelessness didn't bother me because the film depends more on mood and character than many of the others, and key actions seem to be alarmingly taking place off-screen. Our three heroes have left Hogwarts behind, Quidditch games are a thing of the past, and things have come to such a pass that Harry keeps his white owl in a cramped parrot cage.

The film opens with a frightening meeting of the Death Eaters, plotting the destruction of all three characters. Presiding is Lord Voldemort (Ralph Fiennes), his noseless face disturbingly like a snake's. Harry must be destroyed. That our hero survives after the myriad attacks on his life in the earlier installments does not speak well for Voldemort's minions, but this time they mean business.

Harry (Daniel Radcliffe) moves his family to a safe haven. He joins Hermione (Emma Watson) and Ron (Rupert Grint) in flight, sometimes literally. They seek counsel from old friends, and spend a great deal of time in wilderness isolation. They have the ability to materialize anywhere, and we find them in forbidding forests, beside mirrorlike lakes ringed by mountains, and in a harsh landscape where the rocks have been riven by deep cracks. That some of these locations are actual and others are CGI is usually not noticeable, although I doubt that Harry would have skipped so casually over these cracked stones if they were real.

This isolation serves two purposes. It helps conceal them from Voldemort. And, especially after Ron Weasley seems to live up to his name and weasel out, it allows Harry and Hermione to become closer friends than ever, confidants, and even, yes, in love. They share a kiss so chaste that passion seems a stranger to them; they might as well be observing a formal ritual. And they are nude, or almost nude, as they stand close to each other and ghostly CGI mists obscure all the naughty bits as efficiently as fig leaves.

Much has to do with tracking down missing pieces of Voldemort's soul. The late beloved Dumbledore (Michael Gambon) has left obscure clues to their whereabouts, leading to two observations: (1) Beyond a certain level of obscurity, a clue lacks usefulness, and (2) how extraordinarily careless of Voldemort to leave missing pieces of his soul lying about.

This installment ends in midstream, which we all knew it would, because Part 2 opens in July. That final installment must at last tie up all the loose ends, dispatch villains, celebrate heroes, and return some stability to the world of magicians. To hope a breeze blows through it and clears away the mists is too much to hope for. Hermione here has grown into an attractive young woman, Harry and Ron are both alert to that, and Harry now even needs to shave (although he has mercifully not graduated to the three-day stubble of the routine action hero).

The final film will be in 3-D. This installment was once planned for retro 3-D, but Warner Bros., a studio that enforces traditional standards, decided against that after observing the disastrous results of other 2-D films converted to 3-D. Presumably the next film will have 3-D done well. It will suffer in brightness and clarity, and that is a shame. Look closely at the 2-D opening Warner Bros. logo here and you will swear it's 3-D.

As we approach the end of a decade of Harry Potter, it's clear how wisely (and luckily) the studio cast the series. Radcliffe, Grint, and Watson have grown from children to young adults, still retain the qualities they had when younger, are practiced professionals, and carry the series. And they are surrounded by a supporting cast that's like an honor roll of great recent British actors.

Setting aside actors from earlier films who have passed away (Richard Harris) or are no longer needed (Emma Thompson), let me just make a list for those who know their actors: Helena Bonham Carter, Robbie Coltrane, Ralph Fiennes, Michael Gambon, Brendan Gleeson, Richard Griffiths, John Hurt, Rhys Ifans, Jason Isaacs, Bill Nighy, Alan Rickman, Fiona Shaw, Timothy Spall, Imelda Staunton, David Thewlis, Warwick Davis, Tom Felton, Toby Jones, Simon McBurney, Peter Mullan, and Julie Walters. Rather awesome.

I make it a custom to avoid becoming expert on the endless characters and plot strands of series movies. Life is too short to become an authority on all of the movies about James Bond, *The Lord of the Rings,* and so on. I'm sure students of Harry Potter will comprehend *Harry Potter and the Deathly Hallows* better than I was able to. They'll see a character and recall scenes from a movie made seven years ago. For me, it's more about the immediate experience. The important thing is that the characters know what's happening. At least by the end, anyway.

Harry Potter and the Half-Blood Prince ★ ★ ★

PG, 153 m., 2009

Daniel Radcliffe (Harry Potter), Rupert Grint (Ron Weasley), Emma Watson (Hermione Granger), Jim Broadbent (Horace Slughorn), Helena Bonham Carter (Bellatrix Lestrange), Robbie Coltrane (Rubeus Hagrid), Michael Gambon (Albus Dumbledore), Alan Rickman (Severus Snape), Maggie Smith (Minerva McGonagall), Tom Felton (Draco Malfoy), Evanna Lynch (Luna Lovegood), Bonnie Wright (Ginny Weasley). Directed by David Yates and produced by David Heyman and David Barron. Screenplay by Steve Kloves, based on the novel by J. K. Rowling.

The climactic scene in *Harry Potter and the Half-Blood Prince* takes place in one of those underground caverns with a lake and an ominous gondola as the means of transportation, popularized by *The Phantom of the Opera.* At first I thought—no gondola! But then one appeared, dripping and hulking. In another movie I might have grinned, but you know what? By that point, I actually cared.

Yes, this sixth chapter is a darker, more ominous Harry Potter film, with a conclusion that suggests more alarmingly the deep dangers Harry and his friends have gotten themselves into. There was always a disconnect between Harry's enchanting school days at Hogwarts and the looming threat of Voldemort. Presumably it would take more than skills at Quidditch to defeat the dreaded Dark Lord.

In one of the opening scenes, we find Harry (Daniel Radcliffe) late at night in a café of the London Underground, reading a copy of the *Daily Prophet,* which poses the question: Is Harry Potter the Chosen One? By the film's end, he acknowledges that he has, indeed, been chosen to face down Voldemort (whose name should properly rhyme with the French word for death, *mort.* Also, since their word *vol* can have meanings such as "thief" and "steal," Lord Voldemort is most ominously named).

Harry is distracted from his paper, however, by an instant flirtation with the young waitress, a saucy cutie who informs him, although he asked only with his eyes, that she gets off work at eleven. She indeed waits for him on the platform, but the Chosen One must respond to his higher calling from Dumbledore (Michael Gambon), who either materializes, gets off a train, or has a pied-a-terre right there in the Underground. I for one will be disappointed if that waitress (I think her name is Elarica Gallagher) doesn't turn up again in *Harry Potter and the Deathly Hallows,* whose two parts will conclude the series in 2010 and 2011.

That will be none too soon if Harry doesn't want to steal up on the *Twilight* franchise, since he and his friends, especially poor Ron Weasley, have definitively entered adolescence. Even now he seems to be entertaining thoughts of snoggling with Ron's sister, Ginny (Bonnie Wright). Yes, Harry, so recently a round-eyed little lad, will soon be one of Hogwarts's Old Boys.

Director David Yates suggests the transition in subtle ways, one of them by making Hogwarts itself seem darker, emptier, and more ominous than ever before. Its cheery corridors are now replaced by gloomy Gothic passages, and late in the film an unspeakable fate befalls the beloved dining hall at the hands of Bellatrix Lestrange (Helena Bonham Carter), who seems to function principally as a destructive vixen but no doubt has more ominous goals.

The mission for which Dumbledore summoned Harry at the outset was to visit the London home of Professor Horace Slughorn (Jim Broadbent), who has become reclusive since his Hogwarts days, but is now urgently needed along with his memories of the young student Tom Riddle, who grew up to become the man whose name should rhyme with Death. Dumbledore hopes they can discover a secret vulnerability of Voldemort's, and that is why they find themselves in the underground cavern. When this possible key is discovered, I promise you I'm not spoiling anything by observing that its basic message is "to be continued."

There are really two story strands here. One involves the close working relationship of Dumbledore and Harry on the trail of Voldemort. The other involves everything else: romance and flirtation, Quiddich, a roll call of familiar characters (Hagrid, Snape, McGonagall, Wormtail, Lupin, Filch, Flitwick, and Malfoy, whose name could be French for "bad faith"). With names like that, how do they get through commencement without snickering?

Some of these characters are reprised just as reminders. The giant Hagrid (Robby Coltrane), for example, turns up primarily to allow us to observe, "Look who's turned up!" Snape, as played by Alan Rickman, is given much more dialogue, primarily I suspect because he invests it with such macabre pauses. Radcliffe's Potter is sturdy and boring, as always; it's not easy being the hero with a supporting cast like this. Michael Gambon steals the show as Dumbledore, who for a man his age certainly has some new tricks, so to speak, up his sleeve.

I admired this Harry Potter. It opens and closes well, and has wondrous art design and cinematography as always, only more so. "I'm just beginning to realize how beautiful this place is," Harry sighs from a high turret. The middle passages spin their wheels somewhat, hurrying about to establish events and places not absolutely essential. But those scenes may be especially valued by devoted students of the Potter saga. They may also be the only ones who fully understand them; ordinary viewers may be excused for feeling baffled some of the time.

Hatchet II ★ ½

NO MPAA RATING, 85 m., 2010

Danielle Harris (Marybeth), Tony Todd (Reverend Zombie), Kane Hodder (Victor Crowley), Parry Shen (Justin), Tom Holland (Bob). Directed by Adam Green and produced by Derek Curl, Sarah Elbert, and Cory Neal. Screenplay by Green.

You want gore, you get gore. *Hatchet II* plays less like a slasher movie than like the highlights reel from a slasher movie. It comes billed as, I dunno, satire or homage. Homage it certainly is, to the tradition of movies where everyone starts out alive at the beginning and ends up pretty much dead at the end. If satire means doing what your target does but doing it twice as much, then it's satire, too.

This is the continuation of *Hatchet* (2006), by the same director, Adam Green. Having missed that film, incredibly enough, I learn it ended at the same moment this one begins, with a monstrous swamp creature savaging the heroine, Marybeth (Danielle Harris). Since Marybeth was played by Tamara Feldman in the earlier film, this may cause some confusion if the movies play as a double feature, but hey, if Luis Bunuel could make one movie with two women playing the lead, why can't Adam Green do it with two movies?

As an exercise, let's see how quickly I can summarize the plot. Marybeth escapes from the swamp into the shack of a swamp fisherman (John Carl Beuchler), who offers her a drink from a plastic hospital urinal. He finds out who she is, and throws her out. She appeals to the Reverend Zombie (Tony Todd), who runs Zombie Shop in the French Quarter. He musters a posse of armed men to venture into the swamp, retrieve any leftover body parts of Marybeth's father and brother, and shotgun the Swamp Thing, named Crowley (Kane Hodder). The nonswamp dialogue scenes are dispatched as swiftly as possible, and then Crowley sets about slicing, dicing, slashing, disemboweling, chainsawing, and otherwise inconveniencing the men in the boat.

Man, Adam Green must have run up a bill at the local butcher. Hundreds of dollars' worth of sweetmeats, livers, gizzards, hearts, lungs, and other organs of animals (none of them human, I trust) are seemingly ripped out of Crowley's victims, while blood helpfully obscures our view of the details of these eviscerations.

There is an explanation for Crowley's behavior, a revelation about who he is, an occult connection with Reverend Zombie, and some business involving the bounty hunters, and this information is used by Adam Green as sort of an *amuse-bouche*—you know, the little serving of sorbet that French chefs offer to cleanse your palate between main courses.

There are a number of good movies opening this weekend. *Hatchet II* is not one of them. Tickets are not cheap and time is fleeting. Why would you choose this one? That's a good topic for a long, thoughtful talk with yourself in the mirror.

The Haunting in Connecticut ★ ★

PG-13, 92 m., 2009

Virginia Madsen (Sara Campbell), Kyle Gallner (Matt Campbell), Martin Donovan (Peter Campbell), Amanda Crew (Wendy), Elias Koteas (Reverend Popescu). Directed by Peter Cornwell and produced by Paul Brooks, Daniel Farrands, Wendy Rhoads, and Andrew Trapani. Screenplay by Adam Simon and Tim Metcalfe.

The Haunting in Connecticut isn't based on just any old true story. No, it's based on *the* true story. That would be the case of the Snedeker family, who in the 1970s moved into a ghost-infested house in Southington, Connecticut, and had no end of distress. We know their story is true because it was vouched for by Ed and Lorraine Warren, the paranormal sleuths, who also backed up Bill Ramsey, a demonic werewolf who bit people, *The Amityville Horror*, and the story of Jack and Janet Smurl, who inspired the movie *The Haunted*.

Even so, I doubt it's "based on." More likely it was "loosely inspired by" a story. At the end of the movie, the Snedeker house is consumed by flames, and yet we're told before the credits that it was restored, rehabbed, and lived in happily ever after. So much for any hopes of a sequel. Of course, *Amityville* inspired a prequel, so I may not be safe. I don't believe a shred of this movie is true. Ray Garton, the author of *In a Dark Place*, a book including the case, observed that the Snedekers couldn't get their stories straight. When he reported this to the investigators, Wikipedia says, he was instructed to "make the story up" and "make it scary."

But what does that matter if all you're looking for is a ghost story? *The Haunting in Connecticut* is a technically proficient horror movie, well acted by good casting choices. We have here no stock characters, but Virginia Madsen and Martin Donovan in a troubled marriage, Kyle Gallner as their dying son, and Elias Koteas as a grim priest. They make the family, now known as the Campbells, about as real as they can be under the circumstances.

The movie has an alarming score and creepy photography, and a house that doesn't look like it has been occupied since the original inhabitants . . . died, let's say. So all the elements are there, and one of my fellow critics said he "screamed like a girl three times," although he is rather known for doing so. There are two scream-able elements: (1) surprises and (2) specters.

The surprises are those moments when a hand, a face, a body, a body part, or (usually) a cat leaps suddenly into the frame, and you jump in your seat and then say, "Aw, it was only a cat." Or a face, a body part, a vampire bat, etc. The specters involve some ghostly apparitions that may or may not be physical. There are so many of them that the movie, set in Connecticut but filmed in Canada, has credits for "ghost coordinators" in both Vancouver and Winnipeg. Having seen Guy Maddin's brilliant *My Winnipeg*, I believe the ghosts coordinate themselves there.

Matt, the Campbells' son, is dying of cancer and must be driven many miles for his radiation treatments. Madsen, playing his mother, makes an "executive decision" to buy a house in the distant town so Matt, with radiation burns and nausea, doesn't have to drive so far. She gets a really good deal. Let me ask you something. If you found a terrific price on a three-story Victorian mansion with sunporches, lots of bedrooms, original woodwork, and extensive grounds in Connecticut, and it hadn't been lived in since events in the 1920s, how willing would *you* be to laugh off those events?

If the movie has a flaw, and it does, it's too many surprises. Every door, window, bedroom, hallway, staircase, basement area, attic, and crawl space is packed with surprises, so that it is a rare event in the house that takes place normally. The Campbells are constantly being surprised, so often they must be tuckered out at day's end from all of that running, jumping, and standing real still.

But I must not be too harsh, because surprises are what a movie like this trades in. I also thought Elias Koteas did a great job as the priest, who was not a ghostbuster in a Roman collar but a fellow radiation patient who never looked like he was confident good would win out in the end. (It is noteworthy that the Catholic Church does what it can to discourage exorcism, even though it could have done a lot of business in the boom times after *The Exorcist*.)

So. A preposterous story, so many scares they threaten to grow monotonous, good acting and filmmaking credits, and what else? Oh, what's with the ectoplasm? Didn't Houdini unmask that as a fraud? And the Amazing Randi? And what's it doing still being treated as real in *the* true story?

Henry's Crime ★ ★

R, 108 m., 2011

Keanu Reeves (Henry Torne), Vera Farmiga (Julie Ivanova), James Caan (Max Saltzman), Peter Stormare (Darek Millodragovic), Judy Greer (Debbie Torne), Fisher Stevens (Eddie Vibes), Bill Duke (Frank), Danny Hoch (Joe). Directed by Malcolm Venville and produced by Stephen Hamel, David Mimran, Keanu Reeves, Jordan Schur, and Lemore Syvan. Screenplay by Sacha Gervasi and David White.

Keanu Reeves seems on mild sedation during most of *Henry's Crime*. I think that's intentional. He plays the feckless Henry Torne, an overnight toll booth attendant in Buffalo, who agrees to play in a softball game, drives a car filled with other players, and discovers that what they're actually planning is a bank robbery. Henry gets caught and thrown in the slammer, and takes it philosophically.

Our problem is finding a way to care about these events more than Henry apparently does. He seems to hover above his own life, detached, an observer. Into this life enter people who become more involved in it than he does. There's his conniving friend Eddie Vibes (Fisher Stevens), who tricked him into the bank robbery. His prison cell mate is Max Saltzman (James Caan), a wiseguy from way back who knows all the angles, except how to stay out of prison. Henry's wife, Debbie (Judy Greer), ends their marriage while he's behind bars, becoming preggers in a way that he should find particularly ironic, yet Henry remains calm.

Finally a woman discovers how to really get his attention. This is Julie Ivanova (Vera Farmiga), who hits him with her car. That'll do it. She's an actress rehearsing a production of Chekhov's *Cherry Orchard*, which is being directed by Darek Millodragovic (Peter Stormare—yes, who fed his friend into a wood chipper in *Fargo*). Henry begins to like Julie. Then he discovers that one of the dressing rooms in the theater is connected to an old tunnel that leads to the bank the softball team was trying to rob.

This is perhaps beginning to sound to you like a screwball comedy. Imagine such a comedy if it has gone forty-eight hours without sleep. All the elements are present: Henry needs to be cast in the play to gain access to the tunnel, Max and Eddie get involved, Julie is remarkably accepting, any romance between Julie and Henry hangs in the balance, split-second exits and entrances are called for, and so on. Now imagine everyone sprinting through quicksand.

Keanu Reeves has many strings in his bow, but screwball comedy isn't one of them. Vera Farmiga, James Caan, and Fisher Stevens can do it, but they often seem to be looking back, waiting for Reeves to pass the baton. What you need, I think, is someone nervous to play Henry. A Steve Buscemi, for example. Reeves maintains a sort of Zen detachment. Whatever happens is all right with him.

The film was directed by Malcolm Venville, who seems to muse when he should be fretting. How uninvolved is his direction? A friend of mine in Buffalo went to see the movie, at a premiere, I guess. He wrote me complaining a city block that supplies one of the locations "was shot from a boring angle." When a comedy inspires observations like that, you know you're in trouble.

Hereafter ★ ★ ★ ★

PG-13, 129 m., 2010

Matt Damon (George Lonegan), Cecile de France (Marie LeLay), Jay Mohr (Billy), Bryce Dallas Howard (Melanie), George and Frankie McLaren (Marcus/Jason), Thierry Neuvic (Didier), Marthe Keller (Dr. Rousseau), Derek Jacobi (Himself), Richard Kind (Christos). Directed by Clint Eastwood and produced by Eastwood, Kathleen Kennedy, and Robert Lorenz. Screenplay by Peter Morgan.

Clint Eastwood's *Hereafter* considers the idea of an afterlife with tenderness, beauty, and a gentle tact. I was surprised to find it enthralling. I don't believe in woo-woo, but then neither, I suspect, does Eastwood. This is a film about the afterlife that carefully avoids committing itself on such a possibility. The closest it comes is the idea of consciousness after apparent death. This is plausible. Many near-death survivors report the same memories, of the white light, the waiting figures, and a feeling of peace.

One of the characters seems to have a genuine psychic gift. But is he, in fact, communicating with people beyond the grave? Some form of telepathy might be possible, and he may simply be receiving what his subjects desire or need to be told by their dead loved ones. He brings nothing from beyond the grave that his clients could not have formed in their living minds.

This is a subject that lends itself to sensation and psychic baloney. It's astonishing how many people believe New Age notions, which have the attraction of allowing believers to confer supernormal abilities on themselves and others without the bother of plausibility. Eastwood's film will leave such people vaguely uneasy. It believes most psychics are frauds. It introduced one who seems to be the real thing, but what, exactly, is he real about?

This is a film for intelligent people who are naturally curious about what happens when the shutters close. Eastwood tells three primary stories. The stories meet at the end, in one of those coincidences so beloved by multiple-strand movies. Is this possible? Yes. Is it likely? No. A coincidence never is. That's why we notice them. Throughout the film, the characters behave in ways that seem reasonable enough, and possibilities are left open, which is as it should be. We must live the lives we know and not count on anything beyond the horizon.

Hereafter stars Matt Damon as George, a man who sincerely believes he's able to have communication with the dead, but has fled that ability and taken a low-profile job; Cecile de France as Marie, a newsreader on French television; Bryce Dallas Howard as Melanie, a young cooking student with a fearful dark place inside; Richard Kind as a man mourning his wife; and George and Frankie McLaren as twin brothers, one of whom is struck by a truck and killed.

I won't describe here the traumatic surprises some of them experience. In the surprises as in everything else, *Hereafter* is believable. There are terrifying events, but Eastwood handles them not for sensation but to show how close we all are, at any moment, to oblivion. In the case of Marie, she undergoes the near-death experience we often hear reported, with the white light and the figures. Are people in such a state already dead, or are they experiencing visions generated by the human mind in its final shutdown mode?

The powers of the Damon character seem to be authentic, although what they prove is hard to say. There is a moment handled with love and delicacy in which he says something that is either true or isn't, but is a kindness either way. When he holds a stranger's hands, he experiences a flash of telepathic insight, but the movie never declares that his insights literally come from dead spirits.

Eastwood and his actors achieve a tone that doesn't force the material but embraces it: not dreamlike, but evoking a reverie state. These characters are not hurtling toward the resolution of a plot. There is no "solution" to their stories. There are various degrees of solace, or not. They don't punch the dialogue. They lack the certainty to impose themselves. George in particular is reserved and sad because his power has become a burden to him.

There's a sweet subplot involving Melanie (Howard), whom he meets as a partner in a cooking class. She has experienced loss. George doesn't want to enter her mind. He yearns for a normal life. The ability to read minds would be an unbearable curse. The way his gift affects their relationship is stark and poignant. Marie, the newsreader, is played by Cecile de France in such a fresh and likable way that our sympathy is engaged and we understand that whatever happened to her in the first terrifying scene has fundamentally changed her. George and Frankie McLaren, as the solemn and earnest little boy seeking his dead twin, take a character that could have been pathetic and make him simple and transparent. And notice Richard Kind, so affecting as a man who has lost his wife.

The movie is an original screenplay by Peter Morgan (*The Queen*). Eastwood told me Morgan doesn't believe in an afterlife. I don't know if Eastwood does, either. His film embodies how love makes us *need* for there to be an afterlife. It is the film of a man at peace. He has nothing to prove except his care for the living. ☞

Hesher ★ ★ ½

R, 105 m., 2011

Joseph Gordon-Levitt (Hesher), Devin Brochu (T.J.), Rainn Wilson (Paul), Natalie Portman (Nicole), Piper Laurie (Madeleine). Directed by Spencer Susser and produced by Susser, Lucy Cooper, Johnny Lin, Natalie Portman, Scott Prisand, Win Sheridan, and Matt Weaver. Screenplay by Susser and David Michod.

Hesher assembles a group of characters who aren't sure why they're in the same movie together. One by one they have an attraction, but brought together they're all elbows and angles. The title character (Joseph Gordon-Levitt) is hauled into the movie as a classic deus ex machina, as if he's been lowered by rope into the middle of a situation he has no connection with. He's a fearsome heavy metal creature with charming tattoos: on his back, an upraised middle finger, and on his chest, a man shooting his brains out.

He materializes in the life of young T.J. (Devin Brochu) and moves into T.J.'s house. The film makes no attempt to explain much about who he is, where he came from, or precisely what he thinks about T.J.'s family. At first he seems possibly an imaginary friend for the kid, but then we realize he's quite real, all right. Just inexplicable.

T.J.'s family is desolate. His mother was killed not long ago in an automobile accident. His father, Paul (Rainn Wilson), sits stunned by depression on the sofa, staring at the TV by default, not even really seeing it. His grandmother Madeleine (Piper Laurie) drifts on a cloud of vagueness through their lives, feeding them out of lifelong habit, not asserting herself, asking no questions even when T.J. brings Hesher home for dinner. Well, Hesher essentially brings himself along, but is explained as T.J.'s "friend." How has a ten-year-old acquired a friend who resembles a wasted rocker? Well you might ask, but Paul and Madeleine accept him in their sloughs of passivity.

It's not as if Hesher is really a sweet guy. He's willful, obscene, offensive, and easily angered; the tattoo covering his back must have been chosen after careful consideration. He sets up a camp in the family garage and parks his van in front, from which often pounds heavy metal at full volume. Hesher is not someone you want in your garage.

At the supermarket, T.J. meets the cashier Nicole (Natalie Portman), who has no more reason for being in the film than anybody else. In the store parking lot, she rescues T.J. from a school bully, and he develops a preadolescent crush on her, possibly seeing her as a protective mother substitute. Hesher attempts to subvert this friendship. He's just plain mean.

Portman's character is the most straightforward in the film; she is who she seems to be. Rainn Wilson and Piper Laurie are good actors, and so is, for that matter, Joseph Gordon-Levitt; and here we can see what good actors do with inexplicable situations and undefined characters. In a way, this is pure acting, generated from within, not supported by a narrative framework. Consider Wilson. He has that rare quality in an actor: Uncanny Presence. There are a few like him (Jack Nicholson, Christopher Walken, Bill Murray) who need only to look at something to establish an attitude toward it. Yes, they can get worked up, they can operate on high, but their passive *essence* is the point: dubious, wise, sadly knowledgeable, at an angle to the through-line. Other actors could sit on a sofa and watch TV, but Rainn Wilson makes it a statement. A statement of . . . nothing, which is the point.

In the long history of movies containing encounter groups or twelve-step meetings, few have given us a group inspiring less hope than the one here, where father and son attend a grief counseling session. When did grief counseling become an occupation, anyway? Whenever a demented loner opens fire at a school, grief counselors are platooned in. Just what a kid needs when his schoolmates have been murdered: a session with a stranger who wants to talk about how he feels. Perhaps grief is better dealt with among people one knows and trusts.

But I stray. Wilson brings a sad haplessness to this particular scene, and Devin Brochu's T.J. is throughout a steady, relatively uncomplicated presence. How T.J. will grow up is food for thought. Meanwhile, Hesher acts out in aggressive and offensive ways, directed only by fugitive instincts to help the kid. The film's eventual resolution of the Hesher character perhaps looked promising on the page, but doesn't bring much closure here.

Essentially, Spencer Susser's film is not strong or large enough to contain Hesher. I'm wondering how to evoke him for you. Have you ever seen *Withnail and I*? Hesher is the kind of man about whom Withnail would say: "Jaysus, and I thought I had problems."

He's Just Not That Into You ★ ★

PG-13, 129 m., 2009

Ben Affleck (Neil), Jennifer Aniston (Beth), Drew Barrymore (Mary), Jennifer Connelly (Janine), Kevin Connolly (Conor), Bradley Cooper (Ben), Ginnifer Goodwin (Gigi), Scarlett Johansson (Anna), Justin Long (Alex). Directed by Ken Kwapis and produced by Nancy Juvonen. Screenplay by Abby Kohn and Marc

Silverstein, based on the book by Greg Behrendt and Liz Tuccillo.

Ever noticed how many self-help books are limited to the insight expressed in their titles? You look at the cover, you know everything inside. The rest is just writing. I asked Amazon to "surprise me" with a page from inside the best-seller *He's Just Not That Into You,* and it jumped me to page 17, where I read: "My belief is that if you have to be the aggressor, if you have to pursue, if you have to do the asking out, nine times out of 10, he's just not that into you."

I personally would not be interested in a woman who needed to buy a book to find that out. Guys also figure out that when she never returns your calls and is inexplicably always busy, she's just not that into you. What is this, brain surgery? I have tried, but I cannot imagine what was covered in the previous sixteen pages of that book. I am reminded of the book review once written by Ambrose Bierce: "The covers of this book are too far apart."

The movie version of *He's Just Not That Into You* dramatizes this insight with comic vignettes played by actors who are really too good for this romcom. Jennifer Aniston in particular has a screen presence that makes me wonder why she rarely takes on the kinds of difficult roles her costars Jennifer Connelly, Scarlett Johansson, and Drew Barrymore have played. There are depths there. I know it.

The movie takes place in modern-day Baltimore, where those four, and Ginnifer Goodwin, play women who should ask themselves: Is he really that into me? Aniston, for example, plays Beth, who has been living for years with Neil (Ben Affleck), who is perfect in every respect except that he is disinclined to marry her. "We're happy just the way we are," he argues. The old "if it's not broke, don't fix it" routine. But if a woman knows her loved one won't ever want to marry her, it's her heart that's broke, and there is only one way to fix it. There are even evolutionary theories to explain this.

Gigi (Goodwin), on the other hand, doesn't have a perfect boyfriend, or any at all, and sits by her phone like a penguin waiting for the damn egg to hatch. Why hasn't that dreamy guy who asked for her number called back? Maybe, just maybe, it's because he doesn't want to. I haven't read the book, but I know that much. There was once a girl I didn't call, and she mailed me a book titled *The Dance-Away Lover.* How did I instinctively know the book was about me? Why did I know everything in it without having to read it? Because the book was intended for her, that's why.

Janine (Connelly) is married to Ben (Bradley Cooper), who doesn't share her ideas about home decoration, which are that you always make the more expensive choice. Not a lot of guys are into that. If you get one who is, he may make it a general policy and decide to trade you in for an advanced model. Look for a guy who treats you not as an acquisition but as an angel of mercy, the answer to the prayers of the rat he knows he is.

Mary (Barrymore) is surrounded by great guys, but they're all gay. They're from that subspecies of gay men who learned everything they know about life from Bette Davis. This is true even if they've never seen one of her movies. Then there's Anna (Johansson), who is courted fervently by Conor (Kevin Connolly), who would marry her in a second, except she's "committed" to a married man, who is committed to not marrying her, which is maybe what she likes about him, along with getting the right to constantly be the wronged one in a relationship she, after all, freely walked into.

The problem with most of the movie's women is that they are only interested in (a) the opposite sex, (b) dating, and (c) marriage. Maybe that's because the screenplay only has so much time. But a movie about one insecure woman talking to another can be monotonous, unless you're a masochist looking to share your pain. If you consider a partner who has no more compelling interests than a, b, or c, you're shopping for boredom.

There is one superb monologue in the movie, by Drew Barrymore, who complains that she is driven crazy by the way guys always seem to be communicating in another medium. She calls at home but he doesn't pick up. She calls on his cell, and he e-mails her. She texts him. He Twitters back and leaves coded hints on MySpace. She tries snail mail. He apparently never learned how to open one. She yearns for the days when people had one telephone and one answering machine, and a guy had either definitely called you, or he had not.

This is a very far from perfect movie, and it ends on an unsatisfactory note. Stop reading *now* because I am going to complain that most of the stories have happy endings. Not in the real world, they don't. In the real world, the happy endings come only with a guy who's really into you. I should write a self-help book: *If Some Guy Says He Loves You, Check It Out.*

Hidden Love ★ ★

NO MPAA RATING, 95 m., 2010

Isabelle Huppert (Danielle), Greta Scacchi (Dr. Nielsen), Melanie Laurent (Sophie), Olivier Gourmet (Nielsen's husband). Directed by Alessandro Capone and produced by Massimo Cristaldi and Mark Hammond. Screenplay by Capone and Luca D'Alisera, based on the novel *Madre e Ossa* by Danielle Girard.

Hidden Love is a movie that knows exactly who it is about but doesn't know what it thinks of them. That leaves us four clearly seen characters and a story wandering in the murk of despair. Its principal casualty is Isabelle Huppert, who creates a flawless performance to no particular effect. She gives director Alessandro Capone what few actresses would be capable of, and he leaves her hanging.

Huppert plays Danielle, a woman who has been institutionalized after three suicide attempts. We meet her in therapy sessions with Dr. Nielsen (Greta Scacchi, focusing her attention with growing empathy). As Danielle speaks, it begins to appear she's in the twenty-third year of postpartum depression. All she wants to talk about is the indifference she felt toward her daughter, Sophie (Melanie Laurent), at the moment of giving birth and ever since.

Danielle looks ragged and depressed, makes obsessive hand movements, goes long periods without speaking, stares into space, and assures the psychiatrist that Sophie cannot be believed. Sophie, on the other hand, says her mother is playacting and is a selfish narcissist. What we see of Sophie suggests she is a loving mother to her own little girl. There's a scene where Sophie seems grateful to her mother while being taken to an abortion clinic but angry afterward. So eventually having her daughter was a form of revenge for Sophie, or what?

That and other events in the film go unexplained, or are seen in more than one version, and at the end all we can be sure of is that Danielle is depressed for reasons we can choose from cafeteria-style. The relationship between Dr. Nielsen and her husband (Olivier Gourmet) is, in contrast, briefly but well portrayed, especially during a scene where she confesses her despair over the case.

Isabelle Huppert makes one good film after another, most recently *Home* and *White Material.* She is fearless. Directors often depend on her gift for conveying depression, compulsion, egotism, and despair. She can be funny and charming, but then so can a lot of actors. She is in complete command of a face that regards the void with blankness. She gives her director a valuable asset. He doesn't know how to spend it.

So remorseless is this film that the ending comes like a slap in the face. Presumably it's the original ending, but it feels like nothing so much as one of those upbeat emergency rewrites slapped onto a Hollywood drama a mogul thought was too depressing. The happy nature of this ending is one of the most depressing elements of the film.

Hideaway ★ ★ ★

NO MPAA RATING, 105 m., 2010

Isabelle Carre (Mousse), Louis-Ronan Choisy (Paul), Pierre Louis-Calixte (Serge), Melvil Poupaud (Louis). Directed by Francois Ozon and produced by Chris Bolzli and Claudie Ossard. Screenplay by Ozon and Mathieu Hippeau.

The actress Isabelle Carre was pregnant during the filming of *Hideaway*, and the pregnancy of her character supplies the center of the film. It figures in the plot, but also in the yearning emotions that take uncertain form. Two men are fascinated by her swelling womb, and so is she. It is this promise of new life that overwhelms all of the other elements, and there are a lot of them.

Carre plays Mousse, an enigmatic thirtyish woman, girlish and yet sometimes with tired eyes, who as the film opens is in a room with her lover, Louis (Melvil Poupaud). Their drug dealer arrives and asks, "Is she all right?" Louis: "Now that you're here, she will be." Louis injects them both with heroin, and the next morning, rising early, he gives himself another shot, which is fatal. Mousse discovers he left her pregnant.

There are extraordinary scenes on the day of the funeral, involving Louis's pragmatic mother and his gay brother, Paul (Louis-Ronan Choisy). The family would prefer she not keep the baby. She agrees, then disappears to her "refuge," a lovely chateau overlooking a pastoral sweep of French countryside. There Paul arrives to visit, finding her off drugs and very pregnant. He stays for a time, and indeed connects quickly with Serge (Pierre Louis-Calixte), the young caretaker of the estate.

We have only fragmented information about Mousse's earlier life. Much can be guessed when she tells Paul that the chateau has been loaned to her by a man she slept with when she was sixteen: "He thinks he's my father." Whatever the real story is, that information helps explain her dispassionate approach to life. She's not cold, she's not hostile, but she has been wounded and is emotionally guarded. The camera spends a lot of time on her face, which is pleasant but not forthcoming.

She understands that Paul is gay. No big deal. Romantic formulas suggest Paul and Mousse stay together anyway, but this movie signals that it follows no formulas. Its romanticism is carefully buried, although there are two dream sequences suggesting the ability of a character to imagine ideal outcomes. Meanwhile, life goes on in a casual summertime way, with tea and coffee on the veranda, a trip to a disco in town, desultory conversation, landscape vistas, an idyll financed by the absent man who thinks he's her dad.

The film is by Francois Ozon, who is drawn to parents in awkward forms of love. His suspenseful *See the Sea* (1997) was about a mother staying at the seaside with a baby daughter, and how a woman traveler enters their lives; his strange *Ricky* (2009) was about a couple coping when their baby grows wings. *Hideaway* is deliberately more mundane, settled: It is about a situation that Mousse apparently accepts calmly.

There's an isolated scene. A man in a café boldly asks her to sleep with him. "You like pregnant women?" she asks. "Yes. Except for my wife. I couldn't sleep with her for nine months." There's another movie there. How this scene plays out has something to do with the rest of the film, and of that particular quiet urgency that many men feel about pregnant women. It's a heightened attention, and may be the product of evolution. For a time in her life, a woman's pregnancy is the most important thing about her. That is the subject of *Hideaway.*

Holy Rollers ★ ★

R, 80 m., 2010

Jesse Eisenberg (Sam Gold), Justin Bartha (Yosef), Ari Graynor (Rachel), Danny A. Abeckaser (Jackie), Q-Tip (Ephraim), Mark Ivanir (Mendel Gold), Elizabeth Marvel (Elka Gold). Directed by Kevin Asch and produced by Danny A. Abeckaser, Jen Gatien, Per Melita, and Tory Tunnell. Screenplay by Antonio Macia.

One function of any traditional religious costume is to enforce the wearer's separation from the greater community. Those male Hasidic Jews who choose to dress in black and wear distinctive hats never seem to be anything else than Hasidic Jews. When they dress in the morning, they're making a decision to set themselves apart. This is not required in Jewish law, but is a sign of their devotion.

Apart from the hats, the side curls, and their religious beliefs, Hasidim are, well, a lot like everybody else. Sam Gold (Jesse Eisenberg) is a kid about twenty who is devout, naive, shy around women, loves his mom, respects his dad, and plans to go into the family business. Then his best friend's brother takes advantage of those qualities—and very specifically his dress style—to trick him into being a drug courier.

Holy Rollers is said to be based on a true story, circa 1990, of how Hasidic Jews from Brooklyn Heights were used to smuggle millions of Ecstasy pills from Amsterdam to New York. They weren't stopped by customs because they were so far from the profile of drug runners. In the movie, Sam is frustrated in his plans to build his father's business and accepts $1,000 from the brother to fly to Amsterdam and return with some "medicine."

Come on, you're thinking: How innocent

can this kid possibly be? You should see him tongue-tied, sitting at the other end of a sofa from the girl he hopes to marry. Or even in Amsterdam, trying to avoid any body contact with women in a disco. Yes, the first trip he really does think the pills are medicine, and doesn't ask himself how what he's doing could possibly be legal.

He's a sweet kid as played by Eisenberg, who specializes in that line of work. The brother, Yosef (Justin Bartha), is persuasive, smooth, and hard to refuse. In Amsterdam, Sam meets a man named Jackie (Danny A. Abeckaser) and his girlfriend, Rachel (Ari Graynor), and is brought into their world of late-night clubs and loose living. On his second trip, things click into place, and he begins to put his good business sense to work.

It's that click that throws the movie off. Sam is moral and law-abiding, then changes seemingly overnight into a canny player in the drug trade. Before long he's instructing new Hasidim recruits on how to get past customs: "Act normal and look Jewish." It becomes apparent to his father and indeed his community what he's up to, but he's making good money and it seems so easy. For a long time he never even experiences Ecstasy.

The story may sound sensational, and you're possibly picturing traditional crime scenes: shoot-outs, chases, that sort of thing. But *Holy Rollers* is surprisingly matter-of-fact. Nobody gets shot, nobody gets chased, and Sam's anguish is internal.

The film's failure is to get from A to B. We buy both good Sam and bad Sam, but we don't see him making the transition. The film expects us to assume too much. Eisenberg is convincing as an essentially nice person who sounds confident but turns into a kid again when things start going wrong. But Kevin Asch, the director, keeps his distance from too many scenes; there's no particular suspense involved in getting past customs, for example. The movie relates to its story as Sam relates to women: look, talk, but don't get too close.

Home ★ ★ ★ ½

NO MPAA RATING, 98 m., 2010

Isabelle Huppert (Marthe), Olivier Gourmet (Michel), Adelaide Leroux (Judith), Madeleine Budd (Marion), Kacey Mottet Klein (Julien). Directed by Ursula Meier and produced by Denis Delcammpe, Denis Freyd, Thierry Spicher, and Elena Tatti. Screenplay by Meier, Antoine Jaccoud, Raphaelle Valbrune, Gilles Taurand, and Olivier Lorelle.

There are two questions never answered in *Home*. How did this family come to live here? And why does the mother fiercely refuse to leave, even after a four-lane freeway opens in her front yard? Both are more satisfactory remaining as questions. In any event, as the film opens, they live in a comfortable small home in the middle of vast fields and next to the highway, which hasn't been used for ten years. So much is the road their turf that the story begins with them playing a family game of street hockey on its pavement.

Then big trucks arrive to lay down a fresh coating of asphalt, and steel guardrails are installed on each side and down the middle. Workmen wordlessly clear the highway of their hockey sticks, inflatable swimming pool, satellite dish, charcoal grill, and so on. On the radio, they hear breathless coverage of the road's grand opening, and eventually the first car speeds past their house.

The family seems ordinary enough, if not quite conventional. The parents snuggle, the small boy plays, the sister in her early twenties sunbathes and smokes in the front yard, the teenage daughter wears mostly black and sulks. Michel, the father (Olivier Gourmet), goes off to work every morning in the green Volvo station wagon. Marthe, the mother (Isabelle Huppert), does the laundry ("today is whites day"). There's horseplay in the bathtub, which the family seems to share rather freely.

The opening of the highway wasn't a surprise for them. Maybe they got the house cheap because it was coming. The heavy, unceasing traffic is a big problem. The two younger kids always ran across the bare pavement to cut through a field for school. Dad parked on the other side. Now even getting to the house is a problem. Marion, the smart younger sister (Madeleine Budd) is concerned about CO_2 poisoning. Young Julien (Kacey Mottet Klein) can't safely get to his pals. Judith (Adelaide Leroux) continues to sunbathe in the front yard and gives the finger to honking truck drivers.

Something will have to give, and it does, as the movie grows more and more dark. It's the skill of Ursula Meier, the director and cowriter, to bring us to those fraught passages by rational stages. What happens would not make sense in many households, but in this one it represents a certain continuity, and confirms deep currents we sensed almost from the first.

Do you remember Olivier Gourmet from his performance in the Dardenne brothers' movie *The Son* (2003)? Balding, middle-aged, nimble, and quick. Many secrets. Troubled. Isabelle Huppert you know since forever, usually looking fundamentally the same, always assuming a new character from the inside out. Intriguing us. There's thought in that face, but it's inscrutable. They work with the young actors here to face what it means when a home is not a house.

The Horse Boy ★ ★ ★

NO MPAA RATING, 94 m., 2009

Featuring Rupert Isaacson, Kristin Neff, Rowan Isaacson, Simon Baron-Cohen, Temple Grandin, Roy Richard Grinker, Tulga, and Ghoste. A documentary directed by Michel O. Scott.

The Horse Boy tells a remarkable story. A four-year-old Texas boy with autism has angry seizures, isn't potty-trained, is often distant and hostile. His parents fly with him to Mongolia, drive nine hours into the steppes, and then journey by horseback, with the boy sharing their saddles, to a sacred mountain in reindeer country. There he undergoes a miraculous cure at the hands of shamans.

I have many inclinations, but no reason, to doubt this. At the end of the treatment, the shamans tell the parents that on the next day their boy will stop soiling his pants and throwing tantrums. This happens. Today, back home, little Rowan is now six and for the first time plays with friends his own age.

"Is he cured? No," says Rupert Isaacson, his father. "Is he still autistic? Yes." What happened "seems miraculous," but he is skeptical enough to wonder if the trip itself was part of the cure. Rowan has a strong empathy with animals, especially with horses, but also, we see, with goats—who are docile and affectionate with him. Perhaps the enormity of a long horseback journey with his parents in clearly daunting conditions overwhelmed his defenses and calmed him.

There seems no reason to question that he has improved. In the footage taken after the healing, we never see Rowan except when he is happily playing with his new friends or smiling with his parents. Is that the whole story? You decide. To their credit, Isaacson and his wife, Kristin Neff, a University of Texas psychology professor, do not recommend that parents of other autistic children take them to the wilds of Siberia. All they know is what happened to Rowan.

With any documentary, there is another story that goes unreported: the story of the making of the film. *The Horse Boy* didn't make itself. The parents and their son were accompanied to Siberia by the director/cinematographer Michel Orion Scott, apparently a second cameraman, and sound technicians and a support staff. This cost money, up-front on the bottom line. Airfares, food, lodging, not least insurance for everyone and a completion bond for the film itself.

You may know that the book of the experience, *The Horse Boy,* became a best-seller. The trip and the film were financed by a million-dollar advance on the book Isaacson proposed to write about this experience. He's the author of a successful previous book, *The Healing Land: The Bushmen and the Kalahari Desert,* which includes shamans on another continent. He had heard that the shamans of Mongolia, especially one legendary shaman, had unusual powers.

The stakes are high in such a venture. What if the trip turns into a fool's errand? What if Rowan becomes worse, not better? It was obviously crucial that Rowan undergo some kind of dramatic improvement or there would be no film. It's well to keep that in mind.

The whole enterprise seems to be Isaacson's project. He narrates the film. The wife, Kristin, seems fully in accord with him, and they're both courageous, but I would have liked more insights from the side of her that teaches psychology. I imagine many parents of autistic children, while identifying with the strains autism places upon their marriage, would appreciate more information about his exact state at present.

The film includes expert testimony from autism experts, including the famous Temple Grandin, an autistic professor at Colorado State, who has designed most of the environments used to handle cattle in the worldwide meatpacking industry. Her genius was to be able to identify with the point of view of the cattle.

I've met her. A remarkable woman. She talks in the film about autism in general. The newspaperman in me would have asked her: "Do you feel autistics feel a special empathy and calm with animals? Could the horseback journey itself have brought about some of the improvement?"

Hotel for Dogs ★ ★ ½

PG, 100 m., 2009

Emma Roberts (Andi), Jake T. Austin (Bruce), Kyla Pratt (Heather), Lisa Kudrow (Lois), Kevin Dillon (Carl), Don Cheadle (Bernie), Johnny Simmons (Dave), Troy Gentile (Mark). Directed by Thor Freudenthal and produced by Lauren Shuler Donner, Jonathan Gordon, Ewan Leslie, and Jason Clark. Screenplay by Leslie, Jeff Lowell, Bob Schooley, and Mark McCorkle, based on the book by Lois Duncan.

Hotel for Dogs is a sweet, innocent family movie about stray dogs that seem as well trained as Olympic champions. Friday, the Jack Russell terrier who's the leader of the pack, does more acting than most of the humans and doesn't even get billing. I know, because I searched for one, hoping to mention him by name and call him a good doggie.

What can Friday do? Let himself up and down from a fire escape landing, using a pulley-and-counterweight system. Find his masters anywhere in the city. Steal hot dogs and possibly a whole gyros wheel. Get out of his collar and back in again. Outrace dogs five times his size in a sprint down city streets. And join dozens of other dogs in mastering these abilities: feeding himself, using a doggie fire hydrant, sitting on a toilet, running on a treadmill, activating a bone-throwing mechanism. I'm only scratching the surface.

Friday belongs to Andi (Emma Roberts) and Bruce (Jake T. Austin), a brother and sister in foster care. He is kept a secret from their foster parents, two obnoxious would-be rock musicians (Lisa Kudrow and Kevin Dillon). The kids saved him from the streets, and he has been their secret pal through three years and five foster homes. One day he leads them into an abandoned downtown hotel occupied by two dogs he makes friends with, and soon the kids find themselves running an unofficial animal shelter.

In this they're assisted by Dave (Johnny Simmons) and Heather (Kyla Pratt), two Nickelodeon-cute employees at a pet shop, which they can apparently abandon on a moment's notice to use the store's van on rescue missions. Since they can't possibly care for all those dogs, little Bruce rigs up Rube Goldberg devices to automate the tasks. There's even an automatic door knocker to send the dogs into frenzies of barking and jumping. Good exercise, although sooner or later these dogs will get wise to it.

Don Cheadle plays the dedicated social worker in charge of the kids, who bails them out when they get in trouble with cops and meany attendants at the animal pound. He even has a big speech on the Dog Hotel steps, during which I did my best not to think of *Hotel Rwanda*. What I thought instead was, Marley could learn a lot from these dogs.

Hot Tub Time Machine ★ ★ ★

R, 100 m., 2010

John Cusack (Adam), Rob Corddry (Lou), Craig Robinson (Nick), Clark Duke (Jacob), Crispin Glover (Phil), Lizzy Caplan (April), Chevy Chase (Repairman). Directed by Steve Pink and produced by John Cusack, Grace Loh, Matt Moore, and John Morris. Screenplay by Morris, Josh Heald, and Sean Anders.

Hot Tub Time Machine may sound almost by definition like a bad comedy. I mean, how good can a movie named *Hot Tub Time Machine* possibly be? Yes? That's not what I thought. I saw the stand-up display in a movie lobby and perked up. With a title like that, the filmmakers aren't lacking in confidence. There was also the item of John Cusack in the lead. As a general rule, he isn't found in bad films.

I wasn't disappointed. This is a step or two

below *The Hangover,* but occupying similar turf. It's another guy picture, which is like a buddy picture except usually without cops. The guys bond, they seek to relive their misspent youth, there are women and even wives around but they're strictly in supporting roles.

A forty-something party animal named Lou (Rob Corddry) gets drunk and passes out after he unwisely guns his car engine in time to the music while parked in his garage and listening to Mötley Crüe. This is interpreted as a suicide attempt by his best friends Adam (John Cusack) and Nick (Craig Robinson), and although he tells him they're mistaken, they're not so sure. They're worried about their friend. He's a full-bore, full-time alcoholic without a shred of maturity or caution. What this boy obviously requires is a return to the ski lodge where they all got blasted together in the 1980s. Over Lou's protests, they drag along Jacob (Clark Duke), Adam's nephew. Adam wants to keep him out of trouble (hollow laugh).

Today, this lodge is so shabby it looks not only like a poor excuse for a ski resort but even like a poor excuse for a movie set. That's part of the movie's charm. Did the Marx Brothers ever lavish money on sets? (Well, yes, but never mind.) The check-in routine is from Motel Hell, and the surly one-armed bellboy (Crispin Glover) kicks their luggage around, dumps it on the floor, and sticks out his remaining hand for a tip.

They get the same big room they had before. It's gone downhill. The hot tub seems to harbor growth from the Planet of Mold. But there's a cheerful repairman (Chevy Chase), who plays the role that George Burns used to play when you needed a guy who just looked like he knew the secrets of the universe. Chevy fixes the tub and it starts to bubble with an inner glow, like beer on the simmer. The guys jump in and are magically transported back in time to their youth in the 1980s. Jacob hadn't been born then, but never mind; it's their present selves who are transported.

This then becomes the premise for a comedy contriving more or less every possible problem and paradox, of which the high point is possibly Nick's boozy phone call to his wife, who at the time is still in grade school. A pretty girl named April (Lizzy Caplan) catches Adam's eye, although strict logic suggests they have little future together. And Corddry essentially steals the movie as Lou.

Remember how Corddry was always so earnest and sincere when assuring Jon Stewart of outrageous facts on *The Daily Show*? He brings the same focus to getting drunk. Comedy is a delicate art, with nothing so important as the performer never seeming to believe anything he does is funny. Corddry here achieves a level of comic confidence that seems almost uncanny; Cusack, as coproducer, and Steve Pink, the director (who wrote Cusack's *High Fidelity* and *Grosse Point Blank*), must have intuited this gift and been willing to give him free rein.

I can't be sure, but I think the density of the f-word reaches the saturation point in *Hot Tub Time Machine.* I may have heard it employed as three different parts of speech in the same sentence. One wonders if American spoken English could survive without it. What did we say in the old days? It must have been a quiet land.

The bottom line is, gross-out guy comedies open twice a month, and many of them are wretched excesses. *Hot Tub Time Machine,* which wants nothing more than to be a screwball farce, succeeds beyond any expectations suggested by the title, and extends John Cusack's remarkable run: Since 1983, in fifty-five films, he's never made a bad one. Well, I never saw *Grandview, USA.*

The Housemaid ★ ★ ★

NO MPAA RATING, 106 m., 2010

Jeon Do-yeon (Eun-yi, the maid), Lee Jung-jae (Hoon, the husband), Ahn Seo-hyeon (Nami, the daughter), Seo Woo (Hae-ra, the wife), Park Ji-young (Mother-in-law), Yun Yeo-jong (Miss Cho). Directed and written by Im Sang-soo, based on the 1960 film directed by Kim Ki-young.

The Housemaid takes place almost entirely within the enormous modern house of a very rich man, and centers on the young woman he has hired as a maid. It involves primarily the man, his wife, his daughter, the older woman who runs his household, and his mother-in-law. Within this closed system the husband exercises his will, buying his power because of money and the enabling of the women, who are all subservient.

That something disturbing will happen is a given. Hoon (Lee Jung-jae) is a man who expects all of his wishes to be met without question, and in his hermetic household the introduction of the maid Eun-yi (Jeon Doyeon) creates an imbalance. His wife, Hae-ra (Seo Woo), is content to live in expensive idleness, paging through magazines describing the world of consumer goods she inhabits. She is pregnant with twins, and her focus is on these two latest acquisitions of her marriage. The older servant, Miss Cho (Yun Yeo-jong), hates the family, but is mercilessly efficient in her service. The wife's mother (Park Ji-young) is pleased her daughter married well and wants her to continue to be well married.

Eun-yi is efficient, submissive, and very attractive. We learn little about her except that she needs the job. She is in awe of the man, who comes home from his job as a Master of the Universe and plays flawless classical piano while drinking rare vintages. His wife drifts through in couture designs. The daughter (Ahn Seohyeon) is a mystery, much loved and cared for, but not much needed. The maid and the daughter instinctively bond, because in this home they are the only two with affection to spend.

We know it's inevitable that the husband will attempt to seduce the maid. And it surely is a seduction and a coercion, even though the maid agrees and even seems to appreciate it. Sex is a bad bargain if only one party is free to set the terms. Miss Cho sees what is happening because she sees everything that happens. The mother-in-law also sees. Eventually, the housemaid's pregnancy is obvious.

It is not a problem for the others so long as it doesn't upset the financial equilibrium, in which the husband gets everything he pays for. His wife and her mother are like favored suppliers. The housemaid has opened up a new trading market with unfamiliar producers and negotiable prices. If you sell all the sugar, you don't want to hear about Sweet'n Low.

This story is told by the writer-director Im Sang-soo with cool, elegant cinematography and sinuous visual movements. The dominant mood is gothic, with the persistent sadomasochistic undertones that seem inescapable in so much Korean cinema. Why is that? The situation is obviously explosive, but we have no idea what will set it off.

The central questions are: Who has the most to lose? Who has the most to gain? Whose private agenda is not clearly perceived in the household? Will everyone put up with everything, as the husband expects? The film withholds even hints of the answers to these questions until the final grotesque series of shots, and then all of them are answered in one character's reaction in particular.

The House of the Devil ★ ★ ★

R, 93 m., 2009

Jocelin Donahue (Sam), Greta Gerwig (Megan), Mary Woronov (Mrs. Ulman), Tom Noonan (Mr. Ulman), A. J. Bowen (Victor), Danielle Noe (Mother), Dee Wallace (Landlady). Directed by Ti West and produced by Josh Braun, Larry Fessenden, Roger Kass, and Peter Phok. Screenplay by West.

Has there ever been a movie where a teenage babysitter enjoyed a pleasant evening? And a nondemonic child? Sam gets a break in *The House of the Devil.* She discovers there isn't a baby at all. Only the aged mother of Mr. Ulman, a sinister man played by Tom Noonan, who is my choice to portray The Judge in Cormac McCarthy's *Blood Meridian,* and if you have read that gruesome masterpiece, there is nothing more I need say about Mr. Ulman.

Sam (Jocelin Donahue) is a perky college student saving money for a deposit on her own apartment. She puts up signs around the campus offering her babysitting services, and Mr. Ulman takes one of them. In fact, he takes all of them.

Sam's friend Megan (Greta Gerwig) gives her a lift to the Ulman household, which they find way, way down at the end of a long, long road in the middle of a dark, dark forest. It looks like the House of the Seven Gables with three gables amputated. Mr. Ulman and his wife, Mrs. Ulman (Mary Woronov), greet Sam with hospitality laced with . . . commiseration. The house is furnished in a way to remind you of aged maiden aunts who haven't changed a thing since their parents died.

Mother Ulman is upstairs in her room, Mr. Ulman explains. He only told Sam there was a baby because some babysitters balk at the difficulties of old folks. But not to worry. Mr. Ulman more or less promises she'll be no more problem than Norman Bates's mom. Then the Ulmans depart because they want to observe the full eclipse of the moon and you can't even see the moon so deep in the dark, dark forest, you see.

Left alone on her own (Mother's upstairs in her room and doesn't make a sound), Sam pokes around. It's sort of creepy. Good thing she only snaps on the TV briefly; if *The Addams Family* came on, it might look familiar. And it might come on: This is the mid-1980s, when babysitters had more to fear from their employers than vice versa.

The House of the Devil has been made almost by hand by Ti West, who wrote, directed, and edited. He's an admirer of classic horror films and understands that if there's anything scarier than a haunted house, it's a *possibly* haunted house. The film may provide an introduction for some audience members to the Hitchcockian definition of suspense: It's the anticipation, not the happening, that's the fun.

This is the kind of movie that looks lighted by the full of the moon, which is a good trick during an eclipse. Sam is relieved when Mr. and Mrs. Ulman return, until they don't seem prepared to give her the traditional ride home. She also meets Mother (Danielle Noe), who is considerably more spry than advertised. And there's the family—handyman?—named Victor (A. J. Bowen). And Mother's room turns out to be far, far different than you might expect, and dark, dark.

House of the Sleeping Beauties ★

NO MPAA RATING, 99 m., 2009

Vadim Glowna (Edmond), Angela Winkler (Madame), Maximilian Schell (Kogi), Birol Unel (Mister Gold), Mona Glass (Secretary), Marina Weiss (Maid). Directed by Vadim Glowna and produced by Glowna and Raymond Tarabay. Screenplay by Glowna, based on the novella by Yasunari Kawabata.

House of the Sleeping Beauties has missed its ideal release window by about forty years. It might—*might*—have found an audience in that transitional period between soft- and hard-core, when men would sit through anything to see a breast, but even then, I dunno. It's discouraging to see a movie where the women sleep through everything. They don't even have the courtesy to wake up and claim to have a headache.

I know I am being disrespectful to what is obviously intended to be a morose meditation about youth, age, men, women, children, mothers, hookers, johns, life, death, and the endless possibilities I thought of at sixteen when I heard that song "Behind the Green Door." The movie has been inspired by a 1961 novella by Yasunari Kawabata, who explores the now-obsolete Japanese theory that a woman should be seen but not heard. Even then, they were supposed to wake up sometimes and speak submissively.

The film centers on five scenes in which Edmond, a dying man in his sixties (Vadim Glowna, the director), lies in bed next to sleeping nude women of about twenty, all breathtakingly beautiful, and utters a mournful interior soliloquy about his age, their perfection, his mother, a childhood sexual experience, and his own misery. This is an intensely depressing experience for Edmond and for us, intensified by his robotic smoking habit. Sometimes he shakes a woman or slaps her on her butt, but if anything is going to wake her up, his breath will.

Surrounding these scenes is a plot more intriguing than they deserve, involving Edmond's old friend Kogi (Maximilian Schell), who advised him to visit the brothel in the first place. Kogi is concerned that Edmond is depressed by the death of his wife and young daughter in an auto accident. This happened fifteen years ago. I think the human ability to heal ourselves is such that, after fifteen years, you can expect to be sad and deeply regretful, but if you are still clinically depressed, you need medical attention.

It is also a wonder that this shambling sad sack and secret drinker is still apparently the head of a big corporation and has a full-time driver for his stretch BMW. Here is one tycoon who could definitely not be played by Michael Douglas. We've seen ultrarich Masters of the Universe before, but now we get the first Masturbator of the Universe.

The brothel is a one-bedroom operation supervised by Madame (Angela Winkler), a handsome woman of a certain age, who explains that the women have been "prepared" to sleep the whole night through, and the man is invited to sleep next to them (sleeping pills provided) and feast his eyes, or perhaps caress, but no funny business like sticking his finger in her mouth. Since Madame goes away all night, there's no telling what could happen to these helpless women, of course.

Do you find this premise anything but repugnant? It offends not only civilized members of both sexes, but even dirty old men, dramatizing as it does their dirtiness and oldness. Obvious questions arise, but, no, Madame will not explain why the women sleep so soundly, and the house rules strictly forbid any contact with the women outside the house. How does she find the women? Who are they? Why do they seem to sleep peacefully instead of as if they are drugged? How do they keep their hair and makeup impeccable? Why don't they snore?

Does Edmond get up to nastiness? There is a close-up of his tumescence, which looks younger and healthier than the rest of him, but no explicit sex. It hardly matters; the film is intended as allegory, although I am unsure what the allegory teaches us. Perhaps the message is: "You see what can happen to you if you direct and star yourself in a movie like this."

How Do You Know ★ ★

PG-13, 116 m., 2010

Reese Witherspoon (Lisa), Owen Wilson (Matty), Paul Rudd (George), Jack Nicholson (Charles). Directed by James L. Brooks and produced by Brooks, Julie Ansell, Laurence Mark, and Paula Weinstein. Screenplay by Brooks.

The one thing we don't see Reese Witherspoon doing in *How Do You Know* is playing softball. Considering that she portrays a softball player, this seems strange. To be sure, she's dropped from the team roster early in *How Do You Know*, so that's a reason. But there's something so deeply Witherspoonish about the idea of Reese stealing second that I am unconsoled.

It's established that she's a very good softball player indeed. Her teammates love her, her play is superb, she's a great role model, and her only problem is she's almost thirty. This is apparently past retirement age for women softball players. It's time for her to round third and collect a gold watch.

No sooner does she get some free time on her hands than two would-be lovers complicate her life. Matty (Owen Wilson) is a pro baseball pitcher with a multimillion-dollar contract, and George (Paul Rudd) is a big-time financial wheeler-dealer who works for the firm controlled by his father, Charles (Jack Nicholson). George is the nicer man. Matty is a two-timing, womanizing narcissist. But it looks as if George will be indicted and spend time in prison, and Lisa (Witherspoon) moves into Matty's penthouse, which is large enough for batting practice.

Lisa has sex with Matty and presumably with George, but it's that romcom kind of sex that remains, for an outsider, largely conceptual. Intimate personal behavior doesn't much enter in because all of the characters are limited to sitcom problems. Matty's troubles are shallowness and sex addiction. George is a nice man, ethical, who faces indictment on a technicality. In theory, he should have known every detail about the financial malfeasance of his father's company. It doesn't always work out that way.

I expected this movie to be better. The writer-director is James L. Brooks, and this is the fourth time he's worked with Jack Nicholson (including *Terms of Endearment* and *As Good as It Gets*, for both of which he won acting Oscars). So let's start with Nicholson. Brooks hasn't given him much to work with. He plays a conniving tycoon who doesn't deserve his son's loyalty. It's a heavy role, and there's little to lighten it. In his best roles Jack always seems to be getting away with something. He is here, too, but it's not funny. We like to identify with his onscreen sins, and this is a rare time when Nicholson is simply a creep.

The best-written and funniest role in the film is for Owen Wilson, as the pro pitcher. You know how his characters can have that ingratiating niceness, that solicitude for you while they're serving themselves? Here he plays a man tone-deaf to the feelings of women and clueless about his own behavior. But he's so nice about it that Lisa agrees to move in, and that provides an opening for what every actress should master, the scene where she repacks her bags and marches out.

Rudd's George is very likable. This is the wrong time for him to fall in love. His world is collapsing, and he finds himself in a cheap rented apartment surrounded by packing boxes. He has nothing to offer Lisa, and not enough trust in himself or her to realize she loves him, the big dummy.

All of this whizzes along a few feet off the ground, like most romcoms. Reese Witherspoon is always immensely cuddly, but it's not Lisa's heart that's involved here; it's her story line. Nothing heats up. The movie doesn't lead us; it simply stays in step. Jack Nicholson is one of the few actors who always inspires a quiet chuckle of anticipation when he first appears in a movie. This is a rare movie that doesn't give him a chance to deserve it.

Howl ★ ★ ★

NO MPAA RATING, 84 m., 2010

James Franco (Allen Ginsberg), David Strathairn (Ralph McIntosh), Jon Hamm (Jake Ehrlich), Bob Balaban (Judge Clayton Horn), Alessandro Nivola (Luther Nichols), Treat Williams (Mark Schorer), Mary-Louise Parker (Gail Potter), Jeff Daniels (Professor David Kirk), Todd Rotondi (Jack Kerouac), Jon Prescott (Neal Cassady), Aaron Tveit (Peter Orlovsky). Directed by Rob Epstein and Jeffrey Friedman and produced by Epstein, Friedman, Elizabeth Redleaf, and Christine K. Walker. Screenplay by Epstein and Friedman.

A few days after Allen Ginsberg died in 1997 there was a candlelight memorial service in a coffeehouse in Boulder, Colorado, just down Pearl Street from the Beat Bookshop. Ginsberg was familiar in Boulder as founder of the wonderfully named Jack Kerouac School of Disembodied Poetics at Naropa University. Poets read their work and his, listeners sat on chairs or on the floor, and for that time the beatnik era lived again.

The Beats created poetry, fiction, art, and music, but most of all they created the legend of themselves—"angelheaded hipsters burning for the ancient heavenly connection to the starry dynamo in the machinery of night." After rock 'n' roll they were the first decisive break with the orderly postwar years, and following them were the hippies, Woodstock, flower power, the Me Generation, and adults wearing Levis to the office. For anyone young in the late 1950s—a kid at Urbana High School, for example—to read the opening words of Ginsberg's "Howl" was to know, YES! that they described you: "I saw the best minds of my generation destroyed by madness, starving hysterical naked, dragging themselves through the negro streets at dawn."

Yes. Not that one was, but that one wanted to think of oneself in such terms. You wanted to steal the family car and drive all night and into the burning sun, driven by caffeine, and drive without stopping directly to City Lights bookstore in San Francisco, and have Lawrence Ferlinghetti publish *your* poems, which you would have scribbled on legal pads on the seat next to you as you drove.

The new film *Howl* evokes the first tender birth of that new age. Its Beats still wear jackets and ties. Allen Ginsberg has horn-rim glasses and seems touchingly young, and not at all an angelheaded hipster destroyed by madness. The secret was: He wanted to be one, too. And as the film gently reveals, he was reluctant to have his great early poem published because he wasn't eager to have his daddy find out things about him, such as that he was homosexual.

In years to come Allen Ginsberg would play the role of public poet as Robert Frost had for an earlier and much different generation. He was out when other brave souls were still only opening the closet door and waving. At a National Student Congress I saw him sit cross-legged on a rug and use finger cymbals and chant whatever it was he was chanting, because the act and not perhaps the words seemed to be the point.

What feels right about *Howl* is that it is set before those days, before the beard and the mysticism and Tibet, the public persona and the levitating of the Pentagon. The bold, outspoken man of later days is seen here as still a middle-class youth, uncertain of his gayness, filled with the heady joy of early poetic success, learning how to be himself.

The film is above all about "Howl" the poem. Ginsberg, played by James Franco with restraint and care, reads it as smoke fills a 1955 coffeehouse. There is a re-creation of an early Ginsberg documentary interview. We see scenes from the poem's trial for obscenity, with David Strathairn for the prosecution and Jon Hamm for the defense. (As ludicrous as some of the testimony is, it must be noted it's word for word from the transcript.) There is an uncertain attempt to animate some passages from "Howl," based on the miscalculation that the poem's striking imagery needs visuals, not words, to be realized.

And then there are straightforward biographical scenes involving Ginsberg's friendships with such Beats as Jack Kerouac and Neal Cassady, the charismatic legend who was the inspiration for the Dean Moriarty character in *On the Road*. It is during this time Ginsberg meets the man with whom he would spend the rest of his life, Peter Orlovsky. All of the biographical material is wisely done without the benefit of hindsight: It's possible to forget that "Howl," now a standard, was illegal to sell for a time, and that Ginsberg's own sexuality was against the law in many states. It took some courage to be Allen Ginsberg.

One of the qualities I like about this film is that the writer-directors, Rob Epstein and Jeffrey Friedman, are aware of the time when Beat was new. The coffeehouse reading could be archival footage. The re-created obscenity trial preserves the prim academic standards of the day (even in the 1960s, someone like Auden was not quite acknowledged as gay). The animation could be from an overheated student film. And the Orlovsky scenes focus more on idealized romance. Ginsberg also had a crush on Kerouac, who is seen here in much the same macho way as the early Brando and Newman: a hunk—but perfectly straight, of course.

How to Live Forever ★ ★ ★

NO MPAA RATING, 94 m., 2011

Ray Bradbury, Phyllis Diller, Aubrey de Grey, Pico Iyer, Ray Kurzweil, Jack LaLanne, Buster Martin, John Robbins, Suzanne Somers, and Marianne Williamson. A documentary directed and produced by Mark Wexler. Screenplay by Wexler and Robert DeMaio.

If someone could give you a pill that allowed you to live for five hundred years, would you take it? Not me. Although I'm not keen on dying this minute or this year, I consider death to be the completion of the journey I embarked on at my birth, and do not expect the circle to be unbroken. For one thing, what would I do with all my memories? For another, where would the planet put everybody?

How to Live Forever is a documentary by Mark Wexler about scientific, nutritional, lifestyle, and philosophical approaches to a long life. Humans could once expect to live until about 23, we learn, and there are now 100,000 Americans over the age of 100. The oldest person in this film was 127, and there is a 101-year-old British woman who is quicker and smarter than most of the talking heads on TV.

How do they do it? Good genes, to begin with. Then diet: The key is a satisfying volume of low-calorie foods. Then staying active and taking an interest in things. We meet the Disney animator Tyrus Wong, 98, who flies kites of amazing complexity and beauty on the beach at Santa Monica. And a 101-year-old auto maintenance man in London who runs marathons (he took five rest stops, he explains, for a pint of beer and a smoke). There is a Brit punk rock group whose members, all over 90, put on a good show of destroying their guitars. And a 91-year-old heart surgeon.

Wexler journeys to Okinawa, where heart disease, cancer, and high blood pressure are all but unknown, apparently because of a diet with no meat, limited fish, and large quantities of seaweed and other vegetables. The Okinawans also seem to walk everywhere and keep working; a fisherman in his eighties dives into the sea to place and check his nets.

Back home, Wexler makes the obligatory visit to a cryonics center that promises to thaw you out at some point in the future. I can't think of anything more horrifying. He also learns about laughter yoga, Jack LaLanne's personal regime (he lived until ninety-six), Suzanne Somers's daily intake of hormones, and how Phyllis Diller keeps right on working ("Old age is when your feet are mistaken for alligator shoes"). There is even a Japanese actor in his seventies who stars in "elder porn," a field that seems to contradict Diller's theory that the best contraceptive among the aged is nudity.

Wexler meets a Cambridge biochemist named Aubrey de Grey who believes, with other antiaging experts, that we are approaching a medical "treatment" for aging. Given the undisputed fact that millions of humans live in conditions of starvation, drought, and disease, this strikes me as a mixed blessing. However, I know Wexler's father, the great cinematographer Haskell, and he is ferociously alive at eighty-seven. What keeps him going seems to be diet, exercise, work, and radical outrage. It's worth a try.

How to Train Your Dragon ★ ★ ★

PG, 98 m., 2010

Jay Baruchel (Hiccup), Gerard Butler (Stoick), Craig Ferguson (Gobber), America Ferrara (Astrid), Jonah Hill (Snotlout), Christopher Mintz-Plasse (Fishlegs), Kristen Wiig (Ruffnut), T. J. Miller (Tuffnut). Directed by Chris Sanders and Dean DeBlois and produced by Bonnie Arnold. Screenplay by Sanders and DeBlois, based on the book by Cressida Cowell.

Some movies seem born to inspire video games. All they lack is controllers and a scoring system. *How to Train Your Dragon* plays more like a game born to inspire a movie. It devotes a great deal of time to aerial battles between tamed dragons and evil ones, and not much to character or story development. But it's bright, good-looking, and has high energy. Kids above the easily scared age will probably like the movie the younger they are.

This is another action animation with an improbable young hero. Remember when the heroes in this genre were teenagers? Now it's usually some kid who is ten at the most, revealing himself as stronger, wiser, and braver than older people, and a quick learner when it comes to discovering or mastering a new form of warfare. We are born knowing how to command dragons and spaceships, and we forget as up we grow.

Our hero is Hiccup Horrendous Haddock III (voice by Jay Baruchel), a young Viking who lives in Berk, a mountainside village surrounded by the crags and aeries of hostile dragons. Hiccup tells us that his village is very old, but all of the houses are new. An alarming omen. Led by his father, Stoick (Gerard Butler), and the dragon master, Gobber (Craig Ferguson), the villagers have been in combat with the dragons since time immemorial. It would seem to be an unequal struggle; the dragons are enormous and breathe fire, and the Vikings, while muscular, have only clubs, swords, and spears. They may, however, be smarter than the dragons, although you wouldn't know that just by listening to them.

Butler seems to be channeling his character from *300*, beefed up by many a hearty Viking feast. He joins Ferguson and others in muscular Scottish accents, since as we all know, that dialect of English was widely used among the Vikings. In appearance, the Vikings seem victims of a testosterone outbreak causing enormous sprouty growths of hair. Even the hair from their nostrils might knit up into a nice little sock. Oh, how I tried not to, but as I watched these brawlers saddled up on great flying lizards, I kept thinking, "*Asterix* meets *Avatar*."

The plot: Little Hiccup is ordered to stay inside during a dragon attack. But the plucky lad seizes a cannon, blasts away at the enemy, and apparently wings one. Venturing into the forest to track his prey, he finds a wounded little dragon about his age, already chained up. He releases it, they bond, and he discovers that dragons can be perfectly nice. With his new friend, Toothless, he returns to the village, and an alliance is formed with good dragons against the bad dragons, who are snarly holdouts and grotesquely ugly.

One evil beast is covered all over with giant warlike knobs, and has six eyes, three on either side, like a classic Buick. In one scene, a Viking hammers on an eyeball with his club. Not very appetizing. The battle ends as all battles must, with the bad guys routed and the youngest hero saving the day. The aerial battle scenes are storyboarded like a World War I dogfight, with swoops, climbs, and narrowly missed collisions with craggy peaks and other dragons. For my taste, these continued way too long, but then I must teach myself that I do not have a six-year-old's taste.

Note: The movie is in both 3-D and 2-D. The 3-D adds nothing but the opportunity to pay more in order to see a distracting and unnecessary additional dimension. Paramount has threatened theaters that if they don't clear screens for Dragon *despite the current glut of 3-D films, the studio won't let them show it in 2-D. This displays real confidence in 3-D.*

Hugh Hefner: Playboy, Activist, and Rebel ★ ★ ★

R, 124 m., 2010

Hugh M. Hefner, Joan Baez, Tony Bennett, Pat Boone, Jim Brown, Susan Brownmiller, James Caan, Dick Cavett, Robert Culp, Tony Curtis, Dick Gregory, Jesse Jackson, Bill Maher, Jenny McCarthy, Mary O'Connor, Pete Seeger, Gene Simmons, David Steinberg, Shannon Tweed, Mike Wallace, and Ruth Westheimer. A documentary directed by Brigitte Berman and produced by Berman, Peter Raymont, and Victor Solnicki.

From the moment that Hal Homes and I slipped quietly into his basement and he showed me his father's hidden collection of *Playboy* magazines, the map of my emotional geography shifted toward Chicago. In that magical city lived a man named Hugh Hefner who had Playmates possessing wondrous bits and pieces I had never seen before. I wanted to be invited to his house.

I was trembling on the brim of puberty, and aroused not so much by the rather sedate color "centerfold" of an undressed woman, as by the black-and-white photos that accompanied them. These showed an ordinary woman (I believe it was Janet Pilgrim) entering an office building in Chicago, and being made up for her "pictorial." Made up! Two makeup artists were shown applying powders and creams to her flesh. This electrified me. It made Pilgrim a real person. In an interview she spoke of her life and ambitions.

The photographs that burned into my mind did not reveal any of Miss Pilgrim's wondrous bits. I sensed even then that bits were not what it was about. All depended on context. Miss Pilgrim would disrobe and have her body made up by two other women for her pictorial, and then . . . turning the page . . . and then she would put on a dressing gown and enter a photo studio and meet a serious and respectable-looking photographer . . . and then . . . she would drop the gown to the floor and then . . . I turned the page . . . she would pose for the centerfold.

It was the process that entranced me. I'd seen cheesecake pinups before; my own basement, across the street from Hal's, also contained certain hidden magazines we had studied. That our fathers concealed these magazines from our mothers and that we studied them secretly was surely a rite of passage into manhood. The women we found in those other magazines had no existence apart from their pages. They came into the world full-blown as we saw them, wearing polka-dot bikinis or holding Japanese umbrellas, and after the photo was taken they ceased to exist. They didn't come to work, go home from work, eat, sleep, sneeze, or have any corporeal existence. They were pinups. The women in *Playboy* were real, and lived only 135 miles from Urbana, Illinois, and in some unlikely but thinkable universe, I might meet them. My preteen hormones cried out: Yes! This is what we're hormones for!

In the years to come, Hugh Hefner was often in the news, and rarely in a story I didn't read. He lived in a Mansion. He drove a Mercedes two-seater. He smoked a pipe. In his Mansion, Tony Bennett, Julie London, and Bill Cosby hung out, and there were parties every night, and something was happening that was halfway between a bachelor's pad and a bacchanal.

I promised to myself that if I ever got a job in Chicago, I would get myself invited to the Mansion within six months. It didn't take that long. I was hired by the *Chicago Sun-Times* in the autumn of 1966, and two months later I was assigned to write a feature story about a party at the Mansion. It was a party for the top Chevrolet dealers of America. Julie London was nowhere to be seen. But there was a big buffet, and Hef was in the living room with his dressing gown, his slippers, his pipe, his Pepsi, and his date. I slipped into an alcove and found my way down to the Grotto with its plate-glass window opening onto the aquatic underwater vista of the pool.

And there I met not Miss December, but a

young woman named Royal Kennedy. She worked in broadcasting and was also covering the party. She was amused by the Grotto. We later went out on one or two perfectly respectable dates. She had never met a Playmate. We had that in common. It gradually became clear to me that Bill Cosby might meet Miss December, but I never would.

I went back to the Mansion several more times, for parties and movie nights. When Russ Meyer came through Chicago with his new bride, Edy Williams, Hef had us over for dinner and gave us the tour. Russ shot some of the first Playmates. I covered the opening of the West Coast Mansion in Holmby Hills, and stood at the bar with Tony Curtis. Later, Chaz and I went to some of Hef's New Year's Eve parties out there. In *Playboy,* I'd read about parties at Hef's pad with people like Ray Anthony, Mel Torme, and Miss October of 1967. And now it was 1988, and OMG, there they still were! Ray Anthony, Mel Torme, and Miss October of 1967! And I went to one of Hef's "movie nights" at the Mansion, with Hef using notes on a yellow legal pad to introduce *Treasure Island.*

Many of you will find my comments deplorable. You may believe *Playboy* was the enemy of women. It objectified their bodies. It schooled men to regard them as sex objects. It stood for all that feminists fought to correct. There is some truth to that, but it doesn't impact upon my experience, and the best I can do here is be truthful.

Nobody taught me to regard women as sex objects. I always did. Most men do. And truth to tell, most women regard men as sex objects. We regard many other aspects of another person, but sex is the elephant in the room. Evolution has hardwired us that way. When we meet a new person, in some small recess of our minds we evaluate that person as a sex partner. We don't act on it, we don't dwell on it, but we do it. You know we do. And this process continues bravely until we are old and feeble.

Yes, *Playboy* presented women's bodies for our regard. Yes, they were airbrushed and Photoshopped to perfection. Not a blemish, not a zit, not one single chewed fingernail. This process of perfection doesn't deny nature; it reflects it. When we meditate on the partner of our dreams, the mental image we summon is without flaw. We don't dwell upon a pimple or a bad tooth or a little underarm fat. We meditate on the gestalt. We meditate on being accepted and loved by that wonderful person. Photographers like Diane Arbus photographed people realistically, and were called cruel.

Nor is it only women's bodies that have been objectified and turned into sex objects. Men have undergone the same process. If few women feel they can live up to a Playmate, few men believe they belong in a Ralph Lauren or Calvin Klein ad. *Vogue* doesn't publish seven-hundred-page holiday issues filled with models with zits. I'm not saying this is ideal. I'm saying it's the truth.

So now I move on to a larger view of Hugh Hefner. Yes, he has possibly experienced more orgasms with more different women than any other man who has ever lived. But his relationships have been consensual, and no woman has ever said, "Why, Mr. Hefner! I had no idea you were that kind of man!" It is also notable that in an age where sexual-harassment lawsuits are as common as bankruptcies, Hefner has never been charged with misbehavior. We must conclude that Hefner's behavior is that of a generous gentleman who likes to get laid. That is not the worst thing in the world.

I've just finished watching a new documentary named *Hugh Hefner: Playboy, Activist, and Rebel* by Brigitte Berman, who won an Oscar for *Artie Shaw: Time Is All You've Got* (1985), and also directed *Bix: Ain't None of Them Play Like Him Yet* (1983). My guess is that Hefner and Berman met through their interest in jazz. The film is pro-Hefner, although it supplies Susan Brownmiller and Pat Boone to make the obligatory arguments for the prosecution. It presents Hefner as he would probably want to be seen, as a supporter of civil rights, civil liberties, freedom of speech, and freedom of choice.

His credentials in these areas have cost him some money and trouble. His syndicated TV program *Playboy After Dark,* which he owned and controlled, showcased mixed-race singing groups and blacklisted performers such as Pete Seeger at a time when networks enforced a ban on both. It also showed blacks and whites dancing together on a set supposed to be "Hef's Penthouse." Some stations in the South refused to carry it. The show went on the air not long after Nat King Cole's show left NBC after failing to find advertisers that would buy into a "black" show.

In New Orleans, Hefner franchised one of the first Playboy Clubs, later to learn it was forbidden by law to mix black and white patrons. He bought back the franchise, and reopened it to club members of all races. It was in that club that a black comedian performed before whites for the first time in Louisiana (although black musicians were "legal"). He was a young man from Chicago named Dick Gregory. Gregory appears in the film, recalling that he was a replacement for a white comic, Dr. Irwin Corey, and the *Playboy* event turned out to be a private party for three hundred white businessmen. "Three hours later, I was still talking," Gregory says. "Everything turned around on that day." For his career, it certainly did.

It became an old joke that people said they read *Playboy* because of the articles. But Hefner tried much harder than necessary to maintain a high editorial standard. His issues No. 2 through No. 4 serialized Ray Bradbury's *Fahrenheit 451*. He championed Vladimir Nabokov, Margaret Atwood, James Baldwin, and Jorge Luis Borges. His *Playboy* interviews were newsworthy, and his editors must have smiled when they sent Alex Haley to interview the American Nazi George Lincoln Rockwell. (Haley recalls, "I told him I'd been called 'nigger' many times, but this time I was being well paid to hear it.") *The Hurt Locker* was based on *Playboy* reporting.

Hefner and *Playboy* have been around so long that not everyone remembers what America used to be like. It was sexually repressed and socially restrictive. College students were expelled for having sex out of wedlock. Homosexuality and miscegenation were illegal. Freedom of choice was denied. McCarthyism still cast a pall over the freedom of speech. Many people joined in the fight against that unhealthy society. Hefner was one of them, and a case can be made that *Playboy* had a greater influence on our society in its first half-century than any other magazine.

No doubt *Playboy* objectified women and all the rest of it. But it also celebrated them, and freed their bodies from the stigma of shame. It calmly explained that women were sexual beings, and experienced orgasms, and that photographs of their bodies were not by definition "dirty pictures." Not many of today's feminists (of either gender) would be able to endure America's attitudes about women in the 1950s.

As Hefner speaks, you realize that he believes in civil rights and liberties so deeply that it's instinctive. Many people shared his politics in the 1950s and early 1960s, but not many of them ran corporations that (a) depended on mass audiences, and (b) stood to lose business because of political beliefs. When it came to African-Americans in his clubs or on his TV show (or as his centerfolds), Hefner did the right thing without calculation, and paid a financial penalty. When the (endless) *Playboy* philosophy argued for change, it is unlikely he gained a single reader. But he outlined and defended a progressive philosophy. And when magazine interviews were often revolting puffery about celebrities, he went long and in detail with people such as Malcolm X, Bertrand Russell, Ayn Rand, Jean-Paul Sartre, Elisabeth Kubler-Ross, and Marshall McLuhan. The fact is that sex made money for Hefner, and he used it to produce one of the best magazines in America.

He also spent money to free a man who faced a fifty-year prison term for fellatio. And helped overturn laws that made fellatio and cunnilingus a crime in all fifty states (for which many of us must be grateful). He fought against laws punishing homosexuality and interracial marriage. He supported Lenny Bruce's fight against an obscenity arrest in Chicago. He fought obscenity prosecutions brought by such as Charles Keating, founder of the Citizens for Decent Literature. He won. Berman's doc cannot resist juxtaposing shots of Keating lecturing on morality and Keating in handcuffs being led to prison for bank fraud. Hefner's Playboy Foundation fought for civil liberties in general. The cost for these activities came out of his profits, and that didn't give him a moment's pause.

Some argue, like Brownmiller, that *Playboy* was bad for women—that it made them objects for masturbation. I would suggest *Playboy* was several thousand years behind the curve in doing so. And not only women are used as subjects for meditation during masturbation. Masturbation is an equal opportunity employer. Others argue, like Boone, that *Playboy* promoted immoral behavior. I believe sex in our society, in general, is more moral today than it was when *Playboy* began. I think young people in particular have healthier attitudes toward it than they did when I was in high school. I agree that teen pregnancy and STDs are tragic, but it was Hefner who fought for birth control and protection when they were illegal in some states. I was taught that a woman's body was a possible Occasion for Sin. What kind of morality is that?

Hefner is returning to Chicago this week with his brother, Keith, to revisit their childhood home and their old high school, Steinmetz. I went along with them on their previous return home in 1994. I'd love for him to see the Audience Award winner in this year's Chicago Film Festival, *Louder Than a Bomb.* It's a documentary about the citywide High School Poetry Slam Contest, codirected by Jon Siskel, nephew of Hef's old poker buddy Gene. In its first year of competition, Steinmetz, now a troubled school in a black neighborhood, came out of nowhere and won the event with a gifted group of poet-performers. In the film, it's one of the finalists again. The students of Steinmetz may not much care that Hugh Hefner graduated from their school, but without the social changes he fought for and helped to influence, all of the members of their Poetry Slam team might be in jail today along with the ghost of Lenny Bruce.

The Human Centipede (no stars)

NO MPAA RATING, 90 m., 2010

Dieter Laser (Dr. Heiter), Ashley C. Williams (Lindsay), Ashlynn Yennie (Jenny), Akihiro Kitamura (Katsuro). Directed by Tom Six and produced by Tom Six and Ilona Six. Screenplay by Tom Six.

It's not death itself that's so bad. It's what you might have to go through to get there. No horror film I've seen inflicts more terrible things on its victims than *The Human Centipede.* You would have to be very brave to choose this ordeal over simply being murdered. Maybe you'd need to also be insane.

I'm about to describe what happens to the film's victims. This will be a spoiler. I don't care, because (1) the details are common knowledge in horror film circles, and (2) if you don't know, you may be grateful to be warned. This is a movie I don't think I should be coy about.

OK. Dr. Heiter is a mad scientist. He was once a respected surgeon, but has now retreated to his luxurious home in the forest, which contains an operating room in the basement. His skin has a sickly pallor, his hair is dyed black, his speech reminds us of a standard Nazi, and he gnashes his teeth. He is filled with hatred and vile perversion.

He drugs his victims and dumps them into his Mercedes. When they regain consciousness, they find themselves tied to hospital beds. He provides them with a little slide show to brief them on his plans. He will demonstrate his skills as a surgeon by—hey, listen, now you'd really better stop reading. What's coming next isn't so much a review as a public service announcement.

Heiter plans to surgically join his three victims by sewing together their mouths and anuses, all in a row, so the food goes in at the front and comes out at the rear, you see. They will move on their hands and knees like an insect with twelve limbs. You don't want to be part of the human centipede at all, but you most certainly don't want to be in the middle. Why does Dr. Heiter want to commit such an atrocity? He is insane, as I've already explained.

He also wants to do it because he is in a movie by Tom Six, a Dutch director whose previous two films average 4 out of 10 on the IMDb scale, which is a score so low very few directors attain it. Six has now made a film deliberately intended to inspire incredulity, nausea, and hopefully outrage. It's being booked as a midnight movie, and is it ever. Boozy fanboys will treat it like a thrill ride.

And yet within Six there stirs the soul of a dark artist. He treats his material with utter seriousness; there's none of the jokey undertone of a classic Hammer horror film like *Scream and Scream Again* (1970), in which every time the victim awoke, another limb had been amputated. That one starred the all-star trio of Vincent Price, Christopher Lee, and Peter Cushing, and you could see they were having fun. Dieter Laser, who plays Dr. Heiter, takes the role with relentless sincerity. This is his sixty-third acting role, but, poor guy, this is seemingly the one he was born to play.

Tom Six is apparently the director's real name. I learn his favorite actor is Klaus Kinski, he is an AK-47 enthusiast, and wears RAF sunglasses and Panama hats. Not the kind of guy you want to share your seat on a Ferris wheel. He has said, "I get a rash from too much political correctness." I promise you that after this movie his skin was smooth as a Gerber baby's.

I have long attempted to take a generic approach. In other words, is a film true to its genre and does it deliver what its audiences presumably expect? *The Human Centipede* scores high on this scale. It is depraved and disgusting enough to satisfy the most demanding midnight movie fan. And it's not *simply* an exploitation film.

The director makes, for example, an effective use of the antiseptic interior of Heiter's labyrinthine home. Doors and corridors lead nowhere and anywhere. In a scene where the police come calling, he wisely has Heiter almost encourage their suspicions. And there is a scene toward the end, as the human centipede attempts escape, that's so piteous it transcends horror and approaches tragedy.

The members of the centipede are Ashley C. Williams, Ashlynn Yennie, and Akihiro Kitamura. The Japanese actor screams in subtitled Japanese, perhaps because he will broaden the film's appeal among Asian horror fans. In the last half of the film, the two American actresses don't scream at all, if you follow me.

I am required to award stars to movies I review. This time, I refuse to do it. The star rating system is unsuited to this film. Is the movie good? Is it bad? Does it matter? It is what it is, and occupies a world where the stars don't shine.

Humpday ★ ★ ★ ½

R, 94 m., 2009

Mark Duplass (Ben), Joshua Leonard (Andrew), Alycia Delmore (Anna). Directed and produced by Lynn Shelton. Screenplay by Shelton.

Humpday, a film by a woman about the limits of male bonding, blows the whistle on buddy movies. After the buddies in those movies finish with pounding each other on the back, giving each other Dutch rubs, and chanting, "I love you, man!"—how far are they prepared to take their love? Just about exactly that far, perhaps, and then they draw the line.

The film is a perceptive comedy about how many men, if not homophobic in theory, shudder in practice about the prospect of getting it on with their own sex. It's also about how close friends in school can drift far apart in a decade. That's what has happened to Ben and Andrew. Ben (Mark Duplass) is a married man, using fertility methods to conceive a child with his wife, Anna. Andrew (Joshua Leonard) is a shaggy college friend, who turns up in the middle of the night after living the life of a free spirit in India, Cambodia, Mexico, and other faraway places.

Anna (Alycia Delmore) has never heard of this old buddy. But she's a good sport and invites him to spend the night. Andrew spends more than the night, and Ben, now a straight arrow, feels a certain wistfulness about the freedom he has lost to marriage. Andrew takes him to a party of swingers no longer in the first bloom of youth, where booze, drugs, and sex toys are thrown into the pot, so to speak.

When they're fairly drunk, the two friends hear about a Seattle event named Humpfest, in which amateurs compete to produce the best short porn film. They decide to enter. They will win, they predict, because they have the most daring idea: They will have sex with each other. Two straight guys doing it for the first time. "That's beyond gay!"

As is sometimes the way with drunken vows, these are taken seriously, and Ben and Andrew set about making plans to make the film in a rented hotel room. Meanwhile, Anna grows increasingly uncomfortable with Andrew's omnipresence and his influence on her reliable husband. Anna, you understand, is in no way a conventional movie spouse, but has been imagined by the writer-director, Lynn Shelton, as an open-minded, sex-loving woman who is nevertheless mature and reasonable and expects from Ben an attentive husband and a dependable father.

Anna is, of course, never to learn the truth about what is described as "Andrew's art project." Andrew, of course, lets it slip. Anna's reaction is more complex than you might imagine, and it's at such a moment you appreciate the woman in the writer-director's chair. Women, I suspect, are more likely than men to view sex from the overall perspective of what we may call their lives. In a country like Saudi Arabia, whose citizens express discomfort about men and women even attending movies together, I have little doubt which gender is more concerned.

Ben and Andrew advance doggedly on a trajectory leading them to their Humpfest entry, and there's a rather remarkable scene in the hotel room that involves great perception of word choices, vocal intonations, and body language (what does it mean as both men clasp pillows to their tummies?). I understand most of the dialogue was improvised after extensive discussion, and it sounds real—uncertain, tentative, even bashful. For starters, who's going to pitch and who's going to catch? Not an easy question to answer.

Humpday is funny, yes, but observant and thought-provoking. Buddy movies like *I Love You, Man,* which I loved, can intrigue us with the possibility of an attraction between two men that could threaten a heterosexual romance. But when all bets are called, most guys just don't want to go there. It could be the end of a beautiful platonic friendship.

We will leave Ben and Andrew in their hotel room and pull back to consider Humpfest itself, which I discover is an actual annual event in Seattle. Unlike the porn films described in this film, its entries must be hump films—in other words, depicting an activity common in dogs and Transformers. In fact, the festival has only one rule: "Penetration equals disqualification."

You can find its Web site, which includes a chart of recommended drinking levels, if you want to enter. In the meantime, here is a Humpfest entry of less than sixty seconds. It contains no nudity and no explicit sex, and of course only one protagonist. Be sure to watch until the end: www.youtube.com/watch?v=nRM89nVHyl4.

Hunger ★ ★ ★ ½

NO MPAA RATING, 92 m., 2009

Michael Fassbender (Bobby Sands), Liam Cunningham (Father Dominic Moran), Stuart Graham (Raymond Lohan), Brian Milligan (Davey Gillen), Liam McMahon (Gerry Campbell). Directed by Steve McQueen and produced by Laura Hastings-Smith and Robin Gutch. Screenplay by McQueen and Enda Walsh.

It was a desperate business, and *Hunger* is a desperate film. It concerns the fierce battle between the Irish Republican Army and the British state, which in 1981 led to a hunger strike in which ten IRA prisoners died. The first of them was Bobby Sands, whose agonizing death is seen with an implacable, level gaze in the closing act of the film.

If you do not hold a position on the Irish Republican cause, you will not find one here. *Hunger* is not about the rights and wrongs of the British in Northern Ireland, but about inhuman prison conditions, the steeled determination of IRA members such as Bobby Sands, and a rock and a hard place. There is hardly a sentence in the film about Irish history or politics, and only two extended dialogue passages: one a long debate between Sands and a priest about the utility or futility of a hunger strike, the other a doctor's detailed description to Sands's parents about the effect of starvation on the human body.

There is not a conventional plot to draw us from beginning to end. Instead, director Steve McQueen, an artist who employs merciless realism, strikes three major chords. The first involves the daily routine of a prison guard (Stuart Graham), who is emotionally wounded by his work. The second involves two other prisoners (Brian Milligan and Liam McMahon), who participate in the IRA prisoners' refusal to wear prison clothes or bathe. The third involves the hunger strike.

This is clear: Neither side will back down. Twice we hear Prime Minister Margaret Thatcher describing the inmates of the Maze prison in Belfast as not political prisoners but criminals. The IRA considers itself political to the core. The ideology involved is not even mentioned in the extraordinary long dialogue scene, mostly in one shot, between Sands and a priest (Liam Cunningham) about whether a hunger strike will have the desired effect. The priest, worldly, a realist, on very civil terms with Sands, never once mentions suicide as a sin; he discusses it entirely in terms of its usefulness.

Sands thinks starvation to death will have an impact. The priest observes that if it does, Sands will by then be dead. His willingness to die reflects the bone-deep beliefs of Irish Republicans; recall the Irish song lyric, "And always remember, the longer we live, the sooner we bloody well die."

Sands's death is shown in a tableau of increasing bleakness. It is agonizing, yet filmed with a curious painterly purity. It is alarming to note how much weight the actor Michael Fassbender lost; he went from 170 to 132 pounds. His dreams or visions or memories toward the end, based on a story he told the priest, would have been more effective if handled much more briefly.

Did the hunger strike succeed? After the remorseless death toll climbed to ten, Thatcher at last relented, tacitly granting the prisoners political recognition, although she refused to say so out loud. She was called the Iron Lady for a reason. Today there is peace in Northern Ireland. The island nation is still divided. Bobby Sands is dead. The priest has his conclusions, the dead man has his, or would if he were alive.

The Hurt Locker ★ ★ ★ ★

R, 127 m., 2009

Jeremy Renner (Staff Sergeant William James), Anthony Mackie (Sergeant J. T. Sanborn), Brian Geraghty (Specialist Owen Eldridge), Ralph Fiennes (Contractor Team Leader), Guy Pearce (Sergeant Matt Thompson), David Morse (Colonel Reed), Evangeline Lilly (Connie James). Directed by Kathryn Bigelow and produced by Bigelow, Nicolas Chartier, and Greg Shapiro. Screenplay by Mark Boal.

A lot of movies begin with poetic quotations, but *The Hurt Locker* opens with a statement presented as fact: "War is a drug." Not for everyone, of course. Most combat troops want to get it over with and go home. But the hero of this film, Staff Sergeant William James, who has a terrifyingly dangerous job, addresses it like a daily pleasure. Under enemy fire in Iraq, he defuses bombs.

He isn't an action hero, he's a specialist, like a surgeon who focuses on one part of the body over and over, day after day, until he could continue if the lights went out. James is a man who understands bombs inside out and has an almost psychic understanding of the minds of the bombers. This is all the more remarkable because in certain scenes it seems fairly certain that the bomb maker is standing in full view—on a balcony or in a window overlooking the street, say, and is as curious about his bomb as James is. Two professionals, working against each other.

Staff Sergeant James is played by Jeremy Renner, who immediately goes on the short list for an Oscar nomination. His performance is not built on complex speeches but on a visceral projection of who this man is and what he feels. He is not a hero in a conventional sense. He cares not for medals. He could no doubt recite patriotic reasons for his service, but does that explain why he compulsively, sometimes recklessly, puts himself in harm's way? The man before him in this job got himself killed. James seems even cockier.

The Hurt Locker is a spellbinding war film by Kathryn Bigelow, a master of stories about men and women who choose to be in physical danger. She cares first about the people, then about the danger. She doesn't leave a lot of room for much else. The man who wrote "War is a drug" was Chris Hedges, a war correspondent for the *New York Times*. Mark Boal, who wrote this screenplay, was embedded with a bomb squad in Baghdad. He also wrote the superb movie *In the Valley of Elah* (2007), with Tommy Lee Jones as a professional army man trying to solve the murder of his son who had just returned from Iraq. Also based on fact.

Bigelow and Boal know what they're doing. This movie embeds itself in a man's mind. When it's over, nothing has been said in so many words, but we have a pretty clear idea of why James *needs* to defuse bombs. I'm going to risk putting it this way: (1) bombs need to be defused; (2) nobody does it better than James; (3) he knows exactly how good he is; and (4) when he's at work, an intensity of focus and exhilaration consumes him, and he's in that heedless zone when an artist loses track of self and time.

The most important man in his life is Sergeant J. T. Sanborn (Anthony Mackie), head of the support team that accompanies James. Sanborn and his men provide cover fire, scan rooftops and hiding places that might conceal snipers, and assist James into and out of his heavy protective clothing. Sanborn gives constant audio feedback that James hears inside his helmet. It is Sanborn, who has his eye on everything, who is nominally in charge, and not the tunnel-visioned James.

Sanborn is a skilled, responsible professional. He works by the book. He follows protocol. James drives him nuts. Sometimes James seems to almost deliberately invite trouble, and Sanborn believes that by following the procedure they'll all have a better chance of going home. He isn't a shirker, and he doesn't have weak nerves. He's a realist and thinks James is reckless.

Certainly James behaves recklessly at times, even in his use of protective clothing. He takes risks boldly. But in the actual task of defusing a bomb, he is as careful as if he were operating on his own heart. Bigelow uses no phony suspense-generating mechanisms in this film. No false alarms. No gung-ho. It is about personalities in terrible danger. The suspense is real, and it is earned. Hitchcock said when there's a bomb under a table and it explodes, that's action. When we know the bomb is there, and the people at the table play cards and it doesn't explode, that's suspense.

The Hurt Locker is a great film, an intelligent film, a film shot clearly so that we know exactly who everybody is and where they are and what they're doing and why. The camera work is at the service of the story. Bigelow knows that you can't build suspense with shots lasting one or two seconds. And you can't tell a story that way, either—not one that deals with the mystery of why a man like James seems to depend on risking his life. A leading contender for Academy Awards.

I

I Am ★ ★

NO MPAA RATING, 78 m., 2011

Desmond Tutu, Howard Zinn, Noam Chomsky, Lynne McTaggart, Coleman Barks, and Thom Hartmann. A documentary directed by Tom Shadyac and produced by Dagan Handy.

There is a scene in *I Am* where a laboratory technician embeds sensors in a puddle of yogurt and attaches them to a Bio-Response Meter. When Tom Shadyac directs his thoughts at the yogurt, the needle on the meter bounces back and forth. It is important for you to know that Shadyac is not physically attached to the meter—or to the yogurt, for that matter. When he thinks about his lawyer, the needle redlines.

It's obvious that the yogurt is reading his mind, right? Right? Hello? For Shadyac and the technician, this experiment demonstrates that our minds are wired to the organic world. For me, it raises the following questions: (1) Was the yogurt pasteurized? (2) How did the yogurt know to read Shadyac's mind and not the mind of the technician who was just as close? (3) How did it occur to anyone to devise an experiment testing whether yogurt can respond to human thoughts? (4) Did anyone check to see if the technician was connected to the meter? (5) Is this a case for the Amazing Randi?

You see I am a rationalist. That means I'm not an ideal viewer for a documentary like *I Am*, which involves the ingestion of woo-woo in industrial bulk. When I see a man whose mind is being read by yogurt, I expect to find that man in a comedy starring, oh, someone like Jim Carrey. Since we all understand There Are No Coincidences, it won't surprise you to learn that *I Am* was directed by Tom Shadyac, who earned untold millions by directing Jim Carrey in such films as *Ace Ventura: Pet Detective.*

This documentary is often absurd and never less than giddy with uplift, but that's not to say it's bad. I watched with an incredulous delight, and at the end I liked Tom Shadyac quite a lot. He's a goofball, yet his heart is in the right place. But don't get me started on hearts. Did you know that Shadyac's friend Rollin McCraty, Ph.D., the director of research for HeartMath, has proven that the human heart controls the human brain via various types of biofeedback?

That's not all the heart can do. Try this on for size: When you are shown pleasant or frightening images on a computer screen, your brain (and heart) respond either positively or negatively. That makes sense. But wait. When the images are chosen at random from a big database, the heart sends positive or negative signals to the brain *two to three seconds in advance* of the image being chosen. In other words, the heart knows what the random image is going to be. Yes. Shadyac is grateful for this information. He doesn't ask any questions, like, for example, does the heart tell the brain what signal *would* have been displayed unless the power to the monitor went out in the milliseconds between when it was chosen and was to be displayed?

Dr. McCraty shares another piece of information that's interesting. There are random number generators distributed all over the world. Most of the time the numbers are truly random. But when a global catastrophe like 9/11 or the Japan calamity occurs, our collective minds send out such strong signals that the computers temporarily stop selecting random numbers. Yes. And the screen fills with lots of ones and zeroes to illustrate that.

So I'm thinking, not everybody found out about the Japan earthquake at once. Does McCraty have data showing if the globe's random number calculators failed simultaneously, or were timed to the spread of the news? (I can guess the answer: They all failed at once, because at a Gaia level we all sensed it simultaneously.)

What set Tom Shadyac to gather this information and make a film about it? In 2007 he was a multimillionaire living in a seventeen-thousand-square-foot mansion in Pasadena and flying in a private jet. Then he had a terrible bike accident, breaking bones and suffering a concussion. He became a victim of post-concussion syndrome, which meant the symptoms didn't clear up. He had blinding headaches and debilitating depressions, and contemplated suicide. Mercifully, the symptoms faded, leaving him sadder, wiser, and in search of truth.

He began with two questions: What's wrong with the world? What can we do about it? He traveled the world to pose these questions to many distinguished people, such as the linguist Noam Chomsky; Archbishop Desmond Tutu; Howard Zinn; Lynne McTaggart, an authority on consciousness and the new physics; people at the Institute of Noetic Sciences; his late father, Richard Shadyac, who was CEO of fundraising for St. Jude Hospital; and so on. None of these people necessarily agree with anything the others say. As for Shadyac, hey, he's just listening.

The thing is, he doesn't ask enough. He is not a skeptic. He asks his two questions and mashes together the answers with a lot of fancy editing of butterflies, sunsets, flocks of birds, schools of fish, herds of wild animals, and petri dishes filled with yogurt. From his tour emerges one conclusion: Everything is connected. Our minds, our bodies, our planet, our universe. This happens (you can see this coming) at the quantum level.

Another thing he learns is that money is the root of all evil. Like the fish, birds, animals, and untouched tribes, we have evolved to cooperate and arrive at consensus. By competing to enrich ourselves, we create bad vibes. Give Shadyac credit: He sells his Pasadena mansion, starts teaching college, and moves into a mobile home (in Malibu, it's true). Now he offers us this hopeful if somewhat undigested cut of his findings, in a film as watchable as a really good TV commercial, and as deep.

I leave you with a parting possibility raised by the film: What if your thoughts continue to affect the DNA you leave behind everywhere you go, all through life? At a quantum level, of course.

I Am Love ★ ★ ★ ★

R, 120 m., 2010

Tilda Swinton (Emma), Flavio Parenti (Edoardo Jr.), Edoardo Gabbriellini (Antonio), Alba Rohrwacher (Elisabetta), Pippo Delbono (Tancredi), Maria Paiato (Ida), Gabriele Ferzetti (Edoardo Recchi Sr.), Marisa Berenson (Allegra). Directed by Luca Guadagnino and produced by Guadagnino, Francesco Melzi d'Eril, Marco Morabito, Tilda Swinton, Alessandro Usai, and Massimiliano Violante. Screenplay by Barbara Alberti, Ivan Cotroneo, Walter Fasano, and Guadagnino.

Did she understand when she married her husband what sort of family she was joining? She knew they were rich Italian aristocrats, operators of textile mills in Milan. But did she understand that as a wife from Russia she would serve and provide and even be loved, but would never truly be a member?

When we see Emma (Tilda Swinton), she is preparing the Recchi house for the birthday party of the patriarch. She seems to relate more as a caterer than as a hostess. At the head of the table is the grand old Edoardo (Gabriele Ferzetti). Among those gathered are his son, Emma's husband, Tancredi (Pippo Delbono). The old man makes an unexpected announcement: He is retiring and putting Tancredi in charge. But not Tancredi alone. His grandson, their son, Edo (Flavio Parenti), will also share the responsibility.

Is Emma filled with joy? Her husband and son will inherit the dynasty? She is so calm and expert, it's hard to say. Tilda Swinton is a daring actress who doesn't project emotions so much as embody them. *I Am Love* provides an ideal role for her, in that her actions speak instead of words. We learn she has her own private space, that after launching a family event she likes to leave it running smoothly and retire to her room upstairs.

The opening act of Luca Guadagnino's film establishes the stature of the Recchi family as surely as the Corleones are established in *The Godfather,* or the Salinas in Visconti's *The Leopard.* It may be impossible to write about this film without evoking *The Leopard,* not simply because they both involve Italian aristocrats, but because they involve matters of succession, and the way that love and lust can breach the walls aristocrats live behind. Guadagnino makes the connection inescapable by naming Tancredi; in *The Leopard,* Alain Delon pays the Salina nephew of that name.

The Recchi family has been living in a particular way for a long time. Cushioned by great wealth, working in an industry associated with style, never challenged, well educated, its hungers cloaked in tradition, it occupies its place of privilege effortlessly. Emma speaks Italian fluently, but with a Russian accent, a reminder that she is not . . . quite one of them.

Few actresses can embody urgent sexual desire so well as Swinton. She is realistic about such feelings. When she learns her daughter, Elisabetta (Alba Rohrwacher), is a lesbian, she reacts not as a mother, possibly with shock, but as a woman, in surprise and curiosity. She has heard of such things. The heart has its reasons.

The feast opening the film was prepared by Antonio (Edoardo Gabbriellini), a friend of her Edo's. She consults with this young chef, and a feeling passes into her. Later, on a visit to her daughter in San Remo, she happens to see Antonio, and with decision follows him through the streets. This is all done without dialogue. The camera is pursuer and pursued. The longer she follows him, the more certain they must meet.

Of course they make love. Actresses are often called upon to enact sex in the movies. Swinton does it differently with each character, understanding that sexuality is as distinctive as speech or taste. Emma is urgent as if a dam has burst, releasing not passion but happiness. Of course this affair threatens her relationship with her husband, her son, and her family. But most long-established families have overcome the inconveniences of adultery. Continuity is more important than commitment. The film now observes the ways, not predictable, in which this new sexual fact affects Emma's role.

All this time, Guadagnino has been paying due attention to other important members of the family. There is Allegra (Marisa Berenson), gatekeeper of her husband. There is the long-serving housekeeper, Ida (Maria Paiato), who sees and understands everything and in many ways is Emma's refuge in the household. There is the personality of her son, Edo, as yet untouched by the ordeals of business life, more open in his personal feelings. And there is the overarching sense in which the Recchi family embodies a tradition that, like a church, requires devotion if not belief.

I Am Love is an amazing film. It is deep, rich, human. It is not about rich and poor but about old and new. It is about the ancient war between tradition and feeling. For this role Tilda Swinton learned to speak Italian with a Russian accent, as Tilda Swinton would, but her performance is nothing as trivial as a feat of learning. She evokes Emma as a woman who for years has accepted the needs of the Recchis, and discovers in a few days to accept her own needs. She must have been waiting a long time for Antonio, whoever he would be.

I Am Number Four ★ ½

PG-13, 110 m., 2011

Alex Pettyfer (John), Dianna Agron (Sarah), Callan McAuliffe (Sam), Jake Abel (Mark James), Timothy Olyphant (Henri), Teresa Palmer (Number Six). Directed by D. J. Caruso and produced by Michael Bay. Screenplay by Alfred Gough, Miles Millar, and Marti Noxon.

I Am Number Four is shameless and unnecessary. That's sad, when a movie casts aside all shame, demonstrates itself willing to rip off anything that might attract audiences, and nevertheless fails. What we have here is a witless attempt to merge the *Twilight* formula with the Michael Bay formula. It ends with sexy human teenagers involved in an endless special effects battle with sexy alien teenagers who look like humans, in a high school and on its football field.

Let's pause for a moment to consider this apocalyptic battle. It is all special effects. None of it is physically possible. It might as well be a cartoon; it's essentially CGI animation intercut with brief bursts of inane dialogue. Brief, because the global action market doesn't much care about dialogue, and besides, when people start talking about something, you could run into the hazard of having actual characters in a plot. Minute after relentless minute, creatures both human and alien, whom we care nothing about, wage war and occasionally disintegrate into clouds of tiny pixels for no particular reason.

I like science fiction. The opening shot of *I Am Number Four* holds promise, as John (Alex Pettyfer), the narrator, explains that he is a Mogadorian, no doubt from a planet named

Mogador. Specifically, he is Mogadorian Number Four. Don't expect me to explain the Mogadorian numbering system. He is hiding out on planet Earth, and doing everything possible to disguise himself as a box office attraction like Edward Cullen. They have already killed Numbers One, Two, and Three.

Consider. The *Twilight* movies were about a handsome and sexy teenager who exerted a powerful attraction upon a virginal young girl, and yet held himself aloof because he was a vampire. Here John is a handsome and sexy teenager who is technically unavailable because he is an alien, although it appears that Mogador may luckily have evolved teenage boys indistinguishable from humans to such as Sarah (Dianna Agron). John has been on the lam around America to remain in hiding from those who would kill him, and is accompanied by his fellow Mogadorian Henri (Timothy Olyphant), who poses as his father and cautions him that his real father didn't die only to see John marry an Earth girl. Whether John has the option of returning to Mogador and settling down with a nice Mogadoress to raise Mogadorlings, I am not certain.

The high school elements in the plot revolve around John's popularity in some areas (he's an ace on a Jet Ski) and nonconformity in others (his palms function like high-powered searchlights). He is also free of the ordinary constraints of gravity, and can leap for dozens of yards and even fly. What this means is that the climactic battle scene can take place largely in the air, and Harry Potter's Quidditch games join the honor roll of the plundered.

There is, no doubt, a degree of identification available for the primary audience of *I Am Number Four.* Many teenage girls have perhaps imagined themselves in love with a handsome hunk with tousled blond hair, a three-day stubble, incredible athletic abilities, and hands that glow in the dark. That he is Not From Around Here makes him all the more attractive.

In the film we see native Mogadorians, whose faces are deeply scarred with gill-like extrusions. I am not completely sure if this is how John really looks and he has somehow morphed into teenager form, or if he was forced to flee Mogador because he looked like an alien Edward Cullen. I'm sure this is all spelled out in the movie. Sometimes I find it so very, very hard to care.

Now imagine *I Am Number Four* as a "novelization." There would be the setup, a little dialogue, and then pages and pages of violent action: "John leaped one hundred yards into the air and struck him with a deadly ray! An enemy fighter disintegrated into an ashy gray cloud of pixels! Number Six, her hair flowing in slow motion, whirled around and kicked the Mogadorian commander! 'Look out!' John shouted. 'Behind you!' cried Sarah."

This would quickly grow old. Why audiences enjoy watching protracted sequences of senseless action mystifies me, but they do. There is no strategic or spatial way in which the battle in *I Am Number Four* makes any sense. It is movement and conflict edited together in incomprehensible chaos.

Where is Mogador? Why did nine of its citizens flee to Earth? How did they do so? How is it they breathe our air, eat our food, and make such expert use of our grooming products? Why didn't the other Mogadorians say to hell with it and leave them on Earth? What is a Mogadorian life span? Given what we know about the time and distance involved in space travel, are these the same nine individuals who fled Mogador or their descendants after many generations in an interstellar ark? What's the story on those spotlights in their hands? In all modesty, I think my questions are more entertaining than this movie.

Ice Age: Dawn of the Dinosaurs ★ ★ ★ ½

PG, 93 m., 2009

With the voices of: Ray Romano (Manny), Queen Latifah (Ellie), John Leguizamo (Sid), Denis Leary (Diego), Simon Pegg (Buck), Seann William Scott (Crash), Josh Peck (Eddie), Bill Hader (Gazelle), Kristen Wiig (Pudgy Beaver Mom), Chris Wedge (Scrat), Karen Disher (Scratte). Directed by Carlos Saldanha and produced by Lori Forte and John C. Donkin. Screenplay by Michael Berg, Peter Ackerman, Mike Reiss, and Yoni Brenner.

Ice Age: Dawn of the Dinosaurs is the best of the three films about our friends in the interspecies herd of plucky prehistoric heroes. And it involves some of the best use of 3-D I've seen in an animated feature. It also introduces a masterstroke that essentially allows the series to take place anywhere: There is this land beneath the surface of the earth, you see . . .

Well, if there can be one land, there can be any number of lands, including not only this one, where dinosaurs still roam, but maybe a portal in time leading to the future, or one in space, leading to another planet. We can maybe expect Manny and Ellie in Vegas, or Scrat on Mars. This particular land looks a great deal like a primeval jungle, if such a wilderness had lava falls as well as waterfalls. As it is subterranean, it has sort of a rock roof, although indirect lighting comes from somewhere and sustains lush vegetation.

All of our friends are back, and some new ones, including a ferocious T-Rex and a sexy rival for Scrat the squirrel, named Scrattè, accent grave over the *e*. As befits this land before time, Scrat and Scrattè are saber-toothed squirrels. No wonder the big teeth died out. They're of more use to a carnivore than a vegetarian. But logic like this is of no use in a movie where Sid the sloth (voice by John Leguizamo) adopts three dinosaur eggs and plans to raise the babies.

That's how they all end up underground in the Hollow Earth, the land Edgar Rice Burroughs name Pellucidar, and I guess with a place like that, you can name it anything you want. The mother dinosaur comes looking for her hatchlings, grabs them and Sid, and disappears under the surface. An all-for-one, one-for-all spirit has grown among our friends, who give chase: Manny and Ellie the woolly mammoths (Ray Romano and Queen Latifah), Diego the saber-toothed tiger (Denis Leary), and the possums Eddie and Crash (Josh Peck and Seann William Scott). They meet Buck the weasel (Simon Pegg), who has an eye patch instead of a peg leg and is obsessed with his quest for a Great White Dinosaur, unfortunately not named Moby Dino.

In the Ice Age films the tiger has learned to coexist with such edible species as sloths and gazelles, but dinosaurs aren't covered by the terms of the truce, and this one is so big it could eat even a woolly mammoth in one chomp. That sets us up for the staple of the series—chase scenes involving dizzying falls, catapults into the sky, close shaves, and possible digestion. This is pure invention, and unlike the monotonous chase sequences in some family animation, *Ice Age: Dawn of the Dinosaurs* is tirelessly inventive visually.

Carlos Saldanha, writer of the 2002 film and codirector of the (disappointing) *Ice Age: The Meltdown* (2006), is the director this time, and many of his sequences are in the spirit of the brilliant Scrat-and-acorn scene that opened the first *Ice Age*. That includes one in which Scrat, Scrattè, and the acorn are trapped inside floating bubbles, which is no big deal to the acorn. Still, this is a talented acorn, which sings a tune from the Gilbert O'Sullivan songbook to express how alone an acorn must sometimes feel. An acorn that smart, you don't want to eat all at once.

I thought the 3-D was done well. I remain unconvinced by the process. You have to fool with the glasses, the brightness is dimmed, and so on. But I was surprised how well *Dawn of the Dinosaurs* implements it. It creates much less of a distracting superfluous dimension, and more skillfully makes the whole image seem to belong together. The movie is also widely being shown in 2-D, and if you want to save a few bucks, that's the way to go.

Note: Here's a nice, bright 2-D scene including the new character Buck: www.apple.com/trailers/fox/iceagedawnofthedinosaurs/large_clip. html/.

I Hate Valentine's Day ★ ½

PG-13, 90 m., 2009

Nia Vardalos (Genevieve Gernier), John Corbett (Greg Gatlin), Judah Friedlander (Dan O'Finn), Stephen Guarino (Bill), Amir Arison (Bob), Zoe Kazan (Tammy Greenwood), Rachel Dratch (Kathy Jeemy). Directed by Nia Vardalos and produced by William Sherak, Jason Shuman, and Madeleine Sherak. Screenplay by Vardalos, Ben Zook, and Stephen David.

I Hate Valentine's Day is a romantic comedy with one peculiarity: The heroine is stark staring mad. I will tell you how I arrived at this diagnosis. Genevieve has an unbreakable policy regarding men: Five dates, and she's out the door. She even specifies exactly what each of the dates must be like, leading up to number five, during which she doesn't say so, but going all the way is a possibility.

Why does she impose these draconian measures? Because she likes only the falling in love part of an affair and not the inevitable breaking up. She expects a guy to jump through the hoops and then disappear after number five, remaining, of course, a "friend." When a woman says, "We should stay friends," it translates as, "Take your genitals to a faraway place and limit our contact to sending me flowers on my birthday."

Let's assume conservatively that Genevieve started dating when she was twenty, and that she has met on average three men a year willing to accept her strictures. And that after completing all the requirements, half of them have triumphantly arrived at home plate. Given her age, which a gentlemen does not mention, that works out to thirty-nine sex partners. According to surveys reported by ABC News and the *New York Times,* which I don't necessarily believe, the average American woman has between four and seven sex partners in a lifetime. That means Genevieve is not only an obsessive-compulsive, but a nympho.

Yet she looks so sweet. And knows she does. Yes, this is the second movie in a month, after *My Life in Ruins,* in which Nia Vardalos goes through the entire film smiling brightly and almost continuously. Nobody smiles that much unless they suffer from the rare giocondaphobia, or Constantly Smiling Syndrome, a complaint more often seen among listeners of Bill O'Reilly and field hands in *Gone With the Wind.*

Genevieve is a woman beloved by all who encounter her, when in life I would be terrified of her. She is considered a source of great wisdom about romance, although Dr. Phil might advise protective custody. In *I Hate Valentine's Day,* she runs the cutest little florist's shop in Brooklyn and dispenses invaluable advice to men uncertain about a Valentine's Day gift ("flowers"). She has two gay assistants who think she is about the best thing since Maria Callas. And this cute guy opens a tapas bar next door, named Get on Tapas, ha ha.

The cute guy is played by John Corbett, her costar in *My Big Fat Greek Wedding.* He is way too desirable to have to settle for the five-date rule. The women from *Sex and the City* would be camped out in pup tents on his sidewalk. It should have occurred to someone, maybe Vardalos, the writer and director, that it would have been funnier and way more plausible to make the hero a needy schlub who is lovestruck by her and would agree to waterboarding for even one date. The movie is set up as a valentine to Vardalos. She should try sending herself flowers.

Il Divo ★ ★ ★ ½

NO MPAA RATING, 117 m., 2009

Toni Servillo (Giulio Andreotti), Anna Bonaiuto (Livia Andreotti), Giulio Bosetti (Eugenio Scalfari), Flavio Bucci (Franco Evangelisti), Carlo Buccirosso (Paolo Cirino Pomicino), Giorgio Colangeli (Salvo Lima). Directed by Paolo Sorrentino and produced by Nicola Giuliano, Francesca Cima, and Andrea Occhipinti. Screenplay by Sorrentino.

They would seem to be opposites, but on the basis of two recent films, the longtime Italian prime minister Giulio Andreotti and the longtime fashion emperor Valentino were surprisingly similar. Both are seen as intensely private, rarely happy, single-minded in pursuit of their ambitions, cool in their personal relationships, and ruling as if by divine right. A difference is that Valentino was never accused of criminal activities.

Another difference is that they've inspired radically different films. *Valentino: The Last Emperor* is reverential; *Il Divo* is fascinated by what it presents as Andreotti's lifelong career of skullduggery. Still serving the Italian state as a senator for life at the age of ninety, he entered politics in 1946 and was prime minister during most of the years between 1972 and 1992. During much of that time he was widely believed to have associations with the mafia, and *Il Divo* shows him imagining a confession to his wife in which he links himself to 236 deaths. One of those might include the murder of Aldo Moro, his election rival, who was kidnapped by the Red Brigades and killed after fifty-four days when Andreotti shockingly refused to negotiate a ransom.

What you would not guess from this history is that *Il Divo* is a deadpan, horrified comedy. The writer-director Paolo Sorrentino is fascinated by Andreotti's wicked intelligence, his awareness that so many believe the worst of him, his enigmatic mask. He fascinated his contemporaries; Margaret Thatcher once said of him: "He seemed to have a positive aversion to principle, even a conviction that a man of principle was doomed to be a figure of fun." He said of himself: "Power is a disease one has no desire to be cured of." He knew where all the strings were attached, and once told a pope: "Your Holiness, forgive me, but you don't know the Vatican like I do."

What is astonishing is that a film like this could be made about a man still living. One imagines Andreotti reflecting that it only enhances his larger-than-life image. His Christian Democrats ruled postwar Italy until 1992, by which time the party was in such disrepute that it no longer survives. Yet he prevails. He prevails, and the legend is only enhanced by the great performance here by Toni Servillo, an actor who succeeds in making him hypnotizing by supplying him with an almost cheerful lack of the slightest magnetism. Here was a man who suppressed the usual charm of a politician, perhaps aware he worked better as an enigma. Was he thinking of himself when he famously said, "You sin in thinking bad about people; but often, you guess right"?

The film proceeds like a black comedy version of *The Godfather,* crossed with Oliver Stone's *Nixon.* It assembles a roll call of figures in postwar Italian politics, society, and crime, uses an abundance of names and dates in captions, and makes us despair of keeping track until we realize we're not intended to—the purpose of all these facts is simply to evoke the sheer scope and breadth of Andreotti's machinations. The more we learn, the more fascinated we become, as Servillo portrays him as poker-faced, hunched, impassive, observing all, revealing little, wise, and cynical beyond measure. Imagine Dick Cheney without the jolly charisma.

After I saw *Il Divo,* I suppose I should have felt indignation. I suppose I should also have felt that way after *The Godfather.* But such films present such mesmerizing figures that I simply regard them, astonished. I wonder if just before a snake strikes you, you think, "What an amazing snake!" The Italians, you have to admit, get good value for their money. Who could possibly follow Andreotti as prime minister? Try Silvio Berlusconi.

Note: "Il Divo" was also the nickname of Julius Caesar, a name suggesting "the divine one." Andreotti's other nicknames, per Wikipedia: Beelzebub, the Hunchback, the Sphinx, and the Black Pope.

The Illusionist ★ ★ ★ ★

PG, 90 m., 2010

With the voices of: Jean-Claude Donda (Illusionist), Eilidh Rankin (Alice). Directed by Sylvain Chomet and produced by Chomet and Bob Last. Screenplay by Chomet and Jacques Tati.

The Illusionist represents the magically melancholy final act of Jacques Tati's career. Tati, of course, was the tall Frenchman, bowing from the waist, pipe in mouth, often wearing a trench coat, pants too short, always the center of befuddlements. If you've seen *Mr. Hulot's Holiday,* you know who he was, and if you haven't, it belongs in your holding pattern.

Tati, who died in 1982, wrote the screenplay for this film but never made it. He intended it for live action. As the story goes, his daughter Sophie Tatischeff still had the script and handed it to Sylvain Chomet, who made the miraculously funny animated film *The Triplets of Belleville* (2003). Chomet has drawn it with a lightness and beauty worthy of an older, sadder Miyazaki story. Animation suits it. Live action would overwhelm its delicate fancy with realism.

The story involves a magician named Tatischeff who fails in one music hall after another, and ends up in Scotland, where at last he finds one fan: a young woman who idealizes him, moves in with him, tends to him, cooks and cleans, and would probably offer sex if he didn't abstemiously sleep on the couch. He's a good magician on a small scale, flawless at every trick except producing a rabbit from a hat. His problem there involves his frisky rabbit, which likes to sleep on Tatischeff's stomach at night. The rabbit makes it a practice during the act to pop up and peep around at inopportune moments.

Tatischeff finally ends up in Edinburgh, a city that has never looked more bleak and beautiful in a film. Time has passed him by. Audiences prefer pop groups to aging magicians. He reaches the lowest stage in his career, performing in a shop window. He remains quiet, reflective, almost indifferent to the girl (although he buys her a pretty frock).

If you recall the opening scenes of *Up*, you know that animation is sometimes more effective than live action for conveying the arc of a life. This magician does what he does very well, but there's no longer a purpose for him. Did Tati feel the same when he wrote this in the 1950s, before *Hulot* was a worldwide success?

Important to the charm of *The Illusionist* is the grace with which the character of Tatischeff has been drawn. He looks like Tati, but much more important, he has the inimitable body language. The polite formality, the deliberate movement, the hesitation, the diffidence. His world is an illusion, which he produces nightly from a hat.

Tati became a legendary man of the cinema, a perfectionist producing a small body of enormously ambitious films that can be described as meticulous silent comedies with sound. The major works are *Jour de Fete* (1949), the worldwide hit *Mr. Hulot's Holiday* (1953), *Mon Oncle* (1958), *Play Time* (1967), *Trafic* (1971), and *Parade* (1974). He was admired and beloved.

He was also flawed, and one area of concern involves his family. After *The Illusionist* played at Cannes 2010, I received a letter from his middle grandson, Richard Tatischeff Schiel McDonald, telling me that the Chomet version "greatly undermines both the artistry of my grandfather's original script whilst shamefully ignoring the deeply troubled personal story that lies at its heart."

Briefly, he writes of Tati, "in the script he wrestles with the notion of publicly acknowledging his eldest daughter, my mother, who he had under duress from his elder sister heartlessly abandoned during the Second World War." It is a fraught family story, and the full and fascinating letter is here: http://bit.ly/dkigRT.

Becoming aware of these facts, and how they were apparently sublimated in Tati's more fanciful tale, only adds interest to *The Illusionist.* However the film stands on its own, and however much it conceals the real life events that inspired it, it lives and breathes on its own, and as an extension of the mysterious whimsy of Tati.

I Love You, Beth Cooper ★ ★

PG-13, 102 m., 2009

Hayden Panettiere (Beth Cooper), Paul Rust (Denis Cooverman), Jack Carpenter (Rich Munsch), Lauren London (Cammy Alcott), Lauren Storm (Treece Kilmer). Directed by Chris Columbus and produced by Columbus, Michael Barnathan, and Mark Radcliffe. Screenplay by Larry Doyle, based on his novel.

The writer of *I Love You, Beth Cooper* says the story is based on a dream. I believe him. This is one of the very few movies where I *wanted* the hero to wake up and discover it was only a dream. But it's a dream all the way through—a dream evoking just another teen romcom.

The situation is so universal. The high school nerd harbors a secret crush on the most popular girl in school. He chooses the occasion of his valedictory speech to publicly proclaim this love. We can believe that, all the way up to the valedictory speech. But, yes, this is another movie hailing a hero with the courage to say what he really believes and accept the consequences.

Sometimes, as in a dream, doing that will pay off abundantly by focusing the popular girl's attention on how unique and special you are. Sometimes the popular girl will reveal herself as actually a warm and cuddly human being. Sometimes. More often, the nerd will confirm everyone's belief in his nerdhood, humiliate himself, selfishly derail the whole graduation exercise, and discover that the most popular girl really *is* a bitch. Lots of wonderful girls fall in love with nerds. They may not become the most popular girl in school, but they don't care. That honor carries with it a terrible lifetime price tag.

So what I wish is that *I Love You, Beth Cooper* had awakened from its dream and been a smart high school comedy, even one subscribing to an alternate set of clichés in which the hero discovers he really loves the nerdy girl once she takes off her glasses.

I am also tiring of the way high school movies insist that all nonheroic characters travel in posses of three. All Most Popular Girls arrive flanked by two girlfriends who follow them by half a step. And all macho villains have two underlings who follow their orders. In *I Love You, Beth Cooper*, the girlfriends are nice enough, because the heroine is. But the villain, "Muncher" Munsch (Jack Carpenter), is a uniformed ROTC officer who, along with his sidekicks, is a muscular master of the martial arts, a skilled gymnast, and a vicious bully. When he whistles, his minions snap to attention. And they attack with coordination worthy of a dance troupe.

The movie also goes over the top with special effects, where the theory "less is more" must be in an incomprehensible language. I know that fierce struggles over romance can break out in high school, but with these kids, I doubt they would threaten to be lethal. Nor is driving an SUV into a house commonplace. Scene after scene is on autopilot.

I'm thinking of films that remember what it's like to be a teenager with a hopeless love. *Almost Famous, Lucas, Say Anything, The Man in the Moon.* If I were a filmmaker like Chris Columbus, who has directed two of the Harry Potter films, I don't know if I'd bother with this genre unless I felt I could make a film aspiring to that kind of stature.

Of the two costars, what I can say is that I'm looking forward to their next films. Hayden Panettiere (Beth) is professional and lovable and convincingly projects emotions and has a face the screen loves. Paul Rust (Denis the valedictorian) can be very earnest and sincere, and seems to actually take the plot seriously, which is more than I could do.

I Love You, Man ★ ★ ★ ½

R, 104 m., 2009

Paul Rudd (Peter Klaven), Jason Segel (Sydney Fife), Rashida Jones (Zooey), Andy Samberg (Robbie), J. K. Simmons (Oz), Jane Curtin (Joyce), Jon Favreau (Barry), Jaime Pressly (Denise). Directed by John Hamburg and produced by Hamburg and Donald De Line. Screenplay by Hamburg and Larry Levin.

I would like to have a friend like Sydney Fife. I think a lot of guys would. Even though it's funny, charming, and lighthearted, that may be the basic appeal of *I Love You, Man*. Sydney represents the freedoms most men hesitate to give themselves, maybe through fear of ending up alone, arrested, or locked inside behavior that looks fun when you're young but crazy when you're older. The great thing about Sydney is that he lives your fantasies so you don't have to yourself.

Peter needs a Sydney (Jason Segel) in his life. He has been told this by Zooey (Rashida Jones), the girl he plans to marry. She would, however, have preferred a less extreme case than *this* Sydney. Peter (Paul Rudd) is a Realtor who is hopelessly, even touchingly, clueless when it comes to seeming the least bit cool. One of those really nice guys who, when the chips are down, has no idea where to look, what to say, how to move, or how to extricate himself gracefully from an impossible situation. He gets along great with women but has no male best friend, and actually needs to find one to be best man at his wedding.

Because this is a romcom, various obligatory scenes are necessary; Peter goes shopping for a best friend on some man-dates with guys met on the Internet, with predictable results. The movie feels locked into formula until the appearance of Sydney, met while scarfing free food at Peter's open house for the home of Lou Ferrigno. Jason Segel brings sunshine into the movie; we like his character even more quickly than Peter does.

Sydney lives in a little frame cottage a block up the street from the Venice Beach boardwalk. This house was cheap in, oh, say, the Depression. Now it only looks cheap. We never see its interior; Sydney escorts Peter directly to his "man cave," a converted garage in the backyard where he keeps all his toys: drum set, guitars, music system, flat-screen TV, movie posters, lava lamps, weird souvenirs, recliner chairs, wet bar, fridge, wall hangings, even an area dedicated to . . . well, never mind.

Jason Segel plays Sydney as a man thoroughly comfortable within his own skin, an unapologetic hedonist who uses his intelligence as a comic weapon. Essentially, the whole movie is based on the fact that he is able to create an actually plausible, human best friend. Incredibly, this is the first time I'm aware of seeing him in a movie. I apparently saw him in *SLC Punk!* and *Slackers* (zero stars), but never saw his recent *Forgetting Sarah Marshall.* I think he's a natural for Walter Matthau, and both Segel and Rudd would be perfect for a SoCal retread of the classic British one-upmanship comedy *School for Scoundrels.*

Rudd is also very good and very funny, using delicate timing to create a man who is never quite right for the room. Observe his attempts to look loose and casual. He even pulls off sincere scenes with the lovely Rashida Jones, and sincerity, as we know, is the downfall of many a romcom and almost all buddy movies. I believe my Little Movie Glossary even contains an entry about an obligatory moment in all buddy movies in which one of the characters says, you guessed it, "I love you, man."

John Hamburg, who cowrote and directed, populates his film with many other gifted comedy actors, including J. K. Simmons as Peter's father, Jane Curtin as his mother, Andy Samberg as his gay brother, and Jon Favreau and Jaime Pressly as a married couple from hell—their own. Lou Ferrigno finds the right note as the client about to fire his Realtor, who has asked himself the question, "How many people want to buy a mansion in Beverly Hills with a statue of the Incredible Hulk in the garden?"

I Love You, Man is above all just plain funny. It's funny with some dumb physical humor, yes, and some gross-out jokes apparently necessary to all buddy movies, but also funny in observations, dialogue, physical behavior, and Sydney Fife's observations as a people watcher. I heard a lot of *real* laughter from a preview audience, not the perfunctory laughter at manufactured payoffs. You feel good watching the movie. That's what comedies are for, right? Right?

I Love You Phillip Morris ★ ★ ★ ½

R, 98 m., 2010

Jim Carrey (Steven Russell), Ewan McGregor (Phillip Morris), Leslie Mann (Debbie), Rodrigo Santoro (Jimmy), Michael Mandel (Cleavon). Directed by Glenn Ficarra and John Requa and produced by Andrew Lazar and Far Shariat. Screenplay by Ficarra and Requa, based on the book by Steve McVicker.

If you wanted to make a movie about the life of Steven Russell, you might start with this question: Can we get Jim Carrey? You would need an actor who can seem both instantly lovable and always up to no good. That *I Love You Phillip Morris* is based on a true story is relevant only because it is too preposterous to be fiction. Russell is a con man, and his lifelong con is selling himself to himself.

That process begins when he discovers he isn't who he thought he was. His parents tell him he is adopted. My notion is that if you love your parents and they tell you you're adopted, you'd love them even more. It doesn't work that way for Steven Russell. Once that rug has been pulled from beneath his feet, he sets about creating a new reality for himself. He becomes a police officer. He marries Debbie (Leslie Mann), as wholesome as a toothpaste model. They have two children. He plays the church organ. He is a poster boy for truth, justice, and the American Way.

Continuing to seek truth, he discovers the identity of his birth mother. Shall we say she is a disappointment. After a traumatic accident, he has time in the hospital to reflect that his entire life has been constructed out of other people's spare parts. Who is he *really*? He decides he is gay. Not only gay but flamboyantly, stereotypically gay, and soon living with a Latin lover (Rodrigo Santoro) on Miami's South Beach. He begins to pass checks and defraud credit cards to finance their heady lifestyle.

Now when I wrote "he decides he is gay," did some of you think you don't "decide" to be gay—you simply are, or are not? I believe that's the case almost all the time. I'm not completely sure about Steven Russell. The movie reveals him as an invention, an improvisation, constantly in rehearsal to mislead the world because he has a *need* to deceive. Who could be less like a churchgoing cop and family man than a South Beach playboy? Does he like gay sex? Yes, and very energetically indeed. Does he like straight sex? You bet he does. He can sell himself on anything. I think gay sex is the easier sell.

The method of *I Love You Phillip Morris*

provides great quantities of plot and then holds them at arm's length. It isn't really about plot. Plots are scenarios that characters are involved in. Steven Russell improvises his own scenario, so that most of what happens is his own handiwork in one way or another. Carrey makes the role seem effortless; he deceives as spontaneously as others breathe.

The authorities have a supporting role. He keeps breaking the law, and they keep arresting him. After he's imprisoned for theft and fraud, life changes when he's assigned a new cell mate: Phillip Morris (a blond Ewan McGregor as we've never seen him before). Steven falls in love. Or perhaps, as the song has it, he falls in love with love. After he's released, he creates a new persona, a lawyer, and floats this deception with a single shred of proof to pull off a stunt that gets Phillip out of prison. McGregor rises to this occasion like a dazzled ingénue.

Phillip is in love with Steven; that's not in doubt. But he is slow to understand the depth and complexity of Steven's fabrications. He's a sweet kid with a naive Southern accent, and not the brightest bulb on the tree. He's a bystander as Steven steals a fortune from a health care organization that has possibly never even employed him. Steven is soon back behind bars, and the movie unfolds into a series of increasingly audacious and labyrinthine confidence schemes.

All of this, as I said, is based on Russell's own story, as written by Steve McVicker of the *Houston Press.* Russell impersonated doctors, lawyers, FBI agents, and the CFO of a health care company. He convinced prison officials he had died of AIDS and later successfully faked a heart attack. He escaped from jail four times (hint: always on Friday the 13th). He is now serving 144 years in Texas in maximum security and solitary confinement, which seems a bit much for a man who never killed anyone and stole a lot less money than the officers of Enron.

The Imaginarium of Doctor Parnassus ★ ★ ★

PG-13, 122 m., 2010

Heath Ledger (Tony), Johnny Depp (Imaginarium Tony 1), Jude Law (Imaginarium Tony 2), Colin Farrell (Imaginarium Tony 3), Christopher Plummer (Dr. Parnassus), Andrew Garfield (Anton), Verne Troyer (Percy), Lily Cole (Valentina), Tom Waits (Mr. Nick). Directed by Terry Gilliam and produced by Amy Gilliam, Terry Gilliam, Samuel Hadida, and William Vince. Screenplay by Terry Gilliam and Charles McKeown.

The traditional motto at Second City is Something Wonderful Right Away, and maybe Terry Gilliam has the words displayed on his mirror when he shaves every morning. He has never faltered. *The Imaginarium of Doctor Parnassus* could be seen as a sideshow version of his own life, with him playing the role of the pitchman who lures you into his fantasies. That they may seem extravagant and overheated, all smoke and mirrors, is, after all, in the nature of a pitchman's fantasies.

The story in Gilliam's fevered new film is all over the map as usual, but this time there's a reason for it. His wild inventions in character, costumes, and CGI effects are accounted for by a plot that requires revolving worlds. Elements of this plot were made necessary by the tragic death of Heath Ledger halfway into the shooting, but the plot itself, I think, was in place from the first.

It involves a bizarre, threadbare traveling show that unfolds out of a rickety old wagon in rundown pockets of London occupied mostly by drunks and grotesques. The show consists of the (very, very) old Dr. Parnassus (Christopher Plummer) perching ominously on a stool while his barker, Anton (Andrew Garfield), his daughter, Valentina (Lily Cole), and his angry dwarf, Percy (Verne Troyer), try to perform for an unruly handful of lager louts.

Percy and Anton save the life of a man hanging from a bridge. Why only they can perform this task is wisely not explained. The man on the rope is Tony (Heath Ledger). I know. He joins the show, is appalled by its archaic form, and suggests updates. The reason it's creaky is that Dr. Parnassus is many centuries old, having made a pact with Satan (Tom Waits, as usual) to live forever on condition that Satan can possess his daughter when she turns sixteen. You have to admit, Dr. Parnassus didn't rush into reproduction. Of course, he wants out of the deal. Satan frequently runs into credit payment risks.

Tony, it develops, can enter/evoke/control/create strange worlds on the other side of a looking glass on the shabby stage. In these worlds anything goes, which is always to Gilliam's liking. CGI allows the director and his designers to run riot, which they do at a gallop, and some wondrous visions materialize.

I believe Ledger was intended to be the guide through all of these. But Gilliam apparently completed filming all the outer-world London scenes, Ledger returned to New York for R&R, and the rest is sad history. Gilliam replaced him by casting Johnny Depp, Jude Law, and Colin Farrell as the Tonys of Imaginariums 1 through 3 and offering no other explanation, as indeed with Imaginariums he isn't required to do. Depp looks the most like Ledger, but it's a melancholy fact that Farrell steals the role.

My problem with Terry Gilliam's pictures is that they lack a discernible story line. I don't require A-B-C, Act 1–2–3, but I do rather appreciate having some notion of a film's own rules. Gilliam indeed practices Something Wonderful Right Away, and you get the notion that if a bright idea pops into his head, he feels free to write it into his screenplay under the Cole Porter Rule (Anything Goes). Knowing my history with Gilliam, whom I always want to like more than I do, I attended the Cannes screening of *Dr. Parnassus* in order to be baffled, which I was, and then the Chicago press screening, where I had an idea what was coming and tried to reopen my mind. Gilliam is, you understand, a nice man, and has never committed the sin of failing to amaze.

Now what I see are a group of experienced actors gamely trying to keep their heads while all about are losing theirs. Can it be easy to play one-third of a guide to one-third of an arbitrary world? You just have to plunge in. Ledger himself, who makes Tony relatively grounded in the "real" world, must have been prepared to do the same, and would have lent the story more continuity. Still, this movie is an Imaginarium indeed. The best approach is to sit there and let it happen to you: See it in the moment and not with long-term memory, which seems to be what Dr. Parnassus does. It keeps his mind off Satan's plans for his daughter.

Imagine That ★ ★ ½

PG, 107 m., 2009

Eddie Murphy (Evan Danielson), Thomas Haden Church (Johnny Whitefeather), Yara Shahidi (Olivia Danielson), Nicole Ari Parker (Trish), Ronny Cox (Tom Stevens), Martin Sheen (Dante D'Enzo), DeRay Davis (John Strother). Directed by Karey Kirkpatrick and produced by Ed Solomon and Lorenzo di Bonaventura. Screenplay by Solomon and Chris Matheson.

Eddie Murphy's new family comedy is a pleasant and unassuming fantasy in which a high-powered investment adviser gets advice from his daughter's imaginary friends. We never see the friends, but we see a great deal of the daughter, and it's a charming performance from newcomer Yara Shahidi.

She plays Olivia, seven years old, who doesn't see nearly enough of her daddy. He is Evan Danielson (Murphy), who is competing for a big promotion at his Denver investment firm. Olivia is being raised by his former wife, Trish (Nicole Ari Parker), who insists it is time for the child to spend some quality time with her father.

Evan is not well equipped to handle this, or much of anything else apart from his job. He can't find babysitters, takes the kid to the office, and to his horror discovers she has drawn with water paints all over his notes and charts for a crucial meeting. It does not go well. He's upstaged by Johnny Whitefeather (Thomas Haden Church), a Native American who evokes the great spirits and Indian legends to convince the clients the force is with him.

In response, Murphy does one of his semi-comic riffs, desperately improvising advice from the stories Olivia told him about her drawings. He returns to his office expecting to be fired but amazingly the advice turns out to be solid gold. But how did he do that? What did Olivia know? She knew what a fairy princess told her, and she can see her imaginary world when she has her precious blue blankie over her head. Evan doesn't know what else to do, so he starts turning to Olivia for more investment tips, and she's right again and again.

The movie is amusing without ever being break-out funny—except for one scene, loudly appreciated by the kiddies in the audience, when he makes pancakes and Olivia insists he eat them covered with gobs of ketchup, mustard, chocolate sauce, and hot sauce. Kids may not get all the verbal jokes, but playing with food, they understand.

Murphy stays interestingly in character, not going over the top. He does his usual rapid-fire dialogue and desperate invention, but more sanely than usual. The film is really about the father-daughter relationship, and Murphy comes through as sincere, confused, lonely, and with a good heart.

The key to the chemistry between them is Yara Shahidi's work as the daughter. Apparently she really is seven, and her previous experience is limited to three episodes of *In the Motherhood.* She's a natural. I never caught her trying to be "cute." She played every scene straight and with confidence, and she's filled with personality. I've been noticing recently how good the child actors are in movies. Maybe they grow up inputting acting from TV. I wonder why not all young actors can bring this gift with them into adulthood. To paraphrase e.e. cummings: And down they forgot as up they grew.

The third major role, by Thomas Haden Church, is an interesting invention: an Indian con man, trading on his background to score points in the boardroom, steamrollering the clients with his people's lore. This is funny. Is it offensive? Not when we find out more about Johnny Whitefeather.

So all of these elements are present in the film and supply nice moments, but director Karey Kirkpatrick, the writer of animated films such as *Chicken Run* and *Over the Hedge,* never brings them to takeoff velocity. They rest on the screen, pleasant, amusing, but too predictable for grown-ups and not broad enough for children. I couldn't believe *Imagine That* counts on one of the most exhausted clichés in the movies, the parent making a dramatic late entrance to a child's big concert.

Still, think about this: If the investment gurus of Wall Street had turned to their kids for advice, we might not be in such a mess.

IMAX: Hubble 3-D ★ ★ ★

G, 45 m., 2010

Leonardo DiCaprio (Narrator). Featuring the astronauts Scott D. Altman, Andrew J. Feustel, Michael T. Good, John M. Grunsfeld, Gregory C. Johnson, Michael J. Massimino, and K. Megan McArthur. Directed, written, and produced by Toni Myers.

When I think of space travel, I get a sort of mental tingle. It intrigues and frightens me. I have nightmares, possibly illustrated by *2001,* in which the astronaut Poole has his tether clipped by HAL 9000 and goes tumbling away into the immensity. Mercifully, his oxygen tube has been cut, so he will quickly be dead. I remember, too, a science fiction story that curdled my blood about an astronaut who is lost in space *with* a full tank of oxygen, and drifts into the void, his vision field filled with the universe.

Then you would know how small you were, how powerless and insignificant. When the end comes, it would be good to be set adrift into space, I think, with time for reflection, or perhaps madness. Fatal, yes, but so much less boring than the ceiling of a hospital room. I have always been intensely interested in thoughts of space.

IMAX: Hubble 3-D offers two categories of images, both awesome. One involves footage filmed on board the space shuttle Atlantis on a mission to repair the Hubble Space Telescope one last time. The other involves a 3-D rendering of some of Hubble's photographs of the cosmos. It's remarkable how casual the astronauts are, joking and performing for the camera. Then we see space walks in which they drift weightless to replace, adjust, and tune up Hubble. There is nothing there but the shuttle, Hubble, Earth, and the abyss. If they lose a tool, it is lost . . . forever, or until it is found millions and millions of years from now in a galaxy far away.

The fact that this footage exists at all is enough to justify it. Someone like me would need to see it. I would be happier if the astronauts had been less confident and casual. I suppose that's the astronaut culture. Could they have acted? Pretended to be tense, scared, deadly serious? They're like the crew on the *Star Trek* command deck, which most of the time might as well be controlling the traffic grid of a subway system.

The important thing to understand about the 3-D photography of stars is that they are too far away to give any true idea of their distance. Almost all of the objects in the universe are very, very far apart. What they did was take Hubble photographs of small and old (therefore young) slices of the sky and use spectrum analysis and a computer to separate the stars according to their distance. Although the narration by Leonardo DiCaprio doesn't mention this, the third dimension we're regarding is really time, not space. As the viewpoint moves forward toward galaxies, we are hurtling at unimaginable speed toward light that originated longer and longer ago.

Beyond the most distant stars, at the end of our ability to see, there is black nothingness. If you stood there and looked outward, what would you see? A logical question. The answer is: more universe. Not another universe, but this one, because space is curved, you see, and therefore has no edge. This answer satisfies me, although I do not understand it and cannot picture how space can be curved. I understand how a circle has no beginning and no end, and that helps.

So these are thoughts I had while watching *IMAX: Hubble 3-D.* A movie like this can get you thinking.

I'm Still Here ★ ★ ★

NO MPAA RATING, 108 m., 2010

Joaquin Phoenix, Antony Langdon, Sean Combs, David Letterman, and many others. A documentary directed by Casey Affleck and produced by Affleck, Joaquin Phoenix, and Amanda White.

A mind is a terrible thing to waste. The tragedy of Joaquin Phoenix's self-destruction has been made into *I'm Still Here,* a sad and painful documentary that serves little useful purpose other than to pound another nail into the coffin. Here is a gifted actor who apparently by his own decision has brought desolation upon his head. He was serious when he said he would never act again. He was serious when he announced a career as a hip-hop artist. He wasn't goofing when he was on the Letterman show. He was flying into pieces.

For reasons that are unclear and sidestepped, this process was documented on video by the actor Casey Affleck, who is married to Joaquin's sister Summer. It's not well done technically—the image and sound are bad—but it has the advantage of access to private and tormented moments. After Phoenix imploded during a famous appearance on Letterman, we see him leaving a limousine in Central Park, crawling up an embankment into some shrubbery, and screaming that he has destroyed his life, his music sucks, he will never be able to act again, and "I'm totally f—ked!"

All of this is true. At least we must assume it is. If this film turns out to *still* be part of an elaborate hoax, I'm going to be seriously pissed. Actually, there are subtle signs it might be. The scene in Central Park: Is it a little too perfect dramatically? The scenes of cocaine sniffing, the nude parties including Joaquin's assistant Antony Langdon and two hookers: Were they really possible with a director, cinematographer, and sound man in the room? Would Casey Affleck release this devastating film with the acquiescence of his wife?

Apparently so. It exists, it was released, I've seen it, and Joaquin Phoenix, as the title assures us, is still here. One doubts he will be walking the red carpet if the film has a premiere. It documents a train wreck. A luxury train—one carrying Phoenix, his several personal assistants, his agent, his publicist, and apparently not one single friend who isn't on salary. A train that flies off the tracks and tumbles into the abyss.

Phoenix comes across as a narcissist interested only in himself. He is bored with acting. He was only a puppet. He can no longer stand where he's told, wear what he's given, say what is written. It's not him. He has lost contact with his inner self. He allows that true self to emerge here as a fearsomely bearded, deliberately shabby, chain-smoking egotist who screams at his patient assistants, blames himself on everyone else, and has deluded himself into thinking that there is a future in his dreadful hip-hop lyrics.

He thinks fame and fortune are due him. He earned them in his acting career, yes, but he will no longer act. He expects Sean Combs to *want* to produce his CD, although Combs has worked hard to earn the respect that Phoenix manifestly doesn't deserve. He's a little surprised that Combs remains sensible during their negotiations, expecting to be *paid* for his services and oh, you know, studios, musicians, sound engineers, those kinds of things. He stands in the middle of an airport, puzzled that no limousine awaits. He flies to Obama's inauguration, not invited, and doesn't make it outside of his hotel room. He is mystified that he may no longer be able to afford his Los Angeles home.

Phoenix's hip-hop performances are incomprehensible. The lyrics that we hear are lead-footed and stupid. During one performance he races from the stage and vomits copiously. He is enabled by his saintly staff, including Langdon, who has been with him for years and appears to be paid as a twenty-four-hour companion, since it's doubtful anyone would want to be with this man for free. Antony, we learn, has recently become a recovering alcoholic.

Which leads us to Phoenix's substance abuse problems. He doesn't drink much in the film. He smokes a great deal of what looks like pot. He says he scored cocaine in New York, and hardly seems to be using it for the first time. He has no onscreen moment when he appears clean or sober. Whether drugs alone could account for his condition, or whether mental illness is also involved, is not for me to say.

But I will say this: Joaquin Phoenix is a good actor. I was astonished by his performance as Johnny Cash in *Walk the Line* (2005). He was so good in other films, including the superb *Reservation Road* (2007), *Two Lovers* (2008), and *Gladiator* (2000), although I was unenthusiastic about the film. Whether he wants to be an actor is his business. Many great and worthy people have been, and in this film we see or hear about Paul Newman, Sean Penn, Jack Nicholson, and for that matter Danny DeVito (whom Phoenix dismisses).

I have hope that if Phoenix ever cleans up his body and mind, he can be restored and can be happy again. See how Robert Downey Jr. and Dennis Hopper came back from the edge of the grave. We do not desperately need another actor, but Joaquin is imprisoned within his illness, and he desperately needs to get well. If he wants a career as a singer—well, why not country music? In *Walk the Line* he proved he has a talent for it. In *I'm Still Here* all he proves is that he is hurtling toward the same pointless oblivion that killed his brother River. It is a waste of the privilege of life.

Note: Regarding the film's three-star rating: It could be one, it could be four. What do stars have to do with it?

In a Better World ★ ★ ½

R, 113 m., 2011

Mikael Persbrandt (Anton), Trine Dyrholm (Marianne), Ulrich Thomsen (Claus), Markus Rygaard (Elias), William Johnk Nielsen (Christian), Kim Bodnia (Lars), Evans Muthini (Big Man). Directed by Susanne Bier and produced by Peter Aalbaek Jensen. Screenplay by Anders Thomas Jensen.

A new book by a Cambridge University scholar suggests that a lack of empathy is at the root of all cruelty. People are not intrinsically evil, argues Simon Baron-Cohen, but some lack the ability to identify with what others are feeling: "People who lack empathy see others as mere objects."

Although I doubt Susanne Bier knew of this book when she made *In a Better World*, it plays like a demonstration of the same insight. In parallel stories set in Denmark and Africa, it considers characters who act with cruelty and those who deliberately seek to act with empathy, and poses some moral choices for those who fall somewhere in the middle of the spectrum.

In a Better World, which won this year's Academy Award for best foreign film, centers on two boys and their fathers. Elias (Markus Rygaard) and Christian (William Johnk Nielsen) meet at the school where Christian has just transferred. Elias is a cute kid with braces, and when he's picked on by the school bully, Christian defends him in a sudden and bloody way. "Nobody will pick on me again," he explains.

Now pull back a step to their fathers. Elias's dad is Anton (Mikael Persbrandt), who commutes between Denmark and an unnamed African country, where he operates a free medical clinic. To his care come victims of all sorts, including women savagely sliced by the powerful local Big Man (Evans Muthini). Christian's dad is Claus (Ulrich Thomsen), whose wife has died of cancer and left Christian resenting his father.

Anton is often in Africa, and Claus is often in London. The two boys bond. One day when Anton is home, he and Elias see a foul-tempered local man named Lars (Kim Bodnia) pushing around people who innocently offended him. Anton steps in, and Lars slaps him. Thinking this over, Anton decides to set an example to his son, and takes him to Lars's auto shop for what is intended as a nonviolent confrontation. Lars is incapable of such a thing.

Christian, very inward, very intense, earlier defended Elias against the schoolyard bully, and now devises a plan for them to gain revenge against Lars. Meanwhile, back in Africa, Anton's clinic receives an emergency patient: Big Man, with an ugly, festering leg wound.

No more about the plot. What Susanne Bier does is cut between all of these stories to contrast the kinds of people who are instinctively cruel and those who are instinctively kind. The outcomes of the parallel stories are unpredictable, although they follow a certain logic.

I admired her *Things We Lost in the Fire* and her Danish and American versions of *Brothers*, but here her method is too foregrounded. The African events in particular don't fit organically into the rest of the film, playing more like a contrived contrast. The story of the boys works well (they're both good actors), and their fathers are well drawn and seen with sympathy. There's also an estranged mother who is drawn into the unhappiness.

There are two strong stories here, in Africa and Denmark. Either could have made a film. Intercut in this way, they seem too much like self-conscious parables. No doubt the film's noble intentions appealed to the Academy voters, but this seems to me the weakest of the five nominees. What does the title suggest? That in a better world there would not be such cruelty? True, no doubt.

Incendies ★ ★ ★ ½

R, 130 m., 2011

Lubna Azabal (Nawal Marwan), Melissa Desormeaux-Poulin (Jeanne Marwan), Maxim Gaudette (Simon Marwan), Remy Girard (Notary Jean Lebel). Directed by Denis Villeneuve and produced by Luc Dery and Kim McCraw. Screenplay by Villeneuve, based on the play by Wajdi Mouawad.

After the death of their mother, twins in Montreal are called to the office of her employer. She had gone to work for him some twenty years ago in Canada after escaping sectarian violence and rage in a nation not unlike Lebanon. She left for her children, they learn, two letters. Jeanne (Melissa Desormeaux-Poulin) is asked to give hers to the father they never knew. Simon (Maxim Gaudette) is told to give his to a brother they didn't know they had.

This is a plot for a thriller, really, and Denis Villeneuve's Oscar-nominated *Incendies* doesn't shy away from that truth. But it wants to be much more than a thriller, and succeeds in demonstrating how senseless and futile it is to hate others because of their religion. Most people do not choose their religions but have them forced upon themselves by birth, and the lesson of *Incendies* is that an accident of birth is not a reason for hatred.

The heroine who comes to this conclusion is the author of the two letters, Nawal (Lubna Azabal), the twins' mother. Jeanne travels to the Middle East to carry out her mother's wishes. Simon stays resentfully in Canada until later in the story. In flashbacks spurred by Jeanne's meetings and conversations, we learn of Nawal's early life. Born a Christian, she fell in love with a Muslim. This was impossible for both of them in that time and place. It led her on a romantic, religious, and political odyssey, and inspired her to do unthinkable things.

All about her, others were also doing the unthinkable. People who were not murderers in their nature killed others and justified it, on both sides, in the names of their gods. And when enough people had died, they no longer needed their gods because they sought personal or tribal revenge. A season of murder by fanatics broadened into years of retribution by bystanders who took up their guns. Villeneuve is especially chilling when he shows young adolescents with rifles, killing others their own age when neither shooter nor target is old enough to understand the gift of life.

The plot of *Incendies* is based on a play by Wajdi Mouawad, described as consisting of poetic monologues. The screenplay by Villeneuve refashions the action in a way more suited to a film, where it is often better to show something than to evoke its mental image. The underlying story here could, with a few adjustments, be a noir set in any country, taking its choice of all the sad justifications men find for murder.

In its Middle Eastern setting, the film takes on a contemporary feel, and the scenes of battle, rape, and torture are concise and pitiless. The performance of Lubna Azabal, who plays Nawal over a range of years, is never less than compelling; she helps us understand in a visceral way why she acts as she does—as she must—under the circumstances she is unlucky enough to inherit. And Villeneuve's writing and direction do an effective job of making clear events that might have become cloudy. The specific way, in cryptic dialogue, that he reveals his film's shocking secret is flawless.

The film's ending, which you will not learn from me, is stunning in its impact. I am not sure it quite works out in terms of strict logic, but logic can be forgotten when the purpose is revelation. And that revelation, when it comes, lays bare the pathos of "justified" murder and the pathology of cruelty.

I am left with a question you might want to ask yourself after seeing the film: What was the mother's purpose in leaving the letters for her children? Yes, we can see, they deserve to know the truth about their father and their brother. She could have told them—either in life or, for that matter, in the letters. By sealing the letters she assigns them a mission that could easily have failed. If they had not found the recipients, they would not have learned the truth. Then what purpose did the letters serve?

Well, of course they provided the motive for Jeanne's journey, and later for Simon's. They're essentially MacGuffins. That's why I'm not so bothered by the device. A MacGuffin is a way of setting a story into motion, and *Incendies* tells a shocking one.

Inception ★ ★ ★ ★

PG-13, 148 m., 2010

Leonardo DiCaprio (Dom Cobb), Ken Watanabe (Saito), Joseph Gordon-Levitt (Arthur), Marion Cotillard (Mal), Ellen Page (Ariadne), Tom Hardy (Eames), Cillian Murphy (Robert Fischer), Tom Berenger (Browning), Michael Caine (Miles), Dileep Rao (Yusuf). Directed by Christopher Nolan and produced by Nolan and Emma Thomas. Screenplay by Nolan.

It's said that Christopher Nolan spent ten years writing his screenplay for *Inception.* That must have involved prodigious concentration, like playing blindfold chess while walking a tightwire. The film's hero tests a young architect by challenging her to create a maze, and Nolan tests us with his own dazzling maze. We have to trust him that he can lead us through because much of the time we're lost and disoriented. Nolan must have rewritten this story time and again, finding that every change had a ripple effect down through the whole fabric.

The story can either be told in a few sentences, or not told at all. Here is a movie immune to spoilers: If you knew how it ended, that would tell you nothing unless you knew how it got there. And telling you how it got there would produce bafflement. The movie is all about process, about fighting our way through enveloping sheets of reality and dream, reality within dreams, dreams without reality. It's a breathtaking juggling act, and Nolan may have considered his *Memento* (2000) a warm-up; he apparently started this screenplay while filming that one. It was the story of a man with short-term memory loss, and the story was told backward.

Like the hero of that film, the viewer of *Inception* is adrift in time and experience. We can never even be quite sure what the relationship between dream time and real time is. The hero explains that you can never remember the beginning of a dream, and that dreams that seem to cover hours may last only a short time. Yes, but you don't know that when you're dreaming. And what if you're inside another man's dream? How does your dream time synch with his? What do you really know?

Cobb (Leonardo DiCaprio) is a corporate raider of the highest order. He infiltrates the minds of other men to steal their ideas. Now he is hired by a powerful billionaire to do the opposite: to *introduce* an idea into a rival's mind, and do it so well he believes it is his own. This has never been done before; our minds are as alert to foreign ideas as our immune system is to pathogens. The rich man, named Saito (Ken Watanabe), makes him an offer he can't refuse, an offer that would end Cobb's forced exile from home and family.

Cobb assembles a team, and here the movie relies on the well-established procedures of all heist movies. We meet the people he will need to work with: Arthur (Joseph Gordon-Levitt), his longtime associate; Eames (Tom Hardy), a master at deception; Yusuf (Dileep Rao), a master chemist. And there is a new recruit, Ariadne (Ellen Page), a brilliant young architect who is a prodigy at creating spaces. Cobb also goes to touch base with his father-in-law, Miles (Michael Caine), who knows what he does and how he does it. These days Michael Caine need only appear on a screen and we assume he's wiser than any of the other characters. It's a gift.

But wait. Why does Cobb need an architect to create spaces in dreams? He explains to her. Dreams have a shifting architecture, as we all know; where we seem to be has a way of shifting. Cobb's assignment is the *inception* (or birth, or wellspring) of a new idea in the mind of another young billionaire, Robert Fischer Jr. (Cillian Murphy), heir to his father's empire. Saito wants him to initiate ideas that will lead to the surrender of his rival's corporation. Cobb needs Ariadne to create a deceptive maze space in Fischer's dreams so that (I think) new thoughts can slip in unperceived. Is it a coincidence that Ariadne is named for the woman in Greek mythology who helped Theseus escape from the Minotaur's labyrinth?

Cobb tutors Ariadne on the world of dream infiltration, the art of controlling dreams and navigating them. Nolan uses this as a device for tutoring us as well. And also as the occasion for some of the movie's astonishing special effects, which seemed senseless in the trailer but now fit right in. The most impressive to me takes place (or seems to) in Paris, where the city literally rolls back on itself like a roll of linoleum tile.

Protecting Fischer are any number of gun-wielding bodyguards, who may be working like the mental equivalent of antibodies; they seem alternatively real and figurative, but whichever they are, they lead to a great many gunfights, chase scenes, and explosions, which is the way movies depict conflict these days. So skilled is Nolan that he actually got me involved in one of his chases, when I thought I was relatively immune to scenes that have become so standard. That was because I cared about who was chasing and being chased.

If you've seen any advertising at all for the film, you know that its architecture has a way of disregarding gravity. Buildings tilt. Streets coil. Characters float. This is all explained in the narrative. The movie is a perplexing labyrinth without a simple through-line and is sure to inspire truly endless analysis on the Web.

Nolan helps us with an emotional thread. The reason Cobb is motivated to risk the dangers of inception is because of grief and guilt involving his wife, Mal (Marion Cotillard), and their two children. More I will not (in a way, cannot) say. Cotillard beautifully embodies the wife in an idealized way. Whether we are seeing Cobb's memories or his dreams is difficult to say—even, literally, in the last shot. But she makes Mal function as an emotional magnet, and the love between the two provides an emotional constant in Cobb's world, which is otherwise ceaselessly shifting.

Inception works for the viewer like the world itself worked for Leonard, the hero of *Memento*. We are always in the Now. We have made some notes while getting Here, but we are not quite sure where Here is. Yet matters of life, death, and the heart are involved—oh, and those multinational corporations, of course. And Nolan doesn't pause before using well-crafted scenes from spycraft or espionage, including a clever scheme on board a 747 (even explaining why it must be a 747).

The movies often seem to come from the recycling bin these days: sequels, remakes, franchises. *Inception* does a difficult thing. It is wholly original, cut from new cloth, and yet structured with action movie basics so it feels like it makes more sense than (quite possibly) it does. I thought there was a hole in *Memento*: How does a man with short-term memory loss remember he has short-term memory loss? Maybe there's a hole in *Inception*, too, but I can't find it. Christopher Nolan reinvented *Batman*. This time he isn't reinventing anything. Yet few directors will attempt to recycle *Inception*. I think when Nolan left the labyrinth, he threw away the map.

The Informant! ★ ★ ★ ★

R, 108 m., 2009

Matt Damon (Mark Whitacre), Scott Bakula (Brian Shepard), Joel McHale (Robert Herndon), Melanie Lynskey (Ginger Whitacre), Patton Oswalt (Ed Herbst), Allan Havey (Dean Paisley), Tom Papa (Mick Andreas). Directed by Steven Soderbergh and produced by Gregory Jacobs, Jennifer Fox, Michael Jaffe, Howard Braunstein, and Kurt Eichenwald. Screenplay by Scott Z. Burns, based on the book by Eichenwald.

Mark Whitacre was the highest-ranking executive in U.S. history to blow the whistle in a case of corporate fraud. He ended up with a prison sentence three times longer than any of the criminal executives he exposed. To be sure, there was the detail of the $9 million he embezzled along the way for his personal use. What we discover toward the end of *The Informant!* may help explain that theft, although he apparently didn't want that used in his defense.

Whitacre, persuasively played by Matt Damon in Steven Soderbergh's new thriller, was a top vice president of Archer Daniels Midland in Decatur, Illinois, one of the fifty largest corporations in America. Sprawling at the edge of the small central Illinois city, it is surrounded by miles of soybean fields, and if you buy Japanese tofu at Whole Foods, it probably passed through ADM on its way to Japan. It's also involved in several other crops, produces sweeteners, sells ethanol.

Whitacre knew that ADM and its competitors were engaged in global price fixing that cost consumers billions. This largesse was passed on invisibly to executives and stockholders, yet created a surprisingly small footprint in central Illinois. Yes, executives lived in very nice houses (Soderbergh shot in Whitacre's mansion in tiny Moweaqua, Illinois), but they were low profile compared to Manhattan high rollers, and ate at the local restaurants just like ordinary folks.

Whitacre is put under pressure to discover the source of contamination, possibly industrial sabotage, in one of ADM's operations. He engages in unofficial conversations with key competitors overseas and thinks he may be onto something. Then FBI agents swoop down as part of an espionage probe. He clears himself, but as the agents (Scott Bakula and Joel McHale) are leaving, he calls after them.

He has something he wants to say. They're blindsided. He tells them ADM has been fixing prices for years, that he has been involved, that he has the details and wants to clear his conscience. His wife, Ginger (Melanie Lynskey), helped him arrive at the decision to do the right thing.

The FBI recruits him as an informant, taps phones, teaches him to wear a wire, and even videotapes price-fixing meetings, building an airtight case. Eventually three officials, including vice chairman Michael Andreas, son of the founder, were found guilty; the company was fined $100 million and paid another $400 million in a class action lawsuit.

If only it were that simple, *The Informant!* might have been a corporate thriller like Michael Mann's *The Insider* (1999), with Russell Crowe as a whistle-blower in the tobacco industry. But during the investigation Mark Whitacre reveals himself as a man of bewildering contradictions. Who would think to attempt an embezzlement and phony check-cashing scheme while literally working under the noses and at the side of FBI accountants? What was the full story of the industrial espionage he halted? Did he really expect that by exposing those above him, it would clear the way for him, one of the key price fixers, to take command of the company?

What did Whitacre think about *anything*? Not even his wife was sure. All is explained, sort of, in *The Informant!* and as Soderbergh lovingly peels away veil after veil of deception, the film develops into an unexpected human comedy. Not that any of the characters are laughing.

The film is fascinating in the way it reveals two levels of events, not always visible to each other or to the audience. A second viewing would be rewarding, knowing what we find out. Matt Damon's performance is deceptively bland. He comes from a world of true-blue downstate people, without affectations, surrounded by some of the richest farmland in the world. Whitacre's determination to wear the wire leads to situations where discovery seems inevitable, but he's seemingly so feckless that suspicion seems misplaced. What he's up to is in some ways so very simple. Even if it has the FBI guys banging their heads against the wall.

Mark Whitacre, PhD, released a little early after FBI agents called him "an American hero," is now an executive in a high-tech start-up in California and is still married to Ginger. Looking back on his adventure, he recently told his hometown paper, the *Decatur Herald and Review*: "It's like I was two people. I assume that's why they chose Matt Damon for the movie because he plays those roles that have such psychological intensity. In the *Bourne* movies, he doesn't even know who he is."

The Informers ★ ★ ½

R, 98 m., 2009

Billy Bob Thornton (William Sloan), Kim Basinger (Laura Sloan), Winona Ryder (Cheryl Moore), Mickey Rourke (Peter), Jon Foster (Graham Sloan), Amber Heard (Christie), Austin Nichols (Martin), Lou Taylor Pucci (Tim Price), Brad Renfro (Jack), Chris Isaak (Les Price), Mel Raido (Bryan Metro), Rhys Ifans (Roger). Directed by Gregor Jordan and produced by Marco Weber. Screenplay by Bret Easton Ellis and Nicholas Jarecki, from the novel by Ellis.

The Informers is about dread, despair, and doom, and its characters are almost all about to be hit with more reasons for dread and despair, and a shared doom. It takes place in the Los Angeles showbiz drug subculture circa 1983, when AIDS didn't have a name and cocaine looked like the answer to something. It demonstrates the eerie ways that music and movies connect people from vastly different lives in a subterranean way where desire is the common currency.

What do they desire? Drugs, sex, power, wealth, and fame or its proximity. These things have made their lives hollow daily punishments, treatable only by oblivion. One character, in a moment of desperate need, says, "All I want is someone to tell me what is good, and someone to tell me what is bad." Hemingway told him, if he had been listening: "What is moral is what you feel good after, and what is immoral is what you feel bad after."

As nearly as I can recall, none of the characters ever feels happy. They're all pitiful, some are evil, the rest are helpless. There may be a few who are bystanders, like the anchorwoman, but even she's guilty of sleeping with a married studio chief primarily because of who he is. Almost everyone in this film is connected by sexual partners, sometimes in ways they never suspect.

The film, based on work by Bret Easton Ellis, takes place in his usual world of hedonistic excess. It tells many interweaving stories and is skillfully cast with actors who embody precisely what their roles call for. What common needs can link characters played by Billy Bob Thornton, Kim Basinger, Mickey Rourke, Winona Ryder, Lou Taylor Pucci, Amber Heard, Chris Isaak, Jon Foster, Brad Renfro, and Rhys Ifans? See paragraph two.

The scenes cycle through parties, famous restaurants, studio offices, TV news sets, Mulholland Drive, beaches, and beds. A lot of beds, often populated by bisexual threesomes. Thornton is the studio head, Basinger is his pill-popping wife, Ryder is the newswoman. Basinger uses a male prostitute who is one of the threesomes. Thornton's children despise him.

There is a wasted rock singer in the film (Mel Raido) who thinks he might once have lived in L.A. He vaguely realizes at times where he is and what he is doing. A father (Isaak) who takes his son to Hawaii, suspects the kid might be gay, approves when he invites a girl to dinner, then tries to pick her up. A wasted night clerk (Brad Renfro) who hopes to be an actor ends up being victimized by his loathsome uncle (Rourke) into possibly (not certainly) committing a monstrous act. A young girl (Heard) who sleeps with anyone, more or less out of indifference.

There is no hope in this world. No frogs falling from the sky. I have met a few people like this and imagine they tend to meet one another. Their humanity has been burnt right out. Bret Easton Ellis is sometimes described as the poet of beautiful blond people whose lives are devoted to making themselves and others miserable. True enough. The most intimate, and startling, scene between Thornton and Basinger involves him requesting something disgusting (not sexual) and her providing it, while they're both preoccupied with whether they can ever live together again, or even want to. The fact that this service she provides takes place without discussion suggests the numbness of their souls.

If *The Informers* doesn't sound to you like a pleasant time at the movies, you are right. To repeat: dread, despair, and doom. It is often, however, repulsively fascinating, and has been directed by Gregor Jordan as a soap opera from hell, with good sets and costumes. If he finds no depths in the characters, well, what depths are there? What you see is what you get. Sometimes less than that. Some viewers of *The Informers* criticize it for lacking a third act, but these lives are all two-act plays.

Note: Brad Renfro, who once played Huck Finn, died of a heroin overdose on January 15, 2008. He was twenty-five. He is actually very good here, in a role he possibly never dreamed of playing.

Inglourious Basterds ★ ★ ★ ★

R, 152 m., 2009

Brad Pitt (Lieutenant Aldo Raine), Christoph Waltz (Colonel Hans Landa), Michael Fassbender (Lieutenant Archie Hicox), Eli Roth (Sergeant Donny Donowitz), Diane Kruger (Bridget von Hammersmark), Daniel Bruhl (Frederick Zoller), Til Schweiger (Sergeant Hugo Stiglitz), Melanie Laurent (Shosanna Dreyfus), B. J. Novak (Private First Class Smithson Utivich), Samm Levine (Private First Class Hirschberg). Directed by Quentin Tarantino and produced by Lawrence Bender. Screenplay by Tarantino.

Quentin Tarantino's *Inglourious Basterds* is a big, bold, audacious war movie that will annoy some, startle others, and demonstrate once again that he's the real thing, a director of quixotic delights. For starters (and at this late stage after the May 2009 premiere at Cannes, I don't believe I'm spoiling anything), he provides World War II with a much-needed alternative ending. For once the bastards get what's coming to them.

From the title, ripped off a 1978 B-movie, to the Western sound of the Ennio Morricone opening music to the key location, a movie theater, the film embeds Tarantino's love of the movies. The deep, rich colors of 35 mm film provide tactile pleasure. A character at the beginning and end, not seen in between, brings the story full circle. The "Basterds" themselves, savage fighters dropped behind Nazi lines, are an unmistakable nod to the Dirty Dozen.

And above all there are three iconic characters, drawn broadly and with love: the Hero, the Nazi, and the Girl. These three, played by Brad Pitt, Christoph Waltz, and Melanie Laurent, are seen with that Tarantino knack of taking a character and making it a Character, definitive, larger than life, approaching satire in its intensity but not—quite—going that far. Let's say they feel bigger than most of the people we meet in movies.

The story begins in Nazi-occupied France, early in the war, when the cruel, droll Nazi Hans Landa (Christoph Waltz) arrives at an isolated dairy farm where he believes the farmer (Denis Menochet) is hiding Jews. He's right, and a young woman named Shosanna (Melanie Laurent) flees into the woods. It is for this scene, and his performance throughout the movie, that Christoph Waltz deserves an Oscar nomination to go with his Best Actor award from Cannes. He creates a character unlike any Nazi—indeed, anyone at all—I've seen in a movie: evil, sardonic, ironic, mannered, absurd.

The Hero is Brad Pitt, as Lieutenant Aldo Raine, leader of the Basterds. Tarantino probably wants us to hear "Aldo Ray," star of countless war films and B pictures. Raine is played by Pitt as a broad caricature of a hard-talking Southern boy who wants each of his men to bring him one hundred Nazi scalps. For years his band improbably survives in France and massacres Nazis, and can turn out in formal evening wear at a moment's notice. Pitt's version of Italian is worthy of a Marx brother.

The Girl is Shosanna, played by Laurent as a curvy siren with red lipstick and, at the end, a slinky red dress. Tarantino photographs her with the absorption of a fetishist, with close-ups of shoes, lips, a facial veil, and details of body and dress. You can't tell me he hasn't seen the work of the Scottish artist Jack Vettriano and his noir paintings of the cigarette-smoking ladies in red. Shosanna calculatingly flirts with Frederick Zoller (Daniel Bruhl), a Nazi war hero and now movie star, who convinces Joseph Goebbels to hold the premiere of his new war film in her theater. This sets up a plot that includes Tarantino breaking several rules in order to provide documentary footage about how flammable nitrate film prints are.

A Tarantino film resists categorization. *Inglourious Basterds* is no more about war than *Pulp Fiction* is about—what the hell *is* it about? Of course nothing in the movie is possible, except that it's so bloody entertaining. His actors don't chew the scenery, but they lick it. He's a master at bringing performances as far as they can go toward iconographic exaggeration.

After I saw *Inglourious Basterds* at Cannes, although I was writing a daily blog, I resisted giving an immediate opinion about it. I knew Tarantino had made a considerable film, but I wanted it to settle and to see it again. I'm glad I did. Like a lot of real movies, you relish it more the next time. Immediately after *Pulp Fiction* played at Cannes, QT asked me what I thought. "It's either the best film of the year, or the worst film," I said. I hardly knew what the hell had happened to me. The answer was: the best film. Tarantino films have a way of growing on you. It's not enough to see them once.

Inkheart ★ ★

PG, 105 m., 2009

Brendan Fraser (Mo Folchart), Paul Bettany (Dustfinger), Helen Mirren (Elinor Loredan), Jim Broadbent (Fenoglio), Andy Serkis (Capricorn), Eliza Hope Bennett (Meggie), Rafi Gavron (Farid), Sienna Guillory (Resa). Directed by Iain Softley and produced by Softley, Cornelia Funke, and Diana Pokorny. Screenplay by David Lindsay-Abaire, based on the novel by Funke.

I never knew reading was so dangerous. No child seeing *Inkheart* will ever want to be read to again, especially if that child loves its mother, as so many do. Here is a film about a man named Mo who, when he reads aloud, has the power of liberating fictional characters into the real world. The drawback is that real people are trapped within the same book. Tit for tat. A law of physics must apply.

The film opens with its best scene, for me, anyway: the professional book buyer Mo (Brendan Fraser) and his twelve-year-old daughter, Meggie (Eliza Hope Bennett), poking through an open-air book market. As always I was trying to read the titles on the spines. Not realizing that *Inkheart* is based on a famous fantasy novel, I had the foolish hope the movie might be about books. No luck. Wait till you hear what it's about.

At the edge of the market is a dark little bookstore presided over by a dark little man. As Mo prowls its aisles, he hears the faint chatter of fictional characters calling to him. (Dictionaries must be almost impossible to shut up.) Sixth sense leads him to discover, on an obscure shelf, the novel *Inkheart,* in the format of a Penguin mystery from the 1950s. He buys it, slips it into his pocket, and the two of them are followed by a mysterious skulking man.

We discover this is the very book Mo was reading when his wife, Meggie's mother (Sienna Guillory), was sucked into its pages, and that is the true story, Meggie, of how your mom suddenly disappeared when you were little. Yeah, right, Dad. At the same time, various demonic creatures were liberated from the book's pages. They have now set up shop in a mountaintop castle and are conspiring to command Mo's power now that he has discovered their book again. Do they want to return to its pages, or be reunited with old chums in the real world? And how do you get a mortgage to buy a castle when you're a demonic creature and your résumé mentions only fictional adventures in an out-of-print book? The banks must have been lending carelessly there awhile back.

Mo and Meggie take refuge in a cliffside mansion occupied by her great-aunt Elinor (Helen Mirren). Mansion? Looks to me like a dreamy tourist hotel from a Merchant-Ivory production. Elinor is a nasty scold who always wears a turban, the reliable standby of the actress tired of having her hair fussed over every second. I hope good Dame Helen passed this tip along to young Eliza Hope Bennett, who shows every sign of becoming an accomplished actress.

The movie now descends into the realm of your basic good guys vs. wrathful wraiths formula, with pitched battles and skullduggery. The villains are Dustfinger (Paul Bettany) and the ambitious Capricorn (Andy Serkis), and there is always the threat of Mo and Meggie being transmogrified into the pages of the book. There they'd at least have the company of the missing mom and the shabby author Fenoglio (Jim Broadbent), who wrote the novel within *Inkheart,* and apparently was only set free to rise up one level, to the novel containing his novel. Thanks for nothing.

Lots of screams, horrible fates almost happening, close scrapes, cries for help, special effects, monomania, quick thinking, pluck, fear, and scrambling. You know the kinds of stuff. I learn there are two more novels in this series by Cornelia Funke, both of which will remain just as unread by me as the first. It is hard to guess what they will involve, however, because this one closes with a curiously cobbled-together ending that seems to solve everything, possibly as a talisman against a sequel.

In Memoriam ★ ★ ★

NO MPAA RATING, 101 m., 2011

Ian Forester (Jonathan), Kelly O'Sullivan (Kelly), Sadie Rogers (Sadie), Chris Carr (Ernest), Annabel Armour (Deborah), H. B. Ward (Tom), Hanna Dworkin (Nancy), Gerrit O'Neill (Jay Sr.). Directed by Stephen Cone and produced by Cone, Kathleen Cardoza, Keith Cardoza, and Gina LoPiccolo. Screenplay by Cone.

Someone sends Jonathan a snarky e-mail. Two naked students, apparently making love at the time, fell off the roof of a campus building in Chicago and were killed. Jonathan is appalled that anyone could find this funny. In the painfully true opening scenes of *In Memoriam*, he cannot get the deaths out of his mind. He's driven to begin what he calls an "investigation" into who the students were and what led them to the rooftop.

Stephen Cone's film *In Memoriam* never steps wrong in its first half hour, which I watched in fascination. Jonathan (Ian Forester) talks to the friends of the dead students and even to their parents (one set more willing than the other). It seems to him *wrong* that two people would die like that, in the midst of happiness. Forester is particularly effective in finding the right notes for his sorrow, which is not personal but existential.

I thought I vaguely recalled a real news item about deaths like that, but I couldn't find it online. What I did find were stories about four other students dying after falls from various campus buildings—one while doing a class project on "filming from high places." Those stories permitting comments included equally heartless snark. On the Internet, trolls can indulge the rotten festering of their shallow minds.

Jonathan eventually decides to reenact the last hours of the dead couple in the film. And that's where Cone's own film goes—not wrong, exactly, but in a less compelling direction. Jonathan recruits helpers, he finds a cameraman, he auditions actors, they all pitch in together on a tiny budget. They seem to be reasonable people engaged in a plausible undertaking. These elements are possibly not a million miles distant from what Cone himself did.

He's a sure-minded director, and *In Memoriam* is a touching film. Its final hour has convincing performances and avoids any horrors along the lines of "Hey, gang! Let's make a movie!" The scenes with the two sets of parents are acutely seen. There are some subplots, one involving a possible romance and the other a sublimated one, which are handled with admirable subtlety. A couple of moments with music seem somewhat obtrusive. The reality level is otherwise convincing.

And yet Cone never quite regains the force of his opening scene. I was thinking about that. How could he? I think perhaps Jonathan's initial obsession is so absorbing that we almost don't want it to find a release. If the opening Jonathan sequences were combined with one particular later moment, you would have an incredibly effective short film. Here is a paradox: Cone opens so well that he sets the bar too high for the rest of the film. "People die," one of his characters says. Yes, and mankind has spent a long time trying to deal with that fact, which has such an irrefutable finality.

Inside Job ★ ★ ★ ★

PG-13, 108 m., 2010

A documentary narrated by Matt Damon. Directed by Charles Ferguson and produced by Ferguson and Audrey Marrs. Screenplay by Chad Beck and Adam Bolt.

I don't fully understand the workings of the derivatives and credit swaps we've heard so much about. But I'm learning. These are ingenious computer-driven schemes in which good money can be earned from bad debt, and Wall Street's Masters of the Universe pocket untold millions at the same time they bankrupt their investors and their own companies.

This process is explained in Charles Ferguson's *Inside Job*, an angry, well-argued documentary about how the American financial industry set out deliberately to defraud the ordinary American investor. The crucial error (in administrations of both parties) was to allow financial institutions to trade on their own behalf. Today many large trading banks are betting against their own customers.

In the real estate market, banks aggressively promoted mortgages to people who couldn't afford them. These were assembled in packages. They were carried on the books as tangible assets when they were worthless. The institutions assembling them hedged their loans by betting against them. When the mortgages failed, profits were made despite and because of their failure. This process has been targeted by financial reform measures, which many in both parties oppose because—well, lobbyists have persuaded them. There is no moral justification for how Wall Street functions today.

A Chicago group named Magnetar was particularly successful in creating such poisoned instruments for the sole purpose of hedging against them. Most of the big Wall Street players knew exactly what the "Magnetar Trade" was and welcomed it. The more mortgages failed, the more money they made. They actually continued to sell the bad mortgages to their clients as good investments. There was a famous exchange on C-SPAN as Senator Carl Levin grilled Daniel Sparks, head of the Goldman Sachs Mortgages Department, on why the company aggressively sold investments its own traders described to one another as "shitty." It was entertaining to watch Sparks maintain a facade of studious probity as Levin socked him with the word "shitty" again and again.

This Wall Street climate helps to explain one session of Senate testimony I have been fascinated by for almost two years: How Richard Fuld, CEO of Lehman Brothers, was able to defend the $484 million bonus he received after leading his firm into bankruptcy. Yes, the firm failed. But it failed because of poisoned investments it hedged against, and paid its executives bonuses on the profits from those hedges.

Lawrence McDonald, who wrote a book on Lehman's collapse, said on the *PBS NewsHour*: "Richard Fuld's driver would call Lehman Brothers, and one of the elevators in the southeast corner of the building would become frozen. A security guard would come over and hold it until Mr. Fuld arrived in the back door. . . . There's only fifteen feet where King Richard Fuld is exposed to the rabble, I guess you'd call us."

Some may say, well, he was the boss. I say, who the hell did he think he was? I've waited for elevators with my bosses, including Marshall Field and Rupert Murdoch. They seemed content enough that there *was* an elevator.

One of the most fascinating aspects of *Inside Job* involves the chatty on-camera insights of Kristin Davis, a Wall Street madam, who says the Street operated in a climate of abundant sex and cocaine for valued clients and the traders themselves. She's not talking about a few naughty boys. She says it was an accepted part of the corporate culture that hookers at $1,000 an hour and up were kept on retainer, that cocaine was the fuel, and that she and her girls didn't understand how some traders could even function on the trading floor after most nights.

That leads me to the matter of financial reform. We need it. We need to return to an era of transparency. We need to restore a market of investments that are what they seem to be. We need to deprive investment banks of the right to trade on behalf of their own accounts. We need to require them to work on behalf of their customers. In the days before deregulation, it was hard to get a mortgage from a bank that didn't believe you could make the payments. In recent years it was hard not to get one.

The bad mortgages were sliced and diced into so many derivatives that the banks themselves had no idea what paper they were holding. In one of the more refreshing moments during the housing meltdown, Representative

Marcy Kaptur of Ohio advised her constituents: "If a bank forecloses on you, don't move, and demand they produce a copy of your mortgage. In many cases, they can't." She was prophetic; banks are now halting foreclosures all over the country.

Gene Siskel, who was a wise man, gave me the best investment advice I've ever received. "You can never outsmart the market, if that's what you're trying to do," he said. "Find something you love, for reasons you understand, that not everyone agrees with you about, and put your money in it." The stocks I thought of were Apple, Google, and Steak 'n Shake. I bought some shares. That was a long time ago. Reader, if I had invested every penny I had on Gene's advice, today I would be a Master of the Universe.

Insidious ★ ★ ½

PG-13, 101 m., 2011

Patrick Wilson (Josh Lambert), Rose Byrne (Renai Lambert), Barbara Hershey (Lorraine Lambert), Lin Shaye (Elise Rainier), Ty Simpkins (Dalton Lambert), Angus Sampson (Tucker), Leigh Whannell (Specs). Directed by James Wan and produced by Jason Blum, Oren Peli, and Steven Schneider. Screenplay by Leigh Whannell.

Insidious is an affectionate visit to the Haunted House Movie, a genre that seems classic in contrast to queasy-cam gorefests. It depends on characters, atmosphere, sneaky happenings, and mounting dread. It's not terrifically good, but moviegoers will get what they're expecting. This is a new collaboration between director James Wan and writer Leigh Whannell, who launched the *Saw* franchise.

As the movie opens, an unsuspecting family is moving into a big old house they must have found through the Amityville Multiple Listing Service. It's the kind of house you require for a haunting movie, with lots of rooms, nooks, crannies, corridors, staircases, closets, and shadows—and an attic, of course. Although more modern houses were used in the *Paranormal Activity* movies, you really require all the creaky old bells and whistles.

The Lambert family seems to have been happy before this real estate transaction. Josh (Patrick Wilson) is a teacher, Renai (Rose Byrne) writes songs, and young Dalton (Ty Simpkins) is the most curious of the kids. That's why he sneaks into the attic, falls off a treacherous ladder, and immediately goes into a coma. Brain scans reveal no head injury. Could it be . . . something else?

Renai is positive something snaky is happening. Her boxes get moved around by unseen hands. Doors and windows open by themselves. We are even more sure than Renai is because we begin to see the stark apparition of a fearsome specter. Imagine a beast from Hades.

Dad begins to stay at work late. The movie probably wants us to blame him for not caring and trying to avoid the problems at home. We know better. We identify an example of the Absent Father Syndrome, that screenwriter's convenience for getting Dad out of the way so Mom can be home alone and told she's imagining things.

This is a family that needs help. They hire a psychic named Elise Rainier (Lin Shaye), who sends over two ghostbusters (Angus Sampson and the writer Leigh Whannell). These two seem singularly incompetent and provide some nice chuckles. Since the whole film teeters on the edge of being a comedy, it's probably a good idea that when Lin Shaye turns up, she brings in some cause for serious alarm. She's seen these cases before.

What is the malevolent presence? Why is it there? What does it want? What can it gain from the hapless Lamberts? The answers to such questions must necessarily remain theoretical at a metaphysical level, but at a practical level, the purpose of the presence is to generate startling bangs at frequent intervals, materialize unexpectedly, look horrifying, and be a nuisance. Its purpose, in short, is to go BOO!

Inspector Bellamy ★ ★ ★ ½

NO MPAA RATING, 110 m., 2011

Gerard Depardieu (Paul Bellamy), Clovis Cornillac (Jacques Lebas), Marie Bunel (Francoise), Jacques Gamblin (Gentil/Leullet/Leprince). Directed by Claude Chabrol and produced by Patrick Godeau. Screenplay by Chabrol and Odile Barski.

Paul Bellamy is large, unkempt, sweet, blissfully married, and very calm for a police inspector. He doesn't solve a case so much as observe it with interest as it solves itself by the working of human nature. If you, like me, are a lover of Georges Simenon's Inspector Maigret, you will find his nature embodied here in the performance of Gerard Depardieu. If you are not, get your hands on a Maigret novel and thank me for the rest of your life.

As Claude Chabrol's *Inspector Bellamy* opens, Paul is on holiday with Francoise Bellamy (Marie Bunel), who, like Madame Maigret, understands her husband profoundly and is his sounding board as a case first baffles him and then unfolds under the gentle pressure of his low-key snooping. A man has been following them for days, and even now is creeping about in the garden. This man is named Gentil, and later will turn out to be Leullet, whom Gentil killed, *sort of*, while actually killing Leprince, who was in a sense only technically a victim. All three men are played by Jacques Gamblin. This is not at all confusing because of the ordered precision of Bellamy's approach, and Chabrol's.

Besides, it doesn't matter so much who did what and to whom. As in a Simenon novel, the solution is less interesting than the people encountered along the way and the sometimes sad lessons learned. *Inspector Bellamy* is only technically a murder mystery, and the critic Armond White is correct in observing, "Genre is Chabrol's MacGuffin." After hooking the audience with the mystery, Chabrol uses it as his avenue into the relationships between Bellamy and his wife, his loutish half-brother, Jacques (Clovis Cornillac), and two spritely local women who are mistresses, but not always the mistresses of those who claim them.

Chabrol, as always, shows a tenderness toward the lives of people who are exceptional only because crime touches them. He pays great attention to domestic details, and to the tone of the pillow talk between the Bellamys. He suggests that in their marriage, and perhaps in every marriage, things are not as simple as they seem. (Here he departs from Simenon; in Maigret's marriage, I believe things *are* as simple as they seem.) He introduces an extra character in Jacques—who is unnecessary in terms of the murder—really, not merely "seemingly" unnecessary. And Chabrol explores the unhappy history of Paul and Jacques, involving Francoise. In their relationship he uses the detective genre just as White says he does, as a device to involve us in another story thread.

Chabrol began making films at the dawn of the New Wave, in 1958. Depardieu began in 1970. Both worked prolifically. Hard to believe this was the first time they worked together. Chabrol and Odile Barski wrote the screenplay especially for Depardieu, and deliberately as homage to Simenon and Maigret; now that I see Depardieu as the famous inspector, I agree, yes, he makes a convincing Maigret, although at least two dozen other actors have played him. He is bulkier than I picture Maigret, and I've assumed the inspector's nose was less exceptional, but there is the inner quiet, the tranquillity in the face of violence, the curiosity and acceptance of human nature.

Here is a movie about a cop and a crime in which not one shot is fired. The only person who gets slapped is Bellamy. The movie ends with wisdom and resignation, not an orgasm of hyperactive computer effects. People talk about considerable things. They speculate about motives, even their own. They are articulate. Chabrol made many such films. He died on September 12, 2010, a survivor from the idealism of the New Wave, which he outlived. Which we have all outlived.

The International ★ ★ ★

R, 118 m., 2009

Clive Owen (Louis Salinger), Naomi Watts (Eleanor Whitman), Armin Mueller-Stahl (Wilhelm Wexler), Brian F. O'Byrne (The Consultant). Directed by Tom Tykwer and produced by Charles Roven, Richard Suckle, and Lloyd Phillips. Screenplay by Eric Warren Singer.

Not since the days of silent movies have bankers as a group been cast so ruthlessly as villains. They used to wear waxed mustaches and throw widows and orphans out into the storm. Now the mustaches are gone. "Banker" has been incorporated into the all-embracing term "Wall Street." The bankers in *The International* broker arms deals, sell missiles under the counter, and assassinate anyone who gets too snoopy. First they throw you out into the storm, then they blow you up.

Whether this is a fair portrait is not the purpose of a movie review to determine. It is accurate of the bankers on view here, and given the face of Armin Mueller-Stahl, once familiar as a good guy, now enjoying a new career as a ruthless villain. His bank, based in Luxembourg, as so many schemes are, has been assassinating Nosy Parkers for getting too close to their operations, which involve investing in African rebels and nuclear weaponry, and arming both sides of the Israeli-Palestinian conflict.

Does it seem to you that a bank with headquarters in Luxembourg is asking for it, just as a nice girl shouldn't rent a room in a whorehouse? In the opening scenes we meet the Interpol agent Louis Salinger (Clive Owen), keeping watch in Berlin as his partner meets with an insider of the bank. The partner is killed by mysterious means, and that, as they say, makes it personal. Salinger is joined by Eleanor Whitman (Naomi Watts), a district attorney from Manhattan, for cloudy law enforcement reasons but excellent dramatic ones: It's great to have a plucky blonde in the plot.

The movie has a scene in it Hitchcock might have envied, a gun battle ranging up and down the ramps of the Guggenheim Museum in New York. Why there? Because the visuals are terrific. After Salinger and Whitman follow their quarry there, how do dozens of the bank's killers turn up? Because they're needed. Why do assassination squads in the movies always dress in matching uniforms? Makes them easier to identify. You don't ask questions like that. You simply enjoy the magnificent absurdity of the scene. (It was filmed, by the way, on an enormous interior set in Germany.)

A lot of the remainder of the movie involves dialogue and plotters skulking around colorful international locales including even Istanbul, that traditional setting for intrigue. I found the unfolding of the plot sort of fascinating. The ads will no doubt play up the shoot-out, but you may be relieved to discover this isn't another hyperkinetic exercise in queasy-cammery. It's more interested in demonstrating that a bank like this transcends national boundaries and corrupts everyone it deals with.

How does it do this? With money. As David Mamet so usefully informs us: "Everybody needs money. That's why they call it money." In the film, everything is secondary to the bank's profits, and an Italian political candidate, not unlike Berlusconi, is shot during a speech. Why the bank, so efficient, isn't better at going after Salinger and Whitman isn't hard to explain: They're needed for the whole movie. The Berlusconi type has a big dialogue scene in which he explains, succinctly and objectively, how banks, armies, and governments interact. Apparently our Wall Street was a babe in the woods, being motivated merely by arrogance, avarice, and ego.

I enjoyed the movie. Clive Owen makes a semi-believable hero, not performing too many feats that are physically unlikely. He's handsome and has the obligatory macho stubble, but he has a quality that makes you worry a little about him. I like heroes who *could* get killed. Naomi Watts wisely plays up her character's legal smarts and plays down the inevitable possibility that the two of them will fall in love.

The director is Tom Tykwer (*Run, Lola, Run*). Here he's concerned not merely with thriller action but with an actual subject: the dangers of a banking system that operates offshore no matter where your shoreline is. We're gradually getting it into our heads that in the long run your nuclear capability may not be as important as your bank balance. Banks are not lending much money these days, but if you want to buy some warheads, they might take a meeting.

The Invention of Lying ★ ★ ★ ½

PG-13, 99 m., 2009

Ricky Gervais (Mark Bellison), Jennifer Garner (Anna McDoogles), Jonah Hill (Frank), Louis C. K. (Greg), Jeffrey Tambor (Anthony), Fionnula Flanagan (Martha Bellison), Rob Lowe (Brad Kessler), Tina Fey (Shelley). Directed by Ricky Gervais and Matthew Robinson and produced by Gervais, Dan Lin, Lynda Obst, and Oly Obst. Screenplay by Gervais and Robinson.

In its amiable, quiet PG-13 way, *The Invention of Lying* is a remarkably radical comedy. It opens with a series of funny, relentlessly logical episodes in a world where everyone always tells the truth, and then slips in the implication that religion is possible only in a world that has the ability to lie. Then it wraps all of this into a sweet love story.

Ricky Gervais plays a pudgy everyman named Mark, who's a writer for a company that produces movies of stunning tedium. There's no comedy or drama in its productions because, of course, fiction requires lies. Mark fails to turn the Black Plague into box office and is fired, but not before his secretary (Tina Fey) tells him she has loathed every day she worked for him. Mark takes this agreeably enough; one is not easily insulted when everyone tells the truth all the time.

What would such a world be like? In *The Invention of Lying*, a retirement home is called "A Sad Place Where Homeless Old People Come to Die." Pepsi ads say: "For when they don't have Coke." When Mark goes on a blind date with Anna (Jennifer Garner), she opens the door and starts right off with a hilarious line that Garner reportedly improvised on the spot. Then she says she finds him unattractive, there will never be any possibility of sex, and he is too short and fat to make a good genetic sperm source. At a restaurant, the waiter tells them he hates working there, and that Anna is out of Mark's league. Mark and Anna agree.

You see how it goes. Mark lives in a typical little city with bland people and no anger. Everyone always believes everyone else. I wonder if politics are even possible. We see this isn't an ideal situation. There are no consolations. Nothing eases the way.

Mark is a nice man, in that sneaky-smooth Gervais way, and would like to console his mother (Fionnula Flanagan), who is dying in a Sad Place Where Old People, etc. One day he undergoes an astonishing revelation. He knows his bank balance is $300. The camera zooms into his brain to show mental lightning bolts, and he tells the teller he has $800. She hands him the money and apologizes for the bank's computer.

He can lie! His world lacks even a word for this. Nor does it have the word "truth." Something is either "so," or "not so." With his new power, Mark is able to tell his mother that death doesn't lead to oblivion, but to a wonderful afterlife. Of course she, and everyone else, believes him. The word races around the world, and people beg for more details. Anna tells him how happy he could make everyone.

Then, in one of the funniest satirical scenes I can remember, Mark stands on his front steps and informs the world there is a Man in the Sky, and they will be happy up there with him after death. The world is ecstatic. This Man, Mark explains, is responsible for everything. "Even my cancer?" a woman asks. Yes, that too, but Mark asks his audience not to get bogged down in the details.

What we have here, in microcosm, is the paradox of a benevolent god creating a world of evil. Mark is hard-pressed to explain it, but greater men than he have tried. Think of the power you'd possess if everything you said was believed without question. Mark, under the circumstances, behaves reasonably well.

I saw the movie with a large audience, which laughed a lot and had a good time. I have no idea what they thought of its implications. It isn't strident, ideological, or argumentative; it's simply the story of a guy trying to comfort his mother and perhaps win the woman he loves. Gervais, who codirected and cowrote with Matthew Robinson, walks a delicate tightrope above hazardous chasms.

He's helped greatly in his balancing act by Jennifer Garner's inspired, seemingly effortless, performance as a great beauty who isn't conceited or cruel but simply thinks Mark, with his pug nose, is the wrong genetic match for her children. She plans to marry Brad (Rob Lowe), who is as conventionally handsome (and boring) as Clark Kent. The film has one of those scenes at the altar ("Do you, Brad, agree to stay with Anna as long as you can?") that avoids obvious clichés by involving profound philosophical conclusions.

I saw the trailer for *The Invention of Lying* and expected to dislike it. It's a much better movie than the trailer dares to admit. Today's trailers would make *Sophie's Choice* into a feel-good story. Watching the movie, I thought—oh, yeah, that's right: It's October. Good movies are allowed again.

Invictus ★ ★ ★ ½

PG-13, 134 m., 2009

Morgan Freeman (Nelson Mandela), Matt Damon (Francois Pienaar), Jason Tshabalala (Tony Kgoroge), Louis Minnaar (Springbok Coach), Shakes Myeko (Minister of Sport), Patrick Lyster (Francois's Father), Leleti Khumalo (Mary). Directed by Clint Eastwood and produced by Eastwood, Robert Lorenz, Lori McCreary, and Mace Neufeld. Screenplay by Anthony Peckham, based on the book by John Carlin.

Morgan Freeman has been linked to one biopic of Nelson Mandela or another for at least ten years. Strange that the only one to be made centers on the South African rugby team. The posters for Clint Eastwood's *Invictus* feature Matt Damon in the foreground, with Freeman looming behind him in shadowy nobility. I can imagine marketing meetings during which it was lamented that few Americans care much about Mandela, and Matt Damon appeals to a younger demographic.

Screw 'em, is what I would have contributed. The achievement of Nelson Mandela is one of the few shining moments in recent history. Here is a man who was released after twenty-four years of breaking rocks in prison and sleeping on the floor to assume leadership of the nation that jailed him. His personal forgiveness of white South Africa was the beacon that illuminated that nation's Truth and Reconciliation Commissions, one of the very few examples in history of people who *really* had much to forgive, and forgave it. Let us not forget that both black and white had reasons to grieve, and reasons to forgive, and that in many cases they were facing the actual murderers of their loved ones.

Compared to that, what really does it matter that an underdog Springbok team, all white with one exception, won the World Cup in rugby in the first year of Mandela's rule? I understand that in a nation where all the races are unusually obsessed by sport, the Cup was an electrifying moment when the pariah state stood redeemed before the world—even if soccer is the black man's game there, and rugby is the white's. It was important in the way the Beijing Olympics were important to China.

Clint Eastwood I believe understood all of these things and also sought to make a film he believed he could make, in an area where he felt a visceral connection. Eastwood is too old and too accomplished to have interest in making a film only for money. He would have probably read the screenplays for the previous Mandela projects. They all had one thing in common: They didn't get made. It was universally agreed that Morgan Freeman was the right actor (Mandela and he met and got along famously), but the story, financing, and deal never came together. Eastwood made the film that did get made.

It is a very good film. It has moments evoking great emotion, as when the black and white members of the presidential security detail (hard-line ANC activists and Afrikaner cops) agree with excruciating difficulty to serve together. And when Damon's character Francois Pienaar, as the team captain, is shown the cell where Mandela was held for those long years on Robben Island. Chaz and I were taken to the island early one morning by Ahmed Kathrada, one of Mandela's fellow prisoners, and yes, the movie shows his very cell, with the thin blankets on the floor. You regard that cell and you think, here a great man waited in faith for his rendezvous with history.

The World Cup was a famous victory. The Springboks faced a New Zealand team so dominant it had crushed every opponent—Japan by around ninety points, which in rugby is a *lot.* South Africa won in overtime. About that team name. The South African national teams have been called the Springboks since time immemorial (New Zealand is known as the All Blacks). A springbok is on the tail of every South African Airlines airplane. It's the national logo. Would Mandela change the name to one less associated with the apartheid regime? He would not. Join me in a thought experiment. An African-American is elected mayor of Boston. He is accepted, grudgingly in some circles. How would it go over if he changed the name of the Red Sox?

Freeman does a splendid job of evoking the man Nelson Mandela, who is as much a secular saint as Gandhi. He shows him as genial, confident, calming—over what was clearly a core of tempered steel. The focus is on his early time in office. I believe there may be one scene with a woman representing Winnie Mandela, but the dialogue is vague. Damon is effective at playing the captain Francois, an Afrikaner, child of racist parents, transformed by his contact with "the greatest man I've ever met." Clint Eastwood, a master director, orchestrates all of these notes and has us loving Mandela, proud of Francois, and cheering for the plucky Springboks. A great entertainment. Not, as I said, the Mandela biopic I would have expected.

Ip Man 2 ★ ★ ★

R, 108 m., 2011

Donnie Yen (Ip Man), Sammo Hung (Hung Chun-nam), Huang Xiao-ming (Wong Leung), Xiong Dai-lin (Cheung Wing-sing), Simon Yam (Chow Ching-chuen), Darren Shahlavi (The Twister). Directed by Wilson Yip and produced by Wong Bak-Ming. Screenplay by Edmond Wong.

Ip Man 2 is a reminder of the pleasure of classic martial arts films in which skilled athletes performed many of their own stunts. In its direct and sincere approach, it's a rebuke to the frenzied editing that reduces so many recent action movies into incomprehensible confusion. I'm not saying deceiving camera angles and crafty stunt work isn't involved in the fight scenes here, but basically we see fighters in real time and space. That enormously increases the impact.

The movie is a sequel to an international 2008 hit that told the story of the legendary grandmaster who was Bruce Lee's teacher. In the first film, he fought against the Japanese occupiers of China, and this time his big showdown is with the Twister, a boxing champion of the British forces occupying Hong Kong. In both cases, his philosophy and strategy involve Wing Chun, the martial arts school adopted by Bruce Lee, which is now dominant in the West.

Ip Man (Donnie Yen) is a serious young family man with a second child on the way when he decides to open his own martial arts academy in Hong Kong. This is opposed by the syndicate that controls the sport, and that sets up an extended sequence where he must fight a series of their best fighters. The setup for these fights is daunting: A round table is balanced in the center of dozens of wooden stools turned upside down. The first fighter who is forced off the table loses the match, and lands on the waiting wooden legs. "I've seen this done with knives instead of stools," the head man sniffs.

I'm not naive. I don't believe Donnie Yen and his opponents were actually balanced on a teetering table while filming all of these scenes. You can work miracles with close-ups and camera angles. What I do appreciate is that the logic of time and space is respected, and there is a convincing illusion of realism. It's also obvious that you must be very skilled and experienced to act in such scenes, unlike the Hollywood stars who do all of their fighting with CGI.

Movies in this genre depend on an outsize villain for the climactic fight, and in the Twister (Darren Shahlavi) we get a character so over the top that he would have to dial down to become a pro wrestler. He's the champion of the British forces—symbolically defending British imperialism—and Ip Man is fighting for Chinese home rule.

The fight seems odd. The Twister is a boxer, wearing gloves. Ip Man, dressed in his usual quasi-clerical floor-length black costume, is a martial artist using his feet, elbows, fists, and so on. Midway in the match, the referee abruptly announces that kicking will no longer be allowed. That seems a fairly casual way to approach a championship.

I learn from online experts on this art form that Sammo Hung, who portrays the master of the Hong Kong martial arts syndicate, is himself a famous choreographer of these films, and that in fact he filmed his big scene here not long after having heart surgery. Sometimes the story behind a movie is the best one.

Donnie Yen makes an interesting martial arts star. He comes across as pleasant, sincere, never angry. His discipline involves control of mind and body. (He loves his wife, but isn't an ideal family man; she goes into labor and his duty is to his next fight.) He doesn't scream or make threats or seem to hate anyone, even The Twister. At the end of the film a five-year-old boy is brought to him as a possible student.

He asks the kid for his name. "Bruce Lee," the kid says. He is destined to carry the Ip Man's message to the world.

Irene in Time ★ ½

PG-13, 95 m., 2009

Tanna Frederick (Irene Jensen), Andrea Marcovicci (Helen Dean), Victoria Tennant (Eleanor Jensen), Karen Black (Sheila Shiwers), Lanre Idewu (Jacob), Jack Maxwell (Mikey). Directed by Henry Jaglom and produced by Rosemary Marks. Screenplay by Jaglom.

Henry Jaglom's new film, *Irene in Time,* is dedicated to "my daughter." A curious note to end on, since it is about a woman whose personality and selfhood have been destroyed by an absent, unreliable father. So much is she obsessed by this long-gone parent that her life is consumed by talking about her father, relating her childhood memories, hanging around with his old friends, and dating men she hopes will fill the gap in her life.

Irene's dating strategy is so inept and needy, however, it's a wonder one guy lasted for what she says is three months but he precisely times at two and a half months. Another poor guy, an architect, doesn't last though their first dinner together. She asks if he uses a protractor and compass in his drawing, and he says he does. And pencils and erasers? Yes, he says, all the tools. "And what is your favorite tool?" He doesn't have one. "Come on," she says, "close your eyes and concentrate! Name your favorite tool!" By now he's looking desperate, and asks: "What is your problem?"

Her Daddy's Little Girl act isn't helped by the books she studies about how to behave on dates, attract men, and so forth. If any of you, my dear readers, are women studying such books as *The Rules,* I offer this free advice: A wise man will stay far away from a woman playing him like a fish, and only a needy one will respond well if you are coy about returning his calls.

Irene (Tanna Frederick) is such an insecure flywheel that any man (repeat, any man) should know enough to start edging away after two minutes of conversation. A woman's stock of small talk shouldn't center on how magical her father was, especially when she's in her thirties and hasn't seen him since she was young.

Irene in Time follows Jaglom's "women's trilogy" of films about women's issues such as childbearing, weight, and compulsive shopping. I guess it's the women's quartet now. Irene hangs around with a posse of female friends who gossip, offer sometimes heartfelt advice, receive massages, have lunch, and attend parties. They're all apparently independently wealthy, well divorced, or kept women, since work never seems to interrupt their busy schedules. True, Irene has a job of sorts, making a recording with a band, but their woeful material seems well suited for the lounge of a cruise ship.

There's a dramatic revelation in the film, inspired by a trail of clues in the form of messages that Irene's father apparently left behind years ago for her to discover only now. Good thing she finds them. Note to disappearing fathers: If you want to communicate in twenty years with a daughter, write it down in a letter and leave it with your lawyer.

The revelation does, however, lead to two of the better scenes in the movie, involving older women played by Victoria Tennant and Andrea Marcovicci. Tennant plays her mother, and I must not tell you whom Marcovicci plays.

Jaglom has been producing his own films since 1971 and has made some good ones, notably *Deja Vu* (1997). This is not a good one. It offers certain pleasures, but suffers from an inability to structure events or know when to end a shot. And it has an ending that is simply, perhaps ridiculously, incomprehensible. That's if it means what I think it means, and I fear it does.

Note: Strolling around the Internet, I found a review of Irene in Time *by Tommy Garrett of the* Canyon News. *He compares Jaglom with Wilder and Hitchcock, then writes: "In Frederick's case, he has given her a vehicle which has propelled her into a category that no actress in the past 50 years could be placed. Frederick makes the list of very talented women in Hollywood: Garbo, Davis, Crawford and Hepburn."*

(I'm grateful to Tommy Garrett, who has achieved the feat of writing praise so astonishing we at last have someone to compare to the critic who said I Am Legend *was one of the greatest movies ever made.)*

Iron Man 2 ★ ★ ★

PG-13, 124 m., 2010

Robert Downey Jr. (Tony Stark), Gwyneth Paltrow (Pepper Potts), Don Cheadle (Lieutenant Colonel "Rhodey" Rhodes), Scarlett Johansson (Natasha Romanoff), Sam Rockwell (Justin Hammer), Mickey Rourke (Ivan Vanko), Samuel L. Jackson (Nick Fury), Clark Gregg (Paul Coulson), Garry Shandling (Senator Stern). Directed by Jon Favreau and produced by Kevin Feige. Screenplay by Justin Theroux, based on the Marvel comic by Stan Lee, Don Heck, Larry Lieber, and Jack Kirby.

Iron Man 2 is a polished, high-octane sequel, not as good as the original but building once again on a quirky performance by Robert Downey Jr. The superhero genre doesn't necessarily require good acting, but when it's there (as in *Iron Man* and *The Dark Knight*), that takes it up a level. Downey here gives us a Tony Stark who is cockier and more egotistical than ever. Or, and here's the key, he seems to be.

All heroes have a fatal flaw. That's one of the rules of the road in fiction. Tony Stark's flaw is that he is dying. The megalomaniac act comes naturally, but now it's useful as a cover-up. His chest-mounted battery pack, or life source, or whatever it is, is running low and poisoning his blood. It works by using the rarest element in the periodic table, and to renew it would require discovering or inventing a new element. Not easy.

So Tony stands aside at big events and uses a little blood monitor—helpfully named the "Stark Blood Monitor," in case anybody sees it—that tells him his blood toxicity is relentlessly climbing toward death. This is his private fear, not even shared with the loyal Pepper Potts (Gwyneth Paltrow), who is running his company.

Stark is sponsoring a Stark Expo at the site of the New York World's Fair, and he flies in for an appearance in the Iron Man suit and promises world peace. The arena is thronged with adoring fans. Imagine Steve Jobs announcing iPad 3. But trouble is brewing. His archrival Justin Hammer (Sam Rockwell) plans an army of rival iron suits. A congressional committee headed by the fatuous Senator Stern (Garry Shandling) wants Stark to make Iron Man the exclusive property of the Defense Department. And in Russia, the bitter Ivan Vanko (Mickey Rourke) believes Stark's father stole the Iron Man secrets from his own father.

Hammer hires Vanko to design a better suit than Stark's, the two suit designs go to war, we get half an hour of sensational special effects, and Bob's your uncle. But you also have a niece, a sexy martial arts expert played by Scarlett Johansson, who may be more than she seems. The character was named Black Widow in the comic books, never a good sign. Fighting at Stark's side is his comrade Lieutenant Colonel "Rhodey" Rhodes (Don Cheadle); while rocketing through a blizzard of enemy missiles, the two find time to talk. How slow must a missile be moving if your buddy has time to warn you to dodge it?

The best CGI sequence in the movie comes at midpoint, when Tony Stark decides to drive his own car in the Monaco Grand Prix, and Ivan Vanko stands fearlessly in the middle of the race, dressed like a kinky gladiator and wielding electric whips that can slice a car in two. He nearly destroys Stark, which is so exciting that we forget to wonder how he knew that Tony was driving his own car. It's after this race that Hammer signs him up.

Mickey Rourke gives us all the Ivan Vanko we could possibly wish for, unless he had a third arm to provide space for more tattoos. His performance features flashing his gold teeth in mirthless laughter, and lots of growling. Sam Rockwell gives a wry comic performance as Hammer, a querulous whiner who seems in over his head in the super weapons business.

You want a sequel, you got a sequel. *Iron Man 2*, directed like the first one by Jon Favreau, gets the job done. Since both movies have essentially the same story arc, there aren't a lot of surprises, however, which started me to wondering how the guys survive inside those suits. Sure, the suits are armored, but their bodies aren't. How many dizzying falls and brutal blows and sneaky explosions can you survive without breaking every bone in your body? Just askin'. At the end of a long day, those suits should be filled with bloody pulp.

Is Anybody There? ★ ★ ½

PG-13, 92 m., 2009

Michael Caine (Clarence), Bill Milner (Edward), Anne-Marie Duff (Mum), David Morrissey (Dad), Elizabeth Spriggs (Prudence), Leslie Phillips (Reg), Ralph Raich (Clive), Rosemary Harris (Elsie). Directed by John Crowley and produced by David Heyman, Marc Turtletaub, and Peter Saraf. Screenplay by Peter Harness.

Sir Michael Caine makes acting look as natural as running water. I have never sensed an ounce of egotism in his makeup. The videos he made to teach film acting are plain-spoken and practical. Of course, you need inspiration and talent. But what can he tell you about that? He tells you that you have to look out of the same eye all during a close-up. Or if you don't, that's what they mean by shifty-eyed.

Look at him here in *Is Anybody There?* Caine is seventy-six years old, but this is the first movie where he looks it. He doesn't give a damn. He's supposed to be old. That's why he has checked himself, reluctantly, into an old folks' home. It's called Lark Hall; it's close to the sea and inhabited by dotty seniors who have little to entertain them apart from territorial battles and simmering resentments.

He plays a retired magician named the Amazing Clarence, who drives up in a van painted like an ice cream wagon and almost runs down Edward (Bill Milner), who is about ten and whose parents run the operation. Edward likes living in Lark Hall because he's fascinated by ghosts, and he reasons that a home for the aged would be a good place to find some. He sneaks his tape recorder under the bed of a dying patient, hoping to capture some spirit manifestations.

The Amazing Clarence is spiteful, hostile, and unfriendly. Edward doesn't much notice. He's a force of nature and bowls over Clarence with his curiosity. The old magician is persuaded to put on a magic show for the other retirees; he pretends great reluctance, but I doubt it because if you're still tooling around the countryside in a van and doing one-night stands at seventy-six, it may be because you like to.

The rest of *Is Anybody There?* doesn't measure up to the Amazing Clarence and his young acolyte. Lark Hall seems less like a retirement home than a failed pilot for a sitcom, with old folks who behave in relentlessly obvious comic shtick. It reminded me nostalgically of *Mrs. Palfrey at the Claremont* (2005), with Joan Plowright and Anna Massey among the inhabitants of an establishment where the evening meals were an exercise in thrilling nonverbal communication. The folks in Lark Hall should spend more time eyeing one another and less time acting out.

I can't really recommend the film, unless you admire Caine as much as I do, which is certainly possible. Let's say I somehow found myself retired, and I was informed that the movie was shallow, clunky, and sitcomish, but that Michael Caine played an old magician named the Amazing Clarence in it. I would take the remnants of my latest Social Security check and hobble down to the theater, because my sixth sense would tell me Caine would be worth the price of admission. I would, however, demand a full refund if the Amazing Clarence didn't attempt at least one magic trick that went spectacularly wrong. Reader, the theater would be able to keep my money.

I Spit on Your Grave (no stars)

NO MPAA RATING, 108 m., 2010

Sarah Butler (Jennifer Hill), Jeff Branson (Johnny), Daniel Franzese (Stanley), Rodney Eastman (Andy), Chad Lindberg (Matthew), Andrew Howard (Sheriff Storch), Tracey Walter (Earl Woodason). Directed by Steven R. Monroe and produced by Lisa M. Hansen and Paul Hertzberg. Screenplay by Stuart Morse, based on a 1978 screenplay by Meir Zarchi.

This despicable remake of the despicable 1978 film *I Spit on Your Grave* adds yet another offense: a phony moral equivalency. In the original, a woman foolishly thought to go on holiday by herself in a secluded cabin. She attracted the attention of depraved local men, who raped her, one after the other. Then the film ended with her fatal revenge. In this film, less time is devoted to the revenge and more time to verbal, psychological, and physical violence against her. Thus it works even better as vicarious cruelty against women.

First let's dispatch with the fiction that the film is about "getting even." If I rape you, I have committed a crime. If you kill me, you have committed another one. The ideal outcome would be two people unharmed in the first place. The necessity of revenge is embedded in the darker places of our minds, and most hate speech is driven by "wrongs" invented in unbalanced minds. No one who commits a hate crime ever thinks his victim is innocent.

That set aside, let's see what this movie does. The woman, Jennifer (Sarah Butler), is a writer who rents a cabin in the woods where she plans to stay by herself. Once we know this, we start waiting for the gas station occupied by demented rednecks. There's always one. Of course that's where Jennifer stupidly asks directions and reveals where she's going to ignorant, leering phallus carriers.

There are four. One is their "ringleader." One is his sidekick. One compulsively makes video recordings. The fourth is mentally handicapped and they treat him as their pet "retard." After many scenes involving alarming noises in the night and the usual Woman in Fear sequences, the men enter her cabin and terrorize her.

They use words and guns. They insinuate. They toy with her answers. They enjoy her terror. This is rape foreplay, and they stretch it out as long as they can. There is a reason for this. Rape is a crime of violence, not sex, and the male rapist typically savors the fear he causes more than the sex. Indeed, if he enjoyed sex more, he might not be a rapist. The true pornography in this film involves the dialogue and situation in the cabin *before* the physical assault. It is well done. This is a professionally made film. The audience is very, very quiet. Some share Jennifer's terror. Some, I am afraid, may be aroused or entertained by it.

When the rape inevitably arrives, it is the hapless mental deficient, Matthew (Chad Lindberg), who is forced by the others to go first. Otherwise he crouches whimpering in a corner. The movie's exploitation of his handicap is on a par with the cruel sadism of the film. Eventually Jennifer is thoroughly raped and runs away into the woods barefoot and almost naked and, when they approach with a shotgun to eliminate her as a witness, jumps from a high bridge and disappears.

We will slip past the movie's nonexplanation for her survival and reappearance to consider her revenge. I choose not to describe her methods. Let me suggest that if you recall any of the torture scenes described in the novels of Cormac McCarthy or Larry McMurtry, I suspect the director and writer of this film remember them as well. Jennifer's methods are elaborate, bizarre, and cruel.

Oh, sure, they have it coming to them—except for the pathetic Matthew, who has been a victim all his life and is now punished by Jennifer even though she witnessed his grief and innocence. He is a man and must die. A couple of tortures here inspired groans from the audience, but this stuff isn't a novelty for connoisseurs of horror movies. Consider *Saw* and anything with *chainsaw* in its title.

No, it's the first half of the movie that's offensive. It implicitly assigns us the POV of the men as they taunt and terrorize Jennifer in plausible ways—which are different from her killing methods, which are implausible, probably impossible, and offered and received as entertainment.

Now here's an interesting thing: There were walkouts from the packed screening I attended. Not many, maybe eight or nine. Nobody walked out in the second half; they all left in the first half. And . . . they were all men. Most of the audience looked like they were on dates. For conversation afterward, if you see this loathsome film, here are some suggestions:

Men, ask your dates: What bothered you more, the first or second half? Would you recommend this movie to your girlfriends? Did you enjoy it? (It's OK; you can be honest.)

Women, ask your dates: What part did you like the most, the first or second half? Would you recommend this movie to your sister? Why did we go to this particular film? Did you know there were two new four-star films playing in the same multiplex?

Both men and women may find some food for thought in the answers. Certain answers may cause you to ask yourself if you have any future with this other person. ☞

It's Complicated ★ ★ ½

R, 120 m., 2009

Meryl Streep (Jane), Steve Martin (Adam), Alec Baldwin (Jake), John Krasinski (Harley), Lake

Bell (Agness), Mary Kay Place (Joanne), Rita Wilson (Trisha). Directed by Nancy Meyers and produced by Meyers and Scott Rudin. Screenplay by Meyers.

It's Complicated is perfectly plausible if you are only willing to believe that Meryl Streep sells a whole lot of muffins. She plays a bakery and restaurant owner who lives in a sprawling hacienda on a bluff overlooking the Pacific in Santa Barbara, set on grounds approached by a sweeping circular drive. I've been to Oprah's place, which is only a little nicer. Life is sweet, although she hires an architect to give her a new kitchen. Her current one tragically has only two ovens.

Give the sainted Meryl a lot of credit. Living alone, she occupies this space as if it makes perfect sense for her. There's an actress for you. Her children love her, her son-in-law adores her, and life would be perfect if it weren't that her husband, Jake (Alec Baldwin), left her ten years ago. You'd think she'd be able to get over the loss of Baldwin in ten years. A lot of women have.

Jake married the much younger Agness (Lake Bell), another of those people who mess with the spelling of their names to make it hard on everybody. Agness (rhymes with "ssss") has a perfect body but a petulant expression, and for the life of us we can't figure out why Jake left the merry Meryl for her. Neither can he. Running into his first wife at their son's graduation, he's moved by memories of their past. At the bar of her hotel, she unwisely orders a Tanqueray martini, dry, with a lemon twist, just before Jake walks in. That's like disarming before the battle.

They experience something between love and tantric rapture. She's not merely more exciting than he remembered, she's the next generation of Viagra. Alec Baldwin, it must be said, was born to play a man blissful in bed, and few other actors could so perfectly deliver his line, "Home, sweet home." Miss Streep, in one of her rare (and nonexplicit, of course) sex scenes, inspires as so often our belief that she's good at everything she does. Maybe she does bake great muffins.

Adam (Steve Martin), her architect, is meanwhile forging ahead with plans for the new addition on a house already spacious enough to accommodate a youth hostel. He visits a lot, and it is clear he's smitten. But he's recovering from a painful breakup and fearful of starting something new. Jane finds herself in the position of starting to like this architect while at the same time carrying on an affair with a married man, her ex-husband. She keeps this a personal secret, confiding only in her best girlfriends, which is accurate enough about the way women keep secrets.

It's Complicated was written and directed by Nancy Meyers, who after *Something's Gotta Give* (2003), *What Women Want* (2000), and *The Holiday* (2006), has established a cottage industry in movies about romantically inclined middle-aged people. Pairing Diane Keaton and Jack Nicholson, Mel Gibson and Helen Hunt, and now Streep, Baldwin, and Martin, she favors tush-baring scenes from her stars, although it's a sign of the times that Baldwin finds himself hooked up with Martin via iChat, with the camera and screen-sharing options unfortunately enabled.

There's funny stuff here. We like everybody. We enjoy the way Harley the future son-in-law (John Krasinski) finds himself in possession of much more information than he desires. At the same time, we're aware that the scene of a character sneaking up to peek through a window, losing his footing, and crashing to the ground was not fresh when it was used so well in *The Lady Eve* (1941). And while it can be funny when a respectable lady gets stoned on pot, it's difficult for even Streep to make it funny for ten minutes.

It's Complicated is a rearrangement of the goods in Nancy Meyers's bakery, and some of them belong on the day-old shelf. Oh, how I hate food analogies in reviews. In a season of blessings, there are several better choices than this one. Truth in criticism: I must report that I expect *It's Complicated* will be terrifically popular with its target demographic, which includes gal pals taking a movie break after returning Christmas presents. Not everybody is in a mood for *Avatar.*

I Will Follow ★ ★ ★ ½

NO MPAA RATING, 83 m., 2011

Salli Richardson-Whitfield (Maye), Michole White (Fran), Omari Hardwick (Troy), Dijon

Talton (Raven), Tracie Thoms (Tiffany), Damone Roberts (Himself), Blair Underwood (Evan), Beverly Todd (Amanda). Directed by Ava DuVernay and produced by DuVernay and Molly M. Mayeux. Screenplay by DuVernay.

I Will Follow doesn't tell a story so much as try to understand a woman. Through her, we can find insights into the ways we deal with death. In one way or another, every emotion in this wonderful independent film is one I've experienced myself. Grief, of course. But also anger, loneliness, confusion, and a sense of lost direction. Above all, urgent conversations you have in your own mind with someone who is no longer alive to have them with you. How many people, now dead, have you wanted to ask questions you should have asked when they were alive?

The film takes place during one day in a home in Topanga Canyon, just a short drive above Los Angeles but with a sort of woodsy feeling. This is where a woman named Amanda (Beverly Todd) spent the last year of her life. She had breast cancer, she refused chemo, she wanted to die on her own terms in her own house, and died not long ago. We spend the day with her favorite niece, Maye (Salli Richardson-Whitfield), who lived with her for that last year.

Maye feels as if she's taking her next step into thin air. Amanda was a powerful and charismatic woman, a recording session drummer for rock 'n' roll and jazz groups. Maye has had success as a makeup artist in Hollywood, but it was her aunt who seemed glamorous and enchanting above everyone else. Now Maye is left behind.

The film opens with an argument with the movers. There's that tension you feel when someone touches anything left behind by the dead person, and it's like they're killing them just a little more. To help her pack up things, Maye has her nephew Raven (Dijon Talton), who is distracted, annoyed, unhelpful. People come by the house all day: two guys from the Goodwill, a woman repairman from the satellite company, a neighbor. All of these small roles are cast and written to create characters who are small but very human.

The key visitor is Amanda's daughter and Raven's mother, Fran (Michole White). Through her, we get an insight into Raven's attitude toward his grandmother. Fran always believed Maye was her mother's favorite. At the end, it was Maye whom Amanda chose to live with, Maye who nursed her, Maye who supported Amanda's desire to die at home without chemo. Fran blames Maye for Amanda's death—or at least for it coming so soon.

We're familiar with the five stages of grief: denial, anger, bargaining, depression, and acceptance. Are there also stages of mourning? One of them might be blame. We feel it's wrong for a person to die, and we want someone or something to blame. It must be someone's fault. By living with Amanda and sharing her feelings, Maye has accepted her death. But as her daughter, Fran feels closed out and blames the "favorite niece." A lifetime of resentment wells up in a powerful scene between the two women.

What is particularly human about *I Will Follow*, which was written and directed by Ava DuVernay, is that she understands why Fran feels that way. There's no attempt to make Maye the good character and Fran the bad one. They both have valid reasons for their emotions. And all the people who pass through the house that day (there are about twelve) come with feelings we understand and perhaps have shared. One who particularly struck me was the neighbor, maybe contemplating his own mortality, who didn't know Amanda that well. They apparently talked only over the fence. It's clear to me that as they talked about their gardens and the pleasant weather, they shared unspoken feelings that they were comrades in the process of leaving life. Another important visitor is Troy (Omari Hardwick), as Maye's sorta boyfriend. As they speak, we understand instinctively their fondness and also a certain reserve; these two don't easily give away their hearts.

Beverly Todd, a beautiful woman who has been in countless movies and TV shows since the late 1960s, has an important presence here in many flashbacks, some of them dreamy or fragmented, as Amanda. She easily evokes the magic Maye must have felt, and that gives weight to the present-day scenes. For Salli Richardson-Whitfield, the role of Maye is a great performance, as she embodies emotions the script wisely doesn't spell out. *I Will Follow* is an invitation to empathy. It can't have a traditional three-act structure, because every life closes in death, and only supporting characters are left onstage at the end. What goes unsaid, but not thought, is that we will all pass this way eventually.

Amanda's family is African-American. The neighbor and some of the visitors are white. Why do I mention race? I wasn't going to. This is a universal story about universal emotions. Maybe I mention it because this is the kind of film black filmmakers are rarely able to get made these days, offering roles for actors who remind us here of their gifts. Ava DuVernay, a documentarian making her first feature, has made *I Will Follow* as the first of a group of new indie African-American films.

J

Jack Goes Boating ★ ★ ★

R, 91 m., 2010

Philip Seymour Hoffman (Jack), Amy Ryan (Connie), John Ortiz (Clyde), Daphne Rubin-Vega (Lucy). Directed by Philip Seymour Hoffman and produced by Beth O'Neil, Peter Saraf, Marc Turtletaub, and Emily Ziff. Screenplay by Bob Glaudini, based on his play.

Philip Seymour Hoffman has a gift for playing quickly embarrassed men who fear rejection. He can convey such vulnerability in some roles that we're on his side without the screenplay needing to persuade us. We want to finish his sentences, clap him on the back, cheer him up. In other roles, such as *Synecdoche, New York*, he projects enough ego to enforce his will for years on end. There's an actor for you.

In *Jack Goes Boating*, Hoffman is not only the star but also the director. He is merciless in using himself as an actor. His face is often seen in close-up, sweaty, splotchy, red as if he suffers from rosacea. He seems perpetually blushing. In life Hoffman's skin is perfectly normal; not every actor would stand for this, but vanity is not one of Hoffman's sins.

In the movie he plays a limousine driver for a company owned by his uncle, which gives us an idea of his stature in the family. At dawn he meets for coffee with his best friend, Clyde (John Ortiz), and they sit in a parked limo and regard the unattainable towers of Manhattan. Jack is clueless. Clyde is effortless. Even in their forties, they have a student-teacher relationship. Clyde is going to teach Jack how to chat up a girl, make himself likable, swim, row a boat, even eventually cook a meal for her—which may be asking for too much.

Clyde is married to Lucy (Daphne Rubin-Vega). She works in a funeral home with Connie (Amy Ryan). Connie is the kind of person who you'd describe as sweet but terribly shy. Clyde and Lucy decide these two people belong with each other, perhaps by default because they appear to belong with nobody else.

This leads into a dinner that reminds me a little of Mike Leigh's *Abigail's Party*, in the sense that the wrong people are in the wrong room at the wrong time, and social embarrassment is the main course. The movie is based on an off-Broadway play by Bob Glaudini that Hoffman and Ortiz produced and acted in with Rubin-Vega. It has a touch of Leigh and more than a touch of kitchen sink drama; its stage origins are suggested by the way Jack lives in a flat where the kitchen, dining area, and living area are essentially one space—that works beautifully when his dinner for Connie goes wrong, as it must.

It's expected in a four-character play that all four characters will come into play, and they do, in an unexpected way. The interplay between Jack and Connie is awkward and initially promising, but it's clear they have a lot of shyness to overcome in catching up to Clyde and Lucy. Still, even happy marriages have secrets.

You can sense the familiarity the actors have with their roles, but there's not the sense they've been this way before. What has traveled this path is the screenplay, which follows a familiar pattern and is essentially redeemed by the meticulous performances. The actors make it new and poignant, and avoid going over the top in the story's limited psychic and physical space. Even at their highest pitch, the emotions of these characters come from hearts long worn down by the troubles we see.

Jane Eyre ★ ★ ★ ½

PG-13, 118 m., 2011

Mia Wasikowska (Jane Eyre), Michael Fassbender (Rochester), Jamie Bell (Saint John Rivers), Sally Hawkins (Mrs. Reed), Judi Dench (Mrs. Fairfax). Directed by Cary Joji Fukunaga and produced by Alison Owen and Paul Trijbits. Screenplay by Moira Buffini, based on the novel by Charlotte Bronte.

Gothic romance attracts us with a deep, tidal force. Part of its appeal is the sense of ungovernable eroticism squirming to escape from just beneath the surface. Its chaste heroines and dark, brooding heroes prowl the gloomy shadows of crepuscular castles, and doomy secrets stir in the corners. Charlotte Bronte's *Jane Eyre* is among the greatest of Gothic novels, a page-turner of such startling power it leaves its pale, latter-day imitators like *Twilight* flopping for air like a stranded fish.

To be sure, the dark hero of the story, Rochester, is not a vampire, but that's only a technicality. The tension in the genre is often generated by a virginal girl's attraction to a dangerous man. The more pitiful and helpless the heroine the better, but she must also be proud and virtuous, brave and idealistic. And her attraction to the ominous hero must be based on pity, not fear; he must deserve her idealism.

This atmospheric new *Jane Eyre*, the latest of many adaptations, understands those qualities, and also that the very architecture and landscape embodies the Gothic notion. The film opens with Jane Eyre fearfully fleeing across the bleak moors, where even nature conspires against her. This is not the opening we expect, with Jane already fully grown, but later in flashbacks we'll be reminded of her Dickensian girlhood, her cruel aunt, her sadistic boarding school, and her need as a girl without means to earn her own way as a governess.

Jane is described in the novel as a plain girl; is that where the phrase "plain Jane" comes from? Here she's played by Mia Wasikowska (of Tim Burton's *Alice in Wonderland*), who is far from plain, but transforms herself into a pale, severe creature who needs to be watered with love. She is employed by the intimidating Rochester (Michael Fassbender) to supervise the care of his "ward," Adele Varens (Romy Settbon Moore), who is being raised in his isolated manor, Thornfield. How he came into the possession of a young girl as his "ward" is an excellent question, one among many that could probably be answered by Thornfield's dedicated housekeeper, Mrs. Fairfax (Judi Dench).

The classic *Jane Eyre* is the 1944 version with Joan Fontaine and Orson Welles. Fontaine was twenty-seven; Welles was twenty-nine. Mia Wasikowska is twenty-two and Michael Fassbender is thirty-four. In the novel, Jane is scarcely twenty and Rochester is . . . older. Whether in any version he is old enough to accomplish what he has done in life is a good question, but this film is correct in making their age difference obvious; Jane in every sense must be intimidated by her fierce employer. No version I know of has ever made Rochester as unattractive as he is described in the book.

Rochester is absent a good deal of the time, although represented by the foreboding atmosphere of Thornfield, the enigmatic loyalty of Mrs. Fairfax, and the sense that something is amiss in the enormous manor. Here Judi Dench's contribution is significant; the tone of her voice conveys so much more about Rochester than her words.

Either you know the plot or not. Its secret is a red herring with all the significance of "Rosebud." It functions only to provide Rochester with an honorable reason to propose a dishonorable thing, and thus preserve the moral standards of the time. The novel is actually about forbidden sexual attraction on both sides, and its interest is in the tension of Jane and Rochester as they desire sex but deny themselves. Much of the power comes from repressed emotions, and perhaps Charlotte Bronte was writing in code about the feelings nice women of her time were not supposed to feel.

The director here is Cary Joji Fukunaga, whose *Sin Nombre* was one of the best films of 2009. Its story, based on fearsome Mexican gangs, scarcely resembles *Jane Eyre*, but it showed an emotional intensity between characters who live mostly locked within themselves. He's a director with a sure visual sense, here expressed in voluptuous visuals and ambitious art direction.

Michael Fassbender is an Irish actor who can have a threatening charm; did you see him in *Fish Tank* (2009), a quite different film about a seductive man who takes advantage of a teenage girl? Mia Wasikowska, from Australia, is a relative newcomer who must essentially carry *Jane Eyre* and succeeds with restraint, expressing a strong moral compass. Judi Dench is firm, as a housekeeper must be firm, and observes everything, as a housekeeper must. All of the rest is decoration. Without the costumes, sets, locations, sound design, and the wind and rain, gothic cannot exist.

Jennifer's Body ★ ★ ★

R, 102 m., 2009

Megan Fox (Jennifer Check), Amanda Seyfried (Needy Lesnicky), Johnny Simmons (Chip Dove), Adam Brody (Nikolai Wolf), J. K. Simmons

(Mr. Wroblewski), Amy Sedaris (Toni Lesnicky), Chris Pratt (Officer Duda), Juno Ruddell (Officer Warzak), Kyle Gallner (Colin Gray). Directed by Karyn Kusama and produced by Daniel Dubiecki, Mason Novick, and Jason Reitman. Screenplay by Diablo Cody.

Just what we were waiting for, *Twilight* for boys, with Megan Fox in the Robert Pattinson role, except that I recall Pattinson was shirtless. Diablo Cody's next screenplay after *Juno* is a 180-degree reversal, with the heroine now transformed into a fiend who eats the flesh of teenage boys. Can you imagine Juno's poor boyfriend, Michael Cera, with steak sauce?

The film opens on a deceptively light note in high school, introducing Jennifer Check (Fox) and Needy Lesnicky (Amanda Seyfried) as lifelong best friends. Jennifer is the hottest and most popular babe in school, and Needy is—well, needy. Surely that's her nickname. What parents would name a child Needy?

Jennifer is your classic teen queen who rules the school. Boys lust after her, she's the head cheerleader, and maybe it does her ego good to have needy Needy trailing along. But then she's transformed into, not a vampire exactly, although she does go after throats with bared teeth. She's some kind of demon or monster, sort of undefined, whose mission in life becomes attacking teenage boys.

Her image gives her a valuable weapon in satiating her unwholesome appetites. Timid lads who would never dream of dating Jennifer now find her unexpectedly friendly, even seductive. One kid even gets invited to her home. This turns out to be a creepy empty house. Why do characters always enter creepy empty houses and feel their way in the dark, when they should stand outside on the sidewalk and whistle?

Jennifer gets away with murder because, well, who would expect the sexy and popular cheerleader to be a secret drinker of blood and quite possibly a devourer of flesh? Only Needy suspects the horrifying reality, and finally it is she who stands between Jennifer and more victims, including a nice kid like Chip Dove (Johnny Simmons), who you know is a nice kid because his name, after all, is Chip Dove, and what kind of name is that for a villain?

It's easy to go on like this, but I'd be missing something. There is within Diablo Cody the soul of an artist, and her screenplay brings to this material a certain edge, a kind of gleeful relish that's uncompromising. This isn't your assembly line teen horror thriller. The portraits of Jennifer and Needy are a little too knowing, the dialogue is a little too off-center, the developments are a little too quirky. After you've seen enough teen thrillers, you begin to appreciate these distinctions. Let's put it this way: I'd rather see *Jennifer's Body* again than *Twilight.*

Megan Fox is an interesting case. We think of her as a star, but this is actually her first leading role. She didn't get named number 18 on *Maxim*'s Hot 100 list of 2007 for acting. (The top post went to Lindsay Lohan. How quickly times change.) She is also famous for her many tattoos, but in researching that aspect of her image I made an encouraging discovery. Anyone can have a tattoo of a butterfly. Been there, done that. But Megan Fox has a tattoo that quotes *King Lear*: "We will laugh at gilded butterflies." How cool is that? Plus, so far, there are no tiresome rumors about booze and drugs.

Fox did her career a lot of good with the two *Transformer* movies, but this is her first chance to really perform, and you know what? She comes through. She has your obligatory projectile vomiting scene and somehow survives it, she plays the role straight, and she looks great in a blood-drenched dress with her hair all straggly. Amanda Seyfried makes a plucky heroine.

The film is directed by Karyn Kusama, who in the splendid *Girlfight* (2000) introduced Michelle Rodriguez. She handles this material efficiently and with a certain relish. It's not art, it's not *Juno,* it's not *Girlfight* for that matter, but as a movie about a flesh-eating cheerleader, it's better than it has to be.

Jerichow ★ ★ ★

NO MPAA RATING, 91 m., 2009

Benno Furmann (Thomas), Nina Hoss (Laura), Hilmi Sozer (Ali), Andre M. Hennicke (Leon), Claudia Geisler (Administrator), Marie Gruber (Cashier), Knut Berger (Policeman). Directed by Christian Petzold and produced by Florian Koerner von Gustorf and Michael Weber. Screenplay by Petzold.

In a district where unemployment and poverty are common, it may not seem like wealth to own a snack shop. But if you own a string of them, you've got it made. Ali owns a string. He also owns a beautiful blond wife, whom he acquired by paying off her debts, just like he got the snack shops and a shiny new Mercedes.

Yet Ali is not a happy man. Born in Turkey but raised in East Germany, he moans, "I am in a country where nobody wants me, with a wife I bought." He needs a friend. Also a driver, after he loses his license for drunk driving. He hires Thomas, who has troubles of his own: He has been dishonorably discharged from the German forces in Afghanistan, his wife has just died, his savings have been stolen in a settlement of a gambling debt, he was knocked out in the process, and he is homeless and broke. Sure, he'd like to be Ali's driver.

This is the setup for Christian Petzold's *Jerichow,* named for the East German locale. Petzold may ring a bell for you from last year's weirdly intriguing thriller *Yella,* about a woman on the lam from an abusive husband and hoping to embezzle a fortune in her new job. Yella was played by Nina Hoss, who plays Ali's wife, Laura, here. She would be sexy if she didn't have that quality of edgy desperation. Ali (Hilmi Sozer), who looks a little like a Turkish Bob Hoskins, is a very untrusting man, convinced he is being cheated for an excellent reason: He is.

Thomas (Benno Furmann), who shows in one scene he is very confident with brutal hand-to-hand fighting, is the kind of man Ali is looking for—a collector, enforcer, spy, and dependent on Ali. He is also taller than Ali, younger, and better-looking, which doesn't escape Laura's attention. We can see trouble coming.

Ali likes to flash his money and hint at big plans, but he leads a narrow life. He and Laura live at the end of a forest road, next to the warehouse where they load a van with milk, soda, chips, and candy for daily deliveries. He is half-crazy with paranoia, sneaking around corners to catch his shop managers stealing. He also fears catching Laura and Thomas together, and when he makes a business trip to Turkey, is he almost setting them up?

It may not be that simple. Nothing in this movie may be that simple. Petzold doesn't make level-one thrillers, and his characters may be smarter than us or dumber. It's never just about the plot, anyway. It has to do with random accidents, dangerous coincidences, miscalculations, simple mistakes. And the motives are never simple.

It's easy to compare *Jerichow* with the films of *The Postman Always Rings Twice,* with the grimy gas station owner, the sexy wife, and the rugged drifter, but people have a way of not behaving according to their superficial qualities. And there may be something going on here about the complexities of being a stranger in a very strange land.

Joan Rivers: A Piece of Work ★ ★ ★ ½

R, 84 m., 2010

Featuring Joan Rivers. A documentary directed by Ricki Stern and Annie Sundberg and produced by Seth Keal and Sundberg.

No one is ever too old. You may have that idea about Joan Rivers, who is seventy-five in this film and never tires of reminding us of that fact. Is that too old? It's older than she would prefer, but what are you gonna do? She remains one of the funniest, dirtiest, most daring and transgressive of stand-up comics, and she hasn't missed a beat.

Joan Rivers: A Piece of Work covers the events in about a year of her life. If the filmmakers didn't have total access, I don't want to see what they missed. In one stretch in this film she closes a show in Toronto, flies overnight to Palm Springs, does a gig, flies overnight to Minneapolis and performs another one. Try that sometime.

She has the energy, stamina, and aggression that a great stand-up needs. She assaults the audience. She pounds laughter out of us. If you've seen her only on television, you have no idea. I saw her in Vegas, and she had people weeping with laughter. I saw her at a memorial service in Toronto for a friend of hers, and she brought down the house. Was that wrong at a memorial service? Brian Linehan, her friend, wouldn't have expected anything less, and she knew it. If you need devout solemnity, Joan Rivers is not your girl.

The way she is funny is, she tells the truth

according to herself. She hates some people. She has political opinions. Her observations are so merciless and her timing so precise that even if you like that person, you laugh. She is a sadist of comedy, unafraid to be cruel—even too cruel. She doesn't know fear. She seems to be curious about how far she can go and still get a laugh. That must feel dangerous on a stage with a live audience. Maybe she feeds on that danger.

This documentary began filming before she had her latest fifteen minutes of fame on Donald Trump's *Celebrity Apprentice.* God help Rod Blagojevich if he'd been on the show that season. Rivers has had hours of those fifteen minutes of fame. Her life is like a comeback tour. She is frank about her setbacks. She was Johnny Carson's resident cohost (and gave young Siskel & Ebert their first spot on *The Tonight Show*). She left Carson to begin her own nightly show on Fox. Carson never spoke to her again. NBC banned her from all of its shows until two years ago. The Fox show eventually failed, and it was discovered that her husband, Edgar, the show's manager, had been stealing from her. He killed himself. She never forgave him—for the suicide, not the other stuff.

She was down. She was up. Her daughter, Melissa, says, "Her career was like me having a sister." I wonder if Melissa appears with her on red carpet shows because it's a chance for some quiet time with Mom. She hardly mentions the red carpets for which she is now widely known. For her, it all comes down to this week: Does she have bookings? She looks at blank pages in her engagement calendar and says they're so white she needs sunglasses to read them.

What makes Joannie run? They say if a shark stops swimming, it dies. She's not a shark. She's a woman who for various reasons depends on making audiences laugh. They walk in knowing all of her problems, knowing her age, eagle eyed for the plastic surgery, ready to complain, and she *forces* them to laugh because she's so damned funny. I admire that. Bernard Shaw called it the Life Force. We see her in the film's first shot, without makeup. A minute later, *Joan Rivers* is before us. Her life is a performance of herself.

Yes, she's had plastic surgery. Well, why not? I think it's wrong for most people. But show business is cruel and eats its old, and you do what you have to do. She talks about it. She talks about everything. A portrait emerges of a bright little girl who walked onto a stage and never wanted to get off. If she can't have a network show, she'll work a dinner club.

There's that need in a lot of comics. Once in the Merchandise Mart, I was riding down in an elevator with Henny Youngman. The doors opened at the private club on the second floor, and there was a big placard there pointing to the room for a wedding. Henny didn't miss a beat. He walked off, asked to be introduced to the father of the bride, and told him, "My name is Henny Youngman. I'll do ten minutes for two hundred dollars."

I think *Joan Rivers: A Piece of Work* is fascinating and has a lot of laughs in it. It's more than that. It's the portrait of a woman who will not accept defeat, who will not slow down, who must prove herself over and again. A brave and stubborn woman, smart as a whip, superbly skilled. You want to see what it looks like to rage, rage against the dying of the light? Joan Rivers will not go gentle into that good night.

Jonah Hex ★ ★

PG-13, 80 m., 2010

Josh Brolin (Jonah Hex), John Malkovich (Quentin Turnbull), Megan Fox (Lilah), Michael Fassbender (Burke), Will Arnett (Lieutenant Grass), Michael Shannon (Doc Cross Williams). Directed by Jimmy Hayward and produced by Akiva Goldsman and Andrew Lazar. Screenplay by Mark Neveldine and Brian Taylor, based on the DC Comics characters by John Albano and Tony Dezuniga.

Jonah Hex is a Western set around the town of Stunk Crick, although that doesn't entirely explain why the climactic scene involves an attack on the U.S. Capitol building in Washington. Using my powers of logic, I deduce that the characters traveled there from Stunk Crick. The movie is not precise in its geography. Most of the location filming was in Louisiana, which is not named, perhaps because that might make it hard to explain its vast deserts and dusty frontier town.

The thriller involves a man named Jonah Hex (Josh Brolin), who is bent on vengeance. During the Civil War, the evil Quentin Turnbull (John Malkovich) strapped him to a cross and made him watch as a house containing his family was set afire. Then Turnbull branded Jonah's face with a hot iron, causing difficulties with leaks when he tries to throw back a shot of whiskey. You can see why Jonah would want his revenge. To be sure, Turnbull mutters something about Jonah having previously murdered HIS family, meaning he isn't entirely without motive.

Stunk Crick is your standard frontier town with a wide Main Street, a saloon, and a room over the saloon occupied by Lilah, a sexy hooker. The presence of Lilah in the film is easily explained: She is played by Megan Fox. If you want a woman in an old western town, there are only three occupations open to her, hooking, schoolmarming, and anyone called Ma.

Lilah and Jonah are in love, for reasons unexplained. It certainly isn't because of the quality of their conversation. The only hooker in a Western I've ever believed in was in *Lonesome Dove,* but I've seen *Lonesome Dove,* and *Jonah Hex* is no *Lonesome Dove.*

It's based on some DC Comics characters, which may explain the way the plot jumps around. We hear a lot about graphic novels, but this is more of a graphic anthology of strange occult ideas. Consider, for example, that Jonah was once so close to death that he wandered around on the Other Side and made valuable contacts there. He can even talk to the dead, and one corpse revives long enough to tell him precisely where Quentin Turnbull can be found.

In what is possibly a confused stab at allegory, Jonah finds himself trying to prevent Turnbull from blowing up the Capitol building with a terrorist super weapon. In scenes set in the Oval Office, the U.S. president is concerned about this threat by Turnbull, who is an embittered Confederate general, and decides that the wanted outlaw Hex is the only man who can prevent the plot from being carried out.

A climactic battle scene takes place in the Potomac River between two ironclad ships. In U.S. history, you will recall, there was such a battle between the USS *Monitor* and the Confederate ship *Virginia.* One of these ships looks like the *Monitor*, but I'm unclear. Anyway, Turnbull is onboard, directing the Weapon, which is a big cannon. He's previously tested it by blowing up a Western town. Now he trains it on the Capitol, depicted in special effects that suggest the Capitol and the Washington Monument were the only two structures in Washington at that time, at least for purposes of being fired on.

After Hex saves the day, he's invited into the Oval Office, thanked, and then presented with a big badge. What is this badge? The president tells Hex: "America needs a sheriff." This provided the audience with a big laugh, which sounded like it might have been bottled up for a while.

The Joneses ★ ★

R, 96 m., 2010

Demi Moore (Kate Jones), David Duchovny (Steve Jones), Amber Heard (Jennifer Jones), Ben Hollingsworth (Mick Jones), Gary Cole (Larry), Glenne Headly (Summer), Lauren Hutton (KC). Directed by Derrick Borte and produced by Borte, Doug Mankoff, Andrew Spaulding, and Kristi Zea. Screenplay by Borte.

Everyone wants to keep up with the Joneses. They're good-looking, friendly, popular, affluent, and they always seem ahead of the curve when it comes to what they drive, wear, play, and consume. They never boast. They never have to. People just plain want to be just like them. And you had better stop reading now, because it's impossible to say more without a spoiler.

OK, for those still in the room, I wonder how many will really be surprised by the big plot "reveal." From the first moments of dialogue, there seems to be something off about the Joneses. Nothing is made explicit for a time, but they don't seem to relate to one another as family members. There's something they understand and we don't.

The fact is, they aren't a family; they're a marketing unit. Marketing people talk about "early adopters": People who influence a peer group by being the first to know about, use, wear, or attend something. At a conference I attended in Boulder, Colorado, total strangers followed Andy Ihnatko and his iPad around like a man with a T-bone at a dog pound. The Joneses are professional early adopters, paid to impersonate a family unit and consume the sponsor's products.

Among other advantages to this story idea, it makes product placement necessary, not merely venal. If you don't leave this movie more aware of the new Audi models, you slept through it. The Joneses never make a point of anything. It's just that Steve Jones (David Duchovny) makes great shots with his new golf clubs. Kate Jones (Demi Moore) entertains so brilliantly. Their teenagers, Jennifer (Amber Heard) and Mick (Ben Hollingsworth), wear such cool stuff. If the Joneses don't have a dog, maybe that's because there's not enough money in dog retailing.

It would seem to be a comfortable existence, consuming the best products ahead of the market and never having to pay for them. It's not that easy. It means denying your own impulses to be honest and confiding. Suppressing your own tastes. Not feeling genuine. Ask yourself who in your crowd insisted you had to see *How to Train Your Dragon* in 3-D, when you wanted to see it in 2-D, and what you *really* wanted to see was *My Son, My Son, What Have Ye Done.* That person is a Jones.

You, on the other hand, are a Larry or Summer (Gary Cole and Glenne Headly), the next-door neighbors who are always playing catch-up. You have ceded control of your taste to someone you admire for superficial reasons. This is a doomed enterprise, for you will never, ever catch up, and by definition you can never take the lead because the Joneses define the race.

The Joneses not surprisingly finds troubling flaws in the lives of this professional family. Try as they will to be disciplined and on message, they have emotions of their own. Some of them involve sex. Others involve a feeling of inner worthlessness. The strongest is Kate, played by the great-looking Demi Moore as a capable team leader aiming for a promotion. Steve is a former golf pro, so no stranger to the challenge of playing a role model, but his decency runs deeper than Kate's.

As for the kids, Jennifer and Mick, well, even their names are popular; Jennifer is the sixty-seventh most popular name in the nation and Michael is the third. But they're teenagers, and you know how that goes. So many raging hormones, either to follow or suppress. That Jennifer and Mick are so attractive, and so . . . advanced . . . for their age complicates their inner lives. At that age, you haven't been completely tamed by the corporate mind-set.

The Joneses was directed and cowritten by Derrick Borte, an advertising man, and contains a good deal of dark cynicism. It also hopes to entertain, and those two goals don't fit together easily. Either this is a tragic family or a satirical one, and the film seems uncertain which way to jump. In a perfect film, the noose of their inauthentic lives would draw more tightly, more swiftly, around the Joneses, and the movie might be angrier.

Still, Demi Moore is good as a corporate team player with no conscience (she could have played the George Clooney role in *Up in the Air*), and the others adequately act around the problems of the screenplay. It's just that somehow this movie should acknowledge how very close to life it is, and how in our society you don't have to pay the Joneses. They learn their roles from television and work for free.

The Joy of Singing ★ ★ ★

NO MPAA RATING, 96 m., 2010

Marina Fois (Muriel), Lorant Deutsch (Philippe), Jeanne Balibar (Constance), Julien Baumgartner (Julien), Nathalie Richard (Noemie), Caroline Ducey (Anna), Guillaume Quatravaux (Joseph), Evelyne Kirschenbaum (Eve). Directed by Ilan Duran Cohen and produced by Anne-Cecile Berthomeau and Edouard Mauriat. Screenplay by Cohen and Philippe Lasry.

Don't get the wrong idea. *The Joy of Singing* could also be titled *The Joy of Singing Rather Than Being Murdered.* One of the meetings of Madame Eve's voice class begins with her tearful announcement that two of the group have been found dead. Her students eye one another uneasily. Who will be killed next? We wonder, too.

This is the goofiest thrill-sex-music-spy movie in many a moon, with a surprising amount of nudity and an even more surprising amount of singing, ranging from opera to "Amazing Grace" to "I'll Stand by You." Its MacGuffin is a missing USB memory stick containing unspecified uranium secrets.

I fully believe no one in the movie has any idea what these secrets could consist of, where they came from, and how they went missing, but never mind. The information belonged to the late husband of Constance (Jeanne Balibar), a student in the class. Therefore, French undercover agents *and* terrorists *and* possible Israeli and Russian agents enroll in the class to keep an eye on her. I'm trying to remember if anyone in the class has enrolled to improve their voice.

This is all done with a straight face. The students with their nefarious secrets all have to sing. Some aren't half bad. A couple are damn fine. Maybe there's something about singing in a small group of fellow spies that elevates the libido. Soon many, if not all, of these people (except for Madame Eve) are screwing like rabbits. Even the young hustler Julien (Julien Baumgartner), who doesn't give freebies for ethical reasons, is astonished to find himself growing tender about Noemie (Nathalie Richard). If there's one thing fatal to spying, it's sincerity.

At a different velocity this could be a screwball comedy, especially with those big apartments where people are always coming into and going out of rooms, but then it would be less fun. Death and sex are sort of serious, you see, and these people don't treat them lightly. They also have underlying concerns about growing old and never having children. The French agents, Muriel (Marina Fois) and Philippe (Lorant Deutsch), have a problem: She wants him to sleep with her, and he wants to be respected for more than his body. If Inspector Clouseau wandered in, he'd be out of his league and soon out of his pants.

I'll award a shiny new dime to anyone who watches the film once and can tell me who is doing what and to whom and for what reason. It just doesn't matter. We get the basic idea, and realize we know more about what's happening than anyone on the screen. I doubt if anyone in the movie, in the audience, or among the filmmakers can offer a plausible explanation for why all these people have to attend music class, especially considering its fatality rate.

Judy Moody and the NOT Bummer Summer ★ ★

PG, 91 m., 2011

Jordana Beatty (Judy Moody), Heather Graham (Aunt Opal), Parris Mosteller (Stink), Jaleel White (Mr. Todd), Garrett Ryan (Rocky), Preston Bailey (Frank), Janet Varney (Mom), Kristoffer Winters (Dad). Directed by John Schultz and produced by Gary Magness and Sarah Siegel-Magness. Screenplay by Kathy Waugh and Megan McDonald, based on the books by McDonald.

Judy Moody and the NOT Bummer Summer is a film that little kids might find perfectly acceptable. Little, little, little kids. My best guess is above fourth-grade level you'd be pushing it. The kids, on the other hand, might enjoy its zany adaptation of Megan McDonald's bestseller. That makes this a good candidate for watching on video. I doubt many parents would enjoy it much, and I can't see grown-ups attending unless they're on duty.

The movie tells the story of red-headed Judy Moody (Jordana Beatty), who learns in disbelief that while all her friends will be spending the summer doing neat things, her own parents will be away from home on an important trip. They plan to abandon Judy and her kid brother, Stink (Parris Mosteller), to the care of her dreaded Aunt Opal (Heather Graham). That information immediately reminded me that one of my mother's best friends was named Opal Hollingsworth. I heard the name "Opal Hollingsworth" so often that it's difficult for me to think of an Opal not named Hollingsworth.

What, you may ask, does that possibly have to do with *Judy Moody and the NOT Bummer Summer*? I must be honest. Both while watching the movie and again while writing this review, when I got to the name "Aunt Opal," my mind veered off on a tangent. There was little in the film to draw it back on course. It may seem unfair of me to change the subject so arbitrarily, but I am trying to signal my grown-up readers that they may find themselves looking for stuff to think about while watching this film.

Anyway, Aunt Opal turns up and is not nearly so bad as Judy Moody fears. She draws up a Thrill Chart, a weirdly unconnected checklist of things to keep Judy and Stink occupied during the summer, and the film works its way through some of these topics with lots of bright colors and jolly music. There are also some jokes about those basic bodily functions that little kids seem to find hilarious.

Jordana Beatty is capable here, sweet and spirited, and my wish for her is that life brings her screenplays that I will find more interesting. She might excel in *The Life of Opal Hollingsworth*, who was quite a character.

Julia ★ ★ ★ ★

R, 140 m., 2009

Tilda Swinton (Julia), Saul Rubinek (Mitch), Kate del Castillo (Elena), Aidan Gould (Tom), Jude Ciccolella (Nick), Bruno Bichir (Diego), Horacio Garcia Rojas (Santos), Gaston Peterson (Miguel). Directed by Erick Zonca and produced by Francois Marquis and Bertrand Faivre. Screenplay by Zonca and Aude Py.

Tilda Swinton is fearless. She'll take on any role without her ego, paycheck, vanity, or career path playing a part. All that matters, apparently, is whether the movie interests her, and whether she thinks she can do something interesting with the role. She almost always can. She hasn't often been more fascinating than in *Julia,* a nerve-wracking thriller with a twisty plot and startling realism.

We have not seen this Tilda before—but then, we haven't seen most of the Tildas before. This one is an alcoholic slut who lacks what we are pleased to call normal feminine emotions. She's just been fired from another job. Her pattern is to get sloppy drunk every night and drag a strange man to bed. She needs money. Her neighbor Elena (Kate del Castillo) comes to her with an offer. Elena's young son is now living with his millionaire grandfather, who won't allow her to see him. She needs somebody to help her kidnap the child.

This is the beginning of Julia's nightmare journey through a thorn thicket of people you do not want to meet. If there's one thing consistent about her behavior, it's how she lies to all of them. This is not one of those tough heroines you sort of like. You don't like her. She makes not the slightest effort to be liked. She doesn't give a damn. She cuts back on the drinking, however, perhaps because she is constantly fleeing—both away from and toward.

You have to give a lot of credit to Erick Zonca, the fifty-two-year-old French director who cowrote the film with Aude Py. He makes it move relentlessly. He skillfully buries it in seedy American and Mexican locations that never, ever, feel like sets. He uses a child actor and uses him well. He makes no attempt to sentimentalize the kid, who is spoiled and hostile. He puts Tilda Swinton at the center of this, and she plays Julia as a tough broad who is in way over her head, and desperately invents stories to mislead those who want the money involved—which starts out at $50,000 before she cheats her way up to $2 million.

The plot of *Julia,* its twists and turns and surprises and rotten luck, is, shall we say, not very plausible. I believed it. That's because everything that happens seems inevitable, not contrived—the inescapable outcome of what has gone before, growing out of the greed and evil of the characters, which Julia, who is herself greedy and evil, is blindsided by. I could summarize the plot for you in one sentence, but I don't think I will, and when you see the film you will understand why.

Do we hate this woman Julia? When you see how she treats the boy Tom (Aidan Gould), we want to, except that she's all that stands between Tom and much worse things, including death. No matter what her motive for keeping him alive, there comes a moment when she shields him with her body from a man with a gun, and an utterly amoral woman would have made a deal.

Oh, she offers lots of deals. She's not to be trusted. There are times here when only her quick powers of invention keep her and the boy alive, and Swinton does a magnificent job with a tough acting challenge: letting us see how desperate she is without another character being able to tell. This movie lives on the edge all the way through, right up until an astonishing final scene on the median strip of a superhighway. What she does then shows that she's a better woman than she was when she started out, but you can't call it a false happy ending because it's more wrung-out than happy, and after all, what choice did she have?

This movie should have a big ad campaign and be making a lot of noise, stirring up word of mouth. It's being treated as an art film. It's good enough to be an art film, but don't let anyone pigeonhole it for you. It's one doozy of a great thriller. And the acting here is as good as it gets—not just from Swinton but from Saul Rubinek as her one remaining friend, and by Bruno Bichir as Diego, whom she meets in Tijuana. You want to be careful who you meet in Tijuana. Swinton here is amazing. She goes for broke and wins big time.

Julie and Julia ★ ★ ½

PG-13, 123 m., 2009

Meryl Streep (Julia Child), Amy Adams (Julie Powell), Stanley Tucci (Paul Child), Chris Messina (Eric Powell), Linda Emond (Simone Beck), Mary Lynn Rajskub (Sarah), Jane Lynch (Dorothy McWilliams), Frances Sternhagen (Irma Rombauer). Directed by Nora Ephron and produced by Ephron, Laurence Mark, Amy Robinson, and Eric Steel. Screenplay by Ephron, based on books by Julie Powell and Julia Child.

Did you ever want to take a three-day bus trip sitting next to Julia Child? Just asking. In thirty-minute programs on TV, she was priceless. But to live with her, I suspect, must have taken the patience of a saint. Her husband, Paul, in *Julie and Julia* is portrayed as a saint, so that explains her marriage.

Now about Julie Powell. That's the woman who wrote a blog documenting her vow to cook all the way through Child's *Mastering the Art of French Cooking*, 524 recipes in 365 days. She is also married to a patient man, although he retains enough self-respect to walk out for a few days halfway through her project. Together, they make just about enough money to live above a pizza parlor in Queens. How do they pay for all those groceries?

The performances go a long way toward selling the characters. Meryl Streep creates an uncanny version of Julia Child, of course with a spot-on accent. She seems to have grown several inches to play the great six-foot-two-inch chef. Stanley Tucci, playing her diplomat husband, stands five foot eight in real life. The movie somewhat diminishes this difference, but at no point, however, does he seem capable of denying anything to his beloved goddess.

Amy Adams could make anyone lovable, but with Julie Powell it's sometimes a stretch. Julie is so single-minded about her obsession that it comes to dominate her married life. Having cooked a few of Julia's recipes myself, I doubt there are many you can start on after getting home, some nights, as late as eight or nine. The dinner bell seems to have rung at the Powell household after midnight, although the wait was mellowed by a remarkable number of martinis.

The film, written and directed by Nora Ephron, cuts back and forth between the two women, showing how their dedication to cuisine shaped their lives and marriages. A fair number of no doubt delicious recipes are prepared and served, but there is never a moment our mouths water as they did over the Japanese noodle soup in *Tampopo.*

Nor are the leads seen as great eaters. They put a forkful in their mouth, close their eyes, and say "Mmmm," and that's about it. If Paul likes a dish, it is because it gives him the opportunity to tell Julia what a genius she is. Poor Eric simply gobbles everything like pizza after a softball game; having to wait so late for his meals perhaps gives him anxiety.

Julia Child was a rarity, an American woman studying haute cuisine at a French school for professional chefs, and was obviously a gifted student and a natural chef, even if she was driven to cooking because of her impatience with bridge. Ephron chooses to show her education in scenes so broad we could be watching *I Love Lucy.* If you came home and found your wife savagely dicing so many onions she had a pyramid two feet high, would you wonder about her?

As for Julie Powell, her project is undertaken to boost her self-esteem; she's a telephone call taker in a cubicle, dealing with insurance questions involving 9/11, although "really" she's a novelist. Someone once said, "What you do all day instead of your real job *is* your real job."

This movie is not lacking in entertainment value, especially from the Streep performance. But if the men had been portrayed as more high-spirited, it might have taken on intriguing dimensions. Both husbands are, frankly, a little boring: They've been assigned their supporting roles in their marriages and are reluctant to question the single-mindedness of their wives.

All the same, credit is due. Julia Child really did write a cookbook that changed American culinary history. And Julie Powell really did cook her way through 524 recipes in 365 days. I am currently writing a cookbook titled *The Pot and How to Use It,* about how you can cook almost anything in a rice cooker. Take my word for it, it's not going to take anyone a year to cook their way through this one.

Jumping the Broom ★ ★ ★

PG-13, 107 m., 2011

Angela Bassett (Mrs. Watson), Paula Patton (Sabrina Watson), Laz Alonso (Jason Taylor), Loretta Devine (Mrs. Taylor), Meagan Good (Blythe), Tasha Smith (Shonda), Romeo Miller (Sebastian), DeRay Davis (Malcolm), Valarie Pettiford (Aunt Geneva), Mike Epps (Willie Earl). Directed by Salim Akil and produced by Tracey E. Edmonds, Elizabeth Hunter, T. D. Jakes, Michael Mahoney, Glendon Palmer, and Curtis Wallace. Screenplay by Hunter and Arlene Gibbs.

The groom's mother is a postal worker in Brooklyn. The bride's family lives in a seaside compound on Martha's Vineyard so spacious no neighbors are visible. The bride and groom are in love, but their families are not. That was good enough for *Romeo and Juliet,* and it still sorta works with *Jumping the Broom.*

This is one of those films during which I notice things I simply decide to disregard. It's a good time at the movies, and an excellent demonstration of why I dislike the word "flawed," which critics use as if they were gazing through jewelers' eyepieces. It's not a perfect movie. The mothers are exaggerated to the point of easy sitcommery. So OK: We're not going for the sociology. We're going for fun, and if characters are too broad, that, too, can be fun. There's such a thing as being picky, picky, picky, and in this case Angela Bassett and Loretta Devine have such good timing with their performances that to hell with nuance.

The marriage takes place across the class divide between two old African-American families. The Taylors are working class. The Watsons are members of the ruling elite; Mr. Watson basically just stands around posing like a sleek master of the universe.

We meet the Watson girl, Sabrina (Paula Patton), after another of the one-night stands apparently not unknown to her. She's fed up with these hit-and-run guys and tells her best friend, Shonda (Tasha Smith), from now on she's going to save her cookies like a good Girl Scout until she meets Mr. Right. The film was coproduced by Bishop T. D. Jakes, who possibly finds even retroactive abstinence to be commendable. It was Oscar Levant who said, "I go back so far, I knew Doris Day before she was a virgin."

Mr. Right is Jason Taylor (Laz Alonso), who may come from a blue-collar home but is a hot shot on Wall Street, and the kind of chap any mother should be proud to have her daughter marry. Not Angela Bassett's Mrs. Watson. As for Loretta Devine's Mrs. Taylor, she is affronted that the bride's mother contacts her by e-mail. E-mail! How insulting is that?

The mothers meet for the first time on the wedding day. Their meeting is not a masterpiece of subtle dialogue, but let it be said that Devine and Bassett slug it out boldly, as everyone present (and in the audience) winces. What saves this from being a bloodbath of social mayhem is the leavening presence of some amusing supporting characters.

It is written that couples who meet at weddings are under a special star, and young Sebastian (Romeo Miller) easily believes that when he lays eyes (and would like to lay so much else) on Sabrina's best friend, Shonda. She isn't quite old enough to be his mother, but easily old enough to be his mother's younger sister. He's love-struck, sincere, inexhaustible. She flees him and lectures him and is touched by his devotion and might secretly like to be touched by more than that.

There's an even broader romance between the bridesmaid Blythe (Meagan Good) and the chef (Gary Dourdan), which results in one of the most original explanations I can imagine for keeping flour off the knees of your pants.

The title *Jumping the Broom* comes from an ancient custom of slavery days, passed down in the Taylor family. When Mrs. Watson hears of this, she declares, "Our family weren't slaves. We owned slaves." While I have no doubt that was sometimes the case, I submit that neither Mrs. Watson nor any other African-American in the past century or more would choose to make that announcement in public.

The movie is elegantly photographed. There is something about a wedding that bestows a pleasing structure upon a film. We anticipate that inevitable moment when all happiness seems doomed. The cast is large, well chosen, and diverting. The ceremony is delightful. Sabrina and Jason make a lovely couple. Someday they will laugh in remembering their mothers. Not someday real soon.

Just Another Love Story ★ ★ ★ ½

NO MPAA RATING, 104 m., 2009

Anders W. Berthelsen (Jonas), Rebecka Hemse (Julia), Nikolaj Lie Kaas (Sebastian), Charlotte Fich (Mette), Dejan Cukic (Frank), Karsten Jansfort (Poul), Flemming Enevold (Overlaege Dichmann), Bent Mejding (Hr. Castlund). Directed by Ole Bornedal and produced by Michael Obel. Screenplay by Bornedal.

Apart from a little nudity, *Just Another Love Story* could have been inspired, almost shot by shot, from a 1940s film noir from RKO, when it would have started with Robert Mitchum dying on the sidewalk in the rain. This is a vigorous thriller from Denmark that tells the classic noir story of a flawed cop trapped between a good wife and a bad woman. The twist is, the woman doesn't know she's been bad, since she has amnesia. It gets better.

Jonas is a Copenhagen homicide scene photographer, happily married, two kids. One day his car stalls, another car slams into him, runs head-on into a third car, and flips into the ditch. The other driver, Julia, is critically injured. He visits her in the hospital and is greeted with joy by her family, who assumes he must be the Sebastian she told them about, the new fiancé she met in Vietnam. He had to return on a later flight.

At this point, if Jonas (Anders W. Berthelsen) had seen any noirs at all, he would say: "I don't know who Sebastian is, but my name is Jonas." He pauses for a fatal instant and is swept into another life. Because Julia (Rebecka Hemse) doesn't remember much and can't see well, she has no choice but to agree with her family that this is Sebastian. Her father gives him a blank check, her family embraces him, and Jonas topples into a double life.

Oh, but it's more than that. Most noirs are. One thing about them is that they're rigidly moralistic. If you cheat on your wife, you're going to pay for it. This is true even if your wife knows nothing about it, the other woman can scarcely be blamed, and you start out only trying to accommodate an accident victim and her worried family.

Ole Bornedal, the film's writer and director, works at a considerably quicker pace than traditional noirs and ingeniously introduces ironies and complications I will not even hint at. The closing scenes of the plot spring one surprise after another. They seem laid on thick, but we have to admit, given all that leads up to them, they make sense.

Just Another Love Story works in nice little touches. I liked Jonas's partner in photographing crime scenes, who deals with the violence and gore by laughing about it. There's a scene where a horrifying situation is described, and the guy shakes, he's chuckling so hard. Why is this shown? Well, if you photograph murder scenes, you deal with it the best you can. The whole movie flavors its plot with quirky observations and asides.

It's interesting that two of the best thrillers of the last several months, *Tell No One* and *Just Another Love Story*, have come from Europe. Both movies gain because they star actors unfamiliar to us. They gain because there's room in them for close observation of the characters. They gain most of all because they don't slow down the plot for unnecessary special-effects scenes—fights, chases, things like that. Unless such scenes are necessary or very well done, essentially they just put the plot on hold while the filmmakers flex their muscles. Here the plotting has all the muscle that's required.

Just Go with It ★

PG-13, 116 m., 2011

Adam Sandler (Danny), Jennifer Aniston (Katherine), Brooklyn Decker (Palmer), Nick Swardson (Eddie), Nicole Kidman (Devlin Adams), Bailee Madison (Maggie), Griffin Gluck (Michael), Dave Matthews (Ian Maxtone Jones), Kevin Nealon (Adon). Directed by Dennis Dugan and produced by Jack Giarraputo, Heather Parry, and Adam Sandler. Screenplay by Allan Loeb and Timothy Dowling.

The people in this movie are dumber than a box of Tinkertoys. One fears they're so unfortunate it's not politically correct to laugh at them. That's not a problem because *Just Go with It* is so rarely funny. Here is a story that began as a French farce. Then it was adapted into a Broadway play named *Cactus Flower.* Then the play was made into a movie. Now it has been made into another movie. This process has diluted it like a homeopathic medicine, so that not an atom of the original formula can be found.

Consider. Danny (Adam Sandler) broke off his wedding at the last minute, but continues to wear the wedding ring. Women find the ring seductive and cannot resist having sex with a married man. Therefore, most (not all) of the women in his life are stupid. This works for him for approximately twenty-five years. In the meantime, he becomes a famous plastic surgeon in Beverly Hills. He is assisted by Nurse Katherine (Jennifer Aniston), who has two kids.

On the one day he isn't wearing his ring, he spends an idyllic night at the beach with the delicious twenty-three-year-old Palmer (Brooklyn Decker). Then she finds the ring in his pocket and thinks he is married, and he lies and says yes, but his divorce is almost final. She insists on meeting his wife. He makes Nurse Katherine pretend to be his wife. He buys her several thousand dollars' worth of clothes for her one (1) meeting with Palmer.

For reasons having to do with Palmer's love of children, they all fly to Hawaii together with Nurse Katherine's two kids and Danny's high school buddy Eddie (Nick Swardson), who pretends to be the nurse's fiancé. Eddie disguises himself with thick glasses and the worst German accent since the guy who worshipped Hitler in *The Producers.* He also brandishes a meerschaum pipe because everyone who has seen *Inglourious Basterds* knows all Germans smoke meerschaum pipes.

This might work as a farce. Maybe it did, in France. It worked as a Broadway play by Abe Burrows. It worked as a 1969 movie with Walter Matthau, Ingrid Bergman as the nurse, and Goldie Hawn as the young girl. It doesn't work now. The problem is the almost paralytic sweetness of the characters. Nobody is really trying to get away with anything. They're just trying to do the right thing in an underhanded way. Walter Matthau was crafty in the cradle. Goldie Hawn was the definitive ditz. Ingrid Bergman was *sigh.* The 1969 screenplay was by I. A. L. Diamond, who knew a thing or two about farce when he wrote *Some Like It Hot.* They made a good movie.

So nice is everyone here that even the completely surplus character played by Nicole Kidman is undermined. She plays the old standby, the popular girl who was mean to Nurse Katherine in high school. We know the cliché. Kidman could have done something with it, but the screenplay gives her nowhere to go. It's painful to endure the cloying scene where they kiss and make up.

Just Go with It is like a performance of the old material by actors who don't get the joke. The movie doesn't even have the nerve to caricature the Kidman character, who is presented as a true-blue, sincere Bo Derek clone. Adam Sandler stays well within the range of polite, ingratiating small-talk artists he unnecessarily limits himself to. Jennifer Aniston is alert and amused, but by giving her the fake boyfriend with the meerschaum the film indicates that she, too, is one tinker short of a toy.

There is one funny scene in the movie. It involves a plastic surgery victim with a roaming right eyebrow. You know the movie is in trouble when you find yourself missing the eyebrow.

Just Wright ★ ★ ★

PG, 99 m., 2010

Queen Latifah (Leslie Wright), Common (Scott McKnight), Paula Patton (Morgan Alexander), James Pickens Jr. (Lloyd Wright), Phylicia

Rashad (Ella McKnight), Pam Grier (Janice Wright). Directed by Sanaa Hamri and produced by Debra Martin Chase, Shakim Compere, and Queen Latifah. Screenplay by Michael Elliot.

One reason people like Queen Latifah is that she likes herself. In most of her roles, she radiates cheer. She can play grim, as in *Bringing Out the Dead,* but she has a natural sunniness that makes me, at least, feel good. And she is a real woman, not a skinny woman with too many sharp angles. Jennifer Aniston, who looks perfectly great, makes me worry about her mental health when she publicizes her new baby food diet.

Latifah has never been fat. She has always been plus size. There is a difference. She is healthy, fit, carries herself with confidence, and looks terrific in *Just Wright* in the kind of clothing a physical therapist might feel comfortable wearing. If you're dragging around feeling low about yourself, you want to know her secret.

This is not a discussion of the Queen's body, however; it's about the whole gestalt. One of the reasons she's the star of *Just Wright* is that few people, and certainly no one in this film, can hold the screen against her. In common with many other stars, when she's in a shot, it's about her.

Sure, we go along with the fiction that Scott (Common), the handsome pro basketball player in the movie, is going to marry Morgan (Paula Patton), Queen Latifah's BFF. Sure, we think Patton looks terrific and is a beauty. But, come on. Once Scott injures his knee and hires Miss Wright (Latifah) as his live-in physical therapist, we know he's going to fall in love with her. It's so much easier to fall in love with someone who is necessary to you than someone you are necessary to.

The plot involves Leslie Wright and Morgan as obsessed fans of the New Jersey Nets—Leslie because she loves basketball, and Morgan because she wants to be a player's wife. After Leslie has a Meet Cute with the handsome Nets star Scott McKnight at a gas station, she gets invited to his birthday party, and, of course, takes Morgan along. Scott zooms in on Morgan. Leslie, as loyal best friend, is accustomed to this.

After Scott gets a knee injury and Leslie becomes his special duty therapist, the trick is to not rush in the direction the movie is obviously moving. Director Sanaa Hamri accomplishes this. She and writer Michael Elliot add enough detail and actual dialogue (you know, people talking about things in more than one syllable) that we enjoy the growing-closer process. Paula Patton's Morgan is a self-centered egotist and no good at caregiving, but hey, that's built into the role.

Sanaa Hamri is herself an actor-director, with an interesting background; she directed two of Prince's TV specials and the very good *Something New* (2006), starring Sanaa Lathan (no relation). That was another film about a woman and man gradually discovering they're in love, which is always more fun than the first-sight deal. Here Common isn't called upon to do much heavy lifting in the acting department, but he plays well with Queen Latifah. Sure, the movie is a formula. A formula that works reminds us of why it became a formula.

K

Kaboom ★ ★ ½

NO MPAA RATING, 86 m., 2011

Thomas Dekker (Smith), Haley Bennett (Stella), Chris Zylka (Thor), Roxane Mesquida (Lorelei), Juno Temple (London), Andy Fischer-Price (Rex), Nicole LaLiberte (Red-Haired Girl). Directed by Gregg Araki and produced by Araki, Sebastien Lemercier, and Andrea Sperling.

Kaboom exists entirely in and for the moment. It brings some intriguing college students onscreen, watches them have sex with one another, and involves them in a plot in which there is not much difference between hallucination and everyday life. It raises only one question: Since the characters devote so much time to it, why don't they seem to care much about sex? It seems more like a pastime for idle hands and genitals.

The movie has been cast, designed, clothed, scored, and edited to the bleeding edge of hip, but it hasn't exactly been written. There's some nice dialogue, but sometimes it sounds like lines left over from other screenplays that were too good to throw away. The director, Gregg Araki, enjoys material of this sort; his characters draw the line only at heterosexual monogamy. What's curious is that his central character, Smith (Thomas Dekker), is filled with sexual yearnings despite the abundance of opportunities at hand.

Smith describes his sexuality as "undecided." As the film opens, he lusts for his hunky roommate Thor (Chris Zylka), who reminds me that the generation of kids named after Marvel superheroes must be approaching thirty. Thor isn't gay, he just plays gay in his life. His best friend, Stella (Haley Bennett), is a lesbian. Into her life comes Lorelei (Roxane Mesquida), who is a practicing witch—and I don't mean a Wiccan Earth goddess, but the kind of witch Aleister Crowley would approve of, with actual wicked powers. Lorelei and the character named the Red-Haired Girl (Nicole LaLiberte) appear in his dreams, even before he meets them. (Note: Nicole LaLiberte might have made a good wife for Rockets Redglare, had they overlapped in life.)

There are many other characters, including a pothead resident adviser and three hostile male figures wearing animal masks. Some of these figures are real, some dreams, some imposters, and then the line blurs and this microcosm of campus sex hobbyists turns out to be linked to the sort of secret global conspiracy that could inspire lots of Dan Brown novels.

None of this matters. If the events in *Kaboom* are anything, they're arbitrary. That helps justify the film's ending, which nobody can claim doesn't tie up all the loose threads. But this movie isn't about beginnings and endings—or middles, for that matter. If anything can happen, does it much matter? You could watch it like you listen to an album, not paying much attention to which cut you're on.

There's one thing that confuses me. *Kaboom* is as indulgent as a film school exercise. I thought Gregg Araki had outgrown messing about like this. His *Mysterious Skin* (2004) was lovingly controlled and mysteriously spellbinding. Now he engages his shallow and narcissistic characters on their level, not his.

The Karate Kid ★ ★ ★ ½

PG, 131 m., 2010

Jaden Smith (Dre Parker), Jackie Chan (Mr. Han), Taraji P. Henson (Sherry Parker), Han Wenwen (Mei Ying), Wang Zhenwei (Cheng), Rongguang Yu (Master Li). Directed by Harald Zwart and produced by James Lassiter, Jada Pinkett Smith, Will Smith, Ken Stovitz, and Jerry Weintraub. Screenplay by Christopher Murphey.

If you've seen *The Karate Kid* (1984), the memories will come back during this 2010 remake of the original. That's a compliment. The original story was durable enough to inspire three sequels, and now we have an entertaining version filmed mostly on location in China, with fifty-six-year-old Jackie Chan in the role of Mr. Miyagi.

The original film was one of its year's best movies. The new one lacks the perfect freshness of that one; there aren't many surprises as it follows the 1984 almost point by point. But here is a lovely and well-made film that stands well on its own feet. The Chinese locations add visual interest, there are scenes of splendor in mountains and on the Great Wall, and the characters are once again engaging.

The original film's greatest asset was the Oscar-nominated performance by Pat Morita as Mr. Miyagi. Jackie Chan is so famous that it can come as no surprise here when Mr. Han, a reclusive janitor, reveals a hidden talent for the martial arts. But Chan has never been a strutting, macho fighter onscreen; his charm comes from a self-kidding quality. Here he does a good job of cooling down his usual cheerfulness and keeping his cards hidden.

In the role of his young pupil, Jaden Smith, son of Will and Jada Pinkett Smith, has a natural screen presence that glows. Dre Parker is calmer than the skitterish kid played by Ralph Macchio, but so much smaller than his opponents that we can well believe his fear of a bully at school. And when that happens, we can forget obsessing about the 1984 film and enjoy this one. That was then; this is now.

The story once again involves a kid being packed up by his divorced mom and forced to leave his hometown and friends and move far away—from Detroit to Beijing, this time. He hates it. Then a cute young violinist named Mei Ying (Han Wenwen) smiles at him, and life looks more promising—if it weren't for the school bully, Cheng (Wang Zhenwei). This creature is so hateful and sadistic it's hard to explain, until we meet his brutal kung fu coach, Master Li (Rongguang Yu). The monstrous Li teaches a new form of child abuse: kids beating up on each other.

The story proceeds, as it must, with Dre slowly softening the heart of Mr. Han, who saves him from a beating by Cheng and agrees to teach him the secrets of kung fu. Training goes well, and Dre and Mei Ying make a pact to attend each other's big days: his kung fu tournament, her recital. There's the usual nonsense about her parents disapproving of him. Gee, why in the world would the parents of a world-class classical musician disapprove of a kung fu student from Detroit who doesn't speak Chinese?

Luckily for Dre and the movie, everyone in China who needs to speak English can do so, even the little monster Cheng. Many Americans not only have small interest in learning another language, they have small interest in reading subtitles of their own. We believe, as Mark Twain put it in *The Innocents Abroad,* that any foreigner can speak English if only it is spoken slowly enough and loudly enough.

It goes without saying that the whole film leads up to a climactic kung fu tournament, and that Dre is pitted against Cheng for the championship. The lineage of the film is distinguished; the '84 version was directed by John Avildsen, director of *Rocky.* This film's climax is unusually well handled; the tension is constructed in a careful way, the characters are developed, and use of a scoreboard makes it seem orderly, not rushed. It's one of the better Obligatory Fight climaxes I've seen.

The director, Harald Zwart, has not been one of my favorites; he made last year's *Pink Panther 2.* But here, with a robust script by Christopher Murphey and cinematography by Roger Pratt (who filmed two Harry Potters), he makes a handsome, absorbing movie. It runs a little long, but during the championship, that's the last thing you're thinking of.

Katyn ★ ★ ★ ½

NO MPAA RATING, 121 m., 2009

Maja Ostaszewska (Anna), Artur Zmijewski (Andrzej), Andrzej Chyra (Jerzy), Jan Englert (General), Danuta Stenka (General's Wife), Magdalena Cielecka (Agnieszka), Agnieszka Glinska (Irena). Directed by Andrzej Wajda and produced by Michal Kwiecinski. Screenplay by Wajda, Wladyslaw Pasikowski, and Przemyslaw Nowakowski.

In 1940, some fifteen thousand officers of the Polish army were rounded up, transported in sealed buses to a forest named Katyn, shot in the back of the head by the Russian KGB, and buried in mass graves. That is the simple truth. When the nation was occupied by both the Nazis and Soviets, their deaths were masked in silence. Then the Nazis dug up the graves and blamed the deaths on the Soviets. After the defeat of Hitler and the Soviet occupation of Poland, history was rewritten and the official version blamed the massacre on the Nazis.

One of the officers murdered that day was Jakub Wajda, whose son Andrzej would become a leading Polish film director and one of the chroniclers of the Solidarity movement. Now eighty-two, Andrzej has evoked what happened that day and how it infected Polish society for fifty years. Reflect that everyone in Poland knew the truth of the massacre, but to lie about it became an official requirement under the Soviet-controlled regime. Thus, in some cases, to gain immunity or advancement in postwar Poland required parents and children, brothers and sisters of the dead to remain silent about their fates.

This poor bruised nation, trapped by time and geography between the two dark evils of twentieth-century Europe, has prevailed, and its survival is embodied in the career of Wajda, who in key films starting in the 1950s found a way to say what he needed even with Communist national film censorship. His early films *Kanal* (1957), about the Warsaw Uprising, and *Ashes and Diamonds* (1958), about the Polish Resistance during the war, involved Poland's two oppressors.

A single image at the beginning of *Katyn* expresses the nation's dilemma. A bridge is crowded by fleeing civilians—from both ends. Some flee advancing Nazis. Some flee advancing Russians. As the two armies, in concert under the Hitler-Stalin pact, acted together, such situations took place. The refugees are not tattered stragglers, but ordinary civilians, torn so quickly from domestic security that they carry suitcases, although they could have little idea of the journey ahead for them.

Wajda tells his story through a few characters. We meet Anna (Maja Ostaszewska), traveling in search of her husband, Andrzej (Artur Zmijewski), a Polish officer. They are clearly intended as Wajda's parents; movingly, he has named his father after himself. His father, like many of the Polish officer corps, was not a professional military man, but a reservist, called up from the professional, scientific, educational classes. The 1940 massacre would exterminate many of a generation's best and brightest.

Lives hang by a thread. Anna succeeds in finding her husband at a deployment camp and begs him to escape with her. He feels his place is with his fellow officers. Neither of them suspect he will be executed. Wajda broadens his canvas to include others, including Andrzej's own father; his mother, like his wife, waits for word. We meet two other women: the wife of an executed general, who refuses to toe the Soviet line, and the sister of a dead officer, who commissions a plaque in his memory. Her crime is to add the date of the Katyn massacre, since the Soviets played with time to make it correspond to a later period when the Nazis were enemies, not friends.

The actresses playing these roles are all well known in Poland, where I assume they are easy to distinguish. To an outsider like myself, they tended to resemble one another, and I was able to follow them by story and plot more easily than facially. This is not really a problem because all are facets of the same experience.

Anna remains the central figure, refusing to accept that her husband is dead until she finally receives the truth from an eyewitness to his remains. So did many loved ones cling to hope, as the POW/MIA relatives do in this country. The dead had no peace. They were dug up by the Nazis to expose Soviet crimes, then dug up again, and metaphorically dug up in revisionist history.

The film ends with a scene of relentless horror, showing the assembly line of execution. Men are taken from the sealed buses one by one, their names checked off a list, then quickly walked to their place of death and killed with a bullet to the back of the skull. Their bodies fall or are heaved into mass graves in orderly progress, falling side by side and buried by bulldozer. Now Wajda has brought some small measure of rest to their names, to Poland, and to history.

Note: Katyn *was one of 2008's Oscar nominees for best foreign language film.*

Kick-Ass ★

R, 117 m., 2010

Aaron Johnson (Dave/Kick-Ass), Christopher Mintz-Plasse (Chris/Red Mist), Mark Strong (Frank D'Amico), Chloe Grace Moretz (Mindy/Hit Girl), Nicolas Cage (Damon/Big Daddy). Directed by Matthew Vaughn and produced by Vaughn, Adam Bohling, Tarquin Pack, Brad Pitt, David Reid, and Kris Thykier. Screenplay by Vaughn and Jane Goldman, based on the comic book by Mark Millar and John S. Romita Jr.

Shall I have feelings, or should I pretend to be cool? Will I seem hopelessly square if I find *Kick-Ass* morally reprehensible, and will I appear to have missed the point? Let's say you're a big fan of the original comic book, and you think the movie does it justice. You know what? You inhabit a world I am so very not interested in. A motion picture camera makes a record of whatever is placed in front of it, and in this case it shows deadly carnage dished out by an eleven-year-old girl, after which an adult man brutally hammers her to within an inch of her life. Blood everywhere. Now tell me all about the context.

The movie's premise is that ordinary people, including a high school kid, the eleven-year-old, and her father, try to become superheroes in order to punish evil men. The flaw in this premise is that the little girl *does* become a superhero. In one scene, she faces a hallway jammed with heavily armed gangsters and shoots, stabs, and kicks them all to death, while flying through the air with such power it's enough to make Jackie Chan take out an AARP membership.

This isn't comic violence. These men, and many others in the film, are really stone-cold dead. And the eleven-year-old apparently experiences no emotions about this. Many children that age would be, I dunno, *affected* somehow, don't you think, after killing eight or twelve men who were trying to kill them?

I know, I know. This is a satire. But a satire of what? The movie's rated R, which means in this case that it's doubly attractive to anyone under seventeen. I'm not too worried about sixteen-year-olds here. I'm thinking of six-year-olds. There are characters here with walls covered in carefully mounted firearms, ranging from handguns through automatic weapons to bazookas. At the end, when the villain deliciously anticipates blowing a bullet hole in the child's head, he is prevented only because her friend, in the nick of time, shoots him with a bazooka shell at ten-foot range and blows him through a skyscraper window and across several city blocks of sky in a projectile of blood, flame, and smoke. As I often read on the Internet: Hahahahaha.

The little girl is named Mindy (Chloe Grace Moretz). She adopts the persona of Hit Girl. She has been trained by her father, Big Daddy (Nicolas Cage), to join him in the battle against a crime boss (Mark Strong). Her training includes being shot at point-blank range while wearing a bulletproof vest. She also masters the martial arts—more, I would say, than any other movie martial artist of any age I can recall. And she's gifted with deadly knife-throwing skill; a foot-long knife was presented to her by her dad as, I guess, a graduation present.

Big Daddy and Mindy never have a chat about, you know, stuff like how when you kill people they are really dead. This movie regards human beings like video game targets. Kill one, and you score. They're dead, you win. When kids in the age range of this movie's home video audience are shooting each other every day in America, that kind of stops being funny.

Hit Girl teams up with Kick-Ass (Aaron Johnson), the narrator of the film, a lackluster high school kid who lives vicariously through comic books. For reasons tedious to explain, he orders a masked costume by mail order and sets about trying to behave as a superhero, which doesn't work out well. He lacks the training of a Big Daddy. But as he and Hit Girl find themselves fighting side by side, he turns into a quick learner. Also, you don't need to be great at hand-to-hand combat if you can just shoot people dead.

The early scenes give promise of an entirely different comedy. Aaron Johnson has a certain anti-charm, his problems in high school are engaging, and so on. A little later, I reflected that possibly only Nic Cage could seem to shoot a small girl point-blank and make it, well, funny. Say what you will about her character, but Chloe Grace Moretz has presence and appeal. Then the movie moved into dark, dark territory, and I grew sad.

The Kids Are All Right ★ ★ ★ ½

R, 104 m., 2010

Julianne Moore (Jules), Annette Bening (Nic), Mark Ruffalo (Paul), Mia Wasikowska (Joni), Josh Hutcherson (Laser). Directed by Lisa Cholodenko and produced by Gary Gilbert,

Philippe Hellmann, Jordan Horowitz, Jeffrey Levy-Hinte, Celine Rattray, and Daniela Taplin Lundberg. Screenplay by Cholodenko and Stuart Blumberg.

The Kids Are All Right centers on a lesbian marriage, but is not about one. It's a film about marriage itself, an institution with challenges that are universal. Just imagine: You're expected to live much, if not all, of your married life with another adult. We're not raised for this.

The married couple involves Jules (Julianne Moore) and Nic (Annette Bening). They're raising a boy named Laser (Josh Hutcherson) and a girl named Joni (Mia Wasikowska). Each mother has one of the children, and because the same anonymous sperm donor was used, they're half-siblings. Home life is casual and happy, upper middle class. Nic is a doctor, Jules is unfocused and lately thinking she might go into landscape gardening. Like many couples, they're going through a little midlife crisis.

That's nothing compared with what awaits them, in a smart comedy by Lisa Cholodenko, whose *High Art* and *Laurel Canyon* showed those particular slices of Los Angeles we think we might find ourselves in for a period, before we got our acts together. The imperfect but stable home life of their family is disturbed by the decision of the children to seek out their birth father. Jules and Nic are staunchly liberal and approve of this in theory. In practice they find it disturbing.

The father turns out to be Paul (Mark Ruffalo), the kind of onetime hippie who says things like, "Sure, I mean . . . sure, yes, of course . . . I mean, why not? Sure . . ." He's with the program. He runs a cozy little organic restaurant with food from his own organic garden, has never married, has no other children, and is way cool in a way that involves no conscious effort. He thinks it's cool to meet his kids, it's cool their moms are married, it's cool they invite him for dinner. I mean . . . sure, yes, of course . . . I mean, why not? Sure.

Learning that Jules is taking up landscape design, he hires her to design the garden area sloping down behind his house in what looks like the Hollywood Hills. And what with bringing in bags of soil and standing in the rain with him discussing plans, Jules and Paul like, have sex. I mean, why not?

This causes a great deal of unhappiness when it's discovered, but not operatic grief and passion. More feelings of betrayal on Nic's part, and confusion from Jules and Paul, who didn't expect their secret to be discovered and, like, were not thinking of getting *married* or anything, and are really, truly sorry. So are the kids, because they love their moms, and they like Paul a lot, too.

Cholodenko, writing with Stuart Blumberg, is wise to keep her tone light. *The Kids Are All Right* isn't a laffaminit comedy, but it is a comedy, and fondly satirical of Nic's tendency to be quite serious. I refuse to call it a "gay film." I toyed with the idea of not even using the word "lesbian" and leaving it to you to figure out that the couple was female. This is a romantic triangle happening to involve these three people.

What interests Cholodenko is who they are. Moore and Bening are superb actors here, evoking a marriage of more than twenty years and all of its shadings and secrets, idealism and compromise. Nic is more of the mind, Jules is more of the heart. The film gives them convincing, intelligent dialogue, mannerisms that fit, and children who, having been raised outside homophobic hysteria, are nice and well adjusted. And with Mark Ruffalo's Paul, the film creates a slightly exaggerated version of characters like many we may have met: casually progressive, a little unfocused, pleasant, and agreeable. I mean, why not?

The Killer Inside Me ★ ★ ½

R, 109 m., 2010

Casey Affleck (Lou Ford), Kate Hudson (Amy Stanton), Jessica Alba (Joyce Lakeland), Ned Beatty (Chester Conway), Elias Koteas (Joe Rothman), Tom Bower (Sheriff Bob Maples), Simon Baker (Howard Hendricks), Bill Pullman (Billy Boy Walker). Directed by Michael Winterbottom and produced by Andrew Eaton, Chris Hanley, and Bradford L. Schlei. Screenplay by John Curran, based on the novel by Jim Thompson.

What we desire is not a happy ending, so much as closure. That often means simply that a film knows what it thinks about itself. *The Killer Inside Me* is expert filmmaking based on a frightening performance, but it presents us with a character who remains a vast, empty, lonely, cold space. The film finds resolution there somewhere, perhaps, but not on a frequency I can receive.

Michael Winterbottom's film is inspired by a 1952 pulp novel by Jim Thompson, perhaps the bleakest and most unrelenting of American crime novelists. The book is considered by some his finest work; other Thompson novels were filmed as *The Grifters, The Getaway, After Dark, My Sweet,* and *Coup de Torchon.* Stephen King wrote: "Big Jim didn't know the meaning of the word stop. There are three brave *lets* inherent in the forgoing: He let himself see everything, he let himself write it down, then he let himself publish it."

What Thompson saw in his character Lou Ford (Casey Affleck) was a mild-spoken, intellectual psychopath with no understanding of good and evil. He murders people he loves, *while* loving them, and has no idea why. The story's insights into this seem limited to the title. There is a killer inside him. The killer is not him. He doesn't understand that killer. He has no control over him and no doubt sincerely regrets the killer's crimes.

The story is set in West Texas in the early 1950s. Lou Ford, narrating his own story, is a deputy sheriff in a small town. He still lives in the home where he was raised. In the evenings he plays classical piano, reads books from his father's library, plays opera recordings. His voice, high-pitched but rough, bespeaks innocence. He has a girlfriend named Amy (Kate Hudson). He has the respect and affection of his alcoholic boss, Sheriff Bob Maples (Tom Bower). He is unfailingly calm and pleasant.

One day Maples gives him a job: Drive a few miles outside town and have a word with a prostitute, Joyce (Jessica Alba). A powerful local developer, Chester Conway (Ned Beatty), is concerned about her influence on his son, Elmer (Jay R. Ferguson). Ford pays the visit, has some words, and soon the two of them are urgently having rough sex. Why? Because this is the pulp universe, where a woman may be a prostitute with other men but she finds *you* irresistible. Female psychology is not the strong point with many pulp writers. Psychology in general is sketchy, based on simplified and half-understood Freudian notions. With Lou Ford, for example, we're given fragmented glimpses of childhood sexual abuse. Not the sort of abuse we've seen before: His mother liked Lou to slap her.

Indeed, Lou seems to attract women who like to be beaten. One apparently even likes to be nearly killed. The film attempts to account for this no more than it explains Lou's own nature. The best explanation probably is: When you buy a cheap paperback with a lurid cover, these are the sorts of events that will be described inside. In prose, the focus is through the point of view. In the film, we see the violence happening, and the first time it comes as a gut punch because we're not remotely expecting it.

Not from Lou Ford, anyway. Casey Affleck, an effective actor, is so convincing with his innocent, almost sweet facade that the movie sets us up to expect he'll be solving a crime, not causing one. He maintains that facade in the face of the most compelling challenges, not only from his own violence, but from two people with excellent reasons to suspect him: a labor leader (Elias Koteas) and the county attorney (Simon Baker). When Lou actually confesses to a kid who admires him (Liam Aiken), even what happens then doesn't faze him.

There is a point beyond which his implacability brings diminishing returns. While I admire Affleck's performance, I believe Winterbottom and his writer, John Curran, may have miscalculated. The reader of a pulp crime thriller might be satisfied simply with the prurient descriptions, and certainly this film visualizes those and has as its victims Jessica Alba and Kate Hudson, who embody paperback covers, but the dominant presence in the film is Lou Ford, and there just doesn't seem to be anybody at home.

The King's Speech ★ ★ ★ ★

R, 118 m., 2010

Colin Firth (Bertie), Geoffrey Rush (Lionel Logue), Helena Bonham Carter (Elizabeth), Guy Pearce (Edward VIII), Jennifer Ehle (Myrtle Logue), Derek Jacobi (Archbishop Cosmo Lang), Michael Gambon (George V), Timothy Spall (Winston Churchill), Anthony Andrews (Stanley

Baldwin). Directed by Tom Hooper and produced by Iain Canning, Emile Sherman, and Gareth Unwin. Screenplay by David Seidler.

The King's Speech tells the story of a man compelled to speak to the world with a stammer. It must be painful enough for one who stammers to speak to one other person. To face a radio microphone and know the British Empire is listening must be terrifying. At the time of the speech mentioned in the title, a quarter of the earth's population was in the empire, and of course much of North America, Europe, Africa, and Asia would be listening—and with particular attention, Germany.

The king was George VI. The year was 1939. Britain was entering into war with Germany. His listeners required firmness, clarity, and resolve, not stammers punctuated with tortured silences. This was a man who never wanted to be king. After the death of his father, the throne was to pass to his brother Edward. But Edward renounced the throne "in order to marry the woman I love," and the duty fell to Prince Albert, who had struggled with his speech from an early age.

In *The King's Speech*, director Tom Hooper opens on Albert (Colin Firth) attempting to open the British Empire Exhibition in 1925. Before a crowded arena and a radio audience, he seizes up in agony in efforts to make the words come right. His father, George V (Michael Gambon), has always considered "Bertie" superior to Edward (Guy Pearce), but mourns the introduction of radio and newsreels, which require a monarch to be seen and heard on public occasions.

At that 1925 speech, we see Albert's wife, Elizabeth (Helena Bonham Carter), her face filled with sympathy. As it becomes clear that Edward's obsession with Wallis Simpson (Eve Best) is incurable, she realizes her Bertie may face more public humiliation. He sees various speech therapists, one of whom tries the old marbles-in-the-mouth routine first recommended by Demosthenes. Nothing works, and then she seeks out a failed Australian actor named Lionel Logue (Geoffrey Rush), who has set up a speech therapy practice.

Logue doesn't realize at first who is consulting him. And one of the subjects of the film is Logue's attitude toward royalty, which I suspect is not untypical of Australians; he suggests to Albert that they get on a first-name basis. Albert has been raised within the bell jar of the monarchy and objects to such treatment, not because he has an elevated opinion of himself, but because, well, it just isn't done. But Logue realizes that if he is to become the king's therapist, he must first become his friend.

If the British monarchy is good for nothing else, it's superb at producing the subjects of films. *The King's Speech*, rich in period detail and meticulous class distinctions, largely sidesteps the story that loomed over this whole period: Edward's startling decision to give up the crown in order to marry a woman who was already divorced three times. Indeed the Duke and Duchess of Windsor (as they became) would occupy an inexplicable volume of attention for years, considering they had no significance after the duke's abdication. The unsavory thing is that Wallis Simpson considered herself worthy of such a sacrifice from the man she allegedly loved. This film finds a more interesting story about better people; Americans, who aren't always expert on British royalty, may not necessarily realize that Albert and his wife, Elizabeth, were the parents of Queen Elizabeth II. God knows what Edward might have fathered.

Hooper makes an interesting decision with his sets and visuals. The movie is largely shot in interiors, and most of those spaces are long and narrow. That's unusual in historical dramas, which emphasize sweep and majesty and so on. Here we have long corridors, a deep and narrow master control room for the BBC, rooms that seem peculiarly oblong. I suspect he may be evoking the narrow, constricting walls of Albert's throat as he struggles to get words out.

The film largely involves the actors Colin Firth, formal and decent, and Geoffrey Rush, large and expansive, in psychological struggle. Helena Bonham Carter, who can be merciless (as in the Potter films), is here filled with mercy, tact, and love for her husband; this is the woman who became the much-loved Queen Mother of our lifetimes, dying in 2002 at 101. As the men have a struggle of wills, she tries to smooth things (and raise her girls, Elizabeth and Margaret). And in the wider sphere, Hitler takes power, war comes closer, Mrs. Simpson wreaks havoc, and the dreaded day approaches when Bertie, as George VI, will have to speak to the world and declare war.

Hooper's handling of that fraught scene is masterful. Firth internalizes his tension and keeps the required stiff upper lip, but his staff and household are terrified on his behalf as he marches toward a microphone as if it is a guillotine. It is the one scene in the film that *must* work, and it does, and its emotional impact is surprisingly strong. At the end, what we have here is a superior historical drama and a powerful personal one. And two opposites who remain friends for the rest of their lives.

Note: The R rating refers to Logue's use of vulgarity. It is utterly inexplicable. This is an excellent film for teenagers.

Knight and Day ★ ★ ★

PG-13, 109 m., 2010

Tom Cruise (Roy Miller), Cameron Diaz (June Havens), Peter Sarsgaard (Fitzgerald), Viola Davis (Director George), Jordi Molla (Antonio), Paul Dano (Simon Feck), Maggie Grace (April Havens), Marc Blucas (Rodney), Celia Weston (Molly). Directed by James Mangold and produced by Todd Garner, Cathy Konrad, Steve Pink, and Joe Roth. Screenplay by Patrick O'Neill.

Knight and Day aspires to the light charm of a romantic action comedy like *Charade* or *Romancing the Stone*, but would come closer if it dialed down the relentless action. The romance part goes without saying after a Meet Cute contrived in an airport, and the comedy seems to generate naturally between Tom Cruise and Cameron Diaz. But why do so many summer movies find it obligatory to inflict us with CGI overkill? I'd sorta rather see Diaz and Cruise in action scenes on a human scale, rather than have it rubbed in that for long stretches they're essentially replaced by animation.

Have summer audiences been so hammered down by special effects that they require noise and fragmented visuals to hold their interest? Is it still possible to delight in a story unfolding with charm and wit? How many machine guns do you need in a romantic comedy? If you have charismatic stars like Cruise and Diaz and an A-list director, do you have to hedge your bet?

The movie is entertaining but could have been better. The director is James Mangold, whose previous two films were *Walk the Line* and *3:10 to Yuma*. I have a hunch there was an early draft of Patrick O'Neill's screenplay that was more in the Cary Grant romcom tradition, and then somebody decided the effects had to be jacked up. From the ads, you could get the notion this was a Michael Bay film.

The wonder is that Cruise and Diaz are effective enough in their roles that they're not overwhelmed by all the commotion surrounding them. They make the movie work because they cheerfully project that they know it's utter nonsense and pitch in to enjoy the fun. I've been reading that movie stars can no longer "sell" a blockbuster movie. Audiences buy the concept, brand name, packaging, whatever. If that's true, which I doubt, it would mean a victory of technology over humans. If it comes true, it will be because movies have lost interest in creating and shaping characters we care about—because they're using actors as insert shots in special effects.

The plot makes splendid use of a MacGuffin, the device that explains everything by explaining nothing. Roy Miller, the Cruise character, has something and there are bad guys who want it. I could tell you what it is, but what difference does it make? That's the whole point of a MacGuffin. Anyway, Roy *happens* to run into June Havens, the Diaz character, at an airport, for reasons you will discover. That's the manipulated Meet Cute. Now this next part you will want to follow closely.

They both end up on the same airplane, which has no other passengers except some men scattered here and there. She goes to the rest room. He kills all the men and both pilots, and sits the dead passengers upright, *Weekend at Bernie's* style. She comes out of the rest room, not having heard the gunshots. He crash-lands the plane in a field, and urges her to follow him in escaping FBI agents who are after them.

But . . . but . . . was there no other way for the bad guys to get the MacGuffin than by taking over a scheduled flight? Maybe, I dunno, snatch him on the ground? How did the FBI know the plane would crash—and where? Also, if you track who has possession of the MacGuffin during various times at the airport, you'll go crazy. Mind you, I'm not complaining. The movie knows this sequence is monumentally silly, and so do Cruise and Diaz, and Cruise keeps up a reassuring line of patter all during it, even while trying to crash-land safely.

That stuff is entertaining. There's also a running joke about how much ground they cover in an international chase. The movie was shot on location in Massachusetts, Spain (where they are chased by bulls), California, Jamaica, Austria, and Kankakee, Illinois, which has an excellent Steak 'n Shake out on I-57. Whether the actors were actually there on all those locations is a good question. Maybe only the green screen stuff was shot on location.

Such matters are irrelevant in a movie that makes not the slightest pretense of realism. Cruise and Diaz are fully scripted throughout with nonstop bantering and one-liners. They never seriously discuss their situation. They spend half the movie in dire danger. Thousands of bullets miss them. By motorcycle, car, train, airplane, and parachute, they survive anything.

That girl June, she's a trouper. She follows Roy everywhere and believes everything he says. But . . . but . . . why does she need to come along? Roy has the MacGuffin. She was a witness, you say? To what? I'll tell you why she has to be along. It's because this is a romantic action comedy starring Tom Cruise and Cameron Diaz, that's why.

So all of that I accept and even applaud, and I observe that Diaz has one of the most winning grins in the movies. Basically, what I wanted was more of it. Some of that Cary Grant dialogue. More flirtation. More of a feeling the characters, not the production, were the foreground. More of the stars. Because movie stars really do make a difference. I insist on it.

Knowing ★ ★ ★ ★

PG-13, 122 m., 2009

Nicolas Cage (John Koestler), Rose Byrne (Diana Wayland), Chandler Canterbury (Caleb Koestler), Lara Robinson (Lucinda Embry/Abby Wayland), Ben Mendelsohn (Phil Beckman). Directed by Alex Proyas and produced by Proyas, Todd Black, Jason Blumenthal, and Steve Tisch. Screenplay by Proyas, Ryne Pearson, Juliet Snowden, and Stiles White.

Knowing is among the best science fiction films I've seen—frightening, suspenseful, intelligent, and, when it needs to be, rather awesome. In its very different way, it is comparable to the great *Dark City*, by the same director, Alex Proyas. That film was about the hidden nature of the world men think they inhabit, and so is this one.

The plot involves the most fundamental of all philosophical debates: Is the universe deterministic or random? Is everything in some way preordained, or does it happen by chance? If that question sounds too abstract, wait until you see this picture, which poses it in stark terms: What if we could know in advance when the earth will end?

Nicolas Cage, in another wound-up, edgy performance, plays Koestler, a professor of astrophysics at MIT. He votes for deterministic; as he tells his class, he believes "shit happens." His wife has died, and he's raising his young son, Caleb (Chandler Canterbury). A time capsule is opened at Caleb's grade school, containing the drawings of students in 1959 predicting the sights of 2009. But the sheet Caleb gets isn't a drawing; it's covered with rows of numbers. In a prologue, we've seen the girl with haunted eyes, Lucinda (Lara Robinson), who so intensely pressed the numbers into the paper.

What do these numbers mean? You already know from the TV ads, but I don't believe I should tell you. I'll write another article that will contain spoilers. Let me say that Koestler discovers almost by accident a pattern in the numbers, and they shake his scientific mind to its core. His obsession is scoffed at by his MIT colleague, a cosmologist named Beckman (Ben Mendelsohn), who warns Koestler against the heresy of numerology—the finding of imaginary patterns in numbers. Beckman's passionate arguments in the film, which are not technical yet are scientifically sound, raise the stakes. This is not a movie about psychic mumble-jumble; Koestler is a hard-headed scientist, too, or always thought he was, until that page of numbers came into his hands.

By "scientifically sound," I don't mean anyone at MIT is going to find the plot other than preposterous. So it is—but not while the movie is playing. It works as science fiction, which often changes one coordinate in an otherwise logical world just to see what might happen. For Koestler, it leads to a rejection of what he has always believed, to his serious consideration of the paranormal, and to his discovery of Diana (Rose Byrne), the daughter of little Lucinda who wrote down the numbers, and Abby, the granddaughter (Lara Robinson again).

He believes the two children are somehow instrumental in the developing scenario, and he bonds with Diana to protect them from evil Strangers in the woods—who are mostly kept far enough away in long shots to prevent them from seeming more Strange than they must. The logic of the story leads us to expect something really spectacular at the end, and I was not disappointed visually, although I have logical questions that are sort of beside the point.

With expert and confident storytelling, Proyas strings together events that keep tension at a high pitch all through the film. Even a few quiet, human moments have something coiling beneath. Pluck this movie, and it vibrates. Even something we've seen countless times, like a car pursuit, works here because of the meaning of the pursuit and the high stakes.

There are sensational special effects in the film, which again I won't describe. You'll know the ones I mean. The film is beautifully photographed by Simon Duggan, the Marco Beltrami score hammers or elevates when it needs to, and Richard Learoyd's editing is knife-edged; when he needs to hurtle us through sequences, he does it with an insistence that doesn't feel rushed.

You may have guessed from the TV ads that something very bad is unfolding for the earth, and you may ask, not unreasonably, how these two nice parents and their lovable kids can possibly have any effect on it. Ah, but that would be in a random universe, and *Knowing* argues that the universe is deterministic. Or . . . *does* it? Your papers will be due before class on Monday.

Kung Fu Panda 2 ★ ★ ★ ½

PG, 90 m., 2011

Jack Black (Po), Angelina Jolie (Tigress), Dustin Hoffman (Shifu), Jackie Chan (Monkey), Seth Rogen (Mantis), Lucy Liu (Viper), David Cross (Crane), James Hong (Mr. Ping), Gary Oldman (Lord Shen), Michelle Yeoh (Soothsayer). Directed by Jennifer Yuh Nelson and produced by Melissa Cobb. Screenplay by Jonathan Aibel and Glenn Berger.

Kung Fu Panda 2 is exactly as you'd expect, and more. The animation is elegant, the story is much more involving than the original, and there's boundless energy. I enjoyed it as fully as I possibly could, given the horror of its 3-D. The original film, in 2-D widescreen, was just fine. But never mind. Hollywood has brainwashed us (or itself) that 3-D is an improvement and not an annoyance.

What's best about this sequel is that it's not a dutiful retread of the original, but an ambitious extension. Of the many new elements, not least is the solution of the mystery of how Mr. Ping, a goose, could be the biological father of Po, a panda. In the original film, as nearly as I can recall, every character represented a different species, so I thought perhaps inscrutable reproductive processes were being employed. But no, Po's parenthood is explained here, and it has a great deal to do with new developments in the kingdom.

As we rejoin events in this mythical Chinese kingdom, Po (Jack Black), having attained the status of Dragon Warrior in the first film, still leads the Furious Five: Tigress (Angelina Jolie), Mantis (Seth Rogen), Monkey (Jackie Chan), Viper (Lucy Liu), and Crane (David Cross). Of these Tigress is clearly the most formidable, and Mantis remains the enigma; even though he sounds like Seth Rogen, how does he get past the weigh-in?

The kingdom now faces the prospect that it will be conquered and ruled by the evil peacock Lord Shen (Gary Oldman), whose minions have designed a new weapon that causes him to scour the land of scrap iron. This Shen is a wicked foe, hurling sharp, pointed feathers from his tail like a circus knife-thrower. It turns out that the mystery of Po's parentage is explained by Lord Shen's paranoia after a soothsayer (Michelle Yeoh) tells him to beware of pandas, so their destinies are linked more deeply than Po can imagine.

This is a film from Dreamworks, which is locked in competition with Pixar, and is swinging for the fences. The animation is much superior to your average 3-D feature about cute little animals, although the distortion caused by 3-D effects does it no favors. The story gets a lot of humor out of Po; Jack Black's voicing invests him with more personality than you'd expect from a character who resembles a balloon in the Macy's Thanksgiving Day Parade. (*Kung Fu Panda 3* could possibly open with Po working out with a personal trainer, maybe Tigress.) The director, Jennifer Yuh Nelson, broadens the scope of the animation to include more styles than your basic cartoon animals, and the imaginary sequences involving Po's history are rather beautiful.

Doing voice-over work must now count as an important part of every actor's repertory, and that has created a demand for actors who have distinctive voices. Dustin Hoffman is especially successful as a guru named Shifu. As he grows older, Hoffman is more and more mastering the timing and inflection of a smart stand-up comic. It's a gift.

Speaking of *Panda 3*, I wonder if the relationship between Po and Tigress will advance from its current status as what might be called a warm friendship. Tigress seems to occupy a favored position in Po's heart, reopening the possibility of cross-species pollination.

L

La Mission ★ ★ ½

R, 117 m., 2010

Benjamin Bratt (Che Rivera), Erika Alexander (Lena), Jeremy Ray Valdez (Jes), Jesse Borrego (Rene), Talisa Soto Bratt (Ana), Max Rosenak (Jordan), Kevin Michael Richardson (Dee). Directed by Peter Bratt and produced by Peter Bratt, Benjamin Bratt, and Alpita Patel.

He is an admirable man, well liked in the Mission District of San Francisco. A single father whose son is headed for UCLA. A bus driver whose love is working on customized low-riders. A longtime recovering alcoholic. He got in trouble as a young man, did prison time, but now in his forties, he's put all that behind him.

This is the Che Rivera we meet at the beginning of *La Mission,* played by Benjamin Bratt as in a tattooed macho role—a man who isn't afraid to face down unruly passengers on his bus. He loves his son Jes (Jeremy Ray Valdez). After some disagreements with his upstairs neighbor Lena (Erika Alexander), he's beginning to see her in a new light. He's the anchor of a group of friends who work together on their lovingly customized cars.

Then he discovers his son is gay. That isn't part of his world, his culture, his comprehension. There is always violence coiled inside him, and he throws his son out of the house, fights with him on the sidewalk, and as a result assures that everyone in the neighborhood and at Jes's school knows the secret. They both sense a lot of stares and giggles and negative feelings from the Latino community.

Lena, as it turns out, works at a shelter for abused women. She is firm and unyielding in her distaste for violence. She'd started to like Che—there's a lot to like about him—but now she fears he's a type she's seen too often. He doesn't have a way to process anger. He explodes. He loves his son but hates homosexuality more.

This story is told earnestly and with some force in *La Mission,* written and directed by Benjamin's brother Peter. They worked together earlier on Peter's *Follow Me Home* (1996), an in-your-face film about a car full of minority graffiti artists on a cross-country odyssey. Here their hearts are in the right place, but the film tries to say too many things for its running time.

I believe Che's outrage at his son's personality. I do not believe his son would challenge him by suggesting Che found out something about gay sex in prison. At that moment I felt a screenplay talking, not a character. The film's treatment of Che's alcoholism is perfunctory—used for plot points, not character revelation. I believe an African-American woman and a Mexican-American man could certainly come together in the way the movie shows, but I was puzzled that the movie scarcely seemed to get deeper into that than the casting.

And Jes's lover is not simply too good to be true; he's too good to be interesting. This is Jordan (Max Rosenak), who is clean-cut, wholesome, and supportive, and of course has loving parents. I would have liked him a little more complex. I don't even know how they met; he's simply there because the story requires him.

Some crucial scenes take place in a hospital. These scenes, I think, overplay Che's feelings. I don't require acceptance and reconciliation, and the film is forthright in avoiding easy answers. But does the screenplay shortchange Che by painting him more broadly at the end than he seemed at the beginning? If experience does anything, it leaves us wiser.

Land of the Lost ★ ★ ★

PG-13, 93 m., 2009

Will Ferrell (Dr. Rick Marshall), Danny McBride (Will Stanton), Anna Friel (Holly Cantrell), Jorma Taccone (Chaka). Directed by Brad Silberling and produced by Jimmy Miller and Sid and Marty Krofft. Screenplay by Chris Henchy and Dennis McNicholas.

Land of the Lost is a seriously deranged movie. That's not to say it's bad, although some of its early critics consider it a hanging offense ("a pot of ersatz dinosaur piss"—Peter Keough, *Boston Phoenix*). Marshall Fine even apologizes for prematurely predicting that *Night at the Museum: Battle of the Smithsonian* would be "the most witless, humor-challenged movie of the summer." The release inspires fervent hatred, which with the right kind of movie can be a good thing. Amid widespread disdain, I raise my voice in a bleat of lonely, if moderate, admiration.

The film involves a gloriously preposterous premise, set in a series of cheerfully fake landscapes that change at the whim of the art director. How else to explain a primeval swamp within walking distance of a limitless desert? Or to explain a motel sign from another dimension that appears there, with all of the motel missing but plenty of water still in the pool? And dinosaurs walking the earth at the same time as early man, just like in *Alley Oop* and *The Flintstones*?

Will Ferrell plays Dr. Rick Marshall, a scientist who assures Matt Lauer of the *Today* show that he has discovered a way to solve the energy crisis by importing fossil fuels from a parallel dimension. Lauer informs him that respectable scientists think he's mad. Like who? "Stephen Hawking," Lauer says. Dr. Rick goes nuclear: "You promised you wouldn't mention that!"

Marshall has, in fact, invented a machine that will transport him to one of those other worlds, and he is encouraged to try it by the only scientist in the world who agrees with him, Holly Cantrell (Anna Friel), who was thrown out of Cambridge for saying so. For reasons far too complicated to enumerate, they are joined in their journey by a fireworks salesman and part-time guide to a mysterious cave named Will (Danny McBride). Their cave tour strangely includes a river that seems to originate in thin air and flow into an artificial mountain before sucking them into a vortex and depositing them in . . . the Land of the Lost.

There they become friends with Chaka (Jorma Taccone), who belongs to a tribe of Missing Links and offers convincing evidence that in his land the straightening of teeth had not been developed. Luckily, Holly speaks his language. Yes, speaks his language, indicating that the movie will do anything to get to the next scene.

There are many jokes about dinosaur manure, dinosaur urine, dinosaur intelligence, dinosaur babies, and dinosaurs' hurt feelings. Also blood-sucking insects, carnivorous trees, and the sound track from *A Chorus Line*. The use of the songs is utterly wacky, of course, which is why I liked it.

The movie is inspired by the 1974 TV series and has the same producers, Sid and Marty Krofft. The two will never be confused, but they share one thing in common: deliriously fake locations, props, and special effects. The dinosaurs are so obviously not really there in shots where they menace humans that you could almost say their shots are *about* how they're not really there. Confronted with such effects, the actors make not the slightest effort to appear terrified, amazed, or sometimes even mildly concerned. Some might consider that a weakness. I suspect it is more of a deliberate choice, and I say I enjoyed it.

I guess you have to be in the mood for a goofball picture like this. I guess I was. Marshall Fine says it's worse than *Night at the Museum*, but I've seen *Night at the Museum*, and Marshall, this is no *Night at the Museum*.

Larry Crowne ★ ★

PG-13, 99 m., 2011

Tom Hanks (Larry Crowne), Julia Roberts (Mercedes Tainot), Brian Cranston (Dean Tainot), Cedric the Entertainer (Lamar), Taraji P. Henson (B'Ella), Gugu Mbatha-Raw (Talia), Wilmer Valderrama (Dell Gordo), Pam Grier (Frances). Directed by Tom Hanks and produced by Hanks and Gary Goetzman. Screenplay by Hanks and Nia Vardalos.

Larry Crowne has Tom Hanks and Julia Roberts and a good premise and a colorful supporting cast, but what it doesn't have is a reason for existing. The screenplay carries blandness to a point beyond tedium. At some point the sinking realization sets in that Larry Crowne was born a nice guy, will always be a nice guy, will find few bumps in his road, and is destined for a happy ending. We watch not in suspense but in envy.

Hanks produced and directed the film, and cowrote the screenplay with Nia Vardalos, his pal since the days when Hanks's wife, Rita Wilson, produced Vardalos's *My Big Fat Greek Wedding* (2002). That was a good movie. Since then Vardalos wrote and starred in the awful *Connie and Carla* (2004), starred in the dismal *My Life in Ruins* (2009), and wrote and directed the train wreck *I Hate Valentine's Day* (2009). As a writer she seems drawn toward banality.

In *Larry Crowne*, Hanks plays a nice guy who gets fired from his retail job because he lacks the education to qualify him for a management position. This happens despite his countless awards for employee of the month. Larry cashes in his possessions, trades his car for a scooter, and decides to enroll in a local community college. As his economics teacher, he draws Dr. Matsutani (George Takei), the only character in the film interesting enough to have a movie made about him. As his public speaking teacher, he gets Mercedes Tainot (Julia Roberts), a character who seems to have drifted over from the auditions for *Bad Teacher*.

The story arc is simplicity itself: Larry Crowne is a nice man who becomes nicer with the encouragement of other nice people. He eventually inspires the bad teacher to become a good teacher, abandon her porn-surfing loser of a husband, cure herself of alcoholism, and fall in love with him. More than this a nice guy cannot be expected to do.

I watched the movie with all the pleasure I bring to watching bread rise. Don't get me wrong. I enjoy watching bread rise, but it lacks a certain degree of interest. You look forward to it being finished.

Larry is assisted in his lifestyle transition by the fetching Talia (Gugu Mbatha-Raw), who supervises a makeover; he ditches the regular-guy duds for basic black and gets a cool haircut. There is also character interest from his neighbors, Lamar (Cedric the Entertainer) and B'Ella (Taraji P. Henson), but that's what they're in the movie for: character interest. They don't seem essential. At the neighbor's garage sale, Larry buys a motor scooter and ends up as a member of a scooter club, which is like a motorcycle gang of environmentalists. How many scooter clubs are there in Los Angeles? Don't tell me. I don't want to know.

What we have here is a screenplay lacking in conflict. I often complain about screenwriters who slavishly follow the story arcs taught in screenwriting classes. Nia Vardalos might benefit from one of those classes. In place of conflict, the story substitutes cutesy whims. Tom Hanks on a motor scooter! Neat!

Julia Roberts is fine here, to the degree that the film permits it. She's pretty and has that warm smile and is transformed under the gentle pressure of Larry's sunny influence. Surely her marriage must be more deeply troubled than we ever see, but the movie's still waters don't run deep.

The Last Airbender ½ ★

PG, 103 m., 2010

Noah Ringer (Aang), Nicola Peltz (Katara), Jackson Rathbone (Sokka), Dev Patel (Prince Zuko), Shaun Toub (Uncle Iroh), Aasif Mandvi (Commander Zhao), Cliff Curtis (Fire Lord Ozai), Seychelle Gabriel (Princess Yue). Directed by M. Night Shyamalan and produced by Shyamalan, Scott Aversano, Frank Marshall, and Sam Mercer.

The Last Airbender is an agonizing experience in every category I can think of and others still waiting to be invented. The laws of chance suggest that *something* should have gone right. Not here. It puts a nail in the coffin of low-rent 3-D, but it will need a lot more coffins than that.

Let's start with the 3-D, which was added as an afterthought to a 2-D movie. Not only is it unexploited and unnecessary, but it's a disaster even if you like 3-D. M. Night Shyamalan's retrofit produces the drabbest, darkest, dingiest movie of any sort I've seen in years. You know something is wrong when the screen is filled with flames that have the vibrancy of faded Polaroids. It's a known fact that 3-D causes a measurable decrease in perceived brightness, but *Airbender* looks like it was filmed with a dirty sheet over the lens.

Now for the movie itself. The first fatal decision was to make a live-action film out of material that was born to be anime. The animation of the Nickelodeon TV series drew on the bright colors and clear-line style of such masters as Miyazaki, and was a visual pleasure to observe. It's in the very nature of animation to make absurd visual sights more plausible.

Since *Airbender* involves the human manipulation of the forces of air, earth, water, and fire, there is hardly an event that can be rendered plausibly in live action. That said, its special effects are atrocious. The first time the Waterbender Katara summons a globe of water, which then splashes (offscreen) on her brother Sokka, he doesn't even get wet. The Firebenders' flames don't seem to really burn, and so on.

The story takes place in the future, after man has devastated the planet and survives in the form of beings with magical powers allowing them to influence earth, water, and fire. These warring factions are held in uneasy harmony by the Avatar, but the Avatar has disappeared, and Earth lives in a state of constant turmoil caused by the warlike Firebenders.

Our teenage heroes Katara and Sokka discover a child frozen in the ice. This is Aang (Noah Ringer), and they come to suspect he may be the Avatar, or last Airbender. Perhaps he can bring harmony and quell the violent Firebenders. This plot is incomprehensible, apart from the helpful orientation that we like Katara, Sokka, and Aang, and are therefore against their enemies.

The dialogue is couched in unspeakable quasi-medieval formalities; the characters are so portentous they seem to have been trained for grade-school historical pageants. Their dialogue is functional and action driven. There is little conviction that any of this might be real even in their minds. All of the benders in the movie appear only in terms of their attributes and functions, and contain no personality.

Potentially interesting details are botched. Consider the great iron ships of the Firebenders. These show potential as steampunk, but are never caressed for their intricacies. Consider the detail Miyazaki lavished on *Howl's Moving Castle*. Try sampling a Nickelodeon clip from the original show to glimpse the look that might have been.

After the miscalculation of making the movie as live action, there remained the challenge of casting it. Shyamalan has failed. His first inexplicable mistake was to change the races of the leading characters; on television Aang was clearly Asian, and so were Katara and Sokka, with perhaps Mongolian and Inuit genes. Here they're all whites. This casting makes no sense because (1) it's a distraction for fans of the hugely popular TV series, and (2) all three actors are pretty bad. I don't say they're untalented; I say they've been poorly served by Shyamalan and the script. They are bland, stiff, awkward, and unconvincing. Little Aang reminds me of Wallace Shawn as a child. This is not a bad thing (he should only grow into Shawn's shoes), but doesn't the role require little Andre, not little Wally?

As the villain, Shyamalan has cast Cliff Curtis as Fire Lord Ozai and Dev Patel (the hero of *Slumdog Millionaire*) as his son, Prince Zuko. This is all wrong. In material at this melodramatic level, you need teeth-gnashers, not leading men. Indeed, all of the acting seems inexplicably muted. I've been an admirer of many of Shyamalan's films, but action and liveliness are not his strong points. I fear he takes the theology of the bending universe seriously.

As *The Last Airbender* bores and alienates its audiences, consider the opportunities missed here. (1) This material should have become an A-list animated film. (2) It was a blunder jumping aboard the 3-D bandwagon with phony 3-D retrofitted to a 2-D film. (3) If it had to be live action, better special-effects artists should have been found. It's not as if films like *2012* and *Knowing* didn't contain "real-life" illusions as spectacular as anything called for in *The Last Airbender*.

I close with the hope that the title proves prophetic.

Last Chance Harvey ★ ★ ★

PG-13, 92 m., 2009

Dustin Hoffman (Harvey Shine), Emma Thompson (Kate Walker), Eileen Atkins (Maggie), Liane Balaban (Susan), James Brolin (Brian), Kathy Baker (Jean). Directed by Joel Hopkins and produced by Tim Perell and Nicola Usborne. Screenplay by Hopkins.

Last Chance Harvey is a tremendously appealing love story surrounded by a movie not worthy of it. For Dustin Hoffman, after years of character roles (however good) and dubbing the voices of animated animals, it provides a rare chance to play an ordinary guy. For Emma Thompson, there is an opportunity to use her gifts for tact and insecurity.

For both, their roles project warmth and need.

When the film gets out of their way and leaves them alone to relate with each other, it's sort of magical. Then the lumber of the plot apparatus is trundled on, and we wish it were a piece for two players. One subplot, scored with funny-bumpy-scary music, is entirely unnecessary. And even with the two stars on screen, there is too much reliance on that ancient standby, the Semi-Obligatory Lyrical Interlude.

But what's good is very good. Hoffman plays Harvey, a failed jazz pianist who has found success writing jingles for TV ads. Thompson plays Kate, an airport interviewer for a British agency. Hoffman flies to London to attend his daughter's wedding, and in the space of twenty-four hours he learns that he has been fired and that his daughter would prefer her stepfather gave her away. At the same time, Thompson is ignored on a blind date and has to deal with a mother who fears her new neighbor is a vivisectionist.

They met briefly when Harvey was rude to her at the airport. The next day, when both are deep in misery, they find themselves the only two people in a pub. Harvey recognizes her, apologizes, and out of desperation tries to start a conversation. She resists. But notice the tentative dialogue that slowly allows them to start talking easily. It's not forced. It depends on his charm and her kindness.

Pitch perfect. But then the dialogue fades down and the camera pulls back and shows them talking and smiling freely, and the music gets happier, and there is a montage showing them walking about London with lots and lots of scenery in the frame. The movie indulges the Semi-OLI more than once; it uses the device as shorthand for scenes that should be fully transcribed. In *Before Sunrise* and *Before Sunset,* Richard Linklater sent Ethan Hawke and Julie Delpy talking all through a night in Vienna and all through a day in Paris, and never let them stop, and kept his camera close. Why didn't Joel Hopkins, the writer-director of *Last Chance Harvey,* try the same? He had the right actors.

He gets one thing right. They stay outdoors. Going to his hotel or her flat would set the stage for body language neither one is ready for. They avoid the issue by walking around London, although unfortunately Hopkins sends them mostly up and down the Victoria Embankment and the South Bank, so he can hold the Thames vista in the background. We get more montages of them walking and talking, as substitutes for listening to a conversation we've become invested in.

One subplot works well. After she starts him talking about why his relationship with his daughter failed, she tells him he *must* attend her wedding reception. He says she must go with him. He will buy her a dress. There is a gratuitous and offensive montage of her trying on dresses, including one frilly gown that looks perfect for a fancy dress ball in *Gone with the Wind.* Not only is this montage an exhausted cliché, they're in a hurry, remember? But when they get to the reception, Harvey is touching in a carefully worded speech.

The subplot that doesn't work involves Kate's mother (Eileen Atkins). She peers through the curtains at the suspicious neighbor, thinks she sees him carrying a body to the woodshed, and speed-dials her daughter every five minutes. Every time we cut to her, we get that peppy suspense music, as the movie confuses itself with light comedy.

Last Chance Harvey has everything it needs and won't stop there. It needs the nerve to push all the way. It is a pleasure to look upon the faces of Hoffman and Thompson, so pleasant, so real. Their dialogue together finds the right notes for crossing an emotional minefield. They never descend into tear-jerking or cuteness. They are all grown up and don't trust love nearly as much as straight talk. Hopkins deserves credit for creating these characters. Then he should have stood back and let them keep right on talking. Their pillow talk would have been spellbinding.

The Last House on the Left ★ ★ ½

R, 100 m., 2009

Tony Goldwyn (John Collingwood), Monica Potter (Emma Collingwood), Sara Paxton (Mari Collingwood), Garret Dillahunt (Krug), Spencer Treat Clark (Justin), Riki Lindhome (Sadie), Aaron Paul (Francis), Martha MacIsaac (Paige). Directed by Dennis Iliadis and produced by Wes Craven, Sean Cunningham, and Marianne Maddalena. Screenplay by Adam Alleca and Carl Ellsworth, based on the 1972 film by Craven.

I have seen four films inspired by the same thirteenth-century folk ballad: Ingmar Bergman's *The Virgin Spring* (1960), Wes Craven's *The Last House on the Left* (1972), David DeFalco's *Chaos* (2005), and now Dennis Iliadis's remake of the 1972 film, also titled *The Last House on the Left.*

What I know for sure is that the Bergman film is the best. Beyond that, it is a confusion of contradictions. I gave the 1972 film 3½ stars, describing it as "a tough, bitter little sleeper of a movie that's about four times as good as you'd expect." I gave the 2005 film zero stars, describing it as "ugly, nihilistic, and cruel—a film I regret having seen." What do I think about the latest story about a girl who goes walking in the woods, is raped and in some versions is killed, and whose attackers then seek shelter in the house of her parents, who realize who they are and take revenge?

Would I still admire 1972 today? Can I praise 2009 after savaging 2005? Isn't it all more or less the same material? Not quite. In the Bergman film, the father asks God's forgiveness for taking vengeance and says: "I promise You, God, here on the dead body of my only child, I promise you that, to cleanse my sins, here I shall build a church. On this spot. Of mortar and stone . . . and with these, my hands."

And such a church was built in the 1300s, and still stands at Karna in Sweden. No churches will be built because of the other films, no parents will ask forgiveness, and few members of the audience will think they should. These are in the horror genre, which once tried to scare the audience but now invites the audience to share the fear and pain of the characters. It is the one genre that can lead the box office without name stars, perhaps because its fans know that big stars very rarely appear in one (I'm not thinking of films where story is first but those in which graphic violence is first).

Horror films have connoisseurs, who are alert to gradations in violence. The well-informed critic "Fright" at the Web site Horror Movie a Day writes: "In the original, EVERYTHING was just so depraved, the rape barely stuck out as anything worse than the other things they endured. Not the case here, and so while some may cry foul that the movie is too toned down, I think it's a good decision." Not many unseasoned audience members will find the 2009 rape scene "toned down," and indeed I found it painful to watch. In the 2005 film, it was so reprehensibly and lingeringly sadistic I found it unforgivable. So now my job as a film critic involves grading rape scenes.

I don't think I can. I wrote that original *Last House* review thirty-seven years ago. I am not the same person. I am uninterested in being "consistent." I approach the new film as simply a filmgoer. I must say it is very well made. The rape scene appalled me. Other scenes, while violent, fell within the range of contemporary horror films, which strive to invent new ways to kill people so the horror fans in the audience will get a laugh.

This film, for example, which as I write has inspired only one review (by "Fright"), has generated a spirited online discussion about whether you can kill someone by sticking their head in a microwave. Many argue that a microwave won't operate with the door open. Others cite an early scene establishing that the microwave is "broken." The question of whether one *should* microwave a man's head never arises.

Let's set that aside and look at the performances. They're surprisingly good, and I especially admired the work of Monica Potter and Tony Goldwyn as the parents of one of two girls who go walking in the woods. It is no longer only the father who takes revenge; both parents work together, improvising, playing a deadly chess game in their own home, which they know better than the villains. We are only human, we identify with the parents, we fear for them, and we applaud their ingenuity.

There is also sound work by Krug (Garret Dillahunt), the convincingly evil leader of a pack of degenerates. He isn't just acting scary. He creates a character. And Sara Paxton, who has been acting since eight and was twenty when the movie was made, shows, as so many sexy young blondes do, that they are better than the bubblehead roles they are mostly given.

It is also true that director Dennis Iliadis and his cinematographer, Sharone Meir, do a smooth job of handling space and time to create suspense. The film is an effective representative of its genre, and horror fans will like it, I think, but who knows? I'm giving it a 2½ on the silly star rating system and throwing up my hands.

The Last Mountain ★ ★ ★

PG, 95 m., 2011

William Sadler (Narrator), Maria Gunnoe, Bo Webb, Robert F. Kennedy Jr., Jennifer Hall-Massey, Joe Lovett, Bill Raney, Don Blankenship, Ed Wiley, Lorelei Scarbro, David Aaron Smith, and Susan Bird. A documentary directed by Bill Haney and produced by Haney, Clara Bingham, and Eric Grunebaum. Screenplay by Haney and Peter Rhodes.

Is there another state in the union more cruelly defaced than West Virginia? Its mountains have been blown up, its forests ripped out and thrown away, and the green new land that the settlers discovered now includes a wasteland of a million dead and toxic acres. Nationally, one in one hundred thousand people get brain tumors. In a small West Virginia town surrounded by strip mining, six neighbors have developed brain tumors. What are the odds of that?

The Last Mountain is a blunt and enraged documentary about how such things came to be. It is about Coal River Mountain, the site of a last stand against Massey Energy, a company it says disregarded environmental concerns, compromised the political process, and poisoned great stretches of the state in the name of corporate profits. Now lakes of sludge loom above towns, rivers are dead and dying, and heavy metals invade the bloodstreams and brains of the inhabitants.

Yes, we need coal. Yes, West Virginia has a lot of it and once had a lot more. Coal is a major contributor to global warming, but those very words, "global warming," are anathema to those whose minds have been bought and paid for by Big Energy. I would like to see a comparison of the dollars spent on (1) greener energy and (2) political lobbying by a company like Massey, the villain in *The Last Mountain*. Corporations by their nature exist to maximize profits. Their executives are compelled to enact draconian measures to further them. It's how they work.

The bad guy in *The Last Mountain* is Don Blankenship, who was chairman and CEO of Massey from 2000 until 2010. He doesn't believe in climate change and once equated energy conservation with communism. It was on his watch that twenty-nine miners were killed in the explosion at Massey's Upper Big Branch mine on April 5, 2010. Wikipedia: "In 2005, Blankenship wrote a memo to employees telling them that maximizing coal production was more important than spending time constructing things like support beams or ventilation shafts." Also Wikipedia: "When groundwater pollution from coal slurry injection by Massey Energy began contaminating wells around Blankenship's home, Massey paid to build a water line to his home from a neighboring town. Blankenship did not offer to provide uncontaminated water to any of his neighbors."

He fits my notion of a bad man. My notion of a heroine is Maria Gunnoe, a West Virginia woman who is one of the leaders of a campaign to defend Coal River Mountain. Articulate, plain-spoken, she has been transformed by the campaign.

A film like *The Last Mountain* fills me with restless anger. I have seen many documentaries like this, all telling versions of the same story: When there is money to be made at the cost of the environment, it is the environment that will suffer. And the suffering will be justified by denying global warming and "defending free enterprise." I understand that corporations exist to make profits, but I believe government exists to regulate them. Another hero in this film is Robert F. Kennedy Jr., who visits West Virginia frequently on behalf of the environmental activists, and lobbied Obama to reverse some (not all) of the Bush administration's moves to weaken green laws.

Still, it all comes back to the fact that we need energy. As I watched the film's aerial shots flying over the harsh and ugly landscapes left behind by Massey, it occurred to me that something was missing. No, not simply trees and other living things. I would have liked to see some wind turbines.

The Last Song ★ ★ ½

PG, 107 m., 2010

Miley Cyrus (Ronnie Miller), Greg Kinnear (Steve Miller), Liam Hemsworth (Will Blakelee), Bobby Coleman (Jonah Miller), Kelly Preston (Kim Miller). Directed by Julie Anne Robinson and produced by Jennifer Gibgot and Adam Shankman. Screenplay by Nicholas Sparks and Jeff Van Wie, based on a novel by Sparks.

Now that Miley Cyrus is seventeen, it's about time she played a sixteen-year-old. That she does fetchingly in *The Last Song,* and wins the heart of a beach volleyball champion a foot taller than she is. Well, actually 12.5 inches. She also learns to love her dad, played by Greg Kinnear, whose aura suggests a man easier to love than, say, Steve Buscemi. She does this on an idyllic island paradise offshore from Savannah, Georgia, where her dad is a classical composer whose pastime is restoring stained glass windows.

I was trying to remember the last time I felt the way about a girl that Miley Cyrus's fans feel about her. That would have been in 1959, when I saw Hayley Mills in *Tiger Bay.* Oh, she was something. A brave tomboy. She was twelve, but I could wait. It's a bit much to ask for the same innocence from Miley, who has already had her first world tour, but the fact is, she does a good job of making her character, Ronnie, engaging and lovable. That's despite her early Alienated Teen scenes. You know it's an Alienated Teen when it's a lovely day on an island paradise, but she has her hands pulled up inside the sleeves of her sweater and huddles against the chill of the cold, cruel world.

I like Miley Cyrus. I like her in spite of the fact that she's been packaged within an inch of her life. I look forward to the day when she squirms loose from her handlers and records an album of classic songs, performed with the same sincerity as her godmother, Dolly Parton. I think it'll be a long, long time until she plays a movie character like the freestanding, engaging heroines of Ashley Judd, but I can wait.

The Last Song is about how Ronnie (Miley) and her little brother, Jonah (Bobby Coleman), are taken by their mother (Kelly Preston) to spend the summer with their dad, Steve (Kinnear). She blames her dad for the divorce, is sullen and withdrawn. Ten minutes after she hits the beach (dressed in Gothic black), her milk shake is spilled by a flying volleyball player named Will (Liam Hemsworth). Talk about your Meet Cutes. Gradually she overcomes her hostility to men and realizes Will is a nice and honorable kid, even though he lives in a vast Southern mansion with insufferable rich parents.

Ronnie and Will make an attractive couple, possibly because Miley is standing on a box below camera range. I suspect Hemsworth may have been cast for his appeal to fangirls, rather like Robert Pattinson in *Twilight.* He's a little too tall, blond, blue-eyed, and hunky to be super plausible. He can definitely become a star, but it may be in the Peter O'Toole tradition; I can more easily imagine him in a remake of *Lawrence of Arabia* than as a settled spouse in a domestic drama.

Miley Cyrus, on the other hand, is attractive in the way of a girl you might actually meet. Her acting is unaffected, she can play serious, and she works easily with a pro like Kinnear, whose light comedy skills are considerable and undervalued. She even seems sincere in the face of a plot so blatantly contrived it seems like an after-school special. Would you believe that she and Will bond over sea turtle eggs?

Yes, she scares off a raccoon trying to raid a nest of eggs buried in the sand and mounts an all-night vigil over them. Then she calls the aquarium, and who do you think is the handsome volunteer who responds to the call? Standing watch together the second night, Ronnie and Will start talking, and it's only a matter of time until they regard together the itty bitty turtles hurrying toward the sea.

The other big crisis of her summer is that she's a trained classical pianist, but has just turned down a scholarship to Juilliard because her dad, you see, is such a snake. In a world containing divorce, what's the use of Mozart? The film's title relates to this situation, I believe, in some obscure way. Miley does, however, sing in the movie. She's mad at her dad, but not her fans.

The Last Song is based on the novel by Nicholas Sparks, who also wrote the screenplay. Sparks recently went on record as saying he is a greater novelist than Cormac McCarthy. This is true in the same sense that I am a better novelist than William Shakespeare. Sparks also said his novels are like Greek tragedies. This may actually be true. I can't check it out because, tragically, no really bad Greek tragedies have survived. His story here amounts to soft porn for teenage girls, which the acting and the abilities of director Julie Anne Robinson have promoted over its pay scale.

The movie is intended, of course, for Miley Cyrus admirers, and truth compels me to report that on that basis alone, it would get four stars. But we cannot all be Miley Cyrus fans, and these days you rarely hear Hayley Mills mentioned. Yet I award the film two and a half stars.

To be sure, I resent the sacrilege Nicholas Sparks commits by even mentioning himself in the same sentence as Cormac McCarthy. I would not even allow him to say, "Hello, bookstore? This is Nicholas Sparks. Could you send over the new Cormac McCarthy novel?" He should show respect by ordering anonymously. But it seems unfair to penalize Miley Cyrus fans, Miley, and the next Peter O'Toole for the transgressions of a lesser artist.

The Last Station ★ ★ ★

R, 110 m., 2010

Helen Mirren (Sofya), Christopher Plummer (Tolstoy), Paul Giamatti (Chertkov), Anne Marie Duff (Sasha), Kerry Condon (Masha), James McAvoy (Valentin). Directed by Michael Hoffman and produced by Bonnie Arnold, Chris Curling, and Jens Meurer. Screenplay by Hoffman, based on the novel by Jay Parini.

Watching *The Last Station,* I was reminded of the publisher Bennett Cerf's story about how he went to Europe to secure the rights to James Joyce's *Ulysses.*

"Nora, you have a brilliant husband," he told Joyce's wife.

"You don't have to live with the bloody fool."

If Joyce was a drunk and a roisterer, how different was the Russian novelist Leo Tolstoy, who was a vegetarian and pacifist, and recommended (although did not practice) celibacy? *The Last Station* focuses also on *his* wife, Sofya, who after bearing his thirteen children thought him a late arrival to celibacy and accused him of confusing himself with Christ. Yet it's because of the writing of Joyce and Tolstoy that we know about their wives at all. Well, the same is true of George Eliot's husband.

The Last Station focuses on the last year of Count Tolstoy (Christopher Plummer), a full-bearded Shakespearian figure presiding over a household of intrigues. The chief schemer is Chertkov (Paul Giamatti), his intense follower, who idealistically believes Tolstoy should leave his literary fortune to the Russian people. It's just the sort of idea that Tolstoy might seize upon in his utopian zeal. Sofya (Helen Mirren), on behalf of herself and her children, is livid.

Chertkov, who as the quasi-leader of Tolstoy's quasi-cult, hires a young man named Valentin (James McAvoy) to become the count's private secretary. In this capacity, he is to act as a double agent, observing moments between Leo and Sofya when Chertkov would not be welcome.

It may be hard for us to understand how seriously Tolstoy was taken at the time. To call him comparable in stature to Gandhi would not be an exaggeration, and indeed, Gandhi adopted many of his ideas. Tolstoy in his eighty-second year remained active and robust, but everyone knew his end might be approaching, and the Russian equivalent of paparazzi and gossips lurked in the neighborhood. Imagine Perez Hilton staking out J. D. Salinger.

Tolstoy was thought a great man and still is, but in a way his greatness distracts from how good he was as a writer. When I was young the expression "reading *War and Peace*" was used as a synonym for idly wasting an immense chunk of time. Foolishly believing this, I read Dostoyevsky and Chekhov but not Tolstoy, and it was only when I came late to *Anna Karenina* that I realized he wrote page-turners. In *Time* magazine's compilation of 125 lists of the ten greatest novels of all time, *War and Peace* and *Anna Karenina* placed first and third. (You didn't ask, but *Madame Bovary* was second, *Lolita* fourth, and *Huckleberry Finn* fifth.)

The Last Station has the look of a Merchant-Ivory film, with the pastoral setting, the dashing costumery, the roomy old country house, the meals taken on lawns. But did Merchant and Ivory ever deal with such a demonstrative family? If the British are known for suppressing their emotions, the Russians seem to bellow their whims. If a British woman in Merchant-Ivory land desires sex, she bestows a significant glance in the candlelight. Sofya clucks like a chicken to arouse old Leo's rooster.

The dramatic movement in the film takes place mostly within Valentin (James McAvoy), who joins the household already an acolyte of Tolstoy. Young and handsome, he says he is celibate. Sofya has him pegged as gay, but Masha (Kerry Condon), a nubile Tolstoyian, pegs him otherwise. Valentin also takes note that Tolstoy, like many charismatic leaders, exempts himself from his own teachings. The thirteen children provide a hint, and his private secretary cannot have avoided observing that although the count and countess fight over his will, a truce is observed at bedtime, and the enemies meet between the lines.

As the formidable patriarch, Christopher Plummer avoids any temptation (if he felt one) to play Tolstoy as a Great Man. He does what is more amusing; he plays him as a Man Who Knows He Is Considered Great. Helen Mirren plays a wife who knows his flaws, but has loved him since the day they met. To be fair, no man who wrote that fiction could be other than wise and warm about human nature.

Some women are simply sexy forever. Helen Mirren is a woman like that. She's sixty-four. As she enters her seventies, we'll begin to develop a fondness for sexy septuagenarians.

Mirren and Plummer make Leo and Sofya Tolstoy more vital than you might expect in a historical picture. Giamatti has a specialty in seeming to be up to something, and McAvoy and Condon take on a glow from feeling noble while sinning. In real life, I learn, Tolstoy provided Sofya with more unpleasant sunset years, but could we stand to see Helen Mirren treated like that?

Last Train Home ★ ★ ★ ★

NO MPAA RATING, 87 m., 2010

Chen Suqin, Zhang Changhua, Zhang Qin, and Zhang Yang. A documentary directed by Lixin Fan and produced by Mila Aung-Thwin and Daniel Cross.

This is inevitable: Painful social conflict will arise between those Chinese citizens who produce consumer goods for the world, and those Chinese who want to consume them. *Last Train Home*, an extraordinary documentary, watches that conflict play out over a period of three years in one family. It's one of those extraordinary films, like *Hoop Dreams*, that tells a story the makers could not possibly have anticipated in advance. It works like stunning, grieving fiction.

The film opens like a big-picture documentary, showing us a huge crowd being directed by police as it grinds its way forward. We are informed that these are some of the 130 million Chinese citizens who make an annual train journey from urban centers to their provincial villages—"the largest human migration in the world." Umbrellas of every description protect them. They carry enormous bundles—gifts, perhaps, or food for the journey. They're headed home for Chinese New Year.

We gradually center on Zhang Changhua and Chen Suqin, a married couple. Years ago they left their home in the Szechuan province to take low-paying jobs in a textile factory in Guangzhou, which is the huge industrial city on the mainland next to Hong Kong. Here, in row after row, they work bent over sewing machines, assembling perhaps the jeans I'm wearing right now. They live in dormitories—married adults, with next to no privacy.

They save every yuan they can to send home. They left their children behind to be raised by a grandmother. Their dream is that by fifteen years of this toil, they will pay for the children to finish school and live better lives. For that dream they have sacrificed the life of parenthood, and are like strangers at home to children who know them as voices on the telephone, seen on the annual visit.

This is a reality Dickens could hardly have imagined. The fruit of their toil has contributed to China's emergence as a global economic power. But their lives are a grim contrast to the glittering Beijing of the Olympics, the towers of Shanghai, the affluent new business class. And here is the part you may sense coming: Are their children grateful for what amounts to the sacrifice of two lifetimes?

The filmmaker, Lixin Fan, follows this family for three years, in the city and in the village. We hear much about how Chinese parents pressure their children to study hard and excel. Overseas, they frequently do succeed. But China is a huge nation, so large that a generation may not be long enough to rise from poverty.

Their daughter, Zhang Qin, is in high school, and comes to regard her parents as distant strangers—and nags. She's had enough of it. But what she does is beyond heartbreaking. She moves to Guangzhou and gets a factory job. She does the math. If she keeps her wages instead of sending them home, she'll have them to spend on herself. Does it occur to her to suggest her parents move back home with her brother, while she helps support and repay them? Not a chance.

There is so much to say about this great film. You sense the dedication of Lixin Fan and his team (he did much of the cinematography and editing himself). You see once again the alchemy by which a constantly present camera eventually becomes almost unnoticed, as people live their lives before it. You know the generations almost better than they know themselves because the camera can be in two places and they are usually in one or the other.

There is a quiet moment in a mall. On their day off, Zhang Qin and her friends go shopping. They like a pair of jeans: "Are these made in our factory?" No, in another. Of course they want them. Of course their generation wants them. But their generation doesn't want to work years leaning over a sewing machine and sleeping in a dorm.

We read about the suicides in Apple's plants in China. Seeing this film, you suspect there are many suicides among workers in factories whose brands are less famous than Apple. Chinese peasants no longer live without television and a vision of another world. They no longer live in a country without consumer luxuries. *Last Train Home* suggests that the times they are a-changin'. The rulers of China may someday regret that they distributed the works of Marx so generously.

Law-Abiding Citizen ★ ★ ★

R, 122 m., 2009

Jamie Rice (Nick Rice), Gerard Butler (Clyde Shelton), Colm Meaney (Detective Dunnigan), Bruce McGill (Jonas Cantrell), Leslie Bibb (Sarah Lowell), Michael Irby (Detective Garza), Gregory Itzin (Warden Iger), Regina Hall (Kelly Rice), Emerald-Angel Young (Denise Rice), Christian Stolte (Darby), Annie Corley (Judge Laura Burch), Viola Davis (Mayor). Directed by F. Gary Gray and produced Gerard Butler, Lucas Foster, Mark Gill, Robert Katz, Alan Siegel, and Kurt Wimmer. Screenplay by Wimmer.

Law-Abiding Citizen is a taut thriller about a serial killer in reverse: He's already in prison when he commits all but one of his many murders, and in solitary for most of that time. So the story is a locked-room mystery: How does he set up such elaborate kills? Does he have an accomplice outside the walls, or what?

Jamie Foxx stars as Nick, the Philadelphia district attorney, and Gerard Butler is Clyde, the ingenious killer. He begins the film as a loving husband and father, but then his wife and daughter are savagely murdered. Nick arranges a plea bargain: One of the guilty men will be executed, and the other, in return for his testimony, will get a murder conviction but not death.

Clyde can't believe this. He saw his family murdered. Both men are guilty. On this everyone agrees. Why is one allowed to live? Because, Nick explains, the case isn't airtight without the testimony, and if they lose, both men walk free. That's not good enough for Clyde, who has ten years to plot, plan, and simmer in his hatred.

That's the prologue. I won't go into detail about what happens next, except to observe that Clyde's first killing involves his penetration of the death row execution chamber itself—and that's before he's in prison. Is this guy Houdini, or does he have supernatural powers?

As his methods are uncovered, it's clear he's a nonmagical human being, but a clever one with remarkable resources. So remarkable, in fact, that they fly in the face of common sense. Movie super villains have a way of correctly predicting what everyone will do and making their plans on that basis. The explanation of Clyde's methods is preposterous, but it comes late enough that F. Gary Gray, the director, is first able to generate considerable suspense and a sense of dread.

Foxx and Butler make a well-matched pair in their grim determination. Colm Meaney is underused as Foxx's partner; we suspect he may be the accomplice, given the Law of Economy of Characters, but perhaps he has a different role to play. Leslie Bibb works well as Foxx's partner, Regina Hall as his wife, Annie Corley as the judge who experiences some surprises in her courtroom, and the powerful Viola Davis as the city mayor.

Law-Abiding Citizen is one of those movies you like more at the time than in retrospect. I mean, *come on,* you're thinking. Still, there's something to be said for a movie you like well enough at the time.

Leap Year ★ ★ ★

PG, 97 m., 2010

Amy Adams (Anna), Matthew Goode (Declan), Adam Scott (Jeremy), John Lithgow (Jack). Directed by Anand Tucker and produced by Gary Barber, Chris Bender, Roger Birnbaum, and Jake Weiner. Screenplay by Deborah Kaplan and Harry Elfont.

Amy Adams and Matthew Goode have the charm necessary to float a romantic comedy like *Leap Year,* and this is a story that needs their buoyancy. A sort of conspiracy forms between the audience and the screen: We know what has to happen, and the movie knows what has to happen, and the point is to keep us amused. *Leap Year* did better than that: It made me care. It did that by not being too obvious about what it was obviously trying to do.

Let's start off on the same page. A sweet but over-organized young woman named Anna (Amy Adams) has been dating a high-powered heart surgeon named Jeremy (Adam Scott) for four years. He's pleasant, attentive, presentable, and shares her goal of buying a condo in the best building in Boston. He does nothing, absolutely nothing wrong. For veteran filmgoers, he has one fatal flaw: He has a healthy head of hair, and every strand is perfectly in place. No modern movie hero can have his hair combed.

When, oh when, will Jeremy ask Anna to marry him? After dashing her hopes once again, he hurries off to Dublin for a cardiologists' convention because as we all know it's a professional necessity for cardiologists to meet in faraway places. Anna is told that in Ireland on Leap Day, every four years, a woman can ask a man to marry her. Anna double-checks on the Web, somehow not discovering that this is believed nearly everywhere, and if a man in Denmark turned her down, he would have to buy her a pair of gloves.

Anna flies off to Ireland. The flight lasts only long enough for her to survive severe turbulence. The plane is diverted to Cardiff. Is there *anyone* in the theater surprised that she didn't arrive in Dublin on schedule? Despite canceled ferry boats, she makes her way to Ireland by hiring a tugboat. The skipper says they can't land at Cork but must head for Dingle. Dingle in Ireland is more or less as far as you can get from Wales (or Dublin), but never mind.

We know what's coming. Anna must meet her costar, Declan, played by Matthew Goode as the owner of the local pub. I suspect business has fallen off there ever since Robert Mitchum left after filming *Ryan's Daughter* in 1969. Anna is now wet and tired, but still plucky. In the pub, she asks Declan how she can get to Dublin. Turns out Declan is not only the publican but the taxi driver and runs the local hotel. They get a good smile out of this, but wouldn't you be asking yourself why neither one mentions "Local Hero"?

OK, enough fooling with the plot. Let's agree it stays firmly on course, and that Anna and Declan argue all the way to Dublin through adventures that, by law, must include getting all muddy and being forced to share a bedroom together. Therefore, the success of the film depends on the acting and direction.

Amy Adams and Matthew Goode sell it with great negative chemistry and appeal. Adams has an ability to make things seem fresh and new; everything seems to be happening to her for the first time, and she has a particularly innocent sincerity that's convincing. (Who was it that said if you can fake sincerity, you can fake anything?) Goode is wisely not made too handsome. Oh, you could shoot him as handsome; he's good-looking, let's face it. But the director, Anand Tucker, shoots him as annoyed, rude, and scruffy. Hair not too well combed.

Then take another look at Jeremy (Adam Scott). I'm not going to say he's too handsome. All I have to say is that in a silent movie he could simply walk on the screen and you'd know he's not going to get the girl. The movie carefully avoids making him a heavy. It's rather clever: He smoothly does more or less exactly what she's trained him to do, and what he doesn't understand is that she no longer believes in that version of him.

Bottom line: This is a full-bore, PG-rated, sweet romantic comedy. It sticks to the track, makes all the scheduled stops, and bears us triumphantly to the station. And it is populated by colorful characters, but then, when was the last time you saw a boring Irishman in a movie?

Leaves of Grass ★ ★ ★ ★

R, 105 m., 2010

Edward Norton (Bill Kincaid, Brady Kincaid), Tim Blake Nelson (Bolger Tim), Susan Sarandon (Daisy Kincaid), Keri Russell (Janet), Richard Dreyfuss (Pug Rothbaum), Steve Earle (Buddy Fuller). Directed by Tim Blake Nelson and produced by Nelson, Elie Cohn, Kristina Dubin, John Langley, William Migliore, and Edward Norton.

Tim Blake Nelson's *Leaves of Grass* is some kind of sweet, wacky masterpiece. It takes all sorts of risks, including a dual role with Edward Norton playing twin brothers, and it pulls them off. It is certainly the most intelligent, philosophical, and poetic film I can imagine that involves five murders in the marijuana-dealing community of Oklahoma and includes John Prine singing "Illegal Smile."

Sometimes you can't believe your luck as a movie unfolds. There is a mind behind it, joyful invention, obvious ambition. As is often the case, I had studiously avoided reading anything at all about *Leaves of Grass* before going to see the movie, although I rather doubted it would be about Walt Whitman. What I did know is that the actor Tim Blake Nelson has written and directed three films I enormously admired: *Eye of God* (1997), *O* (2001), and *The Grey Zone* (2001), all three dealing in a concrete dramatic way with important questions: religion, redemption, race, the Holocaust; and that the actor Edward Norton has never agreed to appear in a film he didn't believe he had reason to respect.

The film opens with Norton as a philosopher named Bill Kincaid giving a lecture on Socrates to a packed classroom of starstruck students at Brown. It's a measure of Nelson's writing and Norton's acting that this lecture isn't a sound bite but is allowed to continue until the professor develops his point, and it's an interesting one. Only as I think back do I realize what an audacious way that is to open a movie about the drug culture of rural Oklahoma.

SPOILER WARNING: Kincaid is on the fast track. He's published books, is a crossover intellectual superstar, is offered a chance to open his own department at Harvard. Then he gets a telephone call telling him his twin brother, Brady, is dead. He has long since severed his old family ties, but he flies home for the funeral to Little Dixie, Oklahoma, and is met at the airport by his twin's best friend (Nelson). As it turns out, Brady is not dead, and the story was a lie designed to lure him back home for two purposes. One is to force him to see his mother, a 1960s pothead played by Susan Sarandon. The other is to act as his double to establish an alibi while Brady goes up to Tulsa for a meeting with the region's dominant marijuana dealer, Pug Rothbaum (Richard Dreyfuss).

Now I will abandon synopsis and consider the pleasures of the film. First there's the dual performance by Norton, who is flawless as both an elite intellectual and a good ol' boy. In appearance, movement, and dialect he's for all intents two different people, one who has reinvented himself and shed his down-home roots, the other who is growing the best marijuana around. I like the way the film makes the twins equally brilliant; Brady has designed and built a hydroponic farm that is producing its seventh generation of top-quality weed. He is also something of a philosopher himself. In writing his dialogue, Nelson doesn't condescend. He is a Tulsa native who dismisses the widespread notion that a man's "hick" accent (the movie's word) provides a measure of his intelligence. Brady sounds like a semiliterate redneck, but he's very smart.

Faithful readers will know I am much occupied with the various definitions of God. Here is Brady's theory, as explained to his best buddy: There is a God, but man can never conceive of him or know him, because God is perfect and we cannot know perfection. Take for an example parallel lines extending to infinity. There can never be indefinitely parallel lines demonstrating themselves in the real, physical world, because it does not admit of parallelism. That is widely understood. Ah, but man can conceive of parallel lines, and prove them absolutely by mathematics. Just so with Brady's God. We can form an idea of perfection reaching into infinity, but we live in a universe that will never—can never—intersect with his. Rather elegant thinking, wouldn't you say, as expressed in Brady's own pothead barroom vernacular in the cab of a pickup truck with a shotgun rack.

I suspect there's a lot of Tim Blake Nelson in this film that is buried out of sight. Some elements are visible. That would include the Jewish community of Tulsa, which Nelson affectionately describes as "wildly eccentric, unlikely, and exotic." The plot includes not only Rothbaum, the drug lord and well-known charitable benefactor, but Ken Feinman (Josh Pais), the financially desperate orthodontist who finds himself bizarrely drawn into the plot. As is Rabbi Zimmerman (Maggie Siff), who explains to Billy Kincaid her belief that the world is broken and our duty is to try to fix it.

Another valuable character is Janet (Keri Russell), a local English teacher and poet, who quotes Whitman to Billy and entrances him in a way he has never before allowed. I suspect Janet has personal meaning to Nelson. In a press conference he said he is grateful to have been raised around books and rhetoric, and much of his dialogue here may be payback. Yes, but also always perfectly appropriate and in tune.

The plot involves as many dead and severely wounded bodies lying around as in *Blood Simple*, and Nelson weaves it expertly without a lot of visible "plotting." The story is the terrain the characters move through, and they are always the foreground. What stands out is the ability of both Billy and Brady (perhaps even more Brady) to understand the world philosophically and deal with it intellectually.

Here's a quote for the video box: "One of the year's best!" No, Tim Blake Nelson . . . thank *you*.

Leaving ★ ★

NO MPAA RATING, 85 m., 2010

Kristin Scott Thomas (Suzanne), Sergi Lopez (Ivan), Yvan Attal (Samuel). Directed by Catherine Corsini and produced by Michel Seydoux and Fabienne Vonier. Screenplay by Corsini and Gaelle Mace.

The French are considered, especially by themselves, to be expert in the arts of romance. Their films about love are often adult, thoughtful, perceptive, and observant. In order to preserve that reputation, they should have refused an export license to *Leaving*. Here we have characters who couldn't figure their way out of a Dr. Phil show.

We begin with the premise that sexual passion is sufficient to compel a French woman in her forties to abandon her husband and two children, her home, her profession, her reputation, and her credit cards in order to recline in the arms of a Spanish handyman who is an ex-con with no funds. He must be very handy indeed. She experiences love at first sight, a *coup de foudre*.

Suzanne (Kristin Scott Thomas) is in a loveless marriage with Samuel (Yvan Attal), a doctor. He is proper and polite, expects his meals on time, takes pride in his possessions, and agrees to remodel a room in one of their outbuildings so she can resume her practice of reflexology. Ivan (Sergi Lopez) turns up to perform this task, and soon they are reflexing to the same drummer.

Oh, it is love. Mad, heedless love. She can hardly wait to confess to her husband, because she cannot lie. Perhaps this compulsion can be understood because Suzanne is British. It explains something about the two nations that in the United Kingdom people sometimes have tea between five and seven, and in

France they sometimes have *cinq à sept*, which you're going to have to look up for yourself. Suzanne could have avoided much unhappiness if she had only been able to keep a secret.

Suzanne is not only impetuous, but doesn't seem to know her husband very well. Samuel isn't a good sport. He demands his wife back. She should get out in that kitchen and rattle those pots and pans. He cuts off her allowance, freezes the bank account, cancels the credit cards, pulls strings to make both Ivan and Suzanne unemployable, and otherwise inconveniences them.

This makes no difference. In Ivan's arms she's like a teenager with her first boyfriend. He takes her to visit a ruined stone cottage on a remote hillside, and she dreams that they'll build a little love nest. Ivan keeps a cool head. He usually has good advice. He's in love, but he's not nuts. Now with Suzanne: I knew you could get galloping pneumonia, but I hadn't heard about galloping erotomania.

Still, I want to say a word in praise of Kristin Scott Thomas. She is a splendid actress. Because she's perfectly bilingual, she finds challenging roles in France while Hollywood would reduce her to playing Magical Women. (These are like Spike Lee's Magical Negroes—wise and kind characters who have nothing to do in the plot but stand around being wise and kind.) Sometimes in the past Thomas has seemed to be, well, a little brittle. Here she is warm, soft, and lovable. When she cuddles Ivan he purrs. Thomas walks around in jeans and a T-shirt and has that Isabelle Huppert lifelong little girl look. She's good. Pity about the movie.

Le Quattro Volte ★ ★ ★ ½

NO MPAA RATING, 88 m., 2011

Giuseppe Fuda (Shepherd), Bruno Timpano and Nazareno Timpano (Charcoal Workers). Directed by Michelangelo Frammartino and produced by Philippe Bober, Marta Donzelli, Elda Guidinetti, Gabriella Manfre, Susanne Marian, Gregorio Paonessa, Andres Pfaffli. Screenplay by Frammartino.

Here is a film that invites philosophical musing. Made without dialogue and often in long shots, it regards the four stages of existence in a remote Italian village. Those stages, as set down 2,500 years ago by Pythagoras, are animal, vegetable, mineral, and intellectual. It's not necessary to know that or anything else to watch *Le Quattro Volte*, which doesn't require active interpretation but invites meditation and musing. I drifted pleasantly in its depths.

The camera usually keeps a certain distance, so it isn't telling a story but observing daily life. A very old shepherd climbs with effort after his goats on a hillside, while his dog barks and is a busybody. The shepherd returns to the village and waits as an old woman sweeps the dust from the church floor. Some of this dust he mixes with water and drinks as a remedy.

Events unfold slowly. In one unbroken shot of some duration, we see the dog somehow sets into motion a truck, which rolls down an incline and breaks open an enclosure holding the goats. The goats wander into the village. In another shot, the dog hurries down a road, encounters some walkers, and hurries back. Usually trained animals don't perform at such a distance from their masters. That's not the point of the shots, but of course you think of things like that.

Other shots. A smoldering coal-black heap, tamped down by workers. A tall tree felled. The erection of the tree in the town. Processions. A funeral. The sudden and unceremonious birth of a goat. The adventures of this kid. Human affairs seen at such a distance they seem isolated by the objectivity of history. Goat affairs seen closely as the mother licks her newborn.

The director, Michelangelo Frammartino, has made a serene and beautiful film. Its visuals cover the animal, vegetable, and mineral stages in our infinitesimal bit of the universe. Our thoughts, and his, supply the fourth stage. The title can be translated as *The Four Realms*. The four realms . . . of what? It doesn't say. Perhaps the four realms of everything that is.

Often I felt no need to bring the images up to the level of verbal thought. I observed the old shepherd's difficult passage through life, I noticed how quiet and empty the village seems to be, I actually thought about what it would be like to live there, who one would talk with, how one could find books or movies, and whether all the citizens are as ritual-bound as those we see.

I also thought about charcoal. I had no idea how it was created. Then I thought about goats. I like to visit them in their enclosure in the farm at the Lincoln Park Zoo. Their step is so nimble, their behavior so alert. They are tactful animals, ever so much more graceful than pigs or sheep. I started thinking, forgive me, about goat curry. Then I started thinking about what I was thinking. You might be surprised how absorbed you become during this film.

Let Me In ★ ★ ★ ½

R, 115 m., 2010

Chloe Grace Moretz (Abby), Kodi Smit-McPhee (Owen), Richard Jenkins (The Father), Elias Koteas (The Policeman), Cara Buono (Owen's Mother), Sasha Barrese (Virginia). Directed by Matt Reeves and produced by Alexander Yves Brunner, Guy East, Donna Gigliotti, Carl Molinder, John Nordling, Simon Oakes, and Nigel Sinclair. Screenplay by Reeves, based on the screenplay and novel *Let the Right One In* by John Ajvide Lindqvist.

"I've been twelve for a very long time."

Let Me In, like the Swedish film that inspired it, deals brutally with the tragic life of the vampire. It's not all fun, games, and Team Edward. No lifestyle depending on fresh human blood can be anything but desperate. A vampire, like a drug addict, is driven by need. After a certain point, all else is irrelevant and the focus is on the craving.

The film is remarkably similar in tone and approach to *Let the Right One In*, and it is clear the American writer-director, Matt Reeves, has admiration for the Swedish writer-director, John Ajvide Lindqvist. He understands what made the first film so eerie and effective, and here the same things work again. Most U.S. audiences will be experiencing the story for the first time. Those who know the 2008 version will notice some differences, but may appreciate them.

The core story remains similar. Owen, a boy on the brink of adolescence, lives a lonely life in a snowbound apartment complex with an alcoholic mother, hardly seen. He is bullied at school by a sadistic boy, much larger. A girl named Abby and her father move into the next apartment. She announces, "I can never be your friend," but some latent kindness causes her to feel protective toward the lonely and abused child. Abby is a vampire, but vampires have their reality forced upon them and, having lived for a long time, may have seen much to make them pity the living.

The story focuses tightly on Owen (Kodi Smit-McPhee) and Abby (Chloe Grace Moretz, of *Kick-Ass*). Two other adults are of consequence: Her "father" (Richard Jenkins), who can hardly be her father and was probably, long ago, in Owen's shoes. In vampire lore he is her Familiar. The other adult is a local policeman, played by Elias Koteas as a saturnine and solemn man. He's investigating a serial killer in the region. Where there are vampires, there must always be serial killers.

The night and the cold are also characters. The film is shot in chill tones of blue and gray, Owen and Abby have uncanny pale skin, there is frost on his breath, but not on hers. She doesn't feel the cold, we gather. Or the warmth. Many of the events are the same in both films, although the U.S. version adds one surprise that comes at a useful time to introduce frightening possibilities: This is not a safe world, and bad things can happen.

Both films end with scenes set in a swimming pool at night. The windows, high up under the ceiling to admit sunlight, are dark and cold. We can imagine the clammy tiles, the chill in the locker room where Owen is so often picked on. The bullies call him a "girl," and seem obsessed with seeing his genitals—homophobic cruelty that casts a sad light on the first film's revelation about Abby's body. Both these characters feel sexually threatened or inadequate. It may only be me, but as I recall indoor swimming pools at night in winter (at high school, or the YMCA), they always had a whiff of mournful dread.

In the *Twilight* films, sexuality is treated as a tease. The handsome Edward is cast as a sexy but dangerous threat, who manfully holds back from sex with Bella Swan. She's tempted, but the films are cautionary fables about the danger of teenage sex. In *Let Me In*, sex is seen more as a troubling encroachment on privacy. Owen and Abby for their own reasons quail from intimacy and contact, and their only sensuous moments involve the comfort of close, tender hugs.

Where this will lead is easy to guess. Owen will move into Abby's life as her next Familiar. She will protect him. Among the things she will save him from is the necessity of growing up and functioning as a normal male. She will control everything. Thus Bella's sweet masochism will become Owen's hunger to give over control. To be a servant is the price for not being a victim. Those hoping to see a "vampire movie" will be surprised by a good film.

Letters to Juliet ★ ★ ★

PG, 101 m., 2010

Amanda Seyfried (Sophie), Vanessa Redgrave (Claire), Christopher Egan (Charlie), Gael Garcia Bernal (Victor), Franco Nero (Lorenzo Bartolini). Directed by Gary Winick and produced by Ellen Barkin, Mark Canton, Eric Feig, Caroline Kaplan, and Patrick Wachsberger. Screenplay by Jose Rivera and Tim Sullivan.

I know *Letters to Juliet* is soppy melodrama, and I don't mind in the least. I know the ending is preordained from the setup. I know the characters are broad and comforting stereotypes. In this case, I simply don't care. Sometimes we have personal reasons for responding to a film.

Letters to Juliet is about Sophie (Amanda Seyfried), an American girl who visits Verona with the man she's engaged to marry (Gael Garcia Bernal). He's always leaving her behind to investigate wine and truffles for his New York restaurant. She visits the house allegedly inhabited by Shakespeare's Juliet. Below the balcony there, lovelorn women for years have posted "letters to Juliet" asking for advice.

Sophie finds a letter fifty years old, written by a young British girl about a Tuscan boy she met, fell in love with, and allowed to fall out of her life. Sophie writes to the girl, the letter amazingly finds its way, and soon Claire (Vanessa Redgrave) and her grandson, Charlie (Christopher Egan), arrive in Verona. So now, if we're experienced moviegoers, we know what must happen by the end of the story.

All of this is wrapped up in unimaginably beautiful shots of the Italian countryside, the warmth of the friendship between Sophie and Claire, and visits to many men named Lorenzo Bartolini, which was the name of the boy Claire loved so long ago. A hard-hearted realist would suggest that Sophie help Claire check out the possible Lorenzo Bartolinis on the phone, but no. *Letters to Juliet* requires the three of them to visit the candidates in person, leading to a series of false leads and at last, of course, to the real Lorenzo Bartolini (Franco Nero).

As it happens, this story stirred romantic memories in my own life. Once in a small hill town outside Rome, under a full moon, I stood before the balcony being used by Franco Zeffirelli for his great film *Romeo and Juliet* (1968), and heard Nino Rota hum his theme music to Zeffirelli. Some years later, I stood beneath Juliet's balcony in Verona itself with a woman dear to my heart, and saw the notes pinned to the wall.

And the very first movie set I ever visited, before I was yet a movie critic, was *Camelot* (1967). On that set I met and interviewed Vanessa Redgrave, who was not yet thirty, and Franco Nero, who was twenty-six. They played Guenevere and Lancelot. They fell in love on the set and had a child. They took separate paths for years, but on New Year's Eve 2006, they married. Even earlier, Franco walked Vanessa's daughter Natasha Richardson down the aisle when she married Liam Neeson.

So you see, when Vanessa marries Franco forty years after falling in love with him, and they are playing characters who meet after fifty years, and this all has to do with Juliet's balcony—reader, what am I to do? I am helpless before such forces.

Vanessa Redgrave recently lost her sister, Lynn. I met Lynn once in London. I went to her house for tea. This was not long after the success of *Georgy Girl.* My interview has been lost in the past, but I remember the feeling of the day, Lynn sitting cross-legged on the carpet beside her coffee table, smoking and jolly, a famous actress friendly to an unknown kid her own age.

I have strayed far from the film. But I've told you what you need to know about it. I also want to observe that our response to every film depends on the person we bring to it. Pauline Kael said she went to a movie, and the movie happened, and she wrote about what changed within her after she saw it. This is quite valid. Sometimes, however, we go to a movie, and our lives have happened, and we write about what hasn't changed.

Life As We Know It ★ ★

PG-13, 113 m., 2010

Katherine Heigl (Holly Berenson); Josh Duhamel (Eric Messer); Josh Lucas (Sam); Alexis, Brynn, and Brooke Clagett (Sophie); Hayes MacArthur (Peter Novack); Christina Hendricks (Alison Novack). Directed by Greg Berlanti and produced by Paul Brooks and Barry Josephson. Screenplay by Ian Deitchman and Kristin Rusk Robinson.

Awww. Their best friends are killed in an auto accident, leaving behind their cute little one-year-old daughter, Sophie. Holly and Messer are appointed in the will as Sophie's joint custodians. Alas, Holly and Messer (Katherine Heigl and Josh Duhamel) can't stand each other. But the will specifies they should move into their friends' home, so Sophie won't miss her own room.

Awww. Sophie is just as cute as most one-year-old babies. She's always ready to roll, maybe because she's got backup; the character is played by triplets (Alexis, Brynn, and Brooke Clagett). Holly and Messer know nothing 'bout raisin' no babies. The first emergency comes when Sophie does do-do in her diaper.

Awww. This is really sad. Holly and Messer have to share the same enormous Atlanta mansion. I think it has room for an indoor one-hundred-yard dash. Although their friends Peter and Alison (Hayes MacArthur and Christina Hendricks) were young, they must have been loaded. "The mortgage is prepaid for a year," the lawyer tells Holly and Messer. How many people can say that?

Awww, this is never gonna work out. Messer is a tomcat on the prowl. Hell, that first night he met Holly on a blind date set up by Peter and Alison, he had another date lined up for later. And Holly—well, she's one of your organized types, spic and span, not a mess like Messer. Plus, she maybe has a crush on Sam (Josh Lucas), the handsome pediatrician.

Awww, I gotta admit, I liked the actors. Katherine Heigl and Josh Duhamel do what they can with this off-season TV material, and Josh Lucas is awfully nice, which of course a kindly young pediatrician would have to be to almost win the heart of Katherine Heigl. But the film is so clunky. It's not every rom-com that starts out with the tragic deaths of the parents of a one-year-old and moves right on to the poop jokes.

So anyway, what happens in the movie? You'll never guess in a million years. Never. You might just as well give up. I don't like spoilers, so just let me say Holly and Sam adopt Sophie and live happily in the mansion forever after. Awww.

Life During Wartime ★ ★ ½

NO MPAA RATING, 98 m., 2010

Shirley Henderson (Joy Jordan), Ciaran Hinds (Bill Maplewood), Gaby Hoffman (Wanda), Allison Janney (Trish Maplewood), Michael Lerner (Harvey Weiner), Chris Marquette (Billy Maplewood), Rich Pecci (Mark Weiner), Charlotte Rampling (Jacqueline), Paul Reubens (Andy), Ally Sheedy (Helen Jordan), Dylan Riley Snyder (Timmy Maplewood), Renee Taylor (Mona Jordan), Michael Kenneth Williams (Allen). Directed by Todd Solondz and produced by Derrick Tseng and Christine K. Walker. Screenplay by Solondz.

There's always rationing in wartime. What's rationed in Todd Solondz's *Life During Wartime* are feelings of hope, kindness, and optimism. His people are disturbed, pleading, and often perverse, and indeed some of them are so badly off they're dead and must appear as ghosts to make their complaints. Always the kvetching, from beyond the grave yet.

Solondz describes the film as "a quasi-sequel" to his great *Happiness* (1998). If ever there was a film where the characters' lives were over at the end, it's that one. Solondz brought closure. Now, twelve years later, wondering what happened to his people after that film ended, he approaches entropic collapse.

Well, they aged at different rates. They turned

into different people, played by different actors, while keeping the same names. Allen, played by Philip Seymour Hoffman in the first film, morphed into a black man (Michael Kenneth Williams), although Hoffman and Williams are still two of the three actors in either film with three names. The genders of the various characters are the same, although the gender behavior is far from conventional. These people are stuck in their minds and can't bring happiness to themselves or others. Only the children can be happy, and in the Solondz world their innocence is a time bomb.

I could supply here a listing of the major characters in the 1998 film and the actors who played them. Can you remember the names of movie characters for twelve years? I can't, not unless they're named Marge Gunderson or Anton Chigurh, but in this film, Joy (Shirley Henderson) talks like a middle-age little girl, and once again finds herself stuck in restaurants in mutual misery with a man. This time it's Allen (Williams), who has moved on from dirty phone calls and wankery to gangbanging and despair.

The man Joy had her agonizing date with in the first film has now become the dead Andy (Paul Reubens), whose ghost torments her (again in a restaurant booth) with piteous pleas. Later, Williams also appears to her as a ghost, urging her to kill herself. Her men have a way of not getting everything done in one lifetime.

Trish (Alison Janney) has moved to Florida to help her children escape the reputation of their pedophile father. They think he's dead. But Bill (Ciaran Hinds) is on parole and unwisely wants to meet his older boy at college. Trish is dating Harvey (Michael Lerner), so devastated by a divorce he fears he's forgotten how to perform sex. To the degree that he remembers, he's sure that he can't. Trish's younger son, Timmy (Dylan Riley Snyder, in a performance that evokes great sympathy), is preparing for his bar mitzvah when he discovers his father was a pedophile—not good news on the day he becomes a man.

Trish has tried to break with her past and start anew in Florida. Her sister Helen (Ally Sheedy) is a thriving Hollywood screenwriter, driven and unfulfilled. Joy is the third sibling. For these three sisters, Chekhov would be the Marx Brothers. One of the best performances in the film is by Charlotte Rampling as the last woman in the world who Bill, the reforming pedophile, should choose as his partner in grown-up sex. These people live in interiors as barren as demonstration homes. They don't have much stuff around. Ed Lachman, the cinematographer, almost sees them as on a stage set, "suggesting" the rooms where they live.

This is the Solondz world. I think he's a brilliant filmmaker. He evokes so effectively his own point of view, which is appalling and compulsive. You can imagine his screenplays being read aloud in his distinctive voice, which seems to embed in every word a querulous complaint against—well, everything. When he's good (*Palindromes*, *Storytelling*, *Welcome to the Dollhouse*), few can touch him. Here he's made a film that is sad without energy, dead without life. As a sequel to *Happiness*, it regards the same lives, then as tragedy, now as farce.

Limitless ★ ★ ½

PG-13, 105 m., 2011

Bradley Cooper (Eddie Morra), Abbie Cornish (Lindy), Robert De Niro (Carl Van Loon), Anna Friel (Melissa), Andrew Howard (Gennady). Directed by Neil Burger and produced by Leslie Dixon, Ryan Kavanaugh, and Scott Kroopf. Screenplay by Dixon, based on a novel by Alan Glynn.

I know how Eddie Morra feels. Like him, I know almost everything but have forgotten most of it. We are told time and again that we use only a small portion of our brains and have enough left over to run nations in our down time. *Limitless* is about Eddie's adventures after his ex-brother-in-law gives him a pill that suddenly puts his entire brain online.

He finishes his novel at typing speed. He wins at poker, invests in the market, and runs it up to millions. He fascinates a woman who had rejected him as a loser. He knows intuitively how to handle situations that used to baffle him. He is hailed as the Wall Street guru of the age.

Eddie is played by Bradley Cooper as a schlub who becomes a king. This sort of mental rags-to-riches progression has inspired a lot of movies; ever see Cliff Robertson in *Charly* (1968)? The difference here is that Eddie Morra remains himself before and after, and all that changes is his ability to recall everything he ever saw or heard. *Limitless* assumes that would be a benefit and make him rich, but what if most of what he ever saw or heard about Wall Street was wrong (as it usually is)?

The movie sidesteps the problem that what we need is more intelligence and a better ability to reason, not a better memory. For memory, modern man has Google. There's no need to stumble over such technicalities, however. Given its premise, *Limitless* is passably entertaining. Abbie Cornish plays Lindy, the successful young professional woman who dumps Eddie as a loser and falls for him all over again when he becomes a winner. This is not sneaky on her part; there is every reason to dump the original Eddie and many good ones to return.

Eddie grows entangled in three problems. One has to do with the source of the magic pills; the ex-brother-in-law is no longer in a position to reveal it. The second has to do with a mob loan shark who liked being smart and wants to get that way again.

The third involves Carl Van Loon, played by Robert De Niro as one of the richest men in America. He hires Eddie as an investment magician, Eddie loses his touch when he runs out of pills, he regains it, and so on. De Niro is not well used in the role because he plays Van Loon straight and in one dimension. Don't you suppose he could have been supplied with a quirk of his own? The twist at the end comes too late.

Bradley Cooper fits well into the two versions of Eddie Morra, and director Neil Burger does inventive visual effects in showing how time telescopes for Eddie and the answers to problems seem to materialize before his eyes. A subplot about a murder, however, raises questions it doesn't answer, and all the quasi-criminal stuff seems a little perfunctory. The movie is not terrifically good, but the premise is intriguing; it doesn't really set out to explore what such a pill might really do to a person. *Limitless* uses only 15, maybe 20 percent of its brain. Still, that's more than a lot of movies.

The Limits of Control ★ ½

R, 116 m., 2009

Isaach De Bankole (Lone Man), Alex Descas (Creole), Jean-Francois Stevenin (French), Luis Tosar (Violin), Paz de la Huerta (Nude), Tilda Swinton (Blonde), Youki Kudoh (Molecules), John Hurt (Guitar), Gael Garcia Bernal (Mexican), Hiam Abbass (Driver), Bill Murray (American). Directed by Jim Jarmusch and produced by Stacey Smith and Gretchen McGowan. Screenplay by Jarmusch.

I am the man in *The Limits of Control.* I cannot tell you my name because the screenplay has not given me one. There's only room for so many details in 116 minutes. Call me The Man With No Name. I wander through Spain saying as little as possible, as Clint Eastwood did in films I enjoyed as a boy. Now I am a man, handsome, exotic, cool, impenetrable, hip, mysterious, quiet, coiled, enigmatic, passive, stoic, and hungry.

On my journey, I enter cafés and always specify the same order: "Two espressos, in two separate cups." In each café, I am met by a contact. I exchange matchboxes. The one I hand over is filled with diamonds. The one I am given contains a note on a small piece of paper, which I eat. I meet strange people. I do not know them. They know me. I am the one with two espressos in two separate cups. One is a beautiful young woman, always nude, whom I would like to get to know better, but not in this movie.

The writer and director of the film is Jim Jarmusch. I've seen several of his movies and even appeared in a couple. This one takes the cake. He is making some kind of a point. I think the point is that if you strip a story down to its bare essentials, you will have very little left. I wonder how he pitched this idea to his investors.

As an actor, my name is Isaach De Bankole. I have the opportunity to appear in scenes with actors who are known for the chances they take. Sometimes an actor like that will prove nothing except that he is loyal to his friends or a good sport. Bill Murray is appearing so frequently in such films I think it is time for him to star in a smutty action comedy. The other good sports include Tilda Swinton, Gael Garcia Bernal, John Hurt, and Paz de la

Huerta, who is nude all the time. That's a good sport and a half.

My acting assignment was not so hard. I costarred with Mathieu Amalric in *The Diving Bell and the Butterfly.* He played a man whose movement was restricted to one eye. Now there was a tough assignment. I acted in Lars von Trier's *Manderlay,* where the locations were suggested by chalk lines on the floor of a sound stage. Not as much fun as Spanish cafés. I starred in the Quebec film *How to Make Love to a Negro Without Getting Tired,* and I played the Negro, but I was the one who got tired.

So I'm not complaining. We actors enjoyed Spain. Often we would gather for a dinner of paella and sangria. One night Bill Murray quoted Gene Siskel: "I ask myself if I would enjoy myself more watching a documentary of the same actors having dinner." We all sat and thought about that, as the night breeze blew warm through the town and a faraway mandolin told its tale.

We were pretty sure it would be a good-looking movie. Jarmusch was working with the cameraman Christopher Doyle, and they spent a lot of time discussing their palette, figuring their exposure, and framing their compositions. That reminded me of a silent film named *Man with a Movie Camera,* which some people think is the best film ever made. It shows a man with a movie camera, photographing things. Was Jarmusch remaking it without the man and the camera?

The Lincoln Lawyer ★ ★ ★

R, 118 m., 2011

Matthew McConaughey (Mick Haller), Marisa Tomei (Maggie McPherson), Ryan Phillippe (Louis Roulet), Josh Lucas (Ted Minton), John Leguizamo (Val Valenzuela), Michael Peña (Jesus Martinez), Frances Fisher (Mary Windsor), Bryan Cranston (Detective Lankford), William H. Macy (Frank Levin). Directed by Brad Furman and produced by Sidney Kimmel, Gary Lucchesi, Tom Rosenberg, Scott Steindorff, and Richard S. Wright. Screenplay by John Romano, based on the novel by Michael Connelly.

I like movies about smart guys who are wiseasses and think their way out of tangles with criminals. I like courtroom scenes. I like big old cars. I like *The Lincoln Lawyer* because it involves all three, and because it matches Matthew McConaughey with a first-rate supporting cast while so many thrillers these days are about a lone hero surrounded by special effects. People have words they actually say in this movie. After *Battle: Los Angeles,* that is a great relief.

Let's start with the big old car. It's a Lincoln, and a lawyer named Mick Haller (McConaughey) does most of his work out of the backseat. Apparently he drove it himself until he was socked with a DUI; given how much he drinks in the film, it's amazing he remembered where he parked it. Now he has a chauffeur (Laurence Mason) who ferries him around to the Los Angeles dealers, hookers, bagmen, and lowlifes who are his clientele. Mick's specialty is getting people off, sometimes in a perfectly legal way.

There were decades in the movies when heroes drove new cars, unless it was a period picture. Carmakers used to pay for product placement. We saw Mustangs, GTOs, Chargers. But in recent years, action and thriller heroes have driven mostly classic cars, or oddballs like Hummers. The reason for this is obvious: Modern cars all look mostly the same, and none of them look heroic. Can you imagine James Bond in a Camry? My Ford Fusion gets good mileage, but Mick Haller would just look silly doing business out of the backseat. The only new cars still popular in movies are big black SUVs with tinted windows, which usually prowl in packs.

Anyway, Haller is a streetwise defense attorney with connections who knows how to collect and invest prudent envelopes full of cash. So connected is this guy that a motorcycle gang materializes more or less when he needs one. One day a bondsman (John Leguizamo) comes to him with a higher-class client than usual. Louis Roulet (Ryan Phillippe) is a rich kid from Beverly Hills accused of beating up a woman. He's clean-cut, looks Mick in the eyes, seriously insists he is innocent, and wants to go to trial to prove it.

Mick senses there is something fishy. So do I. If Roulet has unlimited funds and really is innocent, why is he hiring a guy who works out of the backseat of a car? I've seen a lot of crime movies and read my Raymond Chandler and Ross Macdonald. I know, even if Mick doesn't, that he's being used in some way.

Let's not get into the details. Details are interchangeable in movies like this. What you want is a laconic wise guy in the lead, and McConaughey does a nice line in those. You need a good dame in the picture. Marisa Tomei plays his ex-wife, courtroom opponent, and (still) friend. When Tomei walks into a movie, it's like the queen came into the room. I want to stand up. I know why Lady Gaga wants Marisa to play her in a biopic. It's not because they look like sisters. It's because every woman, and many men, would love to have a smile like Marisa Tomei's.

We also meet Mick's opposing attorney (Josh Lucas); a former client he plea-bargained into prison (Michael Peña); a cop who considers him a shyster (Bryan Cranston), and, most valuable, Mick's private investigator (William H. Macy). The PI role isn't very big, but Macy makes it distinctive; he brings it a quirky familiarity that creates a history between the two men without a lot of setup. You care for the hardworking sap.

All of this comes together in a satisfactory way. It isn't brilliant, it's far from foolproof, and the second appearance of the motorcycle gang technically qualifies, I think, as a miracle. The Law of Seemingly Unnecessary Characters comes nicely into play as events from the present turn out to be connected to the past. I did feel undercut by the movie's final revelation—which is, let's face it, completely arbitrary. The plotting seems like half-realized stabs in various directions made familiar by other crime stories. But for what it is, *The Lincoln Lawyer* is workmanlike, engagingly acted, and entertaining.

Little Ashes ★ ★ ★

R, 112 m., 2009

Javier Beltran (Federico Garcia Lorca), Robert Pattinson (Salvador Dali), Matthew McNulty (Luis Buñuel), Marina Gatell (Magdalena), Arly Jover (Gala). Directed by Paul Morrison and produced by Carlo Dusi, Jonny Persey, and Jaume Vilalta. Screenplay by Philippa Goslett.

It was a ripe time to live at the Students' Residence in Madrid and study at the School of Fine Arts. When he arrived from Catalonia in 1922, Salvador Dali met the future poet Federico Garcia Lorca and future filmmaker Luis Buñuel. Dali was a case study, dressed as a British dandy of the previous century with a feminine appearance. No doubt he was a gifted painter. He was to become a rather loathsome man.

Little Ashes focuses on an unconsummated romantic attraction between Dali (Robert Pattinson) and Garcia Lorca (Javier Beltran), who in the flower of youthful idealism and with the awakening of the flesh began to confuse sexuality with artistry. Not much is really known about their romance, such as it was, but in the conservative Catholic nation of the time and given Dali's extreme terror of syphilis, it seems to have been passionate but platonic.

It found release in their roles in the developing Surrealist movement, in which church, state, ideology, landowners, parents, authorities, and laws were all mocked by deliberately outlandish behavior. In 1929, Dali wrote and Buñuel directed probably the most famous of all Surrealist works, the film *Un Chien Andalou* (*The Andalusian Dog*), with its notorious images of a cloud slicing through the moon and a knife slicing through a woman's eyeball. In a time before computer imagery, it was a real eyeball (belonging to a pig, not a woman, but small comfort to the pig).

By 1936, Garcia Lorca was dead, murdered by Spanish fascists. The story is told in the film *The Disappearance of Garcia Lorca* (1997). Buñuel fled Spain to Mexico, then later returned as one of the world's greatest filmmakers. Dali betrayed his early talent, embraced fascism, Nazism, and communism, returned repentant to the Church, and become an odious caricature of an artist, obsessed by cash. "Each morning when I awake," he said, "I experience again a supreme pleasure—that of being Salvador Dali." Yes, but for a time he was a superb painter.

Little Ashes is a film that shows these personalities being formed. Because most audiences may not know much about Dali, Garcia Lorca, and Buñuel, it depends for its box-office appeal on the starring role of Robert Pattinson, the twenty-three-year-old British star of *Twilight*. He is the heartthrob of the teenage vampire fans of *Twilight*, but here shows an admirable willingness to take on a challenging role in direct contrast to the famous Edward Cullen. Is it too much to hope that *Twilight* fans will be drawn to the work of Garcia Lorca and Buñuel? They'd be on the fast track to cultural literacy.

Biopics about the youth of famous men are often overshadowed by their fame to come. *The Motorcycle Diaries,* for example, depended for much of its appeal on our knowledge that its young doctor hero would someday become Che Guevara. *Little Ashes* is interested in the young men for themselves.

It shows unformed young men starting from similar places but taking different roads because of their characters. Garcia Lorca, who is honest with himself about his love for another man, finds real love eventually with a woman, his classmate Magdalena (Marina Gatell). Dali, who presents almost as a transvestite, denies all feelings, and like many puritans ends as a voluptuary. Buñuel, the most gifted of all, ends as all good film directors do, consumed by his work. I am fond of his practical approach to matters. Warned that angry mobs might storm the screen at the Paris premiere of *Un Chien Andalou,* he filled his pockets with stones to throw at them.

The film is absorbing but not compelling. Most of its action is inward. The more we know about the three men the better. Although the eyeball-slicing is shown in the film, many audiences may have no idea what it is doing there. Perhaps Dali's gradual slinking away from his ideals, his early embrace of celebrity, and his preference for self-publicity over actual achievement makes better sense when we begin with his shyness and naivete; is he indeed entirely aware that his hair and dress are those of a girl, or has he been coddled in this way by a strict, protective mother who is hostile to male sexuality?

Whatever the case, two things stand out: He has the courage to present himself in quasi-drag, and the other students at the Residence, inspired by the fever in the air, accept him as "making a statement" he might not have been fully aware of.

I have long believed that one minute of wondering if you are about to be kissed is more erotic than an hour of kissing. Although a few gay sites complain *Little Ashes* doesn't deliver the goods, I find it far more intriguing to find how repressed sexuality expresses itself, because the bolder sort comes out in the usual ways and reduces mystery to bodily fluids. Orgasms are at their best when still making big promises, don't you find?

Looking for Eric ★ ★

NO MPAA RATING, 116 m., 2010

Steve Evets (Eric Bishop), Eric Cantona (Himself), Stephanie Bishop (Lily), Gerard Kearns (Ryan), John Henshaw (Meatballs), Lucy-Jo Hudson (Sam), Stefan Gumbs (Jess). Directed by Ken Loach and produced by Rebecca O'Brien. Screenplay by Paul Laverty.

Looking for Eric is the last film I would have expected from Ken Loach, the great British director of films about working-class lives. His strength is social realism and a critique of the limited options within a class system. He works close to the earth and to his characters.

Here now is a most unexpected comedy, appealing to world soccer fans and based on a common enough daydream: A man's sports hero appears in his life and carries on friendly conversations with him. I call it a fantasy, but Loach approaches it as if it were quite real. He uses Eric Cantona, a famed star of Manchester United, and places him right there in the room with Eric Bishop (Steve Evets), a Manchester postal worker badly in need of encouragement.

The outlines of Eric's life are grim. The film begins after he survives a car crash and involves his two worthless grown sons, Ryan and Jess, and his lingering feelings for his estranged wife, Lily (Stephanie Bishop), who has refused to speak to him in seven years.

Into this sad man's life steps Cantona, a superstar in all the soccer-playing world, who becomes his confidant and confessor. Cantona, it must be said, is quite successful in his role: warm, persuasive, a source of common sense. He diagnoses Eric's problem: He should get back together with Lily. This is also the plan of Sam (Lucy-Jo Hudson), Eric and Lily's grown daughter.

This counsel provides a reason for flashbacks showing Eric and Lily's romance in earlier years, very touching, causing us to hope they'll fall in love all over again. But, excuse me, why does this require brokering by an imaginary sports star? Cantona himself produced the film and may have been involved in the financing, which could explain how it came to be made. What I can't explain is why Loach chose to make it. Maybe after so many great films he simply wanted to relax with a genre comedy. It has charm and Loach's fine eye and an expected generic payoff. But it doesn't make any sense.

I had another problem I'm almost ashamed to admit. Loach has always made it a point to use actors employing working-class accents, reflecting the fact that accent is a class marker. I've usually been able to understand the characters in his movies; it's the music as much as the words to begin with, and then I start to hear the words. This time his star, Steve Evets, uses a Manchester accent so thick many of the English themselves might not be able to understand it. Ironically Eric Cantona, who is French, is easier to understand.

Looking for Eric is inexplicable. It has elements of a Loach social drama, which might have been better used as the entire story. Cantona is nice enough, but so what? If there seem to be any comic possibilities in the story, Loach doesn't find them. If your world doesn't revolve around Eric Cantona, he'll come over as just a nice enough guy, no big deal. And can the great Ken Loach actually have fallen prey to the Obligatory Action in the Third Act virus?

Lorna's Silence ★ ★ ★ ½

R, 105 m., 2009

Arta Dobroshi (Lorna), Jeremie Renier (Claudy), Fabrizio Rongione (Fabio), Alban Ukaj (Sokol), Morgan Marinne (Spirou). Directed by Jean-Pierre Dardenne and Luc Dardenne, and produced by Jean-Pierre Dardenne, Luc Dardenne, and Denis Freyd. Screenplay by Jean-Pierre Dardenne and Luc Dardenne.

The Dardenne brothers focus intently on individuals in their films, which are among the best in recent years. In such films as *Rosetta* (1999), *Le Fils* (*The Son*, 2002), and *L'Enfant* (*The Child*, 2005), their cameras scarcely allow the protagonists to escape the frame. *Lorna's Silence* begins that way but allows shots in which Lorna is not even present. A plot begins to unfold that she isn't aware of.

Lorna (Arta Dobroshi) is a young woman of about thirty from Albania, now living in Belgium. She is a beneficiary and exploiter of the marriage-for-sale racket. A pathetic drug addict named Claudy has married her for money, a vermin named Fabio has arranged this marriage, Fabio plans to arrange Claudy's death, a Russian will pay Lorna to marry him so he can obtain a passport, and then, Lorna believes, she will be free to marry her lover, Sokol. They even know the little storefront where they talk of opening a café.

It is all so shabby and sad. And dominating the early scenes is the character of Claudy (Jeremie Renier), who wants to quit heroin cold turkey and is a wretched, needy, trembling creature. Renier's performance is the best thing in the movie, although all the actors, cast partly for their faces, are part of creating this desperate world.

Lorna treats Claudy coldly. He telephones her incessantly. He is afraid to be left alone. Eventually his pathos wears her down; she's not an evil woman, just an opportunist. She wonders if it might not be possible for her to divorce Claudy, rather than clear the stage with an overdose—Fabio's plan.

The gift of Jean-Pierre and Luc Dardenne is to show their characters as trapped in personal human situations; they're not creatures of a plot. Fabio (Fabrizio Rongione), for example, isn't a "villain"; he is simply a man, brutal and heartless by nature and driven entirely by money. He has a callow flunky named Spirou (Morgan Marinne), who is as servile as a cur. Both Rongione and Marinne have the hard faces of bullies; you would feel wary of them on sight.

That's not to say they're that way in person. They may be jolly good chaps for all I know. Here they are reptilian. That's partly because the Dardennes shoot them mostly in profile; a full face seems open to us, but a side shot from an oblique angle can seem sinister. If everyone has a "good side," the Dardennes must figure out which it is, in order to avoid it.

All centers on Lorna. She is a pleasant-enough young woman, crisp, direct. I've seen photos of Arta Dobroshi with a warm smile.

In *Lorna's Silence,* she plays a woman who is deprived of her bodily integrity even more than a prostitute might be; she hasn't been bought and sold because of sex, but simply because of her gender. Claudy married her for money, the Russian doesn't care if he sleeps with her, and Sokol is a snaky man who is out of the country most of the time. His qualities exist mostly in her mind.

The Dardennes do something I haven't seen them do before. There is a considerable time lapse in the story, while basic changes take place with the characters. Lorna's nature shifts. I'm not saying this is bad, but it releases the tension they generate when they stay close in time and space. Still, what power is here. What affecting acting by Dobroshi, Renier (who in *L'Enfant* played the father who sold and desperately tried to rebuy his child), and Marinne (who was the apprentice with the dark past in *The Son*). In the cold, harsh world of the Dardennes, they feel sympathy but can grant little mercy.

The Losers ★ ★ ★ ½

PG-13, 98 m., 2010

Zoe Saldana (Aisha), Jeffrey Dean Morgan (Clay), Chris Evans (Jensen), Idris Elba (Roque), Columbus Short (Pooch), Oscar Jaenada (Cougar), Jason Patric (Max). Directed by Sylvain White and produced by Kerry Foster, Akiva Goldsman, and Joel Silver. Screenplay by Peter Berg and James Vanderbilt.

The Losers is a classical action movie based on a comic strip. It does just enough nodding toward the graphics of drawn superheroes, and then gets that out of the way and settles down into a clean, efficient, and entertaining thriller. It's a reminder of how exhausting this kind of material can be when it's brought to a manic level by overwrought directors. It looks, feels, and plays like a real movie. There is another reason to be grateful: It's not in 3-D. You have to treasure movies like this before they're entirely eaten away by the marketing gimmicks.

Story, straightforward, no gargoyles. Five tough guys on a mission against a drug lord in Bolivia. They abort the mission when they see a bus full of little kids arrive at the target. No luck. A voice named "Max" orders a plane to carry out a bombing run. The tough guys break in and rescue the kids just in time. A helicopter is sent for them. No room on the copter except for the kids. The copter is shot down, the kids die.

"That was supposed to be us," they say, regarding the smoldering wreckage. Close-up of flames still licking at a toy bear that was established earlier as belonging to a cute kid. Note: Whenever a kid gets on a copter in an action film and is told to take good care of his bear, the kid and the bear will go down in flames.

The tough guys rip off their dog tags and throw them on the flames. Now they're The Losers, dedicated to bringing the mysterious Max to justice. Who is he? They guess maybe CIA–Special Forces–Black Ops . . . nobody knows. Meanwhile, they're officially dead and stranded in Bolivia with no passports and no money.

Think I'm giving away too much? That's only the pre-title sequence. Then we meet them one by one: Clay (Jeffrey Dean Morgan), Jensen (Chris Evans), Roque (Idris Elba), Pooch (Columbus Short), and Cougar (Oscar Jaenada). Each has a specialty: command, ordnance, rockets, sniper, etc. They're rugged, macho, wisecracking. Clay is the highest-ranking officer, but he keeps saying, "We're not in the military now." Later, of course, he pulls rank.

Then we meet Aisha (Zoe Saldana). Saldana is a seriously beautiful woman. You didn't notice that so much in *Avatar.* She poses as a bar girl to seduce her way into Clay's room, and then they have a deadly fight, destroy the room, and burn down the hotel, and after that they're friends on the same side and Clay is convincing the others to trust her. I didn't quite follow this every step of the way.

Aisha knows who Max really is, where he is, and how to get him. And she has the resources to get The Losers into the United States, arm them, rent them helicopters, and so on. They want to avenge those kids. Can Aisha be trusted? It's not always clear. Nor is it clear at first exactly what Max is up to, although here's a first: He demonstrates the first green weapon of mass destruction. It totally destroys a target, yet adds no pollution to the atmosphere. How's that for progress? How he plans to use the weapon and what his super-secret computer files are for provide the movie's MacGuffin.

Max is played by Jason Patric, who can make a very snaky snark. The director, Sylvain White, contrives a nice little scene on the beach where Max's curvaceous servant shades him with an umbrella. The wind blows the umbrella aside for a second, and the shot becomes a perfect steal of that butler on the beach in the Jack Vettriano painting that became the largest-selling poster in British history. Then Max shoots her. That's not in the Vettriano.

The Losers knows what it's doing and how to do it. Sylvain White doesn't have a lot of credits, but he knows how to direct and not trip over his own feet. The movie gets the job done, and the actors show a lot of confidence in occupying that tricky middle ground between controlled satire and comic overkill. It's fun.

I noted that Zoe Saldana is beautiful. I noted something else. In keeping with the current popularity of cafe au lait complexions, the movie uses lighting and filters to bathe the romantic scenes in a kind of golden glow, so that Saldana and Morgan come out looking about the same. We're no longer making people of color look whiter in the movies; we're tinting people of whiteness. Time marches on.

The Loss of a Teardrop Diamond ★ ★ ★

PG-13, 102 m., 2010

Bryce Dallas Howard (Fisher Willow), Chris Evans (Jimmy Dobyne), Ellen Burstyn (Miss Addie), Mamie Gummer (Julie), Ann-Margret (Aunt Cornelia), Will Patton (Old Man Dobyne), Jessica Collins (Vinnie). Directed by Jodie Markell and produced by Brad Michael Gilbert. Screenplay by Tennessee Williams.

Soft summer nights, the moon low above the river, "Alice Blue Gown" drifting on the breeze, a rich Southern girl who tasted freedom in Paris and now pretends to desire Memphis society, a poor but honest boy, bitchy debutantes in pastel gowns, wary old ladies in wide-brimmed hats, an opium addict in agony, a good but drunken father, and down by the levee the ghosts of sharecroppers drowned by a rich man's dynamite.

The voice of Tennessee Williams calls to us across the twenty-six years since his death. It is not strong and fierce, but it is his. *The Loss of a Teardrop Diamond* is an original screenplay he wrote in the 1950s, never produced, long forgotten. It has been filmed in a respectful manner that feels like a touring production of an only moderately successful Broadway play. Understand that, accept it, and the film has its rewards and one performance of great passion.

That would be by Ellen Burstyn, Miss Addie, who plays it all in bed in her sickroom in a Tennessee country mansion with a debutante party going on downstairs. She has snared Fisher Willow (Bryce Dallas Howard) away from the party and ordered her to lock the doors. Addie lived for many years in Hong Kong, consoled by opium for her lost dreams. She remembers Fisher from a brief visit home. The girl struck her as hard and brave. Now she asks her to do something for her. Give her the pills that will allow her to die.

Fisher is very agitated, a word Tennessee might have liked. She has hired Jimmy Dobyne (Chris Evans), the good-looking poor boy whose alcoholic father manages her father's commissary, to be her escort to the party. She even measured him for his evening wear. Jimmy's grandfather was governor, but the family has fallen back to its knees. Addie senses all has not gone well on their date, discovers Jimmy didn't want to kiss Fisher when she parked on the riverbank, advises her to escape and go back to Europe.

These are all Williams tropes. The paralyzing stupidity of genteel society. The lure of Europe and the "arts," and escape itself. The drink, the drugs, the decay. The not-as-young woman hiring a gentleman caller and hoping for the kindness of strangers. Bryce Dallas Howard is affecting as Fisher, but not electrifying because the material doesn't have it in it. Chris Evans, as Jimmy, is reserved to the point of oddness: a straight arrow without the arrowhead. He may think he's channeling Paul Newman, but he evokes instead the new male lead on a soap opera.

There are extended scenes involving the party downstairs, everyone perfectly dressed. No one talks unless they have dialogue provided. They stand around murmuring like extras. Remember the party scene in Visconti's

The Leopard, all told in one shot, establishing characters and relationships? This party is as lifeless as the "pageant" staged earlier in a garden by drilled girls for bored old ladies.

And yet I relax and take it for what it is. I feel Tennessee's yearnings. I saw something of his life indirectly, at a remove. His brother Dakin lived in Chicago and was a frequent player on the newspaper drinking circuit; he announced his candidacy for governor at a press conference at Riccardo's. He wore a white pinstripe suit and a Panama hat. He had a platform, but the only plank you ever heard about was that he was the brother of Tennessee—and of Rose, you remember, the sister. He was a friendly man, courteous, sharing I suspect the joke of his several runs for office. He was the comedy, Rose was the tragedy, and Tennessee was the recording angel.

You will want to see this film if Tennessee means anything to you. Does he, to most people, anymore? And do Albee and Miller? A nonmusical play can hardly open on Broadway these days, and the twentieth century's playwriting history flourishes elsewhere in places like Chicago. But this *is* a Tennessee Williams screenplay. And in it one of the great Williams women, Miss Addie, and one of the great Williams actresses, Ellen Burstyn. That ought to mean something. Well, shouldn't it?

Louder Than a Bomb ★ ★ ★ ½

NO MPAA RATING, 100 m., 2011

Kevin Coval, Adam Gottlieb, Elizabeth Graf, Kevin Harris, John Hood, Lamar Jorden, Peter Kahn, Jesus Lark, Nate Marshall, She'Kira McKnight, Preye Porri, James Sloan, Charles Smith, Robbie Q. Telfer, and Nova Venerable. A documentary directed and produced by Greg Jacobs and Jon Siskel.

Poetry slams began in Chicago in 1984 and have become an international phenomenon without most people probably having heard of them. They're poetry readings as a spectator sport. Individuals and teams are scored by judges on the Olympic ten-point scale, but while Olympic diving judges claim to be looking at specific elements in a dive, slam judges are responding to emotion, charisma, and—well, poetry. Some slammers are also rap artists, but slam and rap are different art forms, and slammers rely only on their voices.

Louder Than a Bomb is about the 2008 Chicago-area slam of the same name, the nation's largest. Teams and soloists from sixty high schools compete, and the finalists face off in a citywide slam that fills a theater usually used for rock concerts. The suspense that year initially centered on Steinmetz, a troubled inner city school that had never entered before it won the 2007 Bomb in a thrilling upset. Can Steinmetz and its coach, James Sloan, repeat?

The film was directed by Greg Jacobs and Jon Siskel (Gene's nephew), who followed several competitors for months and guessed well in choosing those they focused on. The 2008 Steinmetz team had some gifted repeaters, and we also meet three outstanding solo talents:

—Nova Venerable from Oak Park/River Forest High School, who helps her mom with the complex needs of a disabled kid brother and then writes about that and her absent father.

—Nate Marshall from Whitney Young Magnet High School, whose parents were addicts but who, when asked to choose between basketball and poetry, chooses words, and masters them with almost bewildering fluency.

—Adam Gottlieb, from Northside College Prep, whose poems are so joyous and whose performances so charismatic that he makes it possible to think of a slammer as a rock star.

—The Steinmetz team, calling themselves the Steinmenauts, are Lamar Jorden, Kevin Harris, Jesus Lark, Charles Smith, and She'Kira McKnight. They develop artistic and personal differences, which Coach Sloan helps them work out during tense scenes. When they triumphantly appear onstage, their very presence is a tribute to their poetry.

Siskel and Jacobs focus on the performances, which are inspiring and electrifying. Their film left me wondering why American television must be so gutless and shallow. If these kids and others like them were programmed against *American Idol* or *Dancing with the Stars*, the shabbiness of those shows would be placed in dramatic contrast. Here are real performers with real feelings and important things to say.

I hesitate to hint about the outcome of the contest, nor to steal some of the thunder and surprises from the performers. I'll end on this: After *Louder Than a Bomb* plays theatrically, it will air on the Oprah Winfrey Network. Why doesn't Oprah consider it a pilot for a series? America's got talent, all right, but maybe we've been looking for it in the wrong places.

Love and Other Drugs ★ ★ ½

R, 112 m., 2010

Jake Gyllenhaal (Jamie Randall), Anne Hathaway (Maggie Murdock), Oliver Platt (Bruce Winston), Hank Azaria (Dr. Stan Knight), Josh Gad (Josh Randall), Gabriel Macht (Trey Hannigan). Directed by Edward Zwick and produced by Pieter Jan Brugge, Marshall Herskovitz, Charles Randolph, Scott Stuber, and Zwick. Screenplay by Randolph, Zwick, and Herskovitz, based on the book *Hard Sell: The Evolution of a Viagra Salesman* by Jamie Reidy.

Love and Other Drugs stars Jake Gyllenhaal as Jamie Randall, a pharmaceutical salesman who sells love, Zoloft, Viagra, and other products with equal sincerity. He's a charmer, determined to sell his way out of Ohio and into the big Chicago market, and if that involves flirting with the receptionists in doctors' offices, it's a tough job but somebody's got to do it.

The movie takes place at that point in the 1990s when Viagra was tumescing in the marketplace, and Jamie is riding the success of his employer, Pfizer. He infiltrates hospitals, befriends doctors, pushes drugs, and sabotages the best efforts of his aggressive rival, Trey Hannigan (Gabriel Macht), whose product Prozac is outselling Zoloft. Whether these products, or any of their products, work very well is not a concern of the salesmen. They sell.

Jamie is egged on by his supervisor, Bruce Winston (Oliver Platt), and it seems quite possible he'll make it to Chicago when his life makes an unexpected course correction. He's buddies with Dr. Stan Knight (Hank Azaria), who introduces him as his intern and allows him to observe as he palpates the breast of his lovely patient Maggie Murdock (Anne Hathaway). Strictly speaking, doctors aren't supposed to do that. Maggie discovers the fraud, and in the course of an argument with Jamie about it they both grow so passionate that, well, they rip off each other's clothes and fall upon the bed in a confusion of sheets and moans.

Maggie and Jamie discover that they really, really like each other. She has something she wants to tell him. She is in the early stages of Parkinson's disease. This introduces an unexpected note into what seemed to be a screwball comedy. Hathaway brings such tenderness and solemnity to her role that she moves the film away from comedy and toward *Love Story*, and from then on we never quite know where we're headed.

The emotional tug-of-war intensifies because of the presence of Jamie's brother, Josh (Josh Gad), who seems to have been imported directly from an Odd Buddy Movie. Josh is helpless in the area of appropriate behavior, seems to have selected his wardrobe in high school for the rest of his life, has made millions of dollars in the markets, and has a disastrous personal life. Although he could buy a hotel, he lacks the skill or the courage to check into one, and seems intent on living for the rest of his life on the sofa in Jamie's small apartment.

That would be permissible in another kind of movie. Not in this one, where matters grow serious between the two lovers—so serious, indeed, that they begin to discuss how their love will prevail through the difficult road ahead. The movie gives full weight and attention to the subject of Parkinson's and doesn't trivialize it or find jokes in it (how could it?).

But the more weight the story of Maggie and Jamie takes on, the more distracting is the screenplay's need to intercut updates on the pharmaceutical wars. Nor do we continue to care much about Bruce and Trey. The most effective single scene in the movie takes place at a meeting of people with Parkinson's and their loved ones. The husband of a victim describes to Jamie in stark, realistic detail the possible course of the disease, and how it may affect the woman he loves. After this scene, the movie has definitively introduced a note that makes the rest seem trivial.

The director is Edward Zwick, a considerable filmmaker. He's essentially working with a screenplay (by Charles Randolph, Marshall Herskovitz, and himself) that doesn't work.

Given that problem, you have to observe that he is a capable filmmaker even in bad weather. He obtains a warm, lovable performance from Anne Hathaway, and dimensions from Gyllenhaal that grow from comedy to the serious. The scene with the husband of the Parkinson's survivor has a simple grandeur. As a filmmaker by nature, Zwick gives that scene its full weight, no matter that it's not a good fit in his movie. That counts for something. ☞

Loveless ★ ★ ★

NO MPAA RATING, 104 m., 2010

Andrew von Urtz (Andrew), Cindy Chastain (Joanna), Genevieve Hudson-Price (Ava), Gary Wilmes (Tad), Kendra Hurley (Kendra), Sabin Streeter (Sabin), Scott Cohen (Ricky), Ramin Serry (Ramin), Shauna Lyon (Shauna). Directed by Ramin Serry and produced by Shauna Lyon. Screenplay by Serry.

We all know someone like Andrew, with his intense vagueness. It's important for him to convey to you that he has something important to tell you. The precise nature of that always seems to reside in his next unspoken sentence. He's like a fortune-teller, trying to get you to reveal what you want to hear him say.

Andrew, the hero of Ramin Serry's *Loveless*, is a midthirties office worker in Manhattan, who tirelessly drinks and tries to pick up women and has a low-key cluelessness that some women find attractive. Besides, anyone this unskilled at claiming he's looking for an actress for his new movie might possibly be telling the truth. Andrew is played by Andrew von Urtz in his movie debut, and played so easily and convincingly that you not only believe such a person might exist, but that you are probably looking at him.

Half-drunk, he tries out the actress routine on Ava (Genevieve Hudson-Price), whom he meets in a bar. She stalks out to go to a party, he follows her, and finds himself at her brother's birthday. Her brother, Ricky (Scott Cohen), has many other brothers (I counted three), and they all worship the memory of their dead father. Indeed, Ava and Ricky believe they talk to him and receive daily guidance.

Andrew finds himself at another party, this one given by friends, where he meets his ex-girlfriend Joanna (Cindy Chastain). That isn't surprising because Andrew is the kind of man whose friends would possibly rather stay in touch with his ex-girlfriend than with him. Not that he's obnoxious. It's more that he's perfectly nice, but wearying. He and Joanna start up again, sort of, and, meanwhile, Ava's brothers decide to finance Andrew's movie, Ava smothers him in lust, Joanna meets her, and Andrew, who would possibly like to be left in peace to drink, finds himself loveless but not loverless.

Loveless is a movie about behavior, not plot. It doesn't much matter which woman, if either, Andrew ends up with, or whether his movie (or Ricky's movie) ever gets made. Andrew is a character whose life is about process, not plot. He doesn't get from A to C but spends his best years circling B. He wanders. He wanders in his drinking, in his sex life, in his plans. He's indulged by his boss, who is a friend, and probably has a gift for inspiring indulgence. Certainly the women in his life accept a lot.

Although Andrew von Urtz and Cindy Chastain are in their first film and Genevieve Hudson-Price has only two previous credits, all three have a natural ease on camera. In genre, *Loveless* is a romantic comedy, and their comfort level in the form is a contrast to the tense energy you often sense in romcoms. Nobody is obsessed with an imaginary finish line, least of all Andrew, who ends as he begins, circling B.

The Lovely Bones ★ ½

PG-13, 136 m., 2010

Mark Wahlberg (Jack Salmon), Rachel Weisz (Abigail Salmon), Susan Sarandon (Grandma Lynn), Stanley Tucci (George Harvey), Michael Imperioli (Len Fenerman), Saoirse Ronan (Susie Salmon), Rose McIver (Lindsey Salmon). Directed by Peter Jackson and produced by Jackson, Carolynne Cunningham, and Fran Walsh. Screenplay by Jackson, Walsh, and Philippa Boyens, based on the novel by Alice Sebold.

The Lovely Bones is a deplorable film with this message: If you're a fourteen-year-old girl who has been brutally raped and murdered by a serial killer, you have a lot to look forward to. You can get together in heaven with the other teenage victims of the same killer and gaze down in benevolence upon your family members as they mourn you and realize what a wonderful person you were. Sure, you miss your friends, but your fellow fatalities come dancing to greet you in a meadow of wildflowers, and how cool is that?

The makers of this film seem to have given slight thought to the psychology of teenage girls, less to the possibility that there is no heaven, and none at all to the likelihood that if there is one, it will not resemble a happy gathering of new Facebook friends. In its version of the events, the serial killer can almost be seen as a hero for liberating these girls from the tiresome ordeal of growing up and dispatching them directly to the Elysian Fields. The film's primary effect was to make me squirmy.

It's based on the best-seller by Alice Sebold that everybody seemed to be reading a couple of years ago. I hope it's not faithful to the book; if it is, millions of Americans are scary. The murder of a young person is a tragedy, the murderer is a monster, and making the victim a sweet, poetic narrator is creepy. This movie sells the philosophy that even evil things are God's will and their victims are happier now. Isn't it nice to think so. I think it's best if they don't happen at all. But if they do, why pretend they don't hurt? Those girls are dead.

I'm assured, however, that Sebold's novel is well written and sensitive. I presume the director, Peter Jackson, has distorted elements to fit his own vision, which involves nearly as many special effects in some sequences as his *Lord of the Rings* trilogy. A more useful way to deal with this material would be with observant, subtle performances in a thoughtful screenplay. It's not a feel-good story. Perhaps Jackson's team made the mistake of fearing the novel was too dark. But its millions of readers must know it's not like this. The target audience may be doom-besotted teenage girls—the *Twilight* crowd.

The owner of the lovely bones is named Susie Salmon (Saoirse Ronan, a very good young actress, who cannot be faulted here). The heaven Susie occupies looks a little like a Flower Power world in the kind of fantasy that, murdered in 1973, she might have imagined. Seems to me that heaven, by definition outside time and space, would have neither colors nor a lack of colors—would be a state with no sensations. Nor would there be thinking there, let alone narration. In an eternity spent in the presence of infinite goodness, you don't go around thinking, "Man! Is this great!" You simply *are*. I have a lot of theologians on my side here.

But no. From her movie-set Valhalla, Susie gazes down as her mother (Rachel Weisz) grieves and her father (Mark Wahlberg) tries to solve the case himself. There's not much of a case to solve; we know who the killer is almost from the get-go, and, under the Law of Economy of Characters, that's who he has to be because (a) he's played by an otherwise unnecessary movie star, and (b) there's no one else in the movie he *could* be.

Here's something bittersweet. Weisz and Wahlberg are effective as the parents. Because the pyrotechnics are mostly upstairs with the special effects, all they need to be are convincing parents who have lost their daughter. This they do with touching subtlety. We also meet one of Susie's grandmothers (Susan Sarandon), an unwise drinker who comes on to provide hard-boiled comic relief, in the Shakespearean tradition that every tragedy needs its clown. Well, she's good, too. This whole film is Jackson's fault.

It doesn't fail simply because I suspect its message. It fails on its own terms. It isn't emotionally convincing that this girl, having had these experiences and destined apparently to be fourteen forever (although cleaned up and with a new wardrobe), would produce this heavenly creature. What's left for us to pity? We should all end up like her, and the sooner the better; preferably not after being raped and murdered.

Lymelife ★ ★ ★ ½

R, 95 m., 2009

Alec Baldwin (Mickey Bartlett), Kieran Culkin (Jimmy Bartlett), Rory Culkin (Scott Bartlett), Jill Hennessy (Brenda Bartlett), Timothy Hutton (Charlie Bragg), Cynthia Nixon (Melissa Bragg),

Emma Roberts (Adrianna Bragg). Directed by Derick Martini and produced by Steven Martini, Barbara DeFina, Jon Cornick, Alec Baldwin, Michele Tayler, and Angela Somerville. Screenplay by Derick Martini and Steven Martini.

Lymelife sometimes cuts to the tiny buildings and inhabitants of a model suburb, the kind you might find on display in a Realtor's office. Just as frequent are its shots of actual homes in a Long Island suburb, of the sort occupied by the Bartlett and Bragg families. The film is about the distance between the ideal and the real.

Unhappy suburban families are more familiar in the movies than real ones—perhaps because, as Tolstoy believed, all happy families are the same. The sickness of these two families emanates from the parents. Two are committing adultery with each other. A third has Lyme disease and regards life with fatigue and depression.

The movie isn't about Lyme disease, but it serves as a theme: "Isn't it amazing that your whole life can be changed by a bug the size of a pimple on your ass?" A tick has destroyed the spirit of Charlie Bragg (Timothy Hutton) and left his sluttish wife, Melissa (Cynthia Nixon), open to the predations of her business partner, Mickey Bartlett (Alec Baldwin). Mickey's wife, Brenda Bartlett (Jill Hennessy), knows what's going on but tries to stand above it.

Their children are directly affected, and much of the film is seen through the eyes of two kids around fifteen, Scott Bartlett (Rory Culkin) and Adrianna Bragg (Emma Roberts). In a film of good actors, these are two finely realized performances. Scott has an inarticulate crush on Adrianna and is wounded when he sees her with an older, more studly boy. Adrianna likes him—they've been lifelong friends—but likes to date "more mature" men, which at that age may mean seventeen. Both of them know what Mickey and Melissa are doing. Adrianna is cynical; he's betrayed.

But those are only the outlines of a tender, sometimes painful, sometimes blackly comic story. The film's characters are not types but particular people, and if the adults protect themselves in one way or another, the children are wide open. That includes Scott's older brother, Jimmy (Kieran Culkin), who is getting out while he can and has enlisted in the service. (The film has misplaced the Falkland Islands conflict in the 1970s, but how many even remember it? Nor was it a U.S. war.)

Rory Culkin's performance is the mainspring. Apart from the misfortune that they all look angelic, the Culkin family is rich in gifted actors. Here Rory plays a sexually inexperienced, bullied, sensitive kid, wounded by the loud arguments of his parents. His mother, played by Hennessy, is a strong, good woman, keeping a brave face for her kids, loathing her husband. He lives through his work (a new suburban home development), buys a new home for them without even mentioning it to her, and has sex with Melissa because she is there.

Now look at the Timothy Hutton character, the sick one. Exhausted, emasculated, hopeless, he stares at a blank television screen, watches unseen as his wife and Mickey have sex in the basement, develops a strange obsession with a deer he often sees in a forest near his house. Such a low-energy character might seem to offer little for an actor to "do," but Hutton brings the film a level of defeat and despair that shadows everything. They could all end up like him; Brenda wraps Scott's neck, wrists, and ankles with duct tape and searches his hair for ticks.

The film is by Derick Martini, written with his brother Steven. I met them at Toronto 1999, with their screenplay for the quirky indie *Goat on Fire and Smiling Fish.* This is their first feature—showing confidence enough, despite a heavyweight cast, to build carefully to their unexpectedly appropriate conclusion. Martini is especially good with Alec Baldwin, an actor whose power is used here to create an intense mano a mano with Jimmy. He and Hennessy are lacerating together in a scene of mutual hate.

A buried subject is parenting. There are two good parents here. Brenda has a warm scene with Scott the morning after his confirmation (and, she doesn't know, his first sexual experience); Adrianna, the young girl, who knows more about life than Scott, sees him with sympathy, and handles him with almost maternal care. Emma Roberts's performance is far deeper than the sexpot we first seem to see.

Lymelife doesn't have the sheer power of *The Ice Storm,* but it's not just another recycling of suburban angst. By allowing their characters complexity, the Martinis spill open those tiny model homes as thoroughly as a dropped Monopoly game.

M

Made in Dagenham ★ ★ ★ ½

R, 113 m., 2010

Sally Hawkins (Rita O'Grady), Bob Hoskins (Albert Passingham), Miranda Richardson (Barbara Castle), Geraldine James (Connie), Rosamund Pike (Lisa Hopkins), Rupert Graves (Peter Hopkins), Andrea Riseborough (Brenda), Daniel Mays (Eddie O'Grady), Kenneth Cranham (Monty). Directed by Nigel Cole and produced by Elizabeth Karlsen and Stephen Woolley. Screenplay by William Ivory.

Ford is having a great year, and I just bought one of their new Fusions. How would I feel if I discovered the women building it had been paid less than the men simply because they were . . . well, women? If a woman does the same job as a man, should she receive the same pay? Yes, says common sense. No, say corporations that will disregard anything in the search for profits.

Ford, let me hasten to add, has a policy of equal pay for equal work. It was not always that way, with Ford and, to be fair, most corporations. *Made in Dagenham* takes place so recently as 1968, when the British Ford plant in Dagenham paid women significantly lower wages than men—with the agreement of their own unions and the Labour government of Harold Wilson.

Why was this so? Did they do less work? No. In fact, they were highly productive. It was so because the unions, the company, and the government were run by men and, I dunno, I guess they just weren't used to thinking about women in that way. *Made in Dagenham* is a delightfully entertaining movie based on fact. The women went on strike, annoyed their unions and their husbands, and embarrassed Wilson, who was caught with his principles down.

Sally Hawkins, that emerging dynamo of British acting, stars as Rita O'Grady, who sews automobile seat covers in what is literally a sweatshop; she and her coworkers have to strip down to bra and panties because of the unbearable heat. Her union organizer, Albert Passingham (Bob Hoskins), is a left-winger whose principles run deeper than his union's. He was raised by a brave mother, instinctively admires women, and sees with his own eyes that unequal pay is wrong.

Rita is a quiet woman who almost by accident becomes the shop steward. Albert spots the way her spontaneous humanity cuts through politics. Using her first as a surrogate, he encourages the idea of a strike. The head of the union at Ford (Kenneth Cranham) "works closely with management," as they say, and the government is also not eager to alienate a big corporate employer. All Rita O'Grady knows is that she works hard and believes that what's fair is fair.

A brief strike escalates into a much larger one. Her own husband, Eddie (Daniel Mays), is against her. The usual alarms circulate about left-wing influences. But when Rita is seen on the telly (and she is), she makes it all seem so simple (because it is). The strike at Dagenham changed history, in England and America, at Ford and many other manufacturers, and elsewhere in the developed world. It's one reason so many jobs are outsourced to places where labor unions and equal pay do not find favor.

The struggle is far from over. Only last week, a Republican filibuster in the U.S. Senate prevented passage of the Paycheck Fairness Act, which would have added teeth to measures for equal pay. You don't see many GOP ads saying it's against equal pay, but it is. So are corporations, and there may be a connection, but it's harder to say now that corporate political contributions can be secret.

But back to Dagenham. Although Albert set the ball rolling, Rita quickly found tons of support, some of it in unlikely places. One backer of the strike was the government's minister for labor, Barbara Castle (Miranda Richardson). A "fiery redhead" (Why are all redheads "fiery"?), she defied the pipe-puffing Wilson, who didn't want to alienate Ford. She explained her reason: "Harold, you are wrong." Probably the movie's best scene is when Castle receives O'Grady and her coworkers in her office and astonishes them by giving her support. Her decision put the Labour party on the spot.

Another ally is much more unlikely. She is Lisa Hopkins (Rosamund Pike), who is married to a top executive at Ford. She received a first-class education, could have had a career, but now finds herself playing the role of a well-trained and tamed corporate wife. Her husband, Peter (Rupert Graves), assumes that of course she opposes the striking women. Not so fast there, Pete.

Niki Caro's 2005 film *North Country* starred Charlize Theron in a similar story about a woman who won the first American sexual-harassment lawsuit. That was in 1984. Some men are slow to figure these things out. The unexpected thing about *Made in Dagenham* is how entertaining it is. That's largely due to director Nigel Cole's choice of Sally Hawkins for his lead. In Mike Leigh's *Happy Go Lucky* (2009) and again here, she shows an effortless lightness of being. If she has a limitation it may be that she's constitutionally ill adapted for playing a bad person.

Make Believe ★ ★ ★

G, 90 m., 2011

Siphiwe Fangase, Hiroki Hara, Bill Koch, Krystyn Lambert, Derek McKee, Nkumbuzo Nkonyana, Jeff McBride, and Lance Burton. A documentary directed by J. Clay Tweel and produced by Steven Klein. Screenplay by Cleven S. Loham.

Oh, I wanted to be a magician. I memorized a biography of Houdini and mailed off to Johnson Smith Co. for boxes that made coins disappear, trick card decks, and wands that contained weights to make tassels rise and fall. I ordered the neighborhood kids into the basement and staged a laborious performance by The Great Ebertini. Tassels rose and coins disappeared, but the cards needed more work.

A lot more work, I learn in *Make Believe.* This is a charming documentary about the finalists in the Teenage Magician Contest at the annual World Magic Seminar in Las Vegas. From Malibu, Chicago, Colorado, Japan, and South Africa they come, dreaming of being presented with first place by the great Lance Burton. The documentary visits their homes, gets their stories, talks to their friends and parents, and follows them backstage in Vegas.

But mostly it watches them practice, over and over and over. Hiroki Hara, who lives in Kitayama, Japan, uses the village hall and rehearses relentlessly all day, every day, mentioning that he grows lonely there all by himself, but his goal makes it worthwhile. The others practice, too, and one sheds a few tears when two coaches tell him he's not ready for the finals. He rehearses some more, and on the big day, he is ready and then some.

Not a single rabbit is pulled from a hat. Most of the tricks are small-scale—locking rings, disappearing scarves, card production. A deck of cards in their hands seems to have a life of its own. One kid turns cards into iPods while they're fanned between his fingers. We see him in his basement, building the props.

Hara is the most inventive. He appears as a ghost monster with flashing green eyes, and presents an elegantly choreographed act. Siphiwe Fangase and Nkumbuzo Nkonyana, from a township in Cape Town, are the most entertaining, with their act based on music, dance, and magic soccer balls in honor of the World Cup held in South Africa.

For one contestant, everything goes wrong. A ball drops during a ball-production trick, and a trap in a hat doesn't work. It's not the magician's fault; both tricks *always* work. It's one of those days. The other contestants, backstage, discuss this with a kind of dread, knowing that no matter how often they practice, the same thing could happen to them.

One question not really addressed by the movie is whether these kids are wise to skip classes and put social life and college on hold in order to focus single-mindedly on magic. Apparently they all think they'll find professional careers, maybe not in Vegas, but at conventions and so forth. I hope so.

One thing we don't find out is how any of the tricks are done. The secrets in some cases (the steel rings, the vanishing scarves) are pretty widely known. In card manipulation, most of the people in the audience know in theory exactly how it's done, but are connoisseurs judging how well they are performed. Magicians have a saying: "The trick is told when the trick is sold." These kids are sold on tricks.

Malls R Us ★ ★ ★

NO MPAA RATING, 78 m., 2009

A documentary directed by Helene Klodawsky

and produced by Ina Fichman and Luc Martin-Gousset. Screenplay by Klodawsky.

Is a shopping mall a sacred place? Not a question often asked. A provocative new documentary named *Malls R Us* seriously argues that malls serve similar functions today that cathedrals, temples, parliaments, arenas, and town squares did in earlier times. Then it slowly works its way around to the possibility that they may be a plague upon the earth.

One thing is clear. From its uncertain beginnings in the 1950s, led by a developer named Victor Gruen, the mall concept has expanded relentlessly until it is essentially the template for a city-state such as Dubai, in the United Arab Emirates. They've become so omnipresent, we learn, that in all of North America there remains only a single location suitable for a new megamall—outside Montreal. In China and Japan they're reshaping cities and traditional ways of life, and in India they've inspired class conflicts and street protests in Delhi. You can buy Nikes, Sony TVs, and Louis Vuitton luggage in pretty much all of them, and dine at McDonald's.

I'm conflicted. I like malls. My favorite is the Ala Moana in Honolulu. I never buy much of anything. I like to sit in the enormous food court and feel the hum of the city. On the other hand, I love meandering through the busy local streets of London, Paris, or Toronto, where one little shop after another is lined up, often with a real live owner on the premises.

Ray Bradbury shares my conflict, I learn in *Malls R Us*. The great science fiction writer is interviewed in the film. He likes the futuristic vision of the new supermalls, and at the same time yearns for a simpler time when he was growing up in Waukegan and folks walked downtown to do their shopping and see a movie.

Helene Klodawsky, the director, is also of two minds. She's traveled the globe to assemble footage of malls so spectacular that we in North America have little idea of their scope. In Osaka, Delhi, Warsaw, they sprawl across city blocks and devour traditional neighborhoods. They center on fountains, spires, waterfalls, roller coasters, nature preserves.

Rubin Stahl, who is developing the Montreal project, is like a kid delighting in his gargantuan existing projects, like the Scottsdale Galleria, where he take us on a tour of its nature diorama, including a real (i.e., stuffed) polar bear. He says his Montreal project will be the world's first environmentally friendly mall, complete with fully stocked trout streams; he hopes Al Gore will visit to open it.

Thinking even bigger than Stahl is Eric Kuhne, an American architect who finds malls an outlet for his fantasies. He's building a million-square-foot project in Dubai. At a brainstorming session, we see him seeking inspiration in the Tower of Babel and an artichoke.

If Minneapolis and St. Paul have the Mall of America, Dubai is proposing itself as the Mall of the World. Jets fly in from everywhere loaded with affluent consumers, who wander through an air-conditioned desert oasis with wall-to-wall luxury brands. Thousands of workers are imported from Third World countries to build these fantasies. Their average wage: forty-five cents an hour.

It's that income disparity that concerns Klodawsky. She considers India as a case study of a land where malls may not be a perfect fit. She interviews Vikram Soni, an environmentalist who walks us through the Delhi Ridge Wilderness Preserve, a watershed that renews itself annually and provides drinking water better than in bottles. Now it is being destroyed for a mall. There don't seem to be permits, but Indian bureaucracy is notoriously unreliable, and the developers are bulldozing anyway.

Anyone who has been to India pictures the endless streets of small shops piled upon shops, each one with an owner and a family to support. Seeking to modernize, or something, Delhi has condemned tens of thousands of these little stores and torn them down. Klodawsky has footage of an event not much covered in the news: Thousand of Indians blocked the city streets for days in protest. In a land where 50 percent lack reliable drinking water, most will never be able to afford to enter a mall.

There seems to be a life cycle for malls. Most run down after about thirty years. There's even a Web site, deadmalls.com, devoted to the thousands that have closed. What happens to them? Apparently they just sit there empty. This used to be the most wonderful fountain, says a nostalgic visitor to one of them.

Mammoth ★ ★ ★

NO MPAA RATING, 125 m., 2009

Gael Garcia Bernal (Leo), Michelle Williams (Ellen), Marife Necesito (Gloria), Run Srinikornchot (Cookie), Sophie Nyweide (Jackie). Directed by Lukas Moodysson and produced by Lars Jonsson. Screenplay by Moodysson.

Our health care rests to a sizable degree upon the shoulders of Filipino doctors, nurses, patient care specialists, and caregivers. There is a reason for this. Medical schools in the Philippines produce many graduates whose eyes are set on such jobs in North America, where there is a perennial shortage. During my adventures since 2006, I've been helped by a great many Filipinos, who were without exception cheerful, hardworking, and skilled—not least when on three occasions they were racing me to emergency surgery in the middle of the night.

One of the central stories in *Mammoth* involves a Filipino nanny who cares for rich children in Manhattan while her own children at home live in relative poverty and tell her on the phone how much they miss her. The film is intended to make us feel guilty that such people care for us and not for their own. I don't buy that. At least in the case of the Filipinos I've known, they worked hard to win jobs over here, are sending much of their income back home, are saving to bring over their kids, and are urging them to get an education to help them find jobs when they get here. It certainly helps that English is one of the national languages.

In a world of massive inequality, they're at least taking those direct measures available to them to improve their family situations. Only superficial thinking about global reality would lead a Swedish-born director such as Lukas Moodysson to offer the sentimental simplifications in *Mammoth,* which cuts back and forth between a lucky American kid at the planetarium and her nanny's children telling her they love her in a phone call. This is hard, but it's harder to be unable to feed your children or offer them a future.

These matters don't make this a bad movie. It's very well acted and is about a good deal more than the nanny. As the parents, Leo and Ellen, it stars Gael Garcia Bernal and Michelle Williams (in her first lead since *Wendy and Lucy*). The two other leads are Gloria (Marife Necesito), as the nanny, and Cookie (Run Srinikornchot), as a bar girl Leo meets while on a business trip to Thailand.

Understand Leo isn't looking for trouble. He's a happily married video game author, very rich, in Bangkok to sign off on details of a major deal. But his business partner handles the negotiations, he's bored and lonely, he jets off to a coastal resort for a break, and he meets Cookie—who is very nice. No, really. In Thailand some parents know their children are working in the sex industry and happily accept the money. That's sad, but it's the way things are.

Nor does Leo mistreat or exploit Cookie (an adult), other than accepting her basic situation. Suppose he doesn't do business with her. Will she then leave prostitution? She may well be better off with a nice guy like him than the next sex tourist who wanders into the bar. Money has a way of dictating our decisions. If Leo weren't rich, for example, maybe he'd be back home where he's needed.

His wife, Ellen, is a surgeon specializing in pediatrics, which brings her into touch with a young patient who—but you can guess how this world simply isn't fair. There are so many reasons to be outraged and depressed in this film, indeed, that it all but distracts from the real and immediate qualities of the four fine actors.

Lukas Moodysson, working for the first time in English, has made some good films, including *Together* (2000), *Lilja 4-Ever* (2002), and *Show Me Love* (1998), which used a little English in its Swedish title (cough). What he finds from Michelle Williams here is interesting. *Wendy and Lucy* was so effective at establishing her as a helpless innocent that it's sort of a shock to see her here as a cool and competent ER surgeon. It shows her range at a time when many actresses are cast over and over in the same role. *Mammoth* is a perfectly decent film. Too bad it isn't a little more thoughtful. It's easy to regret misfortune, if all you do is regret it.

Note: What does the title mean? If refers to the movie's $3,000 fountain pen made from ivory from a frozen mammoth. Not coincidentally, it's also the word for "mother" in Tagalog, a national language of the Philippines.

Management ★ ★ ★

R, 93 m., 2009

Steve Zahn (Mike), Jennifer Aniston (Sue), Woody Harrelson (Jango), Fred Ward (Jerry), Margi Martindale (Trish). Directed by Stephen Belber and produced by Marty Bowen, Wyck Godfrey, and Sidney Kimmel. Screenplay by Belber.

Sometimes casting has everything to do with a movie. In the usual course of events, a high-powered company sales executive wouldn't have much to do with Mike, the hapless loser who works and lives at the Arizona motel where she plans to spend one night. But cast Steve Zahn as the loser and it becomes thinkable.

The sales rep is Sue, played by Jennifer Aniston, who is upward-bound, successful, sharply dressed, and reduced to spending her evenings in remote motels, playing games on her laptop. Sue is every woman Mike has ever wanted but has never had, which is easy because he wants all women and has never had any. He's a nice guy, often stoned, under the thumbs of his parents, who own the motel, and looks at her with the love-struck eyes of a wet puppy.

Why and how they end up in the laundry room doing the rumpy-pumpy on a dryer is something *Management* takes for granted. Sometimes, apparently, high-powered Manhattan career women swoon in the presence of a guy who looks like he should be pumping their gas. His courtship technique is cute: He checks her in, carries her bags, brings her flowers, knocks again with the "customary" house bottle of champagne, uncorks it, gets two plastic-wrapped glasses from the bathroom, and struggles to say several coherent words in a row.

We can more or less predict where all of this will lead. Mike is obviously the fish out of water, so he must travel to New York to dramatize his unsuitability. Then Sue must travel to Washington, where she sees Jango (Woody Harrelson), a former punk rocker who has become a yogurt millionaire (for Harrelson, this is typecasting). Then Mike must follow her there.

He's not a stalker, you understand. He only wants to lick her hand, curl up at her feet, and be thrown a Milk Bone when he's been a good boy. It is Aniston's task to make us believe Sue might be won over by this, and because she succeeds, the movie works as a sweet romcom with some fairly big laughs.

What's nice is to see Zahn playing a guy who's not the dimmest bulb in the chandelier. For some reason he's often typecast as a stoner dimwit, maybe because he was so good at playing such roles early in his career. Here he's smart enough, just extremely socially challenged. Watch Aniston play off him with her pert intelligence; she could demolish him but is touched by his lack of defenses.

Fred Ward has a good role here as Mike's father, a perfectionist stuck with a slacker as an heir. Eventually he, too, is touched. That only leaves one question, which first-time writer-director Stephen Belber wisely doesn't mine for a subplot: Why did Sue's office travel manager book her into this motel?

The Marc Pease Experience ★

PG-13, 84 m., 2009

Ben Stiller (Jon Gribble), Jason Schwartzman (Marc Pease), Anna Kendrick (Meg Brickman), Jay Paulson (Gerry), Zachary Booth (Craig), Ebon Moss-Bachrach (Gavin), Gabrielle Dennis (Tracey). Directed by Todd Louiso and produced by Michael London, Bruna Papandrea, and David Rubin. Screenplay by Louiso and Jacob Koskoff.

The Marc Pease Experience is a cheerless and almost sullen experience. Not even its staging of a high school production of *The Wiz* can pep it up. It's badly written and inertly directed, with actors who don't have a clue about what drives their characters. This is one of those rare films that contains no chemistry at all. None. The actors scarcely seem to be in the same scenes together.

For that matter, I can't think of many titles that are worse. "Marc Pease" is a name that looks like a typo, and Marc has no "experience" other than allegedly existing during the events of this film. Oh, at the end he becomes more philosophical and human, but that's just the screenplay jerking his chain. There is no sense that a human is involved.

The movie involves two unpleasant men. There is a young woman who is intended as pleasant but lacks all dimension on the screen, so she is simply filling a blank space labeled "pleasant character." Both unpleasant men are attracted to this young woman, but there is not a single scene between her and either of them that has the slightest joy, playfulness, affection, credibility, or humanity. All three are like bad witnesses who have been coached.

Eight years ago, when he was in high school, Marc Pease (Jason Schwartzman) panicked onstage while playing the Tin Man, and ran offstage and out of the school screaming. His drama coach, who has the Dickensian name of Mr. Gribble (Ben Stiller), has never forgiven him. Both have designs on Meg Brickman (Anna Kendrick), who is a little young for Marc and inappropriately young for Mr. Gribble. She has a nice singing voice and is coached by Gribble, the letch.

Marc Pease, now a limo driver, lives with the dream that his eight-member a cappella singing group, now reduced to four members, will cut a demo tape and become famous. He believes Mr. Gribble will produce this demo. He sells his condo to finance the recording session. The people who made this movie presumably know someone in the recording business, who could have advised them that even in this housing market, you don't have to sell a condo to pay for a demo. Don't you kind of guess every member of the audience can figure that out?

This year Mr. Gribble is producing *The Wiz* again. Same costumes, etc. There is a crisis on opening night, involving behavior bordering on lunacy by Marc Pease and on the malevolent by Mr. Gribble. Nevertheless, Marc Pease saves the production, in a way I will not spoil for you in case someone kidnaps you, takes you to a theater, straps you to a seat, props your eyes open with toothpicks, and forces you to watch this film.

I learn that Ben Stiller had another job coming up and shot all of his scenes in two weeks. Perhaps he suspected this film was not his shot at an Academy nomination. Stiller, Schwartzman, and Anna Kendrick will all work again. My advice: as soon as possible.

Marmaduke ★ ★

PG, 87 m., 2010

Lee Pace (Phil Winslow), Judy Greer (Debbie Winslow), William H. Macy (Don Twombly). With the voices of: Owen Wilson (Marmaduke), Emma Stone (Mazie), George Lopez (Carlos), Christopher Mintz-Plasse (Giuseppe), Steve Coogan (Raisin), Stacy Ferguson (Jezebel), Kiefer Sutherland (Bosco). Directed by Tom Dey and produced by Dey and John Davis. Screenplay by Tim Rasmussen and Vince di Meglio, based on the comic strip by Brad Anderson and Phil Leeming.

Dogs cannot talk. This we know. Dogs can talk in the movies. This we also know. But when we see them lip-synching with their dialogue, it's just plain grotesque. The best approach is the one used by *Garfield* in which we saw the cat and heard Bill Murray, but there was no nonsense about Garfield's mouth moving.

The moment I saw Marmaduke's big drooling lips moving, I knew I was in trouble. There is nothing discreet about a Great Dane with a lot on his mind, especially when he's the narrator of the film and never shuts up. And when his master, Phil, moves the Winslow family from Kansas to Orange County and he joins the crowd at the dog park of a vegetarian pet food company, well, what can I say about a movie that has more speaking parts for dogs (and a cat) than for humans?

This is a congenial PG-rated animal comedy. If you like the comic strip, now in its fifty-sixth year, maybe you'll like it, maybe not. Marmaduke's personality isn't nearly as engaging as Garfield's. Then again, if personality is what you're in the market for, maybe you shouldn't be considering a lip-synched talking-animal comedy in the first place.

The plot. In California, Marmaduke likes his new backyard, but gets in hot water with his family for a dumb reason and runs away. Mazie, the collie he's been romancing at the park, goes searching for him, and it rains, and Marmaduke gets lost, and his family piles in the station wagon and searches, and—long story made short—they all end up where a burst sewer has caused a big sink hole (although not as big as the one in Guatemala). Mazie falls in, Marmaduke leaps in after her, they're swept into a sewer, they come out in an aqueduct, Phil Winslow (Lee Pace) leaps in, and so on and so forth.

Great Danes can be your best friends, but they are not gifted comedians. Mazie is typecast as a sexy collie; just once couldn't a pug play the female lead, in a little nontraditional casting? And speaking of that, what's with William H. Macy as the owner of the pet food company? If you admire Macy as I do, you can imagine dozens of ways he could be funny as a pet food tycoon. The movie sidesteps all of them and has him play the role right down the middle as a businessman. Then why hire Macy in the first place?

And then . . . but enough. Why am I writing, and why are you reading, a review of a talking-animal movie? Little kids may like it. It's not offensive. I don't find Marmaduke particularly photogenic, but that's just me. Great Danes look like they have extra elbows. The movie gets two stars. It could have done a little better if Marmaduke had kept his mouth shut.

Me and Orson Welles ★ ★ ★ ★

PG-13, 109 m., 2009

Zac Efron (Richard Samuels), Claire Danes (Sonja Jones), Christian McKay (Orson Welles), Zoe Kazan (Gretta Adler), James Tupper (Joseph Cotton), Leo Bill (Norman Lloyd), Eddie Marsan (John Houseman), Ben Chaplin (George Coulouris), Al Weaver (Sam Leve), Kelly Reilly (Muriel Brassler). Directed by Richard Linklater and produced by Ann Carli, Linklater, and Marc Samuelson. Screenplay by Holly Gent Palmo and Vince Palmo, based on the novel by Robert Kaplow.

Remember that Orson Welles himself didn't always look like Orson Welles. He was a master of makeup and disguise, and even when appearing in the first person liked to use a little putty to build up a nose he considered a tad too snubbed. The impersonation of Welles by Christian McKay in *Me and Orson Welles* is the centerpiece of the film, and from it all else flows. We can almost accept that this is the Great Man.

Twenty-four years after his death at seventy, Welles is more than ever a Great Man. There is something about his manner, his voice, and the way he carries himself that evokes greatness, even if it is only his own conviction of it. He is widely thought of as having made one masterpiece, *Citizen Kane*, and several other considerable films, but flaming out into false starts, uncompleted projects, and failed promise. Yet today even such a film as *The Magnificent Ambersons*, with its ending destroyed by the studio, often makes lists of the greatest of all time.

Oh, he had an ego. He once came to appear at Chicago's Auditorium Theater. A historic snowstorm shut down the city, but he was able to get to the theater from his nearby hotel. At curtain time he stepped before the handful of people who had been able to attend. "Good evening," he said. "I am Orson Welles—director, producer, actor, impresario, writer, artist, magician, star of stage, screen, and radio, and a pretty fair singer. Why are there so many of me, and so few of you?"

Richard Linklater's new film is one of the best movies about the theater I've ever seen, and one of the few to relish the resentment so many of Welles's collaborators felt for the Great Man. He was such a multitasker that while staging his famous Mercury Theater productions on Broadway he also starred in several radio programs, carried on an active social life, and sometimes napped by commuting between jobs in a hired ambulance. Much of the day for a Welles cast member was occupied in simply waiting for him to turn up at the theater.

Most viewers of this film will not necessarily know a lot about Welles's biography. There's no need to. Everything is here in context. The film involves the Mercury's first production, a *Julius Caesar* set in Mussolini's Italy. It sees this enterprise through the eyes of Richard Samuels (Zac Efron), a young actor who is hired as a mascot by Welles and somehow rises to a speaking role. He is starstruck and yet self-possessed, and emboldened by a sudden romance that overtakes him with a Mercury cohort, Sonja Jones (Claire Danes).

The film is steeped in theater lore. The impossible hours, the rehearsals, the gossip, the intrigue, the hazards of stage trapdoors, the quirks of personalities, the egos, the imbalance of a star surrounded entirely by supporting actors—supporting onstage, and in life.

Many of the familiar originals are represented here, not least Joseph Cotten (James Tupper), who costarred with Welles in *Citizen Kane* and *The Third Man*. Here is John Houseman (Eddie Marsan, not bulky enough but evocative), who was Welles's long-suffering producer. And the actor George Coulouris (Ben Chaplin), who played Mr. Thatcher in *Kane*. All at the beginning, all in embryo, all promised by Welles that they would make history. They believed him, and they did.

McKay summons above all the unflappable self-confidence of Welles, a con man in addition to his many other gifts, who was later able to talk actors into appearing in films that were shot over a period of years, as funds became available from his jobs in other films, on TV, on the stage, and in countless commercials ("We will sell no wine before its time."). Self-confidence is something you can't act; you have to possess it, and McKay, in his first leading role, has that in abundance.

He also suggests the charisma that swept people up. People were able to feel it even in his absence; I recall having lunch several times at the original Ma Maison in Beverly Hills, where no matter whom I was interviewing (once it was Michael Caine), the conversation invariably came around to a mysterious shadowy figure dining in the shade—Welles, who ate lunch there every single day.

Efron and Danes make an attractive couple, both young and bold, unswayed by Welles's greatness but knowingly allowing themselves to be used by it. Linklater's feel for onstage and backstage is tangible, and so is his identification with Welles. He was thirty when he made his first film, Welles of course twenty-five, both swept along by unflappable fortitude. *Me and Orson Welles* is not only entertaining but an invaluable companion to the life and career of the Great Man.

The Mechanic ★ ★

R, 92 m., 2011

Jason Statham (Arthur), Ben Foster (Steve), Donald Sutherland (Harry), Tony Goldwyn (Dean), Mini Anden (Sarah). Directed by Simon West and produced by Rene Besson, Robert Chartoff, John Thompson, David Winkler, Irwin Winkler, William Chartoff, Rob Cowan, Marcy Drogin, and Avi Lerner. Screenplay by Richard Wenk and Lewis John Carlino.

The Mechanic tells a story as old as *Hamlet* in a style as new as unbaked bread. What's the point? An intriguing plot is established, a new character is brought on with a complex set of problems, and then all the groundwork disintegrates into the usual hash of preposterous action sequences. Is there an action director left who knows it isn't all about the sound and the fury?

The movie is a remake of sorts of the 1972 Charles Bronson film, which seemed fairly good at the time and might only seem better today. It follows a cool professional killer, "The Mechanic" (Jason Statham), who works for a sinister killing corporation and specializes in murders that don't seem like murders or are deliberately misleading in other ways.

My guess is that in real life such operators are lonely, brutal, and tending toward paranoia. Statham's character, Arthur Bishop, on the other hand, is a hedonist and esthete who lives alone in elegance, prizes his classic car, and apparently believes a hooker isn't a hooker if you overpay her. For twenty bucks, you're buying sex, but for thousands you are identifying yourself as a consumer of the highest degree.

Bishop is, then, a worthless creature who prizes himself highly. It is assumed we make no moral judgment on his murders because nothing in this film has human meaning and few of its viewers will expect any. It's all an exercise in technique. George Clooney played a similar character in *The American*, an infinitely superior film that was also about an untraceable solo killer working for a murder corporation. But that film was fascinated by the Clooney character, whose attempts to deal with sex without feeling got him into trouble.

There are two human elements in *The Mechanic*. Donald Sutherland plays another killer under contract to the same company—a veteran in this line of work, who is wise and bearded and was Bishop's mentor. This would be touching if their field was science or the law, but less so since their field is killing people for money. That we are expected to be moved by what are presented as Sutherland's ethical instincts is a peculiarity best not meditated upon. The fact is that Sutherland pulls it off on the surface level, and brings more humanity than the character deserves.

The other character is Steve (Ben Foster), the son of a character I will not name. Bishop has killed this man, the son doesn't know that, and Bishop takes the kid under his arm and teaches him the theory and practice of the trade. Steve has problems with immaturity, substance abuse, and other issues that the suave, shaven Bishop is a stranger to, but Bishop works with him and has faith that the young man will grow up into a killer to make his father proud.

The film is well made by Simon West (*Tomb Raiders*), a technician in the tradition of Michael Winner, who made the Bronson film. Directors like this must be very good, regardless of whether their films are worth making in the first place. Audiences have been drilled to accept noise and movement as entertainment. It is done so well one almost forgets to ask why it has been done at all.

Medicine for Melancholy ★ ★ ★ ½

NO MPAA RATING, 88 m., 2009

Wyatt Cenac (Micah), Tracey Heggins (Joanne). Directed by Barry Jenkins and produced by Justin Barber. Screenplay by Jenkins.

Medicine for Melancholy is nothing more or less than the story of a man and a woman spending twenty-four hours together. It has no other agenda, which is part of its charm. Haven't we all spent some interesting time together with a stranger, talking a little about our lives, sharing a certain communion, with no certainty that we will ever see them again?

Micah and Joanne are African-Americans in their late twenties who wake up next to each other in a bed in an expensive home on San Francisco's Nob Hill. They are hung over. They don't know each other's names. She wants to go home and forget. He persuades her to have breakfast. In a perhaps symbolic walk across a hill into a less posh neighborhood, he tries to cheer her up. It becomes clear that in a city with a 7 percent black population, he sees her as intriguing: a single, hip black woman in what he describes as the "indie world."

They talk. They take a taxi to her neighborhood—not to her door. She leaves her wallet in the cab. He discovers she is Joanne, not "Angela." He tracks her down on his bike. He kids her. They bike to an art gallery. Then they go through a couple of museums. They're getting to like each other.

Micah is interested in stereotypes. He observes that two black people spending Sunday at art museums does not fit the stereotype. Whose? His, I think. She asks what race has to do with it. He says his identity, in the eyes of the world, is as a black man. "That's what people see." Who would speculate he supplies and maintains upscale private aquariums? And Joanne? Her expensive condo in the Marina belongs to her lover, a white man now in London on business. He is an art curator, although Micah observes there is not a single artwork in the condo.

"Does it matter that he's white?" she asks. "Yes and no," Micah says. A good answer. The day does not continue their discussion of interracial dating. It becomes more of a test-drive of a possible life together. Neither seriously expects to lead such a life, but it's intriguing to play. At one point they go to Whole Foods. When a newly met couple go grocery shopping together, they're playing house.

Micah is concerned with demographics and residential patterns. He passionately loves San Francisco and has seen gentrification push out the populations and neighborhoods that gave it flavor. All men need a lecture topic when trying to impress a woman, and this is his. At one point the film drops in on a completely unrelated discussion group about housing policy; it's the sort of detour you might find in *Waking Life*.

The actors are effortlessly engaging. Tracey Heggins plays skittish at first, then warmer and playful. Is she having a better time than she usually has with her white lover? Yes. Well, maybe yes and no. She doesn't talk enough about him for us to be sure. Wyatt Cenac plays a smart charmer; the urban facts he cites are a reminder of his comedy alter ego, the "Senior Black Correspondent" on Jon Stewart's *The Daily Show.*

Medicine for Melancholy is a first, but very assured, feature by Barry Jenkins, who has the confidence to know the precise note he wants to strike. This isn't a statement film or a bold experiment in style; it's more like a *New Yorker* story that leaves you thinking, yes, I see how they feel. The film is beautifully photographed by James Laxton; much of the color is drained, making it almost black and white. The critic Karina Longworth writes: "I guessed that the entirety of the film had been desaturated 93 percent to match the racial breakdown, but in a recent interview, Jenkins said the level of desaturation actually fluctuates." The visual effect is right; McLuhan would call this a cool film.

Meek's Cutoff ★ ★ ★ ½

PG, 104 m., 2011

Michelle Williams (Emily Tetherow), Bruce Greenwood (Stephen Meek), Paul Dano (Thomas Gately), Zoe Kazan (Millie Gately), Will Patton (Solomon Tetherow), Shirley Henderson (Glory White), Neal Huff (William White), Tommy Nelson (Jimmy White), Rod Rondeaux (The Indian). Directed by Kelly Reichardt and produced by Elizabeth Cuthrell, Neil Kopp, Anish Savjani, and David Urrutia. Screenplay by Jon Raymond.

To set aside its many other accomplishments, *Meek's Cutoff* is the first film I've seen that evokes what must have been the reality of wagon trains to the West. They were grueling, dirty, thirsty, burning, and freezing ordeals. Attacks by Indians were not the greatest danger; accidents and disease were. Over the years from movie Westerns I've developed a composite image of wagon trains as Conestoga parades led by John Wayne, including lots of women wearing calico dresses, and someone singing "Red River Valley" beside the campfire.

Not here. Director Kelly Reichardt's strategy is to isolate her story in the vastness of the Oregon Trail, where personalities seem to weaken in the force of the wilderness. She shows three families who bring reality to Robert Frost's phrase "vaguely realizing westward." They are gradually understanding that they are hopelessly lost. Their guide, Stephen Meek (Bruce Greenwood), boasts of his accomplishments, but members of the group sense that he is pushing ahead blindly in the hope that somehow the way through the Cascade Mountains will reveal itself.

The group includes Emily Tetherow (Michelle Williams), her husband, Solomon (Will Patton), the young couple Millie and Thomas Gately (Zoe Kazan and Paul Dano), and the Whites: Glory, William, and Jimmy (Shirley Henderson, Neal Huff, and Tommy Nelson). In their wagons they bring a few household furnishings, some clothes, and a forlorn bird in a cage, whose pathetic smallness echoes their own in this landscape. The men withdraw to discuss their mistrust of Meek, and it is significant that Reichardt identifies with the women as they attempt to overhear what's said.

Her focus in general is on the "womenfolk," as Westerns liked to call them. She centers on Michelle Williams as Emily, and of course Reichardt and Williams worked together on *Wendy and Lucy*, the evocative 2008 film about a drifter and her dog. Both films were written by Jonathan Raymond. Michelle Williams appears at first to be a slight, unprepossessing person, but in *Meek's Cutoff* she then reveals inner certainty. She is sure their guide is lost, she is certain they face death by thirst, and it is she who determines how they must use an Indian (Rod Rondeaux) they capture: He will find water.

The Indian, first seen alone on a high ledge watching them, is portrayed in a particular way. Unlike the fierce close-ups of Indian warriors we've been trained on in many Westerns, he is an enigmatic man, self-contained, observing, mostly held in the film's usual long and medium shots. We don't know what he's thinking. Why should we? In circa 1845, the two races were alien to each other.

At a time when many directors fall contentedly into the rhythm of a standard visual language, Reichardt devises a strategy that suggests the distance and isolation of these travelers. This is the first new feature film I've seen in a long time that has been photographed in the 1:1.33 screen ratio (as all movies were before the early 1950s). That's the ratio of many, maybe most, classic Westerns, but we expect widescreen these days, and her frame encloses her characters—not in the landscape (it appears limitless) but in their dilemma. They are such a small, helpless group, bound up with their hopes and fears. Imagine what it involved 165 years ago to set out in an ox-drawn covered wagon and trek across a continent in search of rumors.

I'm sure the women of the period wore hooded sunbonnets. They're always seen that way in Westerns. But Hollywood costume departments made sure the bonnets didn't obscure the famous faces of their stars (Joanne Dru, for example). The bonnets in *Meek's Cutoff* bury faces deep in shadow, are hard to see into, and must create tunnel vision. They not only protect women, but limit them. The men are also hidden; Meek's biblical beard and the deep shadow of his hat make him concealed and enigmatic.

The distinctive thing here is the subservience of the characters to the landscape. These pioneers do not stand astride the land; they wander it in misery and exhaustion. The wheels of their wagons are little match for the terrain. There is a heartbreaking accident. The peeps of the caged bird become a mocking reminder of the domesticity they've left behind.

Meek's Cutoff is more an experience than a story. It has personality conflicts, but isn't about them. The suspicions and angers of the group are essentially irrelevant to their overwhelming reality. Reichardt has the courage to establish that. She doesn't make it easy for us with simplistic character conflict. She's genuinely curious about the hardly educated pioneers who were brave, curious, or hopeful enough to set out on such a dangerous journey. It goes without saying that they had nothing to keep them home where they started from. Many started from hopelessness and died on the journey toward hope. Or wandered in the mountains. I learn that *Meek's Cutoff* was based on a true story. I didn't need to be told that.

Note: Although you'll see the movie in 1:1.33, Steve Kraus of the Lake Street Projection Room in Chicago writes me: "It was true 1.37:1 Academy Ratio. By 'true' I mean similar on-screen results could be had by pillar boxing 1.33 within the conventional cropped widescreen 1.85:1 aperture, which would make it easier for mainstream theaters to show such films correctly, but Meeks *was the real deal, in the format of films from before the widescreen era. Correct lenses and aperture plates are required to show."*

Of course, Steve has the lenses and plates. If you see this movie projected in widescreen, it is being projected wrongly.

Megamind ★ ★ ★

PG, 95 m., 2010

With the voices of Will Ferrell (Megamind), Tina Fey (Roxanne Ritchi), Jonah Hill (Hal/Tighten), David Cross (Minion), Brad Pitt (Metro Man). Directed by Tom McGrath and produced by Lara Breay and Denise Nolan Cascino. Screenplay by Alan Schoolcraft and Brent Simons.

Megamind was the third 3-D movie I'd seen in a row, and as I struggled to free my glasses from their industrial-strength plastic envelope, I wasn't precisely looking forward to it. Why do 3-D glasses and DVDs come so securely wrapped they seem like acts of hostility against the consumer? Once I freed my glasses and settled down, however, I was pleased to see a 3-D image that was quite acceptable. Too dim, as always, but the process was well used and proves again that animation is incomparably more suited for 3-D than live action is.

I'd just been rewatching *Superman* (1978), and felt right at home with the opening, narrated by a bright blue alien over flashbacks to his infancy. Born on a distant planet, he's packed into a rocket ship and blasted off to Earth, just like the Man of Steel. En route he meets his lifetime nemesis, a golden child who also lands on Earth in the lap of wealth. The blue child, alas, lands in a prison and is raised by hardened convicts.

As they grow up, these two super beings are destined to play crucial roles in nearby Metro City, where they're named Megamind (voice by Will Ferrell) and Metro Man (Brad Pitt). We may remember that Superman was given his name by Lois Lane, and here the story of the two super beings is covered by a TV reporter named Roxanne Ritchi (Tina Fey). Roxanne's cameraman Hal (Jonah Hill, looking rather Jonah Hill-like) later morphs into yet a third super being named Tighten.

This setup is bright and amusing, even if it

does feel recycled from bits and pieces of such recent animated landmarks as *The Incredibles* with its superpowers and *Despicable Me* with its villain. *Megamind* even goes so far as naming Megamind's fishy sidekick Minion (David Cross), a nod to the Minions who serve the despicable Gru. I enjoyed Megamind's conclusion, after being bullied as a child, that if he can't get credit for doing anything good he might as well become a villain.

It is a truth universally acknowledged that a hero requires a villain, and *Megamind* has some fun by depriving Megamind of Metro Man. Left without an opponent, he loses his zeal for evildoing, and actually clones Tighten to cure his loneliness. All of this of course is accomplished with much slapstick and sensational action, in a population that consists entirely of super beings, plus Roxanne, the prison warden, and cheering thousands of anonymous humans.

Tina Fey does a spirited job with Roxanne, and again I was reminded of *Superman* and Margot Kidder's high-spirited, unafraid Lois Lane. This time Roxanne isn't smitten by anyone, which is just as well because these guys are aliens, after all.

Megamind is an amusing family entertainment and gains some energy from clever dialogue and the fun Will Ferrell has with his character. I like the way he pronounced Metro City like "metricity," for example. The 3-D is well done, if unnecessary. Nothing in the movie really benefits from it, and if you can find it in 2-D that's the best choice. Save the surcharge and see those colors nice and bright.

The Men Who Stare at Goats ★ ★ ★ ½

R, 93 m., 2009

George Clooney (Lyn Cassady), Jeff Bridges (Bill Django), Ewan McGregor (Bob Wilton), Kevin Spacey (Larry Hooper), Stephen Lang (General Hopgood), Nick Offerman (Scotty Mercer), Tim Griffin (Tim Kootz). Directed by Grant Heslov and produced by Heslov, George Clooney, and Paul Lister. Screenplay by Peter Straughan, based on the book by Jon Ronson.

Bear with me here. Imagine *Ghostbusters* is based on a true story. Imagine the Big Lebowski as a real-life U.S. Army general. All factual, right? That's what *The Men Who Stare at Goats* sort of wants us to believe. I think I sort of do—to a small degree, sort of. "More of this is truer than you would believe," the movie says in an opening title. I'm waiting for the review of this one in *Skeptic* magazine.

We begin with a newspaperman named Wilton (Ewan McGregor) from Ann Arbor. That's a poignant note because Ann Arbor recently lost its daily newspaper. He interviews a goof who tells him he was a member of the New Earth Army, a supersecret army team of paranormals who were being trained as stealth weapons. In theory, they could spy at a distance, kill by the power of their sight alone, and penetrate enemy lines in spirit, not in body.

Wilton hungers to hunt where the headlines are. In 2002 he flies to Kuwait, hoping to cross into the war zone. He runs into a legendary guy he heard about from the crackpot back home. This is Lyn Cassady (George Clooney), said to be the best of the New Earth trainees. Wilton pumps him and learns of an acidhead Vietnam veteran named Bill Django (Jeff Bridges), who sold the army the notion of fighting men who could transcend physical limitations. We see Django in flashbacks; Bridges essentially plays him *as* the Big Lebowski. Members of the Church of Lebowskism will be able to enjoy this film as apocrypha.

The movie flashes between the recent Middle East and events twenty years earlier, when Cassady trained under Django to become, he explains, a Jedi Warrior. Clooney doesn't overplay and is persuasive, playing Cassady as a sensible, sane man who has seen the impossible and has no choice but to believe it. He shows Wilton videos of a goat and a hamster killed by brain power. In theory, mind power can even allow men to run through walls—if, of course, they believe they can.

The two of them unwisely journey into wartime Iraq, where they run into hostility. Cassady attempts to deal with it using paranormal techniques. He explains his theory of Jedi Warriordom to Wilton, who has apparently never seen *Stars Wars* episodes I, II, and III. Little joke. Their troubles are intercut with scenes of Cassady's early training, which included such self-persuasion exercises as fire walking. *I think* it is impossible that a flywheel like Bill Django could survive in the army, but then again, he has top-security clearance in a crucial secret program, so maybe he gets a pass. It may be that psychotropic drugs are justified as a pathway to higher powers. Whatever.

Kevin Spacey, who has been absorbed recently in London theatrical adventures, comes back in a good role as Hooper, who hates everything that Cassady stands for, whatever that is. All of the actors play without winks and spins, unless you consider Lebowskism itself a wink and spin. And then we're faced with the fact that the movie is based on the 2004 book by Jon Ronson, a writer for the *Guardian,* who wrote it humorously but (he said) truthfully about an army experiment. It was this real program, he says, that inspired playing the *Barney the Dinosaur* theme as a torture technique.

It actually doesn't matter if the book is truthful. It doesn't claim the paranormal powers are real. Ronson simply says some officials thought they might be—and that if they were, we had to get there first. The movie is funny either way.

But figure this out. The book inspired a BBC-TV series that interviewed the real retired general Albert Stubblebine III, who explains on camera exactly how men could walk through walls.

Mercy ★ ★

NO MPAA RATING, 87 m., 2010

Scott Caan (John Ryan), Wendy Glenn (Mercy Bennett), Troy Garity (Dane), John Boyd (Erik), James Caan (Gerry Ryan), Dylan McDermott (Jake). Directed by Patrick Hoelck and produced by Scott Caan, Vince Palomino, and Phil Parmet. Screenplay by Caan.

I have a problem with movies about men whom women cannot resist. If a man knows that, how did he find it out? By succeeding with one woman after another? If he's thirty-five, never been married, and doesn't like to date the same woman twice, he probably has a problem, and he probably *is* a problem. Even in a town as big as Los Angeles, word would get around. You wouldn't want to be the woman watched by everyone in the room to see if you fall for the Irresistible Man.

John Ryan is apparently such a man. Played by Scott Caan as a man who is surgical in his focus, he sees, decides, and moves in. He seems to succeed. If the woman is gone when he wakes up in the morning, that was a successful date. If they go to his place, they can't even feel a kindly urge to help him clean up a messy bachelor pad. Unless there is a toothbrush in the bathroom, there seems to be nothing in his apartment that didn't come with the demonstration unit.

One night at a party his moves don't work. It must be said he uses hopelessly outdated lines. When a man says, "You are the most beautiful woman I have ever seen," a woman should reply: "I know. But why would that make me want to sleep with you?" At the party, where he has already lined up a date with a waitress, he zeroes in on Mercy Bennett (Wendy Glenn), a classy woman with a British accent. "Mercy?" he asks. "Is that a joke?" He explains that (*cough*) the party is in his honor.

He thought it might be a joke because his new novel is named *Mercy.* He chats her up, gets nowhere, and the next day is horrified to read Mercy Bennett's review of the novel. She hated, hated, hated it. He's intrigued. He calls her up and asks her to meet, not for a date, but for a talk about the book. (It doesn't occur to him, then or ever, that if she reviewed his book and was invited to the party she probably knew who he was.)

These scenes are in the half of the film titled "Before." It also establishes his married best friend (Troy Garity) and his agent (Dylan McDermott). There is his lovelorn pal Erik (John Boyd), whose own girl is manifestly trying to dump him. John tutors Erik on the theory and practice of picking up women and dumping them.

In the film's second half, titled "After," we meet a changed John Ryan. He hasn't been shaving, he's deeply depressed, for the first time in years he goes to visit his father (James Caan), an English professor. His dad says he hasn't read his books, which is probably as well; he writes "romance novels" and, as we have seen, knows nothing about romance. Father and son share the same jaundiced view of women. The apple has not fallen far from the tree.

The time shifting (in a screenplay written by Scott Caan) may leave you adrift at times. There are flash-forwards, flashbacks, and possibly imagined scenes. The point is the same. They add up to a playboy getting his comeuppance. This story arc is predictable and not very satisfying, and the film's strengths are in the performances. Scott Caan is effective as a heartless creep, Wendy Glenn is devastating as a woman so assured she can perform verbal emasculation, and James Caan relates with his (own) son in scenes that inspire speculation the screenplay might be a little autobiographical.

What's lacking is a little more depth. This is a movie that covers a lot of distance in only eighty-seven minutes. We know the basics: The pickup artist gets hurt and becomes sadder but wiser. What we'd like to know is more about the people, especially Mercy Bennett. She never has a scene without Ryan. The women in the film don't seem to talk to one another about him, or themselves. And how does a bad novelist become a good one at the age of thirty-five after one life-changing experience?

The Merry Gentleman ★ ★ ★ ½

R, 99 m., 2009

Michael Keaton (Frank Logan), Kelly Macdonald (Kate Frazier), Tom Bastounes (Dave Murcheson), Bobby Cannavale (Michael), Darlene Hunt (Diane), Guy Van Swearingen (Billy Goldman), William Dick (Mr. Weiss). Directed by Michael Keaton and produced by Ron Lazzeretti, Steven A. Jones, and Tom Bastounes. Screenplay by Lazzeretti.

Good actors sometimes despair of finding worthy opportunities. They cheerlessly attend a premiere of their new film and think, "I could direct better than this dingbat." Sometimes they're right. I give you Michael Keaton, whose *Merry Gentleman* is original, absorbing, and curiously moving in ways that are far from expected. Michael Keaton once starred in *Jack Frost* as a boy's father imprisoned in a snowman. Think about that.

Keaton is one of the most intelligent men I have met in the acting profession, where you don't have much success these days if you're dumb. His mind is alive and present in many of his characters, and sometimes you get the impression the character is thinking, "I could say a lot more if the screenplay allowed me." What is uncanny about *The Merry Gentleman* is the way he implies that his character sometimes wishes he had said less.

Keaton plays Frank Logan, a Chicago hit man who is efficient and deadly, but suicidal. But no, this isn't a crime movie. Nothing as easy as that. It's a character study as Georges Simenon might have written, and Logan isn't the most important character. That is Kate Frazier, an abused wife newly employed in an office. A crime movie requires a skillful actress, but *The Merry Gentleman* requires a gifted one, and Keaton as director correctly places his focus on Kelly Macdonald, who played Josh Brolin's small-town wife in *No Country for Old Men*. Keaton wisely allows her to use a mid-Atlantic version of her Scots accent, because why not? She gets another aspect to her character for free.

These two first encounter each other through what is technically a Meet Cute, but they don't collide while entering a revolving door. Logan has just used a sniper scope to murder a man in an office window across the street. The job performed, he stands on the ledge of a rooftop and prepares to jump off. Kate, emerging from the street door of the building, looks up, sees him, and screams. He is startled and falls back onto the roof. He knows she has seen him. Now they will have to meet.

Is the movie about his intention to kill her before she can identify him? It's legitimate for us to think so. Although Logan goes through the motions of preparing for that, there is the possibility that he might have murdered for the last time. Yet how can we know? Kate reports the incident to the police, who file a routine report. Then the dead man is found, and a policeman named Murcheson (Tom Bastounes) realizes she must have seen the killer.

Murcheson, a recovering alcoholic, is immediately attracted to her. He invites her for "a coffee or something." Recovering from marriage, she is not eager to make a new friend. Murcheson, who is not a bad person, persists. Logan must realize the woman who saw him is dating the policeman on the case. There are other elements in play, but discover for yourself.

What is so good about the movie is the way Kate relates to these two men, who both hunger for care and sympathy. The screenplay is by Ron Lazzeretti, who writes dialogue of a very high order: subtle, cautious, aware. We understand this will not be a movie about a triangle and will not hurry to a neat conclusion. It will be about a worthwhile woman trying to relate to two difficult puppies left on her doorstep.

The Merry Gentleman isn't jolly. There are undercurrents of sadness and dread. Both men are frightened of their flaws. What will happen may be unforeseeable. Watch Keaton. His is a complex performance, evoking a damaged man who has, somewhere inside, ordinary emotions. As a director, he is attentive to the inner feelings of all three main characters, and it is there that a lot of the film really resides.

Of Lazzeretti I know little, except that he directed a feature in 1999 named *The Opera Lover*, and it also starred Tom Bastounes, an intriguing actor. I believe they met through Second City. Lazzeretti set out to write a film about humans, not genre stereotypes, and I suspect that's what attracted Keaton. The hit man–possible victim situation provides a reason for this unsocial man to need to meet her and adds potential suspense, but I was pleased the movie ended in the way it did.

Mesrine: Killer Instinct ★ ★ ★ ½

R, 113 m., 2010

Vincent Cassel (Jacques Mesrine), Cecile de France (Jeanne Schneider), Gerard Depardieu (Guido), Roy Dupuis (Jean-Paul Mercier), Gilles Lellouche (Paul), Elena Anaya (Sofia). Directed by Jean-Francois Richet and produced by Thomas Langmann. Screenplay by Abdel Raouf Dafri.

Jacques Mesrine was a brutal man who shot dead thirty-nine victims during his twenty-year run as a bank robber and kidnapper. That total doesn't include the prisoners, possibly dozens, he executed point-blank after they'd been tortured during France's war against Algeria. He escaped from two high-security prisons, kidnapped a millionaire, broke back into one of the prisons in an attempt to free his friends, and went on the lam in Quebec, Arizona, and Florida.

Yes, but he was a particularly French criminal who claimed he was an anarchist, protested prison conditions, described all his killings as acts of revolution against the state, and wrote two best-sellers that were compared by some to Camus. When he was France's Public Enemy Number One and every police officer in the nation was participating in a manhunt, he granted exclusive interviews and wrote tender love poems to his lawyer.

This is too much man for one movie, and so he has gotten two, *Mesrine: Killer Instinct* and *Mesrine: Public Enemy No. 1.* They're rolling out one after the other in North America, which usually doesn't work at the box office, but *Killer Instinct* ends with his car trapped behind a truck when its back canvas goes up and French cops open fire, killing his girlfriend, Jeanne Schneider (Cecile de France), and his dog, and wounding him fourteen times in the chest and head. Only wounding him? Yes, and then the screen promises *Mesrine: Public Enemy No. 1.* (I'm assuming he wasn't murdered; if he was, the second movie would have to be in reverse chronology or extremely slow motion.)

Mesrine, played with rough intensity by Vincent Cassel, was the most famous criminal in French history, and he came to that role only late in his career, after he was already famous in Canada and the United States. The Montreal papers called him and Jeanne "the French Bonnie and Clyde," he outdid Dillinger by robbing two banks across the street from each other within ten minutes, and like Dillinger he was an expert in self-publicity. Was the police ambush an assassination attempt? The police denied it, but he predicted it, and he promised he would never be taken without gunfire. He was known as a master of disguise, moved boldly in public when his face was on every TV screen, and in a touch too good for fiction, he took Jeanne to Cape Kennedy to watch the Apollo moon launch.

Jean-Francois Richet's *Mesrine: Killer Instinct* has parallels with Michael Mann's *Public*

Enemies, particularly in the suggestion that both men began to feed on their publicity. They walk into banks almost as celebrities making guest appearances. But Dillinger tried to stay out of shooting situations, and Mesrine seemed addicted to danger. He wrote a newspaper explaining that after he committed his first robbery he felt free because he had crossed a line separating him from control of the state. He declared war, and when authorities raided his apartment they found an arsenal, including automatic weapons and grenades.

Vincent Cassel in his forties is France's leading hard-boiled actor. Have you seen *The Crimson Rivers, Read My Lips, Irreversible,* or *Eastern Promises*? As Mesrine he affects the sideburns and mustache of a bad guy who studies himself in the mirror and doesn't know his look isn't working. He makes Mesrine self-absorbed, arrogant, and detached from the meaning of his murders. He depends on the charisma of his evil to attract women, and it does—although it didn't work for his first wife, the mother of his two children. Well, he wasn't very famous then. Unlike some American stars, Cassel makes no attempt to protect his image. Gaspar Noe's *Irreversible,* in particular, would be unthinkable for most of them. In it Cassel stars in a story I described as "so violent and cruel that most people will find it unwatchable."

Don't get the wrong idea. Cassel isn't his characters. He also plays nice guys and did the voice of the French hoodlum in *Shrek.* Here he even seems a sympathetic underdog until you reflect he has chosen the role for himself and murdered innocent people along his road to romance. He had an ordinary enough start in life, but then was attracted to the petty criminals who infest the Paris district called Clignancourt—that's where the tourists go to shop in *les puces,* the flea market. By then, his father believed, he had already been morally destroyed by his experiences in Algeria.

Yes, but some people become addicted to being bad. If you're trained as a paratrooper, you don't routinely seek work as a torturer and executioner. Mesrine seems to have had little concept of other people; life for him perhaps contained no more emotion than a point-and-shoot video game. The director Richet, who made the Ethan Hawke–Laurence Fishburne *Assault on Precinct 13* (2005), treats him as an insect more than a psychological case study.

The acting is macho understatement. Mesrine is a character who might have been played years ago by Gerard Depardieu, who appears here as Guido, a bullet-headed impresario of larceny. The two are business partners, not friends, and there's the suggestion none of his underworld pals understand the depth of Mesrine's pathology. They know they're bad guys, but Jacques takes it to another level.

Note: I obtained information on Mesrine from an article by John Lichfield in the Independent.

Mesrine: Public Enemy No. 1 ★ ★ ★ ½

R, 133 m., 2010

Vincent Cassel (Jacques Mesrine), Ludivine Sagnier (Sylvie Jeanjacquot), Mathieu Amalric (Francois Besse), Samuel Le Bihan (Michel Ardouin), Gerard Lanvin (Charlie Bauer), Olivier Gourmet (Commissaire Broussard), Anne Consigny (L'avocate de Mesrine). Directed by Jean-Francois Richet and produced by Thomas Langmann, Maxime Remillard, and Andre Rouleau. Screenplay by Abdel Raouf Dafri.

Because *Mesrine: Public Enemy No. 1* covers essentially the same material in the same style as *Mesrine: Killer Instinct,* there's not much to add in reviewing the second film of the pair. There are some personnel changes; Ludivine Sagnier replaces Cecile de France as the woman in Mesrine's life, Mathieu Amalric appears as a jumpy accomplice, the stout-hearted Olivier Gourmet is the prosecutor, and Anne Consigny is the attorney he has much need of. She was the one he wrote love poetry to.

The central enigma remains the same: Jacques Mesrine was born in a stable middle-class home, well educated, then sent to Algeria as a paratrooper who soon became a torturer and executioner and found he liked the work. He escaped from four prisons, killed perhaps forty people, kidnapped in France and Quebec, and stuck up banks the way other people use ATM machines.

Women were inexplicably willing to commit themselves to him. *Killer Instinct* ended with Mesrine and Sylvie being sprayed with a hail of police bullets, and *Public Enemy No. 1* opens with the same ambush. Since Mesrine was always heavily armed and had promised he would not be taken alive, Sylvie must, or should, have known that being attached to him placed her in the fire zone. Why did she do it? Was it love? After the gunfire, she doesn't even look to see what happened to Jacques, but starts screaming at the cops because they killed her dog.

Both of these films are directly and forcibly made, and indeed won Cesars for best director (Jean-Francois Richet) and best actor (Vincent Cassel). They have an impact recalling the days when gangster movies and action pictures in general had a meaty realism and weren't weakened by absurd CGI. No cars, guns, or people do anything here that cars, guns, and people cannot do in real life. If there's ever a film titled *Bourne vs. Mesrine*, the bout will end in the first round and the crown will return to Paris.

Vincent Cassel is the overwhelming fact of both films. He doesn't give Mesrine great depth, because how can he? The man was a psychopath, immune to movie psychology. But he gives him great presence. He is brutal, ugly, powerful, and inscrutable. In other roles Cassel is none of those things; he looks nice when he smiles. But he finds such cold ferocity in Mesrine that he's like a wild animal who kills for survival. I don't think Mesrine likes killing. He just frequently has to.

A great many bullets are fired by Mesrine, who stands up from behind parked cars and starts shooting at the cops in full view. In most movies we know the police bullets will never find their target. With Mesrine (1) sometimes they do, and (2) in real life, he survived an incredible twenty years with the police firing at him at least annually.

Cassel speaks excellent English and appears in many English-language films. Hollywood seems in need of a credible new action star, one who isn't worn out by trekking down red carpets. Here's the man.

The Messenger ★ ★ ★ ½

R, 112 m., 2009

Ben Foster (Will Montgomery), Woody Harrelson (Tony Stone), Samantha Morton (Olivia Pitterson), Jena Malone (Kelly), Steve Buscemi (Dale Martin). Directed by Oren Moverman and produced by Benjamin Goldhirsh, Mark Gordon, Lawrence Inglee, and Zach Miller. Screenplay by Oren Moverman and Alessandro Camon.

Maybe the only way to do it is by the book. You walk up to the house of a total stranger, ring the bell, and inform them their child has been killed in combat. When they open the door and see two uniformed men, they already know the news. Some collapse. Some won't let you finish before they beat their fist on your chest, crying for you to shut up, Goddamn it, that can't be true. Some seem to fall into a form of denial, polite, inviting you in as if this is a social situation. Some tell you it's a mistake. It isn't a mistake.

The Messenger is an empathetic drama about two men who have that job. One is Captain Tony Stone (Woody Harrelson), an old hand at breaking the news. The other is Staff Sergeant Will Montgomery (Ben Foster), who was wounded in combat in Iraq and is serving out the last three months of his tour. Stone, who has never experienced combat, is the more soldierly. Montgomery, in his first days on the job, has a tendency to care about the people—mostly parents—he's informing.

That's a very bad idea, Stone tells him. It is always necessary to go by the book. Don't have physical contact with anyone, let alone hug them. Better for you, better for them. These are their lives. They need the news, not a new best friend. Stone is another of Woody Harrelson's penetrating performances. His hair shaved almost as short as a kid in boot camp, his eyes behind dark glasses, his manner the stubborn fragility of the newly recovering alcoholic, he doesn't care that much about Montgomery, either. This may not be the first soldier he's had to break in on this hard assignment.

Ben Foster has usually played tough guys (*Alpha Dog, 3:10 to Yuma*, the Alaskan vampire thriller *30 Days of Night*). It is a wonderment to me how some actors seem defined by their credits and reinvent themselves in the right role. Here in countless subtle ways he suggests a human being with ordinary feelings who has been through painful experiences and is outwardly calm but not anywhere near healed.

Both of them are time bombs. How close is Stone to taking another drink? Will post-traumatic stress disorder bring down Montgomery? They drive in their rental car through the ordinary streets of America, so recently left by those they bring news of. Stone takes the lead. He sticks to the script. "The Secretary of Defense deeply regrets informing you that your [son, daughter], [military rank], [name], has been killed while on duty."

Everyone takes it differently, and the film develops the two characters as they meet survivors, notably Samantha Morton as a new widow, and Steve Buscemi as an angry father. Following the army way, they would never see these people again. It doesn't work out that way. Montgomery encounters Olivia (Morton) again. He sensed she was hurting.

A tender, frightened romance slowly begins to grow between them, in a series of scenes that are not simply about two people but about these two, and all that we know about them and continue to learn. They meet the angry father again, and Buscemi, as he sometimes does, plays an almost impossible scene in a way we didn't anticipate and cannot improve.

The Messenger is the first film directed by Oren Moverman, a combat veteran in the Israeli army, whose earlier screenplays included the Bob Dylan biopic *I'm Not There* (2007) and the extraordinary *Jesus' Son* (1999). This is a writer's picture, no less than a visceral experience that approaches its subject as tactfully as the messengers do. No fancy camerawork. It happens; we absorb it.

An important element is Kelly (Jena Malone), the girl Montgomery left behind when he shipped out to Iraq. She hasn't remained committed. She isn't heartless; that's her trouble. Her heart found other occupations. Malone treads a careful, not unkind, path with him. Her absence has created a vacuum; he may be too willing for Olivia to fill it.

The Messenger knows that even if it tells a tear-jerking story, it doesn't have to be a tear-jerker. In fact, when a sad story tries too hard, it can be fatal. You have to be the one coming to your own realization about the sadness. Moverman and his screenwriter, Alessandro Camon, born in Italy, have made a very particularly American story, alert to nuances of speech and behavior. All particular stories are universal, inviting us to look in instead of pandering to us. This one looks at the faces of war. Only a few, but they represent so many.

Micmacs ★ ★ ½

R, 104 m., 2010

Dany Boon (Bazil), Andre Dussollier (De Fenouillet), Omar Sy (Remington), Dominique Pinon (Buster), Julie Ferrier (Elastic Girl), Nicolas Marie (Francois Marconi), Marie-Julie Baup (Calculator), Michel Cremades (Tiny Pete), Yolande Moreau (Mama Chow), Jean-Pierre Marielle (Slammer). Directed by Jean-Pierre Jeunet and produced by Jeunet, Frederic Brillion, and Giles Legrand. Screenplay by Jeunet and Guillaume Laurant.

Here's a movie with visual invention and imagination up the wazoo. *Micmacs* is a whimsical fantasy about how a weapons manufacturer is set upon by a man with a bullet in his head and a motley crew of weirdos who live in a cave inside a junkyard. It may be a little too much for one meal.

I say this with reluctance, because this kind of visual energy is rarely found in the movies. I should be grateful for the change after several recent films in which the camera freezes in its tracks and stares stupefied at the action. I suppose I am. But the invention upstages the story without seeming necessary to it.

The director is Jean-Pierre Jeunet. Recall his magical *Amelie* (2001) and *A Very Long Engagement* (2004) and you'll understand its fancies. Recall his *The City of Lost Children* (1995) and you'll understand its problems. In an age when special effects can show us almost anything, there can come a tipping point when a movie is essentially only showing off. I'm not flatly against that, but in general I like to delude myself that the story is in the foreground. It's a judgment call. You may enjoy *Micmacs* more than I did.

The story is about a sad-sack clerk in a video store, named Bazil (Dany Boon). His father was killed with a land mine. As a child, opening a box of his father's effects, he finds the trademark of the manufacturer. He grows up into a feckless young man who passes his time in the video store by reciting the dialogue of movies in synch. One day, after a series of, shall we say, improbable events, he's shot in the middle of the forehead. The bullet lodges. The doc flips a coin and decides to leave it in, even though he could die at any moment.

Naturally, he's replaced at work. He's taken under the wing of a band of scavengers who live in a sort of Aladdin's Cave inside a mound of junk. This may sound sordid, but it's not. Imagine steampunk heaven. These people have the resources of a troupe of itinerant troubadours. They could start their own circus.

There's the contortionist named Elastic Girl (Julie Ferrier). The Guinness book–obsessed type named Buster (Dominique Pinon). A master thief named Slammer (Jean-Pierre Marielle), perhaps because of where he's spent a lot of time. A woman Calculator (Marie-Julie Baup), whose mind does mathematical wonders. A sage from the Congo (Omar Sy), who speaks Fortune Cookie. And Mama Chow (Yolande Moreau), who feeds and mothers them. Oh, and a human cannonball.

These oddballs enlist in Bazil's cause so quickly he hardly realizes he has a cause, and conspire with him to destroy the enterprises of the munitions experts. They zero in on the chief malefactor, Nicolas Thibault de Fenouillet (Andre Dussollier), and conspire against him with schemes so improbably labyrinthine that Rube Goldberg would have advised them to dial down.

The production values of the film are splendid. Jeunet's camera is so liberated that *Micmacs* might as well be animated. But there's a lack of urgency. The characters seem defined by the requirements of the plot. Dany Boon, in the lead, seems to be mostly along for the ride. The villain de Fenouillet is the most compelling character, particularly because of his fondness for collecting spare parts from the cadavers of evil men.

I look at a film like this and must respect it for its ingenuity and love of detail. Then I remember *Amelie* and its heroine played by Audrey Tautou, and I understand what's wrong: There's nobody in the story who much makes us care.

Midnight in Paris ★ ★ ★ ½

PG-13, 94 m., 2011

Owen Wilson (Gil), Rachel McAdams (Inez), Kathy Bates (Gert), Adrien Brody (Salvador), Carla Bruni (Museum Guide), Marion Cotillard (Adriana), Michael Sheen (Paul). Directed by Woody Allen and produced by Letty Aronson, Jaume Roures, and Stephen Tenenbaum. Screenplay by Allen.

This review contains spoilers.

Oh, yes it does, because I can't imagine a way to review *Midnight in Paris* without discussing the delightful fantasy at the heart of Woody Allen's new comedy. The trailers didn't give it away, but now the reviews from Cannes have appeared and the cat is pretty much out of the bag. If you're still reading, give yourself a fair chance to guess the secret by reading through the list of character names in the credits. "Gert." Which resident of Paris does that make you think of?

This film is sort of a daydream for American lit majors. It opens with a couple on holiday in Paris with her parents. Gil (Owen Wilson) and Inez (Rachel McAdams) are officially in love, but maybe what Gil really loves is Paris in the springtime. He's a hack screenwriter from Hollywood who still harbors the dream of someday writing a good novel and joining the pantheon of American writers whose ghosts seem to linger in the very air he breathes: Fitzgerald, Hemingway, and the other legends of Paris in the 1920s.

He'd like to live in Paris. Inez would like to live in an upper-class American suburb, like her parents. He evokes poetic associations with every café where Hemingway might once have had a Pernod, and she likes to go shopping. One night he wanders off by himself, gets lost, sits on some church steps, and as a bell rings midnight, a big old Peugeot pulls up filled with revelers. They invite him to join their party. They include Scott and Zelda Fitzgerald.

Allen makes no attempt to explain this magic. None is needed. Nor do we have to decide if what happens is real or imaginary. It doesn't matter. Gil is swept along in their wake, and finds himself plunged into the Jazz Age and all its legends. His novel was going to be about a man who ran a nostalgia shop, and here he is in the time and place he's most nostalgic for.

Some audience members might be especially charmed by *Midnight in Paris*. They would be those familiar with Fitzgerald, Hemingway, Gertrude Stein, and Alice B. Toklas, and the artists who frequented Stein's famous salon: Picasso, Dali, Cole Porter, Man Ray, Luis Buñuel, and, yes, "Tom Eliot." Allen assumes some familiarity with their generation, and some moviegoers will be mystified because cultural literacy is not often required at the movies anymore. Others will be as charmed as I was. Zelda is playfully daffy, Scott is in love with her and doomed by his love, and Hemingway speaks always in formal sentences of great masculine portent.

Woody Allen must have had a great time writing this screenplay. Gil is, of course, the Woody character (there's almost always one in an Allen film), and his fantasy is an enchanted wish fulfillment. My favorite of all the movie's time-lapse conversations may be the one Gil has with Buñuel. He gives Buñuel an idea for a film: A group of guests sit down to dinner and after the meal is over they mysteriously find themselves unable to leave the house. "But why not?" Buñuel asks. "They just can't," Gil explains. Buñuel says it doesn't make any sense to him. If the story idea and perhaps the name Buñuel don't ring a bell, that's a scene that won't connect with you, but Allen seems aware that he's flirting with Inside Baseball, and tries to make the movie charming even for someone who was texting all during high school.

Owen Wilson is a key to the movie's appeal. He makes Gil so sincere, so enthusiastic about his hero worship of the giants of the 1920s. He can't believe he's meeting these people and they are so nice to him—although at the time, of course, they didn't yet think of themselves as legends; they ran into ambitious young writers like Gil night after night in Miss Stein's salon. Another treasure in the film is Kathy Bates's performance. She is much as I imagine Gertrude Stein: an American, practical, no-nonsense, possessed with a nose for talent, kind, patient. She's something like the Stein evoked by Hemingway in *A Movable Feast*, his memoir of this period. She embodies the authority that made her an icon.

Then there's Adriana (Marion Cotillard), who has already been the mistress of Braque and Modigliani, is now Picasso's lover, and may soon—be still, my heart!—fall in love with Gil. Compared with her previous lovers, he embodies a winsome humility, as well he might. Meanwhile, life in the present continues, with Gil's bride-to-be and future in-laws increasingly annoyed by his disappearances every night. And there's another story involving a journey even further into the past, indicating that nostalgia can change its ingredients at a movable feast.

This is Woody Allen's forty-first film. He writes his films himself, and directs them with wit and grace. I consider him a treasure of the cinema. Some people take him for granted, although *Midnight in Paris* reportedly charmed even the jaded veterans of the Cannes press screenings. There is nothing to dislike about it. Either you connect with it, or not. I'm wearying of movies that are for "everybody"—which means, nobody in particular. *Midnight in Paris* is for me, in particular, and that's just fine with moi.

Modus Operandi ★ ★ ½

NO MPAA RATING, 78 m., 2010

Randy Russell (Stanley Cashay), Danny Trejo (Director Holiday), Mark Borchardt (Dallas Deacon), Michael Sottile (Squire Parks), Barry Poltermann (Casey Thunderbird), Nikki Johnson (Black Licorice). Directed by Frankie Latina and produced by Shalyse Dominique, Laurie Foote, Mark Foote, Sasha Grey, Jon Krill, Zebedee LeTendre, Barry Poltermann, Andrew Swant, Gilbert Trejo, and Sean Williamson. Screenplay by Latina.

You need to have paid your dues to appreciate *Modus Operandi.* Have you marinated in exploitation films? The cheap kind from the '60s and '70s, made by fly-by-night filmmakers on starvation budgets? Where you can almost sense them gasping as they try to accumulate enough footage to qualify as a feature? And where the female characters are wearing bikinis even in business offices?

It's not enough to like such films because they're "so bad they're good." You need to specialize and like the films because they're so good about being so bad, they're good. *Modus Operandi,* a film by Frankie Latina that has won praise on the midnight movie festival circuit, is such a film.

Yes, it has babes in bikinis. Yes, it has a "plot" about spies and assassins. Yes, it's filmed in Cheapo-Color, which is used interchangeably with black and white. Yes, it has scenes set in "Siberia," "Russia," and "Tokyo, Japan." But what makes it special is that it was mostly filmed in Milwaukee, and one of its stars is Mark Borchardt, whom you may recall as the subject of the great documentary *American Movie.* That was about the making of his own bargain-basement horror film, *Coven*, which a British actor informed him he was mispronouncing.

If you have paid those dues, there is a special pleasure to be had in *Modus Operandi* sequences like this one: The evil Dallas Deacon (Borchardt), apparently wearing the same glasses he wore in the doc ten years ago, is being chased in black and white across an open field by a helicopter, in homage to *North by Northwest.* He runs and runs and runs, and then disappears into some trees that didn't exist in the previous shots. The (unseen) pilot shouts, "We lost him down by the river!" Cut to high-quality new color footage of some ducks floating past, but no Borchardt. Cut to unmatched Cheapo-Color footage of three babes in bikinis, feet astride, standing menacingly on the prow of a speedboat on a lake, not a river. One babe means business. A second babe unties the top of the first babe's bikini and she dives in the water—because, of course, she is unable to swim while wearing the top. Cut to Borchardt wading into the (river? lake?) fully clothed.

Do you understand why I enjoyed *Modus Oprandi*? You don't. Millions agree with you. The film is touring the nation in search of those like Quentin Tarantino and John Waters who would stay planted in their seats and watch it a second time.

Often the (satire?) is embedded in the very arrangement of the characters. Know the crime movie cliché in which an evil boss sits enthroned in a restaurant, flanked by hit men and babes? Here they are obviously in the seating area of a Chinese restaurant's waiting room. Know how the bad guy shouts commands in a phone while his babes make out with each other? Here his headquarters is obviously a bench on the balcony of a hotel. His phone is a pastel 1970s desk model. Know how bad guys give orders to those around them? In one shot here, they're lined up parallel, so they have to look sideways to talk.

The plot involves two briefcases, I guess. Who cares? They were stolen from a U.S. presidential candidate. The briefcases are brought up by a scuba diver through a hole in the ice of a frozen lake in "Siberia, Russia" after unmatched footage pretty obviously of Wisconsin ice fishermen. Only CIA agent Stanley Cashay (Randy Russell) can find the briefcases. When we meet him, he's passed out with his head resting in a tavern urinal, with unfortunate results. At one point the search for them involves a mission to fly to "Tokyo, Japan" to shove a letter under the door of the mysterious Black Licorice (Nikki Johnson), who invariably wears huge 1970s sunglasses, even at night or while receiving a massage. Pay close attention to the footage incorporating Black Licorice in shots of crowds crossing a street in Tokyo.

I dunno who's still reading. You know who you are. If the film doesn't sound unique enough, reflect that it's one of the few in its genre to incorporate (1) a full-screen quote by Alexandre Dumas, and (2) a walking-down-the-street shot in homage to *Berlin Alexanderplatz*, and (3) a tavern still using a Blatz Beer sign. The Dumas quote doesn't make clear if it was said by père or fils, but you can't have everything.

Monsters ★ ★ ★ ½

R, 93 m., 2010

Scoot McNairy (Andrew Kaulder), Whitney Able (Samantha Wynden). Directed by Gareth Edwards and produced by Allan Niblo and James Richardson. Screenplay by Edwards.

A movie named *Monsters* must contain monsters. But in its breathtaking final scene, we realize they should not be called monsters but perhaps simply beings. They're aliens from Europa, a moon of Jupiter that has a thin oxygen atmosphere and possibly an ocean of water under its surface. It's one of the prime candidates for life elsewhere in the solar system, and if it's hard to understand how that life might be fifty-foot-high spiders that float and have a pulsing inner glow, well, that's an alien for you. The bastards are always up to something.

I've read some complaints from fanboys that the monsters aren't monstrous enough. You don't hear any complaints about Godzilla, Mothra, or the clicking grasshoppers in *District 9*, but let a filmmaker dare to imagine a truly alien life-form, and it's whine, whine, whine. So let me say that *Monsters* is a rather special achievement. Think of it as a movie that M. Night Shyamalan (and we) would be happy he made. It's based on characters, relationships, fear, and mostly unseen menace, and although its special effects are important, it's not *about* special effects.

I recently came across a collection of covers from a 1950s comic book named *Tales to Astonish!* Each issue featured a different low-rent monster ("Mummex," "Droom," "Titano," "Vandoom," "Rommbu"). The most intriguing was "X," described as "THE THING THAT LIVED!!" The monsters invariably towered high above puny humans who were running for their lives in the foreground. The beings in *Monsters* tower above humans, but that's not because they're giant versions of B-movie clichés. It's because they are different in structure and nature from the life-forms on Earth.

The story, set some years in the future, explains that a probe was sent to Europa to search for life. On its return it crash-landed in Mexico. Whatever was on board found the conditions here suitable. The beings have occupied a wide swath of northern Mexico, known as the Infected Zone, and travel through it is forbidden. The two nations are connected only by boats and airplanes. A massive wall has been constructed to keep the creatures out of the United States, and air force planes fire missiles at them.

Whoops. I just hopped over one allegory and tripped on another one. There's an obvious parallel with our current border situation and the controversy over illegal aliens. And another one with our recent wars, where expensive and advanced aircraft are used to fire missiles at enemies who are mostly invisible. A process of demonization is also going on: Are these beings actually a threat?

Oh, sure, the journey in the film takes us through wastelands of devastation (my guess is they filmed in the aftermath of hurricanes). Boats are in trees, planes are in rivers, and so on. A brief comment, almost a throwaway line, suggests the creatures grow agitated when attacked. Many a creature does. There isn't a single shot on camera of a being actually assaulting anything without provocation.

The story involves Andrew Kaulder (Scoot McNairy) and Samantha Wynden (Whitney Able). He's a freelance photographer. She's the daughter of Kaulder's boss. Her father calls Kaulder and orders him to be sure Sam gets out of Mexico unharmed. He reluctantly agrees. They begin a journey north that, after many setbacks, leaves them trying to navigate a river through the Zone on a boat crewed by hired gunmen.

We see evidence of the aliens. We hear their mournful sounds. We see them unclearly in night-vision images on television news. Apparently they don't come out in daytime. The river journey, like the one in *Apocalypse Now*, often goes smoothly enough, but there's always the invisible threat in the jungle. Andrew and Samantha, like many a movie couple before them, start out antagonistic and gradually lower their guard as they share the journey. But theirs is not a conventional romance. It's more about learning to see another person.

Monsters was written and directed by Gareth Edwards. He also created all the special effects. He shot on location. All of the characters except the leads are played by locals. They're untrained, which means they're all the more convincing. Edwards had a minuscule budget, but he knew how to spend it.

The film holds our attention ever more deeply as we realize it's not a casual exploitation picture. We expect that sooner or later we'll get a good look at the aliens close up. When we do, let's say it's not a disappointment. They're ugly and uncannily beautiful. We've never seen anything like them. And their motives are made clear in a sequence combining uncommon suspense and uncanny poetry. Edwards is brilliant at evoking the awe and beauty he has been building toward, and at last we fully realize the film's ambitious arc. I think the lesson may be: Life has its reasons. Motives are pretty universal. Monsters are in the eye of the beholder.

Monsters vs. Aliens ★ ★ ½

PG, 96 m., 2009

With the voices of: Reese Witherspoon (Susan/Ginormica), Seth Rogen (B.O.B.), Hugh Laurie (Dr. Cockroach, PhD), Will Arnett (The Missing Link), Kiefer Sutherland (Gen. W.R. Monger), Rainn Wilson (Gallaxhar), Stephen Colbert (President Hathaway), Paul Rudd (Derek Dietl). Directed by Rob Letterman and Conrad Vernon and produced by Lisa Stewart. Screenplay by Letterman, Maya Forbes, Wallace Wolodarsky, Jonathan Aibel, and Glenn Berger.

Monsters vs. Aliens is possibly the most commercial title of the year. How can you resist such a premise, especially if it's in 3-D animation? Very readily, in my case. I will say this first and get it out of the way: 3-D is a distraction and an annoyance. Younger moviegoers may think they like it because they've been told to, and picture quality is usually far from their minds. But for anyone who would just like to be left alone to SEE the darned thing, like me, it's a constant nudge in the ribs saying, *Never mind the story. Just see how neat I look.*

The film was made in Tru3D, the DreamWorks process that has been hailed by honcho Jeffrey Katzenberg as the future of the cinema. It is better than most of the 3-D I've seen (it doesn't approach the work on *The Polar Express* and *Beowulf*). But if this is the future of movies for grown-ups and not just the kiddies, saints preserve us. Billions of people for a century have happily watched 2-D and imagined 3-D. Think of the desert in *Lawrence of Arabia*. The schools of fish in *Finding Nemo*. The great hall in *Citizen Kane*.

Now, that flawless screen surface is threatened with a gimmick, which, let's face it, is intended primarily to raise ticket prices and make piracy more difficult. If its only purpose was artistic, do you think Hollywood would spend a dime on it? The superb MaxiVision process is available for $15,000 a screen, and the Hollywood establishment can't even be bothered to look at it. Why invest in the technology of the future when they can plunder the past?

Speaking of the past, *Monsters vs. Aliens* retreads some of the monsters that starred in actual 1950s B-movies: a blob, the fifty-foot woman, and no end of aliens with towering foreheads on their dome-shaped heads. Whether the average kid will get all of the connections is beside the point; if kids could accept Pokemon and the Teenage Mutant Ninja Turtles, these monsters are going to seem like masterpieces of manic personality.

The plot: On her wedding day, sweet Susan (Reese Witherspoon) is mutated by a meteorite; just as she walks down the aisle, she grows to (I learn) just an inch short of fifty feet, maybe because Disney wanted to respect the copyright. Her husband (Paul Rudd) was no match for her anyway, and now he really has small-man complex. After she wreaks havoc with every step, the military names her Ginormica, no doubt sidestepping *Amazonia* so as not to offend the lesbian lobby. She's snatched by the feds and deposited in a secret government prison holding other monsters, who have been languishing since the 1950s. They're old enough that, if they escape, they could terrorize the subway on a senior pass.

Earth is invaded by a robot that has one big eyeball in the middle of its head, like a giant Leggs pantyhose container bred with an iSight camera. Gen. W.R. Monger (Kiefer Sutherland) and the president (Stephen Colbert) are helpless to deal with this threat, and in desperation release the monsters to save the earth. Springing, leaping, skittering, or oozing into battle we have Ginormica at the head of an army including B.O.B., Insectosaurus, Dr. Cockroach, and The Missing Link.

With the exception of Susan, who is perky, these creatures have no personalities in the sense of the distinctive characters in DreamWorks' *Shrek* movies. Basically they express basic intentions, fears, and desires in terms of their physical characteristics. There is a lot of banging, clanging, toppling, colliding, and crumbling in the movie, especially when San Francisco is attacked by Gallaxhar, a squid that is the master of the robot. Conventional evolutionary guidelines are lost in the confusion.

I didn't find the movie rich with humor, unless frenetic action is funny. Maybe kids have learned to think so. Too bad for them. Think of the depth of *Pinocchio*. Kids in those days were treated with respect for their intelligence. *Monsters vs. Aliens* is also lacking in wit.

What is wit? Well, for example, the spirit in which I am writing this review. The dictionary defines it as *analogies between dissimilar things, expressed in quick, sharp, spontaneous observations.* A weak point with the monsters, and way outside Gallaxhar's range.

I suppose kids will like this movie, especially those below the age of reason. Their parents may not be as amused, and if they have several children, may ask themselves how much it was worth for the kids to wear the glasses. Is there a child who would see this movie in 2-D (which has brighter colors than 3-D) and complain?

Monte Carlo ★ ★

PG, 109 m., 2011

Selena Gomez (Grace/Cordelia), Katie Cassidy (Emma), Leighton Meester (Meg), Cory Monteith (Owen), Andie MacDowell (Pam), Brett Cullen (Robert). Directed by Thomas Bezucha and produced by Denise Di Novi, Alison Greenspan, Nicole Kidman, Per Saari, and Rick Schwartz. Screenplay by Bezucha, April Blair, and Maria Maggenti.

Monte Carlo is a harmless, innocuous tweener fantasy that seems constructed out of bits and pieces of movies we must surely have seen before, but can't quite place because there's nothing much to remember. It's chirpy, it's bright, there are pretty locations, and lots happens. This is the kind of picture that can briefly hold the attention of a cat.

It stars Selena Gomez, a Disney discovery who is eighteen but looks fourteen and, let it be said, is cute as a button. I liked her in the movie, with her round-eyed astonishment and unaffected energy. She plays Grace, a new high school graduate who has been saving up for four years to pay for her dream, a graduation trip to Paris.

In another movie, in another universe, this would be a movie about Grace's trip to Paris. *Monte Carlo* is a movie about Grace's trip to a wheezy plot involving mistaken identities, a handsome guy who falls in love with her, and her whirlwind trip through a lifestyle of the rich and famous.

Grace has acquired a stepsister, Meg (Leighton Meester, of *Gossip Girl*), and is devastated when she finds that her mom and stepdad have arranged for Meg to join her on the trip. And Grace will bring along her BFF, Emma (Katie Cassidy, also of *Gossip Girl*). This actually may be prudent because Meg is in her twenties and will perhaps provide a chaperone for Grace and Emma.

Such a possibility is not considered by the movie, which treats the trio more as a unit, bopping through a heady series of adventures after Grace is mistaken for Cordelia Winthrop Scott, a rich little British girl who is heir to a vast fortune and is perhaps not six degrees separated from Paris Hilton. Grace is a dead ringer for Cordelia, and in playing both characters Gomez essentially has only to look like herself.

That sets up the girls for a PG-rated version of *Sex and the City*, except with no sex, one fewer girl, and different cities. Otherwise, the escapism is the same: Through the miraculous intervention of outside forces (a Middle Eastern sheik, or in this case, the mistaken identity), they are whisked off in a private jet and find themselves pampered in a luxurious hotel suite, gowned in haute couture, served thirty-pound lobsters and courted by handsome young guys. And, hey, Owen (Cory Monteith of *Glee*) likes Grace . . . for herself!

There is a puzzlement about the selection of Monte Carlo. Given any role in the decision, what girl in her right mind would want to leave Paris and go to Monte Carlo? Venice, maybe. Monte Carlo is an overbuilt condo tax shelter with bargain-basement royalty. Its sights, in this film anyway, seem to consist mostly of hotel rooms. The adventures of the girls have less to do with traveling in Europe than with conspicuous consumption. The movie gives its tweener target audience credit for little intelligence or curiosity about Europe, and dishes out the same old love-at-first-sight formulas.

I enjoyed two details. One was the budget fleabag hotel they check into. If they had only stayed there, some promising comedy might have been generated. The second was the whirlwind tour by sightseeing bus they take after arriving in Paris. As they trot through the Louvre, their guide seems to be trying to set a speed record. Then again, nothing about these characters suggests they would have ever found the Louvre on their own.

Moon ★ ★ ★ ½

R, 97 m., 2009

Sam Rockwell (Sam Bell), Kevin Spacey (Gerty), Dominique McElligott (Tess Bell). Directed by Duncan Jones and produced by Stuart Fenegan and Trudie Styler. Screenplay by Nathan Parker.

Is *Moon* evoking *2001*, or does its mining outpost on the far side of the moon simply happen to date back to the *2001* era (which was, of course, more than eight years ago)? I lean toward the second theory. After the mission carrying Dave Bowman disappeared beyond Jupiter, mankind decided to focus on the moon, where we were already, you will recall, conducting operations. The interior design of the new moon station was influenced by the *2001* ship, and the station itself was supervised by Gerty, sort of a scaled-down HAL 9000 that scoots around.

At some point in the future (we can't nail down the story's time frame), this station on the far side is manned by a single crew member, Sam Bell (Sam Rockwell). He's working out the final days of a three-year contract and is close to cracking from loneliness. Talking to loved ones via video link doesn't satisfy. The station is largely automated; it processes lunar rock to extract helium-3, used to provide Earth with pollution-free power from nuclear fusion. My guess is, the station is on the far side because you don't want to go gazing at the Man in the Moon some night and see a big zit on his nose.

The station is large and well appointed, and has entertainment resources and adequate supplies. Sam communicates frequently with the home office . . . and so does Gerty. Sam doesn't do any actual mining, but his human hands and brain are needed for repairs, maintenance, and inspection. One day he's outside checking up on something, and his lunar rover smashes up. He's injured and awakens in the station's medical facility. And that, I think, is all I need to say. A spoiler warning would mean secrets are revealed—and you'd look, wouldn't you, no matter what you say.

I want to take a step back and discuss some underlying matters in the film. In an age when our space and distance boundaries are being pushed way beyond the human comfort zone, how do we deal with the challenges of space in real time? In lower gravity, how do our bodies deal with loss of bone and muscle mass? How do our minds deal with long periods of isolation?

The *2001* vessel dealt with the physical challenges with its centrifuge. Dave and Frank had each other—and HAL. Sam is all on his own, except for Gerty, whose voice by Kevin Spacey suggests he was programmed by the same voice synthesizers used for HAL. Gerty seems harmless and friendly, but you never know with these digital devils. All Sam knows is that he's past his shelf date and ready to be recycled back to Earth.

Space is a cold and lonely place, pitiless and indifferent, as Bruce Dern's character grimly realized in Douglas Trumbull's classic *Silent Running*. At least he had the consolation that he was living with Earth's last vegetation. Sam has no consolations at all. It even appears that a new guy may have entered the orbits of his wife and daughter. What kind of a man would volunteer for this duty? What kind of a corporation would ask him to? We, and he, find out.

Moon is a superior example of that threatened genre, hard science fiction, which is often about the interface between humans and alien intelligence of one kind or other, including digital. John W. Campbell Jr., the godfather of this genre, would have approved. The movie is really all about ideas. It only seems to be about emotions. How real are our emotions, anyway? How real are we? Someday I will die. This laptop I'm using is patient and can wait.

Note: The capable director, Duncan Jones, was born Duncan Zowie Heywood Jones. Easy to understand if you know his father is David Bowie, rhymes with Zoe, not Howie. Jones a successful UK commercial director; this is his debut feature.

Morning Glory ★ ★ ★ ½

PG-13, 110 m., 2010

Rachel McAdams (Becky Fuller), Harrison Ford (Mike Pomeroy), Diane Keaton (Colleen Peck),

Patrick Wilson (Adam Bennett), Jeff Goldblum (Jerry Barnes). Directed by Roger Michell and produced by J. J. Abrams and Bryan Burk. Screenplay by Aline Brosh McKenna.

Morning Glory is a funny entertainment to begin with, and then Rachel McAdams transforms it. And Harrison Ford transforms himself. She plays as lovable a lead as anyone since Amy Adams in *Junebug*, and he bestirs himself from his frequent morosity and creates with gusto a TV newsman who is described as a great man, *but* the third worst person of all time. Diane Keaton is pitch-perfect as a morning TV host who can, and must, smile through everything.

Comedies open every week. This is the kind I like best. It grows from human nature, and is about how people do their jobs and live their lives. It is wisely not about a May-October romance between McAdams and Ford. It's more about their love for their work. It isn't deep, and it doesn't approach *Broadcast News* in its examination of the TV producer mentality, but it's the kind of sitcom you can get happily carried along with.

McAdams plays Becky Fuller, a little Energizer bunny of a morning TV producer, who gets fired from her thankless job in New Jersey and then has the good, or bad, luck to be hired to produce a last-place network morning show. Her boss is the dubious Jerry Barnes (Jeff Goldblum), who possibly views himself as the hiring agent for the *Titanic*. Becky plunges with zeal into a show that is not merely stuck in its tracks, but congealed. At the first staff meeting she comes across as a featherbrained lightweight until, in a nice burst of dialogue, she reveals she has heard everything, had strong opinions about it, and fires Keaton's current coanchor.

Her assignment: Turn the show around. The network has one of her heroes hanging around, working off the end of his contract. This is Mike Pomeroy (Ford), who detests what has happened to network news. Becky discovers how much time he has left on his contract and forces him into taking her show's coanchor gig. This involves precisely the kind of news he hates, and he'll have to do some of it, even though Diane Keaton's game enough to kiss a frog.

I suppose the outcome of the story is preordained. And we can hardly stir ourselves to care about the story within the story, about Becky's affair with Paul Newmanish fellow producer Adam Bennett (Patrick Wilson), which forces her to choose between love and her Blackberry. If you think teenagers are tethered to texting, you've never seen a TV producer.

What the movie has is charm and a light-footed smartness. In its version of story meetings and problems with talent, it's not a million miles away from what I've seen taking place. Morning news has a certain caffeinated jollity that's comforting. I sit in grumpy sleepiness and allow myself to be kidded out of it with the on-air "family" and the goofy weathermen. I don't expect hard news and investigative reporting. Pomeroy does. He expects it all the time, which is perhaps why he's sitting out the rest of his contract.

Morning Glory could have been routine. It's Rachel McAdams's life force that illuminates it. She positions herself barely on the right side of manic. She's always on, always optimistic, always hoping. She loves her work. There's a scene where she runs from NBC at Rockefeller Center across town to her network, "IBS," and she does it like a hungry colt. She makes Becky impulsive, determined, frisky, and, yes, cute. She grinds away at Harrison Ford's stone face and carves a smile out of it.

The film was directed by Roger Michell (*Notting Hill*) and written by Aline Brosh McKenna, whose *The Devil Wears Prada* is also about a spunky young woman up against a living legend. They know how to handle this material. They're also fortunate in the casting.

Ford is not a demonstrative actor. Sometimes he can barely rouse himself to growl. Here he's kind of inspired. When he's anchoring with Keaton, his double takes are flawless. When they get into a duel of who says "bye" last, they do it with impeccable timing. Ford doesn't venture beyond his usual acting range, but within it he creates a character with a reluctantly human inside.

I mentioned goofy weathermen. Matt Malloy plays a funny one here. He lives for the weather. He collects weather vanes. He also loves being in TV. Becky is ruthless in how she uses him on outside locations, and those scenes remind us of all the hapless TV people doing absurd things at some risk to their bodies or souls, simply to produce a few minutes of anything to perk us up at home. Back in the studio, the producers like Becky aren't heartless, exactly. It's just that they'll gladly toss human beings on the bonfire of "good TV."

Moscow, Belgium ★ ★ ★

NO MPAA RATING, 106 m., 2009

Barbara Sarafian (Matty), Jurgen Delnaet (Johnny), Johan Heldenbergh (Werner), Anemone Valcke (Vera), Sofia Ferri (Fien), Julian Borsani (Peter). Directed by Christophe van Rompaey and produced by Jean-Claude van Rijckeghem. Screenplay by van Rijckeghem and Pat van Beirs.

She backs up her car. His big truck runs into it. She should have looked first. A truck that size shouldn't have been in a parking lot. They get out and start screaming insults at each other. This is in a Flemish-speaking city in Belgium. We quickly learn that the f-word sounds exactly the same in English and Flemish.

Now here is the intriguing element. They are both livid with anger. Their insults escalate from their driving abilities to their genders. Women are bloodsuckers. Men are—never mind what men are. At some point, very subtle and hard to define, their insults turn into play. No, they don't start grinning. They still both seem angry. But they grow verbally inventive, and we sense, and they sense, a shift in the weather. It ends with him asking her out for coffee.

The buried emotions in this scene play out all through *Moscow, Belgium,* an uncommon comedy that is fairly serious most of the time. She is Matty (Barbara Sarafian), forty-one years old. He is Johnny (Jurgen Delnaet), in his late twenties. Matty's husband has walked out on her and her three kids. Johnny's girlfriend left him for some rich dude. Johnny has fallen helplessly in love with her, possibly because he has met his match in insults, possibly because a woman who can think that fast on her feet can—never mind what she can do.

Their working-class neighborhood of Ghent is named Moucou, with high rises, heavy traffic, rough bars. Johnny lives here in the sleeping compartment of his truck cab. He is friendly, has eyes that smile, hair she would probably love to take a brush to. Her hair is a slightly tidier mess. She has no desire to meet a man, especially one so much younger. Her husband, Werner (Johan Heldenbergh), an art teacher, left her for a little tart who was one of his students. One cradle robber is enough for her family.

Now about her kids. They are individuals intent on their own lives and indifferent to the fact that they are in a movie. Here's what I mean by that. Ever notice how in a lot of movies the family members are playing Family Members? The kids are arrayed around the dinner table smoothly fitting in their dialogue. Matty's kids are Vera, about seventeen, who regards her mother with weary insight; a younger daughter, Fien, who is going through a stage of reading everyone's Tarot cards and relating to you as if you're the Hanging Man or The Fool; and a still younger son, Peter, who is obsessed by airplanes. Johnny comes for dinner, but they're indifferent to him or, in Vera's case, tactfully withdrawn.

Werner turns up when he hears about his wife's young boyfriend, and they all share a family meal that I suspect owes something to Mike Leigh's family occasions of awkward, weird embarrassment. Matty has to choose: the faithless husband who is a handsome jerk, or the love-struck truck driver with a disturbing past and good reasons to never, ever drink again. The audience would advise her against both.

Underneath everything rolls the rhythm of Matty's real life. Men can come and go, but someone needs to put food on the table, do the shopping, be a parent. Matty has a job in the post office, where half the customers seem to know her. This is not the greatest job, but it's what she has. She understands Johnny's pride in his truck. It is all he has, but it is *his.* He can come and go with the freedom of a ranch hand. Werner, on the other hand, sometimes seems like one of the kids. Well, both men do. By the virtue of their continuity through family crises, women maintain a home, which serves as a powerful attraction.

The performances make these characters work. Barbara Sarafian, first seen in a long shot as she looks painfully hostile and withdrawn, is weather-beaten but attractive. Johnny must be the despair of his mother: an unkempt charmer who looks like trouble. Werner is a creep. The only grown-up in the movie is Vera. She puts her mother to an unexpected test, and Matty, after a double take, shows she has instinctive love for her daughter.

I will not be revealing a thing if I say we're not too sure Matty has made the right choice at the end. That's because neither choice would be the right choice. But notice how deeply the director, Christophe van Rompaey, has drawn us into these lives, how much we finally care, and with what sympathy all the actors enter into the enterprise.

The Most Dangerous Man in America ★ ★ ★

NO MPAA RATING, 94 m., 2010

Featuring Daniel Ellsberg (Narrator), Patricia Ellsberg, Anthony Russo, Howard Zinn, Janaki Natajaran, Randy Koehler, Tom Oliphant, Egil Krogh, Max Frankel, John Dean, Leonard Weinglass, Hendrick Smith, and Mike Gravel. A documentary directed and produced by Judith Ehrlich and Rick Goldsmith. Screenplay by Goldsmith, Ehrlich, Lawrence Lerew, and Michael Chandler, partly based on Daniel Ellsberg's *Secrets: A Memoir of Vietnam and the Pentagon Papers.*

I thought I was pretty much familiar with the story about how the Pentagon Papers were leaked to the press in 1971. I knew that Daniel Ellsberg, a high-level analyst at the Pentagon and the Rand Corporation, had Xeroxed the Pentagon's secret history of the war in Vietnam and leaked it to the press, notably the *New York Times.* I recalled his arrest and trial. Ironically, his case was dismissed because White House plumbers broke into his psychiatrist's office and Nixon offered to make Ellsberg's judge head of the FBI. Said Judge William Matthew Byrne Jr.: "The bizarre events have incurably infected the prosecution of this case."

I knew all that. What I never realized was what a high-ranking employee Ellsberg really was, and how secret the Pentagon Papers really were. Locked in safes, their existence was a secret even from President Lyndon B. Johnson, who, it was believed, would have been infuriated by such a history. Ellsberg didn't merely leak the papers; he played a key role in contributing to them.

His first day on the job, cables came in from the celebrated Gulf of Tonkin incident, used by LBJ to justify escalating the war in Vietnam. Later the same day, cables from the commodore in command over the "attacked" ships said there was a "problem" with the reports—which turned out to be false. Johnson didn't want to hear it. He was ready to escalate the war, and he escalated.

His was the latest in a series of presidential decisions beginning with Truman, and continuing through Kennedy, Johnson, and Nixon, who financed France in its Indochinese war, propped up corrupt regimes in South Vietnam, prevented free elections, and eventually wreaked destruction in an unwinnable war.

Ellsberg, a marine company commander in the 1950s, wanted firsthand information. He went to Vietnam personally, shouldered a weapon, and led a patrol. What he learned convinced him that a false portrait of U.S. success was being painted. On a flight back to Washington with Robert McNamara, the defense secretary agreed the war could not be won, and we see the two men leaving the aircraft together before McNamara lied to the press that America was winning it. Later McNamara resigned, for reasons he didn't make clear at the time, nor even later in his confessional Errol Morris documentary, *The Fog of War.*

Ellsberg, in short, could not be dismissed as merely a sneak and a snitch, but a man who had direct knowledge of how the American public had been misled. He saw himself not as a peacenik war protester, but as a government servant exercising a higher moral duty. The documentary *The Most Dangerous Man in America,* by Judith Ehrlich and Rick Goldsmith, traces his doubts about authority back to a childhood tragedy and forward to the influence of young men who went to prison for their convictions.

It is a skillful, well-made film, although, since Ellsberg is the narrator, it doesn't probe him very deeply. We see his version of himself.

A great deal of relevant footage has been assembled, and is intercut with stage re-creations, animations, and the White House tapes of Richard Nixon, who fully advocated the nuclear bombing of Hanoi. Kissinger was apparently a voice of restraint. If you can think of another war justified by fabricated evidence, and another cabinet secretary who resigned without being very clear about his reasons, you're free to, but the film draws no parallels.

Mother ★ ★ ★ ½

R, 128 m., 2010

Kim Hye-ja (Mother), Won Bin (Do-joon), Jin Goo (Jin-tae). Directed by Bong Joon-ho and produced by Choi Jae-won, Park Tae-joon, and Seo Woo-sik. Screenplay by Park Eun-gyo and Bong Joon-ho.

The strange, fascinating film *Mother* begins with what seems like a straightforward premise. A young man of marginal intelligence is accused of murder. A clue with his name on it and eyewitness testimony tie him to the crime. His mother, a dynamo, plunges into action to prove her son innocent. So there we have it, right? He's either guilty or not, and his mom will get to the bottom of things. Or not.

Is it that I've seen so many movies? Is that why I grow impatient with formulas, and am grateful for films that upset my expectations? If you faithfully remade *Mother* for a mass American audience (let's say with Helen Mirren and Ed Norton), mainstream moviegoers would likely be furious because: (a) "You can't do that!" and (b) "Uh, what is it that you did, exactly?"

This is a new South Korean film by Bong Joon-ho, his first after *The Host* (2006). That was a popular thriller about a giant squid created by toxic waste who dragged away a victim. Her family members learn she's still alive, but can't get the authorities to listen. Once again, in *Mother,* blood ties go up against the state.

The mother of the title, played by a respected South Korean actress named Kim Hye-ja, is a force of nature. In a village, she runs a little shop selling herbs, roots, and spices. Her sideline is prescribing herbal cures. Her son, Do-joon (Won Bin), in his late twenties, lives at home and they sleep in the same bed. He's a few slices short of a pie. Early in the film, he's saved from death in traffic when his mother races to the rescue.

Do-joon has a best friend named Jin-tae (Jin Goo). Jin-tae can easily manipulate him, persuade him to his will. Do-joon's mental fogginess may be his most attractive quality. In the town, a shocking murder takes place. A young girl's body is left where all can see. A golf ball with Do-joon's name on it is found near the death site.

Did he do it? We can't be sure. Did Jin-tae do it and plant the evidence? Or persuade Do-joon to do it when he was drunk? Again, we can't be sure. Under the Law of Economy of Characters, Jin-tae must have been involved because there are no other eligible characters. You can't simply produce a killer out of your hat. Of course, Do-joon could be guilty and Jin-tae had no involvement. Or, at least technically, the mother could have done it.

Mother (she's given no other name) marches tirelessly around the village, doing her own detective work. She questions people, badgers them, harasses the police, comforts her son, hires a worthless lawyer. We learn everything she learns. It seems she's getting nowhere. And it's at this point that the movie might become upsetting for a mass audience, because *Mother* creates not new suspects from off the map, but new levels in the previously established story.

The film is labyrinthine and deceptive, and not in a way we anticipate. It becomes a pleasure for the mind. Long after a conventional thriller would have its destination in plain sight, *Mother* is still penetrating our assumptions. So much depends on Kim Hye-ja's performance as a remorseless parent defending her fledgling. Likely she has spent years helping her clueless son escape one dilemma after another, and now she rises to the great occasion of her life. Her struggle is made more difficult because the police found it child's play to extract a confession from him.

Mother, and South Korean films in general, provide a case study of the situation of alternative films in this country. Many Americans have never seen a South Korean film and never will. I once spoke to a class for would-be foreign correspondents at the University of Illinois, and only two of them had ever seen a subtitled film from anywhere.

A film like *Mother*, and the recent *Chaser*, are adult films, not in the sense that they contain x-rated material, but in the sense that they appeal to intelligent grown-ups. A bright ten-year-old can understand most of today's Hollywood films. Disney recently announced it will make only 3-D "event" movies, comic hero stories, and extensions of franchises like *Pirates of the Caribbean*. It has essentially abandoned movies about plausible human beings. It isn't a luxury to see indie and alternative films. It's a necessity.

Mother will have you discussing the plot, not entirely to your satisfaction. I would argue: The stories in movies are complete fictions and can be resolved in any way the director chooses. If he actually cheats or lies, we have a case against him. If not, no matter what strange conclusions he arrives at, we can be grateful that we remained involved and even fascinated. Why do we buy a ticket? To confirm that a movie ends just the way we expect it to?

Mother and Child ★ ★ ★ ½

R, 126 m., 2010

Naomi Watts (Elizabeth), Annette Bening (Karen), Kerry Washington (Lucy), Jimmy Smits (Paco), Samuel L. Jackson (Paul), S. Epatha Merkerson (Ada), Cherry Jones (Sister Joanne), Elpidia Carrillo (Sofia), Shareeka Epps (Ray). Directed by Rodrigo Garcia and produced by Lisa Maria Falcone and Julie Lynn. Screenplay by Garcia.

Three mothers in need of a child. Three children, one not yet born. Three lives that are obscurely linked. Rodrigo Garcia has made his career of films sympathetic to the feelings of women, and *Mother and Child* is so emotionally affecting because it is concerned only with their feelings. The story lines coil and eventually join, but that's just a narrative device. If these characters had no connection, their lives would be equally evocative.

The film is founded on three performances by Annette Bening, Kerry Washington, and Naomi Watts. All have rarely been better. Bening plays Karen, a caregiver at work, where she's a physical therapist, and at home, where she cares for her mother (Eileen Ryan). There will be no one to care for her: When she was fourteen, she gave up a child for adoption, and now she yearns to have that child back. This is not a film about the wisdom of adoption, however, but about Karen's desire for her child.

Kerry Washington plays Lucy, happily married, childless, trying to adopt a child. She finds one she loves, but the baby's birth mother, Ray (Shareeka Epps), is a piece of work. She considers it a seller's market, and is fiercely determined that her unborn baby will find a good home with worthy parents. She's more exacting than an adoption agency. Epps is very good, very focused here.

Naomi Watts plays Elizabeth, a lawyer who is focused not so much on her career but on her power, and how her sexuality can be a part of that. She goes to work for a Los Angeles law firm and makes it her business to have an affair with one of the partners (Samuel L. Jackson). She calls the shots, perhaps because she never knew her own parents, and fears a feeling of abandonment.

A quiet, nurturing person at the intersection of these lives is Sister Joanne (Cherry Jones), a nun at a church adoption bureau. She is childless, of course, but content; she accepts her state as part of her service to God, and is devoted to her clients. The nun is one of several important supporting characters who give *Mother and Child* richness. There is a large cast here, but the actors are gifted and well cast, down to the smaller roles, and each one is important to the development of the story—not just added for diversion or variety.

These include Sofia (Elpidia Carrillo), Karen's maid, who has a daughter who sometimes comes to work with her and embodies some of Karen's regrets. Paul, the Samuel Jackson character, has daughters of his own, as does Paco (Jimmy Smits), Karen's friend at work. They have what she doesn't. Lucy's mother (S. Epatha Merkerson) is a nurturing example of motherhood; not so her mother-in-law, who is cruel about the absence of a grandchild.

Garcia, whose credits include *Things You Can Tell Just by Looking at Her* (2000) and

Nine Lives (2005), has created an interwoven plot here, not just for the purpose of being clever. Each facet revolves to illuminate the others. The characters reflect aspects of the central dilemma of mothers without children. It doesn't argue that all mothers require children, and indeed the nun may be the happiest woman here. It simply argues that these mothers believe that they do.

Of all the performances, Samuel L. Jackson's is the most surprising. It sometimes appears that the busy Jackson will take almost any role to stay working (remember *Black Snake Moan*?). This film provides a reminder of his subtlety. He is a powerful, successful man, relatively helpless with a demanding and sexually skilled woman. They like the sex, there is no love, she doesn't want to be involved in his personal life, and there is something there that disturbs him.

Bening, Watts, and Washington create three distinct beings with three distinct lives. They don't all "share the same problem," but they believe they share the same solution. Garcia embeds their needs in the details of their lives, so we don't emerge with ideas about them, but feelings.

Motherhood ★ ★

PG-13, 89 m., 2009

Uma Thurman (Eliza), Anthony Edwards (Avery), Minnie Driver (Sheila), Daisy Tahan (Clara), David and Matthew Schallipp (Lucas). Directed by Katherine Dieckmann and produced by Rachel Cohen, Jana Edelbaum, Pamela Koffler, Christine Vachon, and John Wells. Screenplay by Dieckmann.

Motherhood is about a conventional family living a conventional life in a conventional way. This life isn't perfect, but whose life is? The father is absent-minded but means well, the kids are normal, the mother is trying to juggle parental duties and her plans for a career. This could be countless families. Why do we require a movie about this particular one?

The film stars Uma Thurman, doing her best with a role that may offer her less than any other in her career, even though she's constantly onscreen. She's Eliza, who takes her laptop along to the playground to work on her blog, which is just a blog. She's not cooking her way through Julia Child or anything. Her husband is played by Anthony Edwards. I didn't remember the character's name after seeing the movie, so I checked with IMDb and he doesn't seem to have one. That tells you something.

The kids are six-year-old Clara (Daisy Tahan) and two-year-old Lucas (twins David and Matthew Schallipp). The tooth-challenged Daisy is pitch-perfect at that demanding age when kids become fixated on their convictions. Watching the movie, it occurred to me that child actors are invariably terrific. Maybe we are all born as great actors, but after a certain age most of us morph into bad ones.

Some effort is made to introduce interest to the cast. Minnie Driver plays a best friend who has an unsatisfactory personal life; the two women go to a sale of women's clothing during which they have tugs-of-war with other women who want the same frocks. Did I mention the movie takes place in Manhattan? That would also explain the crotchety neighbor (Alice Drummond), who is annoyed that a movie crew is using their street as a location. It would also explain Jodie Foster's cameo as a mom being followed by paparazzi. Don't you sort of imagine that if you lived in Greenwich Village you would sometimes have a Jodie Foster sighting?

The movie suggests two directions that might fruitfully have been employed by Katherine Dieckmann, the writer and director. One is in the person of an East Indian delivery man (Arjun Gupta) who begins an intriguing conversation with Eliza. Indian-Americans are appearing in movies much more frequently—for one reason, I suspect, because we like their accents. (An Indian friend told me, "We have been speaking English longer than you have.") Could this meeting have been developed into a subplot?

The other direction might have been fundamental. Instead of jumping through hoops to make Eliza somehow seem unique, special, and besieged by her (utterly commonplace) problems, how about making her desperate with boredom and the desire to break out into the extraordinary? Maybe her blog dives off the high board and she becomes a media creature? I dunno.

The movie is billed as a comedy, but at no point will you require oxygen. There are some smiles and chuckles and a couple of actual laughs, but the overall effect is underwhelming. Meh.

Mr. Popper's Penguins ★ ½

PG, 97 m., 2011

Jim Carrey (Mr. Popper), Carla Gugino (Amanda), Angela Lansbury (Mrs. Van Gundy), Ophelia Lovibond (Pippi), Madeline Carroll (Janie), Clark Gregg (Nat Jones), Jeffrey Tambor (Mr. Gremmins). Directed by Mark Waters and produced by John Davis. Screenplay by Sean Anders, John Morris, and Jared Stern, based on the novel by Richard Atwater and Florence Atwater.

Mr. Popper's Penguins is a stupefyingly dumb family movie proving that penguins have limited charisma as pets. I mean, what do they do? They sit on eggs, they waddle, they eat fish, and they squawk. Sometimes they might snap at you. The movie stars Jim Carrey, who is in his pleasant mode. It would have helped if he were in his manic mode, although it's hard to get a rise out of a penguin.

The movie is inspired by a 1938 children's book, apparently beloved by many. I haven't read it, so I'm trying to imagine why kids might like it. My best guess is that the idea of living in your home with penguins is more delightful than the experience. Penguins look cute in their little tuxedos, and kids can imagine being friends with them. The problem with a movie is that they take on an actual presence that gets old real fast.

This is, perhaps I should make clear, not an animated film. If the penguins were zooming into outer space in 3-D, that might change things. Weighted down by their apparent reality, they're more limited, although sometimes they slide down stuff on their bellies. One goes hang gliding, but not very convincingly. I assumed that all of the penguins in the movie were created with CGI, but no. I learn from IMDb: "Some are, some aren't." Since they all look and behave much the same, either the CGI is very good or the real penguins are well trained.

Jim Carrey plays Mr. Popper, a man involved in architecture and real estate, who must have great wealth because he lives in a Manhattan duplex with a spacious deck and travels in stretch limos. He is divorced from his wife, Amanda (Carla Gugino), although they seem on such good terms it is eerie. The unit of mother and two children is always available to turn up at his co-op at a moment's notice, smiling and cheerful. It's one of those cases, I guess, where the parents are apart only for the good of the children.

Mr. Popper inherits six penguins from his father. Never mind why. At first he doesn't want them in his apartment, which is modern and sleek and looks decorated by a designer with ice water in his or her veins. There is no sign of daily habitation in his living space. What with one thing and another, Mr. Popper comes to love the little creatures; guess how Stinky gets his name. You would think the spic-and-span apartment would soon be deep in penguin poop, but no, Mr. Popper squeezes them over the toilet.

There is a subplot involving Popper's employers, who also move in a unit of three like his family. Also a matter involving the sale of the historic Tavern on the Green by the rich Mrs. Van Gundy (Angela Lansbury). These need concern us no more than they will concern the kiddies in the audience. There is also some weirdly bland courtship by which Mr. Popper attempts to convince Mrs. Popper to return.

Of more interest may be the blessed event when the penguins produce three eggs, a tip-off (given penguin mating habits) that three of them are male and three female. You could have fooled me. Two eggs hatch. The third does not. That is the movie's tragic low point. Mr. Popper seems more distressed than the parents, or perhaps Carrey is the better actor.

Mugabe and the White African ★ ★ ★

NO MPAA RATING, 90 m., 2010

Mike Campbell and Ben Freeth. A documentary directed by Lucy Bailey and Andrew Thompson and produced by David Pearson and Elizabeth Morgan Hemlock.

After the colonial invasions of Africa, all power was held in white hands. Of the colonial powers, the Portuguese were perhaps the best to live under, the Belgians the worst. The British in Southern Africa had a way of doing about as much mischief as everybody else but talking about it in idealistic terms. Cecil Rhodes, whom Northern and Southern Rhodesia were named for, saw himself as a force for civilization. When I visited those two lands in 1962, then not yet independent and renamed Zambia and Zimbabwe, I visited farms not unlike Mike Campbell's in this documentary.

When independence came, many white Rhodesians chose to leave for South Africa or "home," which meant the United Kingdom, even if they'd been born in Africa. Others decided to stay. Campbell bought his farm and regularly made his payments, under the existing law of the black government at the time. He wasn't bothered by the regime of Robert Gabriel Mugabe, which came to power in 1980. Mugabe began land reform, turning many farms over to black control. His government often paid far below market value. In Campbell's case, Mugabe waited until he had made his final payment before claiming the farm. He deemed it would become the possession of a member of his ruling party, and perhaps wanted to free that crony from the task of paying off the mortgage.

Campbell refused to leave. Supported by the five hundred Africans who worked on his farm, he resisted armed raids during which his workers and his family were beaten. This film tells the story of the complaint against Zimbabwe filed in a regional African court. He won, but not until he and his family were nearly beaten to death. After he won, his farm buildings were burned to the ground. Little happens in Zimbabwe without Mugabe's knowledge.

There is an excellent case to be made that whites were guilty of the theft of Africa from its native peoples. There is also a case, which South Africa has been making, that all races should be able to coexist peacefully there. The spirit of Nelson Mandela's Truth and Reconciliation Commission is far from the brutal vision of Mugabe. In a continent where despotic rule is not uncommon, there is little argument that Mugabe is the most monstrous of rulers. He has gladly proclaimed Hitler as his role model.

It seems to me that Campbell has a good case here—good enough, anyway, to convince the judges on the African court. One could understand the government buying his farm at a fair price under eminent domain and installing an African staff to manage it. Mugabe pays pitiful sums and his political cronies, not interested in farming, loot their new properties and deprive the resident laborers of their livelihood. Zimbabwe, which was one of the most prosperous lands in Africa, today has 80 percent unemployment and widespread disease and starvation.

That being said, *Mugabe and the White African* could certainly have looked more deeply. The filmmakers travel to Kent in England to speak with the family of Campbell's son-in-law, but never have any meaningful conversations with the African workers on Campbell's farm. They support him, fight for him, are beaten by Mugabe's thugs for their efforts. What do they think? Possibly their understanding of the situation is less theoretical than ours, and they don't see how they can feed their families without stable employment. Apart from skin color, the difference between Mike Campbell and Robert Mugabe is that Campbell wants to run a farm.

Munyurangabo ★ ★ ★ ★

NO MPAA RATING, 97 m., 2009

Jeff Rutagengwa (Munyurangabo), Eric Ndorunkundiye (Sangwa), Jean Marie Nkurikiyinka (Papa Sangwa), Narcicia Nyirabucyeye (Mama Sangwa), Jean Pierre Harerimana Mulomda (Gwiza), Edouard B. Uwayo (Poet), Etienne Rugazora (Ngabo's Father). Directed and produced by Lee Isaac Chung. Screenplay by Chung and Samuel Gray Anderson.

Perhaps the best way to approach a subject of bewildering complexity is with simplicity. *Munyurangabo* considers the genocide in Rwanda entirely through the lives of two boys who are ten or eleven years old. They are not symbols. They are simply boys, who have been surviving on their own in a big city but are not toughened and essentially good. That's all.

Its story involves one of those miracles that can illuminate the cinema. It was directed by

Lee Isaac Chung, thirty, a first-generation Korean-American who grew up on a small farm in rural Arkansas. It was shot on location in Rwanda in two weeks. It involved only local actors. It is the first film in the Kinyarwanda language (with few, excellent, and easy-to-see subtitles). It is in every frame a beautiful and powerful film—a masterpiece.

An opening shot shows Sangwa and Munyurangabo, called Ngabo, as friends embarking on a cross-country journey. They trek through a pastoral landscape, stricken by drought. There are no dangers along the way. They have been in Kigali, the capital city. They will stop at Sangwa's family farm. He hasn't seen his mother for three years. All seems well, although weighing in our mind is the machete Ngabo carries in his knapsack. Sangwa's mother is joyful to see him, his father reserved and stern: What kind of a boy runs away from home for three years? Why did he not stay to help his family raise his younger siblings? What kind of a thing is that? Who is this boy he is traveling with?

The answers to those questions come in the unfolding of the story, an experience you should have without viewing the trailer, which provides an item of information you don't require. I will discuss instead the rural society Sangwa (Eric Ndorunkundiye) rejoins, and the city boy, Ngabo (Jeff Rutagengwa), sees for the first time. These people are poor. They catch water in plastic jugs from a trickle on the hillside. They till the soil by hand. They live in a house made from mud bricks. But this is not the wretched poverty you imagine. These people possess dignity and have a life they accept on its own terms, which is all they have known. Children run and laugh. Everything is done in its own time.

Sangwa's mother (Narcicia Nyirabucyeye) cherishes her boy and finds food for him when there is none. His father (Jean Marie Vianney Nkurikiyinka) is stern and not quick to forgive, but speaks to his son in reasoned words that obviously sink in. He knows what life is likely to bring Sangwa.

Chung, who cowrote with Samuel Gray Anderson as well as directing, is a born filmmaker. You see that in his eye, his cinematography, and his editing. He avoids pointless reaction shots and obvious payoffs; his strategy is to view a scene, give it weight, and let it stand. Everything is perfectly clear, but nothing is hammered home. We get the point. He knows we do.

The timing and precision of the way Chung explains the boys' journey, and the way he spaces out the information, is so much more effective than crude narrative storytelling. Since all is known between the boys, they never have to tell each other anything simply so we can listen. All dialogue is to the moment, and therefore we understand everything. The playing out of Ngabo's big decision is handled with a perfect sense of the time he takes to arrive at it, and the way it was prepared for and comes about.

There is an extraordinary passage outside a little roadside restaurant. When Ngabo approaches, an older boy is sitting outside in the shade. He sees the machete in the knapsack. He takes a swig from his beer and observes that tomorrow is National Independence Day. He has been asked to recite a poem he wrote. "Would you like to hear me say it?"

He doesn't wait for a reply. He begins with confidence and pride. It is all there, the whole canvas, Rwanda, its past, its future. The poet is played by Edouard B. Uwayo, and this is his own poem. Chung's decision to use it as he does is the right one, and the young poet's face evokes depths of wisdom.

Munyurangabo played in the Un Certain Regard section of Cannes 2007, where *Variety*'s Robert Koehler called it "flat-out, the discovery of this year's batch." It won the Grand Jury Prize at the AFI film festival. The Tomatometer stands at 100. If it seems like I'm trying to convince you on this film, I am. It is rolling out across the country in those few theaters where a film like this is welcomed. You can find it on DVD, and it went to Film Movement subscribers, who receive and can keep a film a month. They certainly got their money's worth.

Must Read After My Death ★ ★ ★

NO MPAA RATING, 76 m., 2009

A documentary directed, produced, and written by Morgan Dews.

Here is a cry from the grave. A woman who

died some eight years ago at the age of eighty-nine left behind about fifty hours of audiotapes, two hundred home movies, and three hundred pages of documents, a record that all ended, thirty years before that, on the death of her husband. The cache was labeled, in bold marker on a manila envelope, *Must Read After My Death.* What an anguished story it tells, of a marriage from hell.

The woman was named Allis. Her grandson, Morgan Dews, has created this film from her archives and understandably represses her family name. She met her husband Charley when they were both married to others. What she wanted was a nice little house with a white picket fence, where she would bear his children, whether or not they were married, because she knew they would have beautiful children together. They were married, and until death did not part.

It was an "open marriage." Charley was away much of the year on business, often to Australia. They decided to exchange Dictaphone recordings, and later tape recordings, and Allis saved hours of taped telephone messages. Charley is forthright about his adventures with "interesting women" he has met in Australia, "good dancers" and obviously good at more than that, "but the international operators listen in." Allis tells only of one weekend affair. She says she thinks she "helped" the man rebuild his self-confidence.

Charley is such a perfect bastard. His dry voice objectively slices through everything. He speaks of love and travel arrangements in the same tone. When he's home, there is always fighting. Always. Not about sex; he sees the real problems in their marriage as housekeeping and finances. Allis says she was meant to be a good mother but was never a housekeeper. She speaks four languages, went to college, was married first to a European, did some kind of unspecified singing. We hear not a word about Charley's first marriage.

Charley and Allis have three sons and a daughter. Charley is relentless with them about their "chores." He's an alcoholic, and it seems to make him a perfectionist. He's tall, balding, handsome in that Harry Smith way. Allis is small, tidy, worried. There are tapes of screaming rages involving Charley and his sons; their daughter, Morgan's mother, not much heard, leaves home at sixteen, following the advice in Philip Larkin's famous poem about destructive families, "This Be the Verse": "Get out as early as you can."

The first line of that poem certainly describes the marriage of Charley and Allis. All four children are angry, miserable, neurotic in various ways. The family falls into the clutches of a psychiatrist named Lenn, who wrongly sends one son to a mental institution, diagnoses Charley as "the worst inferiority complex I've ever seen," and strews misery and anguish as freely as his advice. What we learn of the children later in life is that three of them, anyway, grew up into apparently happy married adults with children.

It was the family itself that was toxic. They needed to get out. Charley is hated by the children, and Allis thinks of herself as not meant for such a life. She and Charley never have a real talk about "open marriage," but it certainly suits good-time Charley, a man without a single moment of introspection in this film.

Home movies and now the ubiquitous videotape mean that everyday lives are now recorded with a detail not dreamed of earlier. We will never hear all of Allis's recordings and see all her images, but this distillation by Morgan Dews might have been what she had in mind when she stored away those records of pain. They act as her justification of her life, her explanation of the misery of her children. I watched this film horrified and fascinated. There is such raw pain here. Allis might have read or seen *Revolutionary Road* and by comparison envied that marriage.

There are things you will see here that will lead you to some conclusions. I will leave you to them. All I can say is that I believe the daughter's guess at the end is correct. We learn that after Charley died, Allis moved to her own small cottage in Vermont and "continued her volunteer work." She lived another thirty years. She never mentioned Charley again.

My Dog Tulip ★ ★ ★ ★

NO MPAA RATING, 83 m., 2011

Voices of: Christopher Plummer (J. R. Ackerley), Lynn Redgrave (Nancy/Grocer's Wife), Isabella Rossellini (Miss Canvenini). Directed by Paul and Sandra Fierlinger and produced by

Howard Kaminsky, Frank Pellegrino, and Norman Twain. Written by Paul and Sandra Fierlinger, based on the memoir by J. R. Ackerley.

My Dog Tulip is the story of a man who finds love only once in his life, for fifteen perfect years. It is the love of a dog. It may be the only love he is capable of experiencing. As other men write books about a woman in their life, J. R. Ackerley wrote a book about a German shepherd bitch he rescued from a cruel home. *My Dog Tulip* has been a private discovery by many readers for years, and now it becomes an animated film combining elating visuals with a virtuoso voice performance by Christopher Plummer.

The film is animated but not intended for children. It is told from and by an adult sensibility that understands loneliness, gratitude, and the intense curiosity we feel for other lives, man and beast. The story is narrated by Plummer, in the voice of a man in his sixties who works for the BBC and lives in London near Putney Common. We know from the book that Ackerley was homosexual, and that is implied without the film making anything of it. For our purposes he is a soloist, cantankerous, crabby, lonely.

Tulip gives him unconditional love. Evolution, which produced humans who could think and were self-aware and knew loneliness, also in an act of serendipity produced dogs that could know us and love us. How strange that an animal could evolve as a wolf, self-select as a wolf that sought human company, and become an animal that values human company and considers its owners to be wonderful gods. People who do not like dogs do not know dogs. It is very difficult to dislike a being who worships you and would gladly die for you—especially when it is handsome and frisky and empathetic, and a good, good doggie, yes it is.

In a sense, *My Dog Tulip* is a natural history. Ackerley is educated by Tulip in the needs and ways of domesticated dogs. He attends to the feeding of Tulip, the training, the grooming, the walking, the territorial marking behavior, the sexual needs, the illnesses, the personality, the life and death. No parents of a child have ever been more observant or taken better care.

To this story, directed and animated by Paul and Sandra Fierlinger, *My Dog Tulip* brings Sandra's watercolors. Fierlinger is the sort of watercolorist one would collect. Her colors, her line, her ability to saturate or wash, are well suited to the story. She makes London with its black cabs and red buses come alive, and then turns pastoral on Putney Common. Her animated paintings have life and impact. She is an original, but if you know of an artist named David Gentleman you'll get the idea.

Given Ackerley's apparent celibacy, it becomes a source of some humor when he struggles to find Tulip a suitable mate. It isn't clear that Tulip much *wants* to become pregnant, but Ackerley is determined that she be impregnated. Perhaps she is a surrogate through which he achieves fertility. Lord knows they struggle together, J. R. and Tulip, through the travails of courtship.

My Dog Tulip has no stupid plot, no contrived suspense. Tulip grows old and dies, as must we all. J. R. Ackerley misses her and writes a book about his loss. Through this dog he knew love. And through J. R., so did Tulip.

My Life in Ruins ★ ½

PG-13, 95 m., 2009

Nia Vardalos (Georgia), Richard Dreyfuss (Irv), Alexis Georgoulis (Poupi), Rachel Dratch (Kim), Maria Adanez (Lena), Maria Botto (Lala), Harland Williams (Big Al), Alistair McGowan (Nico). Directed by Donald Petrie and produced by Michelle Chydzik Sowa and Nathalie Marciano. Screenplay by Mike Reiss.

Nia Vardalos plays most of *My Life in Ruins* with a fixed toothpaste smile, which is no wonder because her acting in the film feels uncomfortably close to her posing for a portrait. Rarely has a film centered on a character so superficial and unconvincing, played with such unrelenting sameness. I didn't hate it so much as feel sorry for it.

Vardalos plays Georgia, an American tour guide in Athens, in rivalry with Nico (Alistair McGowan), who always gets assigned the new bus with the well-behaved Canadians, while our girl gets the beater containing a group of walking human clichés who were old when *If It's Tuesday, This Must Be Belgium* was new.

You got your loud Yankees, your boozy Aussies, your prowling Spanish divorcees, your ancient Brits, and, of course, your obligatory Jewish widower who is laughing on the outside and mourning on the inside.

These characters are teeth-gratingly broad and obvious, apart from Richard Dreyfuss, who brings life, maybe too much life, to Irv, who tells bad jokes even though he is old enough to have learned funnier ones. To him, I recommend the delightful Web site www.oldjewstellingjokes.com, where every single old Jew is funnier than he is. Irv, of course, eventually reveals a sentimental side and does something else that is required in the Screenplay Recycling Handbook. (Interested in reading it? Send in five dollars. I won't mail it to you, but thanks for the money. Rim shot, please.)

The central question posed by *My Life in Ruins* is, what happened to the Nia Vardalos who wrote and starred in *My Big Fat Greek Wedding*? She was lovable, earthy, sassy, plumper, more of a mess, and the movie grossed more than $300 million. Here she's thinner, blonder, better dressed, looks younger, and knows it. She's like the winner of a beauty makeover at a Hollywood studio. She has that "Don't touch my makeup!" look. And if anyone in Hollywood has whiter, straighter, more gleaming teeth, we'll never know it, because like most people they'll usually keep their lips closed.

To speculate on people's motives is risky and can be unfair. Let me gently suggest that when Nia Vardalos made *My Big Fat Greek Wedding* she was an unlikely, saucy movie star who didn't take herself seriously. She was also an incomparably better screenwriter than Mike Reiss, the autopilot sitcom veteran who cobbled together this lousy script.

Now she is rich, famous, and perhaps taking herself seriously after being worked over for one too many magazine covers. She has also made the mistake of allowing herself to be found in one of those situations that only happen in trashy romance novels. The driver of her bus is a surly Greek named Poupi (Alexis Georgoulis), who has a beard that looks inspired by the Smith Brothers. After he shaves it off, he emerges as an improbably handsome, long-locked Adonis of the sort that customarily only dates older women if he has reason to think they are rich. This romance is embarrassing.

There is, in short, nothing I liked about *My Life in Ruins,* except some of the ruins. The tourists are even allowed to consult the Oracle at Delphi. That scene reminded me of when Chaz and I visited an ancient temple at Ise in Japan. Outside the gates, monks sat on platforms inscribing scrolls. "You may ask anything you want," our guide told us. "Will there be peace in our time?" asked Chaz. The monk gave a look at our guide. Our guide said, "Ah . . . I think maybe better question be more like, 'How many monks live in temple?'"

Note: "Poupi" is pronounced "poopy." That would never get past the editor of a romance novel.

My One and Only ★ ★ ★ ½

PG-13, 107 m., 2009

Renee Zellweger (Ann Devereaux), Logan Lerman (George Devereaux), Kevin Bacon (Dan Devereaux), Eric McCormack (Charlie), Chris Noth (Dr. Harlan Williams), Mark Rendall (Robbie), Nick Stahl (Bud), Steven Weber (Wallace McAllister), David Koechner (Bill Massey), Robin Weigert (Hope). Directed by Richard Loncraine and produced by Aaron Ryder and Norton Herrick. Screenplay by Charlie Peters.

I have no idea how closely *My One and Only* follows the facts of George Hamilton's teenage years, but it tells a story that goes a good way toward explaining his years of celebrity and his lifelong attachment to his mother. It's also an appealing comedy, a road movie set in the 1950s and starring Renee Zellweger as his mom, the irrepressible Ann Devereaux.

She's a blond Southern belle, married to Dan, a bandleader (Kevin Bacon) who loves her, after his fashion, but is a compulsive womanizer. Finding him in bed with one woman too many, Ann leaves him, taking her two sons: George (Logan Lerman) and Robbie (Mark Rendall), half brothers from her two marriages. In a sky-blue Cadillac convertible, they set off on an odyssey to find Ann a new husband. That's the only way she can imagine to support them.

Ann is fortyish, comely, attractive to men, but no longer this year's model. Their journeys take them to a series of her old beaus, in Boston, Pittsburgh, and St. Louis, and these hunting expeditions are seen through George's dubious eyes. One is an ex-military sadist, one a playboy, all not suitable candidates. She tries actually working, but being a waitress is beyond her, and then she apparently strikes pay dirt with a proposal from a man whose family owns a big house-paint business.

The paint tycoon is entertaining. As played by the invaluable David Koechner, he sits beside George on a pier and confides that Ann has asked him to have a man-to-man talk with him about women. He explains to the boy that women have a problem with body temperature. They're always too warm or too cool. On a date, always bring along a sweater you can lend them. End of advice. I can't say why, but I suspect George Hamilton really was told this at one time or another in his youth.

Hamilton is the film's executive producer, and although the screenplay is by Charlie Peters, Hamilton must have had substantial input at the story level. His mother was really named Ann. His father was really a bandleader. He had a brother something like the one here. He did get into movies somewhat improbably. The one detail in the film I doubt is that he ever said, "There's too much sun here in L.A. It's not depressing enough."

This is essentially Renee Zellweger's picture, and she glows in it. We've seen the type before, but she's able, beneath Ann's pluck, to suggest her sadness and the love she had for her boys. Yes, she was a lousy mother, as George assures her, but she had a good heart and was determined to provide for them. It struck some as notable that Hamilton remained so close to his mother, even living with her, but this film is a worthy memory, including both her ditzyness and her bravery.

The director, Richard Loncraine, achieves a seemingly effortless early-1950s look, down to the details of Ann's wardrobe and hair, which today look more like costuming than fashion: No matter what she goes through and how much she endures, she's always well turned out. The relationship between her two sons is a little enigmatic, considering Robbie is presented as gay. They never refer to that, except very discreetly. Maybe it was like that in the 1950s.

Basing psychological speculation on a biopic is notoriously risky. All I can say is that after seeing *My One and Only,* Hamilton's persona somehow clicked into place for me. He had the example of a woman who was concerned with making a good impression. I met him only once, in 1971 when he had starred in *Evel Knievel,* and I still recall how nice he seemed.

My Sister's Keeper ★ ★ ★ ½

PG-13, 108 m., 2009

Cameron Diaz (Sara Fitzgerald), Abigail Breslin (Anna Fitzgerald), Alec Baldwin (Campbell Alexander), Jason Patric (Brian Fitzgerald), Sofia Vassilieva (Kate Fitzgerald), Joan Cusack (Judge De Salvo), Heather Wahlquist (Aunt Kelly), Thomas Dekker (Taylor Ambrose), Evan Ellingson (Jesse Fitzgerald), David Thornton (Dr. Chance). Directed by Nick Cassavetes and produced by Mark Johnson, Chuck Pacheco, and Scott L. Goldman. Screenplay by Cassavetes and Jeremy Leven, based on the novel by Jodi Picoult.

My Sister's Keeper is an immediate audience grabber, as we learn that an eleven-year-old girl was genetically designed as a source of spare parts for her dying sixteen-year-old sister. Yes, it's possible: In vitro fertilization ensured a perfect match. And no, this isn't science fiction like Kazuo Ishiguro's novel *Never Let Me Go,* with its cloned human replacements. It's just a little girl subjected to major procedures almost from birth to help her sister live.

So far they have succeeded, and Kate (Sofia Vassilieva) is alive long after her predicted death at five. Her sister, Anna (Abigail Breslin), has donated blood, bone marrow, and stem cells, and now is being told she must donate one of her kidneys. She's had it. It dismays her to know she was conceived as an organ bank, and she wants her chance at a normal life without round trips to the operating room. She may be young but she's bright and determined, and she decides to file a lawsuit against her parents for "medical emancipation."

Hers would be a model family if not for her sister's death sentence. Her mom, Sara

(Cameron Diaz), is a successful Los Angeles lawyer. Her dad, Brian (Jason Patric), is a fire chief. Her older brother, Jesse (Evan Ellingson), is a good student but feels ignored. Anna and Kate love each other dearly. But always there is Sara's relentless drive to keep her daughter alive. Like some successful attorneys, she also wants to win every case in her private life.

Anna goes to an attorney who boasts a 90 percent success rate in his TV ads. This is the polished Campbell Alexander (Alec Baldwin), who drives a Bentley convertible and is known for bringing his dog into courtrooms. Anna offers her savings of seven hundred dollars. This is far under his fee, but he listens and accepts the case.

Although *My Sister's Keeper,* based on the best-seller by Jodi Picoult, is an effective tear-jerker, if you think about it, it's something else. The movie never says so, but it's a practical parable about the debate between pro-choice and pro-life. If you're pro-life, you would require Anna to donate her kidney, although there is a chance she could die and her sister doesn't have a good prognosis. If you're pro-choice, you would support Anna's lawsuit.

The mother is appalled by the lawsuit. Keeping her daughter alive has been a triumph for her all of these years. The father is shocked, too, but calmer and more objective. He can see Anna's point. She has her own life to live, and her own love to demand. The performances don't go over the top, although they can see it from where they're standing. Cameron Diaz has the greatest challenge because her determination is so fierce, but she makes her love evident—more for Kate, it must be said, than for Anna and Jesse. Jason Patric, too, rarely gets sympathetic roles, and he embodies thoughtfulness and tenderness. The young actors never step wrong.

Nicely nuanced, too, is Alec Baldwin as the hotshot attorney. He doesn't have a posh office, and his photo is plastered on billboards, but he's not a fly-by-night, and he has a heart. He also has a sense of humor; in several supporting roles recently, he has stepped in with lines enriched by unexpected flashes of wit. Also navigating around clichés here is Joan Cusack as the judge. She takes that impossible case and convinces us she handles it about as well as possible. The enigma is the underdeveloped brother, Jesse, who runs away for three days.

We're never told what that was all about; in the film, it serves merely to distract us when Taylor (Thomas Dekker), Kate's fellow cancer patient, seems to disappear. The hospital romance between Taylor and Kate is one of the best elements of the movie, tender, tactful, and very touching.

The screenplay by Jeremy Leven and Nick Cassavetes (who directed) is admirable in trusting us to figure things out. Because it's obvious in one beautiful scene that Kate is wearing a wig, they didn't ask, "Will the audience understand that?" and add a jarring line. Routine courtroom theatrics are avoided. We learn of the verdict in the best way. We can see the wheels turning, but they turn well.

My Son, My Son, What Have Ye Done ★ ★ ★

NO MPAA RATING, 87 m., 2010

Willem Dafoe (Detective Hank Havenhurst), Michael Shannon (Brad McCullum), Chloe Sevigny (Ingrid), Michael Peña (Detective Vargas), Udo Kier (Lee Meyers), Brad Dourif (Uncle Ted), Grace Zabriskie (Mrs. McCullum), Irma P. Hall (Mrs. Roberts), Loretta Devine (Miss Roberts), Verne Troyer (Midget). Directed by Werner Herzog and produced by Eric Bassett. Screenplay by Herzog and Herbert Golder.

Werner Herzog's *My Son, My Son, What Have Ye Done* is a splendid example of a movie not on autopilot. I bore my readers by complaining about how bored I am by formula movies that recycle the same moronic elements. Now here is a film where Udo Kier has his eyeglasses snatched from his pocket by an ostrich, sees them yanked from the ostrich's throat by a farmhand, gets them back all covered with ostrich mucus, and tells the ostrich, "Don't you do that again!"

Meanwhile, there is talk about how the racist ostrich farmer once raised a chicken as big as, I think, forty ordinary birds. What did he do with it? "Ate it. Sooner pluck one than forty." Knowing as I do that Herzog hates chickens with a passion beyond all reason, I flashed back to an earlier scene in which the film's protagonist talks with his scrawny pet flamingoes. Is a theme emerging here? And the flamingo who regards the camera with a dubious look: Is it inspired by the staring iguana in Herzog's *Bad Lieutenant*?

For me it hardly matters if a Herzog film provides conventional movie pleasures. Many of them do. *Bad Lieutenant,* for example. *My Son, My Son, What Have Ye Done,* on the other hand, confounds all convention and denies the usual expected pleasures, providing instead the delight of watching Herzog feed the police hostage formula into the Mixmaster of his imagination. It's as if he began with the outline of a stunningly routine police procedural and said to hell with it, I'm going to hang my whimsy on this clothesline.

He casts Willem Dafoe as his hero, a homicide detective named Hank Havenhurst. Dafoe is known for his willingness to embrace projects by directors who work on the edge. He is an excellent actor, and splendid here at creating a cop who conducts his job with tunnel vision and few expected human emotions. It is difficult to conceive of a police officer showing a more measured response to a madman ostrich farmer.

His case involves a man named Brad McCullum, played by Michael Shannon as a man with an alarming stare beneath a lowering brow. He kills his mother with a wicked antique sword as she sits having coffee with two neighbors. He likes to repeat "razzle dazzle," which reminded me of "helter skelter," and yes, the movie is "inspired by a true story." His mother (Grace Zabriskie) is a woman who is so nice she could, possibly, inspire murder, especially in a son who has undergone life-altering experiences in the Peruvian rain forest, as this one has—and why, you ask? For the excellent reason, I suspect, that Herzog could with great difficulty revisit the Urubamba River in Peru, where he shot much of *Aguirre, the Wrath of God* (1972) and part of *Fitzcarraldo* (1982). Perhaps whenever he encounters an actor with alarming eyes, like Klaus Kinski or Shannon, he thinks, "I will put him to the test of the Urubamba River!"

Detective Havenhurst takes over a command center in front of the house where Brad is said to be holding two hostages (never seen), and interviews Brad's fiancée, Ingrid (Chloe Sevigny), and a theater director, Lee Meyers (Udo Kier). Both tell him stories that inspire flashbacks. Indeed, most of the film involves flashbacks leading up to the moment when Brad slashed his mother. Ingrid is played by Sevigny as a dim, sweet young woman lacking all insight and instinct for self-protection, and Meyers is played by Kier as a man who is incredibly patient with Brad during rehearsals for the Greek tragedy *Elektra.* That's the one where the son slays his mother.

The memories of Lee Meyers inspire the field trip to the ostrich farm run by Uncle Ted (Brad Dourif). If you've been keeping track, the film's cast includes almost *only* cult actors often involved with cult directors: Dafoe, Shannon, Sevigny, Kier, Dourif, Zabriskie, and I haven't even mentioned Oscar nominee Irma P. Hall and Verne Troyer. Havenhurst's partner is played by Michael Peña, who is not a cult actor but plays one in this movie. Little jest. For that matter, the film's producer is David Lynch, one of the few producers who might think it made perfect sense that a cop drama set in San Diego would require location filming on the Urubamba River.

There is a scene in this movie that involves men who appear to be yurt dwellers from Mongolia, one with spectacular eyebrow hairs. I confess I may have had a momentary attention lapse, but I can't remember what they had to do with the plot. Still, I'll not soon forget those eyebrows, which is more than I can say for most scenes at the 60 percent mark in most cop movies. I am also grateful for two very long shots, one involving Grace Zabriskie and the other Verne Troyer, in which they look at the camera for thirty or forty seconds while flanked with Shannon and another one of the actors. These look like freeze frames, but you can see the actors moving just a little. What do these shots represent? Why, the director's impatience with convention, that's what.

Herzog is endlessly fascinating and always surprising. I have now performed an excellent job of describing the movie. Can you sense why I enjoyed it? If you don't like it, you won't be able to claim I misled you. I rode on an ostrich once. Halfway between Oudtshoorn and the Cango Caves, it was.

The Mysteries of Pittsburgh ★ ★

R, 95 m., 2009

Jon Foster (Art Bechstein), Peter Sarsgaard (Cleveland), Sienna Miller (Jane), Nick Nolte (Joe Bechstein), Mena Suvari (Phlox). Directed by Rawson Marshall Thurber and produced by Michael London and Jason Ajax Mercer. Screenplay by Thurber, based on the novel by Michael Chabon.

After that summer, nothing would ever be the same again. Where have we seen that movie before? Most recently in *Adventureland*, another movie set in 1980s Pittsburgh. If you think about it, after every summer nothing will ever be the same again. But *The Mysteries of Pittsburgh* has an unusually busy summer, in which a hero who is a blank slate gets scrawled all over with experiences.

The movie is all the more artificial because it has been made with great, almost painful, earnestness. It takes a plot that would have been at home in a 1930s Warner Bros. social melodrama, adds sexuality and a little nudity, and Bob's your uncle. It's based on a 1988 novel by Michael Chabon, still much read and valued, but to call it "inspired by" would be a stretcher. Hardly a thing happens that doesn't seem laid on to hurry along the hero's coming of age.

That hero is Art (Jon Foster), whose voice-over narration does not shy away from the obvious. He is the son of Joe Bechstein (Nick Nolte), a mobster of such stature that he has his own FBI shadows. Joe would like Art to follow him into the family business, but Art wants nothing to do with it. He'll become a broker, which in the 1980s was an honest trade. For the summer he takes a job at a vast surplus bookstore, where the minimum wage allows him to lose himself.

Life comes racing after him. Phlox (Mena Suvari), the store manager, pages him on the intercom for sex on demand in the stock room. At a party, he meets the winsome blonde Jane (Sienna Miller), whose boyfriend, Cleveland (Peter Sarsgaard), is both friendly and disturbing. These two mess with his mind: Jane although she doesn't mean to, Cleveland because he is a sadistic emotional manipulator. The first little "joke" Cleveland plays on Art should have sent Art running as far from Cleveland as he could get. But Art is pathologically passive; the summer happens to him, but he can't be said to happen to it.

Complications from countless other movies. The fraught relationship with his father. Phlox's possessiveness. Jane's ambivalence. Cleveland's odd promotion of an emotional, if not at first sexual, ménage à trois. Then a crime-driven climax that arrives out of thin air and involves a very small world indeed. Finally a bittersweet closing narration that seems to tie up loose ends but really answers nothing about Art except whether he still lives in Pittsburgh.

Complicating this are some well-developed performances for such an underdeveloped screenplay. Peter Sarsgaard is intriguing as the seductive, profoundly screwy Cleveland. Mena Suvari is pitch-perfect in a finally thankless role. Nick Nolte, in expensive suits, hair slicked back, takes no nonsense as the hard mob boss. Sienna Miller is sweet but is never allowed to make clear why she is attracted to either man. Jon Foster, as the feckless protagonist, is the latest in a long line of manipulated male ingénues going back beyond Benjamin in *The Graduate*. This is a guy who hardly deserves the attention of the other characters in the story, with his closed-in, inarticulate, low self-esteem.

At the end, Art is supposed to have learned lessons in life from his "last summer before life begins." The melancholy likelihood is, however, that he learned nothing except the punch line to the old joke, "Don't do that no more." At summer's end he seems poised to graduate directly into the Lonely Crowd. There is an old word: nebbish. It is still a good word.

N

Never Let Me Go ★ ★ ★ ★

R, 104 m., 2010

Carey Mulligan (Kathy), Andrew Garfield (Tommy), Keira Knightley (Ruth), Sally Hawkins (Miss Lucy), Isobel Meikle-Small (Young Kathy), Ella Purnell (Young Ruth), Charlie Rowe (Young Tommy), Charlotte Rampling (Miss Emily). Directed by Mark Romanek and produced by Alex Garland, Andrew Macdonald, and Allon Reich. Screenplay by Garland, based on the novel by Kazuo Ishiguro.

In my will I have left to the next generation such parts of my poor body as it can salvage. That is the Golden Rule. I suppose if you take it literally, you would accept life as a donor in *Never Let Me Go*, since after all, that is the purpose for which you were born. In the film there is a society within the larger one consisting of children who were created in a laboratory to be donors. They have no parents in the sense we use the term. I'm not even sure they can be parents. They exist to grow hearts, kidneys, livers, and other useful items, and then, sadly, to die after too much has been cut away.

When I read Kazuo Ishiguro's novel, the donors' purpose was left murky until midway in the book. In the film, it's clear to us but not, up to a certain point, to the children. They live within a closed world whose value system takes pride in how often and successfully they have donated. They accept this. It is all they have ever known. One of the most dangerous facts of human society is that children believe what they are told. Those who grow out of that become adults, a status not always achieved by their parents.

We meet three donor children, first when young and then later. They are Kathy, Tommy, and Ruth, played in their twenties by Carey Mulligan, Andrew Garfield, and Keira Knightley. They were raised at Hailsham, a progressive boarding school for donors—progressive in the sense that it's an experiment based on the possibility that these test-tube babies are real human beings. Well of course they are, we think. But it doesn't suit the convenience of the larger society to think of them in that way. If you are about to get someone's heart, don't you tend to objectify the source? You should. If you get my heart, I don't want you moping around about me. It's your heart. You pay the bills.

The teachers at Hailsham aren't precisely progressives in the John Dewey tradition, but the school is the last one that still encourages the children at all. The society wants these donors for one purpose and doesn't want to waste resources on them for any other. If you can walk through this plot without tripping over parallels to our own society and educational systems, you're more surefooted than I.

The director, Mark Romanek, wisely follows Ishiguro in burying any meanings well within a human story. The film is about Kathy, Tommy, and Ruth, and their world, and not some sort of parable like *1984*. Essentially it asks, How do you live with the knowledge that you are not considered a human being but simply a consumer resource? Many hourly workers at big box stores must sometimes ponder this question.

Never Let Me Go would have made a serious error in ramping up contrived melodrama toward some sort of science-fiction showdown. This is a movie about empathy. About how Ruth realizes Kathy and Tommy were naturally in love with each other as young adolescents, and how she selfishly upset that process. About how now, when it may be too late, she wants to make amends. About the old rumor at Hailsham that if two donors should fall deeply in love they might qualify for some sort of reprieve—short-term, to be sure. But if their masters can believe they can love, they would have to believe they are human. Two of the requirements for a being with a soul in Thomist philosophy are free will and the ability to love. Donors qualify for both.

This is such a meditative, delicate film. I heard some snuffling about me in the darkness. These poor people are innocent. They have the same hopes everyone has. It is so touching that they gladly give their organs to us. Greater love hath no man, than he who gives me his kidney, especially his second one.

This is a good movie, from a masterful novel. *Remains of the Day*, also inspired by an Ishiguro novel, was similar: What is happening is implied, not spelled out. We are required to observe. Even the events themselves are amenable to different interpretations. The characters may not know what they're revealing about themselves. They certainly don't know the whole truth of their existence. We do, because we are free humans. It is sometimes not easy to extend such stature to those we value because they support our comfort.

New in Town ★ ★

PG, 96 m., 2009

Renee Zellweger (Lucy Hill), Harry Connick Jr. (Ted Mitchell), J. K. Simmons (Stu Kopenhafer), Siobhan Fallon Hogan (Blanche Gunderson), Frances Conroy (Trudy Van Uuden). Directed by Jonas Elmer and produced by Paul Brooks, Darryl Taja, Tracey Edmonds, and Peter Safran. Screenplay by Kenneth Rance and C. Jay Cox.

We open on a gathering of the Scrappers Club, four women around a kitchen table pasting things into scrapbooks. The moment we hear one of them talking, we're not too surprised to find her name is Blanche Gunderson. Her sister Marge, the trooper, must have been the ambitious one. Not that Blanche isn't, just that she's relentlessly nice.

So are most of the folks in the small town of New Ulm, Minnesota, which is so cold in the winter that scrapping warms you up. Old Ulm (I know you were wondering) is the town on the Danube where Einstein was born. To this frigid outpost flies Lucy Hill, a high-powered exec from Miami, whose mission is to downsize the local food products plant more or less out of existence.

Lucy is the cute-as-a-button Renee Zellweger, so we know she's only kidding when she pretends to be a heartless rhymes-with-witch who hammers around on her stiletto heels and won't smile. That doesn't scare Blanche (Siobhan Fallon Hogan), Lucy's assistant, who invites her home for dinner ("We're only havin' meat loaf"). So uncannily does her accent resemble Marge in *Fargo* that I was trying to remember where I had heard it recently, doncha know?

The extra man at Blanche's table turns out to be Ted Mitchell (Harry Connick Jr.), the widowed dad of a thirteen-year-old girl, whom Blanche obviously thinks would be a great match for Lucy. That Ted, the union guy at the plant Lucy plans to downsize, is perhaps not a perfect match never even occurs to Blanche, who like all Minnesotans and most Dakotans, is just plain nice. I mean that. I've been to Fargo. You should go sometime.

Ted doesn't seem nice at first, but then, jeez, he's originally from out of town, y'know. Ted and Lucy get in such a fight at the table that they both stalk out, which means they miss out on Blanche's famous tapioca pudding. Glossary Rule: Whenever a recipe is much discussed in the first act, it will be tasted in the third.

So firmly do we believe Lucy is visiting relatives of the *Fargo* cast that it's a surprise to learn *New in Town* was actually filmed in Winnipeg, which here looks nothing like the glittering metropolis in Guy Maddin's masterpiece. New Ulm consists of some houses, a VFW hall with a Friday fish fry, the food plant, and not a whole lot else except snow. But the people are friendly, hardworking, and proud of their plant, and soon Lucy softens, begins to like them, and reveals she was Renee Zellweger all along.

Because this is a romcom with no ambition in the direction of originality, Lucy is single, and Ted is the only eligible unmarried man in the cast, so do the math. The only remaining question is whether Lucy can save the plant, if you consider that much of a question. Am I giving too much away? This is the kind of movie that gives itself away. I've used that line before.

The real question is, do you like this sort of romcom? It's a fair example of its type, not good, but competent. The plant workers seem to function like the chorus in an opera, shutting down the line for Lucy's arias from a catwalk and moving as a unit with foreman Stu Kopenhafer (J. K. Simmons) always in the front. Simmons has grown a bushy beard and is wearing a fat suit (I hope), so you may not recognize him as Juno's dad. Let the bushy beard be a lesson: A bushy beard is the enemy of an actor's face unless he is playing Santa or attacking with a chainsaw.

The only question remaining after *New in Town* is, how come there's never a movie where a small-town girl leaves the snarly, greedy, job-ladder-climbing people behind and moves to the big city, where she is embraced by friendly folks, fed meat loaf and tapioca, and fixed up with Harry Connick Jr.?

The New Year Parade ★ ★ ★

NO MPAA RATING, 87 m., 2009

Greg Lyons (Jack), Jennifer Welsh (Kat), Andrew Conway (Mike McMonogul), MaryAnn McDonald (Mike's Wife), Tobias Segal (Curtis), Irene Longshore (Jack's Girlfriend), Paul Blackway (Kat's B.F.), and the South Philadelphia String Band. Directed by Tom Quinn and produced by Quinn and Steve Beal. Screenplay by Quinn.

I'm pretty much paraded out. The high point for me was the Fourth of July twenty-five years ago in Three Oaks, Michigan, where Shriners performed an intricate choreography while riding their power mowers. But I now believe the Philadelphia Mummers Parade must be worth attending every year. The marchers aren't hauling ads for Pepsi or anchoring giant inflated Ronald McDonald balloons. They march because of fierce generational pride.

This I learn from Tom Quinn's movie *The New Year Parade*, an appealing indie feature that weaves together the traditions of the parade and an Irish-American family. If that sounds contrived, it's not; the two flow together in a convincing way. The film, which won top prizes at Slamdance 2009 and (understandably) Philadelphia, introduces us to the McMonogul family, who have been part of the South Philadelphia String Band for three generations.

Mike (Andrew Conway), the father, is captain of the band. He discovers his wife (MaryAnn McDonald) has cheated on him and moves out in a rage. There are subtle hints that she may have had her reasons. Their children, Jack (Greg Lyons), in his early twenties, and Kat (Jennifer Welsh), about sixteen, are devastated—Kat especially, but she decides to stay with her mom. Jack accuses Mike of choosing to destroy the family instead of forgiving his mom, and he contemplates the unspeakable: leaving the band and enlisting with its traditional arch-competitors.

Quinn photographed his film over four years, and yet as his own editor has mastered what must have been hours of material into a story so convincingly embedded in the band and parade that it would have been impossible to create just for a film. His characters all seem to be much of that world; whether his actors are, I can't say. But we see them rehearsing, marching, hanging out, *caring* about the band. For Jack to join the opposition is the most hurtful thing he could do to his father.

On top of that is the enormity of the parade itself. I vaguely imagined it as a bunch of people dressed up funny and playing "Yankee Doodle." The costumes and props cannot even be described. The year's work and no doubt the money involved is almost unimaginable. Yet Quinn does not make the plot rest on that weary old device of who wins the big parade/game/match/bout/election. This is not about winning but about striving.

The New Year Parade is a tad frayed around the edges, no doubt because of the scope of the reality presented. But the story holds strong, the indie approach is more moving than a polished production plugging in big stars, and this is the sort of film a civic resource such as Facets exists to show.

New York, I Love You ★ ★ ★

R, 104 m., 2009

With Hayden Christensen, Andy Garcia, Rachel Bilson, Natalie Portman, Irrfan Khan, Orlando Bloom, Christina Ricci, Maggie Q, Ethan Hawke, Chris Cooper, Robin Wright Penn, Anton Yelchin, James Caan, Olivia Thirlby, Blake Lively, Drea de Matteo, Bradley Cooper, Julie Christie, John Hurt, Shia LaBeouf, Taylor Geare, Carlos Acosta, Jacinda Barrett, Ugur Yucel, Shu Qi, Burt Young, Eli Wallach, and Cloris Leachman. Directed by Jiang Wen, Mira Nair, Shunji Iwai, Yvan Attal, Brett Ratner, Allen Hughes, Shekhar Kapur, Natalie Portman, Fatih Akin, Joshua Marston, and Randy Balsmeyer, and produced by Emmanuel Benbihy and Marina Grasic.

The rules: No more than two days' shooting time. One week of editing. An eight-minute time limit. Ten directors, and one more to consider the ten short films and create transitions. *New York, I Love You* is the second installment in an ambitious project that began with *Paris, Je T'aime* (2006), an anthology with thirteen directors. Rio is said to be next.

Inevitably, the film is a jumble sale, but you can make some nice discoveries. It's not one of those films where all the separate characters come together at the end in a miraculous coincidence, although a few people do turn up, still as themselves, in one another's segments.

I suspect the title isn't intended as a simple declaration, but should be pronounced in a wondering tone, with a wry shake of the head, as in, "Oh, you kid." The film assembles a collection of colorful characters, who find that eight minutes is quite enough to make an impression, as so many New Yorkers would agree.

The very first segment, directed by Jiang Wen and starring Hayden Christensen, Andy Garcia, and Rachel Bilson, begins the film with a deft touch worthy of O. Henry, the master of New York short stories. Bilson and Christiansen meet in a bar, where he finds a cell phone she left behind. He opens a seductive conversation, interrupted by Garcia as her boyfriend, who immediately reads the other guy. The two of them elevate their confrontation to a level of sly expertise, in a way that is rather remarkable.

Another O. Henry twist is in Yvan Attal's segment starring Maggie Q and Ethan Hawke, as two people who meet outside a club. He is determined to seduce her, and launches an impressive improvisation involving his sexual skills and uses. This spiel could work one of two ways: as a serious come-on, or as a display of sheer wit. It fails at both, for reasons he entirely failed to suspect—although it must be admitted he does get her phone number.

In these days after my fractured hip, Joshua Marston's segment starring Eli Wallach and Cloris Leachman struck a chord. They've been married since forever, and now they're taking a walk at Coney Island. "Pick up your feet!" she tells him. "I *am* picking them up!" he says. "You're shuffling!" We intuit this conversation has been going on a very long time. My wife and I exchanged a little smile. Do you have any idea how hard it is to pick up your feet after you've broken your hip? It's not as if shufflers are merely lazy. And it's not as if this is the first time they've been lectured to pick up their feet.

Not all of the stories end in a surprise ending, thank goodness. Some are small slices of life. Mira Nair's segment stars Natalie Portman as a Hassidic woman in dealings with an Indian diamond merchant (Irrfan Khan). She's about to be married and confides that on that day she'll cut off all of her hair. Such a practice is not unknown in India, but the merchant now is simply a man admiring beautiful hair. And she . . . how does she feel?

Look at the cast and credits to form an idea of the directors and actors at work here. By its nature, *New York, I Love You* can't add up. It remains the sum of its parts. If one isn't working for you, wait a few minutes, here comes another one. New Yorkers, I love you.

Next Day Air ★ ★ ★

R, 90 m., 2009

Donald Faison (Leo), Mike Epps (Brody), Wood Harris (Guch), Omari Hardwick (Shavoo), Darius McCrary (Buddy), Yasmin Deliz (Chita), Mos Def (Eric), Emilio Rivera (Bodega), Cisco Reyes (Jesus), Debbie Allen (Ms. Jackson). Directed by Benny Boom and produced by Scott Aronson and Inny Clemons. Screenplay by Blair Cobbs.

Next Day Air is a bloody screwball comedy, a film of high spirits. It tells a complicated story with acute timing and clarity, and it gives us drug-dealing lowlifes who are almost poetic in their clockwork dialogue. By that I mean they not only use the words, they know the music.

Donald Faison stars in a cast of equals, as a pothead delivery man for the Next Day Air firm, who hurls around packages marked "Fragile!" as if he has never seen that word. Drifting in a cloud of weed, he delivers a package to the wrong apartment. Because it contains ten bricks of cocaine, this is a mistake, although perhaps not as fundamental as shipping it from L.A. to Philadelphia in the first place. FedEx and UPS have never lost anything of mine, but then, I've never shipped ten bricks of cocaine, which are likely to attract more attention than a signed copy of *Roger Ebert's Movie Yearbook 2009.*

The drugs are intended for a Latino couple (Cisco Reyes and Yasmin Deliz) and shipped by a cigar-smoking drug lord (Emilio Rivera) who is very annoyed when they are lost. He comes with his sidemen to pound some questions into Faison, who finally leads them to the apartment, where they find a gang of lousy bank robbers (Mike Epps, Wood Harris, Omari Hardwick) who got the shipment, and three men who plan to buy the drugs from them.

This puts, I dunno, nine or ten heavily armed men in a room of limited size. One reason the cops don't respond to the eventual gunfire is that the room simply couldn't hold them. Since a shotgun and an automatic rifle are included with their handguns and one of those gourmet carving knife sets, I'm not sure why the MPAA's R rating mentions "some violence." In the MPAA's coded terminology, the word "some" means "violence, but nothing to get too worked up about." I guess that's fair; there are none of those 3-D X-ray shots showing a bullet inching its way in slow motion through human organ meats.

A plot this complex, with so many characters to keep alive, could easily go astray. Indeed, I could make no sense of this week's *Perfect Sleep* despite a fulsome narration. But the director, Benny Boom, a music video director, knows what he's doing and skillfully intercuts the story strands. The first-time screenplay by Blair Cobbs has a lot of dire dialogue, very sunny, and presents the world's most inept bank robbers along with its most inept delivery man and most imprudent drug lord.

Nice surprise: Debbie Allen plays the manager of the delivery company, and gets a big laugh; no, not just because the audience sees she's Debbie Allen.

The Next Three Days ★ ★ ½

PG-13, 133 m., 2010

Russell Crowe (John Brennan), Elizabeth Banks (Lara Brennan), Brian Dennehy (George Brennan), Lennie James (Lieutenant Nabulsi), Olivia Wilde (Nicole), Ty Simpkins (Luke), Helen Carey (Grace Brennan), Liam Neeson (Damon Pennington). Directed by Paul Haggis and produced by Haggis, Olivier Delbosc, Marc Missonnier, and Michael Nozik. Screenplay by Haggis, based on the film *Anything for Her* (*Pour Elle*), directed by Fred Cavaye.

Russell Crowe slumps comfortably into the role of a junior college teacher in *The Next Three Days*, and then morphs into an unlikely man of action determined to spring his wife from jail. The film might have been more convincing if he'd remained the schleppy English teacher throughout. Once glimmers of *Gladiator* begin to reveal themselves, a certain credibility is lost. The movie is a competent thriller, but maybe could have been more.

That's because the filmmaker is Paul Haggis, director of such powerful films as *Crash* and *In the Valley of Elah* and writer of *Million Dollar Baby*. Here he's remaking a 2008 French film named *Anything for Her*, unseen by me. What he makes of it really doesn't seem worthy of his time, and the performances by Crowe and Elizabeth Banks could have been put to better use.

Crowe and Banks play John and Lara Brennan, a Pittsburgh couple with a young son, who find their world collapses in twenty-four hours. After a nice night out, their doors burst open the next morning, cops charge in, and Lara is hauled away on murder charges. John *knows* his wife did not—could not—commit the crime. But the evidence is compelling: She has the opportunity, it appears she had the motive, and the blood on her coat matches the victim's. Looks bad.

John tries to continue teaching and raising their son. He's conventional, intelligent, settled. The arrest has triggered a deep outrage. First he backs appeals to the sentence. When they all fail, he learns Lara will be transferred to the state penitentiary in three days. The deadline is dire because he plans to break his wife out of the jail she's being held in.

How do you, a bookish English teacher, go about doing that? The movie becomes a prison-break procedural, and the steps John takes and the plans he makes are interesting, as such matters often are in the movies. How he transforms into a man capable of fulfilling them is sort of slipped in. He does them, ergo he could do them. He does a lot of online research, solicits advice from a man who has broken out of a lot of prisons (Liam Neeson), and descends into the Pittsburgh underworld to obtain a weapon.

English teachers are ordinarily not terrifically good at buying guns from dope dealers, and the deal doesn't go smoothly, shall we say. But by now Russell Crowe the hero of *Master and Commander* has surfaced, almost on command. It's not his fault the role requires such a stretch. It's perfectly possible for ordinary people to cleverly break into and out of things, which they do all the time. But there's a requirement in the marketplace that there must be action scenes; Haggis supplies them, and Crowe rises to the occasion, as he must.

There are intriguing subcurrents. Did Lara Brennan perhaps actually commit the murder? There are indistinct black-and-white flashback scenes that are ambiguous. They raise the possibility. I consider them cheating: A movie knows whodunit. If it includes scenes that deliberately mislead us and then later clears up our confusion, that's a form of cheating, and the movie knows it. Better if you can use POV scenes in which another observer (John, say) misleads himself. Here, that's not possible.

Elizabeth Banks plays many of her scenes behind bars and begins to despair. Her son, picked on at school, refuses to talk nicely with her. The family's money is gone. She has little reason to think John can do anything at this point and sinks into depression. Then we get to the third act, and personalities take second place to action.

It's not a bad movie. It's sort of slow, because it spells out a lot of details, but it kept me involved. It's just that, after it was over, I felt it was a waste of the talent involved. I'd like to see Crowe and Banks in a smart Haggis original that wasn't about a jailbreak. I'm not sure, unfortunately, that the people financing the film would agree with me.

Nick Nolte: No Exit ★ ★

NO MPAA RATING, 74 m., 2010

Featuring Nick Nolte, Jacqueline Bisset, Rosanna Arquette, Barbara Hershey, Ben Stiller, Paul Mazursky, Alan Rudolph, Powers Boothe, James Gammon, F. X. Feeney, Mike Medavoy. A documentary directed and produced by Thomas Thurman.

Nick Nolte is an interesting actor. Perhaps too interesting to appear in an independent documentary about himself. Perhaps too interesting to be interviewed by someone else. In *Nick Nolte: No Exit*, he interviews himself. The way he does this does what it can to assist a fairly pointless documentary.

Seated behind a silver laptop, well groomed and wearing a big white Stetson, Nolte asks questions. Seated behind a black desktop computer and looking disheveled and squinty-eyed (well, all right, hungover), Nolte replies to them. It would be going too far to say he "answers" them.

Here is a fine actor who has made many very good films. On the wall behind him is the poster for Paul Schrader's *Affliction* (1997), the one he and James Coburn both won Oscar nominations for (Coburn won). His credits include *Hotel Rwanda, The Thin Red Line, Who'll Stop the Rain, North Dallas Forty, Lorenzo's Oil, Q&A,* and many others.

He mentions several of these films, and others, but doesn't really discuss them. He's proud of them, and of his work, as he should be. He admires Marlon Brando, who encouraged him. He has nothing to say about his private life. He mentions "the most famous celebrity mug shot," which he posed for after a DUI arrest in 2006, but doesn't go into details.

Nolte is intercut with sound bites about him by Nick Nolte, Jacqueline Bisset, Rosanna Arquette, Barbara Hershey, Ben Stiller, Paul Mazursky, Alan Rudolph, Powers Boothe, James Gammon, F. X. Feeney, Mike Medavoy. He's worked with them all, but doesn't go into detail. Most of them he doesn't mention.

Yet despite everything, the film has a certain fascination because Nolte is such a charismatic enigma. I've interviewed him several times, including at Telluride, which he attended in a bathrobe, and at Cannes, where we did a Q&A that was light on the A's. I enjoyed his company. Can't say that he confided many secrets.

Night at the Museum: Battle of the Smithsonian ★ ½

PG, 105 m., 2009

Ben Stiller (Larry Daley), Amy Adams (Amelia Earhart), Owen Wilson (Jedediah Smith), Hank Azaria (Kahmunrah/The Thinker), Christopher Guest (Ivan the Terrible), Alain Chabat (Napoleon Bonaparte), Ricky Gervais (Dr. McPhee), Steve Coogan (Octavius), Bill Hader (General Custer), Robin

Williams (Teddy Roosevelt). Directed by Shawn Levy and produced by Levy, Chris Columbus, and Michael Barnathan. Screenplay by Robert Ben Garant and Thomas Lennon.

Don't trust me on this movie. It rubbed me the wrong way. I can understand, as an abstract concept, why some people would find it entertaining. It sure sounds intriguing: *Night at the Museum: Battle of the Smithsonian.* If that sounds like fun to you, don't listen to sourpuss here.

Oh, did I dislike this film. It made me squirmy. Its premise is lame, its plot relentlessly predictable, its characters with personalities that would distinguish picture books, its cost incalculable (well, $150 million). Watching historical figures enact the clichés identified with the most simplistic versions of their images, I found myself yet once again echoing the frequent cry of Gene Siskel: Why not just give us a documentary of the same actors having lunch?

One actor surpasses the material. That would be Amy Adams, as Amelia Earhart, because she makes Amelia sweet and lovable, although from what I gather, in real life that was not necessarily the case. I found myself looking forward to the upcoming biopic about Earhart with Hilary Swank. Over the closing credits, Bonnie Koloc could sing Red River Dave McEnery's "Amelia Earhart's Last Flight":

Just a ship out on the ocean, a speck
against the sky,
Amelia Earhart flying that sad day;
With her partner, Captain Noonan, on
the second of July
Her plane fell in the ocean far away.

(Chorus)

There's a beautiful, beautiful field
Far away in a land that is fair,
Happy landings to you, Amelia Earhart,
Farewell, first lady of the air.

Sigh. Sort of floats you away, doesn't it? But then I crash-landed in the movie, where Amelia Earhart has to become the sidekick of Larry Daley (Ben Stiller), who has faked his résumé to get hired as a security guard and rescue his buddies from *Night at the Museum* (2006).

What has happened, see, is that the Museum of Natural History is remodeling. They're replacing their beloved old exhibits, like Teddy Roosevelt mounted on his horse, with ghastly new interactive media experiences. His friends are doomed to go into storage at the National Archives, part of the Smithsonian Institution. We see something of its sterile corridors stretching off into infinity; it looks just a little larger than Jorge Luis Borges's Library of Babel, and you remember how big *that* was.

However, Larry is able to manage one last night of freedom for them before the crates are filled with plastic popcorn. This is thanks to, I dunno, some kind of magic tablet of the villainous Pharaoh Kahmunrah (Hank Azaria). Among the resurrected are Teddy Roosevelt (Robin Williams), General Custer (Bill Hader), Ivan the Terrible (Christopher Guest), Octavius (Steve Coogan), and Albert Einstein (Eugene Levy). Also, the stuffed monkey from our first manned (or monkeyed) satellite, on a flight where the mission controller is played, of course, by Clint Howard, who has played mission controllers in something like half a dozen movies, maybe a dozen. When he gets a job, he already knows all of the lines. I could give you the exact number of the mission controllers he has played, but looking up Clint Howard's IMDb credits for a review of *Night at the Museum: Battle of the Smithsonian* seems like dissipation.

What is the motivation for the characters? Obviously, the video game they will inspire. Wilbur Wright is here with the first airplane, and Amelia pilots the plane she went down in on that sad second of July. Rodin's Thinker (Hank Azaria) is somewhat distracted, his chin leaning on his hand, no doubt pondering such questions as: "Hey, aren't I supposed to be in the Musee Rodin in Paris?"

The reanimated figures are on three scales. Some are life-size. Some are larger-than-life-size, like the statue in the Lincoln Memorial on the National Mall. Some are the size of tiny action figures, and they're creepy, always crawling around and about to get stepped on. Nobody asks Abe Lincoln any interesting stuff like, "Hey, you were there—what did Dick Nixon really say to the hippies during his midnight visit to your memorial?"

I don't mind a good dumb action movie. I

was the one who liked *The Mummy: Tomb of the Dragon Emperor.* But *Night at the Museum: Battle of the Smithsonian* is such a product. Like ectoplasm from a medium, it is the visible extrusion of a marketing campaign.

Night Catches Us ★ ★ ★

R, 90 m., 2010

Anthony Mackie (Marcus), Kerry Washington (Patricia), Jamie Hector ("DoRight" Miller), Tariq Trotter (Bostic), Wendell Pierce (Detective Gordon), Jamara Griffin (Iris), Amari Cheatom (Jimmy). Directed by Tanya Hamilton and produced by Sean Costello, Jason Orans, and Ron Simons. Screenplay by Hamilton.

In the late 1960s revolution seemed to be in the air. Not a revolt powerful enough to topple the government, but one intense enough to threaten its expectations. Then the war was over, the draft ended, and the moment passed. *Night Catches Us* takes place in Philadelphia at a time when the Black Panthers are still alive in memory.

The film doesn't open with that large canvas, however, but with a small one. Marcus (Anthony Mackie) walks past a Cadillac in a driveway and into a house, and is told "your father is in the living room." The father's introduction is an example of one shot doing the work of much dialogue. Marcus has a brother, Bostic (Tariq Trotter), who harbors much anger against him, and slowly we learn that Marcus is believed in the neighborhood to have betrayed a Panther comrade and been responsible for his death.

So deep was this belief that Marcus left town for some years, and it's still not comfortable for him to walk in the neighborhood. One person who doesn't hold him accountable is the dead man's widow, Patricia (Kerry Washington). She's a lawyer, a widow with a daughter, and we sense immediately that there's unfinished passion between them. Perhaps people suspected that and tied it to the dead Panther's betrayal.

This is not an action movie. It is a movie about loss, sadness, and regret, and the feeling that history has moved on. Bostic, the brother, symbolizes that by having joined the Black Muslims, a group that by then represented a similar rejection of white society and even a somewhat similar iconography. Bostic is finished with the past. He can't wait to sell the family house.

Night Catches Us wisely avoids many of the situations this setup might suggest—situations that have been played out in countless other films. It doesn't turn into a street war or a whodunit. Its emotional center is the understanding that grows between Marcus and Patricia. They're good people, capable of useful lives, trying to free themselves from the chains of the past. She never believed he was a snitch. Perhaps they can find reconciliation and acceptance.

The film leads to no showy conclusion, no spectacular climax. It is about movement possible within the soul even in difficult times. The writer-director, Tanya Hamilton, faces the problem of all directors of period films, and solves them here by re-creating the Black Panther period in black-and-white news photos. That's about right. Even a few years later, that's somehow how it's remembered in the mind. The Panthers feeding kids breakfast. The Panthers in their black berets. The fiercely identical anger and resolve in their faces. All over with. Leaving Marcus and Patricia to get on with things.

A Nightmare on Elm Street ★

R, 95 m., 2010

Jackie Earle Haley (Freddy Krueger), Kyle Gallner (Quentin Smith), Rooney Mara (Nancy Holbrook), Katie Cassidy (Kris Fowles), Thomas Dekker (Jesse Braun), Kellan Lutz (Dean Russell). Directed by Samuel Bayer and produced by Michael Bay, Andrew Form, and Bradley Fuller. Screenplay by Wesley Strick and Eric Heisserer.

Forget about the plot, the actors, and the director. What you require to make a new *Nightmare on Elm Street* are these three off-the-shelf sound effects:

1. A sudden, loud clanging noise mixed with a musical chord.
2. Snicker-snack sounds, which Freddy Krueger's steel finger claws make every time they are seen.
3. A voice deepener, to drop Freddy's speaking voice to an ominous level.

On top of that, you need your sudden cuts, your lighting from below, your thump-thump-thumps, and, of course, a dog that barks at something unseen in the night, so that your teenage heroine can go out onto the lawn in bare feet and flimsy PJs and call, "Rufus! Rufus! Here, boy!" You know in your bones that Rufus is now checking into Doggie Heaven.

Oh, and actors. Lots of Dead Teenagers, seen in the last moments of their lives, when they enjoy a farewell Moment of Deceptive Safety just before there's a sudden, loud clanging noise and the snicker-snack claws disembowel them and Freddy rumbles, "You have nothing to worry about. This won't hurt one . . . little . . . bit."

The 2010 edition of *A Nightmare on Elm Street* is number 8½ in the series. I arrive at that number not out of a desperate desire to be seeing the Fellini film instead, but because *Freddy vs. Jason* (2003) should in all fairness count for half a film on this list, and half a film on the *Friday the 13th* list.

It is sad to think of all those Dead Teenagers. They were played by ambitious, talented young actors, some of them now in their forties, who survived grueling auditions for the honor of being slashed by Freddy. Some of them are now successful: Johnny Depp, for example. Robert Englund became famous playing Freddy, but where can that lead when you're always wearing a mask of makeup? Now Jackie Earle Haley plays the role. For what purpose? He might as well play Santa Claus.

It was twenty-six long years ago when Freddy first began to haunt the nightmares of the children of Elm Street in Springwood, Ohio. At least 137 victims have been claimed by Freddy in the years since then, but the shady little street is still lined with handsome homes and hasn't been leveled, covered with ashes and sprinkled with holy water. The franchise was founded by Wes Craven, the Ray Kroc of horror, who made the excellent *Wes Craven's New Nightmare* (1994), about Freddy haunting the dreams of the *makers* of the *Nightmare* movies.

Freddy is not a good argument for a supernatural existence. He can live inside wallpaper, appear anywhere, and has no need of physical existence except, arguably, when he inflicts actual physical damage. Yet he's such a bore, always growling away with his deep-voiced *hahahahaha*. If a man leads an interesting life he ought to be able to make good conversation, is what I say.

I stared at *A Nightmare on Elm Street* with weary resignation. The movie consists of a series of teenagers who are introduced, haunted by nightmares, and then slashed to death by Freddy. So what? Are we supposed to be scared? Is the sudden clanging chord supposed to evoke a fearful Pavlovian response? For Rufus, maybe, but not for me. Here, boy.

9 ★ ★ ★

PG-13, 79 m., 2009

With the voices of: Elijah Wood (No. 9), Jennifer Connelly (No. 7), Christopher Plummer (No. 1), Crispin Glover (No. 6), Martin Landau (No. 2), Fred Tatasciore (No. 8), John C. Reilly (No. 5). Directed by Shane Acker and produced by Tim Burton, Timur Bekmambetov, and Dana Ginsburg. Screenplay by Pamela Pettler and Jim Lemley.

The first images are spellbinding. In close-up, thick fingers make the final stitches in a roughly humanoid little rag doll, and binocular eyes are added. This creature comes to life, walks on tottering legs, and ventures fearfully into the devastation of a bombed-out cityscape.

This visionary world was first created as a short subject by Shane Acker, a student at UCLA, and was nominated for a 2006 Oscar. At the time I found it "an atmosphere of creeping, crashing, menace . . . elaborated as a game of hide-and-seek, beautifully animated and intriguingly unwholesome." So it is still, as the first figure, named 9, meets his similar predecessors, No. 1 through No. 8, and they find themselves in battle against a Transformer-like red-eyed monster called the Beast.

One might question the purpose of devising a life-form in a world otherwise without life, only to provide it with an enemy that wishes only to destroy it. The purpose, alas, is to create a pretext for a series of action scenes, an apocalyptic battle that is visually more interesting than, but as relentless as, similar all-action-all-the-time movies. This is a disappointment. Remembering the promise of his original short, I looked forward to what Acker would do at feature length, especially with a producer like Tim Burton to watch his back.

The characters look similar but are easy enough to tell apart, not least because they have their numbers stitched on their backs. They also have different visual characteristics and are voiced by distinctive actors, including Christopher Plummer as their fearful leader, No. 1, and Jennifer Connelly as the token female, No. 7. The usefulness of gender in a species without genitalia is not discussed, not even wistfully.

Nine is the youngest, probably the smartest, and certainly the most daring, leading the others, against No. 1's wishes, to poke around the ruins. These look left over from a city from the past, not the future, and a 1940ish newsreel reports on a devastating global war triggered by a Hitleresque dictator. Was the Beast left behind to wipe out any survivors and assure final victory even in the absence of victors?

Such questions, I submit, are intriguing. But the dialogue is mostly simplified Action Speak, with barked warnings and instructions and strategy debates of the most rudimentary kind. Since this movie is clearly targeted not at kiddies but at teens and up, is it now Hollywood theory that eloquence and intelligence are no longer useful in action dialogue?

One of the benefits of the pre-CGI era was that although action scenes might be manifestly artificial, they had to be composed of details that were visually intelligible. Modern CGI artists, intoxicated by their godlike command of imagery, get carried away and add confusing complexity. If I were pressed to provide the cops with a detailed description of the Beast, the best I could do would be: "You'll know it when you see it. Also, it has a big glowing red eye."

Contrast that to the enormous construction in Miyazaki's *Howl's Moving Castle.* It is awesomely complex, but I have a large print of one of Miyazaki's still drawings from the film, and you can clearly see that it's all *there.*

9 is nevertheless worth seeing. It might have been an opportunity for the sort of challenging speculation that sci-fi is best at, however, and the best reason to see it is simply because of the creativity of its visuals. They're entrancing.

Nine ★ ★

PG-13, 112 m., 2009

Daniel Day-Lewis (Guido Contini), Marion Cotillard (Luisa), Penelope Cruz (Carla), Judi Dench (Lilli), Stacy Ferguson (Saraghina), Kate Hudson (Stephanie), Nicole Kidman (Claudia), Sophia Loren (Mamma). Directed by Rob Marshall and produced by Marshall, John DeLuca, Marc Platt, and Harvey Weinstein. Screenplay by Michael Tolkin and Anthony Minghella, based on the book for the musical *Nine* by Arthur Kopit.

My problem may be that I know Fellini's *8½* too well. Your problem may be that you don't know it well enough. Both of us may be asking, who exactly was *Nine* made for? This is a big-scale version of the 1982 Broadway production, which won the Tony for best musical. It's likely that most who saw it had either seen the Fellini or made that their business.

I didn't see the musical, but I'm sure it greatly benefited from being live and right there onstage, where the energy in the performance compensated for its lack of a single great song. All the songs sound exactly like standard boilerplate Broadway show tunes, except for composer Maury Yeston's "Finale," which evokes the original Nino Rota sound track for Fellini, which is the problem.

Fellini's great films are essentially musicals. Like most Italian directors of his generation, he didn't record live dialogue and sound. He depended on dubbing. On a set, he usually had an orchestra playing and asked his actors to move, not in time with the music, but "in sympathy." Everyone in a Fellini film evokes an inner body rhythm. Then there's Rota's music itself, my favorite sound tracks. I could watch a Fellini film on the radio.

The story, recycled by Rob Marshall for *Nine,* involves aspects of Fellini's own life: his vagueness about screenplays and deadlines, his indifference to budgets, his womanizing, the guilt about sex instilled by his Catholic upbringing, his guilt about cheating on his wife and about bankrupting his producers. It was said that *8½* wasn't so much a confessional as an acting-out of the very problems he was having while making the film, including how to use a gigantic outdoor set he constructed for no clear purpose.

It's a great film, some say his best. *Nine* the musical "adapts" it, true enough, but doesn't feel it. Consider Fellini's most famous scene. The many women in the life of the hero, Guido (played by Marcello Mastroianni), assemble in a fantasy harem and greet him: the Swedish air stewardess, his wife, his mistress, his mother, Saraghina the local whore of his childhood, and above all his muse (Claudia Cardinale), a reassuringly perfect woman, encouraging, never critical. In the harem they caress him, bathe him, soothe him—and then reveal complaints and criticisms, so that he has to take up a whip and threaten them like a lion tamer.

In *Nine* this scene is, of course, reprised, but with an unclear focus. It's less like a vengeful dream, more like a reunion. There's no urgency, no passion, most of all no guilt. In fact, the subtext of Catholic guilt, which is central to Fellini, is only hinted at in *Nine*. But then *Nine* pays homage to a Broadway musical, and not Fellini at all.

In this connection, consider the odd casting of Daniel Day-Lewis in the Fellini/Mastroianni role, played onstage by Raul Julia. Of course he isn't Marcello; who could be? But he also isn't romantic, musical, comic, baffled, exasperated—and not (even though he apprenticed under a Florentine shoemaker) in the slightest degree Italian. What current movie star could play the role? I think Javier Bardem could. Gael Garcia Bernal? Maybe Alec Baldwin? You need a man who is handsome and never seems to have given it a thought. I'm crazy? Then you tell me.

Nine is just plain adrift in its own lack of necessity. It is filled wall-to-wall with stars (Marion Cotillard as the wife figure, Penelope Cruz as the mistress, Judi Dench as the worrying assistant, Nicole Kidman as the muse, the sublime Sophia Loren as the mother). But that's what they are, stars, because the movie doesn't make them characters. My closing advice is very sincere: In the life of anyone who loves movies, there must be time to see *8½*. You can watch it instantly right now on Netflix or Amazon. What are you waiting for?

9500 Liberty ★ ★ ★ ½

NO MPAA RATING, 80 m., 2010

With Greg Letiecq, Corey A. Stewart, Charlie T. Deane, Guadencio Fernandez, Alanna Almeda, Elena Schlossberg, Frank J. Principi, Martin E. Nohe, and Annabel Park. A documentary directed by Annabel Park and Eric Byler and produced by Chris Rigopulos. Written by Park and Byler.

A few years before Arizona passed its new immigration law, a similar law was passed and then repealed in Virginia's Prince William County. The new documentary *9500 Liberty* tells the fascinating story of how that happened and possibly foretells what lies ahead for Arizona. In Virginia, the law was eventually overturned by a combination of middle-class whites, Republican officeholders, the police chief, Latinos, and economic reality.

When Prince William experienced a major building boom in the 1990s, a shortage of labor created a demand for workers, which led to an increase in the Latino population. Some of the newcomers were legal immigrants. Some were not. A blogger named Greg Letiecq began to write about his unhappiness with hearing Spanish spoken in public places. Finding an audience, he fomented about rising crime rates, rising taxes to pay for services for the newcomers, overcrowded dwellings, music played too loud, fast driving, and so on. He included Latino crime reports from the local police blotter. He even claimed armed members of the Zapatistas Mexican revolutionary group were moving to Prince William.

His organization, Help Save Manassas, issued saucer-sized red lapel stickers and soon they were seen around the town. He and board of supervisors president Corey A. Stewart created a law that would require local police to stop people for "probable cause" and ask them to show their proof of citizenship. This measure seemed to have popular support, and there was resentment against a Mexican-American citizen who erected a large sign on his property (at 9500 Liberty Street) to differ with it.

At about this time filmmakers Eric Byler and Annabel Park (a Filipino-American and a Korean-American) began to post videos on

YouTube that weren't so much political as the raw material for a documentary. They showed discussions and arguments among local residents, testimony before the county board, Stewart, Letiecq and other pro-law figures, and ordinary citizens. As the videos went viral, they inspired another local blog to counter Letiecq, and a growing community discussion about the law.

Among its opponents was Charlie T. Deane, the long-serving, widely respected local police chief, who testified the law would cost about $14 million over five years to enforce, who said his officers had more important things to do, and who said (along with the county attorney) that without video cameras in every police car, the officers and the county would be open to lawsuits. Cameras would cost another $3.1 million.

Ironically, the law was partly to blame for a tax rate increase of 25 percent a year. There was another problem. Latinos began to move out of Prince William or take their business to nearby friendlier areas. There was a retail slump, badly timed to coincide with the collapse of the housing market. The county tax base dropped as taxpaying "legals" left. Restaurants and shops closed. Prince William County and Virginia have sales taxes, income taxes, and other taxes that even noncitizens pay.

Chief Deane met with a Mexican government official and was incredibly accused of treason by the right-wingers (for "negotiating with a foreign power"). This did not go over well. The Republican woman who had hosted a fundraiser for board president Stewart testified against him at a board meeting. There was a rising tide of opposition to the law and the negative image it gave the area. A motion to raise taxes to keep the law and pay for the cameras drew a tie 4–4 vote. Stewart recessed for a caucus and returned with a new "compromise" motion ending the "probable cause" mandate, which resulted in an 8–0 vote. On the board at that time were six Republicans and two Democrats.

The most rewarding element of this deeply involved documentary involves the board meetings. Local citizens stand up to speak their minds, and we hear a great many of them. Some board meetings lasted until well past midnight. They were in the great tradition of New England town meetings. Latinos were united in opposing the law. Many were longtime, well-known American citizens. But the balance was finally tipped by the voices of thoughtful Republicans and their distaste for the hate stirred up by Letiecq and his group. Calling Chief Deane a traitor was the last straw.

Annabel Park and Eric Byler began as objective documentarians who found this story being pressed upon them. They become advocates and are clear about that. They try to show both sides of the debate, but (inevitably, perhaps?) the anti-law faction comes across more positively.

The outcome was this: Passing the law led to higher taxes, not lower ones. The tax base decreased. And as for the crime rate? Chief Deane has charts showing that crime dropped every single year over the past decade.

North Face ★ ★ ★

NO MPAA RATING, 126 m., 2010

Benno Fuermann (Toni Kurz), Johanna Wokalek (Luise Fellner), Florian Lukas (Andi Hinterstoisser), Simon Schwarz (Willy Angerer), Georg Friedrich (Edi Rainer), Ulrich Tukur (Henry Arau). Directed by Philipp Stoelzl and produced by Benjamin Herrmann, Gerd Huber, Danny Krausz, Rudolf Santschi, Boris Schonfelder, Kurt Stocker, and Isabelle Welter. Screenplay by Stoelzl, Christoph Silber, Rupert Henning, and Johannes Naber.

The movies have long been convinced that any story can be improved by adding a romance. Not true. Any story can be improved by leaving out as much as you reasonably can. Consider *North Face*, the bone-chilling, superbly mounted record of an assault on the north face of the Eiger, which is known by the grim understatement as "the last remaining problem in the Alps."

Mountain climbing terrifies me because it has such a ruthless digital simplicity. It is either zero or one: (1) You are holding on. (Zero) You are falling. Time's arrow flies in one direction. Once you aren't holding on, there is nothing you can do. No skill, no courage, no training, nor any rope or piton.

These fears explain why in its scenes on the Eiger itself *North Face* starts strongly and ends as unbearably riveting. They also explain why it was a strategic error to believe this story needed romantic and political subplots. You know something has gone wrong when a story about mountain climbers gives the sorta girlfriend of one of them second billing.

North Face is based on the true story of a May 1936 attempt on the Eiger by four climbers—two Germans and two Austrians who meet on the mountain in the movie but began together in real life. All four are experienced and confident. One is not very wise. Using the long-tested rope-and-piton method, they hope to reach the top after spending only one night in sleeping bags secured to the mountain. They have little petrol burners to heat tea or broth. They are very fit.

One of the Germans has doubts about making an attempt on a peak that has never been scaled and that froze two Germans to death the year before. The Eiger is known for its weather shifts and avalanches of snow and rocks. Meanwhile in Berlin, the Nazi editor (Ulrich Tukur) of a daily newspaper wants to produce German heroes for Hitler in the run-up to the Olympics. The two Germans, Toni Kurz and Andi Hinterstoisser (Benno Fuermann and Florian Lukas), both in the army, are such lackluster Nazis that they're assigned to cleaning latrines.

The editor's secretary, Luise Fellner (Johanna Wokalek), was sweet on Toni when they were young; Toni and Andi took her climbing with them. When her editor discovers she knows them, he orders her to go to the Eiger and convince them it's their patriotic duty to climb. Toni is convinced more by Luise than by Hitler. Setting off from the base, they eye two Austrians, Willy Angerer (Simon Schwarz) and Edi Rainer (Georg Friedrich). Higher up, their climbs will intersect.

The director, Philipp Stoelzl, is uncanny in his ability to convince us these four are actually climbing a mountain. Because the four actors could hardly be climbing themselves, he must use doubles for some shots. That is easier because of sunglasses, hoods, and blowing snow. Some of the shots must have been made on sets. None of that matters. I was on the side of that mountain all the way.

If the film had stayed there, it might have been devastatingly good. It's powerful enough as it is. But consider the 2004 film *Touching the Void,* about a climber who broke his leg, driving a bone through a knee socket, and later fell into an ice crevice, and agonizingly, unbelievably, made his way alone back down the mountain. That semi-documentary by Kevin Macdonald showed only the two climbers. That was more than enough.

In *North Face,* Stoelzl cuts to the luxury hotel at the base and even back to Berlin. There's a lot about the editor's ego and his desire to please Hitler. And much about Luise's fears for her friends and her determination to bring help to them after they disappear from view before the second night. We learn that railway tunnels through the mountain have occasional openings to the surface to admit air, and that the climbers might be approached by that means. Sounds reasonable, although some of her later decisions are dubious.

I believe audiences will enjoy this film. I did. But there's too much baggage along for the ride. It involves not only Luise but also the Nazis. A love story is not needed here, particularly when the reputed lovers got along perfectly well apart for ten years. And as for the Nazis, must every German film set in the '30s involve Nazism? Do you climb a mountain for Hitler and think about him all the way up? Not these climbers. They don't give a damn about Hitler.

Note: Speaking of mountains and special effects, when Clint Eastwood made The Eiger Sanction, *he personally performed in a scene showing him dangling at the end of a rope three thousand feet in the air. A telephoto lens zoomed in on him from a distance to prove it was really him. He told me he attended a sneak preview in disguise and overheard: "It really looked like it was Clint up there. I wonder how they did that."*

No Strings Attached ★ ★

R, 106 m., 2011

Natalie Portman (Emma), Ashton Kutcher (Adam), Cary Elwes (Dr. Metzner), Kevin Kline (Alvin), Greta Gerwig (Patrice), Lake Bel (Lucy), Olivia Thirlby (Katie), Chris "Ludacris" Bridges (Wallace), Ophelia Lovibond (Vanessa). Directed by Ivan Reitman and produced by Reitman, Jeffrey Clifford, and Joe Medjuck. Screenplay by Elizabeth Meriwether.

No Strings Attached poses the question: Is it possible to regularly have sex with someone and not run a risk of falling in love? The answer is yes. Now that we have that settled, consider the case of Emma (Natalie Portman) and Adam (Ashton Kutcher), who met when they were six and now meet when they're maybe twenty-six. Busy people. He's a low-rent TV producer and she's a medical student. She doesn't have time for romance, and he's dating the sexy Vanessa (played by the well-named Ophelia Lovibond).

Still, one must do something about sex, lest the pipes run rusty, as my friend Henry Togna Sr., the London hotelier, instructed me when he was well into his seventies. Adam and Emma see each other at a party, remember each other after all those years, yet do not realize they're having a Meet Cute. Then Adam discovers Vanessa has dumped him and moved in with his father (Kevin Kline). In response, he begins to drink, which is what the Jack Lemmon character always does in these situations, and what with one thing and another he wakes up naked in Emma's apartment while she and three roommates reassure him they're all interns and it's deja vu when it comes to viewing the male netherlands on display.

Is there something a little, I dunno, *dated* about a comedy where a guy clutches a towel to his privates while girls giggle at him? And when he asks if he slept with anyone last night, why does that remind me of Doris Day in *Where Were You When the Lights Went Out?* Here is a titillating sex romp in 2011, when the very words "titillating" and "romp" have outlasted their shelf lives. The movie is rated R, but it's the most watery R I've seen. It's more of a PG-13 playing dress-up.

Anyway, finding out he hasn't slept with Emma, Adam engages in sitcom badinage that quickly leads to the old rumpy-pumpy, and they find the pipes running marvelously clear. What a discovery! They can have sex and remain just friends! This is a great convenience. They proceed to frolic like two bunnies in clover, using their cell phones and texting skills to arrange emergency trysts in roughly anything except a bed.

All of this is fun while it lasts. Then the wheels of Hollywood morality begin to grind. There was a time when the very premise of this film would have been banned, but times change, and now characters can do pretty much anything as long as they don't get away with it. Although *No Strings Attached* might have been more fun if Adam and Emma had investigated the long-term possibilities of casual sex, it is required that the specter of Romantic Love raise its ominous head. Are they . . . becoming too fond? Emma suggests they try sleeping with others so, you know, they won't get too hung up on each other. If you've ever seen a romantic comedy, you know how that works. Experience shows that *not* sleeping with others is the foolproof way of not getting too hung up, etc.

This is a strange film. Its premise is so much more transgressive than its execution. It's as if the 1970s never happened, let alone subsequent decades. Emma and Adam aren't modern characters. They're sitcom characters allowed to go all the way like grown-ups. As the wheels of the plot creak and groan, we're like kids in the backseat, asking, "Are we there yet?" Some diversion is supplied by the subplot involving Adam's dad, Alvin (Kline), an aging TV star trapped forever in his own misspent youth. Alvin is a dedicated hedonist, which Vanessa finds to her liking because hedonists are always happy to pay, one way or another, for their hedonism, and Vanessa is happy to be paid, one way or another.

Natalie Portman won an Academy Award for *Black Swan.* Why she helped produce this I cannot say. Ambitious actors usually do dreck like this in order to afford to produce a movie like *Black Swan.* All the same, she does what she can; she has an edge, aggressive timing, and impressive enthusiasm for sex romping. Of Ashton Kutcher I have less to say. He seems to be a very nice guy, a little too large for agile romping and still too young for a Brendan Fraser role. When I saw him in *The Butterfly Effect* (2004), I registered that he could act, but in this material he's essentially just the Male Unit. There is no character there.

Nothing but the Truth ★ ★ ★ ½

R, 106 m., 2009

Kate Beckinsale (Rachel Armstrong), Vera Farmiga (Erica Van Doren), Matt Dillon (Patton

Dubois), Angela Bassett (Bonnie Benjamin), Alan Alda (Albert Burnside), David Schwimmer (Ray Armstrong), Floyd Abrams (Judge Hall). Directed by Rod Lurie and produced by Lurie, Bob Lari, and Marc Frydman. Screenplay by Lurie.

Alan Alda has a scene in *Nothing but the Truth* where he reads a dissenting Supreme Court opinion defending the right of journalists to protect confidential sources. I assumed the speech was genuine and was surprised to learn that the case inspiring the film was not heard by the Supreme Court. In fact the speech was written by Rod Lurie, the writer and director of the film, who would make an excellent Supreme if writing opinions were the only requirement. It was so soundly grounded in American idealism that I felt a patriotic stirring.

The film is obviously inspired by the case of Judith Miller, a *New York Times* reporter who served eighty-five days in prison for refusing to name her source in the Valerie Plame affair. That was the case in which Vice President Cheney's top aide blew the cover of a CIA agent in order to discredit the agent's husband, who investigated reports that Niger sold uranium to Saddam Hussein. He found no such evidence. The uranium story was part of the web of Bush-Cheney lies about WMDs that were used to justify the Iraq war.

The case is complicated, but if you know the general outlines, you can easily interpret Lurie's fictional story as a direct parallel to Miller/Valerie Plame/Joseph Wilson, though the names and specific details have been changed. In real life, Miller's reporting, accuracy, and objectivity were sharply questioned, and Lurie wisely sidesteps history to focus on the underlying question: Which is more important, the principle of confidentiality or national security? Trying to deal with the real Miller story would have trapped the film in a quicksand of complications.

I'm sure some readers are asking, why don't I just review the movie? Why drag in politics? If you are such a person, do not see *Nothing but the Truth*. It will make you angry or uneasy, one or the other. That Bush lied to lead us into Iraq is a generally accepted fact, and the movie regards a few of the consequences.

Lurie, however, has more on his mind than a political parable. The movie is above all a drama about the people involved, and his actors are effective at playing personalities, not symbols. Kate Beckinsale is Rachel Armstrong, the reporter for the *Capital Sun-Times*. Vera Farmiga is Erica Van Doren, the outed spy. Matt Dillon plays prosecutor Patton Dubois, obviously intended as U.S. prosecutor Patrick Fitzgerald, now so involved in the case of our fascinating former Illinois governor. Alda is the high-priced Washington lawyer hired by the newspaper to defend Rachel. Angela Bassett is the newspaper's editor, under pressure to tart up coverage, trying to stand firm. And this is interesting: There is a wonderful performance by Floyd Abrams as the federal judge; in real life, he was Miller's attorney.

Armstrong and Van Doren are suburban Washington soccer moms whose children attend the same school. They know each other by sight. In possession of the leak, the reporter asks the agent point-blank if it is true, and the agent replies in terms Justice Scalia does not believe decent people use in public. It is a fierce scene.

Dubois, the prosecutor, calls Armstrong as a witness in his investigation of the leak, and she refuses to name her source. That begins her harrowing ordeal in jail, where eventually she has been behind bars longer than any sister prisoner. She will not tell, even though this decision estranges her husband (David Schwimmer), alienates her young son, and paints her as a heartless mother who places job above family.

How she is treated seems to go beyond reasonable punishment. Dillon, as Dubois, is positioned as the villain, but objectively he is only doing his job, and Dillon says he played the role as if he were the film's good guy. Alda comes on strong as a man not above boasting of his expensive Zegna suit, but grows so involved that he goes pro bono. The dire costs to both women are at the heart of things.

Lurie, who is a powerful screenwriter, is freed by fiction to do two very interesting things. (1) He presents the issues involved with great clarity. (2) He shows that a reporter's reasons for concealing a source may be more compelling than we guess. What is deeply satisfying about *Nothing but the Truth* is that the conclusion, which will come as a surprise to almost all viewers, is not a cheat, is plausible, and explains some unresolved testimony.

Nothing but the Truth is a finely crafted film of people and ideas, of the sort more common before the movie mainstream became a sausage factory. It respects the intelligence of the audience, it contains real drama, it earns its suspense, and it has a point to make. In the ordinary course of events, it would have had a high-profile release and plausibly won nominations. But the economic downturn struck down its distributor, the film missed its release window, and its life must be on DVD. It is far above the "straight-to-DVD" category, and I hope filmgoers discover that.

Notorious ★ ★ ★ ½

R, 122 m., 2009

Jamal "Gravy" Woolard (Notorious B.I.G.), Angela Bassett (Voletta Wallace), Derek Luke (Sean Combs), Anthony Mackie (Tupac Shakur), Antonique Smith (Faith Evans), Naturi Naughton (Lil' Kim). Directed by George Tillman Jr. and produced by Voletta Wallace, Wayne Barrow, Mark Pitts, Robert Teitel, and Trish Hofmann. Screenplay by Reggie Rock Bythewood and Cheo Hodari Coker.

He was known as Notorious B.I.G., a man-mountain of rap, but behind the image was Christopher Wallace, an overgrown kid who was trying to grow up and do the right thing. The image we know about. The film *Notorious* is more interested in the kid. He was born in Brooklyn, loved his mother—a teacher who was studying for a master's degree—got into street-corner drug dealing because he liked the money, performed rap on the street, and at twenty was signed by record producer Sean "Puffy" Combs. Four years later, he was dead.

Documentaries about B.I.G. have focused on the final years of his life. *Notorious* tells us of a bright kid who was abandoned by his father, raised by a mother from Jamaica who laid down the rules, and told the kids on the playground he would be famous someday. "You too fat, too black, and too ugly," a girl tells him. He just looks at her. He is sweet-tempered, even after being seduced into the street-corner crack business, but he sounds tough in his rap songs—he is tough, introspective, autobiographical, and a gifted writer.

His demo tape is heard by Sean Combs (Derek Luke), who is seen in the film as a good influence, in part perhaps because he's the executive producer. Combs draws a line between the street as a market and a place where he wants his artists to be seen. B.I.G. leaves the drug business and almost overnight becomes a huge star, an East Coast rapper to match the West Coast artists such as Tupac Shakur.

Tupac was shot dead not long before B.I.G. was murdered, and the word was they died because of a feud between the East and West Coast dynasties and onetime friends B.I.G. and Tupac (Anthony Mackie). Another version, in Nick Broomfield's 2002 documentary *Biggie and Tupac*, is that both shootings were ordered by rap tycoon Suge Knight and carried out by off-duty LAPD officers in his hire. Broomfield produces an eyewitness and a bag man who says on camera that he delivered the money. The film, perhaps wisely, sidesteps this possibility.

Notorious is a good film in many ways, but its best achievement is the casting of Jamal Woolard, a rapper named Gravy, in the title role. He looks uncannily like the original, and Antonique Smith is a ringer for B.I.G.'s wife, Faith Evans. Woolard already knew how to perform but took voice lessons for six months at Juilliard to master B.I.G.'s sound. He performs a lot of music in the film, all of it plot-driven, sure to become a best-selling sound track. As an actor, he conveys the singer's complex personality: a mother's boy, a womanizer, an artist who accepts career guidance from his managers, a sentimentalist, an ominous presence.

The real B.I.G. may have had a harder side, but we don't see it here. Instead, director George Tillman Jr. and his writers, Reggie Rock Bythewood and Cheo Hodari Coker, craft an understated message picture in which B.I.G. eventually decides to accept responsibility for the children he has fathered, and as his mother, Voletta (Angela Bassett), urges him to do, become a man. Shortly before his death, he announces a new direction for his music.

Bassett doesn't play Voletta as a conventional grasping mamma. She believes in tough love and throws her son out of their apartment after she finds cocaine under the bed. Few actors are better at fierce resolve than Bassett, and she provides a baseline for her son's fall and eventual rise. The real Voletta is in the Broomfield documentary, where in 2002 she looks like . . . an older Angela Bassett.

George Tillman and his producing partner, Robert Teitel, are Chicagoans who have, together and separately, been involved in some of the best recent films about African-American and minority characters: *Nothing Like the Holidays, Soul Food, Men of Honor,* both *Barbershop* pictures, *Beauty Shop.* None of these films is sanctimonious, none preaches, but in an unobtrusive way they harbor positive convictions. In *Notorious,* they show how talent can lift a kid up off the street corner but can't protect him in a culture of violence. The whole gangsta rap posture was dangerous, as B.I.G. and Tupac proved.

Note: Tupac: Resurrection, *an extraordinary 2002 documentary, uses hours of autobiographical tapes left behind by Shakur to allow him to narrate his own life story. He also proved his acting ability in* Gridlock'd, *Vondie Curtis-Hall's 1997 film where he costarred with Tim Roth.*

Nowhere Boy ★ ★ ★ ½

R, 97 m., 2010

Aaron Johnson (John), Kristin Scott Thomas (Mimi), Anne-Marie Duff (Julia), Thomas Sangster (Paul), David Morrissey (Bobby), Ophelia Lovibond (Marie), David Threlfall (Uncle George). Directed by Sam Taylor-Wood and produced by Robert Bernstein, Kevin Loader, and Douglas Rae. Screenplay by Matt Greenhalgh, based on a memoir by Julia Baird.

John Lennon wrote the song "Julia" about his mother, and it is a strangely objective love song, as if about a real girlfriend and not a mom. Perhaps that's how he thought of her. When he was very young, he came under the care of his Aunt Mimi, whom he regarded as his mother, and in the telling in *Nowhere Boy,* he didn't see Julia again until the day of his uncle's funeral. The film is based on a memoir written by Julia Baird, his half-sister, who must be presumed to have good information.

"Julia" is a song of longing and regret, written some years after Julia's sudden death. Their relationship was close and did not have the time to grow old. There's a video online of Sean Lennon singing it, in front of back-projected photographs of his father and Julia, and also of his mother, Yoko Ono. "This song is for my mother," he says, and as he sings it, he sounds eerily like his father, in intonation, arrangement, emotion. Perhaps it is for both his parents. He was young when he lost John, and John was young when he lost Julia. Both memories are of interrupted love.

The young man John Lennon (Aaron Johnson) in *Nowhere Boy* was cocky and vulnerable. He was raised in an ordinary lower-working-class home, not far from Strawberry Fields in Liverpool, by an aunt (Kristin Scott Thomas) who loved him, but was reserved and cool. She and her husband had taken the child in after her younger, prettier sister proved incapable of caring for him; John learns the details of his adoption late in the film. He knew Mimi was not his mother, but had no idea that all during his childhood Julia lived only a few blocks away.

She must have seen him often, if he had only known it. Did she stay away out of respect for Mimi? He glimpses her at the funeral of his uncle and instinctively knows who she is. When he discovers where she lives, he knocks on her door and she greets him with instant, embracing love; we get the sense that she was a woman quick to love, impulsive, more spontaneous than the responsible Mimi. Because John and Julia are essentially strangers, their relationship has elements of unrealized romance. There is the tension between joy and sadness we often feel in Lennon's songs, and perhaps we see some of the origin of his place in the flow of British Romanticism.

Nowhere Boy is deliberately *not* about the future John Lennon, Paul McCartney, and George Harrison, nor about the birth of the Beatles. The cataclysm of their future global fame is nowhere on the horizon. It is about a not remarkable childhood and youth in Liverpool, marred by the sudden death of his Uncle George (David Threlfall), also warm and playful, more spontaneous than Mimi. The two men must have formed a club of their own in the Mimi-ordered household.

There are times when I would have liked a little more detail about the gestation of the future musicians. The only actual Beatles note in the film is its opening chord, from the distinctive first sound of *A Hard Day's Night*. We see John meeting Paul, and through Paul, George, in the ways that teenage boys meet. No heartfelt conversations, no elaborate daydreams; music seems to have been a natural way of expression for them. The seminal Beatles moment in the film may be when John goes to the cinema and sees Elvis Presley singing in a newsreel. Later generations can hardly comprehend how, or perhaps even why, Elvis represented a moment of decisive social change.

What do we really learn from *Nowhere Boy*? We don't really learn much about the actual early days of the Beatles as a band. Of course there is no Ringo Starr, who may deserve his own film. What we do learn is that it could be said of the teenage John Lennon that he:

Doesn't have a point of view,
Knows not where he's going to,
Isn't he a bit like you and me?

I think we also learn something more important. We learn that the emotional roller coaster of his formative years probably contributed to the complexity of his lyrics. We learn why there's so often in his music the top level of what seems clear, and then, below, echoes of something else. We feel elation and sadness as simultaneous possibilities. We arrive at the possibility that if Julia had always been there for him, he might not have been there for us. We reflect that even if all you need is love, that isn't always all you get.

Nuremberg: Its Lesson for Today ★ ★ ★

NO MPAA RATING, 78 m., 2011

Liev Schreiber (Narrator). A documentary directed by Pare Lorentz and produced by Lorentz, Budd Schulberg, and Stuart Schulberg.

Of all the many documentaries about the Holocaust, this was the first, made before the term was routinely linked to the event more properly called the Shoah. *Nuremberg: Its Lesson for Today* was edited from many hours of film taken at the eleven-month Nuremberg Trial, which, starting in 1945, placed twenty-two high-ranking Nazis on trial for crimes that together amounted to an outrage against decency. Assembled and edited by Stuart Schulberg with U.S. government funding, the film was exhibited throughout Germany in 1948 and 1949, and then taken from release and never seen in America.

It gave audiences the spectacle of seeing such iconic Nazis as Goring, Bormann, Hess, and Speer now humbled in an international courtroom, earphones clamped to their heads as they listen to the irrefutable evidence of their infamy. The film intercuts statements by the prosecution and defense and brief statements by some of the defendants.

As the record of crimes is read out, the film edits in horrifying footage from other documentaries made for the U.S. Army by such as John Ford. I hadn't seen all of these images before. Jews being marched naked through the streets, gloating mobs empowered by flimsy armbands, skeletal "subjects of medical experiments," the impossibly emaciated survivors of the death camps. An unspeakable sequence of corpses being piled into a mass grave, raising the question of why such film was shot, and why anyone agreed to be seen in it. The systematic extermination of six million Jews and nearly as many others was carried out boldly and openly, without apology, and when the unrepentant Goring is asked in the dock if he ever said human life was worthless, his answer rings out: "*Jawohl!*"

Most of the others seem repentant, and many in their final statements express resentment at what they see as Hitler's betrayal of their values, whatever they thought those were. It is revealing that even then, with the horrifying portrait of their evil deeds laid bare, they instinctively glorified Hitler so much that it was all his fault. Every single one of them was apparently only following orders, even those shown to have personally signed documents ordering the murder of children and those too weak to be useful slaves.

The film is not sophisticated; it is a bludgeon in words and images that cannot be presented otherwise. It was seen as a weapon of "denazification." Some of it feels anachronistic because at Nuremberg, for the first time, evidence was assembled and presented that has later become well known. Many Germans claimed at the time they didn't know what was being done in their names; for some of them it must have been true, and the purpose of this film was to show them their evil leaders, sitting in the dock—never, ever, in the footage here, even looking at one another.

The film, as I said, was never seen in America. This print has been assembled under the supervision of Sandra Schulberg, Stuart's daughter, and Josh Waletzky, who began with an archival print found in Berlin. They have made the decision to restore the original film. Good enough, but there could have been two modern additions. Subtitles would be invaluable to identify the defendants. And there could have been an explanation of why the film was suppressed.

At the time of the Nuremberg trial, it was a growing embarrassment that Stalin, an ally during the war, was as guilty of atrocities as anyone in the dock. And, as Robert McNamara much later said that General Jimmy Doolittle told him after the bombing of Tokyo, that, too, was a war crime.

This point is well made by Salon's film critic, Andrew O'Hehir, who writes: "Even amid all the contradiction and ambiguity of the Nuremberg process, the argument made there was clear: All the nations of the world had to be held to the same standard, and every nation that waged aggressive warfare and committed war crimes, no matter how large or rich or powerful, would be judged accordingly."

The Nutcracker in 3-D ★

PG, 107 m., 2010

Elle Fanning (Mary), Nathan Lane (Uncle Albert), John Turturro (The Rat King), Frances de la Tour (The Rat Queen), Richard E. Grant (Father), Yulia Visotskaya (Mother/Snow Fairy), Shirley Henderson (The Nutcracker), Aaron Michael Drozin (Max), Charlie Rowe (The Prince). Directed by Andrei Konchalovsky. Produced by Konchalovsky and Paul Lowin. Screenplay by Konchalovsky and Chris Solimine.

From what dark night of the soul emerged the wretched idea for *The Nutcracker in 3-D*? Who considered it even remotely a plausible idea for a movie? It begins with an awkward approximation of the story behind the Tchaikovsky ballet, and then turns it into a war by the nutcracker prince against the Holocaust. Am I exaggerating? At one point, the evil Rat King (John Turturro) has his troopers snatch toys from the hands of children so they can be tossed into furnaces, and the smoke will emerge from high chimneys to blot out the sun.

Yes. And the Rats are dressed in fascistic uniforms. And against them stand our heroine, Mary (Elle Fanning), and her Christmas present, a nutcracker (voice of Shirley Henderson) that has imprisoned a handsome prince (Charlie Rowe). And two-legged helicopters swoop low over screaming children, and the city is laid waste, and the Rats dream of world domination.

You may be in disbelief. I was. This is one of those rare holiday movies that may send children screaming under their seats. Their parents, naively hoping to see a sweet version of *The Nutcracker Suite*, will be appalled or angry, take your choice. Yes, there are melodies that began with Tchaikovsky at one point, but now they have (are you sitting down?) lyrics by Tim Rice.

The Nutcracker in 3-D easily qualifies as one of the most preposterous ideas in the history of the movies. It isn't a story; it's a gag line for one of Letterman's "Top 10" lists (No. 9, *It's a Horrible Life;* No. 8, *A Christmas Carol in Hell . . .*).

Andrei Konchalovsky, who wrote and directed it, says this has been a dream project for twenty years. That is tragic. Konchalovsky made the great films *Shy People* and *Runaway Train*, and perhaps he became obsessed with this folly. But what did others think? What about Nathan Lane, who plays a character not previously associated with *The Nutcracker*, Albert Einstein? Yes, he gets to sing a song about the theory of relativity, but not since he played Jacqueline Susann's adoring husband in *Isn't She Great* has a role been more thankless.

Only one thing could have made this premise worse, and they haven't neglected it.

That would be to present it in 3-D. They have. The movie was filmed in Hungary in 2007, and perhaps those screening it sensed a certain lack of enthusiasm. Maybe they thought that by retrospectively "adapting" it to 3-D, it would play better. No luck. I've seen bad retro 3-D. I have never seen 3-D as bad as this. The picture is so dim and dingy you almost wonder if the smoke from those burning toys is drifting between you and the screen.

O

October Country ★ ★ ★

NO MPAA RATING, 80 m., 2010

Featuring members of the Mosher family. A documentary directed by Michael Palmieri and Donal Mosher and produced by Palmieri. Screenplay by Palmieri and Mosher.

"We wouldn't know normal if it fell on us," Donald Mosher says. He sits and smokes on the front porch of one of two adjacent houses that are home to four generations of his family. The Moshers are a sad and dysfunctional family, which they are curiously willing to explain, as if they've spent years rehearsing their mistakes. "Bad taste in men runs in the family," observes Desiree, Donald's eleven-year-old granddaughter.

The Moshers live in the beautiful Mohawk Valley in upstate New York. "Here is where we were born, and here, I guess, is where we'll die," says Dottie Mosher, the matriarch. She and Donald are the enduring centers of a family of a daughter, Donna, who has a history of abusive men; a granddaughter, Daneal, who seems to be following the same pattern; her sister, Desiree, who explains, "I'm a lot smarter than the rest of them"; and Daneal's daughter, Ruby. There is also Don's sister, Denise, who dresses in a black cape, haunts cemeteries to videotape ghosts, and is a Wiccan.

None of the husbands are seen in the film. The only male apart from Donald is Chris, a foster child he and Dottie took in. He's been in jail, explains in one scene how he likes Walmart because it's "easy to steal from," warns the Moshers he'll be trouble for them, and proves it by stealing two computers. Dottie wipes aside a tear as Chris goes back behind bars.

What happened to this family? One of the two codirectors is Donal Mosher, another son, who is never mentioned in the film. His photographs of his family inspired the film, made with his partner, Michael Palmieri, a director of TV commercials. The film is often lovely to regard, and sees the Moshers surrounded by the beauty of the seasons between one Halloween and the next.

The legacy of sadness started when Donald went to serve in Vietnam. Dottie remembers him as a cheerful, upbeat kid when he went away. Something happened there to change him forever. He never talks about it—or about much of anything else. He watches old war movies on TV, makes doll house furniture in his attic workshop, and watches with dour passivity as the generations go awry.

He worked at first in the Remington Arms Factory, the chief employer in the valley, but found his job so boring "an ape could do it." He observes, "Remington executives get an eight-hundred-thousand-dollar Christmas bonus, and the workers get a damn belt buckle after thirty years." He quit, went to work as a police officer, and on his first day on the job covered a suicide that left brains all over a garage wall.

Donna and Daneal seem to move through a cloud of gloom. They know all about abusive men, but seem to feel that is their fate. The spark of hope is Desiree—"Desi"—who is spirited and sarcastic, and seems to have gotten the family's entire allotment of senses of humor. Even at her age, she sees the problems and refuses to enlist in them. I hope her school can set her on a good path in life; she seems ready for one.

One understands how Donal Mosher could obtain access to these moments of stark honesty and bleak truth. One wonders what the family thought of the film when they saw it. This is the face of dysfunction. Apparently alcohol and drugs are not involved, except perhaps with some of the missing men. The drug here is despair. They seem to treat it with cigarettes.

Note: The photographs that inspired the film are here: http://donalmosher.com/.

Of Gods and Men ★ ★ ★

PG-13, 122 m., 2011

Lambert Wilson (Christian), Michael Lonsdale (Luc), Olivier Rabourdin (Christophe), Philippe Laudenbach (Celestin), Jacques Herlin (Amedee), Loic Pichon (Jean-Pierre), Xavier Maly (Michel), Jean-Marie Frin (Paul), Abdelhafid Metalsi (Nouredine), Sabrina Ouazani (Rabbia). Directed by Xavier Beauvois and produced by Pascal Caucheteux and Etienne Comar. Screenplay by Beauvois and Comar.

"Men never do evil so completely and cheerfully as when they do it from religious conviction." So wrote the French philosopher Pascal in the seventeenth century, and his words are quoted by one of the monks in this solemn and engrossing film. *Of Gods and Men* is based on an event in Algeria in 1996, when eight Trappist monks were taken hostage by terrorists. The film centers on the fact that the monks could easily have evaded this but chose not to.

Every scene in the film involves these monks, and most of the scenes are set in their monastery. Several times a day they put on white robes and pray and sing in a little chapel. The rest of the time they tend crops, keep bees, sell honey, treat the sick of the district, eat bread and soup while being read to, and hold community meetings around a table with a candle on it.

They make no attempt to convert anyone to Catholicism. They live peacefully in a Muslim community, attend a service for a child, employ some of the nearby people as workers. There is a deep serenity in their way of life. Although we learn to know the monks by face and name, the film makes no particular attempt to focus on their personalities, except for two: Brother Christian (Lambert Wilson), whom they have elected as leader, and Brother Luc, played by gentle old Michael Lonsdale, whom I first saw in 1962 in Orson Welles's *The Trial*—that time, too, playing a cleric.

Luc is the doctor, himself old, sick, and asthmatic, but seeing countless patients every day and sometimes imparting benevolent advice, as when a village girl questions him about love. Christian is clear-eyed and resolute in his idea of their mission in this place distant from their birthplace in France; they have been called by God to minister to the sick and hungry.

There is revolution in the land. A group of Serbian migrant workers have their throats cut by terrorists. The government urges the monks to leave, the army offers protection, but Christian refuses; there is no place for the army in a monastery. They will deal with what comes.

The most fraught scene comes when terrorists break in on Christmas Eve, demanding that old Luc come with them to care for a wounded comrade. Christian turns them away, after quoting what the Quran has to say in favor of Christians. Their leader, Rabbia (Sabrina Ouazani), is, somewhat unexpectedly, convinced. The next group of terrorists will not be so forgiving.

Of Gods and Men asks us to admire these monks, whose lives are wholly devoted to good works. There is an uplifting scene when they welcome an old friend with a dinner at which wine is served, the music of *Swan Lake* plays, and joy shines from their faces. After some discussion, they follow Christian in deciding to stay at the monastery, no matter what.

The movie has a narration making a sharp distinction between radical Islamic terrorists and the peaceful Muslims who share the district with the monks. But stay. There is another side to the Algerian question, the side of the forcible French occupation and its decades of repressive rule. This land is not France. Technically, which side could be called terrorist?

The film doesn't raise such political questions, except in one enigmatic sentence by a local official. It focuses entirely on the nobility of the monks in choosing to stay with their vocation and their duty in the face of quite probable death. Did they make the right choice? In their own idealistic terms, yes. In realistic terms, I say no. They have the ability to help many who need it for years to come. It is egotism to believe their help must take place in this specific monastery. Between the eight of them they have perhaps a century of life of usefulness remaining. Do they have a right to deprive those who need it of their service? In doing so, are they committing the sin of pride?

I found myself resisting the film's pull of easy emotion. There are fundamental questions here, and the film doesn't engage them. I believe Christian should have had the humility to lead his monks away from the path of self-sacrifice.

Of Time and the City ★ ★ ★ ½

NO MPAA RATING, 77 m., 2009

A documentary directed by Terence Davies and produced by Solon Papadopoulos and Roy Boutler. Screenplay by Davies.

The streets of our cities are haunted by the ghosts of those who were young here long ago. In memory we recall our own past happiness and pain. Terence Davies, whose subject has often been his own life, now turns to his city, Liverpool, and regrets not so much the joys of his youth as those he did not have. Central to these are the sexual experiences forbidden by the Catholic Church to which he was most devoted.

Liverpool was once a shipbuilding capital of the world, later a city broken by unemployment and crime, and now a recovering city named the European Capital of Culture in 2008. For many people, Liverpool's cultural contribution begins and ends with the Beatles, and Davies does little to update that view except to focus on its postwar architecture, which is grotesque, and its modern architecture, much improved, but still lacking the grandeur of the city's Victorian glory.

The way Davies and his cinematographer, Tim Pollard, regard heritage buildings and churches, their domes and turrets worthy of an empire, suggests that he, like me, prefers buildings that express a human fantasy and not an abstract idea. What is it that makes the Hancock magnificent and Trump Tower appalling? Not just the Trump's bright, shiny tin appearance, the busy proportions of its facade, or its see-through parking levels, but a lack of modesty and confidence. It insists too much. On the other hand, there is nothing modest about the grandiloquent civic structures of Liverpool, but their ornate cheekiness is sort of touching. They had no idea they were monuments to the end of an era.

In this city Davies was born into modest circumstances, was shaped and defined by the Church, was tortured by his forbidden homosexual feelings, and gradually grew to reject the Church and the British monarchy. He remembers a boy who put a hand on his shoulder "and I didn't want him to take it away." In his parish, Church of the Sacred Heart, "I prayed until my knees bled," but release never came.

These memories are mixed with those of the city, suggested with remarkable archival footage collated from a century: crowds in the streets and at the beach, factories, shipyards, faces, movie theaters, snatches of song, long-gone voices, an evocation of a city tuned in to the BBC for the Grand National, a long-gone horse and rider falling at the first hurdle, the wastelands surrounding new public housing, children and dogs at play, and, yes, the Beatles.

The sound track includes classical music and pop tunes, and the deep, rich voice of Davies, sometimes quoting poems that match the images. The film invites a reverie. It inspired thoughts of the transience of life. It reminded me sharply of Guy Maddin's *My Winnipeg* (2008), which combined old footage and new footage that looked even older into the portrait of a city that existed only in his imagination. I imagine the city fathers in both places were astonished by what their sons had wrought, although in Winnipeg they would have found a great deal more to amuse them.

O'Horten ★ ★ ★ ½

PG-13, 89 m., 2009

Baard Owe (Odd Horten), Espen Skjonberg (Trygve Sissener), Githa Norby (Mrs. Thogersen), Bjorn Floberg (Flo), Kai Remlov (Steiner Sissener), Henny Moan (Svea). Directed, written, and produced by Bent Hamer.

The thing about a deadpan comedy is it has to think. It must involve us in the lives of its characters so we can understand why they are funny while at the same time so distant. *O'Horten,* a bittersweet whimsy by the Norwegian director Bent Hamer, finds that effortless. It is about a retiring railroad engineer named Odd Horten. *Odd* is a common enough first name in Norway, but reflect that English is widely used in Scandinavia.

O'Horten is a quiet, reflective man, a pipe smoker who lives alone but is not lonely and sets his life by the railroad timetable. He is baffled by retirement. He's not sure when he should be anywhere. After the retirement party thrown by his fellow engineers, who sing him a "choo-choo-choo woo-woo-woo" song, he is uncertain. An evening begins on an inauspicious note when he is unable to get into a colleague's apartment, climbs a scaffolding in freezing weather, lets himself into someone else's window, and finds himself in conversation with a small boy.

O'Horten has his consolations. One is Mrs. Thogersen (Githa Norby), a sweet, silvery-haired widow who lives at the end of the Oslo–Bergen run. He is accustomed to overnighting in her arms. "So . . . this is the end?" she asks on his last run. Apparently so. It doesn't occur to him that they could rendezvous without him driving a train there.

Left to his own devices, O'Horten allows himself to be drawn into uncertain circumstances. There is the case of Trygve Sissener (Espen Skjonberg), a curious old man who informs O'Horten, "Ever since I was young, I have been able to see with my eyes closed." To prove it, he takes O'Horten on a drive through Oslo with a black hood pulled over his head. You would think this would be terrifying for an engineer who once hit a moose on the tracks, but no. He puffs his pipe, interested.

His Oslo resembles the macabre Stockholm of the director Roy Andersson, whose *Songs from the Second Floor* we showed at Ebertfest a few years ago. Inexplicable events seem to be a matter of course. Why, for example, would well-dressed businessmen slide on their fannies down an icy incline? O'Horten is probably wondering the same thing but doesn't inquire.

Odd is played by Baard Owe, a trim, fit man with a neat mustache, who may cause you to think a little of James Stewart, Jacques Tati, or Jean Rochefort. He has some regrets. He was never an Olympic ski jumper like his mother. Too afraid. He never really developed any hobbies. He has few friends. He was on the rails too much. He prides himself in perfection on the job but has no need for perfection in his life. At least a pipe smoker can always count on his pipe.

Old Dogs ★

PG, 88 m., 2009

John Travolta (Charlie), Robin Williams (Dan), Seth Green (Craig), Kelly Preston (Vicki), Matt Dillon (Barry), Rita Wilson (Jenna), Lori Loughlin (Amanda), Ella Bleu Travolta (Emily), Conner Rayburn (Zach), Bernie Mac (Jimmy Lunchbox). Directed by Walt Becker and produced by Peter Abrams, Robert L. Levy, and Andrew Panay. Screenplay by David Diamond and Davis Weissman.

Old Dogs is stupefyingly dimwitted. What were John Travolta and Robin Williams *thinking* of? Apparently, their agents weren't perceptive enough to smell the screenplay in its advanced state of decomposition, but wasn't there a loyal young intern in the office to catch them at the elevator and whisper, "You've paid too many dues to get involved with such crap at this stage in your careers"?

Williams and Travolta play business partners trying to float a big deal with Japan. Meanwhile, they're saddled with baby-sitting six-year-old twins. Be sure your seat belt is visible on the outside of your blanket; you will be awakened for breakfast when this flight is about to land.

The film makes a big business meeting with Japanese investors a study in laugh-avoidance. The Japanese line up on one side of a table in a Las Vegas Japanese restaurant, and Travolta, Williams, their partner Seth Green, and a translator are on the other. Travolta tries to warm them up with the funny story of how Williams just got divorced twice in the last twenty-four hours. The Japanese sit stony-faced. So do we. Then Travolta gets to his big finish, and the Japanese break into helpless laughter. My theory: Since almost all Japanese businessmen in Vegas speak English, they've been playing a practical joke.

This film seems to have lingered in post-production while editors struggled desperately to inject laugh cues. It obviously knows no one will find it funny without being ordered to. How else to explain reaction shots of a dog responding to laugh lines? Or the painfully obvious use of music as glaring as a yellow highlighter to point out comedy? Example: Rita Wilson gets her hand slammed by a car trunk, and the sound track breaks into "Big Girls Don't Cry."

Another clue is when characters break into bad sitcom dialogue. After the Old Dogs end up at camp with their young charges, a muscular counselor (Matt Dillon) asks them, "You girls ready to play a little Ultimate Frisbee?" Williams: "I think so, Mr. Testosterone."

Another clue: "Funny moments" repeated in case we missed them. Example: Robin Williams test-drives a buckled-on, back-mounted device that allows him to fly. It loses power and he drops into a pond. Wow, that was funny! Wait! Here it is again! Same drop, new angle! Twice as funny! Oh, no! A third drop! Ohmigod! Wait—wait—a *fourth* time? Usher, quick! Bring me oxygen!

Seth Green is not a tall man. But hell, he's only three inches shorter than Robin Williams. In this movie, you'd think he was Danny DeVito. He ends up wrapped in the arms of a gorilla. Never mind why. Doesn't matter. First Law of Movie Gorillas: Guy in a gorilla suit is never funny, unless the joke is on him.

To save himself from the enormous beast, Green sings a soothing lullaby. The gorilla dozes off peacefully. Hey, that's good! That's very good! Green gently tries to extricate himself from the gorilla's embrace. Nothing doing! Green desperately starts crooning again. Just think. If the gorilla wakes up, Green will be crushed to death! Man, oh, man!

The release of *Old Dogs* was delayed from April until now because of the death of another of its costars, Bernie Mac. I can think of another way they might have respected his memory.

127 Hours ★ ★ ★ ★

R, 93 m., 2010

James Franco (Aron Ralston), Amber Tamblyn (Megan), Kate Mara (Kristi), Clemence Poesy (Rana), Treat Williams (Aron's Dad), Kate Burton (Aron's Mom), Lizzy Caplan (Sonja). Directed by Danny Boyle and produced by Boyle, Christian Colson, and John Smithson. Screenplay by Boyle and Simon Beaufoy, based on the book *Between a Rock and a Hard Place* by Aron Ralston.

Sometimes a person will make an enormous mistake and get a lot of time to think about it. There was a man who went over Niagara Falls sealed inside a big rubber ball. It never made it to the bottom. The ball lodged somewhere on the way down. He'd counted on his team to cut him out at the bottom. Oops! Aron Ralston, the hero of *127 Hours*, had an Oops! moment. That's even what he calls it. He went hiking in the wilderness without telling anyone where he was going, and then, in a deep, narrow crevice, got his forearm trapped between a boulder and the canyon wall. Oops.

We all heard about this. Ralston stumbled out to safety more than five days later, having cut off his own right arm to escape. He is an upbeat and resilient person and has returned to rock climbing, although now, I trust, after filing a plan, going with a companion, and not leaving his Swiss Army knife behind. The knife would have been ever so much more convenient than his multipurpose tool. I imagine that every time he considers his missing right forearm, he feels that, under the circumstances, he's better off without it.

What would you have done? What about me? I don't know if I could have done it. It involves a gruesome ordeal for Ralston, and for the film's audience, a few of whom have been said to faint. But from such harrowing beginnings, it's rather awesome what an entertaining film Danny Boyle has made here. Yes, entertaining.

For most of the film he deals with one location and one actor, James Franco. There's a carefree prologue in which Ralston and a couple of young women hikers have a swim in an underwater cavern. And during moments of hallucination other people from his life seem to visit. But the fundamental reality is expressed in the title of the book he wrote about his experience: *Between a Rock and a Hard Place.*

Franco does a good job of suggesting two aspects of Ralston's character: (1) He's a cocky, bold adventurer who trusts his skills and likes taking chances, and (2) he's logical and bloody-minded enough to cut through his own skin and bone to save his life. One aspect gets him into his problem, and the other gets him out.

Is the film watchable? Yes, compulsively. Films like this don't move quickly or slowly, they seem to take place all in the same moment. They prey on our own deep fear of being trapped somewhere and understanding that there doesn't seem to be any way to escape. Edgar Allan Poe mined this vein in several different ways. Ralston is at least fortunate to be standing on a secure foothold; one can imagine the boulder falling and leaving him dangling in midair from the trapped arm.

Suddenly his world has become very well defined. There is the crevice. There is the strip of sky above, crossed by an eagle on its regular flight path. There are the things he brought with him: a video camera, some water, a little food, his inadequate little tool. It doesn't take long to make an inventory. He shouts for help, but who can hear? The two women campers have long since gone their way and won't report him missing because they won't realize that he is. For anyone to happen to find him is unthinkable. He will die or do something.

127 Hours is like an exercise in conquering the unfilmable. Boyle uses magnificent cinematography by Anthony Dod Mantle and Enrique Chediak, establishing the vastness of the Utah wilderness and the very specific details of Ralston's small portion of it. His editor, Jon Harris, achieves the delicate task of showing an arm being cut through without ever *quite* showing it. For the audience the worst moment is not a sight but a sound. Most of us have never heard that sound before, but we know exactly what it is.

Pain and bloodshed are so common in the movies. They are rarely amped up to the level of reality because we want to be entertained, not sickened. We and the heroes feel immune. *127 Hours* removes the filters. It implicates us. By identification we are trapped in the canyon; we are cutting into our own flesh. One element that film can suggest but not evoke is the brutality of the pain involved. I can't even imagine what it felt like. Maybe that made it easier for Ralston, because in one way or another his decision limited the duration of his suffering.

He must be quite a man. The film deliberately doesn't make him a hero—more of a capable athlete trapped by a momentary decision. He cuts off his arm because he has to. He was lucky to succeed. One can imagine a news story of his body being discovered long afterward, with his arm only partly cut through. He did what he had to do, which doesn't make you a hero. We could do it, too. Oh, yes we could.

Orphan ★ ★ ★ ½

R, 123 m., 2009

Vera Farmiga (Kate Coleman), Peter Sarsgaard (John Coleman), Isabelle Fuhrman (Esther), CCH Pounder (Sister Abigail), Jimmy Bennett (Daniel Coleman), Aryana Engineer (Max Coleman). Directed by Jaume Collet-Serra and produced by Joel Silver, Susan Downey, Jennifer Davisson Killoran, and Leonardo Di Caprio. Screenplay by David Johnson.

After seeing *Orphan,* I now realize that the Omen was a model child. The Demon Seed was a bumper crop. Rosemary would have been happy to have this baby. Here is a shamelessly effective horror film based on the most diabolical of movie malefactors, a child.

Pity. Esther is such a bright child. So well behaved. Her paintings are so masterful. She sits down at the piano and rips off a little Tchaikovsky. So why does her adoptive mother have such a fearful attitude toward her? Could it be because Kate, the mom, got drunk and almost let her son Daniel drown? Had Max, a darling daughter, but then miscarried a third child? Is an alcoholic trying to stay sober? Just doesn't like the little orphan girl's looks?

There is something eerie about her. Something too wise, too knowing, too penetrating. And why won't she remove those ribbons she always wears? And why does she dress like Little Bo Peep to go to school? Daniel is cool toward her. Max is too young to be sure. Only John, the father, is convinced she's a bright kid and blameless in a series of unfortunate events.

Vera Farmiga is at the film's core as Kate, a onetime Yale music professor who feels she is unfairly targeted by her therapist, her husband, and eventually the authorities. Peter Sarsgaard plays John, the kind of understanding husband who doesn't understand a damned thing except that he is understanding. And Esther, the orphan, is played by Isabelle Fuhrman, who is not going to be convincing playing a nice child for a long, long time.

The movie hinges on a classic thriller device: the heroine who knows the truth and insists on it even though everyone is convinced she's mad and wants to ship her off to rehab or even a mental institution. It's frustrating to know you're right when no one can see the truth you find so obvious.

Things happen around Esther. A child falls from a playground slide. A car rolls down a hill. A nun comes into harm's way. She spreads disinformation. She's secretive. And sometimes she's so perfect you want to wring her neck. When it turns out the orphanage has faulty info on her Russian origins, Kate starts sniffing around in what her husband dismisses as paranoia.

Orphan begins like your usual thriller, with Scare Alerts and False Alarms. You know, like a nice, peaceful shot until suddenly the sound blares and something rushes past the camera and—hey, it's only kids. We even get the old standby when Kate is looking in the medicine cabinet and closes it and—ohmigod!—there's another face in the mirror! But hey, it's only her smiling husband.

Sarsgaard is well cast in the role. He looks normal, sounds pleasant, and yet can suggest something a little twitchy. Not that he's evil. Simply that he really should trust his wife more. Really.

How the movie handles the other children, Daniel and Max, would probably have offended Gene Siskel, who had a thing about movies exploiting children in danger. This one sure does. What with the tree house and the pond and the runaway SUV, it's amazing these kids are still able to function.

The climax of the film is rather startling, combining the logic of the situation with audacity in exploiting its terror. Yet you have to hand it to *Orphan*. You want a good horror film about a child from hell, you got one. Do not, under any circumstances, take children to see this. Take my word on this.

OSS 117: Lost in Rio ★ ★ ★

NO MPAA RATING, 101 m., 2010

Jean Dujardin (Hubert Bonisseur de la Bath), Louise Monot (Delores), Alex Lutz (Heinrich), Rudiger Vogler (Von Zimmel), Reem Kherici (Carlotta), Ken Samuels (Trumendous). Directed by Michel Hazanavicius and produced by Eric Altmeyer and Nicholas Altmeyer. Screenplay by Michel Hazanavicius and Jean-Francois Halin, inspired by the OSS 117 novels by Jean Bruce.

Hubert Bonisseur de la Bath, French Agent OSS 117, looks like a parody of James Bond, British Agent 007, but it may be the other way around. Pretty much unknown over here, he first appeared in print in 1949. I haven't read a single OSS 117 novel (there are more than 250!), but it appears Ian Fleming may have found some inspiration from Jean Bruce, the creator of 117.

The OSS man first appeared in a film in 1957, and was once played by John Gavin, of all people. The character was revived in *OSS 117: Cairo, Nest of Spies* (2006), but while the original stories were played straight, *Cairo* and now *OSS 117: Lost in Rio* are parodies—of the James Bond movies, appropriately enough.

The star is Jean Dujardin, who in some shots looks something like Sean Connery, and who has the same gift of understatement and drollery. He's also surrounded by babes, in particular a sexy Mossad agent named Delores Koulechov (Louise Monot). The movie is set in the early 1960s, and 117 is sent to Brazil to retrieve a secret list of French collaborators with the Nazis. This leads to an action climax atop the right arm of the immense statue of Christ that towers above Rio de Janeiro. Hitchcock set *Notorious* in Rio, but didn't quite have the nerve to use that location.

Imagine that the film looks exactly like a slightly faded thriller from 1967. The makers have gone to a great deal of trouble to get not only the costumes, the sets, the props, and the cars right, but even the film stock; some audience members may wonder if they wandered into a revival house. The stunts are as stagy as 007, the villains as absurd, and 117 as unflappable.

One thing that will strike North American audiences as odd is that 117 is cheerfully racist. Working with an Israeli agent gives him plenty of opportunities to voice his anti-Semitism, which is not intended to hurt, but grows directly out of his ignorance. I think (or hope) the filmmakers are making a commentary on the everyday anti-Semitism of the DeGaulle era.

But 117 is an equal-opportunity offender and makes unbelievably gross statements to women. He somehow gets away with it because Dujardin is a polite charmer with an eager smile and a quick laugh, and you see he doesn't mean to offend; he's only trying to make conversation. That he is clueless is the joke.

There's too much of that for my taste, but the movie depends mostly on wild exaggerations of 007, and here it does something right: It shows stunts and special effects that *look* like they might have been staged in 1967. The movie almost goes out of its way to reveal it's using rear projection on a studio set. The music is appropriate, too: that kind of cheesy pop that has a good time no matter what's happening on the screen. The sound track reminded me of nothing so much as a forced laugh.

I sort of liked the 2006 film, and I sort of like this one, too. I may like it a little more because Dujardin grows on you. The film opens with him singing "Everybody Loves Somebody" in a voice that sounds so much like Dean Martin that maybe it is. But the way he smiles and moves . . . well, surely you've heard of the Trololo Man?

If you haven't, Google him.

Our Family Wedding ★ ★

PG-13, 101 m., 2010

Forest Whitaker (Brad Boyd), America Ferrera (Lucia Ramirez), Carlos Mencia (Miguel Ramirez), Regina King (Angela), Lance Gross (Marcus Boyd), Diana Maria Riva (Sonia Ramirez). Directed by Rick Famuyiwa and produced by Edward Saxon and Steven J. Wolfe. Screenplay by Famuyiwa, Wayne Conley, and Malcolm Spellman.

Our Family Wedding is a perfectly good idea for a comedy: A wedding between a Mexican-American woman and an African-American man leads to culture clash. The film, unfortunately, deals with the situation at the level of a middling sitcom. You almost miss the laugh track. Difficult problems are sidestepped, arguments are overacted, and there are three food fights involving wedding cakes. Well, two, actually, and the destruction of a third cake.

At the center of the wedding are Lucia Ramirez (America Ferrera), who was a law student at Columbia, and Marcus Boyd (Lance Gross), a Columbia med school graduate. The young couple plan to move to Laos, where he will work with Doctors Without Borders. They've been living together in New York, but keeping it a secret from her parents because her mom, Sonia (Diana Maria Riva), expects her to remain a virgin before marriage, and her father, Miguel (Carlos Mencia), would be crushed if he learned she had dropped out of law school. In a plot twist of startling originality, she is not pregnant.

A slimmed-down Forest Whitaker plays Marcus's father, Brad, a popular Los Angeles all-night DJ. He's doing all right and inhabits a huge house in the hills with a pool, stairs leading to a terrace, and a lawn big enough to hold a wedding party. Plus his ride is a Jaguar. Not bad for an all-night DJ.

Miguel is also well off, with the daughter at Columbia, the big luxurious house, and the passion for restoring classic cars. He owns a towing service, which is how he and Brad have a Meet Cute: All his drivers call in sick. Miguel fills in, and he and Brad meet when he tows the Jag.

The dads meet again at dinner when their children pop the big news and are immediately screaming insults and shaking each other by the throat. This scene, like all the stagy arguments between the fathers, is completely unconvincing. Their fights are drummed up for the purposes of the screenplay, and the actors hardly seem to believe them. Their families flutter their hands and beg them to calm down. Their running feud feels phony to begin with, and painfully forced by the end.

All of the family difficulties seem trumped up. Although Lucia is terrified that her mother will discover she had sex before marriage, that revelation, when it comes, is almost a throwaway. Marcus is embarrassed that his dad dates much younger women, but when he turns up at the family dinner with a girl who was Lucia's softball teammate, there's barely a mild stir. Lucia's grandmother faints when she sees Lucia's fiancé is a black man, but when she comes to, this is forgotten. (Didn't anyone tell her?) Oh, and speaking of softball, the game played between the two family teams is so badly staged, I wasn't sure which side many of the players were on, nor who won the game.

The bright spots are America Ferrera, the kind of cuddly beauty who plunges right in and kisses a guy without worrying about her makeup, and Lance Gross as the guy, who has a thankless task as the Perfect Fiancé but doesn't overplay it. Regina King steals many scenes as Brad's longtime lawyer and secret admirer; her character is smart, focused, and sympathetic, and King's costumes showcase those Michelle Obama arms.

Our Family Wedding is a pleasant but inconsequential comedy, clunky, awkward for the actors, and contrived from beginning to end. Compare it with *Nothing Like the Holidays* (2008) to see how well a movie can handle similar material.

Outlander ★ ★

R, 115 m., 2009

Jim Caviezel (Kainan), Sophia Myles (Freya), Jack Huston (Wulfric), Ron Perlman (Gunnar), John Hurt (Rothgar). Directed by Howard McCain and produced by Chris Roberts. Screenplay by McCain and Dirk Blackman.

I am tempted to describe the plot of *Outlander* as preposterous, but a movie about an alien spaceship crashing into a Viking fjord during the Iron Age is *likely* to be preposterous. Two alien life forms survive the crash: Kainan and a monster known as "the Moorwen." Kainan, played by Jim Caviezel, looks exactly like a human being. The Moorwen looks like a giant, speedy, armored hippo-beetle with a toothy front end designed in the same forges of hell that produced the alien in *Alien*.

Kainan was returning from the Moorwen's home planet, which his race had terraformed, not quite wiping out all the Moorwens. The creatures counterattacked, wiping out most of Kainan's fellow settlers; what he doesn't realize is that one Moorwen was onboard ship when he blasted off. Kainan uses a handy device to pump the local Earth language (Viking, spoken in English) into his mind through his eyeball and soon encounters the nearest Viking village.

Having seen more than a few movies, we intuit that this village will contain a venerable king (Rothgar, played by John Hurt), his bodacious daughter (Freya, played by Sophia Myles), a jealous young warrior (Wulfric, played by Jack Huston), and a menacing dissident (Gunnar, played by Ron Perlman). There are also numerous villagers who stand around in the background looking intensely interested.

The village is suspicious of this strange "outlander." Then Vikings start to disappear in the forest, and Kainan realizes he has brought along a passenger. After he saves Rothgar from the Moorwen, he wins royal favor and organizes the village in a plan to lure the beast into a deep pit with stakes at the bottom and burn it alive.

I began my study of science fiction at the age of nine, with *Tom Corbett, Space Cadet*. I grew to love the authors who incorporated as much science as possible: Clarke, Asimov, Heinlein. They would have had questions about Kainan. For example, is he as human as he appears? It seems unlikely from a Darwinian point of view that two human species should evolve independently and contemporaneously on separate worlds. Even more so that they would share common sexual feelings and be able to mate, although that is precisely what Kainan and Freya propose.

But yes, their love flowers, against a backdrop of Arthurian romance. The Moorwen is the dragon, of course. And much depends on a sword mighty enough to pierce its armor. To forge this Excalibur, Kainan dives into the fjord and retrieves scrap steel from the wreckage of his ship, thus bringing the Iron Age to a quick close—in this village, anyway. The climax involves the usual violent and incoherent special effects scenes, after which Rothgar gives Kainan the hand of his daughter, and Kainan and Freya presumably retire to discover if separate evolutionary paths have outfitted them with compatible fixtures.

Outlander is interesting as a collision of genres: The monster movie meets the Viking saga. You have to give it credit for carrying that premise to its ultimate (if not logical) conclusion. It occurs to me, however, that the Moorwen had legitimate reason to be grieved. First Kainan's race appropriated the Moorwen planet for its own purposes, then it massacred the Moorwens, now it was picking off a survivor. Do you think genocide or colonialism are concepts to be found in *Outlander*? Not a chance. That's because Kainan is so human, and the Moorwens are, well, just not our sort.

Outside the Law ★ ★ ★

NO MPAA RATING, 138 m., 2010

Jamel Debbouze (Said), Roschdy Zem (Messaoud), Sami Bouajila (Abdelkader), Bernard Blancan (Colonel Faivre), Chafia Boudraa (Said's Mother), Sabrina Seyvecou (Helene), Assaad Bouab (Ali), Thibault de

Montalembert (Morvan). Directed by Rachid Bouchareb and produced by Jean Brehat. Screenplay by Bouchareb and Olivier Lorelle.

For France, the Algerian War was like our experience in Vietnam, but closer, more personal, and with bloodshed on domestic soil. France had already lost its war to retain French Indochina as a colony when we moved in. At about the same time, it was facing a revolt in French Algeria, which was much more important to it; indeed, many families had members living in either place and supporting either side.

Outside the Law is a big, expensive historical film that considers the war from an Algerian point of view. It assumes in a straightforward manner that the National Liberation Front's attempts to throw the French out of Algeria were directly comparable to the attempts of the French Resistance to throw the Nazis out of France. This is heresy in some circles, and indeed caused right-wing demonstrations against the film, but as attitudes about colonialism shift, this view is gradually becoming more accepted.

Much of the film involves FLN activities in Paris as well as Algeria. But it isn't an explanation of how or why the insurgent tactics were impossible to defeat; *The Battle of Algiers* (1966) has never been improved on for that. This is a more traditional personal melodrama, telling its story through a few characters seen against the backdrop of history. At a reported cost of $25 million, it's unusually expensive for a French film, and it's a sign of changing times that the financing was available.

Rachid Bouchareb, a French director of Algerian descent, tells his story through the lives of three brothers. We meet them first in 1925 when French authorities throw them off the land their family has farmed for generations in Algeria. Homeless and without a livelihood, they form a lifelong resentment, which will express itself in different ways.

They move with their family to Paris. Said (Jamel Debbouze) takes to the streets, works as a pimp, opens a club, and sponsors boxing matches. Messaoud (Roschdy Zem) fights for the French in Indochina, where he observes the Viet Cong firsthand and begins to see parallels between its resistance to colonialism and the struggle for Algeria. He returns to France a revolutionary and joins his brother Abdelkader (Sami Bouajila) in organizing for the FLN in Paris.

Their tactics involve violence. Abdelkader is inspired more by ideas and theory, and Messaoud's energy comes from more basic emotions of resentment and hatred for how the French dispossessed his family. Abdelkader the cerebral is able to kill dispassionately; Messaoud finds it more personal and agonizing. After a certain point it matters not what they think, because they've passed a point of no return and are desperate and wanted armed men, fighting in an invisible army.

We meet Colonel Faivre (Bernard Blancan), who organizes a secret branch of the French police named the Red Hand. He tells those under him that he works on direct orders from the top. They do not officially exist. Their activities will be denied. They will work outside any restraints of the law to do what is necessary to put down the insurgency.

Bouchareb takes these elements and essentially constructs a superior action picture. I'm sure it plays differently here than in France, where emotions on the subject are old and run deep. Imagine the feelings of Americans about a film where the Confederacy is viewed as heroic and the Union as murderous invaders. It all depends on which side you think is the right one. *Outside the Law* votes with the FLN.

The film is very well made. The actors create individual characters, within the limitations of what is essentially a formula. The flaw in the film is that, as Truffaut said, action in movies argues for itself. If we are assigned three protagonists and they're in gunfights with people trying to kill them, we identify with the protagonists. If the cops are the heroes, then we identify with them. So simple action is idea-neutral. If the point is to inspire sympathy for the Algerians, it may be effective, but lacks meaning.

There's a scene early in the film, during a boxing match Said stages for gambling purposes, when the cops raid what they perceive as a dangerous gathering of Algerians and open fire, causing a massacre. I understand this is a fictional version of a real event, about which there is much disagreement. We foreign viewers, not clued in, can only assume we know Said, and so the authorities are wrong.

Compare that with *The Battle of Algiers*, which is much more thoughtful about the methods of the resistance. Its sentiments are on the side of the FLN, but its focus is on the day-to-day reality of the struggle. There is a point in that film where the FLN seems crushed. It is not. The argument is that an indigenous movement cannot be crushed by force because its inexorable causes remain. In *Outside the Law*, the matter seems more simply about strategy and victory.

Outside the Law is at the very least a superior action film, in which the action sequences are plausible and grounded in reality. It is also a parable in support of anticolonialism. What it isn't, at the end of the day, is a film about the larger picture. It's about these characters and their stories. Well, most films are. It's just helpful to be clear that you're not finding out much about the larger issue.

P

Page One: Inside the *New York Times* ★ ★ ★

R, 88 m., 2011

David Carr, Brian Stelter, Bruce Headlam, Tim Arango, Bill Keller, Michael Hirschorn, Shane Smith, Gay Talese, David Remnick, Andrew Ross Sorkin, Larry Ingrassia, Markos Moulitsas, Seth Mnookin, Nick Lemann, Carla Baranauckas, Katherine Bouton, Katrina vanden Heuvel, Nick Denton, Jimmy Wales, Rick Lyman, Dean Baquet, Ken Auletta, Brian Lam, Charles Strum, Carl Bernstein, John Carr. A documentary directed by Andrew Rossi and produced by Alan Oxman and Adam Schlesinger. Screenplay by Rossi and Kate Novack.

When the *New York Times* started to charge for Web access to more than twenty articles a month, I signed up. I can't imagine a month when I wouldn't exceed that number. The paper remains, as it has long been, the most essential source of news in this country. *Page One: Inside the New York Times* sets out to examine its stature in these hard times for print journalism, but ends up with more of the hand-wringing that dominates all such discussions. People who are serious about the news venerate the past, hope for the future, and don't have a clue about the present.

Andrew Rossi's documentary had unlimited access to limited areas within the paper. There is extensive coverage of the staff of the *Times*' media desk, which covers other media, but the film lacks the skill of that staff in covering the *Times*. Nor does it eavesdrop on any strategic conversations among *Times* managers about the bottom line and the hopes for Web revenue.

Instead, what happens is what sometimes happens in many stories: A charismatic hero comes along and distracts from the big picture. That man here is David Carr, the paper's raspy-voiced, oracular star media reporter. I can think of no greater compliment than that he reminds me of the reporters I held in awe when I first went to work for newspapers. Like Mike Royko, he combines cynicism, idealism, and a canny understanding of how things *really* work. As we watch him meticulously report the story that exposed the lamentable "frat house" management of Sam Zell's *Chicago Tribune*, we see the reporter as a prosecutor, nailing down an air-tight case.

Carr is a survivor, an indicted crack addict and single parent who remade himself. We also meet Bruce Headlam, his boss on the media desk, and Brian Stelter, who won a job on the *Times* on the basis of his personal blog (How many bloggers share the dream of winning that lottery?). We follow them through a year in which they write about new media and old, Carr snorts at the idea of media "brands," and Headlam vets the devastating Carr coverage that would bring about regime change at the *Tribune* in a matter of weeks.

What he was essentially covering was the collapse of the print journalism culture. When Sam Zell entrusted the leadership of the *Tribune* to a slaphappy gang of callow radio executives, he revealed he had no idea what he had purchased, or why. There are certain ethical assumptions embedded in traditional journalism that are now being shredded not only by the Zells but by the heady, hit-and-run style of gossip Web sites.

In assuming that they must compete with celebrity gossip and scandal, newspapers abandon what they do well and devote their resources to what they do badly. They do this in pursuit of a "youth demographic" that doesn't read newspapers anyway, and shows symptoms of increasing illiteracy. I suspect that at the bottom of the crisis in print media is a crisis in American education, and that many of today's college graduates cannot read and write as well as grade school graduates did a few decades ago.

But back to the film. You would have to walk into it already knowing a great deal about the *Times*. Moving with no apparent plan, the doc touches on the Pentagon Papers, Judith Miller, Jayson Blair, and Gay Talese's *The Kingdom and the Power*. It doesn't have or find a theme. Attention is paid to Bill Keller, the executive editor, seen at a news meeting to determine the stories for the next day's paper. You won't discover here that he has been replaced by managing editor Jill Abramson (glimpsed a couple of times), whose mission is reportedly to focus on the Internet.

That said, I enjoyed the film very much. It was a visceral pleasure to see a hard-boiled guy like David Carr at its center. There's a scene in a bar, a farewell party for a correspondent going to the Middle East, and the other Timesmen sort of cluster around Carr to hear what he has to say. It was the same with Royko. Some people in this business just seem to *know*.

Paper Heart ★ ★ ★

PG, 88 m., 2009

Charlyne Yi (Herself), Michael Cera (Himself), Jake Johnson (Nicholas Jasenovec). Directed by Nicholas Jasenovec and produced by Sandra Murillo and Elise Salomon. Screenplay by Jasenovec and Charlyne Yi.

To describe Charlyne Yi as a whimsical comedian doesn't quite capture the full flavor. She may be the first female in the history of MySpace to claim she is ten years older than she really is. She appears naive, clueless, a little simple, but she's playing us. She embodies that persona in *Paper Heart,* a quasi-documentary about love that is sweet, true, and perhaps a little deceptive.

Yi is a performance artist who makes standup comedy only one facet of her act. She's short, cute, likes sweat clothes, wears hornrim glasses, isn't assertive, is a poster child for the melting pot: Filipino, Spanish, Korean, Irish, German, French, and Native American. She always seems to be trying to figure things out. *Paper Heart* is about how she has never been able to figure out love.

The movie takes the form of a documentary about her partnership with director Nicholas Jasenovec to travel America seeking insights into romance from all sorts of possible authorities, all of them obviously real, many of them touching, and one of them an inspired choice. That would be the Elvis impersonator who runs a Las Vegas wedding chapel. These people share their own stories, drawn out by Yi's disarming persona.

But wait. Although Nicholas Jasenovec appears in the film, that's not the real Nicholas Jasenovec. It's an actor, Jake Johnson, who is taller and darker and in my opinion more handsome than the real Jasenovec. Photographs reveal the real Jasenovec is shorter, cute, likes sweat clothes, wears horn-rim glasses. Then you have his good friend, the actor Michael Cera (*Juno*'s boyfriend), who looks much more like Jasenovec than Johnson. When Yi goes to a party with Jasenovec, she meets Cera and it's love at first sight.

We see them meeting, and it feels absolutely real: You wonder which of these two diffident and soft-spoken people summoned the energy to speak first. But wait. In real life, before shooting on this film began, Charlyne Yi and Michael Cera were *already* girlfriend and boyfriend, and were celebrated by such gossip sites as Gawker as "America's Twee-hearts." Therefore, their courtship in the film is scripted, although it feels uncannily real, perhaps because Cera and Yi have such enveloping personas that little they do is quite acting.

These matters give *Paper Heart* an intriguing quality on top of its intrinsic appeal. And the onscreen presence of "Nick," as the director, is uncannily well acted by Johnson, who embodies a hungry young L.A. filmmaker who thinks all human considerations are secondary to his film. There are moments when he insists on violating the privacy of Charlyne and Michael with his camera, and these scenes are so well acted and handled that, in retrospect, you realize this is a very well-made film indeed. There's more than meets the eye.

But wait! In real life, the heartless Cera has just dumped Yi! Right in the middle of their national publicity tour for this film! Can this possibly be true, or is it a publicity stunt? Surely he would have been decent enough to keep it private for a couple more weeks? No? Or is it possible that Cera and Yi, like many seemingly passive people, are, in fact, passive-aggressive, and have anger seething just beneath the surface?

Don't ask me. But if the heartbreak is true, I have advice for Charlyne Yi about how to cheer herself up wonderfully: Just go to your MySpace page and take off ten years.

Paranormal Activity ★ ★ ★ ½

R, 96 m., 2009

Katie Featherston (Katie), Micah Sloat (Micah), Michael Bayouth (The Psychic). Directed by

Oren Peli and produced by Peli and Jason Blum. Screenplay by Peli.

Paranormal Activity is an ingenious little horror film, so well made it's truly scary, that arrives claiming it's the real thing. Without any form of conventional opening or closing credits, it begins by thanking "the families of Micah Sloat and Katie Featherston" and closes with one of those "current whereabouts unknown" title cards and a screen of copyright notices. This was apparently a film made without a director, a writer, a producer, grips, makeup, sound, catering, or a honey wagon.

All of the footage is presented as if it had been discovered after the fact. The story device is that Micah shot it himself. There isn't a single shot that violates that presumption, although a few seem technically impossible without other hands on the camera. Those are hard to notice.

Katie is a graduate student of English. Micah is a day trader. They've been together three years and have now moved into a house in San Diego that doesn't seem much lived in. It's well enough furnished, but everything looks new and there's no clutter. Micah greets Katie out front one day by filming her on his new video camera, which she observes looks bigger than his other one.

They've been bothered by indications of some sort of paranormal activity in an upstairs bedroom. Micah's bright idea is to film in the house, leaving the camera running as a silent sentinel while they sleep. Like any man with a new toy, he becomes obsessed with this notion—the whole point, for him, isn't Katie's fear but his film. After one big scare, she asks him incredulously, "Did you actually go back to pick up your camera?"

One benefit of the story device is that for long periods of time the camera is ostensibly left on with no one running it. It's on a tripod at the end of their bed while they sleep, and we see events while their eyes are closed. Some of these events are very minor, and I won't describe any of them. The fact that they happen *at all* is the whole point. That they seem to happen by themselves, witnessed by a static camera, makes them eerie, especially since there are some shots that seem impossible without special effects, and there's no visible evidence of f/x, looking as closely as we can.

He is frequently off camera. She is on cam for almost every shot, and of Katie Featherston's performance it's enough to say it is flawless for the purposes of this film. We're not talking Meryl Streep here; we're talking about a young woman who looks and talks absolutely like she might be an ordinary college student who has just moved in with her boyfriend. There's not a second of "acting."

Micah behaves, shall I say, just like a man. You know, the kind who will never stop and ask directions. Katie has been bothered by some sort of paranormal presence since she was a child, and now she's seriously disturbed, and Micah's response isn't sympathy but a determination to get it all down on film.

They do call in a "psychic expert" (Michael Bayouth), but he's no help. He specializes in ghosts, he explains, and he knows by walking in the door that what's haunting them isn't a ghost but some sort of demonic presence. He recommends a demonologist, but alas this man is "away for a few days." That's the plot's most unrealistic detail. Having spent some time in my credulous days hanging about the Bodhi Tree bookstore in L.A., I would suggest that California is a state with more practicing demonologists than published poets.

I learn from IMDb that *Paranormal Activity* does indeed have a writer-director, Oren Peli, and other technical credits. But like *The Blair Witch Project,* with which it's routinely compared, it goes to great lengths to seem like a film found after the event. It works. It illustrates one of my favorite points, that silence and waiting can be more entertaining than frantic fast-cutting and berserk f/x. For extended periods here, nothing at all is happening, and believe me, you won't be bored.

Paranormal Activity 2 ★ ½

R, 91 m., 2010

Micah Sloat (Micah Sloat), Katie Featherston (Katie Sloat), Sprague Grayden (Kristi), Brian Boland (Daniel), Molly Ephraim (Ali), Vivis (Martine). Directed by Tod Williams and produced by Jason Blum and Oren Peli. Screenplay by Peli and Michael R. Perry.

Paranormal Activity 2 is an efficient delivery system for gotcha! moments, of which it has about nineteen. Audiences who want to be gotchaed will enjoy it. A gotcha! moment is a moment when something is sudden, loud, and scary. This can be as basic as the old "it's only a cat" cliché, or as abrupt as a character being hit by a bus. *PA2* starts slyly with pre-gotcha! teasers, such as a door or a child's toy moving on its own. Then there are obscure offscreen rumbles, like an uneasy stomach. Then loud bangs. Then loud bangs with visible causes. Then all the doors in a room banging open at once. And eventually, well, you can see for yourself, because all the activity is captured by twenty-four-hour security cameras.

The cameras, which function perfectly, never capture the Presence on the screen. For the house is indeed haunted by a ghostlike supernatural presence, I guess. I say "I guess" because there is a scene of a victim being dragged downstairs, and the entity doing the dragging is invisible. On the other hand, the movie ends with a strong suggestion that the malefactor was, in fact, a living human being. So would that be cheating? Hell yes.

But who cares? People go to *Paranormal Activity 2* with fond memories of the original film, which was low-tech and clever in the way it teased our eyes and expectations. It scared them. They want to be scared again. They will be. When there's a loud unexpected bang, it will scare you. The structural task of the gotcha! movie is to separate the bangs so they continue to be unexpected.

Any form of separation will do. The characters include the Sloats (Micah Sloat and Katie Featherston), who are back from the first movie. But this story begins earlier in time than that one and takes place in the home of her sister, Kristi (Sprague Grayden), her husband, Daniel (Brian Boland), teenage daughter, Ali (Molly Ephraim), brand-new baby, Hunter, and his nanny, Martine (Vivis). Martine is ethnic, and we know what that means: She has an instinctive knowledge of ghosts, breaks out the magic incense at a moment's notice, and can't get anyone to listen to her.

There are six speaking roles, not counting the nonspeaking baby and the dog. Good odds, you'd think, that at least one of them would have something interesting to say, but no. The movie isn't about them. They function primarily as gotcha! separators, going through vacuous social motions between gotchas! They are not real swift. The movie numbers the days as they tick away, and along about Day No. 12 I'm thinking, "Why are these people still here?" The screening I attended was treated to a surprise appearance by three stars of that cable show about Chicago's paranormal detectives. These are real Chicago detectives. If the Sloats lived in Chicago, they'd have a SWAT team out there by Day No. 7.

The movie is presented as a documentary with no setup, unless the first movie was the setup. It begins with little Hunter being brought home, and then we get titles like "Day No. 3." Of what? One peculiar title says, "Nine days before the death of Micah Sloat." I probably have the number of days wrong, but you get the idea. What are we supposed to do with this information? I guess we should think, "Sloat, you poor bastard, you only have nine days to go." This knowledge is about as useful as the farmer who tells you to make a left turn five miles before you get to the barn. There are also titles saying things like "1:41:15 a.m.," as if we care.

The character who suffers the most is poor little Hunter. Something is always bothering him in the middle of the night. When a security camera is on the staircase, we hear his plaintive little wail. When it's focused on his bedroom, he's standing up in his wee crib and bawling. The dog is always there barking at something, because dogs, like ethnic nannies, Know About These Things. Hunter screams and screams in the movie. If you were Hunter's parents and your house was haunted, wouldn't you move the poor kid's crib into the bedroom?

My audience jumped a lot and screamed a lot, and then laughed at themselves, even after one event that wasn't really funny. Then they explained things to one another, and I could overhear useful lines like, "She got the $#!+ scared outta her!" I understand they attended in hopes of seeing gotchas! and explaining them to one another. I don't have a problem with *Paranormal Activity 2*. It delivers what it promises, and occupies its audiences. Win-win.

Paris ★ ★ ★ ½

R, 128 m., 2009

Juliette Binoche (Elise), Romain Duris (Pierre), Fabrice Luchini (Roland), Albert Dupontel (Jean), Francois Cluzet (Philippe), Karin Viard (Shop Owner), Julie Ferrier (Caroline), Melanie Laurent (Laetitia), Zinedine Soualem (Mourad). Directed by Cedric Klapisch and produced by Bruno Levy. Screenplay by Klapisch.

At the end of *Paris,* a character whose future is uncertain rides in a taxi through the city and glimpses some of the film's other characters going about their lives. He doesn't know them, but we do, and seeing them so briefly is enough to make the film's point: We are here, we strive, we love, we laugh, we fail, we are sad, sometimes we look at the world and smile for no particular reason.

Here is a film about a group of Parisians. It opens with a sweeping shot of Paris from atop the Eiffel Tower. The characters don't have interlocking lives; it's not that kind of film. They have parallel lives. The purpose of Cedric Klapisch, the writer-director, is to make a symphonic tribute to the city he loves, and each character is a movement.

That said, every character has life and depth. It's unusual for an episodic film to involve us so well in individual lives; as the narrative circles through their stories, we're genuinely curious about what will happen next.

The central character is Pierre (Romain Duris), who is a dancer in his thirties told that he has little time left. Only a heart transplant can save him. His sister Elise (Juliette Binoche) brings her two daughters and comes to live with him, and they try to cheer each other. He spends much time standing on his balcony, observing life in the street. She's rebounding from a bad marriage and considers herself finished with men.

We also meet a famous Parisian historian named Roland (Fabrice Luchini), whose lectures are so literate and certain he seems to be reading from a TelePrompTer scrolling in his mind. He is very alone. Well into his fifties, he becomes obsessed with a pretty student and anonymously sends her florid romantic compliments by text. Then he lurks nearby to watch her reading them. Creepy. Meanwhile, he's starring in a TV documentary series about the city.

His younger brother is Philippe, played by Francois Cluzet, the Dustin Hoffmanish star of *Tell No One* (2006). Philippe is an architect, a father-in-waiting, an encourager who senses Roland's discontent. Elise finds herself attracted to Jean (Albert Dupontel), a vendor in one of the many Paris street-food markets. Jean is divorced from Caroline (Julie Ferrier), but they're still friendly. Still, they don't seem to have a future.

There are several smaller characters, including a bakery owner (Karin Viard) who has outspoken prejudices about people from any part of France that is not Paris, and yet is open-minded enough to praise a young employee from North Africa who is a reliable worker. I've met French people like that: not racist, but tactlessly opinionated—or particular, as they might prefer.

All of these stories are told against the backdrop of Paris, a city Klapisch loves with a passion. He hasn't made a travelogue with beauty shots, however, but set his story in very specific places: streets, a university, cafés, restaurants, dawn at the vast Rungis, the wholesale food market that replaced Les Halles. There is even a scene set in the catacombs, the bones and skulls of Parisians past neatly stacked behind the professor.

The characters have love, fear it, or seek it. Only one has a desperate problem. None is quite satisfied. They have a daily reprieve from illness or death but never think in those terms—except for Pierre, who is forced to. They go to work, home again, to their spouses or lovers or empty flats. They move easily through the city, and we are reminded that in Paris, traditionally a city of tiny apartments, the cafés serve as living rooms. You're not buying a coffee, you're renting a table, and it's yours for as long as you sit there.

I love Paris in the same way Klapisch does, for the concentration and intensity of its daily life and street theater. A modern place like downtown Houston seems to me an unlovely prospect, all concrete, no shadows. Why do modern corporations envision their headquarters as freestanding tombstones instead of friendly neighbors?

Viewing the film's city, I was reminded of another film, *When the Cat's Away* (1996). That was the one about the young woman who leaves town and entrusts her cat with a neighboring cat lady. When she returns, this old lady is heartbroken: The cat has run away. The entire neighborhood gets caught up in the search, including a simple-minded fellow who helpfully risks his life on rooftops, usually in search of the wrong cat. I looked up the film, and discovered it was by Cedric Klapisch. There you go.

Paris 36 ★ ★ ½

PG-13, 120 m., 2009

Gerard Jugnot (Pigoil), Clovis Cornillac (Milou), Kad Merad (Jacky), Nora Arnezeder (Douce), Pierre Richard (Monsieur TSF), Bernard-Pierre Donnadieu (Galapiat), Maxence Perrin (Jojo), Elisabeth Vitali (Viviane). Directed by Christophe Barratier and produced by Nicolas Mauvernay and Jacques Perrin. Screenplay by Barratier.

Sometimes you get the feeling that if a movie had been made years ago, it would now be considered a classic. *Paris 36* is like that—an old-fashioned story set around a music hall. Cutting-edge, it's not. But if taken in the right spirit, enjoyable.

In the 1930s, in no particular neighborhood in Paris, an ancient music hall named the Chansonia wheezes along with performers who are past their sell-by dates. It's a time of social upheaval in France; the Popular Front, a left-wing coalition, has taken power, and the rise of Hitler is stirring up French right-wingers. The Chansonia's cast and crew are solidly socialist.

For Pigoil (Gerard Jugnot), the left-wing stage manager, things are going badly. The Chansonia's fascist landlord has padlocked the doors for rent in arrears, Pigoil and his friends are all out of work, his wife has left him, and a silence has fallen upon the neighborhood. The burden, he feels, rests on his shoulders. Jacky (Kad Merad), a man who wears a sandwich board for the theater but believes he can do impressions, becomes a supporter. Also Milou (Clovis Cornillac), a young radical, who helps him to reopen the doors again. But it is not enough to have the doors open; customers must use them.

The day is saved by the miraculous appearance of Douce (Nora Arnezeder), a chantoozie who is not only said to be a future star, but actually has the charisma to prove it. She's an overnight success, the show comes together, but the day is only apparently saved. The situation is fraught with complications. There is the problem of Pigoil's gifted young son Jojo (Maxence Perrin), an accordionist now in the custody of his faithless mother, and the schemes of the fascist landlord Galapiat (Bernard-Pierre Donnadieu).

Paris 36 takes place in a neighborhood known locally simply as the Faubourg (the street). Remarkably, I learn, this entire neighborhood—streets, facades, cafés—was built as a set outside Prague. It's one of those movie neighborhoods not crowded with extras. Like the street in Spike Lee's *Do the Right Thing*, it's a place where everyone knows one another; the street's a stage, and the neighbors are players on it. And they all know about Monsieur TSF (Pierre Richard), nicknamed after a French broadcasting station. He never leaves his room, but the jazz on his radio keeps everyone humming.

It is inevitable that the movie ends with a smashing song-and-dance number starring Douce and, of course, young Jojo. It's one of those numbers where the size of the cast (even including Pigoil) seems improbable. Not to mention the sound of the orchestra. The theater is too small to possibly support such a production, but never mind: Hey, gang, let's rent the old Chansonia and put on a show!

The movie otherwise lacks a certain energy, advances somewhat creakily through its plot, and contains mostly obligatory surprises. Still, it's pleasant and amusing. If I had seen it before I was born, I would have loved it.

Passing Strange ★ ★ ★

NO MPAA RATING, 135 m., 2009

De'Adre Aziza (Edwina/Marianna/Sudabey), Daniel Breaker (The Youth), Eisa Davis (Mother), Colman Domingo (Mr. Franklin/Joop/Mr. Venus), Chad Goodridge (Reverend Jones/Terry/Christophe/Hugo),

Rebecca Naomi Jones (Sherry/Renata/Desi), Stew (Narrator). Directed by Spike Lee and produced by Elizabeth Ireland McCann. Screenplay by Stew, based on his stage play.

Passing Strange is one of the best musicals I've seen. It tells the story of a young black man from Los Angeles, rebelling against a loving, churchgoing family and breaking out on his own in the late 1960s to follow the call of art, or "art," to Amsterdam and Berlin. Starting with a garage band, he moves through psychedelic, punk, and rock stages in a journey toward the meaning of life. But can that meaning be found in art? His life builds toward that question.

The movie is moving and exciting not only because of the book, music, and performances, but because of its intelligence, passion, and heart. A Tony Award winner from the Public Theater and on Broadway, it has been filmed by Spike Lee, whose work is the very model of how to record a live performance.

This is the semi-autobiographical story of the rock musician Stew, who wrote the book and lyrics and is onstage throughout as the Narrator. He is surrounded by a gifted, high-energy cast, in a production that certainly works as a musical but also, particularly, as a drama. Often the story of a musical will be only a clothesline to hang the songs from. This story has depth and weight.

The hero is a young man known only as The Youth (Daniel Breaker), who when we meet him is being sent by his loving mother (Eisa Davis) to try out for a church choir. He joins after a comely choir member catches his eye, but church doesn't turn out as his mother intended, after he samples pot for the first time under the tutelage of the pastor's son (Colman Domingo). The son, who calls himself a coward under his father's thumb, instills in The Youth a vision of Europe and its freedoms, art films and cafés, a refuge for such black American exiles as James Baldwin.

Once in Amsterdam, embraced (sometimes literally) by a more color-blind society, The Youth finds not only personal freedom but a new understanding of his own roots. The scenes in Holland and Germany are rich with satire of the times, as the hash bars of Amsterdam are replaced by the radicalism of Berlin. The Dutch and Germans are played with droll accents by the cast members De'Adre Aziza, Rebecca Naomi Jones, Chad Goodridge, and Domingo, who, with a few costume details and attitude changes, effortlessly evoke three characters apiece.

Stew's lyrics, sometimes funny, sometimes edgy, come with a twist. Having warmed the fleshpots of Amsterdam, The Youth encounters a new kind of sex in Berlin. "Celibacy," he is informed by a female German erotic entrepreneur, "is the only sane response to a world gone wild. My porno films feature fully clothed men making business deals."

The hero feels he has embarked on a new kind of life in the Old World, and when entreated by his mother to come home for Christmas, he hems and haws and says that "maybe after" his next show he can "start thinking about" visiting home. Her song advises him "don't forget your own people." And indeed, he poses as culturally much "blacker" in Europe than he really is, because it works for him. It's as foretold by the preacher's son: "We're blacks passing as blacks."

This progress from youthful rebellion to eventual disillusionment and a search for deeper meaning is one that Stew himself possibly made. Today a forty-eight-year-old guitarist, studiously nonhip, he transforms himself with his guitar into the whole catalog of musical poses but emerges as a man who has learned something. Toward the end he makes this devastating observation: "Some of us spend our entire adult lives acting on the decisions of a teenager."

Spike Lee attended the opening night of *Passing Strange* at the Public, determined to film it, and shot at several performances at the Belasco Theater on Broadway, including closing night. With great skill and craft, he allows the material to speak for itself. He uses several cameras for many simultaneous angles, and with his editor, Barry Alexander Brown, seamlessly composes close-ups and longer shots to convey both character emotion and the exuberance of the choreography.

I can't single out a performance. This is a superb ensemble, conveying that joy actors feel when they know they're good in good material. This is not a traditional feature, but it's one of Spike Lee's best films.

Paul ★ ★ ½

R, 104 m., 2011

Seth Rogen (Paul), Simon Pegg (Graeme Willy), Nick Frost (Clive Gollings), Jason Bateman (Agent Zoil), Kristen Wiig (Ruth Buggs), Bill Hader (Haggard), Blythe Danner (Tara Walton), John Carroll Lynch (Moses Buggs), Joe Lo Truglio (O'Reilly), Jeffrey Tambor (Adam Shadowchild), Sigourney Weaver (The Big Guy). Directed by Greg Mottola and produced by Tim Bevan. Screenplay by Simon Pegg and Nick Frost.

Here's a movie that teeters on the edge of being really pretty good, and loses its way. I'm not quite sure what goes wrong, but you can see that it might have gone right. Maybe Paul, its alien hero, should have been sent back to the shop for a rewrite. He isn't merely voiced by Seth Rogen, he *is* Seth Rogen, if Seth Rogen looked like your usual bulb-headed, big-eyed being from outer space.

The premise is lovable. Graeme and Clive (Simon Pegg and Nick Frost) play two average fanboys from England who breathlessly embark on their dream trip to America. Their destination: Comic-Con in San Diego, and then they plan to rent an RV and tour such American landmarks as Roswell, New Mexico, where (as we all know) a flying saucer landed years ago and the event has been covered up ever since, becoming famous for allegedly being covered up.

The Comic-Con scenes are priceless, as our lads vibrate with excitement in the presence of the legendary sci-fi author Adam Shadowchild, whom Jeffrey Tambor invests with a dour impatience for the species of fanboys. I don't know where Tambor got the inspiration to wear that hat, but sometimes you see a prop and your heart leaps up because it is so right.

After San Diego, the boys drive to Area 51 in Nevada, the first leg of their odyssey. Pegg and Frost bring a wide-eyed innocence and sweetness to their characters, for whom just about everything in America is more or less alien. That includes Paul, whose van crashes in front of them on the highway. If you are an alien and a bad driver, Graeme and Clive are the first two humans you want to meet. They've been inflamed for so long by images of creatures that look exactly like you, that they aren't particularly surprised when you appear. So you join them in their RV and enlist them in your trip toward a rendezvous with your Mother Ship.

Along the way they all meet Ruth Buggs (Kristen Wiig), an intelligent-design advocate with a black lens in her glasses, who finds most of what they say shocking, but joins them in the RV for excellent reasons, even though the existence of an alien poses a considerable challenge to her creationism.

As you expect with a movie that begins at Comic-Con, *Paul* revels in its geekdom. The movie is wall-to-wall with references to other sci-fi movies, some overt, some subtle, as we gradually catch on that this one little creature, Paul, must have been single-handedly behind most of the close encounters of the last seventy years. The movie even supplies a new ending for one sci-fi classic, which brings it to a total of three.

But Paul himself may be a miscalculation. He is Seth Rogen in every aspect except physical appearance. His voice, his vocabulary, his thinking, even his wardrobe (such as it is). And he uses even more four- and ten-letter words than Seth Rogen characters usually do. I think that's a mistake in two ways: (1) If you're going to involve Seth Rogen in a live-action movie, put him on the screen. (2) Paul isn't alien enough. The joy in characters like *E.T.* and *Starman* is that they *are* aliens. Their thinking is strange. Their reactions are unexpected. Paul is somehow too . . . ordinary.

So the movie's a miss, but not without its pleasures. One of them is the appearance of Sigourney Weaver, who knows a thing or two when it comes to aliens who are not ordinary.

Paul Blart: Mall Cop ★ ★ ★

PG, 87 m., 2009

Kevin James (Paul Blart), Jayma Mays (Amy), Keir O'Donnell (Veck Sims), Bobby Cannavale (Commander Kent), Stephen Rannazzisi (Stuart), Shirley Knight (Mom Blart), Raini Rodriguez (Maya Blart). Directed by Steve Carr and produced by Adam Sandler, Jack Giarraputo, Barry Bernardi, Todd Garner, and Kevin James. Screenplay by James and Nick Bakay.

Paul Blart: Mall Cop is a slapstick comedy with a hero who is a nice guy. I thought that wasn't allowed anymore. He's a single dad, raising his daughter with the help of his mom; he takes his job seriously; he may be chubby but he's brave and optimistic. And he's in a PG-rated film with no nudity except for a bra strap, and no jokes at all about bodily functions.

What's even more amazing, the movie isn't "wholesome" as a code word for "boring." It's as slam-bang preposterous as any R-rated comedy you can name. It's just that Paul Blart and the film's other characters don't feel the need to use the f-word as the building block of every sentence. They rely on the rest of the English language, which proves adequate.

Kevin James stars as Officer Blart, who looks like the result of an experiment combining the genomes of Jackie Gleason and Nathan Lane. He dreams of making it into the state police, and indeed is in great physical shape but tends to collapse because of hypoglycemia. He carries around little sugar packets the way some people pack nitro for angina. He's a veteran security officer at a giant mall in West Orange, New Jersey, which he patrols aboard a Segway, a vehicle he has so mastered that he can even go in reverse without looking.

It is Black Friday, the day after Thanksgiving, busiest shopping day of the year. He turns up pitifully hung over. Paul doesn't drink, but the night before, assaulted by hot sauce during a nacho-eating contest, he chugged a pitcher he mistakenly thought contained virgin margaritas. His behavior alienated a pretty mall salesclerk named Amy (Jayma Mays), and his heart has been broken, far from the first time.

The mall is seized by a tightly organized crew of thieves, and customers are ordered outside, but Blart was playing free video games and didn't notice. Now he's locked inside, the only person who might be able to save Amy, his daughter, Maya (Raini Rodriguez), and their fellow prisoners. Yes, it's a hostage situation, with the mall already surrounded by cops and a SWAT team. The plan of the thieves is sensationally stupid, guaranteed to call attention to their scheme, easy to thwart, and possibly inspired by watching *Dog Day Afternoon* while drunk.

Everything is a sitcom until Officer Blart goes into action in an astonishingly inventive cat-and-mouse chase past myriad product placements, all of which find uses. The movie even discovers a new angle on the old hiding-in-the-ventilation-shaft routine.

Paul Blart emerges as a hero and something else: Kevin James illustrates how lighting and camera angles can affect our perception of an actor. In the early scenes, he's a fat schlub, but after he goes into action, the camera lowers subtly, the lighting changes, and suddenly he's a good-looking action hero, ready for business. He demonstrates what fat men have secretly believed for a long time. Should Daniel Craig someday retire, I am supporting Kevin James for the next James Bond.

Percy Jackson and the Olympians: The Lightning Thief ★ ★ ★

PG, 119 m., 2010

Logan Lerman (Percy), Alexandra Daddario (Annabeth), Brandon T. Jackson (Grover), Uma Thurman (Medusa), Sean Bean (Zeus), Pierce Brosnan (Chiron), Steve Coogan (Hades), Catherine Keener (Sally Jackson), Joe Pantoliano (Gabe Ugliano), Melina Kanakaredes (Athena), Rosario Dawson (Persephone), Kevin McKidd (Poseidon). Directed by Chris Columbus and produced by Michael Barnathan, Thomas M. Hammel, Guy Oseary, Mark Radcliffe, and Karen Rosenfelt. Screenplay by Craig Titley, based on the novel by Rick Riordan.

Every movie involving superheroes requires an origin story, and *Percy Jackson and the Olympians: The Lightning Thief* has a doozy. The Greek gods on Mount Olympus sometimes descend to Earth to have children, you see, and these half-god, half-humans are demigods. They live among us. One is Percy Jackson (Logan Lerman), who is the teenage son of Poseidon and Sally Jackson (Catherine Keener). He doesn't know this. I wonder if his mom noticed. Kind of a letdown to discover Greek gods are runaway dads.

Percy finds he can think best when underwater for ten minutes at a time. Poseidon was the god of the sea, you will recall. His best buddy is Grover (Brandon T. Jackson), who is revealed as a sort of assistant-demigod assigned to watch over him. His teacher is Mr. Brunner

(Pierce Brosnan), who is actually Chiron, a centaur. Give Brosnan a lot credit for wearing the back half of a horse as if he'd been doing it for years.

The movie, based on a novel by Rick Riordan, has fun working out modern parallels for Greek mythology. Percy, for example, thinks he is dyslexic, but it's only that his eyes instinctively turn English into Greek letters. No help in class. After learning of his real identity, he goes off to Chiron's demigod training camp with Grover, and he becomes friends with Annabeth (Alexandra Daddario), a demigoddess if ever I've seen one.

The plot heats up. Zeus (Sean Bean) and Poseidon (Kevin McKidd) meet atop the Empire State Building to discuss Zeus's missing lightning bolt, which he believes Poseidon's son Percy has stolen. (The story requires a certain suspension of disbelief.) Why, when, or how he allegedly might have done so begins as a mystery to Percy, but eventually the situation leads to slam-bam special effects sequences, as the gods and demigods do battle.

Undoubtedly the biggest attraction among the gods is Medusa, and Uma Thurman demonstrates she can wear a snake-filled head as gracefully as Pierce Brosnan can trot around with a horse's netherlands. There is also the advent of Steve Coogan as Hades. Yes, Steve Coogan. Hades, you recall, is the brother of Zeus and Poseidon.

Or maybe you don't recall. It's one of my weaknesses that I was never able to work up much of an interest in the Greek gods, who made for discouraging fiction because they were entirely defined by their attributes. They had no personalities to speak of, but simply went about doing what they did. You can understand why Zeus is so upset about losing his lightning bolt. That's what he does, is hurl that lightning bolt. What is Zeus without his bolt?

Director Chris Columbus has fun with this goofy premise, but as always I am distracted by the practical aspects of the story. Does it bother the Greek gods that no one any longer knows or cares that they rule the world? What are the genetic implications of human-god interbreeding? And, forgive me, I'll have to double back to Sally Jackson, Percy's mother. How did she meet Poseidon? At the beach, I suppose. Did he reveal his true identity? If a guy picks you up at the beach and says he's Poseidon, do you say, fine, let's not date, let's just mate? And then when the bastard dumps you and disappears leaving you pregnant, what way is that for a god to behave?

My remaining question involves the title. Call me foolish, but I don't consider *Percy Jackson and the Olympians: The Lightning Thief* an ideal title. The movie's original title was *Percy Jackson and the Lightning Thief,* which at least has the advantage of sounding less like a singing group.

Note: This is the first film I recall with end credits including the names of the actors who played Parthenon Janitors. I know, it's the Parthenon in Nashville, but even so.

The Perfect Game ★ ★ ★

PG, 118 m., 2010

Clifton Collins Jr. (Cesar Faz), Cheech Marin (Padre Estaban), Jake T. Austin (Angel Macias), Ryan Ochoa (Norberto), Emilie de Ravin (Frankie), Moises Arias (Mario), Patricia Manterola (Maria), Louis Gossett Jr. (Cool Papa Bell), Bruce McGill (Tanner). Directed by William Dear and produced by Daniel de Liege, Michael O. Gallant, Mark W. Koch, David Salzberg, Christian Tureaud, and W. William Winokur. Screenplay by Winokur.

Once upon a very long time, a film "based on a true story" was both true and almost too good to be a story. Perhaps anticipating any suspicion, William Dear intercuts newsreel footage from 1957 with *The Perfect Game,* frequently piping into the past for black-and-white and then segueing into the color of the present day. These players really lived, and this game was really played.

The film begins in Monterrey, Mexico, seen here as an impoverished town with many baseball fans, who follow the Brooklyn Dodgers on the radio with nearly religious intensity. We meet young Angel Macias (Jake T. Austin), who aims at a bucket fastened to a wall as a strike zone and dreams of greatness on the mound. His father is not so enthusiastic.

The setup is traditional. The town's boys have time on their hands and need an activity to keep them out of mischief. Enter wise, gentle Padre Estaban (Cheech Marin), who thinks a baseball team might help. Newly returned to town is Cesar Faz (Clifton Collins Jr.), who was a prospect for the St. Louis Cardinals but was devalued and shunted aside, possibly because he was Mexican. Unable to take more of the racism of management, he returned home and is recruited by Padre Estaban, not without difficulty, to coach the kids' team.

Because the film is titled *The Perfect Game*, you expect one to be pitched. You do not expect it to be pitched in Monterrey. You sort of know how these underdog sports movies turn out. Doesn't matter. *The Perfect Game* so expertly uses the charisma and personalities of the actors, especially the young ones, that it's thrilling anyway.

The scenes at the Little League World Series in Williamsport, Pennsylvania, make the contrast seem so dramatic between the teams in the final game—the Mexicans seemingly a foot shorter on average than their American counterparts. William Dear cannot, by the very nature of his story, avoid certain clichés, but the way he orchestrates the big game is sure and confident, and there's that life we often feel at the end of an underdog story.

In the years since, the Little League World Series has become blown out of proportion, verging on the exploitation of the players. They're trained within an inch of their lives, placed under enormous pressure, and subjected to punishing media scrutiny. It's not a game anymore. In 1957, these kids were *playing*. And it was a perfect game.

A Perfect Getaway ★ ★ ★

R, 97 m., 2009

Steve Zahn (Cliff), Timothy Olyphant (Nick), Milla Jovovich (Cydney), Kiele Sanchez (Gina), Marley Shelton (Cleo), Chris Hemsworth (Kale). Directed by David Twohy and produced by Robbie Brenner, Mark Canton, Ryan Kavanaugh, and Tucker Tooley. Screenplay by Twohy.

Man, am I glad I knew nothing about *A Perfect Getaway* going in. There are two things Hollywood can't resist in making a trailer: showing the best jokes in a comedy, and revealing the secrets of thrillers. Oops, did I say "thriller"? If you see ads on TV, I suppose you already knew that, but I didn't, and on the basis of the opening minutes, I thought this was a comedy. Honest.

So here was a thriller that worked for me. I didn't see revelations approaching because I didn't expect any. At one point in the film, I wondered about something, and then thought, "Nahhh, couldn't be." Could be.

The movie is about two couples and a suspicious third couple. The two main couples are Cliff and Cydney, honeymooners in Hawaii, and Nick and Gina, hikers. They meet on a difficult wilderness trail on the beautiful island of Kauai. The trail is spotted with signs warning of narrow paths, steep drops, sudden rains, and falling rocks. I love warnings about falling rocks. How do you avoid them? The Hawaii Park Service is famous for its helpful signs. My favorite is "Caution: Lava flow."

Cliff and Cydney (Steve Zahn and Milla Jovovich) are burdened with half the contents of an outdoor store for their couple of days of camping. Nick and Gina (Timothy Olyphant and Kiele Sanchez) travel lighter; indeed, the first time we see Nick he's carrying only a canteen, although later he produces a tent and a hunting bow. The third couple (Marley Shelton and Chris Hemsworth) are hitchhikers; she's friendly, he sends out bad vibes to both of the other men.

News comes of the brutal murder of a honeymooning couple in Honolulu. But Kauai should be safe, right? Maybe not. It's a rule of a thriller that if you warn the audience about a brutal killing, the killer(s) must turn up. This would be true if hikers in Iceland learned of a brutal killing in Hawaii. You don't bring the gun onstage unless it fires.

The director, David Twohy, allows creepiness to steal into the film slowly, but soon the jungle shadows seem filled with menace. Also, there is a narrow path with a steep drop, although Nick helps the newlyweds to negotiate it. Nick is a former Special Ops man, first into Iraq; Gina helpfully mentions he's "impossible to kill." Soon his macho posture begins to eat away at the less capable Cliff. They all travel together, which may or may not be a good idea, although—are they being followed? Whether they are or not I will leave you to decide. I will also leave the obligatory murderer(s) unrevealed. Let me just mention that Cliff says he's a screenwriter, and Nick finds out the screenplay is being rewritten and busts his chops about that, and then Nick mentions "red snappers" and Cliff says the correct term is "red herrings," and let us say that although the dinner menu includes mountain goat and macaroni and cheese, there is no fish course.

I enjoyed the acting. Steve Zahn is at last being liberated from the doofus characters he specialized in and allowed into the I.Q. mainstream. Milla Jovovich sure does a mighty fine rural Georgia accent for a girl from Ukraine. Timothy Olyphant is convincing as a man who is impossible to kill, and Kiele Sanchez as a woman who likes that aspect of his character.

The plot will require some discussion after the film is over. Is it misleading? Yes. Does it cheat? I think not. It only seems to cheat. That's part of the effect. All's fair in love and war, and the plots of thrillers.

The Perfect Sleep ★ ½

R, 105 m., 2009

Anton Pardoe (Narrator), Roselyn Sanchez (Porphyria), Patrick Bauchau (Nikolai), Peter J. Lucas (Ivan), Tony Amendola (Dr. Sebastian), Sam Thakur (The Rajah). Directed by Jeremy Alter and produced by Alter, Keith Kjarval, and Anton Pardoe. Screenplay by Pardoe.

The Perfect Sleep puts me in mind of a flywheel spinning in the void. It is all burnished brass and shining steel, perfectly balanced as it hums in its orbit; yet because it occupies a void, it satisfies only itself and touches nothing else. Here is a movie that goes about its business without regard for an audience.

Oh, it is well crafted, I grant you that. The cinematography contains fine compositions, looking down steeply on angled shadows and seeking down lost corridors. It has interiors that look like nineteenth-century landmarks of architecture just after the movers left with the furniture. It has grim men, a seductive woman, guns, knives, garrotes, scalpels, needles, cudgels, feet, fists, and baseball bats. It even has Patrick Bauchau, with the most insinuating voice since Orson Welles. But what in God's name is it about?

The Perfect Sleep does not lack explanation; in fact, the unnamed hero (Anton Pardoe) provides a narration that goes on and on and on, perhaps because the screenplay is by Anton Pardoe. He has returned to an unnamed city after ten years of fleeing men who would kill him, one who may be his father, a woman named Porphyria (Roselyn Sanchez), whom he loves and who has always loved him, a child he raised or fathered—or is an orphan, I'm unclear—an ambitious crime boss named The Rajah, a sinister physician named Dr. Sebastian (Tony Amendola), empty streets, wicked staircases, not many cars, and lots of streetlights.

It's all here. And after telling you so much about what's in it, wouldn't you think I could tell you the plot? I know the Narrator is back, he wants revenge, people want revenge on him, everybody is getting killed, and he personally is beaten, stabbed, kicked, thrown down stairs, skewered, hammered with karate, strangled, whipped, and shot point-blank in the head, and, what a guy, he just keeps on narrating, narrating, and narrating.

There are many unique ways of delivering mayhem in the film, some of them described in clinical detail by Dr. Sebastian while he is administering them. "Jugular . . . carotid? Carotid . . . jugular?" he debates with himself, his scalpel poised. At another point, he walks cheerfully up to two guys and stabs them in a lung apiece. Then he explains to them that they each have a collapsed lung. Dreadfully painful but not fatal.

He suggests it would be appalling for one to have two collapsed lungs. And he delivers this speech: "Our very biological structure promises us that, if it be now, 'tis not to come; if it be not to come, it will be now; if it be not now, yet it will come: Good sirs, the readiness is all." If this sounds like part of a famous speech, you are correct. I fancy the two collapsed lung guys are trying to remember where they heard it when he stabs them in the remaining two lungs. Now I know a lot about collapsed lungs, but I'm not entirely sure who Dr. Sebastian is.

Maybe it doesn't matter. Maybe if it did, the plot would give us a place to dig in our claws and hold on. The movie seems more interested in behavior. Many scenes take place in vast empty spaces like abandoned rehearsal halls or hotel function rooms. Major characters are discovered along an office corridor behind glass doors with their names stenciled on (more fun than captions). There are shadows on top of shadows. It's the film noir universe, all right. What does the title refer to? Perhaps to what you will enjoy during the film.

The Pink Panther 2 ★ ★

PG, 92 m., 2009

Steve Martin (Jacques Clouseau), Jean Reno (Ponton), Emily Mortimer (Nicole), Andy Garcia (Vincenzo), Alfred Molina (Pepperidge), Yuki Matsuzaki (Kenji), Aishwarya Rai Bachchan (Sonia), John Cleese (Dreyfus), Lily Tomlin (Mrs. Berenger). Directed by Harald Zwart and produced by Robert Simonds. Screenplay by Scott Neustadter, Michael H. Weber, and Steve Martin.

I was smiling all the way through the opening credits of *The Pink Panther 2*. They made me miss the golden age of credits, when you actually found out who the actors were going to be and maybe saw a little cartoon in the bargain: this time, one about the misadventures of the Pink Panther, of course. And then the names in the cast!

Imagine these appearing one after another: Steve Martin, Jean Reno, Emily Mortimer, Andy Garcia, Alfred Molina, Aishwarya Rai Bachchan, John Cleese, Lily Tomlin, Jeremy Irons, Johnny Hallyday . . . wait a minute! Aishwarya Rai Bachchan! That's the Indian actress Aishwarya Rai! The most beautiful woman in the world!

As the movie began, my smile faded. The actors are let down by the screenplay and direction, which don't really pop the supporting characters out into strong comic focus. Maybe the cast is simply too star-studded? There's sometimes the feeling they're being cycled onscreen by twos and threes, just to keep them alive.

Then there's the albatross of the Blake Edwards and Peter Sellers films. Edwards was a truly inspired director of comedies (*The Party, SOB, Victor/Victoria*). Peter Sellers was a genius who somehow made Inspector Clouseau seem as if he really were helplessly incapable of functioning in the real world, and somehow incapable of knowing that. Steve Martin is a genius, too, but not at being Inspector Clouseau. It seems more like an exercise.

The plot: "The Tornado" has stolen the Magna Carta, the Japanese emperor's sword, and the Shroud of Turin. Next may be the Pink Panther, the pink diamond that is, for some reason, the symbol of France's greatness and not merely an example of carbon under great pressure. Clouseau is chosen, despite the apoplectic agitation of Chief Inspector Dreyfus (John Cleese), to join an international police Dream Team to thwart the possible deed.

Also onstage is Clouseau's assistant, Nicole (Emily Mortimer), a fragrant rose; she and Jacques are so in love with each other they cannot even bring themselves to admit it. The Italian team member, Vincenzo (Andy Garcia), family name Doncorleone, moves in on Nicole and tells Clouseau that Sonia (Aishwarya Rai) likes him. That creates a romcom situation that's sort of muted because of Jacques and Nicole's shyness, and because the film seems reluctant to foreground Sonia very much. Aishwarya Rai is breathtaking in Bollywood films, where they devote a great deal of expertise to admiring beauty, but here she's underutilized and too much in the background.

Molina plays Pepperidge, a Sherlockian type who claims to be a great deducer of clues. Clouseau takes one look at him and they start a deducing showdown, sort of funny. Reno is Ponton, Clouseau's associate inspector, whose considerable presence never really pays off. Yuki Matsuzaki, as the Japanese cop Kenji, seems to be projecting ideas about the character that were edited out or never written in. Tomlin is the departmental expert on P.C. behavior, whom Clouseau argues with ("But . . . blondes *are* dumb!").

Opportunities to better develop all of these characters are lost, and we're left with the sight and stunt gags, which are central to the Panther movies, of course, but feel recycled: This time, little kids are the kung fu experts, for example, instead of Cato.

Too many of the stunt gags are performed without payoffs; Buster Keaton, the master, always gave you reaction shots. When Clouseau is mistaken for the pope, for example, and seems to fall from his balcony to his death, why isn't there a crowd to contemplate the fallen Frenchman with his black moustache, maybe lurching to his feet, blessing them, and intoning *dov'e la toilette*? Or after Clouseau sets the restaurant on fire, why not make him struggle to get back inside, telling the firemen he insists on paying his check?

The first two Panther movies, *The Pink Panther* (1963) and *A Shot in the Dark* (1964), were a serendipitous coming together of Edwards and Sellers. Truth to tell, none of their others were as inspired. The moment had passed. And it still hasn't come back round again. Zut!

Pirate Radio ★ ★ ★

R, 116 m., 2009

Philip Seymour Hoffman (The Count), Bill Nighy (Quentin), Rhys Ifans (Gavin), Tom Sturridge (Carl), Kenneth Branagh (Dormandy), Emma Thompson (Charlotte). Directed by Richard Curtis and produced by Curtis, Hilary Bevan Jones, Tim Bevan, and Eric Fellner. Screenplay by Curtis.

Before we get to the movie, let's assume you're near a computer that has iTunes. Go to "radio," look under "alternative rock," and go down to Radio Caroline. I'll tell you why in a moment. Don't turn it up so loud that it drowns out my review.

Incredible but true: From the birth of rock 'n' roll, through the rise of the Beatles and the Stones, all the way until the late 1960s, the BBC used to broadcast only about thirty minutes per day of pop music. "Thought for the Day" did almost as well. The old maids on the BBC board of governors thought it was, in the words of a Conservative minister depicted in this movie, "immoral."

Boredom abhors a vacuum. From pirate radio stations anchored offshore, a steady stream of rock was broadcast from powerful transmitters to the British mainland, where at a given moment, more than half of the radios may have been tuned in. The most famous of these pirates was Radio Caroline. Yes, the very station we're listening to right now. Webcasting is sort of piratical, no? (Right now on Radio Caroline: Bob Dylan's "Just Like a Woman.")

Caroline is the inspiration for Radio Rock, the floating transmitter in *Pirate Radio*. Richard Curtis, who wrote and directed the film, was ten years old in Radio Caroline's heyday, but he must know people who worked on board because the film has a real feel for the shipboard combination of excitement and desperation. Think about it. You're at the cutting edge of a cultural revolution, but you're anchored outside the U.K. territorial waters. It's the Swinging '60s, but the only woman on board is a lesbian. Nobody is swinging, anyway. (Now playing: The Who, "Won't Get Fooled Again.")

The shipboard culture involves a mixed bag of oddballs and egomaniacs who hold sway over millions of listeners and then go back to their grotty cabins and smoke weed. Well, it's not a crime outside territorial waters. Life really only happens for them when they're on the air. The best known of them is The Count (Philip Seymour Hoffman), an American who has a focus on his work that can only be described as reverential. The ranks of his rivals are peopled by a menagerie of British character actors, led by the Steve Buscemis of England, Bill Nighy and Rhys Ifans. Hold on, Ifans is Welsh. ("I Want You All to Myself," Joan Armatrading.)

Shifts on Rock Radio are long: More than a month, I think, and I get the impression some DJs never went ashore. Everybody is stir-crazy. Nobody is a happy camper. ("Free Bird," Lynyrd Skynyrd.)

Aboard this ship of fools arrives one day a young man named Carl (Tom Sturridge), who is the godson of the station's aloof and preoccupied manager, Quentin (Nighy). What's Carl doing aboard here? He's on summer holiday and is rather uncertain in the midst of this hotbed. It's possible he may find the solution to a personal question on board. ("Complicated," Avril Lavigne.)

Richard Curtis is good at handling large casts, establishing all the characters, and keeping them alive. His credits include *Love Actually* and the scripts for *Four Weddings and a Funeral, Notting Hill,* and *Bridget Jones's Diary.* Here the plot doesn't require a reason for the characters to keep running into one another; there's nowhere they can hide. No coincidences means more development. And the wall-to-wall '60s rock keeps things bright.

Meanwhile, back in Parliament, a tight-arsed Sir Alistair Dormandy (Kenneth Branagh) denounces pirate radio as "a sewer of dirty commercialism and no morals." As the threat of a shutdown looms, the prospect grows dire, and we begin to realize that among these pirates, as among the original ones, the shipboard community holds their identity and validates their stubborn dreams.

The government vows to sink the pirates and finally forces through the required legislation. This is highly unpopular. Just imagine an American administration turning off your rock and forcing you to listen only to NPR. Wow, I'm sorry I wrote that. There are probably fringers who think Obama is plotting to do just that.

No Beatles. No, I don't mean Obama would outlaw the Beatles. I mean I noticed Radio Caroline didn't play their records.

Pirates of the Caribbean: On Stranger Tides ★ ★

PG-13, 136 m., 2011

Johnny Depp (Jack Sparrow), Penelope Cruz (Angelica), Geoffrey Rush (Barbossa), Ian McShane (Blackbeard), Kevin R. McNally (Gibbs), Sam Claflin (Philip), Astrid Berges-Frisbey (Syrena), Stephen Graham (Scrum), Keith Richards (Captain Teague). Directed by Rob Marshall and produced by Jerry Bruckheimer. Screenplay by Ted Elliott and Terry Rossio.

Before seeing *Pirates of the Caribbean: On Stranger Tides*, I had already reached my capacity for Pirates of the Caribbean movies, and with this fourth installment, my cup runneth over. Indeed, so doth Captain Jack Sparrow's, as he obtains two chalices to use while drinking from the Fountain of Youth, and seeks a mermaid's tears to invest them with magic. There's always a catch-22. You fight Spanish conquistadors and the British Navy to find the bloody fountain, and now you need a weepy mermaid.

I had fleeting hopes for this episode of the Disney franchise. An opening sequence is fun, as Captain Jack impersonates a British judge, is chased through London, and discovers his old amour Angelica (Penelope Cruz) attempting to impersonate him while raising the crew for a ship. That anyone would still want to sail under Jack's command is a tribute to the daring of British seamen. The movie is fun until they set sail.

Johnny Depp, who confesses he's rather tired of playing his relentless hero, nevertheless does a plucky job here. He plays Jack Sparrow as an insouciant wise guy, rarely ruffled, always ready with a quip. Whether he is a competent swashbuckler is hard to say because the fight sequences here are composed in the editing room and do not seem to exist in an actual space-time continuum. We no longer see truly great sword fighting, the kind performed by Liam Neeson and Tim Roth in *Rob Roy* (1995). It's all impossible leaping and incomprehensible cutting, giving us all of the movement of action and none of the excitement.

The best way to describe the plot is by explaining that the Fountain of Youth is the MacGuffin. Angelica and Jack set sail for the New World aboard a ship commanded by Blackbeard (Ian McShane), who is said to be her father. The ship's crew includes zombies, which is a step up from previous crew members in the series, skeletons. Blackbeard is in a race to find the fountain before Captain Barbossa (Geoffrey Rush), who is being financed by King George, who needs to drink from the fountain none too soon. Rush is as always a dependable actor, but his sandpapery skin complexion is rather alarming here. Get this sailor some Lubriderm.

Also in the race is a boatload of Spanish sailors sent by their king. All three boats pitch up on the same beach and fight one another to the fountain. But wait. The mermaids. Yes, a special reflector used in an old lighthouse casts light on one of the longboats, and light attracts mermaids, and it's a nasty sight. We get to meet only one of the mermaids, the well-named Syrena (Astrid Berges-Frisbey), who is comely and doe-eyed, and has one of those official hairdos that cleverly conceals the delightful bits.

Syrena and Philip (Sam Claflin), a cleric, lock eyes and hearts, but Syrena is needed for her tears, and is held captive and transported through the jungle in a large water tank, wherein she nearly drowns because she cannot breathe, establishing at last what I have always argued, that mermaids are amphibians.

One improvement this time is the dropping of the superfluous nonpirate characters played earlier by Orlando Bloom and Keira Knightley. I was never sure what essential function they fulfilled; Depp and Cruz are so over-the-top they function as their own supporting characters.

Even in his first Pirates movie, Depp seemed to be channeling large parts of the persona of Keith Richards, not to mention all of the eyeliner. Here the Rolling Stone himself turns up again, playing Jack Sparrow's father. The hairdressers for these two characters seem to have involved themselves in some sort of a grudge bet.

Pirates of the Caribbean: On Stranger Tides is about what you'd expect. It is long, expensive, and bombastic, and the beautiful mermaid has a tantalizing way of not coming quite far enough out of the water. For me, it's too much of a muchness. The whole series was inspired by a ride at Disney World. There's a bright side to that. At least no movie has yet been inspired by "It's a Small World."

Planet 51 ★ ★ ½

PG, 91 m., 2009

With the voices of: Dwayne Johnson (Captain Chuck Baker), Justin Long (Lem), Jessica Biel (Neera), Gary Oldman (General Grawl), Seann William Scott (Skiff), John Cleese (Professor Kipple), Freddie Benedict (Eckle), Alan Marriott (Glar). Directed by Jorge Blanco and codirected by Javier Abad and Marcos Martinez; produced by Guy Collins and Ignacio Pérez Dolset. Screenplay by Joe Stillman.

The 1950s Hollywood tradition was that an alien spaceship landed on Earth and was surrounded fearfully by military troops. *Planet 51* is true to the tradition, but this time the ship comes from Earth, and it lands on a planet inhabited by little green men. It's still the 1950s, however.

Yes, on *Planet 51* they speak English, "Lollipop" is on the jukebox, and they speed around in little cars that look like a cross between '50s gas guzzlers and those bubble-domed cars of the future. Planet 51, in fact, is a lot like the black-and-white parts of *Pleasantville.* Everybody is sweet and friendly, except for militaristic warmongers like General Grawl (Gary Oldman), and it's hard to figure out who he's afraid of because as far as we can tell, this is a civilization without any enemies.

Although not bowling me over, this is a jolly and good-looking animated feature in glorious 2-D. It doesn't make the slightest effort to explain why an English-speaking clone of the world of *American Graffiti* could exist elsewhere in the universe. How could it? Besides, under the emerging theory of the multiverse, I think (but am not sure) such a thing is entirely possible. Somewhere. As long as it's consistent with the laws of physics. I am not sure how they explain that the rain is made of rocks. You'd think the rocks would eventually bury everything. Maybe they melt?

Not that science on Planet 51 has reached the level of explaining such things. Its hero, Lem (Justin Long), has just won a job as a lecturer at the astronomical observatory, where he explains the universe is "hundreds of miles wide." He is gently filled in by Chuck Baker (Dwayne Johnson), an American astronaut who lands on the planet. At first he and Lem are frightened of each other, but after they bond and Chuck discovers he can breathe Planet 51's atmosphere, he settles down to the puzzle of using his lander to return to its orbiter. He has arrived with Rover, possibly intended to stay and look around, who is a cross between a Mars lander, WALL-E, and a friendly dog, and he loves to scamper around and collect rocks, as all good Rovers do.

Apparently there is no way a family animated cartoon can avoid ending in action scenes, and General Grawl leads his troops against the menacing Chuck. At least the battle is slapstick and not very violent. And all ends happily. Oops, was that a spoiler?

The movie was written by Joe Stillman, who wrote *Shrek.* It was beautifully animated in Spain and uses the voice talents of Jessica Biel, Seann William Scott, and John Cleese. It's perfectly pleasant as kiddie entertainment, although wall-to-wall with pop references to the American 1950s. I believe there may be millions of kiddies who, hard as this is to conceive, have never heard of Elvis. As that decade recedes in our rearview mirror, it more and more seems to signify something big and enduring. What, I am not sure.

Play the Game ★ ★

PG-13, 105 m., 2009

Andy Griffith (Grandpa Joe), Paul Campbell (Dave), Liz Sheridan (Edna Gordon), Doris Roberts (Rose Sherman), Marla Sokoloff (Julie), Clint Howard (Dick), Rance Howard (Mervin), Geoffrey Owens (Rob), Juliette Jeffers (Carrie). Directed, written, and produced by Marc Fienberg.

The Andy Griffith Show meets *Seinfeld* in the sack, in *Play the Game,* which shows Andy is not too old to star in a sex comedy. I guess. Griffith plays Grandpa Joe, who lost his beloved wife two years ago. Now his grandson Dave (Paul Campbell) thinks it's time for him to start dating again. After all, he isn't getting any younger.

Grandpa Joe is pretty much on standby in his retirement home. He'd like to get cozy with Rose (Doris Roberts). But he's unprepared for the wiles of Edna (Liz Sheridan, who played Seinfeld's mom). She supplies Joe with Viagra, and he more or less seduces her on autopilot.

Dave considers himself a babe magnet. He's a genius at fast-talking himself into relationships that, alas, have a way of ending once he's run through his prepared material. He's also a whiz at selling cars, but at least when he makes a sale the victim drives it off the lot.

The screenplay, written by first-time director Marc Fienberg, fervently stays true to an ancient sitcom tradition. We somehow suspect Grandpa Joe will end up with the adorable Rose, and whaddaya know, Dave finds genuine love with Rose's granddaughter, Julie (Marla Sokoloff).

And that's about it, except for a close-up of Andy Griffith that I could easily have lived without. I've admired Griffith ever since *No Time for Sergeants,* but the one thing I must admit I've never wanted to do was regard his face while he's enjoying oral sex from Seinfeld's mom. I have a good friend whose own dad discovered Viagra in a retirement home and would call his son almost daily to recount his latest adventures. He called once when I was in the room with my friend, who urgently told him, "Dad, I've told you, I don't want to know!" I told him the old one about the old lady who runs naked into the TV room of her retirement village shouting, "Super sex! Super sex!" One of the guys perks up and says, "I'll have the soup, please."

Please Give ★ ★ ★ ½

R, 91 m., 2010

Catherine Keener (Kate), Amanda Peet (Mary), Oliver Platt (Alex), Rebecca Hall (Rebecca), Ann Morgan Guilbert (Andra), Sarah Steele (Abby). Directed by Nicole Holofcener and produced by Anthony Bregman. Screenplay by Holofcener.

There is an evil-tempered old woman in *Please Give* whose greatest accomplishment is having survived into her nineties without being pushed down a steep flight of stairs. She finds fault with everyone and everything, is ungrateful, is a whiner, and brings nothing to the party. How do people like this live with themselves?

Her next-door neighbors are waiting for her to die so that her apartment will become available and they can break down some walls. This is in New York, the city that drains a cruel price per square foot of living space from its inhabitants. I know New Yorkers happy to find an apartment that for a somewhat poor Chicagoan would be the bedroom. It is one of the pleasures of Nicole Holofcener's new film that everyone, including the old lady, knows this.

The couple next door are Kate and Alex (Catherine Keener and Oliver Platt). They run an antique-furniture store specializing in furniture from the 1950s—you know, the kind your family accumulated at great expense, which sat there in the house looking superior. They often obtain their stock from grandchildren who consider a 1952 coffee table to be the graceless blotch it surely is, but which metrosexuals consider an ironic statement on how cool they are.

The old lady, Andra, is played by Ann Morgan Guilbert with exact cunning: She makes Andra expert at seeming unaware of her monstrous selfishness. Andra is looked after by two granddaughters, Mary (Amanda Peet) and Rebecca (Rebecca Hall). Rebecca is constant and kind, Mary is a distracted heavy drinker, both are attractive, and they live together in one of those roommate arrangements that can be explained only by madness or the cost of apartments.

Kate is another of those Catherine Keener characters you feel like you've known somewhere before. She and her husband have a nice life as a couple who seem to be winning their own version of *Antiques Roadshow.* They have a daughter, Abby (Sarah Steele), who is pudgy, has skin problems, and is a little antisocial right now but is smart, has good timing, and will eventually get life sorted out. Abby is incredulous at the way her mom is a pushover for street beggars, as if she's making some kind of amends. Kate can hardly enjoy a meal without taking a doggie bag to a homeless man. She's an innocent; she's shocked to find that another dealer bought a table from her and marked it up in his own store.

Kate and Alex are reasonably happy. They run errands for old Andra to calm their consciences, and decide to have a dinner party for the old lady and her granddaughters. This scene shows Holofcener demonstrating that recognizable life is almost always more engrossing than fantasy; it's an exercise in social embarrassment, one of those Bunuelian scenes in which people unexpectedly tell the truth and say what should not be said.

Nicole Holofcener, who made the great *Lovely and Amazing,* pays close attention to women. She doesn't define them by their relationships with men. In a Holofcener movie, women actually have their *own* reasons for doing things—and these are even allowed to be bad reasons, and funny ones. The movie is about imperfect characters in a difficult world, who mostly do the best they can under the circumstances, but not always. Do you realize what a revolutionary approach that is for a movie these days?

Poetry ★ ★ ★ ½

NO MPAA RATING, 139 m., 2011

Yun Jung-hee (Mija), Lee David (Wook), Kim Hira (M. Kang). Directed, produced, and written by Lee Chang-dong.

There is perhaps something in the river. It floats slowly closer on the current. It is the body of a young woman. *Poetry* opens with this extended shot, so that our realization can slowly grow. Then we meet an old woman named Mija. She learns from her doctor that she is in the early stages of Alzheimer's. It is difficult to be sure what effect this news has. She continues with her life.

Mija (Yun Jung-hee) lives in a South Korean city where she looks after her grandson, Wook (Lee David), and is a caregiver for an old man who is half-paralyzed by a stroke. She is a small, unremarkable woman, cheerfully dressed, quiet, getting things done. She signs up for an adult class in poetry writing at a local community center. The teacher is not a bad teacher, maybe even a good one, although he acts as if you can be taught to write poetry. All you can do is write it. Whether it is good or not isn't up to you.

The teacher encourages his students to look, *really* look, at things. He asks them if they have ever *really* looked at an apple. Mija goes home and really looks at an apple. It is such a perfect fruit. But then, every fruit is perfect. Mija's grandson is a sullen lout, a layabout with worthless friends. She is told one day that he has been implicated with five other boys in the rape of a young woman. That was the young woman in the river.

She carries on. She still attends class. It is very difficult to be sure what she is thinking, and this kind of film is more absorbing than those with characters who wear their emotions on their sleeves. We peer at her, we want to see into her. Yun Jung-hee's performance is delicately given, in that she seems to be concealing nothing and yet we remain outside. Aware of her diagnosis, we look for signs of memory loss, but she remembers, all right. It's just that she is more focused on poetry at the moment.

There is a scene here that is heartrending. The fathers of the other boys meet with Mija and explain they're getting up a fund to pay off the dead girl's mother. Mija is made to feel she must raise the money as a duty to her grandson. She deals with this in her own way, which I will not specify, except by saying that she begins to *really* look. And the poetry class, with its promise of transcendence, takes a place in her soul that we sense, rather than see.

This is the second of Lee's films I've seen after *Oasis* (2002). That film also approached extreme cruelty with outward composure. It deals with a disturbed and worthless ex-con who killed a man in a hit-and-run accident.

After prison, he meets the severely disabled daughter of his victim, he assaults her, and this begins a relationship that seems somehow to meet their mutual needs. Believe me, I know how horrifying that sounds. But Lee doesn't make exploitation films and he doesn't find conventional answers. He is puzzled by the mysteries of inexplicable behavior.

In *Poetry*, we have a movie that is outwardly more calm. It is not seeking answers, either. It begins with events and sees how they develop. Mija, at the center, is perhaps determined not to fill her remaining memories with despair, and to avoid adding to the sum of the world's misery. Maybe it's as simple as that. And I must add that the film contains certainly the most poignant badminton match I can imagine.

Note: Poetry *won the prize for best screenplay at Cannes 2010.*

Police, Adjective ★ ★ ★

NO MPAA RATING, 115 m., 2009

Dragos Bucur (Cristi), Vlad Ivanov (Anghelache), Irina Saulescu (Anca), Ion Stoica (Nelu), Marian Ghenea (Prosecutor). Directed, written, and produced by Corneliu Porumboiu.

Police, Adjective is a peculiar title for a film. The posters at Cannes 2009 read "*Politist, adjectiv.*" With a period and a gun on top of a dictionary. A critic from Romania, sitting next to us before the screening, explained that the purity of the language is enforced as fervently in Romania as in France, and "police," of course, is properly a noun.

And there you have the movie. Its hero is a young cop assigned to nab drug users, and its surprisingly effective key scene involves an argument with his captain over the dictionary definitions of the words "conscience" and "justice." This may not sound exciting, but it was welcome after legions of cop movies in which such arguments are orchestrated with the f-word (good luck finding that in the dictionary).

The cop's name is Cristi (Dragos Bucur), and he's been assigned to follow a sixteen-year-old schoolboy suspected of smoking pot. The kid does smoke pot. He often smokes it with a pal and a girlfriend. Does he "supply" it? If he has it and offers a toke to them, I suppose the definition of that would be supplying.

The cop is recently married, and he and his wife spent their honeymoon in Prague. He doesn't want to follow this kid. If he arrests him, the kid gets locked up for eight to sixteen years. "That would ruin his life," he tells the captain. "Did you force him to smoke pot?" No, the cop says, but in Prague it's smoked openly on the streets and the cops look the other way.

The captain patiently explains that in Romania smoking pot is against the law, and the duty of the police is to enforce the law. "I don't want to arrest him," Cristi says. "It's against my conscience." Then the dictionary comes out. My dictionary, which I believe the captain was also using, although in Romanian, has only one definition: *conscience. noun. An inner feeling or voice viewed as acting as a guide to the rightness or wrongness of one's behavior.*

You know the rest. It isn't a policeman's job to act on his inner voices and feelings. It's his job to enforce the law.

This movie I suspect comes with a lot of baggage. Romania under the Ceausescu regime (1965–89) started out promisingly but grew into a repressive police state under which perhaps two million people were killed. Ceausescu's police were often only enforcing the law. Romania has a population of twenty-one million, but it's in the nature of things that many people knew the cops, who were sometimes arresting them or their neighbors. What choice did a cop have?

I speculate that Corneliu Porumboiu, born 1975, who wrote and directed the film, grew up in a nation shadowed by those memories, and that his film to some degree is about that time. It is also a low-key, observant record of a universal dilemma among people in authority: How do you do your duty when your inner voice tells you it's wrong?

The visual style, foregrounding drab areas of a small industrial city, is flat and realistic. We never really meet the young suspect. Cristi doesn't confide in his wife. His office mate knows what he feels but stays out of it. Only the captain and a prosecutor will discuss it with him. Both are more than willing. Both are of an age when they would have started their careers under Ceausescu. They depend on the strict definition of the law because they can use that as a refuge from their inner voices. Cristi understands this, and that's why the debate over the dictionary is so intense. They aren't talking about definitions. They're talking about the past, present, and future of their nation.

Note: The film won both the Un Certain Regard jury prize and the Critics' Prize at Cannes 2009.

Ponyo ★ ★ ★ ★

G, 101 m., 2009

With the voices of: Noah Cyrus (Ponyo), Frankie Jonas (Sosuke), Matt Damon (Koichi), Cate Blanchett (Gran Mamare), Tina Fey (Lisa), Kurt Knutsson (Newscaster), Cloris Leachman (Yoshie), Liam Neeson (Fujimoto), Jennessa Rose (Kumiko), Lily Tomlin (Toki), Betty White (Noriko). Directed by Hayao Miyazaki and produced by Steve Alpert, Kathleen Kennedy, and Frank Marshall. Screenplay by Miyazaki.

There is a word to describe *Ponyo,* and that word is "magical." This poetic, visually breathtaking work by the greatest of all animators has such deep charm that adults and children will both be touched. It's wonderful and never even seems to try: It unfolds fantastically.

The G-rated feature tells a story both simple and profound. Sosuke, a five-year-old who lives in a house on a seaside cliff, finds a goldfish trapped in a jar on the beach. This is Ponyo. Freeing her, he is rewarded by a lick on a finger that heals a cut. And by tasting human blood, we learn, Ponyo gains the ability to transform between fish and human.

This begins a friendship. Sosuke (voice by the Jonas brother Frankie) protects Ponyo (Noah Cyrus, Miley's kid sister) in a pail until arms and legs pop spontaneously from her body and she becomes a little girl who speaks his language. He takes her to school and to the nursing home next door where his father works, and all is wonderful until we discover that by crossing the divide between land and sea, Ponyo has triggered ecological changes that unleash a dangerous tsunami that floods Sosuke's village right up to the doorstep of his house.

This begins an exciting escape in a toy boat that Ponyo magically enlarges, and a dreamlike journey among flooded treetops in search of Sosuke's mother. From the surface they can see giant prehistoric fish, awakened by the great wave, that cruise the highways his mother once drove.

This cannot help but sound like standard animated fare. But I have failed to evoke the wonder of Hayao Miyazaki's artistry. This sixty-eight-year-old Japanese master continues to create animation *drawn by hand,* just as *Snow White* and *Pinocchio* were. There is a fluid, organic quality to his work that exposes the facile efficiency of CGI. And, my God!—his imagination!

The film opens with a spellbinding, wordless sequence beneath the sea, showing floating jellyfish and scampering bottom-dwellers. The pastels of this scene make *Ponyo* one of the very rare movies where I want to sit in the front row, to drown in it. This is more than "artistry." It is art.

And consider Miyazaki's imagination as he creates a human protector of this seascape, Fujimoto (Liam Neeson). He is the father of Ponyo and her countless baby sisters (the biology involved is wisely not explained). And although he seems sinister at first, his desire to keep Ponyo in the sea is eventually explained because of his concern for the balance of Earth's nature.

Already it is threatened by the debris of human civilization; we see a bottom-scooping ship dredge up tons of waste. Sosuke's happy life on the cliff top and the peace of his friends at the old folks' home are belied by the pollution so near at hand. Of course, it is up to Ponyo and Sosuke to set things back in balance.

Miyazaki is the Japanese creator of *My Neighbor Totoro, Spirited Away, Howl's Moving Castle,* and many other beloved films. Already I have heard from a few people who don't want to see it "because it's Japanese." This is solid gold ignorance. "Is it only dubbed?" I was asked. You dummy! *All* animated films are dubbed! Little Nemo can't really speak! Miyazaki is known as the god of American animators, and Disney has supplied *Ponyo* with an A-list cast of vocal talents, including also Cate Blanchette, Matt Damon, and Tina Fey.

The English-language version has been adapted by John Lasseter (*Toy Story, Up*) and, believe me, he did it for love, not money. There are so few movies that can delight both a small child and the adult in the next seat. Here is one of them.

Post Grad ★ ★ ★

PG-13, 89 m., 2009

Alexis Bledel (Ryden Malby), Zach Gilford (Adam Davies), Rodrigo Santoro (David Santiago), Jane Lynch (Carmella Malby), Fred Armisen (Pitchman), Bobby Coleman (Hunter Malby), Michael Keaton (Walter Malby), Carol Burnett (Grandma Maureen). Directed by Vicky Jenson and produced by Jeffrey Clifford, Joe Medjuck, and Ivan Reitman. Screenplay by Kelly Fremon.

The Malbys are just plain nice. That's the only word for them. They're a goofy, strange California suburban family who love one another and share the same sunny sense of humor and nothing terrible ever happens to them and it's all for one and one for all.

Post Grad, the story of how Ryden Malby graduates from college and tries to enter the job market, shows them coping with hard times with good cheer. It's a screwball comedy. It's also, I have to say, a feel-good movie that made me smile a lot. The Malbys are just so darned lovable.

Take Ryden. She's played by Alexis Bledel, who is beautiful in a blue-eyed, open-faced kind of way, and awfully hopeful she'll get a job in publishing because she likes to read more than anything. Dad is Walter (Michael Keaton), the district manager for a luggage retailer, who isn't worried that things will work out fine for her, and even offers her a job helping him sell mail-order belt buckles that he doesn't know are stolen goods.

Ryden's mom, Carmella (Jane Lynch), is sort of the sane center of gravity. Her grandma (Carol Burnett) is a hip baby boomer who gives her frank sex advice. Her much younger little brother, Hunter (Bobby Coleman), is a cuddly goof. Her best friend, Adam (Zach Gilford), is admiring and loyal, and accepts that she's not in love with him. Even David (Rodrigo Santoro), Adam's sexy older Brazilian rival from across the street, is not a letch and doesn't take advantage of her.

To these good people happen unfortunate things. A job is lost. A cat is mashed. Coffins are damaged. Dad is arrested. The brakes fail on Hunter's car in the soap box derby, and it runs into the lake. But the mashed cat is successfully buried, not without a struggle, which brings to mind the observation of a pet grave digger in *Gates of Heaven*: "Make it too small, and you can't get 'em in there."

There's no doubt Alexis Bledel is the star of this show, an adorable young woman. You may recall her from the *Sisterhood of the Traveling Pants* movies or *Bride & Prejudice*. Hard to believe she was in *Sin City*. Keaton and Lynch somehow seem like the logical parents for this phenomenon of niceness.

Apart from a few words and attitudes, this movie, directed by Vicky Jenson and written by Kelly Fremon, could be a throwback to more innocent times. It contains no drugs, no angst, no bitterness, no generation gap, no big family problems, and it doesn't even seem to know how blessed it is. Sometimes you get out of a movie and feel like you've just worked a desperate overnight shift on homicide. You get out of this movie and you have a good feeling.

Oh, it's not a great movie. It won't alter the course of cinema. It won't make any best ten lists. If you're cynical or jaded, it might not get past you. But here is the first movie in a long time that had me actually admitting I wouldn't mind seeing a sequel.

Potiche ★ ★ ½

R, 103 m., 2011

Catherine Deneuve (Suzanne Pujol), Gerard Depardieu (Maurice Babin), Fabrice Luchini (Robert Pujol), Karin Viard (Nadege), Judith Godreche (Joelle), Jeremie Renier (Laurent Pujol). Directed by Francois Ozon and produced by Eric Altmeyer and Nicolas Altmeyer. Screenplay by Ozon, adapted from a play by Pierre Barillet and Jean-Pierre Gredy.

It has been years since I sensed that Catherine Deneuve and Gerard Depardieu were acting. They are, of course, and as a wide variety of characters. But they give their directors what Billy Wilder once asked Jack Lemmon to do:

"Nothing." There is never a note wrong, never the slightest strain, always such an unforced ease in the sight of the camera that they might have been born onscreen.

Here they are in Francois Ozon's comedy *Potiche*. The title is a French word that combines aspects of "trophy wife" and "status symbol." Here she comes now, the *potiche*, jogging down a forest path in a red running suit: Suzanne (Deneuve), the bourgeois wife of a provincial factory owner.

Her father created the factory, which manufactures umbrellas. Her husband, Robert (Fabrice Luchini), became the boss after the old man's death. It appears that she brought the factory into their marriage, but Robert behaves as if he built it from the ground up with his own hands, one *parapluie* at a time. He is an arrogant man, the ruler of his little kingdom, who cheats on his fragrant wife with his secretary—who herself seems not very pleased by him.

Suzanne lives a serene and comfortable life, loves her adult son and daughter, understands that her husband has a mistress and is perhaps happy to have the mistress relieve her of some of her duties. That Deneuve so convincingly inhabits this character is a demonstration of effortless skill.

It is 1977. France is shaken by strikes. I recall Cannes in those years, annually shut down for a day or two by striking workers who took their own strolls on the red carpet. The workers go on strike at the umbrella factory, Robert marches out to denounce them, and they make him a hostage. Suddenly all the labor problems have become the business of Suzanne.

She has been depicted as just slightly bubble-brained. She carries around a little pocket notebook in which she writes little poems that are more than a little banal. The method of Deneuve's approach to the role is not to pretend Suzanne becomes suddenly serious, but to show Suzanne as still exactly the same person, as only the circumstances change.

She needs help. She calls upon the town mayor, Maurice (Gerard Depardieu). He is a communist, as many French mayors were at that time. He is also a fond man in late middle age, running a little to seed, who remembers Suzanne warmly from his past. (Their unforced onscreen affection must owe something to the fact that they have appeared in eight films together, and have lived in each other's pockets for decades as glories of the French cinema.) They work together to find a way past the stupidity of her husband and the anger of the workers. Along the way Suzanne reengages in life; we sense her strategy for dealing with her unbearable husband was to partition him into a soundproof room in her mind.

The film is a whimsical comedy, based on a popular Parisian stage success of some years ago. It plays like one, although Ozon uses more locations than a play would find possible. There's little effort at psychological depth, and the characters float along on the requirements of comedy. But it's sweet comedy, knowing about human nature, and Deneuve and Depardieu, who bring so much history to the screen, seem to create it by their very natures.

Precious: Based on the Novel *Push* by Sapphire ★ ★ ★ ★

R, 109 m., 2009

Gabourey "Gabby" Sidibe (Precious), Mo'Nique (Mary), Paula Patton (Ms. Rain), Mariah Carey (Ms. Weiss), Lenny Kravitz (Nurse John), Sherri Shepherd (Cornrows). Directed by Lee Daniels and produced by Daniels and Sarah Siegel-Magness. Screenplay by Geoffrey Fletcher, based on the novel *Push* by Sapphire.

Precious has shut down. She avoids looking at people, she hardly ever speaks, she's nearly illiterate. Inside her lives a great hurt, and also her child, conceived in a rape. She is fat. Her clothes are too tight on her. School is an ordeal of mocking cruelty. Home is worse. Her mother, defeated by life, takes it out on her daughter. After Precious is raped by her father, her mother is angry not at the man, but at the child for "stealing" him.

There's one element in the film that redeems this landscape of despair. That element is hope. Not the hope of Precious, but that of two women who want better for her. It's not that Precious "shows promise." I think it's that these women, having in their jobs seen a great deal, can hardly imagine a girl more obviously in pain.

That is the starting point for *Precious,* a great American film that somehow finds an authentic way to move from these beginnings to an inspiring ending. Gabourey "Gabby" Sidibe, a young actress in her debut performance as Precious, says: "I know this girl. I know her in my family, I know her in my friends, I've seen her, I've lived beside this girl." We may have seen her, too, if we looked. People often don't really look. They see, evaluate, dismiss.

Sidibe is heartbreaking as Precious, that poor girl. Three other actresses perform so powerfully in the film that Academy voters will be hard-pressed to choose among them. Audiences may be hard-pressed to recognize them. Mo'Nique plays Mary, Precious's chain-smoking couch potato of a mother, treating her daughter like a domestic servant and turning a blind eye on years of abuse. Paula Patton is Ms. Rain, Precious's teacher, who is able to see through the girl's sullen withdrawal and her vulgarities and wonder what pain it may be masking. Mariah Carey is Ms. Weiss, a social worker.

This casting looks almost cynical on paper, as if reflecting old Hollywood days when stars were slipped into "character roles" with a wink. But Lee Daniels, the director, didn't cast them for their names and actually doesn't use any of their star qualities. He requires them to act. Somehow he was able to see beneath the surface and trust they had within the emotional resources to play these women, and he was right. Daniels began his career by producing *Monster's Ball,* in which Halle Berry shed her glamour and found such depths that she won an Oscar. Daniels must have an instinct for performances waiting to flower.

Carey and Patton are equal with Sidibe in screen impact; the film holds the girl in the center of their attempt to save her future. Why would a teacher and a social worker go to such lengths to intervene? They must see tragic victims of abuse every day. Mary, the mother, is perhaps not a bad woman but simply one defeated by the forces she now employs against her daughter. Mo'Nique is frighteningly convincing.

The film is a tribute to Sidibe's ability to engage our empathy. Her work is still another demonstration of the mystery of some actors, who evoke feelings in ways beyond words and techniques. She so completely creates the Precious character that you rather wonder if she's very much like her. You meet Sidibe, who is engaging, outgoing, and ten years older, and you're almost startled. She's not at all like Precious, but in her first performance she not only understands this character but knows how to make her attract the sympathy of her teacher, the social worker—and ourselves. I don't know how she does it, but there you are.

Predators ★ ★

R, 106 m., 2010

Adrien Brody (Royce), Topher Grace (Edwin), Danny Trejo (Cuchillo), Alice Braga (Isabelle), Walton Goggins (Stans), Oleg Taktarov (Nikolai), Laurence Fishburne (Noland). Directed by Nimrod Antal and produced by Elizabeth Avellan and John Davis. Screenplay by Alex Litvak and Michael Finch.

Predators may be the first film in history to open with a deus ex machina. Yes, the entire plot and all the human characters drop into the movie from the heavens. The last thing they remember is a blinding flash of light. Now they're in free fall, tumbling toward the surface, screaming, grabbing for rip cords on the parachutes they didn't know they had.

The first to land, with a mighty thump, is Royce (Adrien Brody). The others start dropping all around him. These people are savage professional killers from all over: a mercenary, a Japanese samurai, an Israeli markswoman, a mass murderer, an African warlord, and so on. How did they get in this thick jungle, and why?

They discover they're on another world: a perfectly terraformed world, it would seem. The gravity allows them to walk normally, and they can breathe the air and drink the water. Royce notices something odd: The sun never moves. They arrive in a clear space and realize there are three or four moons in the sky, which are either very close or very huge, since their discs are many times that of our moon.

Now hold on here. As every science-fiction fan knows, if a planet always presents the same face to its sun, and is ringed by bodies apparently larger than it is, it will quickly become molten lava pulled hither and yon by vast tidal forces. But never mind. After the visitors are attacked by humongous beasts of prey, Royce figures it out: They're in a game preserve. He figures out a lot of things in the movie, which might have been more fun if he hadn't.

Who runs this game preserve, and why? If you recall the first *Predator* (1987), Arnold Schwarzenegger and other killers found themselves in the Amazon fighting an unseen predatory alien. Has that race of aliens imported humans to its solar system for a rematch? Is it a wise use of resources to transport several mammals untold light-years through space just so you can watch them getting their asses predatored?

No time to think about them. Here come some really vicious warthog-looking creatures. They weigh about half a ton apiece, move as fast as lions, and have so many horns and spikes sticking out of them that fornicating must have to be a sometime thing.

Look at an illustration of one of these fearsome beasts. Can you spot the design flaw? Its horns or fangs, whatever they are, extend too far in front of its mouth! After they kill their prey, how do they eat it? I thought, maybe they lie on their backs and shovel the food in with their feet. But no, how's that gonna work with all the spikes on their backs?

Never mind. The movie is mostly about our nasty heroes being attacked by terrifying antagonists in incomprehensible muddles of lightning-fast special effects. It lacks the quiet suspense of the first *Predator*, and please don't even mention the *Alien vs. Predator* pictures, which lacked the subtlety of *Mothra vs. Godzilla*. The resident aliens view everything in POV shots through what looks like a video monitor with a haywire color adjustment, and they appear in ways I will not go into.

There are always a few characters who get killed in attack movies like this. What confuses me is why they don't all get killed. Look at the illustration again. If that thing hit you at 20 mph and got you down on the ground and all you could do was stab it with your knife, would you expect to have dialogue later in the movie?

There is, of course, one woman in the film, Isabelle (Alice Braga). She and Royce slowly bond, and eventually at the end . . . but no, I can't tell you if they kiss. That would be a spoiler. One thing you know for sure: The alien warthogs don't spend a lot of time frenching.

Prince of Persia: The Sands of Time ★ ★

PG-13, 116 m., 2010

Jake Gyllenhaal (Dastan), Gemma Arterton (Tamina), Ben Kingsley (Nizam), Alfred Molina (Sheikh Amar), Steve Toussaint (Seso), Toby Kebbell (Garsiv), Richard Coyle (Tus), Ronald Pickup (King Sharaman). Directed by Mike Newell and produced by Jerry Bruckheimer. Screenplay by Boaz Yakin, Doug Miro, and Carlo Bernard, based on the video game by Jordan Mechner.

Prince of Persia: The Sands of Time is a children's story beefed up to appeal to young teens. It's based on a video game, but don't make me play it, let me guess: The push-button magic dagger is used in the game to let you rewind and try something again, right? Since anything in the story (any death, for example) can be reversed, the stakes are several degrees below urgent. And there's a romance in which the boy and girl spend endless moments about to kiss for every nanosecond they actually do. If I were the Prince of Persia, I'd push the button, go back in time, and plant a wet one on Tamina's luscious lips.

The movie is set in ancient Persia, which is now named Iran. This is a land with truly astonishing landscapes: deserts, canyons, craggy monument valleys, and a mountain range that resembles the Himalayas. Fair enough, since Persia reaches "from the steppes of China to the shores of the Mediterranean," but even more impressive since it's all within a day's journey of the capital city.

That city, whose name escapes me, is ruled by the noble King Sharaman (Ronald Pickup). One day in the marketplace he sees a brave young urchin defend a boy being beaten and escape pursuit by running across rooftops. This is Dastan, who will grow up to be played by Jake Gyllenhaal. He's an orphan; his birth parents are two movies, the Douglas Fairbanks (1924) and Michael Powell (1940) versions of *The Thief of Bagdad*.

Dastan is adopted by the king and raised with two brothers, Garsiv (Toby Kebbell) and Tus (Richard Coyle). The names of the movie's characters seem to have been created by a random-word generator. The king has a brother named Nizam (Ben Kingsley), first seen in a sinister close-up that could be subtitled, "I will turn out to be the villain." He has a Vandyke beard and eyes that glower smolderingly.

Dastan is good at running on rooftops. He can also leap from back to back in a herd of horses, jump across mighty distances, climb like a monkey, and spin like a top. This is all achieved with special effects, ramped up just fast enough to make them totally unbelievable. Fairbanks has a 1924 scene where he hops from one giant pot to another. He did it in real time, with little trampolines hidden in the pots, and six pots in that movie are worth the whole kitchen in this one.

Anyway, the evil Nizam insists that the Persian army invade the peaceful city of Alamut. This is a beautiful city surrounding a towering castle. King Sharaman has ordered the city not be sacked, but nooo. Nizam has secret information that Alamut is manufacturing weapons of mass destruction for Persia's enemies. Poor Dick Cheney. He can't even go to a Disney swashbuckler without running into finger wagging.

Anyway, Dastan climbs the city walls, pours flaming oil on its guards, etc., and then encounters the beautiful Princess Tamina (Gemma Arterton). She possesses the Dagger of Time, which is an honest-to-God WMD, since if it's switched on too long, all the sands of time will run out, and it's back to the Big Bang.

The plot involves portentous dialogue ("The only way to stop this Armageddon is for us to take the Dagger to the Secret Guardian Temple"), which separates tiresome CGI sequences in which clashing warriors do battle in shots so brief we can see people getting whacked, but have no conception of actual physical space. Of course, this must all lead to Tamina and Dastan fleeing from the evil Nizam, who has framed the lad for regicide.

Their flight brings them under the sway of the film's obligatory Comic Supporting Character, Sheikh Amar (Alfred Molina), a con man who runs rigged ostrich races, and those who have tried to fix an ostrich race will know that the bloody ostriches are impossible to reason with. My interest perked up with the prospect that Dastan and Tamina might try to flee by ostrich-back, but no luck. Imagine the scene! Gemma in foreground, Jake right behind her, compressed by telephoto, jerking up and down at terrific speed while sand dunes whiz past on the green screen in the background.

The irritating thing about special effects is that *anything* can happen, and often you can't tell what the hell it is. Dastan, for example, seems to fall into a vast sinkhole as the sand is sucked from beneath him at dizzying speed. Exactly how he is saved of this predicament isn't exactly clear.

Other key events are obscure. It looked to me as if Garsiv was killed on two occasions, yet is around for the end of the movie, and I don't think the Dagger of Time was involved in either of them. The workings of the Dagger are in any event somewhat murky; when you push the button in its base, it makes you light up like Sylvester the Puddy Cat sticking a paw in an electric socket, and everyone fast-reverses into their starting positions. How do people in movies always know how to do this stuff without practice?

The two leads are not inspired. Jake Gyllenhaal could make the cover of a muscle mag, but he plays Dastan as if harboring Spider-Man's doubts and insecurities. I recall Gemma Arterton as resembling a gorgeous still photo in a cosmetics ad. If the two actors had found more energy and wit in their roles (if they'd ramped up to the Alfred Molina level, say), that would have been welcome. Oh, almost forgot: Molina's ostrich racer is outraged at government taxes. If big government can't leave a man alone to race his ostriches, they're all Alamutist sympathizers.

The Princess and the Frog ★ ★ ★

G, 95 m., 2009

With the voices of: Anika Noni Rose (Tiana), Bruno Campos (Prince Naveen), Keith David (Dr. Facilier), Michael-Leon Wooley (Louis), Jennifer Cody (Charlotte), Jim Cummings (Ray), Peter Bartlett (Lawrence), Jenifer Lewis (Mama

Odie), Oprah Winfrey (Eudora, Tiana's Mother), Terrence Howard (James, Tiana's Father), John Goodman ("Big Daddy" La Bouff). Directed by John Musker and Ron Clements and produced by Peter Del Vecho. Screenplay by Musker, Clements, and Rob Edwards.

The opening scenes of Disney's *Princess and the Frog* are like a cool shower after a long and sweaty day. This is what classic animation was like! No 3-D! No glasses! No extra ticket charge! No frantic frenzies of meaningless action! And . . . good gravy! A story! Characters! A plot! It's set in a particular time and place! And it uses (calm me down here) lovingly hand-drawn animation that proceeds at a human pace, instead of racing with odd smoothness. I'm just gonna stand here and let it pour over me.

The movie, which is sweet and entertaining, doesn't quite live up to those opening scenes. But it's a demonstration that the Walt Disney Studios still shelters animators who know *how* to make a movie like that, in an age when too many animated films are like fast food after memories of Mom's pot roast. My guess is that afterward the poor kids won't feel quite so battered by input overload. It dances on the screen and doesn't come into the audience and shake you to make you like it.

The story is set mostly in an African-American community in New Orleans, America's most piquant city, before and after World War I. We meet a young girl named Tiana, who is cherished by her mother Eudora (voice by Oprah Winfrey) and father James (Terrence Howard). Her mom is a seamstress, her dad a hardworking restaurant owner who stirs up a mighty gumbo. He goes off to the army and . . . doesn't return. For Tiana as an adult (Anika Noni Rose), life is a struggle, but she holds fast to her dream of opening a restaurant and serving up her dad's gumbo (with just a soupçon more red sauce).

This is all shown in flowing, atmospheric animation and acted with fetching voices, but the songs by Randy Newman are—I dunno, do you think he's getting sort of Randy Newmaned out? And the absence of a couple of terrific musical numbers is noticeable, I think, although younger viewers will probably be drawn into the story.

SPOILER WARNING: You've heard it before. A princess kisses a frog, and it turns into her handsome Prince Charming. But what if instead *she* turns into a frog? That's what happens. So now Tiana and the visiting Prince Naveen of Malvonia (Bruno Campos) are both amphibians, although they retain, of course, all of their moral principles and do not perform that act of which frogs are more fond than anything apart from croaking and eating flies.

They're captives of a spell cast by the evil voodoo villain Dr. Facilier (Keith David). But life in the swamp is enlivened by two friends, Louis (Michael-Leon Wooley), an alligator who plays jazz saxophone, and Ray (Jim Cummings), a firefly who fills the Jiminy Cricket slot. They seek the occult Mama Odie (Jenifer Lewis), who may have the power to offset Facilier, and whether Tiana and Prince Naveen are restored and settle down to happy lives of slurping gumbo, I will leave for you to discover.

It is notable that this is Disney's first animated feature since *Song of the South* (1946) to feature African-American characters, and if the studio really never is going to release that film on DVD, which seems more innocent by the day, perhaps they could have lifted "Zip-a-Dee-Do-Dah" from it and plugged it in here. Although the principal characters are all black (other than the rich man Big Daddy and the prince, who is of undetermined race), race is not an issue here because Disney adroitly sidesteps all the realities of being a poor girl in New Orleans in the early 1920s. And just as well, I suppose.

The Princess and the Frog inspires memories of Disney's Golden Age that it doesn't quite live up to, as I've said, but it's spritely and high-spirited and will allow kids to enjoy it without visually assaulting them.

Princess Kaiulani ★ ★ ½

PG, 97 m., 2010

Q'orianka Kilcher (Princess Ka'iulani), Barry Pepper (Thurston), Will Patton (Sanford Dole), Shaun Evans (Clive Davies), Jimmy Yuill (Archie), Julian Glover (Theo Davies). Directed by Marc Forby and produced by Forby, Lauri Apelian, Ricardo S. Galindez, Nigel Thomas, and Roy Tijoe. Screenplay by Forby.

In the late nineteenth century, American corporations backed by U.S. Marines overthrew the legitimate monarchy of Hawaii. One of the conspirators was Sanford B. Dole, of pineapple fame.

Princess Ka'iulani, niece of King David Kalakaua, was in England at the time, getting a thorough Victorian education. After Kalakaua's death, Queen Lydia Lili'uokalani became his successor to the throne and resisted the outsiders. Then Ka'iulani returned and took up the doomed struggle.

Princess Ka'iulani (Q'orianka Kilcher) is much remembered in Hawaii, much forgotten on the mainland, and the subject of this interesting but creaky biopic. She was the child of a Hawaiian mother who died when she was young, and a Scottish father, Archibald Cleghorn (Jimmy Yuill). It was he who feared his young daughter's life was in danger from the Americans, and returned her to Britain and to the household of his friend Theo Davies (Julian Glover). In the United Kingdom she attended a rigorous boarding school, where there was some rudeness but the children of foreign royalty were not unknown. And she fell in love with Davies's son, Clive (Shaun Evans).

News of the uprising was withheld from her, but when she learned, she blamed the Davies family for concealing telegrams, hurried home, and moved into the Iolani Palace. (The film opens with her throwing a switch to illuminate the place and bring electricity to Honolulu; it had electric lighting before the White House.)

The real Iolani Palace, usually closed to the public but handsomely maintained, was made available to the filmmakers, and is one of a wealth of Hawaiian locations that make the film effortlessly authentic. Indeed, in production values the film is flawless. But it plays too sedately, moves too slowly, and contemplates the occupation of a sovereign kingdom with a curious impassivity.

The presence of Q'orianka Kilcher in the lead is a suggestion of what might have been. You may recall her as the tall, grave fourteen-year-old playing the somewhat similar historical figure Pocahontas in Terrence Malick's *The New World* (2005). In both films a native princess sees her nation conquered by Europeans and is removed to England, educated, and falls in love with a Brit. The difference is that Malick finds mystery, poetry, and beauty in his film, and *Princess Kaiulani* plays more like a history lesson.

When the film was premiered at the 2009 Hawaiian Film Festival, there was much complaint about its original title, *The Barbarian Princess*. For so she was called, just as Pocahontas was sometimes described as a savage. She seems to have been a woman of uncommon intelligence and strength of will, and so loyal to her land that in the film she breaks off with Clive Davies and chooses Hawaii over love.

Princess Kaiulani shows the European business community conspiring against King David's efforts to secure Hawaiians' title to their own land, and indeed the rights were stripped away and the Doles and other old white families converted much of Hawaii into their own private plantation. The film's treatment of these results seems somewhat muted; more drama would have been welcome.

Q'orianka Kilcher seems an intriguing Ka'iulani, as she was a Pocahontas. Of Peruvian and German descent, she was raised in Hawaii, was a hula dancer by five and a student of classical voice at the University of Hawaii by six. Unlike a standard young starlet, she evokes great depth and sympathy in her role, and seems to have created Ka'iulani from the inside out. That she has admired the character since childhood is a help. It's a shame more help didn't come from greater passion in the filmmaking.

The Princess of Montpensier ★ ★ ★ ½

NO MPAA RATING, 139 m., 2011

Melanie Thierry (Princess Marie), Lambert Wilson (Comte de Chabannes), Gregoire Leprince-Ringuet (Prince de Montpensier), Gaspard Ulliel (Henri de Guise), Raphael Personnaz (Duc d'Anjou), Judith Chemla (Catherine de Guise), Philippe Magnan (Marquis de Mezieres), Michel Vuillermoz (Duke of Montpensier). Directed by Bertrand Tavernier and produced by Frederic Bourboulon, Laurent Brochand, and Eric Heumann. Screenplay by Tavernier, Jean Cosmos, and Francois-Olivier Rousseau.

The Princess of Montpensier enters the field of the swashbuckling romance so littered with our memories of other films, and conquers it with a startling freshness. So well does Bertrand Tavernier suggest the period that he evokes tangible physical qualities: the warmth of flesh, the coldness of steel, the green fields on which men fight and die. This world of France in 1562 might be idyllic, if it were not being torn by the need of Catholics and Protestants to kill one another.

We meet a fierce soldier, the Count of Chabannes (Lambert Wilson), who after unknowingly plunging his blade into the belly of a pregnant woman decides he is disgusted by war. That places him outside the pale, a traitor to one side, a deserter to the other. He's redeemed by an affectionate student and becomes the tutor to the beautiful Marie de Mezieres (Melanie Thierry), a rich and famous beauty who in short time is forced into an arranged marriage with the callow Philippe de Montpensier (Gregoire Leprince-Ringuet). The negotiations between the fathers of these two young people are a straightforward business contract involving the transfer of lands, with not the slightest thought of Marie's desires.

On her part, she's indifferent to Philippe, but drawn passionately to Henri de Guise (Gaspard Ulliel), a rugged and arrogant man who proudly displays his scarred face. The de Guise family is also powerful and also desires Marie; a cardinal in their family represents the only appearance of religion in this film, and he is a politician, not a man of prayer. Ironic that although France is in a civil war over religion, it comes down to tribes rather than theology.

Establishing the major players and some minor ones slightly impedes the early scenes, but soon the characters are vivid and the intrigue begins. It centers on Marie, and on Melanie Thierry, who looks a decade younger than her thirty years, a classic heroine with a fresh, proud beauty. She is duly handed over to the attentions of her husband for a humiliating wedding night attended by witnesses to testify that the sheet is bloody, and then her husband hurries off to a new war and she responds quickly to the tutoring of Chabannes.

He falls in love with her and admits it, although neither is moved to act on the fact. Henri de Guise comes back into her life, and so does the powerful Duc d'Anjou (Raphael Personnaz). She makes it clear she's drawn to both. Her husband becomes a monster of jealousy, and one night during a masked ball she unwisely confides in the wrong masked figure. Of course, this is 1562, and Marie hasn't seen many movies demonstrating how hazardous it is to confide in anyone at a masked ball without being absolutely sure who is behind the mask.

Tavernier has an uncanny success in showing the life within a medieval castle, which provides staircases, nooks, crannies, closets, corners, and retreats for intrigues. One night there is a compelling set piece during which Chabannes the tutor tries to prevent a disastrous discovery. We realize that for all the massive size of a medieval castle, its inhabitants lived more or less in earshot of footfalls and passion.

Bertrand Tavernier's career has been a celebration of many kinds of films. He began in 1974 with *The Clockmaker of St. Paul*, one of the best films ever made from a Simenon novel, and has made films about war (*Coup de Torchon*), jazz (*'Round Midnight*), biography (*Daddy Nostalgia* with Dirk Bogarde), an old artist (*A Sunday in the Country*), young cops (*L.627*), and French filmmaking under the Nazis (*Safe Conduct*). He is one of the most prolific and generous of directors, and there is no word that summarizes a Tavernier film except, usually, masterful.

All the dramatic mechanism he sets in motion here hinges on the reality that the princess of Montpensier is, at the same time, a possession and an object of desire. The moment she is officially sold off into marriage, powerful men feel free to disregard that contract, and so does she. To our modern eyes her natural romantic partner should be her tutor, but neither Marie nor Chabannes, who buy into the norms of their world, thinks of acting on that. There are only three possible partners in her constrained world, and she prefers the two who are more desirable than her husband.

Princess Marie becomes quite a sympathetic figure in the story: smart, yearning for knowledge, resentful that she has no personal choice, not valued for her mind, with no sympathy even from her own mother. Tavernier takes leave of her in a beautiful shot where she is alone. All alone. As all rich women then were, unlike the lucky poor.

A Prophet ★ ★ ★ ★

R, 154 m., 2010

Tahar Rahim (Malik el Djebena), Niels Arestrup (Cesar Luciani), Adel Bencherif (Ryad), Reda Kateb (Jordi le Gitan), Hichem Yacoubi (Reyeb), Jean-Philippe Ricci (Vettorri). Directed by Jacques Audiard and produced by Lauranne Bourrachot, Martine Cassinelli, and Marco Cherqui. Screenplay by Audiard and Thomas Bidegain.

There is a murder at the center of Jacques Audiard's *A Prophet* that is unlike most murders I've seen in films. It's clumsy, messy, and brutal, and leaves the killer shaking. Whether he shakes with grief, relief, or anger we cannot say. That's the key to this film. We look, we see, but we cannot say. It often must be that way when we witness violence. Those capable of murdering live in another country.

The movie follows the life of Malik, a young Frenchman of Arab descent, who enters prison as a naive outsider and is shaped into an evil adult criminal. He wasn't born evil; he was born a shy, passive loser. Prison made him all that he can be. He seems an unlikely protagonist for a prison movie. Played by Tahar Rahim, he's skinny, insecure, trying to raise a mustache. He's behind bars for unclear reasons; he says he's innocent, although it doesn't matter. Prison efficiently strips him of privacy and self-respect and serves him over to the Corsican gang that controls everything behind bars through violence and bribes.

This gang is run by Cesar Luciani (Niels Arestrup), a man who has the presence of Don Corleone but colder eyes. He walks everywhere followed by bodyguards. His spies see all that happens. He gives an order, and it is followed out. He makes it his business to intimidate the new man, who is useful because he provides entrée into the wing housing the Arabic prisoners.

There is a prisoner there (Hichem Yacoubi) whom Cesar wants killed. This man must not live to testify. Malik is instructed by Cesar's lieutenant how to conceal a razor blade in his mouth and slit the man's throat. It is very simple. If Malik doesn't do this, he will die. When Malik seeks help from the warden, he quickly sees that Cesar is right: Kill or die.

Well, it's an unforgiving Darwinian choice. Malik has never killed. He makes a botch of it. There is a horrible struggle. Everything is covered in blood. Malik escapes only because Cesar has had the wing cleared out. It is a baptism. Now that he has killed, he is not a "man," but he is a survivor who will do what is necessary.

In the years to come, Malik undergoes a transformation. He's a quick learner. Outside society never got a chance to fashion him. Now he learns how to observe, how to measure motives, how to devise strategy, how to rise. He also learns to read, although that's more important for his self-confidence than for anything he learns. It's not as if he becomes Jean Genet. He is an outsider to the Corsicans, a "dirty Arab," but there is no purpose in resenting that. He keeps his own counsel.

Eventually he becomes Cesar's most trusted confidant, perhaps because he is Arab, cannot band with the other Arabs, and has no other place to turn. Prisoners sometimes are given a few days' leave. He performs a task for Cesar on the outside, and it also allows him to better position himself. *A Prophet* becomes a young man's bleak, remorseless coming-of-age story.

The best performance in the film is by Niels Arestrup, as Cesar Luciani. You may remember Aerstrup from Audiard's *The Beat That My Heart Skipped* (2005), where he played a seedy but confident father who psychically overshadows his son. That one was very loosely inspired by James Toback's *Fingers*, with Harvey Keitel as the vulnerable son of a gangster.

Aerstrup sees but does not want to be perceived. He keeps his own deep counsel. He rules by passive aggression. He has held absolute power over life and death for so long that he acts as if it's innate. Most of his big moments involve silent reaction shots: decisions and realizations.

The newcomer Tahar Rahim is an enigma. What is he thinking? I believe that's the quality Jacques Audiard wants. He's a newly poured man, and when the mold sets, it happens inside. He learns from Cesar to reveal nothing. Many movies and actors are too ready to inform us what everyone is thinking, and why. It's more absorbing for us to read significance from mystery. An actor who reveals nothing, like Alain Delon in Melville's *Le Samourai,* is fascinating.

But what does go on inside Malik? That's the frightening part. We can only judge by what he does. Now he is prepared to kill. If we must be killed, don't we all rather hope it will be by someone for whom the act has meaning? For whom our life has importance? Malik was such a man once, but that ended in the bloody mess of the prison cell. Now prison has prepared him to return to the streets.

Note: A Prophet *swept all major categories in this year's Cesar Awards, the "French Oscars." It won the Grand Jury Prize at Cannes 2009.*

The Proposal ★ ★ ★

PG-13, 107 m., 2009

Sandra Bullock (Margaret Tate), Ryan Reynolds (Andrew Paxton), Mary Steenburgen (Grace Paxton), Craig T. Nelson (Joe Paxton), Betty White (Grandma Annie), Denis O'Hare (Mr. Gilbertson), Malin Akerman (Gertrude), Oscar Nuñez (Ramone). Directed by Anne Fletcher and produced by David Hoberman and Todd Lieberman. Screenplay by Pete Chiarelli.

The Proposal is a movie about a couple who start out hating each other and end up liking each other. It's a funny thing about that. I started out hating the movie and ended up liking it.

It opens on a rather cheerless note, as the portrait of Margaret (Sandra Bullock), a tyrannical book editor, and Andrew (Ryan Reynolds), her long-suffering assistant. Known on office instant messages as The Witch, she terrorizes underlings, fires the man who wants her job, and orders Andrew to marry her.

How that happens is, she's a Canadian in danger of being deported, she imperiously ignored the law, and now she figures if she gets married she'll get her green card. They blackmail each other in their prenuptial hostage negotiations and fly off to Sitka, Alaska, to meet his folks. Sitka turns out to be a charming waterfront town, filled with chic little shops like the Fudgery, no fast-food stores or franchise chains, and a waterfront that looks less like a working fishing harbor than a tourist resort. Perhaps that's because the movie was filmed not in Alaska, but in Massachusetts and Rhode Island. Alaska might have been too real for this fantasy.

So I was sitting there cringing, knowing with uncanny certainty where the story was going. No movie begins with scenes of a man and a woman who are utterly incompatible unless it ends with them in love, unless perhaps it might be one about Hitler and Eleanor Roosevelt. They will fly to Alaska, she will be charmed by his family, she will be moved by the community spirit, she will love the landscape after the skyscraper towers of Manhattan, and they will have misadventures, probably involving unintended nudity and someone falling off a boat. So it is written.

But slowly, reluctantly, disbelievingly, they will start to warm up to each other. And it was about at that point when reluctantly, disbelievingly, I began to warm up to them. Bullock is a likable actress in the right roles, which she has been avoiding frequently since *Speed 2: Cruise Control* (1997), which I liked more than she did. She is likable here because she doesn't overdo it and is convincing when she confesses that she has warmed to his family's embrace—and who would not, since Andrew's mother is the merry Mary Steenburgen and his grandmother is the unsinkable Betty White. His father, Craig T. Nelson, is not quite so embraceable, but only because he is protective.

The key scene involves Steenburgen and White fitting Granny Annie's wedding dress for Bullock, and the presentation of a family heirloom. I don't care how much of a witch a woman is, when she sees herself in the mirror wearing her grandmother-in-law's gown, she's going to cave in. For that matter, Bullock was never that convincing as the office witch; she couldn't have touched Meryl Streep's work in *The Devil Wears Prada.*

The Proposal is much enhanced by all of the supporting performances. Betty White, at eighty-seven, makes her character eighty-nine and performs a Native American sunrise ceremony beside a campfire in the forest, which is not easy, especially in the Alaskan summer when the sun hardly sets. And look for a character named Ramone (Oscar Nuñez), who will remind you of an element in *Local Hero*.

The Proposal recycles a plot that was already old when Tracy and Hepburn were trying it out. You see it coming from a great distance away. As it draws closer, you don't duck out of the way because it is so cheerfully done you don't mind being hit by it.

The Providence Effect ★ ★ ★

PG, 92 m., 2009

With Paul Adams III, Jeanette DiBella, John W. Fountain. A documentary produced and directed by Rollin Binzer.

One of the great success stories in American education is Providence St. Mel Catholic High School, at 119 S. Central Park on Chicago's West Side. This is a far from advantaged area where gangs and drugs are realities, and yet the school reports that for twenty-nine straight years, it has placed 100 percent of its graduates in colleges. Of course, this figure benefits from the school's policy of expelling troublemakers, but it also reflects its commitment to providing deserving students with a quality education.

The Providence Effect, a new documentary, charts the school's growth from a time when an existing Catholic high school was scheduled for closure by the Archdiocese of Chicago. A remarkable educator named Paul J. Adams III began at the school as a counselor, was named principal, and raised funds to keep the school open as a private academy dedicated to college prep. It boasts that in the most recent seven years, half its students have gone to first-tier, even Big Ten and Ivy League, schools.

About five years ago, Providence St. Mel opened Providence Englewood Charter School, starting at kindergarten to begin on students at the dawn of their school days. The results are impressive. They draw from the same neighborhood pool. Their test scores are above the state average.

A documentary about this achievement is certainly appropriate. The new film *The Providence Effect* is impressive, although not quite the film it could have been. It asks few hard questions. It's concerned primarily with charting the school's achievements through a series of testimonials from current and former teachers, community leaders, and national figures (Ronald Reagan visited the school twice). These witnesses are impressive, but the film's lack of traditional documentary footage leads to a certain beneficent monotony. The doc observes but doesn't probe.

How do the students survive the toxic neighborhood in their personal lives? What is the process by which a misbehaving or counterproductive child can be expelled? What is the selection process? How are non-Catholic students regarded? How do teacher salaries rank? Do gangs take a negative interest in the school or its children?

The film's powerful message is that inner-city black and Hispanic children are fully capable of competing with anyone on an intellectual level. But potential and practice are two different things. What kinds of homes do the students come from? Presumably their parents are highly motivated on their behalf and maintain family discipline. Can the process of becoming a Providence St. Mel success story be said to begin at birth?

What prevents the public school system from producing results such as these? The film suggests that public schools spend too many resources on administration and bureaucracy, and not enough on education itself. Also, of course, they have to take all applicants—those suited for school and those already temperamentally not suited. Guns and drugs are a problem. Self-image and school spirit are also. If there's one thing we learn for sure about Prov-St. Mel's in this film, it's that the students and teachers are united in a fierce belief in the school.

Public Enemies ★ ★ ★ ½

R, 140 m., 2009

Johnny Depp (John Dillinger), Christian Bale (Melvin Purvis), Marion Cotillard (Billie Frechette), Billy Crudup (J. Edgar Hoover), Stephen Dorff (Homer Van Meter), Stephen Lang (Charles Winstead), Branka Katic (Anna Sage). Directed by Michael Mann and produced by Mann and Kevin Misher. Screenplay by Mann, Ronan Bennett, and Ann Biderman, based on the book *Public Enemies: America's*

Greatest Crime Wave and the Birth of the FBI, 1933–34 by Bryan Burrough.

"I rob banks," John Dillinger would sometimes say by way of introduction. It was the simple truth. That was what he did. For the thirteen months between the day he escaped from prison and the night he lay dying in an alley, he robbed banks. It was his lifetime. Michael Mann's *Public Enemies* accepts that stark fact and refuses any temptation to soften it. Dillinger was not a nice man.

Here is a film that shrugs off the way we depend on myth to sentimentalize our outlaws. There is no interest here about John Dillinger's childhood, his psychology, his sexuality, his famous charm, his Robin Hood legend. He liked sex, but not as much as robbing banks. "He robbed the bankers but let the customers keep their own money." But whose money was in the banks? He kids around with reporters and lawmen, but that was business. He doesn't kid around with the members of his gang. He might have made a very good military leader.

Johnny Depp and Michael Mann show us that we didn't know all about Dillinger. We only thought we did. Here is an efficient, disciplined, bold, violent man, driven by compulsions the film wisely declines to explain. His gang members loved the money they were making. Dillinger loved planning the next job. He had no exit strategy or retirement plans.

Dillinger saw a woman he liked, Billie Frechette, played by Marion Cotillard, and courted her, after his fashion. That is, he took her out at night and bought her a fur coat, as he had seen done in the movies; he had no real adult experience before prison. They had sex, but the movie is not much interested. It is all about his vow to show up for her, to protect her. Against what? Against the danger of being his girl. He allows himself a tiny smile when he gives her the coat, and it is the only vulnerability he shows in the movie.

This is a very disciplined film. You might not think it was possible to make a film about the most famous outlaw of the 1930s without clichés and "star chemistry" and a film-class screenplay structure, but Mann does it. He is particular about the way he presents Dillinger and Billie. He sees him and her. Not them. They are never a couple. They are their needs. She needs to be protected because she is so vulnerable. He needs someone to protect in order to affirm his invincibility.

Dillinger hates the system, by which he means prisons, which hold people, banks, which hold money, and cops, who stand in his way. He probably hates the government, too, but he doesn't think that big. It is him against them, and the bastards will not, *cannot*, win. There's an extraordinary sequence, apparently based on fact, where Dillinger walks into the "Dillinger Bureau" of the Chicago Police Department and strolls around. Invincible. This is not ego. It is a spell he casts on himself.

The movie is well researched, based on the book by Bryan Burrough. It even bothers to try to discover Dillinger's speaking style. Depp looks a lot like him. Mann shot on location in the Crown Point jail, scene of the famous jailbreak with the fake gun. He shot in the Little Bohemia Lodge in the same room Dillinger used, and Depp is costumed in clothes to match those the bank robber left behind. Mann redressed Lincoln Avenue on either side of the Biograph Theater and laid streetcar tracks; I live a few blocks away and walked over to marvel at the detail. I saw more than you will; unlike some directors, he doesn't indulge in beauty shots to show off the art direction. It's just there.

This Johnny Depp performance is something else. For once, an actor playing a gangster does not seem to base his performance on movies he has seen. He starts cold. He plays Dillinger as a fact. My friend Jay Robert Nash says 1930s gangsters copied their styles from the way Hollywood depicted them; screenwriters like Ben Hecht taught them how they spoke. Dillinger was a big movie fan; on the last night of his life, he went to see Clark Gable playing a man a lot like him, but he didn't learn much. No wisecracks, no lingo. Just military precision and an edge of steel.

Christian Bale plays Melvin Purvis in a similar key. He lives to fight criminals. He is a cold realist. He admires his boss, J. Edgar Hoover, but Hoover is a romantic, dreaming of an FBI of clean-cut young accountants in suits and ties who would be a credit to their mothers. After the catastrophe at Little Bohemia (the FBI let Dillinger escape but killed three civilians), Purvis said to hell with it and made

J. Edgar import some lawmen from Arizona who had actually been in gunfights.

Mann is fearless with his research. If I mention the Lady in Red, Anna Sage (Branka Katic), who betrayed Dillinger outside the Biograph when the movie was over, how do you picture her? I do, too. We are wrong. In real life she was wearing a white blouse and an orange skirt, and she does in the movie. John Ford once said, "When the legend becomes fact, print the legend." This may be a case where he was right. Mann might have been wise to decide against the orange and white and just break down and give Anna Sage a red dress.

This is a very good film, with Depp and Bale performances of brutal clarity. I'm trying to understand why it is not quite a great film. I think it may be because it deprives me of some stubborn need for closure. His name was John Dillinger, and he robbed banks. But there had to be more to it than that, right? No, apparently not.

Push ★ ½

PG-13, 111 m., 2009

Chris Evans (Nick Gant), Dakota Fanning (Cassie Holmes), Camilla Belle (Kira Hudson), Cliff Curtis (Hook Waters), Djimon Hounsou (Henry Carver). Directed by Paul McGuigan and produced by Bruce Davey, William Vince, and Glenn Williamson. Screenplay by David Bourla.

Push has vibrant cinematography and decent acting, but I'm blasted if I know what it's about. Oh, I understand how the characters are paranormals, and how they're living in a present that was changed in the past, among enemies who are trying to change the future. I know they can read minds and use telekinesis to move things. I know they're a later generation of a Nazi experiment gone wrong, and the U.S. Army wants them for supersoldiers.

But that's all simply the usual horsefeathers to set up the situation. What are they *doing*? The answer to that involves a MacGuffin that would have Hitchcock harrumphing and telling Alma, "Oh, dear, they really have allowed themselves to get carried away." The MacGuffin is a briefcase. Yes, like in *Pulp Fiction*, but this time we know what's in it. It's a drug or serum that (is the only thing that?) kills paranormals. And the Division desperately wants it.

I'm not sure if the Division is part of the army or against it. I know that the telekinetic Nick (Chris Evans) is hiding from it in Hong Kong, and that the Pusher Cassie (Dakota Fanning) finds him there and brings along the briefcase (I think), and that she's followed there by most of the other characters, including Kira (Camilla Belle) and the Division agent Henry (Djimon Hounsou), who is another Pusher. Pushing involves not drugs but Pushing into other people's minds.

Kira is said to be the only paranormal who ever survived the deadly serum. But why did they want her dead? And who are they? And why is it so urgent to find the briefcase, which contains a syringe filled with the serum? This is an especially perplexing question for me because when the syringe was being filled to kill Kira, it looked to me like the label on the bottle of medicine clearly said "B-12," an excellent curative for anemia, which none of the characters has a problem with.

Apart from the MacGuffin, the movie is wall to wall with the Talking Killer Syndrome. Never have more people pointed more guns at more heads and said more words without anyone getting shot. Even if they are telekinetic and can point the guns without holding them.

All of these people, and others, speak very earnestly about Pushing, and they plot to outwit and outthink enemy Pushers, and clearly they are in a lot deeper than the audience is ever likely to get. It's like you're listening to shop talk in a shop that doesn't make anything you've ever seen.

Dakota Fanning's Cassie claims at one point that she's "older than twelve," but I dunno. Her mother would probably not have allowed her to fly off to Hong Kong alone, wearing a miniskirt and with purple streaks in her hair, but her mother has been killed, which is part of her problem. She does get a little drunk, which provides the movie's only laugh. Dakota's real mother probably told her, "Dakota, honey, why don't you take the role and get to see Hong Kong?" If that's what happened, she has the best reason of anybody for being in this movie.

Putty Hill ★ ★ ★ ★

NO MPAA RATING, 85 m., 2010

Sky Ferreira (Jenny), Zoe Vance (Cory's older sister), James Siebor Jr. (Cory's brother), Dustin Ray (Cory's best friend), Cody Ray (Dustin's brother), Charles Sauers (Tattooist), Cathy Evans (Cory's mom), India Streeter (Cory's girlfriend). Directed by Matthew Porterfield and produced by Eric Bannat, Steve Holmgren, Joyce Kim, and Jordan Mintzer. Screenplay by Mintzer and Porterfield.

In a way rarely seen, *Putty Hill* says all that can be said about a few days in the lives of its characters without seeming to say very much at all. It looks closely, burrows deep, considers the way in which lives have become pointless and death therefore less meaningful. It uses fairly radical filmmaking techniques to penetrate this truth and employs them so casually that they seem quite natural.

Matthew Porterfield's film, which takes place in a poor, wooded suburb of Baltimore, involves the death by overdose of a young man named Cory. We never meet him, although we see his portrait at a memorial service. The portrait tells us nothing: He projects no personality for the camera. His family and friends gather for his funeral, and we meet them in unstructured moments that tell us much about them but little about Cory.

The sad truth is, nobody knew Cory that well. There seems to have been little fierce love for him, even from his girlfriend (whose identity I only learned from the Web site), because little is made of her in the film as she sits quietly at a memorial gathering, impassive. Everyone knows he died from an overdose of heroin; no one is much surprised. One conversation is philosophical about how he "wasn't able to handle it."

Sometimes Porterfield's camera steps aside with some of the characters, and an off-screen voice (his?) is heard interviewing them. How old are you? Do you have brothers and sisters? Have you come back for the funeral? Have you attended many funerals? This voice seems to come from outside; it doesn't necessarily know who these characters are. The illusion is that the film is an ongoing narrative, and the interviewer is asking characters questions in order to clarify it for himself. Oddly, this seems perfectly natural.

So do all the actors. None of them, I learn, are professionals. Only the lead, Sky Ferreira, as Cory's sister Jenny, has any performing experience; she's a C&W singer. Few experienced actors could be this convincing, sound this authentic, seem to be there in the moment and not in any way acting. The dialogue isn't "written"; everything feels spontaneous, and it *just sounds right*, if you know what I mean.

Cory lived in a mostly lower-class white neighborhood, although at his memorial service there are a fair number of blacks, including his unidentified girlfriend, a woman possibly her mother, and others. His mourners mostly seem people without resources. The only occupation we see onscreen is held by a tattoo artist, who learned his trade while in prison for second-degree murder after revenging the rape of his wife ("and you can fill in the rest").

The film opens with contemplative shots inside a barren apartment we later learn was Cory's. It returns there at the end, as two of the mourners break in, sit in the dark and smoke, and are surprised he could live like that. Where is all his stuff? Probably sold to buy drugs, we suppose. Only a miserable life could have been lived in these rooms.

Casually, we meet Jenny as she arrives back in town. She hasn't seen Cory much in recent years. Doesn't miss home: "God, no." We follow four girlfriends as they hang out in an aboveground pool, go walking in a woods, meet two cops with rifles, watch TV, smoke, are bored. Later they go to a swimming hole but don't seem to have as much fun as they should. Notice the body language as a boy and girl lie on a rock, hands idly entwined; why do we feel eroticism is behind them and has been played out?

The most extraordinary scene is the memorial service. Everyone sits crowded together passing around pitchers of beer. A professional karaoke emcee has been employed along with his equipment. Family members sing standard songs—in Cory's memory, I guess. Some of the mourners say a few awkward words about the deceased. The karaoke man asks, "Does anyone else want to say something at this time?" His words "at this time," reflecting a dutiful solemnity, attempt to lend a sense of ceremony. Tributes are inarticulate and trail off into uncompleted thoughts.

No one seems to know exactly where Cory was or what he was doing. He made little impression. No one has learned anything from his death other than, perhaps, that it was to be expected. None of these people seem to have hopes and plans. A grandmother in "sheltered living" won't attend the funeral because "I simply can't take it. I want to remember things as they were."

Porterfield takes no cheap shots. He respects these people, their lives, their unspoken hopelessness. He doesn't go for dire colorful dialogue. He has no social commentary. *Putty Hill* makes no statement. It looks. It looks with as much perception and sympathy as it is possible for a film to look. It is surprisingly effective. I know what the budget was, but the figure is irrelevant. He had all the money he needed to make this film, his cinematography by Jeremy Saulnier always simply and evocatively visualizes; there is not one wrong shot. He has internalized his characters, knows them, understands them, shows them in just such a way that we can, too. If there had been a real Cory, this would be his memorial. Watching *Putty Hill,* we don't have to be told there are real Corys.

Q

Queen of the Sun: What Are the Bees Telling Us? ★ ★ ★

NO MPAA RATING, 82 m., 2011

A documentary directed by Taggart Siegel and produced by Siegel and Jon Betz.

In the Central Valley of California, there are five hundred thousand acres of almond trees. All almond trees. Nothing but almond trees. This is wrong. It is not natural. For these trees to bear almonds, they must be pollinated. But bees cannot live there, for there is nothing to sustain them when the trees are not in blossom. So hives containing millions of bees must be trucked more than a thousand miles, and then trucked back again.

Almonds are an agribusiness, run by corporations concerned only with their profits. In *Queen of the Sun*, you will learn that bees would prosper in the valley if there were year-round nectar for them. Would it kill a corporation to set aside some tracts of land for flowers and vegetables? Wouldn't that be easier and more pleasant than mile after mile and row after row of almond trees? Easier for the corporations and easier for the bees?

From time to time a bee truck will be involved in a highway accident. These aren't cute little yellow trucks, but long, flatbed trailer-trucks. The bees escape, motorists panic, the cops are called, TV helicopters circle, exterminators swarm in, and no one asks—why in the *hell* are we trucking bees across the country?

We need bees. If bees were to become extinct, animals would be threatened because so much plant life would cease to exist. On your table you would find limited choices and high prices. Yet when I mentioned this on my Facebook page, the first reader was prompt to comment: "I could care less they're creepy I'm allergic sooner they go the better."

There are other kinds of pollination, by the wind, by ladybugs, by the coats of animals, but bees do the heavy lifting. We have native bees, but our beloved honeybee was imported from Europe and thrived here until recently. Now they're suffering from colony collapse disorder, in which the beekeeper goes out in the morning and finds his bees are dead or have disappeared. One culprit seems to be the use of insecticides. Bees do a marvelously complex dance to communicate distance and direction to one another, and insecticides can apparently so confuse their navigation that they fly out one morning and forget the way home.

This I have learned from Taggart Siegel's *Queen of the Sun: What Are the Bees Telling Us?*, a remarkable documentary that's also one of the most beautiful nature films I've seen. In exquisite photography by Siegel, we go inside hives and follow bees as they sip on flowers. We also meet beekeepers in sylvan settings (Illinois, Germany, New Zealand, Italy) and even on rooftops in Manhattan. Yes, there's a movement supporting rooftop hives and gardens.

It's true that bees sting. A wasp sting is worse, but a bee sting is no fun. Since the bee dies, it's even less fun for the bee. The beekeepers in *Queen of the Sun* often wear masked hoods, gloves, and so forth, but just as often they seem unprotected. One guy with a luxuriant mustache even runs it across the backs of bees on a honeycomb and says, "They like it." He was a brave man who first found this out.

Honey and beeswax are valuable cash crops, but if bees didn't make honey or wax, they would still be essential to the environment. Bees moved around by truck pollinate $15 billion in crops every year, including your next honey almond. The value of the crops that are naturally pollinated by bees is incalculable.

Bees, the film argues, are part of an intricately choreographed ecosystem that we meddle with at our peril. The same almond trees that must be pollinated via interstate commerce have so depleted their soil that they must be fertilized by chemicals. Crops in rotation have worked for millions of years. Why do corporations poison the environment in order to produce inorganic produce?

Taggart Siegel is known to me as the director of an earlier documentary, *The Real Dirt on Farmer John*, about an eccentric but inspiring organic farmer in Illinois. I was looking for Farmer John and his Dr. Seuss hat in this film, but no luck. Siegel's message remains the same: We need to trust the earth to its own hands. The campaign to legalize beekeeping in Manhattan is an example. Are you putting out some flowers this summer, and maybe planting a garden? The bees are ready to pitch in for free.

Queen to Play ★ ★ ★ ½

NO MPAA RATING, 96 m., 2011

Sandrine Bonnaire (Helene), Kevin Kline (Dr. Kroger), Francis Renaud (Ange), Valerie Lagrange (Maria), Alexandra Gentil (Lisa), Jennifer Beals (American Woman), Dominic Gould (American Man). Directed by Caroline Bottaro and produced by Dominique Besnehard and Michel Feller. Screenplay by Caroline Bottaro and Caroline Maly, based on the novel *The Chess Player* by Bertina Henrichs.

I'd like to be playing a game of chess right now. I'd like to be sinking down into its cool depths and staring infinity in the face. I'd like to be competing with the player across the board from me in terms of implacable logic rather than motor skills and hand-eye coordination. When I play chess, I temporarily leave time.

I wonder if someone who doesn't love chess as much as I do would like *Queen to Play* as much as I did. Such a person could enjoy the transformation of a Corsican chambermaid into a strong chess player. It might be read as a story of female empowerment, of a woman asserting herself in her marriage and in her job. That would be fair enough.

But what I enjoyed was the way the film summons up the pure obsessive passion that chess stirs in some people. I never got to be very good (although I could maybe beat you), but I spent 1965 partly sidetracked by chess. I bought books. I played through classic games. I joined a chess club. I became a fan of queen-side strategies because I figured most of my opponents would know a lot more about kingside. These thoughts gave me much pleasure. Then I fell back into being what I really was, a mediocre patzer, because when you get to a certain point in chess you realize what a very long way you still have to go.

Queen to Play stars Sandrine Bonnaire as Helene, a hotel maid who cycles to work through the pastoral beauty of Corsica, where Napoleon no doubt played chess many years ago. She is married to Ange (Francis Renaud), who works at a boatyard. One morning at work she sees, through a filmy white curtain, two of the guests (Jennifer Beals and Dominic Gould) seated on the terrace and playing a game of chess that looks for all the world like foreplay. They seem so in love they're on their honeymoon—or cheating.

Something in the scene sends an arrow through her heart. Ange is an all-right guy—she thinks of him as handsome—but they no longer look at each other like that couple. For his birthday she buys him one of those computer chess game boards that will play against you if you can't find anyone else. "I don't play chess!" he says in astonishment. "Maybe you will learn," she says.

Awake in bed, her eyes still open, she knows he never will. In the middle of the night she takes out the game and reads the rules of chess. She finds it grand that the most powerful piece is the queen and holds it protectively.

Her other job is cleaning for an American, a widower named Dr. Kroger (Kevin Kline). She sees a fine wooden chess set on his shelf and asks him to play. Of course he checkmates her in a few moves. But they continue to play, he teaches her fundamentals, and it turns out that she's a natural. Some people are. Not people like me.

Where this all leads I will leave for you to enjoy. The film has some sly fun with the way chess consumes Helene's mind: Even bread crumbs begin to represent chess pieces for her. The floors in hotel lobbies are often black and white squares, and the tablecloths in Italian restaurants are red and white, and so on.

The most observant element of the movie is the way it handles the changing relationship between Helene and Dr. Kroger (with Kevin Kline speaking his own French). The story is based on the novel *The Chess Player* by Bertina Henrichs, and what it knows is the way the minds of two players can become engaged, not in a romantic way, but in the pure contact of their thinking. There are often no words in the mind during a chess game. Just rules of spatial relationships. It can get pretty intimate.

R

Rabbit Hole ★ ★ ★ ½

PG-13, 91 m., 2010

Nicole Kidman (Becca), Aaron Eckhart (Howie), Dianne Wiest (Nat), Tammy Blanchard (Izzy), Miles Teller (Jason), Giancarlo Esposito (Auggie), Jon Tenney (Rick), Sandra Oh (Gaby). Directed by John Cameron Mitchell and produced by Nicole Kidman, Gigi Pritzker, Per Saari, Leslie Urdang, and Dean Vanech. Screenplay by David Lindsay-Abaire, based on his play.

In *Rabbit Hole*, Becca and Howie are trying their best to get on with things. This is the tricky and very observant story of how a married couple is getting along eight months after their four-year-old ran out into the street and was struck dead by a car. They were leveled with grief. Their sex life stopped. They lived for a time in a daze, still surrounded in the house by the possessions of the child who no longer lived there.

But their lives are no longer a daily agony. Life is beginning again. *Rabbit Hole*, based on an acclaimed play by David Lindsay-Abaire, occupies the drafty spaces between the clichés of this situation. Becca (Nicole Kidman) and Howie (Aaron Eckhart) are rattling unhappily in an emotional emptiness. As a couple they attend a group therapy session for mourners, and Becca finds it's a room full of self-righteous therapy addicts while Howie finds a sympathetic ear from Gaby (Sandra Oh). And that's just what he finds—an ear. He finds someone who can hear him, and he feels he must have been speaking past Becca.

She is also not hearing her mother (Dianne Wiest) or a younger sister (Tammy Blanchard). She's not even on good terms with the dog. Sadness for her has settled into discontent. As a couple, they've reached that point of touchiness where nothing ever seems to be the right thing to say. What makes John Cameron Mitchell's film so interesting is that it bravely investigates what you say then.

I know all this sounds like a mournful dirge, but in fact *Rabbit Hole* is entertaining and surprisingly amusing, under the circumstances. The film is in a better state of mind than its characters. Its humor comes, as the best humor does, from an acute observation of human nature. We have known people something like this. We smile in recognition.

I was interested in Nicole Kidman's performance. I've always believed her to be talented, since all those years ago when she and Thandie Newton starred in the wonderful *Flirting* (1991). She seems to be two people: the glamorous star of *Moulin Rouge* and *Nine*, and the risky, daring actress in *Birth*, *The Hours*, and *Eyes Wide Shut*. Celebrity has clouded her image; if she were less glamorous, she would be more praised. Age will be only an asset to her.

Here she plays the character who changes: the balance point of the story. Aaron Eckhart's Howie has things that happen in his life, but he essentially remains the same man. Becca is troubled and disturbed beyond the depths created eight months ago, and *Rabbit Hole* is about how she's pulled by inner tides.

The wonder is that Mitchell and his screenplay see her confusion fairly clearly. Apart from anything else, *Rabbit Hole* is a technical challenge. It is simple enough to cover the events in the story, not so simple to modulate them for humor and even warmth. I knew what the movie would be about, but I was impressed by how it was about it.

Race to Witch Mountain ★ ★ ½

PG, 98 m., 2009

Dwayne Johnson (Jack Bruno), AnnaSophia Robb (Sara), Alexander Ludwig (Seth), Carla Gugino (Dr. Alex Friedman), Ciaran Hinds (Henry Burke), Garry Marshall (Dr. Donald Harlan), Tom Everett Scott (Matheson). Directed by Andy Fickman and produced by Andrew Gunn. Screenplay by Matt Lopez and Mark Bomback.

Before the sneak preview of *Race to Witch Mountain*, they had a little quiz show and gave away T-shirts. One question: "Who plays Jack Bruno?" Half the audience roared, "The Rock!" Not one lonely vote for Dwayne Johnson. The other famous movie "Rock" was born Roy Harold Scherer Jr. It's a name that stays in the mind.

I think Dwayne Johnson has a likable screen presence and is a good choice for an innocuous family entertainment like this, and also he once sent me some Hawaiian Macadamia Nut Brickle. I would have mailed it back because film critics are not supposed to accept gifts from movie stars, but I accidentally ate it first. What Johnson does here is provide a credible tough-guy action hero in a nonthreatening mode. He rules over chases, fights, explosions, and an Ooze Monster, yet never seems nasty, so the kids can feel safe around him.

Young audiences will like the kids in the movie, played by AnnaSophia Robb and Alexander Ludwig. And in using kids as the costars, the movie has its cake and eats it too, because Sara and Seth may look like they're fifteen or sixteen, but actually, you see, they're aliens whose flying saucer crash-landed and is being held at a secret government UFO facility inside Witch Mountain—so secret, the mountain is not shown on Google Maps. I suspected right away it was a mountain made for this movie because it is shaped like a sawed-off version of the mashed potato sculpture that Richard Dreyfuss kept sculpting in *Close Encounters of the Third Kind*—the one that resembled, you remember, the outcrop where the flying saucer landed.

Anyway, Dwayne Johnson plays a former driver for a Las Vegas mob boss who goes straight after he gets out of prison and starts driving a taxi. In his backseat one day, Sara and Seth materialize, explain they are aliens, and ask him to drive them to a remote desert location. They talk like an artificial intelligence program that got a D in English, although later they gradually start to sound more like Disney teenagers. They're later joined by Dr. Alex Friedman (Carla Gugino), an expert who was in Vegas lecturing to fanboys and girls at a combination UFO convention and costume party.

On their tail is a pursuit team of federal agents led by a hardnose named Burke (Ciaran Hinds). Burke moves in a caravan of three black SUVs with tinted glass, although when necessary he can materialize dozens of heavily armed SWAT team members. The chase leads deep into Witch Mountain, although not before the kids enter a buried chamber beneath a miner's shack and there obtain some kind of extraterrestrial cell phone extracted by Seth after plunging his arm up to the elbow into a pulsating mass of gelatinous goo.

Further details I will leave for your discovery. Since Seth and Sara only appropriated the bodies of human teenagers, I was left with a couple of questions. (1) Did they displace real teenagers, or only clone themselves? (2) They're cute, but what do they actually look like as aliens? Not quivering gobs of mucilaginous viscidity, I trust.

Radical Disciple: The Story of Father Pfleger ★ ★ ★

NO MPAA RATING, 58 m., 2009

Featuring Father Michael Pfleger, Carol Marin, Reverend Jeremiah Wright, and Tom Roeser. A documentary directed by Bob Hercules and produced by Hercules and Terrie Pickerill.

The most significant image of Fr. Michael Pfleger may be an old snapshot taken in the basement of his childhood home. It shows him in front of an altar made of orange crates and a white sheet, with candles and a Bible on it. My mother used to implore me to pray for a vocation to the priesthood. With little Mike Pfleger, there was never any doubt.

Michael Pfleger is well known in Chicago and elsewhere as an outspoken liberal and civil rights advocate. The Roman Catholic hierarchy doesn't concern itself with his politics but in the very public way he weaves them into his priesthood. He advocates politics in his sermons, shares his pulpit with others, leads demonstrations, speaks out. He invited the controversial Reverend Jeremiah Wright to speak from his altar before a reading by the poet Maya Angelou. At the height of the controversy in autumn 2008, he preached from Wright's altar.

Politics are not to be discussed from the pulpit. Nobody but a Catholic priest is to give a sermon. There is another problem. In the archdiocese of Chicago, a priest is assigned to a parish for six years, renewable once. Pfleger has been the pastor at St. Sabina's Church on Chicago's South Side since 1981. When he went there he was the youngest Catholic pastor in Chicago. Now he has been there longer than any other priest has served in one parish in America. That has made a series of cardinals increasingly unhappy. Now sixty, Pfleger seems to consider St. Sabina's a lifetime pastorate, and his congregation agrees. He walks a tightrope. "Somebody is in my church every Sunday waiting to trip me," he says in this doc.

Pfleger feels a deep affinity with his parishioners. When he first came to the parish, the church was desolate, run-down, sparsely attended, scheduled for closure. Soon it was packed for services. He led campaigns to restore the church. He rebuilt St. Michael's Academy, opened an employment resource center and social services center, and built residences for senior citizens.

The elder housing is on land once occupied by bars, porno stores, and hookers. Pfleger led campaigns against such stores, singling out merchants who sold alcohol or tobacco to minors, leading campaigns against billboards targeting teenagers, selling malt liquor and cigarettes. He was behind twenty Chicago billboards advising "Stop Listening to Trash," and attacking several rappers for their songs, often violent, that were disrespectful to women. He and the Reverend Jesse Jackson led demonstrations against gun shop owners selling to inner-city youths.

I have attended Mass at St. Sabina's three or four times. The South Side congregation is predominantly African-American, with a good sprinkling of other races. Father Pfleger is a gifted, impassioned orator. A black parishioner in this documentary says when she started going to the church she sat in the back and couldn't see him. By his voice, she thought he sounded black.

Pfleger was an outspoken supporter of Barack Obama. It's not that he told his congregation it would be a sin to vote against him, it's more that he considered it unthinkable. The archdiocese fears his sermons will threaten its tax-exempt status. He has been reprimanded more than once by the current Francis Cardinal George, who would dearly love to reassign him and once put him on leave for two weeks to "meditate and reconsider."

"He keeps a distance" from the official church, says *Sun-Times* columnist Carol Marin in the doc. She covered Pfleger for years as a TV reporter. He also doesn't bond readily with other priests. His focus is on his pastorate, not the church structure. However, Pleger's theology remains orthodox. He is arguably the most loved white man in the Chicago African-American community. Among mainstream Catholics, not so much. "He is a follower of Marx," says Tom Roeser, head of the Catholic Citizens of Illinois.

This documentary by Bob Hercules assembles archival and new footage and interviews into a comprehensive portrait. If you've heard of Father Pfleger and want to know more, here is the place. What seems to be lacking is a fuller examination of the church's differences with its priest. Archdiocesan spokesmen are judicial. Roeser seems more concerned with his politics than his theology. The most helpful view comes from Marin, who has covered him for thirty years, approves of him, but questions some of his choices and strategies.

One thing seems certain. More than most priests, he has brought material change to the community and transformed his parish. Some of his most passionate actions can be seen as practicing the teachings of Jesus quite literally.

Ramona and Beezus ★ ★ ★

G, 103 m., 2010

Joey King (Ramona), Selena Gomez (Beezus), John Corbett (Robert), Bridget Moynahan (Dorothy), Ginnifer Goodwin (Aunt Bea), Josh Duhamel (Hobart), Sandra Oh (Mrs. Meacham), Hutch Dano (Henry Huggins). Directed by Elizabeth Allen and produced by Denise Di Novi and Alison Greenspan. Screenplay by Laurie Craig and Nick Pustay, based on the novels by Beverly Cleary.

Kids who started reading anytime between the 1950s and today may know the books of Beverly Cleary, and at ninety-four she's still writing. Her books are set on Klickitat Street in Portland, Oregon, which is a real street not far from her childhood home; she must have filed it away for future reference.

On that street, those readers will know, live a nine-year-old girl named Ramona, her fifteen-year-old sister, Beatrice, their parents, Robert and Dorothy, their Aunt Bea, and

Ramona's friend Henry Huggins. Life has stayed lively for these characters for sixty years because of the inexhaustible Ramona (Joey King), who gets up to so much mischief that I think she must have indirectly inspired *Leave It to Beaver.*

It's not that Ramona is a bad girl. Winningly played by King, no one can look more innocent, and indeed even think herself more innocent. She's a virtuoso of the "But I was only standing here!" routine. Yet every day in an astonishing number of ways she disrupts her family more than that insurgent Labrador in *Marley and Me.* Considering that the story revolves around her father losing his job, I don't even want to think about the bills for property damage.

Without ever meaning to, of course, Ramona survives as chaos erupts around her, and in her daydreams she dangles by precarious handholds over a roaring gorge, for starters. She was causing mischief even when she was too young to know better: She saddled her sister Beatrice with the hated nickname Beezus.

This is a featherweight G-rated comedy of no consequence, except undoubtedly to kids about Ramona's age. Joey King and the Disney star Selena Gomez are both appealing, and the movie is wisely populated with grown-ups who are content to play straight men; Sandra Oh is a calming presence as Ramona's sensible teacher. The adults hint that normality exists in some form on Klickitat Street, and prevent the movie from going totally wacko and running off the rails.

It's surprising that these books by Beverly Cleary didn't inspire a TV series in the 1950s or 1960s like *Leave It to Beaver.* (Sarah Polley played Ramona in a 1980s PBS series.) Maybe they'd still work on Nickelodeon or the Disney Channel, but not these days on general TV. We no longer all watch the same TV shows, we are no longer as innocent, and the world of Klickitat is fading into timeless nostalgia. *Ramona and Beezus* is a sweet salute.

Rango ★ ★ ★ ★

PG 107 m., 2011

With the voices of: Johnny Depp (Rango), Isla Fisher (Beans), Abigail Breslin (Priscilla), Alfred Molina (Roadkill), Bill Nighy (Rattlesnake Jake), Harry Dean Stanton (Balthazar), Ray Winstone (Bad Bill), Timothy Olyphant (Spirit of the West), Ned Beatty (Mayor). Directed by Gore Verbinski and produced by Verbinski, John B. Carls, Graham King, and Jacqueline M. Lopez. Screenplay by Verbinski, John Logan, and James Ward Byrkit.

Rango is some kind of a miracle: an animated comedy for smart moviegoers, wonderfully made, great to look at, wickedly satirical, and (gasp!) filmed in glorious 2-D. Its brilliant colors and startling characters spring from the screen and remind us how very, very tired we are of simpleminded little characters bouncing around dimly in 3-D.

This is an inspired comic Western, deserving comparison with *Blazing Saddles*, from which it borrows a lot of farts. The more movies you've seen, the more you may like it; it even enlists big bats to lampoon the helicopter attack in *Apocalypse Now.* But let's say you haven't seen lots of movies. Let's say you're a kid. *Rango* may surprise you because it's an animated film that plays like a real movie and really gets you involved.

The title character is a lizard, voiced by Johnny Depp. Just an ordinary lizard. You know, green and with scales and pop eyes. But to this humble reptile comes the responsibility of bringing civilization to Dirt, an untamed Western town tormented by villains and running desperately short on water.

The other characters are outsize versions of basic Western types. There is, for example, Rattlesnake Jake (Bill Nighy), the bad man whose gang holds the town in a grip of terror. After Rango accidentally kills the eagle that has been dining on Dirt's citizens, he is persuaded by the mayor (Ned Beatty) to wear the sheriff's badge and bring law to Dirt. This involves tough talk in saloons, face-downs on Main Street, and a chase sequence between high canyon walls that's a nod in the direction of *Star Wars.*

Rango loves Westerns. Beneath its comic level is a sound foundation based on innumerable classic Westerns, in which (1) the new man arrives in town, (2) he confronts the local villain, and (3) he faces a test of his heroism.

Dirt has not only snakes but vultures to contend with, so Rango's hands are full. And then there's the matter of the water crisis. For some reason, reaching back to the ancient tradition of cartoons about people crawling through the desert, thirst is always a successful subject for animation.

The movie is wonderfully well drawn. The characters are wildly exaggerated, yes, but with an underlay of detail and loving care. The movie respects the tradition of painstakingly drawn animated classics, and does interesting things with space and perspective with its wild action sequences. The director is Gore Verbinski, who directed Johnny Depp in all three of the *Pirates of the Caribbean* movies. I think he benefits here from the clarity of animation drawings, as compared with the tendency of the *Pirates* to get lost in frenzies of CGI. Yes, animation is also computer-generated imagery these days, but it begins with artists and drawings and paintings and a clearly seen world.

The movie is rated PG. I hope it will be huge at the box office. Godard said that the way to criticize a movie is to make another movie. *Rango* is a splendid and great-looking entertainment with a strong story, limitless energy, and a first-rate voice cast, including Abigail Breslin, Ned Beatty as the disabled mayor, Alfred Molina, Bill Nighy, Stephen Root, Timothy Olyphant, Ray Winstone, and, yes, Harry Dean Stanton. No Sam Elliott, but you can't have everyone.

Here's what I hope: Lots of families will see this. They won't have a single thought about it being in 2-D. They will pay ordinary ticket prices. They will love the bright colors and magnificent use of space. In a few weeks, they'll go to a 3-D movie and wonder, why did we have to pay extra for this? ☞

Rare Exports: A Christmas Tale ★ ★ ★ ½

R, 84 m., 2010

Onni Tommila (Pietari), Jorma Tommila (Rauno), Per Christian Ellefsen (Riley), Tommi Korpela (Aimo), Rauno Juvonen (Piiparinen), Ilmari Jarvenpaa (Juuso), Peeter Jakobi (Santa). Directed by Jalmari Helander and produced by Anna Bjork, Francois-Xavier Frantz, Petri Jokiranta, and Knut Skoglund. Screenplay by Helander.

Rare Exports: A Christmas Tale is a rather brilliant lump of coal for your stocking hung by the fireside with care. How else to explain an R-rated Santa Claus origin story crossed with *The Thing*? Apart from the inescapable fact that the movie has Santa and reindeer in it, this is a superior horror film, a spot-on parody of movies about dead beings brought back to life. Oh, and all the reindeer are dead.

I need to help you picture this. It is the day before Christmas in the far Arctic north. Young Pietari lives on a reindeer ranch with his dad and other men who would feel right at home shooting reindeer from a helicopter. Yes, they are hunting food. The Scandinavians eat reindeer. God knows they do. I once visited Finland, Norway, and Sweden on a tour for the Scandinavian Film Institute, and at every single meal some sort of reindeer appetizer was served as a "delightful surprise." Between meals or when lost in the snow, they gnaw on reindeer jerky.

I stray. Nearby, there is a huge mound that looks vaguely sinister. The Americans have been blasting away up there with dynamite. Very sinister. Pietari (Onni Tommila) and his friend Juuso have been sneaking through the fence to spy on the Yanks. Pietari is a dead ringer in every way for Ralphie in *A Christmas Story*.

There is a legend that centuries ago the citizens were threatened by fearsome monsters. They were able to trick them onto the lake, where they froze. One of them was cut out inside a giant block of ice and buried deep beneath the mound. And now . . .

It's an idea from *The Thing*, where an alien was found in Antarctica and brought frozen into a hut, where drip . . . drip . . . drip . . . it began to thaw. We approach this possibility on the Night Before Christmas. Pietari's mother is dead (lots of lumps of coal in this stocking), and his dad, Rauno (Jorma Tommila), keeps telling him to stay in the house, and Pietari, an earnest, stubborn Ralphie type, keeps sneaking out. He's the only one who figures out what's happening: Inside the mound, inside the ice, is Santa Claus.

Well, not Santa precisely. A savage, scrawny

beast of a man with a beard, who eventually does admittedly end up wearing a Santa suit, but strictly for warmth. This creature is, however, arguably of the species *Santus clausium.* The director of *Rare Exports: A Christmas Tale,* the Finnish Jalmari Helander, has made two *Rare Export* short subjects about the capture and taming of wild Santas, who are then supplied to the worldwide market for Santas. Those Finns, what cutups.

Don't let it get lost in the confusion that this is a fine film. An original, daring, carefully crafted film that never for one instant winks at us that it's a parody. In its tone, acting, location work, music, and inexorably mounting suspense, this is an exemplary horror film, apart from the detail that they're not usually subtitled *A Christmas Tale* and tell about terrifying wild Santas.

Note: The R rating was earned by the F word and a nekkid Santa. Did I mention the reindeer slaughter?

RED ★ ★

PG-13, 110 m., 2010

Bruce Willis (Frank Moses), Morgan Freeman (Joe Matheson), John Malkovich (Marvin Boggs), Mary-Louise Parker (Sarah Ross), Helen Mirren (Victoria), Karl Urban (William Cooper), Brian Cox (Ivan Simanov), Rebecca Pidgeon (Cynthia Wilkes), Ernest Borgnine (Henry), James Remar (Gabriel Singer), Richard Dreyfuss (Alexander Dunning). Directed by Robert Schwentke and produced by Lorenzo di Bonaventura and Mark Vahradian. Screenplay by Jon Hoeber and Erich Hoeber, based on the graphic novel by Warren Ellis and Cully Hamner.

This would have been a hell of a cast when we were all younger. *RED* plays like a movie made for my Aunt Mary, who was always complaining, "Honey, I don't like the pictures anymore because I don't know who any of the actors are." If the name Ernest Borgnine sounds familiar, here's the movie for you.

Borgnine at ninety-three is still active and has a project "in development," I learn from IMDb, even if it's ominously titled *Death Keeps Coming.* Says here it's a supernatural Western being produced by Tarantino. Borgnine himself is a heck of a guy. I flew out of Cartagena with him one morning with a terrible hangover, and we got stranded in some forgotten Colombian airport where he fed me aspirin crushed in milk. An actor like that is a role model.

Bruce Willis stars in the title role of *RED,* which refers to his alert level ("retired: extremely dangerous") and not his hair. He's a former CIA agent who discovers bad guys want to kill him. So he summons the members of his old killing squad and they prepare a defense. The team includes Joe Matheson (Morgan Freeman), Marvin Boggs (John Malkovich), Victoria (Helen Mirren), and Ivan (Brian Cox).

(Notes: Victoria requires no second name because she is a woman in a thriller; Ivan is a Russian because the Russian in every thriller is named Ivan; Malkovich may have taken the role because he is never considered for characters named Boggs; and Freeman reveals early that he is dying of liver cancer. We know that as the black member of the team he must die first, because that's how he would have wanted it. So once again poor Morgan Freeman is hung out to dry. He'd rather play the villain. As he once explained to me: The villain is usually the most interesting character in the movie, and one thing you *know* is, he'll still be around for the last scene.)

In addition to his old comrades, Frank Moses takes along Sarah Ross (Mary-Louise Parker), a telephone operator, for his retirement plan. He's fallen in love with her voice. He explains she has to go on the run with him because her life is in danger. Like any federal employee, she finds this reasonable. Her life will be much safer with a man who is the target of thousands of rounds of automatic weapon fire. The villains in thrillers are such bad shots they'd suck at video games.

The bad guys are in the upper reaches of the CIA, and the conspiracy reaches all the way to a vice president with connections to a huge private defense contractor. This man is played by Richard Dreyfuss, who subtly signals to us, "You only *think* this is my Dick Cheney imitation, but if the studio let me loose, I could nail this role." Are sinister Dick Cheney roles growing uncommonly frequent? Hollywood is always fearful of running out of villains and, having run through Russians, Chinese, Nazis, and Mongols, seems to have fallen upon poor Cheney with relief.

RED is neither a good movie nor a bad one. It features actors we like doing things we wish were more interesting. I guess the movie's moral is, these old people are still tougher than the young ones. You want tough? I'll show you tough. In one scene, Helen Mirren is gut-shot and a blood stain spreads on her white dress. In a closing scene not a day later, she's perfectly chipper, and has had time to send the dress out to the cleaners.

The Red Machine ★ ★ ★ ½

NO MPAA RATING, 84 m., 2010

Lee Perkins (F. Ellis Coburn), Donal Thoms-Cappello (Eddie Doyle), Meg Brogan (Aggie Driscoll), Maureen Byrnes (Stella Snyder), Eddie Lee (Ichiro Shimada), Madoka Kasahara (Naomi Shimada), David Ross Paterson (Admiral McAdams). Directed by Stephanie Argy and Alec Boehm and produced by Argy, Boehm, and Ken Cortland. Screenplay by Argy and Boehm.

The Red Machine is a lean, intense thriller about a disgraced spy for the U.S. Navy and a jailed safecracker who team up to steal the secret of the Japanese version of Enigma, the Nazi cryptography machine. It's set in Washington in the 1930s when Japan and the United States still had diplomatic relations, and the target is a red cipher machine.

Something happened to Lieutenant F. Ellis Coburn (Lee Perkins) in Tokyo seven years earlier to turn him into the man we see. He looks to be a flawlessly turned-out navy officer, but he's locked behind a stone face and a reputation all his superiors know about. In a climate of expanding promotions as the navy prepares for war, everyone notices he's stuck at lieutenant.

Eddie Doyle (Donal Thoms-Cappello) is a cocky young thief straight from a 1930s pulp crime magazine. He approaches his craft as a science, noiselessly breaking and entering, cracking combinations, slipping into the night. He can pick locks and pockets, and works within a tight criminal fraternity ruled by Stella Snyder (Maureen Byrnes), a wise-talking hard case.

Navy intelligence has broken all the Japanese codes but this one. The red machine baffles them. They assign Coburn to the task because of his undoubted skills, and get Eddie released from jail for his particular specialty. Eddie will get them into the guarded embassy, and when Coburn sees the machine he'll know what he's looking at. The machine itself can't be stolen; the Japanese must never suspect it has been compromised.

The drama also involves the Japanese ambassador Shimada (Eddie Lee) and his wife, Naomi (Madoka Kasahara), who, almost inevitably, have links to the mysterious events in Tokyo seven years ago. And that's about it. These people, this stage, the red machine.

The movie, written and directed by the married pair of Stephanie Argy and Alec Boehm, doesn't fall back on stunts, chases, or extended gun battles; it's in the honorable tradition of the heist movie. That involves blueprints, plans, and the need to be very, very quiet. There's a nice scene when a safe is opened just behind an open door in Shimada's office. The Coburn character becomes so desperate to stall that he plays every card in his hand, including personal secrets.

The Red Machine is deeper than it first seems. The plot has hidden levels, and so do the characters, particularly the unlikely team of Doyle and Coburn. They don't like each other and don't like working together, and any possible personal progress is shut down by Coburn's fearsome reserve. He is taciturn to the point of aggression.

Neither actor overplays. Perkins's role doesn't allow him. Donal Thoms-Cappello's thief is supposed to be brash and dubious, which he is, but within reason. There's some subtle shifting going on that the directors suggest with visuals, not dialogue; an unspoken agreement to conspire takes place below the surface.

Here's a film with an elegant simplicity. Not a shot doesn't do its work. It may remind you of a 1940s B crime movie, and I mean that as a compliment. When you don't have a lot of explosions and special effects to exploit, you have to turn to the imagination—yours and the audience's.

Red Riding Hood ★

PG-13, 120 m., 2011

Amanda Seyfried (Valerie), Gary Oldman (Solomon), Billy Burke (Cesaire), Shiloh Fernandez (Peter), Max Irons (Henry), Virginia Madsen (Suzette), Lukas Haas (Father Auguste), Julie Christie (Grandmother). Directed by Catherine Hardwicke and produced by Leonardo DiCaprio, Jennifer Davisson Killoran, Alex Mace, and Julie Yorn. Screenplay by David Leslie Johnson.

Of the classics of world literature crying out to be adapted as a sexual fantasy for teenage girls, surely *Red Hiding Hood* is far down on the list. Here's a movie that cross-pollinates the *Twilight* formula with a werewolf, and adds a girl who always wears a hooded red cape, although I don't recall her doing any riding. It's easy to imagine a story conference in which they said: "Hey! Let's switch the vampires with a werewolf and recycle the theme of a virgin attracted to a handsome but dangerous hunk, only let's get two hunks!"

What this inspiration fails to consider is that while a young woman might toy with the notion of a vampire boyfriend, she might not want to mate with a wolf. And although she might think it was, like, cool to live in the woods in Oregon, she might not want to live in the Black Forest hundreds of years ago because, like, can you text from there?

Red Riding Hood has the added inconvenience of being dreadfully serious about a plot so preposterous it demands to be filmed by Monty Python. The only scene that amused me was a dream sequence where Grandma says, "The better to eat you with." I'm asking myself, "How can Red Riding Hood dream about dialogue in her own fairy tale when she hasn't even gone over the hill and through the dale to Grandmother's house yet?"

The movie was directed by Catherine Hardwicke, who made *Twilight.* It opens with aerial shots of hundreds of square miles of forests, dotted here and there by stubby, grim castles. Then we meet the narrator, Valerie, who always wears a red cape. She is but a lass when she steals away with her prepubescent boyfriend, Peter, so they can trap a bunny rabbit and possibly slit its throat, although the camera moves away from the bunny at the crucial moment to focus upon their faces as the young actors think, "OK, this is where they flash forward and we are replaced by Amanda Seyfried and Shiloh Fernandez."

They live in a village which is one of the most peculiar nonplaces in the history of production design. Because the original fairy tale was by the Brothers Grimm, I suppose there's a chance the village is in Germany, but it exists outside time and space and seems to have been inspired by little plastic souvenir villages in airport gift shops. You know, populated mit Hansel und Gretel.

Valerie (Seyfried) wants to marry Peter (Fernandez), who is a woodchopper, but her parents have promised her to a rich kid named Henry (Max Irons). The village since time immemorial has been terrorized by a werewolf, who turns up when the moon is full and must be pacified by a pathetic little piggie left chained to a stump, lest it develop an appetite for villagers. Alarmingly, Valerie's sister is found dead, amid distracting cone-shaped haystacks dotted with blue flowers, which is not the sort of detail you want to be noticing when a young girl has been killed but (spoiler) not eaten by a werewolf.

The villagers send off for Father Solomon (Gary Oldman), a famed werewolf fighter, and he arrives with his band of warriors and a very large metal elephant. Solomon, an expert, knows that werewolves are not werewolves all the time, and in between full moons take the form of men. Therefore, one of the villagers must be a werewolf. This has enormous implications for Valerie's possible future love life.

But I know you, my readers. Right now you aren't thinking about Valerie's romance. You're thinking, "Did I just read that Father Solomon arrived with a very large metal elephant?" Yes, he did. A very large metal elephant. I thought the same thing. That must have been a *hell* of a lot of trouble. Even harder than Herzog dragging the boat over the mountain. Showing Father Solomon's men dragging a metal elephant through the woods—there's your movie right there.

Red Riding Trilogy ★ ★ ★ ★

NO MPAA RATING, 302 m., 2010

Andrew Garfield (Eddie Dunford), Paddy Considine (Peter Hunter), Mark Addy (John

Piggott), David Morrissey (Maurice Jobson), Warren Clarke (Bill Molloy), Sean Bean (John Dawson), Peter Mullan (Martin Laws), Robert Sheehan (BJ), Rebecca Hall (Paula Garland), Sean Harris (Bob Craven). Directed by Julian Jarrold (*1974*), James Marsh (*1980*), and Anand Tucker (*1983*) and produced by Wendy Brazington, Andrew Eaton, and Anita Overland. Screenplay by Tony Grisoni, based on the novels by David Peace.

Red Riding Trilogy is an immersive experience like *Best of Youth, Brideshead Revisited,* or *Nicholas Nickleby.* Over the course of 302 minutes, we sink into a virtual world: the corrupt police and establishment figures of West Yorkshire in England, at the time of the real-life Yorkshire Ripper. Peter Sutcliffe, the Ripper, was convicted of killing thirteen women, and may have killed more. The fictional Ripper here enjoys the same inexplicable immunity to police investigation.

This is the sort of undertaking the UK's Channel 4 excels at and is approached in the United States only by ambitious cable TV series. The experience could give you the impression that the three parts were filmed at separate times. The visual style proceeds from 16 mm to 35 mm to high-def video, different actors play some of the characters at different times, and there are three directors, each with a distinctive style. But that was all part of the Channel 4 plan, and the completed trilogy aired in March 2009.

There's a large cast of characters involved in a complex series of events. Few viewers could be blamed for failing a test on what happens and who (in addition to the Ripper) is guilty. Strict continuity is sidestepped to such a degree that some characters do not quite seem to remain dead. This is a way to reflect the shifting nature of reality in which there are many concealed motives and the police version of events is fabricated entirely for their own convenience.

The police have their reasons, chillingly dramatized in a scene where conspirators drink a toast to "the North!" Yorkshire is in northern England, traditionally hostile to the South (London), but what does that have to do with a license for corruption? The toast is an example of the human willingness to excuse behavior by evoking meaningless abstractions (The South! The Young! Party Time! Der Fuhrer!). Where they are is irrelevant to what they do.

They are in a society that seems, to our North American eyes, clearly distinct from other parts of Britain. In some segments, the Yorkshire accents are so pronounced that Channel 4 wisely adds subtitles. We are inhabiting a subculture. In the early scenes, our attention is focused on an investigative reporter, new in town, Eddie Dunford (Andrew Garfield), who looks deeper into the murders, but is unlucky enough to get personally involved with a woman linked to a separate series of crimes. Their intimate scenes together are the closest the trilogy will come to human kindness.

Dunford is an unalloyed hero. Much of the rest of the story involves conspirators who plot among and against themselves. Any sense of objective morality is lacking. We get the sense that no one rises high in the police without knowing the rules and playing by them. They arrange for their own immunity.

There is a public outcry as the Ripper continues to kill and evade capture. It was the same in real life. Scotland Yard was brought in, represented indirectly here by a veteran cop named Peter Hunter (Paddy Considine). He makes little progress, in large part because the officers he's working with have guilt to conceal and much to cover up.

Without revealing anything crucial, the reality is that the Ripper murders are invisibly connected to a police cover-up of a deadly real estate conspiracy, and if you pull a string from the Ripper, the whole ball of yarn of the larger conspiracy may unravel. A central figure becomes a vile chief of police, played by David Morrissey, who is so alarming that one searches the Web to discover he looks a nice enough man in real life. The casting here and throughout is essential to the trilogy's effect.

All this time a mentally challenged suspect has been held as the alleged Ripper. He has even confessed, which after police interrogation in Yorkshire, is a foregone conclusion. His guilt is convincingly challenged, which leads to a reopening of the case, as well it might, because the murders didn't stop with his imprisonment.

One wants to believe no police department in North America has ever been as corrupt as this one from Yorkshire. That may not be true, but the chances of a television trilogy about it are slim. *Red Riding Trilogy* hammers at the dark souls of its villains until they crack open, and it is a fascinating sight. We're in so deep by the final third that there can hardly be a character whose hidden evil comes as a surprise: Can innocence exist in this environment?

The directors, who worked on their segments more or less simultaneously, have impressive credits that do not, however, suggest the different feels they bring to their segments. *Red Riding 1974* is by Julian Jarrold, whose *Brideshead Revisited, Becoming Jane,* and *Kinky Boots* are all some distance from the immediacy of his 16 mm. *Red Riding 1980* is by James Marsh, whose documentaries *Man on Wire* and *Wisconsin Death Trip* don't suggest the 35 mm feature feel of his segment. And *Red Riding 1983*'s Anand Tucker (*Shopgirl, Hilary and Jackie*) is a specialist in clearly delineated ambiguity, at odds with the moral anarchy of his segment. I gather they were not hired to reproduce their strengths, but to find the right approach for this material.

I have given only the sketchiest of plot outlines here. The trilogy isn't so much about what happens objectively (which can sometimes be hard to determine), but about the world in which it takes place, a miasma of greed and evil. I have no idea whether the real Yorkshire police were led by monsters such as these. Someone must have thought so. Channel 4 aired these segments as they stand.

Rejoice and Shout ★ ★ ★

PG, 115 m., 2011

Smokey Robinson, Andrae Crouch, Mavis Staples, Ira Tucker, Marie Knight, Willa Ward, Ira Tucker Jr., Anthony Heilbut, Bill Carpenter, Jacquie Gayles Webb, the Selvey Family, and Darrel Petties. A documentary directed by Don McGlynn and produced by Joe Lauro.

Black gospel music in one way or another created a great deal of the blues, jazz, and rock and roll. Born on the plantations of the South, it merged the Christian hymns of the slave owners with rhythms from Africa and created a new musical form not heard before but reflected everywhere today, even in hip-hop. *Rejoice and Shout* is a consistently entertaining documentary bringing together a remarkable variety of surviving performances on films and records, going back to circa 1900.

Where some of these films came from and how they were preserved isn't a question the film answers, but without them we couldn't see rare 1902 footage of the Dinwiddie Colored Quartet, not the first gospel singers but the first to be filmed. We also see joyous work by the Dixie Hummingbirds, the Staple Singers, the Swan Silvertones, Sister Rosette Tharpe, Mahalia Jackson, and an onstage duel between the Blind Boys of Alabama and the Five Blind Boys of Mississippi.

Smokey Robinson, one of the sources interviewed by Don McGlynn for his film, links the music to his own religious beliefs, which of course is appropriate, but some of the singers, Rosetta Tharpe in particular, seem drawn toward more secular venues. There's even the suggestion that Mahalia Jackson might have liked to do more show tunes and pop music, but was kept in line by her churchgoing mother.

Mavis Staples, whose father links back to the earliest days of gospel, is a warm presence throughout the film, calling on personal memories of many of the artists. Other experts such as Anthony Heilbut, Bill Carpenter, Ira Tucker Jr., and Darrel Petties have a wealth of information, connections, and memories. And *Rejoice and Shout* doesn't show snippets of old performances, but entire songs, so we get a more complete idea of the talents.

My own knowledge of gospel music is limited mostly to what I learned through the (much better) documentary *Say Amen, Somebody*, which told the stories of Thomas A. Dorsey, Willie May Ford Smith, and others. Dorsey wrote an astonishing number of gospel standards (*Precious Lord, Take My Hand* among them), but is only mentioned in passing here. I suppose the footage from *Say Amen, Somebody* wasn't available to McGlynn. Indeed his own footage here is limited to his talking head interviews; all the performance footage is archival. Still, this is an engaging film filled with love for the music.

Note: My review of Say Amen, Somebody *is here: http://bit.ly/iKCje3.*

Remember Me ★ ★ ★

PG-13, 113 m., 2010

Robert Pattinson (Tyler Hawkins), Emilie de Ravin (Ally Craig), Chris Cooper (Sergeant Neil Craig), Pierce Brosnan (Charles Hawkins), Lena Olin (Diane Hirsch), Tate Ellington (Aidan Hall), Ruby Jerins (Caroline Hawkins). Directed by Allen Coulter and produced by Trevor Engelson and Nick Osborne. Screenplay by Will Fetters.

Remember Me tells a sweet enough love story, and tries to invest it with profound meaning by linking it to a coincidence. It doesn't work that way. People meet, maybe they fall in love, maybe they don't, maybe they're happy, maybe they're sad. That's life. If a refrigerator falls out of a window and squishes one of them, that's life, too, but it's not a story many people want to see. We stand there looking at the blood seeping out from under the Kelvinator and ask with Peggy Lee, "Is that all there is?"

You can't exactly say the movie cheats. It brings the refrigerator onscreen in the first scene. It ties the action to a key date in Kelvinator history, one everybody knows even if that's all they know about refrigerators. But, come on. This isn't the plot for a love story; it's the plot for a Greek tragedy. It may be true, as *King Lear* tells us, that "As flies to wanton boys are we to th' gods." But we don't want to think of ourselves as flies, or see fly love stories. Bring on the eagles.

The fact is, *Remember Me* is a well-made movie. I cared about the characters. I felt for them. Liberate them from the plot's destiny, which is an anvil around their necks, and you might have something.

The film opens on a New York subway platform. A young girl witnesses the senseless murder of her mother. We meet her again as a young woman. She is Ally Craig (Emilie de Ravin, from *Lost*), the daughter of a police sergeant (Chris Cooper). She's in college. Having lost his wife, he is intensely protective of her.

We meet a feckless young man named Tyler Hawkins (Robert Pattinson). He slouches about trying to look like a dissipated Robert Pattinson. Drinks too much, smokes too much, has the official four-day stubble on his face, hair carefully messed up, bad attitude. He lives in a pigpen of an apartment with a roommate named Aidan (Tate Ellington), who might have been played by Oscar Levant back in the days when roommates were obnoxious, OK, but bearable.

Tyler gets drunk one night, is thrown out of a club, gets in a fight, the cops are called, and when it's almost all over, he shoves one of the cops—Sergeant Craig, of course. Young drunks: It is *extremely unwise* to shove the cop who is about to let you off with a warning. Tyler is thrown in the slammer. Not long after in school, the snaky Aidan tells Tyler that their pretty classmate Ally is the daughter of that very cop. He dares Tyler to ask her out and then dump her in revenge.

Aidan is a jerk, but logically Tyler is too, because this is morally reprehensible. However, to the surprise of no one in the audience, Tyler falls for Ally and neglects to break up with her. Their courtship is a sensitive, well-acted progression through stages of mutual trust and Tyler's gradual rediscovery of his own real feelings.

There's an intriguing subplot. Tyler's parents are divorced. His father is the immensely wealthy Charles Hawkins (Pierce Brosnan), whose office looks larger than small airplane terminals. His mother, Diane (Lena Olin), has remarried. Tyler's beloved kid sister, Caroline (Ruby Jerins), lives with her. Only with Caroline can Tyler relax and drop the sullen facade, showing warmth and love. Until he meets Ally—and then there are two safe harbors, and his rebirth begins.

Pierce Brosnan plays a key role in the process. He has only a few significant scenes in the movie, but plays them so well that he convincingly takes a three-step character development and makes it into an emotional evolution. Meanwhile, Ally and Tyler encounter fierce opposition to their relationship from her dad, who can't be blamed because as a cop he saw Tyler at his drunken worst.

These people and their situation grow more involving as the movie moves along. Then there's a perfect storm of coincidences to supply the closing scenes. That's what I object to.

If we invest in a film's characters, what happens to them should be intrinsically important to us. We don't require emotional reinforcement to be brought in from outside.

The movie tries to borrow profound meaning, but succeeds only in upstaging itself so overwhelmingly that its characters become irrelevant. I'm guessing the message is: Parents, when you have a rebel child who hates you, someday you will learn what a good person that child really was. It's the dream of every tormented adolescent. Many of them become parents themselves and get their turn at being resented. Such is life.

Repo Men ★ ★

R, 111 m., 2010

Jude Law (Remy), Forest Whitaker (Jake), Liev Schreiber (Frank), Alice Braga (Beth), Carice van Houten (Carol). Directed by Miguel Sapochnik and produced by Mary Parent and Scott Stuber. Screenplay by Eric Garcia and Garrett Lerner, based on Garcia's novel *The Repossession Mambo.*

Repo Men makes sci-fi's strongest possible case for universal health care. In a world of the near future, where they still drive current cars, a giant corporation named the Union will provide you with a human heart, kidney, liver, or other organ. Let's say a pancreas costs you, oh, $312,000. No, it's not covered by insurance, but the sales guy says, "You owe it to yourself and your family." For a guy in need of a pancreas, this is an eloquent argument. Interest rates are around 19 percent.

Now let's say you can't make the payments. If you fall behind more than three months, they send around a repo man who shoots you with a stun gun, slices open your body, reaches in, and repossesses the organ. To be sure, he puts on latex gloves first. I don't believe the gun kills you, but after they leave you on the floor with an organ missing, your prognosis is poor.

Let's say you were conscious during such a procedure. Would it hurt? You bet it would. At one point in the film, our heroes Remy and Beth (Jude Law and Alice Braga) decide the only way to outwit the company's computer is to repossess themselves. He has a donor heart, and as for Beth, her heart is her own, but it is surrounded by guest organs. They don't actually carve themselves open and *remove* the organs. No, that would be fatal. But they have to reach inside each other with a bar-code scanner and scan them in. As Remy carves into his chest with a big old knife, you oughta see the way his fist clenches and he grits his teeth. He's thinking, I wish I had the public option.

I don't know if the makers of this film intended it as a comedy. A preview audience regarded it with polite silence, and left the theater in an orderly fashion. There are chases and shootouts, of course, and a standard overwrought thriller sound track, with the percussion guy hammering on cymbals and a big bass drum. Even then, you wonder.

Remy and Beth find themselves locked in a corridor with a dozen guys from the evil corporation who are well armed. They dodge the bullets and wham some guys with karate, and then Remy pauses, strips off his shirt, reveals his bare (pre-repo) chest, and is wearing kinky leather pants with buckles. From scabbards in the back, he withdraws two long knives that help explain why he wasn't seated earlier in the scene. He slices some other guys. Then he shouts "Hacksaw!" to Beth and she slides it to him on the floor, and he whirls around and *decapitates* three guys, it looked like, although it happened real fast.

What are people supposed to think? Is this an action scene, or satire? Does it make any difference? I dunno. I know the actors play everything with deep, earnest seriousness. The head of the Union corporation is Frank (Liev Schreiber), who demands complete dedication from his repo men and is humorously not humorous. Maybe he's not the head of the whole Union, but only their immediate boss. The Union's headquarters building is maybe one hundred stories high, and Remy stumbles into a room with guys in white suits working at tables that stretch farther than a football field. There are enough props in this movie to clean out the organ department at Moo & Oink's. When I say they're up to their elbows in blood, I mean it. This work takes its toll. Remy's friend at work is a repo man named Jake, played by Forest Whitaker. Like most Forest Whitaker characters and Whitaker himself, he is a warm, nice man. I noticed for the second time in a week (after *Our Family Wedding*) that Whitaker has lost a lot of weight and looks great. I hope the extra pounds weren't repo'ed.

Restrepo ★ ★ ★ ½

R, 94 m., 2010

With Dan Kearney, Lamont Caldwell, Kevin Rice, Misha Pemble-Belkin, and Kyle Steiner. A documentary directed and produced by Tim Hetherington and Sebastian Junger.

"Afghanistan" is a word on the news, debated in terms of our foreign policy. Almost an abstraction. Nobody thinks about foreign policy in *Restrepo*, a documentary shot during the fifteen months an American company fought there under almost daily fire. They were in the Korengal Valley, described on CNN as the most dangerous place in the world.

It is also one of the most desolate, even in the arid land of Afghanistan. Sparse vegetation clings to the rocky, jagged terrain. There is dust everywhere. It is too hot in the summer and too cold in the winter, and in the movie, at least, the troops only actually see one Taliban fighter—and the man who saw him thought it was the last sight he would ever see.

The Taliban is an elusive presence, moving freely through the landscape and population, and there is one point when the company is ambushed and takes fire from 360 degrees. That all of them were not killed seems surprising. The film is named after the first one of their number to die, a twenty-year-old medic, Private First Class Juan S. Restrepo.

Battle Company is led by Captain Dan Kearney, whose plan is to establish an outpost at a key point on Taliban battle routes. The men occupy the position at night and start digging in, using the earth to build fortifications. They catch the enemy off guard. The successful maintenance of Outpost Restrepo, named for their dead comrade, turns the tide of war in the hostile valley and frightens the Taliban. But the hearts and minds of the locals remain an uncharted terrain.

Kearney holds a weekly council with the local elders, a group of men who could not look more aged, toothless, and decrepit if they tried. A portrait of one would be all you needed to suggest the poverty of the region. One elder complains he has lost a cow. It's explained that the cow became tangled in razor wire and had to be put out of its misery. He is offered compensation: the cow's weight in rice, beans, and sugar. He wants cash. His heart and mind are not won.

The location footage is intercut with debriefings of the survivors conducted soon after they've been flown out to Italy. They use understatement to express strong emotions. The deaths of men they fought with are almost impossible for them to speak of. The memory of Restrepo lived on in the guitar lessons he provided and his book of flamenco songs. He was a great favorite. After Outpost Restrepo grew from a dugout into a proper position with shelter and fortifications, they felt right having named it for him.

They all speak with special dread about an operation named Operation Rock Avalanche, through deadly country, where Kearney says the enemy was so close a Taliban fighter once took a man's weapons from him. They come under fire three, four, five times a day. There are many firefights in the film, but they all share one feature: We never see the enemy, and we never see the American targets.

This is hard, hard duty. A fifteen-month tour. Our admiration for these men grows. Their jobs seem beyond conceiving. I cannot imagine a civilian thinking he could perform them. It would take much training—and more important, much bonding. There is the sense they're fighting for each other more than for ideology. At a low point when a nearby company has taken heavy losses, Kearney talks to his men not in terms of patriotism, but in terms of finding the MFs who are shooting at them, and going out and killing them.

The film is nonpolitical. It was filmed at great personal risk by the war photographer Tim Hetherington and the author Sebastian Junger (*The Perfect Storm*). It raises for me an obvious question: How can this war possibly be won? At the end of the film, a title tells us U.S. troops have withdrawn from the Korengal Valley and therefore Outpost Restrepo. No reason is given.

Revanche ★ ★ ★ ½

NO MPAA RATING, 121 m., 2009

Johannes Krisch (Alex), Irina Potapenko (Tamara), Ursula Strauss (Susanne), Hannes Thanheiser (Grandfather), Andreas Lust

(Robert), Hanno Poschl (Konecny). Directed by Gotz Spielmann and produced by Mathias Forberg, Heinz Stussak, and Sandra Bohle. Screenplay by Spielmann.

Revanche involves a rare coming together of a male's criminal nature and a female's deep needs, entwined with a first-rate thriller. It is also perceptive in observing characters, including a proud old man. Rare is the thriller that is more about the reasons of people instead of the needs of the plot.

Alex and Tamara are a sad couple. In a trashy Vienna brothel, she is a prostitute from Ukraine; he is an ex-con who works as a bouncer for the reprehensible pimp Konecny. They are having a secret affair. Neither has the nerve to cross the pimp, the ruler of their world. Konecny has his eye on Tamara, and at one point visits her for sexual purposes while Alex hides humiliatingly under her bed.

Both Alex (Johannes Krisch) and Tamara (Irina Potapenko) are pitiful. They steal moments of love in their grubby rooms, and Alex plots a bank robbery. He brings her along in the getaway car. It will be easy, he says. Nobody will get hurt. Look—his gun isn't even loaded. But it does go wrong, and a cop turns up just as they're driving away.

Alex takes refuge at the only place he can think of, his grandfather's humble farm. And it is here that the story transcends crooks and hookers and bank jobs and becomes so surprisingly human. The catalyst I think is the character of the grandfather, played by Hannes Thanheiser.

He's a proud old man, living alone, mourning his wife, feeding his friends the cows, resisting well-meaning attempts to move him into a "home." When he dies, he wants to be carried out of his farmhouse. He has seen little of his grandson. Alex goes to work, chopping a mountain of firewood for the winter. They eat simple meals of sausage, cheese, and bread. I liked the old man and wanted to give him some mustard.

Susanne (Ursula Strauss), a neighbor's wife, visits him with offers of help. He appreciates her friendliness but not her help. Alex is distant and unfriendly. She takes good notice of him, and out of the blue asks him to visit her that night, when her husband is away. He does. No formalities. They have sex on her kitchen table.

Of course she is the wife of the cop who happened upon the bank robbery, but none of them can know this. We do. We also know that the cop cannot give her a child, and she wants to become pregnant. In this limited world, the old man's son is the only eligible father; she loves the old man and sees the son working hard for him.

The suspense at first involves whether the cop will happen upon them having sex. Then *Revanche* begins to involve a great deal more. It's here that the film's power resides. It seamlessly brings together the possibility of violence, of Alex's exposure, of threats to her marriage, of harm to the old man's well-being, in a way that doesn't seem to manipulate these things for advantage. Instead, it simply tells a good story, very well. Susanne becomes the protagonist. She is taking dangerous risks. All three of the men are unhappy and touchy. In a way, she represents their only hope.

As I watched the film I became grateful that I didn't know the actors. American films often involve actors well known to me, which is fine—but also sometimes stars are chosen primarily because they're "bankable." Few bankable stars could work in this material. The Austrian actors look normal. Unglamorous. Plausible. Ursula Strauss, as Susanne, looks sweet and pleasant but is careworn and not a great beauty. Johannes Krisch, as Alex, looks like a loser marginalized by crime and prison. As the prostitute, Irina Potapenko retails what beauty she has in a buyer's market.

All of these actors create characters who are above all people, not performances. That's why the film is peculiarly effective; it's about their lives, not their dilemmas. And the bedrock is old Hannes Thanheiser, born 1925, as a strong, stubborn, weathered old man who doesn't live through his grandson, his neighbors, or anyone else, but on his own terms, in daily mourning of the wife who shared his long life. That harm or loss could come to him would be a great misfortune.

How often, after seeing a thriller, do you continue to think about the lives of its characters? If you open up most of them, it's like looking inside a wristwatch. Opening this one is like heart surgery.

Note: Revanche *was a 2008 Oscar nominee for Best Foreign Language Film.*

Revolutionary Road ★ ★ ★ ★

R, 119 m., 2009

Leonardo DiCaprio (Frank Wheeler), Kate Winslet (April Wheeler), Kathy Bates (Helen Givings), Michael Shannon (John Givings), Kathryn Hahn (Milly Campbell), David Harbour (Shep Campbell), Zoe Kazan (Maureen Grube), Dylan Baker (Jack Ordway), Jay O. Sanders (Bart Pollock), Richard Easton (Howard Givings). Directed by Sam Mendes and produced by John N. Hart, Scott Rudin, and Bobby Cohen. Screenplay by Justin Haythe, based on the novel by Richard Yates.

Life is what happens to you while you're busy making other plans.

—John Lennon

Revolutionary Road shows the American Dream awakened by a nightmare. It takes place in the 1950s, the decade not only of Elvis but of *The Man in the Gray Flannel Suit.* It shows a young couple who meet at a party, get married, and create a suburban life with a nice house, a manicured lawn, "modern" furniture, two kids, a job in the city for him, housework for her, and martinis, cigarettes, boredom, and desperation for both of them.

The Wheelers, Frank and April, are blinded by love into believing life together will allow them to fulfill their fantasies. Their problem is, they have no fantasies. Instead, they have yearnings—a hunger for something *more* than a weary slog into middle age. Billy Wilder made a movie in 1955 called *The Seven Year Itch* about a restlessness that comes into some marriages when the partners realize the honeymoon is over and they're married for good and there's an empty space at the center.

Frank (Leonardo DiCaprio) and April (Kate Winslet) can't see inviting futures for themselves. Frank joins the morning march of men in suits and hats out of Grand Central and into jobs where they are "executives" doing meaningless work—in Frank's case, he's "in office machines." He might as well be one. April suggests he just quit so they can move to Paris; she can support them as a translator at the American Embassy, and he can figure out what he really wants to do. Translating will not support their Connecticut lifestyle, but Paris! What about their children? Their children are like a car you never think about when you're not driving somewhere.

Frank agrees, and they think they're poised to take flight, when suddenly he's offered a promotion and a raise. He has no choice, right? He'll be just as miserable, but better paid. In today's hard times, that sounds necessary, but maybe all times are hard when you hate your life. Frank and April have ferocious fights about his decision, and we realize that April was largely motivated by her own needs. Better to support the neutered Frank in Paris with a job at the embassy, where she might meet someone more interesting than their carbon-copy neighbors and the "real estate lady," Helen Givings (Kathy Bates).

Helen makes a tentative request. Can she and her husband bring their son John (Michael Shannon) over for a meal? He's in a mental institution, and perhaps some time with a nice normal couple like the Wheelers would be good for him. John comes for dinner, and we discover his real handicap is telling the truth. With cruel words and merciless observations, he chops through their facade and mocks their delusions. It is a wrecking job.

Remember, this is the 1950s. A little after the time of this movie, *Life* magazine would run its famous story about the beatniks, "The Only Rebellion Around." There was a photo of a beatnik and his chick sitting on the floor and listening to an LP record of modern jazz that was cool and hip, and I felt my own yearnings. I remember on the way back from Steak 'n Shake one night, my dad drove slow past the Turk's Head coffeehouse on campus. "That's where the beatniks stand on tables and recite their poetry," he told my mom, and she said, "My, my," and I wanted to get out of that car and put on a black turtleneck and walk in there and stay.

The character John is not insane, just a beatnik a little ahead of schedule. He's an early assault wave from the 1960s, which would sweep over suburbia and create a generation its parents did not comprehend. What he does for the Wheelers is strip away their denials and see them clearly. Do you know these John Prine lyrics?

Blow up your TV, throw away your paper,
Go to the country, build you a home.
Plant a little garden, eat a lot of peaches,
Try an' find Jesus on your own.

Frank and April are played by DiCaprio and Winslet as the sad ending to the romance in *Titanic*, and all other romances that are founded on nothing more than . . . romance. They are so good, they stop being actors and become the people I grew up around. Don't think they smoke too much in this movie. In the 1950s everybody smoked everywhere all the time. Life was a disease, and smoking held it temporarily in remission. And drinking? Every ad executive in the neighborhood would head for the Wrigley Bar at lunchtime to prove the maxim: One martini is just right, two are too many, three are not enough.

The direction is by Sam Mendes, who dissected suburban desperation in *American Beauty*, a film that after this one seems merciful. The screenplay by Justin Haythe is drawn from the famous 1961 novel by Richard Yates, who has been called the voice of the postwar Age of Anxiety. This film is so good it is devastating. A lot of people believe their parents didn't understand them. What if they didn't understand themselves?

Ricky ★ ★

NO MPAA RATING, 89 m., 2010

Alexandra Lamy (Katie), Sergi Lopez (Paco), Melusine Mayance (Lisa), Arthur Peyret (Ricky), Andre Wilms (Doctor), Jean-Claude Bolle-Reddat (Journalist). Directed by Francois Ozon and produced by Chris Bolzli, Claudie Ossard, and Vieri Razzini. Screenplay by Ozon, based on the short story "Moth" by Rose Tremain.

Parables are stories about other people that help us live our own lives. The problem with *Ricky* is that the lesson of the parable is far from clear, and nobody is likely to encounter this situation in their own life. That would be pretty much impossible. The story begins in gritty realism, ends in pure fantasy, and leaves out most of the alphabet as it makes its way from A to Z.

The story begins with Katie (Alexandra Lamy), a morose French factory worker who has been abandoned, she thinks, by the man she lives with. It's hard to pay the rent. We flash back to the beginning, see her living with her peppy seven-year-old daughter, Lisa (Melusine Mayance), and working in a French chemical factory. There she meets a Spanish worker named Paco (Sergi Lopez). He's warm and attracted, they smile, they live together and have a baby.

These events take place in a series of time jumps that are momentarily jolting, but easy enough to follow. Not so easy is what happens to their son, Ricky (Arthur Peyret), as he grows up. In appearance he seems at first like an outtake from *Babies*, but then when Paco cares for him at home alone, Katie discovers bruises on his shoulders. Paco is enraged to be accused of child beating and stalks out, explaining Katie's opening scene.

These scenes are absorbingly created and well acted, and we settle in for a French slice of life. I can hardly deal with any more of the film without revealing details. Here goes, after a spoiler warning.

Those aren't bruises, they're the beginning of wings. Yes. Little wings, which at first look so much like poultry parts that Katie tape-measures a turkey wing at the supermarket, just to get an idea. One night, in slow-mo, the wings begin to sprout tiny feathers, which in close-up look like one of those life forms you don't want to make friends with. Soon the little lad has flapped his way to the top of an armoire.

No, he isn't an angel. Maybe more likely the result of his parents working at the chemical factory, although the movie doesn't make that a point. It doesn't much make anything a point. Katie and Lisa are about as amazed as if the child had a lot of hair on its head. You'd think babies with wings were born every day. Later, after Paco rejoins the family, baby Ricky gets a little injury, and the family doctor seems, to me, insufficiently amazed. Surely this is an OMG case?

Because the film is directed by the esteemed Francois Ozun (*Swimming Pool, Under the Sand, See the Sea*), I waited to see where it would take me. At the end, I wasn't sure. The ending has the form of a statement, but not the content of one. Its last half seems to be building to a life lesson, and perhaps the lesson is: "Parents! If you have a baby with wings, don't be this calm about it!"

I couldn't help myself. All during the film I was distracted by questions of aeronautics. In early scenes, those wings are way too small to allow a healthy baby to fly. Even later, the ratio of wingspan to baby weight seems way off. A scene where Ricky breaks free and flies around a supermarket seems designed for comedy, but doesn't play that way. And what kind of a cockamamie idea is it to hold a press conference and let Ricky fly with only Katie holding a string around his ankle? This is worse than the hot air balloon kid, if there had been one.

The film is bewildering. I don't know what its terms are, and it doesn't match any of mine. I found myself regarding it more and more as an inexplicable curiosity. It's so curiously flat in tone that when a baby grows wings and flies (think about that!), people in the film and in the audience seem to watch with no more than mild interest. *Ricky* makes a good case for lurid melodrama.

The Rite ★ ★ ★

PG-13, 112 m., 2011

Anthony Hopkins (Father Lucas Trevant), Colin O'Donoghue (Father Michael Kovak), Alice Braga (Angeline), Ciaran Hinds (Father Xavier), Toby Jones (Father Matthew), Rutger Hauer (Istvan Kovak). Directed by Mikael Hafstrom and produced by Beau Flynn and Tripp Vinson. Screenplay by Michael Petroni, based on the book by Matt Baglio.

The Rite takes exorcism more seriously than I expected it to. It begins with the supposition that Satan is "alive and active in the world" and assumes that satanic possession takes place and that the rite of exorcism works. Otherwise, we wouldn't have a movie, would we? In metaphysical terms I must immediately jump on the word "alive." In what sense can a being that exists outside of time and space be said to be alive? Active, yes.

The movie is based on the actual experiences of Father Gary Thomas, a California priest who was assigned by his bishop to study exorcism at the Vatican. In *The Rite* he becomes Father Michael Kovak (Colin O'Donoghue) from Chicago, and the closing credits tell us he's now working in a Western suburb. That's a fib. The director, Mikael Hafstrom, should say three Hail Marys and make a good act of contrition.

Father Michael is not a saint. He enters the seminary as a way to get a four-year college education before taking his vows, and then tries to leave the novitiate. Discovering the cost of his education would then roll over into a $100,000 student loan, he reconsiders and agrees to attend a monthlong course in Rome. This sort of detail is more refreshing than shots of him silhouetted against ancient desert structures while monks intone Gregorian chants.

In Rome, he attends classes, debates scripture, and then is advised to spend some time with an experienced exorcist, Father Lucas Trevant (Anthony Hopkins). This, too, is from the book by Matt Baglio, although in the book this priest is Italian. As Hopkins appears onscreen, *The Rite* slips into gear and grows solemn and effective. Hopkins finds a good note for Father Trevant: friendly, chatty, offhand, self-effacing, realistic about demonic possession but not a ranter. He takes the kid along while treating the apparent possession of a pregnant young woman.

That something happens to make people seem possessed I have no doubt. Diagnosing whether Satan is involved is above my pay grade. What I must observe is that demonic possession seems very rare, and the church rejects the majority of such reports. Yet it approaches epidemic proportions in *The Rite*, almost as if it were a virus. The film is like one of those war movies where everybody gets wounded but John Wayne.

Still, I found myself drawn in. It is sincere. It is not exploitative; a certain amount of screaming, frothing, and thrashing comes with the territory. My own guess is that people get the demons they deserve. While true believers go into frenzies, the Masters of Wall Street more cruelly lose joy in their wives and homes.

In Rome, Father Lucas meets a journalist named Angeline (Alice Braga), who like most women in the movies, even journalists, lacks a second name. She follows them on assignment, but it is one of the virtues of the film that she does not get romantically involved. In a correct casting decision, Braga is attractive but not a sexpot. This movie was filmed largely in Hungary. In Hollywood, the role would have had Megan Fox written all over it.

Hafstrom uses what I assume are some Hungarian interiors to go with his exteriors in Rome. A centuries-old library is especially impressive. The ancient presence of the Vatican is evoked to great effect; a reminder that although Satan is in fashion in many denominations, when you want to exorcise, you call in the experienced professionals. The priests are not blind believers. Father Kovak argues at one point that a psychiatrist might be more appropriate. When they get into the trenches with the demons there is spiritual hand-to-hand fighting, but Father Trevant, Father Kovak, and Angeline are as realistic as probably possible.

This is, I suspect, a more realistic film than *The Exorcist*, although not its equal. The real Father Gary Thomas has cited *The Exorcism of Emily Rose* (2005) as more accurate. I admire *The Rite* because while it delivers what I suppose should be called horror, it is atmospheric, its cinematography is eerie and evocative, and the actors enrich it. It has given some thought to exorcism. Grant its assumptions, and it has something to say.

The Road ★ ★ ★ ½

R, 119 m., 2009

Viggo Mortensen (The Man), Kodi Smit-McPhee (The Boy), Charlize Theron (The Woman), Robert Duvall (Old Man), Guy Pearce (The Veteran), Michael K. Williams (The Thief), Garret Dillahunt (Gang Member), Molly Parker (Motherly Woman). Directed by John Hillcoat and produced by Paula Mae Schwartz and Steve Schwartz. Screenplay by Joe Penhall, based on the novel by Cormac McCarthy.

The Road evokes the images and the characters of Cormac McCarthy's novel but lacks the same core of emotional feeling. I am not sure this is any fault of the filmmakers. The novel itself would not be successful if it were limited to its characters and images. Its effect comes above all through McCarthy's prose. It is the same with all of McCarthy's work but especially this one, because his dialogue is so restrained, less baroque than usual.

The story is straightforward enough: America has been devastated. Habitations have been destroyed or abandoned, vegetation is dying, crops have failed, the infrastructure of civilization has disappeared. It has happened in such recent memory that even The Boy, so young, was born into a healthy world. No reason is given for this destruction, perhaps because no reason would be adequate. McCarthy evokes the general apprehension of post-9/11. The Boy and The Man make their way toward the sea, perhaps for no better reason than that the sea has always been the direction of hope in this country.

The surviving population has been reduced to savage survivalists, making slaves of the weaker, possibly using them as food. We've always done that, employing beef cattle, for example, to do the grazing on acres of pasture so we can consume the concentrated calories of their labor. In a land where food is scarce, wanderers seek out canned goods and fear their own bodies perform this work for the cannibals.

Although we read of those who stockpile guns and ammunition for an apocalypse, weapons stores on the Road have grown low. The Man has a gun with two remaining bullets. He is a wary traveler, suspecting everyone he sees. He and The Boy have a few possessions in a grocery cart. He encourages his son to keep walking but holds out little hope for the end of their journey.

I am not sure the characters could be played better, or differently. Viggo Mortensen plays The Man as dogged and stubborn, determined to protect his boy. Kodi Smit-McPhee is convincing as a child stunned by destruction, depending on his father in a world where it must be clear to him that any man can die in an instant. The movie resists any tendency toward making the child cute or the two of them heartwarming.

Flashback scenes star Charlize Theron as the wife and mother of the two in earlier, sunnier days. They show the marriage as failing, and these memories haunt The Man. I'm not sure what relevance this subplot has to the film as a whole; a marriage happy or sad—isn't it much the same in this new world? It has a lot of relevance to The Man and The Boy. In times of utter devastation, memories are all we have to cling to.

The external events of the novel have been boldly solved, and this is an awesome production. But McCarthy's prose has the uncanny ability to convey more than dialogue and incident. It's as dense as poetry. It is more spare in *The Road* than in a more ornate work like *Suttree*; in *The Road* it is evocative in the way Samuel Beckett is. If it were not, *The Road* might be just another film of sci-fi apocalypse. It's all too easy to imagine how this material could be vulgarized into the 2007 version of *I Am Legend*.

How could the director and writer, John Hillcoat and Joe Penhall, have summoned the strength of McCarthy's writing? Could they have used more stylized visuals instead of relentless realism? A grainy black-and-white look to suggest severely limited resources? I have no idea. Perhaps McCarthy, like Faulkner, is all but unfilmable. The one great film of his work is the Coens' *No Country for Old Men*, but it began with an extraordinary character and surrounded him with others. *The Road* is not fertile soil but provides a world with the life draining from it.

McCarthy's greatest novels are *Suttree* and *Blood Meridian*. The second, set in the Old West, is about a fearsome, bald, skeletal man named Judge Holden, who is implacable in his desire to inflict suffering and death. It is being prepared by Todd Field (*In the Bedroom*). The Judge has not been cast; I see him as Tom Noonan—tall, grave, soft-spoken, almost sympathizing with you about your fate. Certainly not as a major star. As for a film based on *Suttree*, the director of *The Road*, John Hillcoat, made a film in 2005 named *The Proposition*, and I wrote in my review:

"Have you read *Blood Meridian*, the novel by Cormac McCarthy? This movie comes close to realizing the vision of that dread and despairing story. The critic Harold Bloom believes no other living American novelist has written a book as strong and compares it with Faulkner and Melville, but confesses his first two attempts to read it failed, 'because I flinched from the overwhelming carnage.'

"That book features a character known as the Judge, a tall, bald, remorseless bounty hunter who essentially wants to kill anyone he can, until he dies. His dialogue is peculiar, the speech of an educated man. *The Proposition* has such a character in an outlaw named Arthur Burns, who is much given to poetic quotations. He is played by Danny Huston in a performance of remarkable focus and savagery."

Perhaps it is significant that Hillcoat's next film would be based on *The Road*. Something in McCarthy's work draws him to it, and you must be a brave director to let that happen. Writing this, I realize few of the audience members can be expected to have read *The Road*, even though it was a selection of Oprah's Book Club. Fewer still will have read his other work. I've been saying for years that a film critic must review the film before him, and not how *faithful* the film is to the book—as if we're married to the book and screen adaptation is adultery. I realize my own fault is in being so very familiar with Cormac McCarthy. That may affect my ability to view the film afresh. When I know a novel is being filmed, I make it a point to not read the book. Yet I am grateful for having read McCarthy's.

Robin Hood ★ ★

PG-13, 131 m., 2010

Russell Crowe (Robin Longstride), Cate Blanchett (Marion Loxley), Mark Strong (Godfrey), William Hurt (William Marshal), Mark Addy (Friar Tuck), Oscar Isaac (Prince John), Danny Huston (Richard the Lionheart), Eileen Atkins (Eleanor of Aquitaine), Kevin Durand (Little John), Scott Grimes (Will Scarlet), Alan Doyle (Allan A'Dayle), Max von Sydow (Sir Walter Loxley). Directed by Ridley Scott and produced by Scott, Russell Crowe, and Brian Grazer. Screenplay by Brian Helgeland.

Little by little, title by title, innocence and joy is being drained out of the movies. What do you think of when you hear the name of Robin Hood? I think of Errol Flynn, Sean Connery, and the Walt Disney character. I see Robin lurking in Sherwood Forest, in love with Maid Marian (Olivia de Havilland or Audrey Hepburn), and roistering with Friar Tuck and the Merry Men. I see a dashing swashbuckler.

That Robin Hood is nowhere to be found in Ridley Scott's new *Robin Hood*, starring Russell Crowe as a warrior just back from fighting in the Third Crusade. Now Richard is dead, and Robin is essentially an unemployed mercenary. This story is a prequel. It takes place entirely *before* Robin got to be a folk hero. The idea of taking from the rich and giving to the poor was still in storyboard form. Grieving Richard the Lionheart and now faced with the tyrant King John, he leads an uprising.

This war broadens until, in the words of the movie's synopsis, "it will forever alter the balance of world power." That's not all: "Robin will become an eternal symbol of freedom for his people." Not bad for a man who, by general agreement, did not exist. Although various obscure bandits and ne'er-do-wells inspired ancient ballads about such a figure, our image of him is largely a fiction from the nineteenth century.

But so what? In for a penny, in for a pound. After the death of Richard, Robin Hood raises, arms, and fields an army to repel a French army as it lands on an English beach in wooden craft that look uncannily like World War II troop carriers at Normandy. His men, wielding broadswords, backed by archers, protected from enemy arrows by their shields, engage the enemy in a last act devoted almost entirely to nonstop CGI and stunt carnage in which a welter of warriors clashes in confused alarms and excursions, and Russell Crowe frequently appears in the foreground to whack somebody.

Subsequently, apparently, Robin pensioned his militia and retired to Sherwood Forest to play tag with Friar Tuck. That's my best guess; at the end the film informs us, "and so the legend begins," leaving us with the impression we walked in early.

Ah, you say, but what of Maid Marian? In this telling, Marion (Cate Blanchett) is not a maid but a widow, and not a merry one. At one point she threatens to unman Robin with her dagger, which is unlike the Maid Marians I've known and loved. Blanchett plays the role with great class and breeding, which is all wrong, I think. She's the kind of woman who would always be asking Robin, "Why do you let that smelly so-called friar hang around you like a fanboy?"

If you listen closely to the commercials, you may hear of a royal edict being issued against "Robin of the Hood." A hood, in medieval English, was, of course, a wood, or forest—a point that may be lost on many of the commercial's viewers.

Robin Hood is a high-tech and well-made violent action picture using the name of Robin Hood for no better reason than that it's an established brand not protected by copyright. I cannot discover any sincere interest on the part of Scott, Crowe, or the writer Brian Helgeland in any previous version of Robin Hood. Their Robin is another weary retread of the muscular macho slaughterers who with interchangeable names stand at the center of one overwrought bloodbath after another.

Have we grown weary of the delightful aspects of the Robin Hood legend? Is witty dialogue no longer permitted? Are Robin and Marion no longer allowed to engage in a spirited flirtation? Must their relationship seem like high-level sexual negotiations? How many people need to be covered in boiling oil for Robin Hood's story to be told these days? How many parents will be misled by the PG-13 rating? Must children go directly from animated dragons to skewering and decapitation, with no interval of cheerful storytelling?

The photography is, however, remarkable, and Crowe and the others are filled with fierce energy. Ridley Scott is a fine director for work like this, although in another world Hollywood would let him make smarter films. God, he must be tired of enormous battle scenes.

Note: The film was the opening night attraction at the 2010 Cannes Film Festival. There must be a reason for that.

The Romance of Astrea and Celadon ★ ★ ½

NO MPAA RATING, 109 m., 2009

Andy Gillet (Celadon), Stephanie Crayencour (Astrea), Cecile Cassel (Leonide), Veronique Reymond (Galathee), Rosette (Sylvie), Rodolphe Pauly (Hylas), Jocelyn Quivrin (Lycidas). Directed by Eric Rohmer and produced by Philippe Liegeois and Jean-Michel Rey. Screenplay by Rohmer, based on the novel by Honore d'Urfe.

The French New Wave began circa 1958 and influenced in one way or another most of the good movies made ever since. Some of its pioneers (Melville, Truffaut, Malle) are dead, but the others (Godard, Chabrol, Rivette, Resnais, Varda) are still active in their late seventies and up, and Eric Rohmer, at eighty-eight, has only just announced that *The Romance of Astrea and Celadon* may be his last film.

It doesn't look like a typical Rohmer. He frequently gives us contemporary characters, besotted not so much by love as by talking about it, finding themselves involved in ethical and plot puzzles, at the end of which he likes to quote a proverb or moral. His films are quietly passionate and lightly mannered.

But then, so is *Astrea and Celadon,* even if it's set in fifth-century Gaul and involves shepherds, shepherdesses, druids, and nymphs. The story was told in a novel by Honore d'Urfe, marquis of Valromey and count of Chateauneuf, who published it in volumes between 1607 and 1627—running, I learn, some five thousand pages. The film version must therefore be considerably abridged at 109 minutes, although it leaves you wondering if the novel ran on like this forever.

The movie does rather run on, although it is charming and sweet, and perhaps too languid. It is about two lovers obsessed with love's codes of honor. That is, curiously, the same subject as Rivette's 2007 film *The Duchess of Langeais,* made when he was seventy-nine. The characters seem perversely more dedicated to debating the fine points than getting down to it. Rivette has them talking to one another; Rohmer has them fretting while separated.

The story is told in pastoral woodlands and pastures and along a river's banks. We meet the handsome Celadon (Andy Gillet) and the beautiful Astrea (Stephanie Crayencour), shepherds and in love, not long before a tragic misperception breaks Astrea's heart, and Celadon hurls himself into the river in remorse. Believed by Astrea to be dead, he is fished out by the statuesque nymph Galathee (Veronique Reymond) and her handmaidens and kept all but captive in her castle. He pines, sworn never to be seen by Astrea's eyes again, while the two lovers debate the loopholes in romantic love with their friends. They also debate such matters as whether the Trinity corresponds to the Roman gods and sing, quote poetry, and mostly seem to ignore sheep.

A druid priest convinces Celadon to disguise himself as a girl and infiltrate Astrea's inner circle, creating much suspense, mostly on my part, as I kept expecting Astrea to exclaim, "Celadon, do you actually think you can fool anyone with that disguise?" But they play by the rules, and then things pick up nicely when they break them.

This would not be the Rohmer film you would want to start with. I've seen most of his films, and my first was *My Night at Maud's* (1969), about a long conversation about everything but love—which is to say, about love. Rohmer, I think, delights in these dialogue passages as allowing him to see his characters more carefully than in your usual formula, where courtships seem to be conducted via hormonal aromas. Sometimes his approach is sexier. The knee in *Claire's Knee* (1970) fascinated me more than entire bodies in countless films. Why Rohmer decided to end with this film I cannot say. Perhaps after forty-five years of features, he had heard it all.

Rudo y Cursi ★ ★ ★

R, 103 m., 2009

Gael Garcia Bernal (Tato), Diego Luna (Beto), Guillermo Francella (Batuta), Dolores Heredia (Elvira), Adriana Paz (Tona), Jessica Mas (Maya). Directed by Carlos Cuaron and produced by Alfonso Cuaron, Alejandro Gonzalez Inarritu, Guillermo del Toro, and Frida Torresblanco. Screenplay by Carlos Cuaron.

I am gradually discovering that soccer is superior to American football: quicker, more athletic, depending on improvisation more than planning. In South and Central America, where American baseball has been embraced, soccer is a way of life. A movie like *Rudo y Cursi* helps explain why: One day, peons on a banana plantation; the next day, playing for big bucks in Mexico City. Just bring your shorts, your shoes, your shirt, and your ability. No shoulder pads.

The movie is a rags-to-beeyaches comedy about two half brothers from a poor rural background who are spotted one day by a talent scout. Why was he even watching their small-town game on a vacant lot? He was stranded there, along with his disabled red sports convertible and his trophy squeeze, by a slow-moving auto shop. He sees them playing and offers them an audition, which hinges ironically on the ancient confusion between audience right and stage right.

This is not a deep movie, but it's a broad one. It reunites three talents who had an enormous hit with *Y Tu Mama Tambien* in 2001: the actors Gael Garcia Bernal and Diego Luna, and Carlos Cuaron, who wrote that film and writes and directs this one. Instead of trying to top themselves with life and poignancy, they wisely do something for fun.

Tato (Bernal) plays the accordion and dreams of a future as a musical star, although nothing about his singing and playing suggests much of a future. Beto (Luna) has a wife and kids and has recently been promoted to foreman of a banana-picking crew. He dreams of being a pro goalie in much the same way we all dream of being Susan Boyle, although without her talent.

Batuta (Guillermo Francella), the talent scout, is a smooth-talking slickster who considers himself a historian and philosopher of soccer. He is the film's narrator and shares the surprising news that soccer was invented by ancient Aztecs while kicking around the severed heads of their enemies. So much for the belief that it originated in China in about 200 B.C. I'm not surprised. To hear them tell it, everything originated in China in about 200 B.C.

The boys travel eagerly to Mexico City, leaving behind Beto's family, their mother, and their mother's assorted worthless husbands. They pick up nicknames. Tato is "Cursi," meaning cornball. Beto is "Rudo," meaning rough-edged. They're dazzled by the bright lights, the big city, and, in Rudo's case, the joys of high-stakes poker. Tato realizes his fantasy of meeting a sexy spokesmodel he's worshipped on TV and tapes his first music video, which, on the basis of its outcome, seems likely to be the last.

Curiously, and wisely, there's not a lot of soccer action in the movie, although it goes without saying there's a Big Match. This isn't a sports movie but a human comedy, and it depends on the effortless chemistry between Luna and Bernal, who evoke, like real brothers, the ability to love and hate each other and push all the right buttons. We are happy for their sudden good fortune, but somehow doubtful it will amount to much; they want success, but not enough to commit their entire lives to the quest.

The movie is the first from the newly formed Cha Cha Cha Productions, a collaboration of the top Mexican directors Alejandro Gonzalez Inarritu (*Amores Perros*), Guillermo del Toro (*Pan's Labyrinth*), and Alfonso Cuaron (brother of Carlos and director of *Y Tu Mama Tambien*). It comes at the end of an exciting decade for the Mexican cinema, which because of its high quality and the growing indie, foreign, and Spanish-speaking markets in the United States, is finding significant success. *Rudo y Cursi* is the sort of high-level buddy movie every national cinema needs for export—along with its masterpieces, to be sure.

Rumba ★ ★ ½

NO MPAA RATING, 77 m., 2009

Dominique Abel (Dom), Fiona Gordon (Fiona). Directed by Dominique Abel, Fiona Gordon, and Bruno Romy, and produced by Abel, Gordon, Charles Gillibert, Marin Karmitz, and Nathanael Karmitz. Screenplay by Abel, Gordon, and Romy.

Rumba is a peculiar deadpan comedy from Belgium, sort of sweet, sort of macabre, about a couple who are out of step with life but not with each other. It's not terrifically funny, but then how could it be? The influence of Jacques Tati abides in the material, without his sunniness.

Dom and Fiona (Dominique Abel and Fiona Gordon) are schoolteachers and competitive rumba dancers, and dangerously out to lunch. Arriving at the dance contest, they realize they've forgotten their costumes, race home to get them, and drive back at top speed while changing their clothes, Dom at one point upside down in the driver's seat while Fiona tugs at his socks. It's one time you're relieved to be able to see it's back projection.

Their luck worsens. Just for starters, they're in a car crash on their way home and Dom loses his memory and Fiona her leg. This doesn't much depress them; they're loving and ebullient and have each other. But then one catastrophe after another besets them, only one of which I will reveal. Abel and Gordon, I learn, have long worked together in cabaret, tilting toward physical comedy. They're essentially silent comedians with no need of a movie with a sound track, and *Rumba* has a bare minimum of dialogue.

They're skilled. A scene when Dom tries to rescue Fiona after a mishap with a trash fire reminded me of that Buster Keaton bit where he tries to help the drunken woman into her bed.

The movie is pleasing and amusing. I think it's intended to be funnier, but it's too laid back to achieve takeoff. Yes, laid back, even after they burn the house down. Those damned wooden legs. Nothing but fire hazards.

The Runaways ★ ★ ★

R, 100 m., 2010

Kristen Stewart (Joan Jett), Dakota Fanning (Cherie Currie), Michael Shannon (Kim Fowley), Stella Maeve (Sandy West), Scout Taylor-Compton (Lita Ford), Alia Shawkat (Robin), Riley Keough (Marie Currie). Directed by Floria Sigismondi and produced by Art Linson, John Linson, and William Pohlad. Screenplay by Sigismondi, based on the book *Neon Angel: The Cherie Currie Story* by Cherie Currie.

An all-girl rock band is named and trained by a rock manager of dubious sexuality, goes on the road, hits the charts, has a lesbian member and another who becomes a sex symbol but crashes from drugs. This is the plot of a 1970 film named *Beyond the Valley of the Dolls,* which inadvertently anticipated the saga of the Runaways five years later. Life follows art.

The Runaways tells the story of a hard-rock girl band that was created more or less out of thin air by a manager named Kim Fowley. His luck is that he started more or less accidentally with performers who were actually talented. Guitarists Joan Jett and Lita Ford are popular to this day, long after the expiration of their sell-by dates as jailbait. The lead singer, Cherie Currie, costarred in the very good *Foxes* (1980) with Jodie Foster, had drug problems, rehabbed, and "today is a chainsaw artist living in the San Fernando Valley." The ideal art form for any retired hard rocker.

The movie centers on the characters of Jett (Kristen Stewart), Currie (Dakota Fanning), and the manager Fowley (Michael Shannon). Jett was the original driving force, a Bowie fan who dreamed of forming her own band. Fowley, known in the music clubs of Sunset Strip as a manager on the prowl for young, cheap talent, told her to give it a shot, and paired her with Currie, whose essential quality is apparently that she was fifteen. That fit Fowley's concept of a jailbait band who would appeal because they seemed so young and so tough. He rehearses them in a derelict trailer in the Valley, writing their early hit "Cherry Bomb" on the spot.

Shannon is an actor of uncanny power. Nominated for a role as an odd dinner guest in *Revolutionary Road* (2008), he was searing as he turned paranoid in William Friedkin's *Bug* (2006). Here he's an evil Svengali, who teaches rock 'n' roll as an assault on the audience; the girls must batter their fans into submission or admit they're losers. He's like a Marine drill sergeant: "Give me the girl. I'll give you back the man." He converts Cherie, who begins by singing passively, into a snarling tigress.

The performance abilities of the Runaways won respect. The rest was promotion and publicity. The film covers the process with visuals over a great deal of music, which helps cover an underwritten script and many questions about the characters. We learn next to nothing about anyone's home life except for Currie, who is provided with a runaway mother (Tatum O'Neal), a loyal but resentful sister (Riley Keough), and a dying alcoholic father. Although this man's health is important in the plot, I don't recall us ever seeing him standing up or getting a clear look at his face.

So this isn't an in-depth biopic, even though it's based on Currie's 1989 autobiography. It's more of a quick overview of the creation, rise, and fall of the Runaways, with slim character development, no extended dialogue scenes, and a whole lot of rock 'n' roll. Its interest comes from Shannon's fierce and sadistic training scenes as Kim Fowley, and from the intrinsic qualities of the performances by Stewart and Fanning, who bring more to their characters than the screenplay provides.

Another new movie this week, *The Girl with the Dragon Tattoo* from Sweden, has a role for a young, hostile computer hacker. Stewart has been mentioned for the inevitable Hollywood remake. Reviewing that movie, I doubted she could handle such a tough-as-nails character. Having seen her as Joan Jett, I think she possibly could.

Note: Many years ago, while I was standing at a luggage carousel at Heathrow Airport, I was approached by a friendly young woman. I'm Joan Jett, she told me. I liked Beyond the Valley of the Dolls.

Just sayin'.

S

Saint John of Las Vegas ★ ★

R, 85 m., 2010

Steve Buscemi (John Alighieri), Romany Malco (Virgil), Sarah Silverman (Jill), Peter Dinklage (Mr. Townsend), Emmanuelle Chriqui (Tasty D Lite), Tim Blake Nelson (Ned). Directed by Hue Rhodes and produced by Mark Burton, Lawrence Mattis, Kelly McCormick, and Matt Wall. Screenplay by Rhodes, based on the story by Dante Alighieri.

If you were to view the trailer of *Saint John of Las Vegas,* it would probably look like a good time. It seems to have so much great stuff. Promise me a movie with Steve Buscemi, Sarah Silverman, Peter Dinklage, and Tim Blake Nelson, and I'm there. But this movie is all elbows. Nothing fits. It doesn't add up. It has some terrific free-standing scenes, but they need more to lean on.

Consider the burning man. This is a sideshow performer who wears a suit designed to burst into flames. Unfortunately, the suit has malfunctioned and he can't take it off until the fuel is exhausted. He waits it out on a folding chair behind the carnival midway, consumed in flames every thirty seconds. That's funny, especially when he's dying for a cigarette. But . . . what? He exists only to be existing.

Well, not quite. The flaming also seems to fit into the movie's overall symbolism. The screenplay, we learn, was written by the director Hue Rhodes, based on the story by Dante Alighieri. That name may not ring a bell with a lot of moviegoers and had better not be a question on the Tea Baggers' literacy test. We all recall that Dante's *Inferno* told the story of a journey into hell, with the poet Virgil as the tour guide.

In the movie, Steve Buscemi plays John Alighieri, an insurance claims adjuster who is assigned a partner named Virgil (Romany Malco) and sets off on a journey through the desert to Las Vegas (hell).

Let's have some fun. Dante's First Circle of Hell was Limbo. In the movie, that would be the main office of the insurance company. People in Limbo have trouble controlling their weaknesses. John's weakness is compulsive gambling. Second Circle is Lust. He lusts for Jill (Silverman), a chirpy coworker who labors in the next cubicle. Later, in a lap-dance bar, he undergoes but resists temptation from a stripper (Emmanuelle Chriqui), who sprained her neck in a car crash but tries to give him a lap dance from her wheelchair. It's her crash the insurance company doesn't want to pay the claim on.

Third Circle, Gluttony. In this circle are rain and hail, which the two drive through. Fourth Circle, Avarice. John dreams of winning the lottery and spends every dollar on scratch cards. Virgil also has greed, revealed later. Fifth Circle, Anger. They argue with a cop and arrive at a senseless flaming gateway in the desert, guarded by Tim Blake Nelson and other naked men with guns. Sixth Circle, Heresy. Virgil seems not to take the insurance company seriously.

Seventh Circle, Violence. In a used car lot, they are led into a trap and John, knocked senseless, barely escapes with his life. The lot is guarded by a savage dog, no doubt based on Cerberus, the watchdog of Hell. Eighth Circle, Fraud. John discovers the nature of a scheme to defraud the insurance company. Ninth and last Circle, Treason against God—or, in this case, Mr. Townsend (Dinklage), who is their boss at the insurance company.

If you recall Dante very well, or jot some reminders on your palm with a ballpoint, you can possibly follow the movie in this way. But if like most people your command of the *Inferno* is shaky, the film may seem disjointed and pointless. There is also this inescapable storytelling dilemma: Once you arrive in the Ninth Circle of Hell, what do you do for an encore?

The acting is first-rate. Buscemi is an apologetic loser who fled Vegas after losing his net worth, and now unwisely returns. Malco's Virgil, now that we think of it, is a guide who seems to have been this way before. Silverman's Jill is part temptress, part saint. It must have taken all of Rhodes's willpower to avoid naming her character "Beatrice," although of course Beatrice was Dante's guide into heaven. That would be the sequel.

And who is Saint John of Las Vegas? That would be John the Baptist or "John of the desert," divine messenger, not to be confused with the brother of Jesus. Why is he "of Las Vegas"? I think the answer must relate to John's gambling history. When Anna Dudak, my landlady on Burling Street, would take a trip to Las Vegas, her husband, Paul, would tell me she had gone to Lost Wages.

Salt ★ ★ ★ ★

PG-13, 100 m., 2010

Angelina Jolie (Evelyn Salt), Liev Schreiber (Ted Winter), Chiwetel Ejiofor (Peabody), Daniel Olbrychski (Orlov), Andre Braugher (Secretary of Defense). Directed by Phillip Noyce and produced by Lorenzo di Bonaventura and Sunil Perkash. Screenplay by Kurt Wimmer.

Salt is a damn fine thriller. It does all the things I can't stand in bad movies, and does them in a good one. It's like a rebuke to all the lousy action movie directors who've been banging pots and pans together in our skulls. It winds your clock tight, and the alarm doesn't go off for one hundred minutes.

It's gloriously absurd. This movie has holes in it big enough to drive the whole movie through. The laws of physics seem to be suspended here the same way as in a Road Runner cartoon. Angelina Jolie runs full speed out into thin air and doesn't look down until she's in the helicopter at the end.

Jolie is one fine-looking woman. You don't need me to tell you that. It's why she gets the big bucks. The movies have celebrated her eyes, lips, profile, biceps, boobs, waist, butt, thighs. *Salt* pays tribute to her ankles. Anyone who can jump from the heights she does here, in the way she does it, may die from a lot of causes, but a sprained ankle won't be one of them.

You know *parkour*? Wikipedia defines it as "the physical discipline of training to overcome any obstacle within one's path by adapting one's movements to the environment." Jolie's character, Evelyn Salt, makes it look as if *Run, Lola, Run* was about walking. There's a scene when she descends eight stories in an elevator shaft by simply jumping across it to one wall support lower than the last. Each time she lands, she says, "Oof," but that's about it.

You're not going to hear much about the plot here. Nothing I could tell you would be necessary for you to know, and everything could be fatal to your enjoyment. Let's just make it simple: She plays a woman determined to single-handedly save the world from nuclear annihilation. Oh, it's not that the plot holds water or makes any sense, but it's a pleasure to be surprised here and there along the way, and it's not like the movie lingers over each twist and turn as if it's just pulled an elephant out of a hat.

No, each revelation is the occasion for another chase scene. Evelyn Salt escapes from, or breaks into, one inescapable and/or impenetrable stronghold after another. And she does it all by herself, and with her bare hands, plus a few guns, grenades, and a homemade rocket launcher. You know how Ginger Rogers did everything Astaire did, except backward and wearing heels? Evelyn does everything James Bond did, except backward and barefoot in the snow.

At one point in the movie, Evelyn is chained to a concrete floor in a North Korean dungeon while a rubber hose is charmingly stuck into her mouth and gasoline is poured in. That's at the *beginning* of the film. I'm not going to tell you what she survives later. She plays a spy for the CIA—but now I'm giving away too many details. Important supporting roles are played by Liev Schreiber and Chiwetel Ejiofor.

The movie has been directed by Phillip Noyce, an Australian whose work ranges from Tom Clancy thrillers to the great and angry drama *Rabbit-Proof Fence*. Here he performs as a master craftsman, aided by the cinematography of Robert Elswit and the editing of Stuart Baird and John Gilroy. The movie has a great many chase scenes, and faithful readers will know that these, in general, have lost their novelty for me. But a good chase scene is a good chase scene. It demands some sense of spatial coherence, no matter how impossible; some continuity of movement, no matter how devised by stunt work and effects; and genuine interest for the audience.

It's in that area that Angelina Jolie really delivers. She brings the conviction to her role that such a movie requires. She throws herself into it with animal energy. Somehow, improbably, she doesn't come off as a superhero (although her immunity suggests one), but as a brave and determined fighter. How does she look? She looks beautiful by default, and there's a scene in an office where she looks back over her shoulder to talk with Schreiber and you think, oh, my. But neither Jolie nor Noyce overplay her beauty, and she gets gritty and bloody and desperate, and we get involved.

Although the movie finds an ingenious way to overcome history and resurrect the Russians as movie villains, neither that nor any other element of the plot demands analysis. It's all a hook to hang a thriller on. It's exhilarating to see a genre picture done really well.

Sanctum ★ ½

R, 109 m., 2011

Richard Roxburgh (Frank), Rhys Wakefield (Josh), Ioan Gruffudd (Carl), Alice Parkinson (Victoria), Dan Wyllie (Crazy George). Directed by Alister Grierson and produced by Ben Browning, James Cameron, Ryan Kavanaugh, Michael Maher, Peter Rawlinson, and Andrew Wight. Screenplay by Wight and John Garvin.

Sanctum tells the story of a terrifying adventure in an incompetent way. Some of it is exciting, the ending is involving, and all of it is a poster child for the horrors of 3-D used wrongly. The film is being heavily marketed as a "James Cameron Production," but if this were a "James Cameron Film," I suspect it would have fewer flaws and the use of 3-D would be much improved.

The movie, based on a true story, involves a scuba-diving expedition into the Esa-ala Caves of New Guinea, said to be the largest cave system in the world. The plan is to retrace an already explored route to reach a "base camp" somewhere far beneath the surface, and then to press on, perhaps to find how the surface water draining into the caves finds its way to the sea. There's no *need* to discover this, you understand, but after some loss of life, Frank (Richard Roxburgh), the leader of the expedition, tells his son, Josh (Rhys Wakefield), that only in a cave does he feel fully alive; the humdrum surface world is not for him and "human eyes have never seen this before."

After awkward opening scenes of almost startling inanity, we find ourselves deep inside the cave system, and our heroes deep in trouble. They are combining dangerous climbing with risky diving, and it's a good question why an inexperienced girlfriend was allowed to come along. Still, tactical errors are not what concerned me. I only wanted to figure out what was happening, and where, and why.

This movie should be studied in film classes as an example of inadequate film continuity. At no point are we oriented on our location in the cave as a whole or have a clear idea of what the current cave space looks like. If you recall Cameron's *Titanic*, its helpful early animation briefed us on the entire story of how the great ship sank. That was a great help in comprehending the events of its final hour. In *Sanctum*, there's a computer animation showing the known parts of the cave, but as the POV whizzes through caverns and tunnels, it achieves only a demonstration of computer animation itself. We learn damn little about the cave. The animated map even flips on its horizontal axis, apparently to show off. Hey, I can do stuff like that on my Mac, and then my hair is parted on the other side!

The movie is a case study of how not to use 3-D. *Sanctum* takes place in claustrophobic spaces with very low lighting, which are the last places you want to make look dimmer than they already are. The lighting apparently comes from battery-powered headlamps, and the characters are half in darkness and half in gloom. Now why put on a pair of glasses and turn down the lights?

One purpose of 3-D is to create the illusion of depth. One way to do this is to avoid violating the fourth wall by seeming to touch it. Let me give a famous example from *Jaws 3-D*. The problem with that movie is that when the shark attacked, it was so big its body touched the sides of the screen, and the 3-D illusion was lost. (The movie has a scene of an eel attack, and *that's* scary.)

Alas, the cinematographer of *Sanctum*, Jules O'Loughlin, consistently touches the side of the screen. He even has the curious practice of framing middle action with large, indistinct blocks of foreground stones and stuff. These are out of focus so that the midrange can look sharp, and 3-D only makes us wonder why the closer objects are less distinct. In close quarters he has to use many close-ups, and those, too, get old in a hurry in 3-D. The Brendan Fraser 3-D movie *Journey to the Center of the Earth* (2008) did a much better job of placing its actors in its spaces. Of course, the spaces were mostly f/x, but there you are.

In its editing continuity, *Sanctum* doesn't make clear how the actions of one character relate to another's. There is great spatial disorientation in the use of the close shots. There is a scene where a character gets in trouble underwater, and I invite anyone to explain exactly what happens. The movie has a tactic to distract from this visual confusion. Three team members follow many of the events from above on a large computer monitor. Alas, we don't see what they see. We only get reaction shots of them seeing it. Where does their screen image come from? Head-mounted webcams? A cam in that submersible lighting device? I dunno. How is the image transmitted? I doubt the cell phone service is great in a cave in the jungles of New Guinea. Maybe they set up a LAN? How is it powered? They even complain about the batteries on their headlamp.

There are a few closing scenes that involve the ruthless reality of who survives in a cave and who doesn't. One of these involves Frank and Josh. We've had a long wait, but the scene works. It has absolutely no need for 3-D. I wonder if people will go to *Sanctum* thinking the James Cameron name is a guarantee of high-quality 3-D. Here is a movie that can only harm the reputations of Cameron and 3-D itself.

Scrappers ★ ★ ★ ½

NO MPAA RATING, 90 m., 2010

A documentary directed by Brian Ashby, Ben Kolak, and Courtney Prokopas.

In the alley I see them at least once a week, the men with their grocery carts, collecting tin cans and other treasure. Some will have a heap as tall as themselves. I learn from the new film *Scrappers* that the same trade happens in Chicago on a larger scale, with men trolling the city for scrap metal and emptying their trucks at scrap-metal yards. For this valuable work they could make a living, until the economy collapsed.

An urban legend has grown up that such men steal copper gutters and the aluminum off the sides of garages. Such theft has been committed, but by desperate creatures of the night, not family men like Otis and Oscar who are the backbone of the scrapper trade. "I paint my name and my phone number on the side of my truck," Otis says. "They know this truck down to 157th Street."

These are happy men. Otis is almost poetic about his joy in cruising alleys and vacant lots for salable metals. He's on his own, alone in the truck, chatting with his wife every half hour or so. Housewives know him and flag him down to carry out an old refrigerator. For one lady he removes two old boilers from her basement, no charge, just for the resale value, and considers himself lucky.

They are strong. With dollies but no forklifts, they lever heavy loads into the backs of pickups with high plywood sides. Their trucks are weighed on the way into a scrapyard and on the way out—they're paid for the difference. They work in all weather, fourteen hours a day, collect cash money at the end, come home to their wives and kids. The film says there are thousands of scrappers in Chicago. I'm reminded of Agnes Varda's great *The Gleaners and I* (2000), about the French vocation of scavenging.

Otis is seventy-three, born in Chicago. Oscar looks to be in his forties and is from Honduras, and I have the impression he may be undocumented. They do useful work. "Mayor Daley is supposed to be a green mayor," says one housewife as she watches a heavy load hauled out of her basement, "but it doesn't seem like they pick up much."

Scrappers look for wire, pipes, aluminum, brass, copper, plain iron, and steel. The scrap yards heap it up, process it into particles about the size of Cheerios, and ship it mostly to China, where it comes back to us and ends up in the alley again. In 2007, we learn, a scrapper could earn $200 to $300 a ton. In 2008, when the market collapsed and new construction ended, the price dropped to $20. Scrappers became desperate.

Fortunate people sneer at them, write them off as bums or thieves. Few in the middle class work as hard all day as these men do—and, quite possibly, work as usefully. You cannot be a drunk and work this hard. You can't support a drug habit. But you can support a family, and *Scrappers* goes into the homes of Otis and Oscar to meet their wives—stable, stalwart women—and their kids. The loyalty in these homes is palpable.

Otis lives in senior housing, but moves out because of bedbugs and water leaking everywhere. He has worked as a scrapper for more than forty years, but it's in his own hallway that he slips on water and gets a concussion. He sits by a hospital window and tells his wife how much he wants to get back to work. I think it's Oscar who compares scrapping to fishing—you go out in the morning hoping for a good catch.

The film was made by Chicagoans Brian Ashby, Ben Kolak, and Courtney Prokopas. They put in the hours in the alleys and brought back a human document. It is necessary we have these films because our lives are so closed off we don't understand the function these men perform. You want green; there ain't nobody greener than Oscar and Otis.

Scre4m ★ ★

R, 111 m., 2011

Neve Campbell (Sidney Prescott), Courteney Cox (Gale Weathers), David Arquette (Dewey Riley), Emma Roberts (Jill Roberts), Hayden Panettiere (Kirby Reed), Rory Culkin (Charlie Walker). Directed by Wes Craven and produced by Craven, Iya Labunka, and Kevin Williamson. Screenplay by Williamson.

The great pleasure in the *Scream* movies is that the characters have seen other horror films. At times they talk as if they're in the chat room of a horror site. Wes Craven's *Scre4m*, the typographically skewed fourth movie in the series, opens with a clever series of horror scenes that emerge one from another like nested Russian dolls, and Kevin Williamson's dialogue is smart and knowing. All through the movie, *Scre4m* lets us know that it knows exactly what it's up to—and then goes right ahead and gets up to it.

The premise is that a psychopath has returned to the town of Woodsboro, which has already seen so many fatal slashings you question why anyone still lives there, let alone watches horror movies. This killer seems at times to be supernormal, is able to appear simultaneously at the front and back doors of a house, and predict precisely where victims will be, and when. As a result, the body count in *Scre4m* mounts relentlessly until you wonder whether everyone in the cast is going to be killed, with the movie ending on an empty room (with the phone ringing—heh, heh).

There is a dark nihilism here that seems to appeal to *Scream* fans. No one deserves to die, but so many do, and horribly, with geysers of blood spurting from their wounds. Why must they die? Why is the killer, "Ghost Face," so driven? The motive is eventually revealed, but I wouldn't go so far as to say it's explained.

Neve Campbell returns as Sidney Prescott, a hometown girl who has written a best-seller and has returned to Woodsboro to promote it. My own inclination would be to stay the hell away from the location of the killings in the original *Scream*, but hey, that's just me. Also back are David Arquette as the local sheriff, and Courteney Cox, the newscaster who is now his wife.

Sidney's cousin Jill (Emma Roberts) has a posse of fellow teenagers who spend most of the time picking up the phone and answering the door when they absolutely shouldn't. They're sophisticated; they know that in a horror movie when you walk past a dark doorway, something is likely to jump out at you. But when they get a call from someone saying, "My face will be the last sight you see," and then the doorbell rings—do they answer it? Of course they do. Survival of the fittest needs another million years to take effect in Woodsboro.

Karl Malden once said the hardest thing he ever had to do as an actor was act as if he didn't know he was about to be hit in the head with a beer can. He could have taken lessons from these girls, who go through the whole movie acting as if they're not about to be stabbed to death.

Wes Craven is a good director, and the film

is done with some wit and style. The actors do what they can in a film that doesn't care about human insights. The characters are almost preternatural in their detachment; if you were embedded in events like these, wouldn't you be paralyzed with panic? Let's say you were the sheriff. Would you act so competent when you were obviously powerless? What about the film's many ambulance drivers? In *Bringing Out the Dead,* Nicolas Cage was in a constant frenzy, and that was supposedly a realistic story. In *Scre4m,* the locals are almost catatonic in their ability to carry on dialogue. How can you dissect a plot when you know you're next on the dissection table?

Maybe that's the point. Perhaps Craven and Williamson are making an ironic and cynical comment on the bloody tradition of the genre. Are they counting on their knowing fans to pick up all their self-aware nods? Could be. Does anyone—*anyone*—watch a movie like this as if it's in any way depicting reality? I dunno. *Scre4m* provides exactly what its audience will expect: one victim after another being slashed, skewered, stabbed, gutted, and sliced, with everyone in on the joke. Maybe that's your idea of a good time.

A Screaming Man ★ ★ ★ ½

NO MPAA RATING, 92 m., 2011

Youssouf Djaoro (Adam Ousmane), Dioucounda Koma (Abdel Ousmane), Emile Abossolo M'bo (District Chief), Hadje Fatime N'Goua (Mariam), Marius Yelolo (David), Djeneba Kone (Djeneba), Heling Li (Madame Wang). Directed by Mahamat-Saleh Haroun and produced by Florence Stern. Screenplay by Haroun.

Adam was the swimming champion of central Africa years ago and now rules over the swimming pool of a luxury hotel. Tall, stately, and middle-aged, he provides towels and services for the mostly white and Asian guests, and cleans up the area at day's end. He's assisted by his son, Abdel, and as *A Screaming Man* opens, the two of them have a contest to see who can hold his breath the longest underwater.

Somewhere offscreen, indirectly alluded to, a civil war is under way in this nation, Chad. Business at the hotel falls off. It has been purchased by a Chinese group, and now Madame Wang, the manager, makes staff cuts. She informs Adam (Youssouf Djaoro) that he will be replaced at the pool by his son, Abdel (Dioucounda Koma), and made a security guard in charge of the hotel gates. He's lucky to have a job. His best friend, David (Marius Yelolo), the hotel chef, loses his.

"But the pool is my life!" Adam says. His long-ago swimming medal validates his existence. Moving sadly to the front gate, he wears a hotel uniform and becomes, in a way, a mirror image of the hero of Murnau's famous *The Last Laugh* (1924). In that film, a hotel doorman measures his worth by his uniform and identity; a similar job is, for Adam, devastating. He regards his son, now holding "his" job, balefully.

The unique quality of the movie is to look at Adam's life, the way he values his job more than his son, and the way status conferred by a Western hotel has bewitched him. He pours out his discontent with his wife, and shares it with the district police chief (Emile Abossolo M'bo), who has been charged with raising troops to fight in the war. These elements play out in an agonizing choice that Adam feels he must make between his son and his "life" as the pool man.

The film was directed by Mahamat-Saleh Haroun, and won the Jury Prize at Cannes 2010 (Haroun himself was a member of the 2011 jury). He is a clear and confident filmmaker. It's easy to imagine how the story, as I have simplified it, could have been a clunky melodrama, but *A Screaming Man* is about what happens within the characters, especially Adam. He never screams, but we feel him screaming.

Haroun was born in Chad, a former French colony, and moved to France at about the age of twenty-one. He has cited Ozu as one of his influences, and like the master he is attentive to the way compositions and body language create dramatic effects. His strategy here is not to have Adam act out his crisis, but to allow us time to empathize with him and understand the emotional choices he is making. One of the crucial events in the film takes place offscreen, and that is the best place for it because what happens isn't as important as its effects.

The movie makes no obvious statements about postcolonial Africa, but it is clear that colonialism in Adam's case requires not so much colonial rulers as those who were ruled. The hotel to begin with, and his job itself, and the Chinese who buy it, are all part of an economic process that dictates his life. He finds his whole value as a man in a job that essentially involves only a title.

A Screaming Man is being released by Film Movement, whose members received their DVDs in the mail quite some time ago. FM is a valuable enterprise that searches festivals and elsewhere for films worthy of being seen, which are perhaps not commercial in today's market. Members get the first (sometimes the only) look. The films are chosen well; I saw this film at Cannes 2010, admired it, and wondered at the time if it would find a release. As we find our way through a troubled time for foreign and art films, enterprises like Film Movement give hope.

Note: Film Movement on the Web: http://www.filmmovement.com.

Season of the Witch ★ ★

PG-13, 95 m., 2011

Nicolas Cage (Behmen), Ron Perlman (Felson), Stephen Campbell Moore (Debelzaq), Claire Foy (The Girl), Stephen Graham (Hagamar), Ulrich Thomsen (Eckhart), Robert Sheehan (Kay), Christopher Lee (Cardinal D'Ambroise). Directed by Dominic Sena and produced by Alex Gartner and Charles Roven. Screenplay by Bragi Schut Jr.

I lost track of the sieges and battles. *Season of the Witch* opens with a series of helpfully labeled sequences in which desert battles are fought, cites are sacked, buttresses stormed, redoubts doubted, enclosures enclosed, and so on. I didn't take notes, but an example might be "The Siege of Synecdoche, April 1, AD 1239."

Anyway, there's a slew of them. Crusaders in armor do battle with fierce desert tribesmen under the blazing sun. Heads are lopped off and roll across the plain. Horses whinny, women scream, children flee, warriors are disemboweled, limbs are severed, dogs would bark if there were dogs. The horror!

After about a dozen years of this, we pause for a discussion between the two hero Crusaders, Behmen (Nicolas Cage) and Felson (Ron Perlman). Yes, Cage and Perlman, so you suspect *Season of the Witch* will not be an exercise in understatement. "The killing of the women and children must stop!" they agree. Having arrived at this conclusion after twelve years of rape and pillage, they do not qualify as quick studies. The comrades abandon the armies of the Crusades, hit the road, and happen across a town somewhere in the vastness.

They have an excellent reason for ending up here, of all places: Why, this is the very same town of the pretitle sequence! Where three women were forced to confess to witchcraft, thrown backward off a bridge with nooses around their necks, hanged dead, and then prudently drowned in the river below! We liberals are earnestly deploring the superstition that forced them to confess Salem-style, until they spring back up from the dark waters and, hey, they *were* witches. Sometimes Glenn Beck is right.

Time has passed since that day (whether the full twelve years, I cannot say), and Behmen and Felson are quickly assigned to convey a surviving (if technically dead) witch (Claire Foy) to a distant monastery where there is a crumbling ancient tome containing the only known incantation that can exorcise her and bring an end to the Black Plague—so hey, we're back in medieval Europe now, specifically Hungary. A possible clue to this film's mind-set as a guy flick is that the Claire Foy character has no name and is known only as The Girl. Not even The Witch.

I am about out of Astonishments for you, but buckle your seat belt for this one: The director, Dominic Sena, has been inspired by Ingmar Bergman's *The Seventh Seal* (1957), that classic tale of a knight who returns from the Crusades and encounters Death on the road. Audiences for *Season of the Witch* may not be thickly larded with students of *The Seventh Seal*, but those few will be rewarded by sundry parallels and allusions. Ever since Bergman's *The Virgin Spring* was remade as *The Last House on the Left*, his work has suggested a rich mine for homage.

You know I am a fan of Nic Cage and Ron Perlman (whose very existence made *Hellboy* possible). Here, like cows, they eat the scenery, regurgitate it to a second stomach found only in actors, and chew it as cud. It is a noble effort, but I prefer them in their straight-through *Human Centipede* mode.

Secretariat ★ ★ ★ ★

PG, 122 m., 2010

Diane Lane (Penny Chenery), John Malkovich (Lucien Laurin), Dylan Walsh (Jack Tweedy), Dylan Baker ((Hollis Chenery), Margo Martindale (Miss Ham), Nelsan Ellis (Eddie Sweat), Otto Thorwarth (Ronnie Turcotte), Fred Dalton Thompson (Bull Hancock), James Cromwell (Ogden Phipps), Scott Glenn (Chris Chenery), Kevin Connolly (Bill Nack). Directed by Randall Wallace and produced by Mark Ciardi, Pete DeStefano, and Gordon Gray. Screenplay by Mike Rich, suggested by *Secretariat: The Making of a Champion* by William Nack.

When Secretariat died at nineteen, my friend Bill Nack told me, the autopsy revealed that his heart was two and a half times the size of an average horse's. Bill had followed the horse for its entire life and wrote the book *Secretariat*, which inspired this film. Bill and I became good friends at Illinois in 1962. I remember him telling me in the 1970s about a racehorse he admired with great passion. I thought it was curious that Nack, who could recite long passages from Fitzgerald and Eliot by heart, had been lured away from literature by a racehorse. Now I understand. He found literature in a racehorse.

Bill has been the close friend of a lifetime. I would call that not a conflict of interest in writing this review, but more of a declaration. I have no fear in suggesting that his twenty years as Secretariat's biographer and his daily presence on the set contributed materially to this film. *Secretariat* just *knows* all sorts of things, and many of them I knew from Bill telling me over the years. They also grow from his love of horses, which began when he was a stable boy. Let me tell a story: When Bill was a reporter at *Newsday*, he climbed on a desk at an office party and recited the names of every Derby winner, correctly, in order. When he climbed down, the editor quietly called him aside and said, "How do you know that?" Then he made Bill the paper's turf writer, in some way setting this movie in motion.

You don't need me to tell you Secretariat was the crowning glory of the Sport of Kings. It is thirty-seven years since he set records in the Kentucky Derby and the Belmont, and those records stand today. It was said by some he was better over shorter distances, and that at the Belmont he would fade against his great rival Sham, who would show more endurance. He won the Belmont by thirty-one lengths. I knew that. Everybody knows that. Bill has shown me video of that race, with the astonishing gap between Secretariat and the rest of the field. So why, when I saw the race in the film, did I have tears in my eyes?

It was because *Secretariat* is a movie that allows us to understand what it really meant. This isn't some cornball formula film. It doesn't have a contrived romance. It's certainly not about an underdog: At the Belmont, Secretariat paid only $2.20 on a $2 bet, and 5,617 holders of winning tickets held them as souvenirs (a wise investment; those tickets go on eBay for as much as $1,000). *Secretariat* takes none of those mundane paths. It is a great film about greatness, the story of the horse and the no less brave woman who had faith in him.

Penny Chenery (Diane Lane) was the daughter of a Virginia horse farm owner. Her father (Scott Glenn) was ill, and his family thought they should sell the farm. But she could read lineages. She flipped a coin with a millionaire and "lost," but won the mare she wanted—and she was there in the stable when the mare gave birth. The groom said he'd never before seen a horse stand up on its legs that soon after birth.

There was something about Secretariat. Bill, who was a regular visitor at Meadow Farm throughout the horse's life, tried to get me to understand: The people around the horse felt it was blessed. Penny Chenery refused to sell the farm, turned down an offer of $7 million for the still-untested horse, and left her husband and family behind in Colorado to commute to Virginia. She had faith. So did the groom, Eddie Sweat (Nelsan Ellis), who was with Secretariat more than any other human being during the horse's life. And so did Lucien Laurin (John Malkovich), the trainer who had been trying to retire when Penny hauled him away from his golf clubs.

The movie focuses closely on the owner, the trainer, and the groom. It has no time for foolishness. When the time comes for the coin flip with millionaire Ogden Phipps (James Cromwell), we understand why Mrs. Chenery wants the mare she does, and director Randall Wallace underlines that with admirable economy, using a close-up of Malkovich studying a breeding chart that works better than five minutes of dialogue.

Gene Siskel used to say his favorite movies were about what people actually do all day. That's what *Secretariat* is. It pays us the compliment of really caring about thoroughbred racing. In a low-key way, it conveys an enormous amount of information. And it creates characters who, because of spot-on casting, are vivid, human, and complex. Consider how it deals with the relationship between Penny and her husband, Jack Tweedy (Dylan Walsh). They became estranged because of her decision, Nack says, but the movie only implies that rather than getting mired in a soap opera.

As a woman, Penny is closed out of racing's all-boys club. If a man neglected his family for a racehorse, that might be common. But a woman is committing some sin against nature. And when she refuses to sell, her whole family—husband, brother, everyone—put enormous pressure on her. They were sure her decision was taking money out of their pockets. How she raises money to keep the farm is ingenious lateral thinking, and best of all, it's accurate.

This whole movie feels authentic. Diane Lane, who is so good in so many kinds of roles, makes Penny as a smart woman with great faith in her own judgment and the courage to bet the farm on it. Every hair in place, always smartly turned out, she labors in the trenches with Lucien and Eddie, negotiates unflinchingly with the Old Boys, eats the stomach-churning meals at the diners where the track crowd hangs out. She looked at the greatest racehorse in the world and *knew* she was right, when all about her were losing their heads and blaming it on her.

Of the actors, I especially enjoyed John Malkovich. He has a way of conveying his reasoning by shorthand and implication. He creates a horse trainer slow to tip his hand, which is correct. No role in Mike Rich's screenplay is overwritten, or tries to explain too much. Like *The Social Network*, another contender for year-end awards, it has supreme confidence in its story and faith that we will find it fascinating. This is one of the year's best films.

To my shame, I used to kid Bill that he wrote stuff like, "Big Red knew it was an important day," as if he could read Secretariat's mind. He wrote nothing of the sort. We would speculate about what a horse does know. W. G. Sebald wrote: "Men and animals regard each other across a gulf of mutual incomprehension." Yes, I think so. But between Secretariat and his human family, something was comprehended. There's a scene here when Penny Chenery and her horse look each other in the eye for a long time on an important morning. You can't tell me they weren't both thinking the same thing. ☞

The Secret in Their Eyes ★ ★ ★ ★

R, 129 m., 2010

Ricardo Darin (Benjamin Esposito), Soledad Villamil (Irene Menendez Hastings), Guillermo Francella (Pablo Sandoval), Pablo Rago (Ricardo Morales), Javier Godino (Isidoro Gomez). Directed by Juan Jose Campanella and produced by Campanella, Mariela Besuievski, and Carolina Urbieta. Screenplay by Campanella, based on the novel by Eduardo Sacheri.

The Secret in Their Eyes opens with the meeting, after many years, of Benjamin (Ricardo Darin) and Irene (Soledad Villamil). She is a judge. He is a retired criminal investigator. They are just a little too happy to see each other. Twenty-five years ago, when she was assistant to a judge and he was an investigator under her, they were involved in a brutal case of rape and murder. Benjamin visited the crime scene, and the corpse of the dead woman spoke eloquently of the brutality of the crime. Two workmen were arrested and convicted. Benjamin was never convinced of their guilt. Now he tells Irene that on his own time he wants to write about the case.

This commences an absorbing back-and-forth journey through time, between Buenos

Aires in 1974 and 2000, which reopens both the crime and the unacknowledged feeling that has remained all these years between Irene and Benjamin. That's where their personal appeal comes into play. The actress Soledad Villamil is, forgive me, my idea of a Woman. Grown-up, tallish, healthy, brunette, sane, and perhaps she was cast for her eyes because the film contains a lot of close-ups and they're required to conceal secrets. Think of Anne Archer. Playing Irene at ages twenty-five years apart, she is never too young or too old, but standing right there.

Ricardo Darin makes her a worthy partner as Benjamin. His rank was too low, his pay too small, her presence too assured for him to trust the signals he must have known she was sending. He's one of those men on whom a beard seems inevitable. There is a sadness about him. He has never stopped thinking about the murder case, and we understand—although the movie is indirect about this—that the investigation was mishandled at the time because of Argentina's diseased right-wing politics.

Without being too obvious about it, the film reassembles the strands of two stories, the murder case and the unfinished emotions between Benjamin and Irene. It is filled with vivid characters. Sandoval (Guillermo Francella) is Benjamin's alcoholic assistant in the investigation, one of those drunks who may be incompetent but is not useless. He and Benjamin, and all the legal side, engage in the droll formality of addressing one another by fanciful titles. Morales (Pablo Rago) is the husband of the dead woman, still obsessed with her death. Gomez (Javier Godino) has always been Benjamin's real suspect, and there is a scene involving him in a soccer stadium that I have no idea how it could have been filmed, special effects or no.

Juan Jose Campanella is the writer-director, and here is a man who creates a complete, engrossing, lovingly crafted film. He is filled with his stories. *The Secret in Their Eyes* is a rebuke to formula screenplays. We grow to know the characters, and the story pays due respect to their complexities and needs. There is always the sense that they exist in the *now*, and not at some point along a predetermined continuum. Sometimes I watch a film unspool like a tape measure, and I can sense how far we are from the end. Sometimes my imagination is led to live right along with it.

The Secret in Their Eyes surprised many by winning the 2010 Academy Award for best foreign-language film. Michael Haneke's *The White Ribbon,* another considerable film, was thought to be the front-runner. The Academy did a good thing when it reformed the foreign language voting, requiring all voters to see all five finalists. In 2009, with the Japanese winner *Departures,* and again in 2010, the voters had an advantage over the rest of us. Who is to say whether they were right? They voted as they felt, and in today's unhappy distribution scene, the Oscar means your chances of seeing this film are much increased. You won't regret it. This is a real movie, the kind they literally don't make very much anymore.

The Secret of Kells ★ ★ ★

NO MPAA RATING, 75 m., 2010

With the voices of: Evan McGuire (Brendan), Christen Mooney (Aisling), Mick Lally (Brother Aidan), and Brendan Gleeson (Abbot Cellach). Directed by Tomm Moore, codirected by Nora Twomey, and produced by Moore, Didier Brunner, Viviane Vanfleteren, and Paul Young. Screenplay by Fabrice Ziolkowski.

When I went to Ireland to visit the set of *Ryan's Daughter,* the studio sent a car to ferry me and my cohort McHugh to the Dingle Peninsula. As we drove along we crossed an old bridge and the driver said, "Leprechauns made their home under this bridge." We stopped for petrol, and I quietly said to McHugh, "He doesn't know you're Irish and is giving us the tourist treatment." "Ebert," said McHugh, "he means it."

Did he mean it? Did McHugh believe that he meant it? With the Irish, the answer is yes and no. McHugh and his brothers told me how as lads they picked up change by discovering the Irish surnames of Yankee tourists and offering to show them where their ancestors lived. They always led them to the same shop in a little cottage, where the owner gave them a "consideration" for any purchases made.

What does this possibly have to do with *The*

Secret of Kells, the new film that was one of this year's Oscar nominees for best animation? Quite a bit, I think. Here is a film about a young and very brave medieval monk named Brendan, a sacred book, a storied monastery, a fairy girl, and an alarming creature, a forest containing little nuts that make brilliant green inks. The fairy girl is quite real, as Brendan can see for himself. If there are any leprechauns, she no doubt knows them. If there are not, how does she know for sure?

The Irish are a verbal people, preserving legends in story and song, and although few Chicagoans may know there's a First Folio of Shakespeare in the Newberry Library, few Dubliners do NOT know that the Book of Kells reposes in Trinity College. I viewed it once. It is a painstakingly illuminated medieval manuscript preserving the four Gospels, and every page is a work of art. Many monks created it over many years.

Perhaps little Brendan was one of them. Perhaps some of that brilliant emerald green was his, extracted from nuts he gathered in the forest. Brendan (voice by Evan McGuire), the youngest and pluckiest monk in the walled monastery, befriends old Brother Aidan (Mick Lally), a traveler who has arrived bearing the precious book. Some pages remain to be created, and Aidan says Brendan must help. He can start by disobeying the Abbot (Brendan Gleeson), venturing outside the walls, and gathering the nuts.

This and his further adventures are related in Tomm Moore's film, which is a little like an illuminated manuscript itself. Just as every margin of the Book of Kells is crowded with minute and glorious decorations, so is every shot of the film filled with patterns and borders, arches and frames, doodads and scrimshaw images. The colors are bold and bright, the drawings are simplified and 2-D. That reflects the creation of the original book in the centuries before the discovery of perspective in the Renaissance.

Like the people in Nina Paley's *Sita Sings the Blues,* these move mostly back and forth within the same plane, which is only correct since perspective hasn't yet created spatial dimension. But there's no feeling of limitation. Indeed, in a season where animated images hurl themselves from the screen with alarming recklessness, I was grateful that these were content merely to be admired.

The movie has a wide appeal, with a gap in the middle. I think it will appeal to children young enough to be untutored in boredom, and to anyone old enough to be drawn in, or to appreciate the artistry. For those in between, the *Transformers*-damaged generation, it will seem to be composed in a quaint, unknown language.

The Secret of the Grain ★ ★ ★ ½

NO MPAA RATING, 151 m., 2009

Habib Boufares (Slimane Beiji), Hafsia Herzi (Rym), Faridah Benkhetache (Karima), Abdelhamid Aktouche (Hamid), Bouraouia Marzouk (Souad), Hatika Karaoui (Latifa), Alice Houri (Julia). Directed by Abdellatif Kechiche and produced by Claude Berri. Screenplay by Kechiche.

A nineteen-year-old actress named Hafsia Herzi steps into the cinema in this film. I have a feeling it will be, like the first film of Isabelle Huppert, not simply a debut, but an announcement: "Here I am, and I am the real thing." She is the energy at the heart of a life-filled portrait of a big family of second-generation immigrants in a shabby French port city, a family that nourishes love, jealousy, discouragement, ambition, and a whole lot of dining and talking.

The Secret of the Grain is the wrong title for this movie. In France, where it was honored for best film, director, screenplay, and most promising actress, the title translates as "Fish Couscous." In England, it opened as *Couscous.* The only secret involving the grain is why it's so late being served. What were you expecting, Napoleon's toenails?

The wave of immigrants from former French colonies such as Tunisia, Morocco, and Algeria began in the late 1950s and continues, but most of the early arrivals are now grandparents, their offspring speaking only a few words of Arabic. We land in the middle of such a family, its patriarch the grave, taciturn Slimane Beiji (Habib Boufares). He's in the process of losing his job at a shipyard and negotiating uneasily between his first wife, Souad (Bouraouia Marzouk), and his lover,

Latifa (Hatika Karaoui), who owns a little hotel. He has two sons, one always in lust, but saves his deepest affection for Latifa's daughter, Rym (Hafsia Herzi). We have to gather these facts from the others, because Slimane doesn't confide.

The Tunisian-born writer-director, Abdellatif Kechiche, isn't interested in a formal story, although he does provide a cliff-hanging third act. He wants us to see these people live. Early in the film, he has a dinner table scene of such virtuosity that we feel we know everyone, even those we haven't seen before. This scene only incidentally sets up plot points; its purpose is to show strong opinions, deep feelings, humor, and a sincere interest in the food. The cook is the first wife, renowned for her couscous; she always sends a plate home to Slimane, who lives in a little room in Latifa's hotel. She also, as a ritual, gives a plate from every meal to the nearest homeless man she can find.

Still waters run deep. Slimane reveals plans to use his severance pay to open a restaurant aboard a rusty ship in the harbor, serving Souad's couscous. His strongest supporter is Rym, and as she talks with Slimane and a group of old musicians who live at the hotel, and to her mother, she reveals herself as an instinctive actress who tells each what they need to hear. She never gets angry, never pushes too hard, and doesn't insist, but it's almost impossible to keep her from having her way.

The film arrives at a big free dinner thrown by Slimane for the town big shots, in hopes of getting planning permission for the restaurant. Here we see race and class discrimination in France; the big shots are happy to wine and dine for free, but in their minds immigrants are not . . . quite . . . French. The younger generation all seem quintessentially French to us, but what do we know?

There are two amazing dialogue scenes in the movie. One involves Rym pleading with her mother to attend Slimane's opening night, despite the couscous being prepared by the other woman. The other involves Alice Houri as Julie, who is married to Slimane's womanizing son and explains with astonishing passion why he is a liar, a worthless scumbag, and a failure as husband and father.

This verbal assault comes to poor Slimane as the latest in a series of disasters, including the delivery of the dinner. Help comes, not from an unexpected source, but certainly in an unexpected way. We leave the movie as we entered, in the middle of things. *The Secret of the Grain* never slows, always engages, may continue too long, but ends too soon. It is made of life itself. Hafsia Herzi has four more films in the can and two in production. Remember her name.

The Secrets ★ ★ ★ ½

NO MPAA RATING, 127 m., 2009

Fanny Ardant (Anouk), Ania Bukstein (Naomi), Michal Shtamler (Michelle), Adir Miller (Yanki), Guri Alfi (Michael). Directed by Avi Nesher and produced by Nesher and David Silber. Screenplay by Nesher and Hadar Galron.

Naomi is a great disappointment to her father. She is his student, the most learned, the most devout student of the respected old rabbi. But she hasn't learned the most important lesson: how to be a submissive woman, to submit herself to the will of her father and her future husband. Even worse, she wickedly thinks she could someday be a rabbi herself.

There are hints in *The Secrets* that she knows well how her father's beliefs worked in the life of her mother: "Often when I came into this kitchen, I found her weeping." Naomi submits to her father the rabbi but not to her father the man. The rabbi has decided that his student Michael will marry Naomi. Naomi has no feeling for this man: She knows more than he does, but he treats her as a silly girl and piously asserts his narrow view of a woman's role.

Naomi buys time. After the death of her mother, she postpones the wedding and convinces her father to let her spend some time in a seminary in a secluded town in Israel. Here she will come into her own as a natural spiritual leader, as a woman, and as someone who discovers the difference between convenient and romantic love.

Avi Nesher's *The Secrets*, a deeply involving melodrama, has all the devices to draw us into this story. In some ways it is a traditional narrative. But it is more. It is gently and powerfully acted. And it is thoughtful about its characters, so that even though they follow a somewhat predictable arc, they contain surprises for us. They keep thinking for themselves.

Naomi (Ania Bukstein) seems at first a subdued, intellectual young woman, who believes explicitly in her father's orthodoxy. But as she sees how it worked in her mother's life and is working in hers, she experiences the basic feminist insight: Why a man but not a woman? It fascinates me that in some religions, men subscribe so eagerly to a dogma that oppresses women, and some women agree with it. Naomi does not agree.

At the seminary, one of her roommates doesn't even think of agreeing. This is Michelle (Michal Shtamler), from Paris, with a chip on her shoulder. The two find themselves assigned to make daily meal deliveries to Anouk (Fanny Ardant), a very ill French woman, just released from prison and living in the town. Michelle discovers on the Internet that Anouk's sentence was for murder. The details of the crime are left murky, but the woman desperately wants to be cleansed and appeals to Naomi and Michelle to help her.

Their help for Anouk is the crux of the film. Even though she is not Jewish, Anouk seeks Jewish healing, and Naomi essentially acts as a rabbi in trying to help her. These scenes are the most moving in the film, involving a secret visit to an ancient cleansing pool, which, of course, is off-limits to women.

Through this process Naomi and Michelle grow close romantically, tension grows between Naomi and the loathsome Michael, Naomi's father reacts with towering rage, and the movie becomes an argument against some elements of his style of Judaism. It will help clarify for some viewers that Judaism incorporates beliefs that are not all in agreement.

The Secrets is, first of all, continuously absorbing, which most good films must be. The performances by the three leading actresses are compelling, although Ardant is required to sustain the note of fatal illness perhaps too long. There's a subplot involving a klezmer clarinetist that's delightful. And one about the older woman in charge of the seminary that evokes an earlier generation's beliefs about the limitations of women.

So *The Secrets* plays as a melodrama and much more: a film about religious and sexual intolerance, about reconciling opposed beliefs, about matching the fervor of feminism against religious patriarchy, and even in some ways a social comedy. It contains an object lesson for the whole genre involving romance and the battle of the generations: Such films can actually be serious about something.

The September Issue ★ ★ ★

PG-13, 89 m., 2009

With Anna Wintour, Thakoon Panichgul, Andre Leon Talley, Grace Coddington, Mario Testino, Patrick Demarchelier, Oscar de la Renta, Stefano Pilati, Vera Wang, Jean Paul Gaultier. A documentary directed by R. J. Cutler and produced by Eliza Hindmarch and Sadia Shepard.

The magazine rack at 7-Eleven doesn't have many real magazines. No *Economist*, *Vanity Fair*, *Discover*, or the *New Yorker*. It's mostly pseudo-magazines, about celebrities, diets, video games, and crossword puzzles. Except for one: *Vogue*. The other day I bought the September 2009 issue, which ran to a little under six hundred pages. That may sound like a lot to you, but actually it's a marker of hard times for the economy.

The September Issue is a documentary about the magazine's September 2007 issue, which set a record at well over eight hundred pages. *Vogue* is ruled by the famous Anna Wintour, who is said to be the single most important person in the world of fashion. When she says yes, it happens. When she says no, it doesn't. She says no frequently. She rarely deigns to explain why, but it would appear that most people believe she is right. She is *always* right about her own opinion, and in fashion, hers is the opinion that matters most.

The documentarian R. J. Cutler followed Wintour for months during the preparation for September 2007, which was expected to set a record. There cannot have been a page in it she wasn't involved with. This seems to be a woman who is concerned with one thing above all: the implementation of her opinion. She is not the monster depicted by Meryl Streep in *The Devil Wears Prada* (2006), but then how could she be? I expect that one to have a sequel titled *Return of the Bitch.*

Perhaps it was *The Devil Wears Prada,* based on a novel by one of her former assistants, that motivated Wintour to authorize this documentary. She doesn't otherwise seem like the kind of woman who craves attention, since after all she is the focus of the eyes of everyone who matters to her. She doesn't throw handbags at her assistants here, as Streep does in the 2006 movie, but then, she knows too much about cameras to make that mistake.

What comes across is that she is, after all, a very good editor. Like Hugh Hefner, William Shawn, Harold Hayes, or Graydon Carter, she knows exactly what she wants, and her readers agree with her. When she cringes at the sight of a dress, we're inclined to cringe along with her. The question arises: What possible meaning is there in haute couture for the vast majority of humans who have ever lived? None, of course. And few of these costumes must actually ever be worn, and then often for photo opportunities like Cannes or the Oscars or charity balls in Palm Beach. A woman cannot live in them. She can only wear them.

Yet there is a very great deal of money involved, because these inconceivably expensive dresses serve as the show cars of designers whose ideas are then taken down-market at great speed by multinational corporations, as was shown happening to Valentino in the 2009 documentary about him. Today Paris, tomorrow Bloomingdale's.

Wintour rules *Vogue* with a regal confidence. No one dares to disagree with her, except for a Julia Childian former British model named Grace Coddington, who has been on the staff as long as Wintour and is as earthy as Wintour is aloof. The two women have a grudging respect for each other, perhaps because each realizes they need someone to push back. Coddington's gift is conceiving many of *Vogue*'s wildly fantastical photo spreads. Wintour's gift is knowing how to moderate her enthusiasm.

We meet other members of her staff, including the court jester, Andre Leon Talley, the editor at large, who specializes in spotting young talent. He's very funny, but I didn't see Wintour smiling at him or very much at anyone else. I think she'd look pretty when she did. Old photographs show she has worn the same hairstyle since time immemorial, perhaps because to change it would be a fatal admission that she cares what people think. In public she always wears the same dark glasses, which provide maximum concealment; "armor," she calls it.

Although we see her taste constantly at work, the only definite things we learn about it are that she approves of fur and disapproves of black. She shows great affection in a scene with her bright daughter, Kathryn. Otherwise, like the Sphinx, she regards.

Seraphine ★ ★ ★ ★

NO MPAA RATING, 126 m., 2009

Yolande Moreau (Seraphine), Ulrich Tukur (Wilhelm Uhde), Anne Bennent (Anne Marie), Genevieve Mnich (Madame Duphot), Nico Rogner (Helmut), Adelaide Leroux (Minouche), Serge Lariviere (Duval), Francoise Lebrun (Mere Superieure). Directed by Martin Provost and produced by Milena Poylo and Gilles Sacuto. Screenplay by Provost and Marc Abdelnour.

You might not look twice at her. Seraphine is a bulky, work-worn housecleaner who gets down on her knees in a roomy print dress and fiercely scrubs the floor. She slips away from work to steal turpentine from the church votive candles, blood from the butcher, and clay from the fields, and these she combines with other elements to mix the paints she uses at night, covering panels with fruits and flowers that seem to look at us in alarm.

Seraphine de Senlis, who died in a French mental institution in 1942, today has her paintings in many museums. She did not paint for money or fame, although she grew heady when they began to come. She painted because she was instructed to by her guardian angel. Sometimes while painting she would loudly sing in praise of the Holy Virgin. In this miraculous film we learn nothing of her low birth or early life; we see only her daily toil and nightly ecstasy.

Seraphine arrives from France as the year's most honored film, winner of seven Cesars from the French Academy, including best film and best actress. The actress is Yolande

Moreau, who combines, as some people do, a plain face with moments of beauty. Notice her fleeting little smile of complicity as she steals fuel from candles before the Virgin. Moreau plays Seraphine as a straight-ahead charger, a little stooped, marching always with energy, plunging into work, not saying much, shy, but very much who she is. Her physical bearing tells us what we need to know about her mental state.

Her life is changed forever when Wilhelm Uhde (Ulrich Tukur) comes as a boarder to the home she works in; it offers a pastoral setting near Chantilly, and she observes that Uhde needs relief from stress. He's a famous German art critic and a Paris gallery owner, already well known as an early champion of Picasso and Braque; he discovered Rousseau. He glimpses one of Seraphine's little paintings of apples, asks to see more, is convinced she is a primitive genius. (In the film, we appear to see her actual paintings.)

She observes everything, worries about Uhde, sees he is sad, offers him some of her homemade "power wine," tells him that when she is sad, she walks in the forest and touches the trees. We even see her climbing one, in her late fifties, for the view.

She lives in bitter poverty, hounded by her landlady, doing laundry for a few francs, doling out her coins at the local store to buy canvas and the paints she cannot mix herself. Uhde admires her work, which she cannot believe, gives her some money, makes her some promises, and then disappears: As a German, he flees France at the outset of World War I. Ten years after the war, he and his sister return to Senlis. He assumes Seraphine is dead. At a town hall exhibition by local artists, he sees a work that is unmistakably hers, but larger and more finished. He is overwhelmed, as many others would be.

Seraphine is not a rags-to-riches story. The director, Martin Provost, who wrote it with Marc Abdelnour, focuses intently on Seraphine's delusions, on the manic state that overtakes her at the prospect of fame and fortune, about how she hides far inside so that Uhde cannot reach her. I've seen many films hoping to understand the nature of great artists; one that comes close is *Vincent,* by Paul Cox. This is another. It "explains" nothing but feels everything. It reminded me of two other films: Bresson's *Mouchette,* about a poor girl victimized by a village, and Karen Gehre's *Begging Naked,* shown at Ebertfest this year, about a woman whose art is prized even as she lives in Central Park.

People like these are not entirely to be pitied. Their art is a refuge. All artists fall into a reverie state while working. Some experience a joy that obliterates their circumstances. The problem is that when they're not creating, they have to go right on living.

Serbis ★ ★ ½

R, 91 m., 2009

Gina Pareno (Nanay Flor), Jaclyn Jose (Nayda), Julio Diaz (Lando), Coco Martin (Alan), Kristofer King (Ronald), Dan Alvaro (Jerome), Mercedes Cabral (Merly), Roxanne Jordan (Jewel). Directed by Brillante Mendoza and produced by Ferdinand Lapuz. Screenplay by Armando Lao.

Although *Serbis* spends a great deal of time following its characters through the corridors and up and down the stairs of a shabby Filipino porno movie theater, we never get a clear idea of the interior layout. And the auditorium looks rather small considering the hulking exterior of the Family Theater. But maybe that's the idea, because the film is a labyrinth of lost and wandering lives.

An extended family runs this failing old theater, lives in it, too, and is even raising a cute little son. The movies on the screen are hetero, but nobody is watching. The dark seats and the bright corridors and staircases are home to gay hustlers and their clientele, everybody knows it, nobody cares, many of them seem to be waiting around for something to relieve their boredom. There is some gratitude when a goat gets loose inside the theater. How it climbed so high without being seen on the stairs is a good question; maybe it's a mountain goat.

Up and down the staff and customers go, like ants in a hill. We get to know the members of the Pineda family of Angeles City pretty well, especially Nayda (Jaclyn Jose), the daughter, whose son is the little boy, and whose mother, Nanay Flor (Gina Pareno), is due in court for her husband's divorce hearing. A strong matriarch, she fiercely wants to be rid of the man. And there is another worry: Merly (Mercedes Cabral), girlfriend of the cousin/projectionist Alan (Coco Martin), has announced she is pregnant, so there will be the expense of a wedding no one wants.

In a film so immersed in sex, there is little actual sex. *Serbis* (the word means "service") is about a closed world in which sex is a commodity and it's a buyer's market. Sexual encounters are hurried, hidden, and never lingered on by the camera of director Brillante Mendoza, who is more absorbed by faces, routine, work, and the passage of time. The body part that receives the most attention is the projectionist's butt, where there is a painful boil. His self-treatment for this affliction reportedly drew groans at the Cannes 2008 press screening, but it seems a quick and relatively painless solution, and I will file it away.

The film opens with a curious scene: Nayda bathes, dresses herself, and applies lipstick in front of a mirror, while telling her reflection, "I love you." Later there is a scene of her mother applying lipstick in preparation for her court appearance. Given the seedy surroundings, there is something touching about these two women preparing their faces to bravely face the world.

This is not a film most people will enjoy. Its qualities are apparent only if one appreciates cinematic style for itself. I enjoyed it because I got into Mendoza's visual use of the corridors and staircases and their life rhythms. Most people will find that annoying. Anyone hoping to see sex will be badly disappointed. Let's put it this way: If you see only one art film this month, this shouldn't be the one. If you see one every week, you might admire it.

A Serious Man ★ ★ ★ ★

R, 104 m., 2009

Michael Stuhlbarg (Larry Gopnik), Richard Kind (Uncle Arthur), Fred Melamed (Sy Ableman), Sari Lennick (Judith Gopnik), Adam Arkin (Divorce Lawyer), Amy Landecker (Mrs. Samsky), Alan Mandell (Rabbi Marshak), David Kang (Clive Park), Fyvush Finkel (Dybbuk), Allen Lewis Rickman (Shtetl Husband), Yelena Shmulenson (Shtetl Wife). Directed, written, and produced by Joel and Ethan Coen.

We learn from the Book of Job: *Man that is born of a woman is of few days, and full of trouble.* Such a man is Larry Gopnik. He lectures on physics in front of a blackboard filled with bewildering equations that are mathematical proofs approaching certainty, and in his own life, what can he be sure of? Nothing, that's what.

His wife is leaving him for his best friend. His son is listening to rock 'n' roll in Hebrew school. His daughter is stealing money for a nose job. His brother-in-law is sleeping on the sofa and lurking in unsavory bars. His gun-nut neighbor frightens him. A student tries to bribe him and blackmail him at the same time. The tenure committee is getting unsigned libelous letters about him. The wife of his other neighbor is sex crazy. God forbid this man should see a doctor.

"This is the kind of picture you get to make after you've won an Oscar," writes Todd McCarthy in *Variety*. I cannot improve on that. After the seriously great *No Country for Old Men*, the Coen brothers have made the not greatly serious *A Serious Man*, which bears every mark of a labor of love.

It is set in what I assume to be a Minneapolis suburb of their childhood, a prairie populated by split-level homes with big garages but not enough trees around them. In this world, Larry Gopnik (Michael Stuhlbarg) earnestly desires to be taken as a serious man and do the right thing, but does God take him seriously? "I read the book of Job last night," Virginia Woolf said. "I don't think God comes out well in it." Someone up there doesn't like Larry Gopnik.

Beginning with a darkly comic prologue in Yiddish, *A Serious Man* inhabits a Jewish community where the rational (physics) is rendered irrelevant by the mystical (fate). Gopnik can fill all the blackboards he wants and it won't do him any good. Maybe because an ancestor invited a dybbuk to cross his threshold, Larry is cursed. A dybbuk is the wandering soul of a dead person. You don't want to make the mistake of inviting one into your home. You don't have to be Jewish to figure that out.

Much of the success of *A Serious Man* comes

from the way Michael Stuhlbarg plays the role. He doesn't play Gopnik as a sad sack or a loser, a whiner or a depressive, but as a hopeful man who can't believe what's happening to him. What else can go wrong? Where can he find happiness? Whom can he please? In the sex department, why are even his wet dreams, starring his brazen neighbor (Amy Landecker), frightening? Why does Sy Ableman (Fred Melamed), his so-called best friend who is taking away his wife, speak to him in terms of such sadness, sympathy, and understanding? Does Fred know Larry is doomed?

Why do his children dismiss him? Why is his no-account brother-in-law (Richard Kind) such a shiftless leech? Why can no rabbi provide him with encouragement or useful advice? Why would a student (David Kang) clearly fail an exam, leave bribe money on his desk, and then act to destroy him?

Why, why, why? I'm sure you've heard the old joke where Job asks the Lord why everything in his life is going wrong. Remember what the Lord replies? If you don't remember the joke, ask anyone. I can't prove it, but I'm absolutely certain more than half of everyone on Earth has heard some version of that joke.

Have I mentioned *A Serious Man* is so rich and funny? This isn't a laugh-laugh movie, but a wince-wince movie. Those can be funny, too. The Coens have found mostly unfamiliar actors, or those like Stuhlbarg, Kind, and Melamed you've seen before, but you're not quite sure where. I imagine (but do not know) that Joel and Ethan have been kicking this story around for years, passing time by reminding each other of possible characters, seeing an actor and observing, "There's our Mrs. Samsky." Their actors weren't cast; they were preordained.

In some ways my favorite is Melamed as Sy Ableman. It's not a big role, but he's so good he establishes a full presence in his first scene, when he's only a voice on the telephone. This is the traitor who has stolen away Gopnik's wife, and he believes it will be good if they have a long, helpful talk. Ableman is not only the grief, but the grief counselor. Such chutzpah, you have to admire.

Amy Landecker, too, is perfect as Mrs. Samsky. She makes the character sexy in a strictly logical sense, but any prudent man would know on first sight to stay clear. Judith Gopnik, as Larry's wife, is able to suggest in only a few scenes that she's leaving him not for passion or out of anger, but because she senses his ship going down and Sy Ableman is a lifeboat.

There is a story told in *A Serious Man* that may seem out of place. I believe it acts as a parable reflecting the film, Gopnik's life, and indeed the Book of Job. It's the one about the Jewish dentist who discovers the words "Help me" naturally occurring in Hebrew on the back of a gentile's lower front teeth. Remember that many parables contain their message in their last lines.

7 Days in Slow Motion ★ ★ ★

NO MPAA RATING, 100 m., 2010

Teja (Ravi), Shiva Varma (Onka), Kunal Sharma (Hamid), Rajeshwari Sachdev-Badola (Ravi's Mom), Ayesha Jalil (Hamid's Mom), Vivek Mushran (Ravi's Dad). Directed and produced by Umakanth Thumrugoti. Screenplay by Thumrugoti.

Ravi, the young narrator of *7 Days in Slow Motion*, is obsessed with movies, and so are his friends Hamid and Onka. So when a professional-quality HD video camera falls into their hands, of course they are compelled to go immediately into production. There are two problems: They have to return the camera at the end of seven days, and on the seventh day they have to sit for final exams at their school.

That's the setup for an unexpected and entertaining look at upper-middle-class life in Hyderabad, a prosperous central Indian city that is the home of many digital industries and a large movie studio. These are privileged kids. Their parents chatter about the Ivy League schools they want them to attend. All depends on the all-important exams, however, and in an opening scene, Ravi (Teja) produces a pie chart picturing how his mother wants him to spend his time: 60 percent for studying, 2 percent for fun.

After the camera literally falls off the proverbial passing truck, they seize their opportunity to secretly produce a film while allegedly studying for exams. They need a story. One suggestion: "The plot from *Indecent Pro-*

posal, the villain from *Terminator,* and the plot from *Titanic.*" They need expertise. Ravi buys *Directing for Dummies.*

And they need a cast. Here there is a problem. Ravi's seventeen-year-old cousin would seem to be ideal, but suddenly she's matched up with a forty-year-old man for an arranged marriage, and their plans (and her hopes of college) are upset.

The movie Ravi eventually edits out of his material turns out to have a much greater effect on his family than anyone could have anticipated. We are also not sure that he could have actually obtained all of those shots, but never mind.

The movie addresses two subjects much discussed in India: the pressure put on children to excel in school, and the unequal opportunities for boys and girls. It's a comedy, not a serious film, but those themes are there. American audiences, long taught to imagine India in terms of Mother Teresa's homeless, may be surprised by this portrait of go-getter, upward-bound Indians; India is said to have a larger middle class than the United States. Another element that goes without comment is that everyone in the movie speaks English fluently (as a great many Indians do).

The adventures of the boys in making the movie would be right at home in a Disney family comedy, and no wonder; Umakanth Thumrugoti, the writer and director, worked at Disney Animation for years, and did visual effects on *Chicken Little, Treasure Planet,* and *Pocahontas.*

The kids, around ten years old, are all good-looking and energetic on camera. Teja, who plays Ravi, and Shiva Varma, who plays Onka, are seasoned veterans of "Tollywood," the Telugu film industry that's sort of a popular, low-rent version of Bollywood. Varma is so good-looking, indeed, that when his cousin forcibly makes him up to step into the female lead, he's almost too comely.

The Indian love of riotous displays of bright colors is everywhere on display. And the film contains several songs and a dance number, which seem to be obligatory in films from India. *7 Days in Slow Motion* is a cheerful family entertainment, completely accessible to English-speaking audiences. Will it get much distribution? As nearly as I can tell, its current engagement at Chicago's Facets Cinematheque is the North American premiere.

17 Again ★ ★ ★

PG-13, 98 m., 2009

Zac Efron (Mike O'Donnell), Matthew Perry (Adult Mike), Leslie Mann (Scarlet), Thomas Lennon (Ned Gold), Michelle Trachtenberg (Maggie), Sterling Knight (Alex), Melora Hardin (Jane Masterson). Directed by Burr Steers and produced by Adam Shankman and Jennifer Gibgot. Screenplay by Jason Filardi.

Mike O'Donnell's wife wants a divorce, his kids are remote, he didn't get the job promotion he expected, and everything else in his life has gone wrong since that magic year when he was seventeen, a basketball star, in love, and looked like Zac Efron instead of Matthew Perry. He's obviously a case for treatment by a Body Swap Movie.

Revisiting the trophy case at his old high school, Mike encounters a janitor who, from the way he smiles at the camera, knows things beyond this mortal coil. If only Mike could go back to seventeen and not make all the same mistakes. In *17 Again,* he can. He falls into a Twilight Zone vortex and emerges as Zac Efron. They say be careful what you wish for, because you might get it. Mike should have been more specific. Instead of wishing to be seventeen again, he should have wished to go back twenty years in time.

Yes, he becomes himself trapped inside his own seventeen-year-old body. Same wife, same kids, same problems. As Old Mike was getting divorced, he'd moved in with his best friend, Ned (Thomas Lennon), and now he throws himself on Ned's mercy: Will Ned pose as his father, so Young Mike can be his son and help out his kids by enrolling in the same high school again? Ned, who is a software millionaire and middle-aged fanboy, agrees, especially after he falls helplessly in love with the high school principal, Jane (Melora Hardin).

Young Mike becomes the new best friend of his insecure son, Alex (Sterling Knight). Then he meets Alex's mom, Scarlet (Leslie Mann), who, of course, before the vortex was his wife, and before that his high school bride (Allison Miller). She thinks it's strange that he looks *exactly* like the boy she married at seventeen. He explains he is the son of an uncle, who I guess would have to be Old Mike's brother, so it's curious Old Scarlet never met him, but if she doesn't ask that, why should I?

In high school, Young Mike again becomes a basketball star, befriends Alex, and attempts to defend his Gothish daughter, Maggie (Michelle Trachtenberg), against the predations of her jerk boyfriend, who as a hot-rodding jock traveling with a posse is, of course, the *last* guy in school who would date, or be dated by, a moody girl who wears black.

I've seen Body Swaps before (Tom Hanks in *Big*). The first act of this movie seemed all retread. Then it started to dig in. There are twin romances; as Shakespeare demonstrated, one must be serious and the other farcical. Young Mike is still seriously in love with his wife, Old Scarlet, and she is powerfully attracted to this boy who's a double for her first love. She thinks that's wrong. He knows it isn't, but how can he explain?

Meanwhile, best buddy Ned courts Principal Masterson, who for the first time in his life has Taught Him What Love Means. Before her, ecstasy was owning Darth Vader's costume. I will not describe what happens the first time they go out to dinner, except to say that it's comic genius, perfectly played by Melora Hardin and Thomas Lennon.

I attended a screening held by a radio station, which attracted mainly teenage girls who left their boyfriends behind. When Zac Efron took off his T-shirt, the four in front of me squealed as if there were buzzers in their seats. Now that he's a little older, Efron has a Tom Cruiseish charm and a lot of confidence. Why Matthew Perry was cast as his adult self is hard to figure; does your head change its shape in twenty years?

17 Again is a pleasant, harmless PG-13 entertainment, with a plot a little more surprising and acting a little better than I expected. Mike is dispatched into that vortex by the bearded old janitor with a delighted smile. The janitor (Brian Doyle Murray) is quite a convenience, supplying vortexes when needed. If his smile reminds you of anyone, he's played by Bill Murray's brother.

Sex and the City 2 ★

R, 146 m., 2010

Sarah Jessica Parker (Carrie Bradshaw), Kim Cattrall (Samantha Jones), Kristin Davis (Charlotte York), Cynthia Nixon (Miranda Hobbes), Chris Noth (Mr. Big), John Corbett (Aidan Shaw), David Eigenberg (Steve Brady), Evan Handler (Harry Goldenblatt), Jason Lewis (Smith Jerrod), Willie Garson (Stanford Blatch), Mario Cantone (Anthony Marantino). Directed by Michael Patrick King and produced by King, John P. Melfi, Sarah Jessica Parker, and Darren Star. Screenplay by Patrick King.

Some of these people make my skin crawl. The characters of *Sex and the City 2* are flyweight bubbleheads living in a world that rarely requires three sentences in a row. Their defining quality is consuming things. They gobble food, fashion, houses, husbands, children, vitamins, and freebies. They must plan their wardrobes on the phone, so often do they appear in different basic colors, like the plugs of a Playskool workbench.

As we return to the trivialities of their lives for a sequel, marriage is the issue. The institution is affirmed in an opening sequence at a gay wedding in Connecticut that looks like a Fred Astaire production number gone horribly overbudget. There's a sixteen-man chorus in white formal wear, a pond with swans, and Liza Minnelli to perform the ceremony. Her religious or legal qualifications are unexplained; perhaps she is present merely as the patron saint of gay men. After the ceremony, she changes to a Vegas lounge outfit and is joined by two look-alike backups for a song-and-dance routine possibly frowned upon in some denominations.

Then it's back to the humdrum married life of our gal Carrie Bradshaw (Sarah Jessica Parker) and the loathsome Mr. Big (Chris Noth). Carrie, honey, how can you endure life with this purring, narcissistic, soft-velvet idiot? He speaks loudly enough to be heard mostly by himself, his most appreciative audience. And he never wants to leave the house at night, preferring to watch classic black-and-white movies on TV. This leads to a marital crisis. Carrie thinks they should talk more. But sweetheart, Mr. Big has nothing to say. At least he's provided you with a Manhattan apartment that looks like an *Architectural Digest* wet dream.

Brief updates. Miranda Hobbes (Cynthia Nixon) is a high-powered lawyer who is dissed by her male chauvinist pig boss. Samantha Jones (Kim Cattrall) is still a sexaholic. Charlotte York (Kristin Davis) has the two little girls she thought she wanted, but now discovers that they actually expect to be raised. Mothers, if you are reading this, run this through your head. One little girl dips her hands in strawberry topping and plants two big handprints on your butt. You are on the cell to a girlfriend. How do you report this? You moan and wail out: "My vintage Valentino!" Any mother who wears her vintage Valentino while making muffin topping with her kids should be hauled up before the Department of Children and Family Services.

All of this is pretty thin gruel. The movie shows enterprise and flies the entire cast away to the emirate of Abu Dhabi, where the girls are given a $22,000-a-night suite and matching Maybachs and butlers, courtesy of a sheikh who wants to have a meeting with Samantha and talk about publicity for his hotel.

This sequence is an exercise in obscenely conspicuous consumption, which the girls perform in so many different outfits they must have been followed to the Middle East by a luggage plane. I don't know a whole lot about fashion, but I know something about taste, and these women spend much of the movie dressed in tacky, vulgar clothing. Carrie and Samantha also display the maximum possible boobage, oblivious to Arab ideas about women's modesty. There's more cleavage in this film than at a pro wrestling wedding.

And crotches, have we got crotches for you. Big close-ups of the girls themselves and some of the bulgers they meet. And they meet some. They meet the Australian World Cup team, for example, which seems to have left its cups at home. And then there's the intriguing stranger Samantha meets at the hotel, whose zipper-straining arousal provokes the fury of an offended Arab guest and his wife. This prodigy's name is Rikard Spirt. Think about it.

Samantha is arrested for kissing on the beach, and there's an uncomfortable scene in which the girls are menaced by outraged men in a public market, where all they've done is dress in a way more appropriate for a sales reception at Victoria's Secret. They're rescued by Arab women so well covered only their eyes are visible, and in private these women reveal that underneath the burka they're wearing Dior gowns and so forth. Must get hot.

I wondered briefly whether Abu Dhabi had underwritten all this product placement, but I learn that *SATC2* was filmed in Morocco, which must be Morocco's little joke. That nation supplies magnificent desert scenes, achieved with CGI, I assume, during which two of the girls fall off a camel. I haven't seen such hilarity since *Abbott and Costello in the Foreign Legion.*

The movie's visual style is arthritic. Director Michael Patrick King covers the sitcom by dutifully cutting back and forth to whoever is speaking. A sample of Carrie's realistic dialogue in a marital argument: "You knew when I married you I was more Coco Chanel than coq au vin." Carrie also narrates the film, providing useful guidelines for those challenged by its intricacies. Sample: "Later that day, Big and I arrived home."

Truth in reviewing: I am obliged to report that this film will no doubt be deliriously enjoyed by its fans, for the reasons described above. Male couch potatoes dragged to the film against their will may find some consolation. Reader, I must confess that while attending the sneak preview with its overwhelmingly female audience, I was gob-smacked by the delightful cleavage on display. Do women wear their lowest-cut frocks for one another?

Note: From my understanding of the guidelines of the MPAA Classification and Rating Administration, Samantha and Mr. Spirt have one scene that far, far surpasses the traditional MPAA limits for pumping and thrusting.

Shall We Kiss? ★ ★ ½

NO MPAA RATING, 102 m., 2009

Virginie Ledoyen (Judith), Emmanuel Mouret (Nicolas), Julie Gayet (Emilie), Michael Cohen (Gabriel), Frederique Bel (Caline), Stefano Accorsi (Claudio), Melanie Maudran (Penelope), Marie Madinier (Eglantine). Directed by Emmanuel Mouret and produced by Frederic Niedermayer. Screenplay by Mouret.

The characters in *Shall We Kiss?* are attractive, wear impeccable clothes, and move easily through minimalist rooms, hotel lobbies, social gatherings, restaurants, and their lives. The sound track is by Schubert and Tchaikovsky. There are discreet paintings on the walls and drawings of composers. They are French, articulate, composed, and dumber than a box of rocks.

That is the only way I can account for their behavior, and since their behavior is the subject of the film, that must be counted as a flaw. They approach the subjects of sex and romance with a naivete so staggering it must be an embarrassment in the greater world. Inside their hermetically sealed complacency, I suppose it's a little exciting.

Gabriel and Emilie are strangers when they have a chance encounter in Nantes. Their eyes meet, there is a connection, they have dinner, and when Gabriel moves as if to kiss Emilie she seems willing, but then pulls back. She is afraid to kiss. Why? She will tell him a story.

Flashbacks to the story involve most of the film, with occasional returns to Emilie (Julie Gayet) relating it to Gabriel (Michael Cohen) in her hotel room. It is about her friends Judith (Virginie Ledoyen) and Nicolas (Emmanuel Mouret, the film's director). They have been best friends since childhood. Judith is happily married. Nicolas has just broken up with a lover of some duration. He is unhappy because he believes he is incapable of fully entering into physical love.

Judith suggests . . . a prostitute? Nicolas tried that. She was perfectly nice but wouldn't kiss him, and without kissing, his engine refused to turn over. What to do? He appeals to Judith. As a dear friend, his very dearest, would she consider . . . you know . . . to . . . She does. They proceed with the shy hesitation of a first game of spin-the-bottle. May I feel? asks he. May I touch here? And here? Shall we undress? I am on record as calling for more foreplay in the movies, but this isn't foreplay; it's the whole spring training season. And the problem is, they both enjoy it. That won't do. The answer is to do it again right away, roughly, on the floor, to break the spell. They enjoy that even more.

Now *Shall We Kiss?* enters into a complex plot involving deception, role-playing, her husband, his new girlfriend, and a twist I won't even hint at. All performed without the slightest concession to actual human nature as many of we humans understand it. In its long, exploratory conversations, the movie plays very much like a film by Eric Rohmer, who, having now allegedly retired at eighty-eight, has left the field free. But Rohmer used artifice to find truth, and Mouret uses it to find artifice.

You say, but perhaps the French—they are like that? And I reply, nooo, I don't think so. What do I really know about French attitudes toward such matters? Very little, although I once knew a French girl who talked no end about romance. We weren't even in spring training. We seemed to be in the Little League. If actual sex had ever entered the picture, I am convinced she would have regarded it as more than a theoretical exercise in platonic friendship.

Is *Shall We Kiss?* without merit? Not entirely. It has a grace, a languid charm, a pictorial elegance. The plot, when it winds up and unwinds, is ingenious. But are we expected in any sense to find these people realistic? What do we learn from them? All I learned was that that will never work. I already knew that.

Sherlock Holmes ★ ★ ★

PG-13, 128 m., 2009

Robert Downey Jr. (Sherlock Holmes), Jude Law (Dr. John Watson), Rachel McAdams (Irene Adler), Mark Strong (Lord Blackwood), Eddie Marsan (Inspector Lestrade), Kelly Reilly (Mary Morstan). Directed by Guy Ritchie and produced by Susan Downey, Dan Lin, Joel Silver, and Lionel Wigram. Screenplay by Michael Robert Johnson, Anthony Peckham, and Simon Kinberg, based on the stories by Sir Arthur Conan Doyle.

The less I thought about Sherlock Holmes, the more I liked *Sherlock Holmes.* Yet another classic hero has been fed into the f/x mill, emerging as a modern superman. Guy Ritchie's film is filled with sensational sights, over-the-top characters, and a desperate struggle atop Tower Bridge, which is still under construction. It's likely to be enjoyed by today's action fans. But block bookings are not likely from the Baker Street Irregulars.

One of the comforts of the Arthur Conan

Doyle stories is their almost staid adherence to form. Villains and cases come and go up the staircase at 221B Baker Street, but within that refuge life stays the same: Holmes all-knowing and calm, Watson fretful and frightened, clues orderly, victims distraught, never a problem not seemingly insoluble. Outside is the fabled Edwardian London, a city we all know in our imaginations. I think I became an Anglophile on those winter nights when I sat curled up in my dad's big chair, a single lamp creating shadows in the corners of the room, reading the Modern Library edition of the stories while in the basement I heard the comforting sounds of my parents doing the laundry.

Every Holmes story is different and each one is the same, just as every day has its own saint but the Mass is eternal. *Sherlock Holmes* enacts the strange new rites of hyperkinetic action and impossible CGI, and Holmes and Watson do their best to upgrade themselves. Holmes tosses aside the deerstalker hat and meerschaum calabash, and Watson has decided once and for all to abandon the intimacy of 221B for the hazards of married life. Both of them now seem more than a little gay; it's no longer a case of, "Oh, the British all talk like that." Jude Law even seemed it be wearing lipstick when he promoted the movie on Letterman.

Well, Holmes, like Hamlet, has survived countless interpretations. The character has been played by Basil Rathbone, Jeremy Brett, Frank Langella, Peter Cushing, John Barrymore, James D'Arcy, Michael Caine, John Cleese, Peter Cook, Rupert Everett, William Gillette, Stewart Granger, Charlton Heston, Anthony Higgins, Raymond Massey, Roger Moore, John Neville, Leonard Nimoy, Christopher Plummer, Jonathan Pryce, Nicol Williamson . . . and now Robert Downey Jr., who is not the least of these.

Downey's Holmes is at once more dissolute and more fit than previous incarnations. Holmes's canonical devotion to the opium pipe is here augmented by other drugs and a great deal of booze. Yet Holmes has the body of a lithe athlete, the skills of a gymnast, and the pugilism of a world champion. He and Watson (who is, you recall, only a doctor, although one with clients who must be puzzled about his office hours) spring readily into action like Batman and Robin.

In a really very good opening sequence, the two burst in upon the fiendish Satanist Lord Blackwood (Mark Strong) in the act of committing a dastardly act. Blackwood is sent to the gallows and sealed in his tomb, only to reappear (to Holmes's undeniable satisfaction) seemingly still alive. This sets off a series of action set pieces in the streets of London, which have never seemed more looming, dark, and ominous; I had the impression Jack the Ripper had just darted out of view.

After the initial apprehension of Blackwood, Holmes retreats to his digs. In Conan Doyle, this is often explained as "a period of study" and implied opium reveries. In Ritchie's version, he trashes his rooms like a drunken undergraduate; they lack only empty pizza boxes. This will not do. My Sherlock is above all fastidious. But never mind. Blackwood's resurrection gives him a new reason for living.

There is also interest from two women: Irene Adler (Rachel McAdams), of course, said to be the only woman to ever touch Holmes's heart, and Mary Morstan (Kelly Reilly), Watson's intended, who may be in for more than she knows. The advent of Mary on the scene sends Holmes into fits of petulance; how dare the doctor prefer a woman to his own fascinating company? Watson has always maintained quarters elsewhere, but in this film the cozy confines of 221B make his other rooms seem more than ever like a beard.

The Conan Doyle stories are still read and probably always will be. Most readers get to at least a few. But among moviegoers on Christmas night (traditionally one of the busiest movie nights of the year), probably not so many. They will be unaware that this *Sherlock Holmes* is cheerfully revisionist. They will be entertained, and so was I. The great detective, who has survived so much, can certainly shrug off a few special effects.

She's Out of My League ★ ★ ★

R, 106 m., 2010

Jay Baruchel (Kirk), Alice Eve (Molly), T. J. Miller (Stainer), Mike Vogel (Jack), Nate Torrence (Devon), Krysten Ritter (Patty), Geoff Stults (Cam), Lindsay Sloane (Marnie). Directed by Jim Field Smith and produced by Eric Gold, David B.

Householter, and Jimmy Miller. Screenplay by Sean Anders and John Morris.

Molly is a perfect ten. Kirk is a five. This scoring is provided by his best friends, who sadly inform him, "You can't jump more than two." Because of reasoning like that, Aristotle Onassis remains a hero to fours and fives everywhere. *She's Out of My League,* which is sortofa good comedy, tells the story of a five who meets a ten who believes there is a ten inside of him fighting to get out.

Kirk (Jay Baruchel) works as a TSA security screener at the Pittsburgh airport. He's competent enough, but the behavior of his colleagues should all by itself raise the national security level to red. Apparently unsupervised, they brighten up their jobs by trying to pick up every cute girl who comes through security. This is made more possible because there never seem to be five hundred impatient passengers waiting in line.

Baruchel looks as if he could indeed be a five, but he has that essential quality of turning into a ten with his attitude alone. Here he will find what I have long observed, that everyone is beautiful when they're looking at you with love in their eyes. Kirk has recently become the victim of the sort of perfect storm that strikes the heroes of movies like this. His girlfriend, Marnie (Lindsay Sloane), has broken up with him. But having lacked a warm family relationship, she latched onto Kirk's family, and now hangs out at his house with her new boyfriend, whom Kirk's parents approve of. Think about that.

Molly is also fresh from romantic disaster. When she loses her iPhone and Kirk finds it and returns it, she asks him out to dinner. He's stunned because, yes, she's out of his league. But it turns out Molly is ready to play in a different league, one where being a ten on the outside is less important than being a ten on the inside. Kirk's innate decency melts her heart.

Jay Baruchel has that quality of seeming like someone we might actually have known outside of a movie. He plays Kirk as apologetic, easily embarrassed, with low self-esteem—plain and simple, a nice guy. Alice Eve, who is despite all evidence British, is pretty, yes, but not actually quite a ten. A 9.5, easy. Isn't that scoring system loathsome? Her best friend, Patty (Krysten Ritter), thinks Kirk is beneath her, possibly because Patty likes to bask in the reflected glow of Molly's tenhood. Kirk's own three best buddies include two party animals and one nice pudgy guy, whose combined wisdom on women is a perfect two.

There are some funny set pieces here, one involving guys rummaging through each other's netherlands, one involving a family trip to Branson, Missouri, in matching sweatshirts. Do you ever get the feeling you're the last American alive who hasn't been to Branson? That *Titanic* attraction sounds great to me. Anyway, much depends on whether Kirk will actually make this journey.

The movie is not a comedy classic. But in a genre where so many movies struggle to lift themselves from zero to one, it's about, oh, a 6.5.

A Shine of Rainbows ★ ★ ½

PG, 101 m., 2010

Connie Nielsen (Maire O'Donnell), Aidan Quinn (Alec O'Donnell), John Bell (Tomas), Jack Gleason (Seamus), Niamh Shaw (Katie), Tara Alice Scully (Nancy). Directed by Vic Sarin and produced by James Flynn, Tina Pehme, and Chris Rudolph. Screenplay by Sarin, Catherine Spear, and Dennis Foon, from the novel by Lillian Beckwith.

As you can possibly guess from the title, *A Shine of Rainbows* is a feel-good movie. Hey, what's not to like about cute orphans, baby seals, sweet moms, and gruff dads with hearts of gold? And rainbows? If your heart is going thumpety-thump at such a prospect, here is the movie for you.

No, I'm serious. And kids may really love it. It's too much of an emotional heart tugger for me, but then I prefer my orphans by Dickens, where the little rascals pick pockets for a living. I'll admit one thing: I wish there were still an Ireland (or anywhere else) where a couple looking like Connie Nielsen and Aidan Quinn could live in an isolated and charming home on a high meadow overlooking the sea, operate a small family farm, and make a living.

The film is set on Corrie Island, off the western coast of Ireland, and I'll grant you one thing: You can find dozens of photos of it at http://j.mp/cnQWBU, and it looks just about the way it does in the film. It is a wonderful place for small Tomas (John Bell), who has become a punching bag for bullies at the orphanage, but is swept up by the heaven-sent Maire O'Donnell (Connie Nielsen), popped aboard a ferry, and carried across to this idyllic setting.

All is fine, except . . . why does his new dad, Alec (Aidan Quinn), glower at him so darkly? Alec confides to his wife that the boy doesn't look sturdy enough. Why didn't she pick a brawnier model? Alec is possibly in the Dickens tradition of a cruel stepfather who demands only a brisk twenty-hour day of hard labor in return for the lad's bowl of gruel. Good thing Tomas is Irish. If he'd been Russian, there'd be no telling.

Maire unfortunately contracts Ali MacGraw's Disease, defined in an ancient edition of the Glossary as that disease of young women whose only symptom is that after they take to a hospital bed they grow more and more beautiful. That leaves Tomas with Alec. Oh, but Tomas finds a new friend, a baby seal stranded down on the beach. He knows another orphan when he sees one.

As Tomas and Alec slowly bond over the seal, Alec's heart melts, as it must. It's the seal I'm worried about. Tomas brings him fish to wolf down, but I dunno . . . how long can a young seal lie helpless on a beach in full sun and remain happy? Couldn't he, like, you know, sort of crawl into the sea? Isn't that kind of programmed into seals? The movie offers some reason for his immobility, which didn't lock into my memory bank. Essentially he stays there day after day because the plot requires him.

I know, I know. I'm being unsentimental. I should make this clear: *A Shine of Rainbows* is a sweet, good-looking film about nice people in a beautiful place, and young John Bell is an appealing performer in the tradition of the Culkins. Quinn and Nielsen are pros who take their roles seriously, and Vic Sarin's direction gets the job done. If I were six . . . but then I'm not, am I?

Shrink ★ ★ ½

R, 110 m., 2009

Kevin Spacey (Henry Carter), Saffron Burrows (Kate Amberson), Jack Huston (Shamus), Keke Palmer (Jemma), Dallas Roberts (Patrick), Robin Williams (Jack), Pell James (Daisy), Mark Webber (Jeremy), Robert Loggia (Robert Carter), Laura Ramsey (Keira). Directed by Jonas Pate and produced by Michael Burns, Braxton Pope, and Dana Brunetti. Screenplay by Thomas Moffett.

Shrink gives us a high-profile Los Angeles psychiatrist whose life has been reduced to smoking as much pot as he possibly can. If the movie contains a surprise, it's that he doesn't find his way to cocaine. Kevin Spacey brings another of his cynical, bitter characters to life—very smart and fresh out of hope—but the movie doesn't give him much of anywhere to take it.

The idea of rich, famous, drug-addled Hollywood flotsam is not precisely original, and this sort of story has rarely been more strongly told than in *Hurlyburly* (1998), with Sean Penn as a cokehead and Spacey himself as a bemused, supercilious witness to the wreckage. As for the behind-the-scenes Hollywood stuff, you can't much improve on Altman's *The Player*.

What director Jonas Pate and his writer, Thomas Moffett, do is sidestep deep characterization and bring in a rather conventional assortment of clients for Spacey's shrink, named Henry Carter. We meet a movie star past his sell-by date (Robin Williams, unbilled), who thinks his problem is sex addiction, although Henry assures him it is alcoholism (the sex addict's running mate). Dallas Roberts plays Patrick, an agent driven by hyperactive compulsions; Patrick's assistant Daisy (Pell James) is preggers; Shamus (Jack Huston) is an Irish actor who is an alcoholic just for starters; and the actress Kate (Saffron Burrows) is a trophy wife who finds her husband's trophy shelf is not yet complete.

These characters are intriguing in their own ways, especially when we sense Williams restraining himself from bolting headlong into his descriptions of sexual improbabilities, but each one is essentially a walk-on act, and even when their lifelines cross it seems an event in the screenplay, not their lives.

One actress who does create a free-standing character is Keke Palmer (Jemma), mourning her mother, finding refuge in the movie revivals she attends as a form of escape. Palmer was the young star of *Akeelah and the Bee* (2006), and is still only sixteen; remember her name.

Directing emotional traffic amid these problems, the Spacey character is coming to pieces. His wife has recently committed suicide, he can barely focus on his clients, and although he's excellent at spotting addiction in others, he rationalizes his own. It takes his father (Robert Loggia) to talk straight to him, and he is stunned to find himself the recipient of an intervention.

Working within the range we frequently find him, Kevin Spacey is a master. Yes, there is a pattern to many of his roles, but there are characters he is suited to and others that would be improbable. Many critics find fault with him for not repeating *American Beauty* in every film, or maybe even for making it in the first place. I sense an acute intelligence at work. When he found few interesting Hollywood projects, he went to the London stage, took over management of the Old Vic, and reinvented himself. Why are some critics snarky toward such an actor? Is it the price they pay for trying?

That said, *Shrink* contains ideas for a film, but no emotional center. A group of troubled characters is assembled and allowed to act out, not to much purpose. Jemma, the young girl, is the most authentic, and Henry relates to her most movingly. Two actors have found something to dig into.

Shutter Island ★ ★ ★ ½

R, 138 m., 2010

Leonardo DiCaprio (Teddy Daniels), Mark Ruffalo (Chuck Aule), Ben Kingsley (Dr. Cawley), Michelle Williams (Dolores), Emily Mortimer (Rachel 1), Patricia Clarkson (Rachel 2), Max von Sydow (Dr. Naehring). Directed by Martin Scorsese and produced by Scorsese, Brad Fischer, Mike Medavoy, and Arnold Messer. Screenplay by Laeta Kalogridis, based on the novel by Dennis Lehane.

Shutter Island starts working on us with the first musical notes under the Paramount mountain, even before the film starts. They're ominous and doomy. So is the film. This is Martin Scorsese's evocation of the delicious shuddering fear we feel when horror movies are *about* something and don't release all the tension with action scenes.

In its own way it's a haunted house movie, or make that a haunted castle or fortress. Shutter Island, we're told, is a remote and craggy island in Boston bay, where a Civil War fort has been adapted as a prison for the criminally insane. We approach it by boat through lowering skies, and the feeling is something like the approach to King Kong's island: Looming in gloom from the sea, it fills the visitor with dread.

To this island in rainy weather in 1954 travel U.S. Marshal Teddy Daniels (Leonardo DiCaprio) and his partner, Chuck Aule (Mark Ruffalo). They're assigned to investigate the disappearance of a child murderer (Emily Mortimer). There seems to be no way to leave the island alive. The disappearance of one prisoner might not require the presence of two marshals unfamiliar with the situation, but we never ask that question. Not after the ominous walls of the prison arise. Not after the visitors are shown into the office of the prison director, Dr. Cawley, played by Ben Kingsley with that forbidding charm he has mastered.

It's clear that Teddy has no idea what he's getting himself into. Teddy—such an innocuous name in such a Gothic setting. Scorsese, working from a novel by Dennis Lehane, seems to be telling a simple enough story here; the woman is missing, and Teddy and Chuck will look for her. But the cold gray walls clamp in on them, and the offices of Cawley and his colleagues, furnished for the Civil War commanding officers, seem borrowed from a tale by Edgar Allan Poe.

Scorsese the craftsman chips away at reality piece by piece. Flashbacks suggest Teddy's traumas in the decade since World War II. That war, its prologue and aftermath, supplied the dark undercurrent of classic film noir. The term "post-traumatic stress disorder" was not then in use, but its symptoms could be seen in men attempting to look confident in their facades of unstyled suits, subdued ties, heavy smoking, and fedoras pulled low against the rain. DiCaprio and Ruffalo both effect this look, but DiCaprio makes it seem more like a hopeful disguise.

The film's primary effect is on the senses. Everything is brought together into a disturbing foreshadow of dreadful secrets. How did this woman escape from a locked cell in a locked ward in the old Civil War fort, its walls thick enough to withstand cannon fire? Why do Cawley and his sinister colleague Dr. Naehring (Max von Sydow, ready to play chess with Death) seem to be concealing something? Why is even such a pleasant person as the deputy warden not quite convincingly friendly? Why do the methods in the prison trigger flashbacks to Teddy's memories of helping to liberate a Nazi death camp?

These kinds of questions are at the heart of film noir. The hero is always flawed. Scorsese showed his actors the great 1947 noir *Out of the Past,* whose very title is a noir theme: Characters never arrive at a story without baggage. They have unsettled issues, buried traumas. So, yes, perhaps Teddy isn't simply a clean-cut G-man. But why are the others so strange? Kingsley in particular exudes menace every time he smiles.

There are thrilling visuals in *Shutter Island.* Another film Scorsese showed his cast was Hitchcock's *Vertigo,* and we sense echoes of its hero's fear of heights. There's the possibility that the escaped woman might be lurking in a cave on a cliff or hiding in a lighthouse. Both involve hazardous terrain to negotiate, above vertiginous falls to waves pounding on the rocks below. A possible hurricane is approaching. Light leaks out of the sky. The wind sounds mournful. It is, as they say, a dark and stormy night. And that's what the movie is about: atmosphere, ominous portents, the erosion of Teddy's confidence and even his identity. It's all done with flawless directorial command. Scorsese has fear to evoke, and he does it with many notes.

You may read reviews of *Shutter Island* complaining that the ending blindsides you. The uncertainty it causes prevents the film from feeling perfect on first viewing. I have a feeling it might improve on second. Some may believe it doesn't make sense. Or that, if it does, then the movie leading up to it doesn't. I asked myself: OK, then, how *should* it end? What would be more satisfactory? Why can't I be one of those critics who informs the director what he should have done instead?

Oh, I've had moments like that. Every moviegoer does. But not with *Shutter Island.* This movie is all of a piece, even the parts that don't appear to fit. There is a human tendency to note carefully what goes before and draw logical conclusions. But—what if you can't nail down exactly what went before? What if there were things about Cawley and his peculiar staff that were hidden? What if the movie lacks a reliable narrator? What if its point of view isn't omniscient but fragmented? Where can it all lead? What does it mean? We ask, and Teddy asks, too.

Shuttle ★

R, 107 m., 2009

Peyton List (Mel), Cameron Goodman (Jules), Tony Curran (Driver), Cullen Douglas (Andy), Dave Power (Matt), James Snyder (Seth). Directed by Edward Anderson and produced by Mark Williams, Todd Lemley, Allan Jones, Michael Pierce, and Mark Donadio. Screenplay by Anderson.

Why do I have to watch this movie? Why does anyone? What was the impulse behind this sad, cruel story? Is there, as they say, "an audience for it"? I guess so. The critic *Tex Massacre* at bloodydisgusting.com rates it four skulls out of five and says, "While gorehounds might not be doing back flips over the blood loss, they should appreciate that director Edward Anderson makes the kills relatively painful and wholly grounded in reality."

I'm not sure if the gorehounds will think there is too much blood loss or too little. Never mind. At least the killings are relatively painful. There's that to be said for it. But I think it's a cop-out to review this movie only as an entry in the horror/slasher genre and not pull back for a larger context. Do images have no qualities other than their technical competence?

Shuttle opens with two young women arriving at an almost empty airport at 2 a.m. It's raining. They can't get a cab. A guy in a van says he'll take them downtown for fifteen dollars. He already has one passenger. Now two young guys also want a ride. Guy says, nothing doing. One girl says, they're with us. Two guys get on board.

Under the driver's window is painted, "No more than three stops." That's strange. Looks like there's room for sixteen, twenty people in the van. The driver takes them on a strange route into no-man's land, pulls a gun, takes all five passengers hostage. OK, so far we're in standard horror territory.

It's what comes next that grows disturbing. The women, played by Peyton List and Cameron Goodman, are resourceful and try to fight back. The young guys help but are neutralized. The other passenger is a crybaby. The film seems set up to empower women. I won't say more about the plot except to say that it leads to utter hopelessness and evil.

That things happen as they do in *Shuttle* I suppose is true, however rarely. But a film can have an opinion about them. This one simply serves them up in hard, merciless detail. There is no release for the audience, no "entertainment," not even much action excitement. Just a remorseless march into the dark.

There is good work here. Peyton List, now twenty-two, working on TV since 2000, is effective as Mel, the more resourceful of the girls. She has a Neve Campbell quality. Tony Curran, as the driver, isn't your usual menacing monster but has more of a workaday attitude inflicting suffering. And the writer-director, Edward Anderson, is reasonably skilled at filmmaking, although it becomes a major distraction when he has the van drive through miles of empty streets when, as the plot reveals, there is little reason.

Last week I reviewed the latest version of *The Last House on the Left.* It had qualities, too, including more developed characters and more ingenious action sequences. But *Shuttle* is uninterested in visual style; it wants to appear nuts-and-bolts, unsentimental, pushing our faces in it. I know the horror genre is a traditional port of entry for first-time directors on low budgets, and I suppose that is Anderson's purpose. All right, he has proven himself. Now let him be less passionately infatuated with despair.

Note: The R *rating proves once again that it is impossible for a film to be rated* NC-17 *on violence alone.*

Silent Light ★ ★ ★ ★

NO MPAA RATING, 136 m., 2009

Cornelio Wall Fehr (Johan), Miriam Toews (Esther), Maria Pankratz (Marianne), Peter Wall (Padre), Elisabeth Fehr (Madre), Jacobo Klassen (Zacarias). Directed by Carlos Reygadas and produced by Reygadas and Jaime Romandia. Screenplay by Reygadas.

Sometimes we are helpless in the face of love, and it becomes a torment. It is a cruel master. We must act on it or suffer, and sometimes because we act, others suffer. *Silent Light* is a solemn and profound film about a man transfixed by love, which causes him to betray his good and faithful wife.

How he fell into this love, we do not know. Certainly Johan isn't the kind of man to go straying. Nor is Marianne, the woman he loves, a husband stealer. That they are both good to the core is the source of their pain. Yes, Johan and Marianne have sex, but it is the strength of the film that not for a second do we believe they are motivated by sex—only by love.

Esther, Johan's wife and the mother of their six children, knows Marianne and knows about the affair. Johan has told her. He is a religious man and has also confessed to his father and his best friend. There is the sense that he will never leave Esther and never stop loving Marianne. He and Esther say they love each other, and they mean it. You see how love brings its punishment.

The director Carlos Reygadas sets this story among the one hundred thousand or so Mennonites living in Mexico. He does not choose such a sect casually. His story involves people who deeply hold their values and try to act upon them and yet who do not seem to be zealots. (It says much about the Mennonites that their clergy are unpaid.) In fact, the film never mentions the word "Mennonite," there are no church services, and all the characters act from their hearts and not simply their teachings.

Reygadas cast the film entirely from the actual Mennonite community, which I believe will feel he played fair with them. If you didn't know these were untrained actors, you would assume they had years of experience. There is not a false instance in the film, and the performances assume an almost holy reality. Cornelio Wall Fehr as Johan, Miriam Toews as his wife, and Maria Pankratz as Marianne are so focused they gather interior power. They take a story of extreme emotions and make it believable. The father (Wall's real father), the friend, all of the actors, are unshakable.

Silent Light has a beauty based on nature and the rhythms of the land. It opens with a sunrise and closes with a sunset, both in long-held shots, and we see corn being gathered by a harvester, wheat being stacked, long dusty roads between soy fields. The cinematographer, Alexis Zabe, evokes some of the unadorned beauty of a film by Bresson or Bergman, and of the Dreyer film this one in some ways resembles, *Ordet.* He keeps a distance that sometimes suggests awe. When Marianne comes to Johan at a critical time near the end, the camera sees them as distant figures across a field. It is not a time for close-ups.

And look at a scene where Marianne tenderly kisses Esther. First we see them from the side, Marianne bending over. Then from directly overhead. When Marianne stands, the camera remains fixed on Esther's face, and we, but only after a time, see that there is a tear on her cheek. Marianne's. What actually happens next is open to discussion. I was reminded of a similar puzzle in Bergman's *Cries and Whispers.*

This film is not short, and it is not fast. There is no score, location sounds seem hard-edged, and when a hymn is sung, it is not a tune but a dirge. The film's rhythm imposes itself. Curious, how a slow and deep film can absorb, and a fast and shallow one can tire us.

"The world is too much with us," Wordsworth says. "Late and soon, getting and spending, we lay waste our powers: little we see in nature that is ours." It is Reygadas's inspiration to set this film among a people whose ways are old and deeply felt, and to cast it with actors who believe in those ways. To set it in "modern times," most places in today's world, would make it seem artificial and false. What the film is really about is people who see themselves and their values as an organic whole. There are no pious displays here. No sanctimony, no preaching. Never even the word "religion." Just Johan, Esther, and Marianne, all doing their best.

A Single Man ★ ★ ★

R, 101 m., 2009

Colin Firth (George Falconer), Julianne Moore (Charley), Matthew Goode (Jim), Nicholas Hoult (Kenny). Directed by Tom Ford and produced by Ford, Andrew Miano, Robert Salerno, and Chris Weitz. Screenplay by Ford, based on the novel by Christopher Isherwood.

Hemingway wrote something years ago that returns to my memory from time to time: "Isn't it pretty to think so." Never mind what he was referring to. The words apply for me to those situations where we imagine the reality to be quite different than it really is. Perhaps our imagination is a protective strategy.

A Single Man is told from the point of view of its hero, George (Colin Firth), the single man. He is single because unmarried and single because homosexual; the phrase was used at one time with a lifted eyebrow. It has been eight months since his lover died, and he still grieves. He is empty. His only friendship is with Charley (Julianne Moore), a sad alcoholic of a certain age with whom he once, briefly, had a try at a heated affair. She gives him gin and sympathy, but it's more ritual than comfort. She tries to kiss him, says maybe "we could still make a go of it," but that's a lie neither one believes.

A Single Man begins on what may be the last day of George's life, in 1962. The sight of a revolver waiting in a drawer makes this unmistakable. He performs his morning toilet of grooming and dressing in impeccable taste, and turns out to the world as the very model of flawless perfection. He teaches a college class on Aldous Huxley (is he still taught?). He works in a subtext about those who do not conform. No student is interested except Kenny (Nicholas Hoult), who may be less interested in the lecture than the lecturer.

Firth plays George superbly, as a man who prepares a face to meet the faces that he meets. He betrays very little emotion, and certainly his thoughts cannot be read in his eyes. He's so good at this it must have been rehearsed since youth. No one will ever see anything in George to complain about. Growing up in Britain as he did in the 1920s and 1930s he must have found few people with whom he could share his true nature. Now, in California, he had only his lover, and his lover is dead. Life is stale and profitless.

His evening is spent with Charley, who is always a little drunk or a little drunker. She has prepared for their date. Her hair is piled up and cemented in place, her makeup perfect, their dinner elegant. They talk in a code long-practiced. She offers sympathy she barely means and he barely feels. It is horrible that this may be the most meaningful relationship right now in either of these lives.

More happens later in the evening, but you will see for yourself. I want to return to those six words. I assume the film faithfully reflects George's idea of who he is, how he behaves, and what it means. The first-time director Tom Ford, the famous fashion designer, has been faulted for over-designing the film, but perhaps that misses the point. Perhaps George has over-designed his inner vision.

He sees himself as impeccable, reserved, ironic, resigned, detached. He projects a cool, impenetrable facade. Charley is seen in his way, which may not be hers. When events take place to interrupt his routine, he tries to maintain his demeanor unchanged. His game plan is apparently to complete this day in an orderly way, and then shoot himself, still above reproach.

Isn't it pretty to think so. It may work for George, but it didn't work for me. I sensed there were shrieks of terror and anger inside, bottled up for years. The last eight months must have been hell. Firth wisely doesn't try to signal this because any attempt to do so would break the facade and reduce his rather awesome performance to acting-out. I think it was Ford's responsibility to suggest it, perhaps through violations of the facade: a stain left overlooked on a tie, a careless remark, a car badly parked. A disintegration.

As Ford's first film, this story, based on a novel by Christopher Isherwood, must have had special meaning. He has another life and wasn't driven to the rigors of filmmaking. Many designers are known for their own faultless appearances. If Ford doesn't scream inside, and I have no reason to believe he does, perhaps the film faithfully reflects his idea of himself and George. Such a man will never kill himself.

Sin Nombre ★ ★ ★ ★

R, 96 m., 2009

Paulina Gaitan (Sayra), Edgar Flores (Willy/Casper), Kristyan Ferrer (Smiley), Tenoch Huerta Mejia (Lil' Mago), Diana Garcia (Martha Marlene), Luis Fernando Peña (Sol), Hector Jimenez (Leche/Wounded Man). Directed by Cary Fukunaga and produced by Amy Kaufman. Screenplay by Fukunaga.

El Norte. The North. It is a lodestar for some of those south of our border, who risk their lives to come here. *Sin Nombre,* which means "without name," is a devastating film about some of those who try the journey. It contains risk, violence, a little romance, even fleeting moments of humor, but most of all it sees what danger and heartbreak are involved. It is riveting from start to finish.

The film weaves two stories. One involves Sayra (Paulina Gaitan), a young woman from Honduras who joins her father and uncle in an odyssey through Guatemala and Mexico intended to take them to relatives in New Jersey. The other involves Casper (Edgar Flores), a young gang member from southern Mexico who joins with his leader and a twelve-year-old gang recruit to rob those riding north on the tops of freight cars. Their paths cross.

This is an extraordinary debut film by Cary Fukunaga, only thirty-one, who shows a mastery of image and story. He knows the material. He apparently spent time riding on the tops of northward trains; hundreds of hopeful emigrants materialize at a siding and scramble onboard, and the railroad apparently makes little attempt to stop them. He is also convincing about the inner workings of the terrifying real-life gang named Mara Salvatrucha.

Before turning to the story, I want to say something about the look and feel of the film. It was photographed by Adriano Goldman, who used not hi-def video as you might suspect, but 35 mm film, which has a special richness. Fukunaga's direction expresses a desire that seems to be growing in many young directors to return to classical compositions and editing. Those norms establish a strong foundation for storytelling; no queasy-cam for Fukunaga. Bahrani is another member of the same generation whose shots call attention to their subject, not themselves.

The story of Sayra, her father, and her uncle is straightforward: They are driven to improve their lives, think they have a safe haven in New

Jersey, and want to go there. Some elements of their journey reminded me of Gregory Nava's great indie epic *El Norte* (1983). The journey in that film was brutal; in this one, it is forged in hell.

That hell is introduced by Fukunaga in the club rooms of the gang, whose members are fiercely tattooed, none more than Lil' Mago (Tenoch Huerta Mejia), the leader, whose face is covered like a war mask. Casper is a member of the gang, more or less by force; he brings twelve-year-old Smiley (Kristyan Ferrer) to a meeting, and the kid is entranced by the macho BS. The three board one of the northbound trains to rob the riders, and that's when Casper meets Sayra and their fates are sealed.

Smiley, so young, with a winning smile, is perhaps the most frightening character because he demonstrates how powerful an effect, even hypnotic, gang culture can have on unshielded kids. In his eyes Lil' Mago looms as a god, the gang provides peer status, and any values Smiley might have had evaporate. The initiation process includes being savagely beaten and kicked by gang members, and then proving himself by killing someone. Smiley is ready and willing.

There are shots here of great beauty. As the countryside rolls past and the riders sit in the sun and protect their small supplies of food and water, there is sometimes the rhythm of weary camaraderie. I was reminded of Hal Ashby's *Bound for Glory*. Kids along the tracks are happy to see the riders getting away with something, and at one place throw them oranges. At stations, the riders jump off and detour around the guards to board the train again as it leaves town.

Sin Nombre is a remarkable film, showing the incredible hardships people will endure in order to reach El Norte. Yes, the issue of illegal immigration is a difficult one. When we encounter an undocumented alien, we should not be too quick with our easy assumptions. That person may have put his life on the line for weeks or months to come here, searching for what we so easily describe as the American Dream. What inspired Fukunaga, an American, to make this film, I learn, was a 2003 story about eighty illegals found locked in a truck and abandoned in Texas. Nineteen died.

Sita Sings the Blues ★ ★ ★ ★

NO MPAA RATING, 82 m., 2009

Directed, written, and produced by Nina Paley.

I got a DVD in the mail, an animated film titled *Sita Sings the Blues*. It was a version of the epic Indian tale of Ramayana set to the 1920s jazz vocals of Annette Hanshaw. Uh, huh. I carefully filed it with other movies I will watch when they introduce the eight-day week. Then I was told I *must* see it.

I began. I was enchanted. I was swept away. I was smiling from one end of the film to the other. It is astonishingly original. It brings together four entirely separate elements and combines them into a great whimsical chord. How did Paley's mind work?

She begins with the story of Ramayana, which is known to every schoolchild in India but not to me. It tells of a brave, noble woman who was made to suffer because of the foibles of an impetuous husband and his mother. Paley depicts this story with exuberant drawings in bright colors. It is about a prince named Rama who treated Sita unfairly, although she loved him and was faithful to him. There is more to it than that, involving a monkey army, a lustful king who occasionally grows ten heads, synchronized birds, a chorus line of gurus, and a tap-dancing moon.

It coils around and around, as Indian epic tales are known to do. Even the Indians can't always figure them out. In addition to her characters talking, Paley adds a hilarious level of narration: Three voice-over modern Indians, Desis, ad-libbing as they try to get the story straight. Was Sita wearing jewelry or not? How long was she a prisoner in exile? How did the rescue monkey come into the picture? These voices are as funny as an *SNL* skit, and the Indian accent gives them charm: "What a challenge, these stories!"

Sita, the heroine, reminds me a little of the immortal Betty Boop, but her singing voice is sexier. Paley synchs her life story and singing and dancing with recordings of the American jazz singer Annette Hanshaw (1901–1985), a big star in the 1920s and 1930s who was known as "the Personality Girl." Sita lived around 1000 BCE, a date that inspires lively debate among the three Indians discussing her. When her husband outrageously accuses her of adultery and kicks her on top of a flaming pyre, we know exactly how she feels when Annette Hanshaw sings her big hit, "Mean to Me."

There is a parallel story. In San Francisco, we meet an American couple, young and in love, named Dave and Nina, and their cat, named Lexi. Oh, they are in love. But Dave flies off to take a "temporary" job in India, Nina pines for him, she flies to join him in India, but he is cold to her, and when she returns home she receives a cruel message: "Don't come back. Love, Dave." Nina despairs. Lexi despairs. Cockroaches fill her apartment but she hardly notices. One day in her deepest gloom she picks up the book *Ramayana* and starts to read. Inspiration begins to warm the cold embers of her heart.

There are uncanny parallels between her life and Sita's. Both were betrayed by the men they loved. Both were separated by long journeys. Both died (Sita really, Nina symbolically) and were reborn—Sita in the form of a lotus flower, Nina in the form of an outraged woman who moves to Brooklyn, sits down at her home computer for five years, and creates this film. Yes, she reveals in her bio that her then-husband "terminated" their marriage while he was in India. No ex-husband has inspired a greater cultural contribution since Michael Huffington.

One remarkable thing about *Sita Sings the Blues* is how versatile the animation is. Consider Sita's curvaceous southern hemisphere. When she sings an upbeat or sexy song, it rotates like a seductive pendulum. Look at those synchronized birds overhead. When they return they have a surprise, and they get a surprise. Regard the marching graybeards. Watch Hanuman's dragging tail set a palace on fire.

The animation style of the scenes set in San Francisco and Brooklyn is completely different, essentially simple line drawings alive with personality. See how Paley needs only a few lines to create a convincing cat. Paley works entirely in 2-D with strict rules, so that characters remain within their own plane, which overlaps with others. This sounds like a limitation. Actually, it becomes the source of much amusement. Comedy often depends on the device of establishing unbreakable rules and then finding ways to break them. The laughs Paley gets here with 2-D would be the envy of an animator in 3-D. She discovers dimensions where none exist. This is one of the year's best films.

Skin ★ ★ ★ ★

PG -13, 107 m., 2009

Sophie Okonedo (Sandra Laing), Sam Neill (Abraham Laing), Alice Krige (Sannie Laing), Tony Kgoroge (Petrus Zwane), Ella Ramangwane (Young Sandra), Faniswa Yisa (Nora Molefe), Hannes Brummer (Leon Laing). Directed by Anthony Fabian and produced by Fabian, Genevieve Hofmeyr, and Margaret Matheson. Screenplay by Helen Crawley, Jessie Keyt, and Helena Kriel.

I remember the story of Sandra Laing. I lived in Cape Town in 1965, the year this film begins, and it was all over the South African newspapers. Sandra (Ella Ramangwane as a child) was the daughter of white Afrikaners, the descendants of the original Dutch settlers. There was no question they were her parents. She didn't look white. They cherished her and were proud of her. She was bright as a button. They enrolled her in school, and there was trouble. The white parents didn't want their children going to school with a black girl.

Given the insanity of the apartheid system, it was unthinkable that white parents could have a black child. Her parents reassure her: Of course she's white. They run a little shop with a black clientele, but that doesn't make them liberal. When Sannie Laing (Alice Krige) gets too friendly with the customers, her husband, Abraham (Sam Neill), tells her, "Be friendly with them, but don't adopt them!"

He's outraged by any suggestion of African blood in his family. Sandra looks "coloured" to the people white and black who see her, but not to her parents. He fights all the way to the Supreme Court to have Sandra officially classified as white. Among his witnesses is a geneticist from Witwatersrand University in Johannesburg who testifies, "many and perhaps most Afrikaners have some non-white blood."

This was a *very* touchy subject in South

Africa. I was aware of an Afrikaner student who hit another student when he was offered a pencil. That was an unmistakable reference to the infamous "pencil test": Stick a pencil through your hair and shake your head. The pencil will usually fall out of white hair, but not from black.

From being a cheerful child, Sandra grows into a troubled adolescent (Sophie Okonedo) who tries to bleach her skin. Her parents set up two disastrous dates with white boys. She falls in love with Petrus (Tony Kgoroge), a young black gardener, and her father chases him away with a rifle. Pregnant, she runs away from home, but now it is a crime for her to live with a black man.

The story of Sandra Laing (her real name) played out into the 1970s and fascinated South Africa like no other. It cut directly into the official fiction that the races were separate and would never meet. She was proof they'd been meeting a lot in the four hundred years since the Dutch landed at Cape Town.

Sophie Okonedo you may remember from *Hotel Rwanda* in 2004, which won her an Oscar nomination. Born in London of a white mother and African father (which is very relevant here), she was in *Dirty Pretty Things* (2002) and *The Secret Life of Bees* (2008)—remember the childlike May Boatwright?—and has completed playing the title role in *Mrs. Mandela*. Here she's magnificent, convincingly spanning Sandra's ages from sixteen into adulthood, and her buffeting by a society where race dictated who you could love, where you could live, how you could work, whether you could study, and who society thought you were. Consider how she handles a scene where she applies to the same clerk who issued her a "white card" and now demands a "black card." Her very existence reveals her society is based on no more than a piece of paper.

This great film by Anthony Fabian tells this story through the eyes of a happy girl who grows into an outsider. This isn't one of those potted stories of uplift and doesn't end quite the way we expect, although we do get to see the real Sandra Laing right at the end. It's not giving away anything to say the film's first scene takes place on the day South Africa elected Nelson Mandela as its first African president. Sandra is cornered by a TV crew that asks for her reaction. She says, "It comes too late for me."

A Small Act ★ ★ ★ ½

NO MPAA RATING, 98 m., 2010

With Chris Mburu, Jane Wanjiru Muigai, and Hilde Back. A documentary directed and written by Jennifer Arnold.

The heartwarming documentary *A Small Act* centers on the life story of Chris Mburu, who as a small boy living in a mud house in a Kenyan village had his primary and secondary education paid for by a Swedish woman. This cost her fifteen dollars a month. They had never met. He went on to the University of Nairobi, graduated from Harvard Law School, and is today a United Nations human rights commissioner.

The film shows Mburu seeking the Swedish woman who "made my life possible." She is Hilde Back. Before even meeting her, in gratitude he started a foundation named the Hilde Back Education Fund to fund scholarships for poor village children. She is now eighty-five years old, a German Jew who was sent to Sweden as a child. Her family died in the Holocaust. She never married, has lived in the same apartment for thirty-five years, was a schoolteacher. She is a tiny woman, but robust and filled with energy. We see them meeting for the first time.

She is flown to Kenya, serenaded by the choir from Mburu's village, feasted, thanked, gowned in traditional robes. She says that her fifteen dollars was an insignificant sum to her, but she kept it up because she thought even a small act was worth performing.

In the film, we see the mud house Chris grew up in. Then we follow Kimani, Ruth, and Caroline—three Kenyan students who hope to win high scores and continue in school. This will depend on winning one of the scholarships. Their families pin all of their hopes on these kids.

One says she would miss her family at a boarding school, but would enjoy being able to study by electric light. In this village the students study by the light of a single oil flame. Most families in Kenya want their children to attend high school, seeing that as the key to success in life. They lack the money, but recently, Kenya has been able to make primary education free.

The schools we see are not physically impressive; the one focused on in the film is a very basic brick structure with no amenities and crowded classrooms with simple board benches and desks. A gym? Don't make me laugh.

Education focuses on reading (in English) and math, with some history and geography. The students are impressed by their ability to be in school at all. Their parents sacrifice to send them; child labor could add to the family income. At the end of primary school, they take tests to qualify for secondary education if they can afford it. The film shows some of the test questions. To me, they look difficult for kids that age. They pass or fail; too many American schools graduate students who are functionally illiterate.

Hilde Back is asked if, since she never had children, she thought of Chris as a son. We see in the film that they stay in close touch. "But I have had children," she replied. "I was a teacher. I had many, many children." And one lived in a mud house in Kenya.

The Social Network ★ ★ ★ ★

PG-13, 120 m., 2010

Jesse Eisenberg (Mark Zuckerberg), Andrew Garfield (Eduardo Saverin), Justin Timberlake (Sean Parker), Armie Hammer (Cameron/Tyler Winklevoss), Max Minghella (Divya Narendra), Brenda Song (Christy Ling), Rooney Mara (Erica). Directed by David Fincher and produced by Dana Brunetti, Cean Chaffin, Michael De Luca, and Scott Rudin. Screenplay by Aaron Sorkin, based on the book *The Accidental Billionaires* by Ben Mezrich.

The Social Network is about a young man who possessed an uncanny ability to look into a system of unlimited possibilities and sense a winning move. His name is Mark Zuckerberg, he created Facebook, he became a billionaire in his early twenties, and he reminds me of the chess prodigy Bobby Fischer. There may be a touch of Asperger's syndrome in both: They possess genius but are tone-deaf in social situations. Example: It is inefficient to seek romance by using strict logic to demonstrate your intellectual arrogance.

David Fincher's film has the rare quality of being not only as smart as its brilliant hero, but in the same way. It is cocksure, impatient, cold, exciting, and instinctively perceptive. It hurtles through two hours of spellbinding dialogue. It makes an untellable story clear and fascinating. It is said to be impossible to make a movie about a writer, because how can you show him only writing? It must also be impossible to make a movie about a computer programmer, because what is programming but writing in a language few people in the audience know? Yet Fincher and his writer, Aaron Sorkin, are able to explain the Facebook phenomenon in terms we can immediately understand, which is the reason five hundred million of us have signed up.

To conceive of Facebook, Zuckerberg (Jesse Eisenberg) needed to know almost nothing about relationships or human nature (and apparently he didn't). What he needed was the ability to intuit a way to involve the human race in the Kevin Bacon game. Remember that Kevin Bacon himself need not know more than a fraction of the people linking through him. Same on Facebook. I probably know 40 of my Facebook friends well, 100 glancingly, 200 by reputation. All the others are friends of friends. I can't remember the last time I received a friend request from anyone I didn't share at least one "mutual friend" with.

For the presence of Facebook, we possibly have to thank a woman named Erica (Rooney Mara). *The Social Network* begins with Erica's date with Zuckerberg. He nervously sips a beer and speed talks through an aggressive interrogation. It's an exercise in sadistic conversational gamesmanship. Erica gets fed up, calls him an asshole, and walks out.

Erica (a fictional character) is right, but at that moment she puts Zuckerberg in business. He goes home, has more beers, and starts hacking into the "facebooks" of Harvard dorms to collect the head shots of campus women. He programs a page where they can be rated for their beauty. This is sexist and illegal, and proves so popular it crashes the campus servers. After it's fertilized by a mundane Web site called the Harvard Connection, Zuckerberg grows it into Facebook.

In theory there are more possible moves on a chessboard than molecules in the universe. Chess masters cannot possibly calculate all of them, but using intuition they can "see" a way through this near-infinity to a winning move. Nobody was ever better at chess than Bobby Fischer. Likewise, programming languages and techniques are widely known, but it was Zuckerberg who intuited how he could link them with a networking site. The genius of Facebook requires not psychological insight but its method of combining ego with interaction. Zuckerberg wanted to get revenge on all the women at Harvard. To do that he involved them in a matrix that is still growing.

It's said there are child prodigies in only three areas: math, music, and chess. These nonverbal areas require little maturity or knowledge of human nature, but a quick ability to perceive patterns, logical rules, and linkages. I suspect computer programming may be a fourth area.

Zuckerberg may have had the insight that created Facebook, but he didn't do it alone in a room, and the movie gets a narration by cutting between depositions for lawsuits. Along the way we get insights into the pecking order at Harvard, a campus where ability joins wealth and family as success factors. We meet the twins Cameron and Tyler Winklevoss (both played by Armie Hammer), rich kids who believe Zuckerberg stole their Harvard Connection in making Facebook. We meet Eduardo Saverin (Andrew Garfield), Zuckerberg's roommate and best (only) friend, who was made CFO of the company, loaned it the money it needed to get started, and was frozen out. And most memorably we meet Sean Parker (Justin Timberlake), the founder of two legendary Web start-ups, Napster and Plaxo.

It is the mercurial Parker, just out of work but basked in fame and past success, who grabbed Zuckerberg by the ears and pulled him into the big time. He explained why Facebook needed to move to Silicon Valley. Why more money would come from venture capitalists than Eduardo would ever raise with his hat-in-hand visits to wealthy New Yorkers. And he tried, not successfully, to introduce Zuckerberg into the fast lane: big offices, wild parties, women, the availability of booze and cocaine.

Zuckerberg was not seduced by this lifestyle. He was uninterested in money, stayed in modest houses, didn't fall to drugs. A subtext the movie never comments on is the omnipresence of attractive Asian women. Most of them are smart Harvard undergrads, two of them (allied with Sean) are Victoria's Secret models, one (Christy, played by Brenda Song) is Eduardo's girlfriend. Zuckerberg himself doesn't have much of a social life onscreen, misses parties, would rather work. He has such tunnel vision he doesn't even register when Sean redrafts the financial arrangements to write himself in and Eduardo out.

The testimony in the depositions makes it clear there is a case to be made against Zuckerberg, many of them sins of omission. It's left to the final crawl to explain how they turned out. The point is to show an interaction of undergraduate chaos, enormous amounts of money, and manic energy.

In an age when movie dialogue is dumbed and slowed down to suit slow-wits in the audience, the dialogue here has the velocity and snap of screwball comedy. Eisenberg, who has specialized in playing nice or clueless, is a heat-seeking missile in search of his own goals. Timberlake pulls off the tricky assignment of playing Sean Parker as both a hotshot and someone who engaged Zuckerberg as an intellectual equal. Andrew Garfield evokes an honest friend who is not the right man to be CFO of the company that took off without him, but deserves sympathy.

The Social Network is a great film not because of its dazzling style or visual cleverness, but because it is splendidly well made. Despite the baffling complications of computer programming, Web strategy, and big finance, Aaron Sorkin's screenplay makes it all clear, and we don't follow the story so much as get dragged along behind it. I saw it with an audience that seemed wrapped up in an unusual way: It was very, *very* interested.

The Soft Skin ★ ★ ★

NO MPAA RATING, 113 m., 2011

Jean Desailly (Pierre Lachenay), Francoise Dorleac (Nicole Chomette), Nelly Benedetti (Franca Lachenay), Daniel Ceccaldi (Clement), Sabine Haudepin (Sabine). Directed by Francois

Truffaut and produced by Truffaut and Antonio da Cunha Telles. Screenplay by Truffaut and Jean-Louis Richard.

Francois Truffaut's *The Soft Skin* is being revived at the very moment when it seems uncannily prophetic. It tells the story of a wealthy and famous French man who has an affair with an airline hostess and foolishly thinks he can keep it a secret from his wife. The difference between Pierre Lachenay and Dominique Strauss-Kahn is that Pierre is timid and guilty, although he would have saved himself a great deal of grief by being even more timid.

This 1964 melodrama was a change of direction for Truffaut, whose *The 400 Blows* (1959), *Shoot the Piano Player* (1960), and *Jules and Jim* (1962) helped define the French New Wave. Here is material more suited to bourgeoisie soap opera, although it is fairly scathing about France's intellectual elite. Pierre (Jean Desailly) is a Parisian literary editor and author, which means that in France he is a good deal more famous than he would be in many countries. So famous that the young air attendant Nicole (Francoise Dorleac) is quite willing to be seduced, and must be considered an accomplice in the process.

Pierre is perhaps forty, an impeccably groomed, well-spoken married man with a delightful wife and a lovable daughter. Truffaut must have cast Jean Desailly for his appearance of ordinary respectability. His hair is always neatly parted, his tie is always in place, he is polite almost to a fault. He isn't a caricature of a lustful, cheating husband; he seems almost abashed by his sexual feelings.

And Nicole? What does she see in him? She sees his fame. She knows who he is. She is staying in his hotel in Lisbon, where he has gone to give a speech about (Truffaut's hero) Balzac. She met his eyes on the airplane, they saw each other again at the airport, and they shared the same elevator at the hotel—he rather pointedly staying on past his floor. Her eyes in the elevator made her willingness clear. He calls her from his room, to, yes, apologize for not helping her with her packages. Although this polite meekness allows their affair to begin, it also contains the seeds of its destruction.

There seems no reason for Pierre to stray. His wife, Franca (Nelly Benedetti), seems an ideal spouse: smart, loving, competent, sexy. They get along in bed. He strays because . . . he can? He is flattered by the company of this younger woman? In the film, Truffaut gives Nicole no particular qualities other than beauty and availability; indeed, it is Pierre's panic and secretiveness that bring out her best qualities, of self-respect and pride.

This happens during the film's centerpiece, Pierre's trip to Reims to introduce a film. He goes only so that Nicole can accompany him. But the chairman of the event is a friend of Pierre's from Paris, so Nicole must be hidden. They check into a different hotel, there is no ticket for Nicole at the screening, and later he's trapped over drinks with the chairman while through the window he sees Nicole being hit on by a creep and does nothing. She will not allow herself to be treated in this way.

What it comes down to is: Pierre is a lousy adulterer. He lacks the desire, the reason, and the skill. Truffaut nicely portrays the crisis of social embarrassment that develops when he tries to keep Nicole out of sight. Part of his dilemma is that he tries so desperately to do the safe and prudent thing. This only leads, as you will see, to catastrophe, in an ending that is perhaps justified but is unconvincing. How could anyone care about mundane Pierre that much?

Note: Francoise Dorleac was the older sister of Catherine Deneuve and costarred with her in Jacques Demy's The Young Girls of Rochefort *(1967). On June 26 of that year, she died in a car crash near Nice.*

Solitary Man ★ ★ ★ ½

R, 90 m., 2010

Michael Douglas (Ben Kalmen), Mary-Louise Parker (Jordan Karsch), Jenna Fischer (Susan Porter), Jesse Eisenberg (Cheston), Imogen Poots (Allyson Karsch), Susan Sarandon (Nancy Kalmen), Danny DeVito (Jimmy Merino). Directed by Brian Koppelman and David Levien and produced by Heidi Jo Markel, Paul Schiff, and Steven Soderbergh. Screenplay by Koppelman.

For an actor with so many films, Michael Douglas hasn't played many conventional heroes. Yes, he did those *Romancing the Stone* roles, and he's been more memorable as a villain (*Wall Street*), but his strongest roles are as sinners: not big or bad enough to be villains, more ordinary men, smart, glib, conniving, trying to get by on short dues. Here is where he best uses his considerable screen presence. And he gets better at it as he grows older because his characters keep on sinning when they just don't have the stamina for it anymore.

In *Solitary Man,* he plays Ben Kalmen, once a regional celebrity as "New York's Honest Car Dealer." Ben is good-looking, still has that great head of hair, and is as persuasive as—well, as a good car dealer. In business he can sense what car to put you in. In sex he can sense what mood to put you in. He closes a lot of deals.

He isn't solitary by choice but by default. He cheated on his good wife, Nancy (Susan Sarandon). He disappointed their daughter, Susan (Jenna Fischer), one time too many. He cheats on his current companion, Jordan (Mary-Louise Parker), in a particularly unforgivable way. He uses the offer of his experience in life to charm Cheston (Jesse Eisenberg), a college student, and then betrays him. He has lied to his customers so often that, as everyone knows, "Honest Ben Kalmen" spent time behind bars.

Yet he's charming and persuasive. He looks like a winner until you look too close. *Solitary Man* follows him for several days after he agrees to accompany Jordan's daughter, Allyson (Imogen Poots), as she goes to Boston to settle in for her freshman year at college. This is the same school he attended. He knows the dean, which may be a help.

You want to like Ben. He works on encouraging that. When he was younger and less of a sinner, he must have been good to know, and there's an effective character in *Solitary Man* who suggests that. This is his old school-years buddy (Danny DeVito) who still runs a greasy spoon diner. On campus, Ben befriends the sophomore Cheston with man-of-the-world advice about sex, success, and how to sell yourself. With women, his approach is solicitous: Do some men misunderstand you? Are your qualities recognized? What are you getting out of the transaction?

The film is all about Ben Kalmen, but one of the strengths of Michael Douglas's performance is that he isn't playing a character. He's playing a character who is playing a character. Ben's life has become performance art. You get the feeling he never goes offstage. He sees few women he doesn't try seducing. As a car dealer, he was also in the seduction trade. His business was selling himself. At a dealership, it's hard to move a lemon. What about in life when you need a recall?

What happens with Ben and the people in his life, especially the women, I should not hint at here. The movie depends on our fascination as we see what lengths this man will go to. Reading in the gossip sheets that Douglas in years past was led astray by lust, we suspect that some of his performance is based on experience. Why is a man a serial seducer? To prove to himself that he can, which to a woman is not a compelling reason to be seduced.

This is a smart, effective film, a comedy in many ways even though it's bookended with reasons for Ben to see it as a potential tragedy. It's a serious comedy, perceptive, nuanced, with every supporting performance well calibrated to demonstrate to Ben that he can run but he can no longer hide. One of the best is by DeVito, who has been standing behind his counter for years and is perfectly content. He doesn't have that hunger that gnaws at Ben.

Imogen Poots is good, too, as the girl going away to school. She could sell Honest Ben the Brooklyn Bridge, and he would think he was talking her into it. As the trip upstate begins to fall apart, so does Ben's shaky financial future, and he has a meeting with a banker (Richard Schiff) that plays out with relentless logic.

Here is one of Michael Douglas's finest performances. Because the other characters, no matter what they think, never truly engage Ben Kalmen, he's on that stage by himself. Everyone else is in the audience. Douglas plays Ben as charismatic, he plays him as shameless, he plays him as brave, and very gradually, he learns to play him as himself. That's the only role left.

The Soloist ★ ★ ½

PG-13, 117 m., 2009

Jamie Foxx (Nathaniel Ayers), Robert Downey Jr. (Steve Lopez), Catherine Keener (Mary

Weston), Tom Hollander (Graham Claydon), Lisa Gay Hamilton (Jennifer Ayers-Moore). Directed by Joe Wright and produced by Gary Foster and Russ Krasnoff. Screenplay by Susannah Grant, based on the book by Steve Lopez.

The Soloist has all the elements of an uplifting drama, except for the uplift. The story is compelling, the actors are in place, but I was never sure what the filmmakers wanted me to feel about it. Based on a true story, it stars Jamie Foxx as Nathaniel Ayers, a homeless man who was once a musical prodigy, and Robert Downey Jr. as Steve Lopez, the *Los Angeles Times* columnist who writes about him, bonds with him, makes him famous, becomes discouraged by the man's mental illness, and—what? Hears him play great music?

"Explaining madness is the most limiting and generally least convincing thing a movie can do," Pauline Kael once wrote. *The Soloist* doesn't even seem sure how to depict it. Unlike Russell Crowe's mathematician in *A Beautiful Mind,* whose madness was understood through his own eyes, the musician here seems more of a loose cannon, unpredictable in random ways. Yes, mental illness can be like that, but can successful drama? There comes a point when Lopez has had enough, and so, in sympathy, have we.

That is no fault of Jamie Foxx's performance creating a man who is tense, fearful, paranoid, and probably schizophrenic. We can almost smell his terror, through the carnival clown clothing and hats he hides behind. When Foxx learned of this role, he might reasonably have sensed another Academy Award. Unfortunately, the screenwriter and director don't set up a structure for Oscar-style elevation, nor do they really want to make a serious and doleful film about mental illness. But those are the two apparent possibilities here, and *The Soloist* seems lost between them.

As the film opens, Lopez is troubled. His marriage has problems, he feels burned out at work, he's had a bike accident. He encounters Ayers almost outside the *Times* building, attracted by the beautiful sounds he's producing on a violin with only two strings. The man can play. Lopez tries to get to know him, writes a first column about him, learns he once studied cello at Juilliard. A reader sends Lopez a cello for him (this actually happened), and the columnist becomes his brother's keeper.

This is a thankless and possibly futile task. *The Soloist* does a very effective job of showing us a rehab center on Skid Row, and the reason so many homeless avoid such shelters. It's not what happens inside, but the gauntlet of street people necessary to run just to get to its doors. Indifference about adequate care for our homeless population was one of the priorities of the Selfish Generation.

As a mentally ill man, Ayers is unpredictable and explosive, yes, but almost as if responding to the arc of the screenplay. Characters have arcs in most movies, but the trick is to convince us we're watching them really behave. Here Foxx is let down, and the disappointment is greater because of the track records of director Joe Wright (*Atonement*) and writer Susannah Grant (*Erin Brockovich*). We see a connection between the two men, but not communication.

As a newspaper columnist, Downey is plausible as his overworked, disillusioned character, finding redemption through a story. And Catherine Keener, like Helen Mirren in *State of Play,* convinces me she might really be an editor. Both actresses bring a welcome change of pace from the standard Lou Grant type. Talk about disillusionment; the old-timers can't believe their eyes these days. The *Los Angeles Times* of this movie is at least still prospering.

As for the music, Beethoven of course is always uplifting, but the movie doesn't employ him as an emotional show-stopper, as Debussy's "Clair de Lune" is used in *Tokyo Sonata.* There's no clear idea of what it would mean should Ayers triumph in a public debut; would it be a life-changing moment or only an anomaly on his tragic road through life? Can he be salvaged? Does he want to be? Or will he always be a soloist, playing to his demons in the darkness under a bridge?

Something Better Somewhere Else ★ ★ ★

NO MPAA RATING, 76 m., 2010

With Christian Stolte, David Pasquesi, John G. Connolly, Stephanie Childers, Naomi Ashley, Tim Polk, and Megan Moore Burns. Directed by

Ron Lazzeretti and produced by Ed Amaya. Screenplay by Lazzeretti.

Something Better Somewhere Else is a delightful film and in some stretches a flawless one. It tells four stories, each one immediately engaging, and gets in and out without overstaying its welcome. In a world of bloated and dumbed-down entertainment, here's a movie with the quickness and acute observation of a good short story.

So what is the flawless part? That would be the execution by director Ron Lazzeretti. Yes, he wrote and directed it, and we'll get back to that. But what I kept noticing was the excellence in details. The acting, the casting, the dialogue, editing, music, and meticulous camera placement. The feeling that not a shot was careless. The film knows what it's doing.

The four stories have one theme: moving on. We live much of our lives, I suspect, in a state of tension between the belief that there must be *Something Better Somewhere Else* and a fear of abandoning what we know and are familiar with. The four segments apply this truth to work, love, marriage, and home.

The first short, *Last Day,* involves a man leaving a job he hates at a place everyone else hates, too. He inspires admiration, envy, and (after farewell drinks) even some hatred. Notice how economically Lazzeretti directs his supporting actors to make each one stand out as an individual. And watch the scene in the bar when his hero uneasily watches one conversation while mired in another.

Wedding Night, the second, is like an O. Henry story, and the ending creates some of the same dissatisfaction he was sometimes guilty of. Still, there's a nice narrative bait and switch.

The third film, *Flowers,* is surprisingly evocative. Set the plot aside for a moment and see how observant the camera is in noticing there is something about a man sitting on a bench at a bus stop and holding a big bouquet of flowers that just makes some women need to smile. This stretch of the film would fail if a single shot seemed "acted," but none does.

The fourth, *Move,* takes place on a family's last day before moving to California. It was the wife who wanted this move, and now she's having second thoughts, and her husband doggedly tries to keep everyone on schedule. In the process we listen to a farewell conversation between the girl and her boyfriend that is written and acted so convincingly we realize we don't hear many authentic teenage voices in teenage movies.

Lazzeretti's perfectionism shows with a shot showing two extras. Observing emotion during the family's departure process, one kid looks at his pal (with the round wire-rim glasses) and that's all that happens, but look at how it's photographed and edited, and realize how much you think you know about those kids. Storytelling is as much a matter of technique as laborious plotting.

Lazzeretti is a Chicago-based commercial director, and that's a form that requires every frame to do heavy lifting. He wrote and produced Michael Keaton's memorable directing debut, *The Merry Gentlemen* (2009). *Something Better Somewhere Else* is only seventy-six minutes long, but three of the four films remain in my mind with as much psychic weight as features.

Something Borrowed ★ ★

PG-13, 112 m., 2011

Kate Hudson (Darcy), Ginnifer Goodwin (Rachel), John Krasinski (Ethan), Colin Egglesfield (Dex), Steve Howey (Marcus), Ashley Williams (Claire). Directed by Luke Greenfield and produced by Broderick Johnson, Andrew A. Kosove, Aaron Lubin, Pamela Schein Murphy, Molly Smith, and Hilary Swank. Screenplay by Jennie Snyder Urman, based on the novel by Emily Giffin.

One of the curious problems with *Something Borrowed* is that Kate Hudson's performance is too effective. She plays Darcy, the lifelong best friend of the heroine, Rachel (Ginnifer Goodwin). Blond, rich, and headstrong, Darcy always gets her way in their relationship. And as the film opens she's about to be married to Dex (Colin Egglesfield), whom Rachel has had a crush on since law school. No good can come of this.

The plot mechanics are more or less inevitable. Thrown together again as the ceremony approaches, Rachel and Dex realize they have always been in love. But what to do?

Rachel doesn't want to hurt her best friend. And Dex has a mother who struggles with depression; only the marriage seems capable of cheering her up.

To be married as an aid to someone else's mental health calls, I think, your own into question. This is especially true because the depressed mother (Jill Eikenberry) doesn't have a single line in the movie, and is seen only looking sad sometimes and happy sometimes. I believe, but cannot be sure, that a surprise decision made late in the film is triggered by her single ambivalent expression.

Now as to Kate Hudson. She plays an alcoholic. This is as clear as day, although I'll bet you won't see her described that way in many other reviews. Among the danger signals of alcoholism must certainly be playing badminton on the beach with a glass of wine in your hand, sitting down in a bar and ordering six shots of tequila, and drinking in every scene where she is not literally being fitted for a wedding dress. If you are marrying an alcoholic and are not one yourself, you shouldn't do it to cheer up your mom.

Kate Hudson plays Darcy so well that she almost forces the film apart at the seams; her character is too strong for it. Dex and Rachel, on the other hand, are sweet, inoffensive, beautiful people, who let others determine key decisions in their lives. As played by Ginnifer Goodwin and Colin Egglesfield, they are also extraordinarily attractive, and I almost held that against them until the story developed some of their depths. Goodwin has one of those faces of which you can think no bad things.

The movie supplies two other male characters, Ethan (John Krasinski) and party animal Marcus (Steve Howey). Ethan is Rachel's confidant during their lunch hours together. He figures out the whole story and pleads with Rachel to express her own feelings for once and not always let Darcy be the winner. It was even Rachel who introduced Darcy to Dex, for criminy sakes, and all but gave him away. Ethan avoids the clutches of their lustful friend Claire (Ashley Williams), a woman whose appearance can only be explained by the need for someone clutchy.

If Dex's mother says nothing, his father (Geoff Pierson) has a speech that is succinct and powerful, essentially ordering his son to go ahead with the wedding. The problem with that is that few fathers order their sons to marry ditzy drunks, but then again, maybe he doesn't know about Darcy's style at badminton.

Something Borrowed gathers an undeniable narrative momentum in its last half because all of the characters are treated sincerely and played in a straightforward style. It's just that we don't love them enough. Dex is too weak, Rachel is too sweet, Ethan has the same problem he accused Rachel of, and only Marcus finally seems to get what he deserves.

Somewhere ★ ★ ★ ★

R, 96 m., 2010

Stephen Dorff (Johnny Marco), Elle Fanning (Cleo), Chris Pontius (Sammy). Directed by Sofia Coppola and produced by Sofia Coppola, Roman Coppola, and G. Mac Brown. Screenplay by Sofia Coppola.

Don't distinguish what he feels with the word "existential." It has nothing to do with philosophy. He believes he's nothing, and it appears he's correct. This is called depression, but it may simply be a realistic view of the situation. Johnny Marco sits in a suite of the Chateau Marmont, that little hotel for generations of Hollywood hideouts, and finds himself a hollow man.

He is a movie star. With that comes such options as money, fame, sex, drugs. Fame is a joke because he gets nothing from it. Sex involves mechanics of the genitals. He drinks and takes drugs and gets a little wound up, but pleasure doesn't seem to be involved. On two occasions he hires twin blond strippers to come to his room, set up their portable equipment, and do choreographed pole dances. No sex is involved. He is demonstrating the truth that if you stare long enough at a wall, it will break the monotony if blond twins do pole dances in front of it.

Sofia Coppola's new film *Somewhere* involves, as did her *Lost in Translation* (2003), a man separated from his family and sitting alone in a hotel room. Its opening resembles Vincent Gallo's *The Brown Bunny* (2003): a long shot of a vehicle tearing around a track.

A man racing madly to nowhere. Bill Murray's Bob in *Lost in Translation* makes dutiful but cheerless phone calls home from Japan. Stephen Dorff's Johnny spends dutiful time with his eleven-year-old daughter, Cleo (Elle Fanning). Neither seems meaningfully connected.

Because so much of *Somewhere* is set at the Chateau Marmont, it might be useful to discuss it. It isn't cheap, but nobody goes there to indulge in conspicuous consumption. What it offers above all is a management that minds its own business. What happens at the Chateau Marmont stays at the Chateau Marmont. It's often linked with another semiresidential legend a few blocks away, the Sunset Marquis. The Chateau, I sense, is more useful for clients who want not so much privacy as retreat. There's a scene where Johnny nods to Benicio del Toro in the elevator. I'll bet you del Toro was staying there at the time. They are both simply waiting for their floors.

The notion of a star sinking into seclusion and depression isn't new. Gus Van Sant's *Last Days* (2005) starred Michael Pitt as a character unmistakably inspired by Kurt Cobain. What distinguishes Coppola's film is the detail in her portrait of celebrity life. Remember that she was a little girl and later a young actress on the sets of her father's movies. Now that we see how observant she is, we can only speculate about what she understood right from the start. She played Michael Corleone's baby.

The movie has, for example, an unusually accurate portrait of how publicists work from the client's point of view. Some become friends, some remain employees, but during work they function as parents and guardians. The star's contract requires him to do some press. The phone rings and the publicist tells the star where to go and what to do. He takes on a certain passivity. The car is there; he takes the car. The press is there; he talks to the press. Some stars are more interested and interesting. Not Johnny. He flies to Milan to accept an award, and the event plays like a bus ride with a Jacuzzi.

He seems to suffer from anhedonia, the inability to feel pleasure. Perhaps he hardly feels anything. The film only indirectly suggests some of the reasons he got this way. It is not a diagnosis, still less a prescription. Johnny stares at the wall and the film stares back. This is more interesting than it may sound. Coppola watches this world. The familiar strangers on the hotel staff are on a first-name basis because a star's world has become reduced to his support. Hookers and sex partners come and go. There are parties filled with strangers, most of them not excited to see a star because they see stars constantly.

Then his daughter. What led to the divorce Cleo probably knows better than he does. The child of an actor, she has learned to play a star. She observes his drinking, his detached attempts at fatherhood, the woman he makes no attempt to explain at breakfast. Why does a man like this inflict partial custody on a blameless child?

Coppola is a fascinating director. She sees, and we see exactly what she sees. There is little attempt here to observe a plot. All the attention is on the handful of characters, on Johnny. He has attained success in his chosen field, and lost track of the ability to experience it. Perhaps you can stimulate yourself so much for so long that your sensitivity wears out. If Johnny has no inner life and his outer life no longer matters, then he's right: He's nothing.

Note: Somewhere *won the Golden Lion at Venice 2010.*

The Sorcerer's Apprentice ★ ★ ½

PG, 108 m., 2010

Nicolas Cage (Balthazar), Jay Baruchel (Dave Stutler), Teresa Palmer (Becky Barnes), Alfred Molina (Maxim Horvath), Monica Bellucci (Veronica), Toby Kebbell (Drake Stone), Alice Krige (Morgana), Jake Cherry (Young Dave), James A. Stephens (Merlin). Directed by Jon Turteltaub and produced by Jerry Bruckheimer. Screenplay by Matt Lopez, Doug Miro, and Carlo Bernard.

Having seen *The Last Airbender* gross untold millions despite the worst reviews in many a year, I confess myself discouraged at the prospect of reviewing *The Sorcerer's Apprentice.* This is a much better film than *Airbender,* which is faint praise, but it's becoming clear that every weekend brings another heavily marketed action "comedy" that pounds tens of millions out of consumers before evaporating.

I use the word "consumer" deliberately. This genre doesn't require an audience in the traditional sense. It attracts children and young teenagers with the promise of cinematic fast food: It's all sugar and caffeine, no nutrition. In place of a plot there's a premise, in place of carefully crafted action there are stupefying exercises in computer-generated imagery, and in place of an ending there's a hook for the sequel and, if all goes well, a new franchise.

The Sorcerer's Apprentice is in small part inspired by the famous sequence in Walt Disney's *Fantasia* (1940) where Mickey Mouse does battle with bewitched brooms and buckets while Leopold Stokowski conducts the famous music by Paul Dukas. Here there's an amusing sequence involving enchanted mops and such, with music that shares most of the same notes as Dukas but none of Stokowski's conducting flair. No matter. Most consumers have likely never heard of the music—or of *Fantasia*, for that matter. Even this shadow of the original is more charming than anything else in the film.

Nicolas Cage is the star, playing Balthazar, a good magician who has long held captive the forces of magical evil. A prologue explains how, 1,300 years ago, the Arthurian magician Merlin (James A. Stephens) warred with the evil magicians Morgana (Alice Krige) and Horvath (Alfred Molina). Merlin sealed them and their despicable minions in the deepest interior of a nested doll. Mankind will be safe as long as they stay there. If Morgana and Horvath escape, the planet will be doomed. They're as bad as BP.

As the story opens, ten-year-old Dave (Jake Cherry) chases a stray love note as it blows through the mail slot of an ancient curiosity shop in New York. This shop is chockablock with weird gimcracks, and presided over by Balthazar, who instantly intuits that Young Dave may have the potential to become the long-awaited Prime Merlinian—the great magician who can vanquish Morgana's forces once and for all.

The purpose of this sequence is crystal clear: It's to establish the protagonist as a kid, before he grows for ten years and becomes the movie's hero (Jay Baruchel). That way gradeschoolers will identify with twenty-year-old Dave. Others can identify with Balthazar, who is played by Cage with his usual admirable energy. It gets a chuckle early in the movie when Young Dave asks Balthazar how he knows something, and Cage spins and snarls: "Because I can read minds!" Next question?

There's a needless subplot involving Dave's crush on the fragrant Becky Barnes (Teresa Palmer), who in grade school all those many years ago was the intended recipient of the love note. Balthazar informs Dave he is The One and commands mighty magical powers. Balthazar then has to leave his shop briefly and asks Dave to guard the Prison Doll with extreme care. Naturally, Dave manages to open it and release the evil magicians. Balthazar should know better than to ever tell the hero of a Jerry Bruckheimer movie about the one thing he should never, never, ever, ever do.

That's it for the story setup. The rest is all centered on special effects. The director, Jon Turteltaub (*National Treasure*) and his several writers devise some clever set pieces, such as a dragon in a Chinatown parade that starts breathing smoke and fire, and it's up to Balthazar and Dave to vanquish the villains. I also liked it when Balthazar brought to life a steel eagle on top of the Chrysler Building and flew around on its back.

Cute Becky Barnes, now a college student, takes it pretty well that this Dave guy who wants to date her is a sorcerer's apprentice. I kept waiting for her to tell Dave she would still be there waiting for him after he finished annihilating the fiends, so maybe he should focus on saving the planet instead of putting the moves on her.

The Sorcerer's Apprentice is a perfectly typical example of its type, professionally made and competently acted. Imagine a graph with one line indicating the consumer's age and the other line representing his degree of enjoyment. These lines would intersect at about the age of Young Dave.

Soul Surfer ★ ★ ½

PG, 106 m., 2011

AnnaSophia Robb (Bethany Hamilton), Helen Hunt (Cheri Hamilton), Dennis Quaid (Tom Hamilton), Lorraine Nicholson (Alana Blanchard), Carrie Underwood (Sarah Hill),

Kevin Sorbo (Holt Blanchard), Jeremy Sumpter (Byron), Ross Thomas (Noah Hamilton), Sonya Balmores (Malina Birch), Chris Brochu (Timmy Hamilton). Directed by Sean McNamara and produced by McNamara, David Brookwell, Dutch Hofstetter, Douglas Schwartz, and David Zelon. Screenplay by McNamara, Deborah Schwartz, Douglas Schwartz, and Michael Berk, from the book by Bethany Hamilton.

Soul Surfer is based on the true story of Bethany Hamilton, a champion surfer who in her early teens was attacked by a shark and lost almost all her left arm. One month later, she was back on a surfboard, has since won several championships, and is at age twenty-one a professional surfer. All of those are remarkable facts.

My problem with the movie is that it makes it look too simple. Bethany has a loving family of professional surfers and a big, friendly dog. She lives in walking distance of the beach. She was and is a committed churchgoer, she got great support from her spiritual leaders, and she was an indomitable optimist with a fierce competitive spirit.

But there had to be more to it than that. I applaud her faith and spirit. I give her full credit for her determination. I realize she is a great athlete. But I feel something missing. There had to be dark nights of the soul. Times of grief and rage. The temptation of nihilism. The lure of despair. Can a thirteen-year-old girl lose an arm and keep right on smiling?

The flaw in the storytelling strategy of *Soul Surfer* is that it doesn't make Bethany easy to identify with. She's almost eerie in her optimism. Her religious faith is so unshaken it feels taken for granted. The film feels more like an inspirational parable than a harrowing story of personal tragedy.

Even its portrait of her recovery and rehabilitation is perfunctory. There's a particularly unconvincing scene where she's fitted with a prosthetic arm and refuses to wear it. They're making remarkable progress in the field of prosthetics. The arm she's offered looks no more useful than the arm she rips off her Barbie doll the same night (in one of the movie's rare moments of depression). Although I can understand a good prosthetic might not help her balance on a surfboard, I believe one might be of use in other situations—and I don't mean cosmetically. Maybe I'm mistaken.

Because Bethany actually was in the water a month after the attack, there can be no quarrel with those scenes in the film. What I missed was more information about her medical condition. What did her doctors advise? What risks were there to the wound? Having totaled almost a year in three trips through the Rehabilitation Institute of Chicago, I've known people who lost limbs, and I know it's very difficult and complicated. Maybe Bethany was so young and resilient, and in such a happy situation with her family and her church, that it was this easy for her. But it feels too simple.

One of the best sequences in the film involves a trip her church group makes to Thailand to bring aid and supplies to the survivors of the tsunami. This episode looks so realistic it's uncanny. It has one detail that made me smile: Bethany packs cans of Spam for the victims. I don't know how you feel about Spam, but I know that in Hawaii it's considered one of the basic food groups. (I like it with Colman's English Mustard—but I'm drifting.)

Soul Surfer is a wholesome movie, intended as inspirational. Whether it will cheer viewers who are not as capable as Bethany is an excellent question. AnnaSophia Robb is a convincing, cheerful heroine. Dennis Quaid and Helen Hunt, as Bethany's parents, are stalwart and supportive, although the screenplay indeed leaves them with no other choice. One character I question is Malina Birch (Sonya Balmores), one of Bethany's competitors, who sneers and is mean and does cruel things and of course always wears black. Why? Does she know she has been cast as the villain?

Source Code ★ ★ ★ ½

PG-13, 93 m., 2011

Jake Gyllenhaal (Colter Stevens), Michelle Monaghan (Christina Warren), Vera Farmiga (Colleen Goodwin), Jeffrey Wright (Dr. Rutledge). Directed by Duncan Jones and produced by Mark Gordon, Philippe Rousselet, and Jordan Wynn. Screenplay by Ben Ripley.

Source Code is an ingenious thriller that comes billed as science fiction, although its science is preposterous. Does that matter, as long as everyone treats it with the greatest urgency? After all, space travel beyond the solar system is preposterous, and we couldn't do without *Star Trek*. The "science" in this case is used to prop up an appealing story of a man who tries to change the past.

His name is Colter Stevens (Jake Gyllenhaal). That he is sure of. That's why it's strange when he finds himself on a Chicago commuter train talking to Christina Warren (Michelle Monaghan), a woman he's never met. It's even stranger when he goes into the toilet and sees a face in the mirror that doesn't belong to him.

How can this be? We are far from sure in the early scenes, which embed us in his confusion. Because some of the pleasure comes from unwinding the mystery, I'd advise you to stop reading now—unless the helpful TV ads have already hinted at the secret.

Spoilers ahead. Colter gains consciousness to find himself (as himself) in a secret army lab talking to a scientist named Goodwin (Vera Farmiga). He gradually understands that the commuter train was destroyed by a terrorist bomb, and that the brain of one of the victims was harvested for memories of the last eight minutes before the explosion. That's a first cousin to the old theory that a killer's image remains imprinted on his victim's retinas.

But listen. Goodwin and her army intelligence team believe that by rerunning those eight minutes, they can discover the identity of the terrorist and prevent a larger explosion that could destroy Chicago. This is because the terrorist unwisely detonated the small bomb as a warning, or something, I dunno. In the movies, evildoers love to pass out alarms and clues so they can be prevented from carrying out their schemes. This is a more sophisticated variation of the Talking Killer Syndrome.

Now comes the human touch. As he returns again and again to those fateful eight minutes, Colter finds that he can remember his previous visits, even though for Christina and others on the train, they are, of course, happening for the first time. This is the *Groundhog Day* paradox: You remember your previous passages through the same span of time. Colter begins to care for Christina, as well he might, as anyone who loved Michelle Monaghan in *Trucker* (2008) will understand. As the conscious occupant of this borrowed body, he apparently possesses free will and need not duplicate exactly what the original memory donor did.

This involves the possibility that he could relive the memories of a man's final eight minutes and act in such a way as to affect the outcome. If the man were to survive—whose memories would he have, his own or his visitor's? (Don't go there.) The army's no-doubt-brilliant Dr. Rutledge (Jeffrey Wright) starts out to account for the experiment, but abandons his explanation, which is our loss. If you had a speech in this movie actually saying in so many words how this was possible, it would rival the findings of such great thinkers as Dr. Moreau, Dr. Jekyll, and Dr. Frankenstein.

No matter. The director and writer, Duncan Jones and Ben Ripley, hurtle ahead with the speed of their commuter train, which, like the man on the Grecian urn, always speeds forward and never gets anywhere. Colter's challenge increases in complexity. The city grows ever closer to destruction. Christina becomes more poignant. The scientists grow more desperate.

What we have here, setting aside the fancy editing involving the time travel, is something that looks like hard science fiction. That's a threatened genre. Movies with plots are threatened in general; much modern "science fiction" involves blowing stuff up. The good classic sci-fi involved starting with an idea and exploring its implications.

Duncan Jones previously made *Moon* (2009), with Sam Rockwell as a character apparently nearing the end of a contract to man a station on the far side of the moon. Characters in Duncan Jones movies should learn not to be so sure of things. But Jones has the right spirit, Gyllenhaal and Monaghan are adept at playing their variations on the eight minutes, and here's a movie where you forgive the preposterous because it takes you to the perplexing.

Splice ★ ★ ★

R, 107 m., 2010

Adrien Brody (Clive Nicoli), Sarah Polley (Elsa Kast), Delphine Chaneac (Dren), Brandon

McGibbon (Gavin Nicoli), Simona Maicanescu (Joan Chorot), David Hewlett (William Barlow), Abigail Chu (Child Dren). Directed by Vincenzo Natali and produced by Steven Hoban. Screenplay by Natali, Antoinette Terry Bryant, and Douglas Taylor.

Well timed to open soon after Craig Venter's announcement of a self-replicating cell, here's a halfway serious science fiction movie about two researchers who slip some human DNA into a cloning experiment and end up with an unexpected outcome, or a child, or a monster, take your pick. The screenplay blends human psychology with scientific speculation and has genuine interest until it goes on autopilot with one of the chase scenes Hollywood now permits few pictures to end without.

In the laboratory of a genetic science corporation, we meet Clive and Elsa (Adrien Brody and Sarah Polley), partners at work and in romance, who are trying to create a hybrid animal gene that would, I dunno, maybe provide protein while sidestepping the nuisance of having it be an animal first. Against all odds, their experiment works. They want to push ahead, but the corporation has funded quite enough research for the time being, and can't wait to bring the "product" to market.

Elsa rebels and slips some human DNA into their lab work. What results is a new form of life, part animal, part human, looking at first like a rounded SpongeBob and then later like a cute kid on Pandora, but shorter and not blue. This creature grows at an astonishing rate, gets smart in a hurry, and is soon spelling out words on a Scrabble board without apparently having paused at the intermediate steps of learning to read and write. Clive thinks they should terminate it. Elsa says no. As the blob grows more humanoid, they become its default parents, and she names it Dren, which is nerd spelled backward, so don't name your kid that.

Dren has a tail and wings of unspecific animal origin, and hands with three fingers, suggesting a few sloth genes, although Dren is hyperactive. She has the ability common to small monkeys and CGI effects of being able to leap at dizzying speeds around a room. She's sweet when she gets a dolly to play with, but don't get her frustrated.

The researchers keep Dren a secret, both because they ignored orders by creating her, and because, although Elsa wanted no children, they begin to feel like her parents. This feeling doesn't extend so far as to allow her to live with them in the house. They lock her into the barn, which seems harsh treatment for the most important achievement of modern biological science.

Dren is all special effects in early scenes, and then quickly grows into a form played by Abigail Chu when small and Delphine Chaneac when larger. She also evolves more attractive features, based on the Spielberg discovery in *E.T.* that wide-set eyes are attractive. She doesn't look quite human, but as she grows to teenage size, she could possibly be the offspring of Jake and Neytiri, although not blue.

Brody and Polley are smart actors, and the director, Vincenzo Natali, is smart, too; do you remember his *Cube* (1997), with subjects trapped in a nightmarish experimental maze? This film, written by Natali with Antoinette Terry Bryant and Douglas Taylor, has the beginnings of a lot of ideas, including the love that observably exists between humans and some animals. It questions what "human" means, and suggests it's defined more by mind than body. It opens the controversy over the claims of some corporations to patent the genes of life. It deals with the divide between hard science and marketable science.

I wish Dren had been more fully developed. What does she think? What does she feel? There has never been another life form like her. The movie stays resolutely outside, viewing her as a distant creature. Her "parents" relate mostly to her mimetic behavior. Does it reflect her true nature? How does she feel about being locked in the barn? Does she "misbehave" or is that her nature?

The film, alas, stays resolutely with human problems. The relationship. The corporation. The preordained climax. Another recent film, *Ricky*, was about the French parents of a child who could fly. It also provided few insights into the child, but then Ricky was mentally as young as his age, and the ending was gratifyingly ambiguous. Not so with Dren. Disappointing, then, that the movie introduces such an extraordinary living being and focuses mostly on those around her. All the same, it's well done and intriguing.

Spoken Word ★ ★ ★

NO MPAA RATING, 116 m., 2010

Kuno Becker (Cruz), Ruben Blades (Senior), Miguel Sandoval (Emilio), Persia White (Shae), Antonio Elias (Ramon), Monique Gabriela Curnen (Gabrielle). Directed by Victor Nuñez and produced by William T. Conway and Karen Koch. Screenplay by Conway and Joe Ray Sandoval.

Spoken Word opens with the startling sound of a gunshot, but the gun appears only in a poem being performed by the hero, Cruz Montoya. He's a star on the San Francisco poetry slam scene and teaches a class for young students at what looks like might be Dave Eggers's 826 Valencia workshop for neighborhood kids. He lives with a warm and loving artist, and his life seems good.

He gets a call from home, in the country outside Santa Fe. His father is dying. He returns not only to his father but to his earlier life. Pops (Ruben Blades) is pleased to see him but reserved. Cruz (Kuno Becker) hasn't stayed in close touch. They're not estranged; it's more that, as Cruz observes, "The men in this family don't talk much." It's clear he has a history in the area; old friends welcome him, but he keeps his distance.

We pick up on his circumstances. His married brother Ramon (Antonio Elias) was given half the family land as a wedding present and sold it to Emilio (Miguel Sandoval), who runs a dance club and sells drugs through it. We've seen Cruz taking pills and being asked about that by his brother and father, in different tones of voice, and we assume they're illegal. We also see Cruz edging reluctantly back into the bar scene, and he begins getting drunk and sleeping all day.

But *Spoken Word* is not at all the expected story you might assume given this setup. Cruz Senior was a local teacher. He is also a painter. Unlike the clichéd patriarch of a Mexican-American family, Pops doesn't oppose his son being a poet, doesn't nag him about grandchildren, is proud of the kid. And Cruz himself is a lot more complex than we assume.

A small but useful supporting role is played by Persia White (of *Girlfriends*) as Shae, the girlfriend back in San Francisco. She worries. Cruz can be remote and fearfully private, but she has some ideas why that is. It would make sense for her to join him in New Mexico—for them, but not for the plot—so she's often on the phone. She doesn't nag. She waits.

Victor Nuñez is a leading American filmmaker who has always worked with stories deeply embedded in American regions. In Florida he made *Gal Young 'Un* (1979), based on the novel by Marjorie Kinnan Rawlings; *A Flash of Green* (1984), based on a John D. MacDonald story and with one of Ed Harris's best performances; *Ruby in Paradise* (1993), which with her first role established Ashley Judd as a great actress; *Ulee's Gold* (1997), which won Peter Fonda an Oscar nomination. Now Nuñez moves to New Mexico and gets far from obvious performances by Kuno Becker and Ruben Blades. He knows his places and the people who live in them.

I met him in 1979, when he was beginning. You can see gaps between those films showing how hard it is to find backing for an independent vision. There was a 2002 film named *Coastlines* that never even got a decent release. Now this rich and textured film. I can easily see alterations that would move it into the mainstream (an abusive father, more addiction, a violent drug dealer instead of a mild businessman, elements of prejudice), but they're all lacking, and the film grows in their absence.

It also grows in the presence of a parallel narrative made of Cruz's poetry and drifting, fragmented images from his past. They're not "flashbacks" but more of meditations on memories. They help to deepen the way we understand his relationship with his father. After all, they don't talk much in their family.

The Spy Next Door ★ ½

PG, 92 m., 2010

Jackie Chan (Bob Ho), Amber Valletta (Gillian), Madeline Carroll (Farren), Will Shadley (Ian), Alina Foley (Nora), Magnus Scheving (Poldark), Katherine Boecher (Creel), Lucas Till (Larry), Billy Ray Cyrus (Colton James), George Lopez (Glaze). Directed by Brian Levant and produced by Robert Simonds. Screenplay by Jonathan Bernstein, James Greer, and Gregory Poirier.

Let's see. Jackie Chan is a spy working for China and the CIA, who falls in love with a widow with three kids. He retires to be with them, but his job follows him home. Mom goes to be with her sick dad. Evil Russians have a plot to control the world's oil supply, and this requires them to chase Jackie and the kids through shopping malls, large empty factories, and so on. Jackie's character is named Bob Ho, which reminds me of someone.

Truth in reviewing requires me to report that *The Spy Next Door* is precisely what you would expect from a PG-rated Jackie Chan comedy with that plot. If that's what you're looking for, you won't be disappointed. It's not what I was looking for.

There are things you learn from movies like this. (1) All kids know how to use weapons better than Russian mobsters. (2) A villainess in a spy movie always dresses like a dominatrix. (3) Hummers are no help. (4) Kids always hate the guy their mom is dating until they survive in battle with him, and then they love him. (5) Whenever an adult turns away, a small child will instantly disappear. The smaller the child, the more agile. (6) Even in New Mexico, Russian gangsters wear heavy long black leather coats, which they just bought in customs at Heathrow. These, added to their six-foot-five-inch heights and goatees, help them blend in. (7) The mole in the CIA is always the white boss, never the Latino.

What else? Oh, (8) if you put a cell phone under a rock with iron in it, it cannot be traced. Only such a rock miles into the desert will work. No good putting it in the stove. (9) Little girls would rather dress in a pink princess outfit than wear a Hulk mask. (10) Spies always have fiery kitchen disasters the first time they cook for kids, and the second time produce perfect French toast with powdered sugar on it. Oh, and (11) no spy has the slightest idea of a reasonable ratio of oatmeal to water.

Such sights made a young Saturday morning audience happy. Nothing to a kid is quite as funny as a food fight. A cat trapped on a roof is a suspense builder. They don't like the guy dating their mom until they save him with their well-timed action moves. And all young audiences find it perfectly reasonable that when a kid runs away from a residential neighborhood on a bike, that kid will, of course, pedal into the large empty factory where Jackie Chan is facing the Russian mob giants.

Jackie Chan is fifty-five. Just sayin'. He no longer runs up walls by using the leverage of a perpendicular surface. Back in the days before CGI, he used to really do that. OK, maybe some wires were involved, but you try running up a two-story wall with wires. I wouldn't even want to be winched up.

Chan was famous for doing his own stunts. He had so many accidents it's a wonder he can walk. Everybody knew to wait for the outtakes during the closing credits because you'd see him miss a fire escape or land wrong in the truck going under the bridge. Now the outtakes involve his use of the English language. What's that? Your name *isn't* Bob Hope?

The Square ★ ★ ★ ½

R, 116 m., 2010

David Roberts (Ray), Claire van der Boom (Carla), Joel Edgerton (Billy), Anthony Hayes (Smithy), Peter Phelps (Jake), Bill Hunter (Gil Hubbard). Directed by Nash Edgerton and produced by Louise Smith. Screenplay by Joel Edgerton and Matthew Dabner.

The Square moves with implacable logic toward catastrophe, as its desperate heroes try to squirm out of a tightening noose. Step by step, mistake by mistake, their delusion is trampled on by reality. More horrible things happen in this film than are probable in any scenario short of a large anvil falling from the sky and flattening the town, but it remains mostly plausible from scene to scene.

Crime doesn't pay. This we all know. Adultery has a way of making itself known. Adulterers who hope to steal cash and live happily ever after are really asking for trouble. Note to adulterers with such a plan: Never try to carry it out until you first join your partner in sin on a seventy-two-hour bus ride.

In a small Australian town, Ray (David Roberts) works as the harried supervisor of a housing development. Carla (Claire van der

Boom) is married to Smithy (Anthony Hayes), a lowlife. Ray and Carla, both unhappily married, have been having an affair for quite some time. In each other's arms they console themselves with the dream that someday they will run away from their lives and live happily ever after—in hiding, I guess.

Carla dreams that this will happen. Ray plays along with it. Note to other women, if younger and without resources: A gray-haired married man with a good job is lying when he says he'll surrender everything for you. Lying. But Carla calls his bluff. She discovers that Smithy has a lot of cash hidden in the house. Enough to finance their flight. It's undoubtedly illegal cash. If they steal it, how can the theft be reported?

Well, sure, yeah, great, Ray says, possibly hoping for something to come up. You know, like maybe Smithy will move the money. Nothing comes up, and Ray finds himself involved in a plan that goes wrong and wronger and wrongest.

The delight of this film, directed by Nash Edgerton and written with his brother Joel Edgerton and Matthew Dabner, is that it never pushes too hard or moves too fast. It lovingly, almost sadistically, lays out the situation and deliberately demonstrates all the things that can go wrong. And I mean *all* the things.

At the center of these things is a very large hole filled with concrete, the "square" of the title. Note to people with dead bodies on their hands: If you cover a corpse with several feet of concrete, it is difficult to dig it up discreetly. It is also hard to keep all of your stories straight, to control what people may notice, to deal with the moment when the cash is found missing, and to say thanks but no thanks when the police try to be helpful.

One of the best elements of *The Square* is how well it establishes the rhythms and layout of its small town, which is in New South Wales, cane toad country. I was waiting for a cane toad to figure in the plot, but Edgerton is admirably disciplined. That's why the movie is so effective. The acting is convincing, the characters are realistic, nobody is looking for trouble, fate plays a role, and we clearly understand who everybody is. There is a shot from a high bluff down to a house on fire, and we already know whose that house is.

The Square has been compared to *Blood Simple* and *A Simple Plan.* High praise, but not undeserved. It's so good to find filmmakers with quiet, firm confidence in story and character. An unseemly number of people die here, but never in "thrilling" scenes, which are so rarely even interesting. They die because, despite their best efforts, something happens to them. Note to thieves and adulterers: Live so as to prevent things from happening to you.

Stake Land ★ ★ ★

NO MPAA RATING, 96 m., 2011

Nick Damici (Mister), Connor Paolo (Martin), Danielle Harris (Belle), Kelly McGillis (Sister Anna), Sean Nelson (Willie), Michael Cerveris (Jebedia). Directed by Jim Mickle and produced by Derek Curl, Larry Fessenden, Adam Folk, Brent Kunkle, and Peter Phok. Screenplay by Mickle and Nick Damici.

Zombies are a great convenience. They provide villains who are colorful and frightening, require no dialogue, motivation, or explanation, and yet function efficiently as a negation of all that is good. Just the very word "zombie" can persuade people to buy tickets for a movie, and "sex" hasn't done that in years. At the risk of using the word "MacGuffin" twice in the same week—well, that's what zombies are, aren't they?

Humans are survivors in an undead world that has gone horribly wrong, where all the good times are past and gone. That's what our modern world feels like to me sometimes; the morning news is filled with more ominous portents than the opening montage of a disaster movie. When Japan is torn by earthquakes and airports are attacked by tornadoes and the economy is melting and radiation is leaking and honeybees are dying, obviously the zombies are only waiting for the globe to warm a little more.

One advantage of zombie movies, and indeed all monster and horror movies, is that they provide a port of entry for new filmmakers. The genre itself is the star. I don't like to say this about David Arquette, who is a jolly nice guy, but I doubt many people went to *Scre4m* to see him; they wanted to see the slasher in the mask.

That said, there are substantial qualities in *Stake Land*, a movie that probably uses zombies as little as it can get away with. Considering that the dialogue calls them *vamps* for short, they're apparently some kind of zombie/vampire hybrid, previously unidentified by horror science. The dead have merged with the undead. You see what spraying with insecticides can lead to.

The movie mercifully focuses on a handful of characters as they journey toward a perhaps mythical New Eden. We begin with the voice of a young narrator, Martin (Connor Paolo), who explains how after his family was massacred he came under the protection of Mister (Nick Damici). How they are driving in a big boat of a classic car through a wasteland of threat and paranoia. How Mister instructs him in the skills of survival. There are echoes here, less eloquent, of *The Road*.

Mister has hard-earned expertise about vamps. A bullet will slow them down, but all that will kill them is the proverbial stake, driven into the base of the skull, where allegedly resides the Reptile Brain. He schools Martin in eternal vigilance, and they survive surprise attacks by zombies that sometimes seem suspiciously well coordinated with one another (given their presumed inability to communicate).

Mister is like a Western hero committed to doing the right thing. When he sees Sister Anna (Kelly McGillis) being attacked by zombies, he rescues her. Their little band grows to include Belle (Danielle Harris), a pregnant young girl, and Willie (Sean Nelson), who was a marine.

On the road they encounter rare safety zones, carefully guarded communities barricaded against strangers. Some of these are run, however, by religious cultists looking forward to the end of days. The scariest is a venomous loony named Jebedia (Michael Cerveris). This is not so unlikely. I just saw a report on CNN about Branch Davidian members looking for the resurrection of David Koresh.

Director Jim Mickle, who cowrote with his star, Nick Damici, has crafted a good-looking, well-played, and atmospheric apocalyptic vision. There are pauses for thoughtful character moments and some nicely written dialogue evoking the looming despair. The cinematography makes this new world look as bleak as—well, as a lot of empty strip malls and seldom-traveled badlands. What with one thing and another, *Stake Land* is, if not precisely entertaining to my taste, certainly attention-getting.

Star Trek ★ ★ ½

PG-13, 126 m., 2009

Chris Pine (James Tiberius Kirk), Zachary Quinto (Spock), Leonard Nimoy (Spock Prime), Eric Bana (Captain Nero), Bruce Greenwood (Captain Christopher Pike), Karl Urban (Leonard "Bones" McCoy), Zoe Saldana (Uhura), Simon Pegg (Montgomery "Scotty" Scott), John Cho (Sulu), Anton Yelchin (Chekov), Ben Cross (Sarek), Winona Ryder (Amanda Grayson). Directed by J. J. Abrams and produced by Abrams and Damon Lindelof. Screenplay by Roberto Orci and Alex Kurtzman.

Star Trek as a concept has voyaged far beyond science fiction and into the safe waters of space opera, but that doesn't amaze me. The Gene Roddenberry years, when stories might play with questions of science, ideals, or philosophy, have been replaced by stories reduced to loud and colorful action. Like so many franchises, it's more concerned with repeating a successful formula than going boldly where no *Star Trek* has gone before.

The 2009 *Star Trek* film goes back eagerly to where *Star Trek* began, using time travel to explain a cast of mostly the same characters, only at a younger point in their lives, sailing the starship *Enterprise*. As a story idea, this is sort of brilliant, and saves on invention because young Kirk, Spock, McCoy, Uhuru, Scotty, and the rest channel their later selves. The child is father to the man, or the Vulcan, and all that.

Don't get me wrong. This is fun. And when Leonard Nimoy himself returns as the aged Spock, encountering another Spock (Zachary Quinto) as a young man, I was kind of delighted, although as customary in many sci-fi films, nobody is as astonished as they should be. "Holy moley! Time travel exists, and this may be me!" It's more like a little ambiguous dialogue is exchanged and they're off to battle the evil Romulan captain Nero (Eric Bana).

Time travel, as we all know, is impossible in the sense it happens here, but many things are possible in this film. Anyone with the slightest notion of what a black hole is, or how it behaves, will find the black holes in *Star Trek* hilarious. The logic is also a little puzzling when they can beam people into another ship in outer space, but they have to physically parachute to land on a midair platform from which the Romulans are drilling a hole to Vulcan's core. And after they land there, they fight with two Romulan guards using fists and swords? The platform is suspended from Arthur C. Clarke's "space elevator," but instead of fullerenes, the cable is made of metallic chunks the size of refrigerators.

But stop me before I get started. I mention these details only to demonstrate that the movie raises its yo-yo finger to the science, while embracing the fiction. Apart from details from the youths of the characters and the Spock reunion, it consists mostly of encounters between the *Enterprise* and the incomparably larger and much better armed Romulan spaceship from the future. It's encouraging to learn that not even explosions and fires can quickly damage a starship. Also that lifeboats can save the crew, despite the vast distance from home base.

That would be because of warp speed, which for present purposes consists of looking through an unnecessary window at bright lights zapping past. This method of transportation prevents any sense of wonder at the immensity of outer space and is a convenience not only for the starship but also for the screenwriters, who can push a button and zap to the next scene. The concept of using warp speed to escape the clutches of a black hole seems like a recycling of the ancient dilemma of the rock and the hard place.

There are affecting character moments. Young Spock is deliberately taunted in hopes he will, as a Vulcan, betray emotion. Because Zachary Quinto plays him as a bit of a self-righteous prig, it's satisfying to see him lose it. Does poor young Spock realize he faces a lifetime of people trying to get a rise out of him? Nimoy, as the elderly Spock, must have benefited because he is the most human character in the film.

Chris Pine, as James Tiberius Kirk, appears first as a hot-rodding rebel who has found a Corvette in the twenty-third century and drives it into a pit resembling the Grand Canyon. A few years later, he's put in suspension by the academy and smuggled on board the *Enterprise* by "Bones" McCoy (Karl Urban) before he becomes the ship's captain. There are times when the command deck looks like Bring Your Child to School Day, with the kid sitting in Daddy's chair.

Uhura (Zoe Saldana) seems to have traveled through time to the prefeminist 1960s, where she found her miniskirt and go-go boots. She seems wise and gentle and unsuited to her costume. Scotty (Simon Pegg) seems to have begun life as a character in a Scots sitcom. Eric Bana's Nero destroys whole planets on the basis of faulty intelligence, but the character is played straight and is effective.

The special effects are slam-bam. Spatial relationships between spaceships are unclear because the Romulan ship and the *Enterprise* have such widely unmatched scales. Battles consist primarily of jumpsuited crew members running down corridors in advance of smoke, sparks, and flames. Lots of verbal commands seem implausibly slow. Consider, at light-warp speeds, how imprecise it would be to say, "At my command . . . three . . . two . . . one."

I understand that *Star Trek* science has never been intended as plausible. I understand that this is not science fiction but an ark movie using a starship. I understand that the character types are as familiar as your favorite slippers. But the franchise has become much of a muchness. The new movie essentially intends to reboot the franchise with younger characters and carry on as before. The movie deals with narrative housekeeping. Perhaps the next one will engage these characters in a more challenging and devious story, one more about testing their personalities than reestablishing them. In the meantime, you want space opera, you got it.

State of Play ★ ★ ★

PG-13, 127 m., 2009

Russell Crowe (Cal McAffrey), Ben Affleck (Stephen Collins), Rachel McAdams (Della Frye), Helen Mirren (Cameron Lynne), Robin Wright

Penn (Anne Collins), Jason Bateman (Dominic Foy), Jeff Daniels (George Fergus). Directed by Kevin Macdonald and produced by Tim Bevan, Eric Fellner, and Andrew Hauptman. Screenplay by Matthew Michael Carnahan, Tony Gilroy, and Billy Ray, based on the BBC series created by Paul Abbott.

State of Play is a smart, ingenious thriller set in the halls of Congress and the city room of a newspaper not unlike the *Washington Post.* It's also a political movie, its villain a shadowy corporation that contracts with the government for security duties and mercenaries in Iraq. The name is PointCorp. Think Blackwater. If an outfit like that would kill for hire, the plot wonders, would it also kill to protect its profits?

Here is Russell Crowe playing an ace investigative reporter for the *Washington Globe.* All the cops and most of the people on Capitol Hill seem to know him; he's one of those instinctive newsmen who connect the dots so quickly that a 127-minute movie can be extracted from a six-hour BBC miniseries. This keeps him so occupied that he has little time for grooming, and doesn't seem to ever wash his hair.

Crowe stepped into the role after Brad Pitt dropped out. Pitt, I suspect, would have looked more clean-cut, but might not have been as interesting as Crowe in this role, as Cal McAffrey, a scruffy hero in a newspaper movie that is acutely aware of the crisis affecting newspapers. He becomes part of a team that involves not two experienced reporters, as in *All the President's Men,* but Della (Rachel McAdams), one of the paper's plucky bloggers. He tries to teach her some ancient newspaper wisdom, such as: If you seem to be on the edge of uncovering an enormous political scandal, don't blow your cover by hurrying online with some two-bit gossip.

In a short span of time, a man is shot dead in an alley, a passing bicyclist, also a witness, is killed, and a woman is shoved or jumps under a subway train. Cal, of course, covers all of these deaths in person. The dead woman was a researcher for Representative Stephen Collins (Ben Affleck), who breaks into tears during a congressional hearing into PointCorp and confesses to conducting an affair with her. His wife, Anne (Robin Wright Penn), plays the brave politician's wife and says their family will stay together. Anne and Cal were lovers in college. The dead man turns out to be carrying a briefcase stolen from PointCorp. Now we connect the dots.

There are many other surprises in the film, which genuinely fooled me a couple of times and maintains a certain degree of credibility for a thriller. The implication is that PointCorp and the administration are locked in an unholy alliance to channel millions of taxpayer dollars into unsavory hands. That this can all be untangled by one reporter who looks like a bum and another who looks like Rachel McAdams (which is no bad thing) goes with the territory.

An important role in their investigation is played by the *Globe*'s editor, Cameron Lynne (Helen Mirren). The paper's new corporate owners are on her neck to cut costs, redesign the venerable front page, get more scoops, and go for the gossip today instead of waiting for the Pulitzer tomorrow. There is, in fact, an eerie valedictory feeling to the film; mother of God, can this be the last newspaper movie? (The answer is no, because no matter what happens to newspapers, the newspaper movie is a durable genre. Shouting, "Stop the presses!" is ever so much more exciting than shouting, "Stop the upload!")

It is a reliable truth that you should never ask an expert how a movie deals with his field of knowledge. Archaeologists, for example, have raised questions about *The Mummy: Tomb of the Dragon Emperor.* When Cal races out of the office at deadline and shouts over his shoulder, "Tell Cameron to kill the story," it is just possible that she would tear up the front page, if the story was so important the paper could not risk being wrong. But when Cal and his sidekick the perky blogger solve the mystery and are back in the office and it is noted, "Cameron has been holding the presses four hours!"—I think her new corporate bosses will want to have a long, sad talk with her, after which she will discover if the company still offers severance packages.

State of Play, directed by Kevin Macdonald (*The Last King of Scotland*), is well assembled and has some good performances. Crowe pulls off the Joaquin Phoenix look-alike; McAdams doesn't overplay her blogger's newbieness; Helen Mirren convinced me she could be a newspaper editor. Robin Wright Penn always finds the correct shadings. If Ben Affleck, as he plays this role, were to have his face carved into Mount Rushmore, people would ask which was the original.

The thing is, though, that the movie never quite attains altitude. It has a great takeoff, levels nicely, and then seems to land on autopilot. Maybe it's the problem of resolving so much plot in a finite length of time, but it seems a little too facile toward the end. Questions are answered, relationships revealed, and mysteries solved too smoothly. If a corporation like PointCorp could have its skullduggery exposed that easily, it wouldn't still be in business.

Still Walking ★ ★ ★ ★

NO MPAA RATING, 114 m., 2009

Hiroshi Abe (Ryota), Yui Natsukawa (Yukari), You (Chinami), Kazuya Takahashi (Nobuo), Shohei Tanaka (Atsushi), Kirin Kiki (Toshiko), Yoshio Harada (Kyohei). Directed by Hirokazu Kore-eda and produced by Yoshihiro Kato and Hijiri Taguchi. Screenplay by Kore-eda.

Most family dramas contain too much drama. In most families, the past and present don't meet and find resolution during a twenty-four-hour period, no matter how many American films you've seen about Thanksgiving. Painful family issues are more likely to stay beneath the surface, known to everyone but not spoken of. *Still Walking,* a magnificent new film from Japan, is very wise about that, and very true.

A dozen years ago, the prized possession of this family was Junpei, the eldest son, doted on by his parents and admired by his younger brother and sister. But Junpei drowned while saving a life, and every year the family gathers, as many Japanese families do, to visit his grave and memory.

These occasions are hated by Ryota (Hiroshi Abe), the second son. His father (Yoshio Harada) almost blames him for not being the one who died. On the drive to his hometown at the seaside, Ryota tells his new wife, Yukari (Yui Natsukawa), they must not even stay the night. This will be her first meeting with the parents; she is a widow with a young son.

The father is a retired physician, slowed with age, still marching joylessly on his daily walk. He stays mostly closed off in his office and greets his son brusquely. The mother has her doubts about this marriage; it is better to marry a divorced woman than a widow because at least the divorcee *chose* to leave her husband.

Also together for this day are Ryota's sister, Chinami, and her husband. It is only slowly that we pick up the suppressed currents of feeling in the family; on the surface, the mother stays cheerful, although the old doctor's bitterness is obvious: The wrong son drowned.

The day arrives at some sort of centerpiece when they welcome a luncheon guest, who is never named. This is the man Junpei died while saving. He is homely, fat, ill at ease, squirmy, apologetic, bursting from his white dress shirt. The doctor clearly doesn't regard him as having been worth saving. Ryota has spent a lifetime feeling shunned by his father and considered inferior to his brother. He has been wounded time and again, and so he is alert to the discomfort of the saved man. Why do they even invite him? He's obviously suffering during these annual visits. They invite him, he learns offhandedly, *because* he suffers.

If anyone can be considered an heir of the great Yasujiro Ozu, it might be Hirokazu Kore-eda, the writer and director of *Still Walking.* In *Maborosi* (1995), *After Life* (1998), and *Nobody Knows* (2004), his first three features released in North America, and now in this film, he has produced profoundly empathetic films about human feelings. He sees intensely and tenderly into his characters. Like Ozu, he pays meticulous attention to composition and camera placement. Acting as his own editor, he doesn't cut for immediate effect but for the subtle gathering of power. His actors look as if they could be such people as they portray.

He feels a strong connection with spouses separated by death or circumstances, and the children who are involved. *Maborosi* involves a widow with a young son, who goes to a new seaside town to marry a virtual stranger. *After Life,* a serious fantasy, is about newly dead people who spend a week in a heavenly waiting room to prepare a film of the one memory they want to carry through eternity. *Nobody Knows* is about the children of a quasi-prostitute who leaves them to fend for themselves in a city apartment.

None of these films elevates the temperature with melodrama. They draw us inward with concern. Kore-eda is a tender humanist, and that fits well with his elegant visual style. In *Still Walking*, he shares something valuable with Ozu: what I call Ozu's "pillow shots," named after the "pillow words" in Japanese poetry, which separate passages with just a word or two, seemingly unconnected, for a pause in the rhythm. These shots may show passing trains (a favorite of both directors) or a detail of architecture or landscape. It isn't their subject that matters; it's their composure.

Stone ★ ★ ★

R, 105 m., 2010

Robert De Niro (Jack Mabry), Edward Norton (Gerald Creeson), Milla Jovovich (Lucetta), Frances Conroy (Madylyn). Directed by John Curran and produced by David Mimran, Jordan Schur, and Holly Wiersma. Screenplay by Angus MacLachlan.

Stone has Robert De Niro and Edward Norton playing against type and at the top of their forms in a psychological duel between a parole officer and a tricky prisoner who has his number. Norton plays Gerald Creeson, imprisoned for his role in a crime that resulted in the murder of his grandparents and the burning of their house. De Niro is Jack Mabry, who plays everything by the book to protect himself from a dark inner nature.

De Niro is an old hand at playing inner demons. His classic weakness was jealousy in *Raging Bull.* Here it is anger, which perhaps leads to lust. The film opens with a younger Jack Mabry enacting a terrifying scene with his young wife and infant. Years later, they are still married, in a loveless gridlock based on passive aggression. He does nothing "wrong." It is his duty to stay married. His wife, Madylyn (Frances Conroy), seems to be hunched against blows that never come. He mechanically sips whiskey and stares at the TV, the wall, anything.

It's time for his retirement. He could pass his caseload on to his successor, but no: He will do his duty to the last detail. That includes handling a parole plea by Creeson, who is very smart, an emotional manipulator whose wife, Lucetta (Milla Jovovich), is such a woman that such a man might use and be used by. Creeson senses that De Niro, the duty-bound straight arrow, might be vulnerable to temptation. Lucetta is smart enough to try, not a bold seduction, but a mental game in which Mabry essentially seduces himself.

This is a process which cannot be dispatched in a neat prison caper package. It involves plotting about personalities. Jovovich's Lucetta has a key role in finding and exploiting an avenue through Mabry's defenses. What does Creeson think about the possibility she will have sex with Mabry? What does he think about her sex life in general? Is her promiscuity useful to him? Does she know it? Apart from whatever she does, she loves her husband without reserve, which is peculiar because he doesn't seem to deserve it, but then you never know.

Stone could have been some sort of a procedural, a straightforward crime movie, but it's too complex for that. It is actually interested in the minds of these characters and how they react to a dangerous situation. De Niro is so good at playing a man who has essentially emasculated himself because of fear of his anger, so that sex and anger may be leashed in precisely the opposite way as in *Raging Bull.* And Norton, the puppet master—it may not even be freedom he requires, but simply the pleasure of controlling others to obtain it.

The Stoning of Soraya M. ★ ★ ★

R, 114 m., 2009

Shohreh Aghdashloo (Zahra), Mozhan Marno (Soraya), Jim Caviezel (Sahebjam), Navid Negahban (Ali), Parviz Sayyad (Hashem), Ali Pourtash (Mullah), David Diaan (Ebrahim). Directed by Cyrus Nowrasteh and produced by Stephen McEveety and John Shepherd. Screenplay by Cyrus Nowrasteh and Betsy Griffen Nowrasteh, based on the book by Freidoune Sahebjam.

The Islamic practice of stoning women and the Christian practice of burning them as witches are both born not from religious reasons but of a male desire to subjugate women and define them in terms of sexuality. Is this in dispute? Are there any theologians who support such actions? Of all the most severe punishments of both religions, this is the one most skewed against women, and the one most convenient for men.

To be sure, no witches have been burned at the stake in many long years, and few ever were. But women are still stoned to death in some Islamic countries, including Iran, where this film is set. The practice survives in backward rural areas, and the law turns a blind eye. It is rare, and Iran denies it, but French journalist Freidoune Sahebjam's best-selling *The Stoning of Soraya M.* (1994) appears to be quite authentic. A woman really was stoned to death on trumped-up adultery charges, brought for the convenience of her husband, who desired to marry a young girl.

Cyrus Nowrasteh's *The Stoning of Soraya M.* does not dramatize this story in a subtle way. You might argue that the stoning of a woman to death is not a subtle subject. But it would be helpful to have it told in a way that shows how almost the entire population of a village allows it to happen, even though most of them know of the woman's innocence and her husband's vile motives. How does a lynch mob form? Instead, we're given a village populated primarily by overacted villains and moral cowards.

Against them is one strong voice: the widow Zahra, Soraya's aunt. She's played by Shohreh Aghdashloo, the Oscar nominee from *House of Sand and Fog* (2004). She knows all the players and all the motives and publicly calls them on it, to no avail. She's a "crazy woman," says the husband, Ali (Navid Negahban). The phrase "crazy woman" can fall easily from the tongue, and it's worth remembering that in Victorian England a wife could be locked in an asylum for life on only her husband's signature (see the great novel *The Quincunx*).

Ali the husband is an immoral monster. His intended child bride has not been asked if she wants to marry him; the marriage has been arranged. The village mullah goes along because Ali threatens to blackmail him about an old prison sentence. The mayor knows it is wrong and doubts Allah desires it, but lacks the courage to do much more than mutter.

The stoning sequence itself is one of the most unbearable experiences I have had at the movies. I learn it lasts nearly twenty minutes. Soraya is buried in a hole up to the waist. Village boys collect stones of a good throwing weight in a wheelbarrow. We see blow after blow, as blood pours from her face and body. She accepts this as her fate, as indeed it is. She did nothing that was not innocent and kind.

The stoning took place in 1986, after the Islamic Revolution. Fundamentalists were in power and enforced their strictures; the measures they introduced are being challenged today in the streets of Iran, and similar extremism is the practice in our dear friend Saudi Arabia. Those with objections fear crushing reprisal. The enforcers have power, position, and wealth to gain, and dare their enemies to go against what they say is God's will.

The message is that if a religion requires practices that seem evil to its members, they should resign from that religion. If it condones a death penalty that is visited unequally on members of a specific gender, race, or class, it is immoral. There cannot be a reward for following it blindly because only a thoughtful choice has meaning. At heaven's gate you cannot say, "I always followed the herd."

The Stoning of Soraya M. has such a powerful stoning sequence that I recommend it if only for its brutal ideological message. That the pitiful death of Soraya is followed by a false Hollywood upbeat ending involving tape recordings and silliness about a car that won't start is simply shameful. Nowrasteh, born in Colorado, attended the USC Film School. Is that what they teach there? When you are telling the story of a woman being stoned to death, you may not be able to use everything you learned in class.

Strongman ★ ★ ★

NO MPAA RATING, 113 m., 2011

Stanley and Michael Pleskun and Stan's girlfriend, Barbara. A documentary directed by Zachary Levy.

Strongman is a tantalizing example of the kind of documentary I find engrossing: a film about an unusual person who invites us into the mystery of a human life. Stanley Pleskun bills himself as "Stanless Steel, the Strongest Man Alive." Whether this is true is beside the point. Stanless, as I will call him, believes it absolutely. His girlfriend, Barbara, and his brother Michael agree, I gather, although they never actually say so.

How does the Strongest Man in the World support himself? He works as a freelancer in the scrap metal industry, collecting scrap and hauling it to a yard. We see him heaving heavy loads into the bed of his truck. Does this help him train? No, I learn from the film's notes, it tires him out and makes it harder to train. Although Zachary Levy, the filmmaker, followed him over a course of years and shot hundreds of hours of film, we see him actually training only twice: once squeezing a hand grip, and again staggering for several yards while carrying heavy concrete blocks.

He is a strict vegetarian who does not smoke or drink, and lives on fruit and vegetable juices. We see him demolish a dozen ears of corn in a single brief sitting. We also see him, perhaps during times of stress, smoking, having a beer, and sharing a pizza. Nobody's perfect. Stanless is convinced he doesn't smoke and advises Barbara to cut it out. He also bums smokes from her.

Barbara is a great mystery to me. She is a good-looking woman about the same age as Stanless. Old photos show her with the facial structure of a model. Her skin remains unlined. She wears her hair in a graying ponytail or braids. She has a presence. She has a beauty. Stanless moves in with her. She rehearses to introduce his act: "Ladies and gentlemen, boys and girls! Presenting Staaaaaanless Steeeel! The Strongest Man in the Woooorld!" He makes appearances at events in New Jersey and New York, bending steel bars, lifting trucks, and so on. He is paid $1,000 and expenses to appear on a British TV show.

He meets with an agent who has "represented all the top strong men." The agent tells him his act lacks a "hook." Indeed, it seems quickly over. Before an audience of maybe two hundred in a parking lot, he positions himself on his back below the rear end of a pickup truck and lifts it high enough with his feet for his brother to slip a sheet of paper under a real wheel. He can also bend pennies and quarters. He puts a bent penny on a chain and gives it to Barbara as a necklace.

What is it with those two? They hug, they kiss, but their relationship seems to center on his strong-man status and her acceptance and support of it. Eventually there's a complex scene in which they argue, although she remains calm and composed, and his complaints seem recycled out of New Age beliefs about the soul and the essence of goodness. He also has moments of offended anger, when he reminded me uncannily of Bruno S., the star of Herzog's *Stroszek*.

Stanless's family life is the stuff of Diane Arbus. Forced to move in with Michael, he shouts: "How can you expect the Strongest Man in the World to live in a space ten by twelve feet?" Michael's living room is an indoor-outdoor carport. Their mother and grandmother live in an ordinary house, where the grandmother, apparently a stroke victim, has to be carried about.

Zach Levy has the deadpan approach of a filmmaker like Errol Morris. You're not sure what he thinks about these people. They are very definitely *themselves*, and we've never seen anyone else like them. Levy's camera simply regards them. The film ends with a flashback to a historic moment: the first meeting between Stanless and Barbara. It solves nothing. I watched the film with quiet fascination.

Submarine ★ ★ ★

R, 97 m., 2011

Craig Roberts (Oliver Tate), Yasmin Paige (Jordana Bevan), Noah Taylor (Lloyd Tate), Sally Hawkins (Jill Tate), Paddy Considine (Graham Purvis). Directed by Richard Ayoade and produced by Mary Burke, Mark Herbert, and Andy Stebbing. Screenplay by Ayoade, based on the novel by Joe Dunthorne.

Craig Roberts, who plays Oliver Tate, the hero of *Submarine*, looks a lot like the very young John Lennon: fresh and hopeful, with the soul of a poet and the self-importance of—well, of a teenage boy who struggles under the weight of his virginity. He also looks so much like young Bud Cort that if you gave him a pair of

Harry Potter glasses he could remake *Harold and Maude.* The British tone of the film helps; it's set in Swansea, Wales.

Oliver seems to be the author of *Submarine*, his own biopic—sometimes literally, sometimes more in the way its tone evokes his preoccupations. Sex is much on his mind, but he sees himself as too serious and cultured to seek it in vulgar ways. True, he rather mistreats Jordana Bevan (Yasmin Paige), a girl in his school, but he immediately regrets that pushing incident, and besides, awkward boys sometimes mask tenderness with roughhouse.

Jordana understands this, and a great many other things about adolescent boys. For example, she knows some of them need leadership or they will stew forever in self-doubt. She isn't a tart, nor is she any more experienced than Oliver, but she's more confident. Their relationship begins with earnest exchanges of searching looks in the school corridor, and soon progresses to having dinner at Oliver's house when his parents aren't home.

His parents are much on his mind. His father (Noah Taylor) is an oddly quiet man, withdrawn, not quite there in the room. His mother (Sally Hawkins) is, like many Sally Hawkins characters, earnestly engaged in whatever occupies her. Right now she is entranced by a self-styled mystic named Graham Purvis (Paddy Considine), who has the gift of holding an audience spellbound with utter nonsense he seems to make up as he goes along.

Oliver is concerned that his mother may be growing too involved with Graham Purvis. He reports to us that his parents have stopped having sex, and explains the ingenious method he used to figure this out. Simultaneously, Oliver very much wants to start having sex—with Jordana Bevan, who for now occupies all the space available in his mind for possible partners.

Submarine isn't an insipid teen sex comedy. It flaunts some stylistic devices, such as titles and sections and self-aware narration, but it doesn't try too hard to be desperately clever. It's a self-confident work for the first-time director, Richard Ayoade, whose purpose I think is to capture that delicate moment in some adolescent lives when idealism and trust lead to tentative experiments. Because Craig Roberts and Yasmin Paige are enormously likable in their roles, they win our sympathy and make us realize that too many movies about younger teenagers are filtered through the sensibility of more weathered minds.

Sugar ★ ★ ★ ½

R, 118 m., 2009

Algenis Perez Soto (Miguel Santos), Rayniel Rufino (Jorge Ramirez), Andre Holland (Brad Johnson), Michael Gaston (Stu Sutton), Jaime Tirelli (Osvaldo), Jose Rijo (Alvarez), Ellary Porterfield (Anne Higgins), Ann Whitney (Helen Higgins), Richard Bull (Earl Higgins). Directed by Anna Boden and Ryan Fleck and produced by Paul Mezey, Jamie Patricof, and Jeremy Kipp Walker. Screenplay by Boden and Fleck.

Sugar approaches with tender care the story of a kid from the Dominican Republic who has a strong pitching arm and a good heart. Miguel Santos, known as "Sugar" because of his sweet personality, is recruited from the fields of dreams in his homeland by Major League Baseball and assigned to an Iowa farm club that is very, very far from home.

I thought I could guess the story. But I couldn't. There isn't a single scene in this film where it really matters which side wins a game, and it doesn't end with a no-hitter. It looks with care at Sugar, and there are a thousand Sugars for every Sammy Sosa. Probably more. Baseball players have become an important export for the Dominican Republic, and poor families like Miguel's dream of the day when sons will be sending home paychecks. A minor league salary represents wealth.

The film is knowledgeable about how the system works. American teams maintain elaborate training facilities in the D.R., send talent scouts to local leagues, and keep recruits under close watch: Room and board is provided, there are security guards to enforce discipline, the kids get a few days off once in a while. This is heaven for them. For years their dreams have been filled with visions of big-time baseball.

Sugar isn't filled with melodramatic developments and a hard landing on American soil. Baseball seems, in fact, a friendly if realistic destination, an income where there was none before. If very few players ever make it into a major league starting lineup, well, they know that going in. What's special about the film—and this is a very special film—is how closely it observes the emotional uncertainties of a stranger in a strange land, not speaking the language, not knowing the customs, beset with homesickness and the dread of disappointing his family.

Algenis Perez Soto, a young baseball player in his acting debut, embodies Sugar with a natural sincerity. The movie regards him with sympathy. Sugar isn't "torn with conflict," as movie ads like to say, but weighed with worry. He finds himself boarding in the friendly Iowa farm home of Helen and Earl Higgins (Ann Whitney and Richard Bull), who have taken in a generation of new players for the local farm club. They know their baseball ("You've been dropping your arm," Helen tells him, and Sugar doesn't disagree).

There is also the presence of their granddaughter Anne (Ellary Porterfield), who sends out mixed messages; she's obviously attracted to him and invites him to meet her friends, evangelicals who would like to get him on board. On the team, he bonds with Jorge (Rayniel Rufino), a more seasoned player from the Republic, and Brad Johnson (Andre Holland), who is the same color but from a different world; if baseball doesn't pan out, he'll go back for an advanced degree from Stanford.

For Sugar, who mumbles he's had "a little" high school, everything depends on baseball panning out. On their regular phone calls, his mother fears she can sense something troubling in his voice. He finds the farm system is supportive, and he gets help from coaches who care, but there is always another player waiting behind him in line.

Anna Boden and Ryan Fleck, who wrote and directed *Sugar,* are serious filmmakers who have no desire to make a "sports movie." They've obviously done their research on the major league farm system and the men who pass through it; at some level, this entire tryout process is for the benefit of a fan in the grandstands with a wise-ass opinion about the "new kid." Remembering a day when Sammy Sosa was booed at Wrigley Field, I see it now in a wholly new light.

The true subject of *Sugar* is the immigrant experience in America. Boden and Fleck are interested in newcomers to this country, doing what they can to make a living and succeed. Whether this happens for Sugar, or how it might happen, you will see for yourself. The filmmakers are too observant to settle for a quick, conventional payoff. For them this film is a chapter in the more interesting story of the lifetime Sugar has ahead of him. Algenis Perez Soto plays the character so openly, so naturally, that an interesting thing happens: Baseball is only the backdrop, not the subject. This is a wonderful film.

Note: The R rating is for relatively inconsequential reasons.

Summer Hours ★ ★ ★

NO MPAA RATING, 103 m., 2009

Juliette Binoche (Adrienne), Charles Berling (Frederic), Jeremie Renier (Jeremie), Edith Scob (Helene), Dominique Reymond (Lisa), Isabelle Sadoyan (Eloise), Kyle Eastwood (James). Directed by Olivier Assayas and produced by Marin Karmitz, Nathanael Karmitz, and Charles Gillibert. Screenplay by Assayas.

Sometimes what holds a family together is custom and guilt. *Summer Hours* begins on the seventy-fifth birthday of Helene, a woman who is joined in the French countryside by her three children and their families. Much of the talk is about how far two of the children had to travel—one from New York, the other from China—and there's the sense they're eager to be going home. Sure, they love their mother. They really do. But you know how it is. They visit less because they should visit more.

Helene understands this. She understands a great deal. She pulls aside Frederic (Charles Berling), her only child still living in France, to talk about the handling of her estate. This makes him unhappy, but she produces an inventory of the sort women often keep, of her valued possessions. Tea sets, vases, paintings.

The house belonged to her uncle, a fairly well-known painter. She has kept it unchanged since his death, as almost a shrine. She has little of his work, but many of his valuable pieces, including a desk. In less than a year, she's dead, and the children gather again. She predicted to Frederic that the house would have to be sold—indeed, she knew them all well enough to foresee everything—but he assumes his sister, Adrienne (Juliette Binoche), and brother, Jeremie (Jeremie Renier), will want to keep it in the family.

He is wrong. Adrienne is getting married to her New York boyfriend (Kyle Eastwood). Jeremie has been offered a promotion in Hong Kong. The film, which has no false sentimentality, is matter-of-fact about how the valuable works are disposed of. They're all sorry they couldn't keep and maintain the house, but, well . . .

There are two long-standing facts of the family that are discussed, really, for the first time. What exactly was the nature of the long relationship between Helene and her uncle? And how is Eloise to be treated—Eloise, the family's cook and housekeeper since time immemorial? Olivier Assayas, the writer-director, doesn't treat these subjects as melodrama but as the sorts of things adult children naturally discuss. They're much more effective that way.

What happens is that the film builds its emotional power by stealth, indirectly, refusing to be a tear-jerker, always realistic, and yet observing how very sad it is to see a large part of your life disappear. A parent, for example. In Errol Morris's *Gates of Heaven,* these perfect words are spoken: "Death is for the living, and not for the dead so much."

The actors all find the correct notes. It is a French film, and so they are allowed to be adult and intelligent. They are not the creatures of a screenplay that hurries them along. The film is not about what will happen. It is about them. The recent American film that most resembles this one is Jonathan Demme's *Rachel Getting Married.* Some audience members didn't know what to think of it because it didn't tell them. Sometimes you just have to figure out what you think for yourself. *Summer Hours* ends on the perfect note, the more you think about it.

Sunshine Cleaning ★ ★

R, 102 m., 2009

Amy Adams (Rose Lorkowski), Emily Blunt (Norah Lorkowski), Alan Arkin (Joe Lorkowski), Jason Spevack (Oscar Lorkowski), Steve Zahn (Mac), Mary Lynn Rajskub (Lynn), Clifton Collins Jr. (Winston). Directed by Christine Jeffs and produced by Glenn Williamson, Jeb Brody, Marc Turtletaub, and Peter Saraf. Screenplay by Megan Holley.

Sunshine Cleaning is a little too sunny for its material. Its heroine, Rose, is a single mom in desperate need of income, trapped in a one-way affair with her high school boyfriend, who fathered her son but married someone else. Her son is always in trouble at school. Her sister, Norah, is a hard-living goofball. Rose starts a new business cleaning up messy crime scenes.

Does this sound sunny to you? The material might have promise as a black comedy, but its attempt to put on a smiling face is unconvincing. That despite the work by Amy Adams as Rose and Emily Blunt as Norah, two effortless charmers who would be terrific playing these characters in a different movie. And Alan Arkin is back, and engaging, in what is coming dangerously close to "the Alan Arkin role." He's their father, Joe, forever hatching new get-poor-quick schemes.

Rose is a good mom. She understands her seven-year-old son, Oscar (Jason Spevack), who is not really troubled but simply high-spirited. I wonder how many little boys are accused of misbehaving simply because they are boys. Why does she still sleep with Mac, the faithless high school quarterback (Steve Zahn) who seduced and abandoned her? She asks herself the same question.

It's Mac, at least, who tips her off on a possible business. He's a cop and notices that people get paid well for mopping up after gruesome murders. So is born Rose and Norah's Sunshine Cleaning, which will clean up the rugs and scrape the brains off the wall, etc. This job by its nature allows them to witness the aftermath of lives unexpectedly interrupted; an ID in a dead woman's purse leads them to make an awkward new acquaintance.

This is promising material. Gene Siskel loved movies about what people actually do all day long. There is even a documentary subject here. But not this film that compromises on everything it implies, because it wants to be cheerful about people who don't have much to be cheerful about. How can you make a feel-good movie about murder-scene cleanups? "Life's a messy business," the poster says. Yes, and death is messier.

There are times when the movie works, but those are the times it (and even we) forget what it's really about. If you could plot it on a curve, it might look like a cross-section of a roller-coaster. The poster also evokes *Little Miss Sunshine*, by the same producers, also with Alan Arkin, and the presence of Amy Adams evokes the sublime *Junebug*. Those were both movies with more consistent tones and, although based on contrivance, felt more natural.

There's one element in the film that does work, and it's sort of off to the side, apart from the rest of the plot. It involves Winston (Clifton Collins Jr.), a one-armed hardware store owner, who babysits Oscar in an emergency and provides an oasis of warmth and common sense. You may remember him as Perry, one of the killers Truman wrote the book about in *Capote* (2005). An actor like this works a lot but doesn't always get ideal roles. Now he's beginning to emerge, with seven more films in postproduction.

You won't have a bad time seeing *Sunshine Cleaning*. You may get a little frustrated waiting for it to take off. It keeps heading down different runways. There's a movie here somewhere. Not this one.

Super ★ ★

NO MPAA RATING, 96 m., 2011

Rainn Wilson (Frank/Crimson Bolt), Ellen Page (Libby/Boltie), Liv Tyler (Sarah), Kevin Bacon (Jacques), Nathan Fillion (The Holy Avenger), Gregg Henry (Detective John Felkner), Michael Rooker (Abe), Andre Royo (Hamilton). Directed by James Gunn and produced by Miranda Bailey and Ted Hope. Screenplay by Gunn.

Super is being sold as a comedy, but I doubt it will play that way. It begins as the portrait of a lovable loser named Frank, and as it ends we're pretty sure he's an insane, ruthless killer. That's not a joke. Maybe the filmmaker, James Gunn, intended it as a joke, but after the camera lingers on the young heroine with a third of her face blown off, it's hard to laugh.

I quite understand that this could all be seen as an ironic commentary on audience expectations; when Ellen Page of *Juno* stars in a movie, we don't much expect to see her brains dripping. But let's face it: Most audiences have little appetite for irony about themselves. One possible way to like the movie might be to observe how unenjoyable it is for people expecting something funny and upbeat, but that would be unkind.

Rainn Wilson stars as Frank, a short-order cook who is married to the lithesome Sarah (Liv Tyler). He's a loser who is content to be a loser. He is also palpably stupid and clueless, a pawn in the hands of the slickster Jacques (Kevin Bacon). Sarah is a recovering addict, a paragon of sweetness until she falls in among low companions, including Jacques, a big-time drug dealer involved with a strip club.

When Jacques comes to Frank's house looking for Sarah, so clueless is Frank that he cooks eggs for his rival. It must be said that Kevin Bacon plays the scene (and praises the eggs) with such wicked comic timing that you can imagine the whole film centering on that scene and flowering in other directions.

It was not to be. Jacques steals Sarah, hooks her on drugs, and requires her for ominous obscure purposes. Frank dissolves into self-pity. While watching a Christian cable channel, he sees a half-witted drama about a superhero and is inspired to imitate it. He goes to a comic book store seeking instructional reading, and meets a clerk named Libby (Ellen Page), who claims she is twenty-two, but has the savvy of a credible eight-year-old.

Frank identifies Jacques with evil in general and reinvents himself as the Crimson Bolt, a masked superhero wearing a tight-fitting red suit he ran up himself on his wife's sewing machine. He then (this is kind of funny) hides behind Dumpsters, hoping to spot crimes being committed, and later, after getting beaten senseless, arms himself with a big wrench and starts pounding drug dealers. The Crimson Bolt becomes a big local news item; Libby figures out who he is and recruits herself as his junior sidekick, Boltie.

This isn't necessarily funny. It approaches humor, however, with the work by Rainn Wilson and Ellen Page, and with the cool, mocking detachment of the Kevin Bacon character, who visits as if an ambassador from another, better movie. There's something I like very much about Wilson, who plays an unaffected klutz with about as much grace and humor as possible. He never seems to be trying to be funny, and that's a strength. But what can he do with this screenplay?

Setting aside the details of the plot mechanics (Jacques, his gated mansion, his henchmen, his drugs, his evil), what we're left with are scenes of Frank the madman appointing himself as the wrath of God and smashing people senseless. When one of the Three Stooges gets beaned with a wrench, it's funny. When presumably actual characters are maimed and possibly killed, not so much.

The movie plunges into nihilistic despair in its third act. This isn't a black comedy because it isn't a comedy. It's a trick played on our expectations, I concede, but to what end? Is there any requirement that a film develop organically from beginning to end? No. There's no rule book. But audiences feel uneasy when they feel toyed with. I'm all for movies that create unease, but I prefer them to appear to know why they're doing that. *Super* is a film ending in narrative anarchy, exercising a destructive impulse to no greater purpose than to mess with us.

Super 8 ★ ★ ★ ½

PG-13, 112 m., 2011

Joel Courtney (Joe Lamb), Kyle Chandler (Jack Lamb), Elle Fanning (Alice Dainard), Riley Griffiths (Charles), Noah Emmerich (Nelec), Ron Eldard (Louis Dainard), Ryan Lee (Cary), Gabriel Basso (Martin), Zach Mills (Preston). Directed by J. J. Abrams and produced by Abrams, Bryan Burk, and Steven Spielberg. Screenplay by Abrams.

With its night skies filled with mystery, its kids racing around town on bicycles, and its flashlights forming visible beams in the air, *Super 8* has the visual signatures of an early Spielberg movie. Its earnest young heroes stumble upon an awesome mystery and try to investigate it themselves. And as a small town in Ohio experiences frightening events, we feel poised between *The Goonies* and a 1950s sci-fi picture with the characters lined up side by side and looking in alarm at an awesome sight.

The associations are deliberate. Steven Spielberg produced the film, and its director, J. J. Abrams, worked in lowly roles on early Spielberg pictures before going on to make *Mission Impossible III* (2006) and *Star Trek* (2009). What they're trying here is to evoke the innocence of an *E.T.* while introducing a more recent level of special effects. There are really two movies here, one about the world of the kids and one about the expectations of the audience, and *Super 8* leads a charmed life until the second story takes command.

Set in the 1970s, it opens with its twelve-year-old hero, Joe Lamb (Joel Courtney), helping his intense friend Charles (Riley Griffiths) make an 8 mm zombie movie for a local film festival. This, of course, must be done in secret, not so much because parents would forbid it, but because it's fun to operate with stealth. Besotted by stories of other young directors (no doubt including Spielberg), they scout locations, improvise costumes, and energetically apply zombie makeup. In this they are greatly assisted by fourteen-year-old Alice (Elle Fanning), who not only plays the zombie mother but, just as importantly, sneaks out with her father's car to drive them all to a midnight shoot at the local train station.

A great opportunity develops when a train comes rumbling out of the night. "Action!" Charles shouts, and Martin and Alice try to perform their dialogue as the train rumbles past. Then a pickup truck appears, racing on the tracks toward the train. The train wreck goes on and on and on, tossing railroad cars around like dominoes. You would think a freight car loaded with heavy metals couldn't fly very high into the sky, but you'd be wrong. This is a sensationally good action sequence, up there with the airplane crash in *Knowing.*

Yes, something ominous is happening, but I'd better not say what. Part of the delicious fun of the film is the way it toys with portents. For example, Joe's dog disappears. He tacks up a card on a notice board. We see that countless dogs have disappeared. Later there's a map of where missing dogs have been found. The dots form a ring around the city. All the dogs ran out of town. This moment reminded me of the great shot in *The Thing* (1952), when the scientists stood on the outline of something in the Antarctic ice and when Howard Hawks's camera drew back, we saw they were in a circle.

Meanwhile, human elements come into play. Joe's mother was killed not long ago in an accident at the steel mill. He mourns her. His father, Deputy Sheriff Jack Lamb (Kyle Chandler), has grown distant and depressive. Joe begins to bond with Alice, who is two years older, but sympathetic and nice. There's an oddly touching scene where he helps her with her zombie makeup.

It is a requirement of these films that adults be largely absent. The kids get involved up to their necks, but the grown-ups seem slow to realize strange things are happening. Here, the mystery centers on the cargo of the cars in the train wreck, and on the sudden materialization of U.S. Air Force investigators and troops in town. If we don't instinctively know it from this movie, we know it from a dozen earlier ones: The authorities are trying to cover up something frightening, and the kids are on the case.

During the first hour of *Super 8*, I was elated by how good it was. It was like seeing a lost early Spielberg classic. Then something started to slip. The key relationship of Alice and her troubled father, Louis (Ron Eldard), went through an arbitrary U-turn. Joe's own father seemed to sway with the requirements of the plot. The presentation of the threat was done with obscure and unconvincing special effects. We want the human stories and the danger to mesh perfectly, and they seem to slip past one another.

All the same, *Super 8* is a wonderful film, nostalgic not for a time but for a style of filmmaking, when shell-shocked young audiences were told a story, not pounded over the head with aggressive action. Abrams treats early adolescence with tenderness and affection. He uses his camera to accumulate emotion. He has the small-town locations right.

And he does an especially good job with Joe, Alice, Charles, and their friends—especially Cary (Ryan Lee). You know how a lot of heist and action movies have an explosives expert? Cary is the kid who is always playing with matches and fireworks. There was always some kid like that in school. The grown-ups said if he kept on like that he'd blow off a finger. We were rather grateful for the suspense.

Surrogates ★ ★ ½

PG-13, 88 m., 2009

Bruce Willis (Thomas Greer), Radha Mitchell (Jennifer Peters), Rosamund Pike (Maggie Greer), Boris Kodjoe (Andrew Stone), James Francis Ginty (Young Canter), James Cromwell (Dr. Lionel Canter), Ving Rhames (The Prophet), Jack Noseworthy (Strickland), Devin Ratray (Bobby), Michael Cudlit (Colonel Brendon). Directed by Jonathan Mostow and produced by Max Handelman, David Hoberman, and Todd Lieberman. Screenplay by John Brancato and Michael Ferris, based on the graphic novel by Robert Venditti and Brett Weldele.

In the future world of *Surrogates*, most of the human population reclines at home without moving, while living vicariously through robot avatars controlled by their minds. They present themselves to the world as younger and more attractive than they really are—and more fit, I assume, since the avatars work out at gyms instead of their owners. No one you meet is really there.

Bruce Willis, looking about thirty-eight and with a healthy mop of hair, stars as Greer, an FBI agent. He and his partner, Jennifer Peters (Radha Mitchell), are assigned to investigate a messy murder late one night outside a club, and are astonished to find that the victim is the son of Dr. Lionel Canter (James Cromwell), the inventor of surrogate technology. But wait a minute, you're thinking. Who dies if only your surrogate is killed? The unsettling answer is that the murder device works by frying the brain of its controller. I hate it when that happens.

Dr. Canter, no longer associated with the corporation that makes surrogates, has indeed grown disillusioned with his invention. As Agent Greer's investigation continues, it leads him into the world of the Dreads—actual human beings who reject surrogates and live on "reservations" with other flesh-and-blood people. The Dread leader is The Prophet (Ving Rhames of the eerie presence), who preaches against avatars as an abomination.

As indeed they are. It's a relief when something goes wrong with Greer's avatar and he must venture onto the streets as himself: middle-aged, bald, and looking, I must say, considerably more attractive than his creepy surrogate.

Unfortunately, *Surrogates,* while more ambitious than it has to be, descends into action scenes too quickly. Why must so many screenplays reduce their ideas to chases and shoot-outs? The concept here, based on a graphic novel by Robert Venditti and Brett Weldele, would lead naturally to intriguing considerations.

Consider plastic surgery. To what extent is Joan Rivers a seventy-six-year-old woman inhabiting a fifty-six-year-old avatar? Consider the problem of sex. After two attractive people meet, flirt, and desire to have sex, there are two possibilities: (1) their avatars have some sort of mechanical encounter while their owners, at home, masturbate; or (2) two real people, God forbid, have to discover how the other really looks. Since evolution suggests that we evaluate potential mates for their reproductive potential, this could lead to setbacks in the process of natural selection.

In this future world, we learn, surrogates mean that crime and racism have been all but eliminated. If anybody can be of any race, that takes care of racism, all right. But crime? How do those humans who are poor and unemployed *pay* for their surrogates? What if you decide you want to trade up to a better model? Sure, your surrogate may have a job, but why would salaries be any better? Especially since robots make poor consumers. What process actually takes place when they have a meal together in a restaurant? Can they eat or drink?

Avatars first came into general consciousness by way of computer games and chat boards. It's well known that people you meet online may not be who they pretend to be. Surrogates sound like an ideal solution for transsexuals. Don't go through the surgery, just switch your avatar's gender. But would that satisfy your hormonal feelings? There are real bodies involved here, and that gets into another issue: If you spend your life reclining, your muscles will atrophy surprisingly quickly, and it will become physically impossible for you to get out of bed and walk, let alone go into action like Bruce Willis does here.

These are areas *Surrogates,* perhaps wisely, doesn't explore. Such a film might have required a Spike Jonze or Guy Maddin. *Surrogates* is entertaining and ingenious, but it settles too soon for formula. One other thing: It ends with the wrong shot. The correct shot would have been the overhead exterior of the street, about four shots earlier. You'll know the one I mean.

Survival of the Dead ★ ★

R, 90 m., 2010

Alan Van Sprang (Sarge Crocket), Kenneth Welsh (Patrick O'Flynn), Kathleen Munroe (Jane O'Flynn), Richard Fitzpatrick (Seamus Muldoon), Devon Bostick (Boy). Directed by George A. Romero and produced by Paula Devonshire. Screenplay by Romero.

For the purposes of watching *Survival of the Dead,* I'm perfectly willing to believe in zombies. It's a stretch, however, to believe in an island off the coast of Delaware where life looks like outtakes from *Ryan's Daughter,* everyone speaks with an Irish accent, and there's a bitter feud between those who believe in capital punishment for zombies, and those who call for their rehabilitation and cure.

How can you kill *or* rehabilitate a zombie, since by definition it is dead? Here's my reasoning: If it can attack you and dine on your throbbing flesh, it isn't dead enough. George A. Romero is our leading researcher in this area, having reinvented zombies for modern times with *Night of the Living Dead* (1968), and returned to them from time to time, most successfully in the excellent *Dawn of the Dead* (1978).

Zombies, as I have noted before (and before, and before), make excellent movie creatures because they are smart enough to be dangerous, slow enough to kill, and dead enough we need not feel grief. Romero has not even begun to run out of ways to kill them. My favorite shot in this film shows a zombie having its head blown apart, with the skullcap bouncing into the air and falling down to fit neatly over the neck. If that doesn't appeal to you, nothing will.

I've seen a whole lot of zombies killed. I've been cordial over the years with Romero, who in addition to reinventing zombies demonstrated how horror movies were a low-cost point of entry for independent filmmakers. To him we possibly owe such directors as David Cronenberg and John Carpenter. *Dawn of the Dead* was a biting indictment of the culture of the shopping mall, with most of its action in a landscape of modern retailing and merchandising. It was also funny.

All true. But after you've seen, oh, I dunno, twenty or thirty zombie movies, you sort of stop caring very much, unless something new is going on, as in *Zombieland.* At this point, I find myself watching primarily to spot and appreciate entertaining new ways to slaughter zombies. That's why the skullcap moment appealed to me. It was new.

Not much else is new in *Survival of the Dead.* After a vaguely explained plague of zombies has broken out, America has descended into post-apocalyptic warfare. The zombie disease is spreading. If one bites you, you become a zombie. That ability to infect others was once the special gift of vampires, and I suspect it has now been bestowed on zombies by gene-splicing at the genetic level. All zombies share one characteristic: They take a lickin' and keep on tickin'.

On the island off Delaware, we meet the O'Flynns and Muldoons, who are in the dependable tradition of the Hatfields and McCoys. The O'Flynns believe zombies exist to be destroyed. The Muldoons, more humane, want to chain them up and keep them around until a cure is discovered. How do you vote? How would you feel if the Muldoon scheme worked, and you were a cured zombie? Would your flesh still look a little decomposed? Would you mention it in your entry on Match.com?

The leader of the O'Flynns is exiled to the mainland via rowboat, and in Philadelphia we encounter paramilitaries who are fighting off zombies and considering going to . . . the island off the Delaware coast. I was unable to stir up the slightest interest in the O'Flynns and Muldoons, the military types reminded me of the better *28 Days Later,* and finally, all that kept my attention were the ingenious ways Romero killed the zombies. The man is a fount of imagination. Scarcely a zombie dies in a boring way. So there's that.

T

Take Me Home Tonight ★ ½

R, 114 m., 2011

Topher Grace (Matt Franklin), Anna Faris (Wendy Franklin), Dan Fogler (Barry Nathan), Teresa Palmer (Tori Frederking), Chris Pratt (Kyle Masterson), Michael Biehn (Bill Franklin). Directed by Michael Dowse and produced by Sarah Bowen, Topher Grace, Gordon Kaywin, James Whitaker, and Dany Wolf. Screenplay by Dowse, Jackie Filgo, and Jeff Filgo.

I follow the Darwin Awards carefully. Those are the mentions given out on the Internet every year of people whose deaths may have improved the species by removing them from the gene pool. Many of the characters in *Take Me Home Tonight* might make a contribution in that way.

Let me run this past you. Your name is Matt (Topher Grace). You are maybe ten years out of high school. You work at a Los Angeles video store. You want to impress a girl named Tori (Teresa Palmer) you lusted after in school. She walks into the video store. You lie and tell her you are a trader with Goldman Sachs. You end up at a party, and she's there. It turns out she's also in banking, and happens to know that Goldman Sachs doesn't have a Los Angeles office.

Everybody then gets drunk and exchanges inane dialogue during the longest scene set at a party since the forty-five-minute formal ball in Visconti's *The Leopard* (1963). Your most hated rival is throwing the party. Your high school class had some kind of cockamamie ritual test involving the Ball (I may have the name wrong, but I'm close). This is a large metal sphere, apparently hammered together out of old junkyard parts. It's in the bed of your rival's dump truck.

You decide one way to regain your self-respect and win esteem in Tori's eyes is to risk the challenge of the Ball. The idea is, you climb inside the Ball, he tilts the truck bed, and the Ball rolls out of control downhill on a canyon road above Los Angeles. To get into the Ball is to qualify yourself as a finalist for the Darwin Award. To aid and abet anyone involved in this process is to act as an accessory to murder.

Now let me get back to that party scene. It is unendurably long. There are endless camera setups to define various groupings of characters who perform badly written dialogue. Among these characters are Matt's twin sister, Wendy (Anna Faris), and her boyfriend, Kyle (Chris Pratt). Wendy got all the brains in the family. Matt got to be Topher Grace. In that family, a trade-off. Wendy is holding an envelope that will tell her if she has been accepted to "Oxford University." Kyle thinks they should get married. He doesn't know where Oxford is. This gives you a notion of the depth of his interest in her.

I put the words "Oxford University" in quotes to mislead you into thinking nobody calls Oxford by that name. Actually, that's its official name, but it is uncool to say "Oxford University." Most people say "Oxford" and people know what you're talking about. You know, like "Berkeley." Anybody tells you they're going to the "University of California at Berkeley," they must think you just got off the train.

Take Me Home Tonight must have been made with people who had a great deal of nostalgia for the 1980s, a relatively underprivileged decade. More power to them. The movie unfortunately gives them no dialogue expanding them into recognizable human beings. They speak entirely in plot points and punch lines, and seem to be motivated only by lust, greed, and ego. Well, we all are, but few bring to this motivation so little intelligence and wit.

Besides, I have news for Tori, who works in banking and thinks she's so smart. If she thinks Goldman Sachs doesn't have a Los Angeles office, she should pay a visit to Suite 2600 in Fox Plaza at 2121 Avenue of the Stars.

Taken ★ ★ ½

PG-13, 91 m., 2009

Liam Neeson (Bryan Mills), Famke Janssen (Lenore), Maggie Grace (Kim). Directed by Pierre Morel and produced by Luc Besson. Screenplay by Besson and Robert Mark Kamen.

If CIA agents in general were as skilled as Bryan Mills in particular, bin Laden would have been an American prisoner since late September 2001. *Taken* shows him as a one-man rescue squad, a master of every skill, a laser-eyed, sharpshooting, pursuit-driving, pocket-picking, impersonating, knife-fighting, torturing, karate-fighting killing machine who can cleverly turn over a petrol tank with one pass in his car and strategically ignite it with another.

We meet Mills (Liam Neeson) in "sort of retirement" in Los Angeles, grilling steaks with old CIA buddies and yearning to spend more time with his seventeen-year-old daughter, Kim (Maggie Grace). Kim now lives with her mom, Mills's ex-wife (Famke Janssen), and her effortlessly mega-rich husband (Xander Berkeley), whose idea of a birthday present is giving Kim, not a pony, but what looks like a thoroughbred.

Mills has seen action in Afghanistan and apparently everywhere else and knows it's a dangerous world for a naive teenage girl. He is against Kim spending the summer in Paris with her girlfriend, even though "cousins" will apparently chaperone. He's right. Kim and her pal succeed in getting themselves kidnapped the afternoon of the same day they get off the plane, although Kim has time for one terrified phone call to Dad before she's taken.

Now listen to this. Using CIA contacts at Langley, Mills is able to use his garbled tape of their conversation to determine the name of his girl's kidnapper (Marko), that he is Albanian, that his ring kidnaps young tourists, drugs them, and runs them as prostitutes; the virgins are auctioned off to Arab sheiks and so on. Headquarters also tells Mills he has ninety-six hours to rescue his daughter before she meets a fate worse than death, followed by death.

With this kind of intelligence, the CIA could be using bin Laden's Visa card in every ATM in Virginia. It's the setup for a completely unbelievable action picture where Mills is given the opportunity to use one element of CIA spy craft after another, read his enemies' minds, eavesdrop on their telephones, spy on their meetings, and, when necessary, defeat roomfuls of them in armed combat. At one point a former colleague in the Paris police says he has left seven bodies behind. Mills is just getting warmed up. How this man and his daughter could hope to leave France on a commercial flight doesn't speak highly of the French police—and the new *Pink Panther* doesn't open for a week. Oh, why does he have only ninety-six hours? To provide the movie with a handy deadline, that's why.

It's always a puzzle to review a movie like this. On the one hand, it's preposterous. But who expects a Bourne-type city-wrecking operative to be plausible? On the other hand, it's very well made. Liam Neeson brings the character a hard-edged, mercilessly focused anger, and director Pierre Morel hurtles through action sequences at a breathless velocity. If Kim is an empty-headed twit, well, she's offscreen most of the time, and the villains are walking showcases for testosterone gone bad. The only tiny glitch is that if one chase scene doesn't use the same ramp down to a construction site that the opening of *Quantum of Solace* did, it sure looks like it does.

The film reopens a question I've had. A lot of movies involve secret clubs or covens of rich white men who meet for the purposes of despoiling innocent women in despicable perversity. The men are usually dressed in elegant formal wear, smoke cigars, and have champagne poured for them by discreet servants. Do such clubs actually exist? Since every member would be blackmailable, how can they survive? If you lost everything in a Ponzi scheme, would you betray your lodge members? Just wondering.

The movie proves two things: (1) Liam Neeson can bring undeserved credibility to most roles just by playing them, and (2) Luc Besson, the cowriter, whose action assembly line produced this film, turns out high-quality trash, and sometimes much better (*The Fifth Element, Taxi, The Transporter, La Femme Nikita,* even *The Three Burials of Melquiades Estrada*). The bottom line is, if you can't wait for the next Bourne thriller, well, you don't have to. I can easily wait, but Truth in Reviewing compels me to confess that if the movie I was describing in the first paragraph sounded as if you'd like this, you probably will.

The Taking of Pelham 1 2 3 ★ ★ ½

R, 106 m., 2009

Denzel Washington (Walter Garber), John Travolta (Ryder), John Turturro (Camonetti),

Luis Guzman (Phil Ramos), Michael Rispoli (John Johnson), James Gandolfini (Mayor). Directed by Tony Scott and produced by Scott, Todd Black, Jason Blumenthal, and Steve Tisch. Screenplay by Brian Helgeland, based on the novel by John Godey.

There's not much wrong with Tony Scott's *The Taking of Pelham 1 2 3* except that there's not much really right about it. Nobody gets terrifically worked up except the special effects people. Oh, John Travolta is angry and Denzel Washington is determined, but you don't sense passion in the performances. They're about behaving, not evoking.

The story, you already know from cable reruns. There are a few changes: The boss hijacker is now an ex-con instead of a former mercenary. The negotiator is now a transit executive, not a cop. The ransom has gone up from $1 million to $10 million. The special effects are much more hyperkinetic and absurd than before, which is not an improvement. When a police car has a high-speed collision, the result is usually consistent with the laws of gravity and physics. It does not take flight and spin head over heels in the air.

The Washington and Travolta roles were played the first time around by Walter Matthau and Robert Shaw. They fit into them naturally. Matthau in particular had a shaggy charm I am nostalgic for. Shaw brought cold steel to the film. Denzel is . . . nice. Sincere. Wants to clear his name. Travolta is so ruthless it comes across as more peremptory than evil.

Since time immemorial, Vehicular Disaster Epics have depended on colorful and easily remembered secondary passengers: nuns with guitars, middle-aged women with swimming medals, a pregnant woman about to go into labor, etc. This time the passengers on the Pelham line disappoint. There's a nice woman who's worried about her child, and an ex–Army Ranger who comes to her aid. That's about it. Few of the juicy ethnic stereotypes of the original.

In fact, the whole film is less juicy. The 1974 version took place in a realistic, well-worn New York City. This version occupies a denatured action movie landscape, with no time for local color and a transit system control room that humbles Mission Control. That may also explain its lack of time to establish the supporting characters, even Travolta's partners. These sleek modern actioners don't give the audience credit for much patience and curiosity. One star or the other has to be on the screen in almost every scene. The relentless pace can't be slowed for much dialogue, especially for supporting characters. It all has to be mindless, implausible action.

Say what you will about the special effects of the 1970s, at least I was convinced I was looking at a *real train.* Think this through with me: Once you buy in to the fact that the train is *there,* the train becomes a given. You're thinking, ohmigod, what's going to happen to the train? With modern CGI, there are scenes where a real train is obviously not on the screen, at least not in real time and space, and you're thinking, ohmigod, real trains can't go that fast. And when cars crash, cars should crash. They shouldn't behave like pinballs.

Note: Here's an interesting thing. Looking up my 1974 review, I found that four of the characters were named Blue, Green, Grey, and Brown. Could it be that when Quentin Tarantino was writing about Mr. White, Mr. Orange, Mr. Blonde, and Mr. Pink in Reservoir Dogs, *he was . . . naw, it's gotta be just a coincidence.*

Taking Woodstock ★ ★ ★

R, 120 m., 2009

Demetri Martin (Elliot Teichberg), Dan Fogler (Devon), Henry Goodman (Jake Teichberg), Jonathan Groff (Michael Lang), Eugene Levy (Max Yasgur), Jeffrey Dean Morgan (Dan), Imelda Staunton (Sonia Teichberg), Paul Dano (VW Guy), Kelli Garner (VW Girl), Mamie Gummer (Tisha), Emile Hirsch (Billy), Liev Schreiber (Vilma). Directed by Ang Lee and produced by Lee, James Schamus, and Celia Costas. Screenplay by Schamus, based on the book *Taking Woodstock: A True Story of a Riot, a Concert, and a Life* by Elliot Tiber with Tom Monte.

Luckily I saw *Woodstock* again in April, so it was fresh in my mind while watching *Taking Woodstock,* Ang Lee's entertaining new film about the kid who made it all possible—in Woodstock, anyway. This was Elliot Teichberg, a young interior designer who leaves a New York City career to return home to upstate New York and help his parents bail out their failing and shabby motel.

He's already held outdoor "music festivals" at the motel, which have involved people sitting on the grass and listening to him play records. Now he learns a nearby town has refused a permit to the organizers of a proposed August 1969 rock concert. As the head of the tiny Bethel Chamber of Commerce, near Woodstock, he calls the organizers and offers a permit. And history is made. What if Woodstock had been named after the town that turned it down, Wallkill?

Lee's movie is so deliberately backstage that we never see any of the performances, although we hear them sometimes in the background. All is seen through the eyes of Elliot, who ignores local fears of a hippie riot and persuades local dairy farmer Max Yasgur (Eugene Levy) to make his acres available as the venue. Max and other people in the film, such as the Port-O-San man and a local couple with one son at Woodstock and another in Vietnam, are familiar from the Woodstock film.

But Lee and his writer, James Schamus, aren't making a historical pastiche. This is a comedy with some sweet interludes and others that are cheerfully over the top, such as a nude theatrical troupe living in Elliot's barn, and Vilma, his volunteer head of motel security, a transvestite ex-Marine played by Liev Schreiber. How does Schreiber, looking just as he usually does except for a blond wig and a dress, play a transvestite? Completely straight. It works.

The backstage cast of characters includes concert organizer Michael Lang (Jonathan Groff) and Elliot's buddy Billy (Emile Hirsch), a returned and strung-out Vietnam veteran. Also loud and omnipresent are Elliot's mother, Sonia (Imelda Staunton), and her long-suffering husband, Jake (Henry Goodman). Sonia, a Russian immigrant paralyzed by fears of poverty, has run the motel into the ground with lack of maintenance and such policies as charging a dollar for a towel. Descended upon by a busload of organizers, she converts rooms into "triples" by hanging sheets from the ceiling. Her shrill greed cuts through all the peace and love until, finally, even she warms up.

Instead of showing much more than glimpses and edges of the concert, Lee shows the local impact as "Woodstock Nation" swamps little Bethel. He also shows the good will of most of the locals and police, who join in the spirit. There's a remarkable shot, which must have been hard to stage, of Elliot getting a ride on a police motorcycle past a backup of hundreds of cars, vans, and pedestrians; this reminded me of the famous traffic jam in Godard's *Weekend.*

I was reminded, too, of another film, Phil Kaufman's *The Unbearable Lightness of Being.* That film made remarkable use of pre-CGI special effects to seamlessly insert its characters into actual footage of the Prague demonstrations against the Russian occupation.

What Lee does, apparently, is use footage from Michael Wadleigh's *Woodstock* (1970) and insert Elliot and others into it. I say "apparently," because the end titles don't mention the Warner Bros. picture. Who knows? It looks remarkably convincing. Perhaps they found some of the miles of additional footage shot by Wadleigh and his big crew. The poignancy of Wadleigh's closing shots of the cleanup effort are mirrored here as Elliot joins in.

Not many events of forty years ago would inspire a feature comedy. Seeing the 1970 film on a big screen in 70 mm in April at Ebertfest, with an audience including many who had never seen it before, was an affirmation of how timeless those "three days of peace and music" have become. *Taking Woodstock* has the freshness of something being created, not remembered. I saw a photo the other day of the young couple shown on the original album jacket. Still married, still with their arms around each other.

Tamara Drewe ★ ★ ★ ½

R, 110 m., 2010

Gemma Arterton (Tamara Drewe), Roger Allam (Nicholas Hardiment), Bill Camp (Glen McCreavy), Dominic Cooper (Ben Sergeant), Luke Evans (Andy Cobb), Tamsin Greig (Beth Hardiment), Jessica Barden (Jody Long), Charlotte Christie (Casey Shaw). Directed by Stephen Frears and produced by Alison Owen, Tracey Seaward, and Paul Trijbits. Screenplay by Moira Buffini, based on the graphic novel by Posy Simmonds.

Tamara Drewe is one of those British comedies in which, one way or another, we envy all of the characters—even, briefly, the one run over by stampeding cows. If one must be vain, lustful, egotistical, or long-suffering, let it be here, at a writers' retreat in the Dorset village of Ewedown, where everyone lives across the street from a field and there are no bank branches to deface the rustic charm.

The writers' colony is run by Nicholas Hardiment (Roger Allam) and his good wife, Beth (Tamsin Greig). He is a best-selling crime novelist and serial adulterer, and she is a saintly helpmate who runs the retreat, befriends the guests, bakes fresh pastries for tea, and is reconciled to his tomcatting because at the end of the day he always returns to her—for the pastries, possibly.

Into this pastoral idyll drops the fragrant Tamara Drewe (Gemma Arterton). Once, long ago, she was a village lass with a big nose. She went off to London to make her fortune and find a plastic surgeon, and has returned to sell the family home. She is now a famous newspaper columnist with a standard-issue nose, the kind of woman men describe as healthy, when they mean so very much more.

The Hardiments are assisted by a robust local lad named Andy Cobb (Luke Evans), who has fallen on bad fortune but cheerfully does odd jobs and harbors a resentment against Tamara, whose family purchased what he still considers *his* family home. Once, in their teen years, Andy and Tamara apparently rummaged a bit among each other's netherlands, notwithstanding her nose.

Nicholas the crime novelist is drawn to Tamara like a cat to tuna. He wears his fame like a backstage pass, and Tamara, after all, is not so very difficult to seduce. She is, in fact, a woman who calls her own shots, and about her lovers is less likely to feel gratitude than pity. Into the mix now comes a famous London rock 'n' roller, Ben Sergeant (Dominic Cooper). I believe it possible that his eyeliner is tattooed.

His presence in town inflames the adolescent girls Jody Long and Casey Shaw (Jessica Barden and Charlotte Christie), who spend their days moping about bored in bus shelters, and lurk behind hedgerows to spy on everyone. Tamara dumps Nicholas for Ben, flirts with Andy, and is one of the many victims of Jody and Casey's meddling with private lives.

The movie was adapted from a graphic novel by Posy Simmonds, and *it* was inspired by Thomas Hardy's *Far from the Madding Crowd*, although there seems to have been an uncredited infusion of French farce along the way. To the game of romantic musical chairs already under way, a new player is added: McCreavy (Bill Camp), a morose American academic who is laboring away at the poetry of Hardy and has come here to Ewedown to be inspired by a village that is indeed far from the madding crowd. He finds a sympathetic ear from Beth, and begins to entertain ambitions about other bits of her anatomy.

Tamara Drewe resembles another British village comedy, *Local Hero*, in which everyone lived in each other's pockets. Its director is Stephen Frears, a master of many genres (*High Fidelity*, *The Grifters*, *Dirty Pretty Things*, *The Queen*). Here he knows exactly what he's dealing with: foolish and flawed people who harbor desires that may not be good for them. Not all of them can be happy, and it must be said that Frears, with his writer Moira Buffini and Simmonds and Hardy lurking in the background, gives us a story in which everyone gets more or less what they deserve. If these people are silly, they are no sillier than most of us. There is admirable craftsmanship at work in the scene of the unfortunate cattle stampede, and although we regret the fate of its victim, we must admit that no one is really to blame, and a rough justice has been served.

There is another pleasure here. All of the characters, except for the two naughty girls, are adults with grown-up ideas and aspirations, however lamentable. I find myself growing weary of the overgrown adolescents who impersonate adult characters in too many recent American films. Even a jolly comedy like this has characters with more depth. For example, at no time in the film does anyone come right out and explain who Thomas Hardy was. The characters are all presumed to already know. Not that you need to know in order to enjoy the film, but it's nice to know stuff you don't need to know, don't you think?

The Tempest ★ ★ ½

PG-13, 110 m., 2010

Helen Mirren (Prospera), Russell Brand (Trinculo), Reeve Carney (Prince Ferdinand), Tom Conti (Gonzalo), Chris Cooper (Antonio), Alan Cumming (Sebastian), Djimon Hounsou (Caliban), Felicity Jones (Miranda), Alfred Molina (Stephano), David Strathairn (King Alonso), Ben Whishaw (Ariel). Directed by Julie Taymor and produced by Taymor, Robert Chartoff, Lynn Hendee, Jason K. Lau, and Julia Taylor-Stanley. Screenplay by Taymor, based on the play by William Shakespeare.

The only way to read Shakespeare's *The Tempest* is as a farewell: a play written, if you will, for his retirement banquet, to be performed before he's handed his gold watch and finally has more time to spend with his family. It is my favorite of all his plays, containing a line I embrace as my consolation: "We are such stuff as dreams are made on, and our little life is rounded with a sleep." The writer who saw more deeply into human nature than any other looked into himself and decided he had finished his work.

Julie Taymor's film *The Tempest* doesn't feel like a farewell. She does not abjure her rough magic. In a film filled with sound and fury, she rages against the dying of the light. There is no reconciliation or closure. What reads as a poetic acceptance of human mortality plays as the defiance of a magician clinging to familiar tricks.

She doesn't capture Shakespeare's tone (or his meaning, I believe), but she certainly has boldness in her reinvention. The best thing she does is change the sex of Prospero, the exiled Duke of Milan who has fled to a remote island with his daughter. Here Prospero becomes Prospera, and is magnificently played by Helen Mirren with more ferocity than resignation. Prospera's daughter, Miranda (Felicity Jones), now seems more suited at her side; Prospera empathizes with her as Prospero never did. Indeed, all the relationships on the island curiously seem more natural when the character becomes a woman.

Consider Ariel (Ben Whishaw), the androgynous sprite who follows Prospera's bidding and performs her magic. Ariel is neither male nor female, and while Prospero seemed to treat the spirit as an extremely skillful pet, Prospera relates more to Ariel's functions as a companion and helpmate. And there is Caliban, the original inhabitant of the island before the first boat arrived from Milan. He resents the usurpers and invokes one of the most terrible curses in literature: "All the infections that the sun sucks up from bogs, fens, flats, on Prosper fall, and make him by inch-meal a disease!" Here, played by Djimon Hounsou as an African, he evokes parallels with colonialism, and Prospera seems more ready to see him beneath her instinctive rejection.

Taymor has gathered a cast that, for the most part, would be ideal for a traditional stage version of the play, and embedded them in special effects that begin with the word "tempest" and build to a frenzy. The dialogue is pure Shakespeare (proving again that he is easier to understand when spoken than read), but these gifted actors sometimes seem to be saying the words as someone with a chainsaw cuts firewood in the next room.

Taymor's stagecraft is bold but not measured. If the top is in sight, she aims for it. This worked with her passionate film *Titus*, based on Shakespeare's *Titus Andronicus*. That's a bloody early play suited to extremes. *The Tempest* contains more resignation; it is a search for sunset. There's a gentle finality to it, despite some quite violent scenes. The best performance I've seen is Barbara Gaines's 2002 production for the Chicago Shakespeare Company, where she used daring rigging to float some actors like performers for Cirque du Soleil. With her you felt love; with Taymor this time, determination.

Many gifted actors join Mirren in finding their own moments within the melee. Felicity Jones as Miranda is hopeful and virginal. King Alonso is played with sad resignation by David Strathairn. Djimon Hounsou plays an angry and almost politicized Caliban. Russell Brand and Alfred Molina are bawdy as two seafarers who wander off and enlist Caliban as a drinking buddy. Alan Cumming and Chris Cooper play Sebastian and Antonio as filled with ominous ill will. Tom Conti is the good king Gonzalo.

They inhabit locations (Hawaii) and remarkable soundstage sets for Prospera's Milan lab and island spaces. Interiors are sensational: her alchemist's workshop and a room with alarming stair steps climbing at an angle. There are all the cliffs you could possibly desire for Prospera to stand atop and howl at the sea.

All of these elements are in place. Taymor might have turned down the heat. You do not have to insist with *The Tempest* because it is a play that puts all assertion behind it and is content to cast its magic staff into the sea. It is the play with which Shakespeare shows that he knew how good he was.

Terminator: Salvation ★ ★

PG-13, 115 m., 2009

Christian Bale (John Connor), Sam Worthington (Marcus Wright), Anton Yelchin (Kyle Reese), Bryce Dallas Howard (Kate Connor), Moon Bloodgood (Blair Williams), Common (Barnes), Jadagrace Berry (Star), Helena Bonham Carter (Dr. Serena Kogan), Jane Alexander (Virginia). Directed by McG and produced by Moritz Borman, Jeffrey Silver, Victor Kubicek, and Derek Anderson. Screenplay by John Brancato and Michael Ferris.

One of Hollywood's oldest axioms teaches us: The story comes first. Watching *Terminator Salvation,* it occurred to me that in the new Hollywood, the story board comes first. After scrutinizing the film, I offer you my summary of the story: Guy dies, finds himself resurrected, meets others, fights. That lasts for almost two hours.

The action scenes, which is to say, 90 percent of the movie, involve Armageddon between men and machines ten years in the future. The most cheerful element of the film is that they've perfected Artificial Intelligence so quickly. Yes, Skynet is self-aware and determines to wipe out humankind for reasons it doesn't explain. A last-ditch resistance is being led by John Connor, or "J.C." for you Faulkner fans.

Christian Bale plays the role of Connor, in a movie that raises many questions about the lines between man and machine. Raises them and leaves them levitating. However, it has many fights between a humanoid cyborg and robotic Skynet men made of steel. How do these antagonists fight? Why, with their fists, of course, which remains a wonderfully cinematic device. They also shoot at each other, to little effect. In fact, one metal man is covered in molten ore and then flash-frozen, and keeps on tickin'. And listen, Skynet buddies, what Bale thought about that cameraman is only the tip of the iceberg compared to what he thinks about you.

There is nothing visible in this world but a barren wasteland. No towns, no houses, no food, no farms, no nothing. Maybe they live on Spam. The Resistance is run from a submarine commanded by General Ashdown (Michael Ironside), who wants to destroy Skynet and all of its human POWs. Connor, who is not even human, vows to save them. Wait. That's Marcus Wright (Sam Worthington), the guy from the past, who looks so much like Connor that maybe he only thinks he's Wright. Marcus is a convicted murderer from the past, awakened from cryogenic sleep.

I know with a certainty approaching dread that all of my questions will be explained to me in long, detailed messages from *Terminator* experts. They will also charge me with not seeing the movie before I reviewed it. Believe me, I would have enjoyed traveling forward through time for two hours, starting just before I saw the movie. But in regard to the answers to my questions: You know what? I *don't care.*

I regret (I suppose) that I did not see the first *Terminator* movie. *Terminator 2: Judgment Day* (1991) was a fairly terrific movie, set in the (then) future, to prevent the nuclear holocaust of 1997. You remember that. It was *about something.* In it, Edward Furlong was infinitely more human as John Connor than Christian Bale is in this film. Think about that.

Schwarzenegger, indeed, reappears in this fourth film, thanks to a body double and a special effects face, which makes him, I think, a cyborg of a cyborg. His famous line "I'll be back" is uttered by one John Connor or another, and I hope it draws more chuckles than it did at the screening I attended. Why, those immortal words are chiseled into granite, or at least into the lobby floor at the AMC River East theaters.

If there is one wholly sympathetic character in this film, that would be Blair Williams, played by the fragrant Moon Bloodgood. She murmurs some tender words at the forty-five-minute mark, representing the most complex dialogue up to that point. Dr. Serena Kogan (Helena Bonham Carter) has a longer speech, but you can't be sure it's really her, and she may have been lying.

Anyway, most of the running time is occupied by action sequences, chase sequences, motorcycle sequences, plow truck sequences, helicopter sequences, fighter plane sequences, towering android sequences, and fistfights. It gives you all the pleasure of a video game without the bother of having to play it.

Terribly Happy ★ ★ ★

NO MPAA RATING, 100 m., 2010

Jakob Cedergren (Robert), Lene Maria Christensen (Ingelise Buhl), Kim Bodnia (Jorgen Buhl), Lars Brygmann (Dr. Zerlang), Anders Hove (Kobmand Moos), Mathilde Maack (Dorthe). Directed by Henrik Ruben Genz and produced by Tina Dalhoff and Thomas Gammeltoft. Screenplay by Genz and Gry Dunja Jensen, based on a novel by Erling Jepsen.

The cow gave birth to a calf with two heads, and they weren't just any two heads. Into the bog it went. All sorts of village problems sink in the bog. No telling what's rotting down there. This beginning may make *Terribly Happy* sound like a modern-day *Motel Hell*, where Farmer Vincent buried people to their necks and fattened them like geese. But no, this is a dour and deadpan film noir from Denmark, and a good one.

Robert (Jakob Cedergren), a young policeman from Copenhagen, has been exiled as punishment to a dismal village in South Jutland. He's about thirty, single, and made a "terrible mistake" he doesn't talk about. The town doesn't look like some cheery Danish hamlet, but more like a rundown grain elevator town in the Old West. When he steps into the bar, he's made to feel not only unwelcome, but in some subtle way threatened. The drinkers regard him with a level, cold gaze. They laugh at him behind his back. When he goes to get a bicycle repaired, he finds the repairman missing. He's told it's not uncommon for folks to go missing.

He asks a young woman for directions. This is Ingelise (Lene Maria Christensen). She has that Shirley MacLaine gamine look. She's not a raving beauty but has undeniable sex appeal. Robert senses it—he feels an attraction—but no, that would be wrong. But what happens when wrong starts to look right?

Something very wrong is happening in this town. The guys in the bar were unfriendly because they have every reason to believe Robert is kidding himself if he thinks he can get anything accomplished as the new town marshal. It gradually develops that Jorgen (Kim Bodnia), the husband of Ingelise, is feared by everyone, not least Ingelise, whom he beats. The film's most eerie detail involves their little daughter. When she parades alone down the abandoned main street with her baby buggy and its squeaky wheels, everyone knows domestic violence is taking place at Jorgen's house.

Bodnia, who plays Jorgen, is alarming in appearance and manner. He isn't one of those jumped-up ex-bouncers who stands six foot six and has big arms and a shaved head. He's alarming not for how he looks but for what he signals he's capable of. If Robert was a bad cop before, he's in way over his head now.

But there's another level. The townspeople seem to have little reason to fear if they'll just go along. They keep their heads low and their thoughts to themselves. Is this intended by the director, Henrik Ruben Genz, as some sort of a parable? I have no idea. It works well enough just at creating an intimidating atmosphere for Robert, who is disoriented when people don't just naturally accept him as, you know, the law.

Genz creates a distinctive look and feel in the film. The town is drab, the people wrung out, and the moments of passion are smoothed back down into the tired routine. You could almost get to feel comfortable in a town like this. Play ball and you won't be disturbed. Jakob Cedergren plays the marshal as a man born to be ordered around. He could only be a policeman in a town where people take cops seriously. Whatever happened to him in Copenhagen has him still in shock, and it's almost like he feels he deserves the way the town treats him. Even in his romantic transgression he seems to be going with the flow.

Terribly Happy at heart plays like a classic Western: the frontier town, the local bad man, the new marshal, the townspeople, cute and vulnerable Ingelise. I've only been to

Denmark twice and have no idea if this is even remotely a Danish situation, but it could fit right fine in the Old West.

Tetro ★ ★ ★

NO MPAA RATING, 127 m., 2009

Vincent Gallo (Tetro), Alden Ehrenreich (Bennie), Maribel Verdu (Miranda), Klaus Maria Brandauer (Carlo/Alfie), Carmen Maura (Alone). Directed, written, and produced by Francis Ford Coppola.

Tetro may be the most autobiographical film Francis Ford Coppola has made. He said at Cannes, "Nothing in it happened, but it's all true." I guess I know what that means. He could be describing any "autobiographical" film or novel. The pitfall is in trying to find parallels: Coppola had a father who was a famous conductor, he has a brother he has sometimes argued with, his sister Talia Shire somewhat resembles the heroine of this film, his nephew Nicolas Cage somewhat resembles the character Tetro, and on and on. All meaningless.

Better to begin with a more promising starting point: The film is boldly operatic, involving family drama, secrets, generations at war, melodrama, romance, and violence. I'm only guessing, but Coppola, considering his father and his Italian-American heritage, may be as opera-besotted as any living American director, including Scorsese. His great epic *Apocalypse Now* is fundamentally, gloriously operatic. The oedipal issues in the *Godfather* trilogy are echoed again in *Tetro*. The emotions are theatrical, not realistic.

For that, he has the right actor, Vincent Gallo, who devotes himself to the title role with heedless abandon. There is nothing subtle about his performance, and nothing should be. He is the son of a famous conductor, he lives in exile in Buenos Aires, he has a wife who loyally endures his impossibilities. There are events in his past that damaged him, and he is unhappy that his younger brother, Bennie (Alden Ehrenreich), knocks unexpectedly at the door. He never wanted to see him again.

Tetro's wife, Miranda (Maribel Verdu), welcomes the young man, who works as a waiter on a cruise ship now in port for repairs. She wishes she knew more about Tetro's family and the reasons for his unhappiness. Tetro is uniformly hostile to almost everyone except Miranda, perhaps because he needs at least one person to speak with. Bennie bunks down in their apartment, is kept at arm's length from Tetro, is left alone in the flat, finds an unfinished play by Tetro, finishes it, and submits it to a festival run by the nation's most powerful critic, Alone (Carmen Maura). Argentina here is a nation that still has a powerful critic.

All hell breaks loose with Tetro, inspiring a series of flashbacks involving his father, Carlo (Klaus Maria Brandauer), a conductor who carries himself as a grand man. There are, of course, terrible secrets in the family past, known to Tetro but not to Bennie, and they are revealed in a final act worthy of Verdi.

Coppola and his cinematographer, Mihai Malaimare Jr., have photographed the central story in black and white, which made me hopelessly desire that more features could be made in this beautiful format. People who dislike b&w movies are, in their sad way, colorblind. The flashbacks are in color, presided over by Brandauer, as a sleek and contended reptile. In a way, this is what his amoral character in *Mephisto* could have turned out like. Without straining or being given a lot of evil dialogue, he communicates egomania and selfishness.

Bennie has always idealized his older brother, picturing him as a brilliant writer in a faraway land, and is shaken to find the reality; Tetro's first entrance, on crutches, flailing at the furniture, is not promising. Gallo is not naturally given to playing ingratiating characters. He brings an uneasy edge to his work, and it's valuable here in evoking the deep wounds of his youth. Alden Ehrenreich, the newcomer playing Bennie, in his first major role, is confident and charismatic, and inspires such descriptions as "the new Leonardo DiCaprio," which remind me of the old showbiz joke.

Perhaps it was because of the b&w photography, but while watching the film I was reminded for the first time in years of Sidney Lumet's *A View from the Bridge* (1962) and Raf Vallone. It has the same feel of too much emotion trapped in a room, and Gallo channels Vallone's savage drive. It was a good memory. Here is a film that, for all of its plot, depends on characters in service of their emotional turmoil. It feels good to see Coppola back in form.

That Evening Sun ★ ★ ★ ½

PG-13, 110 m., 2010

Hal Holbrook (Abner Meecham), Ray McKinnon (Lonzo Choat), Walton Goggins (Paul Meecham), Mia Wasikowska (Pamela Choat), Carrie Preston (Ludie Choat), Barry Corbin (Thurl Chesser), Dixie Carter (Ellen Meecham). Directed by Scott Teems and produced by Terence Berry, Walton Goggins, Ray McHinnon, and Laura D. Smith. Screenplay by Teems, based on the story "I Hate to See That Evening Sun Go Down" by William Gay.

One of the reasons *That Evening Sun* works so well is that the good character isn't all good and the bad character isn't all bad, although they both come close. That leads to a drama set on a Tennessee farm that begins by looking like your standard old-codger story and turns out, as Clint Eastwood's *Gran Torino* did, to be a lot more.

Hal Holbrook, that rock-steady actor with a face off Mount Rushmore, stars as Abner Meecham, an eighty-something who up and walks out of a retirement home one day and takes a taxi to his farm outside of town. It is his farm as far as he's concerned, anyway, although his lawyer son has power of attorney and has rented it to the Choat family. This family is well known to Abner, who dislikes them. He and his neighbor Thurl (Barry Corbin) agree that Lonzo Choat (Ray McKinnon) doesn't amount to much.

While his son, Paul (Walton Goggins), busy with a court case, issues ineffectual commands into his cell phone, Abner sets up an outpost in the bare-boards sharecropper cabin and keeps a hostile eye on the house. Lonzo's sixteen-year-old daughter, Pamela (Mia Wasikowska), comes to visit, is instinctively nice, and sort of disregards Abner's hostility. When she confides that her father hates barking dogs, Abner adopts one of Thurl's barkingest dogs and moves him into the cabin.

Choat has been living on disability, can't make payments on the house, is in no shape to work the farm, and usually has a beer in his hand. If the inside of the farmhouse looks warm and inviting, that's because of two women: Choat's long-suffering wife, Ludie (Carrie Preston), and Abner's own dead wife, Ellen (Dixie Carter). There is poignancy in that role now that Carter, Holbrook's wife, has herself died.

Ellen fixed up the house, Ludie keeps it up, and the two men snarl at each other in the yard. Abner cheerfully calls Choat a white trash redneck, which seems true as we see him drunkenly whipping his wife and daughter with a garden hose. Abner brings this to a stop with a couple of pistol shots. But this situation isn't as simple as who has the gun.

We begin to sense that Choat acts mean but is scared and uncertain inside. By flashbacks and other means, we learn that Abner hasn't always been a sterling husband and father himself. Because both men are flawed, the story takes on an interest and complexity that the setup doesn't hint.

It's a story confined by time and space, adapted by the director, Scott Teems, from the story "I Hate to See That Evening Sun Go Down" by William Gay. Although the setting is a gentle Tennessee landscape and the houses look like illustrations for a calendar of farm life, the situation owes more to Eugene O'Neill or Tennessee Williams. The actors are more than successful at creating deeply plausible characters. There may have been temptations to go broad, but they're all subtle, even McKinnon, in a role that could have gone over the top.

Watching Hal Holbrook, I was reminded again of how steady and valuable this man has been throughout his career. I saw his famous *Mark Twain Tonight* three times in the 1960s, I remember him and Dixie one night at the Royal Court Theater in London where a lamp came crashing to the stage and they handled it with perfect grace and humor, and I remember him most recently as the old man who cares and worries about the doom-seeking hero of *Into the Wild*. Here he incorporates everything he knows about getting to the age of eighty (he's actually eighty-five) and conveys it without the slightest sign of effort. This isn't a performance; it's an embodiment. You know, I think he's about old enough to play Mark Twain.

Note: That Evening Sun *won the Audience Award and a jury prize for ensemble acting at the 2010 SXSW film festival.*

Theater of War ★ ★ ½

NO MPAA RATING, 96 m., 2009

Featuring Meryl Streep, Tony Kushner, George C. Wolfe, Kevin Kline, Jay Cantor, Austin Pendleton, Barbara Brecht-Schall, Oskar Eustis, Jeanine Tesori, Carl Weber. A documentary directed by John Walter and produced by Nina Santisi.

Meryl Streep strikes me as one of the nicest people you'd ever want to meet. Also one of the great actresses, but her down-to-earth quality is what struck me in *Theater of War,* a documentary about the Public Theater's 2006 production of Bertolt Brecht's *Mother Courage and Her Children* in Central Park. She rehearses, she works with the composer, she never raises her voice, she endures full-dress rehearsals during a heat wave. The only complaint she has is that it's not a good idea for audiences to see a performance in "process" because the work looks like "bad acting."

Theater of War, directed by John Walter, does have access to all the rehearsals and intercuts them with documentary material about Brecht, his theatrical career, his life in exile, and his adventures with the House Un-American Activities Committee. There are also interviews with Streep, translator Tony Kushner, Brecht's daughter Barbara Brecht-Schall, and the director George C. Wolfe, a friend of Brecht's, who witnessed the historic 1949 production in East Berlin.

All of this makes an interesting, if not gripping, film about the play, the playwright, and the lead-up work to a stage production. It also leaves me wanting a great deal more. Perhaps in an attempt to emulate Brecht's antiwar theme, Walter devotes too much screen time to footage of antiwar protests during Vietnam, the Israeli invasion of Lebanon, and the war in Iraq. TV news footage means little and still less when it is sometimes seen integrated into graphics representing 1950s all-American families. Nor do we need to see again that familiar footage of U.S. schoolchildren practicing "duck and cover" in case of a nuclear attack.

Walter is trying to make an antiwar doc on top of his primary subject. Not needed, not effective. There could be more of Streep actually changing a stage moment in rehearsal. More from her costar Kevin Kline. Another costar, Austin Pendleton, appears in many shots but is not even mentioned—and he, I believe, would have talked more openly about "process."

The film recounts Brecht's development as a Marxist playwright who deliberately avoided engaging the audience on an emotional level or encouraging it to identify with his characters. He wanted them to rise above the immediate experience to the level of thought and ideology. We are to realize: "War is bad and everyone loses!" At this he is so successful that I suspect the play is impossible to make truly involving. It is sort of a passion play of the left, a work that inspires more piety than enthusiasm.

One peculiar element involves college lectures on Marxism by the novelist Jay Cantor (*The Death of Che Guevara*). If it is explained why he was necessary in the film, I missed it. His comments are generalized and not pertinent. But, oddly, his students are always seen with black bars over their eyes, like patrons being arrested in a brothel. Brecht was famous for distancing strategies that prevented audiences from getting so swept up in his stories that they didn't focus on their messages. Perhaps these distracting and seemingly unnecessary black bars are, dare I say, a Brechtian device?

The doc lacks the usual scene of the company gathered to read their reviews; just as well, because the production was not well received. Oskar Eustis, artistic director of the Public Theater, has said *Mother Courage and Her Children* is the greatest play of the twentieth century. My money's on *Waiting for Godot.*

Thirst ★ ★ ★

R, 133 m., 2009

Song Kang-ho (Sang-hyun), Kim Ok-vin (Tae-ju), Kim Hae-sook (Madame Ra), Shin Ha-kyun (Kang-woo), Park In-hwan (Priest Noh), Oh Dal-soo (Young-du), Song Young-chang (Seung-dae). Directed by Park Chan-wook and produced by Park and Chung Seo-kyung. Screenplay by Park and Jeong Seo-gyeong, inspired by Emile Zola's novel *Therese Raquin.*

Park Chan-wook of South Korea is today's most successful director of horror films, perhaps because there's always more than horror to them. He seems to be probing alarming depths of human nature. Maybe that's why he can simultaneously be celebrated on fanboy horror sites and win the Jury Prize at this year's Cannes Film Festival.

His best-known film is the masterful *Old Boy,* about a man who is taken captive and locked up for years for no reason he can guess and none he is supplied with. Now comes *Thirst,* a blood-drenched vampire film about, unexpectedly, a Roman Catholic priest. The priest is a deeply good man, which is crucial to the story: He dies in the first place because he volunteered as a subject for a deadly medical experiment.

That he is resurrected as a vampire after receiving a transfusion of tainted blood is certainly not his fault. Nor does he set about sinking his fangs into the necks of innocent victims. Given his access to a hospital, he can slurp much of the blood he needs from IV drips leading into unconscious patients, who will hardly complain about a missing pint or two. His slurping, by the way, is very audible; Park has the knack of making the activities of his characters tangible.

This priest, played by the South Korean star Song Kang-ho, is youthful and, despite his vow of chastity, awakened to an urgent carnality by the interloper vampire blood. Perhaps vampires fascinate us because they act not out of a desire to do evil—but by a need. The priest is powerfully attracted to the young wife of a childhood friend of his. We've already seen how willing he is to help the unfortunate, and now his mercy is inspired by this poor girl, who is mistreated by her sick husband and his shrewish mother.

She loves him, too, and is so grateful to him she forgives anything, even the detail of his vampirism. The priest fights against his new undead nature and tries to cause little harm. The girl has no hesitation: in for a dime, in for a dollar. Soon they're so blood-soaked that the film tilts into comedy of a gruesome flavor.

The eventual effect is not as great as it could have been. To begin with a responsible priest is to promise, in some way, to grapple with the philosophical dilemma of vampirism—as *Let the Right One In,* the best modern vampire movie, did. Park descends too enthusiastically into sensation and carnal excess, and it's a disappointment, although it's interesting to see what a quick and willing convert the young wife becomes.

There have long been vampire movies, and Murnau's masterpiece *Nosferatu* (1922) set a high standard for the genre right at the start. What's so attractive about vampires? Perhaps it helps that they tend to be regal in their detachment, familiar with the way of the night, and usually so well dressed. An unflinchingly realistic vampire would be as unattractive as a late-stage addict. There's nothing terrific about living forever if you must do it with the blood of innocents.

No matter. Movies exist to cloak our desires in disguises we can accept, and there is an undeniable appeal to *Thirst.* Park Chan-wook deserves points for mentioning the source of his story, which is *Therese Raquin,* an 1867 French novel by Emile Zola, filmed in 1953 by Marcel Carne and starring Simone Signoret and Raf Vallone. I'll bet if Park hadn't mentioned the Zola novel, no one would have guessed, particularly since it contains no priests and no vampires.

13 Assassins ★ ★ ★ ½

R, 126 m., 2011

Koji Yakusho (Shimada), Takayuki Yamada (Shinrokuro), Yusuke Iseya (Koyata), Goro Inagaki (Lord Naritsugu), Masachika Ichimura (Hanbei Kitou), Mikijiro Hira (Sir Doi), Hiroki Matsukata (Kuranaga), Ikki Sawamura (Mitsuhashi). Directed by Takashi Miike and produced by Minami Ichikawa, Toichiro Shiraishi, and Michihiko Yanagisawa. Screenplay by Daisuke Tengan.

13 Assassins has what many action pictures need, a villain who transcends evil and ascends to a realm of barbaric madness. Against this creature and his private army, a band of samurai is mustered to end his terror. Their heroism against impossible odds is a last hurrah for the samurai code; the film is set in 1844, toward the end of the medieval Edo period, when true samurai warriors were growing rare.

The film is terrifically entertaining, an ambitious big-budget epic, directed with great visuals and sound by Takashi Miike. The last forty-five minutes are devoted to an inventive and ingenious battle scene, but it's not the sort of incomprehensible mayhem we often find in recent action. It's a lesson to the queasy-cam auteurs, because Miike choreographs the action to make it comprehensible—and, more important, has spent his first two acts establishing the characters. We know who the thirteen samurai are, and we understand why many of them behave as they do under threat of death. The care taken with the screenplay and the shot composition deserves comparison to Kurosawa's (even better) *Seven Samurai.*

The film opens with stark, bloody simplicity. A man kneels in a courtyard and disembowels himself in protest against Lord Naritsugu (Goro Inagaki), the half-brother of the shogun. This seppuku was inspired by Naritsugu's cruelty, which we see demonstrated in appalling detail. He amputates some victims, kicks the severed heads of others across rooms, and exercises the right to rape anyone in his domain. He isn't a twisted caricature but a preening narcissist; the shogun inexplicably plans to promote him.

To correct this evil in the land, Sir Doi (Mikijiro Hira) seeks the samurai Shimada (Koji Yakusho), and finds him peacefully fishing atop a ladder in the sea—but with his sword, of course, nearby. Shimada then seeks another dozen warriors to join him, and this process is familiar to us from countless other movies. Each of the recruits has his own personality and backstory, some more elaborate than others, and of course there must be a little comic relief, although Koyata (Yusuke Iseya) grows more serious in the heat of battle.

The odds for these heroes seem impossible; they are only thirteen and Lord Naritsugu fields at least two hundred against them. Miike spares us the whimsy that thirteen good men can defeat two hundred evil ones, and has his samurai rig an entire village as a trap. It's clear this is planned, but the details remain vague, and when the surprises begin it would be logical, I think, to ask exactly how the assassins found the time and resources to marshal such an elaborate ambush. Logical, but not fair; you don't ask questions like that in movies that require your belief.

Samurai films have a rich history, and Miike evokes it elegantly with traditional costumes, idealistic dialogue, sharp characterizations, and a gloriously choreographed fight sequence that must extend in one form or another for forty minutes. I often find fight scenes in movies boring because they substitute movement for drama. But in *13 Assassins*, characters are involved who we know and understand, and the general melee is broken down into structured vignettes. Hollywood action directors could study this film, especially in the way it focuses on story in the midst of violence.

There is a subtext in the film. The thirteen assassins are essentially making a last stand for the traditional samurai code. Modern times are encroaching on Japan, and the shogunate is corrupt, decadent, and a hive of nepotism. I was reminded in a lateral way of Yamata's *Twilight Samurai* (2004), a very good film set in 1868, about a samurai who works for his clan as an accountant and is forced to recall the code of his tradition.

While watching *13 Assassins* I was sure CGI effects must have been used, but I was rarely able to notice them. That's the point, as it always was in traditional special effects: to deceive the eye, not insult it. Most of the movement here is at least somewhat plausible in terms of the real world. Too often CGI is an excuse for what amount to live-action cartoons. Here is a film that could be studied for its lessons by the manufacturers of Friday night action blockbusters.

35 Shots of Rum ★ ★ ★ ★

NO MPAA RATING, 99 m., 2010

Alex Descas (Lionel), Mati Diop (Josephine), Gregoire Colin (Noe), Nicole Dogue (Gabrielle), Julieth Mars Toussaint (Rene), Ingrid Caven (Jo's Aunt). Directed by Claire Denis and produced by Karl Baurmgartner and Bruno Pesery. Screenplay by Denis and Jean-Pol Fargeau.

Here is a movie about four people who have known each other for a long time, and how their relationships shift in a way that was slow in the preparation. The film makes us care for them, and so our attention is held. I've seen films where superheroes shift alliances, and I only yawned. It's not the scope of a story; it's the depth.

Part of the pleasure in Claire Denis's *35 Shots of Rum* is working out how these people are involved with each other. Two couples live across a hallway from each other in the same Paris apartment building. Neither couple is "together." Gabrielle and Noe have the vibes of roommates, but the way Lionel and Josephine obviously love each other, it's a small shock when she calls him "papa."

Lionel (Alex Descas) is a French train engineer. Jo (Mati Diop) works in a music store. Gabrielle (Nicole Dogue) drives her own taxi. Noe (Gregoire Colin) is of uncertain plans. He claims only his much-loved cat is preventing him from moving to Brazil. The four people are in and out of both apartments, and we sense they're a virtual family. Small events take place. A guy flirts with Jo at her store. Gabrielle deals with a talkative customer. Lionel and Jo both bring home rice cookers, so Jo puts hers aside so as not to hurt his feelings.

At work, Lionel attends a retirement party for a longtime engineer, Rene. His fellow workers love him, but Rene is miserable. He has no desire to retire. Afterward on a bus, he confesses to Lionel he has no idea how he got into his life to begin with. He has no desire to be an engineer. Spending his life on trains and buses is no way to live.

Lionel seems content. All four of the neighbors seem content, yes, but not completed. One night they head out together in Gabrielle's taxi to attend a concert. The taxi breaks down, they get out of the rain in a Jamaican café, there's good music on the jukebox, they dance with one another, the woman who owns the café, and others.

And in that long scene with its familiar music, Clare Denis achieves the shift. She does it not with dialogue, not with plot points, but with the eyes. This is what movies are for. They begin happy enough, but . . . incomplete. During the dancing and kidding around, it becomes clear to them, and to us, what must happen for the parts to fall into place.

Denis has long been interested in the former French colonies of West Africa, and in those who came from there to France. Lionel did, and married a German woman; she has died, but they go to visit her sister, Jo's aunt (Ingrid Caven). It is part of Lionel taking care to raise his daughter well and launch her into life. Lionel is handsome, Jo is beautiful, neither one cares.

Nicole Dogue glows in a quiet way as Gabrielle, in her forties, once no doubt stunning, now beautiful in a comfortable way. It's clear she has long been in love with Lionel. No pressure. It's clear Lionel has put that side of his life on hold to be a good father. What does he think about his job? It is a job; he's good at it. The tragedy of the retired Rene will not be his.

You can live in a movie like this. It doesn't lecture you. These people are getting on with their lives, and Denis observes them with tact. She's not intruding; she's discovering. We sense there's not a conventional plot, and that frees us from our interior moviegoing clock. We flow with them. Two are blessed; two are problematic. Will all four be blessed at the end? This is a wise movie and knows that remains to be seen.

This Is It ★ ★ ★ ★

PG, 112 m., 2009

A documentary directed by Kenny Ortega and produced by Ortega, Paul Gongaware, and Randy Phillips.

"This is it," Michael Jackson told his fans in London, announcing his forthcoming concert tour. "This is the final curtain call." The curtain fell sooner than expected. What is left is this extraordinary documentary, nothing at all like what I was expecting to see. Here is not a sick and drugged man forcing himself through grueling rehearsals, but a spirit embodied by music. Michael Jackson was something else.

The film has been assembled from rehearsals from April through June 2009 for a concert tour scheduled for last summer. The footage was "captured by a few cameras," an opening screen tells us, but they were professional high-def cameras and the sound track is full-range stereo. The result is one of the most revealing music documentaries I've seen.

And it's more than that. It's a portrait of Michael Jackson that belies all the rumors that he would have been too weak to tour. That shows not the slightest trace of a spoiled prima donna. That benefits from the limited number of cameras by allowing us to experience his work in something closer to realistic time, instead of fracturing it into quick cuts. That provides both a good idea of what the final concert would have looked like, and a portrait of the artist at work.

Never raising his voice, never showing anger, always soft-spoken and courteous to his cast and crew, Michael, with his director, Kenny Ortega, micromanages the production. He corrects timing, refines cues, talks about details of music and dance. Seeing him always from a distance, I thought of him as the instrument of his producing operation. Here we see that he was the auteur of his shows.

We know now that Michael was subjected to a cocktail of drugs in the time leading up to his fatal overdose, including the last straw, a drug so dangerous it should only be administered by an anesthesiologist in an operating room. That knowledge makes it hard to understand how he appears to be in superb physical condition. His choreography, built from such precise, abrupt, and perfectly timed movements, is exhausting, but he never shows a sign of tiring. His movements are so well synchronized with the other dancers onstage, who are much younger and highly trained, that he seems one with them. This is a man in such command of his physical instrument that he makes spinning in place seem as natural as blinking his eye.

He has always been a dancer first, and then a singer. He doesn't specialize in solos. With the exception of a sweet love ballad, his songs all incorporate four backup singers and probably supplementary tracks prerecorded by himself. It is the whole effect he has in mind.

It might have been a hell of a show. Ortega and special effects wizards coordinate prefilmed sequences with the stage work. There's a horror-movie sequence with ghouls rising from a cemetery (and ghosts that were planned to fly above the audience). Michael is inserted into scenes from Rita Hayworth and Humphrey Bogart movies, and through clever f/x even has a machine-gun battle with Bogie. His environmental pitch is backed by rain forest footage. He rides a cherry-picker high above the audience.

His audience in this case consists entirely of stagehands, gaffers, technicians, and so on. These are working people who have seen it all. They love him. They're not pretending. They love him for his music and perhaps even more for his attitude. Big stars in rehearsal are not infrequently pains in the ass. Michael plunges in with the spirit of a coworker, prepared to do the job and go the distance.

How was that possible? Even if he had the body for it, which he obviously did, how did he muster the mental strength? When you have a doctor on duty around the clock to administer the prescription medications you desire, when your idea of a good sleep is reportedly to be unconscious for twenty-four hours, how do you wake up into such a state of keen alertness? Uppers? I don't think it quite works that way. I was watching like a hawk for any hint of the effects of drug abuse, but couldn't see any. Perhaps it's significant that of all the people in the rehearsal space, he is the only one whose arms are covered at all times by long sleeves.

Well, we don't know how he did it. *This Is It* is proof that he did do it. He didn't let down his investors and colleagues. He was fully prepared for his opening night. He and Kenny Ortega, who also directed this film, were at the top of their game. There's a moving scene on the last day of rehearsal when Jackson and Ortega join hands in a circle with all the others and thank them. But the concert they worked so hard on was never to be.

This is it.

Thor ★ ½

PG-13, 114 m., 2011

Chris Hemsworth (Thor), Natalie Portman (Jane Foster), Tom Hiddleston (Loki), Anthony Hopkins (Odin), Stellan Skarsgard (Erik Selvig), Kat Dennings (Darcy Lewis), Clark Gregg (Agent Coulson). Directed by Kenneth Branagh and produced by Kevin Feige. Screenplay by Ashley Miller, Zack Stentz, and Don Payne.

I didn't attend the critics' screening for *Thor* because it was at the same time Ebertfest was showing *A Small Act*, about an eighty-eight-year-old woman named Hilde Back. She'd flown from Sweden, and I wanted be onstage to present her with the Golden Thumb. Missing *Thor 3-D* was not an inconsolable loss, because I was able to see it in Chicago in nice, bright 2-D. The house was surprisingly well populated for an 8:50 p.m. screening on a Monday, suggesting that some people, at least, will make an effort to avoid 3-D.

Thor is a failure as a movie, but a success as marketing, an illustration of the ancient carnival tactic of telling the rubes anything to get them into the tent. "You won't believe what these girls take off!" a carny barker promised me and my horny pals one steamy night at the Champaign County Fair. He was close. We didn't believe what they left on.

The failure of *Thor* begins at the story level, with a screenplay that essentially links special effects. Some of the dialogue is mock-heroic ("You are unworthy of your title, and I'll take from you your power!") and some of it winks ironically ("You know, for a crazy homeless person, he's pretty cute"). It adapts the original Stan Lee strategy for Marvel, where characters sometimes spoke out of character.

The story might perhaps be adequate for an animated film for children, with Thor, Odin, and the others played by piglets. In the arena of movies about comic book superheroes, it is a desolate vastation. Nothing exciting happens, nothing of interest is said, and the special effects evoke not a place or a time but simply special effects.

Thor, to begin with, is not an interesting character. The gods of Greek, Roman, and Norse mythology share the same problem, which is that what you see is what you get. They're defined by their attributes, not their personalities. Odin is Odin and acts as Odin and cannot act as other than Odin, and so on. Thor is a particularly limited case. What does he do? He wields a hammer. That is what he does. You don't have to be especially intelligent to wield a hammer, which is just as well, because in the film, Thor (Chris Hemsworth) doesn't seem to be the brightest bulb in Asgard.

The land (sphere? state of mind? heaven?) known as Asgard is described in Norse mythology as being near Troy, or perhaps in Asia Minor. In the movie, as nearly as I can gather, it is not of this earth and must be elsewhere in the universe. It consists of towering spires and skyscrapers linked by bridges and buttresses and betraying no sign of a population, except when untold thousands of Asgardians are required to line up at attention like robotic Nazis to receive dictates from the throne of Odin (Anthony Hopkins).

Asgard's ancient enemies are the Frost Giants, whose home is Jotunheim. I believe, but cannot promise you, that Jotunheim and Asgard are linked by a bridge, although this bridge also seems to be the way Thor reaches Earth, so perhaps it's more of a gateway through time and space, which would explain why Asgardians hurtle across intergalactic light-years and land in New Mexico without a hair out of place.

Thor is the first to arrive, and encounters three human scientists. Whether he is human himself is a question the film sidesteps. We know from mythology that gods sometimes mated with humans, which is a hopeful sign. The humans are astrophysicist Jane Foster (Natalie Portman), her friend Darcy (Kat Dennings), and the distinguished Dr. Erik Selvig (Stellan Skarsgard). I mention she's an astrophysicist because she behaves more like a storm chaser, cruising the desert in a van and peering into the skies, which won't get you far in astrophysics. The van hits Thor after he unluckily lands in front of it. This is not a Meet Cute for the gods. Later there's a meteoric event in which Thor's hammer hurtles to Earth and becomes embedded so firmly that it can't be pulled loose by a pickup truck or even the federal government.

So now Thor is on Earth, his hammer is stuck, and I am underwhelmed. Thor luckily speaks English, and Jane and her friends take him to the local diner, where he eats lots of Pop-Tarts and, when he finishes his coffee, smashes the empty cup to the ground. "We don't do that," Jane explains as if to a child, and advises him to simply order another cup, after which he apparently absorbs human behavior and the movie drops the Taming of the Thor angle.

The three scientists are thin soup. Jane flirts demurely with Thor, Darcy stands next to her and does nothing very important, and Dr. Selvig regards them gravely and looms slightly above a low-angle camera while looking on with wise concern. There is also a government agent (Clark Gregg), whose every action is the remedy to an immediate requirement of the plot.

Superhero movies live and die on the quality of their villains. *Thor* has a shabby crew. The Frost Giants spend most of their time being frosty in their subzero sphere of Jotunheim and occasionally freezing their enemies. Thor's brother Loki (Tom Hiddleston) is dark-haired, skinny, shifty-eyed, and sadly lacking in charisma. He might as well be wearing a name tag: "Hi! I can't be trusted!" These villains lack adequate interest to supply a climactic battle, so the movie fabricates a Metal Giant, sends him to the New Mexico town, and has him blast fiery rays that blow up gas stations real good but always miss his targets. He is apparently killed by a sword through his spine, but why does he need a spine, since when his mask lifts we can see his head is an empty cavern?

And what about that town? It seems to be partly a set with two interiors (the diner and Jane's office) and partly CGI. It seems to go for a few blocks and then end abruptly in barren desert. Not even any suburbs or strip malls. I know aliens from other worlds are required to arrive in New Mexico, but why stay there? Why can't the Metal Giant attack the Golden Gate Bridge or scale a Trump Tower somewhere? Who cares if he turns a 7-Eleven into a fireball?

Here is a film that is scoring 79 percent on Rotten Tomatoes. For what? The standards for comic book superhero movies have been established by *Superman*, *The Dark Knight*, *Spider-Man 2*, and *Iron Man*. In that company *Thor* is pitiful. Consider even the comparable villains (Lex Luthor, the Joker, Doc Ock, and Obadiah Stane). Memories of all four come instantly to mind. Will you be thinking of Loki six minutes after this movie is over?

The director given this project, Kenneth Branagh, once obtained funding for a magnificent 70 mm version of *Hamlet*. Now he makes *Thor*. I wonder with a dread fear if someone in Hollywood, stuck with a movie about a Norse god, said, "Get Branagh. He deals with that Shakespeare crap."

Three Monkeys ★ ★ ★

NO MPAA RATING, 109 m., 2009

Yavuz Bingol (Eyup), Hatice Aslan (Hacer), Ahmet Rifat Sungar (Ismail), Ercan Kesal (Servet). Directed by Nuri Bilge Ceylan and produced by Zeynep Ozbatur. Screenplay by Ebru Ceylan, Ercan Kesal, and Nuri Bilge Ceylan.

Nuri Bilge Ceylan's *Three Monkeys* begins on a lonely country road at night in the rain. A middle-aged driver grows sleepy at the wheel. His eyelids droop lower, and then suddenly there is a body in the road behind him, and he is awake now and weeping with fear. That's more action than took place in the whole of *Distant* (2002), Ceylan's oddly seductive film about a cousin who moves in and won't leave. This film is as steamy as the other was dry, an elegant exercise in four characters trapped by class, guilt, and greed.

There is about enough plot here to furnish a thirty-minute TV crime show, if they still made them anymore. What makes the film fascinating is its four central characters. Each one is locked within, hidden from the others, driven by private needs that all come together after the death in the forest. Ceylan films them in painterly widescreen compositions that impose a spectacular landscape, one of lowering clouds, indifferent skies, and lonely vistas. In this world, their best companions are their desires.

The sleepy man at the wheel is a politician named Servet (Ercan Kesal). He's in the middle of an election campaign. In a panic, he wakes his driver, Eyup (Yavuz Bingol), in the middle of the night and asks him to take the rap. If Eyup says he was at the wheel, Servet promises he'll get a short prison sentence, his salary will continue, and there will be cash waiting for him on his release. He agrees.

We meet Eyup's wife, Hacer (Hatice Aslan), and son, Ismail (Ahmet Rifat Sungar). They live in a spartan flat on a top floor of a strikingly narrow building with such a great view they can hardly be bothered to look indoors. She's an attractive woman of not quite a certain age, stuck for life on hold. He is a good-looking kid at an age when poor young men often find there is money to be made from crime. He comes home one night bloodied and beaten, and she decides she needs more money to help him on a career path.

Eyup is opposed to any idea of asking the politician for an advance. His reluctance is that of an employee reluctant to offend a rich and powerful man—even if he holds Servet's reputation in his hands. His wife is not swayed by such class insecurity, approaches Servet, and soon, to their mutual surprise, is having an affair with him. Sounds like the plot of a 1930s pulp crime story, especially when her son finds out.

But Ceylan is intrigued by more than just the spinning out of the story. There is something more going on. His characters are crowded for room. There's no place to escape to in their lives. They're always running up against one another's motives, needs, problems. And when Eyup gets out of prison, everything grows that much more complicated, especially as we learn more about the shaky foundations of the politician's career. Nor must we assume that his affair with the other man's wife happened only because of cash. He and his stature offer her a way out of her dead end.

These themes are always there under the surface, possibly not perceived by his characters. They come into play when the plot takes an ironic direction that places Eyup and his son in a position similar to the one the politician placed them in. That's the kind of moral scorekeeping that film noir specializes in.

The film has extraordinary beauty. Indeed, the visuals by cinematographer Gokhan Tiryaki are so awesome that the characters almost seem belittled, which may be Ceylan's purpose. They scramble about looking for ways out that life has closed to them, while the overarching sky remains indifferent. Words cannot do justice, but there are still photos at http://outnow.ch/Movies/2008/UecMaymun/Bilder/ that will blow your socks off. Click on "Ansehen" to enlarge.

The title? About the monkeys who could see no evil, hear no evil, and speak no evil, of course. Look how far that got them. The film won the Best Director Award at Cannes 2008.

Timecrimes ★ ★ ★

R, 88 m., 2009

Karra Elejalde (Hector), Candela Fernandez (Clara), Barbara Goenaga (Girl), Nacho Vigalondo (Scientist). Directed by Nacho Vigalondo and produced by Esteban Ibarretxe, Eduardo Carneros, and Javier Ibarretxe. Screenplay by Vigalondo.

Time travel in the movies is always about paradox. And it always drives me nuts. Sometimes I enjoy that, in the same way I enjoy chess—and that's a compliment. My mind gets seduced in chess by trains of thought that are hypnotic to me but, if they could be transcribed, would be unutterably boring to anyone else, since you always think of a chess piece in terms of its function, not its name: If this goes here and he moves there and I take that and he takes me back, and I reveal the check and he . . . And if you're a grand master, I don't imagine you think in many words at all. It's more like, "Hmmmm . . . aha!"

Timecrimes is like a temporal chess game with nudity, voyeurism, and violence, which makes it more boring than most chess games, but less boring than a lot of movies. It begins by introducing us to an ordinary sort of Spanish guy named Hector (Karra Elejalde), who is sitting on the lawn of his country place using his binoculars and sees a babe stripping in the woods. Now this is important. What he is witnessing is the outset of an event he has already participated in because of time travel. And when he goes to investigate, he runs the risk of running into himself, which, for paradoxical reasons, he already knows. Not this "he." The other "he."

I guess you can make up the rules of time travel as you go along, but whatever they are, they have to be inexorable, and there have to be dire consequences when a mere mortal rips the fabric of the space-time continuum. The reason we don't get more warnings of this danger, you understand, is that travelers into the past tend to do things that inalterably change the future, so that their present no longer exists for them to return to. I love this stuff.

Hector has a main squeeze named Clara (Candela Fernandez), but leaves her to go into the woods and find the Girl (Barbara Goenaga), who has been assaulted by a certain someone—don't get ahead of me here—and then a little later he meets the Scientist (Nacho Vigalondo, the movie's director), who puts him into what turns out to be a time travel machine, which had earlier or maybe later—now you're getting behind me—done something to lead Hector to sit on the lawn, or maybe see himself sitting on the lawn, or maybe—but now I'm ahead *and* behind—and now (earlier or later?) Hector wraps his bloody head (which I have explained in a review I still haven't written) so he will not be recognized by two of the three Hectors, although I am not sure whether this is Hector One, Two, or Three.

I apologize for the 147-word sentence. In time travel, bad things can happen if you stop for very long. One of the crucial requirements is apparently not to meet yourself coming or going, although if you are physically present twice at the same time, what difference does it make if you see yourself, unless it drives you mad? If I were to see myself walk into this room right now, I would simply nod to myself and ask, "Have you finished writing that review yet?" If I replied no, then I would say, "Well, I have, so why don't we eliminate the middle man and you kill yourself?"

That's not too harsh, because I would only be dying in the past of the unfinished review, see, and be here with my work all done. But then again, in that case, how could I have written it before walking into the room in the first place? I couldn't have, that's how, so that means I couldn't walk into the room, and I would continue writing the review just as I am now, which means the paradox would be solved because nothing happened, which, as nearly as I can tell, would be positive proof that time travel exists.

These problems are dealt with in *Timecrimes* in a thrilling scenario involving possible death by falling off of a roof after getting up there in an unorthodox way, and trying to save the life of a woman one of them loves, maybe two, maybe all three. This is all done in an ingenious and entertaining way. As you might imagine, *Timecrimes* is not a character study. Hector doesn't have the time for that, ha ha. In a time travel saga, by the way, it is considered bad form to wonder what makes somebody tick.

(If, after watching *Timecrimes,* you have the strangest feeling that you have seen some of these problems explored before, you are (a) merely experiencing déjà vu, which is the low-cost and safe alternative to time travel, or (b) remembering Shane Carruth's splendid *Primer* (2004), which, if it didn't drive you nuts, this one will, or has, or vice versa.)

The Time Traveler's Wife ★ ★ ½

PG-13, 107 m., 2009

Rachel McAdams (Clare), Eric Bana (Henry), Arliss Howard (Richard DeTamble), Ron Livingston (Gomez), Stephen Tobolowsky (Dr. Kendrick), Jane McLean (Charise), Brooklynn Proulx (Clare as a Child). Directed by Robert Schwentke and produced by Nick Wechsler and Dede Gardner. Screenplay by Bruce Joel Rubin, based on the novel by Audrey Niffenegger.

Clare is in love with a man who frequently disappears into thin air, leaving behind his clothing in a pile on the floor. "It can be a problem," she observes. Henry is a time traveler, and his trips are out of his control. Another problem is that whenever he arrives at another time, or even returns to the present (whenever that may be for him), he is naked. Well, that makes sense. You wouldn't expect his clothes to travel.

The dilemma of Henry (Eric Bana) and Clare (Rachel McAdams) becomes, in *The Time Traveler's Wife,* a bittersweet love story. The warmth of the actors makes it surprisingly tender, considering the premise that is blatantly absurd. If you allow yourself to think for one moment of the paradoxes, contradictions, and logical difficulties involved, you will be lost. The movie supports no objective thought.

So, OK. It's preposterous. Lots of movies are. What we're given is a lifelong love story that begins when a little girl (Brooklynn Proulx) gives her blanket to a naked man who has appeared in the shrubbery of her family's idyllic meadow. He tells her his name, that he's her friend, and that they'll see each other again. And so they do. When she's grown, she encounters him in a library and introduces herself because at this point in his life he doesn't know who she is. I know what you're asking yourself. Don't even go there.

They fall in love. They get married. Their wedding ceremony is threatened with disaster when he evaporates with minutes to go, but Henry is a stand-up guy and materializes from the future just in the nick of time to stand in for himself. His disappearances strike instantly, for example while he's carrying the dishes to their dinner table. Clare finds herself cleaning up a lot of spills. Although she gets pregnant, if he ever disappears during sex, we don't see it. From a strictly logical point of view, that would be the opposite of *ejaculatio praecox*.

Henry consults Dr. Kendrick (Stephen Tobolowsky), a genetics expert, who finds he has a genetic condition named chrono-impairment. Apparently since this trait is in all of his genes, they travel in time simultaneously, which is just as well, lest he be scattered hither and yon. One thing's for sure. It's hard to explain how a gene for time travel could develop in the Darwinian model, since it's hard to see how an organism could ever find out that was an advantage.

You have to hand it to director Robert Schwentke and screenwriter Bruce Joel Rubin (*Ghost*). They deal with these difficulties by not dealing with them at all. McAdams and Bana play their roles straight and seriously, have a pleasant chemistry, and sort of involved me in spite if myself. They're just so . . . nice. She does get around to asking a logical question: Why did he appear in the first place to that little girl in the meadow and set all of this in motion? Well, maybe he did for the simple reason that he already had, if you see what I mean.

What's remarkable is how upbeat and romantic he's able to remain, considering the difficulties of always rematerializing naked. You'd think he'd be worn down and demoralized. I guess he has some control over where that happens, as in the meadow. But in a crucial opening scene with himself as a child, how does he find two blankets by the side of a road?

He turns up regularly in Chicago—on bridges, on elevated platforms, in alleys—and always breaks and enters to grab clothes, or steals wallets (if a naked man asks you for your wallet, what do you do?). He keeps getting arrested and disappearing from the backs of police cars. The cops should put out a bulletin with an artist's rendition of his face: "If you catch this guy, don't arrest him. It's a waste of time."

Tiny Furniture ★ ★ ★

NO MPAA RATING, 98 m., 2010

Lena Dunham (Aura), Laurie Simmons (Siri), Grace Dunham (Nadine), Alex Karpovsky (Jed), Jemima Kirke (Charlotte), Rachel Howe (Candice), David Call (Keith), Amy Seimetz (Ashlynn), Sarah Sophie Flicker (Julia). Directed by Lena Dunham and produced by Kyle and Alicia Van Couvering. Screenplay by Dunham.

There is a strange space between when you leave school and when you begin work. You are idle as a painted ship upon a painted ocean. You grow restless. You cannot go back, and are uncertain how to proceed. *Tiny Furniture* is about Aura, who is becalmed on that sea.

She has graduated from college in Ohio and returned home to live in her mother's loft in TriBeCa. Her boyfriend called it quits; he had to return home to Colorado and see about the spirits of his ancestors, or something. Four years of education have left her with one video on YouTube and the ability to show approval when a guy says he's reading *The Road* by Cormac McCarthy. Her mother is a famous artist who makes a lot of money selling photographs of tiny furniture, sometimes in the same frame as the feet and legs of Nadine, Aura's sister, who is taller, thinner, and younger than Aura.

Aura (Lena Dunham) is discontented. She hates living at home but has no money to move out. She wants a good job but takes one taking reservations at a restaurant. She wants love and acceptance, and finds it much diluted by her distracted mother (Laurie Simmons) and her competitive sister (Grace Dunham). Of possible boyfriends there are: (1) Jed (Alex Karpovsky), a "big deal on YouTube," who rides a mechanical pony while reciting Nietzsche; and (2) Keith (David Call), who works at the restaurant and has a girlfriend, but asks her out and stands her up.

Aura's life unfolds without plot because there is none. The film seems deliberately motionless, although deep currents are stirring. We see Aura at home, with Jed and Keith, and with her new friend Charlotte (Jemima Kirke), who has a British accent, lends her clothes, and otherwise seems firmly one-up. None of these characters have what you might call chemistry, and that seems deliberate. This is a movie about people who are all passive-aggressive, including Aura. Nobody laughs or tries to say anything funny, and when Aura is happy sometimes, she doesn't trust it.

Aura is played by Lena Dunham, who wrote and directed the film. Her mother and her sister are played by her real mother and sister. The loft in TriBeCa is where her family lives. I have no idea if they're playing themselves, but they're certainly convincing. Dunham, indeed, plays one of the most real people I've seen outside of a documentary. She and the others are unaffected, behave as people we know actually do, live in familiar rhythms.

Visually, the film is simple and direct, as unadorned as the white cabinets that cover a wall of the loft. Dunham's cinematographer, Jody Lee Lipes, doesn't move the camera. It's locked down for a steady, flat gaze. This is correct. It sees like Aura sees. She regards with detached fascination as people behave as people will. Her personality doesn't suggest tracking shots.

Why do I feel such affection for *Tiny Furniture*? It's a well-crafted film, for one thing. For a first picture it shows a command of style and purpose; Dunham knows what she wants and how she needs to get it, and succeeds. Her character Aura is not charismatic or glowing or mercurial or seductive or any of those advertising adjectives, but she believes she deserves to be happy, and we do, too.

The movie has a scene in which sex is enacted. It isn't great sex. It calls into question Woody Allen's statement that the worst sex he'd had wasn't that bad. It happens unexpectedly between two people. It happens in the most depressing place for sex I can imagine. No, worse than whatever you're thinking. It is so desperately dutiful. Two people become seized with the urgent need to create an orgasm together, and succeed, and that exhausts the subject. The scene and what leads up to it define Aura and her partner in terms of what they will settle for. Sometimes that's better than nothing.

I know what the budget of this movie was, but never mind. Lena Dunham had every penny she required. She also had all the talent she needed, and I look forward to her work. It's hard enough for a director to work with actors, but if you're working with your own family in your own house and depicting passive-aggression, selfishness, and discontent, and you produce a film this good, you can direct just about anybody in just about anything.

Today's Special ★ ★ ★

NO MPAA RATING, 99 m., 2010

Aasif Mandvi (Samir), Jess Weixler (Carrie), Madhur Jaffrey (Farrida), Harish Patel (Hakim), Naseeruddin Shah (Akbar). Directed by David Kaplan and produced by Lillian LaSalle and Nimitt Mankad. Screenplay by Aasif Mandvi and Jonathan Bines.

I love cooking and I love Indian food, and so I had a good time during *Today's Special*. That doesn't make it a great movie, but it made it a perfectly enjoyable entertainment for me. Sometimes when you feel strongly enough about certain elements in a movie, they redeem the rest. Nothing wrong with that.

Let's begin with this: India has produced one of the world's great cuisines. You may never have tasted it. Oh, you may have gone to a restaurant like the Tandoori Palace in *Today's Special*, which is a greasy spoon in Queens. The fact is, you may have enjoyed yourself there. I have been to many all-you-can-eat Indian buffets in Chicago, London, and elsewhere, and I knew I wasn't eating great cuisine, but I also knew I was enjoying myself and the price was right.

The movie stars Aasif Mandvi as Samir, a gifted sous chef in a high-falutin' Manhattan French restaurant. He doesn't get the promotion he's counting on, resigns on the spot, and claims he has a job offer in Paris. He never gets there, alas, because his father (Harish Patel) has a heart attack. It's up to Samir to run the Palace on an emergency basis, and he's so incompetent at Indian cooking that he orders out meals from another Indian restaurant.

Enter the enigmatic taxi driver Akbar (Naseeruddin Shah), whom he meets by accident. Akbar gives him an embossed card with only his name on it, nothing else. He claims to have been a great chef back in India. In desperation to find him again, Samir enlists three old-timers who play cards in the restaurant to phone their Indian friends. After a montage of one friend calling another, Akbar is tracked down and appears at the door. I believe this is possible.

Now the film moves into its Mr. Miyagi phase, with Akbar patiently teaching Samir the meaning of cooking and of life. Samir has lost his roots, and must reconnect his cooking with his heart, mind, and stomach. This particularly involves making his own garam masala. Now I'm on the edge of my seat, attentive. Do not make the mistake of so many Westerners in assuming that garam masala is some weird name for some esoteric component of exotic cuisine. No, it is the heart of south Asian cooking. Do not confuse it with "curry."

There is no mystery. It is a yellow spice mixture of various combinations of peppercorns, cloves, malabar leaves, long pepper, black cumin, cumin seeds, cinnamon, cardamom, nutmeg, star anise, and coriander seeds. Every region and every chef has a different recipe. That need not overly concern you. Go to the spice rack, buy a jar labeled "garam masala," and Bob's your uncle. It adds interest to just about everything this side of a wedding cake.

We learn that Samir, whose parents were born in India, who considers himself a great chef, has never mixed garam masala. This is like growing up in New Orleans and having to ask what a bean is. As his father recovers and Akbar teaches him about cooking and life, Samir also begins to fall in love with Carrie (Jess Weixler), a woman he met in the French restaurant's kitchen. Akbar's recipes transform the Tandoori Palace's cuisine, and crowds begin to form. And after an obligatory setback or two, there is a happy ending.

The movie's in-joke is that Samir's mother is played by Madhur Jaffrey. She is not only a considerable actress but a world-famous chef, whose cookbook taught me to seal a pot with flour paste to allow chicken and butter to bake in a sea of spices. Yum. Here she plays a typical Indian mother, despairing of her Westernized son and her impossible husband. It's like having Julia Child play the chef's mother-in-law.

So now you understand why I enjoyed the film. I know it is flawed. I know the story arc is as old as the hills. The romance is cut and dried. Akbar is well acted, but he is a story device. Aasif Mandvi is fun (he plays one of Jon Stewart's senior correspondents on *The Daily Show*). But as a movie, *Today's Special* is only just OK. What saves it, as it saves so very many things, is the garam masala.

Tokyo! ★ ★ ½

NO MPAA RATING, 112 m., 2009

A film in three segments: *Interior Design,* with Ayako Fujitani, Ryo Kase, and Ayumi Ito. Directed by Michel Gondry. Screenplay by Gondry and Gabrielle Bell. *Merde,* with Denis Lavant. Directed by Leos Carax. Screenplay by Carax. *Shaking Tokyo,* with Teruyuki Kagawa, Yu Aoi, and Naoto Takenaka. Directed by Bong Joon-ho. Screenplay by Bong.

Three directors, three films, three reasons to rethink moving to Tokyo: You can't find a place to live, there are earthquakes, and a weird goblin may leap from a sewer and grab your sandwich. *Tokyo!* assigns the French filmmakers Michel Gondry and Leos Carax and the Korean Bong Joon-ho to create their own visions of the megalopolis, which would seem to spawn oddly adapted inhabitants.

The best of the three is *Merde*, the centerpiece by Carax, a director whose films are willfully, sometimes successfully, odd. He stars Denis Lavant as a haywire subterranean denizen who pops off a sewer lid, scrambles to the sidewalk, lurches down the street, and rudely assaults pedestrians. He grabs cigarettes, sandwiches, and arms, alarms a baby, terrorizes the populace, and disappears into another manhole.

He is captured and hauled into court, where a translator is found who allegedly speaks his unknown language. Here he wickedly reviles Japan, its citizens, and specifically its women. It remains unclear why he has chosen to live in sewers. This segment is, oddly enough, similar to some Japanese reality shows, such as *The Screamer,* where a man with an ear-piercing scream is photographed by hidden cameras while he sneaks up behind people and lets loose. What a scream.

Shaking Tokyo, directed by Bong Joon-ho, stars Teruyuki Kagawa as a *hikikomori,* a type so familiar the Japanese have a name for it. A hikikomori, usually male, decides to stay inside one day and essentially never leaves. Some have been reported as hermits for up to ten years, living mostly on pizza deliveries. In America we call these people "software engineers." One day the hero is jarred loose from his isolation by a pretty pizza delivery girl, not to mention an earthquake, which sends others into the unpopulated and barren streets for the first time in months.

Michel Gondry's *Interior Design,* an only slightly more conventional tale, stars Ayako Fujitani and Ryo Kase as young lovers new in Tokyo, who undergo personal and physical changes during the ordeal of apartment hunting. Much more I should not say.

Do these films reflect actual aspects of modern Tokyo? The hikikomori epidemic is apparently real enough, but the other two segments seem more deliberately fantastical. The entertainment value? Medium to high (*Merde*). Tokyo? Still standing.

Tokyo Sonata ★ ★ ★ ½

PG-13, 119 m., 2009

Teruyuki Kagawa (Ryuhei Sasaki), Kyoko Koizumi (Megumi Sasaki), Yu Koyanagi (Takashi Sasaki), Kai Inowaki (Kenji Sasaki), Haruka Igawa (Kaneko), Kanji Tsuda (Kurosu), Koji Yakusho (Thief). Directed by Kiyoshi Kurosawa and produced by Yukie Kito and Wouter Barendrecht. Screenplay by Kurosawa, Max Mannix, and Sachiko Tanaka.

Just as the economic crisis has jolted everyday life, so it shakes up *Tokyo Sonata,* which begins as a well-behaved story and takes detours into the comic, the macabre, and the sublime. All you know about three-act structure is going to be useless in watching this film, even though, like many sonatas, it has three movements.

It opens on a note of routine, of a family so locked into their lives that they scarcely know one another. Ryuhei is a salaryman in a management job. His wife, Megumi, is a source of predictable domesticity, centering on cleaning, sewing, and the preparation of meals. His older son, Takashi, and younger son, Kenji, are filled with unhappiness but seemingly well disciplined, although Kenji gets in trouble at school: The teacher unfairly blames him for passing along a manga, or graphic novel, and Kenji defiantly says he saw the teacher reading a porno manga on the train. Many men in Japan do the same, no big deal, but hypocrisy is the point.

In the opening scene, Ryuhei (Teruyuki Kagawa) is fired. He comes home, hands over his week's wages, says nothing. He is an autocratic father, filled with anger. The older son, Takashi (Yu Koyanagi), announces he has enlisted for the U.S. Army as a way to gain citizenship, as he sees no future for himself in Japan. His father forbids him.

Unable to lose face by admitting his job loss, Ryuhei leaves "for the office" every day and lingers in a cheerless concrete oasis with other jobless men. There is a soup kitchen. His wife sees him there, knows everything, stays quiet. Young Kenji (Kai Inowaki), no longer attending school, spends his money on piano lessons with the beautiful Kaneko (Haruka Igawa). His father, breaking with the Japanese tradition of encouraging children to study, has already forbidden piano lessons. Why? Perhaps he feels so inadequate he's threatened by any success involving his family.

What we seem to have are the outlines of a traditional family drama, in which tensions are bottled up, revelations will occur, and a crisis will result in either tragedy or resolution. But that's not what we're given by director Kiyoshi Kurosawa, best known for upscale horror films. He almost misleads us in the early scenes, by framing the family dinners in sedate and orderly compositions. We believe we know where *Tokyo Sonata* is going. We are wrong.

No, it doesn't turn into another horror film, or a murder-suicide. It simply shows how lives torn apart by financial emergencies can be revealed as being damaged all along. Unemployment is the catalyst—an unspoken reality that makes everyone in the family angrier than they already are. All of the performances have perfect pitch; the young son engages us in the same way as the hero of Truffaut's *The 400 Blows.*

The directions the film takes I should not reveal. But notice how Kurosawa (no relation) allows his train to leave the tracks. Dramatic events occur that demonstrate how a routine, once broken, cannot easily be repaired. The entrance of a completely unexpected character results in an instinctive acceptance of the new situation, providing a sad payoff to what at first seems merely arbitrary.

At the same time, Kurosawa observes the

agony of unemployment in Japan, which, like the United States, has been beset by outsourcing to cheaper labor pools. (The day when China and India begin outsourcing will be a historic turning point.) Ryuhei joins hopeless queues at an employment office. He finds work cleaning toilets in a shopping mall. His humiliation is underlined when all maintenance workers must change into one-piece coveralls at lockers in full view of passing customers. He has an encounter at work that is bizarre.

And then the film finds a form of release in another unexpected scene. Watch it play out. We are blindsided by its beauty. An extended passage is held in a medium-long shot in which nobody moves, and the effect is uncanny. Is there a happy ending? Nothing as simple as that. Simply a new beginning. Debris has been cleared. Old tapes have been destroyed. Freedom has been asserted. Nothing is for sure.

A sonata is a classical form in which two musical ideas are intercut. In the beginning, they are introduced. In the following sections, they are developed in passages revealing the secrets or potentials of both. The conclusion does not resolve them; instead, we return to look at them, knowing what we know now. The "themes" in this movie are the father and his family. At the end they feel the same tensions as at the beginning, but the facade has been destroyed, and they will have to proceed unprotected.

Tooth Fairy ★ ★

PG, 101 m., 2010

Dwayne Johnson (Derek Thompson), Ashley Judd (Carly), Stephen Merchant (Tracy), Julie Andrews (Lily), Billy Crystal (Jerry), Destiny Whitlock (Tess), Chase Ellison (Randy). Directed by Michael Lemback and produced by Jason Blum, Mark Ciard, and Gordon Gray. Screenplay by Lowell Ganz, Babaloo Mandel, Joshua Sternin, Jeffrey Ventimilia, and Randi Mayem Singer.

In the pantheon of such legends as Santa Claus and the Bogeyman, the Tooth Fairy ranks down in the minor leagues, I'd say, with Jack Frost and the Easter Bunny. There is a scene in *Tooth Fairy* when the hero is screamed at by his girlfriend for even *beginning* to suggest to her six-year-old that there isn't a Tooth Fairy, but surely this is a trauma a child can survive. Don't kids simply humor their parents to get the dollar?

The film reveals that there's not one Tooth Fairy anyway, but a whole workforce, tightly scheduled and supervised by the strict head fairy (Julie Andrews). This comes as rather an astonishment to a rugged hockey player named Derek, played by Dwayne (The Rock) Johnson, who is sentenced to a term in Fairy Land for almost spoiling the young girl's faith. It happens so abruptly that he finds himself wearing a pink tutu. Oddly, a still photo of this sight is not included in the movie's press materials.

Derek's nickname in pro hockey is "The Tooth Fairy" because he is a specialist in body-slamming opponents so hard that you can fill in the rest. He hasn't scored a goal in ages. The coach puts him in just so he can take someone out. He spends so much time in the penalty box he has his own recliner installed.

The Rock plays this role straight, which is basically the way he plays every role. He's a pleasant, relaxed screen presence, but a Method Actor he's not. His idea of a tone for the Tooth Fairy is sincerity.

The movie's best scenes involve Fairy Land, where a brisk but very tall fairy social worker named Tracy (Stephen Merchant) adds some quirkiness. Merchant is a six-foot-seven British comedian, inheritor of the possibly genetic trait that populated Monty Python. His great regret in life is that he was never issued wings. Also in Fairy Land is Jerry (Billy Crystal), in charge of magic weapons, who issues Derek visibility sprays and suchlike.

Look, I hate to say this, but Billy Crystal has put on a few pounds. I say it not as a criticism but as an observation. Good for him. He seems more avuncular now, more confiding. Maybe he could start looking for dramatic roles as your favorite wise-guy uncle. Anyway, I've noticed in a lot of movies lately that the stars I've grown old with have, good lord, also grown old with me. There's a kind of fascination in how film so accurately records the passage of time. Julie Andrews, by still looking like Julie Andrews, seems to be swimming upstream.

Derek's girlfriend, mentioned above, is

played by the divine Ashley Judd, thanklessly. I guess as an actor you know that in a movie named *Tooth Fairy* you're going to have a lot of scenes where you're tucking someone in. Fair enough, but where can you go with them dramatically?

The film is rated PG. I wondered why it didn't make Derek a husband instead of a boyfriend, but parents can relax: He seems to sleep on the couch. Uh, huh. The chemistry between the two suggests that they're together primarily because they work so well together at tucking time.

There's no way I can recommend this movie to anyone much beyond the Tooth Fairy Believement Age, but I must testify it's pleasant and inoffensive, although the violence in the hockey games seems out of place. It must be said in closing that given his nickname and reputation, it's a miracle the Tooth Fairy has been allowed to survive with such a dazzling row of pearlies.

The Tourist ★ ★

PG-13, 104 m., 2010

Angelina Jolie (Elise Clifton-Ward), Johnny Depp (Frank Tupelo), Paul Bettany (Acheson), Timothy Dalton (Jones), Steven Berkoff (Reginald Shaw), Rufus Sewell (The Englishman), Bruno Wolkowitch (French Sergeant). Directed by Florian Henckel von Donnersmarck and produced by Gary Barber, Roger Birnbaum, Jonathan Glickman, Tim Headington, and Graham King. Screenplay by Henckel von Donnersmarck, Christopher McQuarrie, and Julian Fellowes.

There's a way to make a movie like *The Tourist*, but Florian Henckel von Donnersmarck doesn't find that way. Here is a romantic comedy crossed with a crime thriller, shot in Paris and Venice, involving a glamorous mystery woman and a math teacher from Wisconsin. The plot is preposterous. So what you need is a movie that floats with bemusement above the cockamamie, and actors who tease one another.

Angelina Jolie does her darnedest. She gets the joke. Here is a movie in which she begins in a Paris cafe, eludes cops by dashing into the Metro, takes an overnight train to Venice, picks up a strange man (Johnny Depp), and checks them both into the Royal Danieli without one wrinkle on her dress or one hair out of place. And is sexy as hell. This is the Audrey Hepburn or Grace Kelly role, and she knows it.

Depp is in the Cary Grant role, of the obliging, love-struck straight man who falls in love and finds himself neck deep in somebody else's troubles. In theory these two should engage in witty flirtation and droll understatement. In practice, no one seems to have alerted Depp that the movie is a farce. I refer to "farce" in the dictionary sense, of course: *A comic dramatic work using buffoonery and horseplay and typically including crude characterization and ludicrously improbable situations.* Depp plays his math teacher seriously and with a touch of the morose.

The plot involves—oh, hell, you know, the usual mystery man who has stolen millions from a gangster and gone into hiding while meanwhile smuggling instructions to Jolie, his lover, instructing her to take the train to Venice, etc. And the cops from Scotland Yard who are tailing her in hopes of nailing the guy. And the gangster and his hit men who are also on the thief's trail. And chases over the rooftops of Venice, and dinner on a train, and a scene in a casino, and designer gowns, and a chase through the canals with Jolie at the controls of a motor taxi, and . . .

Well, there was really only one cliché left, and I was grateful when it arrived. You know how a man in a high place will look down and see a canvas awning that might break his fall, and he jumps into it? Yep. And it's shielding a fruit cart at the open-air market and he lands on the oranges and runs off leaving the cart owner shaking his fist. This is a rare example of the Vertical Fruit Cart Scene, in which the cart is struck not from the side but from the top.

The supporting roles are filled by excellent actors, and it's a sign of the movie's haplessness that none of them make a mark. You have Paul Bettany and Timothy Dalton as cops, Steven Berkoff as the gangster and Rufus Sewell as "The Englishman," who must be important because he hangs around without any apparent purpose. Once in London I saw Steven Berkoff play a cockroach in his adaptation of Kafka's *Metamorphosis.* It might have helped this role if he'd tried the cockroach again.

A depressing element is how much talent *The Tourist* has behind the camera. Florian Henckel von Donnersmarck, the director, made *The Lives of Others*, winner of the Oscar for best foreign film in 2007. The screenplay is by Henckel von Donnersmarck, Christopher McQuarrie (an Oscar for *The Usual Suspects*), and Julian Fellowes (an Oscar for *Gosford Park*). It's based on a French film written by Jerome Salle, which was nominated for a Cesar. All three winners seem to have used their awards as doorstops.

It doesn't matter that the plot is absurd. That goes with the territory. But if it's not going to be nonstop idiotic action, then the acting and dialog need a little style and grace and kidding around. Jolie plays her femme fatale with flat-out, drop-dead sexuality. Depp plays his Wisconsin math teacher as a man waiting for the school bell to ring so he can go bowling. The other actors are concealed in the shadows of their archetypes. Cary Grant would have known how to treat a lady.

The Town ★ ★ ★

R, 124 m., 2010

Ben Affleck (Doug MacRay), Rebecca Hall (Claire Keesey), Jon Hamm (Special Agent Adam Frawley), Jeremy Renner (Jem Coughlin), Blake Lively (Krista Coughlin), Titus Welliver (Dino Ciampa), Pete Postlethwaite (Fergie Colm), Chris Cooper (Stephen MacRay). Directed by Ben Affleck and produced by Basil Iwanyk and Graham King. Screenplay by Affleck, Peter Craig, and Aaron Stockard, based on the novel *Prince of Thieves* by Chuck Hogan.

There's a scene in Ben Affleck's *The Town* that expertly exploits the conversations we have with movie characters. In critical moments we urgently send mental instructions to the screen. Let me set up such a moment here. Doug cares for Claire. There's something she mustn't know about him. If she should see the tattoo on the back of Jem's neck, she would know everything. Jem unexpectedly joins Doug and Claire at a table. With hard looks and his whole manner, Doug signals him to get the hell away from the table. So do we. Jem is a dangerous goofball, and sadistically lingers. He doesn't know the tattoo is a giveaway.

If a film can bring us to this point and make us feel anxiety, it has done something right. *The Town*, Affleck's second film as a director, wants to do something more, to make a biographical and even philosophical statement about the culture of crime, but it doesn't do that as successfully. Here is a well-made crime procedural, and audiences are likely to enjoy it at that level, but perhaps the mechanics of movie crime got in the way of Affleck's higher ambitions.

There are two fairly extended scenes in the film, for example, during which bank robbers with machine guns exchange fire with a large number of cops. My opinion is that when automatic weapons are used by experienced shooters at less than a block's distance, a lot of people are going to get killed or wounded. It becomes clear in *The Town* that nobody will get shot until and/or unless the screenplay requires it, and that causes an audience letdown. We feel the story is no longer really happening, and we're being asked to settle yet once again for a standard chase-and-gunfight climax.

I believe Affleck, his writers, and their source (the novel *Prince of Thieves* by Chuck Hogan) know better, and their characters deserve better. But above a certain budget level, Hollywood films rarely allow complete follow-through for their characters. Consider the widespread public dislike for the year's best crime film, George Clooney's *The American*. People didn't want a look into the soul of an existential criminal. They wanted a formula to explain everything.

In *The Town*, Ben Affleck plays Doug MacRay, the next generation of a bank-robbing family in the Charlestown area of Boston. This square mile, we're told, contains more thieves and bank robbers than anyplace else in the country. It's a family trade, like cobbling or the law. Affleck heads a four-man crew most notably including Jem (a pudgy, loopy Jeremy Renner, miles different than in *The Hurt Locker*). They plan their jobs meticulously, going to lengths to eradicate DNA traces and confiscate security tapes. But Jem has a wild streak. He injures civilians when it's not necessary, and during one job does what is forbidden: He takes a hostage, Claire (Rebecca Hall). Kidnapping is a heavy-duty crime.

They release Claire unharmed. Turns out she lives in Charlestown. Jem gets paranoid. Doug trails her to a Laundromat, meets her by "accident," gets to know and quite unexpectedly gets to like her. This is what *The Town* is really about—how getting to know Claire opens Doug's mind to the fullness of a life his heritage has denied him. The film could have continued to grow in that direction, but instead pulls back and focuses on more crime. We meet Doug's hard-boiled father (Chris Cooper) in prison, and a local crime lord (Pete Postlethwaite, unrelenting). And we follow an FBI team led by Jon Hamm. They have a good idea whom they're looking for; you don't make a career out of bank robbery in Charlestown without the word getting around. But they lack evidence they can take to a jury.

The most intriguing character is Jem. As played by Renner, he's a twisted confusion of behavior, a loose cannon on a team that requires discipline. He's furious when he finds Doug friendly with the woman who could finger them, and the jumpy way he plays friendly is chilling. There's something interesting going on here: Doug is the central character and all interest should move to him, but at about the halfway point it becomes clear that his character has been deprived of impulse and committed to an acceptable ending. Jem, however, remains capable of anything. If you've seen a lot of Jeremy Renner before, you may need to look twice to recognize him; it's like the hero of *The Hurt Locker* moved to Boston and started on a diet of beer, brats, and fries.

The Town shows, as his first film *Gone Baby Gone* (2007) did, that Affleck has the stuff of a real director. Everything is here. It's an effective thriller, he works closely with the actors, he has a feel for pacing. Yet I persist in finding chases and gun battles curiously boring. I realize the characters have stopped making the decisions and the stunt and effects artists have taken over.

A Town Called Panic ★ ★ ★ ½

NO MPAA RATING, 75 m., 2010

With the voices of: Stephane Aubier (Cowboy), Bruce Ellison (Indian), Vincent Patar (Horse), Jeanne Balibar (Madame Longray), Frederic Jannin (Policeman), Benoit Poelvoorde (Farmer). Directed by Stephane Aubier and Vincent Patar and produced by Philippe Kauffmann and Vincent Tavier. Screenplay by Aubier and Patar.

You know how kids play with little plastic action figures that balance their feet on their own little platforms? And how they're not on the same scale? And how kids move them around while doing their voices and making up adventures for them? And how literally anything is likely to happen in those adventures? Then you have a notion of the goofy charm generated by this new animated comedy from Belgium.

A Town Called Panic is well named because it takes place in a town where panic is a daily emotion. Here, in a house on a hill much larger inside than out, live the friendly roommates Cowboy, Indian, and Horse. Their neighbor is Farmer. Law is enforced by Policeman.

It is Horse's birthday, and Cowboy and Indian decide his gift must be a brick barbecue. They go online to order fifty bricks, but order fifty million through a computer error, which causes no end of problems, especially when Cowboy and Indian stack them on top of the house, hoping to conceal their foolishness from Horse. I should explain that Horse seems to be the responsible adult.

Everybody talks like little kids. Indian and Horse are on the same scale, about twice as tall as Cowboy, although nobody notices this. They get around fine on their little platforms, even climbing stairs. Horse, who has four legs and can balance without a platform, takes Farmer's kids to Madame Longray's music lessons and falls in love with Madame, who is also a horse and plays the piano with her hooves, pretty well.

The most frequent line of dialogue in this enchanting world is *Oh, no!* One strange thing happens after another. You wouldn't believe me if I told you how Horse, Indian, and Cowboy all end up perched precariously on a rock slab above a volcano at the center of the earth, or how they get from there to the middle of an ocean and the North Pole, or how they happen upon a mad scientist and his robot, named Penguin, or the excuses Horse uses on his cell phone to explain to Madame Longray why he hasn't turned up for his piano lessons. Or why it rains cows.

A Town Called Panic is the work of Stephane Aubier and Vincent Patar, a Belgian team that first created this world in a group of short films that became enormously popular in 2003 on European television. I've never seen anything like this style. It's stop-action, but *really* stop-action, you understand, because that's the nature of plastic action figures. Cowboy and Indian can move their arms when they need to, but their platforms keep them upright.

I enjoyed this film so much I'm sorry to report it was finally too much of a muchness. You can only eat so much cake. But I don't think that's a problem. Like all animated family films, this one will find a long life and its greatest popularity on video. And because the plot is just one doggone thing after another without the slightest logic, there's no need to watch it all the way through at one sitting. If you watch it a chapter or two at a time, it should hold up nicely.

Now don't get me wrong. I'm glad I saw it on the big screen. It has an innocent, hallucinatory charm. The friendship of the three pals is sweet. I liked Horse's bashfulness when he's smitten with Madame Longray. And his patience with Indian and Cowboy, who get them into one fine fix after another.

Toy Story 3 ★ ★ ★

G, 102 m., 2010

With the voices of: Tom Hanks (Woody), Tim Allen (Buzz Lightyear), Joan Cusack (Jessie), Ned Beatty (Lotso), Don Rickles (Mr. Potato Head), Michael Keaton (Ken), Wallace Shawn (Rex), John Ratzenberger (Hamm), Estelle Harris (Mrs. Potato Head), John Morris (Andy), Jodi Benson (Barbie), Blake Clark (Slinky Dog). Directed by Lee Unkrich and produced by Darla K. Anderson. Screenplay by Unkrich, Michael Arndt, John Lasseter, and Andrew Stanton.

The first two *Toy Story* movies centered on the relationship between a boy and his toys. In Pixar's *Toy Story 3*, young Andy has grown to college age and the story leaves the toys pretty much on their own. In a third act where they find themselves fighting for life on a conveyor belt to a garbage incinerator, we fear it could be renamed *Toy Story Triage.*

The problems all begin with that most dreaded of commands, "Clean out your room!" No mother in history understands that a boy's room has all of his stuff *exactly where he needs it,* even if he dumped it there ten years earlier. Andy's mom gives him three choices: (1) attic; (2) donation to a day care center; (3) trash. Examining his old toys, his gaze lingers fondly on Woody (voice by Tom Hanks), and he decides to take him along to college.

What with one thing and another the other toys find themselves at the day care center, which they think they'll like because there will be plenty of kids to play with them all day long. There seems to be relatively little grieving about the loss of Andy's affections; he did, after all, sentence them to a toy box for years, and toys by nature are self-centered and want to be played with.

Day care seems like a happy choice, until a dark underside of its toy society emerges in the person of an ominously hug-prone bear (Ned Beatty). They pick up, however, some additions to their little band, including Barbie and Ken dolls with extensive wardrobes. If you ask me, Barbie (Jodi Benson) is anorexic, and Ken (Michael Keaton) is gay, but nobody in the movie knows this, so I'm just sayin'.

Buzz Lightyear (Tim Allen) is back, still in hapless hero mode, but after a reboot he starts speaking Spanish and that leads to some funny stuff. I also enjoyed the dilemma of Mrs. Potato Head (Estelle Harris), whose missing eye continues to see independently of her head. This raises intriguing physiological questions, such as, if Mr. Potato Head lost an ear, would it continue to hear, or if he lost a mouth, would it continue to eat without a body? These are not academic questions; at one point, Mister becomes an uncooked taco shell. Mr. and Mrs. Potato Head must be old hands at such dilemmas, since children spend most of their time attaching their body parts in the wrong way, like malpracticing little Dr. Frankensteins.

Man, the toys have a dangerous time of it after they eventually find themselves at a garbage collection center. You have no idea what garbage has to go through before becoming landfill, and even an Indiana Jones toy would have trouble surviving the rotating blades. There is a happy ending, of course, but I suspect these toys may be traumatized for eternity.

This is a jolly, slapstick comedy, lacking the almost eerie humanity that infused the earlier *Toy Story* sagas, and happier with action and jokes than with characters and emotions. But hey, what can you expect from a movie named *Toy Story 3*, especially with the humans mostly offstage? I expect its target audience will love it, and at the box office it may take right up where *How to Train Your Dragon* left off. Just don't get me started about the 3-D.

Transformers: Dark of the Moon ★

PG-13, 154 m., 2011

Shia LaBeouf (Sam Witwicky), Markiss McFadden ("Baby Face"), Rosie Huntington-Whiteley (Carly), Kenneth Sheard (Marc L), Josh Duhamel (Lennox), John Turturro (Simmons), Tyrese Gibson (Epps), Patrick Dempsey (Dylan), Frances McDormand (Mearing), John Malkovich (Bruce Brazos), Kevin Dunn (Ron Witwicky), Julie White (Judy Witwicky), Alan Tudyk (Dutch), Ken Jeong (Jerry Wang), Glenn Morshower (General Morshower). Directed by Michael Bay and produced by Ian Bryce, Tom DeSanto, Lorenzo di Bonaventura, and Don Murphy. Screenplay by Ehren Kruger.

Michael Bay's *Transformers: Dark of the Moon* is a visually ugly film with an incoherent plot, wooden characters, and inane dialogue. It provided me with one of the more unpleasant experiences I've had at the movies.

The series exists to show gigantic and hideous robots hammering one another. So it does. The last hour involves a battle for the universe that for some reason is held at the corner of Michigan Avenue and Wacker Drive in Chicago. This battle is protracted mercilessly beyond all reason, at an ear-shattering sound level, with incomprehensible Autobots and Decepticons sliced up into spurts of action with no sense of the space they occupy.

There is more of a plot in this third *Transformers*. It is a plot that cannot be described in terms of structure, more in terms of duration. When it stops, it's over. We learn that mankind's first mission to the moon was intended to investigate an alien spacecraft that crashed on the dark side. This ship, "the Arc," carried the robots to this solar system from their own, so that the good bots could continue their struggle for "freedom" against the bad bots. It is a bad omen when Lincoln's statue on the National Mall is decapitated.

Humans get involved. These include Sam Witwicky (Shia LaBeouf), who earlier saved the world but now has a job in a mail room, and Carly (Rosie Huntington-Whiteley), who is his sexy girlfriend because the movie requires a sexy girlfriend. There are also such characters as Mearing (Frances McDormand), a government official; Bruce Brazos (John Malkovich), Sam's anal-retentive boss; Carly's former boyfriend Dylan (Patrick Dempsey), whose classic-car collection upstages every robot in the movie; the FBI manipulator Simmons (John Turturro); the peculiar Jerry Wang (Ken Jeong); and the expert warriors Lennox (Josh Duhamel) and Epps (Tyrese Gibson). If you pause to consider for a second, not one of these characters is actually required in the conflict, which is, after all, pretty much between the bots.

Oh, but the humans are needed for us. They are required because bots have no personalities and little intrinsic interest apart from the banging noises they make. They speak in dubbed English that sounds oddly separate from the other voices in the film. And they are so many times larger than the humans that I was reminded of the scale used in *The Incredible Shrinking Man*. We also need people because I, for one, will never care for Optimus Prime any more than for an engine block.

There is no style or wit in the dialogue, except when Malkovich adds his own spin. This is one of those annoying pictures where disembodied voices are heard during chaotic action: "Class dismissed!" "Decepticon punk!" "We've got a Mexican standoff here!" "What do you think you're doing?" "Return what belongs to me!"

Shia LaBeouf is scarcely heroic, and his girlfriend has no particular function except to be in constant peril and (in two hilarious shots) stare thoughtfully into space as if realizing something. The only considerable dramatic scene LaBeouf has is when his mother (Julie White) brings the manic plot to a standstill long enough to urge a self-help book upon her son.

I hesitate to mention another problem with the film because in all fairness it may not be Bay's fault. The framing looks wrong. When you look at enough movies, you develop a sixth sense for what feels correct within the frame. This film seemed too close to its compositions. There was a paucity of headroom, feet were nearly cut off, the sides seemed to squeeze. This wasn't dramatic, but I could feel it.

Of course, I could be mistaken. If I'm correct, here's what may have happened. In the multiplex theater originally set for the screening, it was explained, technicians spent three hours programming the 3-D projector—and then their programming didn't "take." The multiplex resourcefully moved the film to another screen already configured for 3-D. I suspect, however, that the aspect ratio in that room was not quite correct.

Nothing, however, would have repaired the film's lack of narrative coherence. I have a quaint notion that one of the purposes of editing is to make it clear why one shot follows another, or why several shots occur in the order that they do. *Transformers 3* has long stretches involving careless and illogical assemblies of inelegant shots. One special effect happens, and then another special effect happens, and we are expected to be grateful that we have seen two special effects.

Note: Bay is said to have tried to improve the characteristic light level of 3-D. In my screening, it was as dim as usual.

Transformers: Revenge of the Fallen ★

PG-13, 149 m., 2009

Shia LaBeouf (Sam Witwicky), Megan Fox (Mikaela Banes), Josh Duhamel (Captain Lennox), Tyrese Gibson (USAF Tech Sergeant Epps), John Turturro (Gent Simmons/Jetfire), Ramon Rodriguez (Leo), Kevin Dunn (Ron Witwicky), Rainn Wilson (Professor Colan), Julie White (Judy Witwicky), Hugo Weaving (Megatron). Directed by Michael Bay and produced by Ian Bryce, Tom DeSanto, Lorenzo di Bonaventura, and Don Murphy. Screenplay by Ehren Kruger, Roberto Orci, and Alex Kurtzman.

Transformers: Revenge of the Fallen is a horrible experience of unbearable length, briefly punctuated by three or four amusing moments. One of these involves a doglike robot humping the leg of the heroine. Such are the meager joys. If you want to save yourself the ticket price, go into the kitchen, cue up a male choir singing the music of hell, and get a kid to start banging pots and pans together. Then close your eyes and use your imagination.

The plot is incomprehensible. The dialogue of the Autobots, Deceptibots, and Otherbots is meaningless word flap. Their accents are Brooklynese, British, and hip-hop, as befits a race from the distant stars. Their appearance looks like junkyard throw-up. They are dumb as rocks. They share the film with human characters who are much more interesting, and that is very faint praise indeed.

The movie has been signed by Michael Bay. This is the same man who directed *The Rock* in 1996. Now he has made *Transformers: Revenge of the Fallen.* Faust made a better deal. This isn't a film so much as a toy tie-in. Children holding a Transformer toy in their hand can invest it with wonder and magic, imagining it doing brave deeds and remaining always their friend. I knew a little boy once who lost his blue toy truck at the movies and cried as if his heart would break. Such a child might regard *Transformers: Revenge of the Fallen* with fear and dismay.

The human actors are in a witless sitcom part of the time, and a lot of the rest of their time is spent running in slo-mo away from explosions, although—hello!—you can't outrun an explosion. They also make speeches like this one by John Turturro: "Oh, no! The machine is buried in the pyramid! If they turn it on, it will destroy the sun!" "Not on my watch!" The humans, including lots of U.S. troops, shoot at the Transformers a lot, although never in the history of science fiction has an alien been harmed by gunfire.

There are many great-looking babes in the film, who are made up to a flawless perfection and look just like real women, if you are a junior fanboy whose experience of the gender is limited to lad magazines. The two most inexplicable characters are Ron and Judy Witwicky (Kevin Dunn and Julie White), who are the parents of Shia LaBeouf, whom Mephistopheles threw in to sweeten the deal. They take their son away to Princeton, apparently a party school, where Judy eats some pot and goes berserk. Later they swoop down out of the sky on Egypt, for reasons the movie doesn't make crystal clear, so they also can run in slo-mo from explosions.

The battle scenes are bewildering. A Bot makes no visual sense anyway, but two or three tangled up together create an incomprehensible confusion. I find it amusing that creatures that can unfold out of a Camaro and stand four stories high do most of their fighting with fists. Like I said, dumber than a box of staples. They have tiny little heads, except for Starscream, who is so ancient he has an aluminum beard.

Aware that this movie opened in England seven hours before Chicago time, and the morning papers would be on the streets, after writing the above I looked up the first reviews as a reality check. I was reassured: "Like watching paint dry while getting hit over the head with a frying pan!" (Bradshaw, *Guardian*); "Sums up everything that is most tedious, crass and despicable about modern Hollywood!" (Tookey, *Daily Mail*); "A giant, lumbering idiot of a movie!" (Edwards, *Daily Mirror*). The first American review, however, reported that it feels "destined to be the biggest movie of all time" (Todd Gilchrist, Cinematical). It's certainly the biggest something of all time.

The Tree of Life ★ ★ ★ ★

PG-13, 138 m., 2011

Brad Pitt (Mr. O'Brien), Sean Penn (Jack), Jessica Chastain (Mrs. O'Brien), Fiona Shaw (Grandmother), Hunter McCracken (Young Jack). Directed by Terrence Malick and produced by Dede Gardner, Sarah Green, Grant Hill, Brad Pitt, and William Pohlad. Screenplay by Malick.

Terrence Malick's *The Tree of Life* is a film of vast ambition and deep humility, attempting no less than to encompass all of existence and view it through the prism of a few infinitesimal lives. The only other film I've seen with this boldness of vision is Kubrick's *2001: A Space Odyssey*, and it lacked Malick's fierce evocation of human feeling. There were once several directors who yearned to make no less than a masterpiece, but now there are only a few. Malick has stayed true to that hope ever since his first feature in 1973.

I don't know when a film has connected more immediately with my own personal experience. In uncanny ways, the central events of *The Tree of Life* reflect a time and place I lived in, and the young boys in it are me. If I set out to make an autobiographical film, and if I had Malick's gift, it would look so much like this. His scenes portray a childhood in a small town in the American midlands, where life flows in and out through open windows. There is a father who maintains discipline and a mother who exudes forgiveness, and long summer days of play and idleness and urgent, unsaid questions about the meaning of things. The three boys of the O'Brien family are browned by the sun, scuffed by play, disturbed by glimpses of adult secrets, filled with a great urgency to grow up and discover who they are.

I wrote earlier about the many ways this film evoked my own memories of such a time and place. About wide lawns. About a small town that somehow, in memory, is always seen with a wide-angle lens. About houses that are never locked. About mothers looking out windows to check on you. About the summer heat and ennui of church services, and the unpredictable theater of the dinner table, and the troubling sounds of an argument between your parents, half-heard through an open window.

Watching the film, I remembered Ray Bradbury's memory of a boy waking up to the sound of a Green Machine outside his window—a hand-pushed lawnmower. Perhaps you grew up in a big city, with the doors locked and everything air-conditioned. It doesn't matter. Most of us, unless we are unlucky, have something of the same childhood, because we are protected by innocence and naïveté.

As I mentioned the O'Brien family, I realized one detail the film has precisely right: The parents are named Mr. O'Brien and Mrs. O'Brien.

Yes. Because the parents of other kids were never thought of by their first names, and the first names of your own parents were words used only by others. Your parents were Mother and Father and they defined your reality, and you were open to their emotions, both calming and alarming. And young Jack O'Brien is growing, and someday will become Mr. O'Brien, but will never seem to himself as real as his father did.

Rarely does a film seem more obviously a collaboration of love between a director and his production designer, Jack Fisk. Fisk is about my age and was born and raised in downstate Illinois, and so, of course, knows that in the 1940s tall aluminum drinking glasses were used for lemonade and iced tea. He has all the other details right, too, but his design fits seamlessly into the lives of his characters. What's uncanny is that Malick creates the O'Brien parents and their three boys without an obvious plot: The movie captures the unplanned unfolding of summer days and the overheard words of people almost talking to themselves.

The film's portrait of everyday life, inspired by Malick's memories of his hometown of Waco, Texas, is bounded by two immensities, one of space and time and the other of spirituality. *The Tree of Life* has awe-inspiring visuals, suggesting the birth and expansion of the universe, the appearance of life on a microscopic level, and the evolution of species. This process leads to the present moment, and to all of us. We were created in the Big Bang and over untold millions of years molecules formed themselves into, well, you and me.

And what comes after? In whispered words near the beginning, "nature" and "grace" are heard. We have seen nature as it gives and takes away; one of the family's boys dies. We also see how it works with time, as Jack O'Brien (Hunter McCracken) grows into a middle-age man (Sean Penn). And what then? The film's coda provides a vision of an afterlife, a desolate landscape on which quiet people solemnly recognize and greet one another, and all is understood in the fullness of time.

Some reviews have said Mr. O'Brien (Brad Pitt, crew-cut, never more of a regular guy) is too strict as a disciplinarian. I don't think so. He is doing what he thinks is right, as he has been raised. Mrs. O'Brien (the ethereal Jessica Chastain) is gentler and more understanding, but there is no indication she feels her husband is cruel. Of course children resent discipline, and of course a kid might sometimes get whacked at the dinner table circa 1950. But listen to an acute exchange of dialogue between Jack and his father. "I was a little hard on you sometimes," Mr. O'Brien says, and Jack replies: "It's your house. You can do what you want to." Jack is defending his father against himself. That's how you grow up. And it all happens in this blink of a lifetime, surrounded by the realms of unimaginable time and space.

The Trip ★ ★ ★

NO MPAA RATING, 109 m., 2011

Steve Coogan (Himself), Rob Brydon (Himself), Claire Keelan (Emma), Margo Stilley (Mischa), Rebecca Johnson (Sally), Dolya Gavanski (Magda), Kerry Shale (Steve's Agent). Directed by Michael Winterbottom and produced by Andrew Eaton and Melissa Parmenter.

After some movies, Gene Siskel liked to say, "I wish I'd seen a documentary about the same actors having lunch." A whimsical new movie named *The Trip* puts his theory to the test. We've seen Steve Coogan and Rob Brydon costarring in *Tristram Shandy: A Cock and Bull Story* (2005), and now here they are having lunch.

The pretense is that the *Observer* newspaper has assigned Coogan to do an article about dining in the north of England. His qualifications seem to be that he was born in Manchester and eats. When his girlfriend begs off the tour, he recruits his old friend Brydon to drive along, magnanimously offering to give him 45 percent of the fee. Brydon bids farewell to his wife and child, and the two set off in Coogan's Land Rover under gray winter skies.

The film, directed by Michael Winterbottom, consists of (1) Coogan and Brydon talking in the car; (2) Coogan and Brydon talking at breakfast, lunch, and dinner; (3) Coogan's luck at seducing hotel staff members; (4) Coogan standing alone in chilly but lovely landscapes trying to find a signal for his cell phone; (5) food being prepared and served; and (6) shots of the car on motorways and country lanes.

This is a great deal more entertaining than it sounds, in large part because the two actors are gifted mimics—Brydon the better one, although Coogan doesn't think so. They get into a sort of competition that allows them to compete with their versions of such as Michael Caine, Ian McKellen, Sean Connery, Woody Allen, and others. Brydon does a virtuoso impression of Caine's voice evolving from his early days in *The Ipcress File* through decades of whiskey and cigars into its present richness.

There's an undercurrent of rivalry throughout, based on what Coogan sees as his greater fame, success, and talent. What especially bugs him is that he's seen as a comic actor and denied a shot at the heavy-duty A-list material he feels he deserves. He also sees himself as more handsome, fit, and successful than Brydon, and from the way he considers his hair in a mirror, you'd think he wanted it to look that way.

Curiously, they give only perfunctory attention to the many meals they eat, although Winterbottom faithfully goes into the kitchens to show each one being prepared. Scallops are featured in at least half the meals. One breakfast centers on black pudding, which I believe is best eaten with the eyes closed.

Along the way they visit Lake District sites associated with Wordsworth and Coleridge, quote copiously, and speculate on Coleridge's use of opium. Coogan's reaction shot is priceless when one woman recognizes Brydon but not him. And there's an undercurrent: Brydon has a family to return to in a cozy home; Coogan has a son he's distant from and a barren modern apartment.

It's a good question how true to life any of this is. The movie lists no screenwriters, but although it looks like a documentary, it isn't one. Apparently this film is edited down from a longer BBC-TV series during which the food was possibly more discussed. At the end we're left with the intriguing question: Would we rather see the same two actors in a regular story?

TrollHunter ★ ★ ½

PG-13, 99 m., 2011

Otto Jespersen (Hans), Glenn Erland Tosterud (Thomas), Tomas Alf Larsen (Kalle), Johanna Morck (Johanna), Hans Morten Hansen (Finn Haugen). Directed by Andre Ovredal and produced by Sveinung Golimo and John M. Jacobsen. Screenplay by Ovredal.

It is a misery to be a troll. You haunt the forests of Norway, live in clammy caves, and inhabit bodies incapable of processing vitamin D, so that the sun can cause you to crumble into stone. Your obsession is hunting Christians, but because you live in a Norwegian wilderness far from cities, there are few Christians to be found—and since some trolls are taller than trees, they can see you coming.

TrollHunter is a mockumentary allegedly edited from anonymous footage and certainly inspired by *The Blair Witch Project*. It has something going for it: We see a lot of trolls and we saw precious few witches. At first, the filmmakers aren't even looking for trolls; three young students are on the track of a man suspected of poaching bears without a license. We meet Thomas (Glenn Erland Tosterud); his sound person, Johanna (Johanna Morck); and the cinematographer, Kalle (Tomas Alf Larsen); none of whom, of course, is especially competent because a requirement of the genre is a lot of queasy cam.

They're on the trail of a suspect, Hans (Otto Jespersen), who prowls the forest trails in a Land Rover with alarming scratches on its doors. Eventually Hans allows them to trail along, and they discover that the Norwegian government employs troll hunters in a secret program to stop the beasts, who are a threat to power pylons, the environment, and, of course, Christians. They sniff out Christians by their distinctive smell. That leads to some droll scenes in which Hans leads them in smearing their bodies with Troll Stench.

That's funny. A lot of *TrollHunter* (but not enough) is funny. I imagine the best way to see the movie would be the way it was presented at Sundance, at a "secret" midnight screening at which the capacity audience allegedly has no idea what it is about to see.

Trolls are very ugly, except to other trolls. There are various sorts, including mountain trolls and forest trolls. The shortage of Christians in their locales perhaps explains their ill humor. They spend a great deal of time roaring, bleating, squealing, and snorting at a very high volume, which is, after a point, too much of a muchness.

The fake-doc look nicely explains the partial glimpses and incomplete shots during the troll hunt, although we get a nice look at some of the beasts, who have amazingly ugly schnozzolas. There is a scene that seems like a loving tribute to monster movies since time immemorial, in which threatened humans huddle in a cave and monsters can be seen sniffling at the cave mouth. This solves the problem of incorporating effects (and miniatures?) into the shot.

At one point it's explained that trolls cannot be seen in satellite photos. That must be because of their coloration and not their size, because one in particular seems to stand fifty feet tall, easy. Why did I waste time thinking about satellite photos, however, when I was presented with a more pressing problem: If trolls can't stand sunlight, which creates vitamin D and helps with bone calcium, why do they possess so much calcium that a leading cause of death is instant calcification, which is not a pretty sight? Unfortunately, the film ends abruptly before the troll hunters can explain that. Of course, it's a requirement of the genre that all the children of *Blair Witch* end abruptly. But I digress.

Tron: Legacy ★ ★ ★

PG-13, 125 m., 2010

Jeff Bridges (Kevin Flynn/Clu), Garrett Hedlund (Sam Flynn), Olivia Wilde (Quorra), Michael Sheen (Castor/Zuse), Bruce Boxleitner (Alan Bradley/Tron), Beau Garrett (Gem), James Frain (Jarvis). Directed by Joseph Kosinski and produced by Sean Bailey, Steven Lisberger, and Jeffrey Silver. Screenplay by Edward Kitsis and Adam Horowitz.

To the sad story of a father who was trapped inside a snowman for the winter (*Jack Frost*), we must now add *Tron: Legacy*, where the father has been trapped inside a software program for twenty years. Yes, young Sam Flynn has grown up an orphan because his dad was seduced and abducted by a video game. Now a call comes for the young hero to join his old dad in throwing virtual Frisbees at the evil programs threatening that digital world.

This is a movie well beyond the possibility of logical explanation. Since the Tron universe exists entirely within chips, don't bother yourself about where the physical body of Kevin Flynn (Jeff Bridges) has been for the last two decades; it must surely have been somewhere because we can see that it has aged. The solution, I suppose, is that this is a virtual world and it can do anything it feels like, but how exactly does a flesh-and-blood twenty-year-old get inside it? And what does he eat?

Joseph Kosinski's *Tron: Legacy* steps nimbly over such obstacles and hits the ground running, in a 3-D sound and light show that plays to the eyes and ears more than the mind. Among its real-world technology is a performance by Jeff Bridges as Kevin Flynn at two different ages—now, and twenty years ago. The original *Tron* was made twenty-eight years ago, but that would have made young Sam Flynn, his son, nearly thirty, which is too old for the hero in a story of this sort. The ideal age would be around twelve.

In a flashback we see Kevin, lord of a mighty software corporation, taking leave of his son as a child. At first you think Jeff Bridges looks younger in this scene because of makeup or Botox or something, and then you realize this is Bridges's body and voice, but his face has been rendered younger by special effects. They're uncanny. The use of profiles and backlighting makes the illusion adequate for this purpose. The real Bridges turns up later inside the program, whiskery and weathered, but the CGI version of younger Jeff sticks around to play Clu, a program he created, who now desires (you know this is coming) to control the world.

Kevin and Sam reconcile and bond. They join other cyberspace allies, notably including the beguiling Quorra (Olivia Wilde), whom cyber-Kevin has apparently been fathering instead of poor orphaned Sam. Does this symbolize the ways video games can destroy real-life relationships? Just asking. I'm thinking of Quorra and Sam as a possible romantic couple, but there's the pesky problem that she is virtual and he bleeds when he's cut—I think, although maybe not inside the program. This brings us back to a central question about *Avatar*: What or who, precisely, was Neytiri falling in love with?

I'm giving this more attention than the movie does, which is just as well. Isaac Asimov would have attempted some kind of scientific speculation on how this might all be possible, but *Tron* is more action-oriented. (Personal to sci-fi fans: If *2001* is Analog, *Tron: Legacy* is Thrilling Wonder Stories.)

The first *Tron* (1982) felt revolutionary at the time. I'd never seen anything like it. We showed it again at Ebertfest a few years ago. It was the first movie to create a digital world and embed human actors; earlier that had been done with special effects, matte shots, optical printers, blue screen, and so on. *Tron* found a freedom of movement within its virtual world that was exhilarating. The plot was impenetrable, but so what?

Tron: Legacy, a sequel made twenty-eight years after the original but with the same actor, is true to the first film: It also can't be understood but looks great. Both films, made so many years apart, can fairly lay claim to being state of the art. This time that includes the use of 3-D. Since so much of the action involves quick movement forward and backward in shots, the 3-D effect is useful, and not just a promiscuous use of the ping-pong effect. It is also well iterated. (A note at the top informs us that parts of the movie were deliberately filmed in 2-D, so of course I removed my glasses to note how much brighter it was. Dimness is the problem 3-D hasn't licked.)

A long time ago in 1984, Jeff Bridges appeared as an alien inhabiting a human body in John Carpenter's *Starman.* An article in the *New York Times Magazine* called him the perfect movie actor. He wasn't flashy; he was steadily, consistently good. Now that he has won an Oscar for *Crazy Heart* and appearing in *True Grit,* that is still true. Here is an actor expected to (1) play himself as a much younger man, (2) play himself now, and (3) play a computer program (or avatar?), and he does all three in a straightforward manner that is effective and convincing (given the preposterous nature of the material).

Sam, circa twenty (Garrett Hedlund), is well suited to his role, somewhat resembling Bridges. Olivia Wilde makes a fragrant Quorra. In some inexplicable way, these actors and Bruce Boxleitner (Tron) and Michael Sheen (Zuse) plausibly project human emotions in an environment devoid of organic life, including their own.

The artificial world is wonderfully well rendered, building on the earlier film's ability to bring visual excitement to what must in reality, after all, be slim pickings: invisible ones and zeroes. I soon topped off on the thrill of watching Frisbees of light being hurled, but some of the chases and architectural details are effective simply because they use sights and spaces never seen. And the soundtrack by Daft Punk has such urgent electronic force that the visuals sometimes almost play as *its* accompaniment. It might not be safe to play this in the car. The plot is another matter. It's a catastrophe, short-changing the characters and befuddling the audience. No doubt an online guru will produce a synopsis of everything that happens, but this isn't like an opera, where you can peek at the program notes.

I expect *Tron: Legacy* to be a phenomenon at the box office for a week or three. It may not have legs because its appeal is too one-dimensional for an audience much beyond immediate responders. When *2001* was in theaters, there were fans who got stoned and sneaked in during the intermission for the sound-and-light trip. I hesitate to suggest that for *Tron: Legacy,* but the plot won't suffer.

Trucker ★ ★ ★ ★

R, 90 m., 2009

Michelle Monaghan (Diane Ford), Jimmy Bennett (Peter), Nathan Fillion (Runner), Benjamin Bratt (Len), Joey Lauren Adams (Jenny). Directed by James Mottern and produced by Scott Hanson, Galt Niederhoffer, Celine Rattray, and Daniela Taplin Lundberg. Screenplay by Mottern.

There's one of those perfect moments in *Trucker* when I'm thinking, "This is the moment to end! Now! Fade to black!" And the movie ends. It is the last of many absolutely right decisions by the first-time writer-director James Mottern, who began by casting two actors who bring his story to strong emotional life. Both of them show they're gifted and intelligent artists who only needed, as so many do in these discouraging times, a chance to reveal their deep talents.

Michelle Monaghan was on the brink of inhabiting forever the thankless role of the good-looking, plucky female in action movies about men (*Mission: Impossible III*). She was excellent in *Gone Baby Gone*, and here she confirms her talent. Jimmy Bennett, who was eleven or twelve at the time of shooting, has been good in heavy-duty projects before (*Orphan*) and played the young Captain Kirk in *Star Trek* (2009), but here shows a subtlety and command of tone that is remarkable. (It's time for him to start billing himself as "James." He'll be relieved when he's twenty.) Together these actors create an abrasive relationship that sidesteps all sentimentality, in a film that correctly ends when a lesser film would have added half an hour of schmaltz.

Monaghan is Diane Ford, a trucker who just paid off her own rig. She's thirtyish, cold, hard-drinking, promiscuous, a loner. Bennett plays her son, Peter. She left him with his father, Len (Benjamin Bratt), soon after his birth, has stayed away, doesn't like kids—or men, either, although she uses them. One man (Nathan Fillion) has been her best friend for four years, but that involves getting drunk together and never having sex.

Len gets sick. Colon cancer. He's been living for years with Jenny (Joey Lauren Adams), who now needs time to care for him. It's up to Diane to look after the kid. She doesn't want anything to do with him. "Just for a few weeks," Jenny pleads. Just until Len gets better. Sure.

You are anticipating, as I did, that *Trucker* would turn into one of those predictable movies where the mother and son grow to love each other. It doesn't end with mutual hate and abandonment, but it damn near does. The kid is as tough as his mom. "Answer me!" she says. "I don't talk to bitches!" he says. Len and Jenny seem nice enough. Where did he learn to talk like that? Little pitchers have big ears.

I concede the story arc is fairly predictable, assuming neither one murders the other. But Mottern and his actors take no hostages. Diane is hard and tough, and stays that way. Her son is angry and bitter, and stays that way. Do they need to love and be loved? Sure. We know that, but they don't. By the end of the film, she hasn't called him "Peter" and he hasn't called her "Mom." He's "kid" or "dude," and she's "you." They have to be together whether they like it or not, and they know it.

That said, Monaghan makes Diane more sad than off-putting. She isn't a caricature. She works hard, values her independence, is making payments on her small suburban home on an unpaved street, is living up to her bargain with herself. The movie spares us any scenes where she's "one of the guys." It opens after a one-night stand with a guy who tries to be nice, but she doesn't need a nice guy in her life. Nor does she need to be nice with Peter, but one thing she does do: She's always honest with him and speaks with him directly, and I think he knows that. Her performance clearly deserves an Academy nomination.

Peter is loved by his father and Jenny. He hasn't been mistreated. He probably senses how sick his dad really is and knows he wasn't parked with Diane because anyone wanted him there. He's been told things about his mother that are, strictly speaking, true. She did leave him and Len soon after his birth. She does want to avoid seeing him. He says something that reveals he knows of her promiscuity, although he may not quite understand it.

What Mottern does is lock these two characters in a story and see what happens. Something will have to give. The supporting performances by Nathan Fillion, Benjamin Bratt, and Joey Lauren Adams are precisely what is needed: direct, open, no "acting," good tone control. They are good people, but very real people, with no illusions about life.

I value films that closely regard specific lives. I know they usually must have happy endings. Not always. Haven't we all learned to expect certain things in a story about a mother and a son? Aren't those things, in fact, generally true to human nature? I hope to feel elevation at the end. But a film should earn it, not simply evoke it. *Trucker* sets out on a difficult and tricky path, and doesn't put a foot wrong.

True Grit ★ ★ ★ ½

PG-13, 110 m., 2010

Jeff Bridges (Rooster Cogburn), Matt Damon (LaBoeuf), Josh Brolin (Tom Chaney), Barry Pepper (Lucky Ned Pepper), Hailee Steinfeld

(Mattie Ross). Directed by Joel Coen and Ethan Coen, and produced by Joel Coen, Ethan Coen, and Scott Rudin. Screenplay by Joel Coen and Ethan Coen, based on the novel by Charles Portis.

In the Coen brothers' *True Grit*, Jeff Bridges is not playing the John Wayne role. He's playing the Jeff Bridges role—or, more properly, the role created in the enduring novel by Charles Portis, much of whose original dialogue can be heard in this film. Bridges doesn't have the archetypal stature of the Duke. Few ever have. But he has here, I believe, an equal screen presence. We always knew we were looking at John Wayne. When we see Rooster Cogburn in this version, we're not thinking about Jeff Bridges.

Wayne wanted his tombstone to read *Feo, Fuerte y Formal* ("ugly, strong and dignified"). He was a handsome, weathered man when I met him in the 1960s and '70s, but not above a certain understandable vanity. Rooster might be an ornery gunslinger with an eye patch, but Wayne played him wearing a hairpiece and a corset. Jeff Bridges occupies the character like a homeless squatter. I found myself wondering how young Mattie Ross (Hailee Steinfeld) could endure his body odor.

Bridges's interpretation is no doubt closer to the reality of a lawman in those years of the West. How savory can a man be when he lives in saloons and on horseback? Not all riders on the range carried a change of clothes. Of course, he's a lawman with an office and a room somewhere in town, but for much of the movie he is on a quest through inauspicious territory to find the man who murdered Mattie's father.

As told in the novel, Mattie is a plucky young woman with a gaze as level as her hat brim. She hires Marshal Cogburn to track down that villain Tom Chaney (Josh Brolin). She means to kill him for what he done. If Bridges comfortably wears the Duke's shoes, Hailee Steinfeld is more effective than Kim Darby in the earlier film, and she was pretty darn good. Steinfeld was thirteen when she made the film, close to the right age. Darby was a little over twenty. The story hinges on the steel resolve of a young girl who has been raised in the eye-for-an-eye Old West, seen some bad sights, and picked up her values from the kind of old man who can go and get hisself shot.

What strikes me is that I'm describing the story and the film as if it were simply, if admirably, a good Western. That's a surprise to me, because this is a film by the Coen brothers, and this is the first straight genre exercise in their career. It's a loving one. Their craftsmanship is a wonder. Their casting is always inspired and exact. The cinematography by Roger Deakins reminds us of the glory that was, and can still be, the Western.

But this isn't a Coen brothers film in the sense that we use those words. It's not eccentric, quirky, wry, or flaky. It's as if these two men, who have devised some of the most original films of our time, reached a point where they decided to coast on the sheer pleasure of good old straightforward artistry. This is like Iggy Pop singing "My Funny Valentine," which he does very well. So let me praise it for what it is, a splendid Western. The Coens, having demonstrated their mastery of many notes, including many not heard before, now show they can play in tune.

Isn't Rooster Cogburn where Jeff Bridges started out forty years ago? The first time I was aware of him was in *The Last Picture Show* (1971), where he and his friends went to the local movie theater to see *Red River*, starring John Wayne. Since then that clean-faced young man has lived and rowdied and worked his way into being able to play Rooster with a savory nastiness that Wayne could not have equaled.

All the same, the star of this show is Hailee Steinfeld, and that's appropriate. This is her story, set in motion by her, narrated by her. This is Steinfeld's first considerable role. She nails it. She sidesteps the opportunity to make Mattie adorable. Mattie doesn't live in an adorable world. Seeing the first *True Grit*, I got a little crush on Kim Darby. Seeing this one, few people would get a crush on Hailee Steinfeld. Maybe in another movie. But the way she plays it with the Coens, she's more the kind of person you'd want guarding your back.

Matt Damon, Josh Brolin, and Barry Pepper have weight and resonance in supporting roles. Damon is LaBoeuf, the Texas Ranger who comes along for a time to track Tom

Chaney. Glen Campbell had the role earlier, and was right for the tone of that film. Damon plays on a more ominous note. His LaBoeuf isn't sidekick material. He and Cogburn have long-standing issues. Nor, we discover, is LaBoeuf a man of simple loyalty.

As Tom Chaney, Josh Brolin is a complete and unadulterated villain, a rattlesnake who would as soon shoot Mattie as Rooster. In the Western genre, evil can be less nuanced than in your modern movies with all their psychological insights. Barry Pepper plays Lucky Ned Pepper, leader of a gang Chaney ends up with and part of the four-man charge across the meadow into Rooster's gunfire, a charge as lucky for them as the Charge of the Light Brigade.

The 1969 film had glorious landscapes. The meadow and several other scenes were set in the San Juan mountains of Colorado, near Telluride. This film's landscapes are all in Texas, and although some are beautiful, many are as harsh and threatening as the badlands described by Cormac McCarthy or Larry McMurtry.

I expect Bridges and Steinfeld have good chances of winning Oscar nominations for this film. Steinfeld is good the whole way through, but the scene audiences love is the one where she bargains with a horse trader (Dakin Matthews) for the money she feels is owed her. Here the key is the dialogue by the Coen brothers, which never strains, indeed remains flat and commonsense, as Mattie reasons the thief out of his money by seeming to employ his own logic.

I'm surprised the Coens made this film, so unlike their other work except in quality. Instead of saying that now I hope they get back to making "Coen brothers films," I'm inclined to speculate on what other genres they might approach in this spirit. What about the musical? *Oklahoma!* is ready to be remade.

Trust ★ ★ ★ ★

R, 104 m., 2011

Liana Liberato (Annie Cameron), Clive Owen (Will Cameron), Catherine Keener (Lynn Cameron), Viola Davis (Gail Friedman), Chris Henry Coffey (Charlie). Directed by David Schwimmer and produced by Schwimmer, Ed Cathell III, Dana Golomb, Robert Greenhut, Tom Hodges, Avi Lerner, and Heidi Jo Markel. Screenplay by Andy Bellin and Robert Festinger.

The bravest thing about David Schwimmer's *Trust* is that it doesn't try to simplify. It tells its story of a fourteen-year-old girl and a predatory pedophile as a series of repercussions in which rape is only the first, and possibly not the worst, tragedy to strike its naive and vulnerable victim. It's easy to imagine how this story could have been exploited and dumbed down. It works instead with intelligence and sympathy.

At its core is a remarkable performance by young Liana Liberato, who plays Annie Cameron, the happy child of a good home in upper-crust Wilmette, Illinois. The character could have been played in many ways, but Liberato evokes innocence, defiance, idealism, hurt—and trust—without ever seeming to be more aware than she should. We believe above all in her youth. We hear a lot about the premature sexualization of young teens; she creates a "good girl" who isn't advanced, who feels uncomfortable at a party where "popular girls" fake sophistication. She's . . . a nice kid.

She's never had a boyfriend when she meets Charlie online in a chat room. Schwimmer uses titles to show us their conversations. Charlie is in high school. Like her, he plays volleyball. He's a nice kid, too. He understands her. She grows closer to Charlie than any boy she's ever known. They talk for hours on the phone.

Charlie (Chris Henry Coffey) makes a confession. Actually, he's in college. Actually, he's a graduate student. Actually, he's twenty-five. "Why do you keep lying?" she asks. But Charlie is comforting and persuasive. She agrees to meet him in a mall. She must have been warned about cases of online predators like him—but they couldn't have been talking about her Charlie. Yet when Charlie turns up, he's clearly well into his thirties. Annie is crushed. But he is persuasive and compelling, a smooth talker, pushing all the right buttons, exploiting her idealized fantasies about himself. Coffey is very good in the scene.

At this point in the film, I thought I had a pretty good idea where it was going. That's how it surprised me, by being fiercely respectful of Annie's feelings in all their complexities, and providing her with dialogue that reflects her confusion and vulnerability. Schwimmer is an activist in the field of rape awareness, and must have had knowledgeable collaborators, including his writers, Andy Bellin and Robert Festinger.

Rape is a cruel crime. For Annie, the loss of her virginity is not the worst of it. More important is her reputation, her world in New Trier High School, her self-esteem. She might almost have been better off not telling anyone what happened. She confides in a friend, who blabs to the school principal, and she's led away from school by two uniformed officers who come to investigate the crime. In this and countless details for the rest of the film, we realize a psychic rape is being added to the original one. Only a reserved but tactful psychiatrist (Viola Davis) completely understands what is happening.

Annie's parents are good people. Her British father, Will (Clive Owen), is a marketing executive—ironically, catering to the market for sexy teen fashions exploited by the notorious American Apparel. Her mother, Lynn (Catherine Keener), is sensible and loving. The marriage is healthy. What Annie desperately needs is privacy and space. What she gets is an intrusive FBI investigation, brutal gossip at high school, cruel jokes played on the Internet, and the destruction of the idealized vision of Charlie she clings to.

Trust is above all respectful of her feelings. It perhaps goes a shade too far in how it deals with her father's. He becomes obsessed with the FBI investigation, wants personal vengeance against the predator, gets involved in unwise ways. In a crushing scene where his anger leaps out of control, he has the effect of humiliating Annie before hundreds of her classmates.

Trust doesn't offer soothing solutions for Annie. Annie will survive, but has been damaged perhaps more by the aftermath than by the rape itself. The movie is merciless in depicting the methods by which pedophile predators operate. Charlie is the embodiment of evil. But society is lacking in instinctive sympathy and tact for Annie, and society isn't supposed to be evil. Catherine Keener does a warm, unobtrusive job of loving and comforting her daughter, but that's not enough—not when her husband grows more concerned with vengeance than with healing.

It is all too tortuous and complicated. Liana Liberato does such a poignant job of showing how and why. She has three scenes in particular where her wounded feelings spill out in words of anguish, and they are so well written and well acted that they're heartbreaking. David Schwimmer has made one of the year's best films: powerfully emotional, yes, but also very perceptive.

Tulpan ★ ★ ★ ★

NO MPAA RATING, 100 m., 2009

Askhat Kuchinchirekov (Asa), Samal Yeslyamova (Samal), Ondasyn Besikbasov (Ondas), Tulepbergen Baisakalov (Boni), Bereke Turganbayev (Beke), Mahabbat Turganbayeva (Maha). Directed by Sergey Dvortsevoy and produced by Karl Baumgartner and Thanassis Karathanos. Screenplay by Dvortsevoy and Gennady Ostrovskiy.

Tulpan is an amazing film. It shows such an unfamiliar world it might as well be Mars. This is a world where the horizon is a straight line against the sky in every direction. There are no landmarks, no signs, no roads. No vegetation grows much more than a foot or two high. It is dry, dusty, cold, and windy, and nothing seems to be green. This is the world *Tulpan* takes place in, and I can think of only one other story that would feel at home there: *Waiting for Godot.*

Yet the people love it. They are yurt dwellers in Kazakhstan, the largest landlocked nation on Earth. They live on what is named in the credits as the Hungersteppe and raise sheep. We meet a young sailor named Asa, discharged from the Russian navy, who has come here to live with his sister Samal, her husband, Ondas, and their children. As the story opens, Asa, Ondas, and his buddy Boni are negotiating with a poker-faced man and his hostile wife for the hand of their daughter, Tulpan ("Tulip").

Asa enthralls them with tales of the seahorse and octopus. They offer ten sheep and a chandelier. It is to no avail; Tulpan, peeking through the doorway curtains, thinks his ears are too big. There is not one single other potential bride in the district, and how is a man to live here without a wife?

These people are quite familiar with what we call civilization. Their children have been deserting to the cities for years. They do not have electricity, and water must be trucked in. I assume they eat a lot of mutton, and there is a man with an ungainly jeeplike vehicle who comes around selling cucumbers and, I hope, other vegetables. They have a battery-powered radio, which one of the sons listens to eagerly, racing into the yard to announce: "Breaking news! Earthquake in Japan! Seven on the Richter scale!"

They are alarmed that many baby lambs are stillborn. They call out the vet, whose teeth do a thing with his cigarette it is difficult to describe. He travels with a sick baby camel in his motorcycle sidecar. His diagnosis is simple and almost obvious. Asa eventually argues with his taskmaster brother-in-law and walks away from the farm. This consists of disappearing into the void; how do people avoid getting lost here? When Ondas scans the horizon with his binoculars, everything looks the same.

There is humor in the film, some of it involving the cucumber salesman, and tenderness, as when Samal sings a bedtime lullaby to her tired husband and their children. Stark reality, in the difficult birth of a lamb that lives. A shot, long held, of Samal's face, which tells us everything we can ever hope to know about her situation. The film's closing shot is epic in its meaning and astonishing in its difficulty.

This is the first feature by Sergey Dvortsevoy, forty-five, born in Kazakhstan, whose documentaries have been about people in the old Russian republics living between tradition and the future. What does it sound like to you? Ethnographic boredom? I swear to you that if you live in a place where this film is playing, it is the best film in town. You'll enjoy it, not soon forget it, and you'll tell your friends about it and try to convince them to go, but you'll have about as much luck with them as I'm probably having with you. Still, there has to come a time in everyone's life when they see a deadpan comedy about the yurt dwellers of Kazakhstan.

Note: This was the winner of the Un Certain Regard prize at Cannes 2008.

12 ★★★½

PG-13, 153 m., 2009

Sergey Makovetsky (Engineer), Nikita Mikhalkov (Foreman), Sergey Garmash (Cabbie), Valentin Gaft (Elderly Jewish Man), Alexey Petrenko (Transit Worker), Yuri Stoyanov (TV Producer), Sergey Gazarov (Surgeon), Mikhail Efremov (Traveling Actor), Alexander Adabashian (Bailiff), Apti Magamaev (Chechen Accused Man). Directed by Nikita Mikhalkov and produced by Mikhalkov and Leonid Vereschagin. Screenplay by Mikhalkov, Vladimir Moiseenko, and Alexander Novototsky-Vlasov, based on the screenplay by Reginald Rose.

Twelve Angry Men remains a monument of American filmmaking, and more than fifty years after it was made its story is still powerful enough to inspire this Russian version—not a remake, but a new demonstration of a jury verdict arrived at only because one of the men was not angry so much as worried. *12* by Nikita Mikhalkov is a powerful new film inspired by a powerful older one.

You know the story. A jury is sequestered. The men are hot and tired, and impatient to go home. It is assumed that the defendant, a young man accused of murder, is guilty. A quick vote is called for. The balloting shows eleven for convicting, one against. This generates a long and dogged debate in which the very principles of justice itself are called into play.

Perhaps Russia got this film when it needed it. Reginald Rose's original screenplay was written for the CBS drama showcase *Studio One* in 1954 and presented live. Franklin Schaffner (*Patton*) was the director. The telecast took place during the declining days of the hearings held by Senator Joseph McCarthy. CBS also broadcast the army-McCarthy hearings and Edward R. Murrow's historic takedown of the alcoholic witch-hunter. The great film by Sidney Lumet, made in 1957, currently stands at number nine on IMDb's poll of the greatest films, ahead of *The Empire Strikes Back* and *Casablanca.*

If the original story argued for the right to a fair trial in the time of McCarthy's character assassinations, the Russian version comes at a time when that nation is using the jury system after a legacy of Stalinist purges and Communist Party show trials. It also dramatizes anti-Semitism and hatred for Chechens; the youth on trial is newly arrived in Moscow. The issue of overnight Russian millionaires in a land of much poverty is also on many of the jurors' minds.

None of the jurors is given a name, although director Mikhalkov gives himself the role of the jury foreman. One by one, every member of the jury tells a story or reveals a secret. Their set pieces do the job of swaying fellow jurors to reconsider their votes but are effective on their own as essentially a series of one-man shows. There is not a weak member in the cast, and it's a tribute to the power of the actors that the 2½-hour running time doesn't seem labored. The jury is sequestered in the gymnasium of a school next to the courtroom, and they never leave it, but their stories are performed so skillfully that in our minds we envision many settings; they're like radio plays.

Lumet famously began his film with the camera above eye level and subtly lowered it until the end, when the characters loomed above the camera. Mikhalkov, with a large open space to work in, uses camera placement and movement instead, circling the makeshift jury table and following jurors as they wander the room. A sparrow flies in through a window, and its fluttering and chirping is a reminder that the jurors, too, feel imprisoned.

Going in I knew what the story was about, how it would progress, and how it would end. Mikhalkov keeps all of that (writer Rose shares a screen credit), but he has made a new film with its own original characters and stories, and after all, it's not how the film ends, but how it gets there.

Twelve Thirty ★ ★ ½

NO MPAA RATING, 120 m., 2011

Reed Birney (Martin), Jonathan Groff (Jeff), Mamie Gummer (Maura), Portia Reiners (Mel), Karen Young (Vivien), Halley Feiffer (Irina), Barbara Barrie (Eve), Rebecca Schull (Katherine). Directed by Jeff Lipsky and produced by Daniel Sartorius. Screenplay by Lipsky.

Here is an unsuccessful movie with some surprisingly successful scenes. It has moments when it is electrifying and passages where it slows to a walk. Its dialogue is too "written" for the realism of film, but I can easily imagine it working well on the stage. It has more sex than any movie I've seen recently, and gives it much more thought. It doesn't work, but I doubt you'll regret seeing it.

Jeff Lipsky's *Twelve Thirty* involves a twenty-two-year-old named Jeff (Jonathan Groff) and all four members of the Langley family of Iowa City. Jeff claims at the outset he's a virgin and has never even kissed a girl. You're free to believe that if you choose. He's a young man with a lot of nuance behind his conversation, and in the opening scene he falls into conversation with Mel (Portia Reiners). She's his age and they work in the same restaurant. This scene eventually contains a self-contained play of its own. They join the table of two elderly British tourists (Barbara Barrie and Rebecca Schull), and the relationship and story of these two widows creates a lovely moment.

Mel is an intriguing take-charge woman who goes on a drive with Jeff and ends up taking him to bed after overcoming all his (pretended?) objections. But that's that. She enjoyed the sex but won't do it again. Later, we meet her sister, Maura (Mamie Gummer), in a girl-to-girl conversation with her best friend, Irina (Halley Feiffer). At that point we don't know Maura is Mel's sister. So yes, this is one of those interlinking plot movies where everyone (except the widows) ends up connected. But there's a difference: The movie doesn't cut between story lines with clever editing, but is told chronologically, so that we're allowed to make the connection for ourselves.

Jeff and Maura, urged by Irina, slip into a closet at a party, and what happens there you will see—or not see, because it's in the dark. Jeff flees weeping into the night, and goes to Mel's house the next day, where he meets her mother, Vivien (Karen Young). What happens then you will also discover, but let me say Young's acting, here and in an earlier scene with Mel, is quietly, touchingly exact, and her dialogue in various tones is particularly effective.

The father of the girls is Vivien's ex-husband, Martin (Reed Birney), a bisexual who now lives with Robert, never seen. Vivien tells a story about his kindness that is moving; elsewhere in the film, when she and Martin make love, Karen Young's smile of invitation feels uncannily genuine. Toward the end of the film, Martin presides over a discussion with his ex-wife, his daughters, and Jeff, and this is a scene that decidedly doesn't work, no matter how we take it.

So there you are. Ambition, precision, good acting, some acting that doesn't overcome the dialogue, and a scene in the dark that plays as a stunt. Also some distractingly cute repeating jokes about museums and lip balm. I wish all movies that don't work were this interesting.

21 and a Wakeup ★ ½

R, 123 m., 2009

Amy Acker (Caitlin Murphy), Faye Dunaway (Major Rose Thorn), Danica McKellar (Jenny Valentine), Todd Cahoon (Chris Cameron), Ed Begley Jr. (Colonel Ritchie), Ben Vereen (General John Jay Garner), Wes Studi (Doctor). Directed, written, and produced by Chris McIntyre.

I learn that Chris McIntyre served in Vietnam and that *21 and a Wakeup,* set in an army hospital in the waning days of the war, is based on events he experienced and heard about. I'm sure his motivations were heartfelt, but his film is awkward and disjointed, and outstays its welcome.

It stars Amy Acker as a dedicated young army nurse named Caitlin Murphy, assigned to an army combat field hospital. She considers her profession a vocation, as indeed it is. Vocations and an army career don't always go hand in hand, and bureaucracy often wins out. Enforcing the Army Way is the uptight and unfortunately named Major Rose Thorn (Faye Dunaway), who seems opposed to innovation, improvisation, inspiration, and any other inclinations Caitlin might have in mind.

Her character is emblematic of the film's problems. I suspect McIntyre was so happy to enlist a star like Dunaway that it never occurred to him she's inappropriate for the role. God help me if I mention the age of an actress, but let me observe that Dunaway is about my age, and I consider myself beyond the age for optimum combat service.

Even more unfortunately, McIntyre hasn't written a believable character. I doubt Major Thorn as a nurse and as an officer. Her primary function seems to be materializing in a self-contained shot while issuing stiff formal announcements somewhat in the tone of a judge at a debutante charity function. She's stiffly poised in many shots; we can almost hear, "Ready for your close-up, Miss Dunaway."

But let's stop right there. Faye Dunaway is a fine actress and has been miscast in a badly written role. Amy Acker and other leading characters have been well cast in equally badly written roles. In contrast to the energy and life Robert Altman brought to his combat hospital in *M*A*S*H,* this film plays like a series of fond anecdotes trundled onstage without much relationship to one another.

Some of them strain credulity. McIntyre may indeed know about a nurse who went AWOL with a civilian war correspondent (Todd Cahoon) on an unauthorized visit to Cambodia. Such a trip may even have happened. But I didn't believe it.

I also didn't believe the punctuality with which critically wounded soldiers were rushed onscreen at crucial moments in the action in order to punctuate dialogue. These emergencies are tended to by medical personnel who seem like nothing so much as actors impersonating characters they've seen on TV.

McIntyre has enlisted an experienced cast, including Ed Begley Jr., Wes Studi, and Ben Vereen, and while Vereen creates a convincing human, none of them create convincing characters. How can they? They're pawns on a storyboard. The film lacks a sense of time and place. I discover on IMDb that it was actually filmed on location in Vietnam, but its Southeast Asia looks nowhere near as convincing as the locations of Coppola's *Apocalypse Now* and Stone's *Platoon* (shot in the Philippines) or Herzog's *Rescue Dawn* (Thailand).

Maybe I'm being too cynical. Perhaps I'll hear from nurses who served in Vietnam and inform me it was just like this. Even if it was, it plays like an assortment of stories that someone might tell you, "You ought to make a movie about that someday."

The Twilight Saga: Eclipse ★ ★

PG-13, 124 m., 2010

Kristen Stewart (Bella Swan), Robert Pattinson (Edward Cullen), Taylor Lautner (Jacob Black), Bryce Dallas Howard (Victoria), Billy Burke (Charlie Swan), Dakota Fanning (Jane), Peter Facinelli (Dr. Carlisle Cullen), Elizabeth Reaser (Esme Cullen), Jackson Rathbone (Jasper Hale), Kellan Lutz (Emmett Cullen), Ashley Greene (Alice Cullen), Nikki Reed (Rosalie Hale). Directed by David Slade and produced by Wyck Godfrey, Greg Mooradian, and Karen Rosefelt. Screenplay by Melissa Rosenberg, based on the novel *Eclipse* by Stephenie Meyer.

The price for surrendering your virginity is so high in *The Twilight Saga: Eclipse* that even Edward Cullen, the proposed tool of surrender, balks at it. Like him, you would become one of the undead. This is a price that Bella Swan, the virtuous heroine, must be willing to pay. Apparently when you marry a vampire, even such a well behaved one as Edward, he's required to bite you.

This romantic dilemma is developed in *Eclipse,* the third installment in this inexhaustible series, by adding a complication that has been building ever since the first. Jacob Black, the shape-shifting werewolf, is also in love with Bella (Kristin Stewart), and she perhaps with him. Jacob (Taylor Lautner) and his tribe are hot-blooded and never wear shirts, inspiring little coos and ripples of delight in the audience. Here is a fantasy to out-steam any romance novel: A sweet young girl is forced to choose between two improbably tall, dark, and handsome men who brood and smolder and yearn for her.

Nothing is perfect. There is a problem. The flame-tressed vampire Victoria (Bryce Dallas Howard) has been active in Seattle initiating new vampires, or Newbies, who in their youth are ravenous for blood and would have superhuman strength, if they were human. Victoria wants to destroy Bella in revenge for the murder of her boyfriend, James. Edward and Jacob both vow to protect the girl they love, and their fellow vampires and werewolves of course are prepared to fight to the death in this cause. This is true buddy love.

The movie contains violence and death, but not really very much. For most of its languorous running time, it listens to conversations between Bella and Edward, Bella and Jacob, Edward and Jacob, and Edward and Bella and Jacob. This would play better if any of them were clever conversationalists, but their ideas are limited to simplistic renderings of their desires. To be sure, there is a valedictory address, reminding us that these kids have skipped school for three movies now. And Edward has a noble speech when he tells Bella he doesn't want to have sex with her until after they're married. This is self-denial indeed for a 109-year-old vampire, who adds a piquant flavor to the category "confirmed bachelor."

Of Taylor Lautner's musculature, and particularly his abs, much has been written. Yes, he has a great build, but I remind you that an abdominal six-pack must be five seconds' work for a shape-shifter. More impressive is the ability of both Edward and Jacob to regard Bella with penetrating gazes from 'neath really heavy eyebrows. When my eyebrows get like Edward's, the barber trims them and never even asks me first.

There is a problem with the special effects. Many of the mountain ranges, which disappear into the far distance as increasingly pale peaks, look suspiciously like landscapes painted by that guy on TV who shows you how to paint stuff like that. The mountain forests and lakes are so pristine we should see Lewis and Clark just arriving. And the werewolves are inexplicable. They look snarly enough, have vicious fangs, and are larger than healthy ponies, but when they fall upon Newbies, they never quite seem to get the job done. One werewolf is nearly squeezed to death, and another, whose identity I will conceal, hears "he has broken bones on one whole side." Luckily, repairing the damage is only a night's work for Dr. Carlisle Cullen (Peter Facinelli). The problem with the effects is that the wolves don't seem to have physical weight and presence.

Much leads up to a scene in a tent on a mountaintop in the midst of a howling blizzard, when Bella's teeth start chattering. Obviously a job for the hot-blooded Jacob and not the cold-blooded Edward, and as Jacob embraces and warms her, he and Edward have a cloying cringe fest in which Edward admits that if Jacob were not a werewolf, he would probably like him, and then Jacob admits that if Edward were not a vampire—well, no, no, he couldn't. Come on, big guy. The two of you are making eye contact. Edward's been a confirmed bachelor for 109 years. Get in the brokeback spirit.

The audience watched this film with rapt attention. They obviously had a deep understanding of the story, which is just as well, because anyone not intimately familiar with the earlier installments could not make heads or tails of the opening scenes. The *Twilight* movies are chaste eroticism to fuel adolescent dreams, and are really about Bella being attracted and titillated and aroused and tempted up to the . . . very . . . BRINK! . . . of surrender, and then, well, no, no, she shouldn't.

The Twilight Saga: New Moon ★

PG-13, 130 m., 2009

Kristen Stewart (Bella Swan), Robert Pattinson (Edward Cullen), Taylor Lautner (Jacob Black), Dakota Fanning (Jane), Ashley Greene (Alice Cullen), Nikki Reed (Rosalie Hale), Jackson Rathbone (Jasper Hale), Kellan Lutz (Emmett Cullen), Peter Facinelli (Dr. Carlisle Cullen), Billy Burke (Charlie Swan). Directed by Chris Weitz and produced by Wyck Godfrey. Screenplay by Melissa Rosenberg, based on the novel by Stephenie Meyer.

The characters in this movie should be arrested for loitering with intent to moan. Never have teenagers been in greater need of a jump-start. Granted, some of them are more than one hundred years old, but still: Their charisma is by Madame Tussaud.

The Twilight Saga: New Moon takes the tepid achievement of *Twilight* (2008), guts it, and leaves it for undead. You know you're in trouble with a sequel when the word of mouth advises you to see the first movie twice instead. Obviously the characters all have. Long opening stretches of this film make utterly no sense unless you walk in knowing the first film, and hopefully both Stephenie Meyer novels, by heart. Edward and Bella spend murky moments glowering at each other and thinking, "So, here we are again."

Bella (Kristen Stewart) is still living at home with her divorced dad (Billy Burke), a cop whose disciplinary policy involves declaring her grounded for the rest of her life and then disappearing so she can jump from cliffs, haunt menacing forests, and fly to Italy so the movie can evoke the sad final death scene from—why, hold on, it's *Romeo and Juliet*! The very play Edward was reciting narcissistically and contemptuously in an opening scene.

Yes, Edward (Robert Pattinson) is back in school, repeating the twelfth grade for the eighty-fourth time. Bella sees him in the school parking lot, walking toward her in slow-motion, wearing one of those Edwardian Beatles jackets with a velvet collar, pregnant with his beauty. How white his skin, how red his lips. The decay of middle age may transform him into the Joker.

Edward and the other members of the Cullen vampire clan stand around a lot with glowering skulks. Long pauses interrupt longer ones. Listen up, lads! You may be immortal, but we've got a train to catch.

Edward leaves because Bella was not meant to be with him. Although he's a vegetarian vampire, when she gets a paper cut at her birthday party, one of his pals leaps on her like a shark on a tuna fish.

In his absence she's befriended by Jake (Taylor Lautner), that nice American Indian boy. "You've gotten all buff!" she tells him. Yeah, real buff, and soon he's never wearing a shirt and standing outside in the winter rain as if he were—why, nothing more than a wild animal. They don't need coats like ours, remember, because God gave them theirs.

SPOILER WARNING: Those not among that 5 percent of the movie's target audience that doesn't already know this will be surprised that Jake is a werewolf.

> *Bella:* "So . . . you're a werewolf?"
> *Jake:* "Last time I checked."
> *Bella:* "Can't you find a way to . . . just stop?"
> *Jake (patiently):* "It's not a lifestyle choice, Bella."

Jake is influenced, or controlled, or something, by Sam, another member of the tribe. He's like the alpha wolf. Sam and his three friends are mostly seen in long shot, shirtless in the rain, hanging around the edges of the clearing as if hoping to dash in and pick off some fresh meat.

Bella writes long letters to her absent vampire friend Alice (Ashley Greene), in which she does nothing to explain why she is helplessly attracted to these sinister, humorless, and vain men. It can't be the sex. As I've already explained in my review of the first film, *The Twilight Saga* is an extended metaphor for teen chastity, in which the punishment for being deflowered I will leave to your imagination.

The movie includes beauteous fields filled with potted flowers obviously buried hours before by the grounds crew, and nobody not clued in on the plot. Since they know it all and we know it all, sitting through this experience is like driving a pickup in low gear through a sullen sea of Brylcreem.

Two Lovers ★ ★ ★ ½

R, 110 m., 2009

Joaquin Phoenix (Leonard Kraditor), Gwyneth Paltrow (Michelle Rausch), Vinessa Shaw (Sandra Cohen), Moni Monoshov (Reuben Kraditor), Isabella Rossellini (Ruth Kraditor), John Ortiz (Jose Cordero), Bob Ari (Michael Cohen), Julie Budd (Carol Cohen), Elias Koteas (Ronald Blatt). Directed by James Gray and produced by Gray, Donna Gigliotti, and Anthony Katagas. Screenplay by Gray and Richard Menello.

I believe Sandra senses something is damaged about Leonard. *Two Lovers* never puts a word to it, although we know he's had treatment and is on medication. It's not a big, showy mental problem; lots of people go through life like this, and people simply say, "Well, you know Leonard." But Sandra does know him, and that's why she tells him she not only loves him but wants to help him.

Leonard (Joaquin Phoenix) is focused on his inner demons. His fiancée left him—dumped him—and he has moved back to his childhood room, still with the *2001* poster on the wall. He makes customer deliveries for his dad's dry cleaning business. Sandra (Vinessa Shaw) is the daughter of another dry cleaner in the same Brighton Beach neighborhood of Brooklyn. Her father plans to buy his father's business, and both families think it would be ideal if Sandra and Leonard married.

But Leonard meets Michelle (Gwyneth Paltrow) and is struck by the lightning bolt. She's blond, exciting, and in his eyes sophisticated and glamorous. She seems to like him, too. So a triangle exists that might seem to be the makings of a traditional romcom from years ago.

James Gray's *Two Lovers* is anything but traditional, romantic, or a comedy. It is a film of unusual perception, played at perfect pitch by Phoenix, Shaw, Paltrow, and the other actors. It is calm and mature. It understands these characters. It doesn't juggle them for melodrama, but looks inside.

Michelle is the kind of person many of us become fascinated with at some unwise point in our lives. She has enormous charm, a winning smile, natural style. But she is haunted. Leonard is blindsided to discover she has a married lover and that she uses drugs. He is able, like so many men, to overlook these flaws, to misunderstand neediness for affection, to delude himself that she shares his feelings. Sandra, on the other hand, is pretty and nice, but their families have known each other for years, and Michelle seems to offer an entry into a new world across the bridge in Manhattan.

The particular thing about *Two Lovers,* written by Gray and Richard Menello, is that it utterly ignores all the usual clichés about parents in general and Jewish mothers in particular. Both Leonard and Sandra come from loving families, and both of them love their parents. Although Leonard sometimes seems to contain muted, conflicting elements of Travis Bickle and Rupert Pupkin, he tries to get along with people, to be polite, to be sensitive. That he is the victim of his own obsessions is bad luck. It's painful watching him try to lead a secret life with Michelle outside his home, especially when her emergency demands come at the worst possible times.

Leonard's parents are Ruth and Reuben Kraditor (Isabella Rossellini and Moni Monoshov), long-married, staunchly bourgeois, reasonable. Ruth, of course, wants Leonard to find stability in marriage with a nice Jewish girl like Sandra, but her love for him outweighs her demands on him—rare in the movies. Reuben is more narrow in his imagination for his son but not a caricature. And Sandra's father (Bob Ari) wants to buy the Kraditor business and likes the idea of a marriage but would never think of his daughter as part of a business deal. Everyone in the film wants the best for their children.

So the drama, and it becomes intense, involves whether Leonard's demons will allow him to be happy. Michelle represents so many problems she should almost dress by wrapping herself in the yellow tape from crime scene investigations. She has a gift for attracting enablers. We meet her married lover (Elias Koteas), who turns out not to be an old letch, even if he is an adulterer. He's essentially another victim, and a short, tense scene he has with Leonard provides private insights.

Here is a movie involving the kinds of people we know or perhaps have been. It's the third film in which James Gray has directed Joaquin Phoenix (after *The Yards* and *We Own the Night*) and shows them working together to create a character whose manner is troubled but can be identified with. The whole movie is so well cast and performed that we watch it unfold without any particular awareness of "acting." Even the ending, which might seem obligatory in a lesser film, is earned and deserved in this one.

2012 ★ ★ ★ ½

PG-13, 158 m., 2009

John Cusack (Jackson Curtis), Amanda Peet (Kate Curtis), Chiwetel Ejiofor (Adrian Helmsley), Thandie Newton (Laura Wilson), Oliver Platt (Carl Anheuser), Tom McCarthy (Gordon Silberman), Woody Harrelson (Charlie Frost), Danny Glover (President Wilson), Liam James (Noah Curtis). Directed by Roland Emmerich and produced by Emmerich, Larry J. Franco, and Harald Kloser. Screenplay by Emmerich and Kloser.

It's not so much that the earth is destroyed but that it's done so thoroughly. *2012*, the mother of all disaster movies (and the father and the extended family), spends half an hour on ominous setup scenes (scientists warn, strange events occur, prophets rant, and, of course, a family is introduced) and then unleashes two hours of cataclysmic special events hammering the earth relentlessly.

This is fun. *2012* delivers what it promises, and since no sentient being will buy a ticket expecting anything else, it will be, for its audiences, one of the most satisfactory films of the year. It even has real actors in it. Like all the best disaster movies, it's funniest at its most hysterical. You think you've seen end-of-the-world movies? This one ends the world, stomps on it, grinds it up, and spits it out.

It also continues a recent trend toward the wholesale destruction of famous monuments. Roland Emmerich, the director and cowriter, has been vandalizing monuments for years, as in *Independence Day, The Day After Tomorrow*, and *Godzilla*. I still hold a grudge against him for that one because he provided New York with a Mayor Ebert and didn't have Godzilla step on me and squish me.

In all disaster movies, landmarks fall like dominoes. The Empire State Building is made of rubber. The Golden Gate Bridge collapses like clockwork. Big Ben ticks his last. The Eiffel Tower? *Quel dommage!* Memo to anyone on the National Mall: When the earth's crust is shifting, don't stand within range of the Washington Monument. Chicago is often spared; we aren't as iconic as Manhattan. There's little in Los Angeles distinctive enough to be destroyed, but it all goes anyway.

Emmerich thinks on a big scale. Yes, he destroys regular stuff. It will come as little surprise (because the trailer on YouTube alone has 7,591,413 views) that the aircraft carrier *John F. Kennedy* rides a tsunami onto the White House. When St. Peter's Basilica is destroyed, Leonardo's God and Adam are split apart just where their fingers touch (the ceiling of the Sistine Chapel having been moved into St. Peter's for the occasion). Then when Emmerich gets warmed up, the globe's tectonic plates shift thousands of miles, water covers the planet, and a giraffe walks on board an ark.

Also on board are the humans chosen to survive, including all the characters who have not already been crushed, drowned, or fallen into great crevices opening up in the earth. These include the heroic Jackson Curtis (John Cusack) and his estranged wife, Kate (Amanda Peet); the president (Danny Glover), his chief science adviser, Adrian Helmsley (Chiwetel Ejiofor); and his chief of staff, Carl Anheuser (Oliver Platt).

Many gigantic arks have been secretly constructed inside the Himalayas by the Chinese, funded by a global consortium, and they're the only chance of the human race surviving. There are also animals on board, and maybe well-named Noah (Liam James). In theory, ark ticket holders represent a cross-section of the globe, chosen democratically. In practice, Carl Anheuser pulls strings to benefit the rich and connected and wants to strand desperate poor people on the dock. I'm thinking, Emmerich often has a twist when he names villains, like Mayor Ebert from *Godzilla*. So how did this villain get his name? What does "Anheuser" make you think of?

Such questions pale by comparison with more alarming events. The tectonic plates shift so violently scientists can almost see it on Google Earth. This havoc requires stupendous special effects. Emmerich's budget was $250 million. It may contain more f/x in total running time than any other film. They're impressive. Not always convincing, because how can the flooding of the Himalayas be made convincing but impressive? And Emmerich gives us time to regard the effects and appreciate them, even savor them, unlike the ADD generation and its quick-cutting "Bay cams."

Emmerich also constructs dramatic real-scale illusions, as when an earthquake fissure splits a grocery store in half. Cusack is the hero in an elaborate sequence involving his desperate attempts to unblock a jammed hydraulic lift that threatens to sink the ark. He does a lot of heroic stuff in this film, especially for a novelist, like leaping a van over a yawning chasm and flying a small plane through roiling clouds of earthquake dust.

The bottom line is: The movie gives you your money's worth. Is it a masterpiece? No. Is it one of the year's best? No. Does Emmerich hammer it together with his elbows from parts obtained from the Used Disaster Movie Store? Yes. But is it about as good as a movie in this genre can be? Yes. No doubt it will inflame fears about our demise on December 21, 2012. I'm worried, too. I expect that to be even worse than Y2K.

Tyson ★ ★ ★ ★

R, 90 m., 2009

Featuring Mike Tyson. A documentary directed by James Toback.

Some kids beat him up once, and he couldn't stop them. Another kid killed one of his homing pigeons, and he fell upon him with fury. And that is the backstory of Mike Tyson, a boxer known as the Baddest Man on the Planet. When he went into the ring, he was proving he would never be humiliated again and getting revenge for a pigeon he loved. I believe it really is that simple. There is no rage like that of a child, hurt unjustly, the victim of a bully.

James Toback's *Tyson* is a documentary with no pretense of objectivity. Here is Mike Tyson's story in his own words, and it is surprisingly persuasive. He speaks openly and with apparent honesty about a lifetime during which, he believes, he was often misunderstood. From a broken family, he was in trouble at a tender age and always felt vulnerable; his childhood self is still echoed in his lisp, as high-pitched as a child's. It's as if the victim of big kids is still speaking to us from within the intimidating form of perhaps the most punishing heavyweight champion of them all.

Mike Tyson comes across here as reflective, contrite, more sinned against than sinning. He can be charming. He can be funny. You can see why Toback, himself a man of extremes, has been a friend for twenty years. The film contains a great deal of fight footage, of Tyson hammering one opponent after another. We also see a TV interview, infamous at the time, of his ex-wife, Robin Givens, describing him as abusive and manic-depressive. Even then I wanted to ask her, "And who did you think you were marrying?"

Tyson freely admits he has mistreated women and says he regrets it. But he denies the rape charge brought against him by Desiree Washington, which led to his conviction and three years in jail. "She was a swine," he says. He also has no use for boxing promoter Don King, "a slimy reptilian (bleeper)." His shining hero is his legendary trainer Cus D'Amato, the man who polished the diamond in the rough from his early teens and died just before the first heavyweight crown.

"Before the fight even starts, I've won," Tyson says. From Cus he learned never to take his eyes from his opponent's face from the moment he entered the ring. So formidable was his appearance and so intimidating his record that it once seemed he would have to retire before anyone else won the title. But he lost to Buster Douglas in Japan in 1990—the result, he says, of not following Cus's advice to stay away from women before a fight. He went into the ring with a case of gonorrhea. Later losses he attributes to a lack of physical training at a time when he signed up for fights simply for the payday. And there was drug abuse, from which he is now recovering.

This is only Toback's second doc, in a career of directing many fine films (*When Will I Be Loved, Harvard Man, Fingers*). In 1990, he was sitting next to a businessman on a flight and convinced him to finance *The Big Bang,* in which he would ask people about the meaning of life, the possibility of an afterlife, and what they believe in. "Tell me again why I'm financing this cockamamie thing," the man asks him. Toback says, simply, that the film will be remembered long after both he and the man are gone.

Toback is remarkably persuasive. He was offering immortality. It is a tempting offer. In ancient Egypt, an architect named Toback must have convinced a pharaoh to erect the first pyramid. What he offered Tyson was the opportunity to vindicate himself. There is no effort to show "both sides," but, in fact, the case against Tyson is already well known, and what is unexpected about Tyson is that afterward we feel sympathy for the man, and more for the child inside.

U

The Ugly Truth ★ ★

R, 95 m., 2009

Katherine Heigl (Abby Richter), Gerard Butler (Mike Chadway), Eric Winter (Colin), John Michael Higgins (Larry), Nick Searcy (Stuart), Kevin Connolly (Jim), Cheryl Hines (Georgia). Directed by Robert Luketic and produced by Tom Rosenberg, Gary Lucchesi, Steven Reuther, Kimberly di Bonaventura, and Deboray Jelin Newmyer. Screenplay by Nicole Eastman, Karen McCullah Lutz, and Kirsten Smith.

Katherine Heigl and Gerard Butler are so pleasant in *The Ugly Truth* that it's a shame to spoil their party. But toil and try as they do, the comedy bogs down in relentless predictability and the puzzling overuse of naughty words. Once, the movies were forbidden to drop the f-word at all, but in this one, it's only an opening salvo in a potty-mouth bombing run.

Heigl plays Abby, producer of the Sacramento early morning news on a station that is operated like no other station in the history of television. Anchored by a bickering married couple, the broadcast is tanking in the ratings, and so she's forced to bring in Mike Chadway (Gerard Butler), a macho local cable personality whose ideas about the battle of the sexes date back to about *Alley Oop*.

On his first appearance, he departs from his script, diagnoses the anchor as the victim of his control-freak wife, and suggests they've probably stopped sleeping together. "This is great!" the station manager enthuses, despite that the segment runs so long it steps on the first five minutes of the network morning slot.

Abby is a raving beauty who, of course, can't find a man, maybe because her standards are so perfectionist. A handsome young orthopedic surgeon (Eric Winter) comes within her sights, after she twists an ankle falling from a tree outside his bedroom window watching him dry off after a shower while she was trying to rescue her cat. That's the sort of thing, wouldn't you agree, that happens all too rarely in life? Mike, the rugged sex-talk guru, tells her she's making all the wrong moves if she ever wants to catch this guy, and starts coaching her.

So which guy does she end up with? Guess. The movie leaves not a stone unturned, including the semi-obligatory Beauty Makeover Montage, during which Mike advises her on the requirements of a push-up bra and tells her to acquire longer hair. Uh, huh. And when the doc takes her to a ball game, Mike broadcasts instructions to her earphone, just as a producer might speak in an anchor's ear.

There's one scene with real comic possibilities, but it doesn't pay off. Mike gives her a pair of remote-controlled battery-powered vibrating panties. (Yes, they actually manufacture such items. Isn't the Web a useful resource?) Abby, the silly girl, foolishly decides to wear these to a business dinner, and takes along the remote controller for reasons it is hard to explain. A kid at a nearby table grabs the vibrator. We all know what's coming, and Heigl makes a real effort, but I'm afraid Meg Ryan's restaurant orgasm in *When Harry Met Sally* remains the gold standard in this rare but never boring genre.

The TV news as portrayed in the film makes *Anchorman: The Legend of Ron Burgundy* look like a documentary. Every segment can run as long as necessary. Macho Mike ad libs everything. Yes, he's good for ratings, but if after a few days he's really pulling in a twelve in the 5 a.m. hour, in prime time he would outscore the Oscars. And TV cameras do not usually follow newsmen out of the studio and into the street and watch whatever they do then—although if it were funnier, we might not mind.

Katherine Heigl and Gerard Butler are awfully nice here. The movie does them in. Amazing that this raunchy screenplay was written by three women. At its conclusion, I am forced to report, it provides abundant evidence of my belief that a good movie has rarely featured a hot-air balloon.

Uncle Boonmee Who Can Recall His Past Lives ★ ★ ★ ½

NO MPAA RATING, 113 m., 2011

Thanapat Saisaymar (Boonmee), Jenjira Pongpas (Jen), Sakda Kaewbuadee (Tong), Natthakarn Aphaiwonk (Huay), Geerasak

Kulhong (Boonsong). Directed by Apichatpong Weerasethakul and produced by Weerasethakul, Simon Field, and Keith Griffiths. Screenplay by Weerasethakul.

Perhaps our conscious identities exist all the time and occasionally surface into the material world. If we were aware of that, it would make living within real time and space distracting; Wordsworth thought we remember heaven as babies. Later perhaps, if we live carefully and well, as we grow closer to death some tendrils from the other side reach out to greet us.

That is the possibility advanced by *Uncle Boonmee Who Can Recall His Past Lives*, which won the Palme d'Or at Cannes 2010. Don't be put off by its whimsical title, or by the name of its director, which looks strange to Western eyes: Apichatpong Weerasethakul. It's only a movie, and he's only a man. If you are open, even in fancy, to the idea of ghosts who visit the living, this is likely to be a curious but rather bemusing experience.

The movie is easy to understand. I discovered that on my second viewing. The first time through, at one of the morning press screenings at Cannes, I kept expecting for it to declare itself, to be about something. But a dying man like Boonmee is not much for plots, nor does he have an agenda for action. He is taking leave. What happens may seem very odd; the romantic scene with a catfish, for example, which you don't see every day. But to a mind accustomed to the idea of reincarnation, it must be good to meet spirits one has cared for, in whatever their present form.

Uncle Boonmee (Thanapat Saisaymar) spent his life as a farmer in a forested area of Thailand. It was not a perfect life. His nation went through upheaval in his lifetime, and we gather he saw more of that than he desired. Now he is dying of kidney failure, cared for by a male nurse from Laos and some of his family members. He stays in a house in the jungle, open to nature, and at his table is visited by ghosts, including his dead wife (beautiful as when he met her) and his son (who looks as if he got a good price on a gorilla suit with electric red eyes). But this isn't a ghost story, because these aren't ghosts as we understand them. They are as alive and aware as Boonmee.

There is a sequence here that may enthrall you. Boonmee makes a visit to a cave that seems to represent the womb for him. It contains sparkling lights and blind fish and is perhaps not an absolutely real cave. Well, if nature and man are one and interconnected, why would Earth not give birth? Or why would Boonmee in any event not visualize it that way?

At the film's end, there is a measured return to reality as we recognize it. The spirit world recedes. But does the real world have any more substance than visions and hallucinations—when we're having them? At any given moment, what's happening in our minds is all and everything that happens. Here is how Uncle Boonmee spent his final days, and how he recalled his past lives and those who shared them. Simple as that.

The Uninvited ★ ★ ★

PG-13, 87 m., 2009

Emily Browning (Anna), Elizabeth Banks (Rachel), David Strathairn (Steven), Arielle Kebbel (Alex), Maya Massar (Mom), Kevin McNulty (Sheriff), Jesse Moss (Matt), Dean Paul Gibson (Dr. Silberling). Directed by Charles Guard and Thomas Guard and produced by Walter F. Parkes, Laurie MacDonald, and Roy Lee. Screenplay by Craig Rosenberg, Doug Miro, and Carlo Bernard.

Emily Browning's face helps *The Uninvited* work so well. She's a twenty-year-old actress from Australia and has a lot of experience, but looks about fourteen. She makes an ideal heroine for a horror movie: innocent, troubled, haunted by nightmares, persecuted by a wicked stepmother, convinced her real mother was deliberately burned to death. She makes you fear for her, and that's half the battle. Yet she's so fresh she's ready for a Jane Austen role.

I recoiled twice in the opening minutes of *The Uninvited*, and that's a good sign. This is a well-crafted first feature by the Guard brothers (Charles and Thomas) from Britain that weaves a story not as predictable as it might seem. Browning plays Anna, who when we meet her is finishing a stay at a psychiatric clinic under the care of chubby, paternal

Dr. Silberling (Dean Paul Gibson). Her dad (David Strathairn), darkly ambiguous, drives her home to be welcomed by his girlfriend, Rachel (Elizabeth Banks), who is all sunshine and false friendliness.

But Anna yearns only to see her older sister, Alex (Arielle Kebbel). They dive off from their boathouse, make sister-talk on the raft, and then Alex swims away as young Matt (Jesse Moss) arrives on his grocery delivery boat. Matt, the boy who was getting too insistent with Anna when they were making out at the beach campfire. And that was the night her sick mother died, burned up in the boathouse, which had been converted into a sick room, and now, as Anna has just seen, been rebuilt.

What really happened that night? How did Rachel start as her mother's nurse and become Anna's new stepmom? Don't Rachel and her dad know how it disturbs the girls to see them smooching? And who is Rachel, really? Is that her real name? Google can be an insidious resource.

And more about the story I really cannot say. *The Uninvited* gets under your skin. The cinematography has that classy-horror-movie look, the overhead shots of a lonely car driving through ominous trees, the interiors sometimes shadowed, sometimes uncannily sunny, and the—presences—as Emily Dickinson would punctuate, that are half-seen in a half-sleep.

David Strathairn is well cast. Nobody can seem more open and affable, and suggest such hooded menace. Who else is so good at telling his daughter there's nothing to worry about, and making us worry? Elizabeth Banks, as Rachel, is almost convincing when she tells Anna she hopes they can be friends. Almost. Hard to imagine that Banks played Laura Bush *and* Miri of Zack and Miri, but that's acting for you. Here she has moments balanced on a knife edge between being cheerful and being a little too quick to start issuing mom-type orders, like telling Matt not to come to the house anymore.

The Uninvited begins with a classically Freudian situation, moves directly into dream analysis, has blood coming from keyholes and corpses speaking from the grave, and is all set, of course, in a huge, rambling New England shore house with gables, attics, long corridors, and places where anyone, or anything, could be hiding. When a movie like this is done well, it's uncommon. *The Uninvited* is done well.

Note: I'm a little surprised by the PG-13, *more evidence the MPAA awards the rating for what a movie doesn't have (nudity, language, sex) than what it does have, images that could be very troubling for some younger viewers.*

Unknown ★ ★

PG-13, 113 m., 2010

Liam Neeson (Dr. Martin Harris), Diane Kruger (Gina), January Jones (Elizabeth Harris), Aidan Quinn (Martin B.), Bruno Ganz (Ernst Jurgen), Frank Langella (Rodney Cole). Directed by Jaume Collet-Serra and produced by Joel Silver, Leonard Goldberg, and Andrew Rona. Screenplay by Oliver Butcher and Stephen Cornwell.

Is there a term for the paradox of intended accidental consequences? That's when a movie shows something that must be an accident, and it turns out to be part of a plan. Since *Unknown* opens with examples of such events, it won't be a spoiler for me to discuss them. I'll bail out before the tricky stuff.

As the movie opens, we meet Dr. Martin Harris (Liam Neeson) and his wife, Elizabeth (January Jones), who are on a flight to a biotechnology conference in Berlin. I'm thinking all we need to know about biotechnology in a thriller is that it probably involves either genetically altered crops or dangerous plagues. Anyway, at the airport Dr. Harris lets a guy load his luggage and as the taxi leaves, we get a big shot of his briefcase, still on the luggage trolley.

So OK. Was this an accident? If I'm carrying a briefcase that contains a cure for world hunger or a formula of mass destruction, I'm not gonna leave it on the curb. That's like leaving a laptop sitting on the sink when you go into a stall at a public toilet. Anyway, Dr. Harris and his wife get to the hotel, she starts to check in, he realizes his briefcase was left behind, and *without telling her* he grabs another taxi to the airport. He tries to call her but can't get a signal. Ever had that happen to you in Berlin?

A container falls off the truck in front of them, the taxi swerves and plunges through a bridge rail. Dr. Harris is knocked unconscious, but his life is saved by the quick actions of the driver, Gina (Diane Kruger). He's in a coma for four days. He pulls himself together and races to the hotel, only to find that his wife says she has never seen him before and is happily married to the "real" Dr. Martin Harris (Aidan Quinn). Now his ordeal begins: How can he prove his real identity and understand the conspiracy that has taken control of his life?

As a veteran thriller watcher, you can think of several possibilities here. It was all a dream. He has been brainwashed. He only thinks he's Martin Harris. He only imagined he was on a plane with the real Mrs. Elizabeth Harris. The second taxi was waiting to pick him up. And on and on. Or possibly none of the above.

But let's do an instant rewind. Was it an accident he left the briefcase behind? If he hadn't, there would have been no need to return to the airport. Was the falling container an accident? Was it an accident that he got a (beautiful) undocumented Bosnian refugee taxi driver who performed a heroic rescue in icy winter waters? Was it planned that he would be able to walk into the biotechnology conference and find the (real or fake) Dr. Martin Harris?

I'm thinking, if I'm an operative for some sinister secret organization and I want that briefcase and the MacGuffin it contains, here's what I'll do: I'll knock off Liam Neeson, whoever he is, and steal the briefcase. Or break into his hotel room. Or drug him. Anything. Because, think: If he isn't the real Martin Harris, why does he possess the briefcase containing the MacGuffin in the first place? But if he's a fake Martin Harris, who is the real one?

The movie has answers of a sort to some, but not all, of these questions. All the same, it left me rerunning events in my mind and thinking, Wait! Are we dealing with the Paradox of the Intended Accidental Consequences here, or what? *Unknown* is a skillfully photographed and acted film, and few actors are better than Liam Neeson at playing a man who has had the rug pulled out from under him. I was reminded of Roman Polanski's *Frantic* (1988), in which Harrison Ford played a doctor attending a convention in Paris with his wife. In that movie, the wrong briefcase was picked up at the airport, Ford stepped into the hotel shower, and when he stepped out, he found his wife had vanished.

Frantic wasn't watertight, either. The basic situation (an innocent man trapped in a conspiracy he doesn't understand) was a favorite of Hitchcock's, but in his films every consequence is intended. I confess I felt involved in *Unknown* until it pulled one too many rabbits out of its hat. At some point a thriller has to play fair. We're not satisfied when characters find it necessary to come out of nowhere and explain to the hero the underlying reality of his situation. Why does he need to know? Just bump him off. Whenever I hear one of those underlying reality speeches, I think there should be a crawl across the bottom of the screen: "This is actually the voice of the screenwriter desperately trying to explain the plot to himself."

Anyway, maybe this is all just me talking. Maybe I've seen too many movies. *Unknown* isn't really a bad movie, just an absurd one. It has its qualities from moment to moment. It left me with this thought: It's a damn good thing Dr. Martin Harris got that blond Bosnian taxi driver. A lot of taxi drivers, you don't get service like that.

Unmistaken Child ★ ★ ½

NO MPAA RATING, 102 m., 2009

Featuring Tenzin Zopa. A documentary directed by Nati Baratz and produced by Baratz, Ilil Alexander, and Arik Bernstein. Screenplay by Baratz.

To the mind of a Western rationalist, *Unmistaken Child* raises questions so fundamental that they interfere with the film's purpose. Here is a documentary about a very young child who is believed to be the reincarnation of a Buddhist lama, and is taken from his parents to be raised in a monastery. I know this is a practice of traditional forms of Buddhism, but still: Should it go this smoothly? Should the parents be so agreeable? The child so acquiescent? The monks so certain?

There is a tendency for Westerners to accept beliefs such as reincarnation more easily than they might accept some of the fundamentalist beliefs of their own Judeo-Christian tradition. This may be a form of exoticism, the willingness to ascribe to the Mysterious East possibilities we would be dubious about in our own culture.

The documentary, made by Nati Baratz, an Israeli who calls himself an "informal Buddhist," accepts everything in the account at face value. It began, he says, during his visit to a monastery, when he met Tenzin Zopa, a thirtyish Nepalese monk who had recently lost his master of twenty-one years. This man, Geshe Lama Konchog, who had lived a life of solitary meditation in a cave for more than two decades, was respected and beloved, and the Dalai Lama placed Tenzin in charge of the search for his reincarnation.

This search involves observations of the direction of the smoke from Geshe Lama's funeral pyre and the reading of his ashes (a footprint pointing east is discerned, although not by me). An astrologer in Taiwan is consulted and advises that there is a 95 percent chance the reincarnated boy's father will have a name beginning with "A," and that he will be found in a place beginning with "TS."

Thus the search focused on the Tsum Valley of Nepal. Tenzin seeks a child of the proper age, believes he has found the right one, and points to his long ears resembling those of Geshe Lama. The parents, a pleasant and loving couple, are surprisingly willing to part with their child for years. The child is tested to see how he responds to possessions of Geshe Lama and if he seems familiar with his cave, and then transported by SUV to Tenzin's monastery, where he is made much of by throngs of the devout.

This is a ritual that has repeated itself over the centuries. Martin Scorsese's *Kundun* (1997) told the story of the discovery and development of the present Dalai Lama. I know I am expected to believe the tenets of a religion on the basis of faith, not common sense, but during this film I found that very difficult. How reliable are wind directions, the interpretation of ashes, and astrological readings? Would you give over your son on such a basis? Would you trust such a chosen one as your spiritual leader?

These matters aside, *Unmistaken Child* has undeniable interest. It is filmed as events occur, in the actual locations, showing a world of great contrasts between an ancient way of life and a society that uses automobiles and helicopters. Baratz doesn't ask any of the obvious questions, preferring to observe uncritically, and if you can do the same, you may find it worth seeing. I could not, and grew restless.

Unstoppable ★ ★ ★ ½

PG-13, 98 m., 2010

Denzel Washington (Frank Barnes), Chris Pine (Will Colson), Rosario Dawson (Connie Hooper), Ethan Suplee (Dewey), Kevin Dunn (Galvin). Directed by Tony Scott and produced by Scott, Eric McLeod, Mimi Rogers, Julie Yorn, and Alex Young. Screenplay by Mark Bomback.

The freight train pulls out of a siding with no engineer on board and accelerates to 70 mph, and you see how Tony Scott's *Unstoppable* gets its title. The movie is as relentless as the train, slowly gathering momentum before a relentless final hour of continuous suspense. In terms of sheer craftsmanship, this is a superb film.

The trouble begins when an engineer (Ethan Suplee) dismounts after thinking he'd brought the train to a full stop. He hadn't. When he sees the train slowly pulling away, the look on his face is adequate to fuel the next several minutes. At first it's assumed that the train is a "coaster," but no luck. It's under full throttle.

Scott tells the story from several points of view. In the cab of another train, a longtime engineer named Barnes (Denzel Washington) is breaking in a new man, Colson (Chris Pine). In the station yard, a yardmaster named Connie Hooper (Rosario Dawson) is in charge of dispatch and operations. In the railroad's corporate offices, an executive (Kevin Dunn) is concerned mostly about the cost of losing the train, which seems harsh since it is carrying hazardous materials and is rocketing toward the heart of Scranton, Pennsylvania.

Overhead, news choppers circle, providing a live TV feed, which Scott intercuts with the action. That allows him a plausible way to provide an overview and narrate the action; a similar device was used by his brother Ridley Scott to help us follow events in his *Black Hawk Down* (2001).

There isn't a lot of room here for personality development, but Washington and Pine provide convincing characters, the veteran driven by love of his job, the new guy more cynical. This conflict isn't ramped up for dramatic effect in the screenplay by Mark Bomback, but is allowed to play out as naturally as it can, under the circumstances. Rosario Dawson makes her dispatcher aggressively competent, and the hurtling train of course rumbles beneath everything.

Chase scenes involving trains have an unavoidable limitation: Trains require tracks, and can only go forward or in reverse. There are sidings, but getting onto one may not be very simple. Two other films that come to mind are Buster Keaton's *The General* (1926) and Andrei Konchalovsky's *Runaway Train* (1985), which won Oscar nominations for the two men in its locomotive, Jon Voight and Eric Roberts.

How Scott deals with his "chase" is not for me to reveal here, but although the possibilities of two trains on one track would seem to be limited, he and Bomback are truly ingenious. They employ a kind of logical lateral thinking: The trains can only move in certain ways, but those ways may not be as obvious as we assume.

Not that those are terms we're thinking of during the action. The photography and sound here are very effective in establishing that a train is an enormously heavy thing, and once in motion wants to continue. We knew that. But Scott all but crushes us with the weight of the juggernaut. We are spellbound. And we sure hope those little kids are saved.

(Untitled) ★ ★ ★ ½

R, 96 m., 2009

Adam Goldberg (Adrian Jacobs), Marley Shelton (Madeleine Gray), Eion Bailey (Josh Jacobs), Vinnie Jones (Ray Barko), Ptolemy Slocum (Monroe), Zak Orth (Porter Canby). Directed by Jonathan Parker and produced by Catherine DiNapoli and Matt Luber. Screenplay by Parker and DiNapoli.

(Untitled) picks a fight with its very title, which summarizes the f—— you attitude of its hero, a composer of music that sounds like something you'd hear going on in the alley late at night. One of his compositions consists of a chain dropped into a can, loudly ripping paper, a bucket being kicked, the screams of a vocalist, and squawks on a clarinet. He plays the piano with his elbows. Under the circumstances, it seems ungracious for him to complain about an audience member's cell phone.

This musician is named Adrian Jacobs (Adam Goldberg), a bearded thirty-something who seems to have chugged a pint of bile. A good audience for him might consist of two dozen people; some walk out and the rest stare incredulously at the stage. One day, his brother, Josh (Eion Bailey), brings a date to his concert. This is Madeleine Gray (Marley Shelton), who runs a very, very avant-garde art gallery in Soho. Adrian asks if he can borrow her dress. It's made of shiny black plastic, it squeaks when she walks, and he thinks he can use the sound in his music.

(Untitled) is a comedy worthy of the best Woody Allen, and Adrian is not unlike Woody's persona: a sincere, intense, insecure nebbish, hopeless with women, aiming for greatness. He plays classical piano brilliantly and with contempt. If his "serious" work appeals to very few people, that's too many for him. Josh, on the other hand, is raking in the dough with his canvases, which are snatched up in volume for the lobbies of hotels.

The movie plunges fearlessly but not brainlessly into the world of art so cutting-edge it has run out of edges. Remember Damien Hirst, the British artist who inspired a firestorm when he won the Turner Prize for such works as half a shark preserved in formaldehyde? One of Madeleine's clients is Ray Barko (Vinnie Jones), whose art consists of a dead cat splayed on a wall, a goose apparently buried in a wall up to its wings, and a montage for monkey and vacuum cleaner. A rich client (Zak Orth) eats up this stuff. Lots of people do. I don't know if they enjoy it as much as I love my Edward Lear watercolors. Maybe they love it more.

Madeleine hires Adrian and his musicians to perform at her gallery as "conceptual art."

Well, I once attended a poetry reading featuring a revolving fan. Madeleine goes nuts for Adrian, and he finds her hard to resist because everything she wears makes noise. She seems to conceal a sound effects artist in her knickers. Adrian tunes in; the sound track subtly enhances what he hears.

They grow chummy. He attends Madeleine's opening for an artist named Monroe, played by an actor named Ptolemy Slocum, whose own name is a work of art. Meanwhile, Josh's insipid work (pastels of vague shapes adorned by small circles) supports the gallery, but Madeleine keeps them in the back room. He "doesn't need" a gallery opening, she explains. She hates them, is what it is.

It's easy to take cheap shots at conceptual art. *(Untitled)* doesn't do that. It takes expensive shots. Adrian's music has been created for the film by the respected composer David Lang, and Ray Barko's grotesque animals were created by Los Angeles artist Kyle Ng. The thing is, their deliberately (I think) absurd work resembles the real thing, when lesser movies would just ask the art department to drum up something. Barko's "work," given the right setting, would sell. That gives the film plausibility.

Jonathan Parker, who directed and cowrote with Catherine DiNapoli (they collaborated on *Bartleby*), also respects these artists—in a sense. Adrian can manifestly play the piano in a traditional way, so his music is a choice, not a necessity. Ray Barko has so many problems that his art may be a valid expression of his misery. Doubt remains about Monroe (played by Ptolemy Slocum, you will recall), whose pieces include a label reading *Untitled White Wall*, which is displayed on a white wall. Not any old white wall, you understand. It has to be the *right* white wall. I wonder if he'd need to tear up part of your house for its proper installation.

This is a good film, a smart film. It knows a lot about art and wears its knowledge lightly, dealing with its subject in a way even a student at the Art Institute might not find condescending. As so often, casting decisions help enormously in its success. Marley Shelton's gallery owner is like a lot of bright, formidable young women, ambitious, idealistic, bored by most of the men she meets. Vinnie Jones plays Barko as a reunion of pugnacious British eccentrics. Do not overlook the fetching Lucy Punch, as a member of Adrian's band known only as "The Clarinet." Shelton has the confidence and presence of a born comedienne, and as for Adam Goldberg, he plays the role without a shred of humor, which is exactly right. I have put out a Google alert to see if New York gossips identify the original(s) for the rich collector.

Note: Aspects of the film reminded me of Yasmina Reza's Tony Award–winning play Art*—http://en.wikipedia.org/wiki/%27Art%27_(play).*

Up ★ ★ ★ ★

PG, 96 m., 2009

Edward Asner (Carl Fredricksen), Christopher Plummer (Charles Muntz), Jordan Nagai (Russell), John Ratzenberger (Tom), Bob Peterson (Dug). Directed by Pete Docter and produced by Jonas Rivera. Screenplay by Docter and Bob Peterson.

Up is a wonderful film, with characters who are as believable as any characters can be who spend much of their time floating above the rain forests of Venezuela. They have tempers, problems, and obsessions. They are cute and goofy, but they aren't cute in the treacly way of little cartoon animals. They're cute in the human way of the animation master Hayao Miyazaki. Two of the three central characters are cranky old men, which is a wonder in this youth-obsessed era. *Up* doesn't think all heroes must be young or sweet, although the third important character is a nervy kid.

This is another masterwork from Pixar, which is leading the charge in modern animation. The movie was directed by Pete Docter, who also directed *Monsters, Inc.*, wrote *Toy Story*, and was the cowriter and first director on *WALL-E* before leaving to devote himself full time to this project. So he's one of the leading artists of this renaissance of animation.

The movie is in 3-D in some theaters, about which I will say nothing except to advise you to save the extra money and see it in 2-D. One of the film's qualities that is likely to be diminished by 3-D is its subtle and beautiful color palette. *Up*, like *Finding Nemo*, *Toy Story*,

Shrek, and *The Lion King,* uses colors in a way particularly suited to its content.

Up tells a story as tickling to the imagination as the magical animated films of my childhood, when I naively thought that because their colors were brighter, their character outlines more defined, and their plots simpler, they were actually more realistic than regular films. It begins with a romance as sweet and lovely as any I can recall in feature animation.

Two children named Carl and Ellie meet and discover they share the same dream of someday being daring explorers. In newsreels, they see the exploits of a daring adventurer named Charles Muntz (Christopher Plummer), who uses his gigantic airship to explore a lost world on a plateau in Venezuela and bring back the bones of fantastic creatures previously unknown to man. When his discoveries are accused of being faked, he flies off enraged to South America again, vowing to bring back living creatures to prove his claims.

Nothing is heard from him for years. Ellie and Carl (Edward Asner) grow up, have a courtship, marry, buy a ramshackle house and turn it into their dream home, are happy together, and grow old. This process is silent except for music (Ellie doesn't even have a voice credit). It's shown by Docter in a lovely sequence, without dialogue, that deals with the life experience in a way that is almost never found in family animation. The lovebirds save their loose change in a gallon jug intended to finance their trip to the legendary Paradise Falls, but real life gets in the way: flat tires, home repairs, medical bills. Then they make a heartbreaking discovery. This interlude is poetic and touching.

The focus of the film is on Carl's life after Ellie. He becomes a recluse, holds out against the world, keeps his home as a memorial, talks to the absent Ellie. One day he decides to pack up and fly away—literally. Having worked all his life as a balloon man, he has the equipment on hand to suspend the house from countless helium-filled balloons and fulfill his dream of seeking Paradise Falls. What he wasn't counting on was an inadvertent stowaway—Russell (Jordan Nagai), a dutiful Wilderness Explorer Scout, who looks Asian-American to me.

What they find at Paradise Falls and what happens there I will not say. But I will describe Charles Muntz's gigantic airship that is hovering there. It's a triumph of design and perhaps owes its inspiration, though not its appearance, to Miyazaki's *Castle in the Sky.* The exterior is nothing special: a really big zeppelin. But the interior, now, is one of those movie spaces you have the feeling you'll remember.

With vast inside spaces, the airship is outfitted like a great ocean liner from the golden age, with a stately dining room, long corridors, a display space rivaling the Natural History Museum, and attics spacious enough to harbor fighter planes. Muntz, who must be a centenarian by now, is hale, hearty, and mean, his solitary life shared only by dogs.

The adventures on the jungle plateau are satisfying in a *Mummy*/*Tomb Raider*/Indiana Jones sort of way. But they aren't the whole point of the film. This isn't a movie like *Monsters vs. Aliens* that's mostly just frenetic action. There are stakes here, and personalities involved, and two old men battling for meaning in their lives. And a kid who, for once, isn't smarter than all the adults. And a loyal dog. And an animal sidekick. And always that house and those balloons.

Up in the Air ★ ★ ★ ★

R, 109 m., 2009

George Clooney (Ryan Bingham), Vera Farmiga (Alex Goran), Anna Kendrick (Natalie Keener), Jason Bateman (Craig Gregory), Danny McBride (Jim Miller), Melanie Lynskey (Julie Bingham). Directed by Jason Reitman and produced by Jeffrey Clifford, Daniel Dubiecki, Ivan Reitman, and Jason Reitman. Screenplay by Jason Reitman and Sheldon Turner, based on a novel by Walter Kirn.

Ryan Bingham is the Organization Man for the 2000s. He never comes to the office. Technically, he doesn't have an office; he has an address where his employer has an office. His life is devoted to visiting other people's offices and firing them. *Up in the Air* takes the trust people once had in their jobs and pulls out the rug. It is a film for this time.

Bingham describes himself as a "termination facilitator." He fires people for a living. When corporations need to downsize quickly but hate the mess, he flies in and breaks the news to the new former employees. In hard times, his business is great.

This isn't a comedy. If it were, it would be hard to laugh in these last days of 2009. Nor is it a tragedy. It's an observant look at how a man does a job. Too many movie characters have jobs involving ruling people, killing them, or going to high school. Bingham loves his work. He doesn't want a home. He doesn't want a family. He gives self-help lectures on how and why to unpack the backpack of your life.

George Clooney plays Bingham as one of those people you meet but never get to know. They go through all the forms, and know all the right moves and you're "friends," but—who's in there? Sitting in a first-class seat one day, asked where he lives, Bingham says, "Here."

He likes his job because he feels he performs a service. Nobody likes to fire someone. Someone has to. He has protocols. In a curious way, he's like the two army men in *The Messenger*, who notify the next of kin after a soldier is killed. Jason Reitman, the director, auditioned real people who had recently been fired to play some of the fired employees (others are played by actors). He asked them to improvise their words on learning the news. Would you want the job of listening to their pain?

There are two women in Bingham's life. Alex Goran (Vera Farmiga) is also a road warrior, and for some time they've been meeting in dreary "suite" hotels in East Moses, Nowhere—having meals, making love, play-acting at being the happy couple neither one will commit to. Natalie Keener (Anna Kendrick) is a bright, ambitious new graduate who has taken a job with Bingham's company because it's near her boyfriend. Bingham takes her on the road to teach her the ropes. Alex is him now; Natalie is him then.

Farmiga is one of the warmest and most attractive women in the movies, or at least she plays one. You may not guess all she's thinking. Kendrick's Natalie is so brim-full of joy at the dawn of her career that it shines even on ending those of others. Nothing better than making your boss happy.

The isolation of the road life is threatened by the introduction of firing by Web chat. This is in-sourcing, if you will. It may not be warmer than firing someone in person, but it saves a lot of money on airfare. Notice how Reitman likes to start with the way corporations justify immoral behavior and then apply their rationalizations with perfect logic. That method was at the core of his brilliant debut, *Thank You for Smoking* (2005).

Reitman also made the great *Juno*. Still only thirty-two, the son of the Canadian producer-director Ivan Reitman (*Ghostbusters*), he grew up behind the counter of the family store, so to speak. With these three films at the dawn of *his* career, we can only imagine what comes next. He makes smart, edgy, mainstream films. That's harder than making smart, edgy indies. In a pie chart he compiled of questions he's asked time and again during interviews, "How does your father feel about your success?" ranks high. Bursting with pride is my guess.

V

Valentine's Day ★ ★
PG-13, 124 m., 2010

Jessica Alba (Morley Clarkson), Kathy Bates (Susan), Jessica Biel (Kara Monahan), Bradley Cooper (Holden), Eric Dane (Sean Jackson), Patrick Dempsey (Dr. Harrison Copeland), Hector Elizondo (Edgar), Jamie Foxx (Kelvin Moore), Jennifer Garner (Julia Fitzpatrick), Topher Grace (Jason), Anne Hathaway (Liz), Carter Jenkins (Alex), Ashton Kutcher (Reed Bennett), Queen Latifah (Paula Thomas), Taylor Lautner (Willy), George Lopez (Alphonso), Shirley MacLaine (Estelle), Emma Roberts (Grace), Julia Roberts (Captain Kate Hazeltine), Bryce Robinson (Edison), Taylor Swift (Felicia). Directed by Garry Marshall and produced by Mike Karz, Wayne Allan Rice, and Josie Rosen. Screenplay by Katherine Fugate.

I've heard of all-star casts, but *Valentine's Day* has a *complete* star cast. What did other movies do for talent when this one was filming? It has twenty-one actors who can be considered stars, and some are very big stars indeed. It's like the famous poster for *It's a Mad Mad Mad Mad World,* with a traffic jam of famous faces.

That's the movie's problem. Gridlock. It needs somebody like that tough traffic warden who stands under the L at Wabash and Randolph and fiercely wags her finger at drivers who don't shape up. The actors in this movie could populate six romantic comedies with reasonable plots, and a couple of sitcoms. Of course you'd need scripts. *Valentine's Day* is so desperate to keep all the characters alive, it's like those Russian jugglers who run around trying to keep all their plates spinning on poles.

I won't even attempt to describe the plot. Nor will I tell you who the characters are and who plays them. Just the names would come to sixty-three words, and if I described each character in twenty words, I'd run out of space way before I got to Captain Kate Hazeltine (Julia Roberts). I will mention it was nice to see Shirley MacLaine and Hector Elizondo as an old married couple, and of interest that two Taylors (Swift and Lautner) had scenes together.

For the rest, words fail me. The structure of the film involves a large number of couples and additional characters who are not in couples. We wake up with them on the morning of February 14, and all of their stories are completed by midnight, and as Ricky told Lucy, there's a lot of 'splainin to do. Several ancient formulas are employed. (1) Best friends who don't realize they're really in love. (2) Guy who thinks she loves him but she doesn't. (3) Girl who thinks he loves her but he's married. (4) People sitting next to each other on an airplane strike up a conversation. (5) Guy misunderstands phone call, draws wrong conclusion. (6) Fifth-grader's first crush.

The most important characters are a florist named Reed (Ashton Kutcher) and his best friend, Julia (Jennifer Garner). They don't have enough screen time to create three-dimensional characters, but at least they get up to two, leaving everyone else stuck at one or below. They're both attractive, but then all twenty-one stars are attractive, especially if, like me, you think George Lopez is handsome, especially when he smiles.

There's one peculiarity. Usually in formula pictures with this huge a cast, maybe one couple will be African-American, one Latino, and one Asian. No such luck. There are no Asians at all. The black characters include a goofy TV sports reporter (Jamie Foxx) and a wise agent (Queen Latifah). Lopez, a Mexican-American, is relegated to the role of Kutcher's sidekick (i.e., the Tonto role). There are a lot of Indians in the movie, at the next table in an Indian restaurant, revealing that when Indians are out to dinner, they act just like Indians in a movie comedy.

The form of the movie may remind you wistfully of a much better one, *Love, Actually,* which created characters we cared a great deal about. None of the characters here ever get beyond the Look—There's (Name of Star) Threshold. You know, when your mind says, Look—There's Patrick Dempsey! Look—There's Anne Hathaway! Look—There's Topher Grace! Wow—That's Jessica Biel!

Valentine's Day is being marketed as a Date Movie. I think it's more of a First Date Movie. If your date likes it, do not date that person again. If you like it, there may not be a second date.

Valentino: The Last Emperor ★ ★ ★

NO MPAA RATING, 96 m., 2009

Featuring Valentino Garavani, Giancarlo Giammetti, and Matteo Marzotto. A documentary directed by Matt Tyrnauer and produced by Tyrnauer and Matt Kapp.

To be sure, we see Valentino only at times of great stress, while he is designing a new collection, presenting it in Paris, and preparing for a monumental Roman celebration of his career. But as seen in this film, he seems to suffer from anhedonia, the inability to feel pleasure. He is a multimillionaire, has ruled his profession for forty-five years, has a personal and business partner who has been with him all that time, has every whim attended to. But he seems gnawed by dissatisfaction.

Valentino: The Last Emperor is a documentary with privileged access to the legendary designer in his studio, workshop, backstage, his homes, even aboard his yacht and private jet (which he shares with his matched pugs). It is clear that he does not enjoy being filmed and regrets ever having agreed to it. That gives the film an innate fascination. I know next to nothing about haute couture, but I became involved in the buried drama: Valentino, at seventy-seven, with his world of elegant dresses being destroyed by the branded marketing of—belt buckles! purses! sunglasses!—is clearly at the end of his career.

Nobody will ask him about anything else. Whenever he appears in public, he is surrounded by reporters chanting, "When will you retire?" What are the odds Valentino will announce his retirement right there on the sidewalk to a baying pack of vultures?

But Valentino is coming to the end, all the same. His company has been purchased by an Italian millionaire named Matteo Marzotto, and a multinational is currently buying up its stock. I once bought a pair of sweat pants at Marshall Field's with a Pierre Cardin label. Crummy pants. The only labels I trust are Brooks Brothers and L.L. Bean. But sunglasses with a sequined "V" on them are so close Valentino can smell them. He wants out first.

He works very hard. His head seamstress drives a team of skilled dressmakers. No sewing machines for Valentino. Every stitch by hand. Always at his side is Giancarlo Giammetti, his business partner and onetime lover, who guesses they haven't been apart two months in forty-five years. Valentino was hopeless at business; Giammetti was not. Right at the start Valentino dressed Jackie Kennedy, and his name was made. "I know what women want," he says. "They want to be beautiful." There is a forty-fifth anniversary exhibit of his iconic dresses. To my eye, they look timeless and lovely.

But I am looking at Valentino. He carries himself like an emperor. He walks and stands as if always onstage. He speaks and everyone listens. In photos, he poses as if above the rabble. He is surrounded by much taller women, and treats them as if they are invisible. He relates to his models as if they were mannequins; there is no interaction, nothing personal. Even Giancarlo receives only an official hug, an occasional very quiet "Thank you."

I have the impression Giancarlo is the only one licensed to tell Valentino the truth. "How did I do?" he asks in the backseat of their limousine.

"Great."

"Tell me the truth."

"A little too tan," Giancarlo says. This to a man who looks deep orange. How can he design such dresses and not see himself in the mirror? Surely there is a browner spray-on?

Valentino as a boy idolized the goddesses of the silver screen. All he ever wanted to do was dress them, and that is all he has ever done. The sets and spectacles for his forty-fifth anniversary celebration in Rome resemble, he complains, Cirque du Soleil. They do. The models fly high above the crowd. Everyone is there. The film is crowded with stars, and they're all in the background: Sophia, Gwyneth, Mick, Elton, Princess This, Countess That.

But when he appears at the end of a show, watch him walk out only halfway and give his cursory little wave. No big smile. No blowing kisses. No hands up in triumph. Why isn't he happier? Is he driven by a work ethic that gives him no mercy? Is he . . . shy?

Vidal Sassoon: The Movie ★ ★ ½

PG, 94 m., 2011

Vidal Sassoon, Michael Gordon, Mary Quant, John Frieda, Peggy Moffitt, Ronnie Sassoon, and Beverly Sassoon. A documentary directed by Craig Teper and produced by Gordon and Jackie Gilbert Bauer. Screenplay by Teper and Heather Campbell Gordon.

Vidal Sassoon: The Movie might as well be titled *Vidal Sassoon: The Infomercial* for all of the distance it maintains from its subject. Its best quality is that it made me like and admire Sassoon, although if there is anything unlikable and not admirable about him, I wouldn't have discovered it here. The movie is structured around a new book on Sassoon being published by Michael Gordon, who also produced this film and appears in it, and that will give you a notion of its objectivity.

Vidal at eighty-three is alert and superbly fit, a yoga practitioner who still bends into pretzel shapes and lifts weights. The world's most successful hairdresser is the very definition of a self-made man: Born in the Jewish ghetto of London's East End, he was abandoned by his father and placed by his mother in an orphanage for several years—not because she didn't love him, but because she was poor. "She came to see me every week," he says, and in his teens, she apprenticed him to a hairdresser who was a firm disciplinarian. To have unshined shoes or untidy fingernails was a grave offense.

Sassoon never particularly wanted to be a hairdresser. He wanted to be an architect, he tells us, although his spotty education might have put an end to that dream. He was ambitious, and he came to love cutting hair. He worked hard, he was a perfectionist, he soon had a chair in the West End and then his own shop on Bond Street. By then it was the Swinging Sixties, and Vidal Sassoon was at the very epicenter with his revolutionary, architectural haircuts and finally the "five-point cut."

Having never heard of this cut (my ignorances are manifold), I realized on seeing it in this film that I've been looking at it all of my life. To one degree or another, half the women alive must wear their hair differently today because of Vidal Sassoon's scissors. Then came the New York shop, the Vidal Sassoon Academies, the shampoo and hair products line, the daily TV show, the TV commercials for Sassooning, and millions and millions of dollars. Such circles did he move in that once in a health spa, because of a lamentable mix-up, he received an enema intended for Gore Vidal.

It wasn't easy. He was born with a Cockney accent (and demonstrates that very convincingly), and took elocution lessons from a voice coach at the Old Vic. He explained to women why he would not cut their hair the way they wanted it cut. He danced around his clients with a pair of scissors instead of an array of hairdressing hardware. He was married three times, had three children, lost one because of an overdose, is happily married today, and is dedicated to "progressive causes."

There must be more. We will not discover it here. What we will see is a good many classic haircuts and testimonials from current or former employees. There is also an affectionate chat with Mary Quant, who was doing with fashion what Sassoon was doing with hair in the 1960s. It has been a good life. If you know as little about hairdressing as I do, ask yourself two questions: Have you always known Vidal Sassoon was the name of a famous hairdresser? Can you name another one?

Vincent: A Life in Color ★ ★ ★ ½

NO MPAA RATING, 96 m., 2010

Featuring Vincent P. Falk. A documentary directed and produced by Jennifer Burns.

You have never heard of Vincent P. Falk, but if you've been near Chicago's Marina City you may have seen him. He's the smiling middle-aged man with a limitless variety of spectacular suits. He stands on the Michigan or Wabash avenue bridges, showing off his latest stupefying suit. He flashes the flamboyant lining, takes the coat off, spins it in great circles above his head, and then does his "spin move," pivoting first left, then right, while whirling the coat in the air. Then he puts it on again and waves to the tourists on the boat, by now passing under the bridge.

You might be forgiven for suspecting that Vincent is a few doughnuts short of a dozen. I know I did. Then I saw the remarkable documentary *Vincent: A Life in Color*, which unfolds into the mystery of a human personality. Would it surprise you to learn Vincent is a college graduate? A Cook County computer programmer? A former deejay in gay North Side discos? Paying his own rent in Marina City? Buying his own suits? Legally blind?

All of these things are true. I can believe he buys his own suits. What I can hardly believe is that they are sold. We accompany him on a visit to his customary clothing store, which perhaps caters otherwise to members of the world's second oldest profession.

Jennifer Burns, the producer and director of the film, says that like most Chicagoans, she'd seen Vincent and his colorful suits around for years. How could she not? Then one day she was looking out her office window, watching him performing for a tour boat, "and I was struck by the look of sheer joy I saw on his face. I thought to myself, whatever else you have to say about this guy, he has figured out what makes him happy and he does it, regardless of what anyone else thinks." She approached him, and he agreed to be the subject of a film—not surprising, since his pastime is drawing attention to himself. The subtext of the film is how differently life could have turned out for Vincent.

Vincent, whose surname comes from the last of his foster families, was an orphan abandoned by his mother and raised at St. Joseph's Home for the Friendless. There the nuns discovered that Vincent's problem wasn't intellectual but visual and taught him to read, along with the rest of the class, making sure he was always pushed up against the blackboard so he could see. In high school he was picked on relentlessly, and learned to respond with humor. He was a member of the National Honor Society, the chess club, the debate team, and the diving team, luckily never diving into a pool without water. We meet his diving coach, who was as surprised as we are.

Vincent reads with his good eye held less than an inch from a book or computer screen. Sometimes he uses a magnifying glass. He used a cane in high school, then threw it away and walks freely everywhere in Chicago. It is terrifying to think of him crossing a street.

Vincent, a bright student, was accepted at the University of Illinois, where he studied computer science. He eventually wound up at the Illinois Institute of Technology, studying aeronautical engineering. Yes. He became a popular deejay, first for the go-go boys at Stage 618, and then at the gay disco Cheeks. He didn't exactly fit the image, his old boss recalls, and he held the albums an inch from his face, but he was a great spinner. It was during this time he concluded he was gay. For the past twenty years, he's been a computer programmer for Cook County, helping to track billions of dollars in tax revenue. "He's one of the most brilliant programmers I've ever met," his current boss says.

All of which is admirable, but how does it explain the suits? He started wearing the suits in the 1990s, and says he gave his first bridge show in 2000, adding the "spin move" about a year later. He knows the times when every tour boat passes his bridges, and the guides know his name and point him out somewhere between the Wrigley Building and Marina City. To the guides on the Mercury boats, he is "Riverace" (rhymes with "Liberace"). The captain of one of the Wendella boats says you can set your watch by him. Both of his bridges and both of the TV studios are within a short walk of his home.

There is a great deal of discussion in the documentary about Vincent's motivation. It solves nothing. Vincent himself will say only that he likes to entertain people, to cheer them up a little. One expert in the doc speculates that Vincent has spent a lot of his life being stigmatized and isolated, and the suits are a way of breaking down barriers. I confess that the first time I saw him, I saw a man with unfocused squinting eyes and a weird suit, and leaped to conclusions. Having seen this film, I applaud Vincent. Here is a man who likes to buy Technicolor suits and wave them at tour boats. So why not? What are the people on the boats so busy doing that they don't have time for that?

Note: This review is based on my earlier blog entry.

Vincere ★ ★ ★ ½

NO MPAA RATING, 128 m., 2010

Giovanna Mezzogiorno (Ida Dalser), Filippo Timi (Benito Mussolini), Fausto Russo Alesi (Riccardo Paicher), Michela Cescon (Rachele

Mussolini), Pier Giorgio Bellocchio (Pietro Fedele), Fabrizio Costella (Young Benito). Directed by Marco Bellocchio and produced by Mario Gianani. Screenplay by Bellocchio and Daniela Ceselli.

The image of Benito Mussolini has been shifted over the years toward one of a plump buffoon, the inept second fiddle to Hitler. We've seen the famous photo of his ignominious end, his body strung upside down. We may remember his enormous scowling visage trundled out on display in a scene from Fellini's *Amarcord.* What we don't envision is Mussolini as a fiery young man, able to inflame Italians with his charismatic leadership.

That's the man who fascinates Marco Bellocchio, and his *Vincere* explains how such a man could seize a young woman with uncontrollable erotomania that would destroy her life. She was Ida Dalser (Giovanna Mezzogiorno), at first his lover, later his worst nightmare. When she first saw him before World War I, he was a firebrand, dark and handsome, and she was thunderstruck. For Ida, there was one man, and that was Benito (Filippo Timi), and it would always be so.

Her feelings had little to do with his politics. *Vincere* might have been much the same film if Mussolini had been a Christian Democrat. Her feelings spring from a fierce love, which at first is mutual. That he is filled with ideas and ambition makes him all the more attractive, but does she even care what those ideas are? She supports them as a matter of course, selling all she has to support his party newspaper.

They have a son. He leaves to serve in the Italian army in the war. He is possibly lost in combat. She doesn't hear from him. It is an old story. When he reappears after the war, it is impossible for him to lie low; he is Mussolini, in his own mind the chosen one. They are reunited briefly, and the old passion is there. Then she discovers he has a wife. A mistress and a child are decidedly . . . inconvenient for him.

It is revealing how inconvenient Mussolini considers them, and how his values were shaped by bourgeois Catholicism despite his politics. As he makes a strategic alliance with the Vatican, he cannot imagine, and he doesn't believe the public can accept, a leader with a mistress. His wife, Rachele (Michela Cescon), certainly cannot. We might assume Ida could be hidden away or even kept in plain sight, like his friend Hitler's Eva Braun. But no.

If Ida had been capable of staying out of sight and staying quiet, some accommodation can be imagined. A discreet government pension. A home in a city distant from Rome. That is not to be. She considers Mussolini a demigod, and with all the passion of a woman defending her child, she wants her son—hers!—to be acknowledged before all the world as the great man's offspring and heir.

Bellocchio, once himself a fiery young artist (*Fists in the Pocket*), now a legend of the generation of Bertolucci, is concerned with Mussolini's fascism primarily as backdrop. His film is focused on Ida. The last time she sees him in the flesh is the last time we do. Thereafter he's seen only in newsreels—a convenient way for Bellocchio to age and fatten him.

We see Ida's marginal, scorned existence. We see her enacting life scenes that could be staged in opera: She bursts upon Mussolini during public appearances, dragging along the hapless boy as evidence of Benito's heartlessness. The boy himself is bewildered, less concerned with his purported father than with his daily existence with a mother consumed by her obsession.

Was she mad? The term is "erotomania," defined by the conviction that someone is in love with you. It can be a complete delusion, as in the case of celebrity stalkers. But it is not delusional if that person *was* in love with you, held you in his arms night after night, and gave you a son. The fascists instinctively protect Mussolini. When Ida appears in public places, she is surrounded and taken away without Benito even needing to request it. Finally, shamefully, she is consigned to an insane asylum and the boy locked up in an orphanage. She becomes a familiar type: the poor madwoman who is convinced the great man loves her and fathered her child. She writes letters to the press and the pope; such letters are received every day.

Bellocchio bases his film on the performance of Giovanna Mezzogiorno. She is one of those actresses, like Sophia Loren, who can combine passion with dignity. As Mussolini, Filippo Timi avoids any temptation to play with the benefit of hindsight. He is ambitious, hopeful, sometimes unwise of success. The film's title, which translates as "victory," reflects for much of the film a hope, not a certainty.

The film is beautifully well mounted. The locations, the sets, the costumes, everything conspire to re-create the Rome of the time. It provides a counterpoint to the usual caricature of Mussolini. They say that behind every great man there stands a great woman. In Mussolini's case, his treatment of her was a rehearsal for how he would treat Italy.

Vision ★ ★ ★

NO MPAA RATING, 110 m., 2010

Barbara Sukowa (Hildegard von Bingen), Heino Ferch (Brother Volmar), Hannah Herzsprung (Richardis von Stade), Alexander Held (Abbot Kuno), Lena Stolze (Jutta), Sunnyi Melles (Richardis's Mother). Directed by Margarethe von Trotta and produced by Markus Zimmer. Screenplay by Trotta.

Tip O'Neill told us "politics is local," and I suppose that applies as well to a cloistered religious order as to a city. *Vision* is about a remarkable twelfth-century woman named Hildegard von Bingen, who was closed up with a Benedictine order at a young age and rose to become its leader, the author of spiritual books, a composer of music, and an expert in herbal medicine. Although beatified, she was never elevated to sainthood, but is a saint for many feminists and holistic practitioners.

As embodied here by the powerful presence of Barbara Sukowa, she was a considerable woman, and succeeded in gaining almost everything she desired despite a church hierarchy controlled by men. From the age of four she reported visions of God, and as these continued, they gave her authority and won her followers. Indeed, although in a cloister, she was permitted to go on speaking journeys and became quite widely known.

She also succeeded in moving her nuns from within the walls of the male monastery and building their own separate retreat, and then another. This she did despite the fierce objections of her superior, Abbot Kuno (Alexander Held), by appealing over his head to the local archbishop. Still refused permission, she apparently fell into a coma and was revived only by the presence of God. Or that is what she said.

What went on in the mind of this woman, essentially uneducated, who could not read Scripture but learned, wrote her books in her own modified alphabet, and composed one of the largest surviving groups of Gregorian chant? That's what fascinates the German writer-director, Margarethe von Trotta, who makes a choice to view Hildegard's life in its externals and reveal few of the thoughts behind her sometimes forbidding facade. We never know what she's thinking. That's tantalizing.

In the small, closed world where she was raised, she clung to Jutta (Lena Stolze), the child who accompanied her to the cloister. They were "given to the church" as a sort of tithe, their entire lives decided before puberty. It is important to Hildegard to be right, and to be seen as right, and Jutta is her satellite and idolater. A new novice, Richardis von Stade (Hannah Herzsprung), enters the convent and is favored by Hildegard, and an emotional triangle forms that is all the more desperate because none of the three recognize the lesbianism that may be at its core. In another time or place, their interdependent relationships would be recognized as romantic, but here all is sublimated in religion and a struggle for moral supremacy.

Was Hildegard faking her visions and comas? Yes, probably, but she didn't realize it. She seems to have been spellbound by her own legend, and if her deathlike state during one crisis is psychosomatic, it is no less deathlike. She seems to have been an entirely sincere woman, self-deceived to her core. And a good woman, too, whose gifts in so many areas suggest an intelligence that found all the expression it could behind the cloister walls. One of the monks, Brother Volmar (Heino Ferch), recognizes her gifts and helps her to realize them, and so her passion is released in words, music, and church politics rather than in madness.

Trotta is one of the most important feminist directors of recent years. See especially *The Lost Honor of Katharina Blum* (1975), *Marianne and Juliane* (1981), and *Rosa Luxemburg* (1986). Here she declines to impose a set of feminist ideas. She's intrigued by the well-known story of Hildegard. The film is intense, measured, and too slow, but absorbing. What was life like for this brilliant woman in a world entirely without stature or recognition for women? How did she play the cards she was dealt as a child? How did she maneuver? How aware was she of her uniqueness?

Barbara Sukowa never quite lets us know. She carefully avoids modern body and facial language, and stays within the limits of the age. So does Trotta. We must enter these lives with our imaginations, and realize that no matter what rules society lays down for women—for anyone—ways can sometimes be found to prevail on one's own terms.

W

Waiting for Dublin ★ ★

NO MPAA RATING, 83 m., 2009

Andrew Keegan (Mike), Jade Yourell (Maggie), Hugh O'Conor (Twickers), Guido De Craene (Kluge), Britta Smith (Mrs. Kelleher), Des Braiden (Father Quinlan), Karl Sheils (Vito). Directed by Roger Tucker and produced by Paul Breuls. Screenplay by Chuck Conaway.

As nearly as I can tell, *Waiting for Dublin* is having its world premiere on March 13 in (can you guess?) Chicago, Boston, and New York. The timing could not be better. The St. Patrick's Day parades will be over in time for an afternoon matinee. And if you are the kind of person who marches in or attends the parade, you may enjoy this film. Other kinds of people, not so much.

Waiting for Dublin is like a time capsule, a film that, in every detail, could have been made in the 1940s and starred Bing Crosby, Pat O'Brien, Maureen O'Hara, and Edmund Gwenn as dear old Father Quinlan, who has the narcolepsy something fierce. It takes place in an Irish hamlet that has one telephone, in the post office that is also the pub. A horse and cart is the favored mode of transport, especially because there is no petrol in wartime.

The time is 1945. The hero is Mike (Andrew Keegan), an American pilot. He and his copilot, Twickers (Hugh O'Conor), run out of fuel and make an emergency landing in Ireland, where they are taken in, given lodging, and welcomed at the pub. The village has another guest, the German pilot Kluge (Guido De Craene). Ireland is officially neutral, and so such visitors are welcome, so long as they are not English, of course.

The town is inhabited, as the old movie rules required, by only colorful eccentrics, who spend all of their time in the pub waiting to be entertained by strangers. They move as a unit, decide as a unit, observe as a unit, and go to Sunday Mass as a unit to see whether Father Quinlan can get as far as *"Introibo ad altare Dei"* before falling asleep.

They quickly grow sympathetic to Mike's plight. Back home in Chicago, he made a $10,000 bet that he would shoot down at least five German fighter planes in the war. He needs one more, the war is about to end, and there is another problem: He made the bet with Al Capone's nephew, who in the movie is named Vito but in real life was named Ralph (Risky) Capone Jr. The movie was wise to change his name; in Chicago, you probably wouldn't make a bet you couldn't cover with a man named Risky Capone.

Mike is desperate—to make a fifth kill and to have sex with the lovely local lass Maggie (Jade Yourell), who says nothing doing unless he proposes marriage and means it. He comes up with a plan to get his fifth kill, and how he does that and with which weapons, I will leave for you to discover, pausing only to wonder how petrol was obtained. His solution and how it plays out is of course utterly preposterous, beginning from the moment Twickers begs off because he has a "cold."

Look, this is a perfectly sweet and harmless film, and if it were in black and white on TCM on St. Paddy's Day, you might watch it. It's so old-fashioned it's almost charming. It is constructed entirely with clichés and stereotypes, right down to the brotherhood of pilots, which was not original when Jean Renoir used it in *The Grand Illusion* (1937). The actors are pleasant, the locations (County Galway) are beautiful, but the movie is a wheeze.

Waiting for "Superman" ★ ★ ★ ½

PG, 102 m., 2010

Geoffrey Canada, Michelle Rhee, Bill Strickland, David Levin, Mike Feinberg, Daisy Esparza, Bianca Hill, Anthony Black. A documentary directed by Davis Guggenheim and produced by Michael Birtel and Lesley Chilcott. Screenplay by Davis Guggenheim and Billy Kimball.

Toward the end of *Waiting for "Superman,"* there is a sequence that cuts between lottery drawings for five charter schools. Admission to the best of these schools dramatically improves school graduation and acceptance by a college. The applicants are not chosen for being gifted. They come from poor, disadvantaged neighborhoods. But the schools have astonishing track records.

We have met five of these students, talked to them and their parents, and hope they'll win. The cameras hold on their faces as numbers are drawn or names are called. The odds against them are twenty to one. Lucky students leap in joy. The other nineteen of the twenty will return to their neighborhood schools, which more or less guarantee a 50 percent drop-out rate. The key thing to keep in mind is that underprivileged inner-city kids at the magnet schools, such as Kipp LA Prep or the Harlem Success Academy, will do better academically than well-off suburban kids with fancy high school campuses, athletic programs, swimming pools, closed circuit TV, and lush landscaping.

Waiting for "Superman," the new documentary by Davis Guggenheim, says the American educational system is failing, which we have been told before. He dramatizes this failure in a painfully direct way, says what is wrong, says what is right. One of his charts gets a laugh from the audience: Of students in a group of developed nations, Americans rank last in math skills. When the students are asked to guess their standing, Americans put themselves first. Meanwhile, jobs in Silicon Valley go without qualified Americans to fill them, and tech companies must import skilled employees from India and other poor countries.

Guggenheim focuses on an African-American educator named Geoffrey Canada, who deliberately chose the poorest area of Harlem to open his Harlem Success Academy. His formula: qualified teachers, highly motivated, better paid. Emphasis on college prep from day one. Tutoring for those behind in math or reading. There are also charter boarding schools with no TV, no video games. One kid says he wants in, but "my feelings are bittersweet."

One problem with most schools, Guggenheim says, is that after teachers gain tenure in two years it is almost impossible to fire them. In Illinois, for example, one out of 57 doctors loses his medical license, but only one in 2,500 teachers is fired. Some teachers flatly inform their students they have no intention of teaching. Guggenheim blames the powerful American Federation of Teachers, which is the top donor to national Democratic campaigns and state Republican campaigns. Any move to discipline incompetent teachers is met with fierce resistance. A union teacher is a teacher for life. That teachers themselves accept this is depressing.

The film demonstrates (1) that quality education is possible for even the most disadvantaged students; (2) the cost is low, considering that high school dropouts often turn to crime when they can't find good jobs. In ten years, there will be twice as many skilled, well-paid jobs in America as Americans qualified to fill them.

What struck me most of all was Geoffrey Canada's confidence that a charter school run on his model can make virtually *any* first-grader a high school graduate accepted by college. A good education, therefore, is not ruled out by poverty, uneducated parents, or crime- and drug-infested neighborhoods. In fact, those are the very areas where he has success. Consider this: Those lotteries are truly random, as by law they must be. Yet most of the winners will succeed, and half the losers (from the same human pool) will fail. This is an indictment: Our schools do not work.

Our nation is willing to spend trillions on war and billions to support the world's largest prison population rate. Here is a modest proposal: Spend less money on prisons, and more money on education. Reduce our military burden, and put that money into education. In twenty years you would have more useful citizens, less crime, and no less national security. It's so simple.

Note: My review of a doc about a similar school in Chicago, The Providence Effect, *is at http://j.mp/bkqXBZ.*

Waking Sleeping Beauty ★ ★ ★ ½

PG, 86 m., 2010

Featuring Ron Clements, Roy Disney, Jeffrey Katzenberg, Peter Schneider, Rob Minkoff, Michael D. Eisner, Lisa Keene, George Scribner, Gary Trousdale. A documentary directed by Don Hahn and produced by Hahn and Peter Schneider. Screenplay by Patrick Pacheco.

In 1985, when Disney released *The Black Cauldron* to box office disappointment, the animation tradition at the studio was on life support. The studio that began a revolution with *Snow White and the Seven Dwarfs* seemingly no longer knew how to make an animated feature. Roy Disney, Walt's nephew and the largest single stockholder, masterminded an executive shakeup that brought in three men from Paramount: Michael Eisner, Frank Wells, and Jeffrey Katzenberg. That began a second golden age at Disney.

It is enough to name the animated films they made: *Who Framed Roger Rabbit, The Little Mermaid, Beauty and the Beast, Aladdin,* and *The Lion King.* These films proved beyond question that animation was a genre with great international appeal for moviegoers of all ages. Coupled with the home video revolution, they were responsible for literally billions pouring into the studio. Eisner, Katzenberg, and Roy Disney, however, had personal tensions (Michael and Roy thought Jeffrey was getting too much attention as the studio's boy wonder), and after the peacemaker Frank Wells died in a helicopter crash in 1994, the magical period ended.

Waking Sleeping Beauty, made by the studio after all but Disney had left (he died in 2009), is an extraordinary inside look at those ten years. It uses footage and taps into insights, memories, and home movies that only insiders would have access to. Its director and narrator is Don Hahn, who produced *Beauty and the Beast, The Lion King,* and *The Hunchback of Notre Dame,* among others. Another featured narrator is Peter Schneider, who became president of feature animation in 1985, head of Walt Disney Studios in 1999, and left in 2001.

Siskel and Ebert was produced by Disney during all of those years, and I had some contact with these men, and with Rich Frank, studio head before Schneider. Rich would amuse audiences by showing a reel of Siskel and me trashing some of his productions. Michael and Jeffrey insisted that everyone call them—and everyone else at the studio—by their first names. Peter Schneider came on board with a lower profile. One year at Rancho la Puerta, Chaz and I shared a dinner table with a smart, likable young couple from L.A. After a few days, *Siskel and Ebert* came up. "You know I work at Disney," the man said. Really? What do you do? "I'm the president."

It was like that then. I don't know what it's like now. There were rumors that Eisner and Katzenberg didn't get along, and countless articles analyzing why Jeffrey left and/or was pushed after Wells's death. A scene in this film goes a long way to explain the tension. When Jeffrey was in charge of all animation, Eisner announced at a studio meeting that a major new animation building would be constructed. It came as news to Katzenberg.

The most fascinating scenes in *Waking Sleeping Beauty* involve the infamous Disney work ethic. Friends of mine at the studio said the unofficial motto was, "If you didn't come in on Saturday, don't even bother to come in on Sunday." Animators worked so hard they developed anxiety, migraines, carpal tunnel syndrome. The "family studio" required such long hours that some marriages failed. When Katzenberg held a no-holds-barred meeting with the animators, he actually teared up at their stories and relented. But he always came in on Sundays.

The film gives good screen time to the artists who created the films with their own minds and hands and worked in collaboration. There's even a glimpse of young Tim Burton, chained to a drafting board. A tension-breaking Mexican party in the animation department is recalled with the nostalgia of combat veterans given a week of R&R. Whatever happened, happened. The fact remains that those years were revolutionary, and if not for them, it's a good question whether Pixar, DreamWorks, and the other animation production sources—and Disney Animation itself—would still exist. Credit is due.

Wall Street: Money Never Sleeps ★ ★ ★

PG-13, 130 m., 2010

Michael Douglas (Gordon Gekko), Shia LaBeouf (Jake Moore), Josh Brolin (Bretton James), Carey Mulligan (Winnie Gekko), Eli Wallach (Julie Steinhardt), Susan Sarandon (Jake's Mother), Frank Langella (Louis Zabel). Directed by Oliver Stone and produced by Stone, Eric Kopeloff, and Edward R. Pressman. Screenplay by Allan Loeb and Stephen Schiff, based on characters created by Stone and Stanley Weiser.

Oliver Stone's 1987 film *Wall Street* was a wake-up call about the financial train wreck the Street was headed for. Had we only listened. Or perhaps we listened too well, and Gordon ("Greed is good") Gekko became the role model for a generation of amoral financial pirates who put hundreds of millions into their pockets while bankrupting their firms and bringing the economy to its knees. Gekko has been able to cool his heels for many of the intervening years in a federal prison, which is the film's biggest fantasy; the thieves who plundered the financial system are still mostly in power, and congressional zealots resist efforts to regulate the system.

That's my point, however, and not Oliver Stone's. At a time when we've seen several lacerating documentaries about the economic meltdown, and Michael Lewis's *The Big Short* is on the best-seller lists, *Wall Street: Money Never Sleeps* isn't nearly as merciless as I expected. It's an entertaining story about ambition, romance, and predatory trading practices, but it seems more fascinated than angry. Is Stone suggesting this new reality has become embedded, and we're stuck with it?

In some ways Gordon Gekko himself (Michael Douglas) serves as a moral center for the film. Out from behind bars, author of *Is Greed Good?* and lecturer to business students, he at first seems to be a standard repentant sinner. Then he meets a young trader named Jake Moore (Shia LaBeouf) and finds himself edging back into play. Jake wants to marry Gekko's daughter, Winnie (Carey Mulligan), who hasn't spoken to her father for years. Maybe he can be the conduit for their reconciliation. He sincerely loves Winnie, who is a liberal blogger. Jake himself is ambitious, already has his first million, and wants more, but we see he has a good heart because he wants his firm to back alternative energy. Is this because he is green, or only likes it? A little of both, probably.

Jake works for an old-line Wall Street house named Keller Zabel, headed by his mentor and father figure Louis Zabel (Frank Langella). This firm is brought to its knees by a snake named Bretton James (Josh Brolin), who is instrumental in spreading rumors about its instability. Stone doesn't underline the irony that James's firm, and every Wall Street firm, is equally standing on a mountain of worthless debt. In a tense boardroom confrontation, Zabel is forced to sell out for a pittance. The next morning he rises, has his soft-boiled egg, and throws himself under a subway train. It is instructive that although tycoons hurled themselves from windows during the crash of 1929, the new generation simply continued to collect their paychecks, and Gekko expresses a certain respect for Zabel.

The death of his beloved mentor gives Jake a motive: He wants revenge on Bretton James, and suddenly all the parts come together: how he can hurt James, enlist Gekko, look good to Winnie, gain self-respect, and maybe even make a nice pile of money along the way. It has taken an hour to get all the pieces in place, but Stone does it surely, and his casting choices are sound. Then the story hurries along as more melodrama than exposé.

Michael Douglas, of course, is returning in an iconic role, and it's interesting to observe how Gordon Gekko has changed: just as smart, just as crafty, still with cards up his sleeve, older, somewhat wiser, keenly feeling his estrangement from his daughter. Shia LaBeouf, having earlier apprenticed to Indiana Jones and at the beginning of this film with Louis Zabel, falls in step eagerly beside Gordon Gekko, but may discover not everyone in his field wants to be his mentor. Langella has little screen time as Zabel, but the character is crucial, and he is flawless in it. To the degree you can say this about any big player on Wall Street, Zabel is more sinned against than sinner. And then there's Carey Mulligan as Gekko's daughter, still blaming him for the death of her brother, still suspicious of the industry that shaped her father and now seems to be shaping Jake.

Wall Street: Money Never Sleeps is six minutes shorter than it was when I saw it at Cannes, and has a smoother conclusion. It is still, we might say, certainly long enough. But it's a smart, glossy, beautifully photographed film that knows its way around the Street (Stone's father was a stockbroker). I wish it had been angrier. I wish it had been outraged. Maybe Stone's instincts are correct and American audiences aren't ready for that. They haven't had enough of greed.

Walt and El Grupo ★ ★ ★

PG, 106 m., 2009

Featuring Walt and Lillian Disney and sixteen of Disney's employees in 1941. A documentary directed by Theodore Thomas and produced by Kuniko Okubo. Screenplay by Thomas.

Looking back, Walt Disney felt that 1941 was the worst year of his life. He felt betrayed when his animators went on strike and forced him to shut down the new studio he'd just built with the profits from *Snow White and the Seven Dwarfs, Pinocchio,* and *Fantasia.* As labor negotiations dragged on, Disney did what no other Hollywood studio chief would have done. He packed his wife and sixteen important employees on an airplane and embarked on a goodwill tour of South America.

In large part because of Mickey Mouse, Disney had become the world's most beloved Hollywood moviemaker since Chaplin. He'd been asked to make the tour by President Roosevelt, who on the brink of war was alarmed by Nazi inroads on the continent. Walt took the trip partly for patriotic reasons, and partly, I suspect, to get out of Dodge. The employees he took along weren't mostly executives but creative talent; he hoped they'd get ideas for new films in South America. Included was Frank Thomas, one of the "Nine Old Men" credited with the brilliance of Disney's early animated features. Now, sixty-eight years later, Frank's son Theodore has written and directed this labor of love.

No other Hollywood studio has maintained the same corporate continuity since the day it was founded, and Disney is unparalleled in its archives. Long before film preservation became fashionable, Walt enssured that the studio's work was guarded like the family jewels, and no other studio could produce historical treasure like this from its vaults.

To begin with, there is the footage shot on the trip: black-and-white documentary records of "El Grupo" undertaking what was then not a commonplace journey (they left Miami by Pan American seaplane). The continent is all new to them. The costumes, the music, the folklore, the cities, the fabulous night club shows of Buenos Aires. In 1941, the globe was still immense, and electronic media hadn't started to shrink it.

Thomas shows Disney and his group trying to dance the samba, and Walt looking awkward dressed as a gaucho. It intercuts bright, color footage of the films inspired by the trip, including *Saludos Amigos* and *The Three Caballeros.* Thomas retraced the journey for this film; there's a striking dissolve from the view from a balcony to the drawing it inspired seven decades ago. This trip was one of the inspirations for the U.S. explosion of interest in South American costumes and music, and perhaps the many musicals like *Flying Down to Rio.* Disney even brought back composers to work at his studio.

The subtext of the film is: Walt was young once. He was the Spielberg of his time, the boy genius, a mogul not yet forty, already with the familiar mustache but with a thick head of luxuriant black hair. He's affable, diplomatic, always with a cigarette (which earns the PG rating these days—ohmigod, Walt smoked!). Another message is that animated films, then as now, were far more than "cartoons" and often required more art and music design than conventional features. Always you see members of El Grupo taking photos and making sketches.

At a time when Hollywood doesn't remember last year, is obsessed with the bottom line, and is run by men who often have no sense of history, *Walt and El Grupo* evokes a better time. The great Russian filmmaker Eisenstein, on seeing *Snow White,* called it the greatest film ever made. Walt Disney didn't simply invent Mickey Mouse. He created a new genre of films like nothing anybody had seen before.

Waltz with Bashir ★ ★ ★ ½

R, 87 m., 2009

With the voices of: Ari Folman, Ori Sivan, Ronny Dayag, Shmuel Frenkel, Zahava Solomon, Ron Ben-Yishai, Dror Harazi, Boaz Rein-Buskila, Carmi Cna'an. Directed by Ari Folman and produced by Folman, Yael Nahlieli, Bridgit Folman, Serge Lalou, Gerhard Meixner, and Roman Paul. Screenplay by Folman.

Waltz with Bashir is a devastating animated film that tries to reconstruct how and why thousands of innocent civilians were massacred because those with the power to stop them took no action. Why they did not act is hard to say. Did they not see? Not realize? Not draw fateful conclusions? In any event, at the film's end, the animation gives way to newsreel footage of the dead, whose death is inescapable.

The massacre, well documented, took place during Israel's 1982 invasion of Lebanon. The victims were in Palestinian refugee camps. They were killed by a Christian militia. Israelis were in nominal control of the militia but did not stop the massacre. Blame has never been clearly assigned. Certainly the Christians pulling the triggers were guilty. Were the Israelis enablers?

In war, they say, no one sees the big picture, the men at the top least of all. *Waltz with Bashir* opens with a recurring nightmare had by a friend of Ari Folman, who wrote and directed the film. It is described to Folman in the course of his attempt to reconstruct what actually happened during days when he was present; he has the confused impression that the truth of those days was just outside his grasp. He sets out to interview Israeli army friends who were also there, and his film resembles *Rashomon* in the way truth depends not on facts but on who witnessed them and why.

Folman is an Israeli documentarian who has not worked in animation. Now he uses it as the best way to reconstruct memories, fantasies, hallucinations, possibilities, past and present. This film would be nearly impossible to make any other way. Animation will always be identified, no doubt, with funny animals, but is winning respect as a medium for serious subjects. Consider the great success of *WALL-E*, which was greatly entertaining, yet a radical critique of the consumer society.

The film is structured like a conventional documentary, with Folman visiting old army friends and piecing together what they saw and remember. The freedom of animation allows him to visualize what they tell him—even their nightmares. The title refers to an Israeli soldier losing it and firing all around himself on a street papered with posters of the just-assassinated Lebanese president-elect Bashir Gemayel—thus, waltzing with Bashir.

Folman gradually fits together a puzzle with the massacre at the center and his witnesses in concentric rings at various distances. Who knew what was happening? Which Israeli commanders were in a position to stop it? After it was over, it became simply a thing that had happened, seemingly without decision or choice. Had anyone in fact ordered the Christian militia to shoot or had they spontaneously agreed to kill?

It is impossible to pin down the answers. My impression is that some knew, some could have stopped it, but the connections between the two are uncertain. That is almost always the case with genocide. At this moment, for example, the world fully knows that ethnic slaughter is taking place in the Congo. The world stands aside. Eventually we will regret not having acted, as we regret Rwanda, Bosnia, Somalia, and indeed the Holocaust. Those pulling the triggers are the immediate murderers. Those in charge of them are morally guilty. Those who could stop them, even more so. That means us.

The debate still continues about the inaction of the Allies in not bombing the rail lines leading to the death camps, although there were bombs to spare for bombing German civilians. Now *Waltz with Bashir* argues that Israel itself is not guiltless in acts of passive genocide, an argument underlined by the disproportionate Israeli response to the provocations of Hamas. We may be confronted here with a fundamental flaw in human nature. When he said, "The buck stops here," Harry Truman was dreaming. The buck never stops.

Waste Land ★ ★ ★

NO MPAA RATING, 99 m., 2010

Vik Muniz, Fabio Ghivelder, Isis Rodrigues Garros, Jose Carlos da Silva Baia Lopes (Zumbi), Sebastiao Carlos dos Santos (Tiao), Valter dos Santos, Leide Laurentina da Silva (Irma), Magna de Franca Santos, Suelem Pereira Dias. A documentary directed by Lucy Walker, codirected by Joao Jardim and Karen Harley, and produced by Angus Aynsley and Hank Levine.

Across the world's largest garbage dump, near Rio de Janeiro, the pickers crawl with their bags and buckets, seeking treasures that can be recycled: plastics and metals, mostly, but anything of value. From the air they look like ants. You would assume they are the wretched of the earth, but those we meet in *Waste Land* seem surprisingly cheerful. They lead hard lives but understandable ones. They make twenty or twenty-five dollars a day. They live nearby. They feel pride in their labor, and talk of their service to the environment.

While the alleys of Chicago remain cluttered with ugly blue recycling bins that seem to be ignored and uncollected, these pickers rescue tons of recyclables from the dump and sell them to wholesalers, who sell them to manufacturers of car bumpers, cans, plastics, and papers. They raise their children without resorting to drugs and prostitution. They have a pickers' association that runs a clinic and demonstrates for their rights. From books rescued from the dump, one picker has assembled a community library. The head of the association says he learned much from a soggy copy of Machiavelli, once he had dried it out. He quotes from it, and you see that he did.

I do not mean to make their lives seem easy or pleasant. It is miserable work, even after they grow accustomed to the smell. But it is useful work, and I have been thinking much about the happiness to be found by work that is honest and valuable. If you set the working conditions aside (which of course you cannot), I suggest the work of a garbage picker is more satisfying than that of a derivatives broker. How does it feel to get rich selling worthless paper to people you have lied to?

Waste Land, the documentary by Lucy Walker that has been nominated for an Academy Award this year, takes as its entry point into the lives of the pickers the work of the Brazilian artist Vik Muniz. As a youth he had the good fortune to be shot in the leg by a rich kid, who paid him off; he used the money to buy a ticket to America, and now he is famous for art that turns garbage into giant constructions, which he exhibits and photographs.

Perhaps Walker intended to make the film about Muniz. If so, her subject led her to a better one; as he returns to Rio to photograph pickers for a series of portraits, she begins to focus on their lives. We see where they live, we meet their families, we hear their stories, we learn of the society and economy they have constructed around Jardim Gramacho, "Gramacho Gardens." I was especially pleased by a woman named Zumbi, who stirs a huge cauldron of beef stew in her outdoor kitchen constructed at the site.

The workers bring her unspoiled meat and usable vegetables, she says, and that is easy to believe if you have ever been to one of the all-meat restaurants facing the Copacabana beach, where chefs wheel enormous pieces of beef, pork, lamb, and poultry from table to table to carve slices and pile them on your plate. The waste here must be considerable.

Muniz has the advantage of speaking the same language as the pickers, and having come from poverty. When he tells them his portraits will give them and their work recognition, they agree and are happy to cooperate—especially Tiao, who organized their association. Muniz intends to donate all the proceeds from his portraits to the pickers, which is simple enough, but then he and his wife, Janaina Tschape, have a discussion about whether he should invite Tiao to come along when his portrait is auctioned at Phillips.

Can you leave the life of a picker, fly to another country, stay in luxury, and then return to a garbage heap? How do you handle that? It is a matter for endless debate, but eventually Tiao does join Muniz at the auction, where his portrait follows an Andy Warhol, and wins a bid of $50,000. His reaction is to cry, as Muniz embraces him. He feels this is recognition for his life, for his determination to start the association, and for the dignity of his work.

If it makes it difficult for Tiao to return to the Garden, well, it was difficult to be there in the first place. Last year I saw a documentary named *Scrappers*, about the men who travel the alleys of Chicago seeking scrap metal. There is also Agnes Varda's great film *The Gleaners and I* (2000), about those who seek their livings in the discards of Paris. When we see men going through the cans in an alley, some of us tend to distrust and vilify them. They are earning a living. They are providing a service. Incredibly, they're sometimes called lazy. Documentaries like these three help us, perhaps, to more fully appreciate our roles as full-time creators of garbage.

Watchmen ★ ★ ★

R, 163 m., 2009

Malin Akerman (Laurie Jupiter/Silk Spectre II), Billy Crudup (Jon Osterman/Dr. Manhattan), Matthew Goode (Adrian Veidt/Ozymandias),

Carla Gugino (Sally Jupiter/Silk Spectre), Jackie Earle Haley (Walter Kovacs/Rorschach), Stephen McHattie (Hollis Mason/Nite Owl), Jeffrey Dean Morgan (Edward Blake/The Comedian), Patrick Wilson (Dan Dreiberg/Nite Owl II). Directed by Zack Snyder and produced by Lawrence Gordon, Lloyd Levin, and Deborah Snyder. Screenplay by David Hayter and Alex Tse, based on the graphic novel by Alan Moore and Dave Gibbons.

After the revelation of *The Dark Knight,* here is *Watchmen,* another bold exercise in the liberation of the superhero movie. It's a compelling visceral film—sound, images, and characters combined into a decidedly odd visual experience that evokes the feel of a graphic novel. It seems charged from within by its power as a fable; we sense it's not interested in a plot so much as with the dilemma of functioning in a world losing hope.

That world is America in 1985, with Richard Nixon in the White House and many other strange details; this America occupies a parallel universe in which superheroes and masked warriors operate. The film confronts a paradox that was always there in comic books: The heroes are only human. They can only be in one place at a time (with a possible exception to be noted later). Although a superhero is able to handle one dangerous situation, the world has countless dangerous situations, and the super resources are stretched too thin. Faced with law enforcement anarchy, Nixon has outlawed superhero activity, quite possibly a reasonable action. Now the murder of the enigmatic vigilante the Comedian (Jeffrey Dean Morgan) has brought the Watchmen together again. Who might be the next to die?

Dr. Manhattan (Billy Crudup), the only one with superpowers in the literal sense, lives outside ordinary time and space, the forces of the universe seeming to coil beneath his skin. Ozymandias (Matthew Goode) is the world's smartest man. The Nite Owl (Patrick Wilson) is a man isolated from life by his mastery of technology. Rorschach (Jackie Earl Haley) is a man who finds meaning in patterns that may exist only in his mind. And Silk Spectre II (Malin Akerman) lives with one of the most familiar human challenges, living up to her parents, in this case the original Silk Spectre (Carla Gugino). Dr. Manhattan is both her lover and a distant father figure living in a world of his own.

These characters are garbed in traditional comic book wardrobes—capes, boots, gloves, belts, masks, props, anything to make them one of a kind. Rorschach's cloth mask, with its endlessly shifting ink blots, is one of the most intriguing superhero masks ever, always in constant motion, like a mood ring of the id. Dr. Manhattan is contained in a towering, muscular, naked blue body; he was affected by one of those obligatory secret experiments gone wild. Never mind the details; what matters is that he possibly exists at a quantum level, at which particles seem exempt from the usual limitations of space and time. If it seems unlikely that quantum materials could assemble into a tangible physical body, not to worry. Everything is made of quantum particles, after all. There's a lot we don't know about them, including how they constitute Dr. Manhattan, so the movie is vague about his precise reality. I was going to say Silk Spectre II has no complaints, but actually she does.

The mystery of the Comedian's death seems associated with a plot to destroy the world. The first step in the plot may be to annihilate the Watchmen, who are All That Stand Between, etc. It is hard to see how anyone would benefit from the utter destruction of the planet, but in the movie's world there is a nuclear standoff between the United States and the Soviet Union that threatens exactly that. During the Cuban missile crisis, remember "Better Dead Than Red"? There were indeed cold warriors who preferred to be dead rather than red, reminding me of David Merrick's statement: "It's not enough for me to win. My enemies must lose."

In a cosmic sense it doesn't really matter who pushed the Comedian through the window. In a cosmic sense, nothing really matters, but best not meditate on that too much. The Watchmen and their special gifts are all the better able to see how powerless they really are, and although all but Dr. Manhattan are human and back the home team, their powers are not limitless. Dr. Manhattan, existing outside time and space, is understandably remote from the fate of our tiny planet, although perhaps he still harbors some old emotions.

Those kinds of quandaries engage all the Watchmen and are presented in a film experience of often fearsome beauty. It might seem improbable to take seriously a naked blue man, complete with discreet genitalia, but Billy Crudup brings a solemn detachment to Dr. Manhattan that is curiously affecting. Does he remember how it felt to be human? No, but hum a few bars. . . . Crudup does the voice and the body language, which is transformed by software into a figure of considerable presence.

Watchmen focuses on the contradiction shared by most superheroes: They cannot live ordinary lives but are fated to help mankind. That they do this with trademarked names and appliances goes back to their origins in Greece, where Zeus had his thunderbolts, Hades his three-headed dog, and Hermes his winged feet. Could Zeus run fast? Did Hermes have a dog? No.

That level of symbolism is coiling away beneath all superheroes. What appeals with Batman is his humanity; despite his skills, he is not supernormal. *Watchmen* brings surprising conviction to these characters as flawed and minor gods, with Dr. Manhattan possessing access to godhead on a plane that detaches him from our daily concerns—indeed, from days themselves. In the film's most spectacular scene, he is exiled to Mars and in utter isolation reimagines himself as a human and conjures (or discovers? I'm not sure) an incredible city seemingly made of crystal and mathematical concepts. This is his equivalent to forty days in the desert, and he returns as a savior.

The film is rich enough to be seen more than once. I plan to see it again, this time on IMAX, and will have more to say about it. I'm not sure I understood all the nuances and implications, but I am sure I had a powerful experience. It's not as entertaining as *The Dark Knight*, but like the *Matrix* films, *LOTR*, and *The Dark Knight*, it's going to inspire fevered analysis. I don't want to see it twice for that reason, however, but mostly just to have the experience again.

Water for Elephants ★ ★ ★

PG-13, 122 m., 2011

Reese Witherspoon (Marlena), Robert Pattinson (Jacob), Christoph Waltz (August), Paul Schneider (Charlie), Jim Norton (Camel), Hal Holbrook (Old Jacob), Mark Povinelli (Kinko/Walter), Richard Brake (Grady). Directed by Francis Lawrence and produced by Gil Netter, Erwin Stoff, and Andrew R. Tennebaum. Screenplay by Richard LaGravenese, based on the novel by Sara Gruen.

There's something endearingly old-fashioned about a love story involving a beautiful bareback rider and a kid who runs off to join the circus. What makes *Water for Elephants* more intriguing is a third character, reminding us why Christoph Waltz deserved his Academy Award. He plays the circus owner, who is married to the bareback rider and keeps her and everyone else in his iron grip.

The story, based on the best-seller by Sara Gruen, is told as a flashback by an old man named Jacob (Hal Holbrook), who lost his parents in 1931, dropped out of the Cornell veterinary school, hit the road, and hopped a train that happened, wouldn't you know, to be a circus train. Played by Robert Pattinson as a youth, he is naive and excited, and his eyes fill with wonder as he sees the beautiful Marlena (Reese Witherspoon) on her white show horse. The owner, August (Waltz), is prepared to throw him off the train until he learns young Jacob knows something about veterinary medicine.

In an age of prefabricated special effects and obviously phony spectacle, it's sort of old-fashioned (and a pleasure) to see a movie made of real people and plausible sets. The production designer, Jack Fisk, has created a believable one-ring circus here, and even the circus train itself has a personality. (August and Jacob spend an implausible amount of time walking or running on top of it, but never mind.)

The dynamic in the story depends on August's jealousy of Marlena and her stubborn loyalty to their marriage contract. This is where Waltz makes his contribution. Shorter than Pattinson, indeed hardly taller than Witherspoon, he rules everyone as a hard-bitten taskmaster whose easy charm conceals a cold inner core; it's the same dynamic he used as the merciless Nazi in *Inglourious Basterds*. He's much given to offering champagne toasts with a knife hidden inside.

In the early Depression, times are hard and jobs few. The circus is deep in debt, and August produces a new star attraction he thinks can save it. This is Rosie, a middle-age elephant he thinks Marlena can ride and Jacob can train and care for, although neither has worked with an elephant before. Scenes involving the personality and language comprehension of elephants create an intrinsic charm, and the movie surrounds them with a convincing portrait of circus life on the road.

The film's climax involves a series of dire events I will not describe, except to say it's a little unclear how they are started into motion. It's also unclear why Marlena continues to be such a dutiful wife long after August no longer deserves that privilege—but the fact that she does saves the character from dissolving entirely into melodrama.

Water for Elephants was directed by Francis Lawrence, whose *I Am Legend* and *Constantine* were not predictions of this relatively classic film. The screenplay is by Richard LaGravenese, whose *Horse Whisperer* also showed a sympathy for the personalities of animals. Rosie is not as charismatic as a horse, and as Jacob observes, she suffers from dry skin, but you have to concede that her timing is impeccable. This is good, sound family entertainment, a safe PG-13 but not a dumb one, and it's a refreshing interlude before we hurtle into the summer blockbusters.

The Way Back ★ ★ ½

PG-13, 133 m., 2011

Jim Sturgess (Janusz), Ed Harris (Mr. Smith), Colin Farrell (Valka), Sebastian Urzendowsky (Kazik), Gustaf Skarsgard (Voss), Saoirse Ronan (Irena), Mark Strong (Khabarov). Directed by Peter Weir and produced by Joni Levin, Nigel Sinclair, and Duncan Henderson. Screenplay by Peter Weir and Keith R. Clarke, based on the book *The Long Walk: The True Story of a Trek to Freedom* by Slavomir Rawicz.

Not every incredible story makes a compelling movie. *The Way Back* is inspired by a four-thousand-mile foot journey that began with an escape from a Siberian prison camp in the dead of winter and continued across Mongolia and the Gobi Desert, ending finally months later in free India.

At every moment this is astonishing. Mongolia itself was said to be a prison because no one was thought able to walk out of it. Starvation is a daily possibility. So are injuries, disease, death by exposure, or capture by locals eager to collect a reward. Thirst and sun are nearly fatal in the desert. The travelers have only the clothes on their backs. We know some of them reached India, because the saga opens with that news.

But how did they possibly do that? Just as we're told: by walking. Walking and walking. And there lies the weakness of Peter Weir's film, which is nobly staged and has breathtaking cinematography, but frankly, not enough of a story in the vulgar populist sense. Desperation and exhaustion make it difficult for the trekkers to work up much in the way of characters or conflicts, and while that no doubt spares us many clichés, we are left, during their long walk, with too much of a muchness.

The group is often so bearded and weathered that members seem interchangeable. Two who stand out are Ed Harris, an American who claims his name is only "Mr. Smith," and Colin Farrell as Valka, a Russian. Has Harris ever given a bad performance? The group is led by Jim Sturgess as Janusz, who had the idea for the escape. Along the way they meet Irena (Saoirse Ronan), a young Polish woman. Her presence does not inspire romantic rivalries among the men. It's that kind of film.

Peter Weir is a master filmmaker (*Picnic at Hanging Rock, The Year of Living Dangerously, Master and Commander*). His cinematographer, Russell Boyd, works both in tight quarters and with astonishing vistas at the roof of the world. The film is a visual feast. I am far from sorry I saw it.

But there is one area in which it seems to be lacking. Details of survival. How exactly did they survive death by exposure in subzero Mongolia? Why didn't some of their meat spoil? Where did they find water in the desert? How did their footwear hold up—and why, as prisoners, did they have boots?

The answer, I fear, is that although *The Way Back* is described on its poster as "inspired by real events," it is fiction. The saga was first told in a best-selling book by Slavomir Rawicz, which was a European best-seller. But IMDb reports: "In 2006 the BBC unearthed records (including some written by Rawicz himself) that showed he had been released by the USSR in 1942."

There is an irony here. The film exhibits an admirable determination to do justice to a real story, but the story's not real. There's quite an op-ed debate going on right now between those (Neal Gabler) who say the cultural elite is finally being shouted down by populists and vulgarians, and others (A. O. Scott) who say such categories are meaningless. You like movies according to your own tastes.

Some people have bad taste and others have taste more like mine. Yet my taste is large. It contains multitudes. There is room for vulgarity, if it's well done. It's a shame to say so, but perhaps it would have helped *The Way Back* if Peter Weir had relaxed his standards slightly, slipped in some dramatic conflict, and made better use of that pretty Polish girl.

Welcome to the Rileys ★ ★ ★

R, 110 m., 2010

James Gandolfini (Doug Riley), Kristen Stewart (Mallory), Melissa Leo (Lois Riley), Eisa Davis (Vivian). Directed by Jake Scott and produced by Giovanni Agnelli, Scott Bloom, Michael Costigan, Ridley Scott, and Tony Scott. Screenplay by Ken Hixon.

Welcome to the Rileys takes two old plots and makes a rather touching new plot out of them. What we've seen before is (1) the good man who hopes to redeem a prostitute, and (2) the frozen suburban couple who find new hope in their marriage. The film involves such characters in a story that is a little more real and involving than we expect.

James Gandolfini stars as Doug Riley, an Indianapolis plumbing supplies contractor. His wife, Lois (Melissa Leo), hasn't been able to leave their house in years. He's having an affair with Vivian (Eisa Davis), a black waitress at a pancake house, and their two brief scenes together show enormous warmth. He isn't ready to leave his wife, however, perhaps because he knows she would not survive alone. Their daughter was killed at fifteen in a car crash.

Doug goes to New Orleans for a convention, is depressed, wanders into a stripper bar, and finds himself through no desire of his own receiving a hard sell from Mallory (Kristen Stewart). He doesn't want sex. He wants to talk. She thinks he's crazy. She is worn and wounded, hostile and vulnerable. He drives her home and ends up fixing her plumbing, cleaning her shabby shotgun house, and offering her $100 a day to stop hooking.

We think we see where this will lead. That's not where it leads. Ken Hixon's screenplay deliberately avoids most of the obligatory dialogue in a situation like this, and throws some curves at us. One of the surprises involves Lois. Mired in deep depression, Doug decides with a jolt to sell his business and stay in New Orleans. When he informs Lois, she finds the courage to leave the house and drive herself down to New Orleans.

Now watch how she reacts to the reality of her husband's relationship with Mallory. This involves good writing and acting. She is a grown-up. She isn't jealous; she's more concerned that he's crazy. He isn't defensive; he's matter-of-fact. This is Mallory, she's a sixteen-year-old runaway, he's helping her, she doesn't want help. That's how it is.

It's such a relief to be spared the usual clichés here, and observe how Leo so convincingly channels a woman's mothering instinct. It's good, too, to see how director Jake Scott uses the physical presences of his well-cast actors. Stewart is far from the porcelain perfection of the *Twilight* movies, and it's a relief to see that it is, after all, physically possible for a teenager to have complexion problems in a movie. Leo is worn out by loss and worry, but is smart and kind.

And look at what Gandolfini does. He's a mountain of a man, but gentle, not threatening. In terms of body language, he establishes his character in a scene where he crawls into bed with his wife and the mattress sags and he burrows into his pillow and looks—comfortable. When he smokes, his huge hands dwarf his cigarette (there's a subtle tweak: He uses regular cigarettes, not king size, because they make his huge hands look even larger).

I was struck at once by the uncanny accuracy of his central Indiana-Illinois accent. I grew up in downstate Illinois hearing men speak exactly like him. A kind of firm, terse understatement, on a flat, factual note. I could close my eyes and imagine one lifelong friend in particular. Going online, I found that the coastal critics as a group thought he was using a Southern accent, "for some reason." They've never been to the Midwest, and possibly never to the South. We all sound the same to them. Gandolfini has the accent spot on, and it's certainly not one we've heard before from him.

Welcome to the Rileys does a convincing job of evoking its New Orleans locations. Mallory's house is messy and forlorn. Her street is depressing. The city at night seems a contrast between artificial merriment and loneliness, and more evocative than another city known for sin, Las Vegas.

What happens between the three people I will not say. The film introduces them, makes them plausible, and then what happens is pretty much what might happen. These people haven't studied up on their archetypes. Each one is doing the best possible, under the circumstances.

We Live in Public ★ ★ ★ ★

NO MPAA RATING, 91 m., 2009

With Josh Harris, Jason Calacanis, Missy Galore, Anthony Haden-Guest, Douglas Rushkoff. A documentary directed by Ondi Timoner and produced by Timoner and Keirda Bahruth. Screenplay by Timoner.

I'd never heard of Josh Harris, who is billed in this film as "the greatest Internet pioneer you've never heard of." I can be excused for thinking Josh Harris was the fictional hero of a pseudo-documentary, until the film quickly and obviously became authentic. It's not often you see a doc that's been filmed over a period of fifteen years.

Harris was involved in the early days of Prodigy, back in the Compuserve era, and in 1993 founded Pseudo.com, which forecast audio and video webcasting, YouTube, Hulu, and countless other streamers. He was, to put it kindly, ahead of his time. In 1993, 300-baud modems were commonplace, and 1,200 was fast.

Harris was a myopic visionary, a man who saw the future more vividly than his own life. He was a prototype nerd, a lonely kid who raised himself while planted in front of an old black-and-white TV set, using *Gilligan's Island* as a virtual family to supplement his own remote mother. In the 1990s he became one of the early dot-com millionaires, a celebrity in New York, where he threw lavish parties intended not so much for the famous as to attract brilliant and artistic kids to work for him. Pseudo.com is remembered from that time as Nerd Heaven, offering well-paid positions, loaded with perks, equipped with free creature comforts, demanding only your body and soul.

He sold Pseudo for something like $80 million, and that was the end of his good timing. The filmmaker, Ondi Timoner, had already started to document his life and was on the scene when he began a notorious project named Quiet. Try to imagine this: About one hundred of the best and brightest he could find agreed to live twenty-four hours a day in a cavernous space below street level. They would be under video surveillance every moment. Their lives would be streamed on the Web. They shared dining and recreational facilities and even a shooting range. They were given state-of-the-art computers. They lived in cubicles with the square footage of perhaps six coffins. These were stacked atop one another like sleeping cubicles in a Japanese airport.

Yes. And this was to be the future, in which we will all live virtually on the Internet. The film *Surrogates* perhaps owes something to Harris. Remarkably, no murders claimed any of Quiet's eager volunteers; whether any births resulted is not reported. The fire department closed him down in the first days of 2000, but Harris, not missing a beat, moved with his girlfriend into an apartment where every single room was webcast twenty-four hours a day—every meal, every bowel movement, every sexual event, everything, including their (inevitable) ugly breakup. "She was only a pseudo girlfriend," he explained later. I don't knew if she knew that.

By then Harris had spent most of his $80 million and become disillusioned with living in public. He bought an upstate New York apple farm, and Timoner followed him there to find him in work clothes, having returned to the earth. His friends lost touch. He became forgotten as quickly as he became famous. I wonder, and the film doesn't tell us, what he thinks of YouTube. At the end of the film he's living in Africa.

He did, however, fly to Sundance 2009, where the film won the Grand Jury Prize for best documentary. Sundance has recently become a place where the visitors can barely tear their eyes from texting, surfing, e-mailing, or tweeting in order to look at a movie. What did he make of this? Harris saw it coming in the days when a Tandy 100 transmitted text much more slowly than I could read.

This is a remarkable film about a strange and prophetic man. What does it tell us? Did living a virtual life destroy him? When he had a nervous breakdown after the *We Live in Public* Web experiment collapsed, was it responsible?

Remember Jenny Ringley? She was the pioneer of webcams. From April 1996 until 2003, she lived her life online, getting, it was said, tens of millions of hits a week. She never discussed why she shut down Jennycam. Today she says she doesn't even have a MySpace page. And Josh Harris says Sidamo, Ethiopia, is the best place on Earth to live: "People know each other here."

Wendy and Lucy ★ ★ ★ ½

R, 80 m., 2009

Michelle Williams (Wendy), Will Patton (Mechanic), John Robinson (Andy), Larry Fessenden (Man in Park), Will Oldham (Icky), Walter Dalton (Security Guard). Directed by Kelly Reichardt and produced by Neil Kopp, Anish Savjani, and Larry Fessenden. Screenplay by Reichardt and Jon Raymond, based on the story "Train Choir" by Raymond.

I know so much about Wendy although this movie tells me so little. I know almost nothing about where she came from, what her life was like, how realistic she is about the world, where her ambition lies. But I know, or feel, everything about Wendy at this moment: stranded in an Oregon town, broke, her dog lost, her car a write-off, hungry, friendless, quiet, filled with desperate resolve.

Kelly Reichardt's *Wendy and Lucy* is another illustration of how absorbing a film can be when the plot doesn't stand between us and a character. There is no timetable here. Nowhere Wendy came from, nowhere she's going to, no plan except to get her car fixed and feed her dog. Played by Michelle Williams, she has a gaze focused inward on her determination. We pick up a few scraps: Her sister in Indiana is wary of her, and she thinks she might be able to find a job in a fish cannery in Ketchikan, Alaska.

But Alaska seems a long way to drive from Indiana just to get a job in a cannery, and this movie isn't about the unemployment rate. Alaska perhaps appeals to Wendy because it is as far away she can drive where they still speak English. She parks on side streets and sleeps in her car, she has very limited cash, her golden retriever, Lucy, is her loving companion. She wakes up one morning somewhere in Oregon, her car won't start, and she's out of dog food, and that begins a chain of events that leads to wandering around a place she doesn't know looking for her only friend in the world.

When I say I know all about Wendy, that's a tribute to Michelle Williams's acting, Kelly Reichardt's direction, and the cinematography of Sam Levy. They use Williams's expressive face, often forlorn, always hopeful, to show someone who embarked on an unplanned journey, has gone too far to turn back, and right now doesn't care about anything but getting her friend back. Her world is seen as the flat, everyday world of shopping malls and storefronts, rail tracks, and not much traffic, skies that the weatherman calls "overcast." You know those days when you walk around and the weather makes you feel in your stomach that something is not right? Cinematography can make you feel like that.

She walks. She walks all the way to the dog pound and back. All the way to an auto shop and back. And back to what? She sleeps in a park. The movie isn't about people molesting her, although she has one unpleasant encounter. Most people are nice, like a mechanic (Will Patton), and especially a security guard of retirement age (Walter Dalton), whose job is to stand and look at a mostly empty parking lot for twelve hours, to guard against a nonexistent threat to its empty spaces.

Early in the film, the teenage supermarket

employee (John Robinson) who busts Wendy for shoplifting won't give her a break. He's a little suck-up who possibly wants to impress his boss with an unbending adherence to "store policy." Store policy also probably denies him health benefits and overtime, and if he takes a good look at Wendy, he may be seeing himself, minus the uniform with the logo and the name tag on it.

The people in the film haven't dropped out of life; they've been dropped by life. It has no real use for them and not much interest. They're on hold. At least searching for your lost dog is a consuming passion; it gives Wendy a purpose and the hope of joy at the end. That's what this movie has to observe, and it's more than enough.

Whatever Works ★ ★ ★

PG-13, 92 m., 2009

Larry David (Boris Yellnikoff), Evan Rachel Wood (Melody), Patricia Clarkson (Marietta), Ed Begley Jr. (John), Conleth Hill (Leo Brockman), Michael McKean (Joe). Directed by Woody Allen and produced by Letty Aronson and Stephen Tenenbaum. Screenplay by Allen.

Woody Allen said in *Manhattan* that Groucho Marx was first on his list of reasons to keep on living. His new film, *Whatever Works,* opens with Groucho singing "Hello, I Must Be Going" from *Animal Crackers.* It serves as the movie's theme song, summarizing in five words the worldview of his hero, Boris Yellnikoff.

Yellnikoff, played with perfect pitch by Larry David, is a nuclear physicist who was once almost nominated for a Nobel Prize, a statement so many of us could make. His field was quantum mechanics, where string theory can be described in the same five words. He's retired now, divorced from a rich wife who was so perfect for him he couldn't stand it. He lives in a walk-up in Chinatown and works part time as a chess instructor to little "inch worms," whom he hits over their heads with the board.

Mostly what he does is hang out at a table in a coffee shop and kvetch with old pals. These scenes seemed perfectly familiar to me because of my long honorary membership in a group centering on Dusty Cohl at the Coffee Mill in Toronto. Boris doesn't talk with his friends; he lectures them. His speeches spring from the Jewish love of paradox; essentially, life is so fascinating he can't take it any longer.

Midway in his remarkable opening monologue, David starts speaking directly to the camera. His friends think he's crazy. He asks them if they can't see the people out there—us. Allen developed as a standup comic, and the idea of an actual audience often hovers in his work, most literally in *The Purple Rose of Cairo,* where a character climbs down from the screen and joins it.

Boris gets up from the table and walks down the sidewalk, continuing to hector the camera about his own brilliance and the general stupidity that confronts him. It is too great a burden for him to exist in a world of such morons and cretins. He hates everyone and everything—in a theoretical way, as befits a physicist. Later that night he is implored by a homeless waif to give her something to eat, tells her to be about her business, and then relents and invites her in.

This is Melody St. Ann Celestine (Evan Rachel Wood), a fresh-faced innocent from a small town down south, who still believes in the world she conquered in beauty pageants. I've seen Wood in a lot of performances, but nothing to prepare me for this one. She's naivete on wheels, cheerful, optimistic, trusting, infectious. Reader, she wins the old man's heart—and wants it! She proposes marriage, and not for cynical or needy reasons. She believes everything he says, and is perhaps the first person he has ever met who subscribes fully to the theory of his greatness.

This sets in rotation a wheel of characters who all discover for themselves that in life we must accept whatever works to make us happy. Boris and Melody accept each other. Then her parents separately find their way to New York in search of her, and they accept what they discover. They are Marietta (Patricia Clarkson), who is Melody made middle-aged and churchgoing, and John (Ed Begley Jr.), to whom the National Rifle Association ranks just a smidgin higher than the Supreme Court. They are appalled at this human wreckage their daughter has taken to her side.

But whatever works. Both Marietta and John are transformed by the free spirits of

New York, as so many have been, although not, it must be noted, Boris Yellnikoff. The New Yorker and the southerners have never met anyone remotely like one another, but the southerners are open to new experiences. More than that I cannot explain.

It might be complained that everything works out for everyone a little too neatly. So it does, because this is not a realistic story but a Moral Tale, like one of Eric Rohmer's. Allen seeks not psychological insight but the demonstration of how lives can be redeemed. To do this he uses Clarkson's innate exuberance and Begley's congenital probity to get them to where they're going. Once they are free to do so, Marietta indulges her feelings, and John reasons it out.

Larry David is the mind of the enterprise, and Evan Rachel Wood is the heart. David is a verbal virtuoso, playing the "Woody Allen role" but with his personal shtick. He'd be lonely if he couldn't confide in his invisible listeners. His opening monologue would be remarkable from any actor, let alone one without training or stage experience. Wood prevents the plot from descending into logic and reason with her character's blind faith that everything is for the better. *Whatever Works* charts a journey for Allen, one from the words of Groucho to the wisdom of Pascal, who informs us, as Allen once reminded us, that the heart has its reasons.

What's the Matter with Kansas? ★ ★ ★ ½

NO MPAA RATING, 90 m., 2009

With Angel Dillard, Rob Dillard, Pastor Terry Fox, Donn Teske, Brittany Barden, Dawn Barden, and others. A documentary directed by Joe Winston and produced by Winston and Laura Cohen. Inspired by the book by Thomas Frank.

As a liberal, I agree with about a third of the people in *What's the Matter with Kansas?* A conservative would probably agree with the others. What's interesting is that every single person in this film is seen as themselves, is allowed to speak, and seems to have a good heart. I've rarely seen a documentary quite like it. It has a point to make, but no ax to grind.

This is its point: Conservatives in the heartland have persuaded themselves to vote against their own economic and social well-being because they consider hot-button issues more important than their incomes, economic chances, educations, and the welfare of society at large. Their positions dovetail seamlessly with evangelical Christianity, and they accept hardship as the will of God when it seems more clearly to be the working of a top-loaded economy.

No one in the film says that. The film has no narration at all. It is a fascinating series of portraits of Kansans, all of them good people, shown without judgment. In a subtle way, the accumulation of these portraits adds up to this conclusion: They're doing themselves no favors by voting against their own interests and might hold onto their values while still voting more selectively.

The two most likable people in the film are a Christian mother and farmer named Angel Dillard, and a self-proclaimed populist farmer named Donn Teske, both struggling to keep their family farms afloat after two drought years.

Dillard has a story to win our sympathy. After a bad marriage in Los Angeles, she moved back home to Kansas and bought a small homestead. This she planned to farm by herself and probably never remarry ("I must have had one hundred first dates, but when the guys saw this place . . ."). But she did find the right man and has two pretty daughters, one named Reagan.

We see her manning a right-to-life booth at the state fair. She is a loyal follower of Pastor Terry Fox's six-thousand-member Immanuel Baptist Church in Wichita. When Fox is asked by the church deacons to resign because they were uncomfortable with his political sermons about abortion and homosexuality, his followers follow him to exiled services held in a theater at Wild West World, a new theme park.

Along with Fox and other church members, they ask God for guidance and invest their savings in the park. It goes bankrupt without ever thriving, and there are hints that it may have been a Ponzi scheme. But they accept their loss as God's will. At the end of the film, Angel is selling her CD of Christian music at a local event.

She never has the slightest doubt that God wants her to vote conservative. Although she is a fervent pro-lifer, she tells of a disastrous early pregnancy: After her prolonged labor, a doctor braces his foot and pulls out her son with forceps, crushing his skull; although the boy lives until twelve, he never sees, hears, speaks, or eats, and wears diapers.

It took a long time for the doctors to get a heartbeat, she says calmly. "They should have allowed him to die, but they were afraid of a lawsuit." Has it occurred to her to question the difference between allowing a brain-dead child to die and terminating a pregnancy in a similar case?

Donn Teske, head of the Kansas Farmers' Union, is a Wilford Brimley type, plainspoken, "a redneck," and says he was a Republican committeeman but resigned and now considers himself a populist independent. He is eloquent in testifying before Congress, and in Washington goes to visit the modest Franklin Roosevelt Memorial. It was Roosevelt's New Deal, he says, that created the first, and still the best, farm bill.

Another likable figure in the film is Brittany Barden, a bright teenage campaign worker for GOP candidates. Apparently home-schooled, she goes off to college at Patrick Henry University, a conservative Christian school in Virginia. Her mother explains, "Secular schools teach things like evolution." Brittany explains that our nation is Christian, the founding fathers were all Christian, and Christianity is established in the Declaration of Independence and the Constitution. Perhaps at Patrick Henry she will learn that all three of these beliefs are simply untrue.

Kansas at the start of the twentieth century was a staunchly left-wing state. The town of Girard was the home of the socialist *Appeal to Reason*, then the newspaper with the largest circulation in America. Teske goes to visit the Populist Cemetery and speaks of the state's populist roots.

What's the Matter with Kansas? doesn't connect the dots, nor does it need to. It takes no cheap shots. It is all there to see. These good people are voting against themselves. The current hysteria about health care reform is another example. Meanwhile, we see a state that is draining population, with empty sidewalks and vacant parking spaces, boarded storefronts and foreclosures, and a certainty that all is God's will. A billboard outside one town simply says: "Pray for the Election."

Where the Wild Things Are ★ ★ ★

PG, 110 m., 2009

Max Records (Max), Pepita Emmerichs (Claire), Catherine Keener (Mom), Steve Mouzakis (Teacher), Mark Ruffalo (Boyfriend). And the voices of James Gandolfini (Carol), Paul Dano (Alexander), Catherine O'Hara (Judith), Forest Whitaker (Ira), Michael Berry Jr. (The Bull), Chris Cooper (Douglas), Lauren Ambrose (KW). Directed by Spike Jonze and produced by John B. Carls, Gary Goetzman, Tom Hanks, Vincent Landay, and Maurice Sendak. Screenplay by Jonze and Dave Eggers, inspired by the book and illustrations by Sendak.

Where the Wild Things Are reflects so much of a plucky little kid: the flaring up of anger at a parent, the defiant escape into fantasy, the tough talk in a tight situation, the exuberance, and then the fundamental need to return home and be loved and reassured. All of these stages are explored in Maurice Sendak's famous 1963 children's book, which contains only nine sentences. Ah, but what sentences they are when given resonance by his drawings.

Spike Jonze and Dave Eggers have met the challenge of this little masterpiece head-on, by including both a real little boy and the imaginary Wild Things in the same film. It would simply not have done to alter or shrink the monstrous Things, and with an $80 million budget, Jonze has been able to make a movie where any reader of the book should be able to recognize all of the Things in sight.

The creatures in the film are voiced by actors, and given a *great* deal more to say, of course, than in the book. The Things are a considerable technical achievement, combining as they do muppetry and CGI. I don't find them particularly lovely, nor should I; they're not fuzzy toys, but characters in a dream that slides in and out of nightmares.

Max Records, of *The Brothers Bloom*, plays the difficult role of Max, the boy who gets into a stubborn argument with his mom (Catherine Keener) and flees to his room and then to his imagination. In the book, his room transforms itself into a jungle, but the film has him sailing a stormy sea in a little boat that looks like a bathtub toy. It arrives at an island that the Wild Things inhabit in grouchy discontent, and Max finds himself moved to bring the discord under control. Why these creatures, who tower over him, should even consider accepting his leadership is a no-brainer: This is Max's dream.

The plot is simple stuff, spread fairly thin in terms of events but portentous in terms of meaning. It comes down to a question that children often seek answers to: What is right? One of the film's strengths is the way it doesn't soft-pedal sticky situations. For example, Max's mom has a boyfriend (Mark Ruffalo), who isn't painted as an interloper, and affection between the two of them is calmly regarded by Max (whether deeper issues involving his disappeared father are involved in his anger is a good question).

The voice actors and the f/x artists give their fantastical characters personality. When I mention special effects, I don't want to give the impression that the Wild Things are all smoke and mirrors. In close-up they seem tangibly there, and at times I believe human actors are inside costumes. I used to be able to spot this stuff, but f/x have gotten so good that sometimes you just don't know.

The voices belong to Catherine O'Hara as the know-it-all Judith, James Gandolfini as the authoritative boss Thing, Lauren Ambrose as KW, Chris Cooper as Douglas, Forest Whitaker as the pleasant and meek Ira, and Paul Dano as Alexander, who is only a few feet taller than Max. Each of these creatures is one of a kind, leaving open the question of how, and with whom, they reproduce their species.

The movie felt long to me, and there were some stretches during which I was less than riveted. Is it possible there wasn't enough Sendak story to justify a feature-length film? In a way I suppose the book tells a feature-length story just in Sendak's drawings, and Jonze and Eggers have taken those for their inspiration. All the same, I suspect the film will play better for older audiences remembering a much-loved book from childhood, and not as well with kids who have been trained on slam-bam action animation.

Whip It ★ ★ ★ ½

PG-13, 111 m., 2009

Ellen Page (Bliss Cavendar), Marcia Gay Harden (Brooke Cavendar), Kristen Wiig (Maggie Mayhem), Drew Barrymore (Smashley Simpson), Juliette Lewis (Iron Maven), Jimmy Fallon (Johnny), Daniel Stern (Earl Cavendar), Alia Shawkat (Pash), Landon Pigg (Oliver), Andrew Wilson (Coach Razor), Zoe Bell (Bloody Holly), Eve (Rosa Sparks), Ari Graynor (Eva Destruction). Directed by Drew Barrymore and produced by Barry Mendel. Screenplay by Shauna Cross, based on her novel *Derby Girl.*

Whip It is an unreasonably entertaining movie, causing you perhaps to revise your notions about women's roller derby, assuming you have any. The movie is a coming-together of two free spirits, Drew Barrymore and Ellen Page, and while it may not reflect the kind of female empowerment Gloria Steinem had in mind, it has guts, charm, and a black-and-blue sweetness. Yes, it faithfully follows the age-old structure of the sports movie, but what a sport, and how much the derby girls love it.

Page plays Bliss Cavendar, a small-town Texas girl who shares the rebelliousness of Juno but not the stream-of-consciousness verbal pyrotechnics. She's being coached by her smothering mother (Marcia Gay Harden) to compete in a Miss Bluebonnet beauty pageant that squeezes Texas girls into a ghastly caricature of Southern womanhood. Bliss despises it. One day she sees an ad for roller derby in Austin, the nearest town of consequence, and with a friend sneaks off to see a game. She is electrified. She was born to be a derby girl.

She begins a series of secret bus trips to Austin that last for an entire season—much too long for her parents not to notice, but never mind. She auditions in her pink Barbie clamp-ons for the Hurl Scouts team. Lying about her age, against all odds she's allowed by the coach, known as Razor (Andrew Wilson), to give it a try. The team veterans are dubious, but she has pluck and speed and doesn't mind getting knocked around. It's worth noting that Page and the other actresses, some of them real derby stars, do almost all their own skating.

She takes the name Babe Ruthless. Other

competitors are known as Maggie Mayhem (Kristen Wiig), Smashley Simpson (Barrymore herself), Bloody Holly (Zoe Bell), Rosa Sparks (Eve), and Eva Destruction (Ari Graynor). Juliette Lewis is fiercely competitive as the leader of another team, Iron Maven. Such stage names, or track names, are common in roller derby, and one real-life derby girl is known as Sandra Day O'Clobber.

The screenplay is by a Los Angeles Derby Dolls star named Shauna Cross, the original Maggie Mayhem, based on her novel *Derby Girl.* It neatly balances Bliss's derby career and her situation at home, where her dad (Daniel Stern) turns to pro sports on TV to escape his insufferable wife. Well, OK, she's not insufferable, simply an extreme type of stage mother whose values, as her daughter informs her, are based on a 1950s idea of womanhood. Probably her poor mom was dominated by her own overbearing mother.

Bliss is at a hormonal age when she really likes cute boys and is drawn to a young rock band member named Oliver (Landon Pigg). She experiences this relationship in admirable PG-13 terms, and during her season with the Hurl Scouts learns much about her physical and personality strengths. Odd as it may seem, her roller derby experience is a coming-of-age process.

Ellen Page, still only twenty-two, is the real thing. To see her in this, *Juno,* and *Hard Candy* (2005) is to realize she's fearless, completely in command of her gifts, and will be around for a long time. To learn that she will play the lead in a BBC Films production of *Jane Eyre,* being produced by Alison Owen (*Elizabeth*) seems only natural.

Yes, the movie has clichés. Yes, it all leads up to a big game. Yes, there is a character's validating appearance near the end. Yes, and so what? The movie is miles more intelligent than most of the cream of wheat marketed to teenage girls. Funnier, more exciting, even liberating. Barrymore, in her debut as a director, shows she must have been paying attention ever since Spielberg cast her when she was five. She and her team do an especially effective job in staging the derby showdowns.

There *are* rules to roller derby, but the movie doesn't linger over the details. Basically, you go around as fast as you can, try to stay on your feet, protect your teammates, and clobber your opponents. In the last decade, the optional form of the sport has morphed into a sort of gothic-punk-warrior woman hybrid, with much invention going into the outrageous costumes. Which doesn't mean you don't get hurt when you're slammed.

Note: See my review of Unholy Rollers *(1973) and the great documentary* Derby *(1972) at www.rogerebert.com.*

White Material ★ ★ ★ ½

NO MPAA RATING, 105 m., 2010

Isabelle Huppert (Maria Vial), Isaach De Bankole (The Boxer), Christophe Lambert (Andre), Nicolas Duvauchelle (Manuel), William Nadylam (Mayor), Michel Subor (Henri). Directed by Claire Denis and produced by Pascal Caucheteux. Screenplay by Denis and Marie N'Diaye.

Isabelle Huppert is small and slender and embodies the strength of a fighter. In so many films she is an indomitable force, yet you can't see how she does it. She rarely acts broadly. The ferocity lives within. Sometimes she is mysteriously impassive; we see what she's determined to do, but she sends no signals with voice or eyes to explain it. There is a lack of concern about our opinion; she will do it, no matter what we think her reasons are.

In Claire Denis's *White Material,* she plays Maria Vial, a French woman running a coffee plantation in an unnamed African country. The land has fallen into war, both against the colonialists and among the insurgents. In an opening scene, a helicopter hovers above Maria, and French soldiers advise her to evacuate quickly. This she has no intention of doing. As it becomes clear that her life is in danger, she only grows more opaque. Huppert's approach is valuable here because any attempt at a rational explanation would seem illogical. I believe her attachment to the land has essentially driven her mad.

This isn't even her farm. It was owned by her former father-in-law and run by her ex-husband (Christophe Lambert). Now she is in day-to-day charge and moves with confidence. The way she dresses makes a statement: She likes simple sandals and thin print sundresses that make her seem more at home than durable clothing would. She doesn't even much like hats or sunglasses. She runs through fields like a child. She drives the truck, runs errands, goes into town to hire substitute labor when her workers walk away in fear of the war. There's a scene where she all but tries to physically restrain departing workers.

They try to be reasonable with her. Yes, it will be a good crop of coffee beans, but there will probably be no way to get it to market. Anarchy has taken the land. Child soldiers with rifles march around, makeshift army stripes on their shirts, seeking "The Boxer" (Isaach De Bankole), a onetime prizefighter and now the legendary, if hardly seen, leader of the rebellion. When Maria is held at gunpoint, she boldly tells the young gunmen she knows them and their families. Her danger doesn't seem real to her. There is no overt black-white racial tension; the characters all behave as the situation would suggest.

Claire Denis, a major French director, was born and raised in French colonial Africa, and is drawn to Africa as a subject; her first film, the great *Chocolat* (1988), was set there, and also starred the formidable Isaach De Bankole. Both it and this film draw from *The Grass Is Singing*, Doris Lessing's first novel, the idea of a woman more capable than her husband on an African farm. Her 2009 film *35 Shots of Rum* dealt with Africans in France. She doesn't sentimentalize Africa nor attempt to make a political statement. She knows it well and hopes to show it as she knows it. Huppert's impassivity perhaps suits her; the character never expresses an abstract idea about the farm or Africa, and the nearest she comes to explaining why she won't leave is asking, "How could I show courage in France?" No one asks her what that means.

We meet the ex-husband (Lambert) and his father (Michel Subor), but the other major figure in the film is her son, Manuel (Nicolas Duvauchelle). This boy, in his late teens, seems prepared to spend all of his life in his room. While his mother manages the farm, he projects indolence and total indifference. He cares not about her, the farm, or anything. Events cause him to undergo a scary transformation, but it's not one we were expecting. He doesn't move in a conventional narrative direction, but laterally, driven by inner turmoil.

This is a beautiful, puzzling film. The enigmatic quality of Huppert's performance draws us in. She will never leave, and we think she will probably die, but she seems oblivious to her risk. There is an early scene where she runs in her flimsy dress to catch a bus, and finds there are no seats. So she grabs onto the ladder leading to the roof. The bus is like Africa. It's filled with Africans, we're not sure where it's going, and she's hanging on.

The White Ribbon ★ ★ ★ ★

R, 145 m., 2010

Ulrich Tukur (Baron), Susanne Lothar (Midwife), Christian Friedel (Schoolteacher), Burghart Klaussner (Pastor), Leonie Benesch (Eva), Josef Bierbichler (Steward), Rainer Bock (Doctor), Ernst Jacobi (Narrator). Directed by Michael Haneke and produced by Stefan Arndt, Veit Heiduschka, Michael Katz, Margaret Menegoz, and Andrea Occhipinti. Screenplay by Haneke.

Something is wrong in the village. Some malevolent force, some rot in the foundation. This wrongness is first sensed in a series of incidental "accidents." Then the murder of a child takes place. This forces the villagers, who all know one another, to look around more carefully. Is one of them guilty? How can that be? One person couldn't be responsible for all of these disturbing events. Have many been seized in an evil contagion?

After the first screening of Michael Haneke's *The White Ribbon* at Cannes, everybody had theories about who "did it." Well, we're trained to see such stories as whodunits. Haneke is never that simple. It all may have been "done," but what if there seems to be no doer? What if bad things happen to good people who are not as good as they think they are? In Haneke's *Caché* (2005), who shot the alarming videos spying on the family? Are you sure? Haneke's feeling is that we can never be sure.

This great film is set in rural Germany in the years before World War I. All has been stable in this village for generations. The baron owns the land. The farmer, the pastor, the doctor, the schoolteacher, the servants, even the children, play their assigned roles. It is a patriarchal, authoritarian society—in other words, the sort of society that seemed ordinary at that time throughout the world.

We are told the story many years after it took place by the schoolteacher (Ernst Jacobi). In the film, we see him young (Christian Friedel). The old man intends to narrate with objectivity and precision. He'll draw no conclusions. He doesn't have the answers. He'll stick to the facts. The first fact is this: While out riding one morning, the doctor was injured when his horse stumbled because of a trip wire. Someone put the wire there. Could they have even known the doctor (Rainer Bock) would be their victim?

Other incidents occur. A barn is burned. A child is found murdered. Someone did each of these things. The same person could not easily have done all of them. There is information about where various people were at various times. It's like an invitation to play Sherlock Holmes and deduce the criminal. But in *The White Ribbon* there are no barking hounds. The clues don't match. Who is to even say something is a clue? It may simply be a fact seen in the light of suspicion.

Life continues in an orderly fashion, as if a gyroscope tilts and then rights itself. The baron steadies his people. The doctor resumes his practice, but is unaccountably cruel toward his mistress. The teacher teaches and the students study, and they sing in the choir. Church services are attended. The white ribbon is worn by children who have been bad but will now try to be good. The crops are harvested. The teacher courts the comely village girl Eva (Leonie Benesch). And suspicion spreads.

I wonder if it's mostly a Western feeling that misfortune is intolerable and, to every degree possible, death must be prevented. I don't hear of such feelings from Asia or Africa. There is more resignation when terrible things happen. Yes, a man must not harm another. He should be punished. But after he causes harm, they don't think it possible to prevent any other man from ever doing the same thing.

In this German town there is a need to solve the puzzle. Random wicked acts create disorder and erode the people's faith that life makes sense. The suspicion that the known facts cannot be made to add up is as disturbing as if the earth gave way beneath our feet.

Haneke has a way of making the puzzle more interesting than its solution. If you saw *Caché,* you'll remember how, after a certain point, a simple shot by an unmoving camera became disturbing even when nothing happened. It wasn't about what we were seeing. It was about the fact that someone was looking, and we didn't know why.

It's too simple to say the film is about the origin of Nazism. If that were so, we would all be Nazis. It is possible to say that when the prevention of evil becomes more important than the preservation of freedom, authoritarianism grows. If we are to prevent evil, someone must be in charge. The job naturally goes to those concerned with enforcing order. Therefore, all disorder is evil and must be prevented, and that's how the interests of the state become more important than the interests of the people.

I wonder if Haneke's point is that we grow so disturbed by danger that we will surrender freedom—even demand to. Do we feel more secure in an orderly state? Many do. Then a tipping point arrives, and the Berlin Wall falls, or we see the Green Revolution in Iran. The problem, as philosophers have noted, is that revolutionaries grow obsessed with enforcing their revolution, and the whole process begins over.

Haneke's genius is to embed these possibilities in films rooted in the daily lives of ordinary people. He denies us the simple solutions of most films, in which everything is settled by the violent victory of our side. His films are like parables, teaching that bad things sometimes happen simply because . . . they happen. The universe laughs at man's laws and does what it will.

The film is visually masterful. It's in black and white, of course. Color would be fatal to its power. Perhaps because b&w film is hard to find, Haneke filmed in color and drained it away. If a color version is ever released, you'll see why it's wrong. Just as it is, *The White Ribbon* tells a simple story in a small village about little people and suggests that we must find a balance between fear and security.

Who Do You Love? ★ ★ ½

NO MPAA RATING, 90 m., 2010

Alessandro Nivola (Leonard Chess), Jon Abrahams (Phil Chess), David Oyelowo (Muddy Waters), Chi McBride (Willie Dixon), Megalyn Echikunwoke (Ivy Mills), Marika Dominczyk (Revetta Chess), Keb' Mo (Jimmy Rogers), Robert Randolph (Bo Diddley). Directed by Jerry Zaks and produced by Les Alexander, Andrea Baynes, and Jonathan Mitchell. Screenplay by Peter Wortmann and Bob Conte.

The original studios of Chess Records on South Michigan in Chicago are as important to the development of rock 'n' roll as the Sun Records studios in Memphis. You could make a good case, in fact, that without Chess there might have been no Sun, and without Muddy Waters, Willie Dixon, Bo Diddley, and Chuck Berry, there might have been no Elvis Presley, Jerry Lee Lewis, or Carl Perkins. Rock 'n' roll flowed directly, sometimes almost note by note, from rhythm and blues.

Who Do You Love? is the second, and lesser, recent film about the brothers Chess, Leonard and Phil, and the label they founded. It tells the same improbable story of how two Jewish immigrant kids from Poland sold the family junkyard to start a music club on the black South Side, and helped launch the musical styles that have influenced everything since.

Both films are, of course, filled with music. The Chess catalog must have collected some nice royalties. The basic outlines of the films are roughly the same, although *Cadillac Records* (2008) didn't include Phil, the younger and quieter brother. Leonard (Alessandro Nivola) is hopelessly infatuated with black music, Phil (Jon Abrahams) more interested in the business.

It remains a little unclear exactly what Leonard feels about black people. Yes, he supports their rights. But he underpays them. He was fond of Etta James, called Ivy Mills here and played by Megalyn Echikunwoke. Her drug addiction is greatly fictionalized (she is still very much alive, for one thing) and her great hit "At Last" is shifted in time; the equivalent character in *Cadillac Records* is more moving. Leonard historically decided to back her with violins and a full orchestra.

In this movie's telling, Willie Dixon (Chi McBride, very good) was Leonard's scout in finding the best of a new generation of R&B artists. It's Dixon who introduces Chess to Muddy Waters (David Oyelowo) and lends him a guitar for his audition. But Leonard had a good ear and proved it with the stable he built.

He loved the music. In a no doubt exaggerated scene, his family is all packed up in the car and ready to leave on vacation when he explains he has to go on tour with Muddy instead. His wife, Revetta (Marika Dominczyk), is part long-suffering, part perhaps not fully aware from their suburban home of what's going on in the city.

The Chess Records story is part of modern folklore, and both films treat it too much that way: as a well-rehearsed saga. I think more edge is needed, more reality about the racial situation at the time, more insight into how and why R&B and R&R actually did forever transform societies in America and the world. Who had more to do with bringing down the Berlin Wall? Ronald Reagan or Muddy Waters?

Wild Grass ★ ★ ★

PG, 113 m., 2010

Sabine Azema (Marguerite Muir), Andre Dussollier (Georges Palet), Anne Consigny (Suzanne), Emmanuelle Devos (Josepha), Mathieu Amalric (Bernard de Bordeaux), Michel Vuillermoz (Lucien d'Orange), Edouard Baer (Narrator). Directed by Alain Resnais and produced by Jean-Louis Livi. Screenplay by Alex Reval and Laurent Herbiert, based on the novel *L'incident* by Christian Gailly.

Wild Grass is about an unlikely and fateful chain of events that to a young person might seem like coincidence, but to an older one illustrates the likelihood that most of what happens in our lives comes about by sheer accident. This is the new work by Alain Resnais, who may have learned this by experience: There's a springtime in your life when you think it should add up and make sense, and an autumn when you think, the hell with it, anything can happen.

Resnais has been making films since the

dawn of the New Wave: *Hiroshima, Mon Amour* (1959), and *Last Year at Marienbad* (1961). Now he's eighty-eight. Preparing to write, I decided not to mention his age, in fear that some readers might think a director that age couldn't possibly be engaging. But praise must be given. *Wild Grass* is carefree and anarchic, takes bold risks, spins in unexpected directions.

It uses a narrator, which is just as well, because only from an all-knowing point of view can the labyrinth of connections be seen. The narrator begins by telling us that all the subsequent events will take place because the heroine, Marguerite (Sabine Azema), required a shoe size that was hard to find. Therefore on an impulse she went into a shoe store, found the right shoes, and walked out just in time to have her purse snatched by a thief.

Her billfold is later found discarded by Georges (Andre Dussollier), a married man. In the billfold he sees her photograph and learns she is single, a dentist, and a private pilot. He finds it necessary to meet her. This isn't so easy to arrange. Georges in the meantime is the subject of several oblique suggestions that Resnais is never all that clear about. Does he have fearsome secrets? Does he harbor fantasies? Is his mind coming apart?

As we meet these possibilities, we also get to know Marguerite better, with her jolly red hair and her best friend, Josepha (Emmanuelle Devos). You may not place these names, but if you go to French movies you've likely seen both many times; they're very likable, which means Resnais can enlist our sympathy without needing to recruit it. They're not quite sure what to make of this Georges character, and particularly his desire to go up in a plane with Marguerite at the controls.

From time to time we hear narration from characters. We find ourselves in unexpected situations. There are actions that seem objectively impossible. Resnais finds a tone allowing him to incorporate all these detours into the headlong flight of the film itself. Life is like that. In our minds it unfolds straight ahead of us because we remain oblivious to the pianos that didn't fall on our heads, the trucks that didn't hit us in the street, the plague we escaped, and, in this case, the incalculable odds against Marguerite going to that shoe store, and Georges finding her wallet, and her being a pilot, and so on.

I think Resnais's point is that life itself is utterly accidental (beginning with the odds against life arising in the universe, and the odds against our being born). When you look at it that way, everything that happens in *Wild Grass* makes perfect sense. The odds against any two people meeting in Paris almost seem small.

The film is a visual pleasure, using elegant techniques that don't call flashy attention to themselves. The camera is intended to be as omniscient as the narrator and can occupy the film's space as it pleases and move as it desires. Here is a young man's film made with a lifetime of experience.

Winnebago Man ★ ★ ★

NO MPAA RATING, 85 m., 2010

A documentary directed by Ben Steinbauer and produced by Steinbauer, Joel Heller, James Payne, and Malcolm Pullinger. Screenplay by Steinbauer and Pullinger.

There is a video on YouTube that has had millions and millions of hits and made its subject, a man named Jack Rebney, internationally known as Winnebago Man. He is perhaps even as famous as Trololo Man, and that's famous.

Rebney first attracted attention when an old VHS tape surfaced featuring the outtakes of a 1988 session when he was trying without much success to star in a promotional film for Winnebagos. Things were not going well. In take after take, Rebney blew lines, forgot lines, thought lines were stupid, was distracted by crew members moving around, was annoyed by stray sounds, was mad at himself for even doing the damn thing.

Every time the filming breaks down or Rebney calls a halt, he explodes in remarkable verbal fireworks. The only reason "Winnebago Man" doesn't consist of wall-to-wall f-words is that he separates them with other four-letter words. Once it made it onto YouTube, the video was found hilarious by countless viewers. But what were they laughing at really, and who *was* the real Winnebago Man?

A documentary maker named Ben Steinbauer decided to find out. He was curious about the reasons we like footage of real people subjecting themselves (usually unwillingly) to ridicule. Are we laughing at them, with them, or simply in relief that we aren't them? How does their viral fame affect them?

Jack Rebney seemed to have disappeared from the face of the earth. Using methods he shows in his film, Steinbauer finally tracks him down in northern California, where he lives alone in the woods, calls himself a hermit, and wants nothing to do with nobody—never. That's not because of the YouTube video, which he doesn't give a $#!+ about. It's because of the way he is.

Now around eighty, he works as a caretaker for a fishing resort that, it must be said, is never very evident in the film. He has an unlisted phone number and uses post office boxes, and his dog is all the company he wants. He does have a computer; I imagine figures like this feeding the endless comment streams on blogs.

Steinbauer visits him, chats with him, gets first one impression and then another. Rebney more or less agrees to be filmed. His YouTube fame is meaningless to him, but he figures it might be useful if he could parlay it into a way to air his views. Rebney, as you might suspect, has a great many views, including a roster of national figures he believes should be tried as war criminals.

Although we find out a lot about this virtual hermit and develop an admiration for his cantankerous principles, the movie leaves some questions unanswered. We learn that Rebney is threatened with blindness. We wonder how he will get along, at his age, living in a cabin in the woods. We might like to know a little more about Rebney as a young man. We suspect, but can't be sure, that much of his anger is not uncontrolled, but is aimed consciously at what he considers a stupid and corrupt world. He is not a comic character; he's dead serious.

Rebney is not touchy-feely. He is a hardened realist, whose only soft spot may be for his dog. He keeps up with events, feels the nation is going down the drain, and isn't sure why he was so angry while making the Winnebago promotional film. The crew he was cussing out were not good sports, and the outtakes made their way to Winnebago, which fired him. Then it went wide on YouTube.

Steinbauer takes Rebney wider still—all the way to the Jay Leno show, and to a fascinating personal appearance at a Found Film Festival, where he regards himself on the screen and then goes out to speak and proves himself the master of the situation. Steinbauer even sets him up with a Twitter account, but, typically, Rebney loathed it. His most recent Tweet, on March 28, 2009, was: "UP YOUR FERN."

Winter's Bone ★ ★ ★ ★

R, 99 m., 2010

Jennifer Lawrence (Ree Dolly), John Hawkes (Teardrop), Kevin Breznahan (Little Arthur), Dale Dickey (Merab), Lauren Sweetser (Gail), Tate Taylor (Mike Satterfield), Garret Dillahunt (Sheriff Baskin), Sheryl Lee (April), Shelley Waggener (Sonya). Directed by Debra Granik and produced by Alix Madigan and Anne Rosellini. Screenplay by Granik and Rosellini, based on the novel by Daniel Woodrell.

The movie heroes who affect me most are not extroverted. They don't strut, speechify, and lead armies. They have no superpowers. They are ordinary people who are faced with a need and rise to the occasion. Ree Dolly is such a hero.

She is a girl of seventeen who acts as the homemaker for her younger brother and sister. This is in the backlands of the Ozarks. Her mother sits useless all day, mentally absent. Her father, who was jailed for cooking meth, is missing. She tries to raise the kids and feed them, scraping along on welfare and the kindness of neighbors. The children, like all children who are not beaten, are cheerful and energetic and love to play. They have not learned they are disadvantaged.

This world is established with bleak economy in the opening scenes of Debra Granik's *Winter's Bone*, which was a double prize winner at Sundance 2010. Unmistakably filmed on location, this is a society that has been left behind. It looks like Walker Evans's photographs of the rural Depression, brought forward to today. The unanswered question is how Ree Dolly grew up in this world and became strong, self-reliant, and proud. She didn't learn it from her parents.

The sheriff comes to call. Her father, Jessup, has skipped bail. To meet his bond, he put up the house—perhaps the only asset he had. If he doesn't turn himself in within a week, the family will be thrown out. Just like that. "I'll find him," Ree says quietly and firmly. And that's what she sets out to do.

Ree is played by Jennifer Lawrence, a nineteen-year-old newcomer who has already made Jodie Foster's new film. She embodies a fierce, still center that is the source of her heroism. She makes no boasts, issues no threats, depends on a dogged faith that people will do the right thing—even when no one we meet seems to deserve that faith. "Don't ask for what's not offered," she tells her little brother, although the lives of her parents seem to be an exercise in asking and not offering. Did she raise herself?

Everyone in the district knew that Jessup cooked methamphetamine. He is a modern moonshiner. What is obvious is that meth doesn't seem to have made him much money. Perhaps its illegality is its appeal, and its market is among people he feels comfortable with. Ree's travels in search of her father lead her to his brother, Teardrop (John Hawkes), whose existence inflicts a wound on the gift of being alive.

The screenplay, by Granik and Anne Rosellini, based on the novel by Daniel Woodrell, uses the ancient form of an odyssey. At its end will be Ree's father, dead or alive. Most likely dead, she begins to conclude, but unless there is a body her family will be homeless and torn apart. She treks through a landscape scarcely less ruined than the one in Cormac McCarthy's *The Road*. This land seems post-catastrophe. Although it has cars and electricity, running shoes and kitchens, cigarettes and televisions, these seem like relics of an earlier, prosperous time. If thrown-away possessions pile up around the houses of people, it is because they've reached the end of the line. There is no next stop.

There is a hazard of caricature here. Granik avoids it. Her film doesn't live above these people but among them. Ree herself has lived as one of them and doesn't see them as inferior, only ungiving and disappointing. In her father's world everyone is a criminal, depends on a criminal, or sells to criminals. That they are illegal makes them vulnerable to informers and plea-bargainers, so they are understandably suspicious. The cliché would be that they suspect outsiders. These characters suspect insiders, even family members.

As Ree's journey takes her to one character after another, Granik is able to focus on each one's humanity, usually damaged. They aren't attractions in a sideshow but survivors in a shared reality. Do they look at Ree and see a girl in need and a family threatened with eviction? I think they see the danger of their own need and eviction; it's safer to keep quiet and close off.

So the film rests on Ree, counterbalanced by Teardrop, who is aggressive with his hatefulness instead of passive in amorality. A story like this could become mired in despair, but Ree's hope and courage lock us in. How did she get to be the way she is? We are born optimistic, although life can be a great discouragement. In every bad situation, there are usually a few good people. ☞

Win Win ★ ★ ★

R, 106 m., 2011

Paul Giamatti (Mike Flaherty), Amy Ryan (Jackie Flaherty), Bobby Cannavale (Terry Delfino), Jeffrey Tambor (Stephen Vigman), Burt Young (Leo Poplar), Melanie Lynskey (Cindy), Alex Shaffer (Kyle). Directed by Tom McCarthy and produced by Lisa Maria Falcone, Michael London, and Mary Jane Skalski. Screenplay by McCarthy.

I was warming up to describe *Win Win* as a high-level sitcom, and then wondered what's so bad about it being a sitcom if it's high-level? You have a situation, and it's funny. That's a sitcom. You have a funny situation, and there's some truth in it and unexpected characters, well acted, and you may not have a great film, but you enjoy watching it.

Win Win centers on Paul Giamatti, an actor whose motivation often seems to be "I'm fed up and not going to take it anymore." He can play sweet, but he's most at home in a role like this: Mike Flaherty, a mediocre lawyer in a small New Jersey town, who can't make ends meet. He loves his kids and his wife, Jackie (Amy Ryan), but he doesn't like his work, he doesn't have the money to fix the boiler in the basement of his office, and he will happily wait until the dead tree in his front lawn falls on the house before he does anything about it.

Mike volunteers as the wrestling coach for the local high school team. You could not call this a passion. It is more of a task he has stubbornly set himself. Perhaps, years ago and in another body, he was a high school wrestler. He shares his office with an accountant named Stephen (Jeffrey Tambor), who is now also the assistant wrestling coach. It's a good thing the team usually loses because you cannot easily imagine Tambor smiling. Relieved satisfaction is about the limit of his capacity for elation. Joining them in a coaching triumvirate is Mike's best friend, Terry (Bobby Cannavale).

Mike has a client named Leo Poplar (Burt Young; remember him as Rocky's brother-in-law?). Leo is moving into Alzheimer's and refuses to leave his home of many years. When Mike discovers in court that Leo's estate will pay $1,500 a month to a legal guardian, he takes the job himself and immediately double-crosses his client by placing him in a nursing home. This is immoral and dishonest, but Leo will indeed probably be better off there, and Mike needs the money.

All of these scenes remind me of the detail and human qualities of McCarthy's two previous films, which involved sharply defined personalities in situations where their lives were interrupted by strangers. In *The Station Agent* (2003), a movie I would happily stop everything to watch again right now, Peter Dinklage played a dwarf obsessed with trains, who found his privacy invaded by a lonely woman (Patricia Clarkson) and a strange hot dog stand owner (Bobby Cannavale). In *The Visitor* (2007), Richard Jenkins played a withdrawn widower who finds a family of African immigrants has moved into his apartment.

Yes, those are technically sitcom situations. But both are more, and much deeper, than just comedies. He pushes that extra distance to find how his complex, plausible characters might respond. *Win Win* shows similar qualities, but takes fewer chances, and falls back on the ever-reliable Big Game/Match/Fight formula in its third act.

That employs a character who materializes well into the film. Kyle (Alex Shaffer) is old Leo's grandson, who has run away from home and hopes to live with the old man, but ends up living with Leo and Jackie. Mike finds no relatives for Kyle except for a druggie mother in rehab. Wouldn't you somehow know the kid is a champion wrestler? This is where the sitcom stuff clicks in. *Win Win* gathers all the strands (the illegal trusteeship, the wrestling team, the hazardous boiler, the wrestling, the rehabbing mother, Jackie finding out about her husband's misdeeds) and pays them off at the end.

Well, OK. It's too neat. Everything clicks into place. Life seldom has uncomplicated endings. But let it be said that Alex Shaffer, who was cast more for his wrestling than his acting, is effortlessly convincing. That Giamatti and Tambor are funny when they try to out-dour each other. That Amy Ryan does what she can with the loyal-wife-who's-had-enough role. That the ending has simple pleasures, although not those promised by the beginning or by McCarthy's earlier films. I'm happy I saw *Win Win*. It would have been possible to be happier.

The Wolfman ★ ★ ½

R, 102 m., 2010

Benicio Del Toro (Lawrence Talbot), Emily Blunt (Gwen Conliffe), Anthony Hopkins (Sir John Talbot), Geraldine Chaplin (Maleva), Hugo Weaving (Inspector Aberline), Antony Sher (Dr. Hoenneger), Gemma Whelan (Gwen's Maid), David Schofield (Constable Nye), Roger Frost (Reverend Fisk), Clive Russell (MacQueen), Art Malik (Singh). Directed by Joe Johnston and produced by Sean Daniel, Benicio Del Toro, Scott Stuber, and Rick Yorn. Screenplay by Andrew Kevin Walker and David Self.

The Wolfman avoids what must have been the temptation to update its famous story. It plants itself securely in period, with a great-looking production set in 1891. Gothic horror stories seem more digestible when set in once-great British country houses and peopled with gloomy inverts, especially when the countryside involves foggy moorlands and a craggy waterfall. This is, after all, a story set before the advent of modern psychology, back when a man's fate could be sealed by ancestral depravity.

The film's opening and closing shots are of

the full moon, which is correct. An early exterior shows Chatsworth in Derbyshire, perhaps the grandest of all English country houses, as a Gothic shriek. Inside it is derelict and unkempt, inhabited by the sinister old Sir John Talbot (Anthony Hopkins) and his faithful manservant Singh (Art Malik). Gas was well known as a means of illumination in 1891, and indeed electric lights were not uncommon, but Sir John makes do with flickering candles carried from room to room, the better to cast wicked shadows.

Sir John's son Ben and his fiancée, Gwen (Emily Blunt), were living there until recently, when Ben was savagely killed. Gwen writes to his brother Lawrence (Benicio Del Toro), an actor who is appearing in London in *Hamlet* and indeed is holding poor Yorick's skull when we first see him. Lawrence arrives in a foggy, chilly dusk, of course, and his voice echoes in the vast lonely mansion before his father emerges from the shadows.

I love stuff like this. The gloomier and more ominous the better. There is a silent classic named *The Fall of the House of Usher* that actually has dead leaves scuttling across a mansion's floor. Lawrence views his brother's body, which seems to have made a good meal, and then it's off to the obligatory local pub, where the conversations of the locals center on a strange beast marauding in the district. In the nineteenth century, a pub was the evening news.

More plot you do not require. What you might like to know is that *The Wolfman* has been made with care by Joe Johnston, and is well photographed by Shelly Johnson and designed by Rick Heinrichs. The music by Danny Elfman creeps around the edges. Del Toro makes Lawrence sad, worried, fearful, doomy. It's not just the loss of his brother. It's the earlier loss of his beloved mother. The family manse is haunted by his memories. His father, Sir John, however, is played by the bearded Anthony Hopkins as a man holding up perhaps better than you might expect. And he's well turned out for a man who lives almost in the dark.

The film has one flaw, and faithful readers will not be surprised to find it involves the special effects by CGI. No doubt there are whole scenes done so well in CGI I didn't even spot them; but when the wolf-creature bounds through the forest, he does so with too much speed. He'd be more convincing if he moved like a creature of considerable weight. In the first Spider-Man movie, you recall, Spidey swung around almost weightlessly. Adding weight and slowing him in the second film was one of the things that made it great. The wolfman moves so lightly here he almost cries out: Look! I'm animated!

I am not sure of the natural history of wolfmen. Is the condition passed through the blood? Apparently. How exactly does one morph from a man into a wolf? By special effects, obviously. The wolfman has much less pseudo-scientific documentation than the vampire. I understand why he sheds his clothes when he expands into a muscular predator. What I don't understand is how he always succeeds in redressing himself in the same clothes. Does he retrace his path back through the dark woods by moonlight, picking up after himself?

In any event, *The Wolfman* makes a satisfactory date movie for Valentine's Day, which is more than can be said for *Valentine's Day.* Truer love hath no woman, than the woman who loves a wolfman. And vice versa, ideally.

A Woman in Berlin ★ ★ ★

NO MPAA RATING, 131 m., 2009

Nina Hoss (Anonyma), Yevgeni Sidikhin (Andrei), Roman Gribkov (Lieutenant), Irm Hermann (Widow), Rudiger Vogler (Eckhart), Ulrike Krumbiegel (Ilse). Directed by Max Faerberboeck, and produced by Gunter Rohrbach. Screenplay by Faeberboeck, based on the diary *Anonyma: A Woman in Berlin.*

In the final weeks of World War II, the conquering Russian army occupied a Berlin in ruins and did what occupying armies often do, raped and pillaged. There was nothing to stop them—least of all their officers, who knew that after years of relentless battle it was useless to try to enforce discipline, even had they wanted to.

A Woman in Berlin is a diary written at that time and published some fifteen years later. Its author, who identifies herself as a journalist, was anonymous. The book's publication in 1959 inspired outrage in Germany, where the idea of German women cooperating somewhat with the Russians was unthinkable, and in Russia, where it soiled the honor of the Red Army.

In that time, in that place, women were raped. "How many times?" asks one of another, and they both know the subject of the question. The diary and film are about how the author attempted to control the terms of her defilement by deliberately seeking out a high-ranking Russian who would act as her protector. Who is to say this was wrong of her?

The woman, Anonyma, is played by Nina Hoss, who in two other films released here in the past year, *Yella* and *Jerichow*, has emerged as a strong, confident new actress with innate star quality. She is seen here in an early shot at a party, elegantly dressed, ruling the room, a proud Nazi, proposing a toast to the brave boys at the front. At the time it appeared Germany would conquer Europe.

By the end of the war, her husband has disappeared in battle and she is camped out with other women in the remnants of a bombed-out building. They are exhausted, dirty, hungry, frightened. They were all raised in the comfortable middle class, and now find themselves scrabbling like animals for food and shelter. The obvious sources of food, and drink, are the Russians. Most of them are crude, even bestial, but then the women cannot be choosers.

Anonyma has luck seducing a lieutenant and then sets her sights on a major, Andrei (Yevgeni Sidikhin), who is the top-ranking officer in sight. He's also by far the most complex. He resists her come-on at first, perhaps because he's fastidious, more likely because he simply doesn't see himself as that kind of man. Something unspoken passes between them. They grow closer. Yes, she profits from their liaison, and yes, he eventually takes up her offer. But for each there is the illusion that this is something they choose to do.

What little I know about war suggests that sometimes it comes down to a choice between two dismaying courses of action. Some people would rather die than lose their honor. Most people would rather not die, particularly if their deaths would change nothing. Anonyma and Andrei are people with similar sensibilities, similar feelings, now divested of the illusions they presumably brought with them into the war.

That is the movie's insight, and the book's, too, I assume. This isn't a love story in any palpable sense. It is a story about how things were. *A Woman in Berlin* finds no particular point in the story, and no one is heroic in any sense. The woman and man make the best accommodation they can with the reality that confronts them. There are several subplots involving other women and other soldiers, and one involves a woman who is subtly pleased by the power her body gives her. Well, she's not the first such woman, or man.

The film is well acted, with restraint, by Hoss and Sidikhin. The writer and director, Max Faerberboeck, employs a level gaze and avoids for the most part artificial sentimentality. The physical production is convincing. The movie is just enough too long that we realize we've already seen everything it has to observe.

World's Greatest Dad ★ ★ ★

R, 99 m., 2009

Robin Williams (Lance Clayton), Alexie Gilmore (Claire), Daryl Sabara (Kyle Clayton), Evan Martin (Andrew), Geoff Pierson (Principal Anderson), Henry Simmons (Mike Lane), Mitzi McCall (Bonnie). Directed by Bobcat Goldthwait and produced by Tim Perell, Howard Gertler, Sean McKittrick, and Richard Kelly. Screenplay by Goldthwait.

Bobcat Goldthwait makes a daring assault in *World's Greatest Dad* against our yearning to mythologize the dead. But he loses his nerve just before the earth is completely scorched. I have a notion his first-draft screenplay might have been unremittingly dark and cynical. It might not have been "commercial." This version may have a better chance. Audiences think they like bleak pessimism, but they expect the plane to pull put of its dive and land safely.

Robin Williams is the star, demonstrating once again that he's sometimes better in drama than comedy. He has that manic side he indulges, and he works better (for me, anyway) when he's grounded. Here he plays Lance, a high school teacher, the divorced father of a loathsome teenager. His son dies by hanging and becomes the object of a cult of veneration and mourning at the school where he was a student and his dad still teaches.

This premise is well established because of a disturbingly good performance by Daryl Sabara as Kyle, the disgusting son. Kyle is a compulsory masturbator who makes no effort to conceal his pastime from his father. At school, he's a vulgar sexist, insulting girls in the corridors. At all times he is as angry and hostile as he can possibly be, and is genuinely disliked by the student body—with the sad exception of Andrew (Evan Martin), his "friend" and victim.

Lance comes home to find his son has strangled himself. He has loved the boy despite everything, and now he attempts to rewrite the story of his death. He manufactures misleading evidence for the police to find—and although he is a failed author with five rejected novels in the drawer, he now finds his perfect genre by forging a diary allegedly left behind by Kyle at his death.

This diary he posts on the Internet, it goes viral at the high school, and the student body is overtaken with remorse about the way Kyle was treated. Soon he becomes the deity of a death cult, led no doubt by *Twilight* fans, and students start wearing his photo. Lance is now seen as a heroic father.

The way this becomes an obsession is possibly the real point of Goldthwait's film. There's nothing like death to stir the herd instinct. For example, yes, Michael Jackson was a creative and talented artist. But was he as venerated a week before his death as much as a week after? Would anyone have foreseen the state funeral? What, exactly, did it mean when fans staged an all-night vigil at Neverland? Some were motivated by grief, more perhaps by a desire to participate vicariously in fame. Like fanatic sports fans, they seek identities through the objects of their adulation.

The Kyle cult becomes a tiger that Lance, the hero's father, has to ride. As he passes through the corridors, the path clears before him and a hush falls. He becomes much more interesting to his girlfriend, Claire (Alexie Gilmore), a fellow teacher, who had shown alarming signs of growing sweet on Mike (Henry Simmons), a handsome younger faculty member.

The only character who doubts the story about Kyle's death and his diary is Andrew—the only one who knew him, and his onanism, at all well. Lance otherwise triumphs as he creates a fake son in place of his real son, and all leads up to Kyle Clayton Day at the school. It is quite true, as the critic Stephen Holden points out, that the phony death story has brought out the better natures of the survivors. My question is whether Goldthwait, the creator, after all, of *Shakes the Clown*, started out with that intention. There is an inexorably black satire somewhere inside *World's Greatest Dad*, signaling to be saved.

X

X Games 3D: The Movie ★ ½

PG, 92 m., 2009

Featuring Shaun White, Danny Way, Bob Burnquist, Ricky Carmichael, Travis Pastrana, and Kyle Loza. Narrated by Emile Hirsch. A documentary directed by Steve Lawrence and produced by Phil Orlins. Screenplay by Lawrence and Greg Jennings.

Well, it's awesome all right, what these X Games stars achieve. It's also awesome how little there is to be said about it. If you're a fan of extreme skateboarding, motorcycling, and motocross, this is the movie for you. If not, not. And even if you are, what's in the film other than what you might have seen on TV? Yes, it's in 3-D, which adds nothing and dims the picture.

Although *X Games 3D: The Movie* is billed as a documentary, let me mention two things that struck me as peculiar. During the final Mega Ramp extreme skateboarding competition in the Staples Center in Los Angeles, we learn almost accidentally that this is a sport that is scored on a point system, like diving or gymnastics. This is referred to only indirectly by the narrator, Emile Hirsch, who lavishes time on such inanities as "He treats gravity like some people do evolution, as only a theory," and "The present is past; only the future has currency." The flaw in this time theory is that when the future becomes the present it is the past. And gravity is more than a theory when you fall fifty feet onto a hard surface, as one X Gamer does.

We start to notice the competitors glancing up at what must be a scoreboard, but we're never shown it or informed of anybody's score. Why not? The film also has an annoying way of frequently not showing the beginning, middle, and end of a shot in one unbroken take. What's the point? During a two-car motocross "race," it's peculiar that the two cars are only seen together in one brief shot, as one flies off a dirt ramp and over the other, crossing below. Are they on different tracks? The narrator doesn't ever say.

What the athletes do is dangerous and risky. For example, hurtling down an almost perpendicular incline on a skateboard, using your speed to climb another terrifying ramp, and then launching into midair to perform "360s" and even "540s" before landing again on another ramp. Or, flying straight up from a ramp, doing a flip and/or a rotation, and landing again on the same ramp.

On motorcycles, they fly off earthen ramps, twist in the air, and land on another ramp. Or they do a high jump—flying almost straight up in the air to clear a bar at thirty-two or thirty-three feet. Often they fail, fall hard, and there's a tense silence while medics rush to the rescue. One competitor, Danny Way, apparently breaks something at Staples and returns to jump two more times. Earlier, he breaks his ankle in a practice jump and returns the next day to attempt to go over the Great Wall of China on a skateboard.

Athletes are asked why they take such risks and play with such pains (all of them have had broken bones and concussions). Their answers are the usual sports clichés about challenges and "taking the sport to a new level." Their cars and clothing are plastered with commercial endorsements, and at the X Games there are big ads for Pizza Hut, the navy, and so on. I guess they get paid. A lot, I hope.

"Who wants an A in history when you can get an X?" we're asked. Here's my theory about time. Yesterday is history, tomorrow's a mystery—so why get killed today?

X-Men: First Class ★ ★ ★

PG-13, 130 m., 2011

James McAvoy (Charles Xavier/Professor X), Michael Fassbender (Erik Lehnsherr/Magneto), Rose Byrne (Moira MacTaggert), Jennifer Lawrence (Raven/Mystique), Kevin Bacon (Sebastian Shaw), January Jones (Emma Frost), Nicholas Hoult (Hank/Beast). Directed by Matthew Vaughn and produced by Gregory Goodman, Simon Kinberg, Lauren Shuler Donner, and Bryan Singer. Screenplay by Vaughn, Ashley Edward Miller, Zack Stentz, and Jane Goldman.

The best acting in *X Men: First Class* is by President John F. Kennedy, who in his Thanksgiving 1962 message to the nation expresses gratitude for the successful end of the

Cuban Missile Crisis while suppressing what he surely must know, that U.S. and Soviet missiles spent a great deal of time flying back and forth while mentally controlled by the awesome powers of mutants. The movie's use of the missile crisis certainly serves the purpose of establishing this prequel in the early 1960s, and answers a question I've always had: Does the real world overlap with the histories of superheroes?

The movie is high-tech and well acted, with lots of action and noise as it portrays the origins of the X-Men, a group of about a dozen mutants (so far). It begins in a Nazi prison camp, where young Erik Lehnsherr is forced to witness a tragedy and finds he can control metals with his mind—but only when he's angry. He grows up to become Magneto, and is played by Michael Fassbender, the lean German actor who the buzzmeisters say will become a big star off of this film. Heaven help him. He was so good in *Fish Tank*, *Inglourious Basterds*, and *Jane Eyre*; must he play Magneto to become a star? For that matter, Raven/Mystique is played by Jennifer Lawrence, nominated for best actress earlier this year. Now a blue shape-shifter. The price of stardom.

Anyway, at Oxford, we meet the telepath Charles Xavier (James McAvoy) as a young man before he was paralyzed. He will eventually operate a school to shelter and train mutants, and he dreams they can help the world. His archenemy is Sebastian Shaw (Kevin Bacon), Magneto's cruel tormentor in the Nazi camp, now a man who recruits mutants to the dark side, where if they're good, maybe they'll be able to wear a helmet like his and look like a Roman charioteer. If anyone whacks him up alongside the head, he's gonna get a nasty cut from that pointy cheek protector.

Other mutants are gathered into one fold or the other. Each one has a specialty. There is a shape-shifter, a tempest-tosser, a screamer, a fire-blaster, a quick-adapter (named Darwin, of course), and so on. That each would develop a unique ability through simultaneous mutation is a tribute to the intelligent design of Stan Lee and his Marvel Comics crew. Still, it must be confining to have only one trick; you need to move with a crowd to cover all the bases.

The plot involves attempts by CIA agent Moira MacTaggert (Rose Byrne) to use Xavier to battle Shaw, who presents a threat to world peace. Exactly how the CIA discovered the mutants is a little unclear, and indeed the agency exists mostly as a convenience to the plot and the source of Moira, who seems to really like Xavier—and as a telepath, he should realize that if anyone does.

Anyway, the destinies of the good and bad mutants intersect with the Cuban Missile Crisis, which was not quite as we think of it. The scene where the mutants stand on a beach and mentally duel by causing both American and Soviet missiles to shuttle back and forth in the sky is . . . hilarious, I was going to say, but no, I should consider this scene more devoutly.

Director Matthew Vaughn in 2010 gave us *Kick-Ass*, in which an eleven-year-old girl was hammered almost to death for our entertainment. This movie lacks comparable violence, but is louder. At least all the X-Men are old enough to see an R-rated movie without adult supervision. Not that *X-Men* is R-rated; God forbid a comic book movie should turn away a single eager ticket buyer.

This is competent weekend entertainment. It is not a great comic book movie, like *Spider-Man II*, or a bad one, like *Thor*. It is not in 3-D, which is a mercy. The actors all embody their roles convincingly, if somewhat humorlessly, and the special effects cope admirably with those rockets changing directions. The battle scenes involve people having terrible things happen to them in somewhat incomprehensible ways, but they also create an intriguing texture for Raven the shape-shifter; Nicholas Hoult as Beast looks as if he's wearing a shag rug suit, but there you have it.

X-Men Origins: Wolverine ★ ★

PG-13, 107 m., 2009

Hugh Jackman (Wolverine), Liev Schreiber (Sabretooth), Taylor Kitsch (Gambit), Daniel Henney (Agent Zero), Danny Huston (General William Stryker), Kevin Durand (The Blob), will.i.am (Wraith). Directed by Gavin Hood and produced by John Palermo, Lauren Shuler Donner, Ralph Winter, and Hugh Jackman. Screenplay by David Benioff and Skip Woods.

X-Men Origins: Wolverine finally answers the burning question, left hanging after all three previous *Wolverine* movies, of the origins of Logan, whose knuckles conceal long and wicked blades. He is about 175 years old, he apparently stopped changing when he reached Hugh Jackman's age, and neither he, nor we, find out how he developed such an interesting mutation.

His half brother was Victor (Liev Schreiber). Their story starts in "1840—the Northwest Territories of Canada," a neat trick, since Canada was formed in 1867, and its Northwest Territories in 1870. But you didn't come here for a history lesson. Or maybe you did, if you need to know that Logan and Victor became Americans (still before they could be Canadians) and fought side by side in the Civil War, World War I, World War II, and Vietnam. Why they did this, I have no idea. Maybe they just enjoyed themselves.

Booted out of the army in Vietnam, Logan/Wolverine joined a secret black ops unit under General Stryker (Danny Huston), until finally, in Nigeria, he got fed up with atrocities. Nevertheless, he was recruited by Stryker for a *super* secret plan to create a mutant of mutants, who would incorporate all available mutant powers, including those of the kid whose eyes are like laser beams. He wears sunglasses. Lotta good they'll do him.

Am I being disrespectful to this material? You bet. It is Hugh Jackman's misfortune that when they were handing around superheroes, he got Wolverine, who is, for my money, low on the charisma list. He never says anything witty, insightful, or very intelligent; his utterances are limited to the vocalization of primitive forces: anger, hurt, vengeance, love, hate, determination. There isn't a speck of ambiguity. That Wolverine has been voted the number one comic book hero of all time must be the result of a stuffed ballot box.

At least, you hope, he has an interesting vulnerability? I'm sure X-Men scholars can tell you what it is, although since he has the gift of instant healing, it's hard to pinpoint. When a man can leap from an exploding truck in midair, cling to an attacking helicopter, slice the rotor blades, ride it to the ground, leap free, and walk away (in that ancient cliché where there's a fiery explosion behind him but he doesn't seem to notice it), here's what I think: Why should I care about this guy? He feels no pain, and nothing can kill him, so therefore he's essentially a story device for action sequences.

Oh, the film is well made. Gavin Hood, the director, made the great film *Tsotsi* (2005) and the damned good film *Rendition* (2007) before signing on here. Fat chance *Wolverine* fans will seek out those two. Why does a gifted director make a film none of his earlier admirers would much want to see? That's how you get to be a success in Hollywood. When you make a big box-office hit for mostly fanboys, you've hit the big time. Look at Justin Lin with *The Fast and the Furious.*

Such films are assemblies of events. There is little dialogue, except for the snarling of threats, vows, and laments, and the recitation of essential plot points. Nothing here about human nature. No personalities beyond those hauled in via typecasting. No lessons to learn. No joy to be experienced. Just mayhem, noise, and pretty pictures. I have been powerfully impressed by film versions of Batman, Spider-Man, Superman, Iron Man, and the Iron Giant. I wouldn't walk across the street to meet Wolverine.

But wait! you say. Doesn't the film at least provide a learning experience for Logan about his origins for Wolverine? Hollow laugh. Because we know that the modern Wolverine has a form of amnesia, it cannot be a spoiler for me to reveal that at the end of *X-Men Origins: Wolverine,* he forgets everything that has happened in the film. Lucky man.

Y

Year One ★

PG-13, 100 m., 2009

Jack Black (Zed), Michael Cera (Oh), Oliver Platt (High Priest), David Cross (Cain), Hank Azaria (Abraham), Juno Temple (Eema). Directed by Harold Ramis and produced by Judd Apatow, Clayton Townsend, and Nicholas Weinstock. Screenplay by Ramis, Gene Stupnitsky, and Lee Eisenberg.

Harold Ramis is one of the nicest people I've met in the movie business, and I'm so sorry *Year One* happened to him. I'm sure he had the best intentions. In trying to explain why the movie was produced, I have a theory. Ramis is the top-billed of three writers, and he is so funny that when he read some of these lines, they sounded hilarious. Pity he didn't play one of the leads in his own film.

As always, I carefully avoided any of the movie's trailers, but I couldn't avoid the posters or the ads. "Meet Your Ancestors," they said, with big photos of Jack Black and Michael Cera. I assumed it was about Adam and Eve. Cera has smooth, delicate features, and with curly locks falling to below his shoulders, I thought: "Michael Cera in drag. I wonder where Harold will take that?"

But no, even though Cera is sometimes mistaken for a woman, he's all primitive man, banging women on the head. Then he and Black eat of the forbidden apple and make a leap from tribal "hunter-gatherers" (a term they enjoy) to royal security guards. Everyone throughout the film talks like anyone else in a Judd Apatow comedy, somewhere between stoned and crafty.

It must be said that Jack Black and Michael Cera were not born to be costars. Black was fresh and funny once, a reason then to welcome him in a movie, but here he forgets to act and simply announces his lines. Cera plays shy and uncertain, but then he always does, and responds to Black as if Jack were Juno and a source of intimidating wit.

Another leading role is taken by Oliver Platt, as an extremely hairy high priest, who orders Cera to massage his chest with oil. The close-up of Cera kneading his matted chest foliage is singularly unappetizing. There are several good-looking babes in the city (did I mention it is Sodom?), who, as required in such films, all find the heroes inexplicably attractive. Cera and Juno Temple have a good exchange. She plays a slave. "When do you get off?" he asks. "Never."

That and several other of the film's better moments are in the trailer, of which it can be said, if they were removed from the film, it would be nearly bereft of better moments. The movie takes place in the land now known as Israel (then too, I think), although no one does much with that. The Sodomites include in their number Abraham, Cain, and Abel; it's surprising to find them still in action in the Year One, since Genesis places them—well, before the time of the Year One. Sodomy is not very evident in Sodom, perhaps as a result of the movie being shaved down from an R to a PG-13.

The film has shaggy crowds that mill about like outtakes from *Monty Python and the Holy Grail*, and human sacrifice in which virgins are pitched into the blazing mouth of a stone ox, and a cheerful turn when the gods more appreciate a high priest than a virgin. But *Year One* is a dreary experience, and all the ending accomplishes is to bring it to a close. Even in the credit cookies, you don't sense the actors having much fun.

The Yellow Handkerchief ★ ★ ★

PG-13, 102 m., 2010

William Hurt (Brett), Maria Bello (May), Kristen Stewart (Martine), Eddie Redmayne (Gordy). Directed by Udayan Prasad and produced by Arthur Cohn and Terence Rosemore. Screenplay by Erin Dignam, based on the story by Pete Hamill.

The action in *The Yellow Handkerchief* takes place within the characters, who don't much talk about it, so the faces of the actors replace dialogue. That's more interesting than movies that lay it all out. This is the story of three insecure drifters who improbably find themselves sharing a big convertible and driving to New Orleans not long after Hurricane Katrina.

The car's driver is a painfully insecure teenager named Gordy (Eddie Redmayne), who doubts most of what he does and seems to apologize just by standing there. At a rural convenience store he encounters Martine (Kristen Stewart), running away from her life. He says he's driving to New Orleans. No reason. She decides to come along. No reason. They meet a quiet, reserved man named Brett (William Hurt), and she thinks he should come along. No particular reason.

We now have the makings of a classic road picture. Three outsiders, a fabled destination, Louisiana back roads. and a big old convertible. It must be old because modern cars have no style; three strangers can't go On the Road in a Corolla. It must be a convertible because it makes it easier to light and see the characters and the landscape they pass through. They must be back roads because what kind of a movie is it when they drive at a steady seventy on the interstate?

The formula is obvious, but the story, curiously, turns out to be based on fact. It began as journalism by Pete Hamill, published in the early 1970s. In the movie's rendition, Brett fell in love with a woman named May (Maria Bello), then spent six years in prison for manslaughter, although his guilt is left in doubt. Martine slowly coaxes his story out of the secretive man.

You don't need an original story for a movie. You need original characters and living dialogue. *The Yellow Handkerchief*, written by Erin Dignam, directed by Udayan Prasad, has those, and evocative performances. William Hurt occupies the silent center of the film. In many movies we interpret his reticence as masking intelligence. Here we realize it's a blank slate and could be masking anything. Although his situation is an open temptation for an actor to signal his emotions, Hurt knows that the best movie emotions are intuited by the audience, not read from emotional billboards.

Kristen Stewart is, quite simply, a wonderful actress. I must not hold *Twilight* against her. She played the idiotic fall-girl written for her as well as that silly girl could be played, and now that the movie has passed a $200 million gross, she has her choice of screenplays for her next three films, as long as one of them is *The Twilight Saga: Eclipse*. In recent film after film, she shows a sure hand and an intrinsic power. I last saw her in *Welcome to the Rileys*, where she played a runaway working as a hooker in New Orleans. In both films she had many scenes with experienced older actors (Hurt, James Gandolfini). In both she was rock solid. Playing insecure and neurotic, yes, but rock solid.

The story of Eddie Redmayne, who plays Gordy, is unexpected. He fits effortlessly into the role of the scrawny, uncertain fifteen-year-old Louisiana kid. Yet I learn he is twenty-seven, a Brit who went to Eton, a veteran of Shakespeare and Edward Albee. Michael Caine explained to me long ago why it's easier for British actors to do American accents than the other way around. Whatever. You can't find a crack in his performance here.

These three embark on a road odyssey that feels like it takes longer than it might in real life. Their secrets are very slowly confided. They go through emotional relationships expected and not expected. They learn lessons about themselves, which is required in such films, but are so slowly and convincingly arrived at here that we forgive them. There is rarely a film where the characters are exactly the same at the end as they were at the beginning. (Note: Being triumphant is not a character change.)

The filmmaker, Udayan Prasad, made a wonderful British film in 1997, *My Son the Fanatic*. I've seen none of his work since. Now this redneck slice of life. Since the characters are so far from the lives of the actors and the director, this is a creation of the imagination. As it must be. The ending is a shade melodramatic, but what the heck. In for one yellow handkerchief, in for a hundred.

The Yes Men Fix the World ★ ★ ★

NO MPAA RATING, 96 m., 2009

A documentary directed by Andy Bichlbaum and Mike Bonanno and produced by Doro Bachrach, Ruth Charny, Laura Nix, Jess Search, and Juliette Timsit. Screenplay by Bichlbaum and Bonanno.

The Yes Men are a New York political action cooperative specializing in hoaxes that embarrass corporations by dramatizing their evils and excesses. They put up phony Web sites, print fake business cards, and pose as representatives from the companies that are their targets.

It's amazing what they get away with. Maybe not so amazing if you study the faces of some of their audiences. These are people so accustomed to sitting through corporate twaddle that they fail to question the most preposterous presentations.

Consider the "SurvivaBall." This is a fake survival suit, built by the Yes Men but presented as a new product from Halliburton. It's an inflated padded globe completely containing a human body and round as a beach ball. Obviously, if you fell over, you'd have no way to stop yourself from rolling, or be able to stand up on your own. There's a closable face opening, air filters, little extendable gloves, and a port, which, unless I miss my guess, is intended for extra-suit urination. It comes with the big red Halliburton trademark.

The Yes Men seriously pitch this invention at a conference for the security industry. Study the faces in the audience. No one is laughing. People look bored or perhaps mildly curious. There isn't a look of incredulity in the room. The few questions are desultory. Not a single security "expert" seems to suspect a hoax.

Experts in the news business are no more suspicious. The Yes Men faked a BBC interview during which a "spokesman for Dow Chemical" announced a multibillion-dollar payment to the victims of a notorious 1985 explosion at a Union Carbide insecticide factory in Bhopal, India, that killed eight thousand, injured many more, and spread poisons that cause birth defects to this day.

Think of that. Twice as many dead as on 9/11, we know exactly who did it, and Dow (which absorbed Union Carbide) has never paid a dime of reparation. At the news it was finally settling the suit, Dow Chemical's stock price plunged on Wall Street: Things like this could cost money. The Yes Men were unmasked as the hoaxers.

They were also behind a stunt that made the news recently: staging a phony press conference at the National Press Club in Washington, announcing the U.S. Chamber of Commerce was reversing its stand on global warming. Some news organizations double-checked this, but not Fox News, which repeated the story all day.

Another hoax, inspiring the question, Why does the U.S. Chamber of Commerce resist the theory of global warming? What is the USCC, anyway? Is it supported by the dues of countless merchants on Main Street, or is it a front financed by energy companies? Only a month ago, Exelon, the largest U.S. electric utility, announced it would no longer pay dues to support the USCC right-wing agenda.

The Yes Men are represented in this documentary by Andy Bichlbaum and Mike Bonanno. You may have seen them on TV—as themselves or as "corporate spokesmen." It's remarkable no one recognizes them. They don't wear beards or dark glasses. They are disguised, in fact, in a way that makes them above suspicion: Why, they look and talk exactly like middle-aged white men in conservative business suits.

The film is entertaining in its own right, and thought-provoking. Why don't more people quickly see through their hoaxes? Would you believe in a product such as the SurvivaBall? As head of security for your corporation, would you invest in it? It's surprising we don't look outside and see, marching down the street, a parade of emperors without any clothes.

You, the Living ★ ★ ★ ★

NO MPAA RATING, 95 m., 2009

Jessica Lundberg (Anna), Elisabet Helander (Mia), Bjorn Englund (Tuba Player), Leif Larsson (Carpenter), Ollie Olson (Consultant), Birgitta Persson (Tuba Player's Wife), Kemal Sener (Barber), Hakan Angses (Psychiatrist), Gunnar Ivarsson (Businessman). Directed by Roy Andersson and produced by Pernilla Sandstrom. Screenplay by Andersson.

In a sad world and a sad city, sad people lead sad lives and complain that they hate their jobs and nobody understands them. The result is in some ways a comedy with a twist of the knife, and in other ways a film like nobody else has ever made—except for its director, Roy Andersson of Sweden.

Andersson's *You, the Living* is hypnotic. Drab, weary people slog through another depressing day in a world without any bright colors. A bitter, alcoholic woman sits on a park bench hatefully insulting a fat, meek man, screams that she will never see him again, finds out there's veal roast for dinner, and says she may drop by later. A tuba player complains that the bank has lost 34 percent of his retirement fund. He says this while a naked Brunhilda with a Viking helmet has loud sex with him. A carpet salesman loses a sale because someone sold the end off a ten-foot runner.

So it goes. There are fifty vignettes in this film, almost all shot with a static camera, in medium and long shot. Sometimes the characters look directly at us and complain. A psychiatrist says he has spent twenty-seven years trying to help mean and selfish people be happy and asks, what's the point? A girl imagines her marriage with the rock guitarist she has a crush on. The tuba player is hated by his wife and his downstairs neighbor. A bass drum player is also unpopular when he rehearses.

This is the kind of comedy where you don't laugh aloud, I think, although I've not seen it with an audience. You laugh to yourself, silently, although you're never quite sure why. Andersson choreographs the movements of actors who enter and leave rooms, call offscreen or interact with other people we see in other rooms beyond them. He films in bedrooms, living rooms, kitchens, a bar, restaurants, offices, a courtyard, a barber shop, a bus stop in the rain.

Or it looks like he does. I learn that every space in this movie was constructed on a set. It took three years to shoot, was financed from six countries and eighteen sources, and used mostly plain-looking nonactors. It is meticulous, perfectionist in its detail. Andersson's tone has been compared to Jacques Tati's, and certainly they're similar in constructing large, realistic sets that allow them to control every detail of the decor, sound, and lighting.

There's joy in watching a movie like *You, the Living*. It is flawless in what it does, and we have no idea what that is. It's in sympathy with its characters. It shares their sorrow, and yet is amused that each thinks his suffering is unique. The alcoholic woman, who complains over and over that no one understands her, is all too understandable. She calls her mother a sadist for serving nonalcoholic beer with dinner: "What's the point of living if you can't get drunk?"

There are elaborate set pieces that are masterful. One involves long banquet tables lined with joyous people in evening wear who enact a peculiar, traditional ritual involving them standing on their chairs. Another involves a man who proposes to yank a tablecloth out from under all the dishes on a table. And then there's the scene of the young woman imagining her honeymoon with the rock guitarist. This one I won't say a word about: You have to watch it as it plays. Keep in mind that the film was all shot on sound stages. I believe the publicity that says 26,200 screws were used in this production.

Roy Andersson, now sixty-six, has been one of Europe's most successful directors of TV commercials but has made only four features in thirty years. I showed his *Songs from the Second Floor,* winner of the Jury Prize at Cannes 2000, at my Ebertfest. I can only imagine what he must be like. After the failure of his second film, he waited twenty-five years to make the third one. We invited him to Ebertfest, and he sent two of his actors—one who never spoke in the movie and never spoke onstage, either.

You, the Living is a title that perhaps refers to his characters: Them, the Dead. Yet this isn't a depressing film. His characters are angry and bitter, but stoic and resigned, and the musicians (there are also a banjo player and a cornetist) seem happy enough as they play Dixieland. In their world, it never seems to get very dark out, but in the bar it's always closing time.

You Again ★ ★

PG, 118 m., 2010

Kristen Bell (Marni), Jamie Lee Curtis (Gail), Sigourney Weaver (Aunt Ramona), Odette Yustman (Joanna), Betty White (Grandma Bunny), Kristin Chenoweth (Georgia), Victor Garber (Mark), Jimmy Wolk (Will). Directed by Andy Fickman and produced by Fickman, John J. Strauss, and Eric Tannenbaum. Screenplay by Moe Jelline.

If only *You Again* understood that its story was suited for screwball comedy. It labors under the delusion that this assembly of half-baked ideas is destined for a higher comic calling, for example, in the warmhearted romantic weeper category. The movie is so laboriously contrived in every atom of its being that the only interest is in seeing if the characters can avoid the destinies decreed for them by ancient formulas.

No luck. Those who hate each other at the beginning will forgive each other at the end. Those who try to deceive will have their deceptions unmasked. Those destined for love will find it, but not without an obligatory setback at the 66 percent point. If there is a party, it will go wrong. If there is a tree house, it will fall out of the tree. If it is necessary to improvise a wedding at a hospital, a ward will be cleared to make space for a wedding so elaborate it would look unlikely in a church. I hope they save pieces of the wedding cake for the patients whose beds have been wheeled out into the hallway.

The actors are plucky. They're stuck in a movie that gives their characters not even a chance at a human characteristic. Benevolence, jealousy, resentment, charity, wisdom, disappointment, and love are turned on and off like water faucets, often with only a few lines of motivation. Occupations are like name tags: Wise old dad is revealed as a "doctor," mom runs a "bakery," daughter is "vice president of a national public relations firm" in her twenties, brother is a "lawyer," his fiancée is "working with the sick and underprivileged," the fiancée's mother "owns fourteen hotels" and a private jet. None of these jobs figures in any way in the plot, except that the hotelier knows how to say three words in each of six languages (she is played by Sigourney Weaver with such latent energy that I'm sure she would know more words if this movie were not rated PG).

The heroine is Marni (Kristen Bell). In high school she wore braces and glasses, was pimply, and was called "Moo" because her initials were M.O.O. (hint: Don't use your middle name). She is a blonde, of course, and was bullied by a brunette, of course. This was Joanna (Odette Yustman), who has now morphed into Florence Nightingale. Marni's mother is Gail (Jamie Lee Curtis), and wouldn't you know Gail went to high school with Joanna's Aunt Ramona (Sigourney Weaver), and they . . . oh, never mind.

Marni's grandmother Bunny is played by Betty White, whom I urgently advise to start playing against type, because the standard eighty-eight-year-old Betty White, although one hell of a woman, has grown a tad overfamiliar.

There were two parts of the movie I liked. The beginning, with a voice-over by the then unpopular high school sophomore version of Marni, starts out funny before the plot settles in. And there is a moment when Aunt Ramona and mother Gail find out they were on the same cheerleader squad, and do an awesomely physical cheer together, and that is flat-out funny. Aside from that, the movie's pleasures are scant, apart from its observance of Gene Siskel's Rule of Swimming Pool Adjacency, which states that when well-dressed people are near a swimming pool, they will . . . yeah, you got it.

The Young Victoria ★ ★ ★

PG, 100 m., 2009

Emily Blunt (Queen Victoria), Rupert Friend (Prince Albert), Paul Bettany (Lord Melbourne), Miranda Richardson (Duchess of Kent), Jim Broadbent (King William), Thomas Kretschmann (King Leopold), Mark Strong (Sir John Conroy). Directed by Jean-Marc Vallee and produced by Sarah Ferguson, Tim Headington, Graham King, and Martin Scorsese. Screenplay by Julian Fellowes.

Orson Welles allegedly said a movie studio was the best toy train set a child could ever desire. He should have been Queen Victoria. She was crowned in 1837 and ruled until 1901, queen of the greatest empire the world has ever known. She was married to Albert, her great love, from 1840 to 1861, and though she was a widow for the next forty years, at least unlike many monarchs, she wed the man of her choice.

We think of her as the formidable matron of official portraits. She was a girl once. She had teenage crushes. She resented authority. She hated being ordered about. She fell in love with a pen pal, the Victorian equivalent of an online romance. *The Young Victoria* is about those years.

Emily Blunt makes Victoria as irresistible a young woman as Dame Judi Dench made her an older one in *Mrs. Brown* (1997). In seeking fascinating women from that century of the repression of women, we often find them among courtesans or royalty—two classes that need answer to no man. Come to think of it, that answers a question I wrote about twenty-five years ago: Why do so many actresses get their Oscar nominations by playing whores or queens?

The director is Jean-Marc Vallee, and the screenplay is by Julian Fellowes, who in his script for *Vanity Fair* showed a feeling for the same period, and in Altman's *Gosford Park*, a genius for understanding the power struggle within a great household. Their engaging approach is to show Victoria at the center of a mighty struggle that also involved her adolescent emotions.

She is next in line after her uncle, King William (Jim Broadbent), who is gormless. As he approaches death, her mother, the Duchess of Kent (Miranda Richardson), falls under the control of the ambitious Sir John Conroy (Mark Strong). His hope: William will die before Victoria is eighteen, and the duchess will appoint him as regent to rule in her place. Whether William cooperates with this scheme you already know.

Victoria lives in a hermetically sealed world. She meets no one not vetted by the palace hierarchy, has no meaningful independence, is having her life mapped for reasons of state, not the heart. King Leopold of Belgium (Thomas Kretschmann) hopes to marry her to his son, Albert (Rupert Friend). Albert has no enthusiasm for being used as a pawn but is drilled in her likes and dislikes and sent to meet her. Whether deliberately or by misadventure, he reveals he's been coached on her tastes. When she calls him on it, he admits it and begins to win her heart.

But not quite. There are still the attractions of handsome Lord Melbourne (Paul Bettany), the sort of cad most mothers, but not hers, would warn her about. This plays like a Jane Austen story moved from the dollar to the twenty-five-dollar table: We're talking about the heart of the empress of India here.

I'm a pushover for British historical dramas, partly because I'm an Anglophile, partly because it's alarmingly easy for me to identify with these vivid and beautiful characters. The British have a leg up in sets and locations because they often use real ones; nine stately castles and homes get a workout here, and Westminster Abbey, of course.

The *Empire* magazine reviewer Kim Newman writes: "If you're collecting British royal history by installments in the cinema, you'll know exactly how to place this on a shelf with *Elizabeth*, *Restoration*, *The Madness of King George* and *The Queen*." Wouldn't that make a great weekend of videos? Yes, *The Young Victoria* belongs on the same shelf but at the lower end, I'm afraid. It's a charmer but lacks the passion of the others, perhaps because it's so, well, Victorian.

Your Highness ★

R, 102 m., 2011

Danny McBride (Thadeous), James Franco (Fabious), Natalie Portman (Isabel), Zooey Deschanel (Belladonna), Justin Theroux (Leezar), Toby Jones (Julie), (Charles "Dance King" Tallious), Damian Lewis (Boremont), Rasmus Hardiker (Courtney). Directed by David Gordon Green and produced by Scott Stuber. Screenplay by Danny McBride and Ben Best.

Your Highness is a juvenile excrescence that feels like the work of eleven-year-old boys in love with dungeons, dragons, warrior women, pot, boobs, and four-letter words. That this is the work of David Gordon Green beggars the imagination. One of its heroes wears the penis of a Minotaur on a string around his neck. I hate it when that happens.

This is the kind of farce Mel Brooks did ever so much better in *Robin Hood: Men in Tights*, and that was far from a good movie. It takes place in medieval days on a planet that looks like Earth except it has two moons—or maybe it only looks like two moons when the characters smoke that funny-looking pipe. I don't know how much money it cost, but I hope the money all went into sets, costumes, and special effects, because the screenplay cowritten by Danny McBride is so hopeless he doesn't even write himself a good role, and he plays the lead.

Can you believe the film also stars Natalie Portman, James Franco, Zooey Deschanel,

Justin Theroux, and Charles Dance? Why did they do it? Maybe because David Gordon Green's previous film was a nice stoner comedy named *Pineapple Express* and they figured he could do it again? McBride, Green, and Deschanel worked before on a good movie named *All the Real Girls*, but that film came from a different time and a different David Gordon Green.

What calamity has befallen him? He carried my hopes. His first three features were *George Washington* (2000), *All the Real Girls* (2003), and *Undertow* (2004), and I gave all three four stars. I was in the hospital when he released *Snow Angels*, but it got good reviews. Then came *Pineapple Express*, produced by Judd Apatow, which was a pretty good Apatow-style movie, and I figured, all right, David wanted to see how it would feel to have a real budget and work with actors such as Seth Rogen, James Franco, Kevin Corrigan, Rosie Perez, and McBride (his buddy from college days). That was fair enough.

Now comes *Your Highness*. The movie is a perplexing collapse of judgment. Assume for the sake of argument that David thought the time had come for him to direct a farce. Fair enough. One with a severed cyclops head, an emasculated Minotaur, damsels in distress, crowds of witless extras, a castle, hydras, and . . . a mechanical bird? OK, they come with the territory. Not so much the bird. But why this screenplay? What did they think would be funny? They're satirizing a genre that nobody goes to see when it's played straight. It's sad when good actors dress funny and go through material more suitable for a campfire skit on the closing night of summer camp.

One strange thing about the movie is the relentless obscenity in the dialogue. I don't have the slightest difficulty with the f-word or most other words, as themselves. What I don't understand is why almost every single sentence has to be filled with them. Why is that funny? Was I supposed to be "shocked"? Was it intended as daring? It's puerile.

I mentioned boobs. Yes, there are a lot of boobs in this movie. But not much interest in women. Zooey Deschanel plays the intended bride of Franco, the son of the king. She's brought onstage, quickly kidnapped by an evil sorcerer, spends a good deal of time as a captive in his lair, is rescued, and lives happily ever after. She might as well be a mannequin, for all she's given to say and do. This intelligent, nuanced actress, standing there baffled. Used as a placeholder.

Natalie Portman is the Xena clone, a fierce warrior, laid on for anime fans who seem to regard such characters as masturbatory fantasies. She, too, has no personality, although she has more dialogue, all of it expressing clichés of steely determination.

Franco is likable. Likable? That's not good enough for a hero. McBride's character is pathetic, not in a good way. Rasmus Hardiker plays Courtney, the king's aide, who comes along on the quest so he can basically stand there and look at stuff. Oh, what a sad movie this is. David Gordon Green has made great films. He should remind himself of that.

Youssou N'Dour: I Bring What I Love ★ ★ ★

PG, 102 m., 2009

With Youssou N'Dour, Peter Gabriel, Moustapha Mbaye, Kabou Gueye, Bono, and Fathi Salama. A documentary directed, written, and produced by Elizabeth Chai Vasarhelyi.

The Grammy Award–winning Youssou N'Dour is a superstar of world music from Senegal in West Africa, famous in Africa and Europe, now winning a North American following. He also seems to be a nice man, with his heart in the right place. The documentary *Youssou N'Dour: I Bring What I Love* opens with his anthem to Africa, *Wake Up (It's Africa Calling)*, in which he calls on the continent to unify itself, insist on honest leaders, and realize its potential. It follows him on tour at home and abroad, showing him as a charismatic stage presence whose music is powerful, joyous, and danceable; many of his fans may have no understanding of his French, Wolof, and Arabic lyrics, and he also sings in English, which must leave other fans behind. But the music translates itself.

N'Dour, born into a family that encouraged serious study, wanted to be a musician from an early age, hanging out in the music clubs of Dakar and eventually running away from home to perform in the Ivory Coast. His father brought the runaway home and relented to his musical ambitions, and he quickly became a star.

He is one of the creators of the world music genre fusing African, traditional Muslim, Caribbean, and Cuban traditions, and even a flavoring of American jazz and soul. He considers himself a griot singer, and through his grandmother is a member of that West African caste of singers of praise and celebration. We see him at his grandmother's bedside and sense the love flowing between them.

He is popular not only because of his persuasive music, but also because of his unaffected, natural presence, and his closeness with audiences, and his lack of big-star affectations. It also has something to do with his message. N'Dour is Sunni Muslim, reflecting that faith's mystical orientation in contrast with more worldly Muslim traditions. He sings of an African-Arab connection, and that led him into trouble.

In 2004, he made a new album named *Egypt,* which mixed secular and religious music and, worse, was released during the holy month of Ramadan. He was sharply criticized by Sunni leaders for this breach of observance, and although the album sold well abroad, it was his first failure at home. This documentary regards the fallout, as a beloved man fell from local favor despite his intention to bring together religious and musical material.

Then an unexpected thing happened. The album won a Grammy Award. All was forgiven. He was a heroic figure again, paraded through the streets of Dakar, his Grammy held aloft, and invited to a reception at the presidential palace. It's characteristic that N'Dour, a wealthy man, learned the news not at the Beverly Hills ceremony but at home with family and close friends.

This documentary by Elizabeth Chai Vasarhelyi could have used more music for my taste, and fewer talking heads. But it's absorbing all the same. N'Dour is the sort of humanitarian bridge we need in a world so sharply divided.

Youth in Revolt ★ ★ ★

R, 90 m., 2010

Michael Cera (Nick Twisp/Francois), Portia Doubleday (Sheeni Saunders), Zach Galifianakis (Jerry), Ray Liotta (Lance Wescott), Justin Long (Paul Saunders), Jean Smart (Estelle Twisp), Adhir Kalyan (Vuay Joshi), Fred Willard (Mr. Ferguson), Steve Buscemi (George Twisp). Directed by Miguel Arteta and produced by David Permut. Screenplay by Gustin Nash, based on the novel by C. D. Payne.

Michael Cera is not a sissy. It's more like he's unusually diffident. Laid back to a point approaching the horizontal. Yet he yearns. He's so filled with desire it slops over. I speak not of the real Cera, unknown to me, but of the persona he has perfected in such movies as *Superbad, Juno, Nick and Norah's Infinite Playlist,* and *Paper Heart.*

That was the comedy that pretended to be a documentary about his romance with Charlyne Yi, which was also going on in real life. That made for some ambivalent scenes, particularly since Ms. Yi herself is laid back so far the two could star in a movie based on *Flatland.*

Youth in Revolt gives Cera the twee name Nick Twisp, surrounds his aging virgin act with divorced parents who are both shacked up with lustful vulgarians, and then provides him with a dream come true in the person of Sheeni Saunders. She's played by Portia Doubleday, a new actress whose name will always be more melodious than those of her characters. They meet during family vacations at the sublimely named Restless Axles trailer park. For Sheeni, who speaks as if influenced by Juno, virginity is a once-touching affectation, and Nick Twisp is oh-so-eager to join her in this opinion. But there are many obstacles to their bliss, worst of all his family's tragic return home.

His family. His mother, Estelle (Jean Smart), lives with Jerry (Zach Galifianakis), a beer-swilling, belching lout who makes Nick's skin crawl. His father, George Twisp (Steve Buscemi), recently laid off, has robbed the cradle for his live-in, Lacey (Ari Graynor). Both parents all but flaunt their lovers before poor Nick; at Restless Axles, his mom asks Nick to clean up after dinner while she and Jerry (after his post-prandial burp) retire to the bedroom a few feet away for noisy rumpy-pumpy.

Sheeni's parents have much less screen time, so they're cast to make an immediate impression. Try to image M. Emmet Walsh and Mary Kay Place as your parents. OK. Nick is desperate to be reunited with Sheeni, tries to float reasons he needs to take a trip right away, and really inadvertently (honest) sets in motion an explosive, fiery chain of events.

Cera's style lends itself to one note, and the movie wisely gives him another character to play, an imaginary alter ego named Francois Dillinger, inspired by Jean-Paul Belmondo. Of course Nick would know who Belmondo is. I'd believe him if he were inspired by Jean Gabin. In this role, he has a mustache and smokes, but true to character, his mustache is wispy and he always smokes like it's his first cigarette.

It's often observed that comedy never works if an actor signals that he's just said something funny. I don't know if Michael Cera *can* do that. It requires such bold assertion. You'd get suicidal trying to get him to laugh at a joke. This passiveness is why he's funnier than Jack Black, for example, in their movie *Year One*. One of the secrets of *Youth in Revolt* is that Nick Twisp seems bewildered by his own desires and strategies. He knows how he feels, he knows what he wants, but he'd need a map to get from A to B. It's Nick's self-abashing modesty that makes the movie work. Here, you feel, is a movie character who would find more peace on the radio.

You Will Meet a Tall Dark Stranger ★ ★ ½

R, 98 m., 2010

Antonio Banderas (Greg), Josh Brolin (Roy), Anthony Hopkins (Alfie), Gemma Jones (Helena), Freida Pinto (Dia), Naomi Watts (Sally), Lucy Punch (Charmaine). Directed by Woody Allen and produced by Letty Aronson, Jaume Roures, and Stephen Tenenbaum. Screenplay by Allen.

You Will Meet a Tall Dark Stranger is every frame a Woody Allen film, but it isn't very much more. Perhaps the title provides a clue. Its point of view is of an outsider—a fortune-teller, let's say, or the narrator of the film. This person knows about the problems of the characters, knows they hope, knows they lust, knows they dream, and knows that life is a tale told by an idiot, filled with sound and fury, signifying nothing.

That is not such an original observation as when first it was made, but it describes the action of the film well enough. We see several people worriedly scuttling about in search of happiness. These people lead enviable lives. They have money, professions, culture. At the end, for these fortunates and all of us, everything reduces to the hunger for love. It's not really sex they're after; it's to be reflected as valuable in the eyes of somebody new because they need reassurance. It can't all signify nothing, you see, if you're important to someone. This someone must be a new person because (1) you and your current lover know each other too well, and (2) you can project wonderful qualities on the new lover until you get to know that person too well. It is assumed all along, of course, that you are invaluable.

The time is the present. The city, London, where people seem to live in each other's pockets more than in American cities. We meet an old lady named Helena (Gemma Jones), whose husband, Alfie (Anthony Hopkins), has left her for a floozy blonde. She seeks consolation from a medium who sees her floating in clouds of glory and predicts she will meet a very special man.

Helena's daughter is Sally (Naomi Watts). Sally is married to Roy (Josh Brolin), whose first novel was a success and who has been living off her money ever since, while blaming her for writer's block. Meanwhile, the treacherous Alfie is spending a fortune on Charmaine (Lucy Punch), who is an *actress* and reminds me of Ben Hecht's definition of actress: "any woman under thirty who is not actively employed in a brothel, with many exceptions." (His definition of actor: "a waiter.")

Sally and Roy have fought about money and his unwritten second novel for so long they've lost interest in each other. Their eyes stray. Sally is drawn to her magnetic boss, Greg, who, as he is played by Antonio Banderas, makes it hard for us to blame her. Roy finds himself looking into the window of a flat across from his, where on display is the lovely Dia, who, as she is played by Freida Pinto from *Slumdog Millionaire*, makes it hard for us to blame him.

The way Woody Allen handles this is by a

series of conversations in which paradoxes are illustrated by the search for happiness. Dia is remarkably sympathetic with Roy; it's not every subject of a Peeping Tom who introduces him to her parents. Charmaine is a floozy, but not entirely without a heart. The movie is forgiving. But the search for happiness is doomed by definition: You must be happy with what you have, not with what you desire, because the cost of the quest is too high. So consider old Helena. She doesn't meet a tall, dark stranger, but she meets a short, stout one. He owns an occult bookshop, and they determine it was meant for them to be together. What more can you ask? The others are all too smart for their own good.

Z

Zombieland ★ ★ ★

R, 81 m., 2009

Jesse Eisenberg (Columbus), Woody Harrelson (Tallahassee), Emma Stone (Wichita), Abigail Breslin (Little Rock), Amber Heard (Maggie), Bill Murray (Himself). Directed by Ruben Fleischer and produced by Gavin Polone. Screenplay by Rhett Reese and Paul Wernick.

There's no getting around it: Zombies are funny. I think they stopped being scary for me along toward the end of *Night of the Living Dead*. OK, maybe in a few others, like *28 Days Later*. They're the Energizer bunnies of corpses, existing primarily to be splattered. But who would have guessed such a funny movie as *Zombieland* could be made around zombies? No thanks to the zombies.

The movie is narrated by a guy played by Jesse Eisenberg, named after his hometown of Columbus, Ohio, who is making his way back home again across a zombie-infested America. The landscape is strewn with burned-out cars and dead bodies. He encounters another nonzombie survivor, Tallahassee (Woody Harrelson). The two team up, not without many disagreements, and eventually find two healthy women: the sexy Wichita (Emma Stone) and her little sister, Little Rock (Abigail Breslin).

The plot comes down to a road movie threatened by the undead, as countless zombies are shot, mashed, sledge-hammered, and otherwise inconvenienced. Wichita and Little Rock turn out to be con women, dashing the hopes of the love-struck Columbus. Yet eventually they all join in an odyssey to a Los Angeles amusement park, for no better reason than that there's no location like a carnival for a horror movie. Yes, even with a haunted house, the usual ominous calliope music, and a zombie clown. Columbus, like so many others, is phobic about clowns, making Eisenberg an ingrate, since his mother put him through grade school by playing clowns at children's parties.

All of this could have been dreary, but not here. The filmmakers show invention and well-tuned comic timing, and above all there's a cameo by Bill Murray that gets the single biggest laugh I've heard this year. The foursome hauls up at Murray's vast Beverly Hills mansion, so palatial it is surely a grand hotel, and finds him still in residence. More than that I will not say, except that not many zombie comedies can make me think simultaneously about *Psycho* and *Garfield*.

Eisenberg, a good actor, here plays a pleasant nerd who has compiled a seemingly endless survival list for the United States of Zombies. These items are displayed in onscreen graphics that pop up for laughs, and include a tribute to the Back Seat Rule of my Little Movie Glossary, which instructs us—but I'm sure you remember.

Woody Harrelson takes a great deal of relish in killing zombies, often declining to use a gun because he prefers killing them with car doors, tire irons, and whatever else comes to hand. As usual, the zombies are witless, lumbering oafs who dutifully line up to be slaughtered.

Vampires make a certain amount of sense to me, but zombies not so much. What's their purpose? Why do they always look so bad? Can there be a zombie with good skin? How can they be smart enough to determine that you're food, and so dumb they don't perceive you're about to blast them? I ask these questions only because I need a few more words in this review. I will close by observing that Bill Murray is the first comedian since Jack Benny who can get a laugh simply by standing there.

The Best Films of 2010

December 17, 2010—David Fincher's *The Social Network* is emerging as the consensus choice as the best film of 2010. Most of the critics' groups have sanctified it, and after its initial impact it has only grown it stature. I think it is an early observer of a trend in our society, where we have learned new ways of thinking of ourselves: As members of a demographic group, as part of a database, as figures in . . . a social network.

In response to the reader protests of recent years, I've returned to the time-honored tradition of ten films arranged in order from one to ten. After that, it's all alphabetical. The notion of objectively ordering works of art seems bizarre to me.

Here are the year's best feature films:

1. *The Social Network*

Here is a film about how people relate to their corporate roles and demographic groups rather than to one another as human beings. That's the fascination for me; not the rise of social networks but the lives of those who are socially networked. Mark Zuckerberg, who made billions from Facebook and plans to give most of it away, isn't driven by greed or the lust for power. He's driven by obsession with an abstract system. He could as well be a chess master like Bobby Fischer. He finds satisfaction in manipulating systems.

The tension in the film is between Zuckerberg and the Winklevoss twins, who may well have invented Facebook, for all I know, but are traditional analog humans motivated by pride and possessiveness. If Zuckerberg took their idea and ran with it, it was because he saw it as a logical insight rather than intellectual property. Some films observe fundamental shifts in human nature, and this is one of them.

David Fincher's direction, Aaron Sorkin's screenplay, and the acting by Jesse Eisenberg, Justin Timberlake, and the others all harmoniously create not only a story but a worldview, showing how Zuckerberg is hopeless at personal relationships but instinctively projects himself into a virtual world and brings five hundred million others behind him. *The Social Network* clarifies a process that some believe (and others fear) is creating a new mind-set.

2. *The King's Speech*

Here, in a sense, is a first step in a journey that could lead to the world of *The Social Network*. Prince Albert (Colin Firth), who as George VI would lead the British Empire into World War II, is seen in an opening scene confronting a loudspeaker as he opens the Empire Games. He is humiliated by a paralyzing stutter. The film tells the story of how his wife, Elizabeth (Helena Bonham Carter), involves him with a rough-hewn Australian speech therapist (Geoffrey Rush), whose unorthodox methods enable him to eventually face a BBC microphone and forcefully inform the world that the empire is declaring war.

All of the personalities and values in *The King's Speech* are traditional (and the royal values are too traditional, the therapist believes). Tom Hooper's filmmaking itself is crafted in an older style, depending on an assembly of actors, costumes, sets, and a three-act structure. The characters project considered ideas of themselves; *The Social Network*, in contrast, intimately lays its characters bare. From one man speaking at a distance through the radio, to another man shepherding hundreds of millions through a software program, the two films show technology shaping human nature.

A difference between them is that we feel genuinely moved by the events in *The King's Speech*. We identify. While some people may seek to copy the events in *The Social Network*, few, I think, would identify with those characters. Mark Zuckerberg is as much a technology-created superhero as Iron Man.

3. *Black Swan*

And now we leave technology and even reality behind, and enter a world where the cinema has always found an easy match: fantasy. That movies were dreamlike was understood from the very beginning, and the medium allowed directors to evoke the psychological states of their characters. *Black Swan* uses powerful performances by Natalie Portman and Vincent Cassel to represent archetypal attributes: female/male, young/old, submissive/dominant, perfect/flawed, child/parent, good/evil, real/mythical.

Tchaikovsky's *Swan Lake* provides a template for a backstage story that seems familiar enough (young ballerina tries to please her perfectionist mother and demanding director). Gradually we realize a psychological undertow is drawing her away from reality, and the frenzy of the ballet's climax is mirrored in her own life. This film depends more than many others on the intensity and presence of the actors, and Portman's ballerina is difficult to imagine coming from another actor.

4. *I Am Love*

In this film and *Julia* (2008), Tilda Swinton created masterful performances that were largely unseen because of inadequate distribution. Is it an Academy performance if no one sees it? Here she easily clears a technical hurdle (she is a British actress speaking Italian with what I understand is a Russian accent), playing Emma, a Russian woman who has married into a large, wealthy, and guarded Milanese family.

She isn't treated unkindly, at least not in obvious ways, but she doesn't belong. She is hostess, mother, wife, trophy, but never member. Now her husband and son are taking over the family dynasty, and her life is in flux. When she learns her daughter is a lesbian, she reacts not as an Italian matriarch might, but as the outsider she is, in surprise and curiosity. She has heard of such things.

Now she meets a young chef named Antonio (Edoardo Gabbriellini), a friend of her son's. A current passes between them. They become lovers. There are many ways for actors to represent sex on the screen, and Swinton rarely copies herself; here as Emma she is urgent, as if a dam has burst, releasing not passion but happiness. She evokes Emma as a woman who for years has met the needs of her family and discovers in a few days to meet her own needs. She must have been waiting a long time for Antonio, whoever he would be.

5. *Winter's Bone*

Another film with its foundation on a strong female performance. Jennifer Lawrence plays Ree, a girl of seventeen who acts as the homemaker for her younger brother and sister in the backlands of the Ozarks. Her mother sits useless all day, mentally absent. Her father, who was jailed for cooking meth, is missing. She tries to raise the kids, scraping along on welfare and the kindness of neighbors.

When the family is threatened with homelessness, she must find her father, who skipped bail. She sets out on an odyssey. At its end will be Ree's father, dead or alive. Unless there is a body, her family will be torn apart. She treks through a landscape scarcely less ruined than the one in Cormac McCarthy's *The Road*. Debra Granik, the director and coauthor, risks backwoods caricatures and avoids them with performances that are exact and indelible, right down to small supporting roles. Ree is one of the great women of recent movies.

6. *Inception*

A movie set within the architecture of dreams. The film's hero (Leonardo DiCaprio) challenges a young architect (Ellen Page) to create such fantasy spaces as part of his raids on the minds of corporate rivals. The movie is all about process, about fighting our way through enveloping sheets of reality and dreams, reality within dreams, dreams without reality. It's a breathtaking juggling act by writer-director Christopher Nolan, who spent ten years devising the labyrinthine script.

Do dreams have an architecture? Well, they require one for the purposes of this brilliantly visualized movie. For some time now, I've noticed that every dream I awaken from involves a variation of me urgently trying to return somewhere by taking a half-remembered way through streets and buildings.

Sometimes I know my destination (I get off a ship and catch a train, but am late for a flight and not packed). Sometimes I'm in a vast hotel. Sometimes crossing the University of Illinois campus, which has greatly changed. In every case, my attempt is to follow an abstract path (turn down here and cut across and come back up) that I could map for you. *Inception* led me to speculate that my mind, at least, generates architectural pathways, and that one reason I responded to *Inception* is that, like all movies, it was a waking dream.

7. *The Secret in Their Eyes*

This 2009 film from Argentina won the Academy Award for best foreign film. But it opened in 2010 in the United States, and so certainly qualifies. It spans the years between 1974 and 2000 in Buenos Aires, as a woman who is a judge and a man who is a retired criminal investigator meet after twenty-six years. In 1974 they were associated on a case of rape and murder, and the man still believes the wrong men were convicted of the crime. The whole case is bound up in the right-wing regime of those days, and the "disappearances" of enemies of the state.

Although the criminal story is given full weight, writer-director Juan Jose Campanella is more involved in the romantic charge between his two characters. No, this isn't a silly movie love story. These are adults—experienced, nuanced survivors. Love has very high stakes for them, and therefore greater rewards. Soledad Villamil and Ricardo Darin have presence and authority that make their scenes together emotionally meaningful, as beneath the surface old secrets coil.

8. *The American*

George Clooney plays an enigmatic man whose job is creating specialized weapons for specialized murders. He builds them, delivers them, and disappears. Now someone wants him to disappear for good. A standard thriller plot, but this is a far-from-mainstream thriller. Very little is explained. There is a stark minimalism at work. Much depends on our empathy. The entire drama rests on two words: "Mr. Butterfly." We must be vigilant to realize that once, and only once, are they spoken by the wrong person—and then the whole plot reality rotates.

Few of my colleagues admired this film by Anton Corbijn very much. Most of them admired it very little. I received demands from readers that I refund their money, and messages agreeing that there was greatness here. The American reminded me of *Le Samourai* (1967) by Jean-Pierre Melville, which starred another handsome man (Alain Delon) in the role of an enigmatic murder professional. The film sees dispassionately, guards its secrets, and ends like a clockwork mechanism arriving at its final, clarifying tick.

9. *The Kids Are All Right*

There are ways to read that title: Kids in general are all right, these particular kids are all right, and it is all right for lesbians to form a family and raise them. Each mother bore one of the children, and because the same anonymous sperm donor was used, they're half-siblings. The mothers and longtime partners are played by Julianne Moore and Annette Bening, and like many couples, they're going through a little midlife crisis.

Their children (Mia Wasikowska and Josh Hutcherson) unexpectedly contact their birth father (Mark Ruffalo), and the women are startled to find him back in their lives. It was all supposed to be a onetime pragmatic relationship. Ruffalo plays him as a hippie-ish organic gardener for whom "laid-back" is a moral choice. He thinks it's cool to meet his kids, it's cool their moms are married, it's cool they invite him for dinner. I mean . . . sure, yes, of course . . . I mean, why not? Sure. In a comedy with some deeper colors, the film is an affirmation of family values.

10. *The Ghost Writer*

In Roman Polanski's best film in years, a man without a past rattles around in the life of a man with too much of one. A ghost writer (Ewan McGregor) is hired to write the autobiography of a former British prime minister (Pierce Brosnan) so inspired by Tony Blair that he might as well be wearing a name tag. He comes to stay at an isolated country house, reminding us of those Agatha Christie mysteries in which everyone is a potential suspect. His wife, Ruth (Olivia Williams), smart and bitter, met him at Cambridge. His assistant, Amelia (Kim Cattrall), smart and devious, is having an affair with him. The writer comes across information that suggests much of what he sees is a lie, and his life may be in danger.

This movie is the work of a man who knows how to direct a thriller. Smooth, calm, confident, it builds suspense instead of depending on shock and action. The actors create characters who suggest intriguing secrets. The atmosphere—a rain-swept Martha's Vineyard in winter—has an ominous, gray chill, and the main interior looks just as cold. The key performances are measured for effect, not ramped up for effect. In an age of dumbed-down thrillers, this one evokes a classic tradition.

Special Jury Awards

Film festivals like to give Special Jury Prizes for films that they have a special admiration for, beyond the usual parameters of winners. My awards this year go to following:

127 Hours

Aron Ralston went hiking in the wilderness without telling anyone where he was going, and then, in a deep, narrow crevice, got his forearm trapped between a boulder and the canyon wall. Oops. Suddenly his world became very well defined. There was the crevice. There was the strip of sky above, crossed by an eagle on its regular flight path. There were the things he brought with him: a video camera, some water, a little food, his inadequate little tool. It doesn't take long to make an inventory. He shouts for help, but who can hear?

For most of the film Danny Boyle deals with one location and one actor, James Franco. He preys on our own deep fear of being trapped somewhere and understanding that there doesn't seem to be any way to escape. *127 Hours* is like an exercise in conquering the unfilmable. It achieves the delicate task of showing an arm being cut through without ever quite showing it. For the audience the worst moment is not a sight but a sound. Most of us have never heard that sound before, but we know exactly what it is.

Another Year

This year I belatedly decided to award two Special Jury Prizes, because so many readers rightfully wondered why Mike Leigh's *Another Year* was not included. My answer would have been, because it hadn't opened yet. Why stand on ceremony? I love it.

Tom and Gerri are a long-married couple, played by Jim Broadbent and Ruth Sheen, and they seem in complete accord about their life together. They garden, they work, they welcome their friends, they hope their son will find the right girl, they are in love. Their steadfast joy in each other's company is essential, I believe, to provide the film with a center around which the characters revolve. Remarkably, these days, their thirty-year-old son loves them and is happy, and they have no "issues."

Theirs is the home poor Mary (Lesley Manville) comes to when she realizes she has made no home of her own. As Leigh's film grows through spring, summer, autumn, and winter, it involves the lives touched by Tom and Gerri (yes, they smile about their names). In particular they observe Mary, who is single, lonely, getting older, and alcoholic. "It's a shame," Tom says at one point after she's ended yet another sad visit, and that's all he has to say.

These people are not us, and yet we know them. They attend the funeral of Tom's sister-in-law, and we have never been to a funeral quite like it, and yet it is like many funerals. The uninvolved clergyman, the efficient undertakers, the remote father, the angry son, the handful of neighbors who didn't know the deceased all that well, the family skeletons. In particular, notes of social embarrassment that Leigh specializes in—the ways people display their anguish without meaning to.

* * *

And now I add yet another Special Jury Prize Winner. Oh, I'm the first to agree this has grown absurd. I stupidly tripped over the technicality that it had not yet opened in Chicago. Now I must contort myself to find it a place within the arbitrary confines of this list system. Next year I will simply issue an alphabetical list of thirty good films; I vow I will. The idea is to praise films I loved. What do conventions have to do with it?

Somewhere

Sofia Coppola's film gazes dispassionately into the empty eyes of a movie star who has reached the end of his will. Johnny Marco sits in his room at the Chateau Marmont, legendary West Hollywood hotel for generations of Hollywood hideouts, and finds himself a hollow man. Sex is a mechanical process. He uses drinks and takes drugs and gets a little wound up, but pleasure doesn't seem to be involved. He demonstrates the truth that if you stare long enough at a wall, it will break the monotony if blonde twins do pole dances in front of it.

Stephen Dorff plays Marco. He is famous and successful. He is divorced, and when his eleven-year-old daughter (Elle Fanning) spends a few days with him, he is polite and dutiful and seems to feel nothing. He goes through the motions of a publicity tour, an awards ceremony in Milan, and a detailed session for complex makeup, and hardly seems present.

Don't distinguish what he feels with the word "existential." It has nothing to do with philosophy. He believes he amounts to nothing, and it appears he's correct. This is called depression, but it may simply be a realistic view of the situation. Coppola, as always, communicates her feelings by what she looks at and how. It is all gaze and detail. She was a little girl and later a young actress on the sets of her father's movies. We can only speculate about what she understood about this world right from the start. She played Michael Corleone's baby.

* * *

Now for the second ten best films. These are alphabetical, because ranking films in order is pointless after a certain point. They're all worthy of your time.

1. *All Good Things*

In 1982, the wife of a New York real estate investor disappeared without a trace. In 2000, his best friend was found murdered. In 2001, he admitted he killed a neighbor and chopped her up, throwing the pieces away in trash bags. He said it was self-defense. The wife is still missing. No one was ever charged in the death of the friend. He is in jail for the admitted crime, with a sentence adjusted because the jury believed some self-defense may have been involved. *All Good Things* is based on fact.

The facts include the deep involvement of the man's father in operating real estate in the sleazy underbelly of Forty-second Street. The father is played here by Frank Langella, smooth and dangerous, and the son by Ryan Gosling, whose marriage to Kirsten Dunst becomes a country idyll before his father all but orders him back to the city. Andrew Jarecki's film clearly insinuates what really happened, and reminded me of Barbet Schroeder's *Reversal of Fortune*, about the Sunny von Bulow murder. In both cases, what seems to be obvious pathology is impervious to logic.

2. *Carlos*

Carlos came in two versions: One over five hours long, which I saw, and one closer to ordinary feature length, which most people will see in wider release or on cable. Written and directed by Oliver Assayas, a French filmmaker whose projects are usually more tightly focused, this is the epic story of the terrorist known as Carlos the Jackyl (Edgar Ramirez), who operated in the years between 1975, when he led a raid on OPEC oil ministers in Vienna, until 1994, when he was betrayed by former comrades, arrested in Sudan, and returned to France for trial.

The film suggests that much of his behavior wasn't ideological in origin, but grew from megalomania. He kills for many causes, but the primary motive seems to be his own twisted ego, his need to dominate and enforce his will. Assayas uses an enormous canvas and many period locations to portray an elusive man who seemed for a long time to be immune to the law. Recently, from prison, he complained that this film is inaccurate.

3. *Chloe*

Atom Egoyan's film centers on Julianne Moore and Liam Neeson as a Toronto married couple, and Amanda Seyfried as the young call girl who enters their lives. The wife, concerned her husband may be cheating, hires the prostitute to "test" him, and listens avidly to the girl's accounts of her life. Seyfried plays the title character as a powerfully erotic young woman with personal motives that are hidden—from Moore, and from us.

Chloe begins as a film involving eroticism, takes the form of thriller, and then undergoes a sinister transformation into the story of hidden motives that seem to flow counter to the apparent direction of the story. Egoyan is a master of the psychosexual.

4. *Greenberg*

The hero of Noah Baumbach's film was, years ago, part of a rock band on the brink of a breakthrough. Greenberg (Ben Stiller) walked away from it and never explained why. He fled Los Angeles and became a carpenter in New York. Now he's back in L.A., house-sitting his brother's house. His life isn't on hold, it's on stall.

His life is upended when he meets Florence (Greta Gerwig, in a career-making performance). She is on hold: just out of college, and no job. She has health and abundant energy. She's happy with a purpose. On the other hand, we can't stand Greenberg. But we begin to care about him. Without ever overtly evoking sympathy, Stiller inspires identification. You don't have to like the hero of a movie. But you have to understand him—better than he does himself, in some cases.

5. *Hereafter*

Clint Eastwood's film was the sort of inward, spiritual film he doesn't make; it considers the idea of an afterlife with tenderness, beauty, and a gentle tact. It deals with a few characters who all have issues that involve an afterlife. Matt Damon plays a man who sincerely believes he communicates with the dead, but has fled that ability and taken a low-profile job. Cecile de France plays a newsreader on French television. Bryce Dallas Howard is a young cooking student with a fearful dark place inside. Richard Kind is a man mourning his wife. Frankie and George McLaren play twin brothers, one who is struck by a truck and killed.

The Damon character becomes the link between all of them. He seems to have an authentic power, though what it proves is hard to say. Nothing he says need come from the other side. There is a moment handled with love and delicacy in which he says something that is either true or isn't, but is a kindness either way. In that moment perhaps Eastwood is hinting that whether or not there is an afterlife, what we do in this one is what counts.

6. *Monsters*

Gareth Edwards's film is one where the aliens are truly alien. It is so effective precisely because it doesn't showcase them endlessly savaging the earth. It makes them mysterious, sensed but rarely seen, their motives and even their forms incompletely glimpsed. It involves a journey from Mexico to the United States through an "Infected Zone," where fifty-foot-high spidery floaters pulse with an inner glow. It demonstrates that making aliens too literal robs them of their menace and reduces them to special effects.

The film stars Scoot McNairy and Whitney Able as a photographer and the daughter of his publisher. Not by nature compatible, they share a journey that itself becomes the film. It is through wastelands of desolation like those in *The Road. Monsters* are glimpsed but not understood. Then there's a breathtaking final sequence combining uncommon suspense and uncanny poetry, where their motives are made clear. Edwards evokes the awe and beauty he's has been building toward, and we fully realize the film's ambitious arc.

7. *Never Let Me Go*

Mark Romanek's adaptation of Kazuo Ishiguro's novel imagines a society within the larger one consisting of children who were created in a laboratory to be donors of body parts. They know this and accept it. They live within a closed world whose value system takes pride in how often and successfully they have donated. Carey Mulligan, Andrew Garfield, and Keira Knightley star as three doners now in their twenties.

This is a meditative, delicate film, directed sensitively, with actors who find the balancing point between their understanding of reality and ours. These poor characters are innocent. They have the same hopes everyone has. It is so touching that they gladly give their organs to us. Greater love hath no man, than he who gives me his kidney, especially his second one.

8. *Rabbit Hole*

Eight months after the death of their child, a couple remains frozen in sadness and uncertainty. Nicole Kidman and Aaron Eckhart are no longer sleeping together or, actually, feeling married. They try grief counseling and join an encounter group, which she rejects but he returns to. Sandra Oh provides an insightful performance of a woman who seems to have embraced recovery as a lifestyle.

The director is John Cameron Mitchell, adapting David Lindsay-Abaire's play. He treats this situation with respect but with a certain redeeming humor—not comedy, but the kind of deep good humor that can finally creep in late in a period of mourning as life begins to stir again. Kidman and Eckhart are well-suited; good-looking, confident people who suddenly are at a loss about how to live their lives.

9. *Secretariat*

Secretariat was one of the most thrilling and moving entertainments of the year, the story of the greatest race horse of all time. Walking into the theater, everyone knew he would win with the Triple Crown and the historic victory at Belmont. Yet the audience cheered anyway—not in surprise, I think, but in exhilaration. *Secretariat* is a movie that allows us to understand what it really meant.

This isn't a cornball formula film. It doesn't have a contrived romance. It's certainly not about an underdog. It is a great film about greatness, the story of the horse and the no less brave woman who had faith in him. Penny Chenery is played by Diane Lane, and John Malkovich and Nelsan Ellis provide counterpoint as Secretariat's trainer and groom. The best general film of the year.

10. *Solitary Man*

Michael Douglas in the kind of role he plays best, a sinner. His character was once a regional celebrity as "New York's Honest Car Dealer." That went wrong, but he's still as persuasive as—well, as a good car dealer. In business he can sense what car to put you in. In sex he cans sense what mood to put you on. He closes a lot of deals.

He cheated on his wife (Susan Sarandon). He disappointed their daughter (Jenna Fischer). He cheats on his companion (Mary-Louise Parker). He uses the offer of his experience in life to charm a college student (Jesse Eisenberg), and then betrays him. Eventually he is back where he began in college, behind the same counter of a greasy spoon run by an old pal (Danny DeVito). Directed by Brian Koppelman and David Levien, *Solitary Man* is one of Douglas's best performances.

* * *

Overall, 2010 was not a great movie year, but it has many great movies. Also in this book are my picks for the best in the categories of documentaries, foreign, animation, and art films. Why categories? They provide a way to list more good films. If a "best film" list serves any purpose, it's to give you ideas.

The Best Foreign Films of 2010

December 30, 2010—Here are my picks for the year's best foreign films.

Biutiful

Javier Bardem at his most soulful, a man with a good heart doing illegal things. He traffics in the work of illegal immigrants to Spain; Chinese who sleep in a cramped basement and labor in a sweatshop. His character isn't doing this to them; they are both cogs in the same machine. He sees them, he cares for them, he has big problems of his own. One of them is that he is dying.

The man, named Uxbal, has two children he loves tenderly, and a wife who loves them not enough. He moves in unsavory circles but is not unsavory. The undertext of the film is that in this economic world all life is hard and sad, and inhumanity is in the air they breathe. The director, Alejandro Gonzalez Inarritu (*21 Grams, Babel, Amores Perros*) has left behind his usual interlinking cross-plots and focuses on the life and approaching death of this man.

Bardem has a face that can easily show sadness. Some actors risk looking strange when they want to communicate sadness. He has scenes here, one in particular, when his grief is almost frightening.

Cell 211

Juan Oliver (Alberto Ammann), is a serious young man. His wife is pregnant, and his new job as a prison guard will be a big help. Knocked unconscious in an accident, he is carried to a bunk in an empty cell—Cell 211—and then a violent prison riot breaks. He boldly passes himself off as a new prisoner admitted only shortly before. The rioting prisoners are desperate. They're led by a brutal strongman, a lifer with nothing to lose, named Malamadre (Luis Tosar). Juan reads the situation immediately, and instinctively he takes the role of a man siding with his fellow prisoners. When he makes canny strategic suggestions, he seems to prove his worth.

This is a thriller all the more ingenious because Juan's actions are based on desperate calculations and fast thinking, not on heroics. The game he plays is crafty as chess, as he must somehow seem completely plausible on the inside and yet signal his thoughts to police watching every move on closed-circuit TV. Director Daniel Monzon generates a lot of suspense but avoids many prison movie clichés. His parallel story lines inside and outside the prison are well timed and build together.

The term "mounting tension" is an overused cliché. To use it here would be appropriate. Little by little, one development at a time, the situation becomes more critical and the options for Juan and Malamadre grow more limited. And Juan's life always hangs in the balance. There is a moment, indeed, when he says something on a walkie-talkie that would have betrayed him if anyone had been listening. *Cell 211* won eight Goya awards, the Spanish Oscars, in 2010. It has been optioned for a Hollywood remake.

The Chaser

An expert serial-killer film from South Korea, and a poster child for what a well-made thriller looked like in the classic days. Its principal chase scene involves a foot race through the deserted narrow nighttime streets of Seoul. No exploding cars. The climax is the result of everything that has gone before, and not an extended fight scene. This is drama, and it is interesting. Action for its own sake is boring.

The film is a police procedural with a difference: The hero is an ex-cop named Jung-ho, now a pimp, and not a nice man. He is angered because a client of his call-girl service has been, he believes, kidnapping his girls and selling them. When another girl disappears, a phone number raises an alarm, and he sets out to track down the client—who didn't give an address but arranged a street rendezvous.

What we know is that the client is a sadistic murderer. The girl is driven in his car to an obscure address, which she is not intended to ever leave alive. It is a characteristic of South Korean films that they display the grisly details of violence without flinching; the rights to this film have been picked up by Warner Bros., and it's dead certain the violence and the shocking outcome itself will be greatly toned down. Let me simply note that Young-min's tools of choice are a hammer and a chisel, for reasons a police psychiatrist has much to say about.

Father of My Children

We meet Gregoire (Louis-Do de Lencquesaing), a plausible human being. A French film producer, an honest hustler, a loving father and husband, confident of his powers, enjoying his work, making films he believes in. *The Father of My Children* will watch this man come to pieces. It will not be dark melodrama or turgid psychology. It will simply be the story of a good man, well loved, who runs into a dead end.

He is plunging into debt while producing an obscure project of a temperamental auteur not a million miles distant from Lars von Trier. He loves his wife and three daughters. Their country house evokes quiet family togetherness, which is the idea, but his mind is often elsewhere, trying to find a way out of his troubles. Gregoire's office is also a family, in a way, and his employees share his vision. When calamity strikes, even his wife pitches in to help salvage his dream. The second half of the film is the most touching, because it shows that our lives are not merely our own, but also belong to the events we set in motion.

Chiara Caselli, as the producer's wife, is, like many wives of workaholic men, better informed on his business that he can imagine. She believes in him and therefore in his hopes, and touchingly relates with the members of his office family as they all try to move things along. And the film gives due attention to the children, particularly Clemence (played by Louis-Do de Lencquesaing's own daughter), who negotiate unfamiliar emotional territory with their mother. The title (in French, *Le père de mes enfants*) is appropriate.

The story is said to be inspired by the life of the real-life producer Humbert Balsan, who made Lars von Trier's *Manderlay* (2005). Balsan had considerable success; making nearly seventy films, including three by James Ivory, and even acting for Robert Bresson. He committed suicide when his business imploded.

Home

There are two questions never answered in *Home:* How did this family come to live here? And why does the mother fiercely refuse to leave, even after a four-lane freeway opens in her front yard? As the film opens, they live in a small home in the middle of vast fields and next to the highway, which hasn't been used for ten years. So much is the road their turf that the story begins with them playing a family game of street hockey on its pavement.

Then the work crews arrive to prepare for the road to be reopened. The opening of the highway isn't a surprise for them. Maybe they got the house cheap because it was coming. The heavy, unceasing traffic is a big problem. The two younger kids always ran across the bare pavement to cut through a field for school. Dad parked on the other side. Now even getting to the house is a problem.

The movie stars Isabelle Huppert and Olivier Gourmet, two dependably absorbing French stars, as the parents. Madness overcomes them. Something will have to give, and it does, as the movie grows more and more dark. It's the skill of Ursula Meier, the director and cowriter, to bring us to those fraught passages by rational stages. What happens would not make sense in many households, but in this one it represents a certain continuity, and confirms deep currents we sensed almost from the first.

Life, Above All

Oliver Schmitz's film, which hasn't and may not open here, was the best heart-warmer and tearjerker at Cannes 2010. I use the term "tearjerker" as a compliment, because this is a hardened crowd, and when you hear snuffling in the dark you know it has been honestly earned. The film is about deep human emotions, evoked with sympathy and love.

Life, Above All takes place entirely within a South African township, one with moderate prosperity and well-tended homes. It centers on the twelve-year-old Chanda, who takes on the responsibility of holding her family together after her baby sister dies. Her mother is immobilized by grief, her father by drink, and a neighbor woman helps her care for two younger siblings.

Suspicion spreads in the neighborhood that the real cause of the family's problems is AIDS, although the word itself isn't said aloud until well into the film. Let me particularly praise the performances of young Khomotso Manyaka, in her first role, as Chanda; Keaobaka Makanyane as her mother; and Tinah Mnumzana as the neighbor. The film's ending frightens the audience with a dire threat, and then finds an uplift that's unlikely enough in its details to qualify as magic realism.

Life, Above All must have been particularly effective in South Africa, where former president Thabo Mbeki long persisted in puzzling denial about the causes and treatment of AIDS. This contributed to a climate of ignorance and mystery surrounding the disease, which in fact increased its spread. By directly dealing with the poisonous climate of rumor and gossip, the film takes a stand. But in nations where AIDS has been demystified, *Love, Above All* will play strongly as pure human drama, and of two women, one promptly and one belatedly, rising courageously to a challenge.

Mother

The strange, fascinating film *Mother* begins with what seems like a straightforward premise. A young man of marginal intelligence is accused of murder. A clue with his name on it and eyewitness testimony tie him to the crime. His mother, a dynamo, plunges into action to prove her son innocent. So there we have it, right? He's either guilty or not, and his mom will get to the bottom of things. Or not.

The mother of the title, played by a respected South Korean actress named Kim Hye-ja, is a force of nature. In a village, she runs a little shop selling herbs, roots, and spices. Her sideline is prescribing herbal cures. Her son Do-joon (Won Bin), in his late twenties, lives at home, and they sleep in the same bed. He's a few slices short of a pie. Early in the film, he's saved from death in traffic when his mother races to the rescue.

Did he do it? We can't be sure. Mother marches tirelessly around the village, doing her own detective work. She questions people, badgers them, harasses the police, comforts her son, hires a worthless lawyer. We learn everything she learns. It seems she's getting nowhere. And it's at this point that the movie might become upsetting for a mass audience, because *Mother* creates not new suspects from off the map, but new levels in the previously established story.

Mother will have you discussing the plot, not

entirely to your satisfaction. I would argue: The stories in movies are complete fictions, and can be resolved in any way the director chooses. If he actually cheats or lies, we have a case against him. If not, no matter what strange conclusions he arrives at, we can be grateful that we remained involved and even fascinated.

35 Shots of Rum

Two couples live across the hall in the same Paris apartment building. Neither couple is "together." Gabrielle and Noe have the vibes of roommates, but the way Lionel and Josephine love one another, it's a small shock when she calls him "papa." Lionel (Alex Descas) is a train engineer. Jo (Mati Diop) works in a music store. Gabrielle (Nicole Dogue) drives her own taxi. Noe (Gregoire Colin) claims only his much-loved cat is preventing him from moving to Brazil.

The four people are in and out of both apartments so readily, we sense they're a virtual family. One night they head out together in Gabrielle's taxi for a concert. The taxi breaks down, it rains, they shelter in a Jamaican café, there's good music on the jukebox, they dance with one another. During the dancing and kidding around, it becomes clear to them, and to us, what must happen for the parts to fall into place.

Claire Denis, who has two films on this list, has long been interested in the former French colonies of West Africa, and in those who immigrated to France. She has no agenda except interest. You can live in a movie like this. She's not intruding, she's discovering. There's not a conventional plot, and that frees us from our interior movie. We flow with them. Two are blessed, two are problematic. Will all four be blessed at the end?

Vincere

The image of Benito Mussolini has been shifted over the years to one of a plump buffoon, the inept second fiddle to Hitler. We've seen the famous photo of his ignominious end, his body strung upside down. We may remember his enormous scowling visage trundled out on display in a scene from Fellini's *Amarcord*. What we don't envision is Mussolini as a fiery young man, able to inflame Italians with his charismatic leadership.

That's the man who fascinates Marco Bellocchio, and his *Vincere* explains how such a man could seize a young woman with uncontrollable erotomania that would destroy her life. She was Ida Dalser (Giovanna Mezzogiorno), at first his lover, later his worst nightmare. When she first saw him before World War I, he was a firebrand, dark and handsome, and she was thunderstruck. For Ida, there was one man, and that was Benito (Filippo Timi), and it would always be so.

Was she mad? The term is "erotomania," defined by the conviction that someone is in love with you. It is not delusional if that person was in love with you, held you in his arms night after night, and gave you a son. The Fascists instinctively protect Mussolini when she tries to accuse him of abandoning wife and child. When Ida appears in public places, she is surrounded and taken away without Benito even needing to request it. Finally, shamefully, she is consigned to an insane asylum, and the boy locked up in an orphanage. She becomes a familiar type: the poor madwoman who is convinced the great man loves her and fathered her child. She writes letters to the press and the pope; such letters are received every day.

White Material

White Material is the second film on this list (after *35 Shots of Rum*) by Claire Denis, and the second starring Isabelle Huppert (after *Home*). Huppert plays Maria Vial, a French woman running a coffee plantation in an unnamed African country. The land has fallen into war, both against the colonialists and among the insurgents. In an opening scene, a helicopter hovers above Maria, and French soldiers advise her to evacuate quickly. This she has no intention of doing. As it becomes clear that her life is in danger, she only grows more opaque. Huppert's approach is valuable here, because any attempt at a rational explanation would seem illogical. I believe her attachment to the land has essentially driven her mad.

They try to be reasonable with her. Yes, it will be a good crop of coffee beans, but there will probably be no way to get it to market. Anarchy has taken the land. Child soldiers with rifles march around, makeshift army stripes on their shirts, seeking "the Boxer"

(Isaach De Bankole), a onetime prizefighter and now the legendary, if hardly seen, leader of the rebellion. When Maria is held at gunpoint, she boldly tells the young gunmen she knows them and their families. Her danger doesn't seem real to her. There is no overt black–white racial tension; the characters all behave as the situation would suggest.

This is a beautiful, puzzling film. The enigmatic quality of Huppert's performance draws us in. She will never leave, and we think she will probably die, but she seems oblivious to her risk. There is an early scene where she runs in her flimsy dress to catch a bus, and finds there are no seats. So she grabs onto the ladder leading to the roof. The bus is like Africa. It's filled with Africans, we're not sure where it's going, and she's hanging on.

The Best Animated Films of 2010

January 2, 2011—I found some good animated films in 2010, but I didn't find ten. And it's likely that only two of them are titles most moviegoers have had the chance to see. My list reflects a growing fact: Animation is no longer considered a form for children and families. In some cases it provides a way to tell stories that can scarcely be imagined in live action. The classic example is the Japanese *Grave of the Fireflies*, about two children growing up on their own after the Bomb fell.

The first of my best films, unlike some of the others, was primarily intended for children.

Despicable Me

This one begins with the truth that villains are often more fascinating than heroes, and creates a villain named Gru who freeze-dries the people ahead of him in line at Starbucks, and pops children's balloons. Although he's inspired by many a James Bond bad guy, two things set him apart: (1) His vast Mad Scientist lair is located not in the desert or on the Moon, but in the basement of his suburban home, and (2) He dreams not of world control so much as merely dominating the cable news ratings as the Greatest Villain of All Time.

Gru is voiced by Steve Carell, who gives him an accent halfway between a Russian mafioso and a crazed Nazi. His life is made more difficult because his mother (Julie Andrews) sometimes gets on his case. Memories stir of Rupert Pupkin in his basement, yanked from his fantasies by his mother's voice. Gru's most useful weapon is the Insta-Freeze Gun, but now, with the help of his genius staff inventor Dr. Nefario (Russell Brand), he can employ a Shrink Ray. Just as global-scale villainy is looking promising, Gru is upstaged by his arch-rival Vector (Jason Segel), who steals the Great Pyramid.

To make a villain into the hero of an animated comedy is daring, but the filmmakers bring in three cute kids to restore good feelings. Gru finds them at his friendly neighborhood orphanage, run by the suspicious Miss Hattie. His plan is to keep them at his home until his Moon scheme is ready to hatch, and then use them to infiltrate Vector's home by subterfuge—pretending to sell cookies, say. It follows as the night does the day that the orphans will work their little-girl magic on Gru, and gradually force the revelation that the big lug has a heart after all. The refreshing thing about *Despicable Me* is that it violates the convention that children's animation must have a perky, plucky young hero. Carl Frederickson of *Up* put an end to that.

How to Train Your Dragon

Our hero is Hiccup Horrendous Haddock III, a young Viking who lives in Berk, a mountainside village surrounded by the crags and aeries where hostile dragons live. Hiccup tells us that his village is very old, but all of the houses are new. An alarming omen. Led by his father Stoick and the dragon master Gobber, the villagers have been in combat with the dragons since time immemorial. It would seem to be an unequal struggle; the dragons are enormous and breathe fire, and the Vikings, while muscular, have only clubs, swords, and spears. They may, however, be smarter than the dragons, although you wouldn't know that just by listening to them.

Young Hiccup is ordered to stay inside during a dragon attack. But the plucky lad seizes a cannon, blasts away at the enemy, and apparently wings one. Venturing into the forest to track his prey, he finds a wounded little dragon about his age, already chained up. He releases it, they bond, and he discovers that dragons can be perfectly nice. With his new friend Toothless, he returns to the village, and an alliance is formed with good dragons against the bad dragons, who are snarly holdouts and grotesquely ugly.

One evil beast is covered all over with giant warlike knobs, and has six eyes, three on either side, like a classic Buick. In one scene, a Viking hammers on an eyeball with his club. Not very appetizing. The battle ends as all battles must, with the bad guys routed and the youngest hero saving the day. The aerial battle scenes are storyboarded like a World War I dogfight, with swoops, climbs, and narrowly missed collisions with craggy peaks and other dragons. For my taste, these went on way too long, but then I must teach myself that I do not have a six-year-old's taste.

The Illusionist

Jacques Tati played (and was) a tall Frenchman, bowing from the waist, pipe in mouth, often wearing a trench coat, pants too short, always the center of befuddlements. If you've seen *Mr. Hulot's Holiday*, you know all that. Tati, who died in 1982, wrote the screenplay for this film, but never made it. He intended it for live action. His daughter Sophie Tatischeff still had the script, and handed it to Sylvain Chomet, who made the miraculously funny animated film *The Triplets of Belleville* (2003). He has drawn it with a lightness and beauty worthy of an older, sadder Miyazaki story. Animation suits it. Live action would overwhelm its fancy with realism.

The story involves a magician named Tatischeff who fails in one music hall after another, and ends up in Scotland, where at last he finds one fan: a young woman who idealizes him, moves in with him, tends to him, cooks and cleans, and would probably offer sex if he didn't abstemiously sleep on the couch. He's a good magician on a small scale, flawless at every trick except producing a rabbit from a hat. His problem there involves his frisky rabbit, which likes to sleep on Tatischeff's stomach at night. The rabbit makes it a practice during the act to pop up and peep around at inopportune moments.

If you recall the opening scenes of *Up*, you know that animation is sometimes more effective than live action for conveying the arc of a life. This man does what he does very well, but there's no longer a purpose for him. Did Tati feel the same when he wrote this in the 1950s, before *Hulot* was a worldwide success? Important to the charm of *The Illusionist* is the grace with which the character of Tatischeff has been drawn. He looks like Tati, but much more important, he has the inimitable body language: the polite formality, the deliberate movement, the hesitation, the diffidence. His world is an illusion, which he produces nightly from a hat.

My Dog Tulip

Here is the story of a man who finds love only once in his life, for fifteen perfect years. It is the love of a dog. It may be the only love he is capable of experiencing. As other men write books about a woman in their life, J. R. Ackerley wrote a book about a German Shepherd bitch he rescued from a cruel home. *My Dog Tulip* now becomes an animated film combining elating visuals with a virtuoso voice performance by Christopher Plummer.

The film is animated, but not intended for children. It is told from and by an adult sensibility that understands loneliness, gratitude, and the intense curiosity we feel for other lives, man and beast. The story is narrated by Plummer, in the voice of a man in his sixties who works for the BBC and lives in London. He is a soloist, cantankerous, crabby, lonely. Ackerley is educated by Tulip in the needs and ways of domesticated dogs. He attends to the feeding of Tulip, the training, the grooming, the walking, the territorial marking behavior, the sexual needs, the illnesses, the personality, the life and death. No parents of a child have ever been more observant or taken better care.

To this story, directed and animated by Paul and Sandra Fierlinger, *My Dog Tulip* brings Sandra's watercolors. Fierlinger is the sort of watercolorist one would collect. Her colors, her line, her ability to saturate or wash, are well suited to the story. She makes London with its black cabs and red buses come alive, and then turns pastoral on Putney Common. She's an original, but if you know of an artist named David Gentleman you'll get the idea.

The Secret of Kells

Here is a film about a young and very brave medieval monk named Brendan, a sacred book, a storied monastery, a fairy girl, an alarming creature, and a forest containing little nuts that make brilliant green inks. The fairy girl is quite real, as Brendan can see for himself. If there are any leprechauns, she no doubt knows them. If there are not, how does she know for sure?

Perhaps little Brendan was once one of them. Perhaps some of that brilliant emerald green was his, extracted from nuts he gathered in the forest. Brendan (voice of Evan McGuire), the youngest and pluckiest monk in the walled monastery, befriends old Brother Aidan (Mick Lally), a traveler who has arrived bearing the precious book. Some pages remain to be created, and Aidan says Brendan must help. He can start by disobeying the Abbot (Brendan Gleeson), venturing outside the walls, and gathering the nuts.

Tomm Moore's movie is a little like an illuminated manuscript itself. Every shot of the film is filled with patterns and borders, arches and frames, do-dads and scrimshaw images. The colors are bold and bright; the drawings are simplified and 2-D. That reflects the creation of the original book in the centuries before the discovery of perspective during the Renaissance.

The movie has a wide appeal, with a gap in the middle. I think it will appeal to children young enough to be untutored in boredom, and to anyone old enough to be drawn in, or to appreciate the artistry. For those in between, the *Transformers*-damaged generation, it will seem to be composed in a quaint, unknown language.

A Town Called Panic

A Town Called Panic takes place in a town where panic is a daily emotion. Here, in a house on a hill much larger inside than out, live the friendly roommates Cowboy, Indian, and Horse. Their neighbor is Farmer. Law is enforced by Policeman. It is Horse's birthday, and Cowboy and Indian decide his gift must be a brick barbecue. They go online to order fifty bricks, but order fifty million through a computer error, which causes no end of problems. All of these people, by the way, are little action figures.

The movie is the work of Stephane Aubier and Vincent Patar, a Belgian team that first created this world in a group of short films that became enormously popular in 2003 on European television. I've never seen anything like their style. It's stop-action, but really stop-action, you understand, because that's the nature of plastic action figures. Cowboy and Indian can move their arms when they need to, but their platforms keep them upright.

I enjoyed this film so much I'm sorry to report it was finally too much of a muchness. You can only eat so much cake. But I don't think that's a problem. Like all animated family films, this one will find a long life and its greatest popularity on video. Because the plot is just one doggoned thing after another without the slightest logic, there's no need to watch it all the way through at one sitting. If you watch it a chapter or two at a time, it should hold up nicely.

Now don't get me wrong. I'm glad I saw it on the big screen. It has an innocent hallucinatory charm. The friendship of the three pals is sweet. I liked Horse's bashfulness when he's smitten with Madame Longree. And his patience with Indian and Cowboy, who get them into one fine fix after another.

Toy Story 3

In Disney/Pixar's *Toy Story 3*, Andy has grown to college age and the story leaves the toys pretty much on their own. Their problems begin with that most dreaded of commands, "Clean out your room!" Andy's mom gives him three choices: (1) attic; (2) donation to a day-care center; (3) trash. As Andy examines his old toys, his gaze lingers fondly on Woody (voice of Tom Hanks), and he decides to take him along to college.

What with one thing and another, the other toys find themselves at the day-care center, which seems like a happy choice, until a dark underside of its toy society emerges in the person of an ominously hug-prone bear named Lotso. Buzz Lightyear is back, still in hapless hero mode, but after a reboot, he starts speaking Spanish and that leads to some funny stuff. I also enjoyed the plight of Mrs. Potato Head, whose missing eye continues to see independently of her head. This raises intriguing physiological questions, such as, if Mr. Potato Head lost an ear, would it continue to hear, or if he lost a mouth, would it continue to eat without a body? These are not academic questions; at one point, Mister becomes an uncooked taco shell.

This is a jolly, slapstick comedy, lacking the almost eerie humanity that infused the earlier *Toy Story* sagas, and happier with action and jokes than with characters and emotions. Some viewers thought it a masterpiece. I thought it was just fine, but *My Dog Tulip*, it wasn't.

The elephant in the room: This is 3-D, of course. It is the misfortune of contemporary animation that it must mostly be viewed as if through the fog of a peat fire. It is too dim, I tell you, *too dim*! Do I make myself clear? And more expensive—and not worth the extra money. Blast and damn, thundernation, *tonnerre le brest*, rumble, grumble.

The Best Documentaries of 2010

January 12, 2011—Documentaries became a box office factor with the rise of such films as *Hoop Dreams* and *Roger & Me*. Before then, there were hit music documentaries such as *Woodstock*, but most other nonfiction films could expect short runs in few theaters before dutiful audiences. What a small but growing minority of Friday night moviegoers is beginning to discover is that there's a good chance the movie they might enjoy most at the multiplex is a doc.

In alphabetical order, these were the best documentaries I saw in 2010:

The Art of the Steal

Dr. Albert C. Barnes invented a treatment for VD, and he founded the Barnes Foundation, an art museum in the Philadelphia suburb of Lower Merion. The first paid for the second, so the wages of sin were invested wisely. How important was the Barnes Collection? It included 181 Renoirs, 69 Cezannes, 59 Matisses, 46 Picassos, 16 Modiglianis, and 7 van Goghs. Barnes collected these works during many trips to Paris at a time when establishment museums considered these artists beneath their attention. One estimate of the collection's worth is $25 billion.

Barnes hired some Philadelphia lawyers and drew up an iron-clad will, endowing the foundation with funds enabling it to be maintained indefinitely "where it is and how it is." It was his specific requirement that the collection not go anywhere near the Philadelphia Museum of Art. That's where it is today. He hated that museum. He hated its benefactors, the Annenberg family, founded by a gangster, enriched by the proceeds of *TV Guide*, and chummy with the Nixon administration. The Annenberg empire published the *Philadelphia Inquirer*, which consistently and as a matter of policy covered the Barnes Collection story with slanted articles and editorials.

Don Argott's *The Art of the Steal* is a documentary that reports the hijacking of the Barnes Collection as the Theft of the Century. It was carried out in broad daylight by elected officials and Barnes trustees, all of whom justified it by placing the needs of the vast public above the whims of a dead millionaire. The vultures from Philadelphia were hovering, ready to pounce and fly off with their masterpieces to their nest at the top of the same great stairs Rocky Balboa ran up in *Rocky*. It is not difficult to imagine them at the top, their hands in triumph above their heads.

Best Worst Movie

I always intended to view *Troll 2*, which has a Perfect Zero on the Tomatometer, but, I dunno, never found the time. Now comes *Best Worst Movie* to save me the trouble. This is a documentary about what happens to you when you appear in *Troll 2*. It's about the star of the original film, a dentist from Alabama named George Hardy. This is one nice guy. Even his ex-wife says so. He has a Harrison Ford head of hair and a smile so wide it's like a toothpaste billboard. He treats poor kids for free.

He made the movie twenty years ago when he was living in Utah. It was being directed by an Italian named Claudio Fragasso, who didn't "speaka the English" but said he understood Americans better than they understood themselves. The movie was originally named *Goblin*, but the title was changed to *Troll 2* because that sounded more commercial. Don't ask me to explain it. It's about vegetarian goblins who cause their human victims to start growing branches and leaves.

For years, George Hardy forgot all about having made the movie. Then some of his patients started looking at him strangely and asking him if he'd appeared in this horror film they'd seen on cable. The film had been discovered and embraced by the bottom-feeders of horror film fandom. The actors got standing ovations and Hardy started autographing photos, T-shirts, and body parts at conventions. At one point he observes, "There's a lot of gingivitis in this room."

Collapse

Michael Ruppert is a man ordinary in appearance, on the downhill slope of middle age, a chain-smoker with a mustache. He is not all worked up. He speaks reasonably and very clearly. *Collapse* involves what he has to say, illustrated with news footage and a few charts, the most striking of which is a bell-shaped curve. It takes a lot of effort to climb a bell-shaped curve, but the descent is steep and dangerous. He says we are running out of oil fast—faster than anyone knows.

He argues we have passed the peak of global oil resources. Demand is growing larger. It took about a century to use up the first half. Now the oil demands of giant economies India and China are exploding. They represent more than half the global population, and until recent decades had small energy consumption. If the supply is finite, and usage is potentially doubling, you do the math. We will face a global oil crisis, not in the distant future, but within the lives of many now alive. They may well see a world without significant oil.

He recites facts I knew, vaguely. Many things are made from oil. Everything plastic. Paint. There are eight gallons of oil in every auto tire. Oil supplies the energy to convert itself into those by-products. No oil, no plastic, no tires, no gas to run cars, no machines to build them. No coal mines, except those operated by men and horses. That's the heart of Ruppert's message, delivered by a calm guy who could be Wilford Brimley's kid brother, lives alone with his dog, and is behind on his rent. I don't know when I've seen a thriller more frightening. I couldn't tear my eyes from the screen. *Collapse* is even entertaining, in a macabre sense.

Cropsey

Cropsey is a creepy documentary with all the elements of a horror film about a demented serial killer, and an extra ingredient: This one is real, and you see him handcuffed in the film, not merely empty-eyed, shabby, and stooped, but actually drooling. "I've never seen a perp walk like that," says a TV newsman.

The killer's name is Andre Rand, and he's currently doing time in a New York penitentiary. He was the real-life embodiment of *Cropsey*, a bogeyman who figured in the campfire stories and nightmares of many children in Pennsylvania, New Jersey, and along the Eastern Seaboard. In the legends he lived in the woods and ventured out to abduct children. In the early 1980s, Rand was convicted for the kidnapping and murder of two young girls and suspected in the disappearance of three more.

The man fit the legend. Andre Rand was a worker in the Willowbrook State School for the mentally handicapped on Staten Island; Geraldo Rivera won fame for a TV special with footage of its half-naked children scattered on the floor, rocking back and forth in misery. Sanitary facilities were pitiful, filth was everywhere, abuse was common. Willowbrook was shut down, but some of its staff and inmates returned, living in a forgotten network of tunnels under the grounds. Among these were Andre Rand. Rumors spread of Satan worship in the tunnels. Now do I have your attention?

Exit Through the Gift Shop

The speculation that *Exit Through the Gift Shop* was a hoax only added to its fascination. An anonymous London graffiti artist named Banksy arrives to paint walls in Los Angeles. He encounters an obscure Frenchman named Thierry Guetta, who has dedicated his life to videotaping graffiti artists. The Frenchman's hundreds of tapes have been dumped unorganized into boxes. Banksy thinks they might make a film. Guetta makes a very bad one. Banksy takes over the film and advises Guetta to create some art himself. Guetta does, names himself Mr. Brainwash, and organizes an exhibition of his work, through which he makes a fortune in sales.

Surely Guetta cannot be real? With his dashing mustache and Inspector Clouseau accent, his long-suffering wife and his zealous risk taking to film illegal artists by stealth? Surely he didn't rent a former CBS television studio and transform it into an exhibition space?

Surely people didn't line up at dawn to get in—and pay tens of thousands of dollars for the works of an artist who had never held a show, sold a work, or received a review? Surely not if his work looked like art school rip-offs of the familiar styles of famous artists?

Even while I sat spellbound during this film, that's what I was asking myself. But Thierry Guetta surely did. His art exhibition was written up in a cover story in *L.A. Weekly* on June 12, 2008. It mentions this film, which Banksy was "threatening to do." Common sense dictates that no one would rent a CBS studio and fill it with hundreds of artworks in order to produce a hoax indie documentary. Nor would they cast Guetta, indubitably a real person, as himself. Right? Right?

Banksy, the creator of this film, is a gifted filmmaker whose thoughts as he regards Guetta must resemble those of Victor Frankenstein when he regarded his monster: It works, but is it art?

45365

45365 is the zip code of Sidney, Ohio. The brothers Bill and Turner Ross were born there perhaps thirty years ago. They knew everybody in town, and when they spent seven months of 2007 filming its daily life, their presence must have become commonplace. Their film evokes what *Winesburg, Ohio* might have looked like as a documentary.

The film is privileged. No one is filmed with a hidden camera. The camera must have been right there, in the living room, the riverbank, the barbershop, the backseat, the football practice, the front lawn when a man agrees to put up a sign supporting a judge running for reelection. The Rosses must have filmed so much they became trusted and invisible. They know this town without even thinking about it.

Sidney has what can only be described as a great radio station. Local human beings sit before the mics and run the boards. It looks like rain on the day of the big parade, but the station's reporter is on the spot. He's hooked up via his cell phone, and interviews a woman on the street with a tiny mic he holds up to his mouth, and then to hers. Spring, summer, autumn, winter. Music on Radio 105.5. Lawns. Good-looking old buildings. Sidney still looks like a town, not a squatter's camp of fast-food outlets. I could go to Sidney, Ohio, tomorrow and feel right at home.

Inside Job

Derivatives and credit swaps are ingenious, computer-driven schemes in which good money can be earned from bad debt, and Wall Street's Masters of the Universe pocket untold millions while they bankrupt their investors and their companies. This process is explained in Charles Ferguson's *Inside Job*, an angry, well-argued documentary about how the American financial industry set out deliberately to defraud the ordinary American investor. The crucial error was to allow financial institutions to trade on their own behalf. Today, many large trading banks are betting against their own customers.

In the real estate market, banks aggressively promoted mortgages to people who could not afford them. These were assembled in packages. They were carried on the books as tangible assets when they were worthless. The institutions assembling them hedged their loans by betting against them. A Chicago group named Magnetar was particularly successful in creating such poisoned instruments for the sole purpose of hedging against them. Most of the big Wall Street players knew exactly what the "Magnetar Trade" was and welcomed it. The more mortgages failed, the more money they made. They actually continued to sell the bad mortgages to their clients as good investments.

Gene Siskel, who was a wise man, gave me the best investment advice I've ever received. "You can never outsmart the market, if that's what you're trying to do," he said. "Find something you love, for reasons you understand, that not everyone agrees with you about, and put your money in it." The stocks I thought of were Apple, Google, and Steak 'n Shake. I bought some shares. That was a long time ago. Reader, if I had invested every penny I had on Gene's advice, today I would be a Master of the Universe.

Joan Rivers: A Piece of Work

No one is ever too old. You may have that idea about Joan Rivers, who was seventy-five in this film and never tires of reminding us of that fact. Is that too old? It's older than she would prefer, but what are you gonna do? She remains one of the funniest, dirtiest, most daring and transgressive of stand-up comics, and she hasn't missed a beat. *Joan Rivers: A Piece of Work* covers the events in about a year of her life. If the filmmakers didn't have total access, I don't want to see what they missed. In one stretch in this film she closes a show in Toronto, flies overnight to Palm Springs, does a gig, flies overnight to Minneapolis, and performs another one. Try that sometime.

The way she is funny is, she tells the truth according to herself. She hates some people. She has political opinions. Her observations are so merciless and her timing so precise that even if you like that person, you laugh. She is a sadist of comedy, unafraid to be cruel—even too cruel. She doesn't know fear. She seems to be curious about how far she can go and still get a laugh. That must feel dangerous on a stage with a live audience. Maybe she feeds on that danger.

Her life has been like a comeback tour. She is frank about her setbacks. She was Johnny Carson's resident cohost (and gave young Siskel and Ebert their first spot on *The Tonight Show*). She left Carson to begin her own nightly show on Fox. Carson never spoke to her again. NBC banned her from all of its shows until two years ago. The Fox show eventually failed, and it was discovered that her husband Edgar, the show's manager, had been stealing from her. He killed himself. She never forgave him—for the suicide, not the other stuff.

For her, it all comes down to this week: Does she have bookings? She looks at blank pages in her engagement calendar and says they're so white she needs sunglasses to read them. What makes Joanie run? They say if a shark stops swimming, it dies. She's not a shark. She's a woman who for various reasons depends on making audiences laugh. They walk in knowing all of her problems, knowing her age, eagle eyed her for the plastic surgery, ready to complain, and she forces them to laugh, because she's so damned funny. I admire that. Bernard Shaw called it the Life Force. We see her in the film's first shot, without makeup. A minute later, "Joan Rivers" is before us. Her life is a performance of herself.

Last Train Home

It is inevitable that painful social conflict will arise between those Chinese citizens who produce consumer goods for the world, and those Chinese who want to consume them. *Last Train Home*, an extraordinary documentary, watches that conflict play out over a period of three years in one family. It's one of those extraordinary films, like *Hoop Dreams*, that tells a story the makers could not possibly have anticipated in advance. It works like stunning, grieving fiction.

The film opens on a huge crowd being directed by police as it grinds its way forward. These are some of the 130 million Chinese citizens who make an annual Chinese New Year's train journey from urban centers to their provincial villages—"the largest human migration in the world." We center on Changhua Zhan and Suqin Chen, a married couple. Years ago, they left their home in the Szechuan province to take low-paying jobs in a textile factory in Guangzhou, which is the huge industrial city on the mainland next to Hong Kong. They save every yuan they can to send home. They left their children behind to be raised by a grandmother. Their dream is that by fifteen years of this toil, they will pay for the children to finish school and live better lives. For that dream, they have sacrificed the life of parenthood, and are like strangers at home to children who know them as voices on the telephone, seen on the annual visit. Are their children grateful for what amounts to the sacrifice of two lifetimes?

There is so much to say about this great film. You sense the dedication of Lixin Fan and his team. (He did much of the cinematography and editing himself.) You see once again the alchemy by which a constantly present camera eventually becomes almost unnoticed, as people live their lives before it. You know the generations almost better than they know themselves, because the camera can be in two places and they are usually in one or the other.

Chinese peasants no longer live without television and a vision of another world. They no longer live in a country without consumer luxuries. *Last Train Home* suggests that the times they are a-changin'. The rulers of China may someday regret that they distributed the works of Marx so generously.

Restrepo

Restrepo is a documentary shot during the fifteen months an American company fought in Afghanistan under almost daily fire. They were in the Korangal Valley, described as "the most dangerous place in the world." It is also one of the most desolate, even in the arid land of Afghanistan. Sparse vegetation clings to the rocky, jagged terrain. There is dust everywhere. It is too hot in the summer and too cold in the winter, and in the movie, at least, the troops only actually ever see one Taliban fighter—and the man who saw him thought it was the last sight he would ever see. There is one point when the company is ambushed and takes fire from 360 degrees. That all of them were not killed is surprising. The film is named after the first one of their number to die, a twenty-year-old medic, Private First Class Juan S. Restrepo.

Battle Company is led by Captain Dan Kearney, whose plan is to establish an outpost at a key point on Taliban battle routes. The men occupy the position at night and start digging in, using earth to build fortifications. They catch the enemy off guard. The successful maintenance of Outpost Restrepo, named for their dead comrade, turns the tide of war in the hostile valley and frightens the Taliban. But the hearts and minds of the locals remain an uncharted terrain.

This is hard, hard duty. A fifteen-month tour. Our admiration for these men grows. Their jobs seem beyond conceiving. I cannot imagine a civilian thinking he could perform them. It would take much training—and more important, much bonding. There is the sense they're fighting for one another more than for ideology. At a low point when a nearby company has taken heavy losses, Kearney talks to his men not in terms of patriotism, but in terms of finding the mofos who are shooting at them, and going out and killing them. The film is nonpolitical. It was filmed at great personal risk by the war photographer Tim Hetherington and the author Sebastian Junger (*The Perfect Storm*). It raises for me an obvious question: How can this war possibly be won?

Scrappers

In the alley, I see them maybe once a week, the men with their grocery carts, collecting tin cans and other treasures. Some will accumulate a heap as tall as themselves. I learn from the documentary *Scrappers* that the same trade happens in Chicago on a larger scale, with men trolling the city for scrap metal and emptying their trucks at scrap-metal yards. For this valuable work, they made a living, until the economy collapsed. An urban legend has grown up that such men steal copper gutters and the aluminum off the sides of garages. Such theft has been committed, but by desperate creatures of the night, not family men like Otis and Oscar, who are the backbone of the scrapper trade. "I paint my name and my phone number on the side of my truck," Otis says. "They know this truck down to 157th Street."

Otis is seventy-three, born in Chicago. Oscar looks to be in his forties, is from Honduras, and I have the impression he may be undocumented. They do useful work. Scrappers look for wire, pipes, aluminum, brass, copper, iron, and steel. The scrapyards heap it up, process it into particles about the size of Cheerios, ship it mostly to China, where it comes back to us and ends up in the alley again. In 2007, we learn, a scrapper could earn $200 to $300 a ton. In 2008, when the market collapsed and new construction ended, the price dropped to $20 a ton.

Scrappers became desperate. Fortunate people sneer at them, write them off as bums or thieves. Few in the middle class work as hard all day as these men do—or as usefully. *Scrappers* goes into the homes of Otis and Oscar to meet their wives—stable, stalwart women—and their kids. The loyalty in these homes is palpable. The film was made by Chicagoans Brian Ashby, Ben Kolak, and Courtney Prokopas. They put in the hours in the alleys and brought back a human document. It is necessary we have these films because our lives are so closed off we don't understand the function these men perform. You want green, there ain't nobody greener than Oscar and Otis.

A Small Act

This heartwarming documentary centers on the life story of Chris Mburu, who as a small boy living in a mud house in a Kenyan village had his primary and secondary education paid for by a Swedish woman. This cost her fifteen dollars a month. They had never met. He went on to the University of Nairobi, graduated from Harvard Law School, and is today a United Nations human rights commissioner.

The film shows Mburu seeking the Swedish woman "who made my life possible." She is Hilde Back. She is now eighty-five years old, a German Jew who was sent to Sweden as a child. Her family died in the Holocaust. She never married, was a schoolteacher, has lived in the same apartment for thirty-five years, is a tiny woman, but robust and filled with energy.

She is flown to Kenya, serenaded by the choir from Mburu's village, feasted, thanked, gowned in traditional robes. In the village the students study by the light of a single oil flame. The schools are not physically impressive; crowded classrooms with simple board benches and desks. A gym? Don't make me laugh. Hilde Back is asked if, since she never had children, she thought of Chris as a son. We see in the film that they stay in close touch. "But I have had children," she replied. "I was a teacher. I had many, many children." And one lived in a mud house in Kenya.

Vincent: A Life in Color

If you've been near Marina City in Chicago, you may have seen him. He's the smiling, middle-aged man with a limitless variety of spectacular suits. He stands on the Michigan or Wabash Avenue bridges, showing off his latest stupefying suit. He flashes the flamboyant lining, takes the coat off, spins it in great circles above his head, and then does his "spin move," pivoting first left, then right, while whirling the coat in the air. Then he puts it on again and waves to the tourists on the boat, by now passing under the bridge.

The remarkable documentary *Vincent: A Life in Color* unfolds the mystery of a human personality. Would it surprise you to learn that Vincent is a college graduate? A Cook County computer programmer? A former DJ in gay North Side discos? Paying his own rent in Marina City? Buying his own suits? Legally blind? Jennifer Burns, the film's producer and director, says one day, she was looking out her office window, watching Vincent performing for a tour boat, "and I was struck by the look of sheer joy I saw on his face." He agreed to be the subject of a film—not surprising, since his pastime is drawing attention to himself.

Vincent was an orphan abandoned by his mother and raised at St. Joseph's Home for the Friendless. There the nuns discovered that Vincent's problem wasn't intellectual but visual, and taught him to read by making sure he was always pushed up against the blackboard so he could see. In high school, he was a member of the National Honor Society, the chess club, the debate team, and the diving team, luckily never diving into a pool without water. He used a cane in high school, then threw it away and now walks freely everywhere in Chicago. It is terrifying to think of him crossing a street. All of which is admirable, but how does it explain the suits? He started wearing the suits in the 1990s, and says he gave his first bridge show in 2000, adding the "spin move" about a year later. He knows the times when every tour boat passes his bridges, and to the guides he is "Riverace" (rhymes with "Liberace").

Vincent will only say that he likes to entertain people. One expert speculates that Vincent has spent a lot of his life being stigmatized and isolated, and the suits are a way of breaking down barriers. So here is a man who likes to buy Technicolor suits and wave them at tour boats. So why not? What are the people on the boats so busy doing that they don't have time for Vincent?

Waiting for "Superman"

Near the end of *Waiting for "Superman,"* there is a sequence that cuts between lottery drawings for five charter schools. Admission to the best of these schools dramatically improves chances of school graduation and college acceptance. The applicants are not chosen for being gifted. They come from poor, disadvantaged neighborhoods. But the schools have astonishing track records.

We have met five of these students, heard from them and their parents, and hope they'll win. The cameras hold on their faces as numbers are drawn or names are called. The odds against them are twenty to one. Lucky students leap in joy. The other nineteen of the twenty will return to their neighborhood schools, which more or less guarantees they will be part of a 50 percent dropout rate. Underprivileged, inner-city kids at magnet schools such as KIPP L.A. Prep or the Harlem Success Academy will do better academically than well-off suburban kids with fancy high school campuses, athletic programs, swimming pools, closed-circuit TV, and lush landscaping.

Waiting for "Superman," this documentary by Davis Guggenheim, focuses on an African-American educator named Geoffrey Canada, who deliberately chose the poorest area of Harlem to open his Harlem Success Academy. His formula: qualified teachers, highly motivated, better paid. Emphasis on college prep from day one. Tutoring for those behind in math or reading. There are also charter boarding schools, with no TV, no video games. One kid says he wants in, but "my feelings are bittersweet." One problem with most schools, Guggenheim says, is that after teachers gain tenure in two years, it is almost impossible to fire them.

What struck me most of all was Geoffrey Canada's confidence that a charter school run on his model can make virtually any first-grader a high school graduate who's accepted to college. A good education, therefore, is not ruled out by poverty, uneducated parents, or crime- and drug-infested neighborhoods. In fact, those are the very areas where he has success. Consider this: Those lotteries are truly random, as by law they must be. Yet most of the winners will succeed, and half the losers (from the same human pool) will fail. This is an indictment: Our schools do not work.

Winnebago Man

There is a video on YouTube that has had millions and millions of hits and made its subject, a man named Jack Rebney, internationally known as "Winnebago Man." He first attracted attention when an old VHS tape surfaced featuring the outtakes of a 1989 session when he was trying without much success to star in a promotional film for Winnebagos. In take after take, Rebney blew lines, forgot lines, thought lines were stupid, was distracted by crew members moving around, was annoyed by stray sounds, was mad at himself for even doing the damn thing. Every time the filming broke down or Rebney called a halt, he exploded in verbal fireworks. The only reason *Winnebago Man* doesn't consist of wall-to-wall f-words is that he separates them with other four-letter words. The video was found hilarious by countless viewers. But who was the real Winnebago Man?

A documentary maker named Ben Steinbauer found out. He was curious about the reasons we like footage of real people subjecting themselves (usually unwillingly) to ridicule. Are we laughing at them, with them, or simply in relief that we aren't them? How does their viral fame affect them? Jack Rebney seemed to have disappeared from the face of the earth. Steinbauer finally tracks him down in northern California, where he lives alone in the woods, calls himself a hermit, and wants nothing to do with nobody—never. That's not because of the YouTube video, which he doesn't give a $#!+ about. It's because of the way he is.

Now around eighty, he works as a caretaker for a fishing resort. He has an unlisted phone number, uses post office boxes, and his dog is all the company he wants. He does have a computer; I imagine him feeding the endless comment streams on blogs. Rebney more or less agrees to be filmed. He figures a doc might be a way to air his views, of which he has a great many views.

Rebney is threatened with blindness. We wonder how he will get along, at his age, living in a cabin in the woods. He is not a comic character; he's dead serious, a hardened realist, whose only soft spot may be for his dog. He keeps up with events, feels the nation is going down the drain, and isn't sure why he was so angry while making the Winnebago promotional film. Steinbauer takes Rebney wider than YouTube—all the way to the Jay Leno show, and to a fascinating personal appearance at a Found Film Festival, where he regards himself on the screen and then goes out to speak and proves himself the master of the situation. Steinbauer even sets him up with a Twitter account, but, typically, Rebney loathed it. His most recent Tweet in the film, on March 28, 2009, was: "UP YOUR FERN."

The Best Art Films of 2010

February 17, 2011—This is the last of my lists of the best films of 2010, and the hardest to name. Call it the Best Art Films. I can't precisely define an art film, but I knew I was seeing one when I saw these. I could also call them adult films, if that term hadn't been devalued by the porn industry. These are films based on the close observation of behavior. They are not mechanical constructions of infinitesimal thrills. They depend on intelligence and empathy to be appreciated.

They also require acting of a precision not necessary in many mass entertainments. They require directors with a clear idea of complex purposes. They require subtleties of lighting and sound that create a self-contained world. Most of all, they require sympathy. The directors care for their characters and ask us to see them as individuals, not genre emblems. That requires us to see ourselves as individual viewers, not "audience members." That can be an intimate experience. I found it in these titles, which for one reason or another weren't on my earlier lists. Maybe next year I'll just come up with one alphabetical list of all the year's best films, and call it "The Best Films of 2011, A to Z."

Around a Small Mountain

Sometimes a film's message may be no more than that we all have to weather hard times. Maybe that's what Jacques Rivette has in mind with *Around a Small Mountain.* One of the founders of the French New Wave, Rivette is still active at eighty-two. At his film's center is a shabby little circus that becomes the stage on which his two characters live. Kate (Jane Birkin) is returning to the circus after fifteen years. It was her father's. Her lover was killed in a performance. When Vittorio (Sergio Castellitto) meets her, she has a quality that strikes him, and books the room above a local café on the spur of the moment. When the circus leaves town, he follows. It's not that he and Kate begin a love affair. It's that they've both run off to join the circus.

He apparently has nowhere to go and nothing else to do, and the same might be said of her. We learn of the buried past of the circus and the buried careers of its performers. Little one-ring circuses like this set up in town squares in rural districts. They still exist. On the Lido in Venice one night, we attended one smaller than this—so small that after the show, the clown came over to our granddaughter Raven and gave her a ride on his mule.

Jane Birkin has a sculpted, intelligent face. She's a woman who looks like she's up to something. She's had quite a life. Here she exudes the loss of her father, her lover, and the circus. I doubt if she's experienced love since her lover died. Vittorio becomes a sort of passive counselor, coaxing her to face her wounds and let go of them. Their relationship is ever so much more interesting than if Rivette had reduced it to romance. This man and woman, strangers, actually find themselves talking to each other. How often do you see that?

Blue Valentine

They say we get married because we want a witness. Did Dean and Cindy get married because they wanted someone watching? Or was that Dean's need, and did Cindy lose the thrill of the watch? Derek Cianfrance, the film's writer and director, observes the birth and decay of a relationship. Toward the end of the six years, when Cindy is hardly able to remember why she wanted to marry Dean, Cianfrance observes the physical and mental exhaustion that has overcome her. And the way that Dean seems hardly to care—just so long as Cindy remains his wife and his watcher, which in his mind was the deal. Dean thinks marriage is the station. Cindy thought it was the train.

They're played by Ryan Gosling and Michelle Williams as a Pennsylvania working-class couple with a daughter, Frankie. They give us Dean and Cindy at two ages: their age at present, and at the beginning, when they were filled with that dreamy knowledge that the touch of the other brings quick sensuality. It is easier for an actor to play the same character at twenty-four and sixty than at twenty-four and thirty. Though some bodily change occurs, what really happens is a transformation of inner certainty. Williams plays a woman who sits inside her body and no longer knows what it's for and what she wants to do with it.

Dean seems stuck. He seems to stay fixed at the initial stage. Can you see the difference between (1) "He loves me as much as he always did," and (2) "He loves me exactly like he always did"? *Blue Valentine* moves between past and present as if trying to remember what went wrong. From Dean's point of view, maybe nothing did. He wanted to be married to Cindy, and he still does and he still is. Cindy can't stand that. He never signed off on the "grow old along with me" part. He doesn't think the best is yet to be. He thinks it's just fine now.

Catfish

Some filmmakers in New York City, who think they're way cool, get taken apart by an ordinary family in Ishpeming, Michigan. You can view this as a cautionary tale about living your emotional life on the Internet. Or possibly the whole thing is a hoax. To go into detail about that might spoil the film's effect for you. The facts in the film are slippery, but the revelation of a human personality is surprisingly moving.

The film opens in the Manhattan office of Nev, Ariel, and Henry, who make videos of modern dancers. Nev has received a painting of one of his photographs from Abby Pierce, an eight-year-old girl. They enter into a correspondence with Abby's mom, Angela. Nev begins to identify with the whole family. He learns of school plans, pie baking, Sunday family breakfast. Nev and Abby's older sister, Megan, begin a cyber romance. Nev begins to wonder if this could possibly be the girl for him. There are dozens of photos on her Facebook site, and he even starts using software to put himself and Megan in the same photos.

The three videographers have to fly to Vail to shoot a dance event. On the way back east, they decide to make a detour to Ishpeming. They find the Pierce home and family, and I suppose are welcomed with as much grace as possible under the circumstances. Angela Pierce comes across as an essentially good person, as complex as the heroine of a novel. At the end of the day, I believe she humbles Nev and his friends. I wonder if they agree. They all seem to be nice people. Let's agree on this: We deserve to share happiness in this world, and if we supply it in the way it's sought and nobody gets hurt, is that a bad thing?

Chicago Heights

Sherwood Anderson's *Winesburg, Ohio*, is a collection of twenty-two short stories connected by the character George Willard, who comes of age and reflects on the citizens he has grown to know. Perhaps it could inspire twenty-two short films. Daniel Nearing accomplishes the uncanny feat of distilling the book's essence.

Anderson's Winesburg is a town with roads that can be walked along a short distance into the country. His time frame spans the twentieth century's first quarter century. Nearing's Chicago Heights is a distant southern suburb of Chicago, bordering on farmland. His time is the present and recent decades. His central character is Nathan Walker (Andre Truss), also played as Old Nathan by William Gray, and at that age named in the credits as Sherwood Anderson. Anderson's characters were all white. Nearing's characters are all African-American. Race is not a factor. We are concerned with inner selves.

What Nearing does, and it is rather brilliant, is show us Nathan in old age, under a blanket on his bed, remembering, dreaming, or hallucinating about the people he has known. A narrator explains his thoughts. Remarkably for a film of average length, Nearing touches on almost every one of Anderson's characters, and because of his meditative stylistic approach the film never feels rushed or choppy.

Dialogue slips in and out, as it does in the book, but we're not intended to think it's being said now. It's being heard in memory. Nearing succeeds in establishing it as a place like Winesburg where the countryside is always in walking distance, and one can go there with one's complexities and feel at peace.

Daddy Longlegs

Lenny isn't a bad father. He's no father at all. He doesn't understand being an adult. He doesn't understand anything. Why did his former wife think she could trust him with two weeks of child custody? Lenny shouldn't even have custody of himself.

He's in constant motion during *Daddy Longlegs*. If he has role models at all, they're provided by his two sons, Sage and Frey. Lenny acts like their playmate, not their father. He's played by Ronald Bronstein, who projects a relentless upbeat enthusiasm. He tries to babysit the kids, who are five and seven years old, while at the same time working as a movie projectionist and dating, or breaking up, with his current girlfriend (Eleonore

Hendricks). With one kid riding his shoulders and another tagging behind, he rushes out on unclear missions. At one point, he talks a complete stranger into taking the three of them along on a trip with her boyfriend to upstate New York.

The film was written and directed by Ben and Joshua Safdie. Their cinematic father is obviously John Cassavetes, whose own manic heroes ran crazy loops around their lives. If *Daddy Longlegs* is influenced by Cassavetes, that's not a bad thing. Few filmmakers have the nerve to travel that path. Bronstein's performance is crucial. It's difficult to make a manic character plausible, but he does. He never goes over the top. His mania seems devoted more to lifting off from the bottom. How he ever persuaded his wife (Leah Singer) to marry him is hard to explain, most of all, probably, to herself.

Fish Tank

Andrea Arnold's *Fish Tank* is the portrait of an angry, isolated fifteen-year-old girl who is hurtling toward a lifetime of misery. She is so hurt and lonely, we pity her. Her mother barely even sees her. The girl is Mia, played by Katie Jarvis in a harrowing display of hostility. She's been thrown out of school, is taunted as a weirdo by boys her age, has no friends, converses with her mother and sister in screams, and retreats to an empty room to play her music and dance alone. She drinks what little booze she can get her hands on.

And where is her mother? Right there at home, all the time. Joanne (Kierston Wareing) looks so young, she might have had Mia at Mia's age. Joanne is shorter, busty, dyed blond, a chain-smoker, a party girl. The party is usually in her living room. One day, she brings home Connor (Michael Fassbender), a good-looking guy who seems nice enough. Mia screams at him, too, but it's a way of getting attention.

One day Connor takes Mia, her mom, and her little sister, Tyler (Rebecca Griffiths), on a drive to the country. Connor takes Mia wading ("I can't swim") in the river. Walking barefoot, she gets a ride on his back and rests her chin on his shoulder, and what was in the air from the first is now manifest. Some reviews call Connor a pedophile. I think he's more of an immoral opportunist. Arnold sees everything through Mia's eyes and never steps outside to explain things from any other point of view. She knows who the young girl is, and we are left to assume. Whatever she thinks after the visit to Connor's house, we are not specifically told.

Katie Jarvis herself may have been headed for a life similar to Mia's. Her casting in this film, however, led to Cannes, the Jury Prize, and contracts with British and American agents. She is a powerful acting presence, flawlessly convincing here. And Arnold, who won an Oscar for her shattering short film *Wasp* (2003), also about a neglectful alcoholic mother, deserves comparison with British master director Ken Loach.

Jack Goes Boating

Philip Seymour Hoffman has a gift for playing quickly embarrassed men who fear rejection. We're on his side without the script needing to persuade us. We want to finish his sentences, clap him on the back, cheer him up. In *Jack Goes Boating*, Hoffman is not only the star but the director, and is merciless in using himself as an actor. His face is often seen in close-up, sweaty, splotchy, red as if perpetually blushing.

In the movie, he plays a limousine driver. At dawn, he meets for coffee with his best friend, Clyde (John Ortiz), and they sit in a parked limo and regard the unattainable towers of Manhattan. Jack is clueless. Clyde is effortless. Even in their forties, they have a student–teacher relationship. Clyde is going to teach Jack how to chat up a girl, make himself likable. Clyde is married to Lucy (Daphne Rubin-Vega). She works in a funeral home with Connie (Amy Ryan). Connie is the kind of person whom you'd describe as sweet, but terribly shy. Clyde and Lucy decide these two people belong with each other perhaps because they appear to belong with nobody else.

This leads into a dinner at which social embarrassment is the main course. The movie is based on an off-Broadway play by Bob Glaudini, which Hoffman and Ortiz produced and acted in with Rubin-Vega. Its stage origins are suggested by the way Clyde lives in a flat where the kitchen, dining area, and the living area are essentially one space—that works beautifully when his dinner for Connie goes wrong, as it must.

You can sense the familiarity the actors have with their roles, but they make it new and poignant, and avoid going over the top in the story's limited psychic and physical space. Even at their highest pitch, the emotions of these characters come from hearts long worn down by the troubles we see.

Leaves of Grass

Tim Blake Nelson's *Leaves of Grass* is a sweet, wacky masterpiece. It takes all sorts of risks, including a dual role with Edward Norton playing twin brothers, and it pulls them off. It is certainly the most intelligent, philosophical, and poetic film I can imagine that involves five murders in the marijuana-dealing community of Oklahoma.

The film opens with Norton as a philosopher named Bill Kincaid giving a lecture on Socrates to a packed classroom of starstruck students at Brown. What an audacious way that is to open a movie about the drug culture of rural Oklahoma. Kincaid gets a telephone call telling him his twin brother, Brady, is dead. He flies home for the funeral and is met at the airport by his twin's best friend (Nelson). It turns out the story was a lie to lure him back home for two purposes. One is to force him to see his mother, a 1960s pothead played by Susan Sarandon. The other is to act as Brady's double to establish an alibi while Brady goes up to Tulsa for a meeting with the region's dominant marijuana dealer (Richard Dreyfuss).

Norton is flawless as both an elite intellectual and a good ol' boy. He's for all intents two different people: one who has reinvented himself, the other who is growing the best marijuana around. I like the way the film makes the twins equally brilliant; Brady has designed and built a hydroponic farm that is producing its seventh generation of top-quality weed. He is also something of a philosopher himself.

Another valuable character is Janet (Keri Russell), a local English teacher and poet, who quotes Whitman to Billy and entrances him in a way he has never before allowed. The plot involves as many dead and severely wounded bodies lying around as in *Blood Simple*, and Nelson weaves it expertly without a lot of visible "plotting." The story is the terrain the characters move through, and they are always the foreground. What stands out is the ability of both Billy and Brady (perhaps even more Brady) to understand the world philosophically and deal with it intellectually.

Mother and Child

Three mothers in need of a child. Three children, one not yet born. Three lives that are obscurely linked. Rodrigo Garcia has made his career with films sympathetic to the feelings of women, and his *Mother and Child* is so emotionally affecting because it is concerned only with their feelings. The film is founded on three performances by Annette Bening, Kerry Washington, and Naomi Watts. Bening plays Karen, a caregiver at work, where she's a physical therapist, and at home, where she cares for her mother. There will be no one to care for her: When she was fourteen, she gave up a child for adoption, and now she yearns to have that child back. This is not a film about the wisdom of adoption, however, but about Karen's desire for her child. Kerry Washington plays Lucy, happily married, childless, trying to adopt a child. Naomi Watts is Elizabeth, a lawyer who is concentrated not so much on her career but on her power, and how her sexuality can be a part of that.

A quiet, nurturing person at the intersection of these lives is Sister Joanne (Cherry Jones), a nun at a church adoption bureau. She is childless, of course, but content; she accepts her state as part of her service to God and is devoted to her clients. The nun is one of several important supporting characters who give *Mother and Child* richness. In this large cast, the actors are gifted and well-cast down to the smaller roles, and each one is important to the development of the story—not just added for diversion or variety.

Garcia, whose credits include *Things You Can Tell Just by Looking at Her* (2000) and *Nine Lives* (2005), has created an interwoven plot not just for the purpose of being clever. Each facet revolves to illuminate the others. The characters reflect aspects of the central dilemma of the childless mothers. It doesn't argue that all mothers require children, and indeed the nun may be the happiest woman here. It simply argues that these mothers believe that they do.

Please Give

There is an evil-tempered old woman in *Please Give* who finds fault with everyone and everything. Her next-door neighbors are waiting for her to die so they can break through her walls. The old lady, Andra, is played by Ann Guilbert with exact cunning, and looked after by her granddaughters, Rebecca (Rebecca Hall), constant and kind, and Mary (Amanda Peet), a distracted heavy drinker.

The couple next door are Kate and Alex (Catherine Keener and Oliver Platt). They run an antique-furniture store specializing in furniture from the 1950s. Kate is one of those Keener characters you feel like you've known somewhere before. They have a daughter, Abby (Sarah Steele), who is pudgy, has skin problems, and is antisocial, but smart and has good timing. Abby is incredulous at the way her mom is a pushover for street beggars; Kate can hardly enjoy a meal without taking a doggie bag to a homeless man.

Kate and Alex are reasonably happy. They run errands for Andra to calm their consciences, and have a dinner party for the old lady and her granddaughters. This scene by writer-director Nicole Holofcener is an exercise in social embarrassment, one of those Bunuelian scenes in which people unexpectedly tell the truth and say what should not be said. Holofcener pays close attention to women. She doesn't define them by their relationships with men. In a Holofcener movie, women actually have their own reasons for doing things—and these are even allowed to be bad reasons. The movie is about imperfect characters in a difficult world, who mostly do the best they can, but not always. Do you realize what a revolutionary approach that is for a movie these days?

A Prophet

The murder at the center of Jacques Audiard's *A Prophet* is clumsy, messy, and brutal, and leaves the killer shaking. Whether he shakes with grief, relief, or anger we cannot say. That's the key to this film, which follows the life of Malik, a young Frenchman of Arab descent, who enters prison as a naive outsider and is shaped into an evil adult criminal. He was born a shy, passive loser. Prison made him all that he could be. He seems an unlikely protagonist for a prison movie. Prison serves him over to the Corsican gang that controls everything behind bars.

This gang is run by Cesar Luciani (Niels Arestrup), a man who has the presence of Don Corleone but colder eyes. He walks everywhere followed by bodyguards. He makes it his business to intimidate the new man. There is a prisoner whom Cesar wants killed. Malik is instructed by Cesar's lieutenant how to conceal a razor blade in his mouth and slit the man's throat. It is very simple. If Malik doesn't do this, he will die.

In the years to come, Malik undergoes a transformation. He learns how to observe, how to devise strategy, how to rise. *A Prophet* becomes his bleak, remorseless coming-of-age story. But what goes on inside Malik? That's the frightening part. We can only judge by what he does. Now he is prepared to kill. Prison has prepared him to return to the streets.

Rare Exports: A Christmas Tale

How to explain an R-rated Santa Claus origin story crossed with *The Thing*? It is the day before Christmas in the far Arctic north. Young Pietari lives on a reindeer ranch with his dad and other men, and nearby there is a huge mound that looks vaguely sinister. The Americans have been blasting away up there with dynamite. Very sinister. Pietari and his friend Juuso have been sneaking through the fence to spy on the Yanks.

There is a legend that centuries ago the citizens were threatened by fearsome monsters. They were able to trick them onto the lake, where they froze. One of them was cut out inside a giant block of ice and buried deep beneath the mound. And now, Pietari is the only one who figures out that inside the mound, inside the ice, is Santa Claus.

Well, not Santa precisely. A savage, scrawny beast of a man with a beard, who eventually does admittedly end up wearing a Santa suit, but strictly for warmth. Don't let it get lost in the confusion that this is a fine film. An original, daring, carefully crafted film that never for one instant winks at us that it's a parody. In its tone, acting, location work, music, and inexorably mounting suspense, this is an exemplary horror film, apart from the detail that they're not usually subtitled *A Christmas Tale* and tell about wild Santas.

Somewhere

Johnny Marco (Stephen Dorff) sits in a Hollywood hotel suite and finds himself a hollow man. He is a movie star. With that comes money, fame, sex, drugs. Fame is a joke because he gets nothing from it. Sex involves mechanical manipulations of the genitals. He drinks and takes drugs, but pleasure doesn't seem to be involved. Sofia Coppola's film involves, as did her *Lost in Translation* (2003), a man separated from his family and sitting alone in a hotel room. In *Lost in Translation,* Bill Murray's Bob made dutiful but cheerless phone calls home from Japan. Dorff's Johnny spends dutiful time with his eleven-year-old daughter, Cleo (Elle Fanning). Neither seems meaningfully connected.

The notion of a star sinking into seclusion and depression isn't new. What distinguishes Coppola's film is the detail in her portrait of celebrity life. Remember that she was a little girl and later a young actress on the sets of her father's movies. Now that we see how observant she is, we can only speculate about what she understood right from the start. She played Michael Corleone's baby.

Her hero seems to suffer from anhedonia, the inability to feel pleasure. Johnny stares at the wall and the film stares back. Coppola sees, and we see exactly what she sees. There is little attempt here to observe a plot. All the attention is on the handful of characters and on Johnny. He has attained success and lost track of the ability to experience it. Perhaps you can stimulate yourself so much for so long that your sensitivity wears out. If Johnny has no inner life and his outer life no longer matters, then he's right: He's nothing.

Tiny Furniture

Aura has graduated from college and returned home to live in her mother's Tribeca loft. Four years of education have left her with one video on YouTube. Her mother is a famous artist who makes a lot of money selling photographs of tiny furniture, sometimes in the same frame as the feet and legs of Nadine, Aura's sister, who is taller, thinner, and younger than Aura.

Aura (Lena Dunham) is discontented. She hates living at home but has no money to move out. She wants love and acceptance, and finds it much diluted by her distracted mother (Laurie Simmons) and her competitive sister (Grace Dunham). Of possible boyfriends there are: (1) Jed, a "big deal on YouTube," which shows him riding a mechanical pony while reciting Nietzsche; and (2) Keith, who works at the restaurant and has a girlfriend, but asks Aura out and then stands her up.

Aura's life unfolds without plot because there is none. This is a movie about people who are all passive-aggressive, including Aura. Nobody laughs or tries to say anything funny, and when Aura is happy sometimes, she doesn't trust it. Aura is played by Lena Dunham, who wrote and directed the film. Her mother and her sister are played by her real mother and sister. The loft in Tribeca is where her family lives. Visually, the film is as unadorned as the white cabinets that cover a wall of the loft. Dunham's cinematographer, Jody Lee Lipes, doesn't move the camera. It's locked down for a steady, flat gaze. This is correct. It sees like Aura sees. Her personality doesn't suggest tracking shots.

Yellow Handkerchief

This is the story of three insecure drifters who find themselves sharing a big convertible and driving to New Orleans not long after Hurricane Katrina. The car's driver is a teenager named Gordy (Eddie Redmayne), who doubts most of what he does and seems to apologize just by standing there. At a rural convenience store, he encounters Martine (Kristen Stewart), running away from her life. He says he's driving to New Orleans. No reason. She decides to come along. No reason. They meet a quiet, reserved man named Brett (William Hurt), and she thinks he should come along. No particular reason.

We now have the makings of a classic road picture. Three outsiders, a fabled destination, Louisiana back roads, and a big old convertible. William Hurt occupies the silent center of the film. In many movies we interpret his reticence as masking intelligence. Here we realize it's a blank slate, and could be masking anything. Kristen Stewart is a wonderful actress. I must not hold the *Twilight* movies against her. In recent film after film, she shows a sure hand and an intrinsic power. I last saw her in *Welcome to the Rileys,* where she played a runaway working as a hooker in New

Orleans. In both films she had many scenes with experienced older actors (Hurt, James Gandolfini). In both she was rock solid. The story of Redmayne, who plays Gordy, is unexpected. He fits effortlessly into the role of the scrawny, uncertain fifteen-year-old Louisiana kid. Yet I learn he is twenty-seven, a Brit who went to Eton, a veteran of Shakespeare and Edward Albee.

During their odyssey their secrets are slowly confided. They learn lessons about themselves, which is required in such films, but are so slowly and convincingly arrived at here that we forgive them. Prasad made a wonderful British film in 1997, *My Son the Fanatic.* I've seen none of his work since. Now comes this redneck slice of life. Since the characters are so far from the lives of the actors and the director, this is a creation of the imagination. As it must be. The ending is a shade melodramatic, but what the heck. In for one yellow handkerchief, in for a hundred.

Interviews

Casey Affleck

September 22, 2010—The bottom line: Casey Affleck thinks of it as a performance and not as an act, and he thinks of *I'm Still Here* as a film, and not a hoax. In an interview where he revealed details behind the making of his controversial film with and about Joaquin Phoenix, he also said:

• David Letterman was not in on the performance, and what you saw on his show was really happening.

• Phoenix dropped out of character when he was not being filmed or in public.

• The drugs and the hookers were staged. The vomiting was real.

• He would have preferred to remain silent about whether the film was "real" or not, but his distributor urged him to break silence near its opening day.

• Friends and family knew. Ben Stiller was part of the film, and his appearance during the Oscars in "Joaquin" makeup was well meaning and supportive. Natalie Portman, Stiller's co-presenter during the Oscars, also knew.

These and many other revelations emerged as Affleck, director of the film starring his brother-in-law Phoenix, discussed behind-the-scenes realities in making the most-debated film of the year. Based on what he said, *I'm Still Here* must be considered a fiction feature, and Phoenix's work in it must be considered eligible for an Academy Award nomination.

I sent Affleck questions by e-mail, and his replies appear below. Our exchange was a mutual enterprise of *Interview* magazine and RogerEbert.com, and is appearing on both Web sites.

RE: You've now said the whole enterprise was a hoax. So we'll proceed on that basis. Film critics as a group are skilled at judging the authenticity of films. My reading of a group of major reviews of *I'm Still Here* linked at Metacritic indicates that only six stated flatly the film was not genuine. Nine believed it, and the rest were not sure, had doubts, were cagey, or left themselves wriggle room. In terms of your intentions, this counts as a success, right?

CA: I wish people hadn't debated so much the film's veracity or authenticity, hadn't asked only and dully, "Is this real?" But that response is better than apathy, I suppose. Picasso said, "Art is the lie that tells the truth."

My aim was not to fool. My aim was to provoke thought and stir emotion. The enterprise was a film, not a "hoax." The idea that Joaquin was really retiring for good and pursuing a rap career in earnest was an act. Nothing was a hoax. At the Toronto Film Festival someone was walking around to theaters in a beard and wig and glasses and telling journalists he was Joaquin Phoenix. That is a hoax. There was nothing else but the deception.

I was making a movie. In a movie we try to deceive. In theaters, as they say, the deceived are the wisest. I was trying to help the audience suspend their disbelief. That is why the film was released without comment from myself or anyone involved. The reason it was *made* without comment and with Joaquin in character when in public was because the media plays a role in the film and the media would not have played their role as well as they did had it been acknowledged that Joaquin was only performing. When I say "the media" I mean also the unpaid bloggers and vloggers and people all around the world commenting online.

RE: In terms of 20/20 hindsight, many viewers are now pointing to moments when they could see it was staged. Did you deliberately place any "tells" in the film?

CA: No. Not deliberately. I heard of very few tells before I did the interview with the *New York Times* and said that it was a piece of fiction.

RE: I assume you and Joaquin didn't go through this long period of time for frivolous reasons. What was your larger purpose? Your philosophy, dare I say? Joaquin's?

CA: To tell a story. To make a movie. Isn't it

the job of the director to figure out the best way to tell the story they have to tell? This was the best way I could think of to tell this story, about this character. It's a movie about a famous actor who has been acting for a long time and who wants to change paths, to change his life, to peruse a career in music. But he makes mistakes and the world is unforgiving. Things go wrong. He can't recover. He digs himself deeper and deeper.

There are ideas in the film that are interesting to me. I don't have a point to make, though. If it feels like a cautionary tale, what would be the warning? When you have a dream and others tell you, you are no good, give it up? Don't become famous? Prepare, practice, and use stepping-stones? Or maybe don't be incredibly mean to those around you? Some things seems too obvious, some seem lacking. I don't know the point. I only know that it is of course in some way about celebrity culture. It's about fame, in some way. I don't know what it says exactly but I know that it makes me wonder when I watch it. I'm OK with that.

All cultures are different. Some commit genocide. Some are uniquely peaceful. Some frequent bathhouses in groups. Some don't show each other the soles of their shoes or like pictures taken of them. Some have enormous hunting festivals or annual stretches when nobody speaks. Some don't use electricity. We obsess about celebrities. We create them, build myths around them, and then hunt them and destroy them. I don't know where it's taking us or what it means but I know we do it. I have seen a lot of it myself.

RE: Knowing that Joaquin was performing suggests a deeper level of anger against the celebrity-publicity system than a simple psychological meltdown would have. This must be an actor urgently inspired to make a statement.

CA: I think it's more a case of an enormous talent relishing the unique role and broadened parameters of the job.

RE: One thing that surprised me over the time this went on is how little true concern for Joaquin was expressed. He was instead made the butt of jokes. Have we gotten to the point where the press is playing Dunk the Clown with celebrities?

CA: It seems so. There were those willing to lampoon him publicly, who when asked to give an interview for the film said, "I don't want to give you an interview because I don't know what's going on with Joaquin, and if he's having real psychological problems or problems with addiction, I don't know what to say." Yet they felt comfortable mocking him on national TV. I am *not* talking about Ben Stiller and Natalie Portman, who both knew that Joaquin was fine and both knew about the film.

RE: Many of the snarkier Web sites seem to be run by men (hardly ever women) who, I think, take pleasure in the troubles of others. They seem cheered by bad movies, bad box office, arrests, domestic problems, drugs, and even illness—although there they affect a pious sympathy. Would you agree?

CA: I don't know. I don't know who is behind those Web sites. I really have no idea, and until this film I never looked at those sites or read the entertainment sections of those papers much. But the "respected" and "serious" newspapers can be pretty petty and snarky, too.

RE: When Ben Stiller appeared on the Oscars made up as Joaquin, some thought it was cruel. Gwyneth Paltrow told people at the time *Two Lovers* came out that she thought Ben had done a funny performance, and was offended. Now we know that Ben is in *I'm Still Here* pitching a screenplay Joaquin has not read. So Ben knew it was a hoax when he appeared on the Oscars? His performance in a way was helping you two?

CA: Yes. Ben was incredibly supportive. For the guy with the all-time highest box office average, for someone sitting squarely and securely at the top of the heap, he was really gallant in the way he swooped into our little movie and treated us with respect and patience and complete faith. I don't know why. I think he is the real thing, and I mean by that that he does this because he likes it and likes experimenting and challenging himself and growing. And maybe he thought working with a couple knuckleheads was a way of helping himself grow as a philanthropist of the arts. Ben is a very nice guy.

RE: James Gray, the director of *Two Lovers*, was enraged at Joaquin's behavior. I thought *Two Lovers* was a good film and I was in sympathy with Gray. How did you and Joaquin process that whole area?

CA: James just wanted people to see his movie. Magnolia released that as well as my movie, and I don't think a whole lot of people would have seen it if Joaquin didn't have a beard and hadn't told people he was retiring. But maybe I'm wrong. James also was told what was going on.

RE: Did Joaquin go out of character when off-camera? Did he lead an undercover normal life? What was security like?

CA: Yes. When we were not rolling he was out of character. If he was in public he had to behave in a way that didn't contradict the character's personality.

RE: You did a pretty good job of keeping the lid on and the mystery alive. You insisted all through Venice that the film was real, and then revealed it was a hoax when it was just opening. Did Magnolia Pictures think that timing was a good idea?

CA: Yes. From the beginning they said, "we think people should see this film in the same context that we saw it." They saw it knowing nothing. In the end I think it was a mistake, but I agreed at the time.

RE: The drugs, the prostitutes, the vomiting, all real? Some? All staged?

CA: All staged. Vomiting was real. And his hairline is real.

RE: Obviously the public performances in the movie, as in Miami, are real, in the sense that they took place. That must have taken some balls for Joaquin to go through with.

CA: Yes, it was brave.

RE: A Letterman writer has said the Letterman appearance was all planned in advance, and Dave was in on the joke. True?

CA: No. That man seems unreliable. If Dave knew about something it was not because Joaquin or I told him anything. I think David Letterman is a genius. Night after night he is funny and smart. He seems to really enjoy his jokes. They seem connected to who he really is. I like watching him, and there is no one better at turning an awkward moment into something very funny. I am a fan of David Letterman and have been for twenty years. I can't think of many performers, bands, films, political organizations, sports teams, or family members I can say that about.

RE: Even if Letterman was "planned," it was improvisational in the moment. Improv isn't known as part of Joaquin's background. He is however very experienced at being on talk shows. Did you discuss how he would handle it? Any rehearsal? Some viewers say (now) that they can see him almost smiling at some of Dave's lines. Could you?

CA: He didn't break character while in the chair. He was smiling because he (his character) was trying to get along, trying to be in the moment.

RE: Did the subject of Andy Kaufman and his Letterman appearances ever come up, at that time or in general?

CA: Yes. We watched them together. We had seen them, but watched together again. But this was different. That was performance art. This was part of a movie.

RE: You and your small crew must have become adept at creating the illusion of the cinema verité style. And the editing must have been essential. This film, in fact, must have required a lot more work than an actual documentary.

CA: I have never made a documentary. I don't know.

RE: Joaquin was photographed arriving at the dock of the Hotel Excelsior in Venice clean-shaven and neatly dressed. How or why was that picture taken?

CA: In order to get to the festival you have to take a boat and there is only one dock. I wanted him to come to Venice to celebrate the movie. It didn't seem right that he not be there and it didn't seem right that I have to travel alone. I insisted. He wanted to. However, it was decided that he wouldn't walk down a red carpet and have the audience know he was in the theater. It would have influenced the way they reacted.

RE: There were reports that Joaquin sneaked into the Palazzo del Cinema, sat in a back row, and "laughed his ass off." This sounds apocryphal to me.

CA: He laughed while watching the film.

RE: My review of the film expressed concern that Joaquin might be self-destructing. Not many reviews expressed much concern. Even those who thought the film was or might be true didn't seem to care much about the human being. Has the celeb culture vulgarized us so much that stars are now regarded simply as objects?

CA: It seems so. Your review was unique. I appreciated it.

RE: You are Joaquin's brother-in-law. That worked to explain your presence and access even in this period of public meltdown. What did Summer think about it—before, during, and after?

CA: She is next to me. I will ask. She says, "You know exactly how I felt." Me: "How?" Her: "I was excited." Me: "About what?" Her: "I was excited that after all the damn conversations between you two about doing something together you were finally doing it. I am annoyed that all the critics only debate if it's real or not and not what the film is about." Me: "What is it about?" Her: "Ugh, stop it!"

RE: How did you and Summer deal with the concern of friends who weren't in on the secret?

CA: Me: "How did we deal with people who thought Joaquin was really behaving that way for real?" Her: "I would always say he's doing great. But, Casey, do your own stupid interview."

RE: As an actor and director, how do you feel about *I'm Still Here* at the end of the day?

CA: Right now? I feel fine. It changes. My feelings change about every movie I have ever done, every time I think about them.

RE: Do you think Joaquin might smoke too much?

CA: Is there a right amount? It's an awful addiction. Terrible.

Kirsten Dunst

December 28, 2010—In her new film *All Good Things*, Kirsten Dunst plays a character who is murdered, maybe. She certainly disappears. The movie is based on a true story of a poor girl who married into a rich New York City family and vanished into thin air. For an actor, that's a little like playing the Road Runner. You're moving straight ahead and then suddenly the road disappears. Or you do.

The movie costars Ryan Gosling as her husband, who undergoes a Jekyll-and-Hyde transformation, and Frank Langella as his controlling father who owns sleazy Forty-second Street real estate. Dunst's character ends up being married to a stranger. He was a rich kid from Manhattan, they lived a rural idyll in Vermont, and when they moved back to the city, it fell apart.

"When you're enmeshed in a relationship with someone who's so dark, you start to become crazy and dark yourself," she told me. "She was powerful in her own darkness, and I feel like toward the end she wants to kill him inside—just as much as what the real end result was, that he may have killed her."

In real life, the husband has never been charged in connection with her disappearance.

"Whatever happened," she said, "he had something to do with it. I think that if someone is capable of dismembering one person's body, he's certainly capable of murdering someone else. If your daughter-in-law or your wife went missing and you had the money to do whatever you could to go find her, you'd be more proactive. You wouldn't wait a couple of days before you reported her missing to the police."

The film, based on the real-life stories of Robert and Kathie Durst, was directed by Andrew Jarecki, who made the 2003 documentary *Capturing the Friedmans.* That was a film about a family with almost unbelievable secrets. The father and one son were cooperating in the sexual abuse of children, and went undetected for years.

"Andrew and I spent a long time kind of getting into the psychological reasoning for what made her stay in the marriage," Dunst told me in a telephone interview. "Andrew really understands family dynamics, especially the darker side of a family. *In Capturing the Friedmans* and also in this, you have really intense pressures to do what's expected of you. Andrew himself is from a pretty wealthy family and didn't want to go down the path his father wanted him to go down. I think that Andrew understands the real psychological issues within the family unit and how dark they can be."

Dunst will stay on the dark side in her new film, *Melancholia*, by Lars von Trier. It's a science-fiction thriller also starring Charlotte Gainsbourg, who, you will recall, survived the ordeal of *Antichrist*, in which she was an Eve cast out of Paradise. Von Trier, now in postproduction, is keeping plot details of the new film a secret.

"I did talk to Charlotte, actually, a little bit about *Antichrist*," Dunst said, "but I know it was a very emotional, difficult film for her to do. Working with Lars for me was a very wonderful experience. He creates an environment that leaves you with a lot of freedom. He shoots very quickly and even shoots the rehearsals, and it all feels very free. There are no big lighting setups or anything like that, so you really can say it's an intense process for eight hours; there's no big breaks or anything like that, so it keeps the fluidity of the performance on this continual cycle that doesn't break and can make things feel so much more real. We got to improvise a lot. It was very freeing for me."

Also coming out in 2011: *On the Road*, with Dunst joining a cast that reads like a collection of beat images: Steve Buscemi, Kristen Stewart, Viggo Mortensen, Terrence Howard, Amy Adams. The adaptation of Jack Kerouac's American classic road novel will be directed by Brazil's Walter Salles, who made *The Motorcycle Diaries* (2004) about another on-the-roader, Che Guevara.

Robert Redford

April 10, 2011—Who was the first person brought to trial and faced with the death penalty for the assassination of Abraham Lincoln? Most people can be forgiven for thinking it was John Wilkes Booth. They would be mistaken. It was a woman named Mary Surratt, whose connection with the plot against Lincoln remains a matter of debate.

Robert Redford had read a lot about Lincoln, and he knew that Booth, in fact, was never tried at all, but was shot by a Union soldier twelve days after he fled from Ford's Theatre. But he hadn't heard about Mary Surratt, the subject of his new film *The Conspirator*. She was the mother of John Surratt, who met with Booth and others in the Washington boardinghouse she owned. Did she know what they were planning? Was she a co-conspirator?

That's the question at the center of this historical drama, which contrasts her constitutional rights with the desire of Northerners to see someone—almost anyone—found guilty for the crime.

Robin Wright plays Mary Surratt, and Kevin Kline plays Lincoln's power-hungry secretary of war, Edwin Stanton, who pushed for a quick trial. The story is seen through the eyes of her young attorney, Frederick Aiken (James McAvoy), who, as a Union soldier, wants nothing to do with the trial, and is ordered to defend her by the solicitor general.

"I didn't know anything about this until I got the script," Redford told me on the afternoon of the movie's Chicago premiere. "That's what was intriguing. I thought, oh, this is about Lincoln, and that's a road well traveled. But it was the story of Mary Surratt, and I thought, I can get interested in telling a story that people don't know about associated with an event that everybody knows about."

Although Redford will forever be best known as an actor, he has directed eight films and won an Oscar for directing *Ordinary People* (1980). His films have all had particularly American themes; consider *The Milagro Beanfield War*, *A River Runs Through It*, *Quiz Show*, *The Horse Whisperer*, and *The Legend of Bagger Vance*.

The script was written by historian James D. Solomon and came to Redford as the first production of the new American Film Company, started by Omaha billionaire Joe Ricketts, who is also the new owner of the Chicago Cubs. That explains why on the day after the premiere, Redford threw out the first pitch at the Cubs opener.

"Joe wanted to take some of his money and create movies about American history," Redford explained. "Jim Solomon spent fourteen years on this project. All through those years, no one would make this film because they felt Civil War period pieces aren't commercial unless they have a big battle scene. But Joe Rickets put it forward. It's nice to have an independently financed film. On the other hand, he's a businessman, and it was very low-budget. So you have to create Washington, DC, with no money."

What Redford did was go to Savannah, Georgia:

"Ironically, that was the only city in America where we could film Washington in 1865. It was the only city that still had the infrastructure, like the town squares the way they were in those days. We had to put mud and dirt in the streets, and we had to take away all the electrical signs, and we took a small warehouse to create Ford's Theatre. There was a lot of hard work on production design and costumes, and things came together very fast on very little money.

"We spent a lot of time on the palette. I got excited by the idea that in those days, there was no electricity so there was only gas, torch, lantern, and candle, so we experimented with that. The faces of actors when they were in it were almost translucent."

Details surrounding Mary Surratt's case will inevitably remind many viewers of the current controversy about how best to try the Guantanamo prisoners charged with the 9/11 conspiracy.

"Everybody knows the assassination," he said, "but inside that frame is a story that very few people know about. The injustice of Mary Surratt's trial as it relates to our own Constitution was that she was tried by a military tribunal rather than at a civic trial. That wasn't the sole reason for making the movie; that was a good one, but I would not be able to make it unless I could find an emotional core within that story. And that existed with the representation of Frederick Aiken, the lawyer, and because he didn't want the case. He was a Union soldier having to defend a Southern woman whom he thought was guilty. She wasn't going to give him any leeway because she thought he was against her. But he realized the Constitution was under threat, and to me that was the story.

"When you talk about parallels, well, the parallels are there, they're obvious, but it's not for me to point them out. I'm focused on another story, and that's the emotional relationship between the two of them, which takes no political sides whatsoever. How can you not see Guantanamo, how can you not see the Patriot Act, how can you not see habeas corpus being threatened? But I'm not telling that story. That's for people to find out on their own."

What do you think? I asked him. Was Mary Surratt a conspirator?

"No one really knows. The fact was, she ran a boardinghouse, the conspirators met there, her son was one of the conspirators, and certainly she knew. That I do believe. How much she was actually a part of the assassination nobody knows, and neither do I. But I like that; I like the fact that it was never even proven.

"Nobody knows because of the nature of the trial and the way things happened so quickly. The secretary of war, Stanton, says, 'I want these people buried and forgotten quick.' So the trial was rushed.

"Kevin Kline was a little nervous in the beginning, playing such a heavy. I said, 'He's a great heavy because he has a point of view that's totally justifiable.' The country was in such danger at that time of falling apart. A unity that had just been formed was now under threat of breaking apart again; there could be an insurgency from the South that could come into Washington. He had to take control, he had to be strong, he had to be powerful. Very strong similarities to 9/11.

"And so you gotta act quickly, you gotta be bold, you gotta be strong. That's your duty and the belief that the American people want that; that gets into gray territory, but you totally respect the fact that he felt he had to get order quickly. So I wanted that point of view expressed in the movie so those people would understand that no matter how awful he may have been, things he did, that there was a point of view behind it that was understandable."

Robin Wright plays Mary as a woman of a certain degree of stoicism, I said. Another approach might have been to show her as more emotional.

"What was she left with, after all? She was left with nothing but her own integrity, her own pride. So no, I didn't want a bleeding emotionality. It really was, if you wanna boil it all down, I mean, down, down, down to, it was about a mother's love for her son."

Justin Timberlake

October 29, 2010—If he hadn't been selling millions of records when Napster came along, Justin Timberlake thinks he might have been one of its users. Napster was a Web service allowing music fans to rip and exchange their own recordings without observing the niceties of royalties and copyrights, and it inspired a celebrated court battle with users charged as thieves and pirates.

"When Napster hit the scene, I was nineteen or twenty," he told me. "I had mixed feelings about it because I was the same age as all of those college kids that ended up playing the role of defendants in court. Had I not been in the music industry, I probably would have used it. At the same time, I was watching friends in the industry who were songwriters and were forced to take up new jobs. All they do is write songs. They don't have endorsement deals or sold-out shows. They were getting a small piece of the collective pie."

There is an irony, then, to be found in Timberlake playing the role of Sean Parker, the mercurial founder of Napster, in David Fincher's *The Social Network*, one of this year's Academy Award front-runners. The movie is based on the story of Mark Zuckerberg, who launched Facebook as a Harvard undergraduate and soon saw it become a phenomenon. The real Parker had a similar experience with Napster, and materialized in Zuckerberg's life as a Svengali of the fast lane.

The Social Network is on all the lists of Oscar contenders, and Timberlake is often mentioned as a best supporting actor candidate. Justin Timberlake? The perennial Trending Topic on Twitter? Yes, and why not? In one of the best films of the year, he provides a crucial performance, and he does it with confidence, bravado, and heedless energy. It's acting. It is also perhaps like nothing many Timberlake watchers expected, but there you have it: Many performers have talents we never see because they stay within the parameters of their early fame.

For Timberlake, fame was not launched at the Actor's Studio or at Juilliard, but on *Star Search*, when he was eleven. That led to stardom of sorts on *The Mickey Mouse Club*, and then big time when he became the lead singer of 'N Sync. Then he went solo and started winning Grammys and going platinum, and—well, nothing at that point could have predicted his casting as Sean Parker in *The Social Network*.

Parker is a difficult role. Mark Zuckerberg is played by Jesse Eisenberg as a super-intelligent geek who likes to bash people in conversation. Parker sees him and raises him. This requires an actor with a lot of confidence and agility. Eisenberg, at twenty-seven, is very experienced. Timberlake, at twenty-nine, is new to the front ranks of feature films, with all due respect to *The Love Guru* and *Black Snake Moan*. Yet he embodies the Parker role and sells it persuasively. His Parker is a devious manipulator with a private agenda and an instinct for personal openings. He's a spellbinder. The choice of Timberlake is not only good casting by David Fincher and his casting director, Laray Mayfield, but good casting out of left field.

The Zuckerberg-Parker exchanges are often in a rapid-fire tempo that evokes screwball comedies. I asked if that took a lot of rehearsal.

"Our rehearsal process was, in fact, all talking," he said. "We never once got up from the table. We would go through the scene, just reading it. Then David Fincher, [writer] Aaron Sorkin, and the actors who were in the scene would just sit and talk about what our characters were looking to accomplish in each moment.

"For a character like Sean, who was so brilliantly constructed by Aaron, the overall goal was intact. His most convincing trait, as a value for me (and not without irony), was just how literally convincing he could be to a guy like Mark. And when you have the opportunity to do a large number of takes like David likes to do, the dialogue becomes such a part of you. It makes it easier to rattle off a few pages of poetry. Yes, I just referred to Aaron's dialogue as poetry."

I have an additional theory. Later in our e-mail exchange, Timberlake mentioned: "I come from a family of people that THINK that they are really funny. If it was up to my family, I would be doing comedies forever."

To be funny, you have to be smart, think fast, talk fast, and have flawless timing. Those are Sean Parker attributes. Maybe Timberlake began to form them doing stand-up in the family living room.

Judging by photos of the real Zuckerberg and Parker, Timberlake looks something like each of them. "But I sense the Parker role was closer to your inner rhythms," I said. "Wrong?"

"The script was its own song, really," he said. "The rhythm of this film was SO established by Sorkin. He laid the foundation of this world of hyper-smart college kids. I can't think of a writer working today that could have done a more masterful job. If you're asking about which role I would have preferred? Parker. Hands down. The way that character was written was just too much fun.

"But I felt like these two characters probably suffered from the same fears and insecurities. They both invented something to connect with the world comfortably, too. Mark invented Facebook. Sean invented Sean Parker."

I gather no one in the movie met Zuckerberg. Did you meet or did you already know Parker?

"I met him briefly in New York. At the time, I hadn't been cast in the film, but it was speculated that I might be playing the role. We spoke for a second and he seemed like a really nice guy."

I observed that Parker has dialogue where he brags that he brought the music industry to its knees, and put record stores out of business. There's some irony in a multimillion-album seller like Timberlake saying this dialogue, yes?

"To be honest, it really didn't hit me until I screened the film for the first time. When you are embodying a character, you believe every part of what they are feeling and saying and doing. It could have been the iPod that he invented. It was more important for me to find out why he was bragging about it, I felt. I think any bravado that came out of the character was a safety mechanism to hide all of the darker parts of him. But, in my personal opinion, I think it takes more than one person to bring down something like the music industry. Much like it took more than one person to make Facebook a billion-dollar company."

You were a gifted kid who basically overnight found himself a star and then a mogul. Same story with Sean Parker and Mark Zuckerberg. Were there Parker figures in your early career?

"The music industry is full of them. I'll leave it at that."

John Waters

December 7, 2010—The notion of a Christmas show by John Waters is somehow alarming, as if the Big Bad Wolf had decided to perform as the Easter Bunny. Waters has made a career of cheerfully exploiting the transgressive and offensive. He appeared at Chicago's Harris Theater on December 14, 2010, promising to discuss such questions as whether Santa Claus is erotic, whether it's a gay holiday, and why stars on Christmas tours always seem to go crazy onstage when they get to Baltimore.

"My vaudeville show," he calls his performance: "I'm always hoping that my career can end in Baltimore, so I can have a nervous Christmas breakdown onstage in the tradition of Judy Garland."

I've seen him in performance once earlier, with his tribute to the exploitation film pioneer William Castle. Reproducing Castle's promotional stunts, Waters had fake ghosts fly over the audience, stationed a nurse in the lobby to care for anyone who collapsed from fright, and activated buzzers under seats after warning that the Tingler might escape from the screen and crawl under the feet of the audience.

He takes his shows seriously. When I told him he comes across as conversational, he said, "That's a compliment. Every single word is written and rehearsed. However, people think I'm just up there riffing and talking."

Waters has had success making what he calls "exploitation films for art houses." His classics include *Pink Flamingos, Hairspray, Polyester*, and *Cry-Baby*, and his stars have ranged from Johnny Depp and Patricia Hearst to the three-hundred-pound transvestite Divine. He feels some regret that his movies were too funny to play in real grind houses: "To my great shame, they never would have worked at the Loop Theatre in Chicago, my favorite-ever exploitation theater, which played *Vixen* twenty-four hours a day at one point. Because those audiences did not want irony."

Some people have fetishes. I think fetishes themselves are John Waters's fetish. Instead of being turned on by high heels, leather, or rubber, he's turned on by people who are turned on by fetishes, preferably the strangest possible. In his new book *Role Models*, which I read with steadily mounting fascination, the first chapter is about Johnny Mathis, a singer he became fixated on when very young, and finally interviewed for the book.

"I just went to see Johnny Mathis two weeks ago when he was back in Baltimore, first time I'd seen him since the book," he told me, "and he was so hilarious. He joked, 'Oh, you made me famous again.' Really made me laugh because nobody's more famous than Johnny Mathis."

I asked, "Are you more in love with Johnny Mathis, or with the idea of Johnny Mathis?" We were communicating via telephone.

"I'm always in love with the idea of something more than the reality, because then you can't be disappointed. When I say that I stalked Johnny Mathis, I didn't mean it as a boyfriend; I meant it as the fan for all the wrong reasons that I hoped he would take it in the right way, and he did. But the idea of something being such a big influence on me is always the strongest attraction. I never can decide if it's torture to be Johnny Mathis, or great freedom. And everything in my book is about people surviving and leading a more extreme life than I have."

Although he's been a successful professional for years, Waters at sixty-four still has something of the fanboy about him:

"I still go to see movies in movie theaters the Friday they open, and read the reviews that night. I never watch DVDs, and I never watch television. I'm still really old school; I like the art films, I like the foreign films, I like the weirdo ones. I mean, the only magazine that asks me to write my ten best every year is *Artforum.* And I write it for the exact audience that I think would like the movies I like best. This year I liked *Buried* and I liked *Jackass 3-D.* I think *Jackass 3-D* is the only movie in the spirit of my *Pink Flamingos* and my really early films; I think Johnny Knoxville is making his movies in the same spirit that we were making them when we were kids."

Although everyone assumed John Waters was gay, for years he seemed to follow an informal DADT policy. In the new book, he's open and frank about his sexuality, but not Gay PC, if there's such a thing:

"I don't fit in with gay people, either. I'm gaily incorrect. I kinda want gay people to be outlaws again. I don't wanna get married, but I certainly believe that people have the right to be married. I never fit in. There's too many rules in the gay world, too. So if I ever talk about my homosexuality, which I certainly do, I don't do it in a very gaily correct way. I think people should hang around with gay, straight, everybody, completely mixed. Many of my friends are straight. It's just as much fun to me. I don't wanna hang around with everyone that's exactly like me. I went to a wedding in Chicago between a straight man and a straight woman, but they had a gay commitment ceremony, a bad one on purpose—like a bad separatist female folk singer and bad gay music, and it was really good. The relatives were confused."

And for your Christmas show, what will surprise people?

"I talk about how it's even sometimes good to get sticks and stones, and what kind to get."

Oprah Winfrey

May 18, 2011—To borrow a line from *Citizen Kane,* I knew Oprah before the beginning, and now I know her after the end. Her taping of two farewell shows on May 17 at Chicago's United Center brings to a close the most phenomenal run of any talk show host in history, and rings down the curtain on the second act of a life that seems poised to have many more. What lies ahead? Her new cable network, we know. But I suspect she also has a future in high public office.

Gene Siskel and I met Oprah in Baltimore, when she was in her early twenties and hosting a morning talk show. Then she moved to ABC/7 in Chicago, went up against the ruling Phil Donahue, dethroned him in three months, and went on to become a superstar with (for some) elements of Earth mother and deity.

Curious about some of the feelings she was having at this time, I sent Oprah some questions. These are her replies:

RE: The novel *Miss Lonelyhearts* was about the author of an advice column who began to crumble under the weight of his reader's problems. How do you survive the depth of suffering of some of your guests?

OW: I used to take in and *feel everything.* I could literally feel people's energy. Their nervousness. Anxiety, pain. Years ago I complained to the executive producer how feeling everyone's pain was making me sick. And she replied, "Then, you need to stop doing that." So I did. I made a conscious effort to listen and not absorb the pain. Not take it on, but hear it, empathize, and *let it go.*

RE: I believe you started out with a career

and ended up with a vocation. If you agree with that at all, did the transition catch you rather by surprise?

OW: Very much so. Everyone would be surprised at how little I knew about ANYthing when I first came to Chicago. Every decision was made on instinct.

RE: Your Chicago shows began with the standard TV morning show studio format. Today I can't imagine your program without a studio audience. How did the studio audience evolve, and how do you relate to it?

OW: I was accustomed to an audience, though tiny (twenty-four), in Baltimore. I was so thrilled to have the *AM Chicago* job, I forgot to ask my boss, Dennis Swanson, "What is the format? And do you have an audience?" After the first day with no audience we started asking the secretaries to sit in on folding chairs. Then expanded to going on State Street and begging people to come in, "get warm and watch the show." I knew I worked better connecting to real people in front of me. It felt more like sharing the experience rather than being the experience.

RE: Do you monitor your behavior because you are such an influential model for so many people? Many celebrities lead appalling lives. Not you.

OW: Nope. Fame is such an interesting dynamic. It's determined by other people's view of you. I became famous for being myself. I'd be the same self no matter what I was doing. For many years I thought I'd be a teacher. And had visions of getting the teacher of the year award.

RE: Will the Oprah Network broaden out from health and counseling sorts of programs to include news, sitcoms, movies, reality shows?

OW: I want to create programming 24/7 that wakes people up. And use whatever format it takes to do it.

RE: On TV, I saw you weeping at Grant Park during Obama's speech. I sensed at that moment something more than simply joy. I felt something very deep within you had been accessed.

OW: For sure. There's a Negro spiritual, "Wouldn't Take Nothin' for My Journey Now." I was thinking about the journey. His and mine and the collective ours; the sacrifices and prayers, marches, sit-ins, and lynchings. I was thinking about my grandmother, who spent her whole life in acceptance of segregation and oppression not imagining it could be any other way. I was thinking of Martin L. King and the countless others who dared believe it could. I was thinking of the spiritual and emotional impact of his victory on the world.

RE: At the movies, I think many people cry more when they see goodness than when they see sadness. Why is that?

OW: Because we are innately good, and the goodness we see that makes us cry is just a mirror of ourselves. Hits our goodness nerve.

RE: You have created your own environment and never been absorbed into "showbiz" in the sense we associate with the coasts. Did Chicago help your focus?

OW: Chicago represented the very heart of America. If I'd moved the show to L.A., the energy of showbiz would have impacted the show. The "let's do lunch" crowd, agents, wheeling, manipulating, and negotiating. Producers would have had to deal with all of that instead of the steady focus and sacrifice that was required to keep raising the bar for ourselves.

RE: Gene Siskel's invariable question: What do you know for sure?

OW: I know for sure that the third law of motion in physics is real and is the rule of the world: For every action there is an equal and opposite reaction. Being responsible for the energy you put out determines the energy returned. Or to quote Celie, as she finally summoned the courage to leave Mister, in *The Color Purple,* "Everything you even try to do to me, already done to you!"

RE: What do you think happens after death?

OW: You drop your body, and your soul joins the spiritual chorus of *all* there is. Many levels in the chorus. Where you stand in the chorus line is determined by how you live now. I think that Holly Hunter's last words in the movie *The Piano,* when she's sinking to the depths of the ocean with the chain unraveling from the boat, will be true for all of us: "Death. What a surprise!"

In Memoriam

Jill Clayburgh

November 8, 2010—I don't believe Jill Clayburgh would have approved of the headline over her obituary in the *New York Times*, which stated she "starred in feminist roles." They were roles. They were real roles, for a real woman. How did that make them feminist?

Miss Clayburgh, who died Friday at sixty-six, was one of the great stars of the 1970s and 1980s. She was named best actress at Cannes for *An Unmarried Woman* (1978), which won her great acclaim, but her other best role, in *Shy People* (1987), went sadly overlooked.

She was in many other notable movies, including *Starting Over* (1979), which won her second Oscar nomination in two years, and *First Monday in October* (1981), playing the first woman on the U.S. Supreme Court, and although she dealt with leukemia for twenty-one years, she continued to work in movies and on TV, and appears in the 2010 movie *Love and Other Drugs*.

An Unmarried Woman was her breakthrough role. She'd been in the box office disaster *Gable and Lombard* and two comedies, *Silver Streak* and *Semi-Tough*, neither of which offered much opportunity for an actress. Paul Mazursky, the writer and director of *An Unmarried Woman*, told me he cast her on a hunch.

"I had a choice," he said at the time, drinking coffee in his office at Twentieth Century Fox. "I could go with one of the known star actresses, maybe someone like Jane Fonda. Or I could go with a hunch." The hunch was Jill Clayburgh. "I'd had her read for me on two previous films, *Blume in Love* and *Greenwich Village*. She'd read terrifically both times. But both times I wound up casting someone else. And in the work she had done in films, she'd never really come across as well as she'd read for me.

"Some friends saw her on TV, in *Hustling*, based on that Gail Sheehy book. They said she was good. I asked her to come in and read again. She was good. I cast her as my lead. She turned out to be better than I could possibly have expected."

The film became a career milestone for Clayburgh, who was nominated for an Oscar (Fonda won, for *Coming Home*). She won the hearts of audiences right at the beginning. Alone in bed, she hears *Swan Lake* on the radio, and leaps from the bed and dances around the living room in a T-shirt and panties, and before we've quite realized what's happened, she became a star.

In 1987 she filmed *Shy People* for director Andre Konchalovsky, costarring with Barbara Hershey and Martha Plimpton. She played a New York magazine writer who convinces her editor to let her write about her family roots. The assignment takes her into Louisiana bayou country, where she and her daughter (Plimpton) discover a long-lost cousin living in poverty. In one night sequence, Clayburgh is neck-deep in swamp water and has a possible mystical experience. It is one of the great overlooked films.

She worked steadily in movies, on the stage and on TV, where she played Ally's mother on *Ally McBeal*. In 1978 she married the playwright David Rabe, and is survived by her husband, a daughter, Lily Rabe, also an actress; a son, Michael; a stepson, Jason; and a brother, James. Death came at her home in Lakeville, Connecticut.

Tony Curtis

October 1, 2010—When his handsome face and a stroke of luck brought Tony Curtis to Hollywood in 1948, he was twenty-three years old and felt as if he was in heaven. That wasn't because of the acting opportunities. It was because of the women, and Tony was one of the town's best-known lotharios for decades. He loved acting, too, and made great films and bad ones with the same sense of fun. He was also a lifelong artist, whose paintings commanded decent fees, and a party animal until he got clean and sober in 1982. One thing you will not notice in the obituaries is anyone with a bad word to say about him. He was fun, and few had more fun than he did himself.

Curtis, born Bernard Schwartz in 1925

and raised in poverty and in an orphanage, finished navy duty in World War II, took acting lessons in New York, and in 1948 was spotted by a talent agent and signed by Universal Pictures. He was one of the most beautiful men to ever appear in the movies, and stardom came quickly. One day in 1985 at the Cannes Film Festival, he told me of those days:

"Let me tell you a story, sort of a parable. One day in 1948, I went to Hollywood. My name was Bernie Schwartz. I signed a contract at Universal, and I bought a house in the hills. It had a swimming pool. Unheated, but it had water in it. One night I came home late, I jumped in the pool, I swam a few laps, I got out, I dried myself off, I put on my clothes, and I walked directly into this room and sat down and started to talk to you. Do you see what I'm saying? Thirty-eight years, I don't know where they went. Gone like that."

He made four pictures that can certainly be called great, and was crucial to the success of all four: *Some Like It Hot*, *Sweet Smell of Success*, *Spartacus*, and *The Defiant Ones*, for which he received an Oscar nomination. He made perhaps sixty others, some of them huge successes, others best forgotten. He worked on all of them with boundless energy. In an earlier conversation at Cannes 1982, he informed me he was trying to think of a better title for his new movie. The current title was *Othello, the Black Commando.*

"What do you think about *The Othello Conspiracy*? he asked. How about *The Othello File*? *The Othello Connection*?" It was an action picture based on the Shakespeare tragedy. "My name is Colonel Iagovich," he said. "Get it?"

This conversation took place in the suite of the overnight mogul Menahem Golan, whose Cannon Group would distribute the film. From the second floor of the Carlton Hotel, he commanded a view of the sidewalk. Suddenly he jumped to his feet and pressed his nose against the glass.

"Will ya look at the build on that lady!" he shouted. He pushed the curtain aside. "There—the one with the blonde hair and the leopard-skin leotard! See her?" I did not. "Standing in the middle of the intersection, chewing the hell out of that guy? Jesus, I got great eyes!" he said.

Menahem was not impressed. "She's coming this way!" Curtis reported. He moved to another window. An overstuffed chair was in his way. He hurdled the chair. He opened the French doors leading to the balcony and shouted: "*Mon petit*! *Mon petit*! Yoo-hoo! Up here! Come up here, *mon petit*. Up here. Room 241! Two four one!"

The thing about Curtis was, here was a truly great star, a legend, who had a big libido but not a big ego. How many other movie stars would pull up their shirt in a restaurant to show you their scar from heart surgery?

Once, Wolfgang Puck hung an exhibition of Curtis's paintings in his original Spago on Sunset Boulevard. Puck and the director Billy Wilder, who directed *Some Like It Hot*, were both from Vienna and loved talking with each other. One night, Puck told me, he had Billy, a famed art collector, get up and inspect some of the paintings.

"Billy looked at one," Puck said, "and all he said was, 'Lousy actor, lousy painter.' Then he turns around and Tony was standing right there. He doesn't miss a beat. 'Oh, hello Tony,' he says. 'I knew all along you were standing right there.'"

Many people liked his paintings. He wasn't a lousy actor, but he often suffered because of his material. He would joke about bad reviews, but one really stung. It wasn't a review, really, but a myth that grew famous over the years. That was the story that in *The Black Shield of Falworth* his Bronx accent had him saying, "Yonder lies dah castle of my faddah."

"I never said 'Yonder lies da castle of my faddah!'" he told me. "That line has become part of the folklore. You go to see the movie, listen for yourself. What I said was, clear as day, 'father.' See, I was born Bernie Schwartz. I'm a Hungarian Jew from Brooklyn. So they thought I had to pronounce it 'faddah,' because it fit their stereotype. Lawrence Olivier was in the same picture, but nobody thinks he ever mispronounced anything in his whole life."

Actually, Lord Olivier costarred with Curtis only in *Spartacus*, but I got the point.

Bernie Schwartz from Brooklyn, and Tony Curtis from Hollywood died Wednesday, September 29, 2010, at his home near Las Vegas. He was eighty-five. His sixth wife, the horse trainer Jill VandenBerg, was at his side. Together they supported a refuge for abandoned horses in Nevada.

In addition to his wife, Mr. Curtis's survivors include two daughters with Janet Leigh, his first wife: Kelly Lee Curtis and the actress Jamie Lee Curtis. Also Alexandra Curtis and Allegra Curtis, daughters with his wife Christine Kaufmann; and a son, Benjamin Curtis, with his wife Leslie Allen.

Blake Edwards

December 17, 2010—Blake Edwards, the man who gave us Inspector Clouseau, *Breakfast at Tiffany's*, and a perfect *10*, is dead at eighty-eight. A much-loved storyteller and the writer of many of his own films, he was a bit of a performer himself. He directed thirty-eight features and much TV, and was married for the past forty-one years to Julie Andrews, who was at his side when he died. Beginning in the late '40s, he rose through the ranks of television and low-budget movies and produced, wrote, and directed the *Peter Gunn* series. His first great screen success was *Breakfast at Tiffany's* (1961), Audrey Hepburn's iconic role. *Days of Wine and Roses* came in 1962, and provided Jack Lemmon and Lee Remick with two of their best roles.

In 1963 and 1964 came two enormously successful comedies, *The Pink Panther* and *A Shot in the Dark*, beginning his long collaboration with Peter Sellers as the inimitable Clouseau, murderer of the English language. The series had outstayed its welcome by the time Edwards cobbled together the ungainly *Trail of the Pink Panther* (1982) after Sellers's death, using outtakes, doubles, and dubbing.

The honeymoon between Edwards and Sellers faded earlier, although the pictures continued to make money. Sellers was lovable in public but enigmatic in private. "He just got bored with the part," Edwards once said. "He became angry, sullen, and unprofessional. He wouldn't show up for work."

After the 1979 blockbuster *10*, which made Bo Derek an international sex symbol, came *Victor/Victoria* (1982), with a plot only Edwards could have devised: Julie Andrews played a woman playing a man who was forced to become a female impersonator. James Garner falls in love with her, or perhaps him.

Edwards's comedies often embraced farce, perhaps never so boldly as in *Skin Deep* (1989), with an outrageous scene that involved a sort of sword fight taking place in pitch darkness, with dueling glow-in-the-dark condoms.

Edwards and Andrews worked together frequently, bringing *Victor/Victoria* to Broadway in 1995, although their big-budget film musical *Darling Lili* was a notable flop.

In later years they both faced health troubles. Andrews, who was thirteen years younger than her husband, had surgery for benign throat nodules in 1997, which affected her singing voice. Edwards had problems after knee surgery last year, and was confined to a wheelchair. His publicist, Gene Schwam, said the death, at St. John's Health Center in Santa Monica, California, was caused by complications from pneumonia.

His life was filled with laughter, its end, shadowed by illness. He remained productive as long as he could. As Inspector Clouseau once observed, in words written by Edwards, "There is a time to laugh and a time not to laugh, and this is not one of them."

Sidney Lumet

April 11, 2011—Sidney Lumet was one of the finest craftsmen and warmest humanitarians among all film directors. He was not only a great artist but a much loved man. When the news of his death at eighty-six arrived on Saturday, April 9, it came as a shock, because he had continued so long to be so productive.

Of his final film, *Before the Devil Knows You're Dead* (2007), I wrote: "This is a movie, I promise you, that grabs you and won't let you think of anything else. It's wonderful when a director like Lumet wins a Lifetime Achievement Oscar at eighty, and three years later makes one of his greatest achievements." Like many of his films, it went on my list of the year's ten best.

Although he was not as widely known to the general public as directors such as Scorsese, Spielberg, Eastwood, and Spike Lee, his films were at the center of our collective memories. To name only a few of their titles is to suggest the measure of his gift:

Network. Dog Day Afternoon. 12 Angry Men. Serpico. Prince of the City. The Pawnbroker.

Fail-Safe. Long Day's Journey into Night. The Verdict.

Most of his films were set in his native New York City. Although he was nominated four times as best director, he never won an Academy Award until his honorary Oscar; that may have been partly because he was not part of the Hollywood community, but preferred a milieu he understood inside out.

He was a thoughtful director, who gathered the best collaborators he could find and channeled their resources into a focused vision. He shared his thoughts about that in his 1996 book, *Making Movies.* If you care to read only one book about the steps in the making of a film, make it that one. There is not a boast in it, not a word of idle puffery. It is all about the work.

To say he lacked a noticeable visual style is a compliment. He reduced every scene to its necessary elements and filmed them, he liked to say, "invisibly." You should not be thinking about the camera. He wanted you to think about the characters and the story.

Sidney Lumet was born June 25, 1924, in Philadelphia, the son of Polish immigrants who were actors in the Yiddish theater. The boy was onstage from his earliest years. After service in World War II, he began to direct in small New York companies and then moved in on the ground floor in the new medium of television.

Lumet, like such contemporaries as Arthur Penn and John Frankenheimer, was a key director in the golden age of live TV drama. He was an early director for Walter Cronkite's *You Are There.* His first feature was *12 Angry Men,* considered the best of all filmed dramas about a criminal trial. It had a visual style (he slowly lowered the point of view as tension increased), but, typically, audiences were not aware of it.

In 1962 he filmed a historic adaptation of Eugene O'Neill's *Long Day's Journey into Night,* and in 1964 helped launch Rod Steiger's movie career with *The Pawnbroker.* Film followed film, many of them based on ethical issues, although he preferred to deeply embody his messages instead of stating them obviously.

Other strong films followed. In addition to his most famous titles, these had my special admiration: *Daniel, Power, Q&A, Critical Care,* and *Gloria.* He remained remarkably youthful, and in 2006 was able to see the serious dramatic potential of Vin Diesel, dismissed as an action star, and use it for a remarkable performance in *Find Me Guilty,* the story of a Mafioso trial.

Lumet was married four times, to the actress Rita Gam; the heiress Gloria Vanderbilt; Gail Jones, daughter of Lena Horne; and, in 1980, to Mary Gimbel, who survives him. He is also survived by Amy and Jenny Lumet, his daughters by Jones; a stepson, Bailey Gimbel, and stepdaughter, Leslie Gimbel; nine grandchildren and a great-granddaughter. Jenny Lumet went into the family business, as an actress and the author of the award-winning screenplay for Jonathan Demme's *Rachel Getting Married* (2008).

The cause of death, his wife said, was lymphoma. The tears shed at his memorial services will be genuine.

Arthur Penn

September 29, 2010—Arthur Penn, whose *Bonnie and Clyde* was a watershed in American film, died Tuesday, September 28, 2010, at eighty-eight. Gentle, much loved, and widely gifted, he began life in poverty and turned World War II acting experience in the army into a career that led to directing in the earliest days of television and included much work on Broadway.

He was the man who cued Milton Berle to become "Uncle Miltie." A pioneer of live TV drama, his direction of *The Miracle Worker* with Patricia McCormack and Teresa Wright was a milestone. His *Two for the Seesaw* with Henry Fonda and Anne Bancroft was a Broadway hit in 1958.

But his Hollywood debut, *The Left-Handed Gun,* with Paul Newman as Billy the Kid, was a flop. His film *The Miracle Worker* was a success, but his next one, the avant-garde *Mickey One* (1965), with Warren Beatty as a Chicago nightclub comic, laid an egg.

After that film, Beatty was written off as a has-been in a celebrated Rex Reed profile for *Esquire.* Penn had trouble finding work. The two teamed up on *Bonnie and Clyde,* an unusual script by David Newman and Robert Benton; Faye Dunaway costarred in the story of two Depression-era bank robbers. Warner

Bros. mogul Jack Warner saw it and hated it. Legend has it Warner planned to dump it in Texas drive-ins until Beatty got on his knees before him and begged him to allow it to open at the August 1967 Montreal Film Festival.

There, disaster seemed to strike in the form of an angry review by the influential Bosley Crowther of the *New York Times*, who hated it. So did Joe Morgenstern of *Newsweek*, but he famously changed his mind in a later review. When it opened in Chicago, I wrote on September 15, 1967: "This is pretty clearly the best American film of the year. It is also a landmark. Years from now it is quite possible that *Bonnie and Clyde* will be seen as the definitive film of the 1960s." I was right. On October 21, 1967, Pauline Kael praised it in a celebrated *New Yorker* review, her first for the magazine.

The film went on to make an explosive impact on American cinema, causing revolutions in both movies and fashion. "It was the French New Wave washing ashore in Hollywood," the writer-director Paul Schrader told me. Influenced by Truffaut's *Jules and Jim* (1962), it adopted an insouciant tone, combining violence and comedy in a way some viewers found offensive.

Bonnie and Clyde is the only film I know of that returned three times to first-run theaters in Chicago's Loop. The film's 1930s women's fashions came into style after Theodora van Runkle's dresses put *Bonnie and Clyde* on the cover of *Time* for the second time in a few months. And movies for decades after would be populated by Arthur Penn's supporting cast of Broadway actors making their film debuts: Gene Hackman, Michael J. Pollard, Estelle Parsons, and Gene Wilder.

In a London interview at the time, Beatty told me: "Out in the bush leagues, the theater owners, they read the *Times*. For them, Crowther is God. Everybody in the world can like a movie, and if Crowther doesn't, he kills it." Hollywood, he said, "is old, old, old." He posed a question. "I'm twenty-eight years old," he said. "I'll give you five seconds to name me another Hollywood leading man under the age of thirty-five."

After *Bonnie and Clyde* made its impact, Arthur Penn established himself in the top rank of American directors with such films as *Alice's Restaurant* (1969), *Little Big Man* (1970), and the great *Night Moves* with Gene Hackman in 1975. He had less success after that film.

And how did Milton Berle become Uncle Miltie, first superstar of American TV?

"My floor director in those days was Arthur Penn," Berle told me in Toronto in 1980. "He would squat under the camera and give me signals so I knew how much time I had left. One day I think the show is over and look down at Penn, and he's holding up eight fingers. That means I've got eight minutes to fill. I ran out of jokes and started talking to the kids: 'Time to go to bed, kiddies! Uncle Miltie says good night!'" It stuck.

Penn was born September 27, 1922, in Philadelphia. His parents divorced when he was three, and he and his brother, Irving (the famous photographer), lived with their mother in New York and New Jersey as she raised them in poverty. He is survived by his wife, the actress Peggy Mauer, a TV director son, Matthew, a daughter, Molly Penn, and four grandsons. His brother, Irving, died in 2009.

Elizabeth Taylor

March 23, 2011—Elizabeth Taylor, who was a great actress and a greater star, has died at seventy-nine. Of few deaths can it be said that they end an era, but hers does. No other actress commanded more attention for longer, for her work, her beauty, her private life, and a series of health problems that brought her near death more than once.

Death came Wednesday, March 23, 2011, at Cedars-Sinai Hospital in Los Angeles, where she had been hospitalized for six weeks with congestive heart failure. Her publicist, Sally Morrison, said in a statement: "Though she had recently suffered a number of complications, her condition had stabilized and it was hoped that she would be able to return home. Sadly, this was not to be."

Miss Taylor became a star in 1944 with the enduring classic *National Velvet*, although her unique camera presence had already registered onscreen in *Jane Eyre* in 1943, where as one of Jane's young friends she attracted attention. She worked in pictures steadily all her life; her final major starring role was in *Sweet Bird of Youth*, for television, in 1989, although she did some voice-over work, including the voice of Maggie Simpson in *The Simpsons* (1992). Her final onscreen performance was in *These Old Broads* (2001), also for TV, in which she played one of four aging actresses with Shirley MacLaine, Joan Collins, and Debbie Reynolds—significantly, the woman whose husband, Eddie Fisher, Miss Taylor was said to have "stolen" in 1959.

Elizabeth Taylor won Academy Awards for best actress for *Who's Afraid of Virginia Woolf?* (1967) and *Butterfield 8* (1961). She was nominated for *Raintree County* (1957), *Cat on a Hot Tin Roof* (1958), and *Suddenly, Last Summer* (1959). Other major film roles were in *A Place in the Sun* (1951), *Giant* (1956), *Father of the Bride* (1950), *Little Women* (1949), *Cleopatra* (1963), and *Reflections in a Golden Eye* (1967).

In 1993 she won the Academy's Jean Hersholt Humanitarian Award, partly in recognition of her formidable commitment to charity, and in 1999 was appointed Dame Commander of the Order of the British Empire. The BBC reported that although she was the first actress to earn $1 million for making a film, the money she raised for charity surpassed her lifetime earnings as an actress. After her friend Rock Hudson died of AIDS, she began the National AIDS Research Foundation, which later merged into the American Foundation for AIDS Research (AMFAR). Starting in 1985, the annual AMFAR auctions at the Cannes Film Festival became one of the world's largest charity events, with movie moguls bidding against billionaires and arms dealers for prizes that essentially amounted to bragging rights.

Miss Taylor was famously married eight times (twice to Richard Burton) and joked about it, once saying she didn't sleep with any more men than other actresses, but the difference was she married them.

Her first marriage came in 1950, at eighteen, to Conrad Hilton Jr., son of the hotel magnate. Her husband's drinking and physical cruelty put an end to that marriage in eight months. In 1952, she married the actor Michael Wilding, who was the father of her sons Michael Howard Wilding and Christopher Edward Wilding. In 1957 she married the impresario Mike Todd, who died in the 1958 crash of his private plane. They had a daughter, Elizabeth Francis, known as Liza. Todd's best friend was the singer Eddie Fisher, and as he and Taylor comforted each other their feelings blossomed into romance. Fisher left his wife, Debbie Reynolds, to marry Taylor, creating a scandal and setting the stage for her next great romance, when she left Fisher for Richard Burton after they met on the set of the tumultuous production of *Cleopatra* in 1960. That ended Burton's marriage with his wife, Sybil. Fisher, who'd made Debbie Reynolds a scorned wife, now became a scorned husband.

Taylor married Burton in 1964. As "Liz and Dick," the two arguably became the most famous couple in the world. Both passionate, both legendary, both known to drink in excess, they lived on the stage of world publicity. Both at the height of their earning power, they lavished gifts of jewelry upon each other, maintained a famous yacht, helped to define the term "jet set."

Their work together as a bickering couple with an imaginary child in Mike Nichols's *Who's Afraid of Virginia Woolf?* was fancied by some to reflect their own hard-drinking private reality. It was based on the celebrated play by Edward Albee, and the film, in stark black-and-white, won thirteen Oscar nominations, the only film ever to be nominated in every eligible category.

That film, plausibly the peak of Taylor's career, came a year before I began working as a film critic, and I never came into any real contact with her. I did, however, get a backstage glimpse of the Taylor–Burton dynamic in 1969, when he was filming *Anne of the Thousand Days* at Shepperton Studios outside London. They were scheduled to take their yacht to Wales the next day to witness Prince Charles invested as the Prince of Wales. In their dressing room a family reunion was under way, including her daughter, his daughter, and his sister. Elizabeth was showing off an enormous sapphire ring he had just given her.

Taylor didn't star in that film, but they worked together as a rule (their best from that period was Franco Zeffirelli's *The Taming of the Shrew*, in 1967). They were divorced in 1974, decided to remarry a year later, divorced again. Her next husband was John Warner, a handsome Republican from Virginia, and she added Washington to the social circles in which she glittered.

Although she continued to work here and there, Taylor had no need for money and devoted her main energies to charitable fundraising. Her presence at an AMFAR event was royal in tone. But she was never slow to poke fun at herself, and said she was immune to criticism. By the late 1980s she felt her drinking had gotten out of hand and checked into the Betty Ford Clinic in Rancho Mirage, California, where Larry Fortensky, a construction worker, was a fellow patient. They married, and although Fortensky was from a different world than Wilding, Todd, Fisher, Burton, and Warner, the marriage (performed at her friend Michael Jackson's Neverland Ranch) lasted five years.

Her life had been saved with an emergency tracheotomy in 1959 during a battle with pneumonia, and a brain tumor was found in the 1990s. In later years she was unable to walk easily because of back problems.

But oh, she was beautiful. The movie fan magazines celebrated her rare violet eyes, her famous double row of eyelashes, her voluptuous figure, her fiery spirit. Essentially raised in front of a camera, she was a gifted and versatile actress who held the screen against such figures as Spencer Tracy, Paul Newman, Mickey Rooney, Montgomery Clift, James Dean, and Burton.

The dominant actor of her time was Marlon Brando, and she appeared opposite him in one of her best, most overlooked films, John Huston's *Reflections in a Golden Eye* (1967). She played the domineering wife of Brando's closeted army major, in a story of adultery set on a southern military base. They both took big chances, but audiences didn't respond; perhaps they were such great stars they couldn't be accepted in an art film.

In 1965 I was in South Africa, and during a long car journey north from Cape Town to Durban, I found myself in a little coastal town, now forgotten, staying in a hotel with a pool table in the lobby. There was one movie theater in town. It was playing *National Velvet.* I bought a ticket. It was a wonderful movie. Ever after that night, I've never had to wonder why Elizabeth Taylor seemed to be in her own category of stardom.

She is survived by her brother, Howard; her children, Michael Wilding Jr., Christopher Wilding, Liza Todd Livey, and Maria Burton Carson, the daughter she and Burton adopted; and nine grandchildren.

Susannah York

January 17, 2011—Susannah York, the British actress who could plunge deep into drama and then skip playfully in comedies, died January 15, 2011, of bone marrow cancer. She was seventy-two.

Raised in Scotland, a graduate of the Royal Academy of Dramatic Arts, she was twenty when she made her first important film, the classic *Tunes of Glory* with Alec Guinness.

She was to become an icon of 1960s British films in such titles as *Kaleidoscope, A Man for All Seasons, The Killing of Sister George, Oh! What a Lovely War*, and *Battle of Britain.* She memorably played a patient in John Huston's *Freud* (1962), starring Montgomery Clift. But it was as a newlywed struggling to win a marathon dance prize in the American film *They Shoot Horses, Don't They?* (1969) that she won an Academy Award nomination.

In 1972 she won the best actress award at the Cannes Film Festival as a schizophrenic housewife in Robert Altman's *Images.* Altman fulminated for the rest of his life that York and the film never received the respect they deserved.

York starred in films as recently as 2009, and did a great deal of London stage work and television. One success was Piers Haggard's *A Summer Story* (1988), adapted from the John Galsworthy story. Petite and lively all her life, her hair often in a pixie cut, she was a popular guest on British chat and game shows.

Married in 1960 to the actor Michael Wells, she had two children, Sasha and the actor Orlando Wells, before their divorce. She and her children had close-by homes near Clapham Common in South London, and Orlando told the *Guardian*: "She loved nothing more than cooking a good Sunday roast and sitting around a fire of a winter's evening. In some senses, she was quite a home girl. Both Sasha and I feel incredibly lucky to have her as a mother."

In private life she was a political activist, active in the Campaign for Nuclear Disarmament. She is survived by her children and two grandchildren.

Film Festival

Toronto International Film Festival

A Lightbox and the Case of the Manacled Mormon

Toronto, September 10, 2010—I walk out the hotel door and don't know where I am. I've spent almost ten months in Toronto, one film festival at a time, and I know my way around. So where am I? The concierge says the hotel is "near the Entertainment District."

Not far away are some of the big Toronto legit houses. Turn a corner and I realize I'm near both Queen and King, two great streets for walking. And towering over everything is the new Bell Lightbox, the new high-rise home of the Toronto International Film Festival.

The Reitman family, which includes Ivan and Jason, kicked off the Lightbox with a cool $22 million. Toronto developer John Daniels, who essentially underwrote TIFF in its earliest years, built the Lightbox and was a supporter. Among the many other donors was the late Toronto film critic Brian Linehan, in for a million. Those Torontonians. My far-flung correspondent Grace Wang has been inside the Lightbox and loves its theaters, public areas, and festival offices. She has the intriguing title of social media coordinator for the festival. When TIFF was founded, social media did not exist, and neither did Grace. I say we're seeing progress.

I haven't been to the Lightbox yet. Werner Herzog and Errol Morris will hold a discussion there Monday, September 13, and I'll be angling for the front row. In the meantime, all of our festival has taken place at the Scotiabank Cineplex, which replaces the familiar Varsity Cinemas as the venue for most of the press screenings. It's much larger and offers many more seats, which is just as well, because the press corps here is second only to Cannes. This is now a big, brawny film festival, one of the Big Three—or is it Four?—and the unofficial starting line for Oscar season.

Yes, but the true value of TIFF comes in its support for expert, passionate programmers and passionate volunteer screeners, who seem to consider almost every available film from everywhere for the final cut of merely four hundred entries. I've been following the tweets of fest director Cameron Bailey as he jetted from Europe to Africa to India, China, and Japan, looking at movies. Then there was the jigsaw puzzle of finding times and theaters for everything. He says it's like simultaneously holding four hundred birthday parties.

Some of the festival films were previewed in Chicago, New York, and Los Angeles. Some played under the radar at Telluride. A lot played at Cannes. Wherever they came from, they go out from this time and place to bring nurture to a continent of movie lovers starving after the usually cheerless summer drought.

A few early examples, alphabetically:

Buried. (Rodrigo Cortes, Spain). One set, one actor, two props: a cell phone and a lighter. The universal nightmare: being buried alive. Paul Conroy (Ryan Reynolds) has been taken hostage in Iraq and awakens in a coffin. His captors have apparently left the phone and the lighter in aid of their plan to hold him for ransom. He starts telephoning for help, and has infuriating experiences with a 911 operator, the Pentagon switchboard, and the private contractor he drives a truck for.

I knew the premise going in, and wondered if the film would be boring. Not at all. I fell into easy identification with the plot, having been marked for life by a childhood horror comic (adapted from a book?) about a millionaire so terrified of being entombed that he has a bell on his grave with a cord that can be pulled from within his coffin. But then, wouldn't you just know, something goes wrong.

The budget for *Buried* is said to be $3 million. In one sense, low. In another sense, more than adequate for everything director Cortes wants to accomplish, including his special effects and the voice talents of all the people on the other end of the line. Ryan Reynolds has limited space to work in, and body language more or less preordained by the coffin, but he makes the character convincing if necessarily limited. The running time, ninety-five minutes, feels about right. The use of 2:35 wide-screen paradoxically increases the effect of claustrophobia.

Never Let Me Go. (Mark Romanek, United Kingdom). I found Kazuo Ishiguro's 2005 novel completely absorbing and probably difficult to film. The novel doesn't depend on a big surprise reveal at the end, but unfolds its secrets through a point of view that assumes everything is already known. In its alternative present, human beings are cloned to supply body parts. They're raised for this purpose, and after three, sometimes four, donations, they complete. They're not intended to live full lives. They live within a social structure that encourages the full acceptance of their purpose of donors.

Ishiguro's method is to accept that world as a given. His novel is about the meaning of human identity. Are cloned humans persons, or are they simply organisms for the supply of body parts? That's what the novel is about, in the intensely personal terms of the organ donors themselves. There are three central characters, Kathy (Carey Mulligan), Tommy (Andrew Garfield), and Ruth (Keira Knightley). All are cloned. All accept their donor roles. But all have feelings.

The way Mark Romanek (*One Hour Photo*) approaches this material is rather unexpected in terms of the possibilities in this story for sensationalism. He and his writer, Alex Garland, treat it with respect. They seek Ishiguro's melancholy tone. That's inescapable—unless they had turned it into a thriller about a revolt. As in the book, the film's moral questions center on whether the clones have a soul. Form your own opinion. Mine is that to the degree any human has one, all must have one.

Tabloid (Errol Morris, United States) is one of the damnedest films ever made by this artist as documentarian. He presents his "favorite protagonist," Joyce McKinney, who in 1977 was involved in the infamous "Case of the Manacled Mormon." She was alleged to have kidnapped an American Mormon missionary in the United Kingdom, handcuffed him to a bed, and made him a sex slave. In the British tabloid version of the story she became sexually obsessed with him.

The case exploded into a tabloid war at the time, occupying many front pages. It had been all but forgotten when McKinney surfaced again in recent years after finding a South Korean scientist to clone her dog. Morris gains full access to McKinney, then a somewhat shady nude model, now a poised and persuasive sixty-something, who proclaims full innocence and has an explanation for everything. As if often the case with Morris, we can never be sure what he thinks, only that he wants to baffle us with the impenetrable strangeness of reality.

Kurosawa's *Rashomon* will inevitably be evoked in discussions of this film. Morris presents lawmen with boundless reasons to think McKinney guilty of stalking, abduction, and possible rape. He also allows McKinney to offer a perky alternative perspective on the same events. Her alleged victim is portrayed in murky ambiguity; once unshackled, he prudently has refused all interviews. As often, Morris surrounds his story with unexpected asides, blindsides us with surprise revelations, and weaves in an ominously urging score by John Kusiak.

Errol Morris makes intensely personal films, which are neither about his subjects nor himself, but about the intensity of his gaze. No wonder he invented the Interrotron, which allows Morris and the person he is speaking with to peer directly into each other's eyes. He, and we, are constantly asking what we think of this person—and what's really going on here? If *Tabloid* is a love story, it is one only Errol Morris could film.

Hereafter, *Casino Jack*, and Vengeance

September 13, 2010—Clint Eastwood's *Hereafter* considers the possibility of an afterlife with tenderness, beauty, and a gentle tact. I was surprised how enthralling I found it. I don't believe in woo-woo, but there's no woo-woo anywhere to be seen. It doesn't even properly suppose an afterlife, but only the possibility of consciousness after apparent death. This is plausible. Many near-death survivors report the same memories, of the white light, the waiting figures, and a feeling of peace.

The subject lends itself to sensationalizing and psychic baloney. Eastwood has made a film for sensitive, intelligent people who are naturally curious about what happens when the shutters close. He tells three primary stories. Their three central characters meet at the end, but please don't leap to conclusions. This is not one of those package endings where all the threads come together in a coincidence that makes everything clear. They meet in a perfectly explicable and possible way, they behave as we feel they might, and everything isn't tied up neatly. Instead, possibilities are left open in this world, which is as it should be, because we must live the lives we know and not count on there being anything beyond the horizon.

I said the film was made with tact. It is made with the reserve, the reluctance to take obvious emotional shortcuts, that is a hallmark of Eastwood as a filmmaker. This is the film of a man at peace. He has nothing to prove except his care for the story. The original screenplay is by Peter Morgan (who doesn't, Eastwood told me, believe in psychic powers). He gives us Matt Damon as a man who seems actually able to have communication with the dead, but has fled that ability and taken a low-profile job; Cecile de France as Marie, a newsreader on French television; Bryce Dallas Howard as a young cooking student with a fearful dark place inside; Richard Kind as a man mourning his wife; and Frankie McLaren as Marcus, a young boy whose twin brother has been struck by a truck and killed.

I won't describe here the traumatic surprises some of them have. In its surprises as in everything else, *Hereafter* is calmly believable. There are terrifying events, but not the manufactured ones common in lesser films. Eastwood handles them not for sensation but for realism. They lead to experiences that create powerful notions that something—the movie doesn't declare precisely what—happens after death. The powers of the Damon character seem to be authentic, although what they prove is hard to say. There is a moment handled with love and delicacy in which he says something that is either true or isn't, but is a kindness either way.

Eastwood and his actors achieve a tone that never forces the material but embraces it. It is never dreamlike, but it could be described as evoking a reverie state. These people are not hurtling toward the resolution of a plot. There is no "solution" to their stories. There are various degrees of solace, or not. They don't punch the dialogue. They don't "act." They lack the certainty to impose themselves. Damon in particular is reserved and sad, because of a power that has become a burden to him. *Hereafter* is unlike any film Clint Eastwood has ever made, but you'd think he'd been preparing it for years.

* * *

Political movies often play cute in drawing parallels with actual figures. They drop broad hints that a character is *really* Dick Cheney or Bill Clinton and so on. *Casino Jack* is so forthright it is stunning. The film is "inspired by real events," and the characters in this film have the names of the people in those real events: Jack Abramoff, Michael Scanlon, Tom DeLay, Ralph Reed, Karl Rove, George W. Bush, Bob Ney, and John McCain.

This decision to name names by the director George Hickenlooper seems based on boldness, recklessness, or perhaps iron-clad legal assurances. His film uses a fictional sledgehammer to attack the cozy love triangle involving lobbyists, lawmakers, and money. It stars Kevin Spacey in an exact and not entirely unsympathetic performance as Abramoff, once one of the most powerful lobbyists in Washington, who was convicted on charges involving the funds he stole from wealthy Indian casinos while arranging laws for their convenience on Capitol Hill.

The first press screening of the film here at the Toronto International Film Festival was witnessed in a sort of stunned silence by a capacity audience, interrupted slightly by an undercurrent of incredulous murmurs and soft laughter when Spacey, as Abramoff, explodes at a Senate hearing being chaired by McCain. Having evoked the Fifth Amendment repeatedly, he's unable to restrain himself any longer and jumps to his feet to accuse the very members of the panel of having taken campaign contributions and favors from his Indian clients, and voting in their favor.

Astonishingly, Hickenlooper intercuts real footage of the real hearing and the real John McCain with Spacey's performance. Can he get away with this? I guess so. The film is set for a December 2010 release, and the distributors, ATO, have no doubt had the film scrutinized by their attorneys. Apart from that, there's the likelihood (which lawyers may think but cannot say) that no one named in this film is very likely to sue. The Abramoff scandal was called at the time the biggest since Watergate (both were broken by the *Washington Post*), but in the years since his sentencing in 2006, his name has faded from everyday reference, and it's doubtful anyone desires to make it current again.

* * *

The Conspirator by Robert Redford brings drama and clarity to the importance of habeas corpus in American democracy. It's depressing that this cornerstone of freedom doesn't seem to be widely understood. The Latin phrase roughly means "you have the body," and in practice means (1) a lawyer has the right to demand of the state that it acknowledges it holds a prisoner, and (2) that he can demand the state name its charges against the prisoner and bring him to trial or release him. Those seem like elementary demands, but throughout history and in many nations even today, nations act as if they own the rights to the body of a citizen.

Redford's story stars Robin Wright as the strong, calm center of a story we may have vaguely heard about and forgotten. After the assassination of Abraham Lincoln, an outcry goes up for the perpetrators of the deed—those who conspired with John Wilkes Booth. A Washington boardinghouse owner, Mary Surratt, is arrested on conspiracy charges because Booth and others, including her own son, met there to plot the murder. There is no evidence that she met with them or shared their intentions, and she didn't flee as her son did. A lawyer named Frederick Aiken (James McAvoy) is assigned to defend her in a court of military generals, and slowly develops a conviction that she is innocent.

Yet a fever for revenge runs strong in the land, and Mary's rights are brushed aside. Despite a last-minute stay of execution, which is overruled by President Andrew Johnson, she is hanged. But her case resulted in enactment of strong habeas corpus guarantees being written into U.S. law. It cannot have escaped Redford's attention that the prisoners at Guantanamo have been held without charge under both the Bush and Obama administrations, in apparent violation of the principle of habeas corpus as an international standard.

Humans Passed This Way Long Ago

September 14, 2010—About thirty-two thousand years ago, in a limestone cave above the Ardeche River in southern France, humans created the oldest cave paintings known to exist. They spring from the walls with boldness and confidence, as if the artists were already sure what they wanted to paint and how to paint it. Perhaps twenty-five thousand years ago, a child visited the cave and left a footprint, the oldest human footprint that can be accurately dated. At some time after the child's visit, a rock slide sealed the entrance to the cave. In 1994, French archeologists, searching for air plumes that might reveal the presence of a cave, found it again.

They had to descend a narrow opening to its floor, far below on the original entrance level. It is their entry route that Werner Herzog follows in his spellbinding new film *Cave of Forgotten Dreams*, which had its first screening Monday night at the Toronto International Film Festival. Herzog filmed in 3-D, to better convey how the paintings follow and exploit the natural contours of the ancient walls. The process also helps him suggest how the humans of the Upper Paleolithic era might have seen the paintings themselves, in the flickering light of their torches.

Access to Chauvet Cave, named for one of its discoverers, was immediately closed off by the French government, and a locked steel door now bars the way to the air shaft. Behind that door the cave's guardians enforce a strict regime. Herzog is allowed a four-man crew, including himself. They are limited to four cold-panel lights, powered from battery belts. They dare step only on two-foot-wide aluminum pathways that have been installed. They are allowed four hours. If anyone has to leave for any reason—even to get a screwdriver—that day's visit is over; the guardians want to shield the cave's air supply.

Surely men must have been painting somewhere before these cave walls were covered. It is hard to believe that these confident lines and shapes came into being without prelude. Or was there something innate in these forms? Accurate carbon dating suggests that other artists returned to the cave at least two thousand years after the first ones, and continued the work in the same style.

Cave paintings are the earliest evidence we have of our ability for abstract thought, which is what makes us human. They come before any evidence of mathematics, commerce, or political organization above a tribal level. They seem to provide evidence of spiritual thought. There is in the Chauvet Cave a rough raised pillar on which rests the skull of a cave bear, a species now extinct. Its placement cannot be accidental; the arrangement suggests the cave painters thought it deserved special attention or veneration. These early humans coexisted in the same river valley with Neanderthal Men, who left no such evidence; our ability for abstract thought must have allowed us to win that evolutionary struggle, although DNA suggests the two species at some point were able to interbreed.

Only two very small sculptures in the cave show human forms. One is a woman, her sexual organs exaggerated to dramatize her fertility. The paintings themselves are all of animals, an astonishing variety, providing a bestiary of the valley at the time. Mammoths, cave bears, lions, bison, panthers, horses, rhinos. The rhinos have what are surely exaggerated horns, suggesting a desire to emphasize their power. Some of the drawings repeat horns and legs in an obvious attempt to depict movement.

In addition to the footprint, there are poignant signs that humans were here. Near the original entrance, where outside light was still present, many visitors left their palm prints on a wall in red ochre. Were these the artists' marks? Calling cards? Why did many leave them? A palm print stands out: One man had a damaged little finger. Further back in the cave, they found another mark with the same finger. His two visits and a child's footprint remain after thirty millennia.

Herzog's limitation of four small portable light panels works to his advantage; as they move they suggest how the flickering torches might have created an illusion of movement in those repeated features. The space was so limited it was impossible for his crew to stay out of many shots, and their shadows dance on the walls, just as the shadows of forgotten ancestors must have danced in the torchlight. Herzog's inspiration is to show us the paintings as the cave's original visitors must have seen them. I have seen perfectly lighted photographs of other cave paintings that are not so evocative.

Herzog says that in general he dislikes 3-D. He told me this again on Monday. But there are occasions when 3-D is appropriate (he named *Avatar*), and his film is one of them. It was shown with bright, well-focused digital projection. Apart from a one-shot joke at the very end, he never allows his images to violate the theater space; he uses 3-D as a way for us to enter the film's space, instead of a way for it to enter ours. He was correct to realize how useful it would be in photographing these walls. To the degree that it's possible for us to walk behind Herzog into that cave, we do so.

As a documentarian, Herzog is never content to simply document. There's always a transformative element. *Cave of Forgotten Dreams* ends with a "postscript," in which he notes that not very far away France has built its largest nuclear power plant. The water heated by its cooling towers is directed into a huge tropical arboretum, where trees and ferns flourish. Crocodiles were introduced here, "and man, do they like it." Some of them have mutated into albinos. Herzog, in his inimitable accent, pronounces the words lovingly: mutant radioactive albino crocodiles. We see their huge bug eyes popping above the water to regard us. Someday, he speculates, perhaps in thousands of years, the crocs may spread to the cave. What will they make of its paintings?

Is this postscript typical Herzogian whimsy? Yes. But more. There are connections between *Cave of Forgotten Dreams* and at least two other Herzog films, undoubtedly more. Beneath the surfaces of his work coil hidden archetypes, hinting at his conception of our role in the immensity of space and the vastness of time.

Thinking of the cave, I am reminded of another cave, one carved out of ice far beneath the surface of Antarctica. He visits it in *Encounters at the End of the World* (2007). This cave scientists used as a time capsule to store their records. In its walls there are niches that contain small personal possessions—photographs, valued objects, things with meaning to the niche builder. These are talismans saying, "I was here." The low temperature and humidity will preserve these objects indefinitely. Herzog wonders what an alien race, far in the future, might make of them.

The ice cave preserves some part of our nature into a future long after we have disappeared. The Chauvet Cave has preserved part of the nature of these early men far into their future, after they have disappeared. Thus do living beings, bound by time, strive to preserve some expression of their minds. For without abstract thought, animals have little conception of time beyond the evolutionary necessities of earlier, now, and later. So we beat on, boats against the current, borne back ceaselessly into the past.

Now as to the mutant radioactive albino crocodiles. Yes, there goes that Herzog again. We are reminded of the iguanas in his *Bad Lieutenant: Port of Call New Orleans* (2009), and the shot in which Nicolas Cage regards an iguana uneasily, and it returns his stare implacably. There is another shot in which an alligator at the side of a road stares at the corpse of another alligator that has been flattened by traffic.

Ever since I first read them, these words by W. G. Sebald have remained with me: "Men and animals regard each other across a gulf of mutual incomprehension." This is true. Even with an animal as seemingly readable as a dog, what I believe the dog is thinking must be very different from what the dog thinks. Of cats, lizards, whales, and birds, I have no remotest conception.

We see the albino crododile. It sees us. We see a "mutant radioactive albino crocodile." It sees . . . us. Men of thirty-two thousand years ago saw cave bears. They saw their shapes, their movement, their nature. They created meanings for them. They objectified them. They drew them in a representational medium. They depicted three dimensions in two. They suggested movement in static drawings. They crawled far into a cave by torchlight to create these paintings, for reasons that had importance for them. Reasons. Does a cave bear have reasons in this sense?

That we can think in abstractions and imagine one reality in terms of another is what rescues us from the bondage of the present moment. In this ancient cave exist the earliest signs we have found of the abilities that created our history, and the fact that we can even conceive of history. In this cave is enshrined the possibility of you, and me, and Werner Herzog, and everything we can conceive, including aliens visiting to look at some few shabby talismans of our existence.

I'm Still Not All Here

September 17, 2010—We now have it on Casey Affleck's word that *I'm Still Here*, the film about Joaquin Phoenix's apparent descent into self-destruction, was a hoax. We cannot doubt this. Well, perhaps we can; the possibility exists that Affleck caught so much shit after the release that he decided to back off from his devastating portrait of his brother-in-law. But let's agree it is a hoax.

Now the spinning begins. Who fell for it, and who didn't? And why does it matter? I think it matters because it helps establish what the film achieved and how it achieved it. As a documentary it is the sad record of a man lost in the wilderness of drugs, ego, and narcissism. As a fake documentary—a fiction film—it is a rather awe-inspiring record of a piece of high-risk performance art played out in public by Phoenix and Affleck over more than a year. It would be interesting to know which we are watching.

I fell for it. Sure, I expressed some doubts and reservations, but I reviewed it seriously, and even expressed my hope that Joaquin would pull himself together. I was not alone. I've read most of the reviews linked by Metacritic.com, which surveys major critics and publications, and here are the totals I came up with:

Believed it was real (nine): Ebert, Gleiberman, Neumaier, Stevens, Doerksen, Rodriguez, Levy, Puig, Orange.

Not sure, open question, or cagey (fifteen): Persall, Phillips, Rothkopf, Longworth, Williams, Hartlaub, Turan, Baumgarten, Grady, O'Sullivan, Rea, Robinson, Salisbury, Goodykoontz, Travers.

It's a fake (five): Young, Burr, Felperin, Dargis, Edelstein.

If you are one of these critics and believed I have misread you, tell me and I will switch your vote. Some critics believed the film's actual impact was more important than its authenticity. (Stevens: "It's real even if it's a hoax"; Rodriguez: "If the movie is a fake, the filmmakers deserve Oscars for creativity.")

Of those who believed it fake, the one who

did the best job of calling it was David Edelstein in New York: "[The word] 'hoax' strikes me as inapt: Was anyone with half a brain actually deceived? I prefer the word 'act.' In Casey Affleck's drolly poker-faced documentary, *I'm Still Here*, Phoenix's metamorphosis looks less like a scam than a go-for-broke art project, an outlandish psychodrama with a nucleus of truth."

No other critic burned as many bridges as Edelstein. Young in the *Hollywood Reporter* called it a "mockumentary," Felperin said it "blends real and faked," and Dargis said it was "a deadpan satire or a deeply sincere folly (my money is on the first option)," although by calling it an option she leaves the second open. Still, her review can fairly be called nonbelieving.

Of the fifteen in the middle, there is a certain hedging of bets. Both possibilities occurred to them. The rest of us left ourselves no escape route.

This is a compliment to the film, however backhanded. And indeed there is little correlation between how much the critics liked the film and whether they thought it was a hoax. Gleiberman of *Entertainment Weekly* believed it, and Metacritic rates his review at "91." Edelstein didn't believe it, and Metacritic says "80." Writing "Rarely has the question of a documentary's artifice mattered less," Phillips of the *Chicago Tribune* gave it zero stars, because he hated, hated, hated it.

What does all this mean? It means that Phoenix and Affleck have created a risky and quite interesting film. I suspect some of the negative reviews reflect distaste with the way Phoenix presents himself, but that doesn't make the film bad. You don't have to like the central character, and you shouldn't complain if a film makes him as reprehensible as it hopes.

Now that Affleck has spilled the beans, *I'm Still Here* can never be seen in exactly the same way again. I saw it screened in Chicago on September 7, 2010, and my review went online the night of the eighth. Others saw its actual Toronto premiere. No critical consensus had formed when we wrote our reviews. We responded to the visceral experience.

Yes, it's possible today to go back and point to "obvious giveaways." I'm sure to get lots of comments from readers who, of course, were not for one second deceived. It wasn't so easy when you saw it cold. What tilted me was this question: Why in the hell would Joaquin Phoenix go to a year's effort to paint such a repulsive and negative portrait of himself?

On the other hand, there's this question: Why in the hell would Summer Phoenix Affleck not throw every dish in the house at her husband if her brother hadn't been acting?

Both of those questions are tributes to the acting and filmmaking. We can find blips and raise questions about the veracity, but it's hard to believe anyone would voluntarily make this up. In the film, Joaquin hoovers in cocaine, buggers hookers, vomits, appears before a stunned Miami audience as a semiconscious zombie, makes his stupefying appearance on the *Letterman* show, and rages like an egomaniac. If it's acting, it's good acting.

I invite comparison with the work of that great actor Sean Penn in *Hurlyburly* (1998), based on the David Rabe play, in which Penn plays a casting agent stoned out of his mind on cocaine. It's a good performance, but no one would think they were looking at the real Sean Penn. In *I'm Still Here*, on the other hand, even those who thought the movie was a fake had strong personal responses to Phoenix's performance—at least partly based on the assumption that it had to be relatively autobiographical. The charitable speculation was that perhaps Phoenix and Affleck were drawing inspiration from Hollywood people they know, some of whom haven't yet died.

The film's visual and sound style also come into question. This is either a roughly made documentary, or a fiction film brilliantly made to resemble a roughly made documentary. One is reminded of Dr. Johnson's observation, "it is not done well, but one is surprised to find it done at all." For example, there's a shot taken after the disastrous Letterman appearance. Phoenix bolts out of a limo in Central Park and scrambles up a hillside into the shrubbery. It is difficult to believe he really did this. "Is it a little too perfect dramatically?" I asked in my review. Yes, but not too perfect in its visual competence. You can lean either way.

As for the Letterman appearance itself, Affleck says Dave wasn't in on the joke. I believe it. I've watched that video several times. It shows Letterman as the master of his space, dealing with the incoherent Phoenix about as well, and amusingly, as was seemingly possible. But look at Phoenix's body language. As he enters, he conveys a subtle, exact sense of dimly intending to play the role of guest although he's in a clueless state. Throughout the appearance, you don't see him going too far or breaking the reality he's constructing. No matter what we now know, it's a remarkable few minutes of acting and/or behavior.

As I write, there has not yet been an "official" statement from Phoenix himself. All we know for sure is the *New York Times* interview with Affleck in an all-night L.A. diner, a few days after he insisted at Venice that the film was not a hoax. Phoenix is reportedly set to make a return appearance on *Letterman* on September 22, 2010. The only thing I'm fairly sure of is that he won't be contrite.

It Was a Very Good Year

September 20, 2010—"There must be directors at Toronto other than Werner Herzog and Errol Morris," one reader wrote impatiently. "Try reviewing someone else's films for a change." Point taken. I intend to do that below, and say in my defense that I have already written about eight films not by my heroes. Actually, that's not so many, is it? I saw twenty-six of the films but feel no need to write about all of them; in a few cases, I don't want to say negative things about those still searching for buyers.

I know that doesn't reflect the gung-ho spirit of the ravenous packs of journalists at a big festival like Toronto, where bloggers literally sit on the floor outside a screening and start typing to "scoop" one another. I dunno. That's valid for trade-oriented sites and insiders such as Anne Thompson and David Poland (neither of whom I've actually ever seen on the floor), but I'm not suited up for their sport. I find someone or something that really interests me and tend to dwell.

So let me dwell a little on Mike Leigh's *Another Year.* I saw it first at Cannes. I'm pretty confident it's one of those Leigh films that the Academy will love. The Academy is not the final arbiter of taste, although in recent years its taste has grown altogether too good to please the producers of gaseous Oscar bait. *Slumdog Millionaire? The Hurt Locker?* Say what?

I wrote from Cannes: "Mike Leigh has long been a great director, but now he is surely at the top of his form. *Another Year* is beautifully sure and perceptive in its record of one year in the life of a couple happily married, and their relatives and friends, not so happy."

Jim Broadbent and Ruth Sheen play the happy couple. They look like real people, Broadbent with his generous chins and Sheen with her cheery overbite. They don't match conventional ideals of physical beauty, but I love them just the way they are. What others might call flaws I consider enhancements that lift them above convention and make them gloriously themselves. We like them, sincerely and quickly, and it's clear that Leigh does, too. One of the pleasures of the film is simply being around them.

Into their life and home comes a frequent visitor named Mary, who is a forlorn loner and clearly an alcoholic. Tom and Gerri (smile) are kind people, and realize they may actually be the only people Mary has to speak with. The movie occupies itself with Tom and Gerri's happy life—their garden, the son they're proud of, their enduring love—and into this sunshine Mary sweeps down like a storm cloud. She is hopeless, really. She thinks she drinks because of her problems, and in fact her drinking causes them. This is obvious to her friends, and their patience can stretch only so far.

If you know Mike Leigh's films, you can sense this is a story right for his world. If you don't, I wonder how it sounds. It's not a dreary psychodrama, it doesn't preach, it amuses and allows a few tears. The keys are the performances by Jim Broadbent and Ruth Sheen, and Sheen, I suspect, is the one the Academy will be drawn to.

* * *

Darren Aronofsky's *Black Swan* is a joining of ballet, madness, and melodrama, and there are times when ballet itself seems to join the same qualities. How can you be a great dancer and not be a little mad? You have been drilled since childhood, every audition is a measure of your worth, and you are surrounded by people who feed off you and have power over you. There must be times when "break a leg" sounds like well-wishing.

Natalie Portman stars in a big and demanding role as Nina, a young ballerina up for the challenging double role as the White Swan and the Black Swan in *Swan Lake.* Her New York ballet company is a hotbed of intrigue. It's ruled by the sadistic Thomas (Vincent Cassel), who apparently believes a thorough sexual experience with him should be part of any dancer's training. He has cruelly discarded a former lover and prima ballerina (Winona Ryder) to make room for Nina, while insulting Nina's technique: She is too technically good, too cold, to be the Black Swan, although her icy perfection is good for the White Swan.

Now comes a sexy competitor from the West Coast, Lily (Mila Kunis), who seems born to play the Black Swan. Lily's insouciance plays like a rebuff to Nina's years of work. She is deviously, devilishly subversive. And Nina herself is coming apart; a fact clear to her controlling mother (Barbara Hershey), who has perhaps driven her mad with smothering love.

The movie is unafraid of flamboyance. If there is a hint of Aronofsky's previous film *The Wrestler,* in Lily's ability to perform while hurting, it contains more than a hint of the bold imagination of the film before that, *The Fountain* (2006). Although it's better than *The Fountain,* it has the same willingness to go over the top, the ability to follow into fantasy or hallucination. Any dance movie invites comparison with the greatest of all, *The Red Shoes;* and in its Svengali ballet master and its tortured heroine, *Black Swan* has the same heedless ambition.

* * *

There are some roles Hilary Swank might not be right for, and others you can hardly imagine anyone else playing. In Tony Goldwyn's *Conviction,* she plays a working-class woman from a rough childhood. She and her brother, Kenny (Sam Rockwell), had an absent father and a mother who might as well have been absent, and lived in a series of dismal foster homes. But they stuck together and helped each other.

Kenny gets wild when he gets drunk. A local woman is murdered, he's arrested on suspicion, and behaves insultingly to a cop (Melissa Leo, from *Frozen River*). This comes back to haunt him. Two years later a ditzy witness (Juliette Lewis) thinks she might be able to place him at the crime scene, and the cops and prosecutor railroad him behind bars.

The heart of the movie involves Swank dedicating her life to proving her brother's innocence. This eventually costs her her marriage, but she gets a high school diploma, a college degree, and starts law school, where she meets a fellow student named Abra (Minnie Driver), who unofficially signs on as her partner in the cause.

This is all based on a true story, including their lucky break when DNA testing is introduced and proves Kenny innocent. The story generates that kind of urgency we feel when a character is obviously right and is up against stupidity and meanness. It delivers.

* * *

A note on one of the strongest films here, John Curran's *Stone.* It opens October 8, 2010, and a longer review should wait until then. But let me say that there is a union of three performances here that makes its story of psychological maneuvers something special.

Milla Jovovich, Robert De Niro, and Edward Norton are equally compelling, with Jovovich in the most demanding role. She plays the wife of Norton, as a lowlife prisoner, and De Niro plays Norton's parole officer. De Niro is proper, reserved, by the books. Jovovich is a woman unlike he has ever met. She loves her husband without reserve, which is peculiar because he doesn't seem to deserve it, but then you never know.

Stone could have been some sort of a procedural, a straightforward crime movie, but it's too complex for that. It is actually interested in the minds of these characters, and how they react to a dangerous situation.

* * *

Bottom line of TIFF 2010: This is shaping up as a very strong autumn movie season. Sales of films at the festival showed a strong rebound after slumping markets at several recent festivals, and that's an indication of *product* that distributors were willing to bet their money on in an uncertain economy. One of the best kinds of signs.

Ebert's Journal

My Mighty Hammering Over *Thor*

May 14, 2011—If I had my piece on *Thor* to write over again, I think it would be more bemused and whimsical. My tone was off. I brought too much anger to a trivial entertainment. When I described it "as a desolate vastation," I went perhaps one hyperbole too far.

I try to use a generic approach in my reviews. I approach a movie with some idea of its intention and the expectation of its target audience. I compared *Thor* to other movies based on comic book heroes, and found it lacking. But it doesn't really intend to be good in the sense that *The Dark Knight* or *Spider-Man II* are good. It's pitched at the level of a children's movie, although the expensive scope of the production tends to conceal that.

I've found that the fiercest devotees of a movie are likely to be those expert in the material—unless they're the most offended. Members of the Ayn Rand cult, for example, praised *Atlas Shrugged* as a great movie because they worship Ayn Rand. They brought more to that dismal film than it brought to them. In the case of a movie based on comic books, there will be a large fan base who study the original comics with the devout precision of a Randian, a Biblical scholar, or a Shakespearian. Comics are their holy writ, as I discovered even in the process of praising *Watchmen.*

It is impossible for most critics to be familiar with the source material of most movies, and that doesn't bother me. A movie must contain whatever the audience requires in order to enjoy it. It's not required to be "faithful" to its source, as if adaptation were adultery.

After my *Thor* review hit the fan, I was pummeled by outraged comments. A large number cited factual inaccuracies and speculated that I had not seen the movie at all. Some stated that as a fact. One called for me to be fired. Of course I saw the movie. I haven't spent forty-four years at this to start making things up now. I might indeed question how many other movies some of my correspondents have seen, since they confused *Thor* with a good film.

But I did make mistakes. Some of my inaccuracies came from a failure to understand plot points. I wondered, for example, why a giant metal robot chose to attack a small New Mexico town when it could have been attacking the Golden Gate Bridge. I was eviscerated for not knowing that the robot is named the Destroyer, and that of course he attacked the town because that's where Thor was, you see, and Thor was in New Mexico in the first place because that's where the Portal from Asgard leads to. Well, obviously it led to New Mexico, because that's where it took him, but why did it lead there? Because it did in the comic books, I guess. If the name "Destroyer" was used in the movie, and I suppose it must have been, it simply didn't register with me. With some films every frame seems to register. Others have a strange quality of slipping wraith-like through my mind without hitting any brain cells.

If the robot was named the Destroyer, the best reason for my failure to recall its name was that I just didn't give a damn. There were also complaints about my description of the destruction of the Destroyer, because although it is clearly halted by a sword into its spine, it isn't yet finally destroyed. My purpose was to be amused that a robot would have a spine.

I was criticized for my confusion about the physical location of Asgard. There is a "real" Asgard in Norse mythology, but I concluded reasonably that "in the movie it is not of this earth and must be elsewhere in the universe." For this I was told I was a fool. Of course it is on another planet, readers said, because the comics explain all that. I failed to cite holy writ. It was also unclear to me whether the Frost Giants of Jotunheim are on the same planet as Asgard or on another one, because they are linked by the same Portal (which I unwisely called a bridge) that joins Asgard to Earth.

Oh, my errors were many. I said Thor encounters "three human scientists." Jane and Dr. Erik are scientists, but Darcy, who moves with them as a unit, is only Jane's friend. That was a minor error compared with my next one, in writing "Thor's hammer hurtles to Earth and becomes embedded so firmly that it can't be pulled lose by a pickup truck or even the federal government." More proof I didn't see the movie. Didn't I realize it could be lifted only by Thor, after he became worthy of it?

Yes, I realized that, but what I wrote was quite accurate from the POV of the earthlings in the movie, who kept tugging at it. I also realized that the villain, Loki, is not literally Thor's brother but was adopted. Quite a point is made of that in the film. Readers thought I didn't know that. But if your brother is adopted he is still your brother, and in not mentioning that he was adopted I hoped to fend off an attack by the Spoiler Police, because the news that he was adopted comes as a surprise to Loki and many in the audience. Perhaps students of the comic books knew of this so well that mentioning it wouldn't have been a spoiler. I assume most audience members, however, didn't know it.

And so on. Readers attacked me for being unimpressed with Loki's stature as a villain. I asked, "Will you be thinking of Loki six minutes after this movie is over?" Yet six minutes have passed and here I am still thinking about him. I was especially wrong, I learned, for suggesting that (as comic book villains go) Loki was inferior to Doc Ock in *Spider-Man II.* Here I can accuse my critics of being wrong: To say Loki is a better villain than Doc Ock is clearly an error of fact. Did they really see the movies?

Obviously my mistake was to get into the plot at all. One of my weaknesses is to play with the logic of preposterous movies like this. I consider that an amusing exercise, to be read as entertainment and not taken so damned seriously. It even crossed my mind to do a paragraph about the difficulties of agriculture in the subzero kingdom of Jotunheim, speculating that perhaps the Frost Giants raised herds of the kinds of microscopic creatures science has found living under the Antarctic ice shelf. I'm glad that I didn't, because somehow I know the flora and fauna of Jotunheim have been exhaustively explained in the comic books.

There is a larger question here. Does it make a movie "good" because you "like" it? No, it doesn't, and I have liked a lot of bad movies. It is helpful to separate one's immediate amusement from more lasting standards. *Thor* is a minor superhero movie with a boring backstory and an underwhelming weapon (his hammer). Eventually Hollywood will exhaust every last one of its superheroes and start on remakes (there has already been a new version of the Hulk, which is much inferior to the Ang Lee version). The reason we get so many comic book superhero movies is that they all share the same High Concept: "Here is another one of those comic book superhero movies." The TV ads can hammer viewers with a lot of special effects.

Such movies are also useful for marketing purposes. Hollywood lives in thrall to the concept of a franchise. It is difficult to get a movie made in the first place, but more difficult to prevent it from spawning sequels. Some moviegoers have a reluctance to see a film unless they have a very good idea what they're going to get. That's why trailers deliberately give away so much of the story.

What did I learn from this adventure, if anything? I hope I learned to flail less. I don't consider my reviews instructions to readers about whether they should see a film. They're more like a continuing conversation. Nobody enjoys it when people get too wound up and start shouting. I hope to have a good time at a movie, and to provide a good time in writing a review. My guide is Dr. Johnson: "Those who desire to partake of the pleasure of wit must contribute to its production, since the mind stagnates without external ventilation."

A Prayer Beneath *The Tree of Life*

May 17, 2011—Terrence Malick's new film is a form of prayer. It created within me a spiritual awareness and made me more alert to the awe of existence. I believe it stands free from conventional theologies, although at its end it has images that will evoke them for some people. It functions to pull us back from the distractions of the moment and focus us on mystery and gratitude.

Not long after its beginning we apparently

see the singularity of the Big Bang, when the universe came into existence. It hurtles through space and time, until it comes gently to a halt in a small Texas town in the 1950s. Here we will gradually learn who some of the people were as the film first opened.

In Texas we meet the O'Brien family. Bad news comes in the form of a telegram, as it always did in those days. Mrs. O'Brien (Jessica Chastain) reads it in her home, and gives vent to grief. Mr. O'Brien (Brad Pitt) gets the news at work. We gather a child has died. It is after that when we see the universe coming into being, and Hubble photographs of the far reaches.

This had an uncanny effect on me, because Malick sees the time spans of the universe and a human life a lot like I always have. As a child I lay awake obsessed with the idea of infinity and the idea of God, who we were told had no beginning and no end. How could that be? And if you traveled and traveled and traveled through the stars, would you ever get to the last one? Wouldn't there always be one more?

In my mind there has always been this conceptual time travel, in which the universe has been in existence for untold eons, and then a speck appeared that was Earth, and on that speck evolved life, and among those specks of life were you and me. In the span of the universe, we inhabit an unimaginably small space and time, and yet we think we are so important. It is restful sometimes to pull back and change the scale, to be grateful that we have minds that can begin to understand who we are, and where we are in the vastness.

Many films diminish us. They cheapen us, masturbate our senses, hammer us with shabby thrills, diminish the value of life. Some few films evoke the wonderment of life's experience, and those I consider a form of prayer. Not prayer *to* anyone or anything, but prayer *about* everyone and everything. I believe prayer that makes requests is pointless. What will be, will be. But I value the kind of prayer when you stand at the edge of the sea, or beneath a tree, or smell a flower, or love someone, or do a good thing. Those prayers validate existence and snatch it away from meaningless routine.

We all occupy our own box of space and time. We have our memories and no one else's. We live one life, accumulating it in our minds as we go along. Terrence Malick was born in Waco, Texas, and has filmed much of *The Tree of Life* in small Texas towns; the house of the O'Brien family is in Smithville. I felt like I knew this house and this town. Malick and I were born within a year of each other, and grew up in small towns in the midlands. Someone else, without my memories to be stirred, might be less affected by its scenes of the O'Briens raising their three boys.

I know unpaved alleys with grass growing down the center. I know big lawns with a swing hanging from a tree. I know windows that stand open all day in the summer. I know houses that are never locked. I know front porches, and front porch swings, and aluminum drinking glasses covered with beads of sweat from the ice tea and lemonade inside. I know picnic tables. I know the cars of the early 1950s, and the kitchens, and the limitless energy of kids running around the neighborhood.

And I know the imperfect family life Malick evokes. I know how even good parents sometimes lose their tempers. How children resent what seems to be the unforgivable cruelty of one parent and the refuge seemingly offered by the other. I know what it is to see your parents having an argument, while you stand invisible on the lawn at dusk and half hear the words drifting through the open windows. I know the feeling of dread, because when your parents fight, the foundation of your world shakes. I had no siblings, but I know how play can get out of hand and turn into hurt, and how hatred can flare up between two kids, and as quickly evaporate. I know above all how time moves slowly in a time before TV and computers and video games, a time when what you did was go outside every morning and play and dare each other, and mess around with firecrackers or throw bricks at the windows of an empty building, and run away giggling with guilt.

Those days and years create the fundament. Then time shifts and passes more quickly, and in some sense will never seem as real again. In the movie, we rejoin one of the O'Brien boys (now played by Sean Penn) when he grows to about the age his father was. We see him in a wilderness of skyscrapers, looking out high windows at a world of glass and steel. Here are not the scenes of the lawn through the dining room windows. These windows never open. He will never again run outside and play.

What Malick does in *The Tree of Life* is create the span of lives. Of birth, childhood, the flush of triumph, the anger of belittlement, the poison of resentment, the warmth of forgiving. And he shows that he feels what I feel, that it was all most real when we were first setting out, and that it will never be real in that way again. In the face of Hunter McCracken, who plays Jack as a boy, we see the face of Sean Penn, who plays him as a man. We see fierceness and pain. We see that he hates his father and loves him. When his father has a talk with him and says, "I was a little hard on you sometimes," he says, "It's your house. You can do what you want to." And we realize how those are not words of anger but actually words of forgiveness. Someday he will be the father. It will not be so easy.

The Dying of the Light

May 24, 2011—Do you remember what a movie should look like? Do you notice when one doesn't look right? Do you feel the vague sense that something is missing? I do. I know in my bones how a movie should look. I have been trained by the best projection in the world, at film festivals and in expert screening rooms. When I see a film that looks wrong, I want to get up and complain to the manager and ask that the projectionist be informed. But these days the projectionist is tending a dozen digital projectors, and I will be told, "That's how it's supposed to look. It came that way from the studio."

The most common flaw is that the picture is not bright enough. I've been seeing that for a long time. In the years before digital projectors, the problem was often that tight-fisted theater owners weren't setting the xenon bulbs in their projectors at the correct wattage, in the mistaken belief that dialing them down would extend the life of the expensive bulbs.

Not true. If you ran a 3,000-watt bulb at 2,000 watts, you'd extend its life by all of 2.3 percent. Yet when Martin Scorsese used people around the country to actually check theater brightness, he found most of the theaters involved were showing an underlit image. An Eastman Kodak spokesman told me in the late 1990s: "The irony is that their only real achievement is to cheat the customers."

That was then. This is now. Driven by a mania to abandon celluloid in favor of digital, increasing numbers of chains are installing 3-D-ready digital projectors. As everyone can tell simply by taking off their 3-D glasses, the process noticeably reduces the visible light from the screen. I got e-mails from readers saying the night scenes in *Pirates of the Caribbean* were so dim they were annoying.

Ah, but what if you saw the movie in 2-D? As it happens, a lot of people did; Gitesh Pandya of BoxOfficeGuru.com reported: "less than half of the *Pirates* weekend gross came from 3-D screens, with more opting for the 2-D version." He attributes that to moviegoers being "cautious with their dollars." After the weekend, David Poland of MovieCityNews.com ran the numbers and determined 60 percent of sales were in 2-D and 40 percent in 3-D: "Not only is this a clear rejection of 3-D on a major movie, but given how distribution is currently designed, it makes you wonder whether Disney cost themselves a lot of gross by putting their film on too high a percentage of 3-D screens."

There may have been a reason consumers shied away from 3-D. An expertly written article by Ty Burr in the *Boston Globe* reports that some 3-D projectors, particularly those made by Sony, produce "gloomy, underlit" images of 2-D films. His article must have hit a nerve; and I've seen it posted and referred to all over the Web. The newspaper found dark images on eight of the nineteen screens at the high-end AMC Loews Boston Common on Tremont Street.

Burr wrote: "This particular night *Limitless*, *Win Win*, and *Source Code* all seemed strikingly dim and drained of colors. *Jane Eyre*, a film shot using candles and other available light, appeared to be playing in a crypt. A visit to the Regal Fenway two weeks later turned up similar issues: *Water for Elephants* and *Madea's Big Happy Family* were playing in brightly lit 35mm prints and, across the hall, in drastically darker digital versions." His observations indicated the problems centered on Sony projectors: "Digital projection can look excellent when presented correctly. Go into Theater 14 at the Common, newly outfitted with a Christie 4K projector, and you'll see a picture that is bright and crisp, if somewhat colder than celluloid."

He says there is a reason for this: "Many theater managers have made a practice of leaving the 3-D lenses on the projectors when playing a 2-D film." The result is explained by an anonymous projectionist: "For 3-D showings a special lens is installed in front of a Sony digital projector that rapidly alternates the two polarized images needed for the 3-D effect to work. When you're running a 2-D film, that polarization device has to be taken out of the image path. If they're not doing that, it's crazy, because you've got a big polarizer that absorbs 50 percent of the light."

Fifty percent! It can be worse than that. I quote: "Chapin Cutler, a cofounder of the high-end specialty projection company Boston Light & Sound, estimates that a film projected through a Sony with the 3-D lens in place and other adjustments not made can be as much as 85 percent darker than a properly projected film." Your best bet is apparently to (1) find a theater that doesn't use digital at all, (2) doesn't use Sony projectors, or (3) still projects light through celluloid the traditional way.

Digital projectors have been force-fed to theaters by an industry hungry for the premium prices it can charge for 3-D films. As I've been arguing for a long time, this amounts to charging you more for an inferior picture. The winners are the manufacturers of the expensive machines, and the film distributors. The hapless theaters still depend on concession sales to such a degree that a modern American theater can be described as a value-added popcorn stand.

I have an e-mail from a Hollywood professional who writes me: "During the last awards season, I went to an industry screening of *The Social Network* at Sony Studios, in their James Stewart facility—what they said was their best screening room. The movie looked dark and muddy; truly awful. Then I looked back and saw that the picture was emanating from a twin-lens rig. After the show, I complained to the projectionist about the image. He explained that the process of shifting both the lens and changing the silver screen to a white matter screen, which they were equipped to do, was too time-consuming. So he told me that his supervisor authorized showing the movie to Academy voters through the 3-D lens, which looked like shit. And this is at Sony Studios. Just imagine how bad it is in the real world. It is as if the industry is courting self-destruction."

Sony refused to comment on the *Boston Globe* article. At my recent Ebertfest, one seasoned director called the projection in the ninety-year old Virginia Theater in Urbana-Champaign "the best I've ever seen." That's because we use two of the best projectionists in the nation: James Bond, who consults on high-level projection facilities, and Steve Kraus, of Chicago's Lake Street Screening Room.

Ty Burr writes: "So why aren't theater personnel simply removing the 3-D lenses? The answer is that it takes time, it costs money, and it requires technical know-how above the level of the average multiplex employee. James Bond, a Chicago-based projection guru who serves as technical expert for Roger Ebert's Ebertfest, said issues with the Sonys are more than mechanical. Opening the projector alone involves security clearances and Internet passwords, 'and if you don't do it right, the machine will shut down on you.' The result, in his view, is that 'often the lens change isn't made and audiences are getting shortchanged.'"

The problem isn't with all digital projectors, and seems most common with the new Sony 4K projectors, which has lenses too difficult to adjust for most of the (semiskilled) multiplex projectionists. It is possible to project a high-quality digital image, and I've often seen that done. But only if theaters insist on it and manufacturers like Sony make changes allowing their lenses to be changed as needed.

The movie industry feels under threat these days from DVDs, cable movies on demand, a dozen streaming services such as Netflix, Hulu, Fandor, and Mubi, and competition from video games. Decades ago, it felt a similar danger from radio (it introduced talkies) and television (it introduced wide-screen). The irony today is that it hopes to rescue itself with 3-D, which is not an improvement but a step back in quality. The fact that more people wanted to see *Pirates* in 2-D than 3-D is stunning. The fact that 3-D projectors in some theaters are producing murky and dim 2-D pictures makes me very unhappy.

I began by asking if you notice, really notice,

what a movie looks like. I have a feeling many people don't. They buy their ticket, they get their popcorn, and they obediently watch what is shown to them. But at some level there is a difference. They feel it in their guts. The film should have a brightness, a crispness and sparkle that makes an impact. It should look like a movie!—not a mediocre big-screen television.

When people don't have a good time at the movies, they're slower to come back. I can't tell you how many comments on my blog have informed me that the writers enjoy a "better picture" at home on their big-screen TVs with Blu-ray discs. This should not be true. Nobody at Ebertfest confused the experience with sitting at home and watching a video. A movie should leap out and zap you, not recede into itself and get lost in dimness.

I despair. This is a case of Hollywood selling its birthright for a message of pottage. If as much attention were paid to exhibition as to marketing, that would be an investment in the future. People would fall back in love with the movies. Short-sighted, technically illiterate penny-pinchers are wounding a great art form.

What can you personally do to be sure you see an ideal picture? Matthew Humphries at Geek.com writes:

• The title of the movie listed by the theater will have a "D" after it if it is being shown on a digital projector.

• If you are in a "D" movie, look at the projector window when seated. If you see two stacked beams of light it is a Sony projector with the 3-D lens still on.

• A single beam of light means no 3-D lens, or a different make of projector that doesn't have the issue.

• If you see the two beams, then get up and go complain. You paid good money to see the movie, so make a fuss until they either give you back that money or remove the lens. Seeing as that's an involved and time-consuming process, expect a refund.

It's Going to Be a Bumpy Night

June 2, 2011—Jason Pankoke sends me a link from the *Pantagraph* of Bloomington-Normal, Illinois.

"Move over 3-D, here comes D-Box!" says the article by Dan Craft. "Instead of delivering movie thrills straight between the eyes, D-Box lifts and separates, so to speak—detaching the moviegoer from his or her seat via three levels of pitching, rolling, and heaving.

"Moreover, the moviegoer also has control over the intensity of that action, via a control knob that can reduce the movement, or, if it all becomes too much, shut it off."

This new technology will be introduced, I learn, with screenings of *Super 8* at the Starplex Stadium 14 in Normal, "the second location in Illinois to feature the motion seating technology (the other is in suburban Chicago's Rosemont)." Nationally there are eighty cinemas featuring the special chairs.

The dismemberment of the traditional moviegoing experience continues. Can you imagine enduring this atrocity in addition to the horrors of 3-D? Not only are pandas flying out of the screen at you, but you're pitching, rolling, and heaving. I wonder if the seats come with a sick bag. I also wonder what it would be like to watch a movie while seated next to bored kids entertaining themselves with their joysticks.

Of course the D-Box seats involve a higher ticket price. To see *Super 8* from a D-Box seat after 6 p.m. will cost you $16. The next week, if you come back to see *Harry Potter and the Deathly Hallows Part Two*, there will be another $2 surcharge for the 3-D. That said, the Stadium 14 has admirably restrained standard prices; *Kung Fu Panda 2* after 6 p.m. will cost you $10 in 3-D and $8 in 2-D. From this I deduce that the additional fee for D-Box is $8. In Chicago, *Panda* 3-D is $15, which means that as an adult with the fancy seat you'd be looking at $23, and $20 for a child. I have a feeling that for the proverbial family of four, that would get old real fast.

Perhaps this sounds to you like a wonderful thing. You'd enjoy something less like a movie, more like a ride at a theme park. As long as I cannot see or hear you, I don't have a problem with that. I've been to Disney World and strapped myself into seats that shot me into space and dropped me from the tower of terror and so on. So go ahead and enjoy yourself.

For myself, I am a reactionary purist. I dislike 3-D. I also disliked interactive movies, Smell-O-Vision, and the now-forgotten Sensurround, which was introduced for *Earthquake* and quickly discontinued after it shook loose chunks of plaster from the ceiling of a Chicago theater. My needs are few. I hope to see a good movie, well projected, with decent sound, on a good-sized screen, in the company of people who are generally in sympathy with the film. That means I don't object, for example, when people laugh or scream if a movie calls for laughing or screaming. Movies have a way of getting the audiences they deserve.

What I object to is anything in the theater that goes against the flow. I want to give myself up to a movie and even lose myself in it. I don't want people to talk. I don't want to see the evil little screens of cell phones—and with stadium seating, I can see every single one. Among my many quarrels with 3-D is that it removes me from the experience by introducing the unnecessary extra dimension. A 2-D movie creates the illusion of 3-D more effectively, because it allows our minds to cooperate, instead of hammering them with distractions.

There have been indications recently that American audiences may be tiring of 3-D. You may have seen the stories; about 60 percent of the audiences for both *Pirates* and *Panda* chose to see them in 2-D. Wall Street analysts have issued certain sell advisories, and some 3-D–heavy stocks are down in price. This may be, as 3-D defenders say, a blip. *Harry Potter* will provide a test. The Potter movies are often quite dark and very heavy on gloomy interiors that look creepy in 2-D but may simply look obscure with the lower light levels of 3-D.

Time will tell. What depresses me is that mainstream Hollywood seems to be experiencing a crisis of confidence. For decades there was the faith that if you released a good movie, people might very well buy tickets to it. The traditional pattern was to open it slowly, hope for good reviews, and then "roll it out" more widely.

The economics of television advertising put an end to the theory that an audience might find a movie. Now the movies must find an audience. Big new releases open everywhere at once, and everybody knows they will be available before long on DVD or on demand. Theaters offer 3-D as something you can't get at home (apart from "3-D television," about which I am unpersuaded). Now we get rocking and rolling D-Box seats.

The only choice for a reasonably intelligent grown-up, I begin to feel, is to seek out what are called art or independent theaters, where the projection quality is likely to be more closely monitored, and the audience is likely to be civilized. Yes, I'm told, but there's no theater like that within one hundred miles! Then do the best you can. Or wait for the DVD. It hurts me to say that. I feel as if I'm abandoning movie theaters, which I love. Or are they abandoning me?

On the Origin of Transformers

July 4, 2011—As an admirer of Darwin's Theory of Evolution, I have become fascinated by Transformers. These are the grotesque pinheaded robots named Autobots and Decepticons, who pound the hell out of each other in Michael Bay's *Transformers: Dark of the Moon*, a film setting box office records.

They're arguably the least interesting aliens in the history of science fiction, but how much can you expect from an intelligent race that began as a line of Hasbro toys? They have come a long way given their meager beginnings.

In the third installment of their story, we learn that their spacecraft, named the Ark, crashed on the dark side of the Moon after fleeing their home planet of Cybertron. After learning of the existence of the craft, President John F. Kennedy announced a mission to the Moon, and on July 20, 1969, American astronauts took advantage of a period of silence while out of radio contact with Earth to investigate the enormous vessel and (unwisely) awaken one of its passengers. We know this is true because there is actual footage in the film of John F. Kennedy calling for a Moon landing, along with Nixon hailing the success of the mission and even *Apollo 11* astronaut Buzz Aldrin playing himself in the present day. And we wonder why so many people believe the Moon landing was faked.

The film makes no attempt to locate Cybertron, but if we believe the universe is the size it appears to be, it must be many light-years away. If Cybertronians have mastered a way of traveling at the speed of light, one might later wonder why they are otherwise so technically incompetent that the worst they can do on Earth is lay waste to the corner of Michigan Avenue and Wacker Drive in Chicago.

I think I can explain how the Ark made the journey from Cybertron to the Moon. The universe, in fact, is not as large as it appears. As some (not all) Creationists explain, its immensity is only an illusion. While the stars are not necessarily lights fixed in a large globe that circles Earth, they cannot be more than 10,000 years old, since that is the age of the Earth and therefore the universe it inhabits. That requires a universe much smaller than the universe 13.5 billion years old claimed by some. Cybertron would therefore orbit a star much closer than any star in the non-Creationist universe, and an Autobot spaceship could reach the Moon in, oh, maybe a year, tops.

I raise the subject of Creationism because it opens the door to Intelligent Design, which I will require to explain the existence of Autobots. Do you know what Autobots look like? At first appearance they're mild-mannered motor vehicles. They are suddenly capable of unfolding and expanding into gigantic humanoid robots whose size seems optional, since sometimes they can bend over and look a human in the eye, and at other times they are hundreds of feet tall. One might wonder how they pack so much metallic mass into an area the size of a Camaro, and well one might.

They seem to consist mostly of auto parts: fenders, bumpers, grills, hoods, trunks, windshields, and sometimes large tractor tires as shoulders. These parts expand as needed according to scale. They seem to be entirely made of metal, although in this movie an old Autobot has grown a beard, and when another opens its jaws we can clearly see a strand of saliva, which I assume is Pennzoil.

I will avoid the obvious question: How did the inhabitants of Cybertron learn of modern human automobile designs? Since they are capable of such quick morphing, they obviously evolved their auto disguises as a tactic to move unnoticed among humans, and travel around at will. I assume they need gasoline as lifeblood, which explains their interest in the Middle East earlier in the story. Their decision to attack Chicago seems inexplicable, until you take into consideration the generous tax credits offered by the Illinois Film Office.

A more difficult question is: How did intelligent beings evolve from base metals in a nonorganic process? What Autobots and Decepticons look like on Cybertron we cannot know, but logic suggests they look like metal robots, however alien in form. How was the metal mined, refined, shaped, and assembled? Here's where Intelligent Design becomes indispensable.

The advocates of ID, who are arguing that their belief should be included in science classes in Texas, Tennessee, and other states, say that if a living organism has a design that cannot be explained by the theory of natural selection, it is proof of an Intelligent Designer. If you consider a Camaro, for example, wouldn't it obviously have had a Designer? Could its parts have been assembled by a hurricane (or a trillion hurricanes) blowing through a junkyard?

Certainly not. Therefore, this is proof that Autobots were not assembled on Cybertron by hurricanes or any other means envisioned by Darwin, and were Intelligently Designed. That makes the Transformers series a compelling parable for ID, and I expect several of this year's Republican presidential candidates to recommend the movies on that basis alone.

Questions for the Movie Answer Man

Attention Spans

Q. Today was a very discouraging day for me. With a group of intelligent friends, I started watching *Annie Hall* at my home. Unfortunately, as the movie started, people began talking. This continued throughout the movie, much of the conversation unrelated to the movie. Then there was the texting, the visits to the bathroom, the talking to the dog, and so on. I considered walking away or saying something abrupt, but I didn't want to be rude. That's truly ironic, as I've always considered talking during movies to be rude.

When it was over and I was thoroughly annoyed with my friends, one of them told me it was boring. The other said she really liked it. It's hard to trust either opinion as it didn't seem they really watched it. I've noticed similar habits in movie theaters, too: people texting despite the warning before the movie not to, people talking, people going in and out, and the not-so-new problem of the rustling of candy bags. I'm thirty-five, and it sometimes surprises me when my peers can be so obtuse in their movie-watching habits. How can anyone appreciate greatness if they aren't really looking for it?

—Christopher Willson, Carson City, Nevada

A. You've heard about people being killed in car crashes while texting? Some people's attention spans are being killed in the same way.

At the Movies

Q. I've noticed that the official *At the Movies* Web site has been down for some time. Is this somehow related to your upcoming show?

—Kevin Klawitter, Wadena, Minnesota

A. Buena Vista Television took down the site when it stopped producing *At the Movies.* That was fair enough. It contained all the show's reviews over the years—everything by Gene Siskel, myself, Richard Roeper, Michael Phillips, A. O. Scott, Ben Mankiewicz, Ben Lyons, and various guest critics. I understand the archive has been preserved, and I hope it will find a new home somewhere on the Web.

Battle: Los Angeles

Q. Just read your lousy review of the wonderful movie *Battle: Los Angeles,* and the first thing that came to my mind was jawbone of an ass. Fits you perfectly. Grow up!

—Anonymous

A. What was the second thing that came into your mind?

Becoming a Film Critic

Q. I love film. All I have wanted to do was become a film critic. I thought I'd just go for it and ask if you could offer advice. I have a B.A. in English. I am a very good writer, or so I've been told. I was just hoping that maybe, just maybe, you'd read over this and throw a poor dog a bone. Any advice or tips you could give would be appreciated. I just want to know what I need to do, what steps to take, how to get there. I've thought about a master's in film studies, but is it necessary?

—Arthur Gordon

A. There's no easy answer, and not many salaried jobs. Many critics simply open their own Web sites or contribute to others. I think the degree in English is invaluable. Further study is valuable for its own sake, but may not lead any more quickly to work. It would be for your own good, as it should be. Perhaps it might be wise to redefine yourself as a writer and not narrowly as a movie critic. Take someone like George Orwell as a role model.

Best in Film Lists

Q. What do you think about ABC's latest *Best in Film* series? I hate best-film lists because they always leave out some of the best films that other people don't think are great. But then again, who can really define *the* best film? According to ABC, the American public is about to. And this isn't even going to come close to correlating with the Internet Movie Database, and those results are skewed as well. Will there ever be an end?

—Richie Starzec, Middletown, Connecticut

A. It might help if you thought of it this way: ABC is using a formula to create a bogus awards show with no credibility, on a small budget, and depending on lots of film clips to carry the day. All "Best Films of All Time" lists are meaningless and all Internet polls are meaningless, because there has never been a single list to satisfy everyone, or even most people.

In this case the short lists of finalists in several categories were selected, I understand, by various critics and "experts" who made nominations. (Between them, all of those authorities were unable to think of a single silent film that qualified.) The finalists were such suspiciously popular mainstream titles that one wonders how expert the experts were, or how ABC selected from their recommendations.

Let me complain about something, and then explain why complaining is useless. In the category of Best Kiss, one of the nominees was *not* the most famous kiss in movie history, between Cary Grant and Ingrid Bergman in Hitchcock's *Notorious*. That was also for many years the *longest* kiss in movie history. How a list of finalists could forget it is inexplicable.

But that's just me. And that's the flaw. The moment a list is announced, everyone like me works up a lather complaining about what's on it and what got left off. And then when the votes are announced by ABC, there will be learned analysis of the winners and losers and the meaning of it all. All of the analysts will begin with the assumption that they know best, and everybody else is wrong.

Of course, most of the votes will have been cast by the kinds of people who vote in online polls. Those who engage in such a futile enterprise aren't always the brightest bulbs on the Christmas tree. You know what would amuse me? If real movie buffs (like you and I) went online and simply voted for the best films in every category. Then ABC would be stuck with a lot of truly good choices, and its ratings might suffer. Heh, heh.

Black-and-White Films

Q. Once you and Gene Siskel did a show on black-and-white films, and how they should've been preserved back then and forever. You argued the value of the significance of B&W as an added layer and said that movies can only gain from it.

What is your opinion of color films, all of which are created with color in mind, being changed into B&W? Would, for instance, big musicals like *Wizard of Oz* or big epics like *Gone with the Wind* and even contemporary films like *Reservoir Dogs*, *Forrest Gump*, *Being John Malkovich*, or even the Batman films have benefited from that treatment? Would B&W really add something new or interesting in the process? Or should color films not be tampered with?

—Alexander Chatzipantelis

A. The film should be seen as it was originally made. This includes many B&W films of the silent era where some of the scenes were tinted. Of course you can easily watch a color film in B&W simply by adjusting a television, and I did that once as an experiment with *L. A. Confidential*, a film whose noir qualities gave me the notion. It actually looked quite good. I've tried that only two other times, however, with color films whose videos were made from badly faced prints that had turned pink. Then B&W was just making the best of a bad thing.

Black Swan

Q. Many of my friends and I are anticipating the release of *Black Swan* in our town or even close by. Why would such a popular movie restrict its release to only a few theaters? After all, the budget for the film was about $9 to $16 million. Is this a wise move?

—Aviya Ilia, Laredo, Texas

A. Apparently it was. The film racked up the second highest per-screen average of the year in its limited opening weekend (slightly behind *The King's Speech*) and benefited from a lot of publicity. Some films are designed to open wide and make a quick killing. Oscar contenders are designed to open gradually, build an audience, and have staying power. They appeal to a different, somewhat older, audience that thinks it over before going to a movie.

Burlesque

Q. It's probably a coincidence, but I thought I'd check. In your review of *Burlesque*, you ask, "Where did they come from? Where will they go?" about the male dancers who suddenly appear. This isn't an arcane reference to the title of Kitty Carlisle's opening number in *Murder at the Vanities* (1934), which asks the same question about the dancers there?

—Garry Koenigsberg, San Francisco, California

A. I'm afraid not. Great minds think alike.

Criticism of Ebert's Career

Q. Have you listened to Armond White's criticism of your career? It's quite astounding and elitist. It's at: http://j.mp/diVOxc.

—Nathan Kuhl, Bear Creek, Pennsylvania

A. Yes, he says, "I do think it is fair to say that Roger Ebert destroyed film criticism." I was actually quite chuffed to read this. He's the only one of my colleagues willing to admit the power of my influence.

Eat Pray Love

Q. I have watched and read your reviews for years with great honor. I disagree so strongly with your review of *Eat Pray Love* that it makes me sick. You just don't get it, and many others like you don't get it. You do not know at all what it is like being a woman in this day and age (or previously) who did not want to be defined by a man or married off to one. If you think Stephen in the movie was an OK husband, you are out to lunch. He was horrible!!!!!!!!!!!!!! (except on paper to people who do not need emotional sustenance). David was the narcissist from hell that many of us have fallen for . . . do you not get that??????????? Many of the males of the species are frankly overrated and the women's movement has proven this (and frankly not sufficiently). I hope your wife will bring you up to speed.

—Jeanine Carlson, Ph.D.,
licensed clinical psychologist

A. Here is what I wrote about Stephen: "Her first marriage apparently broke down primarily because she tired of it, although Roberts at (a sexy and attractive) forty-three makes an actor's brave stab at explaining they were 'young and immature.' She walks out on the guy (Billy Crudup) and he still likes her and reads her on the Web." Here is what I wrote about David: "She meets a man played by James Franco, about whom, enough said."

My wife???????? She already has me up to speed!!!!!!!!

E-books

Q. You were critical of e-books awhile back. Here's one point in their favor—since I was gifted a Kindle a month ago, I've read eight to ten books (including one of yours), and probably hadn't read that many the entire previous year. Just having so many different books accessible all the time has made the difference. I still read the paper kind, too, but they take longer (they sit on the nightstand).

—Mary Burns, San Mateo, California

A. Reading is an admirable thing to do no matter how you do it. I remain in love with the tactile pleasures of physical books. I've read on a Kindle, and on my iPad, but it's a little like walking on a treadmill: You keep up the pace but don't seem to be getting anywhere.

Film Directors' Credit

Q. It has always puzzled me how a film director can take the complete title credit for directing a film, when it is common practice to employ second unit directors who contribute their own unique vision to complete the shoot. If the director goes on to win a major award such as a Director's Guild Award or ultimately an Academy Award, isn't it a bit of a cheat to take the sole credit without also including the other directors' efforts?

—Kevin Fellman, Phoenix, Arizona

A. True, and Riccardo Muti doesn't play all the instruments in the Chicago Symphony. But the director is responsible for selecting and supervising his team, and many work with the same second unit directors over time. This is well understood. As a general rule, second units don't handle dialogue scenes.

Fun with Yiddish

Q. Russell Crowe's character in *The Next Three Days* couldn't really be a schlepp, because that's a verb of motion. But he could be a schlub, at least to start. Still, the movie lacks credibility, because whoever heard of a schlub who turned into a mensch?

—Jon Paul Henry

A. Now I feel like such a putz.

Harry Potter Fight Scenes

Q. Regarding the latest Harry Potter movie, I was surprised that you didn't mention the fight scenes. This movie and most of the recent movies are seeming to trend to louder, faster, blurrier fight scenes. Is it just me or do the scenes get so confusing that we cannot keep up and give up on trying to follow the action? I find myself saying, OK, fine, I'll wait until it's all over and see who wins. It is wasted film time that could be better used to fill out the story.

—Joel Michello

A. Back in the years when fight scenes were staged using real actors and stuntmen, they were choreographed to make sense. Now that they're largely manufactured with computers, they approach abstract art: assemblies of images and sound cut together so quickly, and with so little attention to angle and POV, that no coherent understanding of them is possible. This is a great loss.

Hereafter

Q. Regarding *Hereafter*: Neither telepathy nor life after death have been proven by science, but you seem to be saying that you and Clint believe in one but not the other. If you are going to make a leap of faith and believe in one, why not believe in both?

—Brian Mier

A. I don't know what Eastwood believes. I don't believe in telepathy, but I think it might theoretically be possible in the physical universe. I don't believe life after death is possible in the physical universe, nor do most believers in it.

Q. In your review of *Hereafter*, you state that you do not believe in "woo-woo." What does this mean, "woo-woo"?

—David Slater, Nashville, Tennessee

A. Man, did that stir up people. Carol Miller of Fargo, North Dakota, wrote: "Come on, you don't believe in 'woo-woo'? Is that a technical word for something? A belief in God? I'm not as concerned if you believe in the afterlife. I want a review of the technical aspects of a film, the acting, story, etc. It's a little condescending, though, to call it 'woo-woo.' Really."

And a reader signed AnyEdge wrote: "I would like to register that I find the phrase 'woo-woo' to be very nearly hate speech. I am a functional skeptic (but not a member of the movement), and have deep concerns with people who believe in disproven things, like homeopathy. But to use a derisive, derogatory term like this to describe other people's beliefs, *even those beliefs we know to be false*, is beneath the dignity of reasonable discourse."

Isn't "woo-woo" pretty general usage? I'm using it in the review to refer to mind reading and psychics in general. Wiktionary.com has two definitions: (1) Supernatural, paranormal, occult, or pseudoscientific phenomena, or emotion-based beliefs and explanations; (2) An alcoholic cocktail consisting of peach schnapps, vodka, and cranberry juice. It is not to be confused with "Woo Hoo," which means (1) great excitement, or (2) In the game Sims 2, sex.

Intelligent Design

Q. I have the utmost respect for your reviews, Mr. Ebert. Frankly, I think you are brilliant in a lot of ways! On the other hand, I cannot and will not support anyone (buying books, etc.) who stands against Intelligent Design!

—Mark Cooper

A. You may run out of reading material and have to turn to video games.

I Spit on Your Grave

Q. I read your review of *I Spit on Your Grave*, a remake of a movie I am familiar with but purposely have never seen. I don't plan on seeing the remake, either. However, I found your comments about revenge interesting and shared them with my dues-paying feminist wife. You wrote: "First, let's dispatch with the fiction that the film is about 'getting even.'

If I rape you, I have committed a crime. If you kill me, you have committed another one."

She quickly pointed out the oversight in your comment. If we understand you, rape is a lesser offense than murder; therefore, if you rape someone and that person murders you, what they have done is escalation, which isn't equal and can't be *even*. My wife, having extensively studied violence against women, will point out that women who are raped are often psychologically damaged for life, and if given the option, would have opted for death. If anything, by murdering her offenders, Jennifer let them off easy. They won't spend the rest of their lives in fear of dark parking lots, empty homes, and being alone with members of the opposite sex.

—James Ford, Ocala, Florida

A. I understand your wife's point, but I was not equating rape and murder or even comparing them. I only used them as an example. If I am harmed, a hurt has been caused me. If I harm in revenge, a hurt has been caused to another. Philosophers have been discussing the moral issues involved for centuries. But in the case of *I Spit on Your Grave*, the film depends on the revenge theme to conceal its real content.

Yes, men rape the heroine. Yes, she devises elaborate and sadistic ways to torture and murder them. So now are they even? No, because in the first half of the film the psychological goading of the women is deliberate and realistic, and for me expresses true hatred of women. In the second half, the woman enacts unlikely and *entertaining* variations on violence that most horror movie fans will feel at home with. So the movie isn't about a woman getting even. It's about a woman horribly mistreated, and then put to work to entertain the goons in the audience who didn't walk out during the first half. The mystery to me is: Why do women watch this movie (or men who love women)?

Kodak Theatre

Q. Since 2001, the Academy of Motion Picture Arts and Sciences has held their Oscar ceremonies at the prestigious Kodak Theatre located in Hollywood. Since the creation of AMPAS, for seventy-eight consecutive years, every single Best Picture has allegedly been shot on Kodak film, thus the chosen name of the venue. Just curious if anyone ever bothered to inform them that last year's Best Picture winner, *The Hurt Locker*, was shot on Fuji film?

—Kevin Fellman, Phoenix, Arizona

A. Gee, it turned out all right. That detail escaped my attention. Actually, the Kodak Theatre was not named because of all the films shot on Kodak, but because Eastman Kodak generously helped support its construction.

Love and Other Drugs

Q. In *Love and Other Drugs*, I was flabbergasted at the way James and Maggie met. Not only is it wrong, but violating and upsetting. As a woman who has had many creepy doctors from adolescence to adulthood, I would like to share my opinion that it is not acceptable in a romantic comedy. I doubted what I saw. Surely the public would be angry with something like this, so it can't be real. When your review of the film came out I thought, "At least Roger Ebert will be angry like me!"

Sure, you commented , "doctors aren't supposed to do that," but I didn't find the passion I was hoping for. This film uses a lighthearted romantic comedy setting and pairs it with the violation of Maggie's body and rights as a human being. It is treated like something cute—as if Jake Gyllenhaal's blue eyes erase something that is not only illegal, but an assault to Maggie's privacy. Then it rewards the "lovable scamp" with sex from the woman he violated. What I find scary is the lack of waves this has caused.

—Megan Coker

A. Jake Gyllenhaal is a drug salesman and the pal of a doctor (Hank Azaria) who disguises him in interns' scrubs and brings him into a private room to observe as he examines Anna Hathaway's breasts. This might be grounds for losing his license. Yes, it was offensive. Yes, perhaps I should have been more angry. So much is permitted in modern movies that sometimes we get desensitized. These days we are desensitized to a lot of things. At the risk of sounding political, I'll ask: If America now feels it can legally commit torture, how much is left?

Make Way for Tomorrow

Q. I just this weekend watched Leo McCarey's *Make Way for Tomorrow* (1937), which you wrote a Great Movies article about. That may be the best 1930s movie I've ever seen. But it's so unbearably sad. Do you think that's maybe why it's relatively obscure? I mean, I've never seen it stated like that, not even by Ozu. My question really is: Why the heck do some of us respond to *really sad* movies so strongly, while others would rather steer clear? I mean, as sad as it was, the movie made me extremely happy, in awe at its wisdom.

—Yancy Jack Berns, Los Angeles, California

A. It refers to the way some younger people put old people like their parents on the shelf and consider them a nuisance. Ozu's masterpiece *Tokyo Story* (1953) told a similar story set in Japan. His screenwriter, Kogo Noda, saw McCarey's film and said he was influenced by it. There's a lot of sentimentality about old folks, but if they fall into sickness or poverty not a lot of modern young couples want to let them move in. They'll be "happier" elsewhere. Regarding your second question: In thinking about "depressing movies," many people don't realize that all bad movies are depressing, and no good movies are.

Monster Movies

Q. In all the giant monster movies I've seen (*King Kong*, *Godzilla*, et al.), the monsters never have the urge to urinate and/or defecate. Even after eating people. Why is that? Do you know of any movies where they do, barring *Jurassic Park?*

—Eric Hodek, Itasca, Illinois

A. Obviously, they must be constipated. That's why they're so short-tempered.

Netflix

Q. I'm a fifteen-year-old who has been reading your Great Movies series for a few years now, but have never had many of the classics at my disposal. However, my family recently got Netflix, and I must say I'm overwhelmed by everything available. Where should I begin? And, if I'm trying to foster an appreciation for classic film in my family, where should they start? Are there any particular directors or titles you would recommend?

—Zachary Trail

A. I could name specific films or directors, but I'd rather encourage you to turn on Netflix, go to Watch Instantly, choose "classics" under genre, and start with the first film that sounds good to you. Just now I tried that and found *Bonnie and Clyde*, *Laura*, *Great Expectations*, and *The Third Man.* Then what happens is you find a director you like and start rummaging around in his work. As to fostering the appreciation of your family for classic films—well, good luck. When it comes to taste, many people are foster-proof. One nice thing about Netflix is if you've given a film a good chance and it's still not working for you, you don't need to feel bad when you stop watching.

Q. I was shocked and appalled this morning to learn that Netflix is refusing to make *Trash Humpers* available on its site. In a statement by the film's distribution company, Drag City, it stated: "We don't expect Netflix to carry anything they don't want to, for whatever reason, but it reminds us that this is the price paid when we allow one entity to control the lion's share of content distribution."

It really is a wake-up call for me. All of the independent video stores are shutting down, and soon it's just going to be Netflix and Redbox. It's chilling and it really makes me want to cancel my Netflix membership, rather than have them try to keep a film away from me that has been to the Toronto Film Festival, New York Film Festival, and London Film Festival, among others. It's worth mentioning that I had no desire to watch *Trash Humpers.* I don't particularly enjoy the work of Harmony Korine, but I certainly support his right to make his films.

—Ryan Sartor, Fairfield, Connecticut

A. The Netflix decision is creating quite a stir. I haven't seen *Trash Humpers*, and it's unlikely to open soon at a theater near you, so video is its only outlet. It doesn't seem to be pornographic. It does appear to be offensive. Is that why Netflix said no to it? I learn it's about a group of actors wearing the masks of old geezers wandering the alleys of Nashville and, according to Rob Nelson of *Variety*, "bashing TVs with sledgehammers, blasting an empty wheelchair with a self-serve car-wash gun, 'killing' various plastic dolls, spanking a trio of women in lingerie, lighting firecrackers, singing, cackling incessantly, and other taste-challenged ephemera. The result, riveting beyond all rationality, is something like *Jackass*, except that here the stunts are dangerous only to standards of good taste—which, of course, is precisely the point."

The statement by Drag City is precisely to the point. The role of Netflix is as a conduit between filmmakers and film viewers. I can understand why they don't handle hard-core pornography. But *Trash Humpers* seems to have merely offended someone's taste. I'm not a member of Netflix for their taste, but for their movies.

Old Film?

Q. I had a facepalm moment tonight and I need commiseration. I loaned my friend and his wife *L.A. Confidential* on Blu-ray a week ago. He returned it tonight and said his wife didn't want to watch it because it was an "old movie." Now, I don't know whether or not that means she didn't like the idea that it took place several decades ago, or that 1997 is "old," but either way I wanted to yell at her. The kicker? They watched *Dance Flick* instead.

—Joseph O'Driscoll, Salt Lake City, Utah

A. He should have said, "Old? How can it be old? It's in color!"

Rango

Q. My wife and I made the mistake of taking our seven-year-old daughter to see *Rango*. I think it should have had a PG-13 rating for the over-the-top sexual innuendos pervasive throughout the movie. The very comparison you made to *Blazing Saddles* would qualify this movie as inappropriate for my daughter. I found *Blazing Saddles* to be funny, though. I guess the difference between G and PG is the adult humor. I guess the smart comment indicates whether you get it or not. Well, in this case not only did we get it, but were saturated with it and finally decided to leave because of our annoyance with it. I agree with Bruce Miller of the *Sioux City Journal* that it is not a movie for the whole family.

—Andrew Reading, Pittsburgh, Pennsylvania

A. It's a film adults enjoy more than kids. I mentioned that in the review. I believe the sexual innuendos probably went over the heads of many children. Lots of animated films sneak in winks for the grown-ups. It all depends on how much you are afraid your daughter picked up on them. The *Blazing Saddles* farts seemed to be much appreciated by kids, and didn't offend me.

Q. I agree with you about how pointless and annoying 3-D is. I was happy to learn in your review that *Rango* was not in 3-D, and that alone was enough to make me go see it, my first animated movie in a few years.

But the relationship between *Rango* and 3-D is more interesting and complicated than it first appears. As you watch the movie, clearly *Rango* was intended to be in 3-D. The characters are constantly thrusting their faces and their implements into the camera. The real question is, why then did the studio decide *not* to release it in 3-D?

—Gregory Berry

A. Of course you can have 3-D-like shots without the process. On Isla Fisher's Web site I found this quote by director Gore Verbinski: "I don't think there's a dimension missing. I don't watch it and go, you know, 'It's flat,' or it's, you know, missing anything. So you know, we talked about it early on and it just didn't seem like we needed to go there."

Red Beard

Q. You said at the end of your Great Movies article about Kurosawa's *Red Beard*: "I believe this film should be seen by every medical student." It might please you to know that my old judo teacher Dr. Paul Harper, who was also a surgeon and researcher at the University of Chicago, required all his surgery residents to watch *Red Beard*. Just reading your description of some of those astonishingly beautiful scenes stirred deep emotional memories of the film.

—Dave Fultz

A. We are drowning in idiotic medical dramas, and *Red Beard* is a rare film that seriously considers a doctor's philosophy about life, death, and health care.

Reflections in a Golden Eye

Q. After the death of Elizabeth Taylor, I read your review of *Reflections in a Golden Eye* again, and noted your comment on the washed-out color palette. It's been years, but I remember John Huston saying in his autobiography *An Open Book* that Aldo Tonti shot the film through a golden filter, the idea being to really give it that golden haze implied by the title. I've never found it on video with the original golden/sepia tone print, but John said it looked better, and who am I to argue?

—Michael Harper

A. I saw the movie in first run as Huston intended. It wasn't quite in B&W; you could see faint greens, golds, reds, and blues. That was unsuccessful at the box office. Audiences saw it as a mistake and not an artistic decision. Since the film was photographed in full color and the "fading" was done in postproduction, most of the video versions have simply restored the color. That's not what Huston intended, and the thing to do with your color adjustment is to fade the color to almost but not quite B&W. Does it work? That's for you to decide.

Scott Pilgrim vs. The World

Q. Why haven't you reviewed *Scott Pilgrim vs. The World*? While it certainly underperformed at the box office, given your (embarrassingly) tumultuous relationship with video games, it would seem like fertile ground for a nuanced and controlled critique of video game culture and its effects on other forms of media.

—Christian Russo

A. Video games rank low on the list of tumultuous relationships I feel embarrassed about, but I've been amazed how often I've been asked your question. I took a month's leave to work on my memoirs, and alas didn't see *Scott Pilgrim.* I still sleep nights.

Secretariat

Q. From a blog entry you wrote about *Secretariat*: "Nor did Penny Chenery, Secretariat's owner, 'luck into' the horse. As the film spells out, she won the horse by *losing* a coin toss, which she wanted to lose." Did you not just describe luck? Did Chenery somehow master the skill of engineering coin tosses to fall the way she desired?

—Tigertooth

A. It wasn't all luck. She counted on her knowledge of bloodlines to know which mare she wanted. She guessed (perhaps luckily) that the millionaire would know less, and choose the wrong mare. Therefore, (1) she wins, and chooses the mare she wants, or (2) she loses, and the millionaire chooses the mare she doesn't want.

Star Ratings

Q. I'm just curious, what led you to give *Black Swan* a rating of 3.5 stars, while *The Wrestler* got 4? The two films have been compared a lot, so I'm interested to hear why you thought one was slightly better than the other.

—Sarah S. Evans, Indianapolis, Indiana

A. And they were directed one after the other by Darren Aronofsky. They're both powerful movies. It's hard to say. The star rating system is the bane of critics because of questions like yours. How's this for an answer: The half-star difference was accounted for by an ineffable difference in the intensity of my emotions.

Star Wars Films in 3-D

Q. Are you looking forward to revisiting the *Star Wars* films in 3-D?

—Ronald Z. Barzell, Los Angeles, California

A. How many different restorations, revivals, refurbishments, retreads, and renovations are we expected to endure? The *Star Wars* films are terrific movies. Why is George Lucas wearing out their welcome?

3-D Movie Technology

Q. Do you remember the audio industry's brief and unsuccessful flirtation with four-channel "quadraphonic" sound? It was a technology that was supposed to deliver surround sound; unfortunately it appeared to have been created by people who knew everything about audio electronics but nothing about how people hear. Similarly, 3-D movie technologies (which, properly speaking, are merely stereoscopy, like an old View-Master) appear to have been created by people who know everything about digital projection but nothing about how people see. In particular, stereo image separation is only one cue that people use to infer depth, and when that cue is inconsistent with other cues—as it often is with 3-D movies—what you get is a headache or, if you're really unlucky, motion sickness.

—Carl Zetie, Waterford, Virginia

A. Man, I've been saying this since day one: 3-D is the waste of a perfectly good dimension. It's been interesting to read several articles in trade publications recently speculating that the latest version of 3-D is already on terminal support. Public acceptance seems to be fading, and the higher prices are causing sticker shock.

What do you really get for the several-dollar surcharge on 3-D? Look at it this way: When toll roads open, the theory is that the tolls are to "pay for the road." Years go by, the roads are paid for, and the tolls go away. Are you "paying for the 3-D projection"? A projector costs maybe $120,000. With a $3 surcharge, that's covered by 40,000 admissions. *The projectors are paid for.* What's more, because they're digital, they allow much lower print costs. There is also the problem that 3-D delivers an inferior picture, noticeably dimmer, not to mention occasional headaches, nausea, and dizziness.

I've argued this year after year after year. Armond, if I can destroy film criticism, why can't I destroy 3-D? What am I doing wrong?

Top-Ten Lists with Gene Siskel

Q. As I recall from all those years when you and Gene did your top-ten special at the end of the year, you'd have many films in common, but never all. I was wondering if the two of you shared notes beforehand—and, if so, whether one or both of you ever made changes to your lists so they wouldn't be that similar? Or are you of a mind that a critic's list should be his list, regardless of what anyone else is going to have on his or hers, and that it's no sin if two guys writing for the same place, doing a podcast together, etc., have that much overlap on such a thing? This is why lists are frustrating. You want to be able to celebrate the best work of the year, but then you start contorting yourself to figure out what goes in and what stays out, how to rank things (if you don't want to just go alphabetical), whether to consider a colleague's rankings, etc.

—Alan Sepinwall, Newark, New Jersey

A. You and a colleague are dealing with the problem of possible list overlap on your Webcast. Gene had an ironclad rule that we never discussed movies or lists in advance. We would send our lists to the producers, who would contrive a show rundown and give us each only the show segments we would be writing.

Trailer Quality

Q. I watched *The Wild and Wonderful Whites of West Virginia* last night at a theater. The previews had the Apple logo in the corner from iDVD, and the movie itself was YouTube quality. The frame rate stuttered, and it was heavily pixelated and compressed. Was this movie distributed everywhere that way? When I see places that aren't movie theaters screening older movies, I expect it to just be a laptop hooked up to an office projector, but this was a first-run theater.

—Drew Zipp, Louisville, Kentucky

A. The picture quality of the trailer is fine. The movie hasn't played here yet, but it was reviewed by A. O. Scott in the *New York Times*, and if I know Tony, he would be inclined to mention an Apple logo from an iDVD. There's your smoking gun right there.

Troll 2

Q. In your review about *Best Worst Movie*, which was *Troll 2*, you said there is no original *Troll*. Actually, there is. It stars Sonny Bono, Michael Moriarty, Noah Hathaway, Julia Louis-Dreyfus, June Lockhart, and Phil Fondacaro. I've seen it dozens of times. It's technically not good at all, but has a bit of style and an occasionally interesting score. *Troll 2* has nothing to do with it, though. Side note, the main character in the film is named Harry Potter, and he encounters a world of magic. Hmmmm?

—Dustin Dear, Austin, Texas

A. Not good at all. Bit of style. Score occasionally interesting. Watched it dozens of times. Does that have anything to do with specials on pitchers at the Alamo Drafthouse?

Winter's Bone

Q. I read your review of *Winter's Bone,* saw the movie, and know the answer to your unanswered question about Ree Dolly (How did she become the person she is?). It's actually pretty simple. She decided. There are many of us out here who have done the same thing.

—Jim Boulton, Albuquerque, New Mexico

A. Think you could offer counseling to Dustin Dear?

Ebert's Little Movie Glossary

These are the year's new contributions to my glossary project. Hundreds of entries were collected in *Ebert's Bigger Little Movie Glossary*, published in 1999. Contributions are always welcome.

* * *

Fish Out of Danger. The escaping character who's running from a following helicopter jumps into the water. All the chasers should have to do is wait until he runs out of air a few feet away and catch him, but instead, he will always manage to escape by submerging and not popping out of the water until he reaches the beach or lake's edge. See Nicolas Cage escaping the ocean prison in *Face/Off* (in plain daylight), Angelina Jolie's lake escape by the end of *Salt*, Kissy's volcano and ocean escape from *You Only Live Twice*, and so on.

—Gerardo Valero, Mexico City, Mexico

Headphone Invincibility Rule. Vacuuming a room while listening to music on large headphones guarantees your survival through natural disasters and other calamities. See *The Day After Tomorrow* and *True Lies*.

—Sam Freedenberg, Rockville, Maryland

It's Not Loaded. Characters brandishing a firearm will often assure others that the weapon is unloaded. Instead of opening the gun to demonstrate this, the character will instead pull the trigger, blasting a hole in something and scaring the bejeezus out of everyone around.

—James Frazier, Cedar Falls, Iowa

Kicking and Entering. Police duos investigating murders inevitably reach a point where the investigation stalls, and then, from nowhere, an obscure clue leads them to an ominous-looking door in a seedy part of town. By-the-Book Cop knocks but turns to leave when no one answers; without a warrant they are powerless. Loose-Cannon Cop promptly kicks open the door (one kick usually does it), and struts in mumbling something about "somebody yelled help" and "probable cause." By-the-Book hesitates, then shrugs his shoulders and follows Loose-Cannon inside. It's OK—the Constitution understands.

—James Arnall, Los Angeles, California

One Bullet Left. Whenever the hero and the villain are involved in an extended gunfight, the hero will open his pistol chamber to check how many bullets he has left. If he does, that number will invariably be one (1), which will be the exact number of bullets he will need to finish the villain off, no more, no less—no matter how difficult the situation or long the odds. See Tom Cruise while rescuing Kerri Russell in *Mission Impossible 3*, Bruce Willis in *Die Hard*, and Michelle Yeoh at the end of *Tomorrow Never Dies*.

—Gerardo Valero, Mexico City, Mexico

The Retort-à-tête Rule. If a character in a movie asks a question, and another character answers with a quick and clever retort, then the first character must use that same comeback in response to another question (asked by the second character), later in the movie. This "Back Atcha" will always be followed by a mandatory Three-Second Delay, to allow less sophisticated members of the audience a little extra time to catch up.

—Randall, Portland, Oregon

Someone Left the Flake Out in the Rain. How to immediately spot the quirky free spirit in a movie: That would be the person standing out in the rain, eyes closed, ecstatic face cast heavenward, arms raised, as if embracing every raindrop. Childlike dancing and twirling are optional.

—Janet Sullivan, Brooklyn, New York

This Is a Hologram Rule. Holograms in science fiction movies always have a blue cast to them and/or an occasional glitch in their display, just to remind us that Liam Neeson is not actually one foot tall.

—Tom Clark, Redwood City, California

The Unbearable Lightness of Beverages. It is obvious that in movies and television all beverages in cups with lids on them are weightless. A 20-ounce coffee that weighs 1.25 pounds in real life, in "reel" life looks to be as light as a feather. And anyone caring a cardboard holder with four large cups, weighing a total of 5 pounds, must have Superman's strength to be able to carry it with just the tips of their fingers. Also, if these cups are filled with hot coffee, the coffee never burns when someone starts gulping it down.

—Keni Miller, Solvang, California

The Well-Thrown Blade. In any action sequence, whenever a knife is thrown but misses its intended target, it will nonetheless lodge itself, blade first, in the wall behind him. It never bounces off the wall and clatters to the ground.

—Mike Dillon, Los Angeles, California

The Writer's Block Rule. Whenever a character must write something under deadline, he can be seen writing in longhand on a pad, then tearing off the sheet of paper, balling it up, and tossing it onto a pile of balled-up pieces of paper, usually overflowing from a wastebasket. Later in the film, after some deeply significant experience, he can be seen confidently typing.

—Dana V. Hatch, Columbus, Ohio

Index

A

D

E

F

G

H

I

J

K

L

M

P

Q

R

S

X

Y

Z